THE

WAR OF THE REBELLION:

A COMPILATION OF THE

OFFICIAL RECORDS

OF THE

UNION AND CONFEDERATE ARMIES.

PREPARED, UNDER THE DIRECTION OF THE SECRETARY OF WAR,

BY

Lieut. Col. ROBERT N. SCOTT, Third U. S. Artillery,

AND

PUBLISHED PURSUANT TO ACT OF CONGRESS APPROVED JUNE 16, 1880.

SERIES I—VOLUME XVII—IN TWO PARTS.
PART II—CORRESPONDENCE, ETC.

WASHINGTON:
GOVERNMENT PRINTING OFFICE.
1887.

28822

PART II.—VOL. XVII.

CORRESPONDENCE, ORDERS, AND RETURNS RELATING TO OPERATIONS IN WEST TENNESSEE AND NORTHERN MISSISSIPPI FROM JUNE 10, 1862, TO JANUARY 20, 1863.*

UNION CORRESPONDENCE, ETC.

SPECIAL FIELD ORDERS, } HDQRS. DEPT. OF THE MISSISSIPPI,
No. 90. } *Corinth, Miss., June 10, 1862.*

I. The order dividing the army near Corinth into right wing, center, left wing, and reserve is hereby revoked. Major-Generals Grant, Buell, and Pope will resume the command of their separate army corps,† except the division of Major-General Thomas, which, till further orders, will be stationed in Corinth as a part of the Army of the Tennessee. General Thomas will resume the immediate command of his division on its arrival at Corinth, and Brig. Gen. T. W. Sherman will report to Major-General Buell for duty with the Army of the Ohio.

*   *   *   *   *   *   *

By order of Major-General Halleck:

J. C. KELTON,
Assistant Adjutant-General.

ORDERS, } HEADQUARTERS FIFTH DIVISION,
No. 36. } *Chewalla, June 10, 1862.*

Commanders of brigades and detachments will at once reduce the baggage of their commands to the minimum.

All officers' trunks, all surplus tents, and extra baggage of every kind, will immediately be deposited in the depot at Chewalla and from there will be sent to Pittsburg Landing and by boat to Cairo, there to await orders.

Hereafter 40 rounds of ammunition must be carried in the cartridge-box, two papers on the person of each soldier, and one box in each company wagon; also the ammunition wagon of each regiment to be full. The remainder on hand, together with surplus arms, will be deposited at the depot for conveyance to Corinth.

By order of Maj. Gen. W. T. Sherman:

J. H. HAMMOND,
Assistant Adjutant-General.

---

*Including operations against Vicksburg subsequent to July 27, 1862, and the Expedition against Arkansas Post, or Fort Hindman, Ark., January 4-17, 1863.

†The Armies of the Tennessee, of the Ohio, and of the Mississippi. See Series I, Vol. X, Part II, pp. 138, 144.

Orders, }   HEADQUARTERS FIFTH DIVISION,
No. 37. }   *Chewalla, June* 10, 1862.

I. General Morgan L. Smith will move his entire command early to morrow morning on the State Line road to Pocahontas and beyond, so as to have a strong working party employed repairing the bridge across Muddy.

II. Colonel McDowell will march his whole brigade about 2 p. m. tomorrow to Pocahontas and then bivouac. He will follow the State Line road.

III. Colonel Dickey, Fourth Illinois Cavalry, will cross the Tuscumbia at Captain Young's, make a circuit to the south and west and reach Pocahontas by night. His trains will follow McDowell's brigade and train.

IV. Commanders of brigades and detachments will hereafter see that in making their encampments they leave the roads entirely clear. Wagons must be parked in the woods and fields, and horses and mules placed so as not to interfere with any trains or column on the march.

By order of Maj. Gen. W. T. Sherman :

J. H. HAMMOND,
Assistant Adjutant-General.

CORINTH, *June* 11, 1862.

Brigadier-General QUINBY, *Columbus, Ky.* :

Island No. 10, and all other works on the river except New Madrid and Columbus, will require only guards to take care of public property. Have the telegraph line repaired to Humboldt as rapidly as possible. The workmen repairing it, guarded by a good cavalry force, can with hand-cars push forward without waiting for the repair of the bridges. I hope to reach Humboldt with supplies within the next two days. Push forward your cavalry force rapidly ; they may be able to save some unburned bridges.

H. W. HALLECK.

GENERAL ORDERS, }   HDQRS. ARMY OF THE TENNESSEE,
No. 54.   }   *In Field near Corinth, Miss., June* 11, 1862.

Col. T. L. Dickey, Fourth Illinois Cavalry, is hereby assigned to the command of a cavalry brigade,* which brigade will be composed of the Fourth Illinois Cavalry Volunteers, Fifth Ohio Cavalry Volunteers, one squadron Second Illinois Cavalry Volunteers, one squadron Thielemann's Independent Cavalry, Eleventh Illinois Cavalry Volunteers, Curtis' Horse, First Nebraska Cavalry Volunteers, Stewart's Independent Cavalry Volunteers, Carmichael's Independent Cavalry Volunteers, O'Harnett's Independent Cavalry Volunteers, and Dollins' Independent Cavalry Volunteers, being the entire cavalry force of the army corps of the Tennessee and District of West Tennessee, except the First Ohio Cavalry, belonging to Major-General Thomas' division. He will immediately assign one company of cavalry to each of the division commanders as an escort. Company A, Fourth Illinois Cavalry, will remain on detached service at these headquarters. All reports and returns required by existing order, and requisitions for supplies will be made through him.

By command of Maj. Gen. U. S. Grant :

JNO. A. RAWLINS,
Assistant Adjutant-General.

---

* Revoked June 20.

CORINTH, *June* 12, 1862.

Major-General McCLERNAND, *Bethel :*

It is reported that some 500 rebel cavalry are marching on Decaturville, Decatur County, to burn the cotton at that place. The gunboat Robb has been ordered down the river for its protection. You will move a sufficient cavalry force, with an infantry and artillery reserve, from Jackson or vicinity in the direction of Decaturville to cut off their retreat. If you capture any of these incendiaries you will order a commission to try them and immediately carry into execution the sentence. Give them summary justice.

Move up to Jackson any part of your division you may require there.

H. W. HALLECK.

CAMP NEAR BOONEVILLE, *June* 12, 1862.

Major-General HALLECK:

A spy whom I sent some days ago to Okolona has just returned. The enemy is scattered along the whole road from Columbus to Tupelo, 16 miles below Guntown. They are disorganized, mutinous, and starving. He reports the woods full of deserters belonging to the northern counties of Mississippi. Nearly the whole of the Tennessee, Arkansas, and Kentucky troops have left. A large rear guard has been strung along perpendicular to the road for 20 miles, driving the stragglers and all the cattle of every description before them. The spy reports that the whole army is utterly demoralized and ready to throw down their arms; the Alabama troops have heard of Wood's and Negley's movements and are clamorous to go home. From all accounts I do not doubt the utter disintegration of Beauregard's army. A small rear guard is at Tupelo, 16 miles south of Guntown, and the nearest troops to us of the enemy. My command is now encamping here and will be in position by sunset.

JNO. POPE,
Major-General.

HEADQUARTERS ARMY OF THE MISSISSIPPI,
Near Danville, June 12, 1862.

Major-General HALLECK :

If any portion of Beauregard's army has left this country, except the numerous deserters who have returned to their homes, the testimony of agents and deserters is worthless. I myself do not doubt that of what is left of his army two-thirds are now scattered along the road to Columbus, for 60 miles, in no condition for service anywhere. Beauregard may possibly have 35,000 reliable troops, though I consider that a large estimate, but they are fully occupied in securing his rear, protecting the artillery and supplies, and preventing the entire dispersion of the remainder. Without abandoning everything they have except their arms no considerable portion of them can now be transferred elsewhere. Such, at least, is my opinion from all the information I can obtain.

JNO. POPE,
Major-General.

HEADQUARTERS ARMY OF THE MISSISSIPPI,
Near Danville, June 12, 1862.

Brig. Gen. A. ASBOTH :

You will take post with your brigade and battery of artillery at Rienzi. As you will probably occupy that position for some time you will be careful to select a strong position for your command, and throw up such earthworks as may be necessary to enable you to make a vigorous defense against any assault until the troops from this place can be advanced to your support. The cavalry is posted in front of you as follows : At Blackland one battalion, with a strong picket at Baldwyn; one battalion at Booneville, with a strong picket at the lower crossing of Twenty Mile Creek, and one cavalry regiment at Jacinto. I send you a sketch* of the country, exhibiting the position of the forces. The commanding officers are instructed to keep you informed of all matters of importance which may become known to them. You will keep me advised fully and frequently of all matters pertaining to your command, and transmit any important news from the cavalry advance by telegraph. I have directed a telegraph operator to report to you, and open an office at Rienzi. Although there is little to be apprehended from a flying and demoralized enemy, I nevertheless enjoin upon you the utmost vigilance. You will keep your command well in hand, and adopt every precaution usual in the face of an enemy.

I am, general, respectfully, your obedient servant,

JNO. POPE,
Major-General, Commanding.

[JUNE 12, 1862.—For Halleck to Stanton, in reference to Beauregard's movements and operations in Arkansas, West Tennessee, North Mississippi, and against Vicksburg, see Series I, Vol. XVI, Part II, p. 14.]

HEADQUARTERS RESERVES, *Camp Bethel, June* 12, 1862.
Brig. Gen. J. A. LOGAN, *Commanding First Division :*

GENERAL : It is reported that some 500 rebel cavalry are marching on Decaturville for the purpose of burning the cotton at that place. The gunboat Robb has been ordered down to prevent it. Although doubting the accuracy of the report as to the existence and movement of such a body of cavalry, yet in order to render compliance with instructions from general headquarters and to meet such a contingency you will immediately cause a detachment of cavalry, supported by infantry and artillery, to move from Jackson in the direction of Decaturville under instructions to cut off the retreat of the enemy and capture him. As distance, character of road, and the importance of rapid movements will make cavalry the most efficient arm of force in the execution of this enterprise you are at liberty to increase the cavalry now at Jackson by transferring a portion of that here to it.

If either you or the officer in immediate command at Jackson should have information showing the inutility and needlessness of sending infantry and artillery, or either, with the cavalry you are at liberty to dispense with both or either of these arms. If you should capture incendiaries of the class described you will immediately order a military commission to try them and promptly execute the sentence of the court, even if it be the extreme penalty of death.

Whatever force may form the expedition will return upon executing its object, or upon proving the report upon which it is founded to be untrue.

JOHN A. McCLERNAND,
Major-General, Commanding.

* Not found.

POST-OFFICE DEPARTMENT, APPOINTMENT OFFICE,
Washington, June 12, 1862.

A. H. MARKLAND, Esq.,
    Special Agent Post-Office Department:
(To be forwarded from Nashville, Tenn.)

SIR: The occupation of Memphis by the United States forces will probably result in changing the transit of military supplies and mails from the Tennessee River to the Mississippi, and via Memphis and Charleston Railroad. In this expectation, as well as for the immediate accommodation of the troops and citizens at Memphis and vicinity, it will be desirable to reopen that office at an early date. It is expected that Col. Lucian Buttles, now at Columbus, Ohio, will be invited to take temporary charge of that office (under your general supervision) until a fit candidate, approved of by Governor Johnson, shall offer for the place.

For the present, military transportation will be employed as heretofore from Cairo, and the Cairo postmaster should be advised by you or by the commanding officer at Memphis of the regiments which will receive mail matter at Memphis in case the entire mails are not sent that way.

Your experience will indicate the further action to be taken for the proper re-establishment of mail service to Memphis. Your past action has been generally warmly approved by the Department.

Very respectfully, your obedient servant,
JOHN A. KASSON,
First Assistant Postmaster-General.

GENERAL ORDERS, }   HDQRS. DEPT. OF THE MISSISSIPPI,
No. 33.   }   *Corinth, Miss., June* 12, 1862.

*   *   *   *   *   *   *

II. The District of West Tennessee will include all that portion of the State west of the Tennessee River and Forts Henry and Donelson.

By command of Major-General Halleck:
J. C. KELTON,
Assistant Adjutant-General.

ORDERS, }   HEADQUARTERS FIFTH DIVISION,
No. 39. }   *Newland's, June* 12, 1862.

The First Brigade will march forward about 12 miles and select a good camping ground on the waters of Spring Creek.

The Third Brigade will move forward about 8 miles and select good ground for camp on the west side of Porter's Creek.

The Second Brigade will move forward about 10 miles and camp on east side of Porter's Creek.

General Hurlbut's division will move its camp forward to the large fields about 3 miles from Newland's, with strong advance guard thrown forward, and will send an expedition toward Jonesborough. More attention must be paid on the march, especially as to the train. Each regimental quartermaster must be with his regimental train and stay with it.

The brigadier will make frequent rests and assure himself against gap in the column, and if any soldier is found in a wagon the teamster will be fined $1, and any soldier who puts his gun in a wagon must be severely punished.

The wagon guards must march by its side, armed and ready to defend the train.

By order of Maj. Gen. W. T. Sherman:

> J. H. HAMMOND,
> *Assistant Adjutant-General.*

ORDERS, }   HEADQUARTERS FIFTH DIVISION,
No. 40. }   *Camp, Spring Creek, June* 12, 1862.

General Denver and Colonel McDowell will march as early as possible in the morning, June 13, and take position respectively on the right and left of the State Line road where it crosses the second branch of Spring Creek, 1½ miles in advance of these headquarters.

General Hurlbut, with one brigade, will at once occupy General Denver's present camp, at Foster's, on the west bank of Porter's Creek. The rest of his command will remain on the Hatchie until the division train arrives, when all of his troops will move by easy marches on the State Line road to Grand Junction.

By order of Maj. Gen. W. T. Sherman:

> J. H. HAMMOND,
> *Assistant Adjutant-General.*

WASHINGTON, *June* 13, 1862.

Col. CHARLES ELLET, JR.,
     Commander of Ram Fleet, opposite Memphis:

The appointments of Dr. Roberts as fleet surgeon and Dr. Lawrence as assistant have been made and forwarded to you by mail, via Cairo. I am glad to learn that you are not entirely disabled, and hope you may be able to give the finishing stroke to the enemy at Vicksburg. Please send me by mail a full description of the vessels composing your fleet; its armament, force, equipment, and where you prepared it, and the cost, suitable for a report to Congress.

> EDWIN M. STANTON,
> *Secretary of War.*

HEADQUARTERS RESERVES, *Camp Bethel, June* 13, 1862.
Maj. Gen. H. W. HALLECK, *Corinth:*

General Wallace reached railroad station on Memphis and Ohio Railroad, 11 miles from Memphis, on the 12th instant. He reports a great scarcity of water from Bolivar to Somerville; chiefly wheat and corn fields on the way. In some districts no cotton burned, and in others nearly all. He chased a party of cotton-burners several miles; captured some horses and equipments, but no victims. Bridges toward Jackson, probably meaning Humboldt, burned. Road from station to Memphis in running order. Saved a passenger and box car and prevented bridge across Wolf River from being burned. Had sent a hand-car to Memphis, and understands there are three locomotives and probably freight cars in Memphis. Was sending his wagons to Memphis for supplies. I am communicating with Bolivar by telegraph. Shall I move my headquarters to Jackson, a more central and convenient point?

> JOHN A. McCLERNAND,
> *Major-General, Commanding.*

POPE'S HEADQUARTERS,
June 13, 1862.

Major-General HALLECK:

General Asboth reports to me from Rienzi that the woods and swamps east of him are swarming with deserters from the enemy. They are making their way homeward. What is to be done with them? Had they not better be suffered to go? It would take reams of blanks to administer oaths to them. I have not hitherto meddled with them. Thousands have passed on their way home, and as many more are coming every day. They endeavor to pass without coming into camp.

JNO. POPE,
Major-General.

—————

CORINTH, *June* 14, 1862.

Major-General POPE:

I think it would be well to make as many of the enemy give their paroles as possible; still it would not be worth while to pursue those who have deserted and are on their way home. I would come to see you, but have for several days been confined to my tent with the "Evacuation of Corinth."

H. W. HALLECK.

—————

U. S. STEAMER SWITZERLAND,
Before Memphis, June 15 [1862].—Via Cairo, 18th.

Hon. E. M. STANTON,
Secretary of War:

SIR: I have received your dispatch informing me of your appointment of Dr. Roberts as surgeon and Dr. Lawrence as assistant surgeon of my fleet, and requesting a detailed report concerning the rams for the last few days. After receiving my wound my mind was not capable of transacting business. Since then great nervous prostration, with pain and fever, have rendered me entirely incapable of mental labor. I now have measles superadded. I will prepare the report you ask for as soon as I am able to dictate it, which I hope will be in the course of two or three days.*

I did not send a detachment to White River to act in conjunction with the gunboats, as Commander Davis requested. Brown, the commander, was not willing to receive my co-operations unless I placed my vessels under the command of one of his officers. This, of course, I could not consent to do. Our success at Memphis was by acting independently.

Mr. Brooks has arrived with supplies for my fleet.

Respectfully,

CHAS. ELLET, JR.,
Commanding Ram Fleet.

—————

HDQRS. FIFTH DIVISION, ARMY OF THE TENNESSEE,
La Grange, Tenn., June 15, 1862.

General LEW. WALLACE, *Memphis, Tenn.:*

SIR: I arrived here with my whole division yesterday, and General Hurlbut is at Grand Junction to-day.

—————————————————————————————
* See Series I, Vol. X, Part I, pp. 906-913, 925-927.

I will start working parties to repair the Memphis and Charleston Railroad immediately, and would like you to examine the Somerville Branch and meet us at Moscow to-morrow with any hand cars that can be found.

I would be obliged to you if you would give me such information as you possess of the position of yours and McClernand's troops.

Respectfully, your obedient servant,

W. T. SHERMAN,
Major-General.

HEADQUARTERS FIFTH DIVISION,
June 15, 1862.

Brigadier-General DENVER,
    Commanding Third Brigade:

SIR: You will march with your command early to-morrow morning on the State Line road to Moscow, examine into the state of damages on the Memphis and Charleston road where it crosses the valley of Wolf River, and do all things possible to restore it to a running condition as soon as possible, to which end you are authorized to call upon planters in the neighborhood for negroes, oxen, wagons, or whatever is necessary to a speedy restoration of the road.

Two companies of Dickey's cavalry will be ordered to report to you this evening for orders.

By order of Maj. Gen. W. T. Sherman:

J. H. HAMMOND,
Assistant Adjutant-General.

HDQRS. FIFTH DIVISION, ARMY OF THE TENNESSEE,
La Grange, Tenn., June 15, 1862.

Brig. Gen. STEPHEN A. HURLBUT,
    Commanding Fourth Division, Grand Junction:

SIR: The chief purpose of our being here is to cover the reconstruction of the Memphis and Charleston Railroad, so as to open up communication from Corinth by way of Jackson, Grand Junction, &c., to Memphis. To this end I have called on the planters here for a force to repair two pieces of trestle-work destroyed here, and to-morrow General Denver will move forward to Moscow to commence the repairs there, and in anticipation of your arrival at Grand Junction I instructed Mr. Smith, an extensive planter there, to call upon his neighbors for a force adequate to repair the road up till he meets a party coming down.

I have already had a messenger at Bolivar, who reports two regiments of Lew. Wallace's command there under command of Colonel Sanderson, but his information about the railroad and telegraph repairs is so scant that I wish you would send up another party on that especial business and to urge forward telegraph as rapidly as possible. I look to you to picket strongly the Ripley road to the southeast and the Holly Springs road at Davis' Mill; also at once open a direct road from your camp to La Grange, if there be not already one.

By order of Maj. Gen. W. T. Sherman:
    I am, with respect,

L. M. DAYTON,
Lieutenant and Aide-de-Camp.

P. S.—I sent to Somerville, where I supposed Lew. Wallace to be.

W. T. S.

HEADQUARTERS RESERVE CORPS,
Bethel, Tenn., June 15, 1862.

Maj. Gen. LEW WALLACE, *Commanding Third Division:*

GENERAL: Your dispatch dated June 12, 1862, announcing your safe arrival at Union Station, was received last evening by courier. I am directed by General McClernand to say that he congratulates you on the success of your expedition and its safe arrival at a point where you can readily reach supplies, you having been advised by a previous dispatch to draw your supplies for that part of your command from Memphis as soon as it was practicable to do so. To-day we are moving our headquarters to Jackson, at which point you will communicate with me by telegraph from the nearest point. At present the telegraph is working to Bolivar.

C. T. HOTCHKISS,
Acting Assistant Adjutant-General.

HDQRS. FIFTH DIVISION, ARMY OF THE TENNESSEE,
La Grange, Tenn., June 16, 1862.

Brig. Gen. STEPHEN A. HURLBUT, *Grand Junction:*

GENERAL: Yours of this morning has been received and read to the general, who is quite unwell and trying to keep quiet. He is glad to know that you have got through so well. Forage you must obtain by purchase from the people of the country; give receipts for the articles taken, which the owner will hand to the division quartermaster and receive vouchers. We can send you a portion of our train to furnish subsistence until communication opens.

General Denver has moved his entire brigade up to Moscow, where he will attend to the repairs of the road.

Move your cavalry and one of your brigades this afternoon toward Holly Springs; take none but the best marching men that you have and as little baggage as possible. Go 10 miles to-night, and to-morrow morning, starting very early, move 15 miles, reaching Holly Springs at 10 o'clock to-morrow morning. General Morgan L. Smith and Dickey's cavalry will move at the same time.

Destroy, if not already destroyed, an important trestle-work which you will find below Holly Springs.

General M. L. Smith will receive similar instructions, and will be directed to meet the commander whom you delegate to carry out these orders at 10 o'clock to-morrow morning at the depot in Holly Springs. When the brigades come together they will act in concert and the senior officer will assume the command, but when the objects are effected the troops will return, each command under its own leader.

General Wallace has gone on to Memphis. Send one section of artillery, picked, with an extra team to each gun.

Very respectfully, your obedient servant,

J. H. HAMMOND,
Assistant Adjutant-General.

HDQRS. FIFTH DIVISION, ARMY OF THE TENNESSEE,
La Grange, Tenn., June 16, 1862.

Brig. Gen. MORGAN L. SMITH, *Commanding First Brigade:*

GENERAL: The general commanding directs me to say that the objects and intentions discussed this morning by him and you will be carried out. General Hurlbut has been instructed to detach his cavalry and one brigade to march 10 miles to-night and 15 in the morning, so as to reach Holly Springs depot at 10 o'clock to-morrow morning. He will take one picked section of artillery. Your instructions are nearly the same as his. You will select your best marching troops and as little baggage as possible. Use your own judgment as to artillery, but the general advises that you take only one section, and that the best, and put to it two extra horses to facilitate movements in case of rough roads. Endeavor to reach Holly Springs at 10 a. m. to-morrow and meet General Hurlbut's troops at the depot there.

After the junction, and until the trestle-work below the town is destroyed and the object of the expedition effected, the troops will act in concert and be under the command of the senior officer present. When the return commences they will march under their own officers.

I have the honor to be, very respectfully, yours,

J. H. HAMMOND,
Assistant Adjutant-General.

HDQRS. FOURTH DIV., ARMY OF THE TENNESSEE,
On Scott's Creek, June 16, 1862.

Brig. Gen. J. C. VEATCH,
Commanding Second Brigade, Fourth Division:

GENERAL: I am directed by General Hurlbut, commanding division, to accompany Special Orders, No. 107, inclosed,* with instructions as follows:

To take none but the best marching men and as little baggage as possible. At Holly Springs, at 10 o'clock to-morrow morning, General Morgan L. Smith and Dickey's cavalry will meet you. The brigades coming together will act in concert, the senior officer assuming command.

You will destroy, if it be not already destroyed, an important trestle-work which you will find below Holly Springs.

When the object of the expedition is effected the troops will return, each brigade or command under its own leader.

I have the honor to be, general, very respectfully, your obedient servant,

HENRY BINMORE,
Assistant Adjutant-General.

HALLECK'S HEADQUARTERS, *June 17, 1862.*

Hon. E. M. STANTON:

The railroad east has been repaired to near Tuscumbia, and troops are at work from that point to Decatur; it is open to the north as far as Trenton, 84 miles, and to the west via Jackson to La Grange, within 49 miles of Memphis. General Quinby is working south from Columbus, and is reported to be within 30 miles of Trenton. Our troops are in possession of the road from Humboldt to Memphis, but cannot yet ascertain its condition. The repair of captured locomotives and cars is progressing rapidly. I am mounting our heavy siege artillery in batteries, so as to enable us to hold this place with a smaller force and to send a part of our troops elsewhere.

H. W. HALLECK,
Major-General.

---

* Not found.

HDQRS. FIFTH DIVISION, ARMY OF THE TENNESSEE,
La Grange, Tenn., June 17, 1862.

Brig. Gen. J. W. DENVER,
Commanding Third Brigade, Moscow:

GENERAL: The general is unwell, but has read your letter. He directs me to say that you can use discretion in making the repairs, but that in forage and provisions the usual custom must be adhered to, viz, give vouchers payable after the war on proof of loyalty. You can explain that the people on the road having permitted the destruction of property must now put up with the inconvenience of our presence while repairing the injury.

Continue to use every precaution against surprise and to learn all that is possible about the country and roads.

General Smith, of this division, and one brigade of Hurlbut's division have gone to Holly Springs. They marched light, each with one section of artillery and extra horses. They were to meet at the depot in Holly Springs at 10 o'clock this morning and jointly to destroy trestlework and bridge or to otherwise render the railroad impassable to the enemy at that point; after that, to return to their respective camps at Grand Junction and this place.

The train from Bolivar arrived last night, but brought no mail or news of any kind. When the regular trains will arrive it is impossible to say, but it will be soon.

There is no further news from Richmond. The town is quiet and the people apparently well satisfied with the conduct of our men. The greater part of Captain Smith's train is up and the remainder is expected to-morrow.

I have signed the requisitions.

Very respectfully, your obedient servant,

J. H. HAMMOND,
Assistant Adjutant-General.

BOLIVAR, *June* 17, 1862.

Maj. Gen. JOHN A. MCCLERNAND:

General Sherman's troops are in Grand Junction and on the road to Holly Springs. The road in good order to Grand Junction.

W. L. SANDERSON,
Colonel, Commanding Post.

HEADQUARTERS DISTRICT OF THE MISSISSIPPI,
Columbus, Ky., June 17, 1862.

Col. JAMES R. SLACK,
Commanding U. S. Forces, Memphis, Tenn.:

COLONEL: The Crescent City has at this moment arrived from Memphis, and by her your dispatch of the 15th is received.* I fully appreciate the difficulties of your position, and wish it was in my power to send you a sufficient force to enable you to overcome them at once and effectually. I have been waiting for the last week for a transport by which to send you five companies of cavalry from this place. The Crescent City will start with them so soon as they can be placed on board and the steamer be coaled.

---

* Not found.

I fully approve your course so far. Be mild but firm, and do not by any means yield your position on the currency question. This policy, if adopted in all the places we occupy in which the Confederate money has obtained circulation by forcing its immense volume within narrow limits, will finally cause the bubble to burst and help to open the eyes of the reflective people of the South to see not only the hopelessness but also the wickedness of their cause.

The insubordination of Colonel Fitch has become too marked and is too clearly intentional to be longer tolerated without serious injury to the service, and it must be instantly checked and punished with even more severity than it would be necessary to show were he a private soldier instead of holding the commission and exercising the functions of the colonel of a regiment. You will if possible send an order of arrest after Colonel Fitch, but if that be not advisable or practicable you will place him in arrest immediately on his return from the expedition undertaken by him in direct violation of your orders.

I am, colonel, very respectfully, your obedient servant,

I. F. QUINBY,
Brigadier-General Volunteers, Commanding District.

[JUNE 17, 1862.—For Johnson to Halleck, see Series I, Vol. XVI, Part II, p. 36.]

CORINTH, *June* 18, 1862.

General W. S. ROSECRANS:

General Nelson seems to be very apprehensive of an attack by Price and Van Dorn from Fulton. Post yourself as to roads and be ready to operate on their flank if they should advance toward Iuka or Tuscumbia. General C. S. H. has been ordered to report to you.

H. W. HALLECK,
Major-General.

HEADQUARTERS ARMY OF THE MISSISSIPPI,
June 18, 1862.

Major-General HALLECK, *Corinth, Miss.:*

Your dispatch received and directions will be attended to.

A guide named Austin left here for Corinth, who knows that country. Please ask Colonel Thom or Major Key to have inquiries made for him there. Please also send down by C. S. H. the positions of your troops east of us. We have information that the rebel rear is covered by all his cavalry massed under Chalmers, base at Tupelo, and hovering around Baldwyn and in the Tippah Hills, west of Blackland. General Elliott knows the Fulton and Iuka road. He says there is a creek 15 miles south of Iuka which is a very strong line of defense.

W. S. ROSECRANS,
Brigadier-General, Commanding.

HEADQUARTERS THIRD DIVISION, RESERVE,
Memphis, Tenn., June 18, 1862.

Captain HOTCHKISS, *Acting Assistant Adjutant-General:*

SIR: On the 16th instant I dispatched my cavalry, scouting from Union Depot toward Germantown, a village 13 miles distant from that point, negroes having informed me that rebel troops had encamped there. At night the party returned, and Captain Burbridge, commanding, informed me that as his advance guard went into the town the enemy's pickets went out of it; that a large force of cavalry were encamped a short distance off; that Union men living in the place had informed him that the force was the advance guard of a heavy body of troops then marching from Holly Springs and other points contiguous, to attack me or burn Memphis.

As several days had passed without receiving dispatches from you—my messengers having gone to Bethel on the Thursday previous, and only this morning returned—I supposed my communication interrupted, and fearing the enemy had designs upon Memphis, defended at the time by but three regiments, two companies of cavalry, and a section of artillery, I at once moved down, arriving here about noon yesterday.

Colonel Slack, commanding at this place, received the same information about the same time. A Rev. Dr. Joseph Warren, chaplain of the Twenty-sixth Regiment Missouri Volunteers, captured at Corinth but released a short time ago, reached the city yesterday and reports rebel pickets within 6 miles.

I concluded that Memphis was a place of greater importance than Union Depot, and that under the circumstances I would be justly subjected to blame if I did not go promptly to the support of Colonel Slack, whose force was hardly sufficient to resist the horde of foes within the city, much less those without. I have no doubt for my own part of the correctness of my action. There is unquestionably a rebel force within striking distance at this moment. Within the hour past citizens have given me notice that they have information of an intention on the part of Forrest and Jackson to make a raid on the town to-night to destroy, if possible, the Government stores now unladen and unloading on the levee in vast quantities. At the same time I was informed that the Government property on the levee was in danger of being burned by the rebels infesting this city. To confirm my opinion, also, since my arrival I have ascertained that there is a scheme on foot to smuggle salt, supplies, clothing, &c., through to the rebel army. Colonel Slack had not the means to stop it. I hardly know whether I have, but will try.

As to the Memphis and Ohio Railroad, I wrote you its condition. The 11 miles of it intact from Union Depot to this city I can as effectually guard from the city as to it.

The government of the city I have not assumed, nor will I until so ordered. Military direction for the security of the post is all I have undertaken.

Very respectfully,

LEW. WALLACE,
General, Third Division.

ORDERS, }   HDQRS. FIFTH DIV., ARMY OF THE TENNESSEE,
No. 43. }   *La Grange, Tenn., June 18, 1862.*

The commanding general must call attention to the duties of officers and men toward the slaves. The well-settled policy of the whole army now is to have nothing to do with the negro. "Exclude them from camp" is General Halleck's reiterated order. We cannot have our trains encumbered by them, nor can we afford to feed them, and it is deceiving the poor fellow to allow him to start and have him forcibly driven away afterward. For these and many good reasons the general now especially directs the colonels of regiments, captains of companies, and regimental quartermasters to give their personal attention to this matter, to remove all such now in camp, and to prevent any more from following our camp or columns of march.

The laws of Congress command that we do not surrender back to the master a fugitive slave. That is not a soldier's business nor is it his business to smuggle him away. Let the master and slave look to the civil authorities and not to us. Also the laws of war make the property of the enemy liable to confiscation if used for warlike purposes, such as horses and wagons hauling stores, slaves making forts, &c. In such cases the commanding officer would rightfully appropriate his labor through the quartermaster and let the title to freedom be tried as soon as a proper civil tribunal can be reached.

If wagon-masters or teamsters carry away in their wagons runaway negroes it is made the duty first of the regimental quartermaster, next of the brigade quartermaster, and last of any commissioned officer, who will cause them to be summarily turned out and the facts reported to headquarters, that the actual offender may be punished by fine and imprisonment as he deserves.

By order of Maj. Gen. W. T. Sherman:

J. H. HAMMOND,
Assistant Adjutant-General.

ORDERS, } HDQRS. FIFTH DIVISION, ARMY OF THE TENNESSEE,
No. 44. }   *La Grange, Tenn., June 18, 1862.*

Too much looseness exists on the subject of foraging. The articles of war make it almost a capital offense for an officer or soldier to pillage, which means taking private property for his own use. It makes no difference if that property be of friend or enemy. Pillaging demoralizes the soldier, allows him to straggle from his ranks and neglect his duty, which in many cases heretofore have proved fatal to whole armies. The general can communicate to any officer the history of many such cases.

When an army moves in an enemy's country it is entitled to draw from that country within limits certain articles of forage and provisions, but as it is a delicate right it must be exercised by as few as possible. Brigade quartermasters needing forage will apply to their commanders for suitable escorts to the wagon train, and will accompany it themselves, and will use all possible forbearance, explaining to the party the necessity, and giving a receipt for quantity and price with a promise to pay at the pleasure of the United States on proof of loyalty at the time; certificate not transferable. In meritorious cases the division quartermaster may pay cash. All forage and provisions thus taken must be taken up on the usual property returns, giving the date and name of the party, that the transaction may be traced in the future settlement of accounts. The regimental quartermaster of the cavalry and the acting quartermaster of batteries of artillery may give receipts and instruct the parties to carry them to the division quartermaster, who will give the formal account. No other persons than those above specified can lawfully take or appropriate private property, except contraband of war, arms, ammunition, &c., which it is the duty of the provost-marshal to collect and deliver to the ordnance officer.

[By command of Maj. Gen. W. T. Sherman:

J. H. HAMMOND,
Assistant Adjutant-General.]

HDQRS. FIFTH DIVISION, ARMY OF THE TENNESSEE,
La Grange, Tenn., June 19, 1862.

General HALLECK, *Corinth:*

The expedition sent to Holly Springs is now returning, having scattered all the loose fragments of the enemy and pushed them toward Grenada, doubtless their center for this field of operations. I will report more in detail when the columns come in. The quiet of a New England Sabbath prevails at La Grange, and our men are pretty well behaved.

There is a point on Wolf River, 6 miles south of Grand Junction, where the Mississippi Central crosses, where there is a good road bridge and three large mills (Davis'). I am satisfied the point from which I can best cover the road lies west of this, and I think we should burn these mills and several of the bridges by which guerrilla parties could dash in and out on this part of the road. Of course I know you do not want any destruction of private property, unless the public service demands it. In the case of Davis' mills I think they should be utterly destroyed.

The people here are known to be secesh, but thus far have made not the least manifestation of it. There are very many highly intelligent and influential men residents of this place.

W. T. SHERMAN,
Major-General.

HDQRS. FIFTH DIVISION, ARMY OF THE TENNESSEE,
La Grange, Tenn., June 19, 1862.

General HALLECK, *Corinth, Miss.:*

Bridges as far as Moscow will be done to-morrow night. I think Grand Junction should be occupied by a small force detached from Bolivar, and that my forces be limited from Moscow to Memphis, in which case I would leave some small guards along the road and take post with my whole force at some point about 25 miles east of Memphis and 4 or 5 miles south of the railroad, commanding Holly Springs on the one hand and Hernando on the other. I will send an expedition to Hernando and break that road at some point south of Hernando, so as to prevent an attempt to run a superior force by cars between me and Memphis. We have provisions on hand to include the 30th instant, and I can easily send into Memphis and have a supply come out and meet me in season. The breaks west of Moscow are all trivial and we can repair as fast as we march, viz, 10 miles a day.

W. T. SHERMAN,
Major-General.

WASHINGTON, *June* 19, 1862.

Major-General POPE, *Saint Louis:*

I am glad to learn from Mr. Horton that you are at Saint Louis to-day. If your orders will admit, and you can be absent long enough from your command, I would be glad to see you at Washington.

EDWIN M. STANTON.

SAINT LOUIS, *June* 20, 1862.

SECRETARY OF WAR:

I leave for Washington in the morning.

JNO. POPE,
Major-General.

SAINT LOUIS, *June* 20, 1862.

Major-General HALLECK:

The Secretary of War telegraphs me that he desires to see me in Washington for a day or two if it will not interfere with your plans by going. I may be detained a few days longer, not more than that. Shall I go? Please answer immediately.

JNO. POPE,
Major-General.

CORINTH, *June* 20, 1862.

Hon. E. M. STANTON,
Secretary of War, Washington, D. C.:

Our forces under Major-General Sherman have occupied Holly Springs, pushing his cavalry as far south as the Tallahatchie River and destroying several railroad bridges. The enemy having appeared in considerable force he fell back to Holly Springs. From captured telegrams it was ascertained that the machinery for manufacturing arms at that place has been removed to Atlanta, Ga. Railroad will be opened to Memphis by Monday and to Columbus by Wednesday of next week. It is reported that Beauregard turned over his command to Bragg on the 15th, but all deserters and negroes say that no troops have been sent south or east. This is positively asserted by a servant of the Confederate master of transportation, who left the enemy's headquarters at Tupelo on Sunday last.

H. W. HALLECK,
Major-General.

HDQRS. FIFTH DIVISION, ARMY OF THE TENNESSEE,
La Grange, Tenn., June 20, 1862.

General HALLECK, *Corinth, Miss.:*

I am afraid of being caught on the question of rations. My orders were for twenty days' from Chewalla. This may prove a little short, but must last till the 30th. I have, say, 14,000 men, including Hurlbut, who eat near 20 wagon loads a day. It is 50 miles to Memphis direct and 65 around by Somerville, the only safe way for a small escort. It will take seven days at the best for a wagon train to make the round trip. I think I can get the track through in all next week, but it is a blind chance, too uncertain to risk, as my facilities for work and progress are of the commonest kind. If you would send me a telegraphic order to the commanding officer at Memphis to work out to meet us our progress would be double. I can send such an order through by courier.

Might it not be well for me to move the bulk of my division half way in, then establish our system of supplies, and return to this neighborhood?

You know that Holly Springs is some 10 miles nearer Memphis than the Junction, and all roads to and from North Mississippi center in

Holly Springs.   We should either hold Holly Springs or select a point whence it could not threaten our road.   We can never expect to be advised of the movements of our enemy, because all the people are with them in heart; we can only endeavor to anticipate them.   I don't think there are 50 organized secesh within 30 miles, but there will be, and this is not the point where the whole road can be guarded.

Am I to understand your telegram of to-day that I hold the bulk of my division in front of the Junction, or merely take it as one of the points under my protection?

The bridges here, and I suppose at Moscow, are done, and my working parties must push west, and the want of provisions may also compel me to move the bulk of the forces westward within reach of supplies. I could leave one regiment at the Junction, one at Moscow, and halt the main army, say 10 miles west of Moscow, whence it would be comparatively safe to dispatch wagons.   Would this meet your approval?

W. T. SHERMAN,
Major-General.

CORINTH, *June* 20, 1862.

Maj. Gen. WILLIAM T. SHERMAN, *La Grange:*

Your forces will guard the road at Grand Junction, while Wallace's division will probably take position near Hernando.   If possible, avoid destroying mills and road bridges.   I hope soon to be able to cut the railroads as far south as the Tallahatchie River.   The forces of McClernand and Quinby have met and are working on the last bridge.   Road to Columbus will be open to Columbus by Wednesday next; McClernand's division will then be available for other duty.   Deserters and contrabands report the main force of the enemy at Tupelo, Okolona, Aberdeen, and Fulton—headquarters at Tupelo.   They have been taking up the rails between Baldwyn and Tupelo and transporting them south, probably to complete road from Meridian to Uniontown.   Telegraph line east still down, and nothing from Washington since 17th.

H. W. HALLECK,
Major-General.

HDQRS. FIFTH DIVISION, ARMY OF THE TENNESSEE,
La Grange, Tenn., June 20, 1862

General DENVER, *Moscow:*

SIR: General Halleck, by telegraph to-day, instructs me to remain in this neighborhood and not move, as I had contemplated, to a point 25 miles from Memphis, where we could have got supplies by wagons; as it is we must push the railroad.

Please send a small guard party to the next break and tell them to use all expedition.   I will send the railroad regiment beyond.   Write me what amount of damage you have heard of, and, if you can, hire some good men to go down the road into Memphis with a letter to the commanding officer asking him to start a party working in this direction. I am still too sick to be of any use, and if you will push this road so we can get out supplies in eight or nine days I will be much obliged. Write me at length.

Yours,

W. T. SHERMAN,
Major-General.

HDQRS. FIFTH DIVISION, ARMY OF THE TENNESSEE,
La Grange, Tenn., June 20, 1862.

General McPHERSON:

General Halleck ordered me to come to this point, which will neces
sitate my utmost energy to reach Memphis with the railroad so as to
draw supplies. Can you possibly spare me a locomotive and a few
platform cars to hurry forward the work? The breaks here and at
Moscow are done, and I must push the Engineer Regiment west on the
track. The bridge at Moscow has been built by soldiers.

I am still 50 miles from Memphis—too far to haul provisions in wagons.
I have sent into Memphis some empty wagons and must order them to
come out loaded, though if possible I must get the track done in five or
six days. Instruct your train each day to go as far west as possible,
but if you give me a locomotive and cars they can meet at the Junction.

W. T. SHERMAN,
Major-General.

GENERAL ORDERS,)   HDQRS. ARMY OF THE TENNESSEE,
No. 56.   )   In Field, Corinth, Miss., June 20, 1862.

General Orders, No. 54, current series, from these headquarters, of
date June 11, 1862, brigading the cavalry of this command and assigning Colonel Dickey, Fourth Illinois Cavalry, to the command thereof, is
hereby revoked, and the cavalry will report to the commanding officers
of the several divisions to which it was attached before the publishing
of said order.

By order of Major-General Grant:

JNO. A. RAWLINS,
Assistant Adjutant-General.

SPECIAL ORDERS,)   HEADQUARTERS,
No. 98.   )   La Grange, Tenn., June 20, 1862.

The Railroad Regiment, Lieutenant-Colonel Wolfe commanding, will
proceed as early as practicable to-morrow morning along the railroad
west, and will make such repairs as may be necessary, according to
orders (verbal) already received from the general commanding.

By command of Maj. Gen. W. T. Sherman:

J. H. HAMMOND.

CORINTH, MISS., June 21, 1862.

Major-General POPE, Saint Louis:

The Secretary of War can order you to Washington if he deems
proper; but I cannot give you leave, as I think your services here of
the greatest possible importance. Your command is directly in the face
of Beauregard, and I think you should be at its head as soon as you
can leave your family.

H. W. HALLECK,
Major-General.

CORINTH, June 21, 1862.

Brigadier-General QUINBY, Columbus, Ky.:

Send all the troops you can spare to Memphis, but keep everything
that will be useful to you in opening the railroad.

H. W. HALLECK.

CORINTH, MISS., *June* 21, 1862.

Brig. Gen. WILLIAM NELSON, *Iuka :*

Trade on the Tennessee River is now free, except for articles contraband. All that is required is a license from a custom-house inspector.

J. C. KELTON,
Assistant Adjutant-General.

CORINTH, MISS., *June* 21, 1862.

Col. W. W. LOWE, *Fort Henry :*

Act of Congress prevents officers from returning slaves to owners, loyal or disloyal. General Orders, No. 3, compels you to turn the negro out of your camp as you would any other vagrant. Negroes who have given you important information concerning the enemy will be protected. Negroes who have worked for the Confederate Government are free by act of Congress.

J. C. KELTON,
Assistant Adjutant-General.

JACKSON, *June* 21, 1862.

Major-General HALLECK:

General Wallace reports that Captain Burbridge made a cavalry reconnaissance from Union Depot, 13 miles, to Germantown on the 16th instant; that as the advance cavalry entered the rebel pickets left the town, and that a large force of the cavalry were reported to be near, supported by a heavy body of troops from Holly Springs; that Colonel Slack, at Memphis, corroborates the report, and that, both hearing that Memphis was to be attacked, he had moved with his detachment from Union Depot to Memphis. I have no corroboration of this report from an officer from Grand Junction, Moscow, La Grange, or Holly Springs; it may be you are more fully advised. Shall I not let General Wallace remain in Memphis for the present, under instructions to continue to guard the roads, and if necessary to take command of post ?

JOHN A. McCLERNAND,
Major-General.

HDQRS. FIFTH DIVISION, ARMY OF THE TENNESSEE,
La Grange, Tenn., June 21, 1862.

General HALLECK, *Corinth, Miss. :*

On a further examination of your dispatches I see you want our force kept as far east as possible. I will therefore have all of Hurlbut's division here and depend on a few supplies from Corinth till the way is opened to Memphis. I will to-morrow move with my division to a point near La Fayette Station, 7 miles west of Moscow, and thence dispatch a wagon train under cavalry and infantry in for supplies. From that point I can better push the repairs, which are represented as trivial, west of Moscow, and as soon as McPherson can promise me a train I can almost undertake to push it through. At present my repair gangs have to march from break to break. When track is down and we establish our base of supplies I can in one day march back to Junction or to such covering point as your judgment will sanction.

W. T. SHERMAN,
Major-General.

CORINTH, *June* 21, 1862.

Maj. Gen. WILLIAM T. SHERMAN, *La Grange:*

Yours of to-day just received. I have anticipated it as well as I could. McPherson will be able to send you two or three car-loads of provis· ions daily. Will not this do with what you have on hand and can get in the country to supply one division till the Memphis road is opened? Of course you must move the other division where you can get supplies. You say the Memphis road will be opened by Monday; if so, you can get supplies from that place. Major reports that he has sent a large amount there. As I cannot know the condition of things as well as you do, you must exercise your own judgment; only don't move farther east than is absolutely necessary.

H. W. HALLECK.

CORINTH, *June* 21, 1862.

Maj. Gen. WILLIAM T. SHERMAN, *La Grange:*

General McPherson will load all the cars he has got with provisions for you to-morrow. As soon as the road to Columbus or Tuscumbia is opened we shall have plenty. In the mean time you must manage the best you can for supplies.

General Grant goes on to-day to take command at Memphis. I think our best line of defense will be Hernando, Holly Springs, Ripley, and Rienzi, if the health of these places should be found suitable. But we must first open the road to Memphis; until that is done, place your troops where they will be most useful and can be best supplied. Noth-ing yet from Washington. Send following to Memphis.

H. W. HALLECK,
Major-General.

CORINTH, *June* 21, 1862.

COMMANDING OFFICER, *Memphis:*

I repeat an order sent some time ago via Columbus: "Employ all your available force in repairing railroad to Grand Junction." This must be attended to in preference to anything else.

H. W. HALLECK,
Major-General.

CORINTH, *June* 21, 1862.

Gov. ANDREW JOHNSON, *Nashville:*

The enemy is driven out of all West Tennessee. East Tennessee will soon be clear of the rebels. Obstreperous women in and about Nash-ville you can easily manage. The regeneration of the entire State is not far off.

I shall call General Buell's attention to your complaints of Captain Greene, the provost-marshal, and others. If he does not afford a remedy soon I will.*

H. W. HALLECK,
Major-General.

---

* See Series I, Vol. XVI, Part II, pp. 36, 44, 47, 48.

ORDERS,)   HDQRS. FIFTH DIV., ARMY OF THE TENN.,
No. 45.)   La Grange, Tenn., June 21, 1862.

I. General Denver will detail one regiment to remain as a guard to the bridge at Moscow and to complete the work beyond there, and with the remaining regiments will move forward about 10 miles and select ground suitable for a camp to the whole division; such ground, if possible, to be south of the road and covered in great part with shade trees, water being of course the first consideration.

Colonel McDowell will move his brigade forward to the same place, beginning his march this afternoon. General Morgan L. Smith will march early to-morrow morning forward to the camp to be selected by General Denver.

II. General Hurlbut will occupy La Grange with his division. The cavalry of each division will on marches constitute its rear guard, and will summarily punish stragglers found committing depredations on private property. We may have to draw pretty freely on the inhabitants for forage and rations, but this must only be done in the manner fixed in orders.

The regiments left at La Grange will be supplied from Corinth until the road to Memphis is open, but the bulk of our army must depend on our wagons, and these must be held ready on arrival at camp to be dispatched into Memphis for supplies.

By order of Maj. Gen. W. T. Sherman:

J. H. HAMMOND,
Assistant Adjutant-General.

CORINTH, *June* 22, 1862.

Hon. E. M. STANTON,
    Secretary of War:

Beauregard left Okolona on the 15th, but whether going to Richmond, Charleston, or Chattanooga is uncertain. According to last advices only 3,000 of his troops had left. Some say they have gone to Mobile, others to Vicksburg, and others to Chattanooga.

I doubt very much if any troops have been or will be sent from here to Richmond. General Nelson reported this morning that General Price, with 10,000 to 15,000 men, was moving from Fulton toward Tusbumbia to fall on Buell's rear to cut off his supplies and destroy railroad. I have sent three divisions against him. We must either fight by the 24th or fall back. The enemy are making demonstrations in various directions to induce us to scatter our forces.

H. W. HALLECK,
Major-General.

CORINTH, *June* 22, 1862.

Brigadier-General NELSON, *Iuka:*

General Thomas' division will immediately march to your relief. General Rosecrans will also throw a force on the enemy's flank by the Jacinto road.

H. W. HALLECK,
Major-General.

HEADQUARTERS ARMY OF THE MISSISSIPPI,
June 22, 1862.

Col. J. C. KELTON,
        Assistant Adjutant-General, Corinth, Miss. : ·

We have all available cavalry on our front now covering the arc southwest around to east of us, more than 50 miles in extent, those toward the east being strong; none available for the arc southwest toward Ripley and Kossuth.

W. S. ROSECRANS,
Brigadier-General, Commanding.

CORINTH, *June* 22, 1862.

Brigadier-General ROSECRANS:

General Nelson reports that the enemy is moving to attack him at Iuka. General Thomas immediately marches to his relief.

You will push forward a division on the Jacinto road to threaten the enemy's flank; also push forward a strong cavalry force to ascertain his position and strength on the east.

H. W. HALLECK,
Major-General.

CORINTH, *June* 22, 1862.

Brigadier-General ROSECRANS:

Arrange your scouts and cavalry movements as you may deem best, and entirely independent of anything that may be done from here.

H. W. HALLECK,
Major-General.

HEADQUARTERS ARMY OF THE MISSISSIPPI,
June 22, 1862.

Major-General HALLECK, *Corinth, Miss.*:

Your dispatch received. Davis' division has been ordered to proceed to Jacinto with instructions to look for and cover the best route to strike the Fulton and Iuka road.

A battalion of cavalry left Jacinto for Fulton at 5 o'clock yesterday morning. If the enemy are moving in force we shall hear from them to-day. Colonel Sheridan has been ordered to prepare three days' rations and be ready to move as soon as the scouts come in. As both is ordered to have three days' rations cooked and ready. He is some miles from Jacinto. It does not seem to me probable that the rebel main force will move on Iuka. Does he not wish to scatter us still more ?

W. S. ROSECRANS,
Brigadier-General, Commanding.

CORINTH, *June* 22, 1862.

Maj. Gen. GEORGE H. THOMAS:

GENERAL : General Nelson telegraphs that the enemy is moving to attack him at Iuka. You will immediately march with your division to his relief and also the protection of the railroad beyond.

General Rosecrans will push a division forward on the Jacinto road to threaten the enemy's flank.

> H. W. HALLECK,
> *Major-General.*

> HDQRS. RESERVE CORPS, ARMY OF THE TENNESSEE,
> *Jackson, June 22, 1862.*

Maj. Gen. LEW. WALLACE,
 Commanding Third Division, Memphis, Tenn.:

GENERAL: Your dispatch of the 18th instant is received. The absence of further instructions from general headquarters has made it unnecessary to communicate with you for a few days past. Major-General Halleck has been advised of your entrance into Memphis and the reasons for it. You will remain there or at any point on the line occupied by your division at your discretion until otherwise directed. It is desired and expected that you will continue your efforts to prevent railroads within your reach from being injured.

A detachment General Sherman's division (General Smith's brigade) has been to Holly Springs and even beyond. No enemy is reported to be there. Maj. Gen. U. S. Grant, commanding district of West Tennessee, is on his way to Memphis, where he proposes establishing his headquarters when Memphis shall have been secured. Would not Bolivar or Grand Junction be a desirable and suitable place for your headquarters?

By command of Maj. Gen. John A. McClernand:

> C. T. HOTCHKISS,
> *Acting Assistant Adjutant-General.*

> HEADQUARTERS RESERVES,
> *Camp, Jackson, June 22, 1862.*

Maj. Gen. LEW. WALLACE, *Memphis:*

It is desirable that you should send your dispatches in future directly to me.

What are General Sherman's men doing that he has called for yours? Your purpose to repair the Mobile and Ohio Railroad is approved.

> JOHN A. McCLERNAND,
> *Major-General, Commanding.*

> MEMPHIS, *June 22, 1862.*

Major-General McCLERNAND:

SIR: Not knowing the telegraph was in operation to your headquarters I have sent dispatches to Colonel Kelton direct; I will forward copies by messenger. Availing myself of your permission, I will remain at Memphis a few days. Hard service has reduced my cavalry force to about 80 effective men, hardly enough to scour clean for guerrillas and cotton burners. At the earnest request of General Sherman I have detached two of my regiments from this post to work out on the Memphis and Charleston Railroad. Soon as General Grant arrives I will detach working detachments on the Memphis and Ohio Railroad.

> LEW. WALLACE,
> *Brigadier-General, Commanding Division.*

WASHINGTON, *June* 23, 1862.
(Received June 28.)
Major-General HALLECK, *Corinth:*

If you have not already given your attention to the practicability of making a cut-off in the rear of Vicksburg I beg to direct your attention to that point. It has been represented to the Department to be an undertaking of easy accomplishment, especially under the protection of gunboats. A dispatch to-day received from General Butler speaks of it as a project contemplated by him, but he may not have a force to spare.

EDWIN M. STANTON,
Secretary of War.

———

CORINTH, *June* 23, 1862.
Major-General GRANT, *Memphis:*

Ascertain condition of railroad from Memphis west toward Little Rock; also the means of sending supplies and re-enforcements to General Curtis. Reports heretofore received from Memphis are entirely unsatisfactory. Let me know about the supplies and means of transportation from that place.

H. W. HALLECK,
Major-General.

———

CORINTH, *June* 23, 1862.
Brigadier-General ROSECRANS:

A citizen from Columbus reports that a rebel force is moving north toward Rienzi or Kossuth with the intention of surprising and capturing your outposts. Be on your guard.

H. W. HALLECK,
Major-General.

(Similar dispatch to Ord.)

———

HEADQUARTERS ARMY OF THE MISSISSIPPI,
June 23, 1862.
Major-General HALLECK, *Corinth, Miss.:*

Your dispatch just received; will be advised at once. A regiment and battery will be sent to take post at Danville and cover the passes of the Tuscumbia, our front and right.

Our cavalry have been employed to the south and east, as I advised Colonel Kelton, so as to have very little disposable for the west and south.

Were it possible for a battalion of the First Ohio Cavalry, which Buell detached from this command, to be sent to Kossuth and Nolin's below it would secure you and our right. We cannot watch that point now, but must content ourselves with drawing in from Blackland and watching the roads near there by light patrols. If that Kossuth scout can be furnished as suggested it will be eminently useful.

W. S. ROSECRANS,
Brigadier-General, Commanding.

HEADQUARTERS ARMY OF THE MISSISSIPPI,
June 23, 1862.

General ASBOTH, *Rienzi, Miss.*:

You are informed by mail to-day that General Davis' division was at Jacinto and a regiment and battery ordered to Danville. The telegram from General Halleck to General Rosecrans would have been sent you if the line had been in working order.

A scout has been ordered from Corinth in the direction of Kossuth and Ripley, so General Rosecrans has been informed.

W. L. ELLIOTT,
Brigadier-General and Chief of Staff.

HDQRS. FIFTH DIVISION, ARMY OF THE TENNESSEE,
La Fayette Station, June 23, 1862.

Col. J. C. KELTON,
Assistant Adjutant-General, Corinth, Miss.:

SIR: The matters herein referred to, being special in their nature, I think should be addressed to you without going through the head-quarters of General Grant, now in motion for Memphis. The general and staff passed my camp this morning and will reach Memphis this evening.

On the 9th instant I received at Chewalla General Halleck's instructions by telegraph to move with my own and Hurlbut's divisions on Grand Junction, thence to detach strong working parties forward to repair the Memphis and Charleston Railroad, to use great care in securing my working parties, and to assure the inhabitants of all proper protection, &c. The bridges across the Tuscumbia and Hatchie had been destroyed by the enemy's cavalry, so I sent forward to those points Denver's brigade and Hurlbut's division, and on Wednesday, June 11, I put in motion my whole division, except the Forty-sixth Ohio left behind as a rear guard to some wagons of provisions which had not yet arrived at Chewalla.

Repairing roads as we marched, we reached Grand Junction after night of the 13th. But there was no water there for troops, and on the morning of the 14th I occupied the town of La Grange, 3 miles west of Grand Junction, with my division, and General Hurlbut encamped his on Scott's Creek, about 2½ miles south of the Junction. There were two pieces of destroyed trestle-work in the town of La Grange which I caused to be repaired as rapidly as possible, and learning that the bridge across Wolf Creek, 10 miles west, was destroyed I sent General Denver's brigade forward to repair it and to ascertain what damage was done beyond. Whilst the work was being done at La Grange and Moscow I dispatched General Veatch's brigade of Hurlbut's division and Morgan L. Smith's of mine, with all our effective cavalry, to Holly Springs, with orders for the cavalry to push on as much farther south as was prudent, and if possible to force the enemy to destroy the bridge across the Tallahatchie River. This expedition was well conducted and cleared our flanks completely of an enemy thus far. Their pickets were at Lamar, retreated, burning a trestle there. At Holly Springs there was the remains of an infantry and cavalry regiment, which escaped in cars and by the railroad. Our cavalry brought in of these about 8 prisoners—officers—whom I paroled.

Our cavalry reached the vicinity of the Tallahatchie Bridge and had quite a brisk skirmish, driving the enemy across the river, where he had cars and re-enforcements, and the officer did not deem it prudent to push his venture farther, as the men of the Fifth Ohio Cavalry have no carbines. Some of the enemy are reported as killed. We had 4 wounded, 2 of whom were doubtless mortally. They were brought some distance to the rear and sent to a farm-house.

The two brigades remained in Holly Springs two days and returned to their respective camps.

On the 21st instant the two pieces of broken trestle-work in La Grange being done, and being unable to hear definite information of breaks west of Moscow, and our stock of provisions being reported to me as expiring the 27th instead of the 30th, I determined to move forward myself from La Grange to hurry up the repairs and send into Memphis for supplies. Even if the track was done the scarcity of cars may prevent our being supplied in that way. Accordingly yesterday, the 22d, I moved forward my whole division to this point, except one regiment left at Moscow to finish up that bridge and guard it. I find two other bridges destroyed, one 3 miles west and another 3 miles east of this point. I now have strong working parties on all, and I feel confident cars may safely come through to-morrow evening. This morning, most agreeably to our surprise, a train of cars arrived at the break 3 miles west of us, from Memphis, with the Fifty-sixth Ohio Volunteers, Col. P. Kinney, with orders to co-operate with us in repairing the road. This now establishes the communication.

We know exactly what is to be done, and not a minute shall be wasted. We labor under difficulties for want of tools, tackle, &c., but I feel confident in promising a through road after to-morrow. This morning, at 3 a. m., I dispatched a heavy train of wagons for Memphis, to bring us out provisions; distance is 30 miles. They should be able to reach there and load to-morrow, and come out in two days, arriving, say, the evening of the 26th, by which date I have no doubt there will be uninterrupted communication between Corinth and Memphis, and then I can move to Coldwater, Holly Springs, Mount Pleasant, or wherever the general thinks best.

There is now great dearth of water in the country, and we have been forced to keep near the Wolf; but our expedition found excellent water in Coldwater, 5 miles north of Holly Springs.

My engineer has been so hard at work on bridges that I have not been able to compile many maps, but I have some sketches, which, at some more leisure moments, I will have him compile and send to Colonel Thom.

I am, with great respect, your obedient servant,

W. T. SHERMAN,
Major-General

HDQRS. FIFTH DIVISION, ARMY OF THE TENNESSEE,
La Fayette Station, June 23, 1862.

General HURLBUT,
Commanding Fourth Division, La Grange, Tenn.:

SIR: Remain with your whole division at or near La Grange. Don't move on Moscow. I expect after getting provisions to effect a junction with you somewhere in front of La Grange, in the neighborhood of Holly Springs. Grant went into Memphis to-day and will order Lew. Wallace out toward Hernando, which will be a threat on the flank.

Keep out your cavalry pickets well, at least to Lamar, always. I have mine to north Mount Pleasant. We must expect all sorts of ruses. I am not certain but that Tallahatchie Bridge was burned; at all events quite a break was made in the trestle near the bridge. If we are threatened we must effect a junction at some point between La Grange and Moscow. Moscow is not a suitable place. I will not remain here an hour after my provision train arrives.

I wrote you to-day where I was, and sent a letter to be forwarded to Halleck. La Grange is the most agreeable and defensible camp thus far discovered, excepting one on Coldwater near Holly Springs.

Hire through Mr. Shelton, the mayor, one or two good spies to go down and stay about Holly Springs and report to you and me any suspicious movements. I had a man who drove the buggy and met General Veatch, who can play the part well.

We are working our very best on the road and will have it done to-morrow night I hope.

My train should be back on the 26th.

Do not move in this direction unless forced, and keep out all possible spies and scouts. I will do the same, and on authentic intelligence of the approach of danger I will use all possible energy to effect a junction.

Yours,

W. T. SHERMAN,
Major-General

COLUMBIA, TENN., *June* 23, 1862.

Hon. E. M. STANTON,
Secretary of War:

Have the following information direct; believe it to be reliable: Rebel forces concentrating in Tupelo, Miss., about 60 miles below Corinth. The division and brigades commanded by Generals Hardee, Polk, Breckinridge, and Van Dorn now there. Price's division reported on the way to East Tennessee. Beauregard, Price, and Breckinridge started for Richmond. All the forces, estimated at 100,000, quite healthy; supplied with two days' bacon, two days' fresh meat, and three days' pickled beef per week, with plenty of flour, rice, sugar, molasses, and coffee. Cavalry in very bad condition; horses do not get over a quart of corn per day; great many dismounted and made to serve as infantry. One Texas regiment of cavalry lately dismounted. All the troops greatly dissatisfied, particularly Tennesseeans. If practicable, most would leave after 16th of July.

JAS. S. NEGLEY,
Brigadier-General, Commanding Post.

HEADQUARTERS ARMY OF THE TENNESSEE,
Memphis, Tenn., June 24, 1862.

Maj. Gen. H. W. HALLECK,
Commanding Department Mississippi, Corinth, Miss.:

I arrived here yesterday afternoon after a warm ride of three days, coming through from La Grange with an escort of 12 men. The entire road is in good order and a very fine one.

Affairs in this city seem to be in rather bad order, secessionists governing much in their own way. I have appointed Colonel Webster commander of the post; Lieutenant-Colonel Anthony, Twenty-third Indiana Volunteers, provost-marshal for the city, and Colonel Hillyer provost-marshal-general. In a few days I expect to have everything in good order.

I inclose you herewith report of J. A. Duble, of gunboat Conestoga, relative to the disaster of the Mound City.* The prisoners spoken of are now here, and such disposition will be made of them as you may direct. I have not been here long enough to determine the practicability of furnishing General Curtis by the way of White River; but on consultation with Captain Phelps, of the Navy, I think it can be done by preparing two light-draught steamers so that the boilers would be proof against musketry, and arming them with two howitzers on the bows. An infantry escort would have to accompany each boat, ready to take the shore and march past threatened points.

On my arrival General Wallace applied for a leave of absence. I granted it to the extent of my authority, the command being left with General Hovey, who is fully qualified to fill the place of the former commander.

U. S. GRANT,
Major-General.

HEADQUARTERS DISTRICT OF WEST TENNESSEE,
Memphis, June 24, 1862.

Brig. Gen. STEPHEN A. HURLBUT,
Commanding Fourth Division, Army of the Tennessee:

I am directed by Major-General Grant to say to you that you can compel all clergymen within your lines to omit from their church services any portion you may deem treasonable, but you will not compel the insertion or substitution of anything.

WM. S. HILLYER,
Aide-de-Camp.

GENERAL ORDERS, }   HDQRS. DIST. OF WEST TENNESSEE,
      No. 57.   }   *Memphis, June 24, 1862.*

Brigade Surg. John G. F. Holston, senior medical officer of this district, is announced medical director of the same.

Col. T. Lyle Dickey, Fourth Illinois Cavalry, is appointed chief of cavalry force of this district. All orders from him will be obeyed and all reports required by existing orders will be made to him.

By order of Major-General Grant:

JNO. A. RAWLINS,
Assistant Adjutant-General.

SPECIAL ORDERS, }   HDQRS. DIST. OF WEST TENNESSEE,
      No. 118.   }   *Memphis, Tenn., June 24, 1862.*

I. For the guidance and control of this city the following orders are published:

Col. J. D. Webster, chief of artillery and chief of staff, is appointed commander of the post. All needful rules and regulations for the government of the city will be made by him, subject to the approval of the general commanding.

---

* Not found.

Col. William S. Hillyer, aide-de-camp, is appointed provost-marshal-general for the district. All local provosts will report to him weekly and will receive instructions from him.

Lieut. Col. D. C. Anthony is appointed provost-marshal for the city of Memphis. He will report to the provost-marshal-general for instructions and assume his duties without delay.

II. The Thirty-fourth, Forty-third, and Forty-seventh Regiments Indiana Volunteers, Col. J. R. Slack commanding, will form the garrison of Memphis and will encamp east of the town.

Company A, Fourth Illinois Cavalry, Captain Osband commanding, is specially assigned to assist the provost-marshal in the performance of his duties.

All the troops in Memphis not enumerated above will immediately go into camp outside of the city on the line of the railroad to Grenada, Miss. They will also picket all the roads leading to the city from the southeast quarters and enforce such orders as have been or may hereafter be published.

*   *   *   *   *   *   *

X. The corps heretofore known as the Reserve Corps of the Army of the Tennessee is hereby dissolved.

Maj. Gen. J. A. McClernand will have immediate command of all troops occupying the country south of Union City and north of the Memphis and Charleston road and on the line of the railroads. He will make all needful rules for the protection of the different lines of road and for the preservation of order within the district commanded by him.

Tri-monthly returns will be required as heretofore. The Third Division will drop from their reports the command at Bolivar, and it will be taken up by General McClernand.

*   *   *   *   *   *   *

By order of Maj. Gen. U. S. Grant:

JNO. A. RAWLINS,
Assistant Adjutant-General.

———

[June 25, 1862.—For Halleck to Stanton, in reference to sanitary condition of the army and future movement, see Series I, Vol. XVI, Part II, p. 62.]

———

La Grange, *June 25, 1862.*

Major-General HALLECK:

My outside cavalry pickets have been driven in or fallen back. I have no doubt a heavy force is concentrating to attack us. I have called in Colonel Cushman's regiment from Grand Junction and concentrated my infantry in this town. If I am satisfied that a considerable force is approaching I shall move in the morning to Moscow to join Sherman; it is a flank movement of 10 miles, and dangerous against so large a cavalry force as the enemy is reported to have. I fear they will cut the Moscow bridge to-night, as it is only defended by a single regiment, the Seventieth Ohio. Unless I receive other orders from you I shall probably move west in the morning.

S. A. HURLBUT,
Brigadier-General.

CORINTH, *June* 25, 1862.

Brigadier-General HURLBUT:

Hold your position and telegraph to General Sherman and General Grant to re-enforce you. I will order a part of General McClernand's force from Jackson to Grand Junction to-morrow morning. Don't yield an inch unless absolutely necessary.

H. W. HALLECK,
Major-General.

CORINTH, *June* 25, 1862.

Major-General SHERMAN, *La Fayette:*

Re-enforce General Hurlbut if necessary; also call on General Grant to assist you.

H. W. HALLECK,
Major-General.

HEADQUARTERS FOURTH DIVISION, *June* 25, 1862.

Maj. Gen. WILLIAM T. SHERMAN, *Moscow, Tenn.:*

Major Ricker reports the enemy advancing on him in force, how great he cannot say. His outside pickets are driven in. I shall be ready for action. I think it is only cavalry. A negro reports that they intend to fortify at Coldwater.

I send this by messenger at 5.30 p. m.

In haste.

S. A. HURLBUT,
Brigadier-General.

LA GRANGE, *June* 25, 1862.

General HALLECK, *Corinth:*

All bridges done except the one at Moscow, which is promised to be ready for the passage of cars to-day. I trust you will order a train through from Corinth. There is a train at Memphis, but they will not permit it to come to my camp; also I have no telegraph, the machine and operator being at La Grange, and all my cavalry is guarding provision trains, so I am cut off from all communication. My provision train will be back to-morrow early. The road will then be done, and I can then take position at Coldwater (6 miles from Holly Springs) or at the Junction or at La Grange, wherever you may order.

We have vague rumors of a heavy force, 30,000 men, coming up from Grenada. I know that the Tallahatchie Bridge is destroyed; that one regiment of infantry and one of cavalry were there last Sunday; that a small detachment of cavalry came into Holly Springs and to Coldwater Creek, 6 miles this side, and then returned to the Tallahatchie, 18 miles south of Holly Springs. Cars come that far north, but no farther.

W. T. SHERMAN,
Major-General.

HDQRS. FOURTH DIV., DISTRICT OF WEST TENNESSEE,
La Grange, Tenn., June 25, 1862.

Col. W. H. W. CUSHMAN, *Commanding Grand Junction, Tenn.:*

COLONEL: Since I have sent and you have received the order of the general commanding division he has received from General Halleck dispatch ordering re-enforcements from Jackson by rail. He agrees with your suggestion to hold your force at Grand Junction as long as possible. Let the baggage train come forward and be parked near the college; throw sentries up the line of the railroad track toward La Grange, and let the engine wait and leave in the morning, taking care to keep out of the way of down train. My instructions are to hold this position at all hazards, and I rely upon you and your command, confidently, to hold them.

Respectfully, your obedient servant,

HENRY BINMORE,
Assistant Adjutant-General.

ORDERS, }
No. 46. }　　　　　　　HEADQUARTERS FIFTH DIVISION,
　　　　　　　　　　　　　　La Fayette, June 25, 1862.

The division will move to-morrow morning to Moscow. General Morgan L. Smith's brigade, in advance, will start as early as possible, to allow the whole division to reach Moscow before the intense heat of the day. He will proceed through Moscow to a point about 1½ miles beyond, and select good ground facing south and near enough Wolf River to obtain from it a supply of water.

General Denver will follow General Smith and select his camp on side of Moscow and near enough the Wolf River to obtain water heretofore.

Colonel McDowell's brigade will bring up the regiments can town of Moscow.

The chief of artillery will distribute Moscow by a road lying on Fourth Illinois Cavalry will bring

The division train and all train.

cross the Wolf River Gen. W. T. Sherman:
the north side
up th

J. H. HAMMOND,
Assistant Adjutant-General.

SPECIAL ORDERS, }
No. 101. }　　　　　　　LA FAYETTE, TENN.,
　　　　　　　　　　　　　　June 25, 1862.

The Fifty-second Indiana Volunteers will move early in the morning to the bridge, 3 miles from this place, and form a junction with the Fiftieth Ohio Volunteers, the senior officer taking command of both regiments.

These regiments will guard the bridges and road to Germantown and draw their supplies from Memphis.

Colonel McDowell, commanding Second Brigade, will detail the Forty-sixth Ohio Volunteers to remain, and with one section of artillery, detached by Major Taylor, protect the depot in La Fayette and the bridge and railroad.

By order of Maj. Gen. W. T. Sherman:

J. H. HAMMOND,
Assistant Adjutant-General.

The railroad having been broken to-day and an attack being imminent great vigilance must be exercised.

J. H. H.,
Assistant Adjutant-General.

CORINTH, VIA CAIRO, *June* 26, 1862—7.40 p. m.

Hon. E. M. STANTON,
Secretary of War:

When I took command of this department the gun and mortar boats were placed under my orders. I am led to infer from one of your telegrams that a change has been made. If so, I have never been notified of it. I received no information of the whereabouts or movements of gunboats. Under such circumstances it is impossible to co-operate. I have no official information of any of our gunboats on Arkansas, and General Curtis telegraphed yesterday that he could hear nothing of them, while a rebel gunboat is destroying large amounts of cotton on White River.

H. W. HALLECK,
Major-General, Commanding.

CORINTH, *June* 26, 1862.

Col. T. J. HAINES, *Saint Louis:*

As there is much scurvy in this army it is important that you supply ... and anti-scorbutics as plentifully as possible.

H. W. HALLECK,
Major-General.

HEADQUARTERS

Brigadier-General ROSECRANS,
Commanding Army of the Mississippi: MISSISSIPPI,
                                                        26, 1862.

GENERAL: General Hurlbut reported last night that the ... moving against him at La Grange. Push a cavalry force through ... ley toward Holly Springs to threaten their flank, and support the movement with infantry and artillery.

Very respectfully, your obedient servant,

H. W. HALLECK,
Major-General.

CORINTH, *June* 26, 1862.

General ROSECRANS:

Send two additional divisions on the road toward Holly Springs via Ripley. Hurlbut reports that Price, Van Dorn, and Breckinridge are at Coldwater with 30,000 men.

H. W. HALLECK,
Major-General.

HEADQUARTERS SECOND BRIGADE, FIRST DIVISION,
CENTRAL ARMY OF THE MISSISSIPPI,
Trenton, Tenn., June 26, 1862.

Brigadier-General QUINBY,
Commanding District of the Mississippi, Columbus, Ky.:

GENERAL: I have the honor to report my arrival at this point yesterday with the First Kansas Regiment, Seventh Wisconsin Battery, and four companies of Sixth Illinois Cavalry. I have divided the Sixty-second Illinois Regiment into three detachments and stationed them with a small cavalry force at Crockett, Kenton, and Rutherford Stations, with instructions to clear the weeds off the track between the stations, and also guard every bridge and trestle-work from Big Obion to and 3 miles south of Rutherford Station.

General Mitchell has ordered me to remain at this place with the balance of my command for the present. He refused to assign the Fifteenth Wisconsin Regiment, Colonel Heg, to my brigade temporarily, as required by instructions from your headquarters at Columbus, dated June 13, 1862.

The Second Illinois Cavalry, Eighth Kansas Regiment, and Second Kansas Battery leave this a. m. for Humboldt.

I was compelled to halt for nearly three days at South Fork of Obion River in order to send some teams back to Union City for supplies.

I will send in a consolidated report of my command in a few days.

I feel it my duty, general, to inform you that the people complain bitterly of the outrages committed by a portion of General Mitchell's brigade; they are charged with jayhawking horses, negroes, &c., from Union and disloyal citizens indiscriminately.

At Union City a foraging party under command of Captain Parrott, formerly a member of Congress from Kansas, arrested Rev. Mr. Koyle, a Union citizen of that locality, and were about to rob him of his mules and buggy, when he told them that he was then in charge of a funeral. They abused him very much, called him a d—d liar and broke open the coffin, and on discovering that it contained a corpse they told Mr. Koyle to go to hell with his d—d secession corpse. Captain Parrott did all he could to restrain the fiends, but failed. He reported the facts to General Mitchell, who declined to take any notice of the case. I have heard of other outrages equally atrocious perpetrated by these wretches. They ought to be punished or mustered out of the service to which they are a disgrace.

I have the honor to be, very respectfully, your obedient servant,

GEO. W. DEITZLER,
Colonel First Kansas, Commanding Brigade.

HEADQUARTERS ARMY OF THE MISSISSIPPI,
June 26, 1862.

General ASBOTH :

The general commanding directs that you send a regiment of infantry and battery of artillery on the Ripley road as far as Nolin's to support a cavalry force ordered through Ripley toward Holly Springs to threaten the flank of the enemy reported to be moving on La Grange. Should you require re-enforcements notify General Davis at Jacinto.

The regiment should be a strong one and under a capable commander, and his troops have three days' rations.

W. L. ELLIOTT.

HEADQUARTERS ARMY OF THE MISSISSIPPI,
June 26, 1862.

General ASBOTH, *Rienzi, Miss.:*

The left wing of this army is ordered to proceed on the Holly Springs road via Ripley. The regiment and battery ordered from your com-

mand will return from Rienzi upon the arrival of the left wing, Genera
C. S. Hamilton.

By order of General Rosecrans:

W. L. ELLIOTT,
Brigadier-General and Chief of Staff.

HEADQUARTERS ARMY OF THE MISSISSIPPI.
June 26, 1862.

General JEFFERSON C. DAVIS, *Jacinto, Miss.:*

The commanding general directs that you report to-morrow with
your division to Brigadier-General Hamilton at Rienzi. The left wing
is ordered to proceed on the Holly Springs road via Ripley, with three
days' rations in their haversacks, two days' rations and extra ammunition to follow by the train; 40 rounds ammunition per man in cartridge-
boxes, 60 rounds in knapsacks. Have wagons, spades, shovels, picks.

W. L. ELLIOTT,
Brigadier-General and Chief of Staff.

(To be forwarded from Rienzi by messenger.)

MEMPHIS, *June 26, 1862.*

General HALLECK:

There is a reported cut in railroad west of Germantown. Wires now
down for two days, with small bodies rebel cavalry through the country
burning cotton and cutting wire as fast as filled up. Additional cavalry would enable me to partially clear the country of these men. There
are five companies of the Sixth Illinois Cavalry at Humboldt and some
here. Can they all come here? Steamer for White River starts this
morning, taking two regiments to re-enforce Colonel Fitch, who will
convey them to General Curtis.

U. S. GRANT.

MEMPHIS, TENN., *June 26, 1862.*

Maj. Gen. H. W. HALLECK,
Commanding Department of the Mississippi:

GENERAL: News has just reached me, or reached me during the
night, that Jackson's forces came in on the railroad near Germantown
yesterday and captured the train with all on board, and also the wagon
train loaded with supplies for General Sherman's division; also cut the
road. Day before yesterday I heard of Jackson being 20 miles southeast from here, intending to make a raid upon this wagon train, with
a view of destroying it, at their camping place for last night. I immediately issued orders for the cavalry here to accompany this train to
their camp ground for last night, and if deemed advisable accompany
them this morning to beyond danger.

The wagon train left the evening this order was published, going out
of the city to encamp. The additional escort followed in the morning,
and with the usual cavalry stupidity took the wrong road, thus leaving
the train protected only with the escort furnished by General Sherman.
As this last force followed on after the capture it is not at all improb
able that they too have been taken.

My information is all from citizens who came in last night, and may
not be strictly reliable.

Accompanying the railroad train was a letter to yourself and one to General Sherman, which I am very sorry to have (these letters), particularly the former, fall into the hands of the rebels. Colonel Grierson, commander of the cavalry sent from here, has just returned from Germantown and discredits the reports of the capture of our trains. He says that Jackson's men have been hovering along the line of the railroad in squads burning cotton; that cotton was burned yesterday at three or four places visited by him.

An impression seems to prevail here that a force is collecting 35 miles southeast from here for the purpose of making an attack on this place and burning it.

My force now here is small, having sent two regiments to re-enforce Colonel Fitch and to protect five steamers loaded with supplies for General Curtis' command. Three steamers are now ready to start. I have had precautionary measures taken to protect the pilots from musketry.

I reported to you the effective strength of this command, but you may not have received it. As my office and quarters have been moved to the suburbs of the city, and all the records are there, I cannot now give you the exact strength. I believe the entire effective force left, after re-enforcing Colonel Fitch, is about 4,000. It seems to me that one of the divisions of the Army of the Tennessee now at Corinth should move west, so as to strengthen this point by another division. This would enable me to hold Hernando or some suitable point on the railroad to Grenada.

Very respectfully, your obedient servant,

U. S. GRANT,
Major-General.

LA GRANGE, *June* 26, 1862.

Major-General HALLECK:

The enemy have not pressed any nearer. My cavalry pickets are 6 miles out, and not disturbed last night or this morning. They are fortifying at Coldwater and impressing all the negroes. There is a strong stampede of them into my lines, and I allow them to pass north to cut off their labor. They claim that in a day or two they will be 30,000 strong, under Breckinridge, Van Dorn, and Price. Refugees say they will be compelled to make a stand there to save utter demoralization. The cavalry moving from Ripley will stampede them, if in force, especially if Wallace threatens their left. My position is strong as regards the front; we are on the right flank. McClernand's force, when it arrives, will secure my left and allow me to amass my force here. I have not heard from General Sherman to-day. We want a machine and operator here, as this one moves to-day.

S. A. HURLBUT,
Brigadier-General.

LA GRANGE, *June* 26, 1862.

Maj. Gen. JOHN A. McCLERNAND:

Your re-enforcement will be in time. There are 15,000 men between Holly Springs and Coldwater. They are fortifying and must be whipped. So, please God, there will be a fight soon.

S. A. HURLBUT,
Brigadier-General.

HDQRS. FOURTH DIV., DISTRICT. OF WEST TENNESSEE,
La Grange, Tenn., June 26, 1862.

Maj. Gen. WILLIAM T. SHERMAN, *Moscow, Tenn. :*

DEAR GENERAL : I shall not send for you unless under pressure. I think I can hold this place six hours against any force they can bring. If you hear my artillery you can start. My opinion is they are fortifying at Coldwater Creek. They have seized all the negroes they can catch. I send you Ricker's last report. My cavalry are behaving well. Unless flanked on the right they cannot hurt me much, and you must feel out that way. Rosecrans is on his way down through Ripley to flank them with a heavy force of cavalry. I expect to hear from him to-night. McClernand will send me troops by 3 p. m. to hold Grand Junction. I shall then concentrate here. My teams are in town and my infantry and artillery posted to command the southern inlets to this place. I think they are well posted and I know they will fight and fight well.

It is evident to me that this nest of thieves must be broken up, and Halleck so understands it from his movements. It will take us about ten days to get at them, as near as I can judge, but they must be cleared out or the road will not be possible to use. I am afraid this cursed move will spoil my chance for going home, which I grievously want to do. Ricker is just in. Nothing of moment in the front. I have relieved him with the other half of my cavalry. I shall keep a very careful watch, but do not now fear an attack. I dreaded a movement last night on Moscow, but it is over.

Yours,

S. A. HURLBUT,
Brigadier-General.

Negroes report that the burnt bridge over the Tallahatchie will be done to-night or to-morrow.

S. A. HURLBUT,
Brigadier-General.

———

CORINTH, *June* 26, 1862.

Major-General MCCLERNAND :

As soon as General Quinby's forces arrive at Jackson your entire division, except one regiment at Bethel and Bolivar, will move on Grand Junction or La Grange.

H. W. HALLECK,
Major-General.

———

HDQRS. RESERVE CORPS, ARMY OF THE TENNESSEE,
Jackson, June 26, 1862.

Brig. Gen. J. A. LOGAN, *Commanding, &c. :*

GENERAL : The troops to be sent by you on the cars this morning will go to Grand Junction and report for orders through their commanding officer to General Hurlbut for the purpose of supporting him in his present position at or near Grand Junction and Moscow, it not being intended that they shall be moved to any distant point without further orders from these headquarters.

By order of Major-General McClernand :

C. T. HOTCHKISS,
Acting Assistant Adjutant-General.

HEADQUARTERS RESERVES,
Jackson, June 26, 1862.

Colonel SANDERSON,
  Commanding Post at Bolivar :

COLONEL : Three regiments will move by rail from this place to Grand Junction and Moscow to-day. Their purpose is to re-enforce General Hurlbut.

You will send all the force with you except a number necessary to guard bridges, &c., under instructions to co-operate in supporting General Hurlbut.

You will be watchful and vigilant in approaching Grand Junction. Fall back on Bolivar if it should become necessary for you to retire.

Keep me continually advised of passing events.

  Yours, &c.,

JOHN A. McCLERNAND,
Major-General, Commanding.

———

HEADQUARTERS ARMY OF THE MISSISSIPPI,
June 26, 1862.

Major-General THOMAS, *Corinth, Miss. :*

Your dispatch just received. Have ordered all the cavalry we have south and west of the Mississippi Central and Ohio Railroad to move at once across the country in columns toward Ripley, and, concentrating there, push forward toward Holly Springs.

Sheridan replaces this force from the recruiting camp in rear.

Asboth sends a regiment of infantry and a battery to Nolin's, intersection of Hatchie pike and Blackland and Corinth road, to support the cavalry. Should the country south of that be clear they may advance still farther. But I do not think it advisable to send the infantry very far in that direction until we know where the rebels lay. Our flank, Davis, with six regiments and two batteries, has gone into camp 1½ miles southeast of Jacinto. His camp equipage went out to-day. He has notice to support Asboth if needed.

There can be no serious move on La Grange.

W. S. ROSECRANS,
Brigadier-General, Commanding.

———

MOSCOW, *June* 26, 1862.

General HALLECK :

I now have an operator here and communicate more to let you know that fact. My division is here; Hurlbut at La Grange, 10 miles apart, and both about the same distance from Holly Springs. I have full ten days' rations and forage on hand. I should have a good strong regiment of cavalry. All the bridges have been repaired and are guarded, the most important one here a large bridge over Wolf Creek. You have heard of the attack on the train west. The train from the east has never come west of La Grange, though all the road is done. This hot weather nearly kills our men on the march. Some are actually dead of sunstroke and very many prostrated and have to be carried in wagons. I have nothing new or authentic from Holly Springs, and my cavalry is so used up that I cannot push them out more than 7 or 8 miles.

W. T. SHERMAN,
Major-General.

Moscow, *June* 26, 1862.

General HALLECK :

On receiving your dispatch to re-enforce Hurlbut I moved my division to Moscow, where I can move promptly to the Junction or forward to Holly Springs. I left a regiment and section of artillery at La Fayette to protect two bridges and the property there. I sent forward to Germantown the Indiana Railroad Regiment to accompany the Ohio Fifty-fourth, [Fifty-sixth ?], which had come over from Memphis to assist in repairing the road. I sent a messenger to Memphis this morning with a letter to General Grant telling him that there was now a force at Holly Springs and that force must be driven away before we can expect to use the railroad here. The train out from Memphis yesterday was thrown from the track by displacing three rails and the soldiers on the train attacked by a force; the strength could not be ascertained by those who reached camp. Judging from your own accounts of the distribution of the enemy's force, will it be safe in marching on Holly Springs; attacking, should McClernand and Grant co-operate?

W. T. SHERMAN,
Major-General.

[JUNE 26, 1862.—General Pope assigned to command of Army of Virginia. See Series I, Vol. XII, Part III, p. 435.]

Moscow, *June* 26, 1862.

General McCLERNAND :

The telegraph office is removed from La Grange to Moscow, where I am with my division. The railroad bridges are all done to Memphis. If General Halleck ordered re-enforcements from you for Hurlbut's he wants them at La Grange. I have no reliable news from Holly Springs, except that there are more than 5,000 of the enemy there and more expected.

The regiments should disembark at La Grange and not the Junction, on account of water.

When will the road to Columbus be done ?

W. T. SHERMAN,
Major-General.

WAR DEPARTMENT, *June* 27, 1862.

Major-General HALLECK, *Corinth :*

No change has been made in the order respecting gunboats, that I am aware of, since I came into this Department. An act of Congress has transferred them to the Navy Department. No report was ever made to this Department by the commander of the gunboats. When Mr. Ellet had his steam-rams ready he wanted to act under your orders, or the orders of this Department, and I requested the President's permission so to direct; but he thought they should be under the command of the officer commanding the gunboats, and instructions were given accordingly. I have always thought you should have command of the gunboats, and will endeavor to procure an order to that effect.

EDWIN M. STANTON,
Secretary of War.

WAR DEPARTMENT, *June* 27, 1862.

Major-General HALLECK, *Corinth :*

The exigencies of the service, in the President's opinion, absolutely require that General Pope should be assigned a command here. It is hoped that among the number of able generals in your command that you can spare him without inconvenience. General Pope desires to have General Schuyler Hamilton and General Granger. The President hopes you will relieve them and send them here, if you can do so without injury to the service.

EDWIN M. STANTON.

MEMPHIS, TENN., *June* 27, 1862.

Maj. Gen. H. W. HALLECK, *Corinth, Miss. :*

I have sent one regiment of infantry and five companies of cavalry to beyond Germantown, in hopes of opening the railroad and telegraph. With the aid of one division from Corinth I think it practicable to occupy Holly Springs, Hernando, and an intermediate point between these places. To intercept and catch M. Jeff. Thompson's and Jackson's cotton-burners I would also like to have the Eleventh Illinois Cavalry sent here.

U. S. GRANT.

HEADQUARTERS DISTRICT OF WEST TENNESSEE,
Memphis, June 27, 1862.

Maj. Gen. H. W. HALLECK,
Commanding Department of the Mississippi :

GENERAL : Between Jackson's and M. Jeff. Thompson's forces, with the weak force here, I fear that it will be impossible for me to keep the railroad open from here to Grand Junction and at the same time keep this city in subjection. There is great disloyalty manifested by the citizens of this place and undoubtedly spies and numbers of the Southern Army are constantly finding their way in and out of the city in spite of all vigilance.

There is every probability that an attempt will be made to burn the city, and no doubt from the extent to be guarded it will prove partially successful. This, however, is a matter which will operate more against the rebels than ourselves.

The regiment sent from here to repair the railroad has just returned. I ordered it to remain as a guard to the road until further orders were received, but as this order was carried by the colonel of this regiment, and he having been taken prisoner before reaching his command, it returned here in obedience to previous orders. I have sent out to Germantown, or to the point where the railroad is broken, to-day a regiment of infantry and five companies of cavalry. They go with three days' rations ; but as some cars and locomotives have just arrived I will keep those troops there if practicable until troops from Bolivar can relieve them. I will make the effort to keep the road and telegraph open.

As I am without instructions I am a little in doubt as to my authority to license and limit trade, punish offenses committed by citizens, and in restricting civil authority. I now have two citizens (prisoners) for murder, whom I shall have tried by a military commission and submit the findings and sentence to you. All communication is prevented south of our lines as far as our guards can prevent it. There is a board of trade established to regulate what goods are authorized to be received and who authorized to sell. I think it will be necessary also to establish some sort of court to settle private claims.

When a direct channel for mails is opened I will submit to you a copy of all orders published for the government of the city.

I would again urge the importance of having here one division of the Army of the Tennessee ordered from Corinth.

I am, general, very respectfully, your obedient servant,

U. S. GRANT
Major-General.

POPE'S HEADQUARTERS, *June* 27, 1862.

General HALLECK:

A picket of our cavalry on the east of the Mobile and Ohio Railroad was surprised, and a Lieutenant Wise, sergeant and two corporals, and 4 men all missing. The rebel force said to be 100 of Forrest's cavalry, with 500 men held in reserve; force said to have gone to Marietta. Darkies from southwest report rebels are going to attack Rienzi.

W. S. ROSECRANS,
Brigadier-General.

MOSCOW, *June* 27, 1862.

General HALLECK:

The country is full of vague rumors, but our pickets and sentinels discover no traces of an enemy. One rumor says that Rosecrans is fighting to-day at Holly Springs; another, that 1,500 cavalry went to attack my wagon train, but mistook and attacked the railroad train. There is no way of reaching the truth at Holly Springs but going there in force. General McClernand telegraphs he will be at Grand Junction as soon as General Quinby relieves him. I fear Rosecrans may attack Holly Springs without communicating with us. I know not the strength and composition of his force; but Hurlbut and I should attack in front if Rosecrans approaches by the flank. There are innumerable roads all centering at Holly Springs, and even Grant might at same time reach Hernando until we occupy line of Coldwater. This railroad cannot be relied on. All very quiet here, and I have sent to Hurlbut for news.

W. T. SHERMAN,
Major-General.

WAR DEPARTMENT, *June* 28, 1862.

Major-General HALLECK, *Corinth:*

The enemy have concentrated in such force at Richmond as to render it absolutely necessary in the opinion of the President for you immediately to detach 25,000 of your force and forward it by the nearest and quickest route by way of Baltimore and Washington to Richmond. It is believed that the quickest route would be by way of Columbus, Ky., and up the Ohio River. But in detaching your force the President directs that it be done in such way as to enable you to hold your ground and not interfere with the movement against Chattanooga and East Tennessee. This condition being observed, the forces to be detached and the route they are to be sent is left to your own judgment. The direction to send these forces immediately is rendered imperative by a serious reverse suffered by General McClellan before Richmond yesterday, the full extent of which is not yet known. You will acknowledge the receipt of this dispatch, stating the day and hour it is received, and inform me what your action will be, so that we may take measures to aid in river and railroad transportation.

EDWIN M. STANTON,
Secretary of War.

———

CORINTH, *June* 28, 1862.

Hon. E. M. STANTON:

Your telegram of the 23d is just received—five days *en route*. It is impossible to send forces to Vicksburg at present, but I will give the matter very full attention as soon as circumstances will permit.

H. W. HALLECK,
Major-General.

———

MEMPHIS, TENN., *June* 28, 1862.

Maj. Gen. H. W. HALLECK, *Corinth, Miss.*:

The effective strength of Wallace's command at present here is 3,800. I have ordered two of the regiments left at Bolivar and one left at Jackson to come here. This will leave at Bolivar one regiment of infantry, two companies of cavalry, and one of artillery.

U. S. GRANT,
Major-General.

———

MEMPHIS, TENN., *June* 28, 1862.

Maj. Gen. H. W. HALLECK, *Corinth, Miss.*:

News has just been received from Commodore Farragut. Gunboats have left here to co-operate in the attack on Vicksburg. A land force of 13,000 is said to be up from New Orleans. One, if not two, gunboats will be here in the morning from mouth of White River. I have sent a force from here, and thus opened again the telegraph communication; will endeavor to keep it so. I have written and telegraphed via Columbus, Ky.

U. S. GRANT,
Major-General.

———

HEADQUARTERS ARMY OF THE MISSISSIPPI,
June 28, 1862.

Major-General HALLECK, *Corinth, Miss.*:

No news from our front, from Jacinto around to Ripley road. Asboth sends statement of man from Rienzi, G. R. Bollard, who left Columbus, confirming the following: Columbus being fortified; used as depot for conscripts; use of slave labor; position of main army between Tupelo and Saltillo; passenger trains come to Tupelo; army, 40,000; many sick, many dispirited; Breckinridge gone to Vicksburg; purchase of teams.

If you think we are secure from a principal attack upon the part of our lines, or, if it comes, may meet its first shock near Rienzi, I will advance another division to some point fit for bivouac beyond Rienzi and threatening an advance on the Ripley, Booneville, and Blackland roads there. Will leave one division in this camp.

W. S. ROSECRANS,
Brigadier-General, Commanding.

HEADQUARTERS ARMY OF THE MISSISSIPPI,
June 28, 1862.
Col. J. C. KELTON,
Assistant Adjutant-General, Corinth, Miss.:

Eight prisoners have arrived from Asboth.   Six deserters from Breckinridge's command.   Left his forces at Abbeville, on the Mississippi Central Railroad, on the 24th instant.   They name only eight regiments, averaging from 200 to 500.   One is a spy.

As soon as the commanding general has decided about the move I mentioned this morning I wish to know in time to have rations cooked, if it be requisite.

W. S. ROSECRANS,
Brigadier-General, Commanding.

MOSCOW, *June 28, 1862.*
General HALLECK:

Your dispatch received.   I keep pickets out to Mount Pleasant.   Will hold my division to march on Holly Springs on the shortest notice, with light baggage, all my artillery, and good men.   Hurlbut and I are about the same distance from Holly Springs, viz, 25 miles.   The place to meet and act in concentration is Coldwater, 6 miles this side of Holly Springs; but we should reach at the same time with Rosecrans.   Had we not better clean Germantown, a dirty hole?   There is where was planned the cutting the wire and destruction of road.   I am told they openly boast the Yankees shall never run a train over the road.

I am preparing a car for a 12-pounder howitzer.

W. T. SHERMAN,
Major-General.

HDQRS. FIFTH DIVISION, ARMY OF THE TENNESSEE,
Moscow, Tenn., June 28, 1862.
General GRANT, *Memphis:*

Your letter by Gould received this a. m.; telegraphed its contents to Halleck.

I sent the Railroad Regiment to Germantown, intending it to make a junction, before starting, with the Fifty-sixth Ohio, but the latter did not wait for it.   I hope both regiments are at Germantown.

I can hear nothing definite from Holly Springs.   No spy can get in and out since Gould went.   I don't like to risk him too much; he has already exposed his life some half dozen times.   I want to move with our forces on Holly Springs, for as long as an enemy occupies that point there can be no safety in running cars on this road.   I am sending a messenger to La Grange to find out if there be any news of Rosecrans, who is moving on Holly Springs from Corinth via Ripley.   I don't know the strength of his forces, but we should act in concert.   Halleck's reiterated orders to me are, "Move not a mile west, unless it be absolutely necessary."

W. T. SHERMAN,
Major-General.

HDQRS. FIFTH DIVISION, ARMY OF THE TENNESSEE,
Moscow, Tenn., June 28, 1862.

Brigadier-General HURLBUT,
          Commanding La Grange:

GENERAL: I am directed by General Sherman to say that situated as we are, cut off from communication with Memphis, you cannot depend on our train for supplies. He therefore wishes you to collect from the surrounding country supplies of meat, meal, and forage; such supplies as you can find and need.

There is a hand-car here that you can have by sending 6 men after it. It will be in repair by to-morrow, and as there are shops at La Grange you can easily keep it going.

There is nothing new here. I send you two papers, the 23d and 27th.

The general further wishes, and indeed the purpose of this letter is, that you send him notice as soon as possible when you hear anything of where General Rosecrans is, or any news of any kind of him.

A letter from General Grant came through this morning by courier. He says that he has no force and cannot assist us at all.

Has any train arrived or any mails? The orderly will await an answer.

Very respectfully, your obedient servant,
                              J. H. HAMMOND,
                              Assistant Adjutant-General.

————

HDQRS. FIFTH DIVISION, ARMY OF THE TENNESSEE,
Moscow, Tenn., June 28, 1862.

General HURLBUT, *La Grange, Tenn.:*

SIR: I have long been impressed with the belief that we could not depend on this railroad till we clear out all traces of an enemy from the northern tier of counties in Mississippi.

Send down 40 wagons and we will share with you the provisions on hand; then make up a train of 60 wagons and send to Memphis by way of Somerville and the Stage road for another supply; that road is more safe than the State Line road. Even with that train send a regiment as escort, to ride in the empty wagons, but to march back as a guard to the loaded wagons. I think Grant will try and protect that road.

As soon as we hear from Rosecrans we must move on Holly Springs, cost what it may.

You must feed McClernand's men. Get corn-meal, beef, &c.

Yours, &c.,
                              W. T. SHERMAN,
                              Major-General.

————

CORINTH, *June* 29, VIA CAIRO, *July* 1.
(Received Washington 8.40 p. m., July 1, 1862.)

Hon. E. M. STANTON,
          Secretary of War:

Official reports received that the expedition from Cassville, under Colonel King and Majors Hubbard and Miller, have captured 2 rebel colonels, 1 lieutenant-colonel, 4 captains, 7 lieutenants, 120 enlisted men, 12 trains, and a large quantity of arms, stores, &c. Railroads to

Memphis, Columbus, and Decatur have been opened. Rebel guerrillas cut the repaired road in two places, through carelessness in guarding it, but damage very slight. Some skirmishing at outpost, but loss incon-siderable. Enemy has been making demonstrations against us for several days, but I think intends no serious attack. The advance of General Buell's army will reach Huntsville to-day. It is believed that the enemy is already evacuating East Tennessee.

H. W. HALLECK,
Major-General.

MEMPHIS, TENN., June 29, 1862.
(By telegraph from Corinth.)

Maj. Gen. U. S. GRANT:

The part of Wallace's division at Bolivar was ordered to Grand Junction. There is no danger of an attack in force on Memphis. It is a mere stampede. The great object now is to protect the railroad against marauders. There was culpable neglect in sending out the train from Memphis till the road was properly guarded. You will report by whose neglect the accident and the capture of telegraph repairers occurred.

H. W. HALLECK,
Major-General..

MEMPHIS, TENN., June 29, 1862.

Maj. Gen. H. W. HALLECK, Corinth, Miss.:

A man through from Okolona reports that there are but 3,000 troops at that place. Columbus is being strongly fortified. Thirty thousand men said to be at Abbeville, intending to march on La Grange as soon as the Tallahatchie Bridge is repaired. This I telegraphed via Columbus, Ky., while the direct line was down.

U. S. GRANT,
Major-General.

CORINTH, June 29, 1862.

Maj. Gen. U. S. GRANT, Memphis, Tenn.:

You say 30,000 men are at Shelbyville to attack La Grange. Where is Shelbyville? I can't find it on any map. Don't believe a word about an attack in large force on La Grange or Memphis. Why not send out strong reconnaissance and ascertain the facts? It looks very much like a mere stampede. Floating rumors must never be received as facts. Order an investigation of the loss of the train and capture of our men by a force of the enemy and report the facts. I mean to make somebody responsible for so gross a negligence.

H. W. HALLECK,
Major-General.

MEMPHIS, TENN., June 29, 1862.

Maj. Gen. H. W. HALLECK, Corinth, Miss.:

I did not say 30,000 troops at Shelbyville, but at Abbeville, which is south of Holly Springs, on the road to Grenada. I made a report of all I knew of the capture of the train, and sent by way of Columbus,

Ky. I have kept all my cavalry force on the road from here to Germantown most of the time since my arrival in Memphis. The balance of the cavalry force here are ordered to make daily reconnaissances to the southeast of the line from here.

I heed as little of the floating rumors about the city as any one. I only gave you the statement of a man from Okolona, who has fled from there with no intention of returning until he can go under the Federal flag. I do not credit his report as to exact numbers, but believe the Tallahatchie Bridge is being repaired, and that a considerable force is at Abbeville. I know, not from rumor, that M. Jeff. Thompson and Jackson are both to the southeast of us. I have asked for the Eleventh Illinois Cavalry, now at Corinth, that I might do effectually what you now ask why I have not done.

Stampeding is not my weakness. On the contrary, I will always execute any order to the best of my ability with the means at hand. Immediately on taking command here I ordered troops from my command at Jackson and Bolivar, where they could be spared, that I might have the force to guard effectually the road from here to where guarded by General Sherman. Your orders have countermanded mine. It will be very difficult, however, to prevent the occasional taking up of a rail or cutting of a wire, as troops of my command passed the scene of the late catastrophe before it occurred and after, on the same day. I do not see that there has been more culpable neglect than was shown by Beauregard in permitting the road from Corinth to Bethel to be cut by my forces on the road south of him, by Colonel Elliott. As all the dispositions of the forces of the Army of the Tennessee have been made without my orders, and in most cases without my being informed of the changes, and as the running of the cars is expressly placed under the control of General McPherson, who had his agent here, and as I have never been directed to place any troops on the road, certainly no blame can attach to me.

U. S. GRANT,
Major-General.

HEADQUARTERS ARMY OF THE MISSISSIPPI,
June 29, 1862.

Col. J. C. KELTON,
Assistant Adjutant-General, Corinth, Miss.:

The following from General Hamilton, beyond Hatchie, 2 p. m.:

Statement of J. E. Yowell.

J. E. Yowell lives in Lincoln County, Tennessee. Went on business to see his brother, a captain in the One hundred and fifty-fourth Regiment Tennessee Militia, who was wounded at Shiloh. Has been at Holly Springs about ten weeks. Left there at 9 o'clock yesterday morning, 27th; just reached here. There are no troops in Holly Springs now. There are two detachments of cavalry out west from Holly Springs—Jackson's regiment and Pinson's six companies—but no infantry or artillery. Heard some six or eight days since that Breckinridge was coming to Holly Springs, but learned Thursday that he had gone to Vicksburg. No trains running from the south to Holly Springs. Bridge burned over the Tallahatchie by the Federals and destroyed entirely by the rebels. General Smith was in Holly Springs last Tuesday morning (one week) with seven or eight regiments of infantry and one of cavalry, and paroled the sick and wounded. Heard that Price had gone to Vicksburg and Beauregard to Richmond. Is a physician and is on his way home. Voted for secession, but it was peaceable secession, not war. The people at Holly Springs were much vexed when they learned that Breckinridge was not coming there.

W. S. ROSECRANS,
Brigadier-General, U. S. A., Commanding.

POPE'S HEADQUARTERS, *June* 29, 1862.
Major-General HALLECK:

Brig. Gen. C. S. Hamilton will bivouac near Ripley to-night, because there is no water on the road for 15 miles beyond toward Salem. He can pass that dry space to-morrow, which will bring him within 13 miles of Holly Springs by to-morrow night. He could therefore reach it by Tuesday morning, if need be. With the partial information in my possession I must wait your instructions about the support to this movement, as called for yesterday morning. If anything serious is to be done at Holly Springs Hamilton must receive special instructions from me to-day, and care will be requisite to insure them supplies for ten days.

W. S. ROSECRANS,
Brigadier-General.

HEADQUARTERS ARMY OF THE MISSISSIPPI,
June 29, 1862.
General HAMILTON, *Commanding, Ripley, Miss.*:

The general commanding directs me to say that Generals Sherman and Hurlbut continue to think that the enemy is in force in front of them. General Halleck does not incline to that opinion; nevertheless, in deference to their views, Sherman has been directed to advance with Hurlbut on Holly Springs, expecting that you will be able to reach there by Wednesday morning; you will proceed accordingly. If you find the enemy reconnoitering closely, put yourself in communication with Sherman. If you can make such dispositions as will secure you, fall back slowly.

Colonel Murphy, with five regiments of infantry and a battery of artillery, will reach Ripley to-morrow night or next day morning, with a view to covering your supplies. He will be subject to your orders. If you find little resistance or no enemy at Holly Springs you will immediately return to Ripley, encamp there, and await further orders; if otherwise, you will of course be governed by circumstances. Report frequently; send efficient officers to keep up your supplies. You have been notified of the means taken to supply you with provisions; further care will be taken to expedite your supply trains. Colonel Murphy will also receive orders to the same effect.

Very respectfully, your obedient servant,

W. L. ELLIOTT,
Brigadier-General and Chief of Staff.

CORINTH, *June* 29, 1862.
Major-General SHERMAN, *Moscow:*

It is reported that Hamilton's forces, from Rosecrans' army, passed the Hatchie River yesterday, and are moving on Holly Springs, but that there is not and has not been any considerable number of rebel troops anywhere near that place, Breckinridge's whole command having gone from Okolona to Vicksburg.

You will co-operate with Hamilton so far as you may deem it advisable, but by no means neglect to guard the Memphis road. The story of a large rebel force in that vicinity looks to me very much like a stampede, caused by two regiments of cavalry. The loss of the train was a matter of serious neglect, and I mean to have the matter thoroughly investigated.

H. W. HALLECK.

CORINTH, *June* 29, 1862.

Major-General SHERMAN, *Moscow:*

You will assume command of Hurlbut's division, and also the part of McClernand's at Grand Junction. Hamilton will reach Holly Springs on Tuesday morning, and will expect your co-operation.

I get no information of McClellan from Washington. Rebels at Chattanooga say he was defeated on the 27th.

H. W. HALLECK,
Major-General.

HDQRS. FIFTH DIVISION, ARMY OF THE TENNESSEE,
Moscow, Tenn., June 29, 1862.

General HALLECK, *Corinth, Miss.:*

I have been studying my maps. If Hamilton passed Hatchie yesterday he had 65 miles to reach Holly Springs. Is he coming by Ripley? On your present order I shall be at Holly Springs Tuesday morning, but I doubt if Hamilton can reach it before Wednesday night. Troops cannot march these hot days. You cannot count over 12 miles a day with trains.

I would go to Holly Springs light, and would therefore march with more rapidity. If possible, it would be well for Hamilton to send a messenger to the Junction announcing his presence at Ripley and fixing the time of his approach to Holly Springs.

W. T. SHERMAN,
Major-General.

HDQRS. FIFTH DIVISION, ARMY OF THE TENNESSEE,
Moscow, Tenn., June 29, 1862.

General HALLECK, *Corinth, Miss.:*

One of my most sucessful scouts, Sergeant Gould, was in Holly Springs five days ago, and he reported one regiment of cavalry and 4,000 infantry in Holly Springs. He saw them and their tents and was certain Breckinridge was there.

I will leave one regiment at the Junction, one at La Grange, and one here, each with a section of artillery, and with the effective force of the remaining regiments I will move on Holly Springs to-morrow afternoon, so as to reach it Tuesday morning.

I have to send a wagon train into Memphis, which I will do by the back road, viz, one leading to the Stage road, which keeps on the north side of Wolf River and enters by Raleigh. I suppose Grant has taken measures to cover his end of the road. I protect it from the Junction to La Fayette. By advancing my whole force south I do not uncover the road. No trains have ever reached me from any quarter.

W. T. SHERMAN,
Major-General.

P. S.—To protect this section of the road a large and efficient cavalry force will be indispensable. There is plenty of forage. Mine and Hurlbut's forces of cavalry are insignificant and are hardly enough for picket duty.

LA GRANGE, TENN., *June* 29, 1862.

Maj. Gen. WILLIAM T. SHERMAN, *Moscow, Tenn.* :

Quite a number of irregular cavalry are reported to me as being on the North Fork of Wolf River, $1\frac{1}{2}$ miles north of the railroad, and north-west of Cromwell's Station, at McCown's Mill. They are within 4 miles of Moscow, and captured 2 of your men yesterday. They were seen yesterday evening by two boys, children of Mr. Woolley, who brings me the information. They have probably come over Ammon's Bridge, and are either waiting for wagon trains or moving across toward the Bolivar Railroad. My wagon train has four companies of infantry as guard, and I have 40 cavalry with forage train on the Somerville road. I cannot state the number they may have nor can I send after them, as my cavalry is all on duty elsewhere.

[S. A. HURLBUT,]
Brigadier-General.

HDQRS. FIFTH DIVISION, ARMY OF THE TENNESSEE,
Moscow, Tenn., June 29, 1862.

General HURLBUT, *La Grange, Tenn.* :

I have a guard at Ammon's Bridge. No cavalry has passed there. No men are reported missing, and our foraging parties have been all along the North Fork. I have only half your force of cavalry, but will send a squad to McCown's Mill; some embryo guerrilla party may have been there.

Have all your forces, except one regiment at the Junction and one at La Grange, with a section of artillery at each place, ready to march to Holly Springs to-morrow at 2 p. m., taking five days' rations and as few traps as possible.

Report to me the number and composition of the regiments that have come from McClernand.

Rosecrans' advance will be at Holly Springs on Tuesday morning and we must march there at same time. Try and keep the movement a secret.

Telegraph me to-day when you dispatch your train to Memphis. I have one ready to start at 3 a. m.

W. T. SHERMAN,
Major-General.

ORDERS, }   HDQRS. FIFTH DIV., ARMY OF THE TENN.,
No. 48. }   *Moscow, Tenn., June* 29, 1862.

The division will be in line and will march at 2 o'clock to-morrow in the order of—Denver's brigade, Smith's brigade, McDowell's brigade.

The cavalry will take the advance, taking the road toward North Mount Pleasant, leaving it to the right, and thence toward Hudsonville. They will halt from time to time to assure that the infantry is on the right road.

Each brigade will carry its cooking utensils and provisions for six days; will leave behind tents and all baggage except the bedding of officers and men. Each regiment will take its ammunition wagon; tools at the rate of 25 axes, spades, and picks per regiment.

The division ammunition train will accompany the expedition. Each brigadier will make arrangements that the sick men left behind be organized to defend the camps against any sudden inroads of cavalry.

General Denver will detail one regiment to remain behind, the colonel of which will be in command and be charged with guarding the railroad bridge and camps. The chief of artillery will designate a section of artillery to remain at Moscow, and be at the disposal of the commanding officer.

By order of Maj. Gen. W. T. Sherman:

J. H. HAMMOND,
Assistant Adjutant-General.

SPECIAL ORDERS,)   HDQRS. DISTRICT OF WEST TENNESSEE,
No. 123.   )   *Memphis, Tenn., June* 29, 1862.

*   *   *   *   *   *   *

IV. Arrests being frequently made on representations of citizens, who afterward decline to appear to give evidence or to furnish names of witnesses to substantiate the charges, it is directed that hereafter in all such cases the prisoner be released and the party causing the arrest be confined or banished from the city, as the case may seem to require. The circulation of unfounded rumors through the city, now so prevalent, being calculated to create uneasiness and fear in the minds of the citizens, will hereafter be prohibited. The provost-marshal will in such cases arrest the parties guilty of violating this order and place them outside our lines, with directions to treat them as spies if ever taken within them thereafter. In all cases where persons are placed outside the lines under this order an accurate description of the person will be recorded in the office of the provost-marshal.

*   *   *   *   *   *   *

By order of Maj. Gen. U. S. Grant:

[JNO. A. RAWLINS,]
Assistant Adjutant-General.

SPECIAL ORDERS,)   HEADQUARTERS,
No. 107.   )   *Moscow, June* 29, 1862.

General Hurlbut will take temporary command of the regiments and detachments of General McClernand's force at Grand Junction. He will designate one regiment and a section of artillery to guard the Junction. He will also send one regiment and a section of artillery to remain at La Grange. With the balance of his force, leaving behind the sick and those unable to march, he will, with five or six days' rations and light wagon trains—leaving behind tents and all baggage except the soldiers' blankets, axes, and intrenching tools and ammunition—march about 2 p. m. of the 30th instant toward Holly Springs, reaching Coldwater by 8 a. m. Tuesday, where he will effect a junction with the Third [Fifth] Division and proceed in concert with it against Holly Springs.

By order of Maj. Gen. W. T. Sherman:

J. H. HAMMOND,
Assistant Adjutant-General.

[JUNE 29, 1862.—For General Orders, No. 38, Headquarters Department of the Mississippi, of this date, in reference to mail facilities, see Series I, Vol. XVI, Part II, p. 74.]

CORINTH, *June* 30, 1862—8 a. m.
Hon. E. M. STANTON,
     Secretary of War :

Your telegram of 26th [27th] is just received. I much regret to lose Pope from this department, but cannot object to his receiving a higher command; but I must protest against the transfer of General Schuyler Hamilton and General Granger unless on their own application or with the object of promotion. I think the former deserves promotion for his operations at New Madrid and Island No. 10.

The sending of new, inexperienced, and inefficient officers to this department has already had a very injurious effect. I am from their rank obliged to assign them to brigades and divisions which have been organized and a long time commanded by others. This creates great dissatisfaction both among the officers and men. In one case this has already amounted almost to a mutiny.

I most respectfully request that as few such transfers be made as possible.

                    H. W. HALLECK,
                      Major-General.

CORINTH, *June* 30, 1862.
Hon. E. M. STANTON,
     Secretary of War : ·

Your telegram of the 28th is just received, but it is so imperfect that parts of it cannot be deciphered till repeated. The object, however, is understood, and measures will be immediately taken to carry it out. The condition of the river and railroads in Tennessee and the want of rolling-stock will render the movement very slow. Cavalry cannot be sent, and it will be exceedingly difficult to transport artillery with horses and guns. If artillerymen are sent can they be supplied with horses and guns there, or shall I send infantry only? I think under the circumstances the Chattanooga expedition had better be abandoned, or, at least, be diminished; if not, I doubt our ability to hold West Tennessee after detaching so large a force as that called for. I will telegraph more in detail as soon as your telegram is repeated, as I cannot understand parts of it.

                    H. W. HALLECK,
                      Major-General.

WAR DEPARTMENT,
June 30, 1862—3 p. m.
Major-General HALLECK, *Corinth :*

Your telegram of this date just received. The Chattanooga expedition must not on any account be given up. The President regards that and the movement against East Tennessee as one of the most important movements of the war, and its occupation nearly as important as the capture of Richmond. He is not pleased with the tardiness of the movement toward Chattanooga, and directs that no force be sent here if you cannot do it without breaking up the operations against that point and East Tennessee. Infantry only are needed; our cavalry and artillery are strong enough. The first reports from Richmond were more discouraging than the truth warranted. If the advantage is not on our side it is balanced. General McClellan has moved his whole force on to the line of the James River, and is supported there by our gunboats;

but he must be largely strengthened before advancing, and hence the call on you, which I am glad you have answered so promptly. Let me know to what point on the river you will send your forces, so as to provide immediately for transportation.

EDWIN M. STANTON,
Secretary of War.

WASHINGTON, D. C., *June* 30, 1862.

Major-General HALLECK, *Corinth, Miss.*:

Would be very glad of 25,000 infantry; no artillery or cavalry; but please do not send a man if it endangers any place you deem important to hold, or if it forces you to give up or weaken or delay the expedition against Chattanooga. To take and hold the railroad at or east of Cleveland, in East Tennessee, I think fully as important as the taking and holding of Richmond.

A. LINCOLN.

TRENTON, TENN., *June* 30, 1862.

Maj. Gen. H. W. HALLECK,
Commanding Department of the Mississippi :

GENERAL: About a week ago I was appointed provost-marshal of this town by Col. G. W. Deitzler, commanding. Since that time my attention has been called to innumerable outrages committed by our troops, especially the First Brigade, under Brig. Gen. Robert B. Mitchell, in passing through this country.

An irregular and perfectly unwarrantable system of foraging is carried on by many of the regiments, which is greatly exasperating some of the inhabitants.

A party under the command of a sergeant or wagon-master goes into the country and takes corn and hay, giving the owner a receipt, of which the following is a specimen :

TRENTON, TENN., *June* 23, 1862.
Received of Robert Green 117 bushels of corn.

WILLIAM ROSS,
Wagon-master Second Battalion, Second Illinois Cavalry.

The original is written in pencil. The country is absolutely full of such papers, which are the only vouchers the owners have for their property. Hundreds of receipts have been presented here within the last week, and among them I have not seen one in proper form.

The brigade quartermaster of General Mitchell has along with him two citizens who sometimes sign the papers of that quartermaster.

The Second Kansas Battery in going through this place turned their horses into a grass lot in town and went off without giving any receipts.

While General Mitchell's brigade was near Union City, at the farm of the mother of the Hon. Emerson Etheridge, a party of men from the Seventh Kansas, Jennison's cavalry, under the charge of Capt. M. J. Parrott, assistant adjutant-general, were out from camp for some purpose and met a funeral procession with the remains of a respectable widow lady of the neighborhood, and, unmindful of the remonstrances of Mr. Parrott, stopped the procession and demanded what they had in the wagon. Being told that it was a dead woman, they burst the coffin and examined the contents and then left, saying, "Go on with your d—d secession b—." This was reported to General Mitchell, but he took no measures to punish it.

Your order excluding negroes from the lines was recently recalled to the troops of that brigade by an order from General Quinby. When the order arrived General Mitchell was absent, and Lieutenant-Colonel Anthony, commanding Seventh Kansas, was temporarily in command of the brigade.

Colonel Anthony had the order read at dress-parade, and then another of his own, threatening punishment to any officer or soldier who should dare to obey yours, and when General Mitchell returned he took no notice of it, so that Anthony's order still stands on the books of the brigade as law. He himself boasted of this to me a few days ago. On Tuesday night, June 24, 1862, a party of cavalry soldiers belonging to Mitchell's brigade—his were the only troops in the vicinity—went to the house of a widow lady, residing not far from this place, Mrs. Emily Tyree. They demanded admittance, but before her son could rise and open the door they burst it open; they then demanded her money, speaking in a most abusive and insulting manner. She gave them all she had, and then they searched the wardrobe for more. Leaving the house they told her that if she informed of the affair they would return and burn her son and herself to death in her own house. They then went to a field and took two horses, all she had, and drove them off.

I believe it was the same night that a party roused the family of a Mr. Harper, residing about 5 miles from this place. They ordered him to open the door and demanded his money. He had $500, which he gave them. After abusing his daughter with rough language they departed.

A Mr. Davis, of this town, one of the oldest citizens and a staunch, outspoken Union man from the beginning, had three valuable negroes taken from him by Jennison's men when they were through here.

I beg leave to submit these plain statements of facts which have come under my own observation within the last two weeks.

I have the honor to be, general, your most obedient servant,

B. P. CHENOWITH,
Captain First Kansas and Provost-Marshal.

MEMPHIS, *June* 30, 1862.

Major-General HALLECK:

A gentleman from Arkansas, who has just made his escape from there and came up on one of our gunboats, says that "General Curtis has lost several foraging parties; the Texas Rangers take no prisoners; thinks the rebel force on White River cannot be less than 5,000 or 6,000; it is estimated by citizens as more than double that number. The troops from Little Rock have all been brought over to the White River; there are some Louisiana troops, between 1,000 and 2,000 from Missouri, four or five regiments Texas Rangers, and a large number of Arkansas conscripts; the number of the latter is estimated very large and increasing daily."

I seriously doubt the force under Colonel Fitch, about 2,200, being sufficient to effect a junction with General Curtis; he cannot be re-enforced from here without the troops coming from elsewhere. Bands of cotton-burners are now within 12 or 15 miles of here, destroying everything and arresting citizens favorable to the Union. I keep the little cavalry at my command constant employed, but they are not sufficient for the task. My instructions to Colonel Fitch are such that he could not permit himself to be cut off, but he may fail in affording relief to General Curtis. I do not doubt the sincerity of my informant, but never estimate numbers to be equal to that reported. Same informant says that he saw letters from men of Pike's command which said they had been ordered into Fort Smith.

U. S. GRANT,
Major-General.

CORINTH, June 30, 1862.

Major-General GRANT:

Report immediately the effective force under command at Memphis and vicinity, exclusive of Sherman's and Hurlbut's divisions; also the parts of Wallace's division which can be concentrated at Memphis. I don't want comments, but facts.

The defeat of McClellan at Richmond has created a stampede at Washington. I want facts as to position, as to troops, and how they can be concentrated, in order to enable me to answer questions and carry out orders. State precisely how many troops you have transportation to Cairo from Memphis for.

I want exact facts.

H. W. HALLECK,
Major-General.

MEMPHIS, TENN., June 30, 1862.

Maj. Gen. H. W. HALLECK, Corinth, Miss.:

The drovers who were captured on their return from La Fayette have got back. One of them has reported to me that they were carried about 10 miles south of Holly Springs. The force at that point was Jackson's cavalry and one regiment besides. He heard the determination expressed not to permit the cars to run or supplies to be carried over the road.

I have re-enforced Colonel Fitch with three cavalry regiments, and sent one regiment of infantry and five companies of cavalry to guard the road. An escort of 150 men is now going via Rolla with beef cattle for Sherman's command.

My present effective force here is five infantry regiments, about 190 cavalry, and four batteries. From this, two companies of infantry and one of cavalry are escorting a wagon train to Germantown, one company guarding a barge to White River, and the 150 men guarding beef cattle.

U. S. GRANT,
Major-General.

CORINTH, June 30, 1862.

Maj. Gen. U. S. GRANT:

Have you steamers at Memphis to transport Wallace's division, except the part at Grand Junction, to Cairo or Saint Louis?

H. W. HALLECK,
Major-General.

MEMPHIS, *June* 30, 1862.

Major-General HALLECK:

There are seven boats here that are ready and could be gotten so in a few hours, capable, the quartermaster reports, of carrying 5,000 men. My command here is four regiments of infantry, numbering 1,879 men; four batteries of artillery, 322 men; seven companies of cavalry, 260 men. There is one regiment of infantry, 429 men, and five companies of cavalry, 382 men, at Germantown; one regiment of infantry of 525 men, one company of cavalry, 45 men, at Bolivar; at Grand Junction three regiments of infantry, 1,700 men, belonging to Wallace's division. The only remaining regiment here would be Colonel Slack's regiment, 699 men. Colonel Fitch has hardly left the mouth of White River or cannot be far up. If the troops from Germantown can march in six hours, those from Grand Junction can come safely with cars by running a hand-car in advance of train. There is also here the Twenty-fourth Indiana Regiment, 536 men strong, just starting for White River. This is a regiment ordered yesterday, but not yet off. A part of the cavalry put down as here is out of the city on duty, but could be gotten back as early as the troops from Germantown. Of the infantry, one company has gone down the river to give safe-conduct to a barge and a detail of 150 men to guard beef cattle for Sherman's command. They have gone via Rolla.

U. S. GRANT,
Major-General.

———

CORINTH, *June* 30, 1862.

Major-General GRANT:

Secure the land side of Memphis by intrenchments and batteries as rapidly as possible. You can impress negroes for that purpose.

H. W. HALLECK,
Major-General.

———

CORINTH, *June* 30, 1862.

Major-General MCCLERNAND, *Jackson:*

The defeat of McClellan near Richmond has produced another stampede in Washington. You will collect as rapidly as possible all the infantry regiments of your division and take advantage of transportation by every train to transport them to Columbus and thence to Washington City. General Quinby will be directed to turn over to you certain troops of his command. The part of General Wallace's division at Memphis will go up the Mississippi and the portion at Grand Junction will follow as soon as relieved. All transports at Pittsburg and Hamburg will be filled with troops from this place.

The entire campaign in the West is broken up by these orders, and we shall very probably lose all we have gained. I will do all I can with the few forces left. You go to a new theater. Success attend you.

H. W. HALLECK,
Major-General.

———

CORINTH, *June* 30, 1862.

General ROSECRANS:

You will immediately recall the expedition to Holly Springs if satisfied that there is no considerable force of the enemy at that place. A brigade will be kept temporarily on this side of the Hatchie River as an outpost and communication kept with it.

H. W. HALLECK,
Major-General.

HEADQUARTERS ARMY OF THE MISSISSIPPI,
June 30, 1862.

Col. J. C. KELTON,
Assistant Adjutant-General, Corinth, Miss.:

I have sent a copy of the commanding general's dispatch directing the recall of Hamilton's forces, in case I am satisfied there is no large rebel force at Holly Springs, to that general, with orders for him to return if he still continues satisfied that there is no rebel force there. He will be at Salem to-night. Dispatch just received, dated this morning, has nothing new or different from what has already been reported from Holly Springs.

W. S. ROSECRANS,
Brigadier-General, Commanding.

HEADQUARTERS ARMY OF THE MISSISSIPPI,
June 30, 1862.

Col. J. C. KELTON,
Assistant Adjutant-General, Corinth, Miss.:

I report the following for the information of the commanding general: Murphy's brigade left yesterday afternoon, as ordered, for Ripley. Colonel Sheridan, from the front, reports that Perkins, railroad engineer, formerly of Corinth, direct from Mobile, with lady from Columbus, just reached his camp, says: The enemy all at Tupelo. Breckinridge's division gone to Vicksburg. Beauregard in Mobile, resigned. Advanced guards 2 miles south of Guntown. Two regiments of cavalry at Saltillo; one more in advance of that. General Villepigue is on the Mississippi Central. Four thousand infantry and 2,700 cavalry reported to have a skirmish with us, where there was a bridge burned.

Another statement from a contraband that ran away from Columbus on the 24th instant: Rebels fortifying Columbus, but not much work done. Forty thousand rebels at Tupelo, south creek, no fortifications. Twenty-four regiments left Tupelo for Fulton on Wednesday. On Thursday at 2 o'clock four regiments of infantry and six pieces of artillery at Saltillo.

W. S. ROSECRANS,
Brigadier-General, Commanding.

POPE'S HEADQUARTERS, *June 30, 1862.*

Colonel KELTON, *Assistant Adjutant-General:*

For the information of the commanding general I telegraph from General Hamilton's dispatch, dated 2.30 p. m. yesterday, the following:

Third Michigan went yesterday to Salem, returning this morning. Reports no rebel troops except cavalry north of the Tallahatchie. One infantry regiment has been at Holly Springs since our troops were there, but had fallen back on the Tallahatchie. Country invested by guerrillas; 200 visited Ripley the night our cavalry were in advance of the place. Two deserters from Breckinridge left him Tuesday. His forces were at Tallahatchie, but had left for Vicksburg on Wednesday morning. Price's and Van Dorn's commands were at same place. The impression there was they were maneuvering to get back into Arkansas. I give this as my opinion also, and I think they will try to get their artillery down the Yazoo. If they are at Tallahatchie it can only be to watch for an advance down the railroad from Grand Junction, not to make an attack on the Mobile and Ohio Railroad. They cannot cross the Tallahatchie in a hurry, coming or going. The little water there is at Ripley will be dried up in a week; wells are scarce. The town could not accommodate more than a brigade. There is no shade for bivouacking within 4 miles. The crossing of the valley of the Tallahatchie is a swamp 1 mile long and might be made very difficult. It is my best route back. The direct road from Corinth to Ripley is not practicable. The Hatchie Bridge is destroyed and the bottom very bad.

I shall send a regiment of Murphy's brigade to guard the Hatchie Crossing and watch Nolin's. The other four regiments go to the best position near Ripley to support Hamilton, who has orders to move on Holly Springs, and if he finds the enemy in force to communicate with Sherman and fight them. If pressed by a superior force, to fall slowly back, command Colonel Murphy, and be governed by circumstances. If no enemy be found requiring his detention he will return to Ripley and report for orders from there.

W. S. ROSECRANS,
Brigadier-General.

CORINTH, *June* 30, 1862.

Maj. Gen. WILLIAM T. SHERMAN, *Moscow:*

Grand Junction must be held by Hurlbut's or your forces. The detachment of Wallace or McClernand there must be sent north.

H. W. HALLECK,
Major-General.

LA GRANGE, TENN., *June* 30, 1862.

Maj. Gen. WILLIAM T. SHERMAN, *Moscow, Tenn.:*

The troops at Grand Junction have no transportation. I shall have to leave them there. It is reported that Breckinridge is moving west toward Memphis.

[S. A. HURLBUT,]
Brigadier-General.

MOSCOW, *June* [30 ?], 1862.

General HURLBUT, *La Grange, Tenn.:*

I will move at 2 p. m., and expect to communicate with you at Lamar and effect a junction at or near Hudsonville. The scarcity of water may force us to Coldwater as soon as possible. I think the afternoon will be cool and fine for the march. Be careful not to encumber yourself with anything but provisions, ammunition, and essentials. From Lamar you could detach a small mounted party to Salem and beyond to hear of Hamilton, whose division is in advance.

Don't think Breckinridge would move on Memphis with its uncertanties, with a heavy force on his flank and another approaching. I doubt if he will remain at Holly Springs, and think he will fall behind the Tallahatchie.

Have you heard whether cars have reached Holly Springs or not? I have nothing from there.

W. T. SHERMAN,
Major-General.

CORINTH, MISS., *July* 1, 1862.
(Received 9.16 p. m.)

Hon. E. M. STANTON,
Secretary of War:

Your corrected telegram of 28th was received last night. I had already acted on the imperfect copy received yesterday morning. General McClernand was ordered to send as many of his division as possible to Columbus by every train. General Quinby has been ordered to detach as many as he can spare from his command near Columbus. Light-draught boats have been ordered from Saint Louis to take one division from this place via Pittsburg. A part of Wallace's division will be sent from Memphis as soon as I can relieve them.

I fear that you have overestimated the strength of the army in West Tennessee. Since the departure of General Buell's army and the detachments to General Curtis' I have less than 65,000 effective men. After sending the detachment ordered to Washington I shall have less than 40,000. We have repaired and have now to guard, between Columbus, Memphis, and Decatur, 367 miles of railroad, besides the posts established on Mississippi River, and many rivers. All scouts, spies, deserters, and prisoners without a single exception report that no troops have been sent from here East. The rebel force in this State is not less than 75,000 or 80,000 men, and Bragg is raising conscripts daily. These are facts of which I have the most reliable evidence. The enemy acts in a friendly country, requiring no guards for his depots, and has an immense rolling stock, so that he can in a few days concentrate on any one point. We cannot so concentrate. I am therefore satisfied that a detachment of 25,000 from this army at the present time will result in the loss of Arkansas or West Tennessee and perhaps both.

Those who have not the proper data have been disposed to underrate the force of the enemy and to overrate that of this army. The facts are precisely as here given. Those who represent otherwise deceive you. Either the Chattanooga expedition must be postponed or a less force sent to Washington, or we have left the alternative of losing much that we have gained here in the West. To surrender any territory we have acquired is certain death to all Union men in that territory. Any loss on our part will be followed by insurrection in Tennessee and Kentucky, and we shall find still greater difficulty in the pacification of those States than we have encountered in Missouri.

H. W. HALLECK,
Major-General.

CORINTH, *July* 1, 1862.
(Received 9.40 p. m.)

The PRESIDENT:

Your telegram, just received, saves Western Tennessee. The former order was positive, and I had no alternative but obedience. The enemy is undoubtedly preparing to attack some point of our lines, supposing our forces diminished. I immediately ordered them all back to their posts. If these troops had been sent East we should have been defeated or forced to retreat.

H. W. HALLECK,
Major-General, Commanding.

CORINTH, *July* 1, [1862]—8.45 a. m.

(Received 9.40 p. m.)

Hon. E. M. STANTON,
Secretary of War :

Telegraph suspending orders for troops is received. If order had been carried out we should have been either defeated or forced to retreat. No forces can be spared at present. The enemy is apparently preparing to make an attack, and his guerrillas have already done us considerable damage.

H. W. HALLECK,
Major-General, Commanding.

———

CORINTH, *July* 1, 1862.

Major-General GRANT:

All accounts confirm the belief that no large force of the enemy has moved west toward Memphis. On the contrary, they are concentrating east of the Tombigbee and opening roads to Marietta. I have very little doubt they are preparing to attack somewhere between here and Decatur. You will perceive the absurdity under these circumstances of moving more of our troops west.

H. W. HALLECK.

———

MEMPHIS, *July* 1, 1862.

Major-General HALLECK:

I will locate the points to be fortified immediately, and as soon as authorized to draw in my cavalry now outside the city will impress negroes to work on them. There are but few negro men in the city.

U. S. GRANT,
Major-General.

———

CORINTH, *July* 1, 1862.

(Received Memphis, July 1.)

Major-General GRANT:

Passes to go South except for military purposes must come from Washington. No forces can be sent you from here. On the contrary, it may be necessary to withdraw Hurlbut or Sherman and abandon the road between here and Memphis. Colonel Kinney will be ordered to report to Colonel Hoffman, superintendent of prisoners of war, to effect the exchange.

I have no engineer officer to send you at present. It is evident that Wallace's division cannot be removed from Memphis till Sherman or Hurlbut is sent to that vicinity, and one is insufficient to defend the road. It is possible that we shall abandon the railroad entirely. I will wait for further orders from Washington. Perhaps the Secretary of War may be induced to revoke his order.

H. W. HALLECK,
Major-General.

———

JACKSON, TENN., *July* 1, 1862.

Major-General HALLECK, *Corinth :*

I started one brigade at day dawn on foot; will send remainder by rail as fast as possible. I will order teams to follow to Columbus unless you direct otherwise. Will turn over camp and garrison equipage to quartermaster.

Had I not better leave the Twelfth Michigan and Sixty-first Illinois here? They are undisciplined, disorganized, and deficient in numbers. They were placed under my command since Shiloh. Will you restore the Eighth Missouri to General Wallace's division.

I will leave artillery and cavalry here unless you direct otherwise.

General Logan is informed of acts of pillage and violence by some of the troops at Humboldt, which must disgrace the army if not repressed. By sending an agent here he could probably get some facts.

I trust you will direct General Wallace's division to halt at Cairo, if it should be ahead of General Logan's, so that I may arrange transportation for both.

> JOHN A. McCLERNAND,
> *Major-General, Commanding.*

CORINTH, *July* 1, 1862.

Major-General McCLERNAND, *Jackson:*

Orders from Washington are suspended. Stop all movements of your troops.

> H. W. HALLECK,
> *Major-General.*

(Similar dispatches to Brig. Gen. R. Allen, Pittsburg Landing, and Col. William Myers, Saint Louis.)

JULY 1, 1862.

Major-General HALLECK:

Nothing from the front save telegraph from Asboth saying it is said Hamilton is encamped 14 miles west; also that the road has been blockaded between Rienzi and Nolin's. I do not credit either.

Orders have been given to send a messenger to Hamilton. We have a regiment of infantry and a section of artillery at the Hatchie Crossing.

Mizner has gone down to Booneville with all his available cavalry. A regiment of infantry and a battery have been sent by Asboth to support Sheridan. I think it would be prudent for Todd to send a cavalry scout out toward Hamilton to meet him and report the condition of the road from Ripley to Corinth in case it should become necessary for him to use it. Would it not be well by way of precaution to advise Sherman to communicate with him, in case my orders have been miscarried, that he is to come back, looking out for his left?

> W. S. ROSECRANS,
> *Brigadier-General.*

HEADQUARTERS SECOND BRIGADE, CAVALRY DIVISION,
July 1, 1862—2.30 p. m.

General ASBOTH, *Rienzi:*

GENERAL: The enemy have ten regiments, under General Chalmers. I am still holding them.

I want supports, particularly artillery. Let me have them at once, if it is possible.

I have been cut up some little, but am still strong. Telegraph this to General Granger immediately.

I am, sir, very respectfully, your obedient servant,

P. H. SHERIDAN,
Colonel, Commanding Second Brigade, Cavalry Division.

HEADQUARTERS SECOND BRIGADE, CAVALRY DIVISION,
July 1, 1862—3 p. m.

Brigadier-General ASBOTH :

GENERAL : Have you not received my dispatches ? I have been holding a large force of the enemy—prisoners say ten regiments—all day, and am considerably cut up. I want Mizner's two battalions and artillery and infantry supports. This is my third dispatch. I am holding my camp.

Telegraph my dispatches to General Granger.

I am, sir, yours, truly,

P. H. SHERIDAN,
Colonel, Commanding Second Brigade, Cavalry Division.

HEADQUARTERS RESERVE,
Rienzi, July 1, 1862.

Brigadier-General ELLIOTT, *Chief of Staff:*

Communication just received from Booneville as follows :

I have received your order to fall back. I have driven the enemy back and hurt them badly. I do not see any necessity of falling back. I will remain until I again hear from general headquarters, as the order was given before it was known I had driven the enemy back. Send down my forage. There was no force in front of me to-day but cavalry, nor is there any this side Guntown.

P. H. SHERIDAN,
Colonel, Commanding Second Brigade.

My messenger sent with dispatches to General Hamilton just returned. He met scouts from General Hamilton, who reported that the general would be here at 8 o'clock to-morrow morning with his command.

The blockade of the road consisted of trees blown over by the wind, which can be easily removed, and so I expect the supply train will reach General Hamilton during the night.

After all these revelations, I ask once more if I shall send the infantry regiment and a battery forward to Booneville, where Colonel Mizner has already arrived with his command and the enemy withdrawn.

ASBOTH,
Brigadier-General, Commanding Reserve.

CORINTH, *July* 1, 1862.

General ELLIOTT:

Sheridan's dispatches received. Asboth must at once re-enforce Sheridan with a good regiment and a battery. Your detail and orders to Asboth are correct. Direct him further, in case this is anything more than a cavalry affair, to prepare to send away all his baggage.

In case a strong advance is made on us, we will withdraw them from Rienzi. Send with all dispatch for Hamilton to return. Advise him of the movements.

W. S. ROSECRANS,
Brigadier-General.

HEADQUARTERS SECOND BRIGADE, CAVALRY DIVISION,
July 1, 1862—5 p. m.

General ASBOTH:

GENERAL: I will not want any infantry supports; I have whipped the enemy to-day. I was attacked by General Chalmers' cavalry, consisting of Brewer's, Adams', Clanton's, and other regiments, amounting to between eight and ten regiments. I have lost some fine officers and men, and have hurt the enemy badly.[*]
I think it would be well to let me have a battery of artillery. I might then be able to follow up the enemy.

I am, general, yours, truly,

P. H. SHERIDAN,
Colonel, Commanding Second Brigade, Cavalry Division.

P. S.—Send down the train.

HEADQUARTERS RESERVE, *July* 1, 1862.

General ELLIOTT:

I directed Colonel Sheridan, according to orders received, to fall back slowly. Shall I, under these circumstances, re-enforce him now with a regiment of infantry and a battery?
The supply train for General Hamilton is moving forward on the Ripley road, and General Hamilton is reported (but not authentically) encamped 14 miles from here, in great want of provisions. Shall I, under these circumstances, order back supply train as directed?
I have sent message to General Hamilton with the required information.

ASBOTH,
Brigadier-General, Commanding Reserve.

WAR DEPARTMENT,
July 2, 1862.

Major-General HALLECK, *Corinth, Miss.:*

Your several dispatches of yesterday to Secretary of War and myself received. I did say, and now repeat, I would be exceedingly glad for some re-enforcements from you; still, do not send a man if, in your judgment, it will endanger any point you deem important to hold, or will force you to give up or weaken or delay the Chattanooga expedition. Please tell me, could you make me a flying visit for consultation, without endangering the service in your department?

A. LINCOLN.

---

* See Part I, pp. 17-20.

CORINTH, MISS., *July* 2, 1862—6 p. m.
(Received 11 p. m.)

The PRESIDENT OF THE UNITED STATES:

The enemy attacked us at Booneville yesterday in considerable force, but were defeated and driven back. Particulars not yet received.* On the line to Memphis they attacked a train and destroyed eight wagons. According to reports of scouts and deserters Bragg is preparing to attack us with the cavalry force of Beauregard's army. Under these circumstances I do not think I could safely be absent from my army, although, being somewhat broken in health and wearied out with long months of labor and care, a trip to Washington would be exceedingly desirable.

H. W. HALLECK,
Major-General.

JACKSON, TENN., *July* 2, 1862.

Maj. Gen. H. W. HALLECK, *Corinth:*

General Grant orders me to take command of the troops and district south of Union City and north of Memphis and Charleston Railroad, excepting, perhaps, Memphis. Shall I proceed to garrison, compose, and command the district according to my own judgment, or hold myself and command ready to move upon being relieved, according to your order by General Quinby?

Please advise me at once.

JOHN A. McCLERNAND,
Major-General, Commanding.

BOLIVAR, *July* 2, 1862.

Maj. Gen. JOHN A. McCLERNAND:

It is currently reported and believed by some of the loyal citizens of this place that about 500 rebel cavalry have made their appearance in this county and have made their threats to burn the cotton now stored at the depots in this place. We have but 40 effective cavalrymen here and 275 infantry, and our camps are situated near the bridges and three-quarters of a mile from the depot.

Is it possible to have any of the cavalry at Grand Junction ordered here? Answer immediately.

W. L. SANDERSON,
Colonel, Commanding.

HEADQUARTERS ARMY OF THE MISSISSIPPI,
July 2, 1862.

Major-General HALLECK:

As telegraphed last night, Hamilton will reach Rienzi at 8 o'clock this morning. What do you think of the propriety of posting him thus: Left division near Jacinto, covering the Marietta, Fulton, and Bay Springs roads; the right between Jacinto and Rienzi, covering Van Dorn's old road to Booneville? From these positions there are two roads leading back to this camp, besides the Glendale, Jacinto, and Farmington road, which is the best for wagons. It is 6 miles only from near

---

* See Part I, pp. 17-20.

Rienzi on the railroad to Jacinto; it would therefore be easy to supply them. The water is good; the roads both south and to their rear offer many strong defensive positions. Their right flank would be secured by Asboth's positions and the Tuscumbia Bottom, which is wide and very difficult, the Jacinto road having had nine bridges connected by a causeway to make good the road across against a demonstration. Asboth could be supported; in case of anything more serious he could be withdrawn. I shall direct Hamilton to hold his troops near Rienzi and examine the ground with a view to this movement and await your decision.

> W. S. ROSECRANS,
> *Brigadier-General.*

> POPE'S HEADQUARTERS, *July* 2, 1862.

Major General HALLECK:

Colonel Sheridan's report via Rienzi this morning confirms the repulse of a very strong cavalry force of ten regiments, names of most being given. He followed them 4 miles on the Booneville and Blackland road, along which he found many dead and wounded. Nine of our wounded have been brought to Rienzi. I have sent him a battery and two infantry companies to support it. Should like to know decision about location of the left wing, now coming from Nolin's to Rienzi. Hamilton has arrived at Rienzi with his staff. Will it not be better to withdraw that brigade from Hatchie Crossing?

> W. S. ROSECRANS,
> *Brigadier-General.*

> CORINTH, *July* 2, 1862.

Major-General ROSECRANS:

Your proposed disposition of Hamilton's division is approved, if the roads and water prove satisfactory on examination.

> H. W. HALLECK,
> *Major-General.*

> HEADQUARTERS SECOND BRIGADE, CAVALRY DIVISION,
> *Booneville, July* 2, 1862—9.30 a. m.

General ASBOTH, *Rienzi:*

GENERAL: I do not wish any further supports. The enemy have " skedaddled."

The artillery and infantry have all arrived, for which I am very much obliged, as well as for the forage you are sending.

I am, sir, very respectfully, your obedient servant,

> P. H. SHERIDAN,
> *Colonel, Commanding Second Brigade, Cavalry Division.*

> HEADQUARTERS ARMY OF THE MISSISSIPPI,
> *July* 2, 1862.

Major-General HALLECK, *Corinth:*

I have just received the following dispatch from Colonel Sheridan:

The enemy have retreated, and in all probability to Guntown and Saltillo. There are none of them to be found between Booneville and Blackland. I have two companies of infantry and a battery of artillery for support furnished by General Asboth, which is all that is necessary at the present time. We were attacked by General Chalmers with the following regiments: Brewer's, 200 strong; Adams', 874; Greer's, 800; First Alabama Battalion, 180; Kentucky Battalion, 180; Clanton's, 800; Balch's, 800, and probably two others.

I have issued an order complimenting Sheridan and his command. More cavalry massed under such an officer would be of great use to us.

Sheridan ought to be made a brigadier. He would not be a stampeding general.

W. S. ROSECRANS,
Brigadier-General.

HEADQUARTERS ARMY OF THE MISSISSIPPI,
July 2, 1862.

General C. S. HAMILTON, *Rienzi :*

The general commanding directs me to say that from the reports of your medical director you seem to be of the impression that only a bivouac of four or five days is intended. Such is not the case. Your command will be put in camp south of the Jacinto and Rienzi road, the left covering the approach from the east, southeast, and south; the right that by the Van Dorn road toward Booneville. Should you find this practicable and a good camping ground you will then open communication with your old camp, repairing the road and blazing the way.

Your supplies will reach you via Rienzi or be procured from there when practicable.

W. L. ELLIOTT,
Chief of Staff.

CAMP NEAR HOLLY SPRINGS,
July 2, 1862.

Major-General GRANT:

I have positive knowledge that Jackson's cavalry have passed to the south of the Tallahatchie, where there is an infantry force. Nothing at Holly Springs. Have not yet heard from Hamilton's division, which ought to have been here from Corinth since yesterday.

Have heard of the attack on my train. Am satisfied with the result. They won't try it again at this point. I cover nearly the whole road east of Germantown. I will take in the country enough mules to make good the loss by the stampede. It is going to cost much to supply us, and it might be better for a time to reoccupy La Grange and Moscow, but Halleck's orders were for me to co-operate with Hamilton; would be at Holly Springs Tuesday morning.

W. T. SHERMAN,
Major-General.

HDQRS. CENTRAL DIVISION OF THE MISSISSIPPI,
Trenton, Tenn., July 2, 1862.

Capt. M. ROCHESTER,
Assistant Adjutant-General, Columbus, Ky :

CAPTAIN: On the return of the Seventh Kansas Cavalry through this place I have turned out of their lines all negroes that I knew were not clearly contraband. Among them were one family of a Mr. Sims and also one of Mr. Davis. I prepared to enforce my order at all haz-ards, and only met with some opposition from one officer, Captain Raf-ferty, who had some difficulty with the provost-marshal, and who I send to you under arrest. The order was enforced by the First Kansas. Infantry.

I am, very respectfully, your obedient servant,

G. M. DODGE,
Brigadier-General, Commanding.

CORINTH, *July* 3, 1862.
(Received July 4, 1.30 a. m.)

Hon. E. M. STANTON,
Secretary of War :

Immediately on the taking of Corinth you informed me that General Mitchel had been ordered to cross locomotives and cars at Decatur. I telegraphed him the number I wanted. I have learned that not one was crossed over and no preparation made to do so. I also ordered locomotives and cars from Louisville. After a whole month two have arrived at Columbus. I can learn nothing of the others ordered. I have demanded an explanation of this neglect from the chief quarter-master at that place. I understand that General Mitchel has been or-dered to Washington. He should be required to give some explanation. These delays and neglect of duty have greatly embarrassed me in sup-plying General Buell's forces *en route* against Chattanooga.

H. W. HALLECK,
Major-General.

CORINTH, *July* 3, 1862.

Maj. Gen. U. S. GRANT :

Deliver to enemy's line all your prisoners not officers, except those guilty of barbarously treating our men, on parole not to serve till ex-changed, as already stated.

No more troops can be sent to Memphis at present. Enemy attacked Booneville but was driven back with considerable loss. Please rescind your orders about districts. They cannot be formed yet. As order to send troops to Washington is suspended, do all in your power to re-en-force Curtis; it is very possible that he has moved to Madison to open communication with Memphis; if not, he is going down east side of White River. We have no telegraph communication with him and can only guess where he is. Do all you can to ascertain.

H. W. HALLECK,
Major-General.

HEADQUARTERS DEPARTMENT OF THE MISSISSIPPI,
Corinth, Miss., July 3, 1862.

Maj. Gen. U. S. GRANT,
Comdg. District of West Tennessee, Memphis, Tenn. :

Other pressing business has prevented me from giving an earlier an-swer to your telegram of the 29th ultimo.

In asking you to report by whose negligence the train which was destroyed by the enemy had been sent over the road before it was prop-erly guarded I made no insinuation that there had been the slightest neglect on your part. Indeed, I supposed the whole thing had been done before you assumed the immediate command at Memphis. What I wanted to know were the facts of the case—who sent it out, and why it was exposed to destruction. This I directed you to investigate and report, and you take offense at the order, as intended to reflect upon you. Nor did I suppose for a moment that you were stampeded; for I know that is not in your nature; but I believed there was a stampede about the enemy threatening our line to Memphis with 30,000 men, and I now have good evidence that he did not have one-tenth of that number.

Again, you complain that troops belonging to your general command received orders direct from me while present with the army here. I shall, whenever occasion requires it, exercise the right of issuing orders direct to any detached command, or to any undetached command, if I deem it necessary. On moving your headquarters to Memphis, where there was only a very small part of the troops of this army, with communications difficult and precarious, you could hardly suppose that I would send orders, which required immediate execution, through you, who were more than a hundred miles away, when my direct orders would reach them in a few minutes. Moreover, I had information of the enemy which you could not possibly have had. I will further add that from your position at Memphis it is impossible for you to exercise the immediate command in this direction.

I must confess that I was very much surprised at the tone of your dispatch and the ill-feeling manifested in it, so contrary to your usual style, and especially toward one who has so often befriended you when you were attacked by others.

H. W. HALLECK,
Major-General.

LA GRANGE, *July* 3, 1862.

Major-General McCLERNAND:

General Sherman's cavalry has reconnoitered toward Memphis, from Holly Springs, and reports that Jackson's cavalry crossed the Memphis and Charleston Railroad in a southerly direction this morning.

M. D. LEGGETT,
Colonel, Seventy-eighth Ohio.

CORINTH, *July* 3, 1862.

General ROSECRANS:

The recall of Hamilton was under an order to immediately send troops to Washington. The rumor of McClellan's defeat was afterward contradicted and the order suspended, but too late to countermand Hamilton's return. Sherman's command was ordered back for same reasons, but he probably did not receive it. Send him this by the courier. I am waiting full report of Sheridan's affair to send to Washington.

H. W. HALLECK,
Major-General.

SPECIAL FIELD ORDERS, } HDQRS. DEPARTMENT OF THE MISS.,
No. 140. } *Corinth, Miss., July* 3, 1862.

I. The commanding officer at Columbus is charged with guarding the railroad from that place to Humboldt, inclusive; the commanding officer at Jackson, from that place to Grand Junction and Bethel, inclusive; the commanding officer of Memphis, from that place to Grand Junction; the commanding officer at Corinth, to Bethel, Iuka, and south and west as far as the roads are opened, except where they come within the limits of other commands; and the commanding officer at Tuscumbia, from Decatur to Iuka, inclusive. Such officers will be under the general orders of their superiors in brigades, divisions, districts, and sub-districts.

II. Military officers not assigned to special duty under the superintendent of the railroad are simply charged with the guarding of the roads and trains; in no case will they interfere with the running of the trains, which will be exclusively under the orders of the superintendent, his assistants, and employés. They, however, will furnish details of working parties, under their own officers, on requisition of the superintendent and his assistants, and such working parties will be under the general direction of the latter, so far as the work itself is concerned.

III. Officers in command of railroad guards or of troops in their vicinity will be held responsible for any injury they may receive. All persons found injuring railroads or telegraph lines will be immediately shot down, and all expenses of repairing such injuries will be assessed upon persons having property or living in the vicinity. Particular care will be taken that our troops do not disturb water-tanks or switches, as serious accidents may result. In no case will any one be permitted to wash in the tanks or to draw off the water. To this end no soldier will be permitted on the track unless as a guard or marching under an officer.

IV. No person, unless traveling on military service, will be allowed a free pass. Military freight will always have the preference. The charges for passage and pr vate freights will until otherwise ordered be the same as fixed by former schedules over the same routes. All freight and passage money collected will be used and accounted for as railroad funds.

By order of Major-General Halleck:

J. C. KELTON,
Assistant Adjutant-General.

GENERAL ORDERS, }   HDQRS. DIST. OF WEST TENNESSEE,
No. 60.   }   *Memphis, Tenn., July 3, 1862.*

The system of guerrilla warfare now being prosecuted by some troops organized under authority of the so-called Southern Confederacy, and others without such authority, being so pernicious to the welfare of the community where it is carried on, and it being within the power of communities to suppress this system, it is ordered that wherever loss is sustained by the Government collections shall be made by seizure of a sufficient amount of personal property from persons in the immediate neighborhood sympathizing with the rebellion to remunerate the Government for all loss and expense of collection.

Persons acting as guerrillas without organization and without uniform to distinguish them from private citizens are not entitled to the treatment of prisoners of war when caught, and will not receive such treatment.

By command of Maj. Gen. U. S. Grant:

JNO. A. RAWLINS,
Assistant Adjutant-General.

WAR DEPARTMENT, *July* 4, 1862.

Major-General HALLECK, *Corinth, Miss.:*

You do not know how much you would oblige us if, without abandon- ing any of your positions or plans, you could promptly send us even 10,000 infantry. Can you not? Some part of the Corinth army are certainly fighting McClellan in front of Richmond. Prisoners are in our hands from the late Corinth army.

A. LINCOLN.

HDQRS. RESERVE CORPS, ARMY OF THE TENNESSEE,
Jackson, July 4, 1862.

Major-General HALLECK, *Corinth:*

Colonel Leggett informs me that General Sherman is relieving the force sent by me to Grand Junction. I will order back the force there unless otherwise ordered by you.

JOHN A. McCLERNAND,
Major-General, Commanding.

COLDWATER, *July* 4, 1862.

Major-General HALLECK:

I came to Coldwater on Tuesday morning and sent a brigade to Holly Springs. About 800 cavalry escaped south. As near as I can learn there are about 4,000 infantry at the Tallahatchie Bridge, 18 miles south of Holly Springs. The railroad bridge was burned, but is being repaired.

I have sent three sets of messengers to Ripley to communicate with the forces sent from Corinth, none of whom have returned, and I have not heard a word of that force yet.

The enemy's cavalry is still between this and Memphis; they at- tacked my train, guarded by the Fifty-seventh Ohio, and were repulsed. The train reached Memphis and I expect it back to Moscow to-morrow. Railroad trains could now run through. Had a car at Moscow fitted up for a gun force here, and another about 20 miles west, in Coldwater, where the Memphis road crosses. It would cover the railroad from Junction. I can hear nothing about an enemy on the Memphis and Grenada road and know nothing of affairs in that quarter.

W. T. SHERMAN,
Major-General.

GENERAL ORDERS, }   HDQRS. DIST. OF WEST TENNESSEE,
    No. 61.   }   *Memphis, July* 4, 1862.

I. Officers and soldiers are hereby prohibited under severe penalties from selling military clothing, arms, or ammunition, whether the same be public or private property, to citizens. In cases where such sales have been heretofore made the citizens who purchased the same will at once return the property so purchased to the commanding officer of the company or regiment to which the soldier belongs of whom the articles were obtained, or to the post quartermaster, under penalty of being arrested and placed in confinement.

II. It is made the duty of all officers to see that this order is strictly enforced, and that all officers, soldiers, or citizens violating the same, by either selling or purchasing, are arrested.

By order of Major-General Grant:

JNO. A. RAWLINS,
Assistant Adjutant-General.

GENERAL ORDERS, }   HDQRS. ARMY OF THE MISSISSIPPI,
　　No. 83.　　　}   *July 4*, 1862.

Soldiers of the Army of the Mississippi:

To-day we celebrate the eighty-sixth anniversary of our national independence. Let the sublime recollections which the day inspires fill our hearts with that fire of patriotism which animated our forefathers in their seven years' contest for the freedom which is now assailed by an arrogant and unscrupulous rebellion.

No love of war, no appeal to passions, no hatred for those whose rights you have been willing to defend, and for which you are now in arms, has exiled you from peaceful pursuits and the endearments of home and friends.

An intelligent patriotism, duly appreciating the priceless value of a Government that covers and protects all that we hold dear in this world, brings you here. Unskilled in using the bowie-knife or plying the lash on the backs of your fellow-men, you did not come boasting you could whip three to one, but modestly and simply offered your lives for the defense of our common liberties; by your docility and patience in inuring yourselves to the toils and hardships of a new profession, and by your courage taught the enemies of our liberties a lesson which, I trust, you will be still more ready to repeat when the occasion offers.

Remember the haughty declaration of the rebels that our Government was at an end! Remember the unscrupulous lies by which they have maligned your character and your motives, calling you thieves, murderers, plundering hordes, who wish to subjugate and destroy! And in reverent fear of the Almighty Ruler of Nations, in whose sight we are but sinners, on this day lift your eyes with hope that He will not permit arrogance, falsehood, treachery, and cruel deception of a peaceful and happy people to triumph; that the tears of the widows and orphans the rebels have made by plunging us into this cruel war may drown them in the day of battle, and that He may give peace and equal rights to all again, under that Government whose natal day we celebrate.

In honor of the day all duties, except the stated roll calls, police, and guard duty, will be suspended. The troops will be paraded under arms, and each brigade will fire a national salute at meridian.

By order of General Rosecrans:

　　　　　　　　　　W. L. ELLIOTT,
　　　　　　Brigadier-General and Chief of Staff.

CORINTH, MISS., *July 5*, [1862]—9 a. m.
(Received July 6, 1862, 1 a. m.)

His Excellency the PRESIDENT:

For the last week there has been great uneasiness among Union men in Tennessee, on account of the secret organization of insurgents to co-operate in any attack of the enemy on our lines. Every commanding officer from Nashville to Memphis has asked for re-enforcements. Under these circumstances I submitted the question of sending troops to Richmond to the principal officers of my command. They are unanimous in opinion that if this army is seriously diminished the Chattanooga expedition must be revoked or the hope of holding Southwest Tennessee abandoned. I must earnestly protest against surrendering what has cost us so much blood and treasure, and which, in a military point of view, is worth three Richmonds. It will be infinitely better to withdraw troops from the Shenandoah Valley, which at this time has no strategic importance. I am doing everything in my power to strengthen our position, and a week or two may change the aspect of affairs here.

H. W. HALLECK,

Major-General.

HDQRS. RESERVE CORPS, ARMY OF THE TENNESSEE,

Jackson, July 5, 1862.

Maj. Gen. H. W. HALLECK, *Corinth :*

Colonel Leggett, commanding at [Grand] Junction and La Grange, informs me that he is actually relieved by a force sent by General Sherman, and is instructed both by Sherman and Hurlbut to report to me for orders.

At the moment of the receipt of your dispatch concerning Colonel Leggett's command I was ordering him to withdraw to Bolivar, and Colonel Sanderson from Bolivar here, intending to send the latter with his regiment to Brownsville, about 26 miles from both Humboldt and Jackson, and west of the latter.

JOHN A. McCLERNAND,

Major-General, Commanding.

COLDWATER, *July* 5, 1862.

Colonel LEGGETT :

I am sadly disappointed at the conduct of that force which came from Corinth, with which I came out to co-operate. It did not come to Holly Springs and retreated to Corinth in confusion, losing its camp equipage, &c. I am sadly deficient in cavalry, and the enemy has a large force, so that they intercept my messengers and attack my trains. I have to send escorts and ambuscades with every train, thereby breaking up the main body into detachments.

The enemy is accumulating at Tallahatchie, 18 miles south of Holly Springs, and will probably attack me at or near Holly Springs. I keep a brigade there, but on account of water my main force is here. If Mc-Clernand is coming to Grand Junction, as he intended, I would like to have all of Hurlbut's and my division off the railroad for maneuver. Halleck and Grant have not given me any orders or support, and I am here in obedience to Halleck's original order, to repair railroad and take position in front of it to protect it.

I would be obliged if you could get to me some message from Halleck, as I have not heard from him in a week, and I ought to have some explanation of the extraordinary movement from Corinth on Ripley. My thanks to Smith, the operator, for his sheet of news.

Yours,

SHERMAN.

LA GRANGE, *July* 5, 1862.

Major-General McCLERNAND, *Jackson :*

I have just received a communication from Sherman. He complains that the force sent from Corinth to co-operate with him has retreated in confusion toward Corinth, leaving their camp equipage. He is without support and can get no word from Grant or Halleck, and desires me to get orders for him. He is in great need of more cavalry, and liable to be attacked by a superior force from Tallahatchie, and wishes to have the balance of his and Hurlbut's division (four regiments) relieved and sent to him. Can you get the attention of either Grant or Halleck and some orders from them?

M. D. LEGGETT,
Colonel Seventy-eighth Ohio.

JACKSON, TENN., *July* 5, 1862.

Major-General HALLECK, *Corinth:*

General Sherman informs Colonel Leggett, and he me, that the former has failed to hear either from you or General Grant.

He says the co-operating force from Corinth has retreated in confusion toward Corinth, leaving their camp equipage; that he needs more cavalry and is liable to be attacked by superior numbers, and wishes to have his and Hurlbut's four regiments (I suppose at or near La Grange and Moscow) sent to him.

If you choose to answer through me and Colonel Leggett, we will forward your answer.

I have sub-districted my district and already sent orders accordingly to different commanders relative to protecting roads, bridges, &c.

JOHN A. McCLERNAND,
Major-General, Commanding.

CORINTH, *July* 5, 1862.

Major-General McCLERNAND, *Jackson:*

Colonel Leggett's dispatch, as reported by you, is all bosh. The Corinth force did not retreat, and left no camp equipage. They were ordered back when they found no enemy in front, and less than 4,000 in front of General Sherman, of which General Sherman has been informed and answered. The disposition of these troops will be ordered as soon as expected dispatches are received from other quarters.

H. W. HALLECK,
Major-General.

HEADQUARTERS ARMY OF THE MISSISSIPPI,
July 5, 1862.

Col. J. C. KELTON,
Assistant Adjutant-General, Corinth:

I forward the following dispatch for information:

RIENZI, *July* 5, 1862.

Major Nelson, of the Seventh Illinois Cavalry, reports the enemy, 411 strong, occupying the Hatchie Bottom. One hundred of their force were at Nolin's this morning. Want of water compelled the major to return to his camp here. He had a slight skirmish with the enemy's advance. Killed one man, took one prisoner, losing one horse killed.

D. M. CALDWELL,
First Lieutenant, Aide-de-Camp.

Sheridan's recent fight has shown the importance of keeping our cavalry massed to the front. Reports from Sheridan of the disappearance of the rebel cavalry from his front lead us to expect it elsewhere. Reported movement of the enemy toward Tuscumbia or east obliged me to direct Sheridan's attention that way for a day or two. Have not cavalry strength left to dislodge or cut off the rebels at Hatchie. Have directed them to be watched and plans laid to cut them off, if their object and strength permit it. Meanwhile think it desirable in every point of view that a small battalion or squadron from Corinth should be posted at Kossuth, with orders to picket down the road toward Nolin's, at least until I can make dispositions to have that road watched. Can and will that be done?

W. S. ROSECRANS,
Brigadier-General, U. S. A., Commanding.

CORINTH, *July* 5, 1862.

General ROSECRANS:

Have this moment received some information about enemy's movements from General Thomas. They seem to threaten Tuscumbia or Decatur, and have again driven in his outposts.

Have your forces ready to move out. Send out strong scouting parties toward enemy's flank to gain positively his movement.

H. W. HALLECK,
Major-General.

HEADQUARTERS ARMY OF THE MISSISSIPPI,
July 5, 1862.

Major-General HALLECK:

Your dispatch received. Hamilton is in position. Davis' division is 1½ miles southeast of Jacinto, on Bay Springs road, and right of brigade covering Marietta road; Buford 2 miles and Sullivan 3 miles to the right. Hamilton has orders to move Third Division early to-morrow morning to position near Adams' Mill, 1½ miles northwest of Jacinto, and to look out for news. All this command have orders to have on hand three days' cooked rations. Will dispatch Sheridan to-night instructions to examine movement southeasterly. He reconnoitered in force beyond Baldwyn to-day. Lieutenant-Colonel Prince will be ordered to push eastwardly from Jacinto. Believe main body of the enemy moving toward Chattanooga or Atlanta by southern main road, cavalry probably covering their left flank and rear, with an intention to make an attack if possible in the direction of Decatur or Tuscumbia; and if not possible it will answer as a demonstration to cover their real movements.

W. S. ROSECRANS,
Brigadier-General.

HEADQUARTERS ARMY OF THE MISSISSIPPI,
July 5, 1862.

General ASBOTH, *Rienzi:*

The general commanding directs that you hold your command in readiness for a move, with three days' cooked rations, two in haversacks and one in wagons; that you inspect and report upon the condition of your command for a move if ordered.

W. L. ELLIOTT,
Brigadier-General and Chief of Staff.

HEADQUARTERS SECOND BRIGADE, CAVALRY DIVISION,
Camp near Booneville, Miss., July 5, 1862.

General GORDON GRANGER,
Comdg. Cavalry Division, Army of the Mississippi:

GENERAL: I inclose herewith some information obtained by a scout sent out by Colonel Hatch last night.* I do not know how much confidence to place in these reports, but think it best to keep you posted.

I have sent out to-day a company in the direction of Marietta to find out something more positive about this.

My impression is that the enemy are making a move and that they are moving into Northern Georgia, and that they have thrown out a column to cover their movement and possibly to make an attack on the railroad to cut off Buell from Corinth.

Warren's Mill, where they are now reported to be in force, is on the east side of the Tombigbee River, a short distance above where Macky's Creek enters into it, and about 2 miles west of the direct road between Fulton and Iuka.

Should this information be correct and their intention be to attack the railroad they have not more than 40 miles to march from Warren's Mill to Iuka.

Everything is quiet here; our pickets undisturbed. No news from the enemy, except that they are still about Tupelo. I don't know where the cavalry have gone to. I have been waiting for that attack that was promised from Blackland by the "likely-looking colored man." They have not yet made their appearance.

Look out for the left flank!

I believe they will go to Atlanta, but it is only an impression.

I am, sir, respectfully, &c.,

P. H. SHERIDAN,
Colonel, Commanding Second Brigade, Cavalry Division.

HEADQUARTERS ARMY OF THE MISSISSIPPI,
July 5, 1862.

General C. S. HAMILTON, *Rienzi and Jacinto Road:*

Colonel Sheridan reports his impression that the enemy is moving into Northern Georgia, and that they have thrown out a column to cover their movement, possibly to make an attack on the railroad, to cut Buell off from Corinth.

The enemy is reported to be at Warren's Mill in force on the east side of Tombigbee, a short distance above where Macky's Creek empties into it, and about 2 miles west of the Fulton and Iuka road. Warren's Mill is about 40 miles from Iuka.

Look for your supplies via Asboth.

W. L. ELLIOTT,
Brigadier-General and Chief of Staff.

LA GRANGE, *July 5, 1862.*

Brig. Gen. JOHN A. LOGAN, *Jackson:*

An officer of the Twentieth Ohio, just arrived from Memphis, reports that 300 of Jackson's cavalry crossed the road in a northerly direction at an early hour this morning 20 miles west of here.

M. D. LEGGETT,
Colonel Seventy-eighth Ohio Infantry.

---

* Not found.

Captain HOTCHKISS,
        Acting Assistant Adjutant-General:

CAPTAIN: That you may be informed of affairs at La Grange the above telegram is sent you.

JOHN A. LOGAN,
Brigadier-General, Commanding.

WAR DEPARTMENT,
Washington City, D. C., July 6, 1862.
Major-General HALLECK, *Corinth, Miss.* :

MY DEAR SIR : This introduces Gov. William Sprague, of Rhode Island. He is now Governor for the third time and Senator-elect of the United States.

I know the object of his visit to you. He has my cheerful consent to go, but not my direction. He wishes to get you and part of your force, one or both, to come here. You already know I should be exceedingly glad of this if, in your judgment, it could be without endangering positions and operations in the Southwest, and I now repeat what I have more than once said by telegraph. "Do not come or send a man if, in your judgment, it will endanger any point you deem important to hold, or endangers or delays the Chattanooga expedition."

Still, please give my friend Governor Sprague a full and fair hearing.

Yours, very truly,

A. LINCOLN.

CORINTH, *July* 6, 1862.
(Received 6.40 p. m.)

Hon. E. M. STANTON,
        Secretary of War :

Official reports just received of a brilliant affair of our cavalry near Booneville, Miss., on the 1st instant. Colonel Sheridan, Second Michigan Cavalry, with two regiments of 728 men, were attacked by parts of eight regiments of rebels, numbering some 4,700 men, which he defeated and drove back after seven hours' fighting. Our loss was 41 killed, wounded, and missing. That of the enemy must have been very great. Left 65 dead on the field. Official reports will be forwarded by mail. I respectfully recommend Colonel Sheridan for promotion for gallant conduct in battle.

H. W. HALLECK,
Major-General.

HEADQUARTERS ARMY OF THE MISSISSIPPI,
July 6, 1862.
General GORDON GRANGER,
        Comdg. Cavalry Division, Army of the Mississippi :

GENERAL : The general commanding directs that you inform Colonel Sheridan of the subject of this dispatch* (Rienzi, July 5, 10 p. m.), and that you instruct Colonel Mizner to watch the movements of this cavalry force with a view if possible to cut them off. Colonel Sheridan should

---

*See report of Lieut. D. M. Caldwell, aide-de-camp, of skirmish on the Hatche River, Miss., July 5, 1862, Part I, p. 21.

send a reconnoitering party on the Ripley road from Dick Smith's around toward Nolin's. If Colonel Sheridan has not a picket on that road in the vicinity of its intersection with the Blackland and Kossuth road one ought to be placed there immediately, and concert of action between Colonels Mizner and Sheridan. You should suggest to Colonel Mizner it is probable he can find a place toward Kossuth, behind Hinkle's Creek, so as to watch the Blackland and Kossuth road, and on the Rienzi and Ripley road, while he can communicate with Rienzi in such a way as to know every movement on either road, and be able to cut off any moderate patroling force of the rebels.

I am, general, very respectfully, your obedient servant,
W. L. ELLIOTT,
Brigadier-General and Chief of Staff.

CORINTH, *July* 6, 1862.

Major-General THOMAS, *Tuscumbia :*

General Rosecrans reports a strong demonstration of the enemy in the direction of Tupelo, also on our right near Kossuth. There is a general movement of the enemy reported. His real design is still in doubt. If threatened by superior forces, move this side of Bear Creek and cover Iuka and Eastport. Under no circumstances permit the enemy to get between you and Jacinto.

H. W. HALLECK,
Major-General.

HEADQUARTERS DEPARTMENT OF THE MISSISSIPPI,
Corinth, July 7, 1862.

Hon. E. M. STANTON,
Secretary of War, Washington :

SIR: Since the Kansas troops entered this department their march has been marked by robbery, theft, pillage, and outrages upon the peaceful inhabitants, making enemies to our cause wherever they went. Brigadier-General Quinby reported that he found it impossible to restrain them, and asked for authority to muster them out of service. On their reaching Major-General McClernand's command he made similar recommendations and reports; and on their way from him to this place they nearly ruined a train of cars by refusing to comply with the orders of the conductor, General Mitchell sustaining them in this disobedience of my orders. It is reported that General Mitchell took no measures whatever to restrain his men from robbery and plunder, while Colonel Anthony actually encouraged his men in committing outrages along the road, on the ground that they were "slaveholders" who were plundered.

I have brought these troops to this place, and shall do my best to reduce them to proper discipline, but am very doubtful of success, so long as bad officers, supported as they allege by political influence at Washington, encourage them in violating laws, regulations, and orders.

I inclose copies of these reports as specimens of the allegations which have been made against these Kansas troops.*

Very respectfully, your obedient servant,
H. W. HALLECK,
Major-General.

---

* See Deitzler to Quinby June 26, Chenowith to Halleck June 30, and Dodge to Rochester July 2, pp. 34, 53, 66.

HEADQUARTERS DEPARTMENT OF THE MISSISSIPPI,
Corinth, July 7, 1862.

Hon. E. M. STANTON, *Secretary of War:*

SIR: I inclose herewith a copy of a report of Brigadier-General Mc-Pherson, superintendent of railroads, from which it will be seen that we opened 367 miles of road in less than one month, besides repairing a number of locomotives and cars which were captured from the enemy greatly injured. Indeed the wood work of most of the cars has been entirely rebuilt, and all this work has been done by details from the army. The men have worked with most commendable industry and energy, and have shown the greatest willingness and alacrity in thus securing the territory we have gained from the enemy. Without these roads our position here would have been untenable for the want of supplies.

We are still greatly in want of rolling stock, but Assistant Secretary Tucker has assured me that he will immediately give his attention to supplying this deficiency. I have made requisition on the Quartermaster-General for the purchase of the Rogers locomotives.

Brigadier-General McPherson deserves great credit for the energy and untiring industry which he has devoted to the repair and organization of these roads.

Very respectfully, your obedient servant,

H. W. HALLECK,
Major-General.

[Inclosure.]

SUPERINTENDENT'S OFFICE,
Corinth, Miss., June 29, 1862.

Maj. Gen. H. W. HALLECK,
Comdg. Department of the Mississippi:

SIR: We have the following lines of railroad now open, and in running order, viz:

	Miles.
From Corinth to Columbus	143¼
From Corinth to Decatur	95
From Corinth to Booneville	20¼
From Corinth to Chewalla	12
From Memphis to Grand Junction	49
From Grand Junction to Jackson	47
Total	367

To operate these roads successfully and do the business required for the army we will need 15 locomotives, besides those already on hand, most of which are old and very much out of repair. I understand that 25 locomotives were ordered for the Mobile and Ohio Railroad (5-feet gauge) from the Paterson Locomotive and Machine Works, Paterson, N. J., and that more than half of them were completed or nearly so, but were never delivered in consequence of the breaking out of the rebellion. These locomotives could most likely be procured and placed upon the road in a short time.

We will also need, in addition to what we now have on hand, 6 first-class passenger cars, 16 second-class passenger cars, 8 mail and express baggage cars, and 100 box freight cars.

Very respectfully, your obedient servant,

JAS. B. McPHERSON,
Brigadier-General and Superintendent.

HDQRS. FIFTH DIVISION, ARMY OF THE TENNESSEE,
Moscow, Tenn., July 7, 1862.

General HALLECK, *Corinth, Miss.:*

I did not get your order of the 1st till yesterday; the messenger fell into the enemy's hands. A second was lost, and the third reached me yesterday. I am at Moscow and Hurlbut at La Grange. As long as I was at Coldwater the cavalry kept below Holly Springs, but they will be again at mischief with our trains. Cannot I have a locomotive? I have never had an hour's use of one even for supplies, except in our trip to Corinth; although my division saved five and have built almost a dozen bridges, a train has never been at my disposal and we have to haul everything from Memphis. Send me a locomotive and I will put her through to Memphis with a gun-car and a strong guard.

To defend the road from Grand Junction to Memphis we should occupy the line of Coldwater, with sufficient infantry and cavalry to pursue the enemy's detachments. To defend it on the line of road McClernand should hold the Junction and La Grange; Hurlbut, Moscow and La Fayette, and my division should be in front of Colliersville and Germantown. It is there all the roads toward Memphis debouch on this line of road.

This is terrible weather for marching; dust and heat insufferable.
W. T. SHERMAN,
Major-General.

MOSCOW, *July 7, 1862.*

General GRANT:

By order of General Halleck I am back at Moscow. The line of Coldwater is the proper line from which to protect this road, but I should have some cavalry. The Fourth Illinois is now a mere squad, and it is worse than toothache to call upon them for hard work. My wagon train again started for Memphis this morning under escort of the regiment that protected it before. I don't think the train will be molested going to Memphis, but coming back it may be different. I think it should take the back road. I want McClernand to hold the Junction; Hurlbut, Moscow and La Fayette, and my division to come to Germantown and Colliersville.

Who should give the order? I have telegraphed to him my return.
W. T. SHERMAN,
Major-General.

MEMPHIS, *July 7, 1862.*

Maj. Gen. H. W. HALLECK, *Corinth, Miss.:*

The following is substance of dispatch just received from General Sherman:

Returned to Moscow. Think Coldwater the line to hold for protection of the railroad. Want McClernand to hold Grand Junction; Hurlbut, Moscow and La Fayette, and my (Sherman's) division to move to Germantown and Colliersville.

Shall I make the order for this position?
U. S. GRANT,
Major-General.

HDQRS. FIRST DIVISION, DISTRICT OF JACKSON,
Jackson, July 7, 1862.
Col. L. OZBURN, Commanding Expedition:

You will proceed at once with your command to Brownsville and make that place the base of your operations and encamp there until otherwise ordered. You will enforce strict discipline and order in your camp by keeping your command together and not allowing them to straggle outside your lines. You will use your utmost endeavors to protect the rights of private property, suffering nothing to be taken except what is absolutely necessary for your command, and then only by paying or agreeing to pay to the owner a just compensation for the same. You will keep a vigilant [guard] posted around your camp to prevent surprise, and also to prevent your command from straggling outside the lines. Information has just been received that a force of some 300 of the enemy (Jackson's cavalry) are in the vicinity of where you will be and beyond you. You will use active measures to take them, if in your power, without hazarding your command, upon receipt of information that you may receive at any time respecting them or their movements, and you will co-operate with Major Wallace, of the cavalry. You will use your endeavors to cultivate a conservative, friendly feeling with the people where you may be. You will report to me your operations from time to time and any other information that you may see proper to communicate to these headquarters.

By command of Brig. Gen. J. A. Logan:

[STEWART R. TRESILIAN,]
Captain and Aide-de-Camp.

HDQRS. FIRST DIV., DISTRICT OF JACKSON, TENN.,
Jackson, July 7, 1862.
Maj. M. R. M. WALLACE, Commanding Cavalry Expedition:

You will proceed at once with your command to Brownsville Landing, by way of Brownsville, and make that place the base of your operations and encamp there until otherwise ordered.

You will enforce strict discipline and order in your camp by keeping your command together and not allowing them to straggle outside your lines.

You will use your utmost endeavors to protect the rights of private property, suffering nothing to be taken except what is absolutely necessary for your command, and then only by paying or agreeing to pay to the owner a just compensation for the same. You will keep a vigilant guard posted around your camp to prevent surprise, and also to prevent your men from straggling outside the lines.

Information has just been received that a force of some 300 of the enemy (Jackson's cavalry) are in the vicinity of where you will be and beyond you. You will take active measures to take them, if in your power, without hazarding your command, upon receipt of information that you may receive at any time respecting them or their movements, and you will co-operate with Colonel Ozburn, who will be stationed at Brownsville. You will endeavor to cultivate a conservative, friendly feeling with the people where you may be. You will report to me your operations from time to time and any other information that you may see proper to communicate to these headquarters.

Respectfully, yours,

JOHN A. LOGAN,
Brigadier-General, Commanding.

ORDERS, }   HEADQUARTERS,
No. 49. }   *Moscow, July* 7, 1862.

Stealing, robbery, and pillage has become so common in this army that it is a disgrace to any civilized people.

No officer other than the general commanding will grant passes beyond the line of pickets, and he will grant none except on extraordinary occasions.

Brigadiers may send out as heretofore the regular foraging parties with guard, strictly according to orders already issued.

Major Gibson will detail a patrol daily of an officer and 10 mounted men, who will patrol the country round about camp. This patrol will fire upon any party engaged in robbery and pillage, or who attempt to escape. All found outside the lines will be delivered to the provost-marshal, who will put them on bread and water until relieved by the commanding general.

This demoralizing and disgraceful practice of pillage must cease, else the country will rise on us and justly shoot us down like dogs and wild beasts.

By order of Maj. Gen. W. T. Sherman :

                                    J. H. HAMMOND,
                                    Assistant Adjutant-General.

———

SPECIAL ORDERS, }   HEADQUARTERS FIFTH DIVISION,
No. 111.   }   *Moscow, July* 7, 1862.

Brig. Gen. J. W. Denver will guard the main road west. Brig. Gen. M. L. Smith will keep one regiment on guard at Ammon's Bridge, over Wolf River, between Moscow and La Grange, to be relieved as he may judge best.

Colonel McDowell, commanding Second Brigade, will guard the railroad, as before the march to Coldwater.

Major Taylor, chief of artillery, will designate a section of artillery to report to General Smith for duty at Ammon's Bridge.

By order of Maj. Gen. W. T. Sherman :

                                    J. H. HAMMOND,
                                    Assistant Adjutant-General.

———

HDQRS. CENTRAL DIVISION OF THE MISSISSIPPI,
                                    Trenton, Tenn., July 8, 1862.

Capt. M. ROCHESTER,
    Assistant Adjutant-General, Columbus, Ky. :

CAPTAIN : I have the honor to submit the following report of the work done by the troops under your command on the Mobile and Ohio Railroad from Columbus to Humboldt :

At Columbus the overflow of the Mississippi River had damaged and destroyed a portion of the track. This was relaid and a new track run to the water's edge for the purpose of unloading cars. At the crossing of Little Obion River was the first bridge out, formerly a Howe's truss, with 90 feet span, the entire wreck of which, bolted together, had to be taken out of the stream. It was replaced by a single bent trestle 110 feet long and 30 feet rise. The danger of a single bent trestle of such height was overcome by placing a crib in the center of the stream, with stringers from bank to bank, on which was built the trestle-work, all above the common stage of water. The next bridge out was at the Bayou Des Shay. This was replaced with a single bent trestle of 90 feet length and 25 feet rise, making a substantial bridge; a water-tank was also built at this bridge. Between this point and Big Obion were some four wooden culverts, partially burnt, and one beam-truss bridge, somewhat damaged; the track was also torn up in places, all of which was repaired. At the Big Obion River a Howe's truss of 120 feet span had been burnt. The height of this bridge and the depth of water precluded replacing it speedily with a permanent structure. The track was therefore changed and a temporary bridge on the lower side of the stream was put in. Three large cribs were built, capped with bolsters and heavy stringers, the whole 130 feet long. A new grade was thrown up around the old trestle-work some 600 feet long, thus lowering the bridge some 10 feet, and leaving the old bridge in such shape that a new truss can be built at any time without the detention or delay of trains. This temporary work was put in in 15 feet of water, and the cribs are very irregular, but at the same time strong and substantial, and would last a long time if the stream at extra high water did not rise above them. All the work was delayed some ten days for want of proper tools. As soon as they arrived the work was pushed and completed in about twelve days; and by the time the rolling stock arrived the road-bed for the entire division was covered with weeds, rendering it impassable for a loaded train. These have all been thoroughly cleaned off. The tanks, all except one, were damaged, and in most cases pumps taken away. These have been replaced and are now all in working order. Section men have been placed on every 12 to 15 miles of the road, and the troops are so distributed that every bridge, trestle, and wooden culvert, every station and switch, are guarded; and this portion of the read is in a condition that good machinery will take over it 25 loaded cars with ease.

I am, very respectfully, your obedient servant,

G. M. DODGE,
Brigadier-General, Commanding.

MEMPHIS, *July* 8, 1862.

Major-General HALLECK:

I commenced gathering contrabands last Saturday to work on fortifications; they are now at work. On account of the limited force here we are only fortifying south end of city to protect stores and our own troops. Colonel Webster has been too unwell to push this matter, and I have no other engineer. Secessionists here have news from Richmond by the south which makes them jubilant. I would like to hear the truth.

U. S. GRANT,
Major-General.

CORINTH, *July* 8, 1862.

Maj. Gen. U. S. GRANT:

McClellan has suffered severe losses, but holds his own. He is being largely re-enforced. Whether troops go from this department is not yet positively determined. You will therefore make no changes in the disposition of troops for the present, unless it may be to assist General Curtis.

H. W. HALLECK,
Major-General.

CORINTH, *July* 8, 1862.

Major-General GRANT, *Memphis:*

The Cincinnati Gazette contains the substance of your demanding re-enforcements and my refusing them. You either have a newspaper correspondent on your staff or your staff is very leaky. This publication did not come from these headquarters.

H. W. HALLECK,
Major-General.

CORINTH, *July* 8, 1862.

Major-General SHERMAN, *Moscow:*

We cannot run the Memphis line at present; we are deficient in rolling stock to bring supplies from Columbus. The river is almost useless. We are very hard pushed, but hope to be better supplied next week. Your supplies must come from Columbus and be switched off at Jackson. Don't get angry; we are doing everything for you in the range of human possibility. If you knew how hard everybody here has been working you would not grumble.

The enemy massed large forces at Tupelo and Fulton. We are not certain of his intention, but believe it to be to cut off our connection with Buell.

McClellan has suffered severe losses, but holds his position, and is being re-enforced. He will now use pick and shovel.

H. W. HALLECK,
Major-General.

MOSCOW, *July* 8, 1862.

General HALLECK:

Excuse my growl. I feel and appreciate the burden you carry, and I know no man in the country able to carry it but you. I have great faith in McClellan, in his dogged perseverance, and if he has got around to James River can occupy the shore from James to Chickahominy, with flanks sure, and then move, as you did on Corinth, with pick and shovel. He must get within command of the city when it becomes attainable. The startle his seeming defeat has given the country must result in re-awakening attention to the large army that still opposes us.

The cars reach La Grange early in the evening, lay over all night, and return next day, but might run down to us ten minutes without loss of time. Still I have teams enough to haul from Grand Junction. I have twenty days' supply on hand.

W. T. SHERMAN,
Major-General.

MOSCOW, *July* 8, 1862.

General HALLECK:

I had dispatched a train for Memphis and escort of a regiment, but upon receiving your dispatch that we could depend for supplies on Columbus I ordered the train from La Fayette. I have just sent a scouting party of 100 cavalry to Mount Pleasant and La Fayette and propose to send a brigade to Rising Sun, where wagon train was attacked, to recover the 6 broken wagons and to take a number of mules from the neighboring planters, according to Grant's orders, to make good the loss. There are small bodies of cavalry all around the country, but I can hear of no large parties or any infantry. If infantry advance from Tallahatchie they will most likely move toward Germantown. Weather is intensely hot and dust very bad. We have abundance of water here in Wolf River.

W. T. SHERMAN,
Major-General.

Hdqrs. Fifth Division, Army of the Tennessee,
Moscow, Tenn., July 8, 1862.

Col. John A. Rawlins,
    Assistant Adjutant-General to General Grant, Memphis:

Sir: My last report of the operations of this and General Hurlbut's (Fourth) divisions was made to Col. J. C. Kelton direct, it being of date June 23, about the time of the change of command from General Thomas to General Grant. My future reports will of course be addressed to your headquarters.

My original orders from General Halleck direct were to move with mine and Hurlbut's divisions from Chewalla to Grand Junction, and thence repair the Charleston and Memphis road west to Memphis. The first repairs were made on some burned trestles in La Grange; next on two large bridges here at Moscow, and lastly two small ones at and near La Fayette. All these bridges were finished and the road ready for cars on June 25, but the accident to the train out of Memphis has prevented its use. For some reason all trains from Corinth and Columbus stop at La Grange, and, as you know, I have been compelled to haul my stores at great labor and risk from Memphis, but General Halleck now informs me that supplies can be had from Columbus, Ky.; I shall not, consequently, send any more teams into Memphis, unless in case of accident to the northern road. I have little confidence in railroads running through a country where every house is a nest of secret, bitter enemies.

On the 29th of June I received a dispatch from General Halleck saying that Hamilton's division of Rosecrans' army corps had passed the Hatchie the day before, and would be at Holly Springs on Tuesday a. m.; ordering me to co-operate as far as advisable, but not to neglect the protection of the railroad. I accordingly ordered General Hurlbut to leave at Grand Junction and La Grange each a regiment of infantry and section of artillery, with all the sick and feeble of his command, and with his effective force to march on Holly Springs, so timing his march as to be at Coldwater at 8 a. m. Tuesday. I made similar dispositions, leaving a regiment and a section of artillery at La Fayette and Moscow, with all the sick and feeble, and with the remainder, about 4,000 men, marched for Holly Springs.

I met Hurlbut's division at Hudsonville, and we moved forward to Coldwater, the first and only point where water can be had between the Wolf River and Holly Springs.

Our cavalry found the enemy's pickets at Hudsonville, drove them across Coldwater, and back toward Holly Springs. About 2½ miles out of Holly Springs the advance guard was drawn into an ambush, was fired on, lost 1 man killed and 3 wounded, all of the Fourth Illinois Cavalry. This cavalry, about 150 men, under command of Major Gibson, was dismounted and drove the enemy out of the woods, killing 1 and wounding others. The enemy's cavalry, three battalions, in all about 1,200 men, under Colonels Jackson and Pinson, formed in front of Holly Springs.

General Denver, commanding the advance brigade, moved forward

Captain Mueller's battery, which by about 18 rounds dispersed the cavalry, which retreated through and beyond the town. General Denver moved to the edge of town and sent pickets through. There was no enemy at Holly Springs but these two regiments of cavalry, about 1,500 strong. These kept away whenever I sent troops into town, but returned in small squads whenever I withdrew the command. I made my chief camp in Coldwater on account of water, which there was abundant, whilst at Holly Springs it is scarce. I sent a brigade daily to picket to Holly Springs. As soon as I reached Coldwater I endeavored to open communication with General Hamilton, supposed to be advancing on the flank in the direction of Ripley. One messenger sent afoot in disguise has never returned; two others mounted followed General Hamilton to Rienzi, and on the 5th of July I received a letter from General Hamilton saying he was on his return to Corinth, having been within 19 miles of Holly Springs. For several days I could get no dispatches or communication from any quarter; but on the 6th I received General Halleck's order by telegraph, of July 1, ordering me not to attempt to hold Holly Springs, but to fall back and protect the railroad. I accordingly ordered General Hurlbut to resume his post at La Grange, and I have come here. Each point is equidistant from Holly Springs, say, 25 miles. Each is on the railroad at vital points, and we are within 10 miles of each other. I think we protect the railroad from Junction to La Fayette, but not beyond. Hurlbut has about 300 cavalry without carbines and much used up. I had eight companies Fourth Illinois, now down to about 200 men, and they and horses much used up. Our infantry has suffered some in marching in the heat and dust, but I think I have on the line about 10,000 good fighting men.

There is no large force of the enemy nearer than Tallahatchie, 18 miles south of Holly Springs, although I have vague reports of large masses moving toward Memphis, and Hurlbut reports 300 cavalry and 5,000 infantry moving toward Davis' Mill, on Wolf River, not more than 7 miles south of the Junction. Of course they must not be allowed to make a lodgment there; but Hurlbut's cavalry have already made so many indefinite reports, which on examination proved unfounded, that I mistrust them. I also found the negroes on our late march and sojourn at Holly Springs full of false and exaggerated rumors. I prefer to be governed by what I think the enemy should attempt. If he has 30,000 men at his disposal he should interpose between Memphis and this command. He can do so perfectly unobserved by an oblique march by way of the Pigeon Roost road or by Hernando, and he could soon repair the railroad to his rear so as to bring forward his supplies; while we, depending on the Columbus road, may be at any moment cut off, as any family along or near that road, being in their interest and constant communication kept up, could break that line of road. I would much prefer the concentration of our whole force on Coldwater, near where the Memphis and Holly Springs [road] crosses and leave but small detachments along the road itself. Along and on the road our every movement is known and reported, while we can hear nothing. I have sent out no cavalry to North Mount Pleasant, a point where several roads meet to the southwest of this. I also picket all bridges and roads near strong with infantry. I don't apprehend attack in this position, but may be drawn out on Hurlbut's alarm or by what would be the enemy's best strategic move, the interposition of a superior force between us and Memphis. They will not in my judgment remain idle, especially if they have gained the advantage over McClellan which they claim, and I doubt if they will move back on Corinth. The destruction of the railroads there have destroyed its importance to them as a point, but Memphis, if recovered, would be a magnificent stroke, and in my opinion they will attempt it. I am told that General Curtis is in imminent danger. These interior operations give our enemy great advantages in their knowledge of country and possession of the hearty co-operation of the people.

I will keep my troops as healthy as possible in this warm and dusty weather, and try and fulfill any plan that you or General Halleck may lay down. We should not be idle these moonlight nights, especially if we detect the enemy in motion.

I am, with great respect,

W. T. SHERMAN,
Major-General.

CORINTH, *July* 8, 1862.

Brigadier-General QUINBY, *Columbus:*

Assistant Secretary Tucker will attend to the purchase of locomotives and cars East. You will purchase in the West if you can.

H. W. HALLECK,
Major-General.

GENERAL ORDERS, }   HDQRS. ARMY OF THE MISSISSIPPI,
    No. 86.   }   *July* 8, 1862.

I. The reasons for continuing the organization prescribed in General Orders, No. 51, May 29, 1862, no longer exist. The organization by wings is therefore abolished.

II. It has been brought to the attention of the general commanding that a practice exists in this army of dividing brigades into demi-brigades, the chiefs of which have staffs and headquarters records independent of those of the regiments composing them. This practice, foreign to our legal organization, and attended with many inconveniences, is prohibited from this date.

III. Division and brigade commanders will cause their respective commands and official papers to conform to this order.

IV. The organization of the army will be as follows:

First Division, Brig. Gen. E. A. Paine.

Second Division, Brig. Gen. D. S. Stanley.

Third Division, late First Division, left wing, Brigadier-General Hamilton.

Fourth Division, late Second Division, left wing, Brig. Gen. J. C. Davis.

Fifth Division, late Reserve, Brigadier-General Asboth.

Cavalry division, Brig. Gen. G. Granger.

V. Division commanders will report at these headquarters at 9 o'clock a. m., when practicable.

VI. The organization of the several divisions into brigades will remain as heretofore ordered.

VII. First Lieutenant Wiles is appointed provost-marshal for this army.

VIII. Capt. L. S. Metcalfe, assistant quartermaster, is assigned to duty as receiving and issuing quartermaster, and will report to Capt. J. W. Taylor, chief quartermaster, for orders.

By order of General Rosecrans:

W. L. ELLIOTT,
Brigadier-General and Chief of Staff.

MEMPHIS, *July* 9, 1862.

Maj. Gen. H. W. HALLECK,
        Corinth, Miss. :

A citizen of this place, reliably vouched for, has just returned from Mobile, via Meridian, Jackson, and Grenada, paying Columbus a visit. He left Mobile on the 3d instant. He says there is no large force left on the Mobile and Ohio road. The largest is at Meridian. At Jackson there is a large force. Between Coldwater and Hernando they are collecting many troops, mostly conscripts. The whole State of Mississippi, capable of bearing arms, seems to be entering the army.

U. S. GRANT,
Major-General.

SPECIAL ORDERS, }   HDQRS. DISTRICT OF WEST TENNESSEE,
No. 133.   }   *Memphis, Tenn., July* 9, 1862.

Complaints of recent irregularities, brought to the attention of the general commanding, render necessary the publication of the following orders:

I. Officers, non-commissioned officers, soldiers, and persons in the service of the United States are forbidden to trespass upon the orchards, gardens, or private grounds of any person or persons, or in any manner whatever to interfere with the same, without proper written authority so to do. Marauding, pilfering, and any unauthorized and unnecessary seizure or destruction of private property is prohibited by General Orders of the department, Nos. 8 and 13, series of 1861, and will be punished with the extreme penalty imposed by the laws of war, which is death.

II. Commissioned officers of companies will not pass their camp lines without written permission of their district, brigade, or regimental commanders, and then only on official business or other urgent and satisfactory reasons, to be given in the letter of permission. Non-commissioned officers and soldiers are prohibited from leaving camp at any time, except when detailed on duty or on written permission of their regimental commanders, who may grant such permission to not more than three men at any one time from each company to be absent under charge of a non-commissioned officer, who will be held responsible for their good conduct.

III. The pickets and guard reliefs will remain at their immediate picket or guard stations, unless in the discharge of proper military duty, and will not straggle therefrom, under penalty of being arrested and severely and summarily dealt with.

IV. No commissioned officer, non-commissioned officer, or soldier will be permitted to be absent from camp after retreat.

V. The military police, patrols, and picket guards will arrest all persons found violating any of the provisions of this order, either by trespassing upon the gardens, orchards, and grounds herein mentioned, or seizure or destruction of private property, or being outside of camp lines or straggling from their guard stations without proper authority. Commissioned officers to be reported to district, division, or brigade headquarters, and non-commissioned officers and soldiers to be taken before the provost-marshal.

VI. Officers of regiments, detachments, and companies, and officers of the day, and of police are enjoined to use their utmost diligence in making known and enforcing all orders necessary for the safety of the command and the city.

By order of Maj. Gen. U. S. Grant:

JNO. A. RAWLINS,
Assistant Adjutant-General.

The foregoing special order, published for the locality of Memphis, is hereby extended to the entire command, and will be strictly enforced.

By order of Maj. Gen. U. S. Grant:

JNO. A. RAWLINS,
Assistant Adjutant-General.

CORINTH, MISS., *July* 10, 1862.
(Received 5 p. m.)

To the President:

Governor Sprague is here. If I were to go to Washington I could advise but one thing: to place all the forces in North Carolina, Virginia, and Washington under one head, and hold that head responsible for the result.

H. W. HALLECK,
Major-General.

MEMPHIS, *July* 10, 1862.

Maj. Gen. H. W. HALLECK, *Corinth, Miss.:*

There are a great many families of officers in the rebel army here who are very violent. Will you approve of sending them all south of our lines?

U. S. GRANT,
Major-General.

CORINTH, *July* 10, 1862.

Maj. Gen. U. S. GRANT, *Memphis, Tenn.:*

Yes, if you deem it expedient.

H. W. HALLECK,
Major-General.

HDQRS. FIFTH DIVISION, ARMY OF THE TENNESSEE,
Moscow, Tenn., July 10, 1862.

General HURLBUT, *La Grange, Tenn.:*

Assure Colonel Leggett of prompt assistance if he needs it. Davis' Mill should be closely watched. No enemy should be allowed to camp there for a single night.

If Jackson's cavalry are about Salem they are watching Halleck's movements about Ripley. Still, as so much now depends on the Columbus road, it should be well guarded.

I can hear or see no enemy about me, and very little of anything between us and Memphis. Very little can be done this hot weather by us or the rebels. Try and prevent petty thieving and pillaging; it does us infinite harm. I hear of some horses taken by your men near Holly Springs and a pair of mules taken by your train from near La Fayette.

Can you hire a good spy to stay at Holly Springs? I can find none here, which is an insignificant place.

W. T. SHERMAN,
Major-General.

HDQRS. FOURTH DIV., DISTRICT OF WEST TENNESSEE,
La Grange, Tenn., July 10, 1862.

Maj. Gen. WILLIAM T. SHERMAN, *Moscow, Tenn.:*

I have fired no guns nor heard any. The country to my south and east is quiet. My cavalry have been at Saulsbury to-day, and report concentration of our forces at Rienzi and Ripley; also that 4,000 cavalry, with infantry and artillery, passed toward Holly Springs night before last, 15 miles below Saulsbury. Everybody, black and white, reports a large force gathering near Holly. Train from north not yet in.

[S. A. HURLBUT],
Brigadier-General, Commanding Fourth Division.

JACKSON, *July* 10, 1862.

Maj. M. R. M. WALLACE, *Commanding Cavalry:*

Your report is received, which is entirely satisfactory.

I desire you to make reconnaissances up the Hatchie River, on this side, as often as you can, and crossing over on the other side if you think it is expedient. You will notify Colonel Ozburn to move up his command to your present camp at Brownsville Landing, and support you in every move that you may make up the river. Send and get six days' more of rations.

Communicate with me often as you can.

I am, major, very respectfully, yours,

JOHN A. LOGAN,
Brigadier-General, Commanding.

SPECIAL ORDERS, }   HDQRS. DISTRICT OF WEST TENNESSEE,
No. 134.   }   *Memphis, Tenn., July 10, 1862.*

*   *   *   *   *   *   *

V. The Thirty-fourth and Forty-third Indiana Infantry, the Sixth Illinois Cavalry, and Rogers' and De Golyer's batteries are hereby temporarily assigned to the Third Division, Army of the Tennessee, commanded by Brig. Gen. A. P. Hovey. All reports and returns and all requisitions for commissary, quartermaster's, and ordnance stores will be made through him.

*   *   *   *   *   *   *

By order of Maj. Gen. U. S. Grant:

JNO. A. RAWLINS,
Assistant Adjutant General.

WAR DEPARTMENT,
July 11, 1862.

Major-General HALLECK, *Corinth:*

The President has this day made the following order, which I hasten to communicate to you:

EXECUTIVE MANSION,
Washington, July 11, 1862.

Ordered, That Maj. Gen. Henry W. Halleck be assigned to command the whole land forces of the United States, as general-in-chief, and that he repair to this capital as soon as he can with safety to the positions and operations within the department under his charge.

A. LINCOLN.

You will please acknowledge the receipt of this order, and state when you may be expected here. Your early presence is required by many circumstances.

EDWIN M. STANTON,
Secretary of War.

CORINTH, *July* 11, 1862.

Major-General GRANT, *Memphis:*

You will immediately repair to this place and report to these headquarters.

H. W. HALLECK,
Major-General.

CORINTH, MISS., *July* 11, 1862—3 p. m.

To the PRESIDENT OF THE UNITED STATES:

Your orders of this date are this moment received. General Grant, next in command, is at Memphis. I have telegraphed to him to immediately repair to this place. I will start for Washington the moment I can have a personal interview with General Grant.

H. W. HALLECK,
Major-General.

MOSCOW, *July* 11, 1862.

General HALLECK:

I want to send an expedition to Rising Sun, 18 miles northwest, where our train was attacked on the 1st and 6th; wagons left broken. Thirty-five mules were lost in the stampede, and, under General Grant's orders, I want to make good the loss by taking a like number from the neighboring planters, who were knowing to the attack. It will take three days. We have had a slight shower, and marching much improved thereby. May I send the expedition?

W. T. SHERMAN,
Major-General.

CORINTH, *July* 12, 1862.

Major-General SHERMAN, *Moscow:*

Send the expedition to Rising Sun to-morrow if you deem it best. General Grant left Memphis yesterday for Columbus. As soon as I can see him you will probably take command at Memphis.

H W. HALLECK,
Major-General.

CORINTH, *July* 12, 1862.
E. M. STANTON,
    Secretary of War:

In leaving this department shall I relinquish the command to next in rank, or will the President designate who is to be the commander?
H. W. HALLECK,
    Major-General.

HEADQUARTERS DEPARTMENT OF THE MISSISSIPPI,
    Corinth, July 12, 1862.
Hon. E. M. STANTON,
    Secretary of War, Washington:

SIR: I inclose herewith a copy of an official report of the commanding officer at Bethel, Tenn., in regard to the conduct of the Seventh Kansas Volunteers on their march to this place. I have similar reports from nearly every town they passed through, and numerous reclamations from the citizens on the road are coming in for payment for property stolen and robbed or destroyed by them. It is said that General Mitchell took no measures to restrain his men, but rather encouraged them in their outrages. Measures have already been initiated to reduce these troops to order and discipline, but I have no doubt that Senator Lane and others will attribute any measures of restraint or punishment which may be adopted to political influences and will heap unmeasured abuses upon any officer who shall attempt to keep them in order. I deem it due to the officers of this army that you should be made aware of the real facts of the case. Either discipline must be maintained or our troops will become a mere band of robbers.

Very respectfully, your obedient servant,
H. W. HALLECK,
    Major-General.

[Indorsement.]

ADJUTANT-GENERAL'S OFFICE,
    August 5, 1862.

The papers within constitute a report from General Halleck, from whom it is now understood that all the measures possible were taken to remedy the evils complained of.
E. D. TOWNSEND,
    Assistant Adjutant-General.

[Inclosure No. 1.]

SAINT LOUIS, *January* 28, 1862.
Major-General HALLECK,
    Commanding Department of Missouri:

GENERAL: In behalf of the loyal citizens of the county of Jackson, Missouri, you honored me with a personal interview in regard to the violent and lawless action of United States military forces in that county, under command of Col. C. R. Jennison and others, and in order that you might fully comprehend and appreciate the mode of warfare practiced by those forces I placed in your hands many petitions of true and loyal men asking for relief at your hands on account of that lawless action; and upon the authenticated facts stated in those petitions I based two propositions:

First. That you would intervene in behalf of the loyal people of my county in order that they should in the future be protected from such wanton outrages on their persons and property.

Second. That you would consider the claim of each petitioner and grant such relief as might be just and proper in that regard.

As to the first proposition you were pleased to inform me that orders had been issued to General Pope to suppress or drive from this State that class of military force of which my people complained. To the second proposition I was informed you had no power or authority to act in the matter, because the loss and injury complained of by each petitioner were done by a military force over which you had no power of control. And at the same time you kindly remarked that you would forward the several petitions to the War Department, at Washington, for advice, orders, &c., thereon; thereupon I requested they should be returned to me in order that I might present them in person, which request you granted.

Above I have given the substance of what passed between us in regard to my mission, and in aid thereof at Washington respectfully ask that you will honor me with a written answer, particularly as to your refusal to take any action on the matters of relief set forth in the petitions, with such reasons, suggestions, &c., in that regard you may deem proper to make.

With respect and esteem,

                                           O. G. CATES.

[Sub-inclosure.]

                    JEFFERSON CITY, *November* 21, 1861.

Hon. O. G. CATES:

DEAR SIR: Yours of the 2d instant came to this place while I was in Washington City, and I have just now upon my return received it. I have received several communications in relation to the depredations committed by Lane's men, and as I read each one I become more and more indignant at the outrages committed upon our people. I had written to the President before I left for Washington, urging that if Kansas should be made a military department Lane should not have the command.

I am happy to know that General Hunter has been assigned to that department. His headquarters will be at Fort Leavenworth. He is a true soldier, hating all robbers and thieves. I have every confidence that he will control Lane, Jennison & Co., and keep them out of this State. Please keep him well informed of the facts. I understand that Lane has no military authority, either from the United States or Kansas, but is robbing on his own account. If he refuses to submit to the authority of General Hunter I will feel myself bound, as the chief executive of the State, to see that the citizens are protected.

Very respectfully, your obedient servant,

                                           H. R. GAMBLE.

[Inclosure No. 2.]

        HEADQUARTERS DEPARTMENT OF THE MISSOURI,
                    Saint Louis, January 29, 1862.

O. G. CATES, Esq., *Saint Louis:*

SIR: Your note of yesterday is received. It correctly states the substance of our conversation. The whole matter must be referred to Washington for such orders as the Government may deem proper to issue.

Very respectfully, your obedient servant,

H. W. HALLECK,
Major-General.

[Inclosure No. 3.]

WASHINGTON, *February* 26, 1862.

Hon. E. M. STANTON,
Secretary of War, United States:

SIR: On the 6th instant you were pleased to acknowledge the receipt of my letter and other papers touching the lawless action of United States military forces in Jackson County, Missouri, which papers you kindly informed me would be submitted to the President for instructions, &c.; since which time, at great inconvenience to my private affairs at home, I have remained anxiously, though patiently, for an answer, satisfied that sickness and other matters of great public interest had so intervened as to preclude on your part a more prompt attention to mere local matters to which I called your aid and kind consideration; hence I now make no complaint of delay in that regard. When I left the city of Saint Louis I had reason to hope from what passed between General Halleck and myself that the good people of my county would be entirely free from all further lawless violence on their property at the hands of United States military forces, and so notified them by letter; but from information since received I regret to inform you I was mistaken in that grateful hope.

It now appears that although the Kansas volunteer troops, in obedience to orders, did leave the State of Missouri, the substituted United States forces in that county have made no change in their mode of warfare for the better; the same wanton and lawless violence on the rights of private property have continued without check or hinderance. Bands of negroes, slave and free, and clans of white men, thief and jayhawker, from the State of Kansas, with the knowledge of that United States force thus substituted, are permitted in open day to enter our county and freely gratify their savage lust of plunder and private revenge on defenseless and terror-stricken people.

One of the great causes of this horrid state of things is the old border Kansas war grudge, aided by a few bad men in our county, who heretofore were rejected from social and political position by the better class of our population, and in order to gratify their malice and revenge become willing informers and guides of the United States forces whenever they enter our county; consequently false representations of the thought, feeling, and action of loyal men and women subject them and their property to violence and outrage.

It is true all this savage mode of warfare is in direct violation of the express rules, orders, &c., of that military department, and certainly does not receive your approbation, yet the question forces itself for consideration, why in that small portion of Missouri where civil law is suspended, no rebel force in arms, the people quiet, peaceful, and submissive to the United States power, such gross wrong, injustice, and outrage are tolerated?

I know and fully appreciate the many and great difficulties you have to contend with in order to crush this great unnatural rebellion, and at the same time satisfy the wants of men of all sections, parties, and factions; hence I ask no intervention on your part in behalf of my county which may seem inconsistent with the general ultimate good of our common country.

With great respect,

O. G. CATES.

[Inclosure No. 4.]

HEADQUARTERS POST,
Bethel, Tenn., July 7, 1862.

Col. J. C. KELTON,
Assistant Adjutant-General, Corinth, Miss.:

The Seventh Regiment of Kansas Cavalry passed through this place yesterday and to-day on their way to Corinth, and ever since their first appearance I have been appealed to to take from them horses they have stolen from the citizens along the route they have traveled from Jackson. I have recovered some of them and handed them over to the owners, but some have eluded me and have gone on to Corinth.

The conduct of this command since it came in this vicinity has been such that it makes one feel ashamed of the volunteer service of the U. S. Army. Complaints come to me of their having robbed the farmers of all their stock and in some cases of their watches and money. I have arrested a corporal of Company F of that regiment who went into a farmer's house and broke open his trunks and stole from them a watch and some money, and will send him to you as soon as I get the testimony in his case.

They have in some instances attempted to force the women to cohabit with them when found at home alone.

Their conduct in this vicinity has been disgraceful to the Army of the United States.

Major Herrick, commanding the regiment, has done all in his power to restore to the owners such property as his men have taken, as have also some others of the officers.

I am, sir, your obedient servant,

W. W. SANFORD,
Lieutenant-Colonel, Commanding Post, Bethel, Tenn.

HEADQUARTERS DISTRICT OF JACKSON,
Jackson, Tenn., July 12, 1862.

Col. J. C. KELTON,
Assistant Adjutant-General:

In obedience to my instructions Colonel Leggett, commanding the third subdivision of my district, has exercised his usual vigilance in the discharge of duty. He reports that one of his most reliable scouts, who returned on the 10th instant, rode with 60 of Jackson's cavalry one whole day, and that he visited several of the enemy's camps, the relations of which to Grand Junction, as also the force occupying them, are illustrated by the accompanying diagram.*

The scout also learned that the rebel cavalry were under orders to make continual forays in the direction of the Memphis and Charleston Railroad for the purpose of harassing us, interrupting our communications, and seizing our supplies. I would add that the rebel cavalry

---

Not found.

frequently visit Davis' Mill, south, Spring Hill, southeast, and Saulsbury, east of Grand Junction. For the space of 30 miles east of the Junction the line of the road is unoccupied by us. These points are within another district and beyond my military jurisdiction, as limited and defined by Major-General Halleck; besides I have not the force adequate to protect them in addition to the different points now guarded by me.

In order to prevent the enemy from crossing the railroad and disturbing the flanks and rear of my position at the Junction frequent reconnaissances should be made over the country indicated by the red dotted line appearing on the diagram. The addition of another regiment of infantry or two or three more companies of cavalry would enable Colonel Leggett to do this. Cannot you place one or both of these at my disposal for that purpose? There can be but little of anything for either the infantry or cavalry now at Humboldt to do. The force now under my command is disposed along the roads from the Junction to Humboldt and from here to Bethel, a regiment of infantry and most of my cavalry being at present at Brownsville.

Very respectfully, your obedient servant,
JOHN A. McCLERNAND,
Major-General, Commanding.

[Inclosure.]

HDQRS. THIRD SUB-DIV. OF THE DIST. OF JACKSON, TENN.,
July 10, 1862.
Capt. O. T. HOTCHKISS,
Assistant Adjutant-General:

CAPTAIN: I have not much of interest to report to-day. Inclosed please find a rough and hasty sketch of the country immediately around me. I have ridden all over the country for some 10 miles about me on the east and south. I sent out a very reliable scout belonging to my command, who returned this evening after an absence of four days. He rode with 60 of Jackson's cavalry one whole day; was in their cavalry camp at Salem, 18 miles from here; also cavalry camp 6 miles west of Salem, 14 miles from here, and into their infantry camp 4 miles southeast of Salem. The numbers at each camp I have marked on the map. He would have gone to Tallahatchie, but he could not in the time I had allotted him, for I more particularly desired to understand what was going on in my immediate front. As near as he could gather from camp talk there is no design to attack with infantry or artillery very soon, but the cavalry are ordered to annoy us and to make a dash at the railroads and our provision and forage trains whenever they can do so. From the map you will see that I am considerably exposed upon my left. The rebels come almost every day to Davis' Mill, south (6 miles from here), and to Spring Hill, southeast, and Saulsbury, east. We have no troops for over 30 miles from here in an easterly direction.

What I most fear is that their cavalry will work north of us by way of Saulsbury and destroy the railroad this side of Middleburg, viz, the trestle-works 10 miles north of here. I keep a squad of men there, but with so much front to protect my force is not fully adequate. I should have either two full companies of cavalry or a regiment of infantry in addition to my present force. As it is, it takes all my cavalry for pickets and forage duty, leaving none to protect the line of railroad. To properly guard the line of railroad and protect myself from any surprise the section of country represented within the red dotted line should be reconnoitered every day.

I will, however, do the best I possibly can with what I have and keep you notified of what is going on here.

A telegraph office is a necessity here, but we have none.

Very respectfully,

M. D. LEGGETT,
Colonel Seventy-eighth Ohio Vol. Infantry, Comdg. Post.

SPECIAL ORDERS, }   HEADQUARTERS FIFTH DIVISION,
  No. 130.   *Moscow, Tenn., July* 12, 1862.

Colonel McDowell, commanding the Second Brigade, will march with the effective strength of his command early to-morrow morning to Rising Sun, Tenn. He will take post at the point where the attack was made by rebel cavalry, supposed to be under the command of Colonel Jackson, of the so-called Confederate Army, on the division train about July 1. He will there levy on the planters in the vicinity for a sufficient number of horses, mules, wagons, &c., to entirely cover the losses sustained by the United States Government in the above-mentioned attack.

An agent of the quartermaster's department will accompany Colonel McDowell, and will receive the property and give receipts, stating that it was taken to compensate the United States for losses sustained from the attacks of guerrillas, and in pursuance of General Orders, No. 60. July 3, 1862, of Major-General Grant.

Colonel Mungen, of the Fifty-seventh Ohio, will send an officer to accompany the expedition, who will point out the road and the position of the trains when the attack was made.

By order of Maj. Gen. W. T. Sherman:

J. H. HAMMOND,
Assistant Adjutant-General.

ORDERS, }   HDQRS. FIFTH DIV., ARMY OF THE TENN.,
  No. 52.   *Moscow, July* 14, 1862.

Pursuant to orders received from general headquarters, Corinth, all the troops at or near Grand Junction belonging to General McClernand's division will move by rail and by land to Bolivar, where they will receive full instructions from headquarters.

I. General Hurlbut will march his division by the State Line road through Moscow and camp on the west side of the bridge and north side of the road, convenient for water, leaving the road clear. He will be careful that nothing is left behind in the way of provisions, tents, or stores of any kind. Before moving he will assure himself that Colonel Leggett has the means to transport by cars to Bolivar the public stores now at the Junction, and such sick and feeble men as cannot march. To this end the train of cars to arrive this p. m. should at once be put to work transporting stores and sick back to Bolivar.

II. After General Hurlbut's division reaches Moscow the Fifth Division will march, followed by General Hurlbut's division, with a suitable interval of time and space. An order for the march will be given by published orders or transmitted through aides-de-camp.

By order of Maj. Gen. W. T. Sherman:

J. H. HAMMOND,
Assistant Adjutant-General.

GENERAL ORDERS, }   HDQRS. ARMY OF THE MISSISSIPPI,
     No. 92.   }   *July* 14, 1862.

For the information of all in this command the following explanations are given in reference to the rights and duties of citizens of the States in which we may be stationed:

I. All citizens of the States claiming the right and holding themselves bound to the duties of citizens of the United States are entitled to the same protection of person and property which we claim for ourselves.

II. We hold citizens to the performance of active duties only when they receive protection; if left without protection they are bound only to good will and abstinence from acts of hostility to the Government.

III. Persons denying that they are citizens of the United States, repudiating the duties of citizens by words or actions, are entitled to no rights save those which the laws of war and humanity accord to their characters. If they claim to belong to a hostile Government they have the rights of belligerents, and can neither justly claim nor have anything more from this army. If they are found making war without lawful organization or commission they are enemies of mankind, and have the rights due to pirates and robbers, which it will be a duty to accord them. It is not our purpose to admit the slaves of loyal masters within our lines, or use them without compensation, or prevent their recovery when consistent with the interests of the service. The slaves of our enemies may come or go whenever they please, provided they do not interfere with the rules and orders of camps and discipline. They deserve more at our hands than their masters.

By order of General Rosecrans:

> W. L. ELLIOTT,
> *Brigadier-General and Chief of Staff.*

> WAR DEPARTMENT,
> *July* 14, 1862.

Major-General HALLECK, *Corinth, Miss.*:

I am very anxious—almost impatient—to have you here. Have due regard to what you leave behind. When can you reach here?

> A. LINCOLN.

> WAR DEPARTMENT,
> *July* 14, 1862.

Major-General HALLECK:

The Secretary of the Navy desires to know whether you have or intend to have any land force to co-operate in the operations at Vicksburg. Please inform me immediately, inasmuch as orders he intends to give will depend on your answer.

> EDWIN M. STANTON.

> CORINTH, *July* 15, 1862.

Hon. E. M. STANTON:

I cannot at present give Commodore Farragut any aid against Vicksburg. I am sending re-enforcements to General Curtis in Arkansas and to General Buell in Tennessee and Kentucky.

> H. W. HALLECK,
> *Major-General.*

CORINTH, *July* 15, 1862.

To the PRESIDENT:

General Grant has just arrived from Memphis. I am in communication with General Buell and Governor Johnson in Tennessee. Hope to finally arrange distribution of troops and to re-enforce Curtis by to-morrow and to leave Thursday morning, the 17th.

H. W. HALLECK,
Major-General.

HDQRS. U. S. FORCES, DISTRICT OF WEST TENNESSEE,
Memphis, July 15, 1862.

Maj. Gen. U. S. GRANT:

Inclosed I send you General Thompson's letter and my reply. As the envelope indicated that the matter was local I took the liberty of opening it and sending a reply.

Trusting that my action will meet your approbation, I have the honor to be, your most obedient servant,

ALVIN P. HOVEY,
Brigadier-General.

[Inclosures.]

SENATOBIA, MISS.,
Monday, July 14, 1862—1 o'clock p. m.

Maj. Gen. U. S. GRANT, U. S. A., *Memphis, Tenn.:*

GENERAL: Upon my return from Grenada this day I find a copy of your Special Orders, No. 14, of July 10, ordering the families of certain parties therein named to leave your lines within five days. If, general, you intend to carry this order into effect, which we of course presume you will, the cause of humanity will require that you make some arrangement with us by which the helpless women and children who will thus be turned out of doors can be provided for; for you must well know by this time that nine-tenths of the people of Memphis come under your law, for there is scarcely a respectable family in that city who have not a father, husband, or brother in our army, or are the widows and orphans of those who have fallen bravely fighting for our cause.

The present terminus of the Mississippi and Tennessee Railroad is at Coldwater Station, which is 34 miles from Memphis, and our regular lines are on the stream of the same name, near the station. We do not know where your regular lines are, and therefore ask that you will please define some point in a southerly direction from Memphis to which the fathers, husbands, brothers, sons, or friends of the exiles can go in safety to meet them, or that you will extend the time for leaving, as it is not possible that the number covered by your order can get transportation to Coldwater within the time granted, and I would not for an instant suppose that you propose that the little feet that will thus be driven from their homes and birth-spots should plod the weary distance of 30 miles.

At the same time, general, that I make this appeal to you I feel it my duty to remark that you must not for a moment suppose that the thousands who will be utterly unable to leave and the many who will thus be forced to take the hateful oath of allegiance to a despised government are to be thus converted into loyal citizens of the United States, or weaned from their affections for our glorious young confederacy; and while to "threaten" were unsoldierly, yet to "warn" is kindness, and therefore, general, I would tell you to beware of the curses and oaths of vengeance which the 50,000 brave Tennesseeans who are still in our army will register in heaven against the persecutor of helpless old men, women, and children, and the general who cannot guard his own lines.

The bearer of the flag and of this letter, Capt. Edward E. Porter, C. S. Army, is authorized to agree with you upon the points asked in the foregoing.

Yours, respectfully,

M. JEFF. THOMPSON, Mo. S. G.,
Brigadier-General on Special Service, C. S. Army.

MEMPHIS, TENN., *July* 15, 1862.

Brig. Gen. M. JEFF. THOMPSON,
C. S. Army, Senatobia:

I have yours of the 14th instant in relation to Special Orders, No. 14,* heretofore issued by Major-General Grant.

I herewith send you Special Orders, No. 15,* which considerably modifies the order to which you allude. You will permit me to say that your sympathies are entirely out of place, as truth and history must record the fact that the Southern people residing in localities where both of our armies have been camped prefer the continuity of the "Northern invaders" to the protection of the Southern chivalry.

You are too well versed in the science of war to be ignorant of the fact that these orders are far more mild than could have been expected after the treatment that helpless Union families have received at the hands of rebels in this city. Add to this the fact that a large part of all the information received by you can be traced directly through the families excluded by these orders, and your application for sympathy in their behalf is somewhat amusing.

The great error that the Federal officers have committed during this war has been their overkindness to a vindictive and insulting foe.

Your threats and intimations of personal danger to General Grant are in bad taste, and should be carefully revised before publication; whether he "cannot guard his own lines" the history of the battles of Shiloh and Donelson will fully show.

Should any families embraced within the orders above alluded to be obstinate and refuse to comply with Orders, No. 15, they shall be escorted to the distance of 10 miles from this city to such points as they may request.

Very respectfully,

ALVIN P. HOVEY,
Brigadier-General, Commanding.

————

SPECIAL FIELD ORDERS, }   HDQRS. DEPT. OF THE MISSISSIPPI,
      No. 160.   }   *Corinth, Miss., July* 15, 1862.

I. Major-General Grant will order the divisions of Generals Sherman and Hurlbut to Memphis. Major-General Sherman will be placed in command of that post and vicinity. The troops at Grand Junction will be withdrawn to Bolivar or the Hatchie River, which will be made the main point of defense from Memphis to Bethel.

—————————

* Not found.

II. A division of infantry will be sent from Memphis to Helena to re-enforce General Curtis. General Grant will make the necessary changes and assignments for carrying out these orders.

III. A division will be ordered by General Grant to replace the division of General Thomas, on the road from Iuka to Decatur, as soon as the latter is ready to move across the Tennessee River to join General Buell.

By order of Major-General Halleck:

N. H. McLEAN,
Assistant Adjutant-General.

CORINTH, *July* 16, 1862.

Major-General SHERMAN, *Moscow:*

You will soon receive orders from General Grant to march yours and Hurlbut's divisions to Memphis. The troops at Grand Junction will fall back to Bolivar, and a new division will be organized and sent to Curtis.

Confidential. I am ordered to Washington, and leave to-morrow, Thursday. I have done my best to avoid it. I have studied out and can finish the campaign in the West. Don't understand and cannot manage affairs in the East. Moreover, do not want to have anything to do with the quarrels of Stanton and McClellan. The change does not please me, but I must obey orders. Good-by, and may God bless you. I am more than satisfied with everything you have done. You have always had my respect, but recently you have won my highest admiration. I deeply regret to part from you.

H. W. HALLECK,
Major-General.

MOSCOW, *July* 16, 1862.

General HALLECK, *Corinth:*

I cannot express my heartfelt pain at hearing of your orders and intended departure. You took command in the Valley of the Mississippi at a period of deep gloom, when I felt that our poor country was doomed to a Mexican anarchy, but at once arose order, system, firmness, and success in which there has not been a pause.

I thank you for the kind expression to me, but all I have done has been based on the absolute confidence I had conceived for your knowledge of national law and your comprehensive knowledge of things gathered, God only knows how.

That success will attend you wherever you go I feel no doubt, for you must know more about the East than you did about the West when you arrived at Saint Louis a stranger. And there you will find armies organized and pretty well commanded, instead of the scattered forces you then had. I attach more importance to the West than the East. The one has a magnificent future, but enveloped in doubt. The other is comparatively an old country. The man who at the end of this war holds the military control of the Valley of the Mississippi will be the man. You should not be removed. I fear the consequences.

Personally you will rule wherever you go, but I did hope you would finish up what you had begun, and where your success has attracted the world's notice.

Instead of that calm, sure, steady progress which has dismayed our enemy, I now fear alarms, hesitations, and doubt. You cannot be re-placed out here, and it is too great a risk to trust a new man from the East. We are all the losers; you may gain, but I believe you would pre-fer to finish what you have so well begun.

With great respect,

W. T. SHERMAN,
Major-General.

SPECIAL FIELD ORDERS,)   HDQRS. DEPT. OF THE MISSISSIPPI,
No. 161.   }   *Corinth, Miss., July* 16, 1862.

I. Brigadier-General McKean is assigned to the command of paroled prisoners at Benton Barracks, Saint Louis.

II. The District of West Tennessee, Major-General Grant command-ing, will include the Districts of Cairo and Mississippi; that part of the State of Mississippi occupied by our troops, and that part of Alabama which may be occupied by the troops of his particular command, includ-ing the forces heretofore known as the Army of the Mississippi.

*　　*　　*　　*　　*　　*　　*

By order of Major-General Halleck:

N. H. McLEAN,
Assistant Adjutant-General.

SPECIAL FIELD ORDERS,)   HDQRS. DEPT. OF THE MISSISSIPPI,
No. 162.   }   *Corinth, Miss., July* 16, 1862.

The major-general commanding the department in giving up the im-mediate command of the troops now in the field and heretofore consti-tuting the Armies of the Ohio, Tennessee, Mississippi, and Southwest desires to express to them his appreciation of the endurance, bravery, and soldierly conduct which they have exhibited on all occasions during the present campaign. As separate corps [they] won the memorable vic-tories of Milford, Mill Springs, Pea Ridge, Fort Donelson, New Madrid, and Island No. 10, and when partially united they defeated the enemy in the bloody battle of Pittsburg and drove him from his intrenchments at Corinth. In the latter of these operations, and in the labor of repairing railroads which the enemy had destroyed, the commanding general bears personal testimony of the good conduct of the troops, and of the cheer-fulness and alacrity with which they endured the fatigues and hard-ships necessary to secure the great objects of the campaign.

The soldiers of the West have nobly done their duty and proved them-selves equal to any emergency. The general commanding desires to express to the commanders of corps and their subordinate officers his warmest thanks for their cordial co-operation on all occasions.

Soldiers, you have accomplished much toward crushing out this wicked rebellion, and if you continue to exhibit the same vigilance, courage, and perseverance it is believed that under the providence of God you will soon bring the war to a close and be able to return in peace to your families and homes.

By order of Major-General Halleck:

N. H. McLEAN,
Assistant Adjutant-General.

SPECIAL ORDERS, }   HDQRS. DISTRICT OF WEST TENNESSEE,
No. 136.   }   Corinth, Miss., July 16, 1862.

I. Brigadier-General Morgan's division of the Army of the Mississippi will hold themselves in readiness to move to the east on the line of the Memphis and Charleston road, to relieve the command of Major-General Thomas, when directed to do so. All supplies that may be left at Eastport by General Thomas will be taken charge of and issued to the troops. For further supplies this place will be looked to. All the points now occupied by the troops of Major-General Thomas' command will be taken possession of by the troops relieving him.

II. Brigadier-General Morgan's division of the Army of the Mississippi will move at an early hour on Monday, the 21st instant, to the east, on the Memphis and Charleston road, and relieve the command of Major-General Thomas on duty guarding said road. The assistant quartermaster and commissary of subsistence of the staff of General Morgan's division will proceed to Iuka and Eastport and relieve the assistant quartermaster and commissary of subsistence of General Thomas' division. Brigadier-General Rosecrans will detach his largest regiment of cavalry to proceed with General Morgan.

By order of Major-General U. S. Grant:

JNO. A. RAWLINS,
Assistant Adjutant-General.

———

GENERAL ORDERS, }   HDQRS. DISTRICT OF WEST TENNESSEE,
No. 62.   }   Corinth, Miss., July 17, 1862.

In compliance with Special Field Orders, No. 161, from Headquarters Department of the Mississippi, Corinth, Miss., July 16, 1862, the undersigned takes the command of all the troops embraced in the Army of the Tennessee, the Army of the Mississippi, and District of Mississippi and Cairo.

All reports and returns required by army regulations and existing orders will be made to the district headquarters, Corinth, Miss.

U. S. GRANT,
Major-General, U. S. Volunteers.

———

ORDERS, }   HDQRS. FIFTH DIV., ARMY OF THE TENN.,
No. 53.   }   Moscow, July 17, 1862.

I. The division will march to-morrow at early daylight on the State Line road westward in the following order: Denver's brigade, McDowell's brigade, Smith's brigade. The head of the column will halt beyond La Fayette at a distance to bring the rear of the column opposite the depot, and will rest until afternoon to enable McDowell's brigade, now at La Fayette, to fall into its appropriate place. The column will hold itself prepared to march the same evening to some point 5 or 6 miles beyond La Fayette for camp.

II. The second day's march will be in the order of McDowell's brigade, Smith's brigade, Denver's brigade. The third day's march, and until we reach our camp, back of Memphis: Smith's brigade, Denver's brigade, McDowell's brigade.

III. More attention must be given to keeping the artillery and trains closed up on the infantry masses. In no case during a march should teamsters attempt to water their teams unless a general halt for noon or night be made.   Should a wagon become disabled it must at once be moved out of the road and the trains pass on. The disabled wagon, with its guard after repairing damages, will fall in and recover its place at the next noon or night halt. Brigade and regimental quartermasters must be with their trains all the time, and will see that the wagon guards keep near their respective wagons and carry their arms and accouterments.

IV. The division train and the ammunition train must follow the train of the first or leading brigade. The rear brigade will send its train in advance of the infantry. The leading brigade will always keep out an advance guard of two companies, with skirmishers in front and on the flanks when there is an appearance of danger ; also a company with axes and spades to repair bridges when necessary. The rear brigade keeps out a rear guard to pick up stragglers. The cavalry will send the wagon train in advance of the last infantry brigade, but will serve as a rear guard during the march. The artillery will be assigned to brigades by the chief of artillery for the purpose of the march, but any battery may at any moment be called out of its place for special service.

V. Officers and men must not leave their ranks on a march or at a halt without the permission of their colonels, and then only for a necessary purpose. The march will be steady and no long stretches. It is far easier for the soldier to keep his place than to follow the winding and rough paths by the wayside or in the adjoining fields; besides, each regiment must at all times be ready for action. Servants and unarmed men must follow in the rear of each regiment, and the time to fill canteens is the night before the march. Should the days be hot it is better to wait for the first halt before making coffee. Each man should have at all times in his haversack bread and meat enough for two days.

With these rules and care on the part of officers having charge of wagon trains there is no difficulty in making the day's march in six or seven hours, divided between the cool of the morning and evening.

By order of Maj. Gen. W. T. Sherman :

J. H. HAMMOND,
Assistant Adjutant-General.

HEADQUARTERS ARMY OF THE MISSISSIPPI,
July 18, 1862.

Major-General GRANT, *Corinth :*

I have just telegraphed Thomas, inquiring if there are not points south of the road where our troops massed could cover the front, preserve discipline, and damage the rebel bands who come up on adventures and mischief. I am fully satisfied that, with a strong nucleus at Tupelo, waiting attack or opportunity for mischief, they have sent considerable to Vicksburg, with an intermediate point above Grenada, and detached a strong column toward Mobile and Richmond, while another under Price has gone toward Chattanooga or Rome. They cover their front by cavalry and guerrillas. They have a desert country of dry ravines and rough ridges on their front below us, and can move much better toward Fulton or westward by their front.

W. S. ROSECRANS,
Brigadier-General, U. S. Army.

BETHEL, TENN., *July* 18, 1862.

Brigadier-General LOGAN:

A man sent in for the purpose reports that a company of guerrillas are in Henderson County, this side of Decaturville. They are there to prevent a company from Farmington joining Union Tennessee regiment, and have killed one Union man and have many under arrest. Wiley Miller or James Farmington, at Decaturville, can show where they can be found. My cavalry is all out on duty or I would send them over there.

W. W. SANFORD,
Lieutenant-Colonel, Commanding Bethel.

JACKSON, *July* 18, 1862.

Colonel SANFORD, *Commanding:*

Your dispatch is received, and forces will be started in the morning to attend to it.

JOHN A. LOGAN,
Brigadier-General, Commanding.

HUMBOLDT, *July* 19, 1862.

General LOGAN:

The information amounts to about this: Colonel Bryant has received word from cotton-buyers and citizens resident that at a place distant about 14 miles from here, in a southwestern direction, and 10 miles from Jackson, in a northwesterly direction, at a place called Poplar Grove or Poplar Corners, is a band of guerrillas 1,600 strong, with three pieces of artillery. He seems strongly impressed that there is a party there, of what number he is not certain. He started one company of cavalry this morning to reconnoiter in that direction. If they arrive before I get a chance to leave I will report.

R. R. TOWNES,
Assistant Adjutant-General.

HEADQUARTERS ARMY OF THE MISSISSIPPI,
July 19, 1862.

General ASBOTH, *Rienzi:*

The brigade of infantry and battery ordered from here to Rienzi has been ordered to return to this camp. The general commanding directs that two good companies of infantry and battery of artillery report to Colonel Sheridan until further orders.

W. L. ELLIOTT,
Brigadier-General and Chief of Staff.

HEADQUARTERS,
Trenton, July 19, 1862.

Brig. Gen. I. F. QUINBY, *Columbus:*

The guerrillas are pressing me, and I am using all my cavalry force against them. We have been without shoes for horses for a long time, and it renders one-half of the force unfit for service. Cannot you push

through on to-morrow's train horseshoes for Second Illinois Cavalry?
My cavalry are on the move from Humboldt, Trenton, Kenton, and
Union City, with orders to wipe out guerrillas and cotton-burners, to
disarm all known rebels in Dyer, Obion, and all the country bordering
the Obion swamps. I have ordered increase of guards at bridges.

G. M. DODGE,
Brigadier-General.

HEADQUARTERS, *Trenton, July* 19, 1862.

Col. GEORGE E. BRYANT, *Humboldt:*

I have ordered a battery to you and one company of cavalry. If the
enemy have a camp within that distance, pitch into them as soon as
forces arrive. In mean time send out your cavalry to get their position.
Use them up before they get settled. Disarm all the known rebels in
the country around you and in the line of march of your cavalry. Have
the arms turned over to you. Look out that your forces do not meet
the forces sent from here west and southwest.

G. M. DODGE,
Brigadier-General, Commanding.

HEADQUARTERS ARMY OF THE MISSISSIPPI,
July 19, 1862.

Col. F. D. CALLENDER,
    Chief of Ordnance, Saint Louis, Mo.:

Our cavalry is diminishing in numbers by contests with the superior
rebel numbers on a front of 60 miles in extent. It is vitally important
that they be mounted and armed well. The latter, if promptly done,
will give temporary relief. Twelve hundred and fifty Colt's army revolvers and 1,100 carbines or revolving rifles are required for the cavalry division. For the country's sake, provide for this without delay.
The cost and risk to which the Government is daily subjected for want
of these arms are such that impossibility or imbecility alone could refuse
or delay the supply.

W. S. ROSECRANS,
Brigadier-General, U. S. Army.

SPECIAL ORDERS, }   HDQRS. ARMY OF THE MISSISSIPPI,
   No. 185. }   *July* 19, 1862

I. Brig. Gen. R. B. Mitchell, U. S. Volunteers, is assigned to First
Brigade, Fourth Division, and will report to Brig. Gen. J. C. Davis,
U. S. Volunteers, for duty.

II. The Eighth Regiment Kansas Volunteer Infantry is assigned to
First Brigade, and the Fifteenth Wisconsin to the Second Brigade,
Fourth Division, and will proceed without delay to that division.

*   *   *   *   *   *   *

IV. The First Division will proceed to relieve General Thomas' division on the Memphis and Charleston Railroad, between Iuka and Decatur. It will take its ammunition and all the forage and subsistence
practicable with its present means of transportation and forward its
camp and garrison equipage by rail, accompanied by a suitable detail
under a competent officer for guard and fatigue duty.

V. To cover as far as practicable the movements of troops the columns will move by road near to or north of the railroad until opposite the positions they are to assume.

VI. General Granger will detail Mizner's brigade of cavalry to move under special instructions to cover the front of Morgan's position, and co-operate with the commander of this division, to whom he will report; but will at the same time report fully through the commander of the cavalry division to these headquarters.

*   *   *   *   *   *   *

By order of General Rosecrans:

C. F. MARDEN,
First Lieutenant and Acting Assistant Adjutant-General.

ORDERS, }   HEADQUARTERS FIFTH DIVISION,
No. 54. }   White's Station, July 19, 1862.

It is manifest that a great many horses, mules, and other private property are now in our camps which have been taken in the country without warrant or authority. All such property will at once be turned in to the division quartermaster, and every regimental quartermaster, commander of a battery, or other officer will cause an actual count of horses and animals in their possession and will make a written certificate that at this date they have on hand that particular number, for which they will account. The count will be verified by the division quartermaster.

All parties who are mounted who are not by law designated and considered as mounted officers or soldiers will have their horses and mules taken away, and those animals treated as public animals. Colonels of regiments will see to the execution of this order, and see that the animals are at once delivered over to the regimental quartermaster and by him to the division quartermaster, who will report as soon as possible the number of animals he has on hand now, and how many are turned over to him by the several regiments and companies.

Every colonel of a regiment or commander of battery and chief of cavalry will to-morrow cause a thorough examination and will report the number of negroes in their camps, and give the names of such as came from their respective States as servants. All other negroes must be registered and put to work on the fortifications as soon as we reach Memphis.

The provost marshal in Memphis will be instructed to put to work in the trenches all soldiers who come to Memphis without leave of the commanding general.

As soon as our camp is established as large an amount of liberty will be given to all good soldiers as is consistent with their duty, and ample opportunity afforded them to see the city with all "its sights."

The commanding general, with the engineer officers and part of his staff, will proceed before daybreak to-morrow morning into Memphis to examine the condition of things there, to see the ground and to select camps. Orders will be sent back for the troops to march into Memphis as soon as camping ground is selected.

Both General Hurlbut's division and my own will remain at or near this camp, at White's Station, until such orders are received, and no officer, soldier, or citizen connected with this marching column will go to Memphis until the two divisions are moved in.

By order of Maj. Gen. W. T. Sherman:

J. H. HAMMOND,
Assistant Adjutant-General.

HDQRS. CENTRAL DIVISION OF THE MISSISSIPI I,
Trenton, Tenn., July 20, 1862.

Capt. M. ROCHESTER, *Asst. Adjt. Gen., Columbus, Ky.:*

There appears to be a general uprising among the guerrillas along the Obion and Hatchie Rivers. The force that threatened Humboldt has been driven south toward Gordonsville, and Brigadier-General Logan has sent his forces after them. The force at Key Corners I have sent five companies of cavalry after, and the force 15 miles west of Troy I have sent three companies of cavalry after. None of the bands had rendezvoused over twenty-four hours before I was aware of their movements, and I immediately sent out my cavalry from all points with instructions to attack, no matter where found or in what force, knowing that quick movements and bold attacks is the most efficient method of breaking them up.

I informed General Logan of the position of those south of us and ordered Colonel Bryant to march on them. They fled the moment Colonel Bryant moved, to escape General Logan's forces. They report that band as a portion of Jackson's cavalry.

I telegraphed in relation to horseshoes. It is almost impossible for me to get along without them.

I am, very respectfully, your obedient servant,

G. M. DODGE,
Brigadier-General.

JULY 20, 1862.

Major-General GRANT:

A dispatch just received informs me that Clarksville is taken by rebels, and that a force, from 600 to 800, is now moving on Fort Henry. Reenforcements are asked for, but I do not have them to spare. Guerrilla bands are forming through Western Kentucky and Tennessee, and unless they are promptly attacked and dispersed they will give us great trouble.

With two good regiments of cavalry, in addition to the infantry and artillery I now have, they could be kept down and the enlisting for the regular rebel service could be suppressed.

I. F. QUINBY,
Brigadier-General.

ROSECRANS' HEADQUARTERS, *July* 20, 1862.

General GRANT:

GENERAL: From a gentleman whom I know, who was imprisoned by the rebels and escaped after two unsuccessful attempts, bringing with him the irons with which he was manacled at Tupelo, I learn the following important facts:

Bragg with a large force left Tupelo on the 7th, the date of his flag-of-truce letter to General Halleck, for the east, marching by Peeksville toward Chattanooga. A small force left Tupelo for Mobile July 1 There has been additional forces sent from Tupelo to Saltillo. Bradfute's cavalry is at Fulton. Thomas Jordan commands at Saltillo. Price is at Priceville, 6 miles east of Tupelo. A brigade is half west of Tupelo. No troops any farther west. Total force in that vicinity will not exceed 20,000. No troops were seen by him north of New Albany except a few strolling cavalry.

W. S. ROSECRANS,
Brigadier-General.

ROSECRANS' HEADQUARTERS, *July* 20, 1862.
Major-General GRANT:

Two dispatches from General Davis, of the Fourth Division, at Jacinto, give contradictory reports. The former that the enemy were moving from Jacinto to Saltillo, the other that they were concentrating at Big Springs Factory, 15 miles southeast of Jacinto, and 25 miles south from Iuka; that they imagine we are reduced in numbers and intend to attack Jacinto and Corinth. They say our guards about Corinth are badly posted and their spies go where they please.

While I do not credit the report of their intended attack on Jacinto I have given Davis orders to be prepared to fight or fall back, sending his baggage before him, on this position.

I have also given Morgan notice of the report. His division will be in Burnsville to-morrow and at Iuka next day and evening. I venture to suggest Davis' division requires caution as to its guard duty.

W. S. ROSECRANS,
Brigadier-General, U. S. Army, Commanding.

HEADQUARTERS ARMY OF THE MISSISSIPPI, *July* 20, 1862.
Major-General HALLECK, *Commander-in-Chief, Washington:*

GENERAL: There is little doubt but that so soon as forage for horses can be got from the corn-crops of the rebels we shall have a host of conscript cavalry and mounted infantry to deal with. Now is the time to strain every nerve to meet this contingency effectually.

1st. What we need is that all the cavalry should be promptly and thoroughly armed. There is no excuse for their being in the field without good arms. I have had offers from private arm manufacturers to supply in four weeks all we need in this army. The utter fatuity of not arming them suitably for service may be inferred from the fact that the cost of maintaining a regiment of cavalry in idleness one month would arm them with revolving rifles.

2d. The regiments should be filled; to which end, all means, official and unofficial, should be used to induce the Governors of States to fill them up. The cavalry are the eyes of the army. Nay, more; I do not hesitate to say that the time will soon be here when a thousand cavalry will do more damage to the rebels by seizing and destroying their means of subsistence than a brigade of infantry.

Having a position on the front, and, for the first time in this war, given development to the working powers of this arm, I take the liberty of urging the necessity of the steps I have indicated, hoping you will be able to bring about the desired ends in time to meet the emergencies to which I have alluded.

W. S. ROSECRANS,
Brigadier-General, U. S. Army, Commanding.

[Indorsement.]

HEADQUARTERS DISTRICT OF WEST TENNESSEE,
Corinth, July 22, 1862.

Respectfully referred to Maj. Gen. H. W. Halleck, with the request that the within suggestions receive early attention. The proper arming of the cavalry in this department is of vital importance and demands prompt action.

U. S. GRANT,
Major-General.

MEMPHIS, *July* 20, 1862.

Major-General GRANT:

Arrived this morning. Left my troops at a good camp 9 miles out. Came in to select good camp. Will dispatch General Hovey's infantry force to Helena, and enforce your orders about rent of stores; also will communicate your request to the senior commander of the Navy as to destruction of all boats from the north line of Tennessee to Vicksburg.

W. T. SHERMAN,
Major-General.

———

ORDERS, }
No. 55. }

HEADQUARTERS,
Memphis, Tenn., July 20, 1862.

In consequence of the total absence of water fit for man or beast at any point near Memphis, save in wells, which are barely adequate to supply the inhabitants, the two divisions under my command will be forced to camp in compact order in and around Fort Pickering, on the river bank, 2 miles south of Memphis.

The Fifth Division will march in the order prescribed early to-morrow into Memphis. On reaching the outer pickets, about 2 miles out, the wagon trains will be ordered to halt and clear the road, and each brigadier will march his brigade in good order straight to the west to Main street, one square east of the levee, then turn south down Main street to Fort Pickering. General Smith's brigade will not enter the fort, but camp some 300 yards to its front or east.

General Denver's and Colonel McDowell's brigades will enter the fort, the former taking the south half and latter the north half of the ground inside the lines of unfinished trenches.

All the brigadiers after selecting the ground for their regiments will send an officer of each regiment back to conduct their train of wagons to camp. General Hurlbut will also pass the column of halted wagons and leave his in like manner behind, to be sent for after the selection of camp, and will pursue the same line of march, viz, down Poplar street to Main, down Main to the fort and camp of Colonel Woods' brigade to the right, and choose camp in the woods next below Colonel Woods' brigade, near the river.

The brigade and regimental quartermasters must remain with their trains, and when the infantry has passed them will, without further orders, follow the column until met by an officer of their respective colonels to conduct them to camp.

There is no use attempting to get water until the river is reached at Fort Pickering, where of course it is abundant in the Mississippi. Every effort should be made to make the march in the cool of the morning as far as possible.

Cavalry will remain and escort the wagon train into camp and then choose their own.

By order of Maj. Gen. W. T. Sherman:

J. H. HAMMOND,
Assistant Adjutant-General.

———

HDQRS. CENTRAL DIVISION OF THE MISSISSIPPI,
Trenton, Tenn., July 21, 1862.

Capt. M. ROCHESTER,
Assistant Adjutant-General, Columbus, Ky.:

I have but one report from my calvary parties sent out; that is a rumor from Big Obion. It is said we have had a small fight 25 miles down the Obion.   Lieutenant-Colonel Hogg, with five companies, is in that vicinity.   At Key Corners they are in force, but by to-night will have left or been attacked.

My fears now are from the Tennessee River.   A large band is forming there, I expect, to clear them out west in time to mass my cavalry and meet that band before they get very near to me.   I am very much opposed to weakening my cavalry force now, if it can be avoided.   We have all the important bridges to hold, with no surplus force at any place, while south of me they have divisions and brigades at points on the road.

I am, very respectfully, your obedient servant,

G. M. DODGE,
Brigadier-General.

HEADQUARTERS,
Trenton, July 21, 1862.

Brig. Gen. I. F. QUINBY, *Columbus, Ky.*:

I have 900 effective cavalry, with the worst guerrilla country to take care of on line of road.   All my cavalry are now out, and it is very dangerous to take any away.   The guerrillas are determined to give us work.   A large force is between here and the Tennessee River, but I have no force to send after them until my cavalry returns.   If you send any, the battalion of Curtis' Horse better go, or three companies of Sixth Illinois.   The Curtis Horse is thoroughly posted around Humboldt, and I do not like to spare them.   Cannot some of the cavalry on the river be pushed out after the guerrillas, or also sent to me.

G. M. DODGE,
Brigadier-General.

BOLIVAR, *July* 21, 1862.

Major-General McCLERNAND:

Colonel Leggett telegraphs me that Jackson's cavalry is within 6 miles of him; that Chalmers is at Burk's Spring, 15 miles, with cavalry and infantry, and that they express intentions of attacking Grand Junction and think of attacking Jackson.

L. F. ROSS,
Brigadier-General, Commanding.

BOLIVAR, *July* 21, 1862.

Major-General McCLERNAND:

Colonel Leggett wants a couple of rifled cannon and infantry to support them.   I have no cannon of that kind and no infantry to spare. Can you furnish them?

How soon can I have additional cavalry force?

L. F. ROSS,
Brigadier-General, Commanding.

ORDERS, }
No. 56. }   HDQRS. FIFTH DIV., ARMY OF THE TENN.,
Memphis, Tenn., July 21, 1862.

The undersigned hereby assumes command in Memphis and vicinity. All orders issued by my predecessor will be respected and enforced.

Staff officers stationed at Memphis will report at once in writing, giving full information as to the condition of their departments and the location of their officers.

W. T. SHERMAN,
Major-General, Commanding.

ORDERS, }   HDQRS. FIFTH DIVISION, ARMY OF THE TENN.,
No. 57. }   *Memphis, July* 21, 1862.

Brigadier-General Hovey, with all the infantry regiments of his former command, will immediately embark for Helena, Ark., there to report for orders to Maj. Gen. S. R. Curtis. The chief quartermaster at Memphis will provide steamboats at once, using boats bound up the river if the nature of their business be not of too much importance. He will notify General Hovey when one or more boats are ready that they at once be freighted.

By order of Maj. Gen. W. T. Sherman :

J. H. HAMMOND,
Assistant Adjutant-General.

ROSECRANS', *July* 22, 1862.

General GRANT:

Have consulted with Granger. We have one brigade cavalry gone to Tuscumbia; the other can muster about 650 or 700, but they are so distributed down on the front toward Booneville and Blackland and Marietta that they could not be assembled in time for a night march before to-morrow night. A day march would defeat our purpose. Seven hundred cavalry can be got ready for a march to-morrow night by stripping our front for the time being. Should you deem this expedient under the circumstances it will be desirable to know from the guide if there be a road by which we can come in below Ripley and avoid the Hatchie Crossing, where they unquestionably have a picket, and, as I was yesterday informed, had burned the bridges. Please send over the guide, from whom we may get some valuable local information.

W. S. ROSECRANS,
Brigadier-General, U. S. Army.

HEADQUARTERS SECOND BRIGADE, CAVALRY DIVISION,
Camp near Rienzi, Miss., July 22, 1862.

Brig. Gen. GORDON GRANGER,
Commanding Cavalry Division :

GENERAL : I posted the Seventh Kansas at Jacinto yesterday. I do not think there is any great necessity for having cavalry stationed at that point. There are only three avenues of approach to Jacinto from the south—one via the Fulton road, intersecting the Tuscumbia road at or near Davenport east of Jacinto. At that point General Davis has a force which would hold with perfect security the largest army the enemy could bring to bear from that direction ; the place is a very strong one. The second approach is by the Booneville and Jacinto road and Marietta and Jacinto road, both of which intersect the Memphis and Tuscumbia road a short distance west of Jacinto, at which point General Davis has a force that is entirely sufficient; this position is also a very strong one. The third approach is an obscure road leading directly south from Jacinto, intersecting the Pontotoc road about 10 miles south of Jacinto. On this last-mentioned road I encamped the Seventh Kansas about 1 mile south of Jacinto.

General Davis has all of these roads so well picketed that it was not deemed necessary to establish cavalry pickets in the advance, and the only work required of the Seventh Kansas would be to send out a scouting party every day, so as to give warning of any advance of the enemy in force. I think that General Davis is abundantly able to hold his position against any force that the enemy can bring on a general battle at that point; in case of an attack he has plenty of roads on which to retreat in case of necessity.

I respectfully offer these remarks as the impressions I received from my observations yesterday, and ask your advice as to the policy of moving the regiment nearer to me, where it would be more in hand.

I am, sir, very respectfully, your obedient servant,

P. H. SHERIDAN,
Colonel, Commanding Second Brigade, Cavalry Division.

[Indorsement.]

HEADQUARTERS CAVALRY DIVISION,
July 22, 1862.

Respectfully referred to the commanding general. I have ordered the Seventh Kansas Cavalry to join the brigade near Rienzi.

G. GRANGER,
Brigadier-General, Commanding.

SPECIAL ORDERS, }   HDQRS. DISTRICT OF WEST TENNESSEE,
  No. 141.   }   *Corinth, Miss., July* 22, 1862.

*   *   *   *   *   *   *

III. Major-General Ord, commanding United States forces at Corinth, Miss., will have all the cavalry in his command in readiness to march to-morrow evening, with three days' rations and one day's forage. He will report to these headquarters as early as practicable the number of such cavalry as are available.

By order of Maj. Gen. U. S. Grant:

JNO. A. RAWLINS,
Assistant Adjutant-General.

ORDERS, }   HDQRS. FIFTH DIVISION, ARMY OF THE TENNESSEE,
  No. 58. }   *Memphis, July* 22, 1862.

All houses inside the new fort must be forthwith vacated by families or persons not constituting a part of its garrison. Under no pretext must any woman or family be allowed to sojourn inside the fort which must be strictly military, all non-combatants excluded.

A military board, to be composed of Lieutenant-Colonel Loudon, Seventieth Ohio; Major Fearing, Seventy-seventh Ohio, and Major Fisher, of the Fifty-fourth Ohio, will assemble immediately in the fort and will examine each house and premises, make a minute of the owner, tenant, and general character of building, such as dwelling, shop, shanty, &c., and affix a value to the house, fences, and immovable improvements. The board will give each owner or tenant a certificate of the value of such improvements, and the fact that he or she has been forcibly dispossessed. The chief quartermaster in Memphis on the presentation of such certificate will cause the party to be put in possession of some vacant house in Memphis of about equal value. The board will make a full report of their action to remain as evidence for the final settlement when made.

The chief quartermaster at Memphis will forthwith, by himself or agent, a commissioned officer, if possible, otherwise by some competent person appointed from civil life to be paid out of rents to be collected, take possession of all vacant storehouses, warehouses, and buildings, and will rent them out if possible to reliable and loyal tenants at fair moderate rents, payable monthly in advance, keeping an accurate account with each piece of property so taken. When the buildings are used by any department of the army the rent will be estimated and charged but not collected; but no building must be occupied by any military person or department without the approval of the commanding general. The buildings inside of the intrenchments will be excepted from the above rule, and be subject to the use and control of the brigadier on whose camping ground they happen to be.

Great care must be taken from the beginning in keeping accounts of rents, &c., and special instructions will be given on this point.

By order of Maj. Gen. W. T. Sherman:

J. H. HAMMOND,
Assistant Adjutant-General.

ORDERS, }
No. 60. }

HEADQUARTERS,
Memphis, Tenn., July 22, 1862.

While negroes are employed on public works, fortifications, driving teams, and such public work, they will be subsisted by the officer in charge by a provision return, specifying number and how employed, which return must be approved at headquarters. As the negro receives no specific wages the commissary may issue to the negroes at the rate of one pound of chewing-tobacco per month, the bills of purchase for which are to be sent to the chief engineer of the district for payment.

The engineer in charge of the fort will purchase necessary clothing, such as shoes and pants, for the negroes, and issue to them, keeping an accurate account of the issues that the value of the clothing may be charged to the proper party on the final settlement of accounts. The bills of purchase will be sent to the chief engineer of the district for payment.

A register and time-table of the negroes employed on the fort will be kept by the engineer in charge or by some one under his orders, giving the name and description of the negro, whether a slave or refugee, and the name of master, that a fair and equitable settlement may be made at the "end of the war."

By order of Maj. Gen. W. T. Sherman:

J. H. HAMMOND,
Assistant Adjutant-General.

HEADQUARTERS DISTRICT OF WEST TENNESSEE,
Corinth, Miss., July 23, 1862.

Maj. Gen. H. W. HALLECK, *Washington, D. C.:*

Since you have left here the greatest vigilance has been kept up by our cavalry to the front, but nothing absolutely certain of the movements of the enemy has been learned. It is certain, however, that a movement has taken place from Tupelo, in what direction or for what purpose is not so certain. Deserters and escaped prisoners concur in this statement, but all concurring so nearly I doubt whether they have not been misled with the view of having information reach us. It would seem from these statements that a large force moved on the 7th of this month toward Chattanooga; that Price was at Tupelo on the 17th, and made a speech to his command, promising to take them back to Missouri through Kentucky; that his ordnance and provision train had moved westward with 17 days' rations, and he has likely followed ere this.

I do not regard this information of special value, except as giving an idea of points to watch and see if these statements are verified.

The changes directed by you before leaving here have all been made. Morgan's division has relieved Thomas. Sherman and Hurlbut have reached Memphis, and the entire Charleston and Memphis road is abandoned by us west of here, except at Chewalla, and a force yet retained at Grand Junction. Should anything occur within this district of a startling or important nature I will inform you by telegraph.

U. S. GRANT,
Major-General.

HDQRS. FIFTH DIVISION, ARMY OF THE TENNESSEE,
Memphis, July 23, 1862.

Dr. E. S. PLUMMER AND OTHERS,
Physicians in Memphis, Signers to a Petition:

GENTLEMEN: I have this moment received your communication, and assure you that it grieves my heart thus to be the instrument of adding to the seeming cruelty and hardship of this unnatural war.

On my arrival here I found my predecessor (General Hovey) had issued an order permitting the departure South of all persons subject to the conscript law of the Southern Confederacy. Many applications have been made to me to modify this order, but I regarded it as a condition-precedent by which I was bound in honor, and therefore I have made no changes or modifications, nor shall I determine what action I shall adopt in relation to persons unfriendly to our cause who remain after the time limited by General Hovey's order has expired. It is now sunset, and all who have not availed themselves of General Hovey's authority and who remain in Memphis are supposed to be loyal and true men.

I will only say that I cannot allow the personal convenience of even a large class of ladies to influence me in my determination to make Memphis a safe place of operations for an army, and all people who are unfriendly should forthwith prepare to depart in such direction as I may hereafter indicate.

Surgeons are not liable to be made prisoners of war, but they should not reside within the lines of an army which they regard as hostile. The situation would be too delicate.

I am, with great respect, your obedient servant,

W. T. SHERMAN,
Major-General.

SPECIAL ORDERS, }   HDQRS. DISTRICT OF WEST TENNESSEE,
No. 142.   }   *Corinth, July* 23, 1862.

*   *   *   *   *   *   *

V. The general hospital at Jackson will be allowed to retain such amount of black labor as the surgeon in charge may decide as being absolutely necessary to perform such menial service as should not be put upon soldiers. In getting this kind of labor such persons will be taken as are free by act of Congress if possible, and if not they will be hired from owners at a reasonable rate of compensation, to be fixed by council of administration, and should owners object they will be pressed into service and not returned or paid for until proof of loyalty is shown.

Proper diet will be procured from the surrounding country for the sick, to be paid for at reasonable rates, fixed by council of administration, if acceded to by the citizens; if not acceded to by them, by forced contribution. This order is made applicable to all general hospitals within this district outside of the loyal States.

By command of Maj. Gen. U. S. Grant:

JNO. A. RAWLINS,
Assistant Adjutant-General.

HDQRS. FIRST DIVISION, DIST. OF JACKSON, TENN.,
Jackson, July 24, 1862.

Colonel NEVINS,
Comdg. Eleventh Illinois Vols. and Cav. Detachment:

You will proceed at once with your command to Lexington, Tenn., and make that place the base of your operations and encamp there until otherwise ordered. You will enforce strict military discipline and order in your camp by keeping your command together and not allowing them to straggle outside your lines. You will use your utmost endeavors to protect the rights of private property, suffering nothing to be taken except what is absolutely necessary for your command, and only then by paying or agreeing to pay to the owner a just compensation for the same. You will keep a vigilant guard posted around your camp to prevent surprise, and also to prevent your men from straggling outside the lines.

Information has just been received that a cavalry force of the enemy is scouring the country on this side of the Tennessee River, opposite Perryville. I desire you to send the cavalry daily in that direction to ascertain what is there, and that you move forward to their support if necessary, using proper precautions, and attack the enemy if there without delay, unless you find them to have a superior force over yours, in which case you will let me know by sending a mounted orderly to report.

The cavalry will be entirely under your control, and you will give them the same instructions as herein given you. I desire you to use your endeavors to cultivate a conservative, friendly feeling with the people where you may be. You will report to me your operations from time to time, and any other information that you may see proper to communicate to these headquarters. You will enlist and swear into service all of the proper age and able-bodied men who may wish to enlist.

I am, colonel, very respectfully, yours,

JOHN A. LOGAN,
Brigadier-General, Commanding.

BOLIVAR, *July* 24, 1862.

Major-General McCLERNAND:

Colonel Leggett moved at dawn this morning. His pickets were driven in last night from La Grange by infantry and cavalry. I have fowarded a strong support and have just received the following:

All well. My command now in motion. I apprehend a little annoyance from cavalry, but nothing serious.

LEGGETT.

The office at Grand Junction is closed. We are out of sugar and meat. Captain Lebo has been unable to have his supplies forwarded. Will you please give us assistance in this matter and have them forwarded to-day if possible?

L. F. ROSS,
Brigadier-General, Commanding.

HEADQUARTERS DEPARTMENT OF THE TENNESSEE,
Memphis, Tenn., July 24, 1862.

SAMUEL SAWYER, Esq., *Union Appeal:*

DEAR SIR: It is well I should come to an understanding at once with the press as well as the people of Memphis, which I am ordered to command, which means control for the interest, welfare, and glory of the whole Government of the United States.

Personalities in a newspaper are wrong and criminal. Thus, though you meant to be complimentary in your sketch of my career. you make more than a dozen mistakes of facts, which I need not correct as I don't desire my biography till I am dead. It is enough for the world to know that I live and am a soldier, bound to obey the orders of my superiors, the laws of my country, and to venerate its Constitution; that when discretion is given me I should exercise it and account for it to my superiors.

I regard your article headed "City Council, General Sherman, and Colonel Slack" as highly indiscreet. Of course no person who can jeopardize the safety of Memphis can remain here, much less exercise public authority, but I must take time and be satisfied that injustice be not done.

If the parties named be the men you describe, the fact should not be published to put them on their guard and encourage their escape. The evidence should be carefully collected, authenticated, and then placed in my hands.

But your statement of facts is entirely qualified in my mind and loses its force by your negligence of very simple facts within your reach as to myself. I had been in the army six years in 1846; am not related at all to any member of Lucas, Turner & Co.; was associated with them six years instead of two; am not colonel of the Fifteenth Infantry, but of the Thirteenth.

Your correction this morning, as to the acknowledged error as to General Denver, is still erroneous.

General M. L. Smith did not belong to my command at Shiloh at all, but was transferred to me just before reaching Corinth.

I mention these facts in kindness, to show you how wrong it is to speak of persons.

I will attend to the judge, mayor, board of aldermen, and pol cemen all in good time.

Use your influence to re-establish system, order, government. You may rest easy that no military commander is going to neglect internal safety as well as to guard against external danger, but to do right requires time, and more patience than I usually possess is necessary. If I find the press of Memphis actuated by high principle and a sole devotion to their country I will be their best friend; but if I find them personal, abusive, dealing in innuendoes and hints at a blind venture, and looking to their selfish aggrandizement and fame, then they had better look out, for I regard such as greater enemies to their country and mankind than the men who, from a mistaken sense of State pride, have taken muskets and fight us about as hard as we care about.

In haste, but in kindness, yours, &c.,

W. T. SHERMAN,
Major-General

SPECIAL ORDERS, }   HDQRS. DISTRICT OF WEST TENNESSEE,
    No. 143.   }   *Corinth, Miss., July* 24, 1862.

*   *   *   *   *   *   *

II. Brig. Gen. J. B. S. Todd, at his own request, is hereby relieved from duty with this army. He will report in person or by letter to the Adjutant-General of the Army. The next officer in rank in his division will immediately take command.

*   *   *   *   *   *   *

By order of Maj. Gen. U. S. Grant:

JNO. A. RAWLINS,
Assistant Adjutant-General.

ORDERS, }   HEADQUARTERS FIFTH DIVISION,
  No. 61. }   *Memphis, July* 24, 1862.

Travel into and out of Memphis by carriage, wagon, horse, or foot in the usual course of business will be as free and unobstructed as is consistent with a state of war. To farmers, planters, and business men, with their families and servants, free intercourse will be permitted without passes or any hinderance, save the right of examination and even search when the officer of the guard judges it proper and necessary.

This travel must be by daylight, and no exception to the rule will be permitted, save to market and supply carts, which may enter an hour before day, provided they are known to the officer of the guard. Wagons leaving town with an undue proportion of any one article of commodity will be stopped, and if found engaged in illicit trade or deception the road guard will send it to his brigadier, who will take the wagon and contents and imprison the parties implicated if he entertain even strong suspicion.

Travel is limited to the following roads:

1. Raleigh road.
2. State Line road.
3. Pigeon Roost and Byhalia road.
4. Hernando road.
5. Horn Lake road.

A small guard charged with this duty will be stationed on each of these roads about 3 miles from the city, at some house by the roadside, where all travelers will pause or stop until they receive a signal to pass. Written instructions from headquarters will be given from time to time to these guards, and when any officer announces to a traveler his decision it must be instantly obeyed, however inconsistent it may appear with the spirit of this order.

Cavalry patrols and pickets and infantry guards posted for other purposes will not molest the regular travel, but all such pickets and guards will promptly arrest and send to the provost-marshal all persons attempting to enter or depart by any other road and at any other time or manner than is herein prescribed.

Brigadier-General Hurlbut is charged with the execution of this order as to the Horn Lake road, the Hernando road, and Pigeon Roost road, and Brigadier-General Smith as to the State Line and Raleigh roads. Details of one commissioned and one non-commissioned officer and three men will be sufficient for each road—details permanent or weekly at the pleasure of the brigadier, who will strengthen the guard under special instructions or when in his judgment it should be necessary.

By order of Maj. Gen. W. T. Sherman:

J. H. HAMMOND,
Assistant Adjutant-General.

GENERAL ORDERS,   HEADQUARTERS,
   No. 62.   *Memphis, Tenn., July 24, 1862.*

The following is announced as the stations of the troops in and near Memphis:

General Denver's brigade in the south half of Fort Pickering, facing east.

Colonel McDowell's brigade in the north half of Fort Pickering, facing east.

General Smith on the State Line road, about 3 miles out from Memphis, facing east, and a regiment detached to the right and left with easy communications to brigade headquarters.

General Veatch's brigade south of Fort Pickering, on a line extending from the Horn Lake road to the river, facing south.

General Lauman's brigade nearly on a line with General Veatch's, toward the east, with its left resting on or near the Hernando road, facing south.

General Hurlbut is charged with guarding the front, from the river around by the south and east to the Charleston and Memphis Railroad.

Brigadier-General Smith is charged with the front, from Wolf River to the Charleston and Memphis road, connecting with General Hurlbut there, at some point hereafter to be designated by the general commanding in person.

One regiment, to be detailed from General Denver's and McDowell's brigades weekly and alternately, will be quartered in the city, to act under special instructions as a provost guard, General Denver making the first detail to-day.

Each brigade will furnish a daily guard of at least 200 men, with a due proportion of officers and a brigade officer of the day. This guard, under the direction of their respective brigadiers, will be posted at some strong position, to be changed from time to time, at least 1 mile from their brigade fronts (excepting the brigades in the fort). From this main guard will be sent forward another mile picket guards to watch roads, paths, or any manner of approach, with vedettes along such avenues of approach.

From the main brigade guards, under the respective officer of the day, will also be frequently sent out active patrols to visit the advance pickets and vedettes, and to scour the country between the brigade pickets. Such patrols must always be compact military bodies, furnished with the countersign that no accident may occur from contact with other guards and patrols. All guards and pickets will be subject to the inspection, visit, and control of a general officer of the day, to be detailed daily from headquarters.

General Hurlbut will regulate his cavalry pickets and patrols and cause them to be advanced well toward the Nonconah.

The Fourth Illinois Cavalry is hereby attached for picket duty to General Smith's brigade, who will cause it to picket and scout well the country forward toward White's Station, on the State Line road.

The commanding general will use the reserve cavalry for scouting in all directions, but this must not be any excuse for relaxation on the part of the officers hereinbefore named. Every officer in command of a regiment or detachment will now see that his men are well provided with clothing, provisions, arms, ammunition, canteens, haversacks, and everything which his own experience has shown him is necessary for the efficiency of the soldiers. Every sentinel must be fully armed and equipped, and to this end regular guard mountings and inspections must precede the posting of all guards.

Officers of the day and commanders of guards have a right, and should not hesitate to use it, of refusing men improperly dressed or equipped. Their duties are very important and they should see that their details are composed of good men, properly provided in all respects.

All officers of this command must now study their books; ignorance of duty must no longer be pleaded. The commanding general has the power at any time to order a board to examine the acquirements and capacity of any officer, and he will not fail to exercise it. Should any officer, high or low, after the opportunity and experience we have had, be ignorant of his tactics, regulations, or even of the principles of the Art of War (Mahan and Jomini), it would be a lasting disgrace.

By order of Maj. Gen. W. T. Sherman:

J. H. HAMMOND,
Assistant Adjutant-General.

HEADQUARTERS ARMY OF THE MISSISSIPPI,
July 25, 1862.
General McPherson, *Corinth:*

The following from General Morgan:

I need 100 wagons in addition to my present regimental wagons. I cannot depend at all upon the railroad for transportation.

We have no wagons to give him, and his move was based on the assumption that the railroad would serve them. What is the matter?

We shall require 900 pounds of forage and rations per day for that command, and the average haul will be the distance from Iuka to Tuscumbia. Can we have it without fail? Please answer.

W. S. ROSECRANS,
Brigadier-General, U. S. Army, Commanding.

HEADQUARTERS ARMY OF THE MISSISSIPPI,
July 25, 1862.
General Morgan, *Tuscumbia:*

Your dispatch does not say where troops were cut off nor where they were. It does not tell us where our cavalry is nor the news to the front.

nor where is General Thomas. Full information is the soul of military life.

As to supplies, provide at once details to load and guard the trains, so as to do it without failure, slackness, or disorder. Organize reconnoitering parties to explore the passes by which your front can be covered. Notify General McPherson and these headquarters what you have done to insure the prompt loading and unloading of the trains.

W. S. ROSECRANS,
Brigadier-General, U. S. Army.

HEADQUARTERS ARMY OF THE MISSISSIPPI,
July 25, 1862.

General U. S. GRANT, *Corinth:*

General Morgan has reached Tuscumbia, and halts there, demanding 100 wagons in addition to his present train before proceeding beyond that point.

General McPherson says he can transfer 50 tons per day along that road, if it be loaded and unloaded promptly and the road protected. But a train was cut off last night from returning by the destruction of a bridge east of Tuscumbia, and a party of infantry, probably Thomas', attacked and probably captured 500 rebel cavalry at Courtland.

W. S. ROSECRANS,
Brigadier-General, U. S. Army.

ROSECRANS', *July* 26, 1862.

General GRANT:

General McPherson says we can supply Morgan on conditions stated. I have telegraphed Morgan that if he cannot protect the railroad train he cannot protect wagon train beyond Tuscumbia; that therefore he should halt at that point, up to which he can so cover his line until such dispositions as are needed can be made. There is no object in pushing his troops beyond the point where he can protect the railroad yet known to me; on the contrary. As soon as I hear from him will telegraph you.

W. S. ROSECRANS,
Brigadier-General.

BOLIVAR, *July* 25, 1862.

Maj. Gen. JOHN A. McCLERNAND:

The cotton speculators are quite clamorous for aid in getting their cotton away from Middleburg, Hickory Valley, &c., and offer to pay liberally for the service. I think I can bring it away with safety, and make it pay to the Government. As some of the Jew owners have as good as stolen the cotton from the planters, I have no conscientious scruples in making them pay liberally for getting it away.

L. F. ROSS,
Brigadier-General.

BOLIVAR, *July* 25, 1862.

Major-General McCLERNAND:

I have information, which I consider reliable, that on the night of 23d about 100 cavalry passed through Estanaula, crossing the ferry at that point; that in the afternoon of same day (23d) from 400 to 500 cavalry-men were at Dancyville. My informant thought they designed making attack at Toone's Station.

L. F. ROSS,
Major-General, Commanding.

HDQRS. FIFTH DIVISION, ARMY OF THE TENNESSEE,
Memphis, July 25, 1862.

Col. JOHN A. RAWLINS,
　　Assistant Adjutant-General, Corinth, Miss.:

SIR: On Tuesday evening of last week, at Moscow, Tenn., I received General Grant's telegraphic dispatch to order the troops belonging to General McClernand's division to Bolivar and to march mine and General Hurlbut's divisions to Memphis, there to assume command, and to send all the infantry of General Lew. Wallace's division to Helena, Ark., there to report to General Curtis.

I immediately telegraphed to General Hurlbut at La Grange the substance of the order, and made my manuscript orders, No. 52, a copy of which will be sent by this mail along with the series, which orders were duly received by General Hurlbut, and a copy to Colonel Leggett, commanding at Grand Junction.

My orders contemplated that all the stores and sick at Grand Junction should proceed by rail to Bolivar and the troops march the distance (21 miles) by land. Colonel Leggett did not move on Wednesday, and when informed of the fact I directed General Hurlbut to see Colonel Leggett to ascertain the reason of his delay. General Hurlbut telegraphed me that Colonel Leggett was waiting to receive his orders from General McClernand. I then notified him we should wait twenty-four hours longer to cover his departure, when we should move.

I telegraphed this fact to General Grant, who approved it, and accordingly General Hurlbut moved his division from La Grange to Moscow on Thursday afternoon.

On Friday I marched my division 15 miles, to Colliersville, Hurlbut halting for water at La Fayette. On Saturday my division moved 15 miles, to White's Station, 9 miles from Memphis, Hurlbut halting at Germantown.

Not knowing the character of country about Memphis as to water, for which our men and animals suffered much, I rode into the city on Sunday morning before daylight, saw General Hovey early in the morning, and notified him to be ready to move to Helena with all his infantry immediately. All Sunday I rode about the city of Memphis examining the site and condition of Fort Pickering, and could find no water except in the Mississippi. Accordingly I sent orders out to White's Station for the troops to march in, and accordingly the whole command marched into Memphis, my division taking post at Fort Pickering and Hurlbut's just below the fort, drawing water out of the river.

On the 21st I issued my Orders, No. 56, assuming command, and same day Orders, No. 57, ordering General Hovey and command to proceed to Helena. General Hovey showed me a dispatch from General Grant, all the infantry regiments of your [his] command. My orders were all the infantry of Wallace's division. There was a regiment here (Slack's) not of Wallace's division, but of Hovey's command. Thinking General Curtis might want as large a force as possible, and there being only five regiments of Wallace's here, I ordered Colonel Slack's regiment also.

I think the good of the service would be advanced by keeping the old divisions entire; Wallace's seems to be broken up in a measure, and some of McClernand's seem to be adrift.

I hesitated long in sending Slack's regiment, and insisted on General Hovey furnishing the original of General Grant's dispatch, of which I kept a copy. All were slow in moving, but got off yesterday morning and are now doubtless at Helena. I have Wallace's artillery and cavalry.

As soon as General Hovey drew in his pickets I sent a brigade (Morgan L. Smith's) out on the State Line road 3 miles, with orders to establish a main guard 1 mile farther out, and pickets and vedettes extending another mile, and cavalry to scout and patrol out to White's Station, 9 miles out.

I quartered two brigades inside of Fort Pickering, with orders to push the work on which they are now engaged. About 750 negroes and all soldiers who are under punishment or are arrested by the provost guard will be made to work on the fortifications.

General Hurlbut's division is encamped south of Fort Pickering, right on the Mississippi, left on the Hernando road, with orders to picket the Pigeon Roost, Hernando, and Horn Lake roads. In this manner I cover all approaches and at the same time push the construction of the fort. Captain Prime, sent here by General Halleck, returned yesterday to Corinth and will have reported to you his opinions as to the mode of making Memphis a secure depot of troops and supplies; he does not contemplate a line of redoubts, but a strong fort on the site of old Fort Pickering, on the southern edge of the city, with a battery looking back upon the city.

On my arrival I was somewhat embarrassed by an order (No. 1) of General Hovey, in regard to persons between the ages of eighteen and forty-five. I doubted the propriety of allowing such to go South, untrammeled by even a parole, whereas they are by the law of the Confederacy conscript soldiers and have doubtless gone to the army. Such should have been made to take a parole and then go South or North.

All in Memphis who are hostile to us should be compelled to leave, for so long as they remain correspondence will go on; and in case of military movements they will manage to convey the information to their friends. But if all who are not our friends are expelled from Memphis but few will be left. I will do nothing hastily; only if any persons manifest any active hostility I will deal with them summarily.

Your orders that when the head of a family is in the South the family too must go I will enforce. And I have said that when any man feels and entertains hostility to us and favor to our enemies it is a breach of honor to remain, and shall, if necessary, be so regarded.

I have issued an order limiting travel to daylight and to the five principal roads, on each of which I will post a small permanent guard, with nothing to do but watch the travel. By giving special instruction to these guards I am satisfied we can protect ourselves against spies and illicit trade more perfectly than by the usual system of provost-marshal passes.

I have, pursuant to your order, ordered the quartermaster to employ a suitable agent to take possession of all vacant buildings, register them and rent them for account of whom it may concern, keeping a true account current with each piece of property and accounting for rents to the quartermaster. I have also had all the negroes registered and will cause a time-table to be kept of their work, so that this matter may also admit of final settlement. There are squads of guerrillas in the country, but I cannot hear of any real force. A negro reports the arrival at

Germantown of about 100 infantry and some cavalry.   As soon as I get things in good shape I will begin to look into these matters.

What about Fort Pillow, its guns, &c.?   Do you expect me to remove these and dismantle the fort?

My adjutant says our tri-monthly reports have been made regularly and sent by mail.

General Hurlbut will be notified as required by your dispatch.

I am, &c.,

W. T. SHERMAN,
Major-General.

GENERAL ORDERS, }   HDQRS. DISTRICT OF WEST TENNESSEE,
No. 64.   }   *Corinth, Miss., July* 25, 1862.

The attention of the major-general commanding having been called to the fact of persons in this district sympathizing with the rebellion, who have cotton for sale, refusing to receive the United States Treasury notes in payment therefor, or anything other than gold and silver which is paid them by speculators whose love of gain is greater than their love of country, and the gold and silver thus paid indirectly affording aid and comfort to the enemy, renders necessary the publication of the following orders:

1st. From and after the 1st of August, 1862, gold and silver will not be paid within this district by speculators for the products of the rebel States.   United States Treasury notes are a legal tender in all cases, and when refused the parties refusing them will be arrested, and such of their crops as are not actually required for the subsistence of their families, stock, &c., may be seized and sold by the nearest quartermaster for the benefit of whom it may concern.

2d. Money so received will be accounted for by the officer receiving it on his next account current, and used for the benefit of Government, only to be paid to the owners of the crops sold on orders from authority above that of district commanders.

3d. Any speculator paying out gold and silver in violation of this order will be arrested and sent North, and the property so purchased seized and turned over to the proper department for the benefit of the Government.

4th. A strict enforcement of this order is enjoined upon all officers in this district.

By command of Maj. Gen. U. S. Grant:

JNO. A. RAWLINS,
Assistant Adjutant-General.

COLUMBUS, *July* 26, 1862.

Maj. Gen. U. S. GRANT:

I have just received the following:

TRENTON, *July* 26.

General QUINBY:

The gold paid out here by cotton buyers finds its way to the Southern army immediately.   Hundreds have left for that army in the counties around here lately, carrying every dollar of gold paid for cotton.

The circulation of gold should be stopped.

G. M. DODGE,
Brigadier-General.

You will pardon me for again bringing this matter before you.

I. F. QUINBY,
Brigadier-General.

BOLIVAR, *July* 26, 1862.

Major-General McCLERNAND:

Captain Townsend has just returned from Middleburg. The enemy, from 500 to 800, but estimated by the citizens and negroes at a much higher number, left Middleburg at about 1 o'clock and moved southwest, toward Moscow. Four of a foraging party were captured by the enemy about 7 miles from here. I cannot suppress them. I have no knowledge of their present location.

L. F. ROSS,
Commanding.

BOLIVAR, *July* 26, 1862.

Major-General McCLERNAND:

I have to-day had a careful examination made into the condition of our cavalry force here. We have total 340 fit for duty; about 103 quite poor.

L. F. ROSS,
Brigadier-General, Commanding.

HEADQUARTERS, *July* 27, 1862.

General GRANT:

Sheridan's cavalry will attack Ripley from three directions to-morrow morning. If the attack from the south, which have the longest road, is a little late it will make no difference, as the rebels will fall back in their road.

W. S. ROSECRANS.

ROSECRANS', *July* 27, 1862.

General GRANT:

Colonel Sheridan sends to-night one regiment cavalry to Hatchie Crossing to dash into Ripley at daylight and then strike the Ripley and Fulton road, 12 miles south of Ripley. The Third, with the battery and two companies infantry, goes to Blackland, and the cavalry advance on the rebel pickets toward Carrollville and Ellistown, while Ord's cavalry goes via Kossuth and Ruckersville, on the Ripley and Pocahontas road, and attacks Ripley from the north. The whole Ripley force then moves south and joins Sheridan at Blackland.

Nothing especial from Morgan, except a terribly grumbling letter at the misbehavior of Thomas' troops at Courtland. Three companies of our cavalry had a skirmish with rebel cavalry southwest of Courtland, in which we lost 23 killed, wounded, and missing. No further particulars, except all safe.

W. S. ROSECRANS,
Brigadier-General.

BOLIVAR, *July* 27, 1862.

General McCLERNAND:

I am surrounded by a large force. Two thousand infantry, said to be the advance guard, were at La Grange yesterday morning. Cavalry are on all sides, said to be 5,000 strong. They have also plenty of artillery. We shall have a fight.

ROSS.

BOLIVAR, *July* 27, 1862.

General McCLERNAND:

My infantry force has just returned safe, but were in sight of 300 cavalry, who kept at a respectful distance. My information as to the infantry at La Grange, to the cavalry, and as to six pieces of artillery is reliable; they were counted. I don't think they will attack us to-day. They say that we escaped them at La Grange and Grand Junction, but they will capture us here if it takes the Army of the Southwest. At present we don't propose being taken.

ROSS,
Brigadier-General, Commanding.

BOLIVAR, *July* 27, 1862.

General McCLERNAND:

Most of the cavalry west of us are reported to be moving northwest, toward Estanaula. I am now sending out additional scouting parties.

ROSS.

JACKSON, *July* 27, 1862.

Captain DOLLINS, *Bolivar:*

You will advance toward Toone's Station to meet Major Stewart, who is moving on the Bolivar road to meet you somewhere about the mouth of Clover Creek. You had better manage to meet him at some point. You can send couriers to cause him to come to Toone's Station.

JOHN A. LOGAN,
Brigadier-General.

Major Stewart will understand that I am consenting to the above order.

JOHN A. McCLERNAND.

BOLIVAR, *July* 27, 1862.

General McCLERNAND:

Dollins has just sent a messenger stating that he tried to capture and destroy the ferry-boat at Estanaula, but was driven back this morning. My forces had not joined him, but were near him. He wants infantry re-enforcements, and says he will whip them before he leaves there.

I can't spare any of my forces.

ROSS.

BOLIVAR, *July* 27, 1862.

General McCLERNAND:

I misunderstood Dollins' messenger. The facts are as follows:

The ferry-boats at Brownsville, Estanaula, and at the steam-mill ferry are destroyed. Dollins' skirmish took place at the ferry known as Lower Post, only 5 miles from Toone's Station.

ROSS.

BOLIVAR, *July 27, 1862.*

General McCLERNAND:

I have all our teams engaged in hauling cotton for fortifications. By morning they will be in good condition for us.

Our pickets have been fired on, on the two roads leading west, but all quiet at present.

The citizens nearly all wish to leave, but I have refused to allow them to do so for fear of their carrying information. I may let them go in the morning. Had I better do so?

ROSS.

HEADQUARTERS ARMY OF THE MISSISSIPPI,
July 27, 1862.

Brigadier-General MORGAN:

I observe by your dispatch to General Elliott that you are pushing your corps eastward, but in your dispatch to me you do not state, so explicitly as I could wish, your grounds. You will observe that your original instructions about relieving General Thomas have been so far modified that you are desired to send your troops only as far east as you can successfully cover and use the railroad. The principle of our movement is that the railroad is made subservient to us, not our forces to the railroad.

Send me some sketch of the country.

Two hundred and seventeen sick and 50 wagon loads of stuff of your division go by train east this morning.

W. S. ROSECRANS,
Brigadier-General, U. S. Army.

FORT HEIMAN, *July 27, 1862.*

ASSISTANT ADJUTANT-GENERAL :

Last night I received the following dispatch, viz:

CHANDIT [?], —— 26.

W. W. LOWE, *Commanding Fort Henry:*

I have just received a communication from reliable Union men of Eddyville, who have fled to the woods, stating that a band of some 150 or 200 are near Eddyville, and contemplate an attack on that place, and that this office and the men guarding the line are in great danger of being attacked immediately. An officer in the rebel army was in Eddyville this p. m. holding a consultation with secesh citizens.

Most of the Union citizens have taken to the woods. I am asked to urge upon you to send a force to that place. I think it very important that the force at this place and Fingo [?] Station should be increased without delay. Strange and suspicious looking persons have been seen near here yesterday and to-day.

R. B. GRIFFIN,
Military Telegraph Operator.

From this it will be seen that the small force here is inadequate to the demands. I at once had all that could be spared sent down 40 miles by boat.

W. W. LOWE,
Colonel, Commanding.

HEADQUARTERS FIFTH DIVISION,
Memphis, Tenn., July 27, 1862.

JOHN PARK, *Mayor of Memphis :*

SIR: Yours of July 24 is before me * and has received, as all similar papers ever will, my careful and most respectful consideration.

I have the most unbounded respect for the civil law, courts, and authorities, and shall do all in my power to restore them to their proper use, viz, the protection of life, liberty, and property.

Unfortunately at this time civil war prevails in the land, and necessarily the military for the time being must be superior to the civil authority, but does not therefore destroy it. Civil courts and executive officers should still exist and perform duties, without which civil or municipal bodies would soon pass into disrespect—an end to be avoided.

I am glad to find in Memphis yourself and municipal authorities not only in existence but in the exercise of your important functions, and I shall endeavor to restore one or more civil tribunals for the arbitrament of contracts and punishment of crimes which the military authority has neither time nor inclination to interfere with.

Among these, first in importance, is the maintenance of order, peace, and quiet within the jurisdiction of Memphis. To insure this I will keep a strong provost guard in the city, but will limit their duty to guarding public property held or claimed by the United States, and for the arrest or confinement of State prisoners and soldiers who are disorderly or improperly away from their regiments.

This guard ought not to arrest citizens for disorder or common crimes. This should be done by the city police. I understand that the city police is too weak in numbers to accomplish this perfectly, and I therefore recommend that the city council at once take steps to increase this force to a number which, in their judgment, day and night, can enforce your ordinances as to peace, quiet, and order, so that any change in our military dispositions will not have a tendency to leave your people unguarded.

I am willing to instruct my provost guard to assist the police force where any combination is made too strong for them to overcome, but the city police should be strong enough for any probable contingency.

The cost of maintaining this police force must necessarily fall upon all citizens equitably.

I am not willing, nor do I think it good policy, for the city authorities to collect the taxes belonging to the State and county, as you recommend, for these would have to be refunded. Better meet the expenses at once by a new tax on all interested. Therefore if you, on consultation with the proper municipal body, will frame a good bill for the increase of your police force and for raising the necessary means for their support and maintenance, I will approve it and aid you in the collection of the tax. Of course I cannot suggest how this tax should be laid, but I think that it should be made uniform on all interests, real estate and personal property, including money and merchandise. All who are protected should share the expenses in proportion to the interests involved.

I am, with respect, your obedient servant,
W. T. SHERMAN,
Major-General, Commanding.

---

* Not found.

SPECIAL ORDERS, }   HEADQUARTERS,
    No. 147.   }   Memphis, July 27, 1862.

The Sixth Illinois Cavalry, Colonel Grierson, will to-morrow morning proceed on a scout toward Germantown, going by the State Line road and returning by the Pigeon Roost or Holly Springs road. The commanding officer will proceed with great caution, falling upon and destroying or making prisoners all in arms, and arresting and bringing in all known to be aiding or abetting the public enemy.

Three days' rations for the men will be taken along, but the horses will be foraged in the country. When forage is taken a receipt may be given, to be settled for in Memphis on the party proving his loyalty.

The scouting party will examine the country from Wolf River to the Pigeon Roost road. The Eleventh Illinois Cavalry will in like manner proceed to scout the country between the Pigeon Roost road and the river, going out well toward Hernando, breaking up and destroying any party they may encounter.

These parties will remain out two or three days and return to their camps, the commanding officers exercising large discretion and making written reports of their scouts on their return to camp. They will be provided with the countersign for three days.

By order of Maj. Gen. W. T. Sherman :

                        J. H. HAMMOND,
                        Assistant Adjutant-General.

                        HUMBOLDT, *July* 28, 1862.
General GRANT :

We have been expecting an attack here all day. Rebels burned trestlework 5 miles below here at 11 o'clock this morning. Forces in line of battle here. Colonel Bryant gone out with re-enforcements of cavalry from Trenton to find enemy. Engagement this morning. Enemy drove in our cavalry on march to Jackson.

                        HOLDREDGE,
                        Operator.

                        JACKSON, [*July*] 28, 1862.
                (Received at Corinth July 28, 1862.)
Major-General GRANT :

My forces have been all sent to Bolivar against my protest; some two small regiments, not enough to do picket duty. My cavalry, including orderlies, have been sent also this morning.

The road has been attacked this side of Humboldt and the bridges burned. I am sending all the force I have to repair and hold it. What will become of this place you can imagine. I shall hold it or be burned in its ashes.

                        JOHN A. LOGAN,
                        Brigadier-General.

                        JACKSON, *July* 28, 1862.
Major-General McCLERNAND :

A large force of cavalry have attacked the road this side of Humboldt, driven our guards away and burned the trestle-work, cut the

wire and destroyed the road. I have ordered a force there with Engineer Regiment to repair. I feared this when I was ordered to send
from here nearly all the troops.

JOHN A. LOGAN,
Brigadier-General.

CORINTH, *July* 28, 1862.

General LOGAN, *Jackson :*

Have we any force now at the burning bridge ? Keep a sharp lookout for rebel forces, and if they are needed I will send you troops from
here at once. I will have all the cars here in readiness to send troops
should they be needed.

U. S. GRANT,
Major-General.

JACKSON, [*July*] 28, [1862].

Maj. Gen. U. S. GRANT:

We have about 50 infantry stationed at the burnt bridge. The Engineer Regiment have gone there, about 300 strong, armed and equipped.

JOHN A. LOGAN,
Brigadier-General.

CORINTH, *July* 28, 1862.

General LOGAN:

What was extent of damage done the road ? How far north of Jackson ? What force was supposed to be engaged ? Did we lose any men,
and what number ? Was the rebel loss anything, or did our men leave
without firing ? Had the train from Columbus passed ?

U. S. GRANT,
Major-General, Commanding.

JACKSON, [*July*] 28, [1862].

Major-General GRANT:

The extent of damages I do not know. The courier left while trestle
was burning. Distance from Jackson, 14 miles. Force supposed to be
some 300 cavalry. Our loss was said to be some 4 or 5 wounded. I did
not learn that any were killed. Rebel loss, 4 killed and 5 prisoners.
The train from Columbus had not passed down. I learn that a large
cavalry force, with perhaps 200 infantry, crossed Hatchie last night
about 18 miles from here. They may be the force.

JOHN A. LOGAN,
Brigadier-General.

JACKSON, *July* 28, 1862.

Major-General McCLERNAND, *Bolivar, Tenn.:*

Colonel Bryant is in pursuit of the enemy and will camp at Poplar
Corners to-night. Where shall I order him ?

JOHN A. LOGAN,
Brigadier-General.

JACKSON, *July* 28, 1862.

Brigadier-General DODGE, *Trenton :*

I am informed by dispatch per messenger that Colonel Bryant is after the rebels and will camp at Poplar Corners to-night. He requests that I should inform you.

JOHN A. LOGAN,
Brigadier-General, Commanding.

ROSECRANS', *July* 28, 1862.

General GRANT :

Sheridan has returned from the front. Has captured a captain of cavalry and some thirty letters on a private mail carrier. They show the enemy moving in large force on Chattanooga. Has sent the letters up. They had 19 miles to come. Will dispatch you when they arrive.

W. S. ROSECRANS,
Brigadier-General, Commanding.

CORINTH, *July* 28, 1862.

Major-General McCLERNAND, *Bolivar,*
Brigadier-General LOGAN, *Jackson:*

Return a portion of the forces to Jackson as soon as possible. The two brigades which will reach Bolivar in the morning will enable you to do this. Answer if this is not so.

U. S. GRANT,
Major-General.

GENERAL ORDERS, }   HDQRS. DISTRICT OF WEST TENNESSEE,
No. 65.   }   *Corinth, Miss., July* 28, 1862.

I. Hereafter no passes will be given to citizens of States in rebellion to pass our lines at any of the stations from Tuscumbia to Memphis, including Bolivar, except to persons employed on secret service, and to those only by generals commanding divisions.

II. Deserters from the rebel army, or those claiming to be such, presenting themselves to the outer guards will be taken prisoners and sent under guard to the nearest commanding officer, who will give them a thorough examination and will only release them on their taking the oath of allegiance and his conviction that the persons so released take the oath in good faith and with the intention of going North.

III. Goods will not be permitted to pass out in any direction where they may be carried south of our lines, nor persons except when employed in secret service, and then only on permits from division commanders.

By order of Major-General Grant:

JNO. A. RAWLINS,
Assistant Adjutant-General.

CORINTH, MISS., *July* 29, 1862.

Maj. Gen. H. W. HALLECK :

Information just in from Colonel Sheridan, who attacked and drove 600 rebels from Ripley this morning, says large force leaving Saltillo for Chattanooga by rail. Wagons moved across the country. General

Cheatham with division had gone west; Withers to follow with division. The Hatchie northwest of Bolivar is now occupied by rebels. McClernand is there with about 6,000 men.

U. S. GRANT,
Major-General.

HDQRS. CENTRAL DIVISION OF THE MISSISSIPPI,
Trenton, Tenn., July 29, 1862.

Capt. M. ROCHESTER,
Assistant Adjutant-General, Columbus, Ky.:

CAPTAIN: I have the honor to submit the following report of the movements of troops in my division for the past ten days:

After the attack on my forces near Humboldt and their dispersion of the enemy I ascertained that a force had been sent from Jackson to attack the enemy near Ripley, Lauderdale County; also that a force of the enemy was threatening Bolivar. I ordered Colonel Bryant to take all the cavalry, with a force of infantry, to follow up the enemy's forces north of the Hatchie River and toward Brownsville, at the same time starting a force from here toward Dyersburg. Last night Colonel Bryant camped in rear of the enemy's force at Poplar Corners, and is still following them. I trust, in connection with the Jackson forces; he will cut off their retreat across the Hatchie and thereby bag them. The enemy's forces are on the increase both north and south of the Hatchie. Those north I believe I shall be able to attend to, but they are so slippery and dodge through such small holes that they may evade me. As I have taken charge of the bridge south of Humboldt I shall endeavor to so guard it that no small band of the enemy can take or destroy it. I have in process of erection there a strong block-house, which when finished will add greatly to the strength of the position. The bridge burned I have had rebuilt, and in one hour after we obtained possession of the road had telegraphic communication south. I must say that the strain upon my health and nerves lately has not added much to the state of my health, though I have full faith that I shall weather it and get through safe. I would be glad to visit Columbus, as the general suggests, but it is not best just at this time.

I am, very respectfully, your obedient servant,

G. M. DODGE,
Brigadier-General.

HEADQUARTERS ARMY OF THE MISSISSIPPI,
July 29, 1862.

General GRANT:

GENERAL: I send accompanying telegrams from Colonel Sheridan, giving information of the movements of rebels and his operations yesterday.

Two divisions left from below for Chattanooga. Cheatham's left last Friday and Saturday. Withers' was to leave Sunday or Monday.

The 600 cavalry escaped from Ripley, retreating toward Salem. The Seventh Kansas pursued them, and have not yet returned; probably foraging.

You will note Sheridan says there are at least 10,000 men at Saltillo. You will also observe that the division of Withers was leaving Saltillo.

W. S. ROSECRANS,
Brigadier-General, U. S. Army, Commanding.

[Inclosures.]

HDQRS. SECOND BRIGADE, CAVALRY DIVISION,
July 29, 1862.

General GRANGER:

I have reliable information from Okolona Saturday, Tupelo Sunday, and Saltillo yesterday. The enemy have been and still are moving in large numbers to Chattanooga, via Mobile and Montgomery, concentrating at Rome, Ga. A large number of troops are at Saltillo, not less than 10,000. The transportation of the troops moving to Rome is going across the country from a point near Okolona. A large train of 200 wagons started across on Saturday. The Second Michigan drove in the enemy's pickets toward Saltillo yesterday, until they could hear the enemy's drums beating. Hicks returned from Tupelo yesterday. I have sent for him this morning and may get additional information.

P. H. SHERIDAN,
Colonel, Commanding Second Brigade.

HDQRS. SECOND BRIGADE, CAVALRY DIVISION,
July 29, 1862.

General GRANGER:

GENERAL: Our cavalry captured Ripley yesterday morning.* Colonel Hatch has just returned, bringing back Judge Thompson and two Confederate soldiers. Our party failed to secure 600 rebel soldiers encamped there, they having made their escape toward Salem. The enemy had decamped just one hour before the arrival of Colonel Lee, who was delayed by bad road and darkness. Colonel Lee has not yet returned. He may bring in some of them. All the male inhabitants of Ripley had fled; the stores and houses all closed. I am sorry to say the soldiers of both regiments were, through carelessness of their officers, permitted to break into and pillage some of the stores and private places. The whole country out here is very much alarmed and stampeded.

P. H. SHERIDAN,
Colonel, Second Brigade.

ROSECRANS', July 29, 1862.

General GRANT:

From perusal of a large number of letters written by members of the Twenty-sixth Alabama and a few others from Richmond, captured by Sheridan, it is clear that there is very considerable movement of troops from Saltillo and vicinage via railroad to Chattanooga; two or three of them say thence to Huntsville, and all speak of a movement in Northern Alabama—of expelling the Yankees from Northern Alabama. One says a considerable force will be left at Saltillo, supposed to be enough to meet the emergency. Two days' cooked rations and the railroad via Mobile is in [sic]. Nearly all of them to leave to-morrow morning. Two or three talk of going from Chattanooga to Huntsville. Unfortunately they are all of the Twenty-sixth Alabama, but the impression is abroad among them that with Bragg on the east and Price in the center, as they say, the Yankees will be made to skedaddle.

W. S. ROSECRANS.

---

* See report of Col. A. L. Lee, Seventh Kansas Cavalry, of expedition from Rienzi to Ripley, Miss., July 27–29, 1862, Part I, p. 25.

JACKSON, *July* 29, 1862.

General McCLERNAND, *Bolivar:*

Have you ordered the men I had at Toone's Station to Medon? If not, I hope you will do it. I have sent one company to Medon to-day.

JOHN A. LOGAN,
Brigadier-General.

———

BOLIVAR, *July* 29, 1862.

Brigadier-General LOGAN, *Jackson:*

I sent 100 men this morning to Medon. There should be at least 150 men to guard there and half way to Toone's. General Ross will guard the other half and from Toone's. You will relieve the men sent by me to-morrow by sending about 70 more men, which, with what are there now, will be 150.

JOHN A. McCLERNAND,
Major-General.

———

BOLIVAR, *July* 29, 1862.

Brig. Gen. JOHN A. LOGAN, *Jackson:*

I ordered you to send a company to Medon and you did not do it. You had more than two regiments at Jackson. You had four companies besides which had been ordered here, and are mistaken in saying they were all delayed as camp guards. The bridges north and south of Jackson within a few miles were destroyed. You have not been asked to re-enforce anybody from your present force. I sent a force to repair the wire and bridge at Medon. The wires are repaired and the bridge nearly. What was your telegram of yesterday but a gratuitous complaint? But enough.

JOHN A. McCLERNAND,
Major-General.

———

JACKSON, *July* 29, 1862.

General McCLERNAND:

I have at all times obeyed orders. The bridge at Medon was not destroyed for want of force at Medon. There were enough to protect it. I understand you ordered to leave 100 men at Toone's Station, and not at Medon; this I ordered Colonel Rhoads to do. I am not mistaken about the camp guards, two companies, you speak of, or provost guard, detached. I had no orders to relieve them. It is true the bridges have been destroyed, and certainly they are not the first ones that have been destroyed; in this case if I am to blame I can bear my part as well as any man. I did not say that I was asked to re-enforce from my present command, but spoke of re-enforcing the points guarded on railroads. I know the wires have been repaired, and I shall repair bridges and will try to do it without much delay. I have no complaints to make of any kind, but will do my duty.

JOHN A. LOGAN.

———

BOLIVAR, *July* 29, 1862.

General LOGAN, *Jackson:*

I found to my surprise that you had not sent an additional company to Medon. The wire was cut in that vicinity. I sent this morning to repair. If you had apprehended an attack on bridge north of Jackson you should have guarded against it. You had not ordered or asked guard for that position before or during the leaving of the troops.

I was ordered to leave but one regiment and left four companies besides. You kept two companies of the Eighteenth and Twenty-ninth, and a regiment was in reach at Bethel. I am satisfied there is no formidable force near you. Report the condition of things.

JOHN A. McCLERNAND,
Major-General.

JACKSON, July 29, 1862.

[General McClernand :]

I cannot say that you should be surprised at my not sending a company to Medon. I did not know of any danger there. When two regiments were going by land to Bolivar the bridge was attacked and burnt. I sent force there. How could I guard against an attack north without anybody to leave here? I had but two small regiments left. The Eleventh got in last night; the rest were guarding the road.

Can I guard all the roads and property here with such a force as is left me, and at the same time re-enforce any of the points when I can have no notice of the attack? The companies that were left from the regiments you spoke of were left as camp guard for their regimental property.

If they don't want their property guarded they can send and take them away. I am doing everything in my power, and if complaints arise from that I am willing to meet the responsibility.

I shall send a force as soon as I can get a train to repair the bridge at Medon, which has been burned. I don't suppose there is any great force near here, and if there is I shall not ask for help until I see the necessity for it.

JOHN A. LOGAN,
Brigadier-General.

BOLIVAR, July 29, 1862.

General LOGAN, Jackson :

The officer at Medon reports otherwise. I ordered the Eighteenth and Twenty-ninth here. You kept four of these companies. I repeat that I have a detail at Medon repairing the bridge or road. If you prefer it I would rather General Ross would guard at Toone's and for you to re-enforce at Medon.

JOHN A. McCLERNAND,
Major-General.

BOLIVAR, TENN., July 29, 1862.

General LOGAN, Jackson :

The company sent by you had not reached Medon at 2 o'clock p. m. The two companies of the Eighth dropped at Toone's day before yesterday at my instance and the detail from Eighteenth previously'sent by you ought to go with these regiments and Colonel Lawler, unless there is an overruling reason to the contrary.

JOHN A. McCLERNAND,
Major-General.

JACKSON, *July* 29, 1862.

General McCLERNAND, *Bolivar:*

Troops were started to Medon about 6 o'clock.   I could not get a car sooner.   You can dispose of the troops at Toone's Station as you see proper.

JOHN A. LOGAN,
Brigadier-General.

JACKSON, *July* 29, 1862.

General McCLERNAND:

I have just heard from Major Stewart; he is moving to Brownsville. Shall I send Colonel Hogg there to meet him?   He reports Jackson's cavalry all crossing the Hatchie at different points.   Has taken two prisoners.   Reports an advance upon Bolivar.

JOHN A. LOGAN,
Brigadier-General.

BOLIVAR, *July* 29, 1862.

General LOGAN, *Jackson:*

Let Colonel Hogg proceed carefully in direction of Medon, thence, if possible, toward Denmark, and inquire for and co-operate with Major Wallace.   Colonel Lawler's brigade, except details, will march toward Estanaula so soon as I hear from Tuttle.

JOHN A. McCLERNAND,
Major-General.

DENMARK, TENN., *July* 29, 1862.

General LOGAN:

I am camped here for the night.   There is evidently a considerable rebel force in the neighborhood.

If we have a fight to-night I will burn the town to make light.   In the morning I will push on toward Brownsville.   I am satisfied that Stewart is cut off.   I will keep you advised, however, if the result should be different.

We are all wide awake and ready for any emergency.

HARVEY HOGG,
Lieutenant-Colonel, Commanding.

P. S.—A force of 150 Mississippi cavalry passed through here toward Brownsville at 2 o'clock p. m.   This force was not the same that fought Stewart.

BOLIVAR, *July* 29, 1862.

Maj. Gen. U. S GRANT:

Major Stewart has had a hard fight with rebel cavalry.   Has taken a number of prisoners and reports that he is pursuing his advantage.

JOHN A. McCLERNAND,
Major-General.

JACKSON, *July* 29, 1862.

General MCCLERNAND, *Bolivar* :

Colonel Hogg is here with cavalry. Where shall I order him?

JOHN A. LOGAN,
Brigadier-General.

BOLIVAR, *July* 29, 1862.

General LOGAN, *Jackson* :

Let Colonel Hogg join Major Wallace and Stewart by the most direct route and move from Brownsville toward Toone's Station, so as to be in supporting distance of this place if the enemy should be approaching, which I now doubt.

JOHN A. MCCLERNAND,
Major-General, Commanding.

CORINTH, MISS., *July* 30, 1862.
(Received 8 p. m.)

Maj. Gen. H. W. HALLECK, *Commander-in-Chief* :

General information obtained by Colonel Sheridan, who has been far to the front and right for several days, shows that Bragg has made headquarters at Rome. Most of the troops from Saltillo and Tupelo have gone to Chattanooga by rail. Wagons move across the country to Rome. Cheatham and Withers have gone west. Price is in command in Mississippi; headquarters at Holly Springs, with force at Grand Junction. Had I not better move Ord's entire command to Bolivar, one division of Rosecrans' to Corinth, and drive the force in front south? They cannot number to exceed 10,000.

U. S. GRANT,
Major-General.

JACKSON, TENN., *July* 30, 1862—2 a. m.

Colonel HOGG, *Commanding Detachment* :

Major Stewart has just arrived. He was attacked close to Denmark this evening by Jackson's cavalry, some 300 or 400 strong, and defeated. His loss is considerable in killed, wounded, and prisoners. He thinks the force is still close there.

It is impossible for any of his men to move to your support in their present condition. He is of the opinion that you had better move in direction of ferry or crossing in direction of Medon, where you can have support of infantry. I have two companies at Medon.

I hope you will move cautiously in whatever direction you go, as a defeat of your force would now insure an attack upon the road at different points. If you think proper you can move so as to watch the crossings of Hatchie, not too far, from where you can give information of a superior force. In fact you can judge best of matters yourself, as you can see the face of the country and can judge of the enemy. I am of opinion that the enemy will have support from nearly all of the citizens in that country. Send my orderlies back and let me know in what direction you move.

JOHN A. LOGAN,
Brigadier-General, Commanding.

TRENTON, TENN., *July* 30, 1862.

General LOGAN, *Jackson :*

Can you inform me at what place they crossed the Hatchie and in what force? Have you heard to-day from my cavalry?

G. M. DODGE,
Brigadier-General.

JACKSON, *July* 30, 1862.

General DODGE, *Trenton :*

They crossed at Estanaula, 600 or 700 strong. Have heard from your cavalry to-day. They are going in the direction of Estanaula, supported by my cavalry.

JOHN A. LOGAN,
Brigadier-General.

HUMBOLDT, TENN., *July* 30, 1862.

General LOGAN, *Jackson :*

Where are Hogg and Brackett?

BRYANT,
Colonel, Commanding.

JACKSON, *July* 30, 1862.

Colonel BRYANT, *Humboldt :*

Moving in the direction of Estanaula, supported by my cavalry.

JOHN A. LOGAN,
Brigadier-General.

HUMBOLDT, *July* 30, 1862.

General LOGAN, *Jackson :*

Are Jackson's forces between Brackett's forces, and where, or by the river?

GEORGE E. BRYANT.

JACKSON, *July* 30, 1862.

G. E. BRYANT, *Humboldt :*

I cannot tell you. It will be necessary to keep a sharp lookout.

JOHN A. LOGAN.

BOLIVAR, TENN., *July* 30, 1862.

Brig. Gen. JOHN A. LOGAN, *Jackson :*

It was Pinson's Mississippi cavalry that Major Stewart engaged yesterday evening.

Slemons' Arkansas cavalry were south of Hatchie and Brownsville yesterday morning. Cotton Jackson's cavalry retired from Estanaula, Tenn., Sunday, immediately after the fight at mouth of Clover Creek, and on Monday were returning toward La Grange. This is what is credibly reported.

JOHN A. McCLERNAND,
Major-General, Commanding.

JACKSON, *July* 30, 1862.

General McCLERNAND, *Bolivar :*

I have the following information, which I give you. It is contained in a note from ———— :

The most of Jackson's cavalry were at Whiteville on last Saturday, 4 miles the other side of Estanaula, and are all this side of the river now, and are directed to cut off communication between here and Columbus and attack points that are weak.

This information I think is reliable.

JOHN A. LOGAN,
Brigadier-General.

———

BOLIVAR, *July* 30, 1862.

General LOGAN, *Jackson :*

Your dispatch concerning Whiteville this minute received. I had a force there late yesterday evening.

Two regiments rebel cavalry are reported to have fallen back in from direction of Estanaula by Whiteville.

I do not think there is much of any rebel infantry east of the Hatchie nor a large cavalry force. This is, however, given as an opinion, but not as a fact.

JOHN A. McCLERNAND,
Major-General.

———

JACKSON, *July* 30, 1862.

General McCLERNAND :

I have sent every cavalryman that is able to ride, under Colonel Mc-Cullough, to support Colonel Hogg. Major Stewart is not able to go. The enemy are in force, I am pretty well satisfied, and I am re-enforcing on the railroad between here and Humboldt, or shall do so as soon as I can get cars. I am satisfied Jackson will make a dash somewhere on the road unless Colonel Hogg can hold him in check.

JOHN A. LOGAN,
Brigadier-General.

———

BOLIVAR, *July* 30, 1862.

General LOGAN, *Jackson :*

You are right in supporting Colonel Hogg as much as possible. I wish Major Stewart, as my chief of cavalry, to accompany the cavalry. You ought to support by an infantry demonstration toward Denmark, if the enemy are still in that direction.

JOHN A. McCLERNAND,
Major-General.

———

BOLIVAR, *July* 30, 1862.

General LOGAN, *Jackson :*

You, being on the ground, must determine whether you will re-enforce your guards by railroad or marching on foot. I would adopt the most expeditious way of doing it. Act boldly, but carefully. You say the enemy are in force; cavalry or infantry, or both ?

JOHN A. McCLERNAND,
Major-General.

JACKSON, TENN., *July* 30, 1862.

General MCCLERNAND, *Bolivar:*

By the enemy being in force I mean cavalry force, though I understand that footmen were engaged against Major Stewart. I think it was citizens collected to support rebel cavalry.

JOHN A. LOGAN,
Brigadier-General.

HEADQUARTERS ARMY OF THE MISSISSIPPI,
July 30, 1862—3.05 p. m.

Major-General HALLECK:

Brigadiers scarce. Good ones scarce. Asboth goes on the month's leave you gave him ten months since. Granger has temporary command. The undersigned respectfully beg that you will obtain the promotion of Sheridan. He is worth his weight in gold. His Ripley expedition has brought us captured letters of immense value, as well as prisoners, showing the rebels' plans and dispositions, as you will learn from district commander.

W. S. ROSECRANS,
JER. C. SULLIVAN,
G. GRANGER,
W. L. ELLIOTT,
A. ASBOTH,
Brigadier-Generals.

ROSECRANS' HEADQUARTERS, *July* 30, 1862.

Major-General GRANT:

A batch of captured letters just in throws a flash of light on the rebel movements. Bragg has gone to North Alabama; headquarters at Rome. Price commands in Mississippi; line extends from Tupelo, via Ripley and Salem, to Holly Springs. Villepigue, with seven regiments, is 10 miles below Grand Junction. Say they could take Corinth when they please. Expect they will leave and will soon occupy the Mobile and Ohio Railroad, &c. When I have finished, will send them to you.

W. S. ROSECRANS,
Brigadier-General, Commanding.

ROSECRANS', *July* 30, 1862.

Major-General GRANT:

I think it best to spare General Stanley at once. I think his purpose, if executed, will be beneficial to the service.

W. S. ROSECRANS,
Brigadier-General.

HEADQUARTERS ARMY OF THE MISSISSIPPI,
July 30, 1862.

Colonel SHERIDAN,
Cavalry Headquarters, Rienzi:

Your dispatch received. Our troops left Grand Junction and La Grange for Memphis some time ago. Our first post north of La Grange is Bolivar. It is reported that a considerable force of cavalry and mounted infantry got up into that angle and threatened Bolivar. Some got across the Hatchie below Grand Junction and Jackson, on the Mobile and Ohio Railroad, and even got in on the Columbus Railroad, but are cleared. It is possible John B. Villepigue has advanced into the gap we left open. Inquire into this. Eastward, four regiments of infantry. Frank Armstrong, with his two regiments of cavalry and two batteries, took the eastward road and arrived at Moulton. Hardee's advance gives the best memoir of map of Hatchie route. You can move up and look for Brown's Creek front, but it may be well for us to scratch this cavalry on our right first. I will ascertain.

W. S. ROSECRANS,
Brigadier-General, U. S. Army.

HDQRS. FIFTH DIVISION, ARMY OF THE TENNESSEE,
Memphis, July 30, 1862.

Col. JOHN A. RAWLINS,
        Headquarters Corinth, Miss.:

SIR: I had the honor to write on the 25th instant, since which nothing has happened here in the vicinity worth reporting. My infantry and cavalry pickets go well out, and I have sent two parties of cavalry, one to Hernando and one to Germantown, to be gone three days. I feel certain that small parties of cavalry and armed citizens are hovering about for mischief, but I have no reliable intelligence of any force being near us. That an attempt may be made on the river at some point north of us is very probable. Should any large force go north of the Hatchie they would be in danger from you; if south of the Hatchie, my forces would be in position.

I am pushing the construction of the fort, and have now at work about 800 negroes, all of which are registered and an account kept of their time and labor. The engineer, Captain Hoepner, will report progress, through Captain Prime. The armament of the fort should be ordered at once from Island No. 10, Saint Louis, or Pittsburg. I am informed there are no guns at Fort Pillow. I sent Colonel Fitch, who was there half a day on his way down, and he asserted all the guns there were disabled and carriages destroyed.

General Curtis, I am informed, goes to Little Rock very soon; indeed, I hear the army moves to-day. I have also learned that the Navy boat Sallie Wood, with about 40 passengers of the fleet and army before Vicksburg, was disabled at Carolina Point, about 90 miles above Vicksburg, and run on shore. All passengers were made prisoners except three, who succeeded in reaching an island and getting on board the Carondelet. One of them, a lieutenant of a Wisconsin regiment, was my informant.

Information has also reached us that our fleet before Vicksburg has raised the siege, the lower fleet returning to Baton Rouge, and upper, on its return, maybe, to this place. This will embolden Van Dorn, and we must soon expect to hear from him.

I have been very busy in answering the innumerable questions of civilians, and hope they are now about through. I found so many Jews and speculators here trading in cotton, and secessionists had become so open in refusing anything but gold, that I have felt myself bound to stop it. This gold has but one use—the purchase of arms and ammunition, which can always be had for gold, at Nassau, New Providence, or Cincinnati; all the guards we may establish cannot stop it. Of course I have respected all permits by yourself or the Secretary of the Treasury, but in these new cases (swarms of Jews) I have stopped it.

In like manner so great was the demand for salt to make bacon that many succeeded in getting loads of salt out for cotton. Salt is as much contraband of war as powder. All the boards of trade above are shipping salt south, and I cannot permit it to pass into the interior until you declare a district open to trade. If we permit money and salt to go into the interior it will not take long for Bragg and Van Dorn to supply their armies with all they need to move. Without money—gold, silver, and Treasury notes—they cannot get arms and ammunition of the English colonies; and without salt they cannot make bacon and salt beef. We cannot carry on war and trade with a people at the same time.

I have had all the vacant houses registered, and the quartermaster will proceed to rent them for account of whom it may concern at once.

Our men have received in great part new clothing, and will soon gain rest and be prepared for the fall campaign. General health good.

I am, with great respect, your obedient servant,

W. T. SHERMAN,
Major-General, Commanding.

HDQRS. FIFTH DIVISION, ARMY OF THE TENNESSEE,
Memphis, Tenn., July 31, 1862.

Col. JOHN A. RAWLINS,
Assistant Adjutant-General, Corinth, Miss.:

SIR: A scouting party returned last night from Colliersville and beyond; captured some officers and guerrillas; also intercepted several letters from Tupelo, from which it appears that the whole army was on the point of starting for Nashville via Chattanooga. I take it for granted you are advised of this, and I merely repeat it as confirmatory. I inclose one of the letters.

All quiet here and hereabouts.

I have supplied General Curtis my extra ammunition. Will you please order the ordnance officer at Saint Louis to fill my requisitions for ammunition and ordnance to arm the fortifications now under construction here, either drawing from Pittsburg or the forts above?

I am, &c.,

W. T. SHERMAN,
Major-General.

HUMBOLDT, *July 31, 1862.*

General LOGAN,
Commanding Post, Jackson:

Have you heard any news from my cavalry to-day? Falkner's guerrilla band was within 2 miles of Cageville last night. There are 75 of them. I shall send out in the morning.

GEORGE E. BRYANT,
Colonel, Commanding Post.

JACKSON, *July* 31, 1862.

Colonel BRYANT, *Humboldt:*

I have not heard from cavalry to-day, though am sure they are moving down the Hatchie, supported by infantry. I have to-night re-enforced the burnt bridge. I do not think there are that many of Falkner's command. If you can send a force against them do so.

JOHN A. LOGAN,
Brigadier-General.

HDQRS. FIFTH DIVISION, ARMY OF THE TENNESSEE,
Memphis, Tenn., July 31, 1862.

General I. F. QUINBY,
    Commanding, Columbus, Ky.:

SIR: I received yours, inclosing dispatches from General Grant, and would be obliged if you would telegraph him the contents of the within letter * and then send it to him by mail.

Colonel Grierson, Sixth Illinois Cavalry, who commanded the scout yesterday to Colliersville, learned that a brigade of the enemy had moved up to within 7 miles of Bolivar and then backed out. There has been a rumor that Bolivar had been attacked, but I do not believe it; it is more probable the bulk of the forces have gone toward Chattanooga and Nashville.

Curtis is preparing to move on Little Rock. He is still at Helena.

I hear the fleet has raised the siege of Vicksburg.

I am fortifying here below Memphis, but dispose my troops to cover the town.

Yours, truly,

W. T. SHERMAN,
Major-General.

WAR DEPARTMENT,
Washington, July 31, 1862.

Major-General GRANT, *Corinth, Miss.:*

Cannot you move on the flank and rear of the rebels on the Hatchie and cut them off? At any rate drive them out of West Tennessee and carefully guard the railroad from Columbus to Decatur.

H. W. HALLECK,
Major-General.

WAR DEPARTMENT,
Washington, July 31, 1862.

Major-General GRANT, *Corinth, Miss.:*

You must judge for yourself the best use to be made of your troops. Be careful not to scatter them too much; also to hold them in readiness to re-enforce Buell at Chattanooga, if necessary.

H. W. HALLECK,
Major-General.

-----

* Probably Sherman to Rawlins, p. 141.

Abstract from Monthly Return of the District of West Tennessee, Maj. Gen. U. S. Grant commanding, for July 31, 1862 (headquarters Corinth, Miss.).

Command.	Present for duty.		Aggregate present for duty.	Aggregate present.	Aggregate present and absent.	Pieces of artillery.		Aggregate present last monthly return.
	Officers.	Men.				Heavy.	Field.	
ARMY OF THE TENNESSEE.								
Department staff	11	....	11	11	11	......	......	11
Jackson, Tenn.—First Division, Major-General McClernand:								
Staff	14	....	14	14	14	......	......	
Infantry	373	6,399	6,772	8,366	12,965	......	......	13,298
Cavalry	26	505	531	696	944	......	......	972
Artillery	19	556	575	630	894	......	......	903
Total	432	7,460	7,892	9,706	14,817	......	......	15,173
Corinth, Miss.—Maj. Gen. E. O. C. Ord:								
Staff	5	....	5	5	5	......	......	5
Infantry	400	7,667	8,067	10,353	16,151	......	......	16,467
Cavalry	21	350	371	574	753	......	......	870
Artillery	24	762	786	918	1,140	......	40	1,149
Total	450	8,779	9,229	11,850	18,049	......	40	18,491
Memphis, Tenn.— Fourth Division, Brig. Gen. S. A. Hurlbut:								
Staff	7	....	7	7	7	......	......	8
Infantry	262	5,092	5,354	6,220	8,059	......	......	7,449
Cavalry	17	256	273	401	497	......	......	498
Artillery	18	328	346	398	454	......	18	459
Total Fourth Division	304	5,676	5,980	7,026	9,017	......	18	8,414
Fifth Division, Maj. Gen. W. T. Sherman:								
Staff	14	....	14	14	14	......	......	14
Infantry	307	5,339	5,646	6,872	8,973	......	......	8,996
Cavalry	42	771	813	1,050	1,290	......	......	842
Artillery	33	873	906	1,013	1,240	......	48	1,108
Total Fifth Division	396	6,983	7,379	8,949	11,517	......	48	10,960
Total Memphis	700	12,659	13,359	15,975	20,534	......	66	19,374
District of Mississippi.—Brig. Gen. I. F. Quinby:								
Staff	14	....	14	14	14	......	......	14
Infantry	144	3,253	3,397	4,128	4,685	......	......	4,719
Cavalry	44	1,137	1,181	1,371	1,598	......	......	1,593
Artillery	11	351	362	428	533	......	18	553
Total	213	4,741	4,954	5,941	6,830	......	18	6,879
District of Cairo.—Brig. Gen. W. K. Strong: Cairo, Ill.:								
Staff	10	....	10	10	10	......	......	10
Infantry	43	865	908	1,230	1,752	......	......	826
Total	53	865	918	1,240	1,762	......	......	836
Paducah, Ky.:								
Staff	7	....	7	7	7	......	......	12
Cavalry	4	115	119	151	160	......	......	180
Artillery	4	119	123	135	188	......	......	191
Total	15	234	249	293	355	......	......	383
Total District of Cairo	68	1,099	1,167	1,533	2,117	......	......	1,219
Total of detached commands	89	1,795	1,884	2,312	3,306	......	......	3,383
Total Army of the Tennessee	1,952	36,533	38,485	47,317	65,653	......	124	64,519

Abstract from Monthly Return of the District of West Tennessee, &c.—Continued.

Command.	Present for duty. Officers.	Present for duty. Men.	Aggregate present for duty.	Aggregate present.	Aggregate present and absent.	Pieces of artillery. Heavy.	Pieces of artillery. Field.	Aggregate present last monthly return.
ARMY OF THE MISSISSIPPI.								
Brig. Gen. W. S. Rosecrans.								
Staff	17		17	17	17			
Cherokee Station, Ala.—First Division, Brig. Gen. J. D. Morgan	221	4,766	4,987	5,878	7,817		14	
Camp Deer Creek, Miss.—Second Division, Brig. Gen. D. S. Stanley	174	3,816	3,990	5,107	6,503		8	
Camp near Corinth.—Third Division, Brig. Gen. C. S. Hamilton	235	5,050	5,285	7,076	8,765		16	
Camp near Jacinto.— Fourth Div., Brig. Gen. J. C. Davis	207	4,143	4,350	5,238	6,433		18	
Fifth Div., Brig. Gen. G. Granger	280	6,088	6,368	7,923	9,829		18	
In charge of siege guns.—Capt. G. A. Williams, First U. S. Infantry	8	219	227	303	364	9	2	
Total Army of the Mississippi	1,142	24,082	25,224	31,542	39,728	9	76	
Total District of West Tennessee	3,105	60,615	63,720	78,870	105,392	9	200	

Troops in the District of West Tennessee, Maj. Gen. U. S. Grant, U. S. Army, commanding, July 31, 1862.

ARMY OF THE TENNESSEE.

FIRST DIVISION.*

Maj. Gen. John A. McClernand.

Infantry.

8th Illinois, Col. Frank L. Rhoads.
11th Illinois, Col. T. E. G. Ransom.
17th Illinois, Lieut. Col. Francis M. Smith.
18th Illinois, Col. Michael K. Lawler.
20th Illinois, Col. C. Carroll Marsh.
29th Illinois, Lieut. Col. Charles M. Ferrell.
30th Illinois, Col. Elias S. Dennis.
31st Illinois, Col. Lyndorf Ozburn.
43d Illinois, Col. Adolph Engelmann.
45th Illinois, Col. John E. Smith.
48th Illinois, Maj. Manning Mayfield.
49th Illinois, Maj. William W. Bishop.
61st Illinois, Col. Jacob Fry.
23d Indiana, Col. William L. Sanderson.
12th Michigan, Col. Francis Quinn.
7th Missouri, Col. John D. Stevenson.
20th Ohio, Maj. Manning F. Force.
68th Ohio, Lieut. Col. Robert K. Scott.
78th Ohio, Col. Mortimer D. Leggett.

Cavalry.

2d Illinois, Company B, Capt. Thomas J. Larison.
4th Illinois (1st Battalion), Maj. M. R. M. Wallace.
11th Illinois, Company I, Capt. Isaac Elwood.
Independent Illinois, Company A, Capt. Berthold Marschner.
Independent Illinois, Company B, Capt. Milo Thielemann.
Stewart's (Illinois) battalion, Company A, Capt. Ezra King.
Stewart's (Illinois) battalion, Company B, Capt. Eagleton Carmichael.
Stewart's (Illinois) battalion, Company C, Capt. James J. Dollins.
Stewart's (Illinois) battalion, Company D, Capt. Morrison J. O'Harnett.
5th Ohio, Co. F, Capt. Phineas R. Miner.
5th Ohio, Co. G, Capt. John G. Curtis.

Artillery.

1st Illinois, Battery D, Capt. Henry A. Rogers.
2d Illinois, Battery B, Capt. Relly Madison.
2d Illinois, Battery E, Capt. George C. Gumbart.
9th Indiana Battery, Lieut. Daniel A. Porter.
14th Indiana Battery, Capt. Meredith H. Kidd.
14th Ohio Battery, Lieut. Homer H. Stull.

* Hdqrs. at Jackson, Tenn. Brigade organizations not given in the original return.

CORINTH, MISS.

Maj. Gen. E. O. C. ORD.

SECOND DIVISION.*

Brig. Gen. RICHARD J. OGLESBY.

7th Illinois, Col. Andrew J. Babcock.
9th Illinois, Col. August Mersy.
12th Illinois, Col. Augustus L. Chetlain.
50th Illinois, Col. Moses M. Bane.
52d Illinois, Maj. Edwin A. Bowen.
57th Illinois, Maj. Eric Forsse.
58th Illinois.
2d Iowa, Col. James Baker.
7th Iowa, Col. Elliott W. Rice.
8th Iowa.

12th Iowa, Lieut. Col. John P. Coulter.
14th Iowa.
14th Missouri,† Col. Patrick E. Burke.
22d Ohio, Lieut. Col. Benjamin T. Wright.
81st Ohio, Col. Thomas Morton.
5th Ohio Cavalry (3d Battalion), Maj. Charles S. Hayes.
1st Missouri Light Artillery (2d Battalion), Capt. George H. Stone

SIXTH DIVISION.*

Brig. Gen. JOHN MCARTHUR.

11th Iowa, Col. Abraham M. Hare.
13th Iowa, Col. Marcellus M. Crocker.
15th Iowa, Col. Hugh T. Reid.
16th Iowa, Col. Alexander Chambers.
15th Michigan, Lieut. Col. John McDermott.
18th Missouri, Capt. Jacob R. Ault.
21st Missouri, Col. David Moore.
25th Missouri, Col. Chester Harding, jr.
16th Wisconsin, Capt. George C. Williams.
17th Wisconsin, Col. John L. Doran.

18th Wisconsin, Capt. Gabriel Bouck.
11th Illinois Cavalry, Col. Robert G. Ingersoll.
2d Illinois Artillery, Battery F, Capt. John W. Powell.
1st Minnesota Battery, Lieut. William Pfaender.
3d Ohio Battery, Capt. William S. Williams.
5th Ohio Battery, Lieut. Bellamy S. Matson.
10th Ohio Battery, Lieut. F. W. Bardwell.

MEMPHIS, TENN.

Maj. Gen. WILLIAM T. SHERMAN.

FOURTH DIVISION.

Brig. Gen. STEPHEN A. HURLBUT.

14th Illinois, Col. Cyrus Hall.
15th Illinois, Col. Thomas J. Turner.
28th Illinois, Col. Amory K. Johnson.
32d Illinois, Col. John Logan.
41st Illinois, Col. Isaac C. Pugh.
46th Illinois, Col. John A. Davis.
53d Illinois, Col. William H. W. Cushman.
25th Indiana, Col. William H. Morgan.
52d Indiana, Col. James M. Smith.
53d Indiana, Col. Walter Q. Gresham.

3d Iowa, Col. Nelson G. Williams.
5th Ohio Cavalry (battalion), Col. W. H. H. Taylor.
2d Illinois Artillery, Battery L, Capt. William H. Bolton.
2d Missouri Battery, Capt. Charles Mann.
7th Ohio Battery, Capt. Silas A. Burnap.
15th Ohio Battery, Capt. Edward Spear, jr.

---

* Brigade organization not indicated in original return.
† Afterward known as the Sixty-sixth Illinois.

FIFTH DIVISION.

Maj. Gen. WILLIAM T. SHERMAN.

40th Illinois, Lieut. Col. James W. Boothe.
55th Illinois, Col. David Stuart.
6th Iowa, Lieut. Col. John M. Corse.
6th Missouri, Lieut. Col. James H. Blood.
8th Missouri, Lieut. Col. Giles A. Smith.
46th Ohio, Col. Thomas Worthington.
48th Ohio, Col. Peter J. Sullivan.
53d Ohio, Col. Wells S. Jones.
54th Ohio, Col. T. Kilby Smith.
57th Ohio, Col. William Mungen.
70th Ohio, Col. Joseph R. Cockerill.
72d Ohio, Col. Ralph P. Buckland.
77th Ohio, Col. Jesse Hildebrand.
4th Illinois Cavalry (eight companies),
     Maj. William L. Gibson.
6th Illinois Cavalry (five companies),
     Col. Benjamin H. Grierson.
11th Illinois Cavalry (four companies),
     Maj. Lucien H. Kerr.
1st Illinois Artillery, Battery A, Capt.
     Peter P. Wood.

1st Illinois Artillery, Battery B, Capt.
     Samuel E. Barrett.
1st Illinois Artillery, Battery E, Capt.
     Allen C. Waterhouse.
1st Illinois Artillery, Battery F, Capt.
     John T. Cheney.
1st Illinois Artillery, Battery H, Capt.
     Axel Silfversparre.
1st Illinois Artillery, Battery I, Capt.
     Edward Bouton.
2d Illinois Artillery, Battery K, Capt.
     Benjamin F. Rodgers.
Independent Illinois Battery, Capt. William Cogswell.
6th Indiana Battery, Capt. Michael Mueller.
1st Michigan Artillery, Battery H, Lieut. Theo. W. Lockwood.
8th Ohio Battery, Capt. Charles H. Schmidt.

DISTRICT OF MISSISSIPPI.*

Brig. Gen. ISAAC F. QUINBY.

Infantry.

54th Illinois, Col. Thomas W. Harris.
62d Illinois, Col. James M. True.
34th Indiana, Company F, Capt. Robert
     B. Jones.
1st Kansas, Col. George W. Deitzler.
5th Missouri, Company F, Lieut. John
     E. Hensler.
12th Wisconsin, Col. George E. Bryant.
13th Wisconsin, Col. Maurice Maloney.
15th Wisconsin, Companies G and I, Capt.
     John A. Gordon.
15th and 16th U. S. Infantry (detachments), Maj. John R. Edie.

Cavalry.

2d Illinois Cavalry, Lieut. Col. Harvey
     Hogg.
6th Illinois Cavalry, Maj. William L.
     Caldwell.
Company E, Illinois Cavalry, Capt.
     William D. Hutchens.

Artillery.

2d Illinois Artillery, Battery G, Capt.
     Frederick Sparrestrom.
2d Illinois Artillery, Battery H, Capt.
     Andrew Stenbeck.
1st Michigan, Battery H (one section),
     Capt. Samuel De Golyer.
7th Wisconsin Battery, Capt. Richard R.
     Griffith.

DISTRICT OF CAIRO.

Brig. Gen. WILLIAM K. STRONG.

63d Illinois, Col. Francis Moro.
71st Illinois, Col. Othniel Gilbert.
6th Illinois Cavalry, Companies B and M.

1st Illinois Artillery, Battery K, Capt.
     Jason B. Smith.
2d Illinois Artillery, Battery C, Capt.
     James P. Flood.

DETACHED COMMANDS.

52d Indiana (one company).
71st Ohio, Col. Rodney Mason.
14th Wisconsin, Lieut. Col. Lyman M.
     Ward.
12th Illinois Cavalry, Company B, Capt.
     Franklin T. Gilbert.
5th Iowa Cavalry, Lt. Col. M. T. Patrick.

4th Ohio Independent Cavalry Company,
     Capt. John S. Foster.
Ford's cavalry (one company), Capt. William Ford.
Engineer Regiment of the West, Col.
     Josiah W. Bissell.

---

* Headquarters at Columbus, Ky.

ARMY OF THE MISSISSIPPI.

Brig. Gen. WILLIAM S. ROSECRANS.

FIRST DIVISION.*

Brig. Gen. JAMES D. MORGAN.

10th Illinois, Col. John Tillson.
16th Illinois, Capt. Charles Petri.
22d Illinois, Maj. Francis Swanwick.
27th Illinois, Lieut. Col. Jonathan R. Miles.
42d Illinois, Lieut. Col. Charles Northrop.
51st Illinois, Col. Luther P. Bradley.
60th Illinois, Col. Silas C. Toler.
10th Michigan, Col. Charles M. Lum.
14th Michigan, Col. Robert P. Sinclair.

Yates Sharpshooters, Maj. Frederick W. Matteson.
1st Illinois Artillery, Battery C, Capt. Charles Houghtaling.
1st Missouri Artillery, Battery G, Capt. Henry Hescock.
1st Missouri Artillery, Battery M, Lieut. Junius W. MacMurray.
10th Wisconsin Battery, Capt. Yates V. Beebe.

SECOND DIVISION.†

Brig. Gen. DAVID S. STANLEY.

First Brigade.

Col. J. L. KIRBY SMITH.

27th Ohio, Maj. Zeph. S. Spaulding.
39th Ohio, Col. Alfred W. Gilbert.
43d Ohio, Lieut. Col. Wager Swayne.
63d Ohio, Col. John W. Sprague.
3d Michigan Battery, Lieut. Carl A. Lamberg.
2d U. S. Artillery, Battery F, Capt. Thomas D. Maurice.

Second Brigade.

Col. ROBERT C. MURPHY.

26th Illinois, Col. John M. Loomis.
5th Minnesota, Col. Rudolph Von Borgersode.
11th Missouri, Col. Joseph A. Mower.
8th Wisconsin, Lieut. Col. George W. Robbins.

THIRD DIVISION.‡

Brig. Gen. CHARLES S. HAMILTON.

First Brigade.

Brig. Gen. N. B. BUFORD.

48th Indiana, Col. Norman Eddy.
59th Indiana, Col. Jesse I. Alexander.
5th Iowa, Lieut. Col. Charles L. Matthies.
4th Minnesota, Col. John B. Sanborn.
26th Missouri, Col. George B. Boomer.
11th Ohio Battery, Capt. Frank C. Sands.

Second Brigade.

Brig. Gen. J. C. SULLIVAN.

56th Illinois, Col. William R. Brown.
10th Iowa, Col. Nicholas Perczel.
17th Iowa, Col. John W. Rankin.
10th Missouri, Col. Samuel A. Holmes.
80th Ohio, Col. Ephraim R. Eckley.
Capt. Henry Hopkins' (Kansas) Battery.
1st Missouri Artillery, Battery I, Capt. William A. Pile.

FOURTH DIVISION.§

Brig. Gen. JEFF. C. DAVIS.

21st Illinois, Col. John W. S. Alexander.
25th Illinois, Maj. Richard H. Nodine.
35th Illinois, Lieut. Col. William P. Chandler.
38th Illinois, Lieut. Col. Mortimer O. Kean.
59th Illinois, Col. P. Sidney Post.
22d Indiana, Col. Michael Gooding.

8th Kansas, Lieut. Col. John A. Martin.
15th Wisconsin, Col. Hans C. Heg.
2d Minnesota Battery, Capt. William A. Hotchkiss.
5th Wisconsin Battery, Capt. Oscar F. Pinney.
8th Wisconsin Battery, Capt. Stephen J. Carpenter.

---

*At Cherokee Station, Ala.   Brigades not indicated on original return.
† Clear Creek, Miss.
‡ Near Corinth, Miss.
§ Near Jacinto, Miss.

FIFTH DIVISION.

Brig. Gen. GORDON GRANGER.

36th Illinois, Col N. Greusel.

44th Illinois, Col. Charles Knobelsdorff.

47th Illinois, Col. John Bryner.

2d Missouri, Col. Frederick Schaefer.

2d Missouri, U. S. R. C., Lieut. Col. Herman Zakrzewski.

15th Missouri, Col. Francis J. Joliat.

7th Illinois Cavalry, Maj. Horatio C. Nelson.

2d Iowa Cavalry, Lieut. Col. Edward Hatch.

7th Kansas Cavalry, Col. Albert L. Lee.

2d Michigan Cavalry, Col. Philip H. Sheridan.

3d Michigan Cavalry, Col. John K. Mizner.

1st Missouri Cavalry, Company F, Capt. James Clifford.

5th Missouri Cavalry, Company C, Capt. Albert Borcherdt.

2d Illinois Artillery, Battery I, Capt. Charles M. Barnett.

2d Iowa Battery, Capt. Nelson T. Spoor.

6th Wisconsin Battery, Capt. Henry Dillon.

In charge of siege guns.

First U. S. Infantry, Capt. George A. Williams.

CORINTH, MISS, *August* 1, 1862.

Maj. Gen. H. W. HALLECK:

It is now almost an absolute certainty that there is but a small force in front of us, most having gone eastward. Bolivar seems to be the most important point to guard and retain troops here to re-enforce Buell if necessary. I would suggest driving the rebels toward Columbus as far as possible preparatory to leaving Corinth with a small garrison.

U. S. GRANT,
Major-General.

ROSECRANS' HEADQUARTERS, *August* 1, 1862.

Major-General GRANT:

Dispatch from Buell; believes not more than two regiments of infantry, brigade of cavalry, and battery at Moulton. Thinks garrison of Decatur not safe; would be made so by a brigade at Courtland. Gives no reasons for holding that road. Morgan has no reliable information, but reports continue to indicate considerable force at Moulton; says commandant at Courtland is informed by cavalry of a force 7 miles from there; strength and kind of troops not stated. Lightning prevents using wires to get answer about this. Granger telegraphed last night from Rienzi all troops have left Tupelo except Price, with 20,000 men; gone east by rail; baggage and artillery by Tuscaloosa toward Rome. Means heavy attack on Buell or Richmond.

W. S. ROSECRANS,
Brigadier-General.

STEAM-RAM SWITZERLAND,
Off Helena, Ark., August 1, 1862.

JAMES BROOKS, *Special Quartermaster, &c.:*

DEAR SIR: I arrived at this place last night with my fleet, in company with the whole gunboat squadron.

We were compelled to move north, owing to the crippled condition of our fleet from so large a proportion of our crews being disabled by sickness. I am happy to state that the movements of the boats have exerted a salutary effect upon the health of the men.

Another reason that influenced me in creating a necessity to do something was the want of subsistence supplies. My fleet was reduced very low indeed for provisions, owing to the supplies sent for not having arrived. I am glad to say that I found them waiting us here. I find myself often limited in the extent and usefulness of my operations from the want of one stronger and better protected boat than any I now have in my fleet. I wish that you would see the honorable Secretary of War and set this matter before him, and if possible obtain his authority to build one strong, heavy iron-plated gunboat and ram for my command, so that I could at all times act efficiently and independently when the service required it, without being under the necessity of applying for co-operation, which when granted comes so slow that it is too late to be effective. A boat for my service must be fast as well as strong, and should not draw more than 7 feet of water—less, if possible. In my opinion the usefulness of such a boat, if properly applied to the service for which it is intended, would well justify the expense to the Government.

I would also suggest that the stern-wheel boats of my fleet, upon which the Government has not been put to much expense, could be employed to very great advantage as tow-boats and for transportation purposes or to carry the mails; being partially protected, they can pass points where boats entirely unprotected could not be expected to venture.

Your very obedient servant,

ALFRED W. ELLET,
Lieutenant-Colonel, Commanding Ram Fleet.

WAR DEPARTMENT,
Washington, August 1, 1862.

Colonel ELLET,
Ram Fleet, Vicksburg, Miss.:

You will employ such negroes as you require on your boats and send the others who are under your protection to Memphis, to be employed by General Sherman. Your prisoners can be sent to Memphis for trial, and a court-martial can be ordered there for their trial as soon as the witnesses can be spared.

H. W. HALLECK,
Major-General, Commanding.

SPECIAL ORDERS, }   HEADQUARTERS,
    No. 156.   }   *Memphis, Tenn., August 1, 1862.*

General Morgan L. Smith will send an expedition for three days, composed of one regiment of infantry, a section of artillery, and the available men of the Fourth Illinois Cavalry, to Raleigh, on the Wolf River. The infantry will scout the country in the neighborhood of Raleigh, destroying or capturing all enemies in arms, and seizing all arms, ammunition, or contraband property found in unsafe hands. The cavalry will scout well forward and to the west, marching over the Randolph road. The cavalry should not operate on the main road, but by cross-roads and by-paths.

II. General Hurlbut will in like manner send ten regiments of infantry, one section of artillery, and the available force of the Fifth

Ohio Cavalry down the Hernando road to Nonconah, the infantry to scout up and down the creek, the cavalry to scout well beyond the Nonconah, sweeping around by the west to the Horn Lake road; the expedition to remain out three days.

The commanding officer of the Sixth Illinois Cavalry will report to General Smith, to do picket duty in front of his brigade during the absence of the Fourth Illinois, and the Eleventh Illinois to General Hurlbut, to picket in front of his division till the return of the Fifth Ohio.

By order of Maj. Gen. W. T. Sherman:

J. H. HAMMOND,
Assistant Adjutant-General.

WAR DEPARTMENT,
Washington City, August 2, 1862.

Maj. Gen. U. S. GRANT,
    Commanding, &c., Corinth :

Your letter of July 28 is just received.* It is very desirable that you should clean out West Tennessee and North Mississippi of all organized enemies. If necessary, take up all active sympathizers, and either hold them as prisoners or put them beyond our lines. Handle that class without gloves, and take their property for public use. As soon as the corn gets fit for forage get all the supplies you can from the rebels in Mississippi. It is time that they should begin to feel the presence of war on our side. Bolivar and the Hatchie River should be well defended, in order to secure our railroad communications.

See that all possible facilities are afforded for getting out cotton. It is deemed important to get as much as we can into market. I see it stated in the newspapers that General Sherman has forbidden the payment of gold for cotton, while General Butler advises the payment of gold, in order to induce planters to bring it to market. I have called the attention of the Secretary of War to this difference, and he directs me to say that the payment of gold should not be prohibited. Instruct General Sherman accordingly.

H. W. HALLECK,
Major-General.

CORINTH, MISS., *August 2, 1862.*

Major-General HALLECK:

I will try and hold the road to Decatur. Think it can be done without much difficulty. Anticipate no serious trouble on the Hatchie; nothing more than an occasional raid from mounted men.

U. S. GRANT,
Major-General.

JACKSON, *August 2, 1862.*

General U. S. GRANT:

I have swept both sides of the Hatchie from Bolivar to Brownsville, on the road to Somerville. The enemy fled precipitately and escaped capture. The force I have on the Hatchie, together with those you are sending and the three regiments here, exclusive of the Eleventh, secures things in these quarters for the present. I will send the Eleventh the

---

* Not found.

first opportunity. I have some 300 negroes at work on the fortifications at Bolivar. I will probably return them on Monday. The 2,400 ammunition has not come.

JOHN A. McCLERNAND,
Major-General.

HEADQUARTERS ARMY OF THE MISSISSIPPI,
August 2, 1862.

Brigadier-General GRANGER, *Rienzi :*

General Mitchell informs me they have had a spy in the rebel cavalry camp near Bay Springs Factory.

The "rebs" have a battalion there; another 3 miles in rear, and reported some infantry support 3 miles in rear of them. Hundred and eighty bales of cotton there, and factory running for rebel use.

Arrange the details of an expedition of infantry from Jacinto and cavalry from your front that will cut off this force unless strongly supported, capture the cotton, and destroy or disable the mills. Give me all the news.

W. S. ROSECRANS,
Brigadier-General, U. S. Army.

HEADQUARTERS ARMY OF THE MISSISSIPPI,
August 2, 1862.

Major-General GRANT, *Corinth :*

No report from the front. General Morgan reports the Town Creek Bridge safe, and the command returned there.

General Davis reports a brisk trade in salt and other contraband goods going on from Pittsburg south through the region east of him. He has seized twelve barrels *in transitu.* It seems to me the provost-marshal and commanding officers at Pittsburg and Hamburg Landings should be held responsible for it. Patrols will be necessary to prevent unprincipled sutlers' clerks and discharged soldiers from selling whatever they please of contraband.

W. S. ROSECRANS,
Brigadier-General, U. S. Army.

CORINTH, *August 3, 1862.*

Maj. Gen. H. W. HALLECK:

Cadwalader has reported for duty here. Order directs him to report to you. Where shall he be assigned? The efficiency of this army is weakened by making commands for so many officers of high rank.

U. S. GRANT,
Major-General.

ROSECRANS' HEADQUARTERS, *August 3, 1862.*
(Received Corinth, August 3, 1862.)

Major-General GRANT:

I have ordered Davis to send Mitchell's brigade to Iuka to relieve Morgan's command, thence to Bear Creek Bridge. Morgan's troops go to Tuscumbia; Davis to be ready to follow him with the remainder so soon as the news from Granger shall show what dispositions are advisable at the front. I have doubts if any operations in force will require support given to Morgan east, from the nature of the country south of Morgan's line, which is generally hilly and poor. It is probable that column was a reconnoitering covering and designed to cut off the Union men from those hilly regions who were flocking to join us.

W. S. ROSECRANS,
Brigadier-General, U. S. Army.

HEADQUARTERS ARMY OF THE MISSISSIPPI,
August 3, 1862.

General MORGAN, *Tuscumbia:*

Mitchell's brigade of Davis' division has been ordered to relieve your troops from Iuka to Bear Creek Bridge, inclusive. On being relieved your troops will join you at Tuscumbia.

By order:

W. L. ELLIOTT,
Brigadier-General.

HEADQUARTERS ARMY OF THE MISSISSIPPI,
August 3, 1862.

Brigadier-General DAVIS, *Jacinto:*

The following from Major Smith, at Iuka,* indicates that it would be well for our troops to start there by crack of day, leaving the train to follow with a suitable guard. Let two days' rations be cooked; ammunition in cartridge-boxes; wagons with enough to make 100 rounds. Instruct the general to inspect everything; move with speed and circumspection, keeping his advance guard well out and good flankers on his left; not to let the head of his column enter a defile until the advance guard has gone clean through and formed on the opposite side to cover his passage against a surprise.

W. S. ROSECRANS,
Brigadier-General, U. S. Army, Commanding.

BOLIVAR, *August 3, 1862.*

General MCCLERNAND:

Letters dated at Tupelo, July 24, and captured by Colonel Lawler, represent the enemy leaving Tupelo and moving toward Chattanooga via Jacksonville, Ala.

L. F. ROSS,
Brigadier-General.

HDQRS. SECOND DIVISION, DISTRICT OF JACKSON,
Bolivar, Tenn., August 4, 1862.

Maj. Gen. JOHN A. MCCLERNAND, *Jackson:*

From information obtained from our scouts we are lead to believe there are no troops at present at either La Grange or Grand Junction.

---

* Not found.

A portion of Bragg's infantry encamped on Wolf River, and there is a rumor that they intend to move to La Grange in a day or two. Thirty of Jackson's cavalry left La Grange on the 2d for the neighborhood of Estanaula. I shall send a force of about 40 after them to-day.

I am, sir, very respectfully,

L. F. ROSS,
Brigadier-General, Commanding.

SPECIAL ORDERS, }   HDQRS. DISTRICT OF WEST TENNESSEE,
No. 154.   }   *Corinth, Miss., August 5, 1862.*

*   *   *   *   *   *   *

Maj. Gen. E. O. C. Ord is hereby relieved temporarily from the command of the Second Division, Army of the Tennessee, and of the town of Corinth.

Maj. Gen. George Cadwalader is assigned to the command of the forces constituting the garrison of Corinth, and will relieve Maj. Gen. E. O. C. Ord.

By command of Maj. Gen. U. S. Grant:

JNO. A. RAWLINS,
Assistant Adjutant-General.

HEADQUARTERS SECOND BRIGADE,
Brownsville, Tenn., August 6, 1862.

Brig. Gen. JOHN A. LOGAN,
Commanding First Division:

GENERAL: I have to report the receipt of Special Orders, No. 214, and also of an order in relation to property of private citizens.

Lieutenant-Colonel Hogg has assumed command of all the cavalry force in this vicinity, and I would respectfully suggest that he be permitted to make his headquarters at a point on the road between here and Brownsville Crossing. This is a central point to the crossings on Hatchie River, and from there communications with all points above and below can be had much more rapidly than at any other point.

Night before last a detachment of the Second Cavalry scouted as far down the river as Green's Ferry; another detachment going north from here met the first detachment at Durhamsville, whence both returned to this point. They report that no organized force can be found in that territory. We shall at once endeavor to communicate down the river with the cavalry scouts from Fort Pillow, and report.

Yours, with respect,

M. K. LAWLER,
Colonel, Commanding Second Brigade.

COLUMBUS, *August 6, 1862.*
Major-General GRANT:

Major-General Sherman sends you, through me, a letter written by a rebel officer on the 24th ultimo, from which it seems that the rebels then were on the point of moving on Nashville via Chattanooga. He wished me to telegraph this much.

I. F. QUINBY,
Brigadier-General.

ROSECRANS' HEADQUARTERS,
Near Corinth, Miss., August 6, 1862—9 a. m.

Maj. Gen. H. W. HALLECK:

Thanks. Please give our cavalry repeating rifles. It will double its force, for experience has shown that repeaters would double the power of an infantry regiment. A simple calculation will show what the peculiar economy of this would be to our army. Five hundred thousand dollars per day is a very fair interest on the difference between the price of repeating and common fire-arms. The calculation is simple, but the data are undoubted by practical men. Am told that some repeating rifles, bought for Berdan's Sharpshooters, are left at the Washington Arsenal.

W. S. ROSECRANS,
Brigadier-General.

HEADQUARTERS ARMY OF THE MISSISSIPPI,
August 6, 1862.

Col. J. K. MIZNER, *Tuscumbia :*

Your orders to cover the railroad line indicated points of station as recommended by General Thomas, but you were informed that it was not designed to restrict you to the occupancy of those stations or to the forces indicated; on the contrary, the general commanding explained to you that he was desirous that you should avoid the distribution of your troops into small detachments; that you should if possible endeavor to cover the road by massing them and striking the enemy in force. You will report to what extent you have carried out these instructions and what are the obstacles. General Morgan reports 400 rebel cavalry at Russellville and 200 at Frankfort. Why can they not be cut off?

By order:

W. L. ELLIOTT,
Brigadier-General and Chief of Staff.

HEADQUARTERS ARMY OF THE MISSISSIPPI,
August 6, 1862.

General MORGAN, *Tuscumbia :*

You will seize all cotton in the name of United States Government; give receipts of division quartermasters to the owners or claimants, specifying the dates, of quantity taken; invoice the same by the most expeditious means; write in duplicate to United States quartermaster, Cairo, Ill., sending a triplicate to these headquarters. Whenever bridges or other damage to the railroad requires repair, the negroes of the neighborhood or others with secession proclivities will be taken for the purpose and returned when no longer required; slaves of persons hostile to the Government to be taken in preference. Notify the inhabitants within reach of your lines that any words or actions hostile to the Government will oblige you to treat the parties as enemies, who can receive only the rights of belligerents, whose property belongs to the United States. The women and children will be ordered beyond our lines, their property seized for the benefit of the United States, and their houses burned.

Supply your command with long forage by cutting corn from the fields and partially drying it in the sun, cutting it up and feeding with salt for your stock, the quartermasters to take up and account for it; use that of rebels in preference.

By order:

W. L. ELLIOTT,
Brigadier-General.

BOLIVAR, [*August*] 6, 1862.

General McCLERNAND:

Do you wish me to occupy Toone's Station and guard the railroad as before your recent order?

L. F. ROSS,
Brigadier-General.

GENERAL ORDERS, }   HDQRS. DISTRICT OF WEST TENNESSEE,
No. 69.   }   *Corinth, Miss., August* 6, 1862.

I. Hereafter no coin will be permitted to pass south of Cairo or Columbus except such as is carried by Government agents and for Government use. The same restriction will be observed at Fort Henry and Fort Donelson.

II. Neither coin, Treasury notes, or goods will be permitted to pass south of Memphis except for the use of the army. The payment of cash for any article of use in aid of the rebellion for Southern products will be discouraged in every way possible.

III. All cotton and other articles coming from points below Memphis will be seized and sold for the benefit of whom it may concern, the proceeds being used by the quartermaster until directed by proper authority to turn them over to other parties, unless the same has been passed by special permit from the Treasury Department.

By order of Major-General Grant:

JNO. A. RAWLINS,
Assistant Adjutant-General.

CORINTH, *August* 7, 1862.

Brig. Gen. LORENZO THOMAS,
          Washington, D. C.:

News from the front continues to indicate movement of the rebels toward Chattanooga. My opinion is that the best troops are being sent to Richmond, and conscripts, with a little leaven from the more disciplined, are left to hold the Western army in check.

U. S. GRANT,
Major-General.

HEADQUARTERS DISTRICT OF JACKSON,
Jackson, Tenn., August 7, 1862.

General ROSS, *Bolivar:*

General Logan is mistaken in telegraphing you that the order for the relief of Lawler's brigade by sending the Twentieth and Twenty-ninth Illinois is countermanded. It was suspended at his suggestion that Lawler's men were unable to travel. I am just informed that he has asked you to relieve his men at Toone's Station. My order was, and is, that he should guard the road from here to Toone's and use the Forty-fifth for that purpose; and until he can accordingly do so his guard at Toone's will remain. If his guard is not strong enough, re-enforce it for the present, according to my telegram of last evening.

JOHN A. McCLERNAND,
Major-General, Commanding.

HEADQUARTERS FIFTH DIVISION,
Memphis, August 7, 1862.

Captain FITCH,
      Assistant Quartermaster, Memphis, Tenn.:

SIR: The duties devolving on the quartermaster of this post, in addition to his legitimate functions, are very important and onerous, and I am fully aware that the task is more than should devolve on one man. I will endeavor to get you help in the person of some commissioned officer, and, if possible, one under bond, as he must handle large amounts of money in trust; but for the present we must execute the duties falling to our share as well as possible. On the subject of vacant houses General Grant's orders are:

Take possession of all vacant stores and houses in the city, and have them rented at reasonable rates; rent to be paid monthly in advance. These buildings, with their tenants, can be turned over to proprietors on proof of loyalty; also take charge of such as have been leased out by disloyal owners.

I understand that General Grant takes the rents and profits of this class of real property under the rules and laws of war and not under the confiscation act of Congress; therefore the question of title is not involved—simply the possession, and the rents and profits of houses belonging to our enemies which are not vacant we hold in trust for them or the Government, according to the future decisions of the proper tribunals.

Mr. McDonald, your chief agent in renting and managing this business, called on me last evening and left with me written questions, which it would take a volume to answer and a Webster to elucidate; but as we can only attempt plain, substantial justice I will answer these questions as well as I can, briefly and to the point:

First. When ground is owned by parties who have gone South and have leased the ground to parties now in the city, who own the improvements on the ground?

Answer. The United States takes the rents due the owner of the land; does not disturb the owner of the improvements.

Second. When parties owning houses have gone South, and the tenant has given his notes for the rent in advance?

Answer. Notes are mere evidence of the debt due landlord. The tenant pays the rent to the quartermaster, who gives a bond of indemnity against the notes representing the debt for the particular rent.

Third. When the tenant has expended several months' rent in repairs on the house?

Answer. Of course allow all such credits on reasonable proof and showing.

Fourth. When the owner has gone South and parties here hold liens on the property and are collecting the rents to satisfy their liens?

Answer. The rent of a house can only be mortgaged to a person in possession. If a loyal tenant be in possession and claim the rent from himself as due to himself on some other debt allow it; but if not in actual possession of the property rents are not good liens for a debt, but must be paid to the quartermaster.

Fifth. Of parties claiming foreign protection?

Answer. Many claim foreign protection who are not entitled to it. If they are foreign subjects residing for business in this country they are entitled to consideration and protection so long as they obey the laws of the country. If they occupy houses belonging to absent rebels they must pay rent to the quartermaster. If they own property they must occupy it by themselves, tenants, or servants.

Eighth. When houses are occupied and the owner has gone South, leaving an agent to collect rent for his benefit?

Answer. Rent must be paid to the quartermaster. No agent can collect and remit money South without subjecting himself to arrest and trial for aiding and abetting the public enemy.

Ninth. When houses are owned by loyal citizens, but are unoccupied?

Answer. Such should not be disturbed, but it would be well to advise them to have some servant at the house to occupy it.

Tenth. When parties who occupy the house are creditors of the owner who has gone South?

Answer. You only look to collection of rents. Any person who transmits money South is liable to arrest and trial for aiding and abetting the enemy; but I do not think it our business to collect debts other than rents.

Eleventh. When the parties who own the property have left the city under General Hovey's Orders, No. 1, but are in the immediate neighborhood, on their plantations?

Answer. It makes no difference where they are so they are absent.

Twelfth. When movable property is found in stores that are closed?

Answer. The goods are security for the rent. If the owner of the goods prefers to remove the goods to paying rent he can do so.

Thirteenth. When the owner lives in town and refuses to take the oath of allegiance?

Answer. If the house be occupied it does not fall under the order; if the house be vacant it does. The owner can recover his property by taking the oath.

All persons in Memphis residing within our military lines are presumed to be loyal, good citizens, and may at any moment be called to serve on juries, *posses comitatus*, or other civil service required by the Constitution and laws of our country. Should they be called upon to do such duty, which would require them to acknowledge their allegiance and subordination to the Constitution of the United States, it would then be too late to refuse. So long as they remain quiet and conform to these laws they are entitled to protection in their property and lives.

We have nothing to do with confiscation. We only deal with possession, and therefore the necessity of a strict accountability, because the United States assumes the place of trustee, and must account to the rightful owner for his property, rents, and profits. In due season courts will be established to execute the laws, the confiscation act included, when we will be relieved of this duty and trust. Until that time every opportunity should be given to the wavering and disloyal to return to their allegiance, to the Constitution of their birth or adoption.

I am, &c.,

W. T. SHERMAN,
Major-General, Commanding.

GENERAL ORDERS, }   HEADQUARTERS FIFTH DIVISION,
No. 66.   }   *Memphis, Tenn., August 7, 1862.*

I. The general commanding announces with shame and mortification that he has discovered a case of bribery in one of the public offices in Memphis, viz, the payment of $100 to a clerk in the office of the provost-marshal-general for a pass to Helena.

II. All officers, soldiers, and employés in the service of the United States are salaried persons and cannot charge a fee for any official act whatever. It is not only a crime but a disgrace to the whole country. In like manner it is a crime for a citizen to offer a bribe; and if any citizen has ever paid or is ever asked to pay a fee, bribe, or has afforded an opportunity to make profit, to corrupt or influence any person in the service of the United States, he is hereby notified that he must give notice thereof to the commanding general forthwith, that justice may be done and the honor of the nation protected against even the suspicion of corruption.

III. To guard against corruption in the future it is ordered that no house taken possession of by the quartermaster under general orders from General Grant, "To take possession of and let to loyal tenants the vacant houses in Memphis," shall be occupied by any officer or employé of the United States Government except by regular assignment under the army regulations by the quartermaster, approved by the commanding general. No rents will be paid except to the quartermaster in person or to one of his clerks on the written receipt of the quartermaster, signed by himself and not by proxy.

IV. Anonymous communications will not be entertained, but any citizen or person having cause for grievance will reduce it to writing, stating names and facts, and signed with the proper name, when redress will be given if necessary. Such communications will be addressed to the adjutant-general of the division, Maj. J. H. Hammond.

By order of Maj. Gen. W. T. Sherman:

J. H. HAMMOND,
Assistant Adjutant-General.

GENERAL ORDERS, }   HDQRS. FIFTH DIV., ARMY OF THE TENN.,
No. 67.   }   *Memphis, August 8, 1862.*

Inasmuch as by law of Congress recently enacted the President of the United States is authorized to receive and employ the labor of slaves or fugitives from slavery, and such fugitives on coming to our camps seeking protection, the following rules will be observed at and near Memphis until the President prescribes other rules, when these will necessarily be superseded and made to conform to the pleasure of the President:

I. All able-bodied negroes who apply for work at Fort Pickering will be received and put to work by the engineer in charge, Captain Hoepner; the names of owners and slaves registered, with date of commencement of work, and a general description by which the negroes can be known. Such negroes will be entitled to rations, to be drawn on provision returns similar to those used for soldiers, and will be supplied with necessary clothing and tobacco at the rate of one pound per month. An account will be opened with each negro, and his wages will be charged with the value of the clothing and tobacco; but no wages will be paid until the courts determine whether the negro be slave or free. The negroes employed on the fort are working as laborers, and will be allowed to return to their masters or mistresses at the close of any week, but masters or mistresses cannot be allowed to enter the fort in search of their slaves, because it is improper that any one not belonging to the garrison should enter Fort Pickering, or even follow its lines and ditches on the outside. A list of negroes so employed will be kept at headquarters, which may be seen by parties interested.

II. The post quartermaster, Captain Fitch, will in like manner employ a force of about 100 negroes out of those who apply to him for work, or he may on occasions take by force when he thinks it absolutely necessary to have an increased force work on the levee, loading and unloading steamboats, coal-boats, and such like labor, a list of whom, similar to that referred in Paragraph I will be kept by the quartermaster and a copy sent to headquarters for reference. These will in like manner be entitled to rations, necessary clothing, and tobacco, but the pay must be reserved until the proper judicial tribunals determine to whom such labor and wages belong.

III. Division quartermasters may employ fugitives to drive teams and attend to horses, mules, and cattle, keeping accurate accounts under the rules of their department applicable to "Persons and articles employed and hired," and subject to the condition of Paragraph I of this order, this list of persons so employed to be sent to headquarters for reference; the number of negroes so hired not to exceed one per team and one to every six span of animals herded or stabled.

IV. The commanders of regiments may cause to be employed as cooks and company teamsters not to exceed 5 per company and 10 per regiment for extra wagons, and 5 for staff wagons; in all, 65 per regiment; which negroes shall be borne on the muster-rolls and supplied with provisions and clothing as soldiers, but in no case will they bear arms or wear the uniform. The quartermaster of the division will supply regimental quartermasters with clothing suitable for such negroes, an account of which will be kept separate and distinct from that of the soldiers. These negroes must be kept to their appropriate duties and place, and the question of wages must remain open and unsettled until the orders of the President are received, or until fixed by subsequent regulations.

V. The commanding general here thinks proper to make known to the people of Memphis the principles by which in the absence of instructions from his superior officers he will be governed in all cases arising under these complicated questions. It is neither his duty nor pleasure to disturb the relation of master and slave; that is for the courts, which, having been destroyed here by our enemy, are inoperative for the present; but in due course of events there must and will be tribunals reestablished here that will judge and decide in cases which have already arisen or may arise under the laws and Constitution of the United States. Then loyal masters will recover their slaves and the wages they have earned during their temporary use by the military authorities; but it is understood that all masters who are in open hostility to the Constitution of their country will lose their slaves, the title to which only exists by force of that very Constitution they seek to destroy.

No influence must be used to entice slaves from their masters, and if fugitives desire to return to their masters they will be permitted to do so; but on the other hand no force or undue persuasion will be permitted to recover such fugitive property.

Officers of the army, from generals to lieutenants, must not employ such fugitives for servants. The Government provides to each officer a distinct pay for his servant, and this is ample for the hire of a free man. Were we to employ such fugitives as servants our motives would be misconstrued, whereas their employment by the Government is in pursuance of law, is clearly within the rules of war, and will increase our effective force by the number of negroes so employed.

By order of Maj. Gen. W. T. Sherman:

J. H. HAMMOND,
Assistant Adjutant-General.

HEADQUARTERS DISTRICT OF WEST TENNESSEE,
Corinth, August 9, 1862.

Maj. Gen. H. W. HALLECK,
General-in-Chief of the Army, Washington, D. C.:

I address you direct, no order yet being received announcing your staff, and not feeling certain that you should be addressed through the Adjutant-General of the Army. All is quiet now north of the Memphis and Charleston road, there being no organized force nearer our line than Holly Springs in the center and Saltillo on the left. There is abundant evidence that many citizens who appear to be quiet non-combatants in the presence of our forces, are regularly enrolled and avail themselves of every safe opportunity of depredating upon Union men and annoying our troops in small bodies.

The guerrillas have been driven entirely south of the Hatchie, and I hope to be able to keep them there. I think of sending the remainder of the Sixth Division of the Army of the Tennessee to Bolivar, which will give a force there sufficient for this purpose.

I am anxious to keep the whole of the Army of the Mississippi together and under the command of Brigadier-General Rosecrans, ready for any emergency, either to move upon any force that may threaten my front or to re-enforce General Buell. Having so many major-generals to provide commands for this may be difficult. I regret that General Rosecrans has not got rank equal to his merit to make this easy.

I have communicated to General Buell several times such information as I had of interest to him, but have never received any acknowledgment. I do not know where he is.

I have sent an additional brigade to hold the line east to Decatur, and ordered another. In accordance with your instructions I will try to hold the communication with General Buell and be in readiness to re-enforce him if it should become necessary.

All intercepted letters from rebel troops show that most of the forces that were in front of us have gone to Chattanooga. I informed you by telegraph that I believed the enemy had no intention of attacking this line in force, but only desire to hold Buell and myself in check, whilst the mass of their disciplined troops are being sent to Richmond. I have no positive evidence of this, but the conviction is strong with me. I give this, however, for what it is worth.

All stores have been removed from Pittsburg Landing, and the regiment that was stationed there I have sent to Jackson. The Sixty-third Illinois Regiment has been brought from Cairo to Jackson and relieved by the Eleventh Illinois, a very much reduced regiment. The Seventy-first Illinois, a new regiment, has also joined, and has been assigned to duty at Columbus. This embraces all the changes made in the position of troops since your departure, except those previously reported.

Recent orders are bringing back great numbers of absentees.

I am, general, very respectfully, your obedient servant,

U. S. GRANT,
Major-General.

HEADQUARTERS,
Trenton, Tenn., August 10, 1862.

Maj. Gen. JOHN A. McCLERNAND, *Jackson, Tenn.:*

A large force of mounted men have gathered between here and the Tennessee River and threaten the road north of this place. I have ordered Lieutenant-Colonel Hogg, with the cavalry belonging to this division, to report here immediately. Porter's company of Jackson's cavalry are north of the Hatchie. Last night they were working north. All my cavalry are after them. The dispatches taken from Falkner show that Porter and Falkner were ordered to burn all cotton between the Tennessee and Mississippi Rivers, and if possible get into Kentucky. Falkner's men are scattered, trying to remount themselves and stealing arms. I got nearly all their horses and some 60 of their arms, with their ammunition. They are working south in squads.

G. M. DODGE,
Brigadier-General, Commanding Division.

BOLIVAR, *August* 10, 1862.

General McCLERNAND:

General Grant telegraphs me to destroy the bridges and ferries on the Hatchie, except such as we can guard. Is Colonel Lawler still at Estanaula, and, if so, am I to use his ferries to carry out the above order, or will Colonel Lawler attend to the matter in his section without my orders? To what point, if any, on the Hatchie toward Estanaula am I expected to defend the crossing? There are two ferries between here and Pocahontas. I will destroy them to-morrow. The bridge at Pocahontas had better be attended to by force from Corinth, as it is nearer

L. F. ROSS,
Brigadier-General.

HEADQUARTERS FIFTH DIVISION,
Memphis, Tenn., August 10, 1862.

His Excellency Gov. ANDREW JOHNSON, *Nashville:*

SIR: Your esteemed favor of August 1 was handed me yesterday by Mr. Smith, cashier of the Memphis Branch of the Union Bank of Tennessee, and I promptly gave him the desired permission to go to Grenada to look up the assets of his bank, but I know full well that his visit will prove unsuccessful. No officer there would dare give up anything of use or value to them. I explained at length my views to Mr. Smith of the duties and obligations of himself and associates in the present strait. The bank has put in circulation notes to the extent of over a million of dollars and are indebted to their depositors for funds to a large amount. These liabilities are of a high and honorable character and the bank must redeem them. As trustees of this debt they will be held to a strict account. They must do all that is possible to secure the property and assets of their bank and apply them honestly to the redemption of their circulation and depositors.

It seems their bullion in coin and assets, notes made here and elsewhere, have been carried away by force and fraud. They deny complicity. They have not the power to retake their coin, which is therefore lost to them, but they can secure the notes. These notes are made payable here and are secured by property in Tennessee. Although the mere pieces of paper are at Grenada, the debts are here, and I must insist that the officers of the bank give public notice that the notes must be paid here by the makers or the securities will be proceeded against. Again, the assets were removed by force and fraud by Beauregard and others, who have property here which is liable for their unlawful acts. Out of these the branch bank can and must recover the means to redeem their notes and pay back to their depositors. They should do so at once, lest tactics be changed and men pay or pretend to pay their notes elsewhere.

The difficulty only is they fear the power of the common enemy and are trembling lest they commit themselves in case our enemy prevails. The branch bank here was vacant or not in use. General Grant ordered me to take possession of all vacant buildings and appropriate them to the use of the United States. I could have taken this building, but have forborne until the directors have time to assume their ground. They must be true to their trust, declare boldly and openly against the parties who robbed them, and at once begin to realize on assets which, though seemingly removed, are still here, else I have no alternative but to conclude that they are in complicity with our enemies and treat them as such.

I know that you agree with me in this—that all men must now choose which king. This by-play is more dangerous than open, bold rebellion. A large amount of the success of our enemies has resulted from their boldness. They have no hair-splitting. We, too, must imitate and surpass their game and compel all men and corporations to at once espouse the cause of their State and National Governments, thereby securing full right to protection, or openly to rebel and forfeit their property and their lives. Please say as much to the president of the bank.

I am, with great respect,

W. T. SHERMAN,
Major-General.

HEADQUARTERS ARMY OF THE MISSISSIPPI,
August 11, 1862.

General GRANGER, *Rienzi:*

General Grant says he has information that 800 to 1,000 conscripts and guerrillas rendezvousing about Ripley are raiding up toward Pocahontas—that is, via Russellville—burning cotton, &c. Can you verify that and if possible cut off and capture a large number of them? "Sharp is the word."

Tell Elliott his orders are here to report to Pope without delay. The Second Missouri Reserve is ordered to Saint Louis to report to Major-General Schofield. Direct them to get ready; the order will be ready in the morning.

W. S. ROSECRANS,
Brigadier-General, U. S. Army.

ROSECRANS', *August* 11, 1862.

General GRANT:

I sent word to Granger to inquire into that matter. Our cavalry were over there on Saturday and captured 25 conscripts. Our spies from there agree in saying there are only 150 of those fellows, who rendezvous

8 miles below Ripley—a spy who went to the Grand Prairie and thence to Grenada, thence back via Ripley. At Grenada, 50 conscripts and the sick. Infantry brigade formerly there gone south to West Landing, 39 miles lower down on the railroad. Breckinridge gone south, to Baton Rouge. No forces except cavalry north of Grenada. Price's force, said to be 12,000 or 15,000, above Tupelo.

W. S. ROSECRANS,
Brigadier-General, Commanding.

ROSECRANS', August 11, 1862.

Major-General GRANT:

I have just received the following from General Granger in reply to my dispatch predicated on yours of to-day:

> I have already captured the guerrilla party referred to. You have probably received, as I forwarded to you, with a free pass to Alton. It consisted of 17 instead of 800.

In reply to my advice he says: "Sharp is our name, game, and practice." It seems so.

W. S. ROSECRANS,
Brigadier-General, U. S. Army.

BOLIVAR, August 11, 1862.

General McCLERNAND:

My scout has returned from Somerville, La Grange, and to camp of enemy, 12 miles below Holly Springs. Total force there reported 18,000, under General Villepigue, of which 900 are cavalry, 24 pieces of artillery; 6 pieces are 24-pounders. They are advancing as rapidly as they can reach the railroad, and expected to be at Holly Springs to-day. He says everybody going into the service able to bear arms. Active preparations going on at every house. It is reported in the Confederate camp and believed by them that the gunboat Arkansas was sunk.

L. F. ROSS,
Brigadier-General.

GENERAL ORDERS, }   HEADQUARTERS FIFTH DIVISION,
    No. 68.   }   Memphis, Tenn., August 11, 1862.

The following orders have been received from department headquarters, and are published for the benefit of all concerned:

> In pursuance of orders from the Headquarters of the Army at Washington all restrictions on the sale of cotton and prohibition of the payment of gold therefor are hereby annulled. Every facility possible will be afforded for getting cotton to market. By order of Maj. Gen. U. S. Grant:

JNO. A. RAWLINS,
Assistant Adjutant-General.

By order of Maj. Gen. W. T. Sherman:

J. H. HAMMOND,
Assistant Adjutant-General.

SPECIAL ORDERS, }   HDQRS. DISTRICT OF WEST TENNESSEE,
    No. 160.   }   Corinth, Miss., August 11, 1862.

I. In accordance with directions from Headquarters of the Army, Brig. Gen. W. L. Elliott is hereby relieved from duty with the Army of the Mississippi, and will report in person without delay to Major-General Pope, commanding the Army of Virginia.

II. The Second Reserve Corps, Missouri Volunteers, Colonel Kallman commanding, will proceed immediately and without delay to Saint Louis, Mo., and report for duty to Brigadier-General Schofield.

*   *   *   *   *   *   *

By order of Maj. Gen. U. S. Grant:

JNO. A. RAWLINS,
Assistant Adjutant-General.

WAR DEPARTMENT,
Washington, August 12, 1862.

Major-General GRANT, *Corinth, Miss.*:

Please telegraph the present position of the several divisions under your command.

H. W. HALLECK,
General-in-Chief.

HDQRS. CENTRAL DIVISION OF THE MISSISSIPPI,
Trenton, Tenn., August 12, 1862.

Captain DAVIS,
Commanding Officer, Sixth Illinois Cavalry:

You will proceed with your command toward Chestnut Bluffs; will join Captain Lynch, who is now scouting in that neighborhood. It is reported that there is a force of rebels in that neighborhood some 200 strong. You will get on track of them and give them no rest till you rout them or drive them out of the country. After disposing of this band you will proceed to Dyersburg and administer the oath to such citizens as desire to come forward and take it. Disarm all known sympathizers with the Southern rebellion and notify the citizens of the consequences of harboring these guerrilla bands. Arrest all persons who are known to have aided Falkner's company. Send them in here with all their property that can be used by the United States Government. Be very strict and allow none of your men to commit any unauthorized depredations upon the person or property of any citizen. If you obtain knowledge of any other band of rebels you will give them no rest till they are either whipped or run out of the country.

By order of Brig. Gen. G. M. Dodge:

GEO. M. REEDER,
Lieutenant, Acting Assistant Adjutant-General.

ROSECRANS', *August 12, 1862.*

Maj. JOHN A. RAWLINS,
Assistant Adjutant-General, Corinth:

The following has been received from Brigadier-General Granger:

RIENZI, *August 12.*

Lieutenant-Colonel KENNETT, *Chief of Staff:*

A deserter from Saltillo, belonging to one of the Missouri regiments, reports as follows:

"Left there yesterday at about 11 o'clock. General Price in command; headquarters at Guntown. Everything has left below except Price's division, which he reports as about 12,000 strong. The movement has been by brigades. The last brigade, under General Jackson, moved about one week ago, infantry and artillery going by cars, their horses by land toward Chattanooga. One division is to return and increase Price's force to 30,000; and that this division is the first one that moved, some four or five weeks ago, and is under command of General Polk. After which the troops on this line are to be attacked."

I give this for what it is worth. The deserter is an intelligent one.

I send the above for the information of the general commanding.

W. S. ROSECRANS,
Brigadier-General.

GENERAL ORDERS, } 　　HDQRS. 5TH DIV., ARMY OF THE TENN.,
No. 70. 　　　　　} 　　　　　　　*Memphis, August 12, 1862.*

The commanding general at Memphis has seen in the newspapers the copy of an order dated War Department, Washington, July 31, 1862, on the subject of absences without proper authority on the part of the officers and soldiers from their proper posts and regiments, which substantially conforms to the orders heretofore issued to this division on the subject of reporting as deserters all who are absent from their posts and regiments, and, convinced that said order is genuine, the following parts thereof are hereby published, and will be complied with by all divisions, brigades, regiments, and detachments stationed at or near Memphis:

WAR DEPARTMENT,
Washington, July 31, 1862.

The absence of officers and privates from their duty under various pretexts while receiving pay at great expense and burden to the Government makes it necessary that efficient measures should be taken to enforce their return to duty, or that their places be supplied by those who will not take pay while rendering no service. This evil, moreover, tends greatly to discourage the patriotic impulse of those who would contribute to support the families of future soldiers.

It is therefore ordered by the President that on Monday, the 11th day of August, all leaves of absence and furloughs, by whomsoever given, unless by the War Department, are revoked, absolutely annulled, and all officers capable of service are required to join their regiments, under penalty of dismissal from the service or such penalty as a court-martial may award, unless the absence be occasioned by a lawful cause.

II. The only excuses allowed for the absence of officers or privates from duty after the 11th day of August are, first, the order of leave from the War Department; second, disability from wounds received in service; third, disability from disease that renders the party unfit for military duty; but any officer or private whose health permits him to visit watering places or places of amusement, or make social visits, or walk about the town, or city, or country in which he may be will be considered fit for military duty and as evading his duty by absence from his command or the ranks.

III. On Monday, the 18th day of August, at 10 o'clock a. m., each regiment and corps shall be mustered, the absentees will be marked, three lists of the same made out, and within forty-eight hours after the mustering one copy shall be sent to the Adjutant-General of the Army and one to the commander of the corps—the third is to be retained; and all officers and privates fit for duty absent at that time shall be regarded as absent without cause, their pay will be stopped, and they will be dismissed from the service, or treated as deserters unless restored, and no officer shall be restored to his rank unless, by the judgment of a court of inquiry to be approved by the President, he shall establish that his absence was not without a cause.

*　　　*　　　*　　　*　　　*　　　*　　　*

II. Commanders of divisions or brigades will designate some one or more officers of their staff as mustering and inspecting officers, and by themselves or such inspectors will, on the 18th day of August, instant, carefully muster each company of their respective commands. The chiefs of artillery and cavalry and the commander of each detachment unassigned to the regular brigade will in like manner muster or cause to be mustered their command, and make and transmit the rolls as required by said order.

III. All orders heretofore issued from these headquarters on this subject are hereby modified so as to conform to the foregoing orders, and all officers and soldiers heretofore reported "deserters" on the muster-roll of June 30, 1862, are hereby declared pardoned as to such muster, and those only will be treated and considered as deserters who remain absent at the muster of August 18, 1862.

By order of Maj. Gen. W. T. Sherman:

J. H. HAMMOND,
Assistant Adjutant-General.

SPECIAL ORDERS, }   HDQRS. DISTRICT OF WEST TENNESSEE,
No. 161.   }   *Corinth, Miss., August 12, 1862.*

*   *   *   *   *   *   *

V. Brig. Gen. J. M. Tuttle is hereby relieved from duty at Bolivar, Tenn., and is assigned to the command of the District of Cairo.

*   *   *   *   *   *   *

By order of Maj. Gen. U. S. Grant:

JNO. A. RAWLINS,
Assistant Adjutant-General.

ROSECRANS', *August* 13, 1862.

Major-General GRANT, *Corinth:*

Your dispatch and the copy from Buell received.* If the rebels will go into Tennessee let them do it; let the general in front, if he cannot successfully fight them, draw them in and destroy the crops as he goes. Let the Government study bear-hunting meanwhile, and learn how even a dog hanging on to the haunches of a bear keeps him from moving till the hunter comes and kills him. Let us fortify and provision needful points so as to be foot and hand free. Your reply to D. C. is good.

W. S. ROSECRANS,
Brigadier-General, U. S. Army.

MEMPHIS, *August* 13, 1862.
(Via Columbus, August 16, 1862.)

General GRANT, *Corinth:*

I hear from Grenada often, and have no idea that there is any movement toward Bolivar or Memphis. I had a letter a few days since from Villepigue, at Abbeville Station, south of Tallahatchie. That bridge is done and cars now run to Davis' Mill, 8 miles from Grand Junction. If Curtis were to move on Panola from Helena all this country would be abandoned save by guerrillas. I have three parties of cavalry out to-night, and will know if there is any movement from the south toward Bolivar; but I don't believe it.

The enemy wants to keep Curtis, myself, and McClernand occupied with reports, whilst they mass their forces on Chattanooga and Nashville. We ought to attack their railroads. Curtis' and my troops moving from Helena and here, striking them near Panola and Oxford.

W. T. SHERMAN, -
Major-General.

---

*See Series I, Vol. XVI, Part II, pp. 315, 316.

HEADQUARTERS ARMY OF THE MISSISSIPPI,
August 13, 1862.

Brigadier-General GRANGER, *Rienzi:*

Make adequate provision for cavalry to scout and watch the front of the Third Division at Jacinto—a battalion under a good commander. The company with Brigadier-General Davis and the two accompanying Mitchell may be disposed of to the best advantage. But the rebel cavalry having returned this way, Mizner might come nearer Iuka, but upon the table lands. Davis' command should have cavalry at Iuka. They need there two companies more than they have, with those sent with Mitchell.

W. S. ROSECRANS,
Brigadier-General, U. S. Army, Commanding.

Have you prepared to support the cavalry if pursued to-morrow?

BOLIVAR, *August* 13, 1862.

Major-General MCCLERNAND, *Jackson:*

General Ord visited this place, by order of General Grant, to examine condition of fortifications and our facilities for ascertaining the movements of the enemy, how far the Hatchie had been explored, &c.

L. F. ROSS,
Brigadier-General.

SPECIAL ORDERS, }   HDQRS. DISTRICT OF WEST TENNESSEE,
No. 162.   }   *Corinth, Miss., August* 13, 1862.

*   *   *   *   *   *   *

IX. In accordance with directions from Headquarters of the Army, Maj. Gen. George Cadwalader is hereby relieved from duty in this district, and will report in person without delay to Maj. Gen. H. W. Halleck, General-in-Chief of the Army, at Washington, D. C.

X. Maj. Gen. E. O. C. Ord is hereby assigned to the command of the post and garrison of Corinth, Miss., and will relieve Major-General Cadwalader.

*   *   *   *   *   *   *

By order of Maj. Gen. U. S. Grant:

JNO. A. RAWLINS,
Assistant Adjutant-General.

SPECIAL ORDERS, }   HEADQUARTERS FIFTH DIVISION,
No. 177.   }   *Memphis, August* 13, 1862.

Colonel Grierson, Sixth Illinois Cavalry, will detail a force of 150 good men, well mounted, armed, and equipped, and provided with three days' rations, for a scout. They will report at headquarters for instructions at 5 p. m. to-day.

Major Kerr, commanding Eleventh Illinois Cavalry, will prepare 150 men ready to embark on board one or more steamboats for a scout of three days, provided in all respects for such service.

The commanding officer of the party will call on the commanding general this evening for written instructions and information not proper to communicate to any other person than himself.

By order of Maj. Gen. W. T. Sherman:

J. H. HAMMOND,
Assistant Adjutant-General.

CORINTH, MISS., *August* 14, 1862.

H. W. HALLECK, *General-in-Chief:*

Two divisions (Sherman's and Hurlbut's), with the Fifty-second Indiana Engineer Regiment, five companies Sixth Illinois Cavalry, Rodgers' battery, one section De Golyer's battery, and the cavalry and artillery belonging to General Wallace's division, except one battery, at Memphis, Tenn.; McClernand's division, four regiments and one battery of Wallace's Third Division, six regiments and one battery of General McArthur's Sixth Division, Seventh Regiment Missouri Infantry, one company cavalry, Fifty-third Illinois, and Captain Foster's Fourth Independent Cavalry, at Bolivar and Jackson; General Davies' Second Division, and the Sixth Division, excepting what is at Bolivar, at Corinth. Divisions of the Army of the Mississippi are stationed as follows: General Paine's First Division, with an additional cavalry regiment, at Tuscumbia; General Davis' Fourth Division on line of roads between Tuscumbia and Corinth; General Stanley's Second Division at Camp Clear Creek; General Hamilton's Third Division at Jacinto; the Fifth Division at Rienzi. The several regiments of cavalry divisions are distributed at the several stations with the infantry division. General Quinby's command remains same as when you were here. The Fourteenth Regiment was not at ———.

U. S. GRANT,
Major-General.

[AUGUST 14, 1862.—For Halleck to Grant, Buell to Grant, and Grant to Halleck, see Series I, Vol. XVI, Part II, p. 333.]

HUMBOLDT, *August* 14, 1862.

General MCCLERNAND:

Governor Johnson telegraphed Captain Young to muster in all Tennessee troops he can under your directions. The captain is at Isaac Hawkins' to-day, where there is a war meeting. Shall I clothe the company and forward them to you? Governor Johnson also says that Morgan attacked Gallatin yesterday and burned twenty subsistence cars, took two companies prisoners, and burned three bridges. My scouts took 4 prisoners yesterday 15 miles east of here; 5 more escaped from them. By letters found on them it appears that several hundred Kentuckians are on their way south, aiming to pass between Humboldt and Jackson, in squads of 5 and 10. Will send you by mail a copy of letters. I thought perhaps you would like these Tennessee troops to guard all the roads and capture these men.

Your obedient servant,

GEORGE E. BRYANT,
Colonel.

ROSECRANS', *August* 14, 1862.

Major-General GRANT, *Corinth :*

Colonel Sheridan with three regiments of cavalry went down last night with orders to take Ellistown and Baldwyn, burn the depot at the latter place, feel of the rebels, and get information generally. The work was to have been begun at daylight this morning.

W. S. ROSECRANS,
Brigadier-General, U. S. Army.

HEADQUARTERS ARMY OF THE MISSISSIPPI,
August 14, 1862.

Major-General GRANT, *Corinth :*

The following dispatch has been received by General Granger from—

RIENZI, [*August*] 14, 1862.

Colonel Sheridan has returned. Captured 4 secesh, also 300 head of mules, horses, and cattle on Twenty Mile Creek, in vicinity of Carrollsville. Twenty Mile Creek is dry. Our horses had no water from the time they left the camp till they returned. Had great trouble to get water for the men, and was obliged to come home during the heat of the day.

W. S. ROSECRANS,
Brigadier-General, U. S. Army.

HDQRS. FIFTH DIVISION, ARMY OF THE TENNESSEE,
Memphis, August 14, 1862.

Maj. JOHN A. RAWLINS,
Assistant Adjutant-General, Corinth :

SIR: It has been physically impossible for me personally to give attention to the thousand of things which had to be done here since my arrival, and at the same time keep you fully advised of their progress. All is well now and matters are progressing favorably, and for the sake of history, and that the major-general may have a clear insight of our situation, I send a variety of papers, some of which need a word of explanation.

1st. Orders, No. 61, abolishes passes on land travel (on the river same as heretofore), and regulates it, confined to five roads and on each road a small guard to inspect each traveler, the wagons, buggies or carriages. Such guards can better prevent illegal traffic or catch spies than any provost-marshal, who must of necessity delegate his power to make out and sign passes to a clerk.*

2d. Orders, No. 62, defines the posts of my brigades and defines the duty of their guard. In that order I threaten incompetent officers with a board of examination, which on inspection I find I cannot appoint. (Section 10, act of Congress, page 521, Army Regulations.) I ask the detail of such a board of five officers, composed of, say, General Hurlbut, General Lauman, General M. L. Smith, Col. D. Stuart, and Col. [Ralph P.] Buckland. If you have granted leaves of absence to any of these, I name Col. [Joseph R.] Cockerill, Lieut. Col. [Charles C.] Walcutt, Major Fearing, and Major Fisher as alternates.*

3d. Orders, No. 67, about negroes. I found about 600 negroes employed here, and daily others come into our works. I have knowledge that a law had passed Congress for using the labor of such negroes, approved by the President and sanctioned by General Halleck. No

---

* See pp. 117, 118.

instructions had come or could come to guide me, and I was forced to lay down certain rules for my own guidance.*

Masters and mistresses so thronged my tent as to absorb my whole time, and necessity compelled me to adopt some clearly-defined rules, and I did so. I think them legal and just. Under this order I must assume to clothe and feed those negroes, but you will observe I make no provisions for any save laboring men. The women and families take refuge here, but I cannot provide for them, but I allow no force or over-persuasion in any case.

4th. Orders, No. 70. I had ordered at the muster of June 30 that all absentees without authority of General Halleck or myself should be reported on the muster-rolls as deserters. I see in the newspapers that the War Department had adopted the same views, only fixing the date August 18, and to put my troops on a footing with all others I have made this order. The official notice has not come to me, but I see it so universally quoted that I cannot doubt that such an order is in existence, and I infer that some accident has prevented its receipt in time to prepare the muster-rolls.*

5th. Instructions to Captain Fitch.† On the receipt of General Grant's telegraphic order about vacant houses and the leases of absent rebels I gave it to Captain Fitch, post quartermaster, with a few instructions. But as he progressed so many points of law and policy arose that he was embarrassed and called on me for further instructions. I made them in the form of a letter, which I authorized him to publish that all the parties might judge for themselves. This has quieted the great mass, but still cases are daily referred to me of the most delicate nature, one of which I inclose with this—the letter of Mrs. Lizzie A. Merwether,‡ whose husband is in the rebel service, and who remained under your orders permitting such ladies to remain on taking or making a parole. I venture to express the opinion that in war the parole of a woman or citizen is not good. From them an oath should be exacted, for the parole is a word of honor which, according to the old Federal code, a soldier alone could make; but apart from this it seems by her own statement her husband deeded this property to her, then rebelled against his Government, and by the fortunes of war now finds himself under one government and his wife under another. In either event the property is safe, let which party prevail. Mrs. Merwether is a lady and has small children dependent on her in the absence of her husband; but Captain Fitch, under my orders, or rather these printed instructions, construed the property to be substantially that of the absent husband and orders the tenants of the property to pay the rents to him.

I think in law and common sense the transfer of property to a wife at such a time and under such circumstances is simply an evasion, and therefore void, but am willing to stretch the rules as wide as possible to favor distressed women and children, although I fear a single departure from the rules of severe justice may lead us into many inconsistencies and absurd conclusions.

6th. I finally inclose a copy of a letter from General Pillow, addressed to S. P. Walker, esq., of this city, and designed for General Grant and myself. It did not come under a flag of truce, but by one of the secret mails which I have not yet succeeded in breaking up. I also inclose a copy of my answer, which I will hand to Mr. Walker and allow him to send as he best may. I do not consider my answer as strictly official, as the matters inquired about are as to the situation of his private property. I have published General Grant's order, based on the one from

---

* See pp. 158, 165.   † See p. 156.   ‡ Not found.

Headquarters of the Army, annulling all restrictions on the purchases of cotton and payment of gold therefor. I cannot see how General Halleck can allow gold, which is universally contraband, thus to pass into possession of an enemy, but I hope his reasons, as usual, are based on a far-seeing policy. I shall of course obey the order and facilitate the trade in cotton and its shipment, but it seems against the grain.

With the exception of small guerrilla bands I hear of no enemy nearer than Holly Springs and Senatobia.

Yours,

W. T. SHERMAN,
Major-General, Commanding.

[Inclosure No. 1.]

OXFORD, MISS., *August* 2, 1862.

SAMUEL P. WALKER, Esq.:

DEAR SIR: The Federal army at Helena have taken off by bodies of armed men all my negroes—men, women, and children—some 400 in number. They have taken off and destroyed everything else I had. They killed one of my overseers and had the other three in jail. I have been informed that many of the women and children are wandering about Memphis suffering for food. I also understand that there are 85 young men and women in a cotton-warehouse or negro-mart in Memphis who are also neglected and are suffering for food. It is difficult for me to realize that such conduct is done by the sanction of the Federal officers of rank; but yet the wholesale robbery which has been carried on below would seem to admit of no other conclusion. My object in this communication is to request of you the favor of ascertaining if the reports I have heard are true, viz, if any of my negroes—men, women, or children—are in Memphis, and to inform me of their condition, and if any of them will be restored to me or to my agent. Please see if any gang of the negroes are confined in the warehouse or negro-mart. I cannot imagine what the Federals want with the women and children.

If you can have access to Generals Grant or Sherman please ascertain if these proceedings have been ordered by them or meet with their approval. The law of confiscation does not take effect for some time to come, and my negroes were in no legal sense liable to seizure. If the Federals intend to seize all the negroes and other property within their power we can only say that the time may come for proper reprisals. My brother James' negroes and L. Long's and Thomas Brown's have all been carried off. Please see if any of these negroes are in Memphis and what is their condition.

I have uniformly in Missouri and Kentucky protected the property of Union men as well as their persons from violence. General Crittenden has a plantation and negroes 25 miles below Columbus, on the river, which I declined allowing to be interrupted when in command at Columbus, though applied to for the purpose.

If you cannot have a personal interview either with Generals Grant or Sherman you will please transmit my letter to them. Your attention to this matter will be gratefully remembered. Please send me through same channel an answer.

Your friend,

GID. J. PILLOW.

If any of my negroes are in Helena will you ascertain if Generals Grant or Sherman will have them restored to me, and all such information as you can get?

[Inclosure No. 2.]

HEADQUARTERS, *Memphis, August* 14, 1862.

General GIDEON J. PILLOW, *Oxford, Miss.*:

SIR: I have received your letter of August 2, 1862, at the hands of Samuel P. Walker, esq. It is not proper in war thus to communicate or to pass letters, but I am willing to admit the extreme difficulty of applying the harsh rules of war when but a few days ago all was peace, plenty, and free intercourse, and on this ground, not officially, I am willing that you should know the truth of the matter concerning which you inquire. It so happens that General Curtis was here yesterday, and I inquired of him the truth concerning the allegations in the first part of your letter touching the seizure and confiscation, the killing of one overseer, the imprisonment of three others, and generally the devastation of your entire estate in that quarter. General Curtis answered no slave was taken by armed men from your or any other plantation unless he had proof that such slaves had been used in war against him; no overseer had been killed or none imprisoned, and the damage to plantation was only such as will attend the armies, such as marked the progress of your and A. Sidney Johnston's columns a year ago in Kentucky.

I understand General Curtis has given letters of manumission to negro applicants who satisfied him they had been used as property to carry on war. I grant no such papers, as my opinion is it is the provision of a court to pass on the title to all kinds of property. I simply claim that I have a right to the present labor of slaves who are fugitives, and such labor is regulated and controlled that it may ultimately be paid for to the master or slave, according to the case. I have no control over General Curtis, who is my superior, but I take it for granted some just and uniform rule will soon be established by our common superior to all cases alike.

I certainly never have known, nor do I believe it possible, that your slaves or those of any other person have wandered about the streets of Memphis in want and destitution. We have abundance of provisions, and no person shall suffer from want here. When we can provide labor it will be done, and thereby they (laborers or slaves) earn their provisions, clothing, and necessaries; but wages are always held in reserve to answer the order of the rightful party. The worst you have to apprehend in case you claim the sixty days under the confiscation law is that your slaves may become scattered. None are allowed to pass up the river save with written passes, and I understand your negroes are either at your plantation or near Helena. I know of none of them here.

General Curtis expressed great surprise at your solicitude for these negroes and at your application that General Grant and myself would have them restored to you or your agent. He says you had sold them all or had transferred them by some instrument of writing for a record to a gentleman near the plantation, who is a loyal citizen of the United States.

I will refer your letter to General Grant, with a copy of this, and have already given a copy to General Curtis, now at Helena. If Mr. Walker can find any of your negroes here the men will be put to work; but Mr. Walker can keep a watch on them and of the women till such times as rules are established for ascertaining and determining the right and title to such kind of property. At present I know of none of your negroes in or near Memphis; certainly none are in the negro-pen or any cotton-shed here.

I am, respectfully, your obedient servant,

W. T. SHERMAN,
Major-General.

SPECIAL ORDERS, }   HDQRS. DISTRICT OF WEST TENNESSEE,
No. 163.   }   *Corinth, Miss., August* 14, 1862.

*   *   *   *   *   *   *

VI. The two divisions of the Army of the Mississippi now guarding railroad east of Corinth will proceed with all dispatch to Decatur, Ala., as soon as relieved by troops to be designated by Brigadier-General Rosecrans. General Rosecrans will designate and order forward sufficient forces to hold the points now held by these two divisions with as little delay as practicable. The troops advancing will carry with them all their camp and garrison equipage, transportation, ammunition, and, if practicable, ten days' rations. At Decatur they will receive supplies from Corinth so long as they remain a part of the command of the District of West Tennessee. Should orders be received by these two divisions from Maj. Gen. D. C. Buell they will be obeyed and supplied thereafter by such means as he may direct.

By order of Maj. Gen. U. S. Grant:

JNO. A. RAWLINS,
Assistant Adjutant-General.

GENERAL ORDERS, }   HEADQUARTERS FIFTH DIVISION,
No. 72.   }   *Memphis, August* 14, 1862.

I. Major Fisher, Fifty-fourth Ohio Volunteers, and Captain Littlefield, provost-marshal of General Hurlbut's division, are announced as assistant provost-marshals of Memphis, and will report for duty to Colonel Anthony. More attention will be given to the quiet and good order of soldiers on the streets. The assistant provost-marshals and the patrols and guards sent out by them have the power and right to suppress all riots and nuisances. Any house where noise, drunkenness, and fighting are either going on or likely to occur is a military nuisance, and will be suppressed by the seizure of its contents and the delivery of the liquors to the hospital department. If the nuisance cannot thus be suppressed the house will be burned or pulled down according to its position. Any brigade provost-marshal may suppress a nuisance in the vicinity of his brigade, but no house will be pulled down or burned without the written order of the commanding general, the provost-marshal, or the commander of a brigade.

Riots on the streets will be promptly suppressed by blows, the bayonet, or firing when necessary. Of course the military are not bound by the licenses issued by the city authorities, as licenses are designed for revenue and not to sanction or encourage crimes and nuisances.

II. In consequence of the abuse of the privilege, passes given to officers and soldiers are hereby limited to the time between guard mounting in the morning and tattoo at night.

When an officer or soldier wishes to remain absent from his regiment and stay in the city overnight he must obtain from his commanding officer and his brigadier a special leave of absence, specifying the reason of his visit to the city.

All officers and soldiers found by the provost guard in the city without passes at any time, or after 10 o'clock at night without special leave from their brigadiers, will be arrested and confined for the night and sent in the morning to the guard of Colonel McDowell's brigade—soldiers to work on the fortification one week, officers to be confined to their tents in arrest. Written lists with charges should accompany each batch of prisoners thus arrested and sent with them to the fort.

It is hereby made the duty of the brigade commander of the Second Brigade, Fifth Division, to organize his guard so as to compel all prisoners confined under this order, as well as such as are or may be sentenced to work by regimental or general courts-martial, to labor nine hours each day on the fortifications. He will cause his guard-house to be carefully repaired and reconstructed, so as to enable the officers of his guard to confine prisoners safely and to control their food. Prisoners who will not work are not entitled to rations, and must be put on short diet.

III. The regiment of infantry on duty as provost guard in the city and the cavalry detailed for the same purpose are hereby declared to be on guard duty the time of their detail, and are subject to the conditions of the forty-fifth Article of War.

By order of Maj. Gen. W. T. Sherman:

J. H. HAMMOND,
Assistant Adjutant-General.

[AUGUST 15, 1862.?]

[General LOGAN:]

GENERAL: I have just received the following telegram:

HUMBOLDT, *August* 15, 1862.

General McCLERNAND:

A messenger from Isaac Hawkins says some 400 or more Kentuckians dressed in citizens' clothes were near Huntingdon last night. They intend to capture Young and his party of 30 men and then cross our lines near Purdy. I have sent out cavalry to captain's assistance.

BRYANT,
Colonel, Commanding.

Instruct Colonel Haynie to take such measures as will enable him to capture enemy if he shows himself in that quarter; also take effectual measures to capture him if he should attempt to pass between Humboldt and Jackson.

JOHN A. McCLERNAND,
Major-General.

[AUGUST 15 and 16, 1862.—For Grant to Buell and reply see Series I, Vol. XVI, Part II, pp. 337, 344, 345.]

SPECIAL ORDERS, ｝ HEADQUARTERS ARMY OF THE MISSISSIPPI,
    No. 211.   ｝   *August* 15, 1862.

I. The Second Division will proceed to relieve the troops of First and Fourth Divisions now guarding the Memphis and Charleston Railroad. They will carry with them all their transportation, arms, ammunition, camp equipage, and baggage, reducing the latter to the quantity allowed by regulations. They will prepare and carry three days' cooked rations.

The First Brigade will move on Sunday morning, the 17th instant; the Second as soon thereafter as practicable.

The First and Fourth Divisions, upon being relieved by the Second Division, will proceed without delay to Decatur.

*   *   *   *   *   *   *   *

By order of General Rosecrans:

C. GODDARD,
First Lieut., Twelfth Infty., Ohio Vols., Actg. Asst. Adjt. Gen.

CORINTH, MISS., *August* 16, 1862—1.20 p. m.

Maj. Gen. H. W. HALLECK:

The rebels have bridge across the Tallahatchie completed and run cars to within 8 miles of Grand Junction. If General Curtis could move on Panola from Helena rebels could be cleared out of Northwest Mississippi. I could send General Sherman at the same time on Oxford. Four divisions of the Army of the Mississippi are now moving to occupy the road to Decatur and to re-enforce General Buell. Reconnaissance far to the front shows the country to be so dry that an attack on this place is hardly to be apprehended.

U. S. GRANT,
Major-General.

CORINTH, MISS., *August* 16, 1862—2 p. m.

Maj. Gen. H. W. HALLECK:

Colonel Sheridan, with three regiments of cavalry, made a forced reconnaissance on the enemy's lines, extending from near Carrollsville and approaching within 6 miles of Guntown, but found no water from the time he left until he returned to Rienzi. Brought back from Butternut 300 head of animals, good mules, fair horses, cattle, a lot of contrabands, and the Mobile Advertiser of the 12th. This paper has very late news from New Orleans and Baton Rouge. Lieutenant Read, of the Arkansas, reports to Mobile Register that the Arkansas went down to co-operate with General Breckinridge in his attack on Baton Rouge and arrived in afternoon; engines gave out in the fight in the morning; commodore Porter attacked her with the Essex, when she ran ashore, was set on fire and deserted, and blew up an hour afterward. Advertiser further states that the New Orleans Delta of the 12th claims great Federal victory; Lovell killed and General Breckinridge lost an arm; two exclamation points. No contradiction. Says large Federal re-enforcements gone from New Orleans to Baton Rouge. Federals expect to save entire army.

W. S. ROSECRANS,
Brigadier-General.

BETHEL, *August* 16, 1862.

General JOHN A. LOGAN:

There are now about 50 rebels, not well armed, near Sampson's Ferry, on the Hatchie. I have some cavalry after them. Tell General Ross to send from Bolivar, around behind them, south. I will attend to them in the north. Let him send from Bolivar. Go behind. I sent this evening infantry to guard the road, and the cavalry force I have is small.

Answer.

I. N. HAYNIE,
Colonel, Commanding.

SPECIAL ORDERS, }   HDQRS. DISTRICT OF WEST TENNESSEE,
No. 165.   }   *Corinth, Miss., August* 16, 1862.

*   *   *   *   *   *   *

II. The following changes in the disposition of the cavalry force of this district is hereby ordered:

The Fourth Illinois Cavalry, excepting Company A, Captain Osband, will report to Brigadier-General Quinby, commanding District of Mississippi, for orders, marching from Memphis and Jackson to Trenton, and from there reporting by telegraph.

Companies F and G, Fifth Ohio, Sixth Illinois, and Thielemann's cavalry will report to Maj. Gen. W. T. Sherman for duty.

The battalion of the Eleventh Illinois Cavalry, now at Memphis, and all of the Second Illinois Cavalry, excepting the force at Paducah and Company B, Captain Hotaling, will report to Major-General McClernand at Jackson.

Captain Osband, Company A, Fourth Illinois Cavalry, will report for duty to these headquarters.

To effect this change troops will march across the country under instructions from their present commanders. The movement will commence from all points on the 23d instant, except Columbus, which will commence on the 25th instant.

*   *   *   *   *   *   *

By order of Maj. Gen. U. S. Grant:

JNO. A. RAWLINS,
Assistant Adjutant-General.

SPECIAL ORDERS, } HEADQUARTERS ARMY OF THE MISSISSIPPI,
  No. 212.   }   *August* 16, 1862.

*   *   *   *   *   *   *

IX. The movement of troops directed by Paragraph I, Special Orders, No. 211, from these headquarters, will be deferred.

The First Brigade will move on Monday as soon as is practicable after the muster ordered by General Orders, No. 71, from district headquarters.

By order of General Rosecrans:

C. GODDARD,
First Lieut., Twelfth Infty., Ohio Vols., Actg. Asst. Adjt. Gen.

CORINTH, MISS., *August* 17, 1862.

Maj. Gen. H. W. HALLECK:

Now that two divisions are on their way to General Buell, would it not be well to abandon railroad from Tuscumbia to Decatur?

U. S. GRANT,
Major-General.

ROSECRANS', *August* 17, 1862.

Major-General GRANT:

Do you understand that two of our divisions are to be sent to Buell, and that we are moreover to try and hold the line through to Decatur? If so, the troops at Danville or other places must go to Iuka. If we cross at Eastport and Tuscumbia, Stanley's division,will go to Iuka and Tuscumbia; Mitchell will cross at Eastport and Paine at Florence. Stanley will try to cover the road till more troops can be got, but we must be careful.

W. S. ROSECRANS,
Brigadier-General.

[AUGUST 17, 1862.—From Grant to Buell see Series I, Vol. **XVI**, Part II, p. 355.]

ROSECRANS', *August* 17, 1862.

Major-General GRANT:

GENERAL: Under the last instructions from you I shall direct Stanley to occupy at Tuscumbia and Iuka; Paine to cross at Tuscumbia, Courtland, and Decatur; Mitchell to cross at Eastport. This will detach the First and Fourth Divisions of the Army of the Mississippi at Farmington and this place. Will require the troops I spoke of at Danville. This army will then extend from Rienzi to Tuscumbia, a distance of 50 miles front, while your entire corps will extend a distance of 30 miles northwestward. A small army covering a front of 80 miles parallel with the enemy's front.

A speedy remedy must be applied or a bad result must be expected.

W. S. ROSECRANS,
Brigadier-General.

ROSECRANS', *August* 17, 1862.

Major-General GRANT:

Have instructed Paine and Mitchell to examine and prepare for crossing, the former at Florence, Courtland, and Decatur, the latter at Eastport; to observe the utmost secrecy and report to me fully without delay. In my instructions do you wish me to say they are detached from this army and will report from Athens to General Buell, or that they will continue a part of this army on detached service, and render reports as usual to these headquarters? Granger reports the arrival of fifteen rebel regiments, 6,000 men, at Guntown within the last two days. Will the troops I asked for be sent him, and will Danville be occupied by a regiment from Davies' command?

W. S. ROSECRANS,
Brigadier-General, U. S. Army, Commanding.

ROSECRANS', *August* 17, 1862.

Major-General GRANT:

The Mackerel—I mean Union Brigade—reported to General Granger, 520. Three hundred for duty advanced as far as Danville, where they bivouacked for the night. They attacked the pigs of Danville, deploying skirmishers for that purpose from the flanks of their column who opened a sharp fire and brought eight of the hairy rascals to the ground before Colonel Tinkham, commanding Twenty-sixth [Illinois], stationed at Danville, arrived and informed the commander of the brigade that these natives were non-combatants, as loyal as possible considering their limited information. The brigade awaits orders there. General Granger by our move loses regiments and battery. Danville covers the crossing of the Tuscumbia in front of Oglesby's camp. It seems to me, general, it would be best to order Granger another regiment, and direct Davies moreover to occupy Danville, which protects the bridge-crossing both of the common and rail road; moreover covers the larger opening on the Memphis and Charleston Railroad left by vacating our camp. Please give the necessary orders.

W. S. ROSECRANS,
Brigadier-General, U. S. Army.

HEADQUARTERS FIFTH DIVISION,
Memphis, August 17, 1862.

Major-General GRANT, *Corinth:*

DEAR SIR: A letter from you of August 4, asking me to write more freely and fully on all matters of public interest, did not reach me till yesterday.

I think since the date of that letter you have received from me official reports and copies of orders telling almost everything of interest hereabouts; but I will with pleasure take every occasion to advise you of everything that occurs here.

Your order of arrest of newspaper correspondent is executed, and he will be sent to Alton by the first opportunity. He sends you by mail to-day a long appeal and has asked me to stay proceedings till you can be heard from. I have informed him I would not do so; that persons writing over false names were always suspected by honorable men, and that all I could hold out to him was that you might release him if the dishonest editor who had substituted his newspaper name to the protection of another would place himself in prison in his place. I regard all these newspaper harpies as spies and think they could be punished as such.

I have approved the arrest of the captain and seizure of the steamboat Saline for carrying salt down the river without permit and changing it off for cotton. I will have the captain tried by a military commission for aiding and abetting the public enemy by furnishing them salt wherewith to cure bacon, a contraband article; also for trafficking on the river without license or permit. I hope the court will adopt my views and stop this nefarious practice. What use in carrying on war while our people are supplying arms and the sinews of war? We have succeeded in seizing a good deal of Confederate clothing, percussion caps, &c., some mails, &c.

At our last regular muster I caused all absentees to be reported "deserted," whereby they got no pay; but inasmuch as the order for the muster for to-morrow, August 18, is universal, I will have the muster to-morrow and all absent then will be treated as deserters, and I will remit the former penalties as they are incurred under my orders.

I have sent out several infantry parties, as also cavalry, and am certain there is nothing but guerrillas between this and Senatobia and Tallahatchie. All the people are now guerrillas, and they have a perfect understanding. When a small body gets out they hastily assemble and attack, but when a large body moves out they scatter and go home.

Colonel Jackson commands at Senatobia, Jeff. Thompson having been ordered away. Villepigue is at Abbeville Station, 18 miles south of Holly Springs. They have guards all along the railroad to Grenada and cavalry everywhere. I think their purpose is to hold us and Curtis here while they mass against you and Buell or New Orleans. Price has been reported coming here, but of this we know nothing. If he comes he can and will take care that we know nothing of it till the last moment. I feel certain that no force save guerrillas have thus far passed north toward McClernand.

All the people here were on the *qui vive* for Baton Rouge and Nashville, but there seems to be a lull in their talk. I find them much more resigned and less presumptuous than at first. Your orders about property and mine about "niggers" make them feel that they can be hurt, and they are about as sensitive about their property as Yankees. I believe in universal confiscation and colonization. Some Union people have been expelled from Raleigh. I have taken some of the richest rebels and will compel them to buy and pay for all the land, horses, cattle, and effects, as well as damages, and let the Union owner deed the property to one or more of them. This they don't like at all. I do not exact the oath universally, but assume the ground that all within our lines are American citizens, and if they do any act or fail in any duty required of them as such then they can and will be punished as spies.

Instead of furnishing a permanent provost guard I give Colonel Anthony two good officers to assist him and change the regiment weekly. All are in tents and have their transportation ready to move. I am also in tents. I think 4,000 men could land opposite Helena, march rapidly to Panola, destroy that bridge, then to Oxford and Abbeville and destroy that, thus making the Tallahatchie the northern limits of their railroad. Afterward, Grenada, Jackson, and Meridian must be attacked. Break up absolutely and effectually the railroad bridges, mills, and everything going to provide their armies and they must feel it. The maintenance of this vast army must soon reduce their strength.

The lines of the Mississippi must be under one command. As it is, Curtis and I are perfectly independent of each other. He was here the other day. I know him well; he is very jealous of interference and will do nothing at another's suggestion. If you want him to do anything you must get Halleck to order it. Fort progresses too slow; 1,300 negroes at work on it. One installment of guns received; balance expected every hour. Weather heretofore unbearably hot, but now pretty cool.

Yours, truly,

W. T. SHERMAN,
Major-General.

WAR DEPARTMENT,
Washington, August 18, 1862.

Major-General GRANT, *Corinth, Miss.*:

As General Buell's communications in Tennessee and Kentucky are seriously threatened your communication with him should be kept open if possible.

H. W. HALLECK,
General-in-Chief.

WASHINGTON, D. C., *August* 18, 1862.

Major-General GRANT:

Letter of General Davis of the 1st instant is just received. You will take stringent measures to prevent all articles deemed contraband of war from reaching the enemy. Arrest and exclude from your lines every sutler or trader engaged in unlawful traffic.

H. W. HALLECK,
General-in-Chief.

COLUMBUS, *August* 18, 1862.

Major-General GRANT:

All persons who bring undoubted proof of loyalty have been permitted to take specie and other money South over the railroad. I do not permit the express company to take packages, except to officers of the army, without a permit. I will not allow my private judgment, however strongly it may condemn unrestricted traffic with the South, to interfere with orders unofficially. I cannot discourage it.

I. F. QUINBY,
Brigadier-General.

BETHEL, TENN., *August* 18, 1862.

Capt. R. R. TOWNES, *Jackson :*

We have captured 17 prisoners and 14 horses. What shall I do with them? Answer.

I. N. HAYNIE,
Colonel, Commanding.

HEADQUARTERS DISTRICT OF JACKSON,
Jackson, Tenn., August 18, 1862.

Col. I. N. HAYNIE, *Bethel :*

Send prisoners and horses by rail under guard to this place. If you can't send the horses by rail turn them over to your quartermaster to be accounted for as other property.

JOHN A. McCLERNAND,
Major-General, Commanding.

HDQRS. FIRST DIVISION, DISTRICT OF JACKSON,
Jackson, Tenn., August 18, 1862.

Col. E. S. DENNIS,
Commanding Post at Estanaula :

SIR : A report has reached General McClernand, and has been transmitted to these headquarters, that a rebel force of cavalry are about crossing at Green's Ferry, 15 miles northwest of Brownsville. To guard against surprise you will detach one regiment of infantry and two companies of cavalry and order them to proceed to Brownsville and remain at that place for such a length of time as you can ascertain the reliability of the above report and in your judgment shall be deemed best. If possible, you will transport the infantry in wagons.

By order of Brigadier-General Logan, commanding post.

HDQRS. CENTRAL DIVISION OF THE MISSISSIPPI,
Trenton, Tenn., August 19, 1862.

Capt. M. ROCHESTER,
Assistant Adjutant-General, Columbus, Ky. :

I have had my cavalry out day and night for two weeks past after different rebel bands, and in this way have so far kept them down and prevented them from joining their forces. I have not reported all the movements but only results, which I suppose the general prefers. The cavalry keep on their track, but it is hard work to catch them. These swamps and canebrakes are almost impenetrable, and when they once get in them it is useless to hunt farther. So far what fights we have had have been decisive and greatly in our favor. I have now some 100 horses and mules taken from them, besides a large number of arms. I have given to well-known Union men some of the arms that they had been robbed of, and have turned over some to the Tennessee troops by request of Governor Johnson. That these bands are being largely re-enforced I have no doubt. They obtained some 500 good arms out of a rebel boat sunk by us in the Tennessee River and have made good use of them.

I now have four companies of cavalry on the Tennessee, in Benton County, following up a force said to be 600 strong; four companies in Dyer and Lauderdale following Porter's band, 300 strong, besides separate companies on the Obion. If it is possible I wish one more company of cavalry could be sent to Colonel Harris, at Union City. He needs another company, but I cannot spare it. If 100 saddles could be sent me I would mount some infantry on the contraband stock and could use them to good advantage.

I am, very respectfully, your obedient servant,

G. M. DODGE,
Brigadier-General, Commanding Division.

FORT HEIMAN, *August* 19, 1862.

ASSISTANT ADJUTANT-GENERAL:

Commanding officer of Donelson telegraphs me yesterday that Clarksville was surrendered yesterday and that Donelson is in danger. He asks me for assistance. I am impressed with the belief that it is a scare, though I know guerrillas are organizing everywhere, and feel that there is necessity for more troops in that section. I need some infantry companies, and the remaining companies of my own regiment I start out to-morrow.

W. W. LOWE,
Colonel, Commanding.

GENERAL ROSECRANS' HEADQUARTERS,
August 19, 1862.

General GRANT:

Mobile Advertiser of 15th here. Breckinridge was whipped at Vicksburg;* General Clark and two colonels killed. They lost 250 men, and say our troops acknowledge loss of 1,000. They mention seventeen regiments cavalry being in the fight; say these numbered 3,500 men when they started, but 500 dropped sick by rain and heat on the way. B. H. Helm was knocked over, contused by their running cavalry; Captain Todd, Mrs. Lincoln's brother, was killed.

Granger's spies say movements eastward. Two sutlers' clerks and a soldier of the Fifty-ninth Illinois taken prisoners last Sunday week returned to-day liberated. They learned or were told that the rebels intended to have Corinth at all cost; that they were getting out timber to repair bridges on the railroad and that conscripts were constantly coming in; they had already 25,000 men. General Haynie has a drover from the South who says that Van Dorn's command, except that with Breckinridge, is at Jackson, and that Bragg is at Chattanooga with 40,000 men; he says he will march to Nashville or fight for it. Granger has sent out a cavalry regiment to attack Marietta at daylight to-morrow morning.

W. S. ROSECRANS,
Brigadier-General.

---

* At Baton Rouge.

BOLIVAR, *August* 19, 1862.

General McCLERNAND:

Scouts which returned from below last night report Villepigue's forces still 12 miles below Holly Springs. I am quite unwell, and would like to be relieved from the command for three or four days and permitted to visit friends in Northern Alabama.

L. F. ROSS,
Commanding.

CORINTH, MISS., *August* 20, 1862—3.45 p. m.

Maj. Gen. H. W. HALLECK, *General-in-Chief:*

The guerrillas are becoming so active in West Tennessee that a large mounted force is required to suppress them. Cannot a portion of General Curtis' cavalry be sent me?

U. S. GRANT,
Major-General.

WAR DEPARTMENT,
Washington, August 21, 1862.

Major-General GRANT, *Corinth, Miss.:*

General Curtis' cavalry is fully employed in Arkansas. Governor Johnson, of Tennessee, was requested some weeks ago to raise some cavalry regiments to act against guerrilla bands. I will send you more cavalry as soon as we can get it. You have charge of everything in your district, but no one has yet been designated to command the old department. It will probably be divided.

H. W. HALLECK,
General-in-Chief.

CORINTH, MISS., *August* 21, 1862—2 p. m.

Maj. Gen. H. W. HALLECK, *General-in-Chief:*

Two steamers are said to have been captured by guerrillas on the Tennessee on the 18th. Steamer Terry has gone down armed with four guns and a company of sharpshooters. General Tuttle informed me that three new regiments were to leave Springfield for Cairo yesterday and to-day. I have directed one of them and the Eleventh Illinois to occupy Paducah and Smithland; one to be sent to Columbus, and the other to remain at Cairo. There is such a demand for cavalry that I will have to mount infantry, making secessionists furnish horses and forage. Should there not be two or three light-draught steamers bought and fitted up, proof against Minie balls, and armed with two guns each, to carry Government freight on the Tennessee from here?

U. S. GRANT,
Major-General.

WASHINGTON, D. C., *August* 22, 1862.

Major-General GRANT, *Corinth, Miss.:*

You will take all possible measures to put down the guerrilla operations on the Tennessee and Cumberland Rivers. Act wherever you can, without regard to district lines. Clarksville should be retaken and occupied as soon as possible. It is believed that most of the enemy's forces have left your front.

H. W. HALLECK,
General-in-Chief.

CORINTH, MISS., *August* 22, 1862.

Maj. Gen. H. W. HALLECK, *General-in-Chief:*

I gave orders yesterday for Colonel Lowe to take command of Donelson in addition to Henry and Heiman; that I would re-enforce him, and he must retake Clarksville. Colonel Webster goes to-morrow with my instructions.

U. S. GRANT,
Major-General.

TRENTON, *August* 22, 1862.

Major-General MCCLERNAND:

Messenger in from Dyersburg reports Jackson's forces within 10 miles of there, on south bank of Forked Deer River. I have sent re-enforcements to Dyersburg; they will attack and follow up. The train of Sixth Illinois leaves here in the morning. Good commanding officers will be given the instructions you suggest. Jackson's whole regiment is north of Hatchie, and all Union men are running from him. The train and two companies of Second Illinois will go direct to Jackson from here; the rest will go direct from Dyersburg or wherever they leave the Sixth, unless you desire them to cross the Hatchie with the Sixth. They are instructed to attack Jackson and drive him south before the two regiments separate.

G. M. DODGE,
Brigadier-General.

FORT DONELSON, [*August*] 22, [1862].

Major-General GRANT:

You are doubtless aware of the fact of the surrender of Clarksville to the forces of Colonel Woodward on Monday last at 2 p. m. No gun fired on either side. The officers and men all paroled, and are now at Paducah or on their way home. It leaves me here at this post with the four remaining companies of the Seventy-first, numbering less than 200 men, with limited rations, no artillery or cavalry, threatened by Woodward and others.

Will you allow me to suggest the importance of re-enforcements as early as possible? Whether re-enforced or not I will hold the place until forced to yield. Can I have the re-enforcements?

JAS. H. HART,
Major Seventy-first Ohio.

BOLIVAR, *August* 22, 1862.

Major-General MCCLERNAND:

Shall I send force to Somerville with cavalry to gather up and bring in horses, mules, negroes, and forage? Everything of use to an army

in that section is being run off South, and unless we act promptly will
be used against us by the rebels.   I wrote you of the matter this morning, but telegraph because it will not admit of delay if anything is to
be done.

L. F. ROSS,
Brigadier-General.

TRENTON, *August* 23, [1862].

Major-General GRANT:
  Have 900 shot-guns, 500 rifles, taken from guerrillas and citizens.

G. M. DODGE,
Brigadier-General.

COLUMBUS, *August* 23, 1862.

General GRANT:
  Twenty-two guerrillas were captured on Monday night and Tuesday
morning 25 miles below here on the Missouri shore.   It is the party
that fired into the Champion Sunday night.   They were not duly enlisted in the rebel service, but were on their way to Arkansas, armed
and mounted.   I propose, with your sanction, to try them by a military
commission.   They are now here.   I have a list of prominent men in
river counties in Missouri, some of which are not within my district,
who are engaged in forwarding recruits to rebel army; proofs undoubted.
Shall I arrest all such, even though without my immediate command ?

I. F. QUINBY,
Brigadier-General.

SUPERINTENDENT'S OFFICE,
Corinth Miss., August 24, 1862.

Maj. Gen. H. W. HALLECK,
  General-in-Chief, Washington, D. C.:

  GENERAL: I can now state to you that the condition of the railroads
between Columbus and this point is quite satisfactory and improving
daily.   I have received five new engines and a number of freight cars
and have repaired several engines and cars so that I can send two
trains daily between Columbus and Corinth and an extra train from
Columbus to Jackson three times a week.   I apprehend no difficulty in
supplying a much larger force over the road than I have to supply at
present.
  Nearly all the public property at Columbus has been brought down
and distributed at different points along the line, and the master of
transportation, Captain Lyman, assures me that the whole of it will be
shipped by the 26th instant.
  If I can once get Columbus clear I shall have no difficulty in keeping
it so.   There have been a good many improvements made at Columbus
which were absolutely necessary for the transaction of a large amount
of business.   Side tracks have been put down in the main street leading to the ordnance and commissary storehouses and two extensive
side tracks to the new quartermaster's storehouses on the south side
of the main depot, the repair shop fitted up, water-tanks arranged, and
everything necessary to facilitate the business.

I am very much pleased with Mr. W. J. Stevens. He is industrious, honest, and shows himself qualified for the position I gave him. General Quinby and all the officers at Columbus speak in the highest terms of him.

Although I have not been able to bring down any private freight from Columbus the passenger and back freight up to the first of this month was over $33,000, and will, I think, reach $40,000 this month; all this of course is entirely independent of Government freight and transportation of troops. On the Memphis and Charleston road I have not been so fortunate. There has been almost constant interruption east of Tuscumbia; bridges and water-tanks burned, trains fired into, track torn up, and two engines run off and badly damaged, which, however, I have in running order again. I have had to rebuild seven bridges this month between Tuscumbia and Decatur.

Last Sunday the train was fired into near Courtland, about 150 shots striking the engine and cars, wounding the conductor mortally, the fireman and one of the brakemen slightly. The engine and train, however, were brought in all right.

Yesterday the train was attacked near Trinity, captured and burned. One of the rails was taken up and the engine run off the track as it was returning from Decatur. There was very little of value in the train and not over seven cars. There was a guard of 25 men, who fought desperately and killed, as I understand, 25 or 30 of the rebels, held them at bay for some time, sent for re-enforcements, and finally drove them off. The firemen and 3 or 4 of our soldiers were taken prisoners. I have sent out a force and got the engine on the track, and it is being brought in to-day. It is badly burned and will require a new set of flues before it can be used. The water was all let out of the boiler and a large fire built in the furnace so that the boiler was made red-hot. Some one had hold of it who evidently knew the most effectual method of using up a locomotive in a short time.

Very respectfully, your obedient servant,

JAS. B. McPHERSON

WASHINGTON, D. C., *August* 25, 1862.

Major-General GRANT, *Corinth :*

The Secretary of War directs that you seize, in the name of the United States, all cotton purchased or shipped by officers or men in the military service of the United States, and turn the same over to the Quartermaster's Department, to be sold on account of whomsoever it may concern.

H. W. HALLECK.

(Same to Generals Buell and Curtis.)

HEADQUARTERS OF THE ARMY,
Washington, D. C., August 25, 1862.

Maj. Gen. WILLIAM T. SHERMAN, *Memphis :*

MY DEAR GENERAL : It was determined before I arrived here that gold and Treasury notes should be paid for cotton, and it was so published in orders by General Butler, in New Orleans. Whether or not this is wise I could not stop to examine. The policy being adopted its operation must be uniform. Hence I directed General Grant to make it so in his district. I understand that tents for the new levies cannot be furnished till we get more cotton, and hence the absolute necessity of encouraging that trade just now.

Money is of no more value to the rebels than cotton, for they can purchase military munitions with the latter as well as the former. Very probably as soon as we get enough cotton for military purposes the policy will be changed.

I found everything here much worse than I anticipated. I am getting Pope, Burnside, and McClellan together, and I think our time of great peril is nearly over. We hope very soon to resume active operations.

I have had no time to attend to matters in the West, and they seem to be going on badly. The administration is very much displeased at the want of energy in Buell's movements, and unless he does something very soon he will be removed. A part of his district has already been assigned to Wright, but he retains nearly all his old army.

As soon as the new troops are organized in the West the fall campaign will be opened there with energy. All we can hope to do for the next month is to hold our positions and prepare for an onward movement.

Yours, truly,

H. W. HALLECK,
General-in-Chief.

GENERAL GRANT'S HEADQUARTERS, *August* 25, [1862],
Via Cairo, Ill., August 28, 1862—8 a. m.

Maj. Gen. H. W. HALLECK, *General-in-Chief:*

Scouts in from the front report all quiet. Rebels are getting out timber to build bridges. Think the main force has gone east, and has not stopped short of Virginia. One division sent forward is on forced march to Nashville. The other is pushing on to Decherd.

U. S. GRANT,
Major-General.

GENERAL GRANT'S HEADQUARTERS,
Corinth, Miss., August 25, 1862—9.10 a. m.

Maj. Gen. H. W. HALLECK :

GENERAL : Colonel Mason, with portion of the Seventy-first Ohio, surrendered Clarksville to the guerrillas. Prisoners were paroled and sent down the river. I ordered them to Benton Barracks, and have put Donelson and Henry under command of Colonel Lowe, and have ordered **six** companies of infantry up to re-enforce him.

U. S. GRANT,
Major-General.

ROSECRANS' HEADQUARTERS, *August* 25, [1862]—8 p. m.,
Via Corinth, Miss., August 26, 1862—11 a. m.

Major-General HALLECK:

Have sent Callender my spare arms, at his request, and promise to replace them with first-class arms in time for the recruits. Now he reports Saint Louis Arsenal bare. We are without either old or new. Recruits are coming in. We cannot arm them. One regiment requires 100 muskets. I beseech you order me 5,000 first-class muskets and some carbines, or revolving arms.

W. S. ROSECRANS,
Brigadier-General, U. S. Army.

WASHINGTON, D. C., *August* 25, 1862.

Major-General GRANT, *Cairo, Ill.:*

General J. A. McClernand will repair to Springfield, Ill., and assist the Governor in organizing volunteers.

H. W. HALLECK,
General-in-Chief.

HEADQUARTERS FIFTH DIVISION,
Memphis, Tenn., August 26, 1862.

Major-General GRANT, *Corinth, Miss.:*

SIR: In pursuance of your request that I should keep you advised of matters of interest here in addition to the purely official matter I now write. I dispatched promptly the thirteen companies of cavalry—nine of Fourth Illinois and four of Eleventh Illinois—to their respective destinations punctually on the 23d instant, although the order only was received on the 22d. I received at the same time from Colonel Dickey the notice that the bridge over Hatchie was burned, and therefore I prescribed their order of march via Bolivar. They started at 12 m. of the 23d, and I have no news of them since. None of the cavalry ordered to me is yet heard from.

The guerrillas have destroyed several bridges over Wolf Creek, one at Raleigh, on the road by which I had prescribed trade and travel to and from the city. I have a strong guard at the lower bridge over Wolf River, by which we can reach the country to the north of that stream, but as the Confederates have burned their own bridges I will hold them to my order and allow no trade over any other road than the one prescribed, using the lower or Randolph road for our own convenience.

I am still satisfied there is no large force anywhere in the neighborhood. All the navy gunboats are below except the Saint Louis, which lies off the city. When Commodore Davis passes down from Cairo I will try to see him and get him to exchange the Saint Louis for a fleeter boat, not iron-clad, one that can move up and down the river, breaking up ferry-boats and canoes, and preventing all passing across the river. Of course in spite of all efforts smuggling is carried on. We occasionally make hauls of clothing, gold lace, buttons, &c., but I am satisfied that salt and arms are got to the interior somehow. I have addressed the board of trade a letter on this point that will enable us to control this better.

You may have been troubled at hearing reports of drunkenness here. There was some after pay-day, but generally all is as quiet and orderly here as possible. I traverse the city every day and night, and assert that Memphis is and has been as orderly a city as Saint Louis, Cincinnati, or New York. Before the city authorities undertook to license saloons there was as much whisky here as now, and it would take all my command as custom-house inspectors to break open all the parcels and packages containing liquor. I can destroy all groggeries and shops where soldiers get liquor just as we would near Saint Louis. Also the newspapers are accusing me of cruelty to the sick—as base a charge as was ever made. I would not let the sanitary committee carry off a boat load of sick because I have no right to. We have good hospitals here, and plenty of them. Our regimental hospitals are in the camps of the men, and the sick do much better there than in the general hospitals; so say my division surgeon and the regimental surgeons. The doctors would, if permitted, take our entire command. General Curtis sends his sick up here, but usually no nurses, and it is not right that nurses should be taken from my command for his sick. I think that when we are endeavoring to raise soldiers and to instruct them it is bad policy to keep them at hospitals as attendants and nurses. I send you Dr. [Nelson R.] Derby's acknowledgment that he gave the leave of absence of which he was charged. I have placed him in arrest, in obedience to General Halleck's orders, but Dr. Derby is still in charge of the Overton Hospital, which is not full of patients. The State Hospital also is not full, and I cannot imagine what Dr. Derby wants with the Female Academy, out on Vance street. I will see him again, and now that he is chief at Overton Hospital I think he will not want the academy; still, if he does, under your orders, I will cause it to be vacated by the children and Sisters of Mercy. They have just made publication for more scholars, and will be sadly disappointed. If, however, this building or any other be needed for a hospital it must be taken; but really in my heart I do not see what possible chance there is under present circumstances of filling with patients the two large hospitals now in use, besides the one asked for. I may, however, be mistaken in the particular building asked for by Dr. Derby, but will go myself and see.

The fort is progressing well, Captain Jenney having arrived. Sixteen heavy guns have arrived, with a large amount of shot and shell, but the platforms are not yet ready; still, if occasion should arise for dispatch, I could put a large force to work; but Captain Prime when here advised that the work proceed regularly under the proper engineer officer and laborers.

    I am, &c.,

                        W. T. SHERMAN,
                    Major-General, Commanding.

                        CORINTH, *August* 26, 1862.
General H. W. HALLECK, *Washington, D. C.:*

    Your dispatch about cotton has been so mutilated in transmission that it is not understood. All cotton seized by Government is sold by quartermaster for the benefit of whom it may concern; names of claimants and amount received kept, so that claims can hereafter be settled by proper tribunals.

                        U. S. GRANT,
                        Major-General.

WASHINGTON, *August* 27, 1862.

Maj. Gen. U. S. GRANT:

My dispatch of the 25th is repeated. The object is to prevent officers and men in the Government service from trading in cotton on their private accounts: "The Secretary of War directs that you seize, in the name of the United States, all cotton purchased or shipped by officers or men in the military service of the United States, and turn the same over to the Quartermaster's Department, to be sold on account of whomsoever it may concern."

H. W. HALLECK,
General-in-Chief.

SPECIAL ORDERS, }   HDQRS. FIFTH DIV., ARMY OF THE TENN.,
   No. 210.   }   *Memphis, August* 27, 1862.

General S. A. Hurlbut will prepare Veatch's brigade with light transportation and two days' rations for a scout; the commanders will report to General Sherman at 7 o'clock this evening for instructions. One hundred of the Fifth Ohio Cavalry will also prepare with two days' rations for a scout; the commanding officer will report in person at these headquarters this evening for instructions.

II. Colonel Grierson, Sixth Illinois Cavalry, will prepare 100 men with two days' rations for a rapid scout; the commanding officer will report in person this evening at 7 p. m. for instructions.

By order of Maj. Gen. W. T. Sherman:

J. H. HAMMOND,
Assistant Adjutant-General.

WAR DEPARTMENT,
Washington, August 28, 1862.

Major-General GRANT, *Corinth, Miss.:*

General Buell asks for re-enforcements. You will give him all the assistance you can spare.

H. W. HALLECK,
General-in-Chief.

CAIRO, ILL., *August* 28, 1862.

Major-General HALLECK:

Two divisions have gone to Buell, and two more are expected to guard the line of railroad without sending there. I do not see how I am to further re-enforce him.

U. S. GRANT,
Major-General.

SAINT LOUIS, MO., *August* 28, 1862—2 p. m

Maj. Gen. H. W. HALLECK, *General-in-Chief:*

Cairo and Columbus being within the Ohio Department have I any longer control over the quartermasters at those places? General Rosecrans urges the purchase of two light-draught steamers to be used for the protection of transports on the Tennessee River. He says it is unsafe to depend upon the railroad for the supplies of his command. Shall I take any steps in the matter?

ROBT. ALLEN,
Chief Quartermaster.

ROSECRANS' HEADQUARTERS,
Iuka, August 28, 1862.

Hon. E. M. STANTON:

I have a disciplined cavalry regiment only half filled. We are in the presence of the enemy superior in numbers, having a cloud of irregulars to do their hard riding and messenger work. It is cruel and impolitic to leave us in this condition, and this is spoken advisedly. You can double our force; that is to say, add five regiments to our cavalry by giving 2,500 revolving rifles and 2,000 revolvers. Even good rifled carbines would add a full regiment to our strength. This is a great matter. You have power. No arms should be given to new troops until old ones are supplied. We are receiving infantry recruits, and the army will need 5,000 Springfield or Whitney rifles within four weeks. Two thousand are wanted to-day to arm those who are in front of the enemy. Wants elsewhere may be pressing; these are extreme. All spare muskets are sent to Saint Louis Arsenal to be issued to new troops, with the distinct understanding that they were to be replaced by first-class arms when required. The public reasons for supplying these troops are strong. I need hardly remind the Secretary it would be one of those things he could do for me personally.

W. S. ROSECRANS,
Brigadier-General.

HDQRS. SECOND DIVISION, DISTRICT OF JACKSON,
Bolivar, Tenn., August 28, 1862.

Colonel CHAMBERS,
Commanding Fifth Brigade:

SIR: I have just received a dispatch from Major-General Grant to the following effect:

It is reported that a rebel force of 6,000 cavalry have been sent to attack our lines. Keep a sharp lookout.

In case of any alarm during the night you will at once send a staff officer to report to these headquarters.

You will please report in person at 7 o'clock a. m. to-morrow.

By order of Col. M. M. Crocker, commanding division:

JAMES WILSON,
Acting Assistant Adjutant-General.

WAR DEPARTMENT,
Washington, August 29, 1862—10.50 a. m.

General ROBERT ALLEN,
Chief Quartermaster, Saint Louis, Mo.:

Columbus is not in the new Department of the Ohio, and Cairo was not intended to be. The arrangement was intended as only temporary in order to get the new troops organized and in the field. If General Grant requires two small-armed boats in the Tennessee River get them for him.

H. W. HALLECK,
General-in-Chief.

IUKA, *August* 30, 1862.

General ROSECRANS:

We have reliable evidence that 100 of the enemy's cavalry are camped within 6 miles of us, and they expect to attack us to-night. Infantry supposed to be following. We are prepared for them and will "welcome them with bloody hands to hospitable graves." When I had arrived here Colonel Harrington was here and had moved the camp to the depot, as I told you we were expecting to do. Colonel Miles not present; consequently I-telegraph.

Yours,

SCHMITT,
Major Twenty-seventh Illinois Volunteers.

SPECIAL ORDERS, }   HDQRS. ARMY OF THE MISSISSIPPI,
No. 225.   }   *Iuka, August* 30, 1862.

I. Brig. Gen. D. S. Stanley, having been instructed to relieve with his the troops of the First Division, is assigned to the duty of occupying the Tennessee Valley, and guarding the railroad from Iuka to Decatur, the road to Eastport, and the depots at that point.

II. He will for the present occupy Iuka with one brigade, covering with these troops everything as far east as Cane Creek.

III. The other brigade will be posted as follows: Two regiments at Tuscumbia, one on the road thence to Decatur, eight companies of infantry at Moulton, eight at Russellville, and four companies at Frankfort.

General Stanley will order block-houses to be erected, after plans to be furnished from these headquarters, at all the bridges and trestle-works requiring guards, in the most suitable position for commanding the points to be guarded. Should time suffice, defensive works, on plans to be furnished, will also be made at Iuka, Eastport, Tuscumbia, Courtland, and Decatur.

IV. Brigadier-General Granger will direct Colonel Mizner to post six companies of cavalry and a section of artillery at Moulton, six companies and a section of artillery at Russellville, and four companies at Frankfort, and to co-operate with the forces of General Stanley fully as heretofore on the same line.

V. Brig. Gen. E. A. Paine, having reported sick, is relieved from duty. He will turn over the command of his division with his instructions to Brig. Gen. J. M. Palmer.

VI. Brig. Gen. J. M. Palmer, having reported for duty, is assigned to the command of the First (Paine's) Division, and will immediately assume command of it, and carry out with the least possible delay the instructions which will be turned over to him by General Paine.

VII. Brigadier-General Paine is allowed to remain at Tuscumbia for a few days to recruit his health and will report by letter to these headquarters.

By command of General Rosecrans:

C. GODDARD,
First Lieut. Twelfth Infty. Ohio Vols., Actg. Asst. Adjt. Gen.

WAR DEPARTMENT,
Washington, August 31, 1862.

Major-General GRANT, *Corinth, Miss.:*

Could you send any more troops into Tennessee or Kentucky, east of the Cumberland, without risking your own positions; if so, from what points can you best spare them?

H. W. HALLECK,
General-in-Chief.

GENERAL GRANT'S HEADQUARTERS,
September 1, 1862—5.30 p. m.

General H. W. HALLECK, *General-in-Chief:*

I am weak and threatened with present forces from Humboldt to Bolivar, and at this point would deem it very unsafe to spare any more troops, except by abandoning railroad east of Bear Creek. In that case could send one division from Tuscumbia, or any point from there to Decatur. Would send Stanley's division.

U. S. GRANT,
Major-General.

HEADQUARTERS,
Trenton, Tenn., September 1, 1862.

Maj. Gen. U. S. GRANT, *Corinth, Miss.:*

The rebel force that crossed the Hatchie at Brownsville camped at Poplar Corners, on Forked Deer River, last night. This is about 12 miles from Humboldt southwest. I have no surplus force, only enough to guard the road and hardly that effectively. At all important bridges I have good block-houses and believe my force guarding them can hold their positions against any cavalry.

G. M. DODGE,
Brigadier-General.

WAR DEPARTMENT,
Washington, September 2, 1862.

Major-General GRANT, *Corinth, Miss.:*

Railroad east of Corinth may be abandoned, and Granger's division sent to Louisville, Ky., with all possible dispatch.

H. W. HALLECK,
General-in-Chief.

HDQRS. CENTRAL DIVISION OF THE MISSISSIPPI,
Trenton, Tenn., September 2, 1862.

Capt. M. ROCHESTER,
Assistant Adjutant-General, Columbus, Ky.:

CAPTAIN: The crossing of the rebel forces at Brownsville and the attack on Bolivar and Medon has kept us busy. The forces that attacked Medon crossed at Cloverfoot and were re-enforced by a portion of the force that crossed at Brownsville. They worked up the Hatchie by keeping in the bottoms. All this time I was aware of their movements, but crossing the Hatchie so far down and in such force convinced me that they meant mischief on my lines, and they still hang along the line from 10 to 12 miles off, ready to make a dash. If I could have had a regiment of infantry and a small force of cavalry I could have stopped the attack on Medon by attacking them the next day, after they crossed at Brownsville, and unless they leave this portion of country before to-morrow night I shall attack them and take the chances. They must have been aware of the movements of our cavalry, as they would not have dared to come so near me if I had my old cavalry force. This now here has only 350 effective men.

I wish to call the attention of the general to the importance of my having one more regiment at least at this place or Humboldt. If one of the new regiments could be obtained to take the place of the Fifty-fourth Illinois Infantry it would be of great benefit to the service. The general must be aware that with a large force of the rebels north of the Hatchie I can only act on the defensive, which is all wrong and sure defeat in fighting these rebels. If I can have any spare force I will follow them whenever they cross, no matter how strong they are. All I want is to feel secure on the railroad. They are now moving a force of 2,000 or more on the Tennessee River under Falkner. It is a part of this force that took Huntingdon. I trust the general will represent these facts to Major-General Grant, and if possible procure a regiment or two for me. I am convinced that General Grant sees the necessity of this. Dyersburg is now in their hands, and it is an easy matter, while they have a lodgment there, to strike the railroad at any point from Humboldt to Big Obion. If I could get arms—rifles or muskets—I could arm three companies of Tennesseeans, who are now at Humboldt.

I am, very respectfully, your obedient servant,

G. M. DODGE,
Brigadier-General.

HDQRS. CENTRAL DIVISION OF THE MISSISSIPPI,
Trenton, Tenn., September 2, 1862.

Capt. M. ROCHESTER,
Assistant Adjutant-General, Columbus, Ky.:

CAPTAIN: There is no doubt but there is a large force of rebel infantry and artillery south of the Hatchie River. They are driving out Union men, who represent them as very strong. I know that they picket all the crossings and that they are much stronger than any force we have this side. Whether they intend to cross any more I cannot surmise. That they have a large force in front of Bolivar I suppose there is no longer any doubt. We as yet have no communication with that place. In the fight near Denmark we lost two pieces of artillery. With the country entirely open east of here, and a chance for them to operate unmolested, they will be able to mass quite a force of renegade Tennesseeans and runaway Kentuckians.

All the prisoners we take agree that Price is moving a force north for the purpose of cutting up our communications and doing what damage he can to keep any of our force going east to Buell. The holding of the road so long between Jackson and Bolivar convinces me that we are underrating their strength. The general may be informed of all their movements from Corinth, but I will keep him posted as far as I can. From the dispatches I get from the south I judge they think that a large force is moving north. Falkner is in command of forces near Dyersburg. The Haywood Rangers are with him. I have spies in his camp, and will know by to-morrow how strong they are.

I am, respectfully, your obedient servant,

G. M. DODGE,
Brigadier-General.

HEADQUARTERS DISTRICT OF JACKSON,
Jackson, Tenn., September 2, 1862.

Brigadier-General LOGAN, *Cairo:*

It is reported that a body of 5,000 cavalry were within 7 miles of this place at sundown—reliable—and intended attacking here—not reliable. My impression is that they intend to cut the road above us. We need more men. Telegraph me on your arrival and departure from Cairo.

R. R. TOWNES,
Assistant Adjutant-General.

HEADQUARTERS DISTRICT OF JACKSON,
Jackson, Tenn., September 2, 1862.

General JOHN A. LOGAN, *Cairo:*

Re-enforcements have been sent. The enemy are still in check.

R. R. TOWNES,
Assistant Adjutant-General.

COLUMBUS, KY.,
Via Cairo, Ill., September 2, 1862.

Major-General HALLECK:

Telegraphic communication is cut off below Jackson. General Ross reports Bolivar invested by a strong rebel force from below. There has been no communication with that place for the last thirty-six hours. He also reports a rebel force of from 6,000 to 8,000 within 7 miles of Jackson, between that place and Denmark. He asks for re-enforcements, but already this place is almost stripped of troops. The new regiments from Illinois do not come forward, it is said, for want of arms. The Seventy-sixth Illinois is now here with but 200 muskets (altered Springfield), half of them useless. Give us arms and we will do more than hold what you have conquered.

I. F. QUINBY,
Brigadier-General.

TUSCUMBIA, *September 2, 1862.*

General GRANT:

Your dispatches received and orders given accordingly. One brigade will cover Iuka and points east. Tuscumbia must be held till the tents of two divisions and other public property are taken away. Iuka covers Eastport and is the surest way of our getting provisions. It must be well held. Have ordered the troops at Iuka to get ready to move. Will move them as soon as they can be replaced. If that is a real attack on Bolivar it will be good for us. We must watch the front. Leave by hand-car to get train at Barton.

W. S. ROSECRANS,
Brigadier-General, U. S. Army.

IUKA, *September 2, 1862.*

General GRANT:

Brand Stout, detailed from the Twenty-fifth Illinois and serving here in some capacity, has deserted, and the circumstances show a bad case for him. He can and will probably tell everything he knows about our lines. We must change them right away. You will not send Granger's cavalry, will you ?

Your dispatch received. I have ordered Stanley to prepare at once with secrecy and dispatch to remove his troops to this place, and instructed not to lose a pound of anything; to cover the movement by an apparent advance southwestward toward Fulton. Similar directions have been given the cavalry under Mizner. It will require four or five days to perfect this.

Please tell me where the Kentucky affair took place.

W. S. ROSECRANS,
Brigadier-General.

JACKSON, *September* 2, 1862.

Major-General GRANT, *Corinth:*

I telegraphed you yesterday that Colonel Dennis' command, moving in from Estanaula, were surrounded by a superior force of rebels. I sent him all the re-enforcements I could spare, and have not heard yet from the expedition. Bolivar is reported invested by a large force under Price. I can spare no force to assist them, being threatened here by largely superior numbers.

Colonel Crocker reports heavy force of enemy at Van Buren and Middleburg and rebel pickets within 4 miles of Bolivar, and has moved all his supplies within the fortifications. A force of rebels, reported 6,000 to 8,000 strong, encamped 7 miles from here last night. General Villepigue is reported to have crossed the Hatchie near Brownsville night before last with infantry and artillery. Can you send me assistance? I send a locomotive with this dispatch, being satisfied that telegrams between here and Corinth are intercepted by the enemy. Being doubtful of this reaching you I telegraphed to General Tuttle to assist us if possible, but have little expectation of help from there.

L. F. ROSS,
Brigadier-General, Commanding District.

GENERAL GRANT'S HEADQUARTERS,
September 3, 1862—12 m. (Via Cairo, Ill., 3 p. m.)

Maj. Gen. H. W. HALLECK, *General-in-Chief:*

Your dispatch for troops to go to Kentucky was received at 12 last night. Arrangements were immediately made to send some troops, but your dispatch could not be made out where they were to go nor what route. They will be sent as promptly as possible. Bolivar has been surrounded for several days, but I think can hold out. Jackson was threatened with strong force of cavalry, estimated at 4,000; I think, however, only four regiments. They were badly handled in our front, again in front of Bolivar, then at Medon, and at last a few miles west from there, which I reported to you. One hundred dead were left on the field. Reports now show that we buried 179 of the enemy's dead. I understand that the whole country around the scene of battle is a hospital for rebel wounded. I have ordered one division from Memphis to Brownsville, and by concentrating the troops west of us at that place I can hold it, if that is important. I will do it at all hazards or be very badly beaten. I immediately telegraphed back for correction of your dispatch.

U. S. GRANT,
Major General.

WAR DEPARTMENT,
Washington, September 3, 1862.

Brigadier-General QUINBY, *Columbus, Ky.*:

I can give you no additional troops at present. All are required in East Kentucky.

H. W. HALLECK,
General-in-Chief.

HUMBOLDT, *September* 3, 1862.

Brigadier-General ROSS:

Messengers in from the force sent from Humboldt report the enemy between Brownsville and Middle Fork of Forked Deer River, at or near Cherry Bluff. Will you send a scout in that direction?

They are reported as infantry and cavalry. If infantry, they must have crossed 15 miles west of Brownsville, at Green's or Whitley's Ferry.

G. M. DODGE,
Brigadier-General, Commanding.

IUKA, *September* 3, 1862.

General GRANT:

If we abandon this line it must be done with great deliberation. We have a large hospital here; commissary stores both here and at Eastport. Everything on the front must appear, if possible, exceedingly strong and have an offensive look. Don't let Granger move till we are all right and our stores and sick cared for. Will be down to see you by cars this morning.

W. S. ROSECRANS,
Brigadier-General.

MEDON, *September* 3, 1862.

Brigadier-General LOGAN:

My pickets were alarmed by approaching cavalry. I sent out a squad of cavalry and infantry and they ran off. A body of about 100 on Bolivar road. I cannot say whether there are more or not.

JOHN D. STEVENSON,
Colonel, Commanding.

WAR DEPARTMENT,
Washington, September 4, 1862.

Major-General GRANT, *Corinth, Miss.*:

My telegram was to send Granger's division to Louisville, Ky., to form the basis for the new troops organizing there. Inform General Wright, at Cincinnati, of the progress of the movement and when they will reach him.

H. W. HALLECK,
General-in-Chief.

GENERAL GRANT'S HEADQUARTERS,
September 4, 1862—3.15 p. m.

Maj. Gen. H. W. HALLECK, *General-in-Chief:*

I am hurrying Granger all practicable. Your dispatch was explained by one from General Boyle.

U. S. GRANT,
Major-General.

HEADQUARTERS DISTRICT OF WEST TENNESSEE,
Corinth, Miss., September 4, 1862.

General JOHN A. LOGAN:

If not already you will soon have a force from Sherman's command in supporting distance of you. Be as quiet as possible with your men, to give them all the rest possible.

Price has not moved toward Saulsbury.

U. S. GRANT,
Major-General, Commanding.

HDQRS. CENTRAL DIVISION OF THE MISSISSIPPI,
Trenton, Tenn., September 4, 1862.

Capt. M. ROCHESTER,
Assistant Adjutant-General, Columbus, Ky.:

CAPTAIN: I desire to call the attention of the general to the importance of keeping a portion of our troops at Brownsville as a point of defense, and to watch the movements of the enemy. It is superior to any north of the Hatchie. Its position is such that no troops could get by it to do any damage north of the Hatchie without our knowledge. From Humboldt to Brownsville there are only two bridges on the railroad out which could be put in in a very short time, giving us railroad and telegraphic communication with the place, and the railroad, running as it does parallel with our present line of communication, can be easily protected. It appears to me as very important that the road should be repaired and the place occupied, as it would keep all small bands of the enemy out of this country and give us due notice of the approach of a large body, with an opportunity to dispute the crossing of the Hatchie. It appears to me that the general commanding the District of West Tennessee, upon proper representation of the importance of a force at that point, would cause it to be occupied.

I am, very respectfully, your obedient servant,

G. M. DODGE,
Brigadier-General.

BETHEL, TENN., *September* 4, 1862.

General JOHN A. LOGAN:

I sent scout out yesterday, and this morning at 3 o'clock started others. I will be advised of the approaches of any force this way and advise you.

I. N. HAYNIE,
Colonel, Commanding.

GENERAL ORDERS, }   HDQRS. ARMY OF THE MISSISSIPPI.
    No. —.   }   *September* 4, 1862.

I. By direction of the general commanding-in-chief Brig. Gen. Gordon Granger will proceed with the infantry division now under his command, the Second Michigan Cavalry, Col. P. H. Sheridan commanding, Hescock's battery and Barnett's battery, to Louisville, Ky., and report for orders to Maj. Gen. H. G. Wright. He will transfer his transportation and spare quartermaster horses to Capt. J. W. Taylor, chief quartermaster Army of the Mississippi.

II. The chronic sick of his division will be sent to a northern hospital most convenient to his new station, those of the Seventh Kansas and Second Iowa Cavalry to the general hospital at Jackson. Dillon's battery will be ordered to report to Brig. Gen. C. S. Hamilton, commanding Third Division.

III. General Granger will make his movements with the utmost secresy and dispatch, covering his front while so doing by the two cavalry regiments he leaves behind. He will relieve Col. P. H. Sheridan from the command of the Second Brigade, Cavalry Division, and direct Col. A. L. Lee to assume command and report by telegraph to Col. J. K. Mizner.

IV. Col. J. K. Mizner, Third Michigan Cavalry, will assume command of the cavalry division, Army of the Mississippi.

                                                W. S. ROSECRANS,
                              Brigadier-General, U. S. Army, Commanding.

                              HEADQUARTERS FIFTH DIVISION,
                              Memphis, Tenn., September 4, 1862.
Col. J. C. KELTON, *Asst. Adjt. Gen., Headquarters of the Army:*

DEAR COLONEL: Please acknowledge to the major-general commanding the receipt by me of his letter, and convey to him my assurances that I promptly modified my first instructions about cotton so as to conform to his orders. Trade in cotton is now free, but in all else I endeavor so to control it that the enemy shall receive no contraband goods or any aid and comfort. Still I feel sure that the officers of steamboats are sadly tempted by high prices to land salt and other prohibited articles at way points along the river. This, too, in time will be checked.

All seems well here and hereabouts. No large body of the enemy within striking distance. A force of about 2,000 cavalry passed through Grand Junction north last Friday, and fell on a detachment of the Bolivar army at Middleburg, the result of which is doubtless reported to you. As soon as I heard of the movement I dispatched a force to the southeast, by way of diversion, and am satisfied that the enemy's infantry and artillery fell back in consequence behind the Tallahatchie.

Weather is very hot, country very dry, and dust as bad as possible. I hold my two divisions ready with original complement of transportation for field service. Of course all things must now depend on events in front of Washington and in Kentucky.

The gunboat Eastport and four transports, loaded with prisoners of war, destined for Vicksburg, have been lying before Memphis for two days, but are now steaming up to resume their voyage.

Our fort progresses well, but our guns are not yet mounted. The engineers are now shaping the banquette to receive platforms. I expect Captain Prime from Corinth in two or three days.

    I am, with great respect,

                                                W. T. SHERMAN,
                                                Major-General.

HEADQUARTERS FIFTH DIVISION,
Memphis, Tenn., September 4, 1862.

Maj. JOHN A. RAWLINS,
　　Assistant Adjutant-General, Corinth:

SIR: I have allowed more time to pass than I should to communicate with the general commanding, but nothing has transpired here worthy of note, and as you know my time is well taken up with the thousand and one little details of necessary duty. The weather has been so hot and roads so dusty that I have been unable to drill as much as should have been done, but generally the brigades are pretty well disciplined and instructed. Our numbers have increased by about 1,000 by absentees joining here, but we are short of arms. Captain Lyford is now here, and has examined all the matters pertaining to his branch of service. I have set apart one brick house inside the fort as an ordnance office and place of issue, and have given him the old brewery under the hill as an ordnance storehouse.

The engineers are constructing four magazines in connection with the fort, and there were two powder-houses on the river bank which we have appropriated, so that I feel assured we will have at Memphis the best possible storage for all the ammunition needed for the fort or for issue to troops.

I have, by board specially appointed, appraised all buildings inside of the fort and for some distance outside, which are already vacated or being so. Tenants thus dispossessed are supplied with other houses in Memphis of equal value. Some of the houses thus taken must be destroyed, but others are put to use either as hospital quarters or storage. By extending the original lines north we take in a large cotton-shed, with a high brick wall. This forms an admirable quartermaster's depot, and a battery erected close by commands the city perfectly. The earthwork of the fort is well progressed and we are now beginning the gun platform. Colonel Bissell has brought down an immense lot of shot and shell, but a small quantity of gunpowder. He has also delivered heavy guns and carriages suited to the work, though not exactly the caliber prescribed by Captain Prime. Colonel Bissell is now operating along the river with the Engineer Regiment, Fifty-second Indiana. He is so energetic and full of zeal that I have not checked him, though I fear he may cause the very thing we endeavor to prevent, viz, the firing on boats. There has been little or none of this of late, and I would favor the condign punishment of any one committing such outrage, but we must be careful not to render ourselves too harsh, or they will naturally seek revenge. He has just destroyed some houses at Hochelrode's, below, and as soon as he gets up I will make him report in writing and send you. He brought up in his last trip some negro women and children. I doubt the policy of burdening ourselves with such, as we can give them no employment and idle negroes of either sex are of no use to us in war. If they seek refuge in our lines we cannot surrender them or permit force to be used in recapturing them, but I doubt the propriety of making them captive. We had over 1,300 negroes on the fort, but since I have allowed the quartermaster and regiments to use contrabands the force at the fort has fallen to 800. The enemy has made herculean efforts to prevent negroes getting to our lines, and they partially succeed, but all say that the negroes everywhere are very saucy and disobedient. I do not think it to our interest to set loose negroes too fast.

On Thursday of last week I learned that a cavalry force was moving up from Abbeville, and inferring their purpose was to attack Bolivar or threaten your communications I at once dispatched Veatch's brigade toward Holly Springs, with cavalry on the State Line and Hernando roads to make a big dust and divert attention. I have reason to believe the movement held back the infantry and artillery that was designed to attack Middleburg and Bolivar. I still think the expedition suggested before, which I know met the general's hearty approval, would counteract any movement northward from the direction of Abbeville or Senatobia.

I will again to-day dispatch my cavalry toward Hernando for the same purpose. The roads are stifling with dust. You already know that I dispatched thirteen companies of cavalry for Bolivar, and have received five companies of the Sixth Illinois, and Thielemann's cavalry, now reduced to 80 men, and only 50 horses. I will not give horses to the cavalry till I impress on them the importance of taking care of what they have. I have sent the Seventy-seventh Ohio, Colonel Hildebrand, to Alton, and now expect hourly the battalion of the Thirteenth Regiment Infantry. Guerrillas now are very quiet, and generally things move along quietly and smoothly. We now await with deep anxiety further news from Virginia and Kentucky.

Yours, truly,

W. T. SHERMAN,
Major-General, Commanding.

MEDON, TENN., *September* 4, 1862.

General LOGAN:

The enemy were discovered since 9 o'clock; the rumors were about 100 within half mile.

They have fled down the Bolivar road. I cannot even conjecture their force, not deeming it prudent with my small cavalry command to pursue at night, and considering it folly to pursue with infantry.

If you are flush of troops an additional regiment will do no harm.

JOHN D. STEVENSON,
Colonel, Commanding.

CORINTH, *September* 5, 1862.

Maj. Gen. H. W. HALLECK, *Washington, D. C.:*

I am now convinced that the steamers Skylark and Callie burned on the Tennessee River about two weeks ago by rebels was done with the connivance of the captains or Treasury agents.* The steamer Terry, just captured on the same river, was probably done with the connivance of her commander, Captain Klinck. I had just ordered the expulsion of Captain Klinck from our lines on the strength of a letter received, sent through Washington, exposing his secession proclivities, the very morning his brother, the quartermaster, sent him in command of the Terry. Klinck is now in Cairo under arrest.

U. S. GRANT,
Major-General.

---

* See Brig. Gen. G. M. Dodge's report of capture and destruction of two steamboats on the Tennessee River, August 18, 1862, Part I, p. 34.

HUMBOLDT, TENN., *September* 5, 1862.

General LOGAN:

Rebels attacked Burnt Bridge this morning, set it on fire, burned camp, and retreated at 4 o'clock. The men put it out, and train is here. I have sent my cavalry after them. Can't you cut them off?

GEORGE E. BRYANT,
Colonel, Commanding.

TRENTON, *September* 5, 1862.

General LOGAN:

The rebels came from Poplar Corners last night at 2 o'clock, and probably returned that way. Can you send your cavalry to head them while I follow?

G. M. DODGE,
Brigadier-General.

HEADQUARTERS,
Bethel, Tenn., September 5, 1862.

General JOHN A. LOGAN:

All is quiet. Work going on vigorously. Information as to the enemy so conflicting I am in uncertainty. Scouts report them on Hatchie, nearly 15 miles from here. Some say a large force; others say small. Have out scouts to-night to know.

I. N. HAYNIE,
Colonel, Commanding.

COLUMBUS, *September* 5, 1862.

General GRANT:

Am I to consider the Thirteenth Wisconsin Volunteers, all of which, except the company at Hickman, part sent to Smithland and Fort Henry, and also Captain Stenbeck's battery of artillery, sent by sections to the same points, as out of my command? The Seventy-sixth Illinois is now armed with the captured Enfield rifles. Major Bigney, commanding at Smithland, telegraphs the guerrilla chief, Johnson, has taken Uniontown and Caseyville and now threatens Smithland. The major asks for cavalry to attack and pursue. I have directed him to mount his infantry as far as practicable.

It is said that 600 horses are at Smithland intended for Buell's army. Ought they not to be removed to safer point, as they cannot be sent forward?

I. F. QUINBY,
Brigadier-General.

RIENZI, *September* 5, 1862.

Major-General GRANT:

Your dispatches received. Granger moves one brigade to-morrow. Hamilton occupies this with two regiments, which come in to-morrow. I am told old Buford learned and blabbed our movements to Major Alger. This is so.

W. S. ROSECRANS,
Brigadier-General, U. S. Army.

RIENZI, *September* 5, 1862.

General GRANT:

I think it a matter of great importance for you to occupy Kossuth by a good regiment of infantry. They will have nothing to meet, but the moral effect on the present movement will be fine. The Seventh Kansas will be there by day after to-morrow morning. A squadron of cavalry might go with infantry.

W. S. ROSECRANS,
Brigadier-General.

SPECIAL ORDERS, }   HEADQUARTERS U. S. FORCES,
No. 227.   }   *Memphis, Tenn., September* 5, 1862.

The Fourth Division, Army of the Tennessee, Brigadier-General Hurl-but commanding, will march via Raleigh, Shelby Station, and the Hatchie Bridge to Brownsville, Tenn., and on arrival General Hurlbut will put himself in communication with the commanding officers at Jackson and Bolivar, and report by letter to Major-General Grant, commanding the District of West Tennessee.

All detachments and extra-duty men from this division are hereby relieved and will join their respective commands.

During the march General Hurlbut will take forage and such supplies as the country affords, giving to the owners receipts payable at the pleasure of our Government. He will carry along ten days' supply of rations. The sick of his command unable to travel will be left at the general hospital at Memphis, each man so left behind to be provided with the necessary descriptive list and account of pay, clothing, &c.

By order of Maj. Gen. W. T. Sherman:

J. H. HAMMOND,
Assistant Adjutant-General.

SPECIAL ORDERS, }   HEADQUARTERS FIFTH DIVISION,
No. 228.   }   *Memphis, September* 5, 1862.

General M. L. Smith will post one of his regiments at a point on the Randolph road near the church, with orders to keep one company at Randolph Bridge as a picket. Another regiment will be posted near the Hernando road, near the point now occupied by General Lauman's left.

General Smith will keep up the road guard on the Raleigh, State Line, Pigeon Roost, and Hernando roads, and General Denver will relieve the road guard on the Horn Lake road.

This order to go into effect at once to enable the movements of Brig-adier-General Hurlbut's division according to orders.

By order of Maj. Gen. W. T. Sherman:

J. H. HAMMOND,
Assistant Adjutant-General.

HEADQUARTERS FIFTH DIVISION,
Memphis, September 6, 1862.

Col. JOHN A. RAWLINS,
Assistant Adjutant-General, Corinth :

SIR : I had the honor to receive at the hands of Colonel Lagow, aide, the letter of General Grant of September 2. I immediately ordered

General Hurlbut's entire division to move to Brownsville by land. The cavalry, eight companies of Fifth Ohio, about 300 effective men, are already advanced to the vicinity of Raleigh, and the remainder of the division will camp there to-night. To-morrow they move to Shelby Station and operate so as to threaten Somerville, and any force that may be near Bolivar or the south of Hatchie. He will then see that he can cross the Hatchie by some bridge or ford on the road toward Brownsville, when he will rapidly cross the Hatchie, take post at Brownsville, and put himself in communication with Jackson and Bolivar.

The Fifty-second Indiana, now operating on the river with Colonel Bissell, will be landed on Monday next at Fort Pillow and reach back to communicate with General Hurlbut, at or near the crossing of Hatchie, and should it be, as I apprehend is the case, that the Jackson and Columbus Railroad is broken, the force in that quarter may be temporarily used from Pillow.

As near as I can learn from a gentleman in whom I confide, General Armstrong, of Price's army, came across to Holly Springs from Tupelo with three regiments of cavalry and two battalions of same. There he was joined by Jackson's and Pinson's regiments, about 1,200 more, making some 3,000 or 4,000 mounted men. This is the force that appeared at Bolivar, it is supposed, for the purpose of breaking up the railroad that supplies you. I fear they will succeed.

Villepigue still remained at Abbeville Depot, 18 miles below Holly Springs, with four regiments of infantry, rather weak, and eight pieces of field artillery. The men talked about a forward movement on Tuesday last, but the only sign of such a movement was that their quartermaster was buying artillery horses at Holly Springs. This gentleman saw the dress-parade last Sunday and counted only 1,200 men.

As soon as I heard cavalry was moving from Coldwater I sent Veatch's brigade toward Holly Springs as a feint, and am satisfied it caused the infantry and artillery to remain; otherwise it would have been at Bolivar. Night before last I dispatched 200 select cavalry of the Sixth Illinois to cross Coldwater on a road between the Holly Springs and Hernando road. They are still out. I learn that about 12 miles out they caught 12 prisoners, whom Colonel Grierson sent in by Lieut. [N. B.] Cunningham, of Company G, Sixth Illinois, and 12 men. About 10 miles out this party was fired on by a party in ambush, by which Lieutenant Cunningham was killed; the party dispersed. Three men are still missing, though it is probable they turned back and joined Colonel Grierson, who had gone on. Five of the prisoners were brought in. As soon as I heard of it I dispatched all my remaining cavalry out to punish the murderers. The body of Lieutenant Cunningham has been brought in dreadfully mangled. I hear the murderers were, as I suspected, citizens, and that the rightful parties have been punished. As soon as my party of cavalry returns I will call for a written report to send you.

Colonel Lagow goes to-day to Columbus and Corinth, and will deliver this and tell all news.

Yours, truly,

W. T. SHERMAN,
Major-General.

SPECIAL ORDERS, } HDQRS. OF THE ARMY, ADJT. GEN.'S OFFICE,
No. 225.   }   *Washington, September* 6, 1862.

*   *   *   *   *   *   *

I. Brig. Gen. Thomas J. McKean, U. S. Volunteers, is hereby relieved from duty at Benton Barracks, Mo., and will immediately report in person to Major-General Grant.

*   *   *   *   *   *   *

By command of Major-General Halleck:

E. D. TOWNSEND,
Assistant Adjutant-General.

HEADQUARTERS, &C.,
Corinth, September 7, 1862.

Col. J. C. KELTON,
Assistant Adjutant-General, Washington, D. C.:

For the information of the general-in-chief I have the honor to report the following changes being made in the disposition of the forces in this district:

The two remaining divisions of the Army of the Mississippi, under command of Major-General Rosecrans, are being collected at this place and form the garrison of Corinth. Rienzi, Jacinto, and Danville will be held for the present. Besides these two divisions there will be here General Davies' division, two brigades of McArthur's, and the cavalry and artillery, with the exception of one battery, of the entire division. The whole will be under the command of General Rosecrans.

The Jackson command, which guards the road from Bethel to Humboldt and from Jackson to Bolivar, will be under Major-General Ord, the forces remaining as now; that is, the former command of General McClernand has been increased by one brigade from General McArthur's division, and one battery. Two brigades from Memphis will occupy Brownsville, probably commanded by Brig. Gen. M. L. Smith. This arrangement gives me Major-General Sherman, commanding on the right; Major-General Ord in the center, and General Rosecrans on the left. With the force at Brownsville the line of the Hatchie will be guarded, and that force will be in readiness to re-enforce Bolivar in case of an attack there, or to occupy that place and leave the present garrison loose to re-enforce Corinth should it become necessary. When this arrangement is entirely completed I will probably move headquarters to Jackson. From that place, with a garrison at Brownsville, I will always be able to communicate with Memphis, by means of courier, in seven or eight hours in case of necessity.

U. S. GRANT,
Major-General.

HDQRS. CENTRAL DIVISION OF THE MISSISSIPPI,
Trenton, Tenn., September 7, 1862.

Capt. M. ROCHESTER,
Assistant Adjutant-General, Columbus, Ky.:

CAPTAIN: The larger part of the rebel force that has been between the Forked Deer Rivers has fallen back to the Hatchie, leaving bands of marauders in Haywood County to do what mischief they can. Their camps extend from Brownsville Landing to Estanaula, and they are reported by our spies and Union men as being from 3,000 to 5,000 strong. They are recruiting a large number of men south of the Hatchie and in the counties bordering it on the north.

Where Colonel McCullough is I know not, but judge by their falling back that he must be scouting in Haywood County. If we could have a force at Brownsville to occasionally dash across the Hatchie we could make it too hot even there for them; all their prisoners and our scouts say that they desire to get north of me. The punishment that I have given them in Dyer, Lauderdale, and Haywood Counties makes them bitter. They take all the property of any Union man or any one who even leans that way, negroes and all, and those men who bought the confiscated property at the sales here they punished terribly. A fight occurred in the streets of Denmark Thursday; what it amounted to I know not. The secesh report that their side lost 30 and that the cavalry cut them up terribly and dispersed them in the fourth charge. I trust it is so.

I am, very respectfully, your obedient servant,

G. M. DODGE,
Brigadier-General.

IUKA, *September 7, 1862.*

General GRANT:

Report from Hamilton says that information leads him to believe that reports are erroneous, and that no immediate attack is intended, but that Price and Van Dorn have united. Cavalry are out on that route to gather further news.

W. S. ROSECRANS,
Brigadier-General, U. S. Army.

IUKA, *September 7, 1862.*

Colonel WEBSTER, *Chief of Staff:*

If possible we ought to have all the information possible of the roads and paths north and southwest of Corinth and east of Purdy. We may find it greatly to our interest to advance, or if Price should try that to let him cross the Hatchie and then cut him off. Can it be got together?

W. S. ROSECRANS,
Brigadier-General, U. S. Army.

SPECIAL ORDERS, }   HDQRS. DISTRICT OF WEST TENNESSEE,
No. 187.   }   *Corinth, Miss., September 7, 1862.*

*   *   *   *   *   *   *

II. The post-office at Corinth, Miss., will hereafter be under the charge and supervision of the post quartermaster, and its employés will be subject to his orders.

*   *   *   *   *   *   *

By order of Maj. Gen. U. S. Grant:

T. S. BOWERS,
Acting Assistant Adjutant-General.

HEADQUARTERS SECOND BRIGADE, CAVALRY DIVISION,
Rienzi, Miss., September 8, 1862.

General C. S. HAMILTON, *Jacinto:*

GENERAL: I last evening assumed command of this brigade, late Colonel Sheridan's, and now composed of Second Iowa and Seventh

Kansas Cavalry, and in compliance with orders from General Granger report to you.

The camps were much disturbed last night by a communication received by Colonel Alexander from yourself, on which he issued an order to strike tents and move baggage to rear. I did not do so, but made preparations to meet an attack. There was no disturbance during the night. My command was so stationed as to guard the roads from Booneville east through Jumpertown to the main crossing of the Hatchie and north above the region of Kossuth. Both regiments had been out with their entire force and are still absent from camp. I have no information which leads me to believe we shall have an immediate attack, though I shall expect one when the enemy learns our situation. Their pickets have been on Twenty Mile Creek for six weeks past. I will try to visit you to-day, though may not be able.

I am, general, respectfully, your obedient servant,

A. L. LEE,
Colonel, Comdg. Second Brigade, Cavalry Division.

IUKA, *September* 8, 1862.

General GRANT:

Hamilton telegraphs news from a deserter that Price and Van Dorn have united for a move into Kentucky, but he thinks they are moving on Corinth. They are working on the railroad. Would it be well for us to take up the rails and haul them off for a mile or two and break up the track-bed down toward Booneville?

W. S. ROSECRANS,
Brigadier-General.

IUKA, *September* 8, 1862.

Major-General GRANT:

The information I sent you is all I have at present. All things considered, it would seem probable that Van Dorn, Breckinridge, and Price should combine, and if we withdraw from the east should hold us in check and move on Buell or make an attempt to dislodge us, if they think they have the power. The best route for them, all things considered, is via Ripley and Chewalla if they have transportation; the railroad by Rienzi is the next best. If we have our troops in hand so as to meet this attack we shall be able to whip them and crush them out. If they move east we shall be able to counteract them. If they should try to penetrate between us and Memphis and cross the Hatchie it would be the best for us of all; they would never return.

W. S. ROSECRANS,
Brigadier-General, U. S. Army.

IUKA, *September* 8, 1862.

General GRANT:

Colonel Mower telegraphed that Colonel Hatch's cavalry reports the enemy in force at Twenty Mile Creek. What force I do not know.

W. S. ROSECRANS,
Brigadier-General, U. S. Army.

HEADQUARTERS FIFTH DIVISION,
Memphis, September 8, 1862.

Brig. Gen. MORGAN L. SMITH,
Commanding First Brigade :

SIR: In continuation of the subject of our conversation of yesterday I now instruct you to march about 1,200 men, selected from the regiments of your brigade, to a point on the other side of the Nonconah where it is crossed by the Pigeon Roost road, where they will bivouac to-night. At that point Colonel Grierson, Sixth Illinois Cavalry, will report to you with about 400 well selected and equipped cavalry and one of our best light batteries. You will then assume command of the whole. See that there are five days' rations on hand and all the tools necessary to effect the object of your expedition.

The object is the destruction of a new bridge under process of construction across Coldwater, about 7 miles below the town of Hernando, and to drive away any force in that neighborhood. To effect this I leave you to act [with] discretion, but suggest that you detach about 100 cavalry to Germantown from your rendezvous with orders to join you afterward by Hernando; with your force then to move rapidly on Hernando, sending the cavalry to the bridge to see if it is guarded by cavalry only or by infantry and artillery. If there be artillery or any large party of infantry the cavalry should not be drawn within range, but return and report to you, when you can act with energy but due caution.

At about the time of the destruction of that bridge you will also cause to be destroyed a large section of the railroad track so effectually that it cannot be repaired, burning ties and bending the iron in such a way as to be utterly useless. The railroad bridge is already broken, but I want it so destroyed that it cannot be repaired this season. If you find surely that only a light force is at Senatobia you may attack that place and destroy it effectually, so as to be useless for the enemy.

Let your movements be rapid and decisive, keeping your own counsels and confiding only in two or three officers next in rank to yourself.

The only force capable of resisting you of which I have any knowledge is at Abbeville or Holly Springs. Therefore if you hear of any advance from that quarter look well to the roads to the fort.

Leave in charge of your camps some responsible officer, who will command the fragment of your brigade, with positive orders to keep all the men in their camps and to see the guard well kept up.

I think you can accomplish all and return to your camp by Saturday, but leave this to you. Having a good force of cavalry you can keep me advised of anything that should be known to me and at the same time watch your own flanks.

I am, &c., your obedient servant,

W. T. SHERMAN,
Major-General, Commanding.

———

GRANT'S HEADQUARTERS,
September 9, 1862—11 a. m.

Major-General HALLECK, *General-in-Chief :*

For two days now I have been advised of the advance of Price and Van Dorn on this place. I presume there is no doubt of the advance of a large force. One division will arrive from Memphis to Bolivar this evening or to-morrow, which will enable me to use all the force now at the latter place whenever required. Should the enemy come I will be as ready as possible with the means at hand. I do not believe that a force can be brought against us at present that cannot be successfully resisted.

U. S. GRANT,
Major-General.

IUKA, *September* 9, 1862.

Major-General GRANT:

Reports from the front show that it is probably four or five regiments of infantry, and that they are in their camp at Baldwyn with no particular sign of movement. I begin very strongly to suspect they are practicing a move on us and intend to cover up a movement on Buell's right and rear via Bluntsville, Gunter's Landing, Huntsville, &c. Is it possible they want to push themselves in a position to foil an attack on Vicksburg?

W. S. ROSECRANS,
Brigadier-General.

IUKA, *September* 9, 1862.

Major-General GRANT:

A private of Thirty-ninth Ohio, captured while straggling from their camp, just returned from Tupelo, paroled, and with a pass to Bay Springs, dated Tupelo, September 6, signed Brigadier-General Cabell, says he was taken to Baldwyn, thence to Guntown, thence to Saltillo and Tupelo, where he saw General Price; heard two citizens tell him "Damned Yankees were coming close, burning, ravishing, and destroying." Price advised them to go home, mind their own business, not shoot any one, as that only made matters worse; he would rectify matters in a week or two. He was told by soldiers he could not leave till after the fight. His remarks to the soldiers that he wanted to know how many engines we had on the Mobile and Ohio Railroad, as he wished them all; that the soldiers could not leave till after the fight; then giving him a pass to go by himself to Bay Springs alone to Mann's company of rebel cavalry; all combined induce me to believe the rebels are playing a game of bluff and are very weak, say 12,000 effectives.

W. S. ROSECRANS.

HEADQUARTERS FIFTH DIVISION,
Memphis, September 9, 1862.

Maj. JOHN A. RAWLINS,
    Assistant Adjutant-General, Corinth:

SIR: I have just heard from General Hurlbut. His column was on Sunday, at 3 p. m., moving in good order near Union Depot, and would move toward Somerville and Bolivar, to a certain point designated in his orders, when he will turn square to the north and move to Hatchie Crossing. The water is very low, and although all the bridges are broken he can easily ford the stream.

I hear of Jackson's and Falkner's cavalry, with other fragments, amounting to about 3,000 men, in his route, but I do not think they will fight him. I think Jackson is waiting for a force from Abbeville, but I have sent Morgan L. Smith's brigade with some cavalry and artillery to the southeast. That will prevent any movement north from that point. The cavalry scout in my last report was fully successful, and I send by this mail Colonel Grierson's report.* I learn that the rebels are constructing a bridge over Coldwater on the Hernando road. To destroy this is a part of General Smith's expedition.

I have just seen a notice in a newspaper that the battalion of the Thirteenth U. S. Infantry is at Cincinnati. That is not hardly fair. I detached one of my regiments to relieve this battalion by your order, with the distinct understanding that I was to receive in lieu this battalion, and it now seems I lose both. This is not fair, and I have written to General Wright to that effect. I hope you will do the same. He should either send the battalion at once or let me have the regiment back, viz, the Seventy-seventh Ohio. You know that I have not too large a garrison to hold Memphis and at the same time make offensive moves along the river and into the interior.

The Fifty-second Indiana Engineer Regiment, still attached to General Hurlbut's division, is now on board the steamer Emelin, ordered to land at Fort Pillow, to open communication with General Hurlbut. I do not understand that this regiment is permanently detached from General Hurlbut, though at present operating under Colonel Bissell on the river.

All well here.

I am, &c.,

W. T. SHERMAN,
Major-General, Commanding.

SPECIAL ORDERS, }   HDQRS. DISTRICT OF WEST TENNESSEE,
No. 190.   }   *Corinth, Miss., September* 10, 1862.

*   *   *   *   *   *   *

IV. The District of Mississippi, commanded by Brigadier-General Quinby, and the District of Cairo, Brig. Gen. J. M. Tuttle commanding, are hereby merged into one district, to be known and designated as the District of Mississippi, to be commanded by Brig. Gen. I. F. Quinby, through whom all reports required by regulations and existing orders will be made.

*   *   *   *   *   *   *

By order of Maj. Gen. U. S. Grant:

T. S. BOWERS,
Acting Assistant Adjutant-General.

---

*See Grierson's report of skirmish at Olive Branch, Miss., Part I, p. 55.

Organization of the Fifth Division, Army of the Tennessee, Maj. Gen. William T. Sherman, U. S. Army, commanding, September 10, 1862.

First Brigade.

Brig. Gen. MORGAN L. SMITH.

55th Illinois, Col. David Stuart.
6th Missouri, Col. Peter E. Bland.
8th Missouri, Col. Giles A. Smith.
54th Ohio, Col. T. Kilby Smith.
57th Ohio, Col. William Mungen.

Second Brigade.

Col. JOHN A. McDOWELL.

40th Illinois, Lieut. Col. Jas. W. Boothe.
6th Iowa, Lieut. Col. John M. Corse.
46th Ohio, Lieut. Col. Charles C. Walcutt.

Third Brigade.

Brig. Gen. J. W. DENVER.

48th Ohio, Col. Peter J. Sullivan.
53d Ohio, Col. Wells S. Jones.
70th Ohio, Col. Joseph R. Cockerill.
72d Ohio, Col. Ralph P. Buckland.

Cavalry.

6th Illinois, Col. Benjamin H. Grierson.
Thielemann's Illinois Battalion, Maj Christian Thielemann.

Artillery.

1st Illinois, Battery A, Capt. Peter P. Wood.
1st Illinois, Battery B, Capt. Samuel E. Barrett.
1st Illinois, Battery E, Capt. Allen C. Waterhouse.
1st Illinois, Battery F, Capt. John T. Cheney.
1st Illinois, Battery H, Lieut. Levi W. Hart.
1st Illinois, Battery I, Capt. Edward Bouton.
Independent Illinois Battery, Capt. William Cogswell.
6th Indiana Battery, Capt. Michael Mueller.
8th Ohio Battery, Lieut. Jacob M. Porter.

Troops in the District of Jackson, Tenn., Brig. Gen. John A. Logan, U. S. Army, commanding, September 10, 1862.

POST OF JACKSON.

Col. MICHAEL K. LAWLER.

Second Brigade.

Col. LYNDORF OZBURN.

18th Illinois, Maj. Daniel H. Brush.
29th Illinois, Lieut. Col. Chas. M. Ferrell.
31st Illinois, Lieut. Col. Edwin S. McCook.

Third Brigade.

Col. C. CARROLL MARSH.

20th Illinois, Maj. Orton Frisbie.
30th Illinois, Col. Elias S. Dennis.
45th Illinois, Lieut. Col. Jasper A. Maltby.

Third Subdivision.

Col. ISHAM N. HAYNIE.

48th Illinois, Lieut. Col. Wm. W. Sanford.
49th Illinois, Lieut. Col. Phineas Pease.

Fourth Brigade.

Col. FRANK L. RHOADS.

8th Illinois, Maj. Robert H. Sturgess.
63d Illinois, Col. Francis Moro.
7th Missouri, Maj. William S. Oliver.

Cavalry.

Maj. LUCIEN H. KERR.

11th Illinois (four companies), Maj. Lucien H. Kerr.
12th Illinois, Company H, Capt. Franklin T. Gilbert.
Ohio Independent Cavalry Company, Capt. John S. Foster.
Stewart's cavalry (four companies).
Tennessee cavalry (one company).

Artillery.

Maj. CHARLES J. STOLBRAND.

1st Illinois, Battery D, Capt. Henry A. Rogers.
2d Illinois, Battery B, Capt. Relly Madison.
2d Illinois, Battery E, Capt. George C. Gumbart.
14th Indiana Battery, Capt. Meredith H. Kidd.
14th Ohio Battery, Lieut. Homer H. Stull.

MISCELLANEOUS.*

Infantry.

17th Illinois.
43d Illinois.
61st Illinois.
23d Indiana.
11th Iowa.
13th Iowa.

15th Iowa.
16th Iowa.
12th Michigan.
20th Ohio.
68th Ohio.
78th Ohio.

Cavalry.

2d Illinois (eight companies).
11th Illinois (two companies).

Artillery.

9th Indiana Battery, Capt. Noah S. Thompson.
3d Ohio Battery, Capt. William S. Williams.

CORINTH, MISS., *September* 10—9.45 p. m.
(Received September 11, 1.40 p. m.)

General H. W. HALLECK, *General-in-Chief:*

With all the vigilance I can bring to bear I cannot determine the objects of the enemy. Everything threatens an attack here, but my fear is that it is to cover some other movement. It may have been instituted to prevent sending re-enforcements to Wright, or to cover a movement on New Orleans by Van Dorn, or to the east on General Buell. Should there be an attack I will be ready.

U. S. GRANT,
Major-General, Commanding.

IUKA, *September* 11, 1862.

Major-General GRANT:

I must think the movement a demonstration to cover a move on Buell: 1st, they ordered up a large quantity of rolling-stock, not needed, for a move on us; 2d, they have been making a great noise about this move, warning us—not usual; 3d, they see us closing in and have known it for many days and yet delayed the move; 4th, they tried to have it as a part of their plan that Price should cross the Tennessee in Buell's rear (this I am sure was a plan of Bragg and Beauregard); 5th, it is their interest to do this, and Roddey has taken post at Courtland.

W. S. ROSECRANS.

---

*Brigade organization and actual commanders not indicated on the original return.

WAR DEPARTMENT,
Washington, September 11, 1862.

Major General GRANT, *Corinth, Miss.* :

Where are the troops sent to General Wright? They should be pushed forward with all possible dispatch to save Louisville and Cincinnati. There can be no very large force to attack you. Attack the enemy if you can reach him with advantage.

H. W. HALLECK,
General-in-Chief.

_____

GRANT'S HEADQUARTERS,
Corinth, Miss., September 11, 1862—7.30 p. m.
(Received September 12, 10.50 a. m.)

General H. W. HALLECK, *General-in-Chief:*

Everything indicates that we will be attacked here in the next forty-eight hours, and at present the route indicated is by the southwest. I will be ready at all points. General Rosecrans is not yet in with all his forces, but will be by to-morrow night. Price's forces are estimated at from 36,000 to 40,000. I cannot believe he has half that number of good troops. He may have conscripts to a large number.

U. S. GRANT,
Major-General.

_____

IUKA, *September* 11, 1862.

General GRANT :

The following is a copy sent to Brig. Gen. C. S. Hamilton :

JACINTO.

Telegraphed you that Mower was at Barnett's. Fourteen companies of cavalry will be on that same point this evening, a little west and south, on the Bay Springs road; two regiments have gone to Burnsville ; two more will follow to-night ; two more to-morrow. Our maps show three roads from Jacinto to Corinth—Glendale road by Mrs. Taylor's and Campbell's Mill, and the two crossing Hurricane at Van Derferd's and Rorey's Mill. Mitchell's Mill commands both, and Hurricane is a bad stream to cross. Should the rebels advance on you in force feel and get them in front and stop their advance guard, and quietly and firmly withdraw by these routes, obstructing their passage at advantageous points. Break down the bridges on Hurricane, fell trees, and fight them, but not to entangle yourself, falling back toward your old camp at Clear Creek, where I think we can find a good battle ground. Your baggage should take the Glendale road, covered by a regiment and section of artillery. Establish at once and maintain an efficient line of communication to headquarters.

W. S. ROSECRANS,
Brigadier-General.

_____

IUKA, *September* 11, 1862.

General GRANT :

Du Bois finds nothing east of the Hatchie. Where are these troops ? I don't believe a large force is in motion, for our reports put them all near old positions on 8th instant. Your orders will be promptly obeyed. We must use trains.

W. S. ROSECRANS,
Brigadier-General.

Iuka, *September* 11, 1862.

Major-General GRANT:

All our troops have orders to have their three days' cooked rations, and all spare regiments move west to-night; those east of Bear Creek to it; those here to Burnsville. I will order those tents to be dumped and wagons to move only with ammunition and provisions.

Please let me know if the move is on the Pocahontas road, for Du Bois says the Ripley front is clear. It is important for me to know all, so as to give orders to Hamilton.

W. S. ROSECRANS,
Brigadier-General, U. S. Army.

Iuka, *September* 11, 1862.

General GRANT:

That force has been at Crockett's for two days, and seems probably to be two regiments of cavalry with a support of two of infantry. Considering all things I see nothing in this to alarm us.

W. S. ROSECRANS.

HDQRS. FOURTH DIVISION, DISTRICT OF WEST TENN.,
In Camp near Hatchie, September 12, 1862.

Maj. JOHN A. RAWLINS:

SIR: Last night at half-past 8 I received through Generals Logan and Ross your orders to move on Bolivar. I had more than half completed a bridge across the Hatchie and should have been in Brownsville to-night.

My march from Raleigh was directed on Somerville, and I showed my head of column on that road as far as Hickory Withe, where I turned toward Brownsville. This was under Major-General Sherman's advice to relieve our forces at Bolivar by showing a strong column on the flank of any attacking force.

We have had to repair bridges and make roads and are delayed, but I expect to be in Bolivar by Saturday night or Sunday morning. My provisions will be out by that time and I shall expect notice where to draw.

One of my regiments, the Fifty-second Indiana, is now, I suppose, at Fort Pillow, and will move thence by land to join me at Brownsville. They will require orders to move on from Brownsville to Jackson, which should be sent from Jackson to Brownsville. If they have not left Fort Pillow I wish orders sent to them either for the overland march or to be moved by boat to Columbus and thus to join the division. There is no force except scattered guerrillas within 20 miles of me.

Very respectfully, your obedient servant,
S. A. HURLBUT,
Brigadier-General, Commanding.

HEADQUARTERS FIFTH DIVISION,
Memphis, September 12, 1862.

Maj. JOHN A. RAWLINS,
Assistant Adjutant-General, Corinth, Miss.:

SIR: I have been waiting for definite news from the interior to convey to the general, and write now lest he may be waiting to hear from me. General Hurlbut's division entire marched from here on Saturday last [6th] for Brownsville. On Monday they were approaching Big Hatchie, east of Shelby Station and west of Somerville, since which time I have no clear account of them, but I feel certain they have reached Brownsville without much trouble. He should have reached that point on Wednesday, and by this time could be at Jackson or Bolivar, according to your orders. When Hurlbut moved I thought it of importance to check Villepigue at or near Abbeville, and also to destroy a bridge said to be under construction over Coldwater, on the road to and beyond Hernando. Accordingly I ordered General Morgan L. Smith, with the effective part of his brigade (about 1,500 men), 400 chosen cavalry, and a battery of artillery, to move about 17 miles toward Holly Springs, and then to turn square off to Hernando and there destroy the bridge in question and effectually tear up about 5 miles of that railroad, so that in no event could the enemy put it in order so as to transport men and materials within one day's march of Memphis. General Smith has not returned, but will be in to-morrow, and I have no doubt has succeeded in making a diversion by which General Hurlbut has reached his destination with little or no molestation, and in destroying effectually that railroad so as to be useless this campaign. I have heard accounts of various little skirmishes along Coldwater, in which we invariably succeeded, but the details can only be had after General Smith's return. According to the best information I can collect Villepigue has moved up to Holly Springs with about 2,000 infantry and twelve guns. Breckinridge's division has also in part moved up from Jackson, Miss. About 4,000 of them have reached Holly Springs. Their cavalry—Jackson's and Porter's and Pinson's cavalry—some 1,500, are encamped along Coldwater. I think their purpose is to pass up between you and Bolivar, or it may be they design merely to hold us in check while Bragg pushes on to Kentucky. But Kirby Smith in his proclamation to the Kentuckians announces that Breckinridge would be there, and I should suppose that he would make an effort to reach Kentucky this fall. As soon as General Smith returns I think I shall be able to arrive at some estimate of the forces that are now at or near Holly Springs. I am satisfied that the movement described by General Smith's brigade has kept this force where it is time enough to enable Hurlbut to co-operate with the force at Bolivar. If Steele would only cross over and destroy those railroads—a thing that two cavalry regiments might achieve—it would relieve you very much from any pressure from the direction of Jackson or Grenada. I am well assured that Breckinridge has come north, but I don't think his force exceeds 5,000 in all. Villepigue has not over 2,000, and the whole cavalry does not exceed 2,000. Hurlbut's forces and those at Bolivar ought to meet this combined movement.

Our fort progresses well; seven guns mounted, and by Saturday I will have fifteen heavy guns in position in addition to forty-two field pieces, all in good order. Matters in the city quiet enough, and the Union men better satisfied, as I have been talking to them a little of their duties.

About 900 negroes work on the fort; many have gone away or to the regiments.

      Yours, &c.,

                            W. T. SHERMAN,
                                Major-General.

ROSECRANS', *September* 16, 1862.

General GRANT:

Do I understand you that I am to go up by rail to support Mower, or that you send up 1,400 men for that purpose? I will consult Du Bois about that move to-night. Hamilton's position is a good support to anything of that sort.

W. S. ROSECRANS.

ROSECRANS', *September* 16, 1862.

General GRANT:

The orders are all out. Colonel Mizner will direct one regiment of cavalry to move this afternoon from Rienzi. Do you not think it would be best to leave one battalion of cavalry to cover that front and conceal movement? I will direct the infantry to begin to move this p. m.

W. S. ROSECRANS.

ROSECRANS', *September* 16, 1862.

General GRANT:

You have the telegram from Du Bois. I have directed Colonel Gilbert to move up the Thirty-ninth Ohio from Johnson's, 4 miles north of Jacinto, to Harvey's Mill, about 2 miles south of Burnsville, where there is a blind road leading to Iuka; to post himself advantageously, then send forward three companies to reconnoiter and cut off the cavalry that burned the train, and send up a company to Burnsville. Prime is to notify General Ross and Colonel Mower of what is coming. I think things will work out. I now find our stores were wagoned down toward Bay Springs; our cavalry heard the train moving down and saw those who had seen the packages with our marks on them. Only one regiment of infantry and one of cavalry has gone from Du Bois. Shall more be moved to-night, or await further instructions?

W. S. ROSECRANS,
Brigadier-General

SPECIAL ORDERS, }   HEADQUARTERS FIFTH DIVISION,
No. 243.   }   *Memphis, September* 16, 1862.

Capt. A. Silfversparre, of the First Illinois Artillery, is hereby selected and detailed to take charge of the fixed and permanent batteries in Fort Pickering. He will see that each gun has its appropriate ammunition—shot, shells, and canister—properly disposed for action, and that the implements are arranged close at hand.

In connection with the ordnance officer of the fort, Lieutenant Neely, he will see that the cartridges, friction-tubes, &c., are properly arranged in the magazines, and will, in connection with Major Taylor, chief of artillery, attach to the light batteries posted in the fort such of the heavy guns as are in position near their batteries, and instruct the officers in the peculiar manual of such guns.

II. General Denver will indicate two companies of his brigade to man the guns of the right flank, not attached to the light batteries as above and station them at the guns on his part of the lines. Such companies to be instructed by or under the direction of Captain Silfversparre, and in case of action to be under his command.

III. Colonel McDowell will, in like manner, designate two companies of his brigade for artillery duty, to be stationed at the heavy guns on the left flank of Fort Pickering. These companies to be instructed daily under the direction of Captain Silfversparre, at such hours as he may designate, and in case of action to be under his immediate command.

By order of Maj. Gen. W. T. Sherman:

J. H. HAMMOND,
Assistant Adjutant-General.

WAR DEPARTMENT,
Washington, September 17, 1862.

Major-General GRANT, *Corinth, Miss.*:

Do everything in your power to prevent Price from crossing the Tennessee River. A junction of Price and Bragg in Tennessee or Kentucky would be most disastrous. They should be fought while separate.

H. W. HALLECK,
General-in-Chief.

ROSECRANS', *September* 17, 1862.

General GRANT:

Stanley's division marches to-night for Davenport's Mill, near Jacinto, where all the regiments meet. Hamilton moves forward to-night. I will not leave here until 8 a. m. to-morrow, in order to get all the news. I will then move to Jacinto and connect my headquarters with Burnsville and Rienzi by lines of vedette posts for prompt and rapid communication with your headquarters. Du Bois could and ought to send a couple of companies to occupy and keep Jacinto in order. The Seventh Kansas will watch the front. It seems our flag-of-truce bearers did not see the troops they report at Baldwyn.

W. S. ROSECRANS,
Brigadier-General.

ROSECRANS', *September* 17, 1862.

Major-General GRANT:

Hamilton has sent out Mizner with a regiment of infantry and all our cavalry, under Mizner, toward Barnett's, on the Jacinto and Iuka road. The only thing we can do to prevent Price passing through the defiles of Bear Creek east is to push that division on him and follow it with all Stanley's force while Ross makes a strong demonstration on his front. This is safe for a day or two if we can keep spies from running to Breckinridge and Van [Dorn and] Price and you can hold your hand against [them]. I can pursue with my entire force, which, including Du Bois and Danville, will be about 13,000 of all arms.

W. S. ROSECRANS,
Brigadier-General, U. S. Army.

ROSECRANS', *September* 17, 1862.

General GRANT:

Mizner's dispatch just in reports that the cannonading of our reconnoitering party ceased at 4.40 last evening, and that about 8 o'clock last evening a very large fire was seen in the direction of Iuka; the distance is 20 miles. Mizner has gone to feel of them since 4 a. m. My suspicions are that some houses and stores have been burned in Iuka, the place abandoned, and that Price has crossed the defiles of Bear Creek, and will pass the Tennessee before it rises—at the Shoals, if possible; if not, will proceed at once to above Decatur, near Whitesburg.

W. S. ROSECRANS,
Brigadier-General.

ROSECRANS', September 17, 1862.

General GRANT:

Am dispatching orders for Hamilton to follow Mizner's advance and hang on the skirts of Price. If you approve I will dispose to follow with my entire force, including Du Bois' command, or Colonel Chambers' regiment in lieu thereof.

W. S. ROSECRANS,
Brigadier-General.

HEADQUARTERS ARMY OF THE MISSISSIPPI,
Jacinto, September 17, 1862.

General GRANT, Corinth:

Have just arrived at Jacinto. There will be a courier line from there to my headquarters at Davenport's Mill. As soon as Stanley comes up we shall move on to near Barnett's, probably to-night. Courier line will be open; stations all the way down from Burnsville. Nothing new from the front. Hamilton has no doubt of Price's being at Iuka.

W. S. ROSECRANS,
Brigadier-General, U. S. Army.

ROSECRANS', September 17, 1862.

General GRANT:

The following just received from Burnsville:

I am going to send in a prisoner who gave himself up to our skirmishers yesterday. He gives some very valuable information. According to his statement Price is trying to draw our troops out from Corinth, when Van Dorn and Breckinridge will attack that place.

J. A. MOWER.

W. S. ROSECRANS,
Brigadier-General.

ROSECRANS', September 17, 1862.

Major-General GRANT:

Have ordered regimental trains and spare baggage of this army to some suitable point within the lines at Corinth, to be parked defensively, guarded by convalescents unfit for duty. March placed under the command of a responsible officer. The sick are to go to the general hospital, where our medical director will see them provided for. I think it would be best to have a few tent-flies to be kept for each company, in view of the storms. The deserter from the rebels at Iuka is an Irishman, from Company F, Second Texas; left last night. He reports Price there with all his force; regiments number from 250 to 350; Armstrong's cavalry, about 1,500; five four-gun batteries, and two heavy rifled pieces captured from us at Shiloh. The two still larger went west. Price was to have left Iuka on yesterday morning, had we not pursued him with our reconnoitering force, destined for up the Tennessee Valley. Rations were ordered for five days. Breckinridge and Van Dorn are to leap in on Corinth from the west as soon as we get out after Price. As to his statement of Price's command and position I have no doubt. Colonel Mower's reconnaissance was ably conducted, and came to within 300 yards of their main line of infantry, Maury's division, in order of battle. The loss of the train was wholly owing to the risk of the conductor, who ran out after Mower had been gone some hours, and was done by Armstrong's entire cavalry force, which came west a few miles south of the railroad to threaten Mower's flank.

W. S. ROSECRANS.

HEADQUARTERS ARMY OF THE MISSISSIPPI,
September 17, 1862.

General GRANT:

Colonel Mizner has returned from his reconnaissance. Road directly east from Jacinto and all south clear as far as Peyton's Mill, and probably altogether so. One company of cavalry proceeded within $2\frac{1}{2}$ miles of Iuka and found no pickets; captured 2 prisoners (captains), one an Englishman and one a school teacher in Bentonville, Ark. He says Price has two divisions (each brigade of four regiments), six batteries, and ten regiments of cavalry, and is aiming to go north through Western Kentucky. A deserter from Iuka says he was there this morning. Great pains ought to be taken to ascertain to-night whether they are gone or not. He says Breckinridge has certainly gone to Holly Springs and will move on Bolivar. If our troops move by Jacinto they will not be ready to fight before day after to-morrow morning; if by Burnsville about the same time, with less fatigue but probably worse roads. I propose to move by Barnett's.

W. S. ROSECRANS,
Brigadier-General, U. S. Army.

SEPTEMBER 17, 1862.

General GRANT:

Have just received the following from General Hamilton:

JACINTO—9.30 p. m.

Price and his whole force are in Iuka. We have captured a lot of prisoners, wagons, mules, and ordnance stores. Some of the prisoners just from Iuka.

W. S. ROSECRANS.

SEPTEMBER 17, 1862.

Major-General GRANT,
　　Commanding Corinth, Miss.:

As Price is an old woodpecker it would be well to have a watch set to see if he might not take a course down the Tennessee, toward Eastport, in hopes to find the means of crossing. Have you any lookout toward Hamburg Landing?

W. S. ROSECRANS,
Brigadier-General.

SPECIAL ORDERS, } HEADQUARTERS ARMY OF THE MISSISSIPPI,
  No. 239.   }   Corinth, September 17, 1862.

I. The troops of this army will move with five days' rations, three cooked, in haversacks, short rations of forage for animals, 100 rounds of ammunition per man (40 in cartridge-boxes), and without baggage. They will take only the necessary transportation to carry the forage and spare rations and ammunition and a few hospital stores. The ambulances will accompany the troops.

The spare transportation of each regiment will be sent with the regimental property neatly packed in it to Corinth, under guard of such convalescent sick as will not be able to endure the fatigues of a march, under the charge of a responsible officer, where the entire transportation of the army will be parked defensively in some suitable position convenient to water. The guards of the train will be organized under the direction of Lieut. Col. H. G. Kennett and placed under the command of the senior officer, who will see that they are armed, attend four daily roll-calls, and perform camp guard duty. Necessary tents for their encampment will be taken from the trains of the regiments to which they belong.

*   *   *   *   *   *   *

The sick will be sent, with their proper papers, under suitable care to Corinth, with orders to report there to Surg. A. B. Campbell, medical director, who will see that they are provided for and who will give receipts to the conductors of the sick-trains, as much suffering results from neglect. Regimental and detachment commanders are enjoined to see that the sick of their commands have their proper papers before they go, holding their medical officers responsible therefor.

Fifty rounds spare ammunition per man will be supplied by Lieut. Charles R. Thompson, ordnance officer. Regimental commanders will direct two wagons to report to Lieutenant Thompson at the ordnance depot in Corinth for the purpose of receiving it. A train guard of 15 men will go with the wagons.

*   *   *   *   *   *   *

II. The commanding officer First Brigade will as soon as practicable comply with General Orders, No. 100, paragraph 11, and forward proceedings to the commanding officer of the division.

*   *   *   *   *   *   *

By order of General Rosecrans:

H. G. KENNETT,
Lieutenant-Colonel and Chief of Staff.

———

WAR DEPARTMENT,
Washington, September 18, 1862.

Major-General GRANT, Corinth, Miss.:

General Butler telegraphs me from New Orleans that the enemy is constructing two iron-clad vessels high up the Yazoo River, and thinks they can be reached by a small land force from Memphis or Helena. Consult with General Steele and the commander of the flotilla, and, if possible, destroy these vessels before their completion.

H. W. HALLECK,
General-in-Chief.

HDQRS. FOURTH DIVISION, DIST. OF WEST TENNESSEE,
Bolivar, Tenn., September 18, 1862.

Maj. JOHN A. RAWLINS,
Asst. Adjt. Gen., Dist. of West Tenn., Corinth, Miss.:

MAJOR : I have the honor to report that in pursuance of order, a copy whereof is hereto annexed, the Fourth Division marched from Memphis, Tenn., on the morning of September 6, 1862, at 11 o'clock.

It accordance with the suggestions of Maj. Gen. W. T. Sherman and in conformity with his advice the line of march was so far changed as to leave Shelby to the north—this for the purpose of throwing the head of column so far toward Somerville as should seem advisable to relieve any force which might be at Bolivar. The course of the march was to Raleigh, northeast; thence almost direct east to Green Bottom; thence to Cypress Creek, where, the prevalence of rain rendering the roads impassable for artillery, the column halted one day. At Cypress Creek the column was turned sharply to the north, passing through Hickory Withe, across the Loosahatchie, the bridge over which had been held by an advance of cavalry. On the 10th the march was continued as far as the Muddy. On the same evening a bridge was built across the Muddy to replace that one which had been heretofore destroyed. An advance force was thrown forward to the Hatchie and to Brownsville and the erection of a bridge over the Hatchie was commenced. On the 11th evening, the bridge over the Hatchie being well-nigh completed, orders for the progress to Brownsville were delivered, but countermanded on the receipt of communication, a copy whereof is hereto annexed.*

Upon the morning of September 12 the column marched southwest to Wesley; thence southeast through Dancyville to Bear Creek, where it bivouacked that night.

On the morning of the 13th September marched at daylight to Clear Creek, where it rested, proceeding at 2 p. m. to Bolivar, where it encamped upon Pleasant Run.

The troops have since been disposed so as best to garrison the city and to supply the deficiency in force caused by the march thence of General Ross' command.

Herewith I have the honor to inclose journal of march, showing roads, water, &c., for the guidance of future operations; also report of the force which marched.*

I have the honor to be, major, very respectfully,

[S. A. HURLBUT],
Brigadier-General, Commanding.

BOLIVAR, *September* 18, 1862.

Maj. Gen. U. S. GRANT, *Corinth, Miss.:*

The roads below me are impracticable for artillery from heavy rain, which is still impending.

General Ross' artillery and wagon trains are here in my charge and without forage. In all we have 4,500 animals, and forage must be sent by rail, as heretofore ordered. The country around cannot support this train except for a day or two.

I assume you do not wish my entire command to demonstrate, and

---

* Not found.

shall therefore send five regiments of infantry, one battalion of cavalry, and twelve pieces as soon as the roads will admit. I wish instructions, however, to proceed, and would prefer them by messenger, as there will be ample time before these clay hills are passable.

[S. A. HURLBUT,]
Brigadier-General.

SEPTEMBER 18, 1862.

General GRANT:

I telegraphed to Capt. [Samuel] Simmons last night to send rations to Colonel Mower, Ross having taken 10,000 which I had ordered, thus preventing Mower's movement until his rations arrived. The telegraph dispatch was not delivered until to-day. Have ordered Mower to move down and join Stanley, making arrangements for his rations to follow him. The rain and darkness prevented Stanley from making progress until this morning. We shall all be concentrated at Jacinto by about 2 o'clock and move forward to the vicinity of the Bay Springs road to-night.

W. S. ROSECRANS,
Brigadier-General, U. S. Army.

HDQRS. ENCAMPMENT, ARMY OF THE MISSISSIPPI,
September 18, 1862.

Maj. Gen. U. S. GRANT,
    Commanding District West Tennessee:

GENERAL: Your dispatch received. General Stanley's division arrived after dark, having been detained by falling in the rear of Ross through fault of guide. Our cavalry 6 miles this side of Barnett's; Hamilton's First Brigade 8, Second Brigade 9 miles this side; Stanley near Davenport's Mills. We shall move as early as practicable, say 4.30 o'clock a. m. This will give 20 miles march for Stanley's division to Iuka. Shall not therefore be in before 1 or 2 o'clock, but when we come in will endeavor to do it strongly. Troops are in good order. Should there be any reason to believe the enemy not in Iuka you will advise us by vedette line, which will follow headquarters at short intervals. Colonel Mizner will establish scouts south and east of us. Everything so far goes to show that their movement has taken place on the road from Marietta that passes above Bay Springs, which he will cause to be examined early to-morrow morning, and the reconnaissance will extend, if practicable, over on to Fulton and Iuka roads.

W. S. ROSECRANS,
Brigadier-General, U. S. Army.

BURNSVILLE, MISS., *September* 19, 1862.

General H. W. HALLECK, *General-in-Chief:*

Your dispatch directing that Price should not be permitted to get into Tennessee is just received. My forces are now here. Enemy's pickets and ours within a few hundred yards. General Rosecrans is south of the enemy moving on him, while Ord attacks from the west. Corinth is well watched at a long distance out, and unless the approach of a large force on that place should call us back I think it will be impossible for Price to get into Tennessee. I will do all in my power to prevent such a catastrophe.

U. S. GRANT,
Major-General, Commanding.

BURNSVILLE, MISS., *September* 19—7.35 p. m.,
Via Cairo, Ill., September 20, 1862.

Maj. Gen. H. W. HALLECK, *General-in-Chief:*

Before leaving Corinth I instructed General Hurlbut at Bolivar to make a great fuss at preparing for a move, and to let word leak out that he expected large re-enforcements there and at Memphis, when a combined movement would be made on Grenada and the Yazoo to destroy boats on that river. The object of this is obvious, but was before your dispatch for this very move to be made real.

U. S. GRANT,
Major-General.

HEADQUARTERS FOURTH DIVISION,
September 19, 1862.

Brig. Gen. J. G. LAUMAN:

GENERAL: In obedience to telegraphic orders from Major-General Grant you will march to-morrow toward Grand Junction. You will make camp below Middleburg (say 12 to 14 miles from here), and push your cavalry forward as far as possible toward Davis' Mill.

It is believed that a force, 2,000 or 3,000, is camped on Wolf River, building a railroad bridge across that stream.

If advisable—that is, safe—destroy that bridge and crush the head of column there.

Give out that this command is about to move, being heavily re-enforced from Columbus; that Sherman, from Memphis, and Steele, from Helena, on the west, are concentrating toward Grenada.

Feel the enemy strongly and ascertain their strength. If they retreat or disperse in front of you destroy the bridge. If they prove too strong to attack safely send me word or draw back if danger is imminent. I need not say to you that the most perfect discipline must be observed and the command in readiness for action at a moment's notice. The movement is a mere demonstration, never letting go your safe return to Bolivar, unless the weakness of the enemy or some favorable circumstances make it advisable to attack in reality.

Much is left to your discretion, and in that I confide.

[S. A. HURLBUT,]
Brigadier-General.

BOLIVAR, TENN., *September* 19, 1862.

Maj. Gen. U. S. GRANT, *Corinth:*

I move Lauman's brigade—five regiments of infantry, twelve pieces of artillery, and two battalions of Second Illinois Cavalry—toward Grand Junction to-morrow morning, with instructions not to engage unless the advantage is on our side; but if an opening occurs to break in and destroy bridge at Davis' Mill. I hold the other brigade to support them if overmatched.

[S. A. HURLBUT,]
Brigadier-General.

HEADQUARTERS FIFTH DIVISION,
Memphis, September 19, 1862.

Brig. Gen. FRED. STEELE, *Helena, Ark.*:

DEAR GENERAL: I take the liberty of inclosing a tracing of a map compiled at my headquarters, which I think is more accurate than any published chart.* I do it to illustrate the importance of a movement of which I wrote you a few days since. Senatobia has been the headquarters of Jackson, who has now gone north and is operating with Armstrong's cavalry about Bolivar. There are few or no troops there now. I caused the new railroad bridge on Coldwater, just above Senatobia, to be effectually broken and destroyed, with the saw-mill that yielded the material, so it cannot be repaired in three months. If you strike in and destroy that at Panola this road is useless for this whole campaign.

Breckinridge has gone over the Central road with his division. That road is in good condition up to Wolf River, at Davis' Mill, 7 miles south of Grand Junction. I think they are engaged in repairing that bridge, which would put them up to Bolivar. Bolivar is of importance, as it covers the railroad back for Grant. Hurlbut's division has gone there from here, leaving me short-handed for building a fort, holding a town, and making expeditions. The breaking of that road (the Central) will have a material effect on the campaign. It would cut off rapid communication with the south from Breckinridge and also prevent his being re-enforced by Van Dorn. I have made close inquiries and find the section from Abbeville to Spring Dale full of high and difficult trestles, which I have indicated on the map. I did propose to General Grant and he to Halleck the breaking of that entire section by a joint expedition from here and Helena; but since that time my force is reduced one-half, and I hardly feel justified in attempting so much, when I know there is a strong force abreast of me anxious to recapture Memphis, which would be as serious to you as to me. My fort is so far progressed that I feel no uneasiness about holding Memphis; but it may be that instead of going to Kentucky, as Breckinridge would, he may linger in the neighborhood until the released prisoners of war join him.

I mention all these points to show you how important it is that these railroads should be interrupted, and as soon as possible.

I am, with great respect, your obedient servant,
W. T. SHERMAN,
Major-General, Commanding.

[SEPTEMBER 19, 1862.]

COMMANDING OFFICER CONFEDERATE FORCES NEAR IUKA:

GENERAL: Inclosed find communication from General Ord and copy of dispatch. The dispatch is reliable. I await your reply to General Ord's suggestion.

I have the honor to be, general, your obedient servant,
M. D. LEGGETT,
Colonel, Commanding Advance.

[Inclosure.]

12 A. M., 19TH.

Colonel LEGGETT:

Can you not get the inclosed dispatch from Cairo to the general commanding the enemy in front? I think this battle decides the war finally,

---
* Not found.

and that upon being satisfied of its truth General Price or whoever commands here will avoid useless bloodshed and lay down his arms.

There is not the slightest doubt of the truth of the dispatch in my
mind.

This by permission of General Grant.

Yours,

E. O. C. ORD,
Major-General, Volunteers.

[Sub-inclosure.]

HEADQUARTERS ARMY OF THE TENNESSEE,
In the Field, September 18, 1862.

Major-General ORD,
Commanding Left Wing:

Following dispatch just received, which you will read early in the
morning to the troops under your command:

CAIRO, September 18, 1862.

General GRANT:

The reports from Washington this evening contain intelligence of general engagement on 16th near Sharpsburg, between rebel army under General Lee and Union
forces.   Hotly contested all day and renewed on morning of 17th, rebels having been
re-enforced during the night by Jackson's army and Union army by 30,000 men from
Washington, and entire force on both sides engaged until 4 p. m., at which time Hooker
gained position, flanked rebels, and threw them into disorder.

Longstreet and his entire division prisoners.   General Hill killed.   Entire rebel
army of Virginia destroyed, Burnside having reoccupied Harper's Ferry and cut off
retreat.

General Hooker slightly wounded.   Action very sanguinary.   Requisitions for surgeons and hospital supplies larger than ever before.

Latest advices say entire rebel army must be captured or killed, as Potomac is rising
and our forces pressing the enemy continually.

J. C. VAN DUZER,
Superintendent.

By command of Major-General Grant:

WM. S. HILLYER,
Colonel and Aide-de-Camp.

HEADQUARTERS CAVALRY ADVANCE,
In the Field, September 19, 1862.

Colonel LEGGETT,
Commanding United States Cavalry:

COLONEL: The commanding officer of the Confederate forces near
Iuka directs me to inform General Ord through you that he does not
credit the dispatches from Cairo which the latter has so kindly forwarded
to him, and that if the facts were as stated in those dispatches they
would only move him and his soldiers to greater exertions in behalf of
their country, and that neither he nor they will ever lay down their
arms—as humanely suggested by General Ord—until the independence
of the Confederate States shall have been acknowledged by the United
States.

I am, very respectfully, your obedient servant,

——— ———,
Colonel, Commanding Cavalry.

BOLIVAR, TENN., *September* 20, 1862.

Brig. Gen. JOHN A. LOGAN, *Jackson, Tenn.:*

I have this morning moved Lauman, with five regiments, twelve pieces of artillery, and 400 cavalry, toward Grand Junction. They will either find and fight the enemy or the rebels will pass our flank or disperse. I want the wagon road to Jackson put in order. Will you see to it in your district?

If they pass us in force it will be downstream toward Brownsville.

[S. A. HURLBUT,]
Brigadier-General.

BOLIVAR, *September* 21, 1862—11 a. m.

Maj. JOHN A. RAWLINS,
    Assistant Adjutant-General:

General Lauman and command 5 miles from Grand Junction. Cavalry advanced as far as Grand Junction, finding no enemy, but best information that portion of force lately in vicinity had left in direction of Corinth, leaving about 2,500 at Davis' Mill. Lauman has orders to attack, if sure of the results, and destroy Davis' Mill and will probably do so this night or to-morrow morning.

I learn from scouts that Villepigue and Jackson's cavalry left day before yesterday for east, probably Corinth. Force at Davis' Mill under command of General Bowen.

S. A. HURLBUT,
Brigadier-General.

BOLIVAR, *September* 21, 1862.

General GRANT:

General Lauman sends me a verbal message by an orderly that the enemy are flanking him on the left, and is rapidly falling back. He is 6 miles below. Shall I move the rest of the division out or wait for him to come in? Stores here are of great value, and I dislike to leave them without guard. Answer at once.

S. A. HURLBUT,
Brigadier-General.

BOLIVAR, *September* 21, 1862.

General GRANT:

General Lauman is attacked 10 miles below here, as I learn by orderly sent in by Colonel Noble with verbal message. I have five regiments here. Shall I move them from this post? Answer at once.

S. A. HURLBUT.

BOLIVAR, *September* 21, 1862.

General GRANT:

General Lauman's command has returned all safe. The cavalry and some infantry followed close up as far as Van Buren, where a few well-directed shots scattered them. Further particulars will be sent by mail to-morrow.

S. A. HURLBUT,
Brigadier-General.

SPECIAL ORDERS, }   HDQRS. DISTRICT OF WEST TENNESSEE,
     No. 199.   }   Corinth, Miss., September 21, 1862.

*   *   *   *   *   *   *

III. Brig. Gen. Thomas J. McKean is hereby assigned to the command of the Sixth Division, Army of the Tennessee.

*   *   *   *   *   *   *

By order of Maj. Gen. U. S. Grant:

JNO. A. RAWLINS,
Assistant Adjutant-General.

GRANT'S HEADQUARTERS,
Near Corinth, Miss., September 22, 1862—10.40 a. m.
General H. W. HALLECK:

Will try to set an expedition on foot for the destruction of rebel boats on the Yazoo. Do I understand that I am to have the co-operation of Steele's forces—cavalry particularly ?

U. S. GRANT,
Major-General, Commanding.

GRANT'S HEADQUARTERS,
Near Corinth, Miss., September 22, 1862.
General H. W. HALLECK, *General-in-Chief:*

I would respectfully request that some of the new regiments now organizing be sent to this command. They could be of great service in guarding railroad and posts that must be occupied, and where they would be behind breastworks. At Memphis one regiment could be well employed, without arms, in manning the siege guns.

U. S. GRANT,
Major-General, Commanding.

BOLIVAR, *September* 22, 1862.
Major-General GRANT :

My cavalry pickets have been to the creek near Van Buren, 8 miles south, and report the camp of rebels broken up. They are supposed to have returned. They were 10,000 strong, as reported. Their precise course not known; went off in three bodies. It would be well to look closely to the railroad to-night. I have every precaution taken against a flank attack and think I am too strong in front. In the morning early I shall report further and ask orders if report is favorable to move down.

S. A. HURLBUT,
Brigadier-General.

BOLIVAR, *September* 22, 1862.
Major-General GRANT :

On yesterday morning at 2 a. m. the Confederate forces in three columns moved out from Davis' Mill—about twenty regiments of infantry, five batteries of artillery, and about 1,000 cavalry. They followed Lauman up to Middleburg, 9 miles from here, and ran trains up there, I think, last night. Van Dorn, Villepigue, Bowen, Rust, and Colonel Helm are along. They may move back to Wolf River for water, but I expect an attack. They started with one day's rations. This information from an intelligent deserter. There is fine water near Van Buren, about 8 miles, and I expect them to camp there to-day. If they do not fall back to Davis' Mill they will of course attack.

I desire orders. I shall of course hold this place, unless ordered to the contrary, to the last extremity. The force, as reported, is very heavy. Breckinridge, with one of his brigades, has gone to Chattanooga.

> HURLBUT,
> *General.*

> NEAR CORINTH, MISS.,
> *Via Cairo, Ill., September 22, 1862.*

Major-General HALLECK:

Bolivar is now threatened with an attack from Villepigue, a portion of Breckinridge's forces, and possibly some other troops. They marched in three columns from Davis' Mill, about 7 miles south of Grand Junction, and will reach to-day, about 8 miles south of Bolivar. They have twenty regiments infantry, 1,000 cavalry, and five batteries artillery. Hurlbut will be so re-enforced to-night as to hold the place if attacked, and to take the initiative if threatened and not attacked. I shall go to Jackson to-morrow, and Bolivar, if necessary.

> U. S. GRANT,
> *Major-General.*

> BOLIVAR, *September* 22, 1862.

General GRANT:

My patrols advise me that the enemy is concentrating in large force 8 miles on the Grand Junction road. I think they will attack early in the morning:

> S. A. HURLBUT,
> *Brigadier-General.*

> JACINTO, *September* 22, 1862, VIA RIENZI.
> (Received September 22.)

General GRANT:

GENERAL: We arrived here to-night. Chickasaw* escaped from the rebels at Bay Springs and rejoined us to-night. He heard one lieutenant say to another that they were going to the place they came from, either Baldwyn, Guntown, or Tupelo. The prisoners were taken to the rear on the morning to be out of the way in the fight which they were told was to come off next day. The train was started out at 3 a. m., and Price went back with a part of the advance guard. When they found out that they were retreating some of the officers said, "Now we have all these forces up here, if Breckinridge and Van Dorn don't attack Memphis we will throw up our commissions."

> W. S. ROSECRANS,
> *Major-General, Commanding.*

---

* L. H. Naron, a scout.

HEADQUARTERS FIFTH DIVISION,
Memphis, September 22, 1862.

Maj. JOHN A. RAWLINS, *Assistant Adjutant-General:*

SIR: Nothing whatever of interest has occurred here since my last. According to the most reliable information up to Wednesday last Breckinridge was at Davis' Mill repairing the railroad and Villepigue at Coldwater. The guerrillas are either getting tired of their vocation or are doing their cause more harm than ours.

Things in town move along quietly and harmoniously, so far as appearances go, and all the world is awaiting news from Maryland, Kentucky, and your quarter. With the defenses of Memphis as now guarded a direct assault is not apprehended; but to be of use I ought to have men enough to operate inland. I think Steele will strike at Grenada, and the quicker we break effectually all railroads the better. We cannot use railroads without having detached guards, and the sooner both belligerents come down to common roads the better. I have a letter from Genera. Steele, at Helena, from which I infer he is also waiting the issue of events above.

I write merely to assure the general that all is well here.

I am, &c.,

W. T. SHERMAN,
Major-General, Commanding.

———

WAR DEPARTMENT,
Washington, September 23, 1862—2.30 p. m.

Maj. Gen. U. S. GRANT, *Corinth, Miss.:*

Arrange with General Curtis at Saint Louis in regard to Steele's cooperation. New troops will be sent you as soon as they can be spared.

H. W. HALLECK,
General-in-Chief.

———

JACINTO, *September* 23, 1862—3 p. m.

Major-General GRANT:

Information shows that only two regiments of Price's troops had reached the railroad last evening. Rear guard at least staid at Bay Springs yesterday. Country all clear and quiet to 4 miles below Blackland and west to the Hatchie. Shall put a brigade of Stanley's division at Rienzi to-morrow. Am getting full information of the routes by which we should march down. Anxiously await news from you.

O, that Corinth could be left to take care of itself!

W. S. ROSECRANS,
Major-General.

———

BOLIVAR, *September* 23, 1862.

Maj. Gen. U. S. GRANT:

Two loads of Ross' troops have come; the others will not be in before night. The enemy have unquestionably, from all reports, fallen back to Davis' Mill, about 10,000 strong. Cavalry are out in pursuit.

I could [not?] move this morning because Ross' troops did not arrive and the enemy have a day's start. Do you wish me to move on La Grange and Davis' Mill with my own division? My stock is out of forage, and I must send this afternoon for a supply into the country.

S. A. HURLBUT,
Brigadier-General.

TRENTON, *September* 23, 1862.

Maj. JOHN A. RAWLINS,
　　U. S. Grant's Headquarters:

A deserter from the Seventh Kentucky, under Breckinridge, [who] came in here this morning, is a man I know. He left Davis' Mill, on Coldwater, Friday morning. Breckinridge was then there with 8,000. Two of the Kentucky regiments had been ordered south, their time being out, and the officers were afraid that they would desert if they came north. He says they were going to Tennessee and Kentucky to join Bragg, there was a large force of conscripts and released prisoners at Jackson when they left that place, and that they had been furloughed sixty days. About 100 left with this man; several have come in. He reports Jackson's cavalry between Somerville and Memphis, and that they caught several of his party.

G. M. DODGE,
Brigadier-General.

HEADQUARTERS DISTRICT OF WEST TENNESSEE,
Jackson, Tenn., September 24, 1862.

General H. W. HALLECK, *Washington, D. C.:*

Your dispatch of the 23d is received. The enemy being driven from his position in front of Bolivar by the rapid return of troops drawn from there to re-enforce Corinth, and everything now promising quiet in our front for a short time, I shall go to Saint Louis in person to confer with General Curtis.

To communicate rapidly with the gunboat fleet and General Sherman at Memphis I would have to visit Columbus, and to go to Saint Louis will keep me away but little, if any, longer from my post than if I should not go. It will also save the possibility of my plan leaking out through the telegraph offices on the route. Another reason for my going is the fact that for several weeks my health has not been good, and although improving for the last few days, I feel that the trip will be of benefit to me. Hoping my course will meet with your approval, &c.,

U. S. GRANT,
Major-General.

SEPTEMBER 24, 1862.

General MCARTHUR:

The enemy who were before Bolivar are reported to have fallen back. Will you please organize all your available cavalry for a scout down to Hatchie to feel if the enemy are approaching Middleton or Pocahontas or are making any attempt to cross the Hatchie and approach the railroad north of us? Send word to commander at Chewalla to be on the alert.

E. O. C. ORD,
Major-General, Volunteers.

HEADQUARTERS FIFTH DIVISION,
Memphis, September 24, 1862.

Col. C. C. WALCUTT,
　　Forty-sixth Ohio Volunteers:

SIR: The object of the expedition you have been detailed for is to visit the town of Randolph, where yesterday the packet Eugene was fired on by a party of guerrillas. Acts of this kind must be promptly punished, and it is almost impossible to reach the actors, for they come from the interior and depart as soon as the mischief is done. But the interest and well-being of the country demands that all such attacks should be followed by a punishment that will tend to prevent a repetition.

Two boats will be placed at your disposal, one, the Eugene, to proceed on the regular trip to Saint Louis when you are done with her, and the other, a chartered boat, wholly at your service. Embark on the Eugene two of your companies and on the chartered boat the remainder of your command, with a section of rifled guns that will be sent to the levee by Major Taylor. Get off by 5 or 6 p. m. at furthest and move up to this bend and make a landing at Cuba Landing; then send the Eugene ahead, moving, under steam without landing, to Fort Pillow and back, till she meets you, following more slowly. You should both be ready to reach Randolph at daybreak or a little before. I think the attack on the Eugene was by a small force of guerrillas from Loosahatchie, who by this time have gone back, and therefore that you will find no one at Randolph; in which case you will destroy the place, leaving one house to mark the place. Let the people know and feel that we deeply deplore the necessity of such destruction, but we must protect ourselves and the boats which are really carrying stores and merchandise for the benefit of secession families, whose fathers and brothers are in arms against us. If any extraordinary case presents itself to your consideration you may spare more than one house; but let the place feel that all such acts of cowardly firing upon boats filled with women and children and merchandise must be severely punished.

It is barely possible that the army of Breckinridge, last heard from at Davis' Mill, designs to reach the Mississippi River at Randolph, in which event the party there yesterday may have been an advance guard. If this be so the Eugene will discover the fact, for they will have artillery; then you should be very careful, as your force would be inadequate; but if the Eugene pass Randolph and return to meet you it is certain that it is a guerrilla raid, when you can safely proceed. Do not land at an accustomed place, but consult with captains and pilots. Approach the shore below the landing, get a couple of companies over as skirmishers, and move rapidly into Randolph. Of course the inhabitants will be all gone, or will be expecting you and be prepared for anything. Keep your men in the reach of your voice, and do your work systematically. Let your quartermaster take a minute account of every house or piece of property destroyed under this order, with the names of owners if possible. If all is clear, you can send parties inland toward Covington, but not over 5 miles.

When done you can take aboard your boat the men from the Eugene and let her proceed on her voyage. If you find men whom you suspect of guilt bring them in, but no women or children. Also you may capture any slaves, horses, or mules belonging to known rebels.

Yours, &c.,

W. T. SHERMAN,
Major-General, Commanding.

COLUMBUS, *September* 24, 1862.

Major-General GRANT:

Fort Pillow is now unoccupied by Federal troops, and there is no gunboat there. You ordered all ordnance and ordnance stores to be moved, and I supposed until to-day that it had been done under the

directio n of Colonel Bissell.   I am just informed that there are still at
the fort several guns spiked—I know not how well—and gun-carriages.
There are many guerrillas in that section of Tennessee; they will probably take possession of the fort, and by mounting the guns would give
our transports trouble.   I think Commodore Davis would be willing to
guard it and the crossings of the rebels with a gunboat.   I am informed
that large amounts of contraband goods are shipped from Saint Louis
for points in the vicinity of Fort Pillow.

I. F. QUINBY,
Brigadier-General.

GENERAL ORDERS, }   HDQRS. DISTRICT OF WEST TENNESSEE,
   No. 83.   }   *Corinth, Miss., September* 24, 1862.

The District of West Tennessee will, until otherwise directed, be divided into four divisions, as follows:

I. The First Division, commanded by Maj. Gen. W. T. Sherman, wil!
embrace all the territory south of the Hatchie and west of Bolivar occupied by our troops; headquarters at Memphis.

II. The Second Division will embrace all territory south of the Kentucky line and to the Hatchie on the west and Bethel Station on the
east, including Bolivar, south of the Hatchie, Maj. Gen. E. O. C. Ord
commanding.   It will be the duty of the commanding officer of the Second Division to guard all the railroads within his district.   Headquarters will be at Jackson or Bolivar, at the option of the commander.

III. The Third Division, Maj. Gen. W. S. Rosecrans commanding,
will embrace all the territory now occupied by the Army of the Mississippi and by the forces at present commanded by Major-General Ord;
headquarters at Corinth, Miss.   It will be the duty of this division to
guard the railroad south from Bethel from Chewalla so far as the country is occupied by our troops.

IV. The Fourth Division, Brig. Gen. I. F. Quinby commanding, will
be composed of what are now known as the Districts of Cairo and of
the Mississippi, including Forts Henry and Donelson, and exclusive of
that portion lying in the State of Tennessee and along the line of the
railroads.

By command of Maj. Gen. U. S. Grant:

JNO. A. RAWLINS,
Assistant Adjutant-General.

SPECIAL ORDERS, }   HEADQUARTERS FIFTH DIVISION,
   No. 250.   }   *Memphis, September* 24, 1862.

Col. J. A. McDowell will prepare a regiment of infantry at 4 p. m.
this day.   He will cause it to be thoroughly inspected, to see that each
man is provided with arms, ammunition (100 rounds), haversacks, canteens, &c.

The quartermaster, Captain Fitch, will charter a good steamboat,
capable of carrying 500 men and two field pieces, to be in service three
days, and also engage passage on this afternoon's packet for 100 men
as far up as Fort Pillow, to be returned by the chartered boat.

Major Taylor, chief of artillery, will have a good section of rifled guns,
with their due proportion of horses and men, at the levee at 2 o'clock
p. m. to embark on the chartered boat.

By order of Maj. Gen. W. T. Sherman:

J. H. HAMMOND,
Assistant Adjutant-General.

COLUMBUS, KY., *September* 24, 1862.

Major-General HALLECK:

I wish to order General Quinby into the field, but before going he says a short leave of absence is necessary to arrange for his family. May I give it?

U. S. GRANT,
Major-General.

WAR DEPARTMENT, *Washington, September* 25, 1862.

Major-General GRANT, *Corinth, Miss.*:

Do as you deem best with General Quinby.

What of Price's army? Do you hear anything from Nashville or Buell's army?

H. W. HALLECK,
General-in-Chief.

SAINT LOUIS, MO., *September* 25, 1862.

Maj. Gen. H. W. HALLECK, *General-in-Chief:*

I do not hear a word from Buell's army. Price was defeated from going east of the Tennessee, but I understand that Breckinridge has gone by way of Mobile and Chattanooga. The rebels came up to within 8 miles of Bolivar, but finding the place so strongly re-enforced fell back to Davis' Mill first, and finding our cavalry in such hot pursuit left there for farther south in great haste. I wrote from Jackson the object of my coming to Saint Louis. Will leave in the morning.

U. S. GRANT,
Major-General.

BOLIVAR, TENN., *September* 25, 1862.

Maj. Gen. U. S. GRANT, *Corinth, Miss.*:

A negro just in from near Grand Junction reports hearing his master say that the enemy have received heavy re-enforcements from Holly Springs and other points in Mississippi, and will move this morning to cut the railroad between Corinth and this place and then attack here. He has evidently heard this. The information is vague as to the proposed point of attack on the road, but the probabilities look toward some point east of Jackson.

There were 300 irregular cavalry in Somerville yesterday.

[S. A. HURLBUT,]
Brigadier-General.

HEADQUARTERS, *Bolivar, September* 25, 1862.

Major-General GRANT:

A large body of cavalry, estimated by the citizens at 2,000 (probably 1,000), passed to-day by Anderson's Mill east, inquiring for Simpson's Ferry, on the Hatchie, half way between Van Buren and here. The force was followed up by my cavalry patrol, who agree that it is a large body of men. I am of the opinion an attack is designed on the railroad, and, if they have taken the direction designated, somewhere in the neighborhood of Bethel or perhaps Purdy. They had four days' rations.

S. A. HURLBUT,
Brigadier-General.

SAINT LOUIS, *September* 25, 1862—10.30 a. m.

Maj. Gen. E. O. C. ORD:

General Hurlbut telegraphs me that rebels are strongly re-enforced and threaten him. Watch in that direction, and, if necessary, re-enforce him all you can. Communicate with General Rosecrans also.

U. S. GRANT,
Major-General.

SAINT LOUIS, *September* 25, 1862.

General STEPHEN A. HURLBUT, *Bolivar, Tenn.* :

I have communicated to Ord and Rosecrans the substance of your telegram, and instructed that you be re-enforced to any extent that may be necessary. Communicate with Ord until my return.

U. S. GRANT,
Major-General.

CORINTH, *September* 26, 1862.

Maj. Gen. H. W. HALLECK,
Commander-in-Chief, Washington, D. C. :

MY DEAR GENERAL: I have received and accepted the appointment of major-general of volunteers, for "meritorious services in Western Virginia," to date from the 17th of September, 1862.

A feeling of shame and indignation came over me as I wrote the acceptance. If fighting successful battles having important results; if successfully defending a mountainous country against an active and powerful foe; if pacifying and restoring law and order to a vast region with 300 miles of mountain frontier, and the successful administration of a department deserved anything from the hands of the Government it deserved my promotion from the date of the close of those services crowned with success. But what do I find? Why, I find myself promoted junior to men who have not rendered a tithe of the services nor had a tithe of the success. I find myself ordered from the command of an army whose confidence I possess—a separate army in the field—to go and take subordinate position in a new and unformed one, where Buell, Granger, Gilbert, Schenck, Lew. Wallace, Tom Crittenden, and Bully Nelson are my seniors.

Were it not a crisis for the country I would not trouble you to intercede in my behalf but would at once resign. As it is a crisis I beg you to intercede for me, that some measure of justice may be done me.

If I have deserved anything for my services in Western Virginia my rank should date from the close of those services, and that is what I ask in the name of justice. I know and the country knows the strength of this demand. I trust it may seem to the administration, as to me, that no statesman or government ever gains by partiality and injustice.

My dear general, amid the great cares and anxieties of your position it is a tax to read a personal letter, but be assured I shall not fail to appreciate and repay, sooner or later, any care or intervention of yours in this matter. I would be most happy to write you, but feel fearful it would tax your time.

W. S. ROSECRANS,
Brigadier-General, U. S. Army, and Major-General, Volunteers.

GENERAL ORDERS, }   HDQRS. DISTRICT OF WEST TENNESSEE,
No. 84.   }   Corinth, Miss., September 26, 1862.

From and after this date the headquarters of the District of West Tennessee will be at Jackson, Tenn., where all reports and returns required by Army Regulations and existing orders will be made.

By order of Maj. Gen. U. S. Grant:

JNO. A. RAWLINS,
Assistant Adjutant-General.

———

GENERAL ORDERS, }   HDQRS. ARMY OF THE MISSISSIPPI,
No. 128.   }   Corinth, September 26, 1862.

I. In compliance with General Orders, No. 83, Paragraph III, Headquarters District of West Tennessee, Corinth, Miss., September 24, 1862, the undersigned hereby assumes command of the third division of the district, which includes all the territory now occupied by the Army of the Mississippi and by the forces at present commanded by Major General Ord.

II. All reports and returns required by Army Regulations and existing orders will be made to these headquarters.

W. S. ROSECRANS,
Major-General, Commanding.

———

BOLIVAR, *September* 27, 1862.
Maj. Gen. U. S. GRANT:

From the best information I can get the forces of the enemy encamped at Davis' Mill, south of Grand Junction, have gone eastward.

S. A. HURLBUT,
Major-General.

———

SPECIAL ORDERS, }   HEADQUARTERS FIFTH DIVISION,
No. 254.   }   Memphis, September 27, 1862.

Whereas many families of known rebels and of Confederates in arms against us having been permitted to reside in peace and comfort in Memphis, and whereas the Confederate authorities either sanction or permit the firing on unarmed boats carrying passengers and goods for the use and benefit of the inhabitants of Memphis, it is ordered that for every boat so fired on ten families must be expelled from Memphis.

The provost-marshal will extend the list already prepared so as to have on it at least thirty names, and on every occasion when a boat is fired on will draw by lot ten names, who will be forthwith notified and allowed three days to remove to a distance of 25 miles from Memphis.

By order of Maj. Gen. W. T. Sherman:

J. H. HAMMOND,
Assistant Adjutant-General.

———

COLUMBUS, KY., *September* 28, 1862.
Maj. Gen. H. W. HALLECK, *General-in-Chief:*

To make a move on the Yazoo River promise success it will be necessary to have some of the new regiments at Memphis to take the place of

Sherman's division. I will want Sherman's division and some of my command at Bolivar to move on Grenada, to attract attention in that direction, while Steele moves across below, from a point not yet determined upon, to do the work designed. Can you send the new troops?

U. S. GRANT,
Major-General.

CORINTH, *September* 28, 1862.

Major-General GRANT, *Columbus :*

Scouts from General McKean confirm my telegraph of Price's movement to Ripley. The seminary building was engaged for his headquarters.

I shall move all Stanley's division to Rienzi, and from thence I think to Kossuth, unless you have views differing from mine.

W. S. ROSECRANS,
Major-General.

STEAM-RAM SWITZERLAND,
Cairo, Ill., September 28, 1862.

Hon. E. M. STANTON,
Secretary of War :

I have the honor to call your attention again to a matter that has before been presented to your notice, and that, in my opinion, is of very grave importance to the public interest, viz : The providing without delay an iron-clad fleet of rams to meet the enemy's new fleet that without doubt will appear upon these waters with the next flood. You are aware of the frail nature of the fleet of wooden boats that I have the honor at present to command. It is no detraction from the eminent services that they have rendered the country to say that it was mainly attributable to the ignorance of the enemy as to their strength and to the bold audacity of their former commander. There seems no room to doubt that the enemy are now busily engaged in building a new fleet of formidable rams and gunboats up the Yazoo River and its tributaries, besides what they may be doing up the Arkansas and White Rivers, with the evident purpose of resuming possession of the Mississippi River with the rise of the water in the winter or spring. The reports to this effect are so constant and uniform that it does seem to me the part of prudence to take warning and make suitable provision while there is yet time to meet the probable emergency. It is a fact that few have the presumption now to dispute that our flat-bottomed slow gunboats are in no way equal to contend against the formidable rams and gunboats that the enemy have heretofore produced and are likely to again bring against us. I trust that it will be regarded as no disparagement to the brave officers and men of the gunboats, nor of the former valuable services of the boats themselves, to say that the latter are in no way suitable to meet the new order of things soon to be produced. It is in view of these, to me, plain facts that I take the liberty of urging upon your notice again the great importance of providing one or more boats of strength and speed equal at least to what we know the enemy have heretofore produced and are capable of reproducing. The disastrous and most mortifying raid of the Arkansas should not soon be forgotten. Recent developments seem to show conclusively that her final destruction was partially, at least, owing to the severe shock she received from the Queen of the West, which disarranged her engine and caused her machinery to break down. If at the time of that action the Queen had been iron-clad, so that she could with partial impunity have for ten minutes longer endured the terrific fire she was exposed to, the Arkansas would never again have left her anchorage.

I trust that you will excuse me for the liberty of thus addressing you, and in apology can only say that the question seems to me of such grave importance, the preparation so far as I can see so small to meet it, that I have felt emboldened, from my knowledge of your energy to provide to meet emergencies, to address you this letter.

With sentiments of highest esteem and unlimited confidence, I remain, very respectfully, your obedient servant,

ALFRED W. ELLET,
Colonel, Commanding Ram Fleet.

CORINTH, *September* 29, 1862.

Major RAWLINS,
Assistant Adjutant-General :

I have not reported to the major-general commanding the details of the Pocahontas capture, because full reports are not in yet. All but about 40 of our men have come in; some 75 or 80 horses and about as many carbines. The rebels are reported to have burned the Pocahontas Bridge completely and left some horses on this side. Eight companies of Third Michigan Cavalry are out there now, and we shall have reports in soon. Stanley will be in Rienzi to-day. Our scouts surprised and routed a party of shot-gun cavalry 5 miles from Ruckersville yesterday. Nothing but general report of Price moving west or south.

W. S. ROSECRANS,
Major-General.

SPECIAL ORDERS, }   HDQRS. DISTRICT OF WEST TENNESSEE,
No. 206.   }   *Jackson, Tenn., September* 29, 1862.

*   *   *   *   *   *   *

III. Brig. Gen. G. M. Dodge is hereby assigned to the command of the Fourth Division, District of West Tennessee, headquarters at Columbus, Ky., during the temporary absence of Brig. Gen. I. F. Quinby.

*   *   *   *   *   *   *

By order of Maj. Gen. U. S. Grant:

JNO. A. RAWLINS,
Assistant Adjutant-General.

SPECIAL ORDERS, }   HEADQUARTERS FIFTH DIVISION,
No. 255.   }   *Memphis, September* 29, 1862.

Brigadier-General Denver will detach one regiment of his brigade and a section of artillery to proceed by river to Randolph and bring away the six guns reported as being at that point abandoned by the rebels. These guns will be either brought away or rolled into deep water of the river.

The officers in command of this detachment will attack any body of guerrillas found at that place or in the neighborhood. The assistant quartermaster, Captain Fitch, will provide a suitable steamboat for the expedition.

By order of Maj. Gen. W. T. Sherman:

J. H. HAMMOND,
Assistant Adjutant-General.

CORINTH, MISS., *September* 30, 1862.

Major-General HALLECK, *General-in-Chief:*

Price is now at Ripley, Van Dorn at Somerville, and Villepigue at Salem. It looks as if Van Dorn was trying to effect a lodgment on the Mississippi above Memphis. Threatened at all other points, I cannot send out forces to drive him away. If Helena troops could now be sent across the river I think they would meet with no difficulty in getting to Grenada, and perhaps down on to the Yazoo.

U. S. GRANT,
Major-General.

CORINTH, *September* 30, 1862.

Major-General GRANT:

News in this a. m. No signs of the enemy at Hatchie Crossing yesterday. Rumors continue to come, as the following from Hamilton: A citizen scout just in says he saw a secesh soldier whom he knew who says Price, Van Dorn, and Breckinridge had effected a junction and would go to Tennessee through Purdy. Stanley says citizen scouts report Price from Ripley, and would rest in Ripley; don't know where he would go from thence. My reasons for proposing to put Stanley at or near Kossuth is that he would cover all the Hatchie crossings, except heavy forces as far as Pocahontas. Hamilton would then move at least one brigade from Rienzi. Look out from southeast from Bolivar.

W. S. ROSECRANS,
Major-General.

BOLIVAR, TENN., *September* 30, 1862.

Major-General GRANT:

My best information is that with the exception of a strong advance guard at Davis' Mill a large portion of the enemy have gone east below Saulsbury. I think Van Dorn is in camp below La Grange, say at Ammon's Bridge, and so down Wolf River to Moscow, with a cavalry advance guard near Somerville. It would be well to look to the bridge partly constructed by me over the Hatchie, 7 miles south of Brownsville. My cavalry patrols go daily within 10 miles of Somerville, but report no force but guerrillas.

S. A. HURLBUT,
Major-General.

HDQRS. FIFTH DIVISION, ARMY OF THE TENNESSEE,
Memphis, September 30, 1862.

Maj. Gen. U. S. GRANT,
Commanding Department of the Tennessee,
(Care of General Quinby, Columbus, Ky.):

DEAR GENERAL: Yours of the 27th is this moment received.* I am not in possession of authentic data as to the exact location of the enemy's fleet of boats in the Yazoo or the road leading thereto. I am certain, however, that General Steele and Captains Phelps and Gwin, of the Navy, know all about it. My study has been mostly confined to the country between this and Grenada. I feel certain that the two railroads that branch from Grenada northward can and should be broken preliminary to operations against any point of the Yazoo near its mouth. Almost the entire force of the enemy about Vicksburg has been moved north except the released prisoners, who are being removed and reorganized back of Vicksburg. If Steele was to move on Panola I could meet him there and we could jointly cross over to the Central road at a point below Oxford, where there are several very high pieces of trestle-work requiring for repairs timbers of a length that could not be replaced in a long time. I have this from undoubted authority, and indicate their several positions on a map herewith.* With these roads broken a comparatively light force could operate between the Mississippi and Yazoo and could destroy the boats lying in the latter. The Yazoo is now very low, and those boats are surely blockaded for five months yet, giving ample time. My force here is now 8,122, of which say 7,000 are good, effective men. I have been drilling these very hard, and the infantry and artillery are in fine order. The cavalry, too, is in better trim and drill than at any former period. Our fort is drawing to completion, and 5,000 new troops could hold the works, leaving me my division for field operations.

You will have heard of the operations of guerrillas on the river. They have done little actual execution, but a good deal of mischief. I am determined to spare no efforts to check all such efforts or attempts on the boats. I send up a regiment to-day to bring from Randolph some guns, which I thought Colonel Bissell had already moved, but which are reported there. The guns are spiked, but still might be repaired and put in position much to our detriment.

Breckinridge has surely gone to Kentucky via Jackson, Meridian, Chattanooga, &c. He took with him only about 3,000 Kentuckians. Van Dorn is near Grand Junction. They are building a bridge there, showing their desire to operate by railroad. This makes it important this Central road should be broken below the Tallahatchie, and Helena is the best point to start from; and the same force can accomplish the other object, viz, the destruction of the boats in the Yazoo. I will write to General Steele for all the information he possesses on this point.

I had a flag of truce yesterday from General Hindman at Little Rock, from which I infer Holmes has gone north from there, although the bearer of the flag said he was at Little Rock sick.

I would be obliged if you would claim the Thirteenth Infantry for me. Wright took it after it had been relieved by my Seventy-seventh Ohio, whereby I lost both; not a fair trade. I doubt not they have enough troops at Cincinnati now and can well spare the battalion.

You know well that this is a magnificent place for assembling and

---

* Not found.

organizing troops and strategically far better than Helena for operations on the river. We are all very healthy, whereas I hear there is much sickness at Helena. I would like to have you send a division of new regiments here; they could soon be made efficient. My own opinion is that after discovering the exact point at which the boats in the Yazoo lie, whilst a force moves from here and Helena against Oxford, the gunboats and transports should threaten Vicksburg, as though an attack was intended, while a comparatively small force can land at some point below Gaines' Landing and strike across to the Yazoo.

Of course the movements of all should be prescribed as to time and kept absolutely secret, so that the enemy could not guess at your purposes—the first Vicksburg, and the real attack on the railroad and Yazoo.

I am, with great respect, your obedient servant,

W. T. SHERMAN,
Major-General, Commanding.

GENERAL ORDERS,　} HEADQUARTERS ARMY OF THE MISSISSIPPI,
No. 131.　　　　} 　　　　　*Corinth, September* 30, 1862.

Col. J. K. Mizner, Third Michigan Cavalry, is announced as chief of cavalry for the Third Division of the District of West Tennessee.

All cavalry serving in the division will be under his command, and all reports and returns required by army regulations and existing orders will be made to him.

By command of Major-General Rosecrans:

H. G. KENNETT,
Lieutenant-Colonel and Chief of Staff.

Abstract from Monthly Return of the District of West Tennessee, Maj. Gen. U. S. Grant commanding, for the month of September 1862.

Command.	Present for duty.		Aggregate present for duty.	Aggregate present.	Aggregate present and absent.	Pieces of artillery.		Aggregate present and absent last monthly return.
	Officers.	Men.				Heavy.	Field.	
Department staff*								
Memphis, Tenn.—First Division, Maj. Gen. W. T. Sherman:								
Staff	15		15	15	15			15
Infantry	285	4,972	5,257	6,701	7,955			8,020
Cavalry	27	676	703	915	966			972
Artillery	24	881	905	1,008	1,151		38	1,129
Grand total	351	6,529	6,880	8,639	10,087		38	10,136
Jackson, Tenn.—Second Division, Maj. Gen. E. O. C. Ord:								
Staff	15		15	15	16			12
Infantry	713	13,713	14,426	17,880	22,278			22,223
Cavalry	103	2,054	2,157	2,794	3,220			2,858
Artillery	43	1,243	1,286	1,449	1,737		40	1,747
Grand total	874	17,010	17,884	22,138	27,251		40	26,840

* Not reported.

Abstract from Monthly Return of the District of West Tennessee– Continued.

Command.	Present for duty.		Aggregate present for duty.	Aggregate present.	Aggregate present and absent.	Pieces of artillery.		Aggregate present and absent last monthly return.
	Officers.	Men.				Heavy.	Field.	
Near Corinth, Miss.—Third Division, Maj. Gen. W. S. Rosecrans:								
Infantry	904	17,992	18,896	22,784	31,303			
Cavalry	118	2,736	2,854	3,499	4,577			
Artillery	37	1,290	1,327	1,553	1,851		65	(*)
Grand total	1,059	22,018	23,077	27,836	37,731		65	
Columbus, Ky.—Fourth Division, Brig. Gen. G. M. Dodge:								
Staff	8		8	8	9			9
Infantry	172	3,498	3,670	4,631	5,310	42	6	4,136
Cavalry	51	1,089	1,140	1,407	1,516			1,490
Artillery	35	856	891	1,051	1,295			1,295
Island No. 10, Tenn.—Maj. Quincy McNeil.	7	216	223	274	315			318
New Madrid, Mo.—Capt. Robert B. Jones.	6	180	186	233	318	12	2	320
Hickman, Ky.—Capt. E. W. Blake	2	123	125	157	167	2		166
Smithland, Ky.—Maj. T. O. Bigney †								
Grand total	281	5,962	6,243	7,761	8,930	56	8	7,734
Jackson, Tenn.—Troops unassigned	19	61	80	685	922			886
Total force in district	2,584	51,580	54,164	67,059	84,921	56	151	45,596

Troops serving in the District of West Tennessee, Maj. Gen. U. S. Grant, U. S. Army, commanding, September 30, 1862.‡

(Headquarters Jackson, Tenn.)

ENGINEER TROOPS.

Bissell's (Missouri) regiment, Col. Josiah W. Bissell.

ESCORT.

4th Illinois Cavalry, Company A, Capt. Embur D. Osband.

FIRST DIVISION.§

Maj. Gen. WILLIAM T. SHERMAN.

Infantry.

40th Illinois, Lieut. Col. James W. Boothe.
55th Illinois, Col. David Stuart.
6th Iowa, Lieut. Col. John M. Corse.
6th Missouri, Lieut. Col. James H. Blood.
8th Missouri, Col. Giles A. Smith.
46th Ohio, Lieut. Col. Charles C. Walcutt.

48th Ohio, Col. Peter J. Sullivan.
53d Ohio, Col. Wells S. Jones.
54th Ohio, Col. T. Kilby Smith.
57th Ohio, Col. William Mungen.
70th Ohio, Col. Joseph R. Cockerill.
72d Ohio, Col. Ralph P. Buckland.

* Not given on return.
† No return.
‡ As indicated by the district and incomplete subordinate returns for that date. For a description of the territorial commands of Sherman, Ord, Rosecrans, and Quinby see general orders of September 24, p. 237.
§ Or Fifth Division, Army of the Tennessee, headquarters Memphis. Brigade organization not given on original return; but see organization September 10, p. 212.

Cavalry.

6th Illinois, Col. Benjamin H. Grierson.
Thielemann's Illinois Battalion, Capt. Berthold Marschner.

Artillery.

1st Illinois, Battery A, Capt. Peter P. Wood.
1st Illinois, Battery B, Capt. Samuel E. Barrett.
1st Illinois, Battery E, Lieut. Abial R. Abbott.
1st Illinois, Battery F, Lieut. Josiah H. Burton.
1st Illinois, Battery H, Lieut. Levi W. Hart.
1st Illinois, Battery I, Capt. Edward Bouton.
Independent Illinois Battery, Capt. William Cogswell.
6th Indiana Battery, Capt. Michael Mueller.
8th Ohio Battery, Lieut. Jacob M. Porter.

SECOND DIVISION.*

Maj. Gen. E. O. C. ORD.

Infantry.

8th Illinois, Col. Frank L. Rhoads.
14th Illinois, Col. Cyrus Hall.
15th Illinois, Col. Thomas J. Turner.
17th Illinois, Col. Addison S. Norton.
18th Illinois, Col. Michael K. Lawler.
20th Illinois, Col. C. Carroll Marsh.
28th Illinois, Col. Amory K. Johnson.
29th Illinois, Lieut. Col. Charles M. Ferrell.
30th Illinois, Lieut. Col. George A. Bacon.
31st Illinois, Col. Lyndorf Ozburn.
32d Illinois, Col. John Logan.
41st Illinois, Col. Isaac C. Pugh.
43d Illinois, Col. Adolph Engelmann.
45th Illinois, Col. John E. Smith.
46th Illinois, Col. John A. Davis.
48th Illinois, Col. Isham N. Haynie.
49th Illinois, Col. William R. Morrison.
53d Illinois, Lieut. Col. Daniel F. Hitt.
54th Illinois, Col. Thomas W. Harris.

61st Illinois, Col. Jacob Fry.
62d Illinois, Col. James M. True.
63d Illinois, Lieut. Col. Joseph B. Mc-Cown.
23d Indiana, Col. William L. Sanderson.
25th Indiana, Col. William H. Morgan.
53d Indiana, Col. Walter Q. Gresham.
3d Iowa, Col. Nelson G. Williams.
1st Kansas, Lieut. Col. Otto M. Tennison.
12th Michigan, Lieut. Col. William H. Graves.
7th Missouri, Col. John D. Stevenson.
20th Ohio, Col. Manning F. Force.
68th Ohio, Col. Robert K. Scott.
78th Ohio, Col. Mortimer D. Leggett.
7th Tennessee, Col. John A. Rogers.
12th Wisconsin, Col. George E. Bryant.

Cavalry.

2d Illinois, Col. Silas Noble.
4th Illinois, Lieut. Col. William McCullough.
11th Illinois, Col. Robert G. Ingersoll.
12th Illinois, Company H, Capt. Franklin T. Gilbert.

Stewart's Illinois Battalion, Major Warren Stewart.
5th Ohio, Col. W. H. H. Taylor.
4th Independent Ohio Company, Capt. John S. Foster.
1st Tennessee, Col. Fielding Hurst.

Artillery.

2d Illinois Light Artillery, Battery L, Capt. William H. Bolton.
9th Indiana Battery.
14th Indiana Battery, Capt. Meredith H. Kidd.
1st Missouri Light Artillery, Battery C, Capt. Charles Mann.
3d Ohio Battery.
7th Ohio Battery, Capt. Silas A. Burnap.

14th Ohio Battery, Lieut. Homer H. Stull.
15th Ohio Battery, Capt. Edward Spear, jr.
7th Wisconsin Battery, Capt. Richard R. Griffith.
1st Illinois, Bat'y D, Capt. H. A. Rogers.
2d Illinois, Battery B, Lieut. Fletcher H. Chapman.
2d Illinois, Battery E, Capt. George C. Gumbart.

---

* At and about Jackson, Tenn.   Division and brigade organizations not indicated on the original return.

THIRD DIVISION.*

Maj. Gen. WILLIAM S. ROSECRANS.

SECOND DIVISION, ARMY OF THE MISSISSIPPI.

Brig. Gen. DAVID S. STANLEY.

First Brigade.

Col. JOHN W. FULLER.

27th Ohio, Maj. Zeph. S. Spaulding.
39th Ohio, Lieut. Col. Edw. F. Noyes.
43d Ohio, Maj. Walter F. Herrick.
63d Ohio, Capt. Charles E. Brown.

Second Brigade.

Col. JOHN M. LOOMIS.

26th Illinois, Maj. Robert A. Gillmore.
47th Illinois, Capt. Samuel R. Baker.
5th Minnesota, Col. Lucius F. Hubbard
11th Missouri, Maj. Andrew J. Weber.
8th Wisconsin, Maj. John W. Jefferson.

THIRD DIVISION, ARMY OF THE MISSISSIPPI.

Brig. Gen. CHARLES S. HAMILTON.

First Brigade.

Col. JOHN B. SANBORN.

48th Indiana, Lieut. Col. Jefferson K. Scott.
59th Indiana, Col. Jesse I. Alexander.
5th Iowa, Lieut. Col. Ezekiel S. Sampson.
4th Minnesota, Capt. James C. Edson.
26th Missouri, Lieut. Col. John H. Holman.

Second Brigade.

Col. SAMUEL A. HOLMES.

56th Illinois, Lieut. Col. Green B. Raum.
10th Iowa, Lieut. Col. William E. Small.
17th Iowa, Col. David B. Hillis.
10th Missouri, Maj. Leonidas Horney.
24th Missouri, Company F, Capt. Lafayette M. Rice.
80th Ohio, Col. Ephraim R. Eckley.

CAVALRY.

Col. JOHN K. MIZNER.

7th Illinois, Lieut. Col. Edward Prince.
11th Illinois,† Col. Robert G. Ingersoll.
36th Illinois, Company A, Capt. Albert Jenks.
2d Iowa, Major Datus E. Coon.
7th Kansas, Lieut. Col. T. P. Herrick.

3d Michigan, Capt. Lyman G. Willcox.
5th Missouri, Company C, Sergeant Alex. L. Mueller.
5th Ohio, Major Charles S. Hayes.
2d U. S., Company C, Capt. Charles E. Farrand.

ARTILLERY.

2d Iowa Battery, Lieut. Daniel P. Walling.
3d Michigan Battery, Capt. Alexander W. Dees.
1st Missouri Light Artillery (four batteries), Maj. George H. Stone.
11th Ohio Battery, Lieut. Henry M. Neil.
2d U. S., Battery F, Capt. Thomas D. Maurice.
6th Wisconsin Battery, Capt. Henry Dillon.
12th Wisconsin Battery, Lieut. Lorenzo D. Immell.

* Headquarters at Corinth, Miss.
† Also reported as in second territorial division.

SECOND DIVISION, ARMY OF THE TENNESSEE.

Brig. Gen. THOMAS A. DAVIES.

First Brigade.

Col. THOMAS W. SWEENY.

12th Illinois, Col. Augustus L. Chetlain.
52d Illinois, Lieut. Col. John S. Wilcox.
22d Ohio, Maj. Oliver Wood.
81st Ohio, Col. Thomas Morton.
Union Brigade, Capt. George W. Kittel.

Third Brigade.

Col. ANDREW J. BABCOCK.

7th Illinois, Lieut. Col. Richard Rowett.
9th Illinois, Col. August Mersy.
50th Illinois, Lieut. Col. Wm. Swarthout.
57th Illinois, Lieut. Col. Fred'k J. Hurlbut.
2d Iowa, Maj. James B. Weaver.
7th Iowa, Col. Elliott W. Rice.
14th Missouri,* Maj. George Pipe.

SIXTH DIVISION, ARMY OF THE TENNESSEE.

Brig. Gen. THOMAS J. McKEAN.†

First Brigade.

Col. BENJAMIN ALLEN.

1st Kansas,‡ Lieut. Col. Otto M. Tennison.
21st Missouri, Col. David Moore.
16th Wisconsin, Maj. Thomas Reynolds.
17th Wisconsin, Col. John L. Doran.

Second Brigade.

Col. JOHN M. OLIVER.

15th Michigan, Lieut. Col. John McDermott.
18th Missouri, Capt. Jacob R. Ault.
14th Wisconsin, Col. John Hancock.
18th Wisconsin, Col. Gabriel Bouck.

Third Brigade.

Col. MARCELLUS M. CROCKER.

11th Iowa, Lieut. Col. William Hall.
13th Iowa, Lieut. Col. John Shane.
15th Iowa, Col. Hugh T. Reid.
16th Iowa, Maj. William Purcell.

Artillery.

Capt. ANDREW HICKENLOOPER.

2d Illinois, Battery F, Lieut. Joseph W. Mitchell.
1st Minnesota Battery, Lieut. G. Frederick Cooke.
3d Ohio Battery, Lieut. Stephen Keith.
5th Ohio Battery, Lieut. Bellamy S. Matson.
10th Ohio Battery, Capt. Hamilton B. White.

POST OF CORINTH, MISS.

Col. AUGUSTUS L. CHETLAIN.

12th Illinois (detachment), Maj. James R. Hugunin.
1st U. S., Capt. George A. Williams.
Engineer detachment, Capt. W. Hill.
Sappers and Miners, Lieut. Christian Lochbihler.

POST OF IUKA, MISS.

Yates Illinois Sharpshooters, Lieut. James C. Cameron.

---

* Afterward known as the Sixty-sixth Illinois.
† McKean reported as commanding on the division return, but Brig. Gen. John McArthur so reported on the district return.
‡ But in a return of the "Central Division, Second Division, District of West Tennessee," this regiment appears as under Colonel Deitzler's command at this date. On return of Sixth Division, Army of the Tennessee, the Twenty-fifth Missouri, Col. C. Harding, is reported as "ordered to Saint Louis."

FOURTH DIVISION.*

Brig. Gen. ISAAC F. QUINBY.†

Big Muddy, Ill.

71st Illinois Companies I and K.

Cairo, Ill.

81st Illinois, Col. James J. Dollins.

Fort Heiman, Ky.‡

Lieut. Col. MATTHEWSON T. PATRICK.

83d Illinois (detachment).
5th Iowa Cavalry (detachment).
2d Illinois Light Artillery, Battery H,
    Capt. Andrew Stenbeck.

Mound City, Ill.

71st Illinois, Companies D and F.

Bird's Point, Mo.

6th Illinois Cavalry, Company M, Capt.
    Isaiah M. Sperry.

Fort Donelson, Tenn.‡

Col. ABNER C. HARDING.

83d Illinois (detachment).
5th Iowa Cavalry (detachment).
2d Illinois Light Artillery, Battery C,
    Capt. James P. Flood.

Fort Henry, Tenn.‡

Lieut. Col. JAMES F. CHAPMAN.

71st Ohio (detachment).
13th Wisconsin, Lieut. Col. James F.
    Chapman.

Paducah, Ky.

Col. T. E. G. RANSOM.

11th Illinois.
6th Illinois Cavalry, Company B, Capt.
    James B. Morray.
Brooks' (Kentucky) cavalry.
1st Illinois Light Artillery, Battery K,
    Lieut. Isaac W. Curtis.
2d Illinois Light Artillery, Battery C.§

HEADQUARTERS NEAR CORINTH, MISS.,
October 1, 1862.

Maj. Gen. H. W. HALLECK, *General-in-Chief:*

For several days there has been a movement of the rebels south of my front, which left it in doubt whether Bolivar or Corinth was to be the point of attack. It is now clear that Corinth is to be the point, and that from the west or southwest. Price, Van Dorn, Villepigue, and Rust are together. Rust commands Breckinridge's forces, the latter having gone to Kentucky, by Mobile and Chattanooga, taking three regiments with him. My position is precarious, but hope to get out of it all right.

U. S. GRANT,
Major-General.

BOLIVAR, *October* 1, [1862].

Major-General GRANT:

There is evidently a movement eastward going on in front of me, the particulars of which I have not yet been able to obtain.

S. A. HURLBUT,
Major-General.

---

* Headquarters at Columbus, Ky. The garrisons at Columbus, Hickman, Smithland, Ky., and at Fort Pillow and Island No. 10, Tennessee, not indicated on original return.

† District return reports Brig. Gen. G. M. Dodge as commanding this division, but the division return so reports Quinby, and reports Dodge as commanding "Central Division" of this division.

‡ Col. William W. Lowe, Fifth Iowa Cavalry, commanding the three posts.

§ Also reported at Fort Donelson.

GENERAL ORDERS, }   HEADQUARTERS BOLIVAR, TENN.,
  No. 108.   }   *October* 1, 1862.

All forces in this command will be held in readiness for action at the shortest notice. One day's cooked rations at all times in haversacks; transportation kept close to the several camps; artillery horses harnessed, except in the case of batteries in forts.

The entire cavalry force will be ready for duty, if required, by sunrise. The greatest vigilance will be observed as to guards and patrols, and rapid reports made to brigade and division headquarters of any movements discovered.

By command of Major-General Hurlbut:

HENRY BINMORE,
Assistant Adjutant-General.

HEADQUARTERS OF THE ARMY,
Washington, October 1, 1862.

Major-General ROSECRANS, *Corinth:*

GENERAL: Your unofficial letter of the 26th ultimo is just received. It would have given me the greatest pleasure if your commission could have been dated back, but the War Department has decided that only in case of reappointments can commissions be dated back of the adjournment of Congress. Whether this is right or wrong I cannot say, but so it is. As soon as I arrived here I tried to get you appointed, but found that there were objections. These I finally succeeded in removing.

I know you are ranked by many of less capacity, and by some who have never rendered any services at all; but this cannot now be helped. I hope, however, that we may not be cursed with the appointment of any more political generals.

We must all do the best we can for the country in our several positions. You have my entire confidence, and if it be possible I will give you a separate command. At present it is difficult to determine what will be done.

Yours, truly.

H. W. HALLECK,
General-in-Chief.

CORINTH, *October* 1, 1862.

General GRANT:

The following just received from Stanley:

RIENZI, *September* 30.

Spaulding just returned. He went to Hatchie. No rebels, and is satisfied from good information that there are none 3 miles beyond. Three prisoners of Fourth Alabama, Breckinridge's command, caught. Breckinridge has gone to Kentucky with three Kentucky regiments. His division is commanded by General Rust. Price, Villepigue, and Rust are all together and camped on the Pocahontas road. Villepigue and Rust brought up 15,000 men. Reported rebel force 40,000. Prisoners don't know where they are going.

W. S. ROSECRANS,
Major-General.

CORINTH, *October* 1, 1862.

Major-General GRANT:

Rebel cavalry have made their appearance at Young's Bridge and upper and lower, from 2 to 5 miles from Chewalla. The bridges were

burned by our troops last night. Your body guard—Ford's cavalry—
are reported to have run in the most disgraceful manner. Have ordered
McKean to send a brigade to sustain the Chewalla command and feel
the enemy if he comes in sight.

W. S. ROSECRANS,
Major-General.

CORINTH, <i>October</i> 1, 1862.

General GRANT:

Report from Chewalla, 4 p. m., infantry and cavalry force of rebels
appeared south of Tuscumbia, at Young's Bridge. If they advance on
Bethel, Stanley, from position near Kossuth, can cut off their retreat;
or if he should be wanted with me, Hurlbut can do the same.

W. S. ROSECRANS,
Major-General.

CORINTH, <i>October</i> 1, 1862.

General GRANT:

Du Bois withdrawn from Rienzi to Danville. Cavalry regiment
camped at Ruckersville, between Clear Creek and Jacinto. No news
from Lee's reconnaissance supported by two regiments of infantry.
Stanley not yet reported himself in position. Hamilton's division concentrated, and Davies and McKean on Chewalla road, except Crocker,
who is near here. How far are the rebels advancing? Demonstration
on Chewalla amounted to nothing.

W. S. ROSECRANS.

HEADQUARTERS FIFTH DIVISION,
Memphis, October 1, 1862.

Hon. JOHN PARK, <i>Mayor of Memphis:</i>

SIR: Your letter of September 29 inclosing two letters from John P.
Trevesant, clerk, dated September 12, is received.* I prefer not by any
action of mine to complicate the machinery of government, and therefore will not sanction the imperfect collection of county and State taxes
by a deputy or clerk.

If the county authorities return to their allegiance and duty I will be
willing to assist them, but to empower a deputy to collect State taxes,
even if these taxes be paid into the city treasury, will give a man in
whom I have not full confidence the power to disturb the merchants
and business men of the city without extending his collections on the
county. I prefer that the city authorities should execute their powers
vigorously, not timidly; suppress crimes, keep your streets guarded,
lighted, and cleaned, and to extend this authority to all who enjoy the
advantages of the city.

If the funds derived from the taxes hitherto provided for are insufficient report to me, and I can levy any species of military contributions. I think it better to have the taxes due the State and county in
the hands of the people till the government of the county and State resume their appropriate functions. I return to you the letter of Mr.
Trevesant.

I am, with great respect, your obedient servant,

W. T. SHERMAN,
Major-General, Commanding.

---

* Not found.

BOLIVAR, *October* 2, 1862—1 p. m.

Maj. JOHN A. RAWLINS,
    Assistant Adjutant-General, Jackson, Tenn. :

I have just received reliable information, as I think, from an intelligent Union man near Grand Junction confirming the previously reported fact that Price, Van Dorn, and Villepigue have united near Ripley and are now at Pocahontas, probably 18,000 strong. He also reports that General Pillow is at Holly Springs with from 6,000 to 8,000 men, principally exchanged prisoners, and is fortifying that place.

The talk among the men with whom he conversed is that they propose an attack on this point, coming in by the way of Spring Creek, which is in fact the weakest part of the line. I send a diagram of the relative positions. If they move on this place they must show their flank to Rosecrans' force, and as they cannot well surprise us are liable to be taken in the act.

As I am liable to be removed at any time would it not be well for Major-General Ord to come down and fully examine the ground ?

    Your obedient servant,
                    S. A. HURLBUT,
                        Major-General.

HEADQUARTERS FOURTH DIVISION,
              October 2, 1862.

Brig. Gen. L. F. ROSS:

By dispatch just received from General Grant I am informed the railroad has been cut 6 miles south of Bethel.

You will re-enforce Engelmann's pickets with another regiment to-night, and use every caution as to the security of our communication north.

The cavalry which went on the north Purdy road went out 18 miles; found no traces of an enemy.

    Your obedient servant,
                    [S. A. HURLBUT,?]
                        Major-General.

BETHEL, TENN., *October* 2, 1862.

Brig. Gen. JOHN A. LOGAN,
    Commanding at Jackson, Tenn. :

Lieutenant Hays with scouts just arrived from within 1 mile of Pocahontas; captured 3 of Price's men and 2 spies, citizens. Lieutenant Hays reports that rebels are building a bridge, and it is almost completed, across the Hatchie. There is no force except pickets on this side of Hatchie. Prisoners report that Price's army are 30,000 or 35,000, under Price, Villepigue, Van Dorn, and Breckinridge. At Tupelo forces of the rebels said to be under marching orders, the bridge just being ready this morning, about 11 o'clock; don't know where their orders were to march to. Prisoners don't know where the rebel cavalry is. Rebels came from Bolivar by Ripley to Pocahontas with three days' rations.

                    I. N. HAYNIE,
           Colonel, Commanding Post at Bethel.

CORINTH, *October* 2, 1862.

General GRANT:

My troops are all concentrated in nearly the position given last night. Have ordered Colonel Lee to examine best point for crossing the Hatchie. What do you think of the plan of my moving with my entire command, save perhaps six regiments, and crossing Hatchie, say near Ruckersville or higher up, as report may show, and push those fellows to the wall?

W. S. ROSECRANS,
Major-General.

———

HEADQUARTERS ARMY OF THE MISSISSIPPI,
Corinth, Miss., October 2, 1862.

Brigadier-General HAMILTON,
Commanding Division:

The general commanding directs that you prepare your command to move by 3 o'clock with three days' rations. Move into the outskirts of town to the north by upper bridge road. Bivouac your troops, columns closed in mass. Your artillery will accompany you. Take post on Purdy road north of the town.

[H. G. KENNETT,]
Lieutenant-Colonel, Chief of Staff.

———

HEADQUARTERS ARMY OF THE MISSISSIPPI,
Corinth, October 2, 1862.

Brigadier-General STANLEY,
Commanding Division:

The general commanding directs that you occupy Kossuth with sufficient force yourself, and relieve Colonel Moore, of Twenty-first Missouri. Let us know when you will be ready.

Very respectfully,

[H. G. KENNETT,]
Lieutenant-Colonel and Chief of Staff.

———

HEADQUARTERS ARMY OF THE MISSISSIPPI,
Corinth, October 2, 1862.

Brigadier-General STANLEY,
Commanding Division:

The meaning of my communication was that you send sufficient force to occupy Kossuth and not proceed there in person; that is to say, Kossuth will be an outpost of your own division and under your own supervision, and will report to you, and you will report what you deem of importance to these headquarters.

Find out by all possible means the best modes of marching our division across the Hatchie.

Very respectfully, your obedient servant,

[H. G. KENNETT,]
Lieutenant-Colone, and Chief of Staff.

HEADQUARTERS ARMY OF THE MISSISSIPPI,
Corinth, Miss., October 2, 1862.
Brigadier-General STANLEY,
    Commanding Division:

The general commanding directs that you prepare your command to move by 3 o'clock with three days' rations. Move by the bridge road, leaving a regiment as a guard at the bridge. Come to near General Grant's old headquarters and report for orders. The outpost at Kossuth will come in.

[H. G. KENNETT,]
Lieutenant-Colonel and Chief of Staff.

GENERAL ORDERS, }   HDQRS. DISTRICT OF WEST TENNESSEE,
    No. 87.   }   *Jackson, Tenn., October* 2, 1862.

I. In pursuance of orders from the Surgeon-General of the Army, Washington, D. C., Surg. Horace R. Wirtz, U. S. Army, is hereby assigned to duty as chief medical director of the District of West Tennessee.

*   *   *   *   *   *   *

By order of Maj. Gen. U. S. Grant:

JNO. A. RAWLINS,
Assistant-Adjutant General.

BOLIVAR, TENN., *October* 3, 1862.
Maj. Gen. U. S. GRANT, *Jackson, Tenn.:*

I have sent a heavy cavalry reconnaissance toward Pocahontas. My own division has only two brigades, each of five regiments. Ross has four brigades. I will hold eight regiments ready to march as soon as I hear from the roads south and west. No further news from Pocahontas. It is reported that the exchanged prisoners from Vicksburg are arriving at Davis' Mill.

[S. A. HURLBUT,]
Major-General.

BOLIVAR, [*October*] 3, 1862.
General GRANT:

I understand it to be my duty to relieve Rosecrans at all hazards if he is still at Corinth. I can't return before Sunday p. m., the distance being 46 miles. On reaching Davis' Bridge I shall of course know whether the enemy are repulsed or not; if not repulsed, I propose to cut through; if repulsed, to destroy their line of retreat in this direction.

S. A. HURLBUT,
Major-General.

BOLIVAR, TENN., [*October*] 3, 1862.
General GRANT:

My column will move at 3 o'clock a. m. in marching order with three days' provisions. I have ordered General Ross to select two regiments from his command; with the two that will arrive will be brigaded to-gether and move at the same hour. A line of couriers will be kept up to General Ross, who will telegraph to you.

S. A. HURLBUT,
Major-General.

BOLIVAR, [*October*] 3, 1862.

General GRANT:

Cavalry have just come in; have been within 4 miles of Pocahontas. Cavalry rear guard of enemy left there at 10 a. m. to-day; the main force crossed the Hatchie at Davis' Bridge yesterday p. m. and last night for Corinth; number not ascertained, but large. Heard no firing from Somerville. It is reported that about 800 cavalry are there. I shall move with my whole division to Pocahontas, or in that direction, early in the morning, but have no expectation that I can do more than demonstrate, unless Rosecrans has beaten Price, in which case I shall be in good position. General Ross remains here with his command.

S. A. HURLBUT.

HEADQUARTERS ARMY OF THE MISSISSIPPI,
Corinth, Miss., October 3, 1862.

Brigadier-General McKEAN:

The general commanding directs me to say, in reply to your dispatch of this date, just received, that if there are no movements on your front he does not see any reason for calling in the regiment at Smith's Bridge, and thinks in that case it advisable that it should remain there for the present, though, as he said in his dispatch, he leaves it to your judg-ment. There is, however, a remote contingency which ought not to be overlooked; should the enemy appear at the bridge the road ought to be obstructed. Nearly everything depends upon the movements on your front.

Very respectfully, your obedient servant,

O. GODDARD,
First Lieut. Twelfth Infty. Ohio Vols., Actg. Asst. Adjt. Gen.

HEADQUARTERS ARMY OF THE MISSISSIPPI,
Corinth, October 3, 1862.

Brig. Gen. D. S. STANLEY,
Commanding Second Division:

I send you map. McKean's left is about a half mile in advance of you and about 1 mile north. You may advance your right up to the road that runs by Battery D, occupying the ridge you are now on; or, if you find better ground, to the road that runs by Mark Suttle's. This will bring you nearer Corinth and put you *en echelon.*

By order of Major-General Rosecrans:

O. GODDARD,
First Lieut. Twelfth Infty. Ohio Vols., Actg. Asst. Adjt. Gen.

HEADQUARTERS ARMY OF THE MISSISSIPPI,
Corinth, Miss., October 3, 1862.
Brigadier-General STANLEY,
Commanding Division:

The general commanding directs you to send a brigade across on to the Chewalla road, through the woods by shortest cut; re-enforce Davies from your left, close in, in conformity with that movement. You had better send Mower. Your guide will show you the road.

[H. G. KENNETT,]
Lieutenant-Colonel and Chief of Staff.

SPECIAL ORDERS, }   HDQRS. DISTRICT OF WEST TENNESSEE,
    No. 210.   }   *Jackson, Tenn., October 3, 1862.*

*   *   *   *   *   *   *

V. Brig. Gen. J. B. McPherson is hereby assigned to the command of the two brigades commanded respectively by Col. M. K. Lawler and Col. John D. Stevenson, and will proceed without delay and with all possible dispatch to Corinth, Miss., and report to Major-General Rosecrans, commanding.

By order of Maj. Gen. U. S. Grant:

[JNO. A. RAWLINS,]
Assistant Adjutant-General.

BETHEL, *October 3, 1862.*
Major-General GRANT:

General McPherson and myself think troops can be sent by rail to Ramer, 11 miles this side of Corinth, and infantry can go by road from there to Corinth. Lawler is *en route* to a point 3 miles below Ramer; will probably be at Ramer by the time your train gets there.

I. N. HAYNIE,
Colonel.

BETHEL, TENN., *October 3, 1862.*
Major-General GRANT:

Passenger train back here; freight train supposed safe through. Three hundred rebels came in to the railroad; freight got by them; rebels then took up rail and cut telegraph; our force, Seventeenth Wisconsin, ran them off. No killed reported as yet.

I. N. HAYNIE,
Colonel, &c.

BETHEL, *October 3, 1862.*
General GRANT:

Burchfield, arrived across from toward Corinth, has just come in on hand-car; reports the track of railroad torn up 5 miles beyond Ramer and 6 miles from Corinth; says there are 800 there of Falkner's cavalry. Three bridges near Chambers said to be burned.

Burchfield says he heard cannon at or below Corinth, or between

Corinth and Chewalla; says they are fighting. Would it not be wel
to send a train here, so in case send down men to Chambers to driv(
out rebels? If you send train, send tools to repair road also; tools ar(
burned.

I. N. HAYNIE.

BETHEL, October 3, 1862.

General GRANT:

Dr. Grimes and Captain House, in charge of scouts sent toward Po
cahontas and Chewalla, confirm reports before made—enemy are mov
ing toward Corinth; are crossing Tuscumbia at Evans' old bridge.
Sharp cannonading not far off from Chewalla to-day for two hours, fron
8 to 10. Scouts captured a contraband from rebel army. He says th(
rebels say they go to Corinth and then to join Bragg's army. The tw
regiments are *en route* as ordered.

I. N. HAYNIE.

BETHEL, October 3, 1862.

Major-General GRANT:

The two couriers sent last night are here; got to Corinth safely; de
livered dispatches; were attacked to-day coming back; lost one horse
wounded. They are fighting at Corinth; rebels investing it close a!
hand. Couriers lost dispatches sent me by General Rosecrans. Th(
general told the courier that if he lost [them] it was not much.

I. N. HAYNIE,
Colonel.

BETHEL, October 4, [1862].

General GRANT:

Courier says General McPherson had not got in, but would be in tc
night; thinks he sent in messengers. This is all he knows. He furthe(
says General Oglesby is getting along finely; also that Price this a. m
was clear into the city, but was driven back up toward the southwes
with terrible loss; ours small.

HAYNIE,
Colonel.

BETHEL, October 4, 1862.

General GRANT:

Courier just in from Corinth reports heavy fighting yesterday; kille(
and wounded quite heavy. Rebels inside of western breastworks. H
brings the following message in cipher.*

I. N. HAYNIE.

BETHEL, October 4, 1862.

General GRANT, *Jackson :*

A message in cipher arrived here from Corinth about 1 o'clock thi(
morning. It was impossible to communicate with the operator at you(
headquarters; we have not yet been able to get him, now 7 o'clock; th(·
line being in good order it must be the fault of the operator. Th(

---

* Probably Rosecrans to Grant, October 3, Part I, v. 160.

cipher message was for this reason sent to Henderson, and from there by courier to you; I feel it to be my duty to call this remissness to your attention.

I. N. HAYNIE.

BETHEL, October 4, [1862].

General GRANT:

This courier left Lawler at 8 o'clock and went into Corinth. When he left Colonel Lawler he (Colonel Lawler) was making for the Blue Cut, 1 mile this side, northwest of the blacksmith's shop. McPherson had not at that time joined Lawler. Courier heard a conversation between a colonel and General Rosecrans; from that he says he learned Van Dorn's forces were up northwest of Corinth, along near to the railroad, on the west side, not far from the blacksmith's shop, in the northwest angle of the railroad. General Rosecrans had ordered at 2 p. m. three regiments and some batteries out in that direction.

Van Dorn's men had not fallen back like Price's. Courier understood from conversation of General Rosecrans with the colonel (don't know his name) that Van Dorn had sixty or seventy guns. General Rosecrans said if Van Dorn held that position he should open on him with his siege guns soon. As courier came on here he heard cannon, about 9 o'clock.

I. N. HAYNIE.

CAMP ON MUDDY, Oct. 4, [1862]. (Received Oct. 5.)

I arrived here this evening at 5 p. m., after an exhausting march of 22 miles. We have driven in the pickets of enemy up to Davis' Bridge, where my cavalry encountered two regiments of rebel cavalry at sunset and fell back. Took 2 prisoners, who report a large force between Davis' and Chewalla. The bridges are deceitful, and if the Hatchie Bridge is destroyed, or the Tuscumbia, I cannot advance. I shall move as rapidly as possible, but see no ground to believe that I can reach Corinth to-morrow. A citizen reports Davis' Bridge destroyed; if so, the game is up, and I shall return to save my own command.

S. A. HURLBUT,
Major-General.

PORTER'S CREEK, TENN., Oct. 4, 1862—11 a. m.

Maj. Gen. U. S. GRANT, Jackson, Tenn.:

The command has reached this place, 12 miles, rather tired. I shall rest and push on to Davis' Bridge to-night.

[S. A. HURLBUT,]
Major-General.

HDQRS. FIRST DIVISION, DIST. OF WEST TENNESSEE,
Memphis, October 4, 1862.

Maj. Gen. U. S. GRANT,
    Commanding District of West Tennessee, Jackson:

SIR: An order calling for a field return makes me fear that the usual tri-monthly reports have not reached you regularly. I believe they have been sent punctually on the dates prescribed, but I will see that the field report is sent. In former letters I have described the condition of affairs here, and will now only repeat, that you may have a full view of our situation.

Morgan L. Smith's brigade is encamped on the outskirts, about 2½ miles from the Court Square (Jackson monument). Three regiments of infantry on the State Line road, one near the bridge over Wolf Creek, and another on the Hernando road. With this brigade I have two good field batteries. I give him daily a detail of 50 cavalry to picket all approaches. I review these troops every Sunday afternoon, and think them as well instructed as any troops in service. They are full of confidence, and only need filling up with recruits to make a No. 1 brigade.

Denver's brigade—four Ohio regiments—occupies the right or south half of the fort, in tents, with posts assigned at the parapet for each company.

McDowell's brigade—three regiments—are in the left or north half of the intrenchments, in tents, with posts fixed. You will remember that out of this brigade, by your order, I detached the Seventy-seventh Ohio to Alton to secure the battalion of the Thirteenth Regulars. I have written again to General Wright on this subject, and hope you too will not forget that I am justly entitled to that battalion. Now that the Cincinnati stampede is passed there can be no just reason why it should not be sent me at once. It is needed to complete this brigade. In the fort I have four field batteries with platforms and embrasures, but the horses are kept in fine order, drills kept up, and they are ready at an hour's call for service.

The fixed batteries—24-pounders, 32-pounders, and 8-inch howitzers—twenty-two in number, are mounted, four on the large mound, three on the small, five on the north battery, and remainder at the salients. I have four infantry companies detailed and instructed to handle these guns, and they have painted the guns and carriages, piled the shot and shell, and are now revetting with brick the breast-height. On the whole the fort (Pickering) is ready for battle. Much work yet remains to be done, but the lines are ready for defense.

I have embraced in the fort an immense cotton-shed, which furnishes fine storage to provisions, forage, camp and garrison equipage, and all things needful for a siege, and I have all my division staff in the lines. I occupy a house just across the street.

A new magazine is substantially done. Two powder-houses under the bluff are full of ammunition, and I have converted an old brewery into an ordnance shop for the repair of arms, by which we can save all broken muskets, &c. Two good roads are finished to the water within the fort, so that steamboats can land our stores there. The brush to the south of the fort is cut down to the extent of a mile. I would like much to show you the amount of work done and its adaption to public wants, and feel satisfied that you will agree with me that Memphis is now the best base of operations on the Mississippi. The citizens who used to talk of our being expelled have ceased to think so. They know we are going to stay.

The civil government also works well now, and the people begin to realize that the Northwest intends to fight till the death for the Mississippi River. This is my hobby, and I know you pardon me when I say that I am daily more and more convinced that we should hold the river absolutely and leave the interior alone. Detachments inland can always be overcome or are at great hazard, and they do not convert the people. They cannot be made to love us, but may be made to fear us, and dread the passage of troops through their country. With the Mississippi safe we could land troops at any point, and by a quick march break the railroad, where we could make ourselves so busy that our descent would be dreaded the whole length of the river, and by the loss of negroes and other property [they] would in time discover that war is not the remedy for the political evils of which they complained. I hold myself prepared to carry out promptly and cheerfully any plan you may make, but I do not believe Halleck will permit you to make any real move till events further develop in Kentucky and Maryland. Of course the troops still south of you must be held in check until Buell tries his strength with Bragg. You have already given Price a hint that he is not to pass north of you. Breckinridge has gone, but mostly for reasons of personal pride, to drink the glory of triumph in his own Kentucky; but I hope Buell and Wright have troops enough to regain all of Kentucky and Tennessee before Christmas. The sad quarrel of Nelson and Davis, and Buell's narrow escape from removal, will make him rash; but still his troops are now so hardy and so well prepared that I have great faith in him and them. I think Halleck will cause McClellan to press on Lee's front whilst he threatens his flank, as also Richmond. He will have every available man at work at once; his apparent silence means work. You know how impetuous he is when he starts, and I expect to hear, by every boat, of regiments by the dozen' pouring on Richmond whilst McClellan holds Lee in check. Same of Buell. We down here will for the time being be lost sight of; but as soon as the Southern Army turns their faces South then look out for squalls. I know you will pardon me for these outspoken thoughts, but I assure you I feel more confidence now than at any former period of the war. The number of men engaged is now commensurate with the game. We know that all the South is in arms and deep in enmity, and we know that every man available for war in the North should now be in motion. We cannot change the hearts of those people of the South, but we can make war so terrible that they will realize the fact that, however brave and gallant and devoted to their country, still they are mortal and should exhaust all peaceful remedies before they fly to war. This is all I hope for, and even this will take time and vast numbers. The scramble for money, for office, of our Northern people makes me sometimes sick, but still we must take them as they are, and I begin to feel that the Northern people will soon realize that words and deeds are different things.

I think I see some symptoms here of favorable change. The guerrillas are less active and offensive. Yesterday 40 wagons with farmers came in, each with a bale of cotton; the guerrillas tried to stop them with threats, but were told that their families were suffering for salt and tea and medicines, shoes, clothing, &c., all of which were abundant in Memphis. When threatened, the guerrillas were told to destroy this cotton they would have to fight, and they let it pass. Now this may or may not be true; but the bearing of the farmers, their plain, simple story impressed me, and I relaxed the usual rules of trade and allowed them to carry back clothing and necessaries for their families. Like events in a more limited scale have occurred on the Arkansas side, and I think many of the farmers are tired of the war, and especially of guerrillas. I have promised if they will take care of the guerrillas they may have trade and that we will deal only with large armies.

Guerrillas have twice attacked boats near Randolph—the Forest Queen and J. J. Roe—on both of which were many lady and children passengers. The attacks were wanton and cruel. I caused Randolph to be destroyed, and have given public notice that a repetition will justify any measures of retaliation, such as loading the boats with their captive guerrillas as targets (I always have a lot on hand), and expelling families from the comforts of Memphis, whose husbands and brothers go to make up those guerrillas. I will watch Randolph closely, and if anything occurs there again I will send a brigade by land back of Randolph and clean out the country. A gunboat is now at Pillow. I have brought away every gun.

General Steele passed up some days ago, and I was in hopes he would find you at Columbus, but I suppose he has gone on to confer with General Curtis. He told me one-half his command was ordered to Iron Mountain, to which he objected. He is anxious to do what you want—strike Grenada; that road should now be destroyed from Holly Springs to below Grenada, so as to be useless for a whole year. Then we, with the river, would have every advantage; but with that road in full operation they can keep pace with us up and down.

I ought to have ten new regiments, when I could organize a good *corps d'armée.* I have enough artillery and only want another regiment of cavalry. Such a force could hold Memphis and check any movement along that road.

Excuse so long a letter.

As ever, your friend,

W. T. SHERMAN,
Major-General.

———

[OCTOBER 4, 1862.—For L. Thomas to Halleck and reply, in relation to the commands of Buell, Grant, and Rosecrans, see Vol XVI, Part II, p. 570.]

———

HEADQUARTERS DISTRICT OF WEST TENNESSEE,
Jackson, October 5, 1862.

Maj. Gen. H. W. HALLECK,
General-in-Chief, Washington, D. C.:

GENERAL: I deem it a matter of great importance in this district to have organized a corps of experienced railroad engineers and builders. Repairs are constantly being required, and if we should penetrate farther into the southern country other roads would have to be fitted up.

To take charge of such a corps a man of experience in superintending such work would be required, and one in whose hands I can place the management of the railroads under my jurisdiction.

I would state in this connection that General McPherson is exceedingly anxious to take an active command, and I think it a great misfortune to have such a man without an important military command. I would feel more strengthened to-day if I could place McPherson in command of a division than I would to receive a whole brigade of the new levies.

I would respectfully ask authority to place Col. George G. Pride in this position. I know that he has the requisite experience and the energy and ability to fill the place admirably. Colonel Pride served on my staff as a volunteer aide at the battle of Shiloh and some time since. I can vouch for his ability. To make Colonel Pride eligible for the position and to entitle him to the position, also to give him the proper command over men, as well as that he may come under proper military restrictions, I would respectfully ask that he be commissioned by the President, with the rank of colonel.

I am, general, very respectfully, your obedient servant,

U. S. GRANT,
Major-General.

BIG MUDDY, TENN.,
October 5, 1862—5 a. m.

Maj. Gen. U. S. GRANT, *Jackson, Tenn. :*

The column is moving toward the Hatchie.   Bridges and levee across the Muddy very bad, and have to be repaired.   Three regiments of cavalry are near Hatchie.   Shall disperse them as soon as infantry and artillery can reach them.

Dispatches from General Ross say that provision train will be here to-day with Major-General Ord.

[S. A. HURLBUT,]
Major-General.

HEADQUARTERS ARMY OF THE MISSISSIPPI,
Corinth, Miss., October 5, 1862.

Brigadier-General HAMILTON,
Commanding Division :

I think it is advisable for you to occupy the ford on the Kossuth road with a good regiment, with orders to ascertain whether the ford is watched on the other side or not, and, if it is watched, to ascertain the nature of the force.   This will be done by deploying a heavy line of skirmishers and pushing them heavily, sending a piece of cannon, if necessary, and making a big noise.   Notify General McKean.

By order of Major-General Rosecrans :
[C. GODDARD,]
First Lieut., Twelfth Infty. Ohio Vols., Actg. Asst. Adjt. Gen.

HEADQUARTERS ARMY OF THE MISSISSIPPI,
Corinth, Miss., October 5, 1862.

Brigadier-General McKEAN :

Halt your train, turn it out, and park it.   I am told it is a mile long. Take nothing with you but ammunition and ration wagons.

You have left our advance guard without a support by your tardy movements.   You are in the way of the other divisions.

By order of Major-General Rosecrans :
[H. G. KENNETT,]
Lieutenant-Colonel and Chief of Guards and Outposts.

HEADQUARTERS ARMY OF THE MISSISSIPPI,
Corinth, Miss., October 5, 1862—2 p. m.

Brigadier-General McKEAN :

Hamilton says you are waiting for orders.   I hear no information from you about the Smith's Bridge road.   You have your orders to push ahead, follow your advance guard closely, and report frequently.

By order of Major-General Rosecrans :
C. GODDARD,
First Lieut., Twelfth Infty. Ohio Vols., Actg. Asst. Adjt. Gen.

HEADQUARTERS ARMY OF THE MISSISSIPPI,
Corinth, October 5, 1862—9 p. m.

Brigadier-General McKEAN,
Commanding Division:

Am coming out to Chewalla with car-load of water. No news from any of you for several hours. Ord has been heavily engaged with the enemy at Davis' Bridge. We must push on as lightly as possible. Baggage has, I understand, interfered with your progress, which certainly has not been remarkable. We must push ahead as soon as the men get a little rest, and be with them by daylight. Send messengers to Chewalla reporting your position.

By order of Major-General Rosecrans:

O. GODDARD,
First Lieut. Twelfth Infty. Ohio Vols., Actg. Asst. Adjt. Gen.

(Generals Davies, Stanley, Hamilton, and McPherson furnished with copies of above.)

HEADQUARTERS ARMY OF THE MISSISSIPPI,
October 5, 1862.

Brigadier-General McPHERSON,
Commanding Advance:

No report from you. If you reach Chewalla ascertain if the enemy passed by Young's Bridge. Halt at that point until Stanley overtakes you. Meanwhile reconnoiter to Young's Bridge. Occupy it with a regiment and reconnoiter beyond. Push an advance guard, but not beyond support, toward Pocahontas.

By order of Major-General Rosecrans:

C. R. THOMPSON,
Lieutenant and Ordnance Officer.

HEADQUARTERS ARMY OF THE MISSISSIPPI,
Corinth, October 5, 1862.

Brigadier-General McPHERSON:

Dispatch received. Sent you word to wait for supports on account of the delay of General McKean; the column has been halted and fallen behindhand. Try to open communication with Bethel and our cavalry, who have been sent to the right.

By order of Major-General Rosecrans:

[H. G. KENNETT,]
Lieutenant-Colonel and Chief of Staff.

HEADQUARTERS ARMY OF THE MISSISSIPPI,
October 5, 1862—1.30 p. m.

Brigadier-General STANLEY,
Commanding Division:

Dispatch received; will send you another guide. You should have taken the road to the right, this side of Cane Creek, which keeps north of the railroad. If you are not too far advanced it would be better for you to face by the rear and do it now, as you will reach Chewalla sooner

The right-hand road turns off 2 miles in rear of Alexander's. Let the advance guard go well ahead, sending its advances forward to report the road back to the head of the column. At Smith's there is a road that runs across the railroad to Concord Meeting-House, about 5 miles from Chewalla, on Hamburg and Chewalla road. Smith's is a mile from Jones'.

By order of Major-General Rosecrans:

C. GODDARD,
First Lieut. Twelfth Infty. Ohio Vols., Actg. Asst. Adjt. Gen.

HEADQUARTERS ARMY OF THE MISSISSIPPI,
Corinth, October 5, 1862—2 p. m.

Brigadier-General STANLEY,
Commanding Division:

You had better take the nearest northern road. I will send you a guide. McKean's halt appears to have interfered with our movements. Advance rapidly, and when you halt close in mass; get out of the road if possible. Overtake McPherson if you can; nothing heard from him. Tell your advance guard to get the names of all the houses on the road, and when you write date your dispatch from the house, and side of the road it is on.

By order of Major-General Rosecrans:

C. R. THOMPSON,
Acting Aide-de-Camp.

HEADQUARTERS ARMY OF THE MISSISSIPPI,
Corinth, October 5, 1862.

Major-General VAN DORN,
Commanding Confederate Forces:

Major-General Rosecrans' compliments to Major-General Van Dorn, commanding officer Confederate forces, and states that provision has been made for the burial of the dead, and a soldier's tribute will be paid those who fell fighting bravely, as did many in Maury's division.

W. S. ROSECRANS,
Major-General, Commanding.

SPECIAL ORDERS, }   HDQRS. ARMY OF THE MISSISSIPPI,
                              THIRD DIV., DIST. WEST TENN.,
No. 252.   }   *Corinth, October* 5, 1862.

I. During the pursuit of Price, Colonel Burke will remain in command of Corinth. The Yates Sharpshooters, Captain Williams' battalion First Infantry, a regiment to be furnished by General Davies, a battalion of cavalry to be furnished by Colonel Mizner, together with his own regiment, the camp of the convalescents and guards of the baggage train will constitute the garrison. Colonel Burke is charged with the defense of the place, the protection of public property, the arrest of all stragglers, the mustering of all prisoners, the supervision of all hospitals, collection of the arms, equipments, and quartermaster stores from the field of battle, and the counting and burial of the dead.

The chief surgeons of hospitals will without delay make and furnish Colonel Burke exact lists of the wounded under their care.

II. The order of the pursuit will be as follows:

Brigadier-General McArthur, with all McKean's division excep. Crocker's brigade, with a good battery and a battalion of cavalry, will advance on the enemy by the route south of the railroad toward Pocahontas. General McKean will follow on this route with the rest of his division and Ingersoll's cavalry.

General Hamilton will follow McKean with his entire force.

McPherson's brigade, with a good battery, will follow the route north of the railroad. Stanley's and Davies' divisions will support him.

Lieutenant-Colonel Lothrop will furnish chiefs of divisions with rockets for signals. Three rockets at intervals of one minute will indicate the head of the advance columns; two at intervals of one minute will indicate the head of the columns supporting the advance, and one will indicate the rear of the entire column on each line. Should the signals of one not be answered by the other they may be repeated every fifteen minutes until answered.

Colonel Mizner, chief of cavalry, will detail a battalion of cavalry to accompany the advance of each column, one battalion to report to Colonel Burke for camp and garrison guard duty; with the remainder of the cavalry, he will join the pursuit, and dispose it according to circumstances, covering the flanks of our columns, and feeling those of the enemy.

The attention of leaders of columns in pursuit is called to the well-known principle of war that it is safe to pursue a flying enemy with a greatly inferior force, and they will take care, while conducting their advance with caution to guard against ambuscade, to push the enemy with vigor and firmness. They are especially instructed on reaching defiles to deploy a very heavy and extended line of skirmishers, with orders to push in, learn the ground, and outflank any opposing force, dispose the artillery so as to sweep the defile and its flanks, and open with rifled shot and shell, endeavoring to strike the retreating column some distance ahead of the defile. The cavalry should deploy right and left beyond the infantry flankers and endeavor to find paths by which the defile may be turned.

The pursuing divisions will provide for prompt communication between each other and these headquarters. As our troops have no great experience, commanders are especially charged to use the precaution of having proper advance guards and flankers, to prevent their columns from falling into ambuscade.

Care will be taken, in carrying rations, to inspect the men and see that they have actually on their persons the required three days' supply. As there will be some men without haversacks it will be necessary for each regiment to have a wagon to supply the deficiencies. These wagons, the spare ammunition wagons, and the ambulances will follow the column in order.

III. Surgeon Holston will take charge of the hospitals at Corinth, establishing a separate one for the enemy's wounded, separating them as far as practicable from our own. He will provide the medical care absolutely necessary for the wounded, sending all regimental surgeons at once to rejoin their commands, as their services will be needed on the march.

The old hospital ground will be reoccupied. Colonel Burke, post commander, will furnish Surgeon Holston with such assistance as may be in his power to render.

*   *   *   *   *   *   *

By command of Major-General Rosecrans:

C. GODDARD,
First Lieut. Twelfth Infty. Ohio Vols., Actg. Asst. Adjt. Gen

BETHEL, *October* 6, 1862.

Major-General GRANT:

Seven prisoners from Price's army, General Moore's brigade, are just brought in by scouts, and they report that the whole brigade, five regiments, Forty-second Alabama, Thirty-fifth Mississippi, Second Arkansas Regiments, and one Texas regiment threw away their arms at Davis' Bridge and every man scattered. This occurred when Hurlbut first attacked their rear. They are a miserable, squalid, starved set. What shall I do with them? Lieutenant Grimes, who is in charge of scouts, reports the woods filled with them.

> I. N. HAYNIE,
> *Colonel, Commanding.*

BETHEL, *October* 6, 1862.

General GRANT:

Prisoners from Price's army, brought in this a. m. by my scouts from near Chewalla, say that rebels admit loss of 4,000, and that a General Martin was killed; they saw his body. They report Price's army in a state of starvation. Really the looks of the men confirm it. No news of the rebels' movements this morning.

> I. N. HAYNIE,
> *Colonel, Commanding.*

HATCHIE, *October* 6, 1862.

Major-General GRANT, *Jackson:*

I am compelled to send back for transportation for my wounded. I am out of rations. The enemy have twenty-four hours' start and are flying light and cannot be overhauled by my command. Rosecrans is in pursuit, as I am told, but my command is too much crippled in wounded men and dead artillery horses to follow.

> S. A. HURLBUT,
> *Major-General.*

HATCHIE, TENN., *October* 6, 1862.

Maj. Gen. W. S. ROSECRANS:

GENERAL: My battery horses are badly cut, ammunition short, and only one day's rations around. I have not wagons and ambulances enough to move my wounded, and must return to Bolivar.

> Your obedient servant,
>
> [S. A. HURLBUT,]
> *Major-General.*

JACKSON, TENN., *October* 7, 1862—2 p. m.

Maj. Gen. H. W. HALLECK, *General-in-Chief:*

If possible, have McPherson made major-general. He should be made at once, to take rank above others who may be promoted for the late battles.

> U. S. GRANT,
> *Major-General, Commanding*

BOLIVAR, *October* 7, [1862]—9.30 p. m.

Maj. Gen. U. S. GRANT:

I have the honor to report that I have returned to this point. My First Brigade is now at Porter's Creek, 13 miles. The Second Brigade, with balance of wounded I captured, artillery, and guns, is at Muddy. Both brigades will be here to-morrow. I received dispatch from General Rosecrans at Ruckersville, dated 10 a. m., urgently requesting me to proceed south, but the state of command and your orders had determined that question.

We had no ink or paper in the division on this trip, so that official reports cannot be made until camp is re-established.

S. A. HURLBUT,
Major-General.

P. S.—My surgeons demand ice for the wounded, say for 200 men. Will you order it from Columbus at once?

SPECIAL ORDERS, }   HDQRS. DISTRICT OF WEST TENNESSEE,
No. 214.   }   *Jackson, Tenn., October* 7, 1862.

*   *   *   *   *   *   *

VII. Major-General Ord, commanding Second Division, District of West Tennessee, having been severely wounded at the battle on the Hatchie, on the 5th instant, is hereby ordered to proceed to Carlisle, Pa., and from there report to the Adjutant-General of the Army, Washington, D. C., and to these headquarters, by letters.

In parting with General Ord the commanding general of the district regrets losing the services of so gallant an officer and so able a commander, and wishes to express the desire, in all sincerity, not only that he may be speedily restored to duty, but that he may be restored to the same field he is now being relieved from. Especially would this be desirable to the commanding general so long as it is his good fortune to command his present armies.

*   *   *   *   *   *   *

IX. Maj. Gen. S. A. Hurlbut is hereby assigned to the command of the Second Division, District of West Tennessee (formerly the command of Maj. Gen. E. O. C. Ord), which embraces all the territory south of the Kentucky line and to the Hatchie on the west and Bethel Station on the east, including Bolivar, south of the Hatchie. It will be his duty to guard all the railroads within his district, and in accordance with General Orders, No. 83, from these headquarters, his headquarters will be at Jackson or Bolivar, at the option of the commander.

By order of Maj. Gen. U. S. Grant.

JNO. A. RAWLINS,
Assistant Adjutant General.

WAR DEPARTMENT,
Washington, October 8, 1862.

Major-General GRANT, *Jackson, Tenn.:*

Prisoners of war will be paroled and delivered to the enemy at some point within his lines. A receipted list must be taken in duplicate, and one copy sent to the Adjutant-General, in order to effect an exchange

General Wright says he has placed seven Illinois regiments at your command. A large body of new levies will be collected as soon as possible at Memphis. General McPherson is promoted. Report others who deserve it.

> H. W. HALLECK,
> *General-in-Chief.*

BOLIVAR, [TENN., *October* 8, 1862].

Major-General GRANT:

Order for Ross' movement received. Two companies Illinois cavalry, one regiment, and one section will move, flying light, to seize and hold Davis' Mill Bridge; the rest of the column will follow rapidly. I think Mack's regiment (Seventy-sixth Illinois) had better remain here, and perhaps the Twelfth Wisconsin. Mack has no haversacks for provisions.

> S. A. HURLBUT.

BOLIVAR, [TENN., *October*] 8, 1862.

Major-General GRANT:

I have just heard from Holly Springs. There are no forces there; all left on Sunday. There is about one company of cavalry at Davis' Mill to destroy the railroad bridge, if no more. Everything in shape of force above Wolf River has moved south. I am of opinion that the rout of Van Dorn's army is complete, and that Pillow's force, late at Holly, has caught the panic. Ross moves to-night and will await further orders at La Grange and Grand Junction, which he is ordered to occupy by morning.

> S. A. HURLBUT,
> *Major-General.*

HEADQUARTERS ARMY OF THE MISSISSIPPI,
October 8, 1862.

Brigadier-General MCARTHUR:

If Hurlbut's division is pushing for Ripley you may follow McPherson by Nolin's toward Hatchie, where there is water, and pushing to Blackland.

By order of Major-General Rosecrans:

> [H. G. KENNETT,]
> *Lieutenant-Colonel and Chief of Staff.*

CAIRO, ILL., *October* 8, 1862—10.35 a. m.

Maj. Gen. H. W. HALLECK, *General-in-Chief:*

General Grant telegraphs me that he wants at least twenty regiments as soon as they can possibly be got. Governor Yates has not got them ready to move. Cannot General Curtis or the Governor of Iowa send some? I have telegraphed General Wright.

> J. M. TUTTLE,
> *Brigadier-General.*

WAR DEPARTMENT,
Washington, October 9, 1862.

Major-General GRANT, *Jackson, Tenn.* :

Governor Johnson is very desirous that troops be sent to Clarksville. How far is the Cumberland navigable, and how could troops be sent to Clarksville?

H. W. HALLECK,
General-in-Chief.

CORINTH, *October* 9, 1862.

Major-General GRANT :

Paroled now 813 enlisted men, 43 commissioned officers, in good health; about 700 Confederate wounded, already sent to Iowa, paroled; 350 wounded paroled here; cannot tell the number of dead yet. About 800 Confederates already buried; their loss about eight or ten to one of ours. Prisoners arriving by every wagon road and train; will send full reports as soon as possible. No return yet from the hospitals. The woods stink yet with unburied dead. Oglesby shot through the breast and ball lodged in the spine; hope for his recovery. No news from Rosecrans.

I understand Hamilton's division, my regiment, and others left Rienzi yesterday at 4 p. m. for the west; nothing authentic from them. Hillyer is here. Shall I send any wounded Confederates to Saint Louis? Our hospitals are full of them. McKean telegraphs me he will be here this night.

P. E. BURKE,
Colonel Western Sharpshooters, Fourteenth Mo. Vols., Comdg.

HEADQUARTERS FOURTH DIVISION,
Bolivar, Tenn., October 9, 1862—3 p. m.

Brig. Gen. L. F. ROSS,
Commanding Expedition :

Report just received. The enemy are in greater force than I expected. You will watch your flanks, especially on the La Grange side. The country around Davis' Mill is very rough, and you may find trouble in working the artillery down. Be as rapid as possible, but cautious, and where you strike, strike hard.

The thing to be done, under General Grant's order, is to destroy the bridge or force them to do so. Listen for cars to-night; reconnoiter closely; finish the work, and return as soon as possible. Even if you whip them severely you must not pursue too far, for they still have the railroad and may have been joined by Van Dorn.

I shall expect you back by day after to-morrow. Keep me advised from time to time of all that is being done.

Yours,

[S. A. HURLBUT,]
Major-General.

BOLIVAR, TENN., *October* 9, 1862.

Maj. Gen. U. S. GRANT, *Jackson, Tenn.* :

I have no camp-kettles or other utensils for prisoners, and suggest that they be removed at once to Alton or some other point, or, if kept here, that necessary utensils be furnished. There are none here.

As soon as Ross returns I shall send the Twelfth Wisconsin back to Humboldt. I expect a report from Ross every moment, which will be forwarded.

What disposition shall I make of the Seventy-sixth Illinois? I am short one regiment in my division, and would like to have them in my Second Brigade. The Fifty-second Indiana has not joined me yet. I suppose it is at Fort Pillow.

[S. A. HURLBUT,]
Major-General.

BOLIVAR, *October* 9, 1862.

Major-General GRANT:

Have just heard from Ross; his advanced guard went into Grand Junction about sunrise, too late for a surprise on Davis' Mill. The main body at 9 a. m. were at Van Buren, 9 miles from Junction. Scouts report 2,000 infantry and 300 cavalry at Davis' Mill; infantry, exchanged prisoners, not well armed. Ross has 3,300 infantry, 400 cavalry, and sixteen pieces of artillery. I have ordered him to crown the heights on Wolf River, near La Grange, and push forward and destroy the bridge or force them to destroy it, and return. I still think they will burn it in presence of Ross' force. I will send his report by train.

S. A. HURLBUT,
Major-General.

HEADQUARTERS ARMY OF THE MISSISSIPPI,

Ripley, October 9, 1862.

Colonel MIZNER:

Having scoured the country toward Oxford, Hickory Flats, Salem, Orizaba, by the scouts now out, and others if necessary, direct your cavalry to report everything to and act in concert with Brigadier-General McPherson. Cover the front south as far east as Rienzi with a force of sufficient strength; the southwestern and western with a force of greater strength.

General McPherson proposes to make a demonstration on the Hickory Flats and Oxford roads to-morrow. I think it will be best for the cavalry to participate in this.

The cavalry had better remain until the night after General McPherson leaves, or longer if deemed prudent, and then move quietly and assemble at a good camp behind the Tuscumbia, to be selected by yourself, where good water and grass are convenient.

Enjoin upon the officers to act constantly in concert with General McPherson and give him a full understanding of all their movements.

By order of Major-General Rosecrans:

C. GODDARD,
First Lieut. Twelfth Infty. Ohio Vols., Actg. Asst. Adjt. Gen.

HEADQUARTERS ARMY OF THE MISSISSIPPI,

Ripley, Miss., October 9, 1862.

COMMANDING OFFICER OF THE TOWN OF RIPLEY, MISS.:

The following instructions are given for your guidance, viz:

Establish your office and appoint an active and reliable man for provost-marshal, and direct him to make his headquarters at the court-house.

You are charged with the enforcement of order, discipline, police regulations, and the preservation of property, both public and private, in the town of Ripley.

Establish police picket guards at the principal entrances of the town, with orders to challenge all persons.

Staff officers and persons mounted or on foot or orderly duty, headquarters dispatch bearers and messengers, and parties on patrol duty and detached service pass in and out by virtue of their orders.

Neither officers, soldiers, nor citizens (except general or staff officers) will be permitted to pass in or out, and all those attempting to do so will be arrested without regard to rank, person, mission, or excuse, and taken to the provost-marshal's office and there detained until their cases can be inquired into. Patrol the town thoroughly and clear it of all our soldiers, arresting every one that is there without a pass signed by a proper officer, and take them to your camp, where they will be held until you have notified the commanding officer of the regiment or company to which they belong that you are directed by major-general commanding to direct them to send a responsible commissioned officer to take charge of them.

All men found with plunder in their possession or in private houses will be separated from the others and immediately tied up and no food furnished them except bread and water. If no rope is to be found, use withes. Report their cases.

When the town has once been cleared and order restored frequent patrols will be sent to arrest such persons as pass into town by other than the principal entrances. The provost-marshal of the army has been directed to order all citizens to immediately report to you all Confederate soldiers at or near their houses, whether disabled or not. You will see those that are well are sent under guard to Crum's Mill, on the Hatchie, thence to be forwarded to Corinth, Miss. A regular descriptive list of the sick will be made, and they will be paroled as prisoners of war, not to bear arms or do anything prejudicial to the interests of the United States Government until regularly exchanged. Your attention is called also to spies, and the major-general commanding hopes that such rigor will be used in their cases as will render it unnecessary for him to be troubled with their examination.

You will be held responsible, and you will hold your officers responsible, that these instructions are enforced in all cases and in the strictest manner.

By order of Major-General Rosecrans:

C. GODDARD,
First Lieut. Twelfth Infty. Ohio Vols., Actg. Asst. Adjt. Gen.

HEADQUARTERS DIVISION OF MEMPHIS,
Memphis, October 9, 1862.

Maj. Gen. U. S. GRANT, *Jackson, Tenn.*:

DEAR GENERAL: You can well understand how glad I was to hear of the successes about Corinth, Chewalla, and Pocahontas. They have had a wonderful effect here, and the secesh have changed their tone very much. I hear through rebel deserters that the rebel army is at Ripley, and therefore out of reach, for they would scatter and escape if pursued.

A few days since I heard that a party of Partisan Rangers were forming on Wolf River, 6 miles from Germantown. I ordered Grierson, with

400 select cavalry, to move out cautiously by night and fall upon them. He did so most successfully, killing 5, wounding 15, and bringing in 6 prisoners and about 20 animals—horses and mules.   He scattered the party and brought in all the papers, commissions, and muster-rolls. There is a small force under a Colonel Ballentine at Byhalia, 5 miles out, and another party under an acting brigadier-general, J. A. Orr, at Holly Springs, but they are too far off to be surprised, so that an expedition against them would simply run down our horses and do no great good.

Since I caused the destruction of the town of Randolph and gave notice if boats engaged in commerce were fired on I should expel rebel families and cause others to take passage on those boats as common targets for the guerrillas, no boats have been molested.

A great deal of cotton has come in of late in small parcels, in single bales, &c., amounting in the aggregate to over a thousand bales, and I have somewhat relaxed the rules as to internal trade.   Farmers have come in gangs, representing their determination to fight guerrillas and carry out to their suffering families the clothing and groceries necessary to their existence.   I have no doubt this is in the main true.   Though in some cases the privilege has been and will be abused, I think it good policy to encourage it, that the farmers and property holders may realize their dependence on other parts of our country, and also realize that a state of war long continued will reduce them to a state of absolute ruin.

The band of guerrillas or partisan rangers are doing us less harm than our enemies, for they in their wants and necessities must take meat and corn, and will take it when and where they please, of friend or foe; the consequence is that the farmers and planters begin to realize that they have to submit to be plundered by these bands of marauders, and are getting heartily tired of it.   Of course some do buy negro shoes for the use of guerrillas and salt for curing bacon.   My own opinion is that all trade should be absolutely prohibited to all districts until the military commander notifies the Government that the rebellion is suppressed in that district, for we know, whatever restraint is imposed on steamboats, that clerks and hands do smuggle everything by which they can make profit.   The great profit now made is converting everybody into rascals, and it makes me ashamed of my countrymen every time I have to examine a cotton or horse case.   I have no doubt that our cause suffers from the fact that not only horses and cotton are bought of negroes and thieves under fabricated bills of sale, but that the reputations of even military men become involved.   Still, as the Treasury authorities think it proper to allow trade and encourage the buying of cotton it is my duty not to interpose any obstacle.   Whenever I do detect fraud I punish it to the fullest extent; and we have made large and valuable prizes, all of which I see go to the use of the United States.

General Steele has passed up the river with half of his Helena command.   General Carr remains at Helena with I suppose 7,000 or 8,000 men, too few to do much good; still I suppose all we can do is to hold fast all we have till the armies of Kentucky and Virginia get abreast of us.

I take it for granted that Price and Van Dorn will renew their efforts on your position, but the terrible punishment they have received will make them timid.   I know and feel that these battles about Corinth have shaken the confidence of their adherents here awfully.

Everything progresses well in my division, and I am putting it in such order that I can add ten infantry regiments and make a corps with which I could reach Grenada and Jackson. I will again sweep with cavalry the country from the mouth of Hatchie and Somerville, so as to clean out all bands now in the country between Wolf and Hatchie Rivers.

All things civil here are also doing well and in good shape.

As ever, your friend and obedient servant,

W. T. SHERMAN,
Major-General.

JACKSON, TENN., *October* 10, 1862—9.30 p. m.

Maj. Gen. H. W. HALLECK, *General-in-Chief:*

Light-draught boats can go to Fort Henry. From there there will be no difficulty in reaching Clarksville. Will go by Donelson should the Cumberland River be too high to ford.

U. S. GRANT,
Major-General.

BOLIVAR, *October* 10, 1862.

Major-General GRANT:

General Ross is on his return, having thoroughly destroyed bridge at Davis'. Only cavalry found, who fled. I regret that the bridge was not saved.

S. A. HURLBUT,
Major-General.

HEADQUARTERS FOURTH DIVISION,
Bolivar, October 10, 1862.

Brig. Gen. L. F. ROSS:

I heard nothing from you last night, and hear no guns this morning. When you have completed your work, if you are satisfied there is no force of considerable size north of Wolf River, push one battalion of cavalry around through Somerville and crush that nest of traitors and guerrillas there.

All is quiet here.

Your obedient servant,

[S. A. HURLBUT,]
Major-General.

WASHINGTON CITY, *October* 10, 1862.

Hon. E. M. STANTON,
Secretary of War :

SIR : As it is possible, perhaps probable, that the debarkation of the Mississippi expedition will be contested by the enemy, it is considered important that it should be formed in part of experienced troops. If the expedition should be limited at first to 20,000 men, one-half or at least one-fourth of that number should be of such troops, and I think they might be taken from the Army of the Tennessee (with which I have been identified) without material detriment to the public service, particularly if their place should be filled by new troops, and since the late defeat and dispersion of the enemy in West Tennessee.

Taking a few regiments from that army, even if they were only skeleton ones, and incorporating them with the expedition would be to impart a martial spirit and tone which would be of great value to it; hence I recommend that the Eighth, Eleventh, Fourteenth, Seventeenth, Eighteenth, Twentieth, Twenty-eighth, and Thirtieth Illinois, and Forty-third Illinois and Thirteenth Iowa, the Seventh and Eighth Missouri, and Seventy-eighth Ohio be assigned to the expedition. Most, if not all, of these regiments are sadly reduced and probably would not average 400 effective men each, giving an aggregate of only 5,200 men.

Some of the regiments named are still more desirable on account of the officers commanding them. Among the number of these officers are Col. T. E. G. Ransom, of the Eleventh Illinois; Colonel Crocker, of the Thirteenth Iowa; Colonel Leggett, of the Seventy-eighth Ohio, and Col. C. C. Marsh, of the Twentieth Illinois, who would make excellent brigade commanders. I would also name Brig. Gen. L. F. Ross and Brig. Gen. Morgan L. Smith, both now in West Tennessee, for division commanders; and ask that First Lieut. James H. Wilson, of the Topographical Corps, be assigned to duty as a member of my staff. I think this would be agreeable to him.

The forces designed for the Mississippi expedition might be concentrated either at Cairo or Memphis, there being comparatively little difference in their eligibility as places of rendezvous and for depots of military supplies.

Your obedient servant,

JOHN A. McCLERNAND,
Major-General.

P. S.—Shelter-tents, capable of being carried by the men, are preferable. Also Springfield muskets (smooth-bore), except for the flank companies of each regiment, which should be armed with the Springfield or Enfield rifled musket.

All the arms of each class should be of the same caliber, and indeed it would be better that all of both classes should be of the same caliber if it were practicable.

SPECIAL ORDERS, }　　HDQRS. DISTRICT OF WEST TENNESSEE,
No. 218. 　　 }　　　　*Jackson, Tenn., October 11, 1862.*

* 　　 * 　　 * 　　 * 　　 * 　　 * 　　 *

VI. Major-General McPherson immediately upon reaching Corinth will turn over his command to Colonel Lawler and report himself in person to these headquarters.

By order of Maj. Gen. U. S. Grant:

[JNO. A. RAWLINS,]
Assistant Adjutant-General.

ROSECRANS' HEADQUARTERS,
October 12, 1862.

Major RAWLINS:

Your orders in reference to McPherson and his troops duly received, and will be carried into effect on the arrival of General McPherson and his command.

W. S. ROSECRANS,
Major-General.

WASHINGTON, *October* 13, 1862.

Maj. Gen. U. S. GRANT, *Jackson, Tenn.*:

GENERAL : Your letter of the 5th instant in relation to the management of railroads in your command has been received and laid before the Secretary of War. General McPherson should be relieved and assigned to his proper command, and if you have no other officer suitable for the superintending of the roads you are authorized to employ a civil engineer, paying him suitable compensation from the proceeds of the roads. It is impossible to give him a military commission, as the law allowing additional aides is repealed. Perhaps it may be revived when Congress meets again. No difficulty is encountered on other roads from the superintendent not having military rank.

Very respectfully, your obedient servant,

H. W. HALLECK,
General-in-Chief.

———

ROSECRANS' HEADQUARTERS,
October 13, 1862.

Major-General GRANT, *Jackson:*

General McPherson arrived last night. No signs of an enemy. Pushed cavalry 17 miles on the Oxford road ; nothing but stragglers. Enemy have gone to Oxford, except a few regiments to Tupelo. A rumor is gaining currency among the secesh that Johnston, with 40,000 men from Virginia, has arrived at Oxford. It must receive prompt attention. Pocahontas is a key which ought to be occupied in case the rebels dispose a portion of their Virginia forces to push in here. It would be a strong move. Tell Sherman to put spies in motion ; I will do the same, to find out all I can.

W. S. ROSECRANS,
Major-General.

———

JACKSON, TENN., *October* 13, 1862—12 noon.

Maj. Gen. H. W. HALLECK, *General-in-Chief:*

General Rosecrans reports a rumor that Johnston, with 40,000 men, has arrived at Oxford. Should reports prove true I will concentrate my forces at Bolivar and be prepared to meet him.

U. S. GRANT,
Major-General, Commanding.

———

SPECIAL ORDERS, } HDQRS. FIRST DIV., DIST. OF WEST TENN.,
    No. 273.   }   *Memphis, October* 13, 1862.

The Sixth Illinois Cavalry and one battery of artillery, to be designated by the chief of artillery, will take post in the city of Memphis, at the depot of the Memphis and Charleston Railroad, and the senior officer will be considered the commanding officer of the whole and be held responsible for the good conduct of all. His attention and the attention of his command is called to the thirty-second Article of War. This property is now substantially that of the United States, and any officer and soldier who damages it can be charged on the muster-roll with the amount of damage, besides being liable to such other punishment as a court-martial may inflict.

II. The post quartermaster, Captain Fitch, will assign specially to Colonel Grierson the property hereby directed, and may include one or more of the vacant cotton-sheds close by for stables, but in no case must any building be taken or appropriated until a specific assignment has been made of it by an officer of the Quartermaster's Department. The regiment will keep in use its wagons and tents and be prepared always for active field service.

III. The provost guard will vacate these premises, and their head-quarters hereafter will be at the Irving Block.

By order of Maj. Gen. W. T. Sherman:

J. H. HAMMOND,
Assistant Adjutant-General.

STEAM-RAM SWITZERLAND,
Mound City, Ill., October 14, 1862.

Hon. E. M. STANTON,
    Secretary of War:

I have the honor to forward you the report * of my nephew, Medical Cadet Charles Rivers Ellet, respecting his late expedition down the river to near Vicksburg. He informs me that his boats were repeatedly fired into by the bands of guerrillas from the shore, and had several sharp engagements. My boats are now all in good repair, and I shall resume my efforts to break up these bands immediately.

Very respectfully, &c.,

ALFRED W. ELLET,
Colonel, Commanding Ram Fleet.

SPECIAL ORDERS, }   HDQRS. DISTRICT OF WEST TENNESSEE,
    No. 221.   }   *Jackson, Tenn., October* 14, 1862.

*   *   *   *   *   *   *

XII. Maj. Gen. J. B. McPherson is hereby assigned to the command of the United States forces at Bolivar, Tenn., and will report to Major-General Hurlbut, commanding Second Division, District of West Tennessee.

*   *   *   *   *   *   *

By order of Maj. Gen. U. S. Grant:

JNO. A. RAWLINS,
Assistant Adjutant-General.

WASHINGTON CITY, *October* 15, 1862.

Hon. E. M. STANTON,
    Secretary of War:

In compliance with your request I have the honor to submit a plan for the organization of the army designed to form the Mississippi expedition:

Twenty-four thousand infantry, 1,000 sharpshooters, 400 Sappers and Miners, 3,000 cavalry, 1,500 light artillery, 100 heavy artillery.

Number and caliber of guns required to arm ten batteries of light

---

* See report of attack on the U. S. steam-ram Queen of the West, near Bolivar, Miss., September 19, 1862, Part I, p. 139.

artillery: Fourteen 10-pounder Parrott guns; twenty-eight Napoleon guns; six 24-pounder howitzers (brass); eight 6-pounder smooth-bore guns (brass); four 12-pounder howitzers (brass).

Number and caliber of guns for siege train: Eight 30-pounder Parrott guns; four 10-inch mortars.

Please assign Lieut. James H. Wilson, Engineers, U. S. Army, who is now here, for duty as a member of my staff.

Your obedient servant,

JOHN A. McCLERNAND,
Major-General.

HEADQUARTERS,
Jackson, October 16, 1862.

Maj. Gen. J. B. McPHERSON,
Commanding Bolivar, Tenn. :

It will be necessary to keep a vigilant lookout to the front and right flank in direction of Somerville. I wish you would see Colonel Johnson, Twenty-eighth Illinois, when he returns; you may rely on the accuracy of his observations. I apprehend nothing of movements in force, but the enemy are strong in cavalry, and the country between La Grange and Somerville and so to Whitesville is fine foraging ground. The Hatchie is fordable still for cavalry at many points, especially near the mouth of Clover Creek, and, if you are satisfied it can be thoroughly done without too large a risk, I wish the nest of irregular cavalry near Somerville broken up, and a sharp lesson taught them not to come too near.

It was my rule not to send out a forage train without a heavy guard, generally a full regiment of infantry and two companies of cavalry. It is good exercise for the men and answers as a reconnaissance.

Yours, truly,

[S. A. HURLBUT],
Major-General.

GENERAL ORDERS, } WAR DEPARTMENT, ADJT. GEN.'S OFFICE,
   No. 159.   }   *Washington, October* 16, 1862.

I. The Department of the Tennessee will include Cairo, Fort Henry, and Fort Donelson, Northern Mississippi, and the portions of Kentucky and Tennessee west of the Tennessee River.

II. Maj. Gen. U. S. Grant is assigned to the command of the Department of the Tennessee.

By order of the Secretary of War:

L. THOMAS,
Adjutant-General.

GENERAL ORDERS, } HDQRS. FIRST DIV., DIST. OF WEST TENN.,
   No. 88.   }   *Memphis, October* 16, 1862.

The engineer in charge of Fort Pickering will lay off a plat of ground of about three acres at some suitable point south or east of the fort for a cemetery, and will inclose it with a good stout fence, with strong gates. The lines should conform as near as may be to the streets and lanes of the survey of the city of Memphis, in order that the ownership of the property may be ascertained at some future time.

II. Hereafter all interments of soldiers or employés about the fort will be made in the fort cemetery, and the bodies which have been buried outside the fort will be removed to the cemetery. Whenever a soldier dies the colonel of his regiment will make requisition on the quarter-master for the necessary lumber, and will see that each grave of his men is marked with a suitable head-board. All funerals must be conducted strictly according to the Army Regulations.

Interments for the general hospital will be made at Elmwood, as here-tofore.

By order of Maj. Gen. W. T. Sherman:

J. H. HAMMOND,
Assistant Adjutant-General.

WAR DEPARTMENT,
Washington, October 17, 1862.

Maj. Gen. U. S. GRANT, *Jackson, Tenn.:*

What is the condition of affairs in your department? Am anxious to know, as Governor Johnson and General Curtis are asking for more troops.

H. W. HALLECK,
General-in-Chief.

JACKSON, TENN., *October* 17, 1862—8.15 p. m.

Maj. Gen. H. W. HALLECK, *General-in-Chief:*

My effective force is 48,500, exclusive of extra-duty men, located as follows: Four thousand eight hundred in Kentucky and Illinois, 7,000 in Memphis, 19,200 from Union City south, besides Corinth forces—latter 17,500. Another attack is soon inevitable. Re-enforcements neces-sary to keep up the confidence of our men as well as to give sufficient strength to meet the enemy. The enemy are largely re-enforced.

U. S. GRANT.

HEADQUARTERS DIVISION OF MEMPHIS,
Memphis, October 18, 1862.

Maj. JOHN A. RAWLINS,
Assistant Adjutant-General, Jackson, Miss.:

DEAR SIR: I am this moment in receipt of the general's letter of the 11th. From some cause there is unusual delay in the letters to and from. I have had several messengers in from the interior of late. Holly Springs is occupied in force, with camps at Davis' Mill, 9 miles south of Grand Junction; at Coldwater, and the Chewalla Creek, east of Holly Springs. Van Dorn and Price were both at Holly Springs yesterday, expecting Pemberton, who is to command all. This is from Ex-Brig. Gen. Ed. Price, son of the rebel general, who has resigned, and whom I have permitted, on certain letters of General Schofield and Gov-ernor Gamble, to return to Missouri. He came in this morning. He came through Oxford a day or two since. There was nothing said of General Joe Johnston being there with 40,000 from the Virginia army. I have heard from many that Ruggles has joined from below with some 4,000 men, supposed to be reorganized regiments of the returned pris-oners sent to Vicksburg by us so opportunely for them.

I have no doubt that in and around Holly Springs is now assembled all the forces they can collect together, and it behooves General Grant to keep his men near enough for concentration.

General Curtis, on the supposition that Missouri was in danger, has taken one-half of the Helena force back to Saint Louis to be sent to the Iron Mountain; the fact is that there is no considerable force in Arkansas threatening Missouri. General Carr has the other half, say 9,000 men, and expects help from me. I will write him to strengthen his defenses, and no force will attempt to storm his fort where he has heavy ordnance. He has a larger force than I have, and I have a much more important place to defend than Helena is. The boats navigating the river are now assailed above and below. I have sent a force above to Island 21, and now comes a call to send some to a post below. We will have to do something more than merely repel these attacks. We must make the people feel that every attack on a road here will be resented by the destruction of some one of their towns or plantations elsewhere. All adherents of their cause must suffer for these cowardly acts.

I propose to expel ten secession families for every boat fired on, thereby lessening the necessity for fighting boats for their benefit, and will visit on the neighborhood summary punishment. It may sometimes fall on the wrong head, but it would be folly to send parties of infantry to chase these wanton guerrillas.

So far as the city of Memphis and neighborhood is concerned all is well. Guerrilla bands are being called into Holly Springs, where the enemy is doubtless concentrating for some effort. We are ready for them here.

I rather fear for Bolivar and Jackson. Pemberton's command, though, is confined to Mississippi and Louisiana, and to assume the offensive he would have to enter Tennessee.

Your obedient servant,

W. T. SHERMAN,
Major-General, Commanding.

[Indorsement.]

HEADQUARTERS DEPARTMENT OF WEST TENNESSEE,
Jackson, October 24, 1862.

Respectfully forwarded to Headquarters of the Army for the information of the general-in-chief, embodying as it does a policy, which I approve but have given no order for, in regard to treatment of rebel families as a punishment to prevent firing into boats; also to show the condition of the Helena force, and for the general information contained therein.

U. S. GRANT,
Major-General, Commanding.

SPECIAL ORDERS, }   HDQRS. FIRST DIV., DIST. OF WEST TENN.,
No. 283.   }   *Memphis, October* 18, 1862.

The Forty-sixth Ohio, Colonel Walcutt, will embark to-night on board of steamboat ———, and before daylight drop down to a point on the Arkansas shore about 15 miles below this, near Elm Grove Post-Office, and there disembark. He will then proceed to destroy all the houses, farms, and corn fields from that point up to Hopefield. The boat will follow him up and communicate with him at such points as he can reach the shore. He will keep an account and except from the execution of this order all parties that he may have reason to believe have not been rendezvousing the guerrillas. This is done to let the guerrillas who attacked the Catahoula feel that certain destruction awaits the country for firing on steamboats engaged in carrying supplies needed by the planters between Memphis and Helena. Major Taylor will send a section of artillery along, subject to Colonel Walcutt's order.

The quartermaster will at once provide a suitable steamboat to drop down to the fort by sunset.

By order of Maj. Gen. W. T. Sherman:

J. H. HAMMOND,
Assistant-Adjutant-General.

JACKSON, TENN., *October* 19, 1862.

Maj. Gen. H. W. HALLECK, *General-in-Chief :*

We have Falkner, 3 of his officers, and 12 men. How shall they be treated? They claim to be regulars in the army and entitled to exchange. I think the officers at least should be held.

U. S. GRANT,
Major-General.

HEADQUARTERS,
Bolivar, Tenn., October 19, 1862.

Colonel NOBLE, *Chief of Cavalry, Bolivar:*

COLONEL: You will send out an expedition of 450 cavalry, under the command of one of your most thorough, active, and intelligent officers, in the direction of Brownsville, to intercept and cut off if possible Colonel Falkner's cavalry force, defeated day before yesterday at Island No. 10. You will direct them to move up on the north side of the Hatchie, ascertain if possible the ford or bridge they are making for, and try and cut them off. The commander of the expedition must move with all possible celerity, but at the same time use due caution against being surprised and cut off himself. Three days' rations must be taken with the men.

Very respectfully, your obedient servant,

JAS. B. McPHERSON,
Major-General.

CORINTH, MISS., *October* 19, 1862—2.10 p. m.

Hon. E. M. STANTON,
Secretary of War:

Our cavalry, in the face of the enemy, and in the best possible season for a campaign, are without arms. Of the 900 revolving arms you ordered sent me, only 439 have been received. One thousand breech-loading or revolving arms and 2,000 pistols are necessary to arm our cavalry, including recruits. Cavalry without arms anywhere is bad enough, but on a hostile frontier it is not only waste but murder. For Heaven's sake do something for us if you can. Please answer.

W. S. ROSECRANS.

WAR DEPARTMENT,
Washington City, October 20, 1862. .

General 'N. S. ROSECRANS, *Corinth, Miss.:*

Dispatch of the 19th in relation to arms received. The 439 Colt's re
volving rifles were all that were on hand.

On the 18th instant, on the requisition of Col. T. L. Dickey, chief of
cavalry General Grant's army, the following breech-loading carbines,
with accouterments and ammunition complete, were ordered to be sent
to Columbus, Ky., with dispatch, for the use of the following regiments
and companies in that army:

Second Illinois Cavalry, 330 Sharps'; Fourth Illinois, 280 Sharps';
Sixth Illinois, 220 Sharps'; Thielemann's, 70 Sharps'; Stewart's Bat-
talion, 70 Sharps'; Ford's company (attached to Fifty-third Illinois), 70
Sharps'; Fifth Iowa, 330 Sharps'; Eleventh Illinois, 630 Smith's; Fifth
Ohio, 750 Burnside's. Total, 2,750 carbines.

On the 14th instant 1,000 army revolvers were ordered from the inspector of contract arms to be sent to Saint Louis Arsenal, and 500 Pet-
tengill army revolvers are now on their way there. These 1,500 pistols
Major Callender has been directed to keep to fill your requisitions. In
making them on him make a separate requisition for each regiment, or
give the designation of each in a consolidated requisition, to enable the
accounts to be kept with the States.

P. H. WATSON,
Assistant Secretary of War.

WAR DEPARTMENT,
October 20, 1862.

Colonel ELLET,
Commanding Ram Fleet, Mound City, Ill.:

The ram fleet was not included in the transfer of the gunboat fleet to
the Navy Department. Its disposition was left for further consideration. You will retain command as heretofore until further orders.

EDWIN M. STANTON,
Secretary of War.

CONFIDENTIAL.]   WAR DEPARTMENT,
Washington City, October 21, 1862.

Ordered, That Major-General McClernand be, and he is, directed to
proceed to the States of Indiana, Illinois, and Iowa, to organize the
troops remaining in those States and to be raised by volunteering or
draft, and forward them with all dispatch to Memphis, Cairo, or such
other points as may hereafter be designated by the general-in-chief, to
the end that, when a sufficient force not required by the operations of
General Grant's command shall be raised, an expedition may be organized under General McClernand's command against Vicksburg and to
clear the Mississippi River and open navigation to New Orleans.

The forces so organized will remain subject to the designation of the
general-in-chief, and be employed according to such exigencies as the
service in his judgment may require.

EDWIN M. STANTON,
Secretary of War.

WAR DEPARTMENT,
Washington, October 21, 1862.

Major-General GRANT, *Jackson, Tenn.:*

I know nothing of Falkner and his officers, and therefore can give no special directions.

To what point do you wish new troops to be sent—Columbus or Memphis?

H. W. HALLECK,
General-in-Chief.

ROSECRANS' HEADQUARTERS,
October 21, 1862—10.30 p. m.

General GRANT, *Jackson :*

My sending away paroled prisoners to Benton Barracks was in conformity with previous custom, and in supposed accordance with your views of the propriety of clearing them out of Corinth as rapidly as possible. As soon as made aware of different orders or views they were promptly carried out. The only person I authorized to leave for Saint Louis was Dr. Scott, not a prisoner, who called on you and took a message from you. Your dispatch complaining of the action is the first intimation I have had of your disapproval. A Captain Tobin was paroled and permitted to go North while I was absent at Ripley, but neither with my consent nor approval. No other instances have come to my knowledge. That part of your dispatch which refers to newspaper reporters and leaky members of my staff showing the existence of any desire or even any sentiment at these headquarters of keeping up a distinction of feeling and spirit between the troops of my command or the rest of your troops, as if they were not an integral part thereof, I answer that no such feeling has ever existed at these headquarters. No countenance, either directly or indirectly, has been given to such an idea, nor was I aware that such an idea was abroad until I saw indications of it from members of your staff and in your own orders.

I regard it as the offspring of sentiments [rather] than those of a desire for justice or the good of the service, and sincerely hope that you do not participate therein. There are no headquarters in these United States less responsible for what newspaper correspondents and paragraphists say of operations than mine. This I wish to be understood to be distinctly applicable to the affairs of Iuka and Corinth. After this declaration I am free to say that if you do not meet me frankly with a declaration that you are satisfied I shall consider my power to be useful in this department ended.

W. S. ROSECRANS,
Major-General, Commanding.

WAR DEPARTMENT,
Washington City, D. C., October 21, 1862.

Major-General ROSECRANS. *Corinth :*

Your requisitions of cavalry arms are filled and are on the way to you. The enormous demand for arms occasions some delay, and the Department has been desirous of supplying you as far as possible with arms of uniform caliber. Every exertion has been made and will be made to supply your demands. I take this occasion to express the great satisfaction which your operations have given to the President and the Department.

EDWIN M. STANTON,
Secretary of War.

CORINTH, MISS., *October* 21, 1862—8.40 p. m.

Hon. E. M. STANTON,
Secretary of War :

Your dispatch announcing the coming of arms for our cavalry was hailed with delight. Profound disappointment followed the receipt of Mr. Watson's dispatch, which shows they all go to little detachments, split up and performing picket duty in our rear. The cavalry for whom I ask are the only ones that are massed, and have had power to chastise and cow the rebel cavalry all summer. For the others, divided up and acting in our rear, the rebels care not a pin. They ought to be well armed, but not until the Second Iowa, Third Michigan, Seventh Kansas, Seventh and Eleventh Illinois have been, for they alone have made the enemy afraid and whipped them in force. Do something for these brave men, who had not less than three fights per week for the last thirty days.

W. S. ROSECRANS,
Major-General.

WAR DEPARTMENT,
October 21, 1862.

Maj. Gen. W. S. ROSECRANS, *Corinth, Miss.* :

Colonel Dickey, accredited by General Grant as chief of cavalry, represented the regiments to whom I telegraphed you the carbines were assigned, as those who had done all the cavalry service in the department. If you will telegraph immediately how many men you have in each of the regiments you mention without carbines, I will do all I can to supply them promptly.

P. H. WATSON,
Assistant Secretary of War.

CORINTH, MISS., *October* 21, 1862.

Hon. P. H. WATSON,
Assistant Secretary of War :

Your dispatch received. Not one of the cavalry command to which you have sent arms has done any real fighting. The Third Michigan, the Second Iowa, the Seventh Kansas, and the Seventh Illinois, who have been in continued combats, say more than fifty fights, this summer, and are the only cavalry that have been massed and managed so as to have power to cow and scourge the rebels effectually, are entirely overlooked in the allotment of arms. They are under my command.

W. S. ROSECRANS,
Major-General.

HEADQUARTERS FIRST DIVISION,
Memphis, October 21, 1862.

Maj. JOHN A. RAWLINS,
   Assistant Adjutant-General, Jackson, Tenn. :

SIR : Since my last, some attacks have been made on the boats navigating the Mississippi River, but in no case have the guerrillas succeeded in getting a boat. They came near firing the Gladiator, but the captain (Irwin) got her off-shore and brought her to Memphis with two dead and many wounded on board. The conduct of the guerrillas was fiendish in the extreme. I ordered parties to Island 21, also to the point where the Catahoula was fired into. At the latter place the officer in command, Colonel Walcutt, Forty-sixth Ohio, found much evidence of complicity with the guerrillas, and he burned their places. I shall compel ten families to leave for every boat fired on, and let them try whether they prefer to live with their own people or with ours. I know from their actions that it is not agreeable, but it is not to be expected that we should feed and clothe the families of men who are engaged in firing upon boats engaged in peaceful commerce. To-morrow I dispatch all my cavalry to Colliersville, then north to Rising Sun, and thence west to Randolph, cleaning up the country of guerrillas. I wish to break up all parties north of Wolf River. At the same time an infantry regiment will march to Raleigh and Union Depot in concert. I will have boats at Randolph to bring them down. I find it difficult to hire regular spies, but I get full information from others who come to Memphis on various pretexts.

Price and Van Dorn are at Holly Springs in force; have received reenforcements from the south; Ruggles, with less than 4,000, and some reorganized exchanged prisoners, about 3,000. I have never heard a word about any from Virginia. Pemberton was expected yesterday, but I have not heard that he is yet there.

Bowen's brigade is at Coldwater, 55 miles out toward Memphis from Holly Springs. General Jackson, with the cavalry, some 2,000, are at Coldwater, 6 miles north of Holly Springs.

Blythe, with quite a force of irregular guerrillas, is at Horn Lake Depot, about 17 miles southeast of Memphis. All other parties of which I hear are small and inconsiderable. They have evidently within a week increased their vigilance, so that less news can be had than heretofore. Now is the time to strike at the Yazoo and Mississippi Central roads, all the troops being north of the Tallahatchie.

My division is now in good health, well equipped, and in good drill. The regiments are small, and I would much like to have some 2,000 recruits for them.

The Thirteenth Infantry has never got to me, though one officer from it has reported to me from Cincinnati via Alton, being ordered to report to his battalion here.

A deserter this moment in confirms the accounts from Holly Springs. Pemberton arrived last Friday with no troops; none even spoken of from Virginia. There was a camp rumor that 9,000 were to come from Arkansas to Mississippi. Confederates expecting you to attack them; some intrenchments near the town. Price's division, with the reorganized prisoners of war, were about to move to Davis' Mill, below Grand Junction. Reorganized prisoners supposed to be 5,000. Deserter knows nothing of Ruggles. Lovell's division on the road out from Holly Springs toward Mount Vernon. Bowen's brigade at Byhalia; Coldwater their line. Nobody at Colliersville or Moscow. No regular troops north of Wolf River. Deserter did not see Pemberton, but heard the boys say he was in town; did not know if Van Dorn was to remain in a subordinate position or go elsewhere. He estimated the aggregate forces at 40,000, but when he attempted to sum up could not make 20,000. My opinion is that Price and Pemberton have not at this time a force larger than attacked Rosecrans. One attack from the river toward Grenada would draw them out of Holly Springs quick. If ever you design to attack, remember La Grange is an admirable place; then Davis' Mill.

I will continue to report as often as I get definite news. I know that Jackson's cavalry is at our old camp at Roberts', 6 miles north of Holly Springs, and that Brown is at Byhalia, and Blythe at Horn Lake Depot.

All very quiet with us on our picket lines, and all town people begin to respect our power. The defeat at Corinth has had a most salutary effect.

Yours,

W. T. SHERMAN,
Major-General, Commanding.

HEADQUARTERS ARMY OF THE MISSISSIPPI,
THIRD DIV. OF THE DIST. OF WEST TENN.,
Corinth, Miss., October 22, 1862.
Hon. E. M. STANTON,
Secretary of War, Washington:

I have the honor to inclose herewith a map of Corinth and vicinity.

Destitute of engineers or topographical engineers, groping our way through an unknown wooded and hostile country, we have been obliged to resort to every possible device to obtain and diffuse information among commanders of troops. Having no copyists, when we get a map we have to resort to an improvised photographer, who, taking likenesses. was required to provide himself with the means of copying maps as the tax for the privilege of staying in camp.

Inclosed I send you two specimens of his handiwork of this place and vicinity.

Very truly, yours,

W. S. ROSECRANS,
Major-General.

CORINTH, *October* 22, 1862.
Maj. Gen. H. W. HALLECK:

MY DEAR GENERAL: I thank you for the kind expressions of confidence contained in your letter replying to mine.

My orders to report for duty to Major-General Wright still stand good.* He says, in a reply to a note I wrote him about the date of my last to you, that he feels fully the weight of my reasons for asking if any arrangements could be made whereby I should not fall under the command of the major-generals of Buell's division, even including General Granger, and will consent to any arrangement that will do away with the difficulties.

Since then we had the stirring times here, and I think it probable will have more of the same, since Bragg has gone over the mountains, and the rivers are low and the roads good; but I am very sorry to say that ever since the battle of Iuka there has been at work the spirit of mischief among the mousing politicians on Grant's staff to get up in his

* Of September 17, 1862.

mind a feeling of jealousy. They have at last so far succeeded that General Grant last evening telegraphed me that he thought certain leaky members of my staff and newspaper correspondents justified his insinuating that he thought I was getting up a spirit of division and trying to make my army appear independent of him. I dispatched, declaring that he had not had a truer friend or more loyal subordinate than myself; that no such sentiment existed or had been countenanced at these headquarters as the one he alluded to; that no headquarters in these United States were less responsible for the sayings of newspaper writers and correspondents than mine, and that I wished it to be distinctly understood that this remark was especially applicable to what had been said about the affairs of Iuka and Corinth. After these declarations I said, "If you do not meet me with the frank avowal that you are satisfied, I shall consider that my ability to be useful in this department has ended." That now is my opinion.

I am bending everything to complete the new defenses of Corinth so that we may hold it by a division against a very superior force. As soon as I finish this work and my report of the late battle and pursuit I shall hope for something that will settle this matter. I am sure those politicians will manage matters with the sole view of preventing Grant from being in the background of military operations. This will make him sour and reticent. I shall become uncommunicative, and that, added to a conviction that he lacks administrative ability, will complete the reasons why I should be relieved from duty here, if I can be assigned to any other suitable duty where such obstacles do not operate.

I forbear speaking of points in the operations here. You will see in my report of the battle of Iuka that I have observed the same thing. But I must close this personal letter, wishing you were here to command.

  Yours, truly,

         W. S. ROSECRANS,
            Major-General.

        CORINTH, MISS., *October* 22, 1862—7 p. m.

Hon. P. H. WATSON:

 Third Michigan Cavalry requires 690 revolvers, 294 Colt's revolving rifles; Fifth Ohio Cavalry, 88 revolvers, 170 Sharps' carbines; Second Iowa, 30 revolving rifles; Seventh Kansas, 250 revolvers, 500 Colt's revolving rifles; Company A, Second U. S. Cavalry, 60 revolvers, 60 carbines—all with slings, pistol-pouches, cap-boxes, and ammunition complete.

         W. S. ROSECRANS,
            Major-General.

         MEMPHIS, *October* 22, 1862.

Miss P. A. FRASER, *Memphis:*

 DEAR LADY: Your petition is received. I will allow fifteen days for the parties interested to send to Holly Springs and Little Rock to ascertain if firing on unarmed boats is to form a part of the warfare against the Government of the United States.

 If from silence or a positive answer from their commanders I am led to believe such fiendish acts are to be tolerated or allowed it would be weakness and foolish in me to listen to appeals to feelings that are scorned by our enemies. They must know and feel that not only will we meet them in arms, but that their people shall experience their full measure of the necessary consequences of such barbarity.

The Confederate generals claim the Partisan Rangers as a part of their army. They cannot then disavow their acts, but all their adherents must suffer the penalty. They shall not live with us in peace. God himself has obliterated whole races from the face of the earth for sins less heinous than such as characterized the attacks on the Catahoula and Gladiator. All I say is if such acts were done by the direct or implied concert of the Confederate authorities we are not going to chase through the canebrakes and swamps the individuals who did the deeds, but will visit punishment upon the adherents of that cause which employs such agents. We will insist on a positive separation; they cannot live with us. Further than that I have not yet ordered, and when the time comes to settle the account we will see which is most cruel—for your partisans to fire cannon and musket-balls through steamboats with women and children on board, set them on fire with women and children sleeping in their berths, and shoot down the passengers and engineers, with the curses of hell on their tongues, or for us to say the families of men engaged in such hellish deeds shall not live in peace where the flag of the United States floats.

I know you will say these poor women and children abhor such acts as much as I do, and that their husbands and brothers in the Confederate service also would not be concerned in such acts. Then let the Confederate authorities say so, and not employ their tools in such deeds of blood and darkness. We will now wait and see who are the cruel and heartless men of this war. We will see whether the firing on the Catahoula or Gladiator is sanctioned or disapproved, and if it was done by the positive command of men commissioned by the Confederate Government, you will then appreciate how rapidly civil war corrupts the best feelings of the human heart.

Would to God ladies better acted their mission on earth; that instead of inflaming the minds of their husbands and brothers to lift their hands against the Government of their birth and stain them in blood, had prayed them to forbear, to exhaust all the remedies afforded them by our glorious Constitution, and thereby avoid "horrid war," the last remedy on earth.

Your appeals to me shall ever receive respectful attention, but it will be vain in this case if General Holmes does not promptly disavow these acts, for I will not permit the families and adherents of secessionists to live here in peace whilst their husbands and brothers are aiming the rifle and gun at our families on the free Mississippi.

Your friend,

W. T. SHERMAN,
Major-General, Commanding.

———

HEADQUARTERS,
Memphis, Tenn., October 22, 1862.

General GRANT:

DEAR GENERAL: A merchant of undoubted character is just in from Holly Springs, which he left yesterday at 10 a. m. He brought many letters from the various officers to Saint Louis and California, some of which were examined. Price is there with all the Missourians, many of whom are known to us personally. Van Dorn and Lovell are ordered to Richmond. No other divisions or brigades have joined them since the battle of Corinth, but they claim that they have received 10,000 men from various quarters. Blythe has about 700 cavalry on the Hernando road and line of Coldwater. Jackson has 4,500 cavalry at my old camp on Coldwater, near Holly Springs. The infantry is camped all about the town, and all seem to be in high spirits. Pemberton is now in command.

On-balancing all accounts received I don't think they can attack, but will await attack. They may occupy Davis' Mill; but if you advance, La Grange is the point. The aggregate force at Holly Springs I should judge to be about 23,000 all told. Cavalry now in good order; infantry only so so; clothing poor and scarce of blankets and shoes; plenty of corn-meal and beef; all else scarce. The letters claim that Bragg whipped Buell, taking 17,000 prisoners.

No firing on our boats since the Gladiator, and I think we should not hesitate to make the country feel the full effects of all such attempts. I am just going to review two of my brigades, which are in fine order.

Yours, truly,

W. T. SHERMAN,
Major-General, Commanding.

SPECIAL ORDERS, }   HEADQUARTERS,
No. 285.   }   *Memphis, October 22, 1862.*

Col. B. H. Grierson, Sixth Illinois Cavalry, will prepare a select battalion of about 400 strong and leave Memphis to-night at about 3 a. m., so as to reach the vicinity of Colliersville about sunrise; then make a feint against Mount Pleasant and Coldwater, and turn north of Wolf River, passing the Somerville road near Rising Sun, and camp the first night so as to deceive the enemy as to his design; then turn upon Shelby Depot and clean out effectually such buildings as have been used for a rendezvous to guerrillas operating thereabouts, and then strike for the Mississippi at Randolph.

II. Colonel Stuart, of the Fifty-fifth Illinois, will with the effective strength of his regiment about the same time move on Raleigh and Union Depot and there destroy the depot buildings and such as are used exclusively by guerrilla bands, and operate in that neighborhood thoroughly.

III. The quartermaster, Captain Fitch, will have two small or one large steamboat at Randolph to take on board the cavalry when it reaches that point, viz, on Friday morning, there to await Colonel Grierson's orders.

IV. These orders will be delivered to each commander by an aide-de-camp, and will be kept strictly secret. Preparations will be made for an absence of three days, and each commander will act with a knowledge and in concert of the movements of the other. The object is to completely destroy Falkner's band of guerrillas, already in confusion from their losses at Island 10.

V. All armed men must be destroyed or captured, their houses and property to be destroyed or brought away. But our officers and soldiers must be informed that already a reaction has begun in Tennessee, of which we should take advantage. The people at large should be made to feel that in the existence of a strong Government, capable of protecting as well as destroying, they have a real interest; that they must at once make up their minds or else be involved in the destruction that awaits armed rebellion against the nation's will.

Subordinates and privates must not pillage, but commanders may do anything necessary to impress upon the people that guerrillas must be driven from their midst, else they must necessarily share the consequences.

By order of Maj. Gen. W. T. Sherman:

J. H. HAMMOND,
Assistant Adjutant-General.

WAR DEPARTMENT,
Washington, October 23, 1862.

Maj. Gen. ROSECRANS, *Corinth:*

The disposition of the arms mentioned in your telegram was occasioned by the Department being misled by a person supposed to be acting for you. The error has been corrected, and a proper direction given, so that they shall be applied to the purpose you desire.

General Halleck will communicate with you on other matters concerning yourself, respecting which orders have been made to-day.

EDWIN M. STANTON,
Secretary of War.

JACKSON, TENN., *October* 23, 1862—10 a. m.

Maj. Gen. H. W. HALLECK, *General-in-Chief:*

It is now certain that the rebels have been largely re-enforced at Holly Springs and are strongly fortifying. Pemberton in command. Tilghman in command of exchanged prisoners. They are re-enforced by conscripts, Alabama and Texas troops. Is it not probable that Bragg will come this way?

U. S. GRANT,
Major-General.

WAR DEPARTMENT,
Washington, October 23, 1862.

Major-General GRANT, *Jackson, Tenn.:*

You will direct Major-General Rosecrans to immediately repair to Cincinnati, where he will receive orders.

H. W. HALLECK,
General-in-Chief.

WAR DEPARTMENT,
Washington, October 23, 1862.

Major-General ROSECRANS, *Corinth, Miss.:*

You will immediately repair to Cincinnati, where you will receive orders. Telegraph your arrival. Go with the least possible delay.

H. W. HALLECK,
General-in-Chief.

CORINTH, MISS., *October* 23, 1862—10 p. m.

Major-General HALLECK:

Your dispatch received, and will be promptly obeyed.

W S. ROSECRANS,
Major-General.

WAR DEPARTMENT, *October* 23, 1862.

Major-General ROSECRANS, *Corinth :*

Orders respecting yourself and your command, which will be communicated to the general-in-chief, render it needless to determine the question of your staff until you receive instructions. I will only say that in respect to your staff I shall be disposed to comply with your wishes entirely.

EDWIN M. STANTON.

CORINTH, *October* 23, 1862.

Major-General GRANT:

I don't value Price's conscripts, but I greatly value those Alabama troops. Beware of Bragg; it is nearly time for a few car-loads of his troops to arrive. Depend upon it unless Buell is sharper than heretofore we shall have the devil to pay here. Please answer my personal dispatch.

W. S. ROSECRANS.

GENERAL ORDERS, } HDQRS. ARMY OF THE MISSISSIPPI,
                      THIRD DIV., DIST. OF WEST TENN.,
No. 143.   }   *Corinth, October* 23, 1862.

It is often the object of a flag of truce to make observations of positions, strength, roads, &c., for the purpose of attack or otherwise; in fact to gain all the information possible.

The following orders regarding the reception of a flag of truce are given for the instruction of officers and men of this command on outpost, vedette, or grand-guard duty, and for all other officers and men who should be acquainted with this as well as other minor details of service.

No person coming from the enemy with a flag of truce must be permitted to advance farther than the outposts or cavalry vedettes.

If a flag of truce approach it will be halted at the usual distance, faced the way it came; the bearer and escort will keep ranks. A messenger will be promptly dispatched to the nearest officer of picket or grand guard, stating the arrival of the flag and rank of officer. He will immediately send a messenger to these headquarters, stating the road, rank of officer, &c. He will then, with one non-commissioned officer and four men, proceed to the flag, see that it is properly halted and faced, and that these instructions are fully carried out until the arrival of a staff officer from these headquarters, who will take charge and give the necessary directions to the officer of the guard.

If the bearer of a flag of truce have papers only he will deliver them to an officer of his rank, who will receipt for them and send the bearer on his way back. If the bearer insists on and can give good reasons for seeing the commanding general he will be met outside the lines, or a staff officer of his rank will have him conducted blindfolded to these headquarters.

Only the officer of the flag will be permitted to enter. The others, if they desire to come just inside our lines, will have their camp guarded by the officer of the guard, but such camp will be in a place where no observations can be made.

No conversation whatever relative to the army is permitted on the part of any officer, soldier, or citizen with any of the party of a flag of truce. All its party shall be treated with the greatest civility and respect.

Any violation of these orders will be promptly and rigorously punished.

Refreshments shall be offered the command and forage furnished for animals.

By order of Maj. Gen. W. S. Rosecrans:

C. GODDARD,
First Lieut. Twelfth Infty. Ohio Vols., Actg. Asst. Adjt. Gen.

[OCTOBER 24, 1862.—For General Orders, No. 168, War Department, Adjutant-General's Office, see Series I, Vol. XVI, Part II, pp. 641, 642.]

JACKSON, TENN., *October* 25, 1862.

General HAMILTON:

I was aware of the destruction of the railroad for a considerable distance south of Rienzi. If practicable, it should be destroyed south of Tupelo. By moving on the small force at that point they will be likely to destroy the road south themselves, as well as the stores they have there. My information is that the enemy have but a small force at Tupelo.

U. S. GRANT.

HEADQUARTERS DEPARTMENT OF THE TENNESSEE,
Jackson, Tenn., October 25, 1862.

General C. S. HAMILTON, *Corinth, Miss.:*

General Quinby will probably be in Corinth to-morrow, and General Dodge as soon as relieved by General Davies.

Can't you get up an expedition to go down the railroad and destroy it far to the south? If done, the cavalry should go in force to Tupelo or farther south, supported by a division of infantry as far down as Guntown or that vicinity.

U. S. GRANT.

JACKSON, *October* 25, 1862.

General C. S. HAMILTON, *Corinth, Miss.:*

Make your preparations and execute the suggestions made in my former dispatch as rapidly as possible.

U. S. GRANT.

CORINTH, *October* 25, 1862.

General GRANT, *Jackson:*

It is believed here that Price has been largely re-enforced from Texas and Arkansas. There are indications that he is moving this way. Deserters say he is going to attack Corinth. I have large cavalry force to scout to the west. Am pushing the fortifications as fast as possible.

C. S. HAMILTON,
Brigadier-General.

HEADQUARTERS DEPARTMENT OF THE TENNESSEE,
Jackson, Tenn., October 25, 1862.
General C. S. HAMILTON, *Corinth, Miss.* :

Price is moving with considerable force toward Bolivar. He is now about 4 miles south of Grand Junction. Hold your troops in readiness for defense where they are or to move with three days' rations in haversacks as may be required. All other moves will be suspended until this blows over.

It may be possible that this is to cover a move on Corinth. Be prepared. I can re-enforce you with ten regiments from here if it becomes necessary.

U. S. GRANT.

———

CORINTH, *October* 25, 1862.
Major-General GRANT:

Dispatch received. Will be ready. A Catholic priest just arrived from Huntsville says the rebels there had news that Mobile was attacked. Price may be causing a movement in that direction.

C. S. HAMILTON,
Brigadier-General.

———

JACKSON, *October* 25, 1862.
Maj. Gen. STEPHEN A. HURLBUT,
Commanding District of Jackson :

You will have two brigades of the troops at this place in readiness to move at a moment's notice with three days' rations in haversacks and 100 rounds of ammunition to each man.

By order of Maj. Gen. U. S. Grant:

JNO. A. RAWLINS,
Assistant Adjutant-General.

———

JACKSON, *October* 25, 1862.
COMMANDING OFFICERS HUMBOLDT, TRENTON, AND COLUMBUS:

Hold one regiment at Columbus, and the regiments not detached on railroad guard from Trenton and Humboldt, with three days' rations in haversacks, ready to move if ordered.

U. S. GRANT,
Major-General.

———

BOLIVAR, *October* 25, 1862.
Major-General GRANT:

Major Hayes has just returned from a scout to Middleburg and reports the cavalry in that vicinity were a couple of companies of cotton-burners.

He also reports the significant fact that the railroad bridge at Davis' Mill has been repaired, and that a very large force of Price's army was 4 miles below Grand Junction last night. No further news could be obtained of them to-day. It looks very much as though Price was making a movement this way. All the appearances and information I can get here indicate it.

JAS. B. McPHERSON,
Major-General.

HEADQUARTERS DEPARTMENT OF THE TENNESSEE,
Jackson, Tenn., October 25, 1862.

Major-General McPHERSON, Bolivar, Tenn. :

GENERAL : Your dispatch received. I have dispatched Hamilton to hold his troops in readiness, with three days' provisions in haversacks, to be ready either for a move or for defense of Corinth.

Hold yours in the same way. The move of Price may be to cover the balance of the army in a move on Corinth. Should either place be attacked ten regiments can be spared from the line of the railroad to reenforce you with.

U. S. GRANT.

GENERAL ORDERS, } HDQRS. DEPARTMENT OF THE TENNESSEE,
No. 1.   }   Jackson, Tenn., October 25, 1862.

I. In compliance with General Orders, No. 159, Adjutant-General's Office, War Department, of date October 16, 1862, the undersigned hereby assumes command of the Department of the Tennessee, which includes Cairo, Fort Henry and Fort Donelson, Northern Mississippi, and the portions of Kentucky and Tennessee west of the Tennessee River.

II. Headquarters of the Department of the Tennessee will remain, until further orders, at Jackson, Tenn.

III. All orders of the District of West Tennessee will continue in force in the Department.

U. S. GRANT,
Major-General, Commanding.

GENERAL ORDERS, } HDQRS. FIRST DIV., ARMY OF THE TENN.,
No. 90.   }   Memphis, October 25, 1862.

To insure harmony in the administration of government in the Division of Memphis the following modifications and changes are made and published for the information of all concerned.

I. Col. D. C. Anthony is announced as the provost-marshal for the city and Division of Memphis, with Major Willard and Lieutenant Edwards as assistants; office on Court street, corner of Third. One regiment of infantry and a squadron of cavalry will compose the provost guard; headquarters in the Irving Block, Second street, opposite Court Square. This guard will be distributed according to the orders of the provost-marshal, and will receive their instructions from him. A military commission, composed of three officers of the army, will sit daily at the office of the provost-marshal and try all offenders under the laws of war. Their sentences, when approved by the commanding general, will be executed by the provost-marshal.

II. The city police, composed of 100 men, will also be under the orders and supervision of the provost-marshal. He will muster and inspect them and satisfy himself that the officers are competent, and that the men are sober, industrious, and of good reputation. He will require each and every one to take the oath of allegiance prescribed by the Congress of the United States. He will, on consultation with the chief of police, divide them into a day and night watch, assigning to each a beat or district, for which he will be held responsible. If a burglary, robbery, riot, or disturbance of the peace occurs on any beat the policeman will be forthwith suspended from duty and pay, and be tried by the military commission or recorder of the city for complicity or neglect, and on the trial the burden of proof will rest with the accused, to show that he was on his post and vigilant. If found guilty he will be punished by dismissal from office, by fine, imprisonment, or such other penalty as the court may impose. The appointment of the city police will remain as now, with the city authorities; but should they fail to fill a vacancy within three days of a notice the provost-marshal will appoint a successor. Their payment will also be made by the city treasurer, and all fines, penalties, and seizures made by the city recorder and police will, as heretofore, go to the city treasury.

III. All soldiers or officers arrested or citizens taken by scouts, pickets, or guards will be sent to the Irving Block, and all offenders against the laws of the State of Tennessee or the ordinances of the city of Memphis will be sent to the city lock-up, at the corner of Third and Adams streets. Military prisoners will be sent under guard daily to their respective brigades; offenders against military law or order will be tried by the military commission. All other offenders will, as heretofore, be tried by the city recorder.

IV. Soldiers will not be arrested by the city police, unless detected in the actual commission of crime, when they will be taken to the nearest camp or provost guard. But if any unlawful assemblage of soldiers or stragglers from camp is discovered it is the duty of the police to send prompt notice to the nearest military guard.

V. Citizens detected in the commission of any grade of crime will be arrested by any guard, civil or military; and all vagrants, thieves, or men of bad reputation, having no visible means of support, or who are known to be dangerous persons to the peace and quiet of the community, will be restrained of their liberty and organized into a gang to work on the trenches, roads, or public streets, under the direction of the chief of police or provost-marshal, at the latter's discretion.

VI. Citizens found lurking about the camps or military lines will be arrested and treated as spies. None will by day approach Fort Pickering nearer than headquarters on Tennessee street or the Horn Lake road, and by night are cautioned that the sentinels have loaded muskets and are ordered to use them if persons are found lurking under suspicious circumstances near their posts.

VII. All citizens will keep to their houses at night, between tattoo and reveille, unless attending church, a place of amusement, a party of friends, or on necessary business, in which cases they will return to their homes by proper streets. After midnight all must be in their houses, except the proper guards, watchmen, or patrols. If found in alleys, by-ways, lots not their own, or unusual places, they will be locked up for the night.

VIII. Negroes will be subject to the laws of the State and city ordinances applicable to free negroes. They can work at any trade or calling, hire out, or, if they choose, return to their former masters, but no force will be used one way or the other. Soldiers not on duty should not meddle in this matter, but guards and sentinels on duty will assist all who appeal to them for protection against violence or undue force. Assemblages of negroes are prohibited, except on permission previously granted by the provost-marshal, setting forth the object, place, time of closing, and probable number to be assembled. If, however, they commit crime of any kind—theft, robbery, violence, or trespass on property—they must be punished according to law.

IX. The object and purpose of this order is to punish or restrain all disorders or crimes against the peace and dignity of this community. In time of war the military authorities must of necessity be superior to the civil, but all officers and soldiers must remember that this state of war is but temporary, and the time must come when the civil will resume its full power in the administration of justice in all parts of the country. The interest and laws of the United States must be paramount to all others, but so far as the laws, ordinances, and performances of the people of this community are consistent with those of the General Government they should be respected.

The provost-marshal and city council will make all proper rules necessary to carry this order into effect and make them public.

W. T. SHERMAN,
Major-General, Commanding.

JACKSON, TENN., *October* 26, 1862—8.40 a. m.
(Received October 27, 12.15 a. m.)

Maj. Gen. H. W. HALLECK, *General-in-Chief:*

The rebel army is again moving, probably on Corinth, They have been re-enforced with the exchanged prisoners, troops from Texas and Arkansas, and conscripts. We will be attacked in a few days. Is it not possible to send the Helena force or some other re-enforcement here?

U. S. GRANT,
Major-General.

HEADQUARTERS DEPARTMENT OF THE TENNESSEE,
Jackson, Tenn., October 26, 1862.

General H. W. HALLECK, *Washington, D. C.:*

You never have suggested to me any plan of operations in this department, and as I do not know anything of those of commanders to my right or left I have none therefore that is not independent of all other forces than those under my immediate command.

As situated now, with no more troops, I can do nothing but defend my positions, and do not feel at liberty to abandon any of them without first consulting you. I would suggest, however, the destruction of the railroads to all points of the compass from Corinth, by the removal of the rails to this place or Columbus, and the opening of the road from Humboldt to Memphis. The Corinth forces I would move to Grand Junction, and add to them the Bolivar forces except a small garrison there. With small re-enforcements at Memphis I think I would be able to move down the Mississippi Central road and cause the evacuation of Vicksburg and to be able to capture or destroy all the boats in the Yazoo River. I am ready, however, to do with all my might whatever you may direct, without criticism.

I see in the papers of Saturday that General Curtis has refused permits to $30,000 worth of liquors which have been authorized to be shipped to Memphis; among it 750 barrels whisky to one of my staff. As no member of my staff has ever been engaged since entering the army in any speculation by which to make a dollar I care nothing for the publication; but as the information could have been derived only from General Curtis' headquarters I think it a matter requiring explanation. I telegraphed General Curtis for the explanation but he has not replied.

The facts are these : I gave a Mr. Farrington, an undoubted Union citizen of Memphis, permission to ship $7,000 worth of liquor to Memphis, subject to Treasury restrictions. Finding that these stores could not be got out of Saint Louis approved, Farrington asked Colonel Pride, who has never been more than a volunteer aide on my staff, to introduce him. From this has sprung the report. I would respectfully suggest that my permits be good for all articles coming into this department, subject only to Treasury regulations and orders of those above me.

I am now holding New Madrid with detachments from troops of this command, which General Curtis has assumed control over, and coolly informs me that he cannot spare them.

I would respectfully suggest that both banks of the river be under one command.

U. S. GRANT,
Major-General.

HEADQUARTERS,
Jackson, October 26, 1862.

Maj. Gen. J. B. McPherson, *Bolivar :*

Watch the secession families in Bolivar closely. They will have notice of any attack on the town. If you find them anxious to get out of town redouble your vigilance and report. Watch especially Neely, Fentress, Bills, and Miller and McNeal. Push strong reconnaissance out to front and heavy cavalry patrol on each flank.

[S. A. HURLBUT,]
Major-General.

GENERAL ORDERS, } HDQRS. DEPARTMENT OF THE TENNESSEE,
  No. 2.   }   *Jackson, Tenn., October 26, 1862.*

I. The geographical divisions designated in General Orders, No. 83, from Headquarters District of West Tennessee, of date September 24, 1862, will hereafter be known as districts. The first division will constitute the District of Memphis, Maj. Gen. W. T. Sherman commanding; the second division, the District of Jackson, commanded by Maj. Gen. S. A. Hurlbut; the third division, the District of Corinth, Brig. Gen. C. S. Hamilton commanding; the fourth division, the District of Columbus, commanded by Brig. Gen. T. A. Davies.

II. The army heretofore known as the Army of the Mississippi, being now divided and in different departments, will be discontinued as a separate army.

III. Until army corps are formed there will be no distinctions known except those of department, districts, divisions, posts, brigades, regiments, and companies.

By command of Maj. Gen. U. S. Grant :

JNO. A. RAWLINS,
Assistant Adjutant-General.

GENERAL ORDERS, }   HDQRS. ARMY OF THE MISSISSIPPI,
                }   THIRD DIV., DIST. OF WEST TENNESSEE,
  No. 151.   }   *Corinth, October 26, 1862.*

By order of the department commander, Brigadier-General Hamilton will assume command of the troops heretofore commanded by Major-General Rosecrans.

The general commanding being called by superior authorities to duty elsewhere, begs leave to bid an affectionate good-by to the officers and men of his command. It is his extreme pleasure to be able to declare truthfully he will not bear away a single painful, personal feeling toward any one of his command, and trusts that for any severity he may have exercised or any feelings he may have wounded he will be pardoned, attributing it to human frailty and sincere desire for the good of the service and the honor of those who serve our country.

By command of Major-General Rosecrans:

C. GODDARD,
First Lieut. Twelfth Infty. Ohio Vols., Actg. Asst. Adjt. Gen.

GENERAL ORDERS, ⎫   HDQRS. ARMY OF THE MISSISSIPPI,
                      ⎬   THIRD DIV., DIST. OF WEST TENNESSEE,
No. 153.   ⎭   *Corinth, October* 26, 1862.

I. By direction of Major-General Grant I hereby assume command of this district and the forces therein. All standing orders of the previous commander will continue in force.

II. Brig. Gen. I. F. Quinby having reported for duty at these headquarters is assigned to the command of the Third Division of the Army of the Mississippi.

[C. S. HAMILTON,]
Brigadier-General, Commanding.

WAR DEPARTMENT,
Washington, October 27, 1862.

Governor YATES, *Springfield, Ill.:*

Helena and other points held by us on the Mississippi are seriously threatened, and you are requested to send there all available troops in Illinois with the least possible delay. They should first report to General Grant, at Columbus, and if not required there they will proceed to Helena.

H. W. HALLECK,
General-in-Chief.

WAR DEPARTMENT,
Washington, October 27, 1862.

Major-General GRANT, *Jackson, Tenn.:*

The Governor of Illinois has been directed to send you as many troops as possible. General Curtis is begging for re-enforcements to be sent to Helena. Be prepared to concentrate your troops in case of an attack. For a cartel-ship to receive deserters is a violation of the laws of war.

H. W. HALLECK,
General-in-Chief.

WAR DEPARTMENT,
Washington, October 27, 1862.

Major-General WRIGHT, *Cincinnati, Ohio:*

All available troops in Illinois should be immediately sent down the Mississippi, reporting first to General Grant, at Columbus, and if not required there they will proceed to Helena.

H. W. HALLECK,
General-in-Chief.

HEADQUARTERS DEPARTMENT OF THE OHIO,
Cincinnati, Ohio, October 27, 1862—1.45 p. m.

Maj. Gen. H. W. HALLECK, *General-in-Chief:*

Governor Yates has been requested, under your instructions, to send all the available troops in Illinois immediately to Columbus, Ky., and General Grant notified accordingly, and that if not needed they are to proceed to Helena. It is not yet known whether Tennessee troops can be spared by General Cox.

H. G. WRIGHT,
Major-General, Commanding.

JACKSON, *October* 27, 1862.

General GRANT:

The following dispatch has just been received from McPherson:

BOLIVAR, [*October*] 27, 1862.

Major-General HURLBUT, *Jackson:*

The reconnoitering party under Colonel Leggett has returned safely. The infantry went 2½ miles south of Van Buren. At this point the cavalry was divided into three detachments; one went to Saulsbury, one to Grand Junction, capturing a picket of 4 men a short distance this side of the Junction and driving the balance out of the town, and the third went through New Castle and within 4 miles of La Grange. The reconnaissance developed the fact that there is no enemy except cavalry this side of Davis' Mill. About 400 cavalry are reported to have gone on to Estanaula, whether for the purpose of crossing the Hatchie and interfering with the railroad or not I have not yet ascertained.

JAS. B. McPHERSON,
Major-General.

JNO. A. RAWLINS,
Assistant Adjutant-General.

HEADQUARTERS,
Bolivar, Tenn., October 27, 1862.

Major-General HURLBUT, *Jackson, Tenn.:*

GENERAL: I have been considering the matter of the disposition of our forces, and respectfully present the following views:

First. Since the battle of Corinth the line of operations on the part of the rebels has changed, and they have practically abandoned the Mobile and Ohio road north of Columbus, if, as was told just before I left Corinth, the enemy had burned a part of their stores at Tupelo. He is now concentrating on the Mississippi Central, in vicinity of Holly Springs. Hence the necessity of a large cavalry force at Corinth has been to a great extent removed and transferred to this section. We have here to scour the country from Somerville to Pocahontas with a force of less than 700 men, many of them badly armed and with poor horses. The cavalry, besides furnishing the patrols for scouring the country, has to furnish escorts for forage trains, advance pickets, orderlies, &c., so that it is with difficulty that I can muster 400 men for any important expedition.

Again, in view of the position which the enemy at present occupies, Pocahontas is an important point, commanding one of the principal crossings of the Hatchie and the roads leading from Ripley, Salem, &c., to other points on the railroad. A force there would also be enabled to guard Davis' Bridge, across the Hatchie, which can be destroyed at any time now when the rebels feel disposed, and which if destroyed would delay the movements of troops from this point to Corinth and *vice versa*. A force at Pocahontas would be within comparatively easy supporting distance of Corinth or this place should either be attacked.

In view of these facts I would respectfully suggest that two divisions now at Corinth—if troops cannot be procured from any other point—be sent to Pocahontas, say the Second and Sixth of the old Army of the Tennessee, and that one of the brigades of cavalry under Colonels Hatch or Lee be divided between Pocahontas and this point. With this arrangement and a proper understanding between the forces at Memphis, Corinth, and this point I feel satisfied that we could clear this section of guerrillas, prevent the raids of regular rebel cavalry, and keep open a line of communication from Memphis to Corinth.

Very respectfully, your obedient servant,

JAS. B. McPHERSON,
Major-General.

BOLIVAR, *October* 27, 1862.

Major RAWLINS, *Assistant Adjutant-General:*

You are a trump. I would rather have Wilson for my engineer than any officer I know. We are old friends; came home from California together last year.

McPHERSON.

SPRINGFIELD, ILL., *October* 28, 1862.

E. M. STANTON, *Secretary of War:*

SIR: At 11.30 o'clock a. m. to-day General Ketchum resigned his functions here to me. I have seen Governor Yates. He says two regiments—the One hundred and eleventh, Col. James S. Martin; the One hundred and third, Col. A. C. Babcock—will leave to-day or to-morrow; that another—the Ninety-fifth, Col. L. S. Church—will probably leave to-morrow, all for Columbus, Ky., and that another—a German regiment, the Eighty-second, Col. Frederick Hecker—will start immediately to Washington.

JOHN A. McCLERNAND,
Major-General.

WAR DEPARTMENT,
October 28, 1862.

Major-General McCLERNAND, *Springfield, Ill.:*

Your telegram was received, and gratifies me. Everything is favorable here for your expedition. I want to know your address so as to communicate by mail facts that will gratify and encourage you. I hope you will exert yourself diligently so as to be on foot without delay.

EDWIN M. STANTON,
Secretary of War.

CORINTH, MISS., *October* 28, [1862].

General GRANT:

Flag of truce has arrived at Chewalla outpost with communication from Van Dorn to Rosecrans. Bearers instructed to deliver dispatch here in person. I send out Colonel Mizner to receive dispatch, which I say will be referred to you.

I wish to avoid their coming to this place.

C. S. HAMILTON,
Brigadier-General.

BOLIVAR, *October* 28, 1862.

Major-General GRANT:

A man by the name of Robinson, who lives near Grand Junction and left there last night, reports to me that infantry were moving south from Holly Springs, though there was a large force of cavalry about Davis' Mill. I have scouts out, and will, I hope, know shortly whether this is the case. I sent Colonel Johnson, with two companies of cavalry, one regiment of infantry, and a section of artillery, yesterday afternoon in the direction of Somerville to make a thorough reconnaissance. He has not returned; will probably be in to-night or to-morrow. My patrols on the Grand Junction road have returned, after going 3 miles south of Van Buren, and report everything quiet and no enemy to be seen or heard from.

JAS. B. McPHERSON,
Major-General.

CORINTH, MISS., *October* 28, 1862.

Major-General GRANT:

I regard it of the first importance to have at least twenty days' forage at this point on hand. Can it be supplied? I want to get the sick and wounded away soon. Please push the hospitals.

C. S. HAMILTON,
Brigadier-General.

CORINTH, *October* 28, 1862.

Major-General GRANT:

Cavalry scouts in to Chewalla to-night report troops have left Holly Springs, going south; also confirmed by one of Price's escort, who left Holly Springs on Sunday.

C. S. HAMILTON,
Brigadier-General.

HEADQUARTERS DEPARTMENT OF THE TENNESSEE,
Jackson, October 28, 1862.

General McPHERSON, *Bolivar, Tenn.:*

Hamilton's scouts, also one of Price's escort, report troops moving south. This would look as if Mobile was threatened. If you can find out anything from the front do it.

U. S. GRANT,
Major-General.

[OCTOBER 28, 1862.—For Rosecrans to Grant see Series I, Vol. XVI, Part II, p. 650.]

WAR DEPARTMENT,
October 29, 1862.

Major-General McCLERNAND, *Springfield, Ill.*:

Your telegram is received. You will receive a dispatch, which will be mailed to-morrow, apprising you of movements here. Every effort should be made to raise all the forces you can. You will see to getting as many cavalry regiments as possible. In respect to arms, do not suffer yourself to be misled by captious and trifling complaints as to their quality. We shall improve them as fast as possible. Additional funds for pay and bounty will be remitted to-morrow. Get the troops forward as fast as possible. Let every hour advance your work.

EDWIN M. STANTON,
Secretary of War.

CONFIDENTIAL.]   WAR DEPARTMENT,
Washington City, October 29, 1862.

Major-General McCLERNAND, *Springfield, Ill.*:

SIR: The importance of the expedition on the Mississippi is every day becoming more manifest, and there will be the utmost endeavor on the part of the Government to give it aid and strength. In conversing with you I indicated the importance of a coastwise expedition against Texas to aid you and create a diversion of the enemy's force. Major-General Banks is now organizing an expedition for that purpose, which will be in a condition to co-operate with any movement that may be made, after you have succeeded in clearing the Mississippi River.

I wish you to report as frequently as possible the progress that you are making in organizing and sending forward troops, specifying the number from each State.

Diligent attention should be given to providing yourself with cavalry. I have authorized, and will give fresh authority if needed, for raising any number of cavalry regiments.

Artillery has already been forwarded to Cairo, and you may raise any number of artillery companies that you deem necessary. These should be organized as independent companies, to be attached to regiments separately or in battalions as circumstances require. Artillery are not designed to have regimental organization.

You will apprise me of your wants, which shall be promptly supplied as far as may be in the power of the Department.

For your success time and diligence are, as you know, important elements. Every confidence is reposed in your zeal and skill, and I long to see you in the field striking vigorous blows against the rebellion in its most vital point.

Yours, truly,

EDWIN M. STANTON,
Secretary of War.

JACKSON, TENN., *October* 29, 1862—4 p. m.
(Received 9 p. m.)

Maj. Gen. H. W. HALLECK, *General-in-Chief*:

Everything now indicates an early attack on Bolivar or Corinth. The rebels have been largely re-enforced, and are moving precisely as they did before the last attack. Price is at Ripley, while a force is in front of Bolivar, with cavalry thrown out in large force toward Somerville. I will be ready to do all that is possible with the means at hand. Re-enforcements not arrived.

> U. S. GRANT,
> *Major-General.*

JACKSON, TENN., *October* 29, [1862]—4.30 p. m.

Major-General HALLECK, *General-in-Chief :*

One hundred and twelve furloughs granted by General Curtis to men of my command are just received. Has authority been granted since General Orders, No. 78, to give furloughs?

> U. S. GRANT,
> *Major-General.*

> WAR DEPARTMENT,
> *Washington, October* 29, 1862.

Governor YATES, *Springfield, Ill. :*

Please send batteries and anything else ready for the field to Columbus or Helena. The security of West Tennessee and Helena is of vital importance to our future operations on the Mississippi.

> H. W. HALLECK,
> *General-in-Chief.*

> HEADQUARTERS DEPARTMENT OF THE TENNESSEE,
> *Jackson, October* 29, 1862.

Brig. Gen. T. A. DAVIES, *Columbus, Ky. :*

Send troops from Paducah and from Cairo, if necessary, under command of General Ransom to Eddyville to attack Morgan at Hopkinsville. Order at the same time all the available forces at Fort Henry and Fort Donelson to co-operate with him. They will act in concert.

You can communicate by telegraph to Paducah and Fort Henry. Have ordered the telegraph operators at these places to remain at their posts.

By order of Maj. Gen. U. S. Grant:

> JNO. A. RAWLINS,
> *Assistant Adjutant-General.*

> COLUMBUS, *October* 29, 1862.

Col. W. W. LOWE,
(*Or Commanding Officer Forts Donelson and Henry :*)

You will take what available force you have at Forts Donelson and Henry and communicate with General Ransom at Paducah, and act in concert with him, and co-operate with him to attack Morgan with 2,500 men at Hopkinsville. Take as little transportation as possible and live off the country as far at practicable.

Answer your disposition.

> THOS. A. DAVIES,
> *Brigadier-General.*

COLUMBUS, *October* 29, 1862.

General RANSOM, *Paducah:*

You will take what available force you have at Paducah to Eddy-ville to attack Morgan with 2,500 men at Hopkinsville. I shall order at the same time the available forces at Fort Donelson and Fort Henry to act in concert with you. Take as little as you can of transportation and subsist as much as possible on the country.

Answer what force you can take and your means of getting to Eddy-ville. Do you want more troops from Cairo? You will communicate with the commanding officer at Forts Henry and Donelson.

THOS. A. DAVIES,
Brigadier-General.

HEADQUARTERS DEPARTMENT OF THE TENNESSEE,
Jackson, Tenn., October 29, 18**.

General HAMILTON, *Corinth, Miss.:*

Immediately on my return from Corinth I telegraphed quartermaster at Columbus to send you forage by every train. He replied that he had no more forage, but telegraphed to Saint Louis for it. Received the reply that they were out there. I telegraphed then to General Allen the necessity for pushing it on rapidly. No reply from him yet. If he cannot send it I will send to Illinois and purchase independently.

Reliable Union men from Brownsville think Bolivar will be the point of attack. We must watch closely. If Bolivar is the point, three divis-ions of your command must march upon them by way of Bethel. If Corinth is attacked you will be assisted from there and ten regiments from along the road. Captain Prime may remain for the present.

U. S. GRANT,
Major-General.

CORINTH, MISS., *October* 29, 1862.

Major-General GRANT:

Flag of truce dispatches were delivered over 6 miles beyond Chewalla. They are from Pemberton and Van Dorn; are of no importance. Will send contents by to-morrow's mail.

Everything confirms the movement of part of Price's and Van Dorn's army south by railroad. I will try and get up a magazine of forage from the country. I think much can be had along the railroad about Bethel, and beyond, if we can have a train of cars to bring it in.

C. S. HAMILTON,
Brigadier-General, Commanding.

CORINTH, MISS., *October* 29, 1862.

Major-General GRANT:

News in, which seems reliable, that part of Price's forces were at Rip-ley yesterday, preparing for another move on this place.

C. S. HAMILTON,
Brigadier-General.

JACKSON, TENN., *October* 29, 1862.

General HAMILTON, *Corinth, Miss.:*

Order one regiment of cavalry from your command to Bolivar. They will march by way of Bethel. It would also be well to occupy Pocahontas with one division and one regiment of cavalry. This would make a good lookout for an attack on either Bolivar or Corinth, and would protect the bridge at Davis' if we should want to use it, or enable us to destroy it for use of the enemy.

U. S. GRANT,
Major-General.

HEADQUARTERS DEPARTMENT OF THE TENNESSEE,
Jackson, Tenn., October 29, 1862.

General HAMILTON, *Corinth, Miss.:*

I am inclined to think that a part of the force from Holly Springs has gone south, either to Mobile or to come around by way of Tupelo to get in on the east of us, and their presence in Ripley is a cover. They might also move a column from there in conjunction with the other.

I have information that a large force of cavalry with some infantry and artillery are now attempting to cross the Hatchie near Brownsville, evidently with the intention of getting on to the river for the purpose of stopping navigation. I will attend to them.

U. S. GRANT,
Major-General.

HEADQUARTERS,
Jackson, Tenn., October 29, 1862.

Maj. Gen. J. B. MCPHERSON, *Bolivar, Tenn.:*

If the railroad bridge at Davis' Mill is not strongly guarded it should be destroyed. No movement, however, will be risked that will bring on a battle. Ascertain, if possible, how things are at the bridge and around it.

[S. A. HURLBUT,]
Major-General.

HEADQUARTERS DEPARTMENT OF THE TENNESSEE,
Jackson, October 29, 1862.

Major-General HURLBUT, *Commanding District of Jackson:*

I am just informed of a movement across the Hatchie of a large force of cavalry with some artillery and infantry under Bowen, evidently with the intention of getting on the river some place to intercept navigation. They are said to be now in the neighborhood of Brownsville. If this is so we will want to send one brigade of infantry with a section of artillery and all the cavalry that can be spared from here and Humboldt to get in their rear and cut them off.

The forces should move toward Brownsville until they found the direction of the enemy, and then pursue them by the most practicable route. They should go with very little baggage, taking three days' rations in haversacks and seven days' in wagons. Forage will have to be obtained on the route, giving receipts as provided for in general orders. This expedition should be conducted by an efficient officer.

U. S. GRANT,
Major-General.

HEADQUARTERS DISTRICT OF JACKSON,
October 29, 1862.

Col. C. C. MARSH, *Jackson, Tenn.*:

You will move at daylight in the morning; will be joined on the march by two companies Fourth Illinois Cavalry from Humboldt. Move rapidly on Brownsville, keeping cavalry well out. If you find that Bowen's force has passed Brownsville you will follow with what force you consider necessary by the nearest practicable road. Push them strongly, capture their artillery, and break up the gang thoroughly. If their trail leads toward the railroad inform me, and cavalry will be ordered from Trenton.

If upon arriving at Brownsville you shall find that they have not gone up the country you will halt your column and your cavalry across Hatchie and ascertain their whereabouts. If within reach of infantry, strike; if not, bring your troops into camp at this post. It is not expected that you will do more than follow vigorously in case they threaten any point on the Mississippi this side the Hatchie. If they shall not have crossed you will not press far to the south of that stream.

Frequent reports are desired, so that dispositions may be made to overtake them from above if they pass you.

You will of course be left largely to your own discretion, and must act independently, according to circumstances which may develop themselves.

[S. A. HURLBUT,]
Major-General.

P. S.—If on arriving at Brownsville you are satisfied that the force is exaggerated or cannot be reached without moving a day's march south of the Hatchie River you will return at once.

JACKSON, TENN., *October* 29, 1862.

Major-General HURLBUT,
Commanding District of Jackson:

SIR: The troops ordered to move under Colonel Marsh need not move until further orders from here. The news we get is that the enemy has not crossed the Hatchie.

By command of General U. S. Grant:

GEO. G. PRIDE,
Aide-de-Camp.

HEADQUARTERS DEPARTMENT OF THE TENNESSEE,
Jackson, Tenn., October 29, 1862.

Major-General MCPHERSON, *Bolivar, Tenn.*:

Hamilton has just learned the following from one of Roddey's men now a prisoner:

Roddey is ordered to Kentucky; will cross the river at Muscle Shoals *en route* to Bragg. Roddey moved from Big Springs on Friday. Joe Johnston is reported at Columbus with large force, and is intending to co-operate with Price, moving to the west of Corinth. No supplies and very little force at Tupelo. Price's movements already commenced.

ELI WHITEHURST.

If it is demonstrated that Bolivar is the point of attack, Hamilton is instructed to move by way of Bethel with three divisions to your support. Should Corinth be attacked, be in readiness to move by same route with all the force that can be spared. I will send ten regiments from the line of railroad to the point of attack.

U. S. GRANT,
Major-General.

JACKSON, *October* 29, 1862.

Major-General McPHERSON, *Bolivar, Tenn.*:

Citizens from Brownsville report Jackson with 9,000 cavalry in neighborhood of Somerville. Your forces in that direction, if not strong enough to meet them, had better be withdrawn.

U. S. GRANT,
Major-General.

HEADQUARTERS DEPARTMENT OF THE TENNESSEE,
Jackson, Tenn., October 29, 1862.

Maj. Gen. WILLIAM T. SHERMAN, *Memphis, Tenn.*:

I am directed by General Grant to acknowledge the receipt of your report of the 21st and letter of the 22d, and to say to you his information is that Bowen is moving north of the Hatchie, with the evident intention of getting on to the Mississippi River to cut off navigation. An expedition will be sent to cut him off from here.

A flag of truce from Corinth went into Holly Springs last week. They allowed our officers to stay in town from Sunday at 3 o'clock p. m. till 10 a. m. Monday. They were taken to the hotel and allowed every liberty. Van Dorn threw no restraint around them, and seemed perfectly indifferent how much they learned. Our officers estimated the force there at not over 25,000.

The enemy are beginning to move now. Price is at Ripley. Information is in that troops are going south, possibly going to Mobile. The general heartily approves your course in expelling secession families as a punishment and preventive example for guerrillas firing into boats. He would also recommend that if it becomes necessary to distribute food to the poor and destitute families, or to unemployed contrabands, to make an assessment on the better provided secession citizens to pay the expenses.

Rosecrans has been ordered to Cincinnati to receive further orders. This is greatly to the relief of the general, who was very much disappointed in him. This matter the general will explain to you when he sees you. He much regrets that Hurlbut is ordered away, and has telegraphed to have the order countermanded.

Adjutant-General Fuller, of Illinois, telegraphed to-day that in addition to eight regiments heretofore sent, one regiment, the One hundred and third, is under orders to move Wednesday; the One hundred and eleventh and Ninety-fifth within four days afterward. He further telegraphs that ten more regiments can be forwarded in next ten days if paid and armed. The general will try and send troops to you; possibly not more than one brigade armed, and one regiment without arms to take charge of siege guns.

The general has abandoned all idea of the expedition. He finds Curtis indisposed to co-operate with him. From the newspaper and other reports it is probable that McClernand will go to Helena and lead whatever expeditions may move from there and report to Curtis. As soon as the promised re-enforcements arrive the general will make arrangements for a forward move, and will then send a staff officer to inform you fully of plans and how he desires your co-operation.

Very respectfully, your obedient servant,

WM. S. HILLYER,
Colonel and Aide-de-Camp.

SPRINGFIELD, ILL., *October* 29, [1862]—10 p. m.

Hon. E. M. STANTON,
Secretary of War:

Everything will be pushed to the uttermost. You say, "Raise all the force you can." Do you mean to give a latitude outside of the call; also to raise cavalry regiments outside of the same; and, if so, in Illinois, Indiana, and Iowa?

JOHN A. McCLERNAND.

WAR DEPARTMENT,
October 30, 1862.

Major-General McCLERNAND, *Springfield, Ill.:*

Your telegram received. I mean to give to the Governors of Indiana, Illinois, and Iowa latitude to raise for operations on the Mississippi all the force they can of artillery, infantry, and cavalry outside of the calls heretofore made; but advanced pay and bounty are allowed only for those raised within the calls and pursuant to previous orders. The local interest and feeling in favor of the Mississippi operations and your personal influence are relied on for the increased force, as the bounty-funds will be exhausted by the previous calls.

EDWIN M. STANTON,
Secretary of War.

SPECIAL ORDERS, } HDQRS. OF THE ARMY, ADJT. GEN.'S OFFICE,
No. 320.   }   *Washington, October* 30, 1862,

I. Maj. Gen. Lewis Wallace, U. S. Volunteers, is assigned to duty in the Department of the Tennessee, and will report in person to Maj. Gen. U. S. Grant, at Corinth, Miss.

    *   *   *   *   *   *   *

By command of Major-General Halleck:

L. THOMAS,
Adjutant-General.

WAR DEPARTMENT,
Washington, October 30, 1862.

Major-General GRANT, *Jackson, Tenn.:*

Re-enforcements for your army are moving from Wisconsin, Minnesota, and Illinois.

Furloughs to men in your command given by General Curtis are null and void; they should not be recognized. Orders, No. 78, are still in force.

H. W. HALLECK,
General in-Chief.

[OCTOBER 30 AND 31, 1862.—For Halleck to Wright and reply, in reference to re-enforcements for Grant, see Series I, Vol. XVI, Part II, p. 656.]

———

WAR DEPARTMENT,
Washington, October 30, 1862.

Governor YATES, *Springfield, Ill.:*

It seems that General Grant is likely to be hard pressed by the enemy, and it is important that troops be sent to him as rapidly as possible.

H. W. HALLECK,
General-in-Chief.

———

OCTOBER 30, 1862.

Maj. JOHN A. RAWLINS,
Assistant Adjutant-General:

SIR: General Ransom reports that he can furnish 250 men (infantry), 60 cavalry, and a section of artillery from Paducah. General Tuttle reports that he cannot furnish any troops—has scarce enough for guard duty. Colonel Lowe, at Fort Donelson, can furnish Thirteenth Regiment and five companies of cavalry; but General Ransom reports that they cannot form a junction except at Hopkinsville. He wishes to know if Lowe shall move out cautiously while he holds the enemy in front in advance of him. He thinks he will be able to hold until Lowe can come up. Will this do?

THOS. A. DAVIES,
[*Brigadier-General.*]

———

JACKSON, TENN., *October* 30, 1862.

General DAVIES, *Columbus, Ky.:*

Where you can suppress guerrillas with the force at your command, do it. This one back of Hale's Landing should be broken up as soon as you can send the troops. Where citizens give aid and comfort to these fellows who amuse themselves by firing into them, arrest them.

U. S. GRANT,
Major-General.

———

COLUMBUS, *October* 30, 1862.

JOHN A. RAWLINS,
Assistant Adjutant-General:

The total force to attack Morgan, 250 infantry, one section of artillery and 60 cavalry, from Paducah; from Fort Henry, 350 infantry and 150 cavalry; from Donelson, about 400 infantry. Total, 1,000 infantry, 200 cavalry, and one section of artillery. Is this force sufficient? The expedition is in motion. All I know of Morgan's forces is what I sent you.

THOS. A. DAVIES,
Brigadier-General.

HEADQUARTERS DEPARTMENT OF THE TENNESSEE,
Jackson, Tenn., October 30, 1862.
General DAVIES, *Columbus, Ky.:*

I doubt much finding Morgan at Hopkinsville, or any other force in or near the number represented. Your forces should move cautiously, however, as if the whole number represented were there, and ascertain from the people as much as they can of the enemy. If Morgan is there he will likely run; it is not his policy to fight, but to plunder and inter-rupt our lines of communication as much as possible.

U. S. GRANT,
Major-General.

CORINTH, *October* 30, 1862.
Major-General GRANT:

Enemy had strong cavalry pickets yesterday 5 miles east of Ripley, on the Rienzi road; too strong to be driven in by our scouts. Thirty-eighth Alabama Regiment was sent to Mobile by Pemberton on the 21st. Another train has been put on the road between Mobile and Tupelo; it looks as though the force at Ripley was covering a movement over to the Mobile and Ohio road.

C. S. HAMILTON,
Brigadier-General.

SPECIAL ORDERS,⎫ HEADQUARTERS DISTRICT OF CORINTH,
⎬   THIRD DIV., DEPT. OF THE TENN.,
No. 5.   ⎭   *Corinth, October* 30, 1862.
*   *   *   *   *   *   *

II. Brig. Gen. G. M. Dodge, having reported for duty, is assigned to the command of the division lately commanded by Brigadier-General Davies.
*   *   *   *   *   *   *

By command of Brigadier-General Hamilton:
[R. M. SAWYER,]
Assistant Adjutant-General.

SPRINGFIELD, ILL., *October* 30, 1862—7 p. m.
Hon. E. M. STANTON,
Secretary of War:

Governor Morton's private secretary inquires when and where to send troops. Governor Morton is on his way to Washington.

JOHN A. McCLERNAND,
Major-General.

WAR DEPARTMENT,
October 31, 1862.
Major-General McCLERNAND, *Springfield, Ill.:*

Orders have been sent Governor Morton to forward his regiments to Columbus, on the Mississippi, as fast as possible.

EDWIN M. STANTON,
Secretary of War.

Abstract from Monthly Return of the Department of the Tennessee, Maj. Gen. U. S. Grant commanding, for the month of October, 1862.

Command.	Present for duty.		Aggregate present for duty.	Aggregate present.	Aggregate present and absent.	Pieces of field artillery.
	Officers.	Men.				
Department staff	15	......	15	15	15	......
DISTRICT OF COLUMBUS.						
Brig. Gen. G. M. DODGE commanding.						
Staff....	8	......	8	8	10	......
Infantry.................................	130	3,192	3,322	4,234	5,532	......
Artillery.................................	67	1,748	1,815	2,266	2,682	......
Cavalry	22	781	803	937	1,061	......
Total	227	5,721	5,948	7,445	9,285	......
DISTRICT OF CORINTH.						
Brig. Gen. C. S. HAMILTON commanding.						
Staff....	904	17,991	18,895	22,783	31,303	......
Infantry.................................	37	1,290	1,327	1,553	1,851	65
Artillery.................................	118	2,736	2,854	3,499	4,577	
Cavalry						
Total	1,059	22,017	23,076	27,835	37,731	65
DISTRICT OF JACKSON.						
Maj. Gen. S. A. HURLBUT commanding.						
Staff....	16	......	16	16	19	......
Infantry.................................	768	15,248	16,016	20,399	25,056	4
Artillery.................................	35	1,149	1,184	1,327	1,549	36
Cavalry	116	2,504	2,620	3,261	3,729	.. ..
Total	935	18,901	19,836	25,003	30,353	40
DISTRICT OF MEMPHIS.						
Maj. Gen. W. T. SHERMAN commanding.						
Staff....	18	......	18	18	18	......
Infantry.................................	318	5,951	6,269	7,424	8,483	.. ..
Artillery.................................	20	847	867	980	1,150	42
Cavalry	25	635	660	884	953	.. ..
Total	381	7,433	7,814	9,306	10,604	42
Grand total...........................	2,617	54,072	56,689	69,604	87,988	147

NOTE.—Department staff not added in on original return.

JACKSON, *November* 1, 1862.

General DAVIES, *Columbus, Ky.:*

Send four regiments of infantry arriving, by steamers suitable for carrying them, to General Sherman, at Memphis. Should any cavalry be sent send that to Memphis.

U. S. GRANT,
Major-General.

HEADQUARTERS DEPARTMENT OF THE TENNESSEE,
Jackson, November 1, 1862.

General HAMILTON, *Corinth, Miss.:*

Start in the morning; move on Grand Junction, keeping a good lookout to the south of you.   If you find the enemy have moved north of that place you can change your direction toward Bolivar.

McPherson will also move to that point, starting next day.

Establish a line of couriers from Chewalla to enable me to communicate with you.

U. S. GRANT,
Major-General.

CORINTH, *November* 1, 1862.

Major-General GRANT:

Your dispatch is received.   Everything will be in readiness.   Please give some instructions about the route to be followed.   Rosecrans carried off the maps that were most needed.

C. S. HAMILTON,
Brigadier-General.

JACKSON, *November* 1, 1862.

General HAMILTON, *Corinth, Miss.*:

The route will be by Pocahontas.   It will be of the utmost importance in case of a move to seize on Davis' Bridge and the bridge at Pocahontas at once with a cavalry force.   Instruct the telegraph operators to keep the offices open until 6 o'clock to-night.

U. S. GRANT,
Major-General.

JACKSON, *November* 1, 1862.

General HAMILTON, *Corinth, Miss.*:

There are indications that Bolivar will be attacked within forty-eight hours.

Have three divisions of your command ready to move to-morrow morning with three days' rations in haversacks and three days' in wagons.   Take as little baggage as can be possibly got along with. Do not move without further directions, but be ready at the time stated.

U. S. GRANT,
Major-General.

JACKSON, *November* 1, 1862.

General HAMILTON, *Corinth, Miss.*:

I have before me a Jackson (Mississippi) paper, which makes no mention of the fall nor even of attack upon Mobile.   It may be so, however.   We will make the move indicated in my former dispatch, and, if practicable, drive the enemy from Holly Springs.   Corinth will then be covered.

U. S. GRANT,
Major-General.

JACKSON, TENN., *November* 1, 1862.

General HAMILTON, *Corinth, Miss.*:

My dispatch should have read north of Grand Junction instead of south of Holly Springs.   My dispatch reads north on examination.

U. S. GRANT,
Major-General.

SPECIAL ORDERS, ⎰ HEADQUARTERS DISTRICT OF CORINTH,
                   ⎱   THIRD DIV., DEPT. OF THE TENNESSEE,
    No. 7   ⎰   Corinth, November 1, 1862.

I. The divisions of Generals Stanley, Quinby, and McArthur will be held in readiness for movement early to-morrow morning with three days' rations in haversacks, three days' in wagons, and 100 [rounds] of ammunition per man. Not more than one tent per company will be taken; no other baggage. Small camp guards will be left, composed as far as possible of non-effectives.

*   *   *   *   *   *   *

By command of Brig. Gen. C. S. Hamilton:
                                    [R. M. SAWYER,]
                        Captain and Assistant Adjutant-General.

                                    BETHEL, [November 1, 1862].
General SULLIVAN:
Lieutenant-Colonel Sanford, with Forty-eighth Illinois, now out on reconnaissance toward Henderson, reports that rebel cavalry, 300 strong, left Henderson and went toward mouth of Duck River. I have no cavalry that can go after them; only one cavalry company here. Other reports say the enemy is in greater force. I doubt it. My scouts are well out toward the river east. Will advise you of anything important if can do so.
                                    I. N. HAYNIE,
                                        Colonel.

                                    JACKSON, November 1, 1862.
Maj. Gen. STEPHEN A. HURLBUT,
        Commanding District of Jackson :
GENERAL: You will have four regiments of infantry ready to move by rail to Bolivar on to-morrow, moving under the command of Brig. Gen. John A. Logan, who on his arrival at that place will assume command of the division lately commanded by Brigadier-General Ross, including the four regiments sent from this place.
By command of Maj. Gen. U. S. Grant:
                                    W. R. ROWLEY,
                                        Aide-de-Camp.

                                    BOLIVAR, November 1, 1862.
Major-General GRANT:
Colonel Leggett has just received the following dispatch :
                                    GRAND JUNCTION.
Colonel LEGGETT:
Large force of infantry and cavalry here. They will attack you; cavalry now moving. I saw you last Tuesday. Can't get to Bolivar.

The dispatch was brought in by a negro about half an hour ago, and Colonel Leggett thinks it is from a man who is perfectly reliable. I shall immediately send four companies of cavalry down on the road to reconnoiter. My patrols that went out this morning have not reported yet.
                                    JAS. B. McPHERSON,
                                        Major-General.

HEADQUARTERS DEPARTMENT OF THE TENNESSEE,
Jackson, November 1, 1862.

Major-General McPHERSON, *Bolivar, Tenn.* :

Prepare to move forward on Monday, leaving four regiments and one battery at Bolivar.   Hamilton starts to-morrow for Grand Junction.

Take three days' rations in haversacks and three days' in wagons. Five regiments will go down to-night and to-morrow to re-enforce you. General Logan will take command of Ross' division.

Preparations should be made for repairing the railroad and telegraph. You give orders for the former and I will attend to the latter.

U. S. GRANT,
Major-General.

HEADQUARTERS DEPARTMENT OF THE TENNESSEE,
Jackson, November 1, 1862.

Major-General McPHERSON, *Bolivar, Tenn.* :

I have ordered Hamilton to hold three divisions in readiness to move toward Bolivar to-morrow morning.   If you ascertain that an attack is threatening inform me of the fact and I will start them at once.   I will send four regiments from here at once.

U. S. GRANT,
Major-General.

BOLIVAR, *November* 1, 1862.

Major-General GRANT:

Dispatches received.   Have telegraphed Major Tweeddale, Engineer Regiment, to send down four companies with arms and tools to repair railroad, if that many men can be spared, and finish the bridge already commenced over the Obion River.   If that many men cannot be spared he is to send as many as he can.

JAS. B. McPHERSON.

BOLIVAR, *November* 1, 1862.

Major-General GRANT :

Major Mudd started at 3.30 this p. m. with four companies of cavalry on reconnaissance toward Grand Junction.   I have heard nothing from him yet.   He was cautioned to be on the alert and to send back couriers if anything important transpired.   My patrol which went out this morning went below Van Buren and returned just before dark without seeing or learning anything of the enemy.   I will advise you immediately if I learn anything important.

JAS. B. McPHERSON,
Major-General.

JACKSON, TENN., *November* 1, 1862.

Major-General McPHERSON, *Bolivar, Tenn.* :

The moment you hear from the front inform me.   If the enemy are moving on you I want to put the troops in motion.

U. S. GRANT,
Major-General.

JACKSON, TENN., *November* 1, 1862.

Major-General SHERMAN, *Memphis, Tenn.:*

Troops from Corinth marched on Grand Junction yesterday; from Bolivar to-day. I go forward with the advance; will push on to Grenada if possible, opening railroad and telegraph as we advance. I have ordered four regiments to Memphis; will order more if the re-enforcements sent me justify it. If communication can be opened with you by courier I will do it.

If you hear of my forces passing Holly Springs, and can put a force on the railroad to repair it, start toward Grenada, repairing the road as the troops advance. A demonstration to the southeast made at once would give the idea of a formidable movement to the front, particularly as you will be receiving re-enforcements and I also in considerable numbers. The amount arrived and to arrive will not amount to less than 30,000 men. The news of these re-enforcements coming cannot be kept from the enemy, of course.

U. S. GRANT,
Major-General, Commanding.

(Sent in cipher to Columbus to forward by first steamer.)

SPECIAL ORDERS,	HDQRS. THIRTEENTH ARMY CORPS,
	DEPARTMENT OF THE TENNESSEE,
No. 5.	*Jackson, Tenn., November* 1, 1862.

I. Brig. Gen. J. D. Webster is hereby appointed general superintendent of the military railroads of this department, and in all matters appertaining thereto he will have, possess, and exercise the same authority as that conferred upon General McPherson by orders from Headquarters Department of the Mississippi. The Engineer Regiment of the West will be under his command, with such officers, soldiers, and citizens as it may be necessary to employ from time to time.

II. Col. George G. Pride is appointed chief engineer of military railroads, and will have charge of the repairs and reconstruction of the road-beds, bridges, and tracks of all railroads in this department.

The mechanics and laborers required will be furnished from the Engineer Regiment, and will be under his command while so engaged. He will have authority to engage citizen employés when necessary. Requisitions for material and funds necessary for repairing and rebuilding railroads will be made by him on the quartermaster's department. All contracts with citizen employés and all requisitions for material and funds will be subject to the approval of the commanding general.

By command of Maj. Gen. U. S. Grant:

JNO. A. RAWLINS,
Assistant Adjutant-General.

JACKSON, TENN., *November* 2, 1862.

General HAMILTON, *Corinth, Miss.:*

Have just heard from Grand Junction. There is a camp of say 2,000 cavalry at La Grange, Tenn., 3 miles from the Junction, and probably a small force at Davis' Mill, 7 miles south. I think the enemy are evacuating Holly Springs; we will ascertain at all events. You should have 200 rounds of ammunition per man with you. Lyford will see that any further supply that may be required is got up.

Further supplies of provisions will be looked after by way of Bolivar.

U. S. GRANT,
Major-General.

JACKSON, *November* 2. 1862.

General C. S. HAMILTON, *Corinth, Miss.*:

I have sent directions to Lieutenant Lyford to forward the ammunition mentioned in your dispatch.

One of my staff is now in Memphis with instructions for General Sherman to move out under certain contingencies, depending on information he may receive. We cannot calculate on his co-operation, however, on account of the length of time it takes to communicate. I am sending re-enforcements to Sherman and also to Bolivar. New regiments are now arriving rapidly.

U. S. GRANT,
Major-General.

CORINTH, *November* 2, 1862.

Major-General GRANT:

My advance will reach the Tuscumbia to-night near Pocahontas. I shall probably stay at Chewalla to-night, and will endeavor to open communication with McPherson to-morrow.

I shall have information to-morrow direct from Jackson, Miss. If the enemy shall prove to be in force at Holly Springs the co-operation of Sherman is of the utmost importance.

C. S. HAMILTON,
Brigadier-General.

CHEWALLA, *November* 2, 1862.

General GRANT:

Troops will come on the Tuscumbia to-night. I shall stop 4 miles beyond this point. Tell me how I can best communicate with McPherson to-morrow.

Negroes bring in the rumor that Price has gone to Mobile.

C. S. HAMILTON,
Brigadier-General.

CORINTH, *November* 2, 1862.

General GRANT:

The three divisions are already gone. I shall move at noon. I have ordered an additional supply of ammunition to follow us but will rely on Bolivar for provisions.

C. S. HAMILTON,
Brigadier-General.

HEADQUARTERS DISTRICT OF CORINTH,
November 2, 1862.

Major-General GRANT,
    Commanding Department, Jackson:

Yours received. Shall reach Porter's Creek to-morrow and Grand Junction the following afternoon. Have communicated with McPherson by telegraph and courier. Will meet him at Van Buren to-morrow. I am very glad you will be on hand. No signs of enemy in front.

C. S. HAMILTON,
Brigadier-General.

BOLIVAR, *November* 2, 1862.

Major-General GRANT:

Will be ready to start at daylight to-morrow (Monday) morning. Shall I start? General Brayman remains in command of the post, with four regiments of infantry, battery of artillery, and the Fifth Ohio Cavalry; also all but three companies of Hurst's First Tennessee Cavalry. I have made three brigades of the Fourth Division, and have two brigades of the Third Division for General Logan. Have put a new regiment into each of the brigades.

JAS. B. McPHERSON,
Major-General.

JACKSON, *November* 2, 1862.

Major-General McPHERSON, *Bolivar, Tenn.:*

Hamilton started this morning. Is moving on Grand Junction. He will put himself in communication with you to-morrow. Start in the morning and try to so arrange as to have both columns reach Grand Junction about the same time. I will join you to-morrow night or the next day. Supplies will be sent from Bolivar as far as possible for further wants.

Two additional regiments will reach Bolivar to-night or to-morrow. This will give a garrison for Van Buren or other available points on the road. Every arrangement will be made to forward other re-enforcements if we should go far south. Re-enforcements are also going to Sherman, and we may look for him. Cavalry should be well thrown out to the west.

Have you any further news from the front?

U. S. GRANT,
Major-General.

BOLIVAR, TENN., *November* 2, 1862.

Major-General GRANT:

Patrols report all quiet on the front. Everything is arranged to start to-morrow morning. Will move so as to reach Grand Junction at the same time with Hamilton.

JAS. B. McPHERSON,
Major-General.

BOLIVAR, *November* 2, 1862.

Major-General GRANT:

Major Mudd reached Grand Junction at 11 p. m. last night; found no rebels there. About 1,000 cavalry passed through Grand Junction a

day or two ago, and it is reported that 1,500 are in camp 1 mile from
La Grange. It is undeniably true that rebel cavalry are in camp there,
but the number is probably exaggerated. I shall be ready to move to-
morrow morning at sunrise. As I understand it we are to move light,
say two wagons to a regiment, one to carry ammunition and the other
provisions, &c. I propose to take along 200 rounds of ammunition
per man.

JAS. B. McPHERSON,
Major-General.

UNITED STATES STEAMER LEXINGTON,
Columbus, November 2, 1862.

Major-General GRANT:

General Sherman asked me to telegraph you that he had confirmatory reports that the enemy were evacuating Holly Springs and going
south to Meridian and toward New Orleans and Mobile, and that he
would send some other news to you in a few days.

JAMES W. SHIRK,
Lieutenant-Commander.

[NOVEMBER 2, 1862—JANUARY 6, 1863.—For correspondence between
Halleck and Grant relating specially to operations on the Mississippi
Central Railroad, see Part I, pp. 467–480.]

DAVIS' BRIDGE,
Hatchie, November 3, [1862]—10.30.

Major-General GRANT, <i>Jackson:</i>

Cavalry scouts from Ruckersville just in report having met a citizen
of Holly Springs who says Price is still there in force, but quiet. We
shall reach Porter's Creek in good season to-day.

C. S. HAMILTON,
Brigadier-General.

HEADQUARTERS DEPARTMENT OF THE TENNESSEE,
Jackson, Tenn., November 3, 1862.

Major-General HURLBUT,
    Commanding District of Jackson:

GENERAL: Inclosed I send you copy of dispatch sent General Davies
last evening.

If Starring's regiment is not among the first two arriving here send
it to Corinth when it does arrive. Send two regiments to Bolivar as
soon as practicable without taking them from here. When that is done
detain all other new regiments at this place. Assign the first one so
detained to Colonel Lawler's brigade and require Lawler to relieve the
Eighth Illinois from road duty. Assign the next one to Colonel Stevenson's brigade, and require him to hold his troops in readiness for a
forward movement at any time. When this is done all other troops can
be assigned to Colonel Lawler's command without being brigaded, leaving them subject to further orders.

U. S. GRANT,
Major-General.

P. S.—In my absence any change you may find necessary for the public safety, even to the re-enforcement of Corinth, which is out of your district, you can make.

I will inform General Dodge that he is to communicate directly with you. A line of couriers will be kept up between my headquarters and the telegraph; through this I desire to be kept informed of everything that it is important should be communicated to me.

[Inclosure.]

JACKSON, TENN., *November* 2, 1862.

General DAVIES, *Columbus, Ky.* :

Are any new regiments on the way here? I want two regiments to go to Bolivar, including any that may be on the road at this time. If there are not two on the road now, send Starring's regiment and detain one to arrive in its place. As previously directed, send four regiments in all arriving, on suitable transports to Memphis. After sending two regiments to Bolivar send one to Trenton and one to Union City to relieve those two regiments, and order them to report here to General Hurlbut. All others arriving will be sent to Jackson for further orders.

U. S. GRANT,
Major-General.

GENERAL ORDERS,) HDQRS. DEPARTMENT OF THE TENNESSEE,
No. 4.   )   *Jackson, Tenn., November* 3, 1862.

It has been reported to the general commanding that many families within the limits of the military guards of this department are in a suffering condition—lacking food and clothing—and without any possible means of earning or procuring support. People not actively engaged in rebellion should not be allowed to suffer from hunger in reach of a country abounding with supplies. The Government, never the cause of this state of affairs, should not be subjected to the burden of furnishing the necessary relief, but the weight should fall on those who by act, encouragement, or sympathy have caused the want now experienced. It is therefore ordered:

I. The necessary expenses for the relief needed must be borne by sympathizers with the rebellion.

II. District commanders throughout this department will cause the extent of these wants to be ascertained and the necessary supplies to be procured and distributed.

III. To this end district commanders will cause all persons known to be disloyal within reach of their respective commands to be assessed in proportion to their relative ability to pay, and cause such assessments to be collected and discreetly applied. Assessments may be paid in money or supplies.

IV. A suitable chaplain or other commissioned officer will be appointed at each post where it may be necessary to distribute supplies under this order, who shall have charge of the distribution of supplies and who shall be held responsible for the faithful performance of his duties, and that no supplies are unworthily bestowed.

V. Commissaries of subsistence will be allowed to sell provisions, at the rates charged officers, to such persons as are designated to distribute them, on certificates that they are for such purpose and are necessary to save suffering.

VI. Officers collecting assessments will keep an accurate account of all moneys and provisions so collected, and from whom, and send their accounts through their immediate commanding officers to the chief commissary of the department to be audited.

The chief commissary of the department will designate in a circular how the abstract of such sales is to be kept and returned.

By command of Maj. Gen. U. S. Grant:

JNO. A. RAWLINS,
Assistant Adjutant-General.

[NOVEMBER 3 and 4, 1862.—For Halleck to Curtis, and reply, in reference to co-operation with Grant, see Series I, Vol. XIII, pp. 778, 779.]

HEADQUARTERS DEPARTMENT OF THE TENNESSEE,
La Grange, November 4, 1862.

General C. S. HAMILTON,
Commanding Left Wing, Army in the Field:

GENERAL: Please get your men in camp as comfortable as you can on the stream 2½ miles south of Grand Junction. McPherson will form a line almost connecting with you, extending down Wolf River, west of this place. Seize on the bridges between you and Holly Springs if they are still standing, and, if not, upon the places where they were, and organize working parties to rebuild them and repair the roads leading to them.

Send out to-morrow a large cavalry reconnaissance, supported by infantry, toward Holly Springs, with a lookout toward Ripley. McPherson will send from here a force to drive out some cavalry that are now in toward Somerville.

Halleck advises me that a large force is moving up from New Orleans; also that Helena force may move toward Grenada. Sherman will also be out. They are now sending me re-enforcements as rapidly as the road can transport them. I have sent some to Sherman. The telegraph and railroad will be complete. I hope to visit your camp some time to-morrow.

Let your teams collect all the forage they can, but in an orderly manner; send in charge of foraging parties officers who can be relied upon to maintain order.

I will probably go around to see you to-morrow.

U. S. GRANT,
Major-General.

NAVY DEPARTMENT,
November 5, 1862.

Hon. E. M. STANTON,
Secretary of War:

SIR I have the honor to inclose herewith a copy of a communication dated the 29th ultimo, received from Acting Rear-Admiral David D. Porter, commanding the Mississippi Squadron, in which he announces his readiness for co-operation with the army.

Very respectfully, your obedient servant,

GIDEON WELLES,
Secretary of the Navy.

[Inclosure.]

UNITED STATES MISSISSIPPI SQUADRON,
Cairo, Ill., October 29, 1862.

Hon. GIDEON WELLES,
Secretary of the Navy, Washington, D. C.:

SIR: Thinking perhaps General Halleck might be under the impression that the navy would not be ready to operate against Vicksburg until February, I beg leave to inform you that I am quite ready to move at any moment. We have been working night and day since I have been here, anticipating an early movement.

The departments are all organized and working well, and I will be able to leave here with the comfort of knowing that everything will be supplied to the squadron.

I have the honor to be, very respectfully, your obedient servant,

DAVID D. PORTER,
Acting Rear-Admiral, Commanding Mississippi Squadron.

GEN'L FIELD ORDERS, } HDQRS. L. W., ARMY OF THE TENN.,
                        In the Field, near Grand Junction,
No. 2.   }   *November 5, 1862.*

I. The plundering and house-burning of the past two day shows that the discipline of this command is becoming seriously impaired. Although these crimes are committed only by those who are "stragglers on the march and skulkers on the battle-field," still all good soldiers share in the odium which such conduct brings upon the army. It is therefore ordered that every effort be made to arrest these thieves and house-burners; that they be immediately tried by a military commission to be detailed by division commanders, and that the sentence, however severe it may be, be promptly executed.

II. Division commanders will hold their regimental commanders strictly responsible for the conduct of their soldiers. Directly after the arms are stacked in camp the roll will be called, and the number of absentees from each regiment will be reported to the division commander. When the army does not march there will be five roll-calls per day, and the absentees reported to the division commander.

III. Officers, of whatever rank or regiment, who do not use all their efforts to repress these gross outrages will be deprived of their commands and confined in the military prison at Alton.

IV. All firing in and about the camps is strictly prohibited; soldiers so offending will be arrested and severely punished. The general commanding regrets that he is forced to use such severity, but it is the only means left him to prevent this army of soldiers from degenerating into an armed mob.

By command of Brig. Gen. C. S. Hamilton:

JOHN V. DU BOIS,
Colonel, U. S. Army, and Chief of Staff.

SAINT LOUIS, MO., *November 6, 1862.*

Col. J. C. KELTON.

Shall I destroy railroad at Grenada if I can?

SAML. R. CURTIS,
Major-General, Commanding.

HEADQUARTERS DEPARTMENT OF THE MISSOURI,
Saint Louis, November 6, 1862.

Col. J. C. KELTON,
Assistant Adjutant-General:

*   *   *   *   *   *   *

I suppose my force on Saturday next will be about 8,000 at Helena. I telegraphed to-night asking you if I shall try to destroy railroad at Grenada. My plan will be to send a cavalry expedition, to travel night and day, destroy, and return. The danger is that bridges may be destroyed to cut off the return. If your dispatch favors the idea I shall direct General Hovey to take all possible precautions to prevent such accidents.*

*   *   *   *   *   *   *

I have the honor to be, very respectfully, your obedient servant,
SAML. R. CURTIS,
Major-General.

HEADQUARTERS DEPARTMENT OF THE TENNESSEE,
La Grange, Tenn., November 6, 1862.

Maj. Gen. WILLIAM T. SHERMAN,
Commanding District of Memphis, Memphis, Tenn.:

A dispatch just received from General Halleck promises me re-enforcements to the number of 20,000 men,† to be sent immediately, and suggests sending them to you. I have asked to have sixteen regiments of infantry and all of the artillery and cavalry that may come to be sent that way. The remainder I want sent here to fill the present organization, at present reduced by taking out railroad guards.

I am also instructed to detail one commissioned officer from each Ohio regiment to report to the adjutant-general of the State, to take charge of drafted men to fill up their respective regiments. You may regard this as an order for making the detail from your command.

The expectation of these re-enforcements will cause a delay in my movements, and will render a demonstration from Memphis unnecessary for the present, unless our reconnaissance should demonstrate that the enemy are evacuating Holly Springs. I will not move from here under a week or ten days, and will try and communicate with you in the mean time.

I have already been re-enforced to such an extent that I feel no doubt of the result if I should advance now, but as so many are coming it is more prudent perhaps to avail myself of our whole strength.

I am also informed by General Halleck that a large force of our troops are moving north from New Orleans. Also that the Helena force is being augmented, and if not practicable to go to Little Rock they will be instructed to cross the Mississippi and march on Grenada. Of course I can make nothing but independent moves with this command, being governed in that by information received from day to day, until I am fully informed of where and how all these other forces are moving, so as to make the whole co-operate.

If you have not yet moved out, under the instructions sent by way of Columbus, it will not be necessary to do so now. If you have moved you can go back to Memphis and await re-enforcements and instructions.

Send me any information you may have received from Holly Springs within the last week. There is no doubt but that Villepigue has left

---

* Portion of letter omitted above appears in Series I, Vol. XIII, p. 780.
† See Part I, p. 467.

there with his command, either for Mobile, Meridian, or Vicksburg. A small force has also been sent to occupy points on the river where the enemy hold both banks, or we hold neither, to prevent desertions. The enemy at Holly Springs is now estimated at 30,000 men, in rather a disorganized condition. I cannot move from here with a force sufficient to handle that number without gloves.

I am, very respectfully, your obedient servant,

U. S. GRANT.

NOVEMBER 6, 1862.

Major-General GRANT:

Lawler has but two regiments in his brigade, the Thirty-first having gone with General Logan. Only one regiment, the One hundred and ninth, has reached Bolivar; the One hundred and nineteenth will come down to-day, assigned by your former order to Bolivar; if they go to Bolivar I must relieve the Twentieth with one of Lawler's regiments. Shall I stop that regiment here and relieve the Eighth with it, so as to send Stevenson forward? No troops are reported yet as coming down, and if I send the Twentieth and Stevenson's brigade it will leave two light regiments of infantry here, not enough for guard duty.

S. A. HURLBUT,
Major-General.

HDQRS. RIGHT WING, ARMY OF THE TENNESSEE,
La Grange, Tenn., November 6, 1862.

Brigadier-General LAUMAN,
Commanding Fourth Division:

GENERAL: You will send Colonel Pugh with his brigade and a section of artillery on a reconnaissance on the Holly Springs road. The infantry and artillery will be preceded by four companies of cavalry, and will go out on the road some 8 or 10 miles, if circumstances permit, to ascertain if possible whether there is any force of the enemy in the vicinity, what it consists of, &c. They will also pay particular attention to the cross-roads, and have them examined before passing the point of intersection. The command will start as soon as it can be got ready.

Very respectfully, your obedient servant,

JAS. B. McPHERSON,
Major-General.

EXECUTIVE MANSION, *November ., 1862.*

Ordered, That Brigadier-General Ellet report to Rear-Admiral Porter for instructions, and act under his direction until otherwise ordered by the War Department.

A. LINCOLN.

HEADQUARTERS DEPARTMENT OF THE MISSOURI,
Saint Louis, Mo., November 7, 1862.

Brig. Gen. A. P. HOVEY, *Helena, Ark.:*

GENERAL: I have written and telegraphed General Halleck in regard to a dash on the railroad at Grenada. Be ready therefore with cavalry and howitzers for a movement which will require great energy, courage, and prudence. The object would be to cut off Price's retreat. At least

1,000 men should go, and I would prefer 2,000. The movement should be supported by a strong force of infantry and artillery, which should follow the expedition in such a way as to guard any crossing of a stream and support the retreat. This reserve should be 1,000 strong, and should be only 30 or 40 miles out from river when cavalry returns. The gunboats would be needed to support the river point, which I suppose would be Friar's Point. Such is the outline. The men must take nothing but provisions and ambulances. They must move night and day. The danger would be burning bridges in our rear, which may be avoided by leaving a company at such bridges. Great care must be taken to cover the movement; an advance of a small trading expedition, of infantry only, to hold Friar's Point and get hold of all the means of sending out intelligence would be necessary. This should be at least twenty-four hours in advance of a general move and should not have the least appearance of a cavalry expedition. The destruction of a bridge or two at or near Grenada is all that I contemplate, so as to prevent the enemy from using the railroad. Vandever or Baker would be a proper man to lead such a movement. I may follow or precede this with a telegraphic communication cautiously worded to prevent outsiders from knowing my purpose. Keep this knowledge very close. Examine the maps at General Washburn's old headquarters and give me early information of your note of preparation.

I am, general, very truly, yours,

SAML. R. CURTIS,
Major-General.

HEADQUARTERS DEPARTMENT OF THE TENNESSEE,
La Grange, Tenn., November 7, 1862.

Maj. Gen. J. B. McPHERSON,
Commanding, &c., La Grange, Tenn.:

SIR: I am directed by Major-General Grant to communicate to you the following:

To-morrow (the 8th instant) you will make a reconnaissance in force with one division in the direction of Holly Springs, with two days' rations in haversacks, taking the westerly roads.

General Hamilton with similar force will co-operate with you, taking the easterly roads, and join you on the main road to Holly Springs, about 10 miles from this place.

You will particularly note the topography of the country, and send a copy of map to these headquarters.

The cavalry of your division will report to Colonel Lee, Seventh Kansas Cavalry, at Davis' Mill, to-morrow at 10 a. m., and the cavalry portion will push as near Holly Springs as possible to ascertain the force, position, and movements of the enemy, as also the location of roads and water.

It is not necessary you should accompany the reconnaissance in person; exercise your own discretion in the matter.

Should you be satisfied Holly Springs is evacuated, and it can be occupied without an engagement, take it and send back couriers for supplies.

You will caution commanders of regiments against acts of vandalism, &c., against straggling, and hold officers to a strict accountability for violation of instructions or neglect of duty.

I am, sir, very respectfully, your obedient servant,

GEORGE P. IHRIE,
Colonel and Aide-de-Camp, U. S. Army.

HDQRS. RIGHT WING, ARMY OF THE TENNESSEE,
La Grange, Tenn., November 7, 1862.

Brigadier-General LAUMAN,
Commanding Fourth Division :

GENERAL : You will hold your division in readiness to move to-morrow morning at 8 a. m. in the direction of Holly Springs on a reconnaissance in force, with the exception of two regiments of General Veatch's brigade, one of which will be left to guard Ball's Bridge, across Wolf River, and the other as a reserve and for picket duty, and one regiment of Colonel Johnson's brigade, which will be left to guard the bridges across Wolf River, on the Holly Springs road. Two batteries will accompany you. The men will go provided with two days' rations in haversacks and 100 rounds of ammunition per man. The command will take the westerly roads to Lamar, where it will be joined by a division from General Hamilton's command.

Commanders of regiments are strictly enjoined to see that there is no straggling from ranks and that no acts of vandalism are committed; and they are notified that they will be held to a strict accountability. Brigadier-General Veatch's brigade I think had better cross at Ball's Bridge and move out from there, joining the balance of the command at a point some 6 miles out, where the two roads come within a short distance of each other. You can, however, after consulting with General Veatch, exercise your own discretion. The hour of marching will be given you as soon as I ascertain the time General Hamilton's division marches.

Very respectfully, your obedient servant,
JAS. B. McPHERSON,
Major-General.

HEADQUARTERS LEFT WING,
November 7, 1862.

Major-General GRANT, *Commanding :*

GENERAL : Quinby's division is selected for the reconnaissance to-morrow. If McPherson does not go in person Quinby will be in command. Will the cavalry be under his orders? What time should the division start, and can it be furnished with a guide? I have none. The movement will have to be postponed unless the provision train gets up to-night. I hear nothing of it as yet. I shall post Stanley's division at Davis' Mill to-morrow, so as to more completely cover the ground between McPherson and me. It will also cover the bridges there and relieve the cavalry now required to hold them. Please let me know if McPherson goes out in command of the reconnaissance. The only thing I get confirmatory of an evacuation is the story of a negro who heard Price say if many more men deserted he would not be able to get his trains off. I somewhat doubt the story.

Send me, if you please, papers of the 5th, if you have them, and also results of elections in the States of New York, Illinois, and Wisconsin. What do you learn of the provision train?

Very respectfully, your obedient servant,
C. S. HAMILTON,
Brigadier-General.

HEADQUARTERS LEFT WING,
November 7, [1862]—7.15 p. m.

[General GRANT:]

GENERAL: Two deserters arrived here from Fifth Kentucky Infantry; left Holly Springs on Wednesday—the day before yesterday—and say the wagons of the army had already gone and that the wagons were removing the sick and that evacuation was the order of the day. They got news of our movement on Tuesday night; that we were 50,000 strong, moving from Bolivar, Corinth, and Memphis, and orders were given to evacuate the next morning. These two men were examined separately, each telling the same story. They were twelve-months' men, whose time was out in September, and this is the first chance they have had to get away.

Quinby will get away by 8 a. m. if we get rations in the night.

Yours, truly,

C. S. HAMILTON,
Brigadier-General.

They report much sickness in Price's army. Please send me papers of the 5th, if any have arrived.

HEADQUARTERS,
Jackson, November 7, 1862.

General GRANT:

Some person must be appointed to take charge of the railroad. As it stands, there is no system nor order. It must be done at once.

S. A. HURLBUT,
Major-General.

JACKSON, *November* 7, 1862.

Major-General GRANT:

The Twentieth are ready to move as soon as the road is open. I will send Stevenson's brigade directly after, or, if you order it, will march them by land. Does General McPherson need Foster's cavalry? If so, will send it through. My cavalry force here is very small. What shall be done with the Engineer Regiment?

S. A. HURLBUT.

SPECIAL FIELD ORDERS, } HDQRS. DEPT. OF THE TENNESSEE,
No. 1.   }   *In Field, La Grange, Tenn., Nov.* 7, 1862,

It is with extreme regret that the general commanding has had his attention called to the gross acts of vandalism committed by some of the men composing the two wings of the army on the march from Corinth and Bolivar to this place. Houses have been plundered and burned down, fencing destroyed, and citizens frightened without an inquiry as to their status in this rebellion; cattle and hogs shot and stock driven off, without any observance of the rules prescribed in general orders for taking such property for public use. Such acts are punishable with death by the Articles of War and existing orders. They are calculated to destroy the efficiency of an army and to make open enemies of those who before, if not friends, were at least non-combatants.

Officers are more to blame for these acts of violence than the men who commit them, and in future will be held to a strict accountability. If they will perform their duty, obedience can be enforced in the ranks.

In future marches all men will be kept in the ranks, and regimental commanders held accountable for their good conduct. It is the duty of regimental commanders, and within their power if they are worthy of the position they hold, to enforce attention to duty on the part of company officers.

All derelictions of duty within any regiment in future will be reported by brigade commanders, through the proper channels, to headquarters of the wing to which they may belong, to the end that the offenders may be brought to trial or immediate dismissal from the service and publicly disgraced.

All men who straggle from their companies and are captured by the enemy will be reported to the general headquarters, so that they may be dishonorably discharged, whereby they will forfeit all future and back pay and allowances, and Government will be protected from exchanging a prisoner captured in actual conflict for one who by his worthlessness and disregard for the good of the service has become a captive.

This order will be read on parade before each regiment and detachment for three successive evenings.

By command of Maj. Gen. U. S. Grant:

JNO. A. RAWLINS,
Assistant Adjutant-General.

WASHINGTON, D. C., *November* 8, 1862.

Major-General CURTIS, *Saint Louis:*

You will immediately place Brigadier-General Steele in command of the troops in Helena, and send with him all the troops from the vicinity of Pilot Knob that can be spared.

H. W. HALLECK,
General-in-Chief.

HEADQUARTERS DEPARTMENT OF THE TENNESSEE,
La Grange, November 8, 1862.

General DODGE, *Corinth, Miss.:*

When you are satisfied the enemy can be attacked and repulsed without endangering the post from other parties, do it. You can judge of the propriety of attacking at Guntown better than I can.

General Wallace will probably relieve you in a day or two. A division then awaits you here.

U. S. GRANT,
Major-General.

LAMAR, MISS., *November* 8, 1862—8.30 a. m.

Major-General GRANT:

One of our men who was taken prisoner near Jackson about five weeks ago made his escape from the rebel lines and came in this morning. He says there are about 30,000 infantry, artillery, and cavalry at Coldwater; that they commenced evacuating Holly Springs, but Pemberton came up on Thursday and put a stop to it, ordering the troops all back. They had out five regiments of cavalry yesterday, which were all driven back. Colonel Lee is advancing his cavalry cautiously to find out the truth of the matter. I cannot hear anything of General Quinby, though I have sent several couriers to find him.

The prisoners are just starting in.

Yours, truly,

JAS. B. McPHERSON,
Major-General.

IN THE FIELD, 5½ MILES FROM LA GRANGE,
November 8, 1862—11.45 a. m.

Major-General GRANT:

My column is all united at this point, where the road from Grand Junction comes in.

The cavalry under Colonel Lee have just arrived, and have gone on in advance. I have established a courier post 4½ miles from La Grange, at the forks of the road. General Quinby's division will not be up for two or three hours. I shall, however, push on cautiously to Lamar or vicinity.

Would it not be well to keep a strong lookout on the Moscow road? Some few of the rebel pickets have been seen.

Very respectfully, your obedient servant,

JAS. B. McPHERSON,
Major-General.

LAMAR, *November* 8, 1862—3 p. m.

Major-General GRANT:

Have just reached this point. The advance under Colonel Lee had some pretty sharp skirmishing with rebel cavalry a short distance beyond here. I shall halt my column here until General Quinby comes up, unless I hear something definite from the front.

JAS. B. McPHERSON,
Major-General.

HEADQUARTERS DEPARTMENT OF THE TENNESSEE,
La Grange, November 8, 1862.

Major-General McPHERSON,
Commanding Reconnaissance:

GENERAL: Your dispatch is received. Well done so far. I hope it will turn out as well throughout. My hope rather favors [their] remaining at Holly Springs. The opportunity of attacking there is better than it would be with the Tallahatchie between. The only particular advantage I can see for us having the rebels abandon Holly Springs is that we would then cover Corinth somewhat better. I will hold two divisions in readiness to-morrow should you require re-enforcements. Take no risks for a general engagement; we are not ready for that. Send in your prisoners in the morning under a proper escort.

U. S. GRANT,
Major-General.

SPECIAL ORDERS, }   HEADQUARTERS DISTRICT OF MEMPHIS,
       No. 311.   }   *Memphis, November* 8, 1862.

A detachment of men, to be composed as follows : Seventy-second Ohio, Colonel Buckland ; Sixth Iowa, Sixth Missouri, six companies Thirty-second Wisconsin, Thielemann's cavalry, and Bouton's battery, all under the command of Colonel Buckland, will rendezvous at the camp of the Fifty-fourth Ohio, on the Hernando road, at 9 a. m. precisely, of Monday the 10th instant, for special service. All will be provided with 60 rounds of ammunition, five days' rations and forage, one wagon and one ambulance for each regiment, squadron, and battery.

Colonel Buckland will receive special instructions, and brigadiers will see that the detachments from their commands are well equipped in all respects for rapid marching.

By order of Maj. Gen. W. T. Sherman :

                               J. H. HAMMOND,
                               Assistant Adjutant-General.

SPECIAL ORDERS, }   HEADQUARTERS LEFT WING,
       No. 11.   }   *Grand Junction, November* 8, 1862.

Brig. Gen. L. F. Ross, having reported for duty with this command, is assigned to the command of a brigade in Brigadier-General McArthur's division.

By command of Brig. Gen. C. S. Hamilton :

                               JOHN V. DU BOIS,
                     Colonel, U. S. Army, and Chief of Staff.

                         HEADQUARTERS LEFT WING,
              Scott's House, November 9, 1862—10.30 a. m.

[General GRANT :]

GENERAL : Stanley's division has been ready to move since dawn. If he moves to support Quinby, McArthur will relieve his pickets at the river-crossings.   My aide, Lieutenant Pearce, has just got back from Corinth, and has brought the printing-press and material from Corinth. You had better take the whole for use at your headquarters; it is on the cars at the Junction.

If Stanley moves I will probably go with him, though on my return last night I was attacked with dysentery and am very weak this morning.   Ought not a depot of provisions to be established at the Junction to-day ?   Only 45 wagons came to my command, and Quinby took all the bread, there being only enough for his division.   We shall get along if we can draw from the Junction this evening or in the morning.

Yours, most respectfully,

                               C. S. HAMILTON,
                               Brigadier-General.

                    LA GRANGE, TENN., *November* 9, 1862.

Brigadier-General HAMILTON, *Commanding, &c. :*

Stanley's division will be required to move only in case the enemy should come out and attack.   Put forces in front in force.   You can send your trains to Grand Junction, as that is probably the most convenient place to draw your supplies, taking in consideration the facilities for unloading the cars.   They will be there to-day without fail.

There is a printing-press connected with these headquarters; you can retain the one you speak of if you need it.

By order of Maj. Gen. U. S. Grant:

JNO. A. RAWLINS,
Assistant Adjutant-General.

LA GRANGE, TENN., *November* 9, 1862.

General HAMILTON:

The following dispatch just received from General McPherson, written 8.30 a. m.:*

*   *   *   *   *   *   *   *

You will send out couriers at once to find Quinby and direct him to Lamar. He should have reported ere this to McPherson. Leave the stores mentioned, to find him and hurry him up. It must be that he has taken Ripley road, which is all wrong.

U. S. GRANT,
Major-General.

HEADQUARTERS LEFT WING,
November 9, 1862—12 m.

[General GRANT:]

GENERAL: I have sent out parties to find Quinby. He camped at Davis' Mill last night. He had a map such as I have; was instructed to join McPherson at Lamar and to pick up a guide on the way. I cannot think he is out of the way, but if it shall prove so, he will speedily be brought back and set right. McPherson probably thought him nearer than Davis' Mill last night. I have little doubt the story brought by our man who escaped is entirely the correct one; it agrees with what McPherson said last night, as coming from the prisoners he had captured.

If the enemy have concluded to stay at Coldwater would it not be well to let them remain there until we can bag them. A big haul now will be of the greatest importance at this juncture of affairs. An officer who came in this morning from Jackson says France and England have formally recognized the Confederacy. If such be the case battles, to have any importance, must be of the most decisive character, and we ought to run no risk, but make sure of great things. Have you heard from Sherman?

A letter from Wisconsin to-day advises me that the Wisconsin regiments in the State, as also those of Pope's command, are ordered to McClernand. Is that so? If I am able to ride I will come over this p. m.

Yours, respectfully,

C. S. HAMILTON,
Brigadier-General.

LA GRANGE, TENN., *November* 9, 1862.

Major-General HURLBUT, *Jackson, Tenn.* :

Refuse all permits to come south of Jackson for the present. The Israelites especially should be kept out.

What troops have you now, exclusive of Stevenson's brigade?

U. S. GRANT,
Major-General.

* See p. 327.

JACKSON, *November* 9, 1862.
Major-General GRANT:

My force at Jackson now consists of the following : Eighteenth Illinois Infantry; Twenty-ninth Illinois Infantry; Ninety-fifth Illinois Infantry; One hundred and nineteenth Illinois Infantry; Fourteenth Ohio Battery; Company D, First Illinois Artillery; Fourteenth Indiana Battery; Third Battalion, Eleventh Illinois Cavalry; Twelfth (Company H) Illinois Cavalry; Company A, Second Illinois Cavalry; Foster's Independent Cavalry.

Colonel Stevenson, Fourth Brigade, will move on Monday morning
                           S. A. HURLBUT,
                                Major-General.

HEADQUARTERS DEPARTMENT OF THE TENNESSEE,
                    La Grange, Tenn., November 9, 1862.
Major-General MCPHERSON :

I have sent word to Hamilton to send out for Quinby, and direct him to you. If the enemy is found in strong force at Coldwater, return, sending Colonel Lee, with the cavalry from Hamilton's column, to hunt Quinby up and direct his return.
                           U. S. GRANT,
                                Major-General.

LAMAR, *November* 9, 1862—1 p. m.
Major-General GRANT, *Commanding :*

We have discovered the enemy drawn up in line of battle, 10,000 strong, on a hill across Coldwater, under Pemberton; 10,000 are under Price, a short distance below Holly Springs, and 13,000 at Abbeville. If our whole army was here we could go to Holly Springs, probably, without much of a fight. As it is, they are disposed to dispute our farther advance. I have made arrangements to fall back and will be in La Grange to-night.

General Quinby came up about 9.30 a. m., having camped at Davis' Mill last night. Colonel Lee, of the cavalry, is a trump and no mistake. He has some more prisoners; altogether I think the number will amount to 150. I am going forward to see Colonel Lee, and will give you more detailed information when I come in.

Very respectfully, your obedient servant,
                           JAS. B. MCPHERSON,
                                Major-General.

SPECIAL FIELD ORDERS,) HDQRS. DEPT. OF THE TENNESSEE,
                       $\rangle$ *In the Field, La Grange, Tenn.,*
       No. 2.   )   *November* 9, 1862.

Hereafter stoppages will be made on muster and pay rolls against divisions for the full amount of depredations committed by any number or numbers of the division unless the act can be traced either to the individuals committing them or to the company, regiment, or brigade to which the offenders belong.

In all cases the punishment will be assessed to the smallest organization containing the guilty parties.

Confiscation acts were never intended to be executed by soldiers, and if they were the General Government should have full benefit of all property of which individuals are deprived. A stoppage of pay against offenders will effect this end, and it is to be hoped will correct this growing evil. It is not only the duty of commissioned officers to correct this evil, but of all good men in the ranks to report every violation, and it is determined now that they shall have a pecuniary interest in doing so. Assessments will also be made against commissioned officers in the proportion of their pay proper.

Where offenses of the nature contemplated in this order are traced to individuals they will be summarily punished to the full extent formerly given to garrison court-martials, or be arrested and tried by a general court-martial, according to the enormity of the offense, and the severest penalties provided imposed and executed.

This order will be read on dress-parades before each regiment and detachment for three successive evenings.

By order of Maj. Gen. U. S. Grant:

JNO. A. RAWLINS, ·
Assistant Adjutant-General.

HEADQUARTERS,
Springfield, Ill., November 10, 1862.

Hon. E. M. STANTON,
    Secretary of War :

I received your order on the 21st ultimo at Washington to proceed to Indiana, Illinois, and Iowa and take measures for the preparation of the Mississippi expedition.

Leaving Washington on the morning of the 22d I arrived at Indianapolis on the 23d, and on the same day had an interview with Governor Morton, who responded cordially to the project of the proposed expedition.

Leaving Indianapolis on the 24th I arrived at this place on the morning of the 25th, and immediately sought an interview with Governor Yates, who also responded with similar assurances.

As soon as the necessary dispatches could be prepared I immediately sent Major Scates, assistant adjutant-general, to Iowa, to see and confer with Governor Kirkwood, who also entered zealously into the project.

When I reached here the impendency of the late election in this State, and the interest felt in it by State officials, in some degree impeded my efforts to forward the troops remaining in the State.

I should also state in explanation of the tardiness attending enlistments that the scarcity of necessary labor caused by the very great number of troops sent from this State has hardly left any of the adult male population behind at liberty to leave their homes. Yet within the short space of sixteen days I have completed the organization, mustered, and forwarded from the different camps in Illinois six regiments of infantry and one six-gun battery to Columbus, Ky., and six regiments of infantry and one six-gun battery to Memphis, Tenn.

From Indiana I have forwarded five regiments of infantry, and from Iowa three, also to Columbus, Ky. In addition to these there is another regiment of infantry in Illinois now under marching orders, and three others in the same State will be mustered by the middle of the current week; and ten more in Iowa, as I am informed, are only lacking overcoats, which I hope soon to furnish. Besides these, probably by the 15th instant twelve or more regiments from Illinois and Iowa may be moved, making twenty regiments of infantry and two batteries gone and twelve nearly ready to go. Four other regiments of infantry, six of cavalry, and four companies of artillery are being enlisted in Illinois, and two other regiments of infantry in Iowa.

Although enlistments in Illinois are less tardy now than before the election, yet the probable delay that will attend the completion of the cavalry and artillery organizations has induced me to recommend to Governor Yates the consolidation of all such deficient organizations after the 20th instant, in order that such as may be completed by this process may be hastened to the field.

Passing from these details to a subject of a more prominent character, I wish to add that the avidity with which the Mississippi expedition is embraced by the people of the Northwest expose all who are charged with carrying it into effect to the consequences of popular fury if they should fail to do so. As for myself I hardly need reiterate the deep and absorbing interest I feel in the enterprise and my entire willingness to do all in my power to promote it. Yet if, from obstacles such as opposed you in the beginning or for other causes, the expedition has become an uncertainty or must be long delayed I trust you will cut my supposed connection with it and order me to other duty in the field at once. In the latter case my familiarity with the old troops of General Grant's command and the country in which he is operating would decide me, if I might be allowed a discretion, to prefer duty with him.

The blockade of the Mississippi River has left to the people of the Northwest but one outlet for their immense surplus of grains and live stock, and that by the lakes and railroads alone, to the East. These channels are closed for the greater portion of the most favorable season for moving these articles to market, leaving the producers and traders at the discretion of exclusive monopolists.

By combinations or otherwise corporations controlling these outlets have raised freights to such high rates as either to stop shipments or sacrifice traders. This evil operates most oppressively upon the energies and enterprise of the people of the Northwest on the one hand and most advantageously to capitalists in the East owning those roads and the manufacturing establishments furnishing the various fabrics required for the use of the Army and Navy on the other. The latter in a pecuniary aspect are deeply interested in continuing it.

What is seen? A comparatively insignificant obstruction has served to continue the blockade of the Mississippi River now for five months, covering a space during which the products of its valley are usually borne upon its waters to market, and the period of the investment of Vicksburg by a strong flotilla of gunboats.

In view of these facts, and the great addition which has been made to our armies under the late calls for volunteers, and the present inertness of the Mississippi Flotilla, the people so deeply interested are illy disposed to receive any excuse for further delay in removing that obstacle. Indeed, any further delay must produce consequences which will seriously complicate our national troubles by adding another geographical question to the one which is now undergoing the arbitrament of arms.

Already are there those who are beginning to look beyond the pale of Federal authority for new guarantees for the freedom of the Mississippi River. The late election, in some instances, affords unmistakable indications of this fact. Not a few of the candidates preferred to office are represented to be opposed to the war and the policy that would continue it. Nor is this altogether surprising, since the earlier inhabitants of the Mississippi Valley, at one time despairing of the Government's willingness or ability to assert their right to a place for tl e deposit of their produce near the mouth of the Mississippi River, began to look with growing favor to the transferring of their allegiance to the Spanish Crown, then holding the outlet of that river.

I am conscious that if something is not soon done to reopen that great highway that a new party will spring into existence, which will favor the recognition of the independence of the so called Confederate States, with the view to eventual arrangements, either by treaty or union, for the purpose of effecting that object.

The resentments of the people will be inflamed by demagogical appeals designed to array the people of the West against the people of the East upon the pretended ground that the latter are in favor of continuing the war and the blockade of the Mississippi, as a means of fostering the interest of their trade, their manufactures, and their capital invested in both. This sentiment is reprehensibly wrong; nay, criminal. Our first and highest duty under Heaven is to preserve the Union and the Government. This we must do; yet wise statesmen will not overlook the difficulties and dangers which surround them, but will avoid them by timely precautions.

In short, delay may bring another separation, and another separation will entail endless collisions, which, after wasting all the States, must sink them in anarchy and wretchedness, like that which drapes Mexico in misery and mourning.

Hence, in conclusion, let me appeal to you, and through you to the President, to do something, and that something quickly, to avert the rising storm, and insure a safe passage to our good and beloved Ship of State through the strait that now threatens her in the distance.

If I have spoken too freely, pardon my boldness. If I have said too much, charge it to an honest zeal for the welfare of my country, and forgive it.

Your obedient servant,

JOHN A. McCLERNAND,
Major-General, U. S. Volunteers.

HEADQUARTERS,
Springfield, Ill., November 10, 1862.

Maj. Gen. H. W. HALLECK, *General-in-Chief:*

I received the order of the Secretary of War on the 21st ultimo at Washington to proceed to Indiana, Illinois, and Iowa and take measures for the preparation of the Mississippi expedition.

Leaving Washington on the morning of the 22d I arrived at Indianapolis on the 23d, and on the same day had an interview with Governor Morton, who responded cordially to the project of the proposed expedition.

Leaving Indianapolis on the 24th I arrived at this place on the morning of the 25th, and immediately sought an interview with Governor Yates, who also responded with similar assurances.

As soon as the necessary dispatches could be prepared I immediately sent Major Scates, assistant adjutant-general, to Iowa, to see and confer with Governor Kirkwood, who also entered zealously into the project.

When I reached here the impendency of the late election in this State, and the interest felt in it by State officials, in some degree impeded my efforts to forward the troops remaining within the State.

I should also state in further explanation of the tardiness attending enlistments that the scarcity of necessary labor caused by the very great number of troops sent from this State has hardly left any of the adult male population behind at liberty to leave their homes. Yet within the short space of sixteen days I have completed the organization, mustered, and forwarded from the different camps in Illinois six regiments of infantry and one six-gun battery to Columbus, Ky., and six regiments of infantry and one six-gun battery to Memphis, Tenn.

From Indiana I have forwarded five regiments of infantry and from Iowa three, also to Columbus, Ky. In addition to these organizations already forwarded there is another regiment of infantry in Illinois now under marching orders, and three others in the same State will be mustered by the middle of the current week; and ten more in Iowa, as I am informed, are only lacking overcoats, which I hope soon to furnish. Besides these, probably by the 15th instant twelve or more regiments from Illinois and Iowa may be moved, making twenty regiments of infantry and two batteries gone and twelve nearly ready to go. Four other regiments of infantry, six of cavalry, and four companies of artillery are being enlisted in Illinois, and two other regiments of infantry in Iowa.

Although enlistments in Illinois are less tardy than before the election, yet the probable delay that will attend the completion of the cavalry and artillery organizations has induced me to recommend to Governor Yates the consolidation of all such deficient organizations after the 20th instant, in order that such as may be completed by this process may be hastened to the field.

Very respectfully, your obedient servant,

JOHN A. McCLERNAND,
Major-General, U. S. Volunteers.

WAR DEPARTMENT,
Washington, November 10, 1862.

Major-General WRIGHT, *Cincinnati, Ohio :*

All spare troops are to be sent to Memphis.

H. W. HALLECK,
General-in-Chief.

LA GRANGE, TENN., *November* 10, 1862.

Maj. Gen. WILLIAM T. SHERMAN, *Memphis, Tenn. :*

GENERAL: Colonel Grierson and company arrived here yesterday about 4 p. m. without accident by the way. Your policies of encouraging trade with the citizens I am satisfied with so long as the Treasury Department throw no more restrictions in the way than they do at present; but I think such articles as are of prime necessity for the supply of an army there should be some restriction in. As we expect to advance southward so soon, however, I do not deem any change from your present policy either necessary or desirable.

McPherson returned last evening from a reconnaissance in force toward Holly Springs. The cavalry had some skirmishing, resulting in the capture of about 130 of the Confederates; 16 killed on their side that our troops saw, and no doubt many wounded. Our cavalry was armed with revolving rifles and dismounted, while the enemy was mostly armed with shot-guns and on horseback.

The reconnaissance was pushed to Coldwater and across it. The facts ascertained from observation, from citizens, deserters, and prisoners, are that on our arrival here Price commenced the evacuation of Holly Springs. Pemberton came up on Wednesday evening and countermanded the order. The enemy now occupy Coldwater, a line in rear, and Abbeville.

The following is the organization:

Pemberton's (four) divisions:

Price—two divisions: Maury, Bowen. Rust, commanding Lovell's division; latter sick at Holly Springs. Tilghman's division—released prisoners.

Rust, 6,000 men—three brigades; five batteries, four guns each.
Tilghman, 4,000 men—two brigades; two batteries, two guns each.
Price, 10,000 men—two divisions; number of guns not known.

At Abbeville there are 12,000 militia. There are no intrenchments at Coldwater; at Holly Springs ordinary rifle-pits. They have no heavy guns. Villepigue has gone to Port Hudson. Directly after the Corinth fight 10,000 men went to Mobile.

General Halleck informed me that there would be a movement north from New Orleans, and that Curtis was directed to re-enforce Helena, and would be directed to move on Grenada if it was impracticable to go to Little Rock. I telegraphed yesterday before receiving your letter to be more definitely informed of their different movements, and particularly that the Helena force be required to co-operate with me.

I am now informed that six regiments have already left for Memphis, and that five or six more will start immediately; this is infantry alone. The Third Regular Cavalry and likely other regiments of cavalry will also join you, besides several batteries.

I think it will not be advisable for you to move until you can do it with two complete divisions of twelve infantry regiments each, with a full proportion of cavalry and artillery. My plan was for you to move on Oxford if the enemy remain where they are now, or some point south of the Tallahatchie; but on reflection I am more inclined to favor your occupying Moscow, and all start together, especially if there should be a movement from Helena as desired.

When you can leave a force of four regiments of infantry with artillery and about four companies of cavalry at Memphis I think you will be ready to move. Re-enforcements may constantly be expected at Memphis after your departure. Hence this opinion.

I will not be able to send you any general officer unless possibly one to take command of the forces that will be left at Memphis. Stuart and Buckland will both command brigades or even divisions as well as if they held the commissions which they should and I hope will hold.

We will of course supply ourselves from the country with everything it affords necessary for the army, giving receipts for the same to be settled at the close of hostilities. These receipts should set forth as far as practicable the status of the parties who are deprived of their property. I will inclose with this some information just this moment received.

I may occupy Holly Springs for the purpose of finishing the railroad as far south as possible and getting our supplies also as far in that direction as possible. We are now getting up rations rapidly and will keep on hand 100,000 ahead. The railroad is completed to Davis' Mill and work progressing rapidly.

There were a number of matters I intended to write you when I commenced, but being interrupted so often I have forgotten them. I will communicate with you again before the final start is made.

Yours, truly,

U. S. GRANT,
Major-General, Commanding.

LA GRANGE, *November* 10, 1862.

General WEBSTER, *Jackson, Tenn.*:

Give orders to all the conductors on the road that no Jews are to be permitted to travel on the railroad southward from any point. They may go north and be encouraged in it; but they are such an intolerable nuisance that the department must be purged of them.

U. S. GRANT,
Major-General.

JACKSON, *November* 10, 1862.

Major-General GRANT:

The Eighty-first Illinois, from Humboldt, is under marching orders for La Grange. General Brayman wants another regiment, and says he has to do railroad duty south. I can send him one in a day or two. The mills at Davis' Mill and the steam mill at Grand Junction ought to be seized for use, also McCown's Mill, near Moscow. They can be made to grind cob-corn, at least, for horses instead of long forage, which will be scarce. The country between La Grange and Somerville has plenty of forage.

S. A. HURLBUT,
Major-General.

Abstract from Tri-monthly Return of the Department of the Tennessee, Maj. Gen. U. S. Grant commanding, for November 10, 1862.

Command.	Present for duty.		Aggregate present for duty.	Aggregate present.	Aggregate present and absent.	Pieces of artillery.		Aggregate present and absent last monthly return.
	Officers.	Men.				Heavy.	Field.	
DISTRICT OF MEMPHIS.								
Maj. Gen. W. T. SHERMAN.								
Staff	14	....	14	14	14	....	....	14
Infantry	813	16,914	17,727	19,513	21,636	....	....	10,224
Cavalry	33	724	757	890	925	....	....	936
Artillery	28	1,046	1,074	1,156	1,232	....	48	1,084
Total District of Memphis	888	18,684	19,572	21,573	23,807	....	48	12,258
DISTRICT OF CORINTH.								
Brig. Gen. G. M. DODGE.								
Infantry	277	5,386	5,663	6,936	8,666	....	....	8,572
Cavalry	14	369	383	489	591	....	....	589
Artillery	11	422	433	517	553	....	....	498
Total District of Corinth	302	6,177	6,479	7,942	9,810	....	....	9,659
DISTRICT OF JACKSON.								
Maj. Gen. S. A. HURLBUT.								
Staff	16	....	16	16	19	....	....	19
Infantry	202	3,834	4,036	5,111	5,891	....	....	5,889
Cavalry	57	1,170	1,227	1,506	1,696	....	....	1,639
Artillery	19	680	699	767	881	74	24	917
Total District of Jackson	294	5,684	5,978	7,400	8,487	74	24	8,464

Abstract from Tri-monthly Return of the Department of the Tennessee, &c.—Continued.

Command.	Present for duty.		Aggregate present for duty.	Aggregate present.	Aggregate present and absent.	Pieces of artillery.		Aggregate present and absent last monthly return.
	Officers.	Men.				Heavy.	Field.	
RIGHT WING.								
Maj. Gen. J. B. McPHERSON.								
Staff	10	....	10	10	10	....	....	10
Infantry	651	12,930	13,581	16,042	18,782	....	....	15,512
Cavalry	59	1,208	1,267	1,550	2,583	....	....	2,272
Artillery	19	731	750	809	942	....	38	912
Total right wing	739	14,869	15,608	18,411	22,317	....	38	18,706
LEFT WING.								
Brig. Gen. C. S. HAMILTON.								
Infantry	537	10,268	10,805	12,228	20,119	....	....	....
Cavalry	76	1,820	1,896	2,263	2,731	....	....	....
Artillery	14	769	783	845	1,279	....	45	....
Total left wing	627	12,857	13,484	15,336	24,129	....	45	....
Grand total department	2,850	58,271	61,121	70,662	88,550	....	155	49,087

Organization of troops in the Department of the Tennessee, Maj. Gen. U. S. Grant, U. S. Army, commanding, November 10, 1862.

RIGHT WING.*

Maj. Gen. JAMES B. McPHERSON.

THIRD DIVISION.

Brig. Gen. JOHN A. LOGAN.

First Brigade.

Col. C. CARROLL MARSH.

20th Illinois, Maj. Orton Frisbie.
30th Illinois, Col. Elias S. Dennis.
31st Illinois, Col. Lyndorf Ozburn.
45th Illinois, Col. John E. Smith.
81st Illinois, Col. James J. Dollins.
124th Illinois, Lieut. Col. John H. Howe.

Second Brigade.

Col. MORTIMER D. LEGGETT.

23d Indiana, Maj. William P. Davis.
20th Ohio, Col. Manning F. Force.
68th Ohio, Maj. John S. Snook.
78th Ohio, Lieut. Col. Zachariah M. Chandler.

Fourth Brigade.

Col. JOHN D. STEVENSON.

8th Illinois, Maj. Robert H. Sturgess.
63d Illinois, Col. Joseph B. McCown.
17th Illinois, Col. Addison S. Norton.
7th Missouri, Lieut. Col. Wm. S. Oliver.

Artillery.

Capt. GEORGE C. GUMBART.

1st Illinois, Battery D, Lieut. James A. Borland.
2d Illinois, Batteries E and F, Lieut. Henry R. Henning.
8th Michigan Battery, Capt. Samuel De Golyer.
3d Ohio Battery, Capt. Wm. S. Williams.

* Headquarters at La Grange, Tenn.

FOURTH DIVISION.

Brig. Gen. THOMAS J. McKEAN.

Infantry. *

14th Illinois, Col. Cyrus Hall.
15th Illinois, Lieut. Col. Geo. C. Rogers.
28th Illinois, Maj. Barclay C. Gillam.
32d Illinois, Lieut. Col. William Hunter.
41st Illinois, Lieut. Col. John Warner.
46th Illinois, Col. Benjamin Dornblaser.

53d Illinois, Maj. Seth C. Earl.
76th Illinois, Col. Alonzo W. Mack.
103d Illinois, Col. Willard A. Dickerman.
25th Indiana, Col. William H. Morgan.
53d Indiana, Col. Walter Q. Gresham.
3d Iowa, Capt. John B. Smith.
12th Wisconsin, Col. George E. Bryant.

Artillery.

2d Illinois, Battery L, Capt. William H. Bolton.
9th Indiana Battery, Lieut. George R. Brown.
1st Missouri, Battery C, Lieut. Edward Brotzmann.
7th Ohio Battery, Capt. Silas A. Burnap.
15th Ohio Battery, Capt. Edward Spear, jr.

Cavalry.

2d Illinois, Lieut. Col. Quincy McNeil.
7th Illinois, Lieut. Col. Edward Prince.
5th Ohio (battalion), † Maj. Charles S. Hayes.

LEFT WING.‡

Brig. Gen. CHARLES S. HAMILTON.

—— DIVISION.

Brig. Gen. DAVID S. STANLEY.

First Brigade.

Col. JOHN W. FULLER.

27th Ohio, Lieut. Col. Zeph. S. Spaulding.
39th Ohio, Col. Edward F. Noyes.
43d Ohio, Col. Wager Swayne.
63d Ohio, Capt. Charles E Brown.

Second Brigade.

Col. JOHN M. LOOMIS.

26th Illinois, Maj. Robert A. Gillmore.
47th Illinois, Col. George A. Williams.
5th Minnesota, Col. Lucius F. Hubbard.
11th Missouri, Maj. Andrew J. Weber.
8th Wisconsin, Lieut. Col. George W. Robbins.
2d Iowa Baty., Lieut. Daniel P. Walling.

—— DIVISION.*

Brig. Gen ISAAC F. QUINBY.

56th Illinois, Lieut. Col. Green B. Raum.
48th Indiana, Col. Norman Eddy.
59th Indiana, Col. Jesse I. Alexander.
5th Iowa, Lieut. Col. Ezekiel S. Sampson.
10th Iowa, Lieut. Col. William E. Small.
17th Iowa, Col. David B. Hillis.

4th Minnesota, Lieut Col. John E. Tourtellotte.
10th Missouri, Col. Samuel A. Holmes.
24th Missouri, Company F, Lieut. W. W. McCammon.
26th Missouri, Col. George B. Boomer.
80th Ohio, Col. Ephraim R. Eckley.

---

* Brigade organizations not indicated on original return.
† But see Districts of Jackson and Corinth.
‡ Headquarters near Grand Junction.

—— DIVISION.*

Brig. Gen. John McArthur.

11th Iowa, Col. William Hall.
13th Iowa, Lieut. Col. John Shane.
15th Iowa, Maj. William T. Cunningham.
16th Iowa, Maj. William Purcell.
1st Kansas, Lieut. Col. Otto M. Tennison.
15th Mich., Lieut. Col. John McDermott.

18th Missouri, Capt. Jacob R. Ault.
14th Wisconsin, Lieut. Col. Lyman M Ward.
16th Wisconsin, Maj. Thomas Reynolds.
17th Wisconsin, Col. John L. Doran.
18th Wisconsin, Col. Gabriel Bouck.

Artillery.†

2d Illinois, Battery F, Lieut. Joseph W. Mitchell.
3d Michigan Battery, Capt. Alexander W. Dees.
1st Minnesota Battery, Lieut. William Z. Clayton.
1st Missouri, Battery M, Lieut. Junius W. MacMurray.
5th Ohio Battery, Lieut. Charles J. Marsh.
10th Ohio Battery, Lieut. Edward Grosskopff.
11th Ohio Battery, Capt. Frank C. Sands.
2d United States, Battery F, Capt. A. S. Molinard.
6th Wisconsin Battery, Capt. Henry Dillon.
12th Wisconsin Battery, Lieut. Lorenzo D. Immell.

Cavalry.

Col. Albert L. Lee.

11th Illinois, Company G, Lieut. Stephen S. Tripp.
2d Iowa, Maj. Datus E. Coon.
7th Kansas, Lieut. Col. T. P. Herrick.
3d Michigan, Maj. Gilbert Moyers.
5th Missouri, Company C, Lieut. John C. Mohrstadt.

DISTRICT OF MEMPHIS, TENN.

Maj. Gen. William T. Sherman.

First Brigade.

Brig. Gen. Morgan L. Smith.

113th Illinois, Col. George B. Hoge.
120th Illinois, Col. George W. McKeaig.
6th Missouri, Col. Peter E. Bland.
8th Missouri, Col. Giles A. Smith.
54th Ohio, Col. T. Kilby Smith.

Second Brigade.

Brig. Gen. J. W. Denver.

40th Illinois, Lieut. Col. Jas. W. Boothe.
100th Indiana, Lieut. Col. Albert Heath.
6th Iowa, Col. John M. Corse.
46th Ohio, Col. Charles C. Walcutt.
13th United States, 1st Battalion, Maj. Daniel Chase.

Third Brigade.‡

97th Indiana, Lieut. Col. Robert F. Catterson.
99th Indiana, Col. Alexander Fowler.
48th Ohio, Col. Peter J. Sullivan.
53d Ohio, Col. Wells S. Jones.
70th Ohio, Col. Joseph R. Cockerill.

Fourth Brigade.

Col. David Stuart.

55th Illinois, Lieut. Col. Oscar Malmborg.
116th Illinois, Col. Nathan W. Tupper.
127th Illinois, Col. John Van Arman.
83d Indiana, Col. Benjamin J. Spooner.
57th Ohio, Col. William Mungen.

Fifth Brigade.

Col. Ralph P. Buckland.

93d Illinois, Col. Holden Putnam.
114th Illinois, Col. James W. Judy.
93d Indiana, Col. De Witt C. Thomas.
72d Ohio, Maj. Charles G. Eaton.
32d Wisconsin, Col. James H. Howe.

Reserve Brigade.‡

117th Illinois, Col. Risdon M. Moore.
130th Illinois, Col. Nathaniel Niles.
33d Wisconsin, Col. Jonathan B. Moore.

---

* Brigade organizations not indicated on original return.
† Assignments to divisions not indicated on original returns.
‡ Commander not indicated.

Artillery.

1st Illinois, Battery A, Capt. Peter P. Wood.
1st Illinois, Battery B, Capt. Samuel E. Barrett.
1st Illinois, Battery E, Capt. Allen C. Waterhouse
1st Illinois, Battery F, Capt. John T. Cheney.
1st Illinois, Battery H, Capt. Axel Silfversparre.
1st Illinois, Battery I, Capt. Edward Bouton.
Cogswell's Illinois Battery, Capt. William Cogswell.
Mercantile Illinois Battery, Capt. Charles G. Cooley.
6th Indiana Battery, Capt. Michael Mueller.
8th Ohio Battery, Capt. Charles H. Schmidt.

Cavalry.

6th Illinois, Col. Benjamin H. Grierson.
Thielemann's Battalion, Maj. Christian Thielemann.

DISTRICT OF CORINTH, MISS.

Brig. Gen. G. M. DODGE.

*Infantry.**

7th Illinois, Col. Andrew J. Babcock.
9th Illinois, Col. August Mersy.
12th Illinois, Col. Augustus L. Chetlain.
50th Illinois, Col. Moses M. Bane.
52d Illinois, Col. Thomas W. Sweeny.
57th Illinois, Col. Silas D. Baldwin.
2d Iowa, Col. James B. Weaver.
7th Iowa, Col. Elliott W. Rice.

Cavalry.

5th Ohio, 3d Battalion.
Stewart's Illinois Battalion.

14th Missouri, † Col. Patrick E. Burke.
22d Ohio, Col. Oliver Wood.
81st Ohio, Col. Thomas Morton.
1st United States, Capt. E. D. Phillips.
Union Brigade.
Yates Sharpshooters, Lieut. Col. John Morrill.

Artillery and Engineers.

1st Missouri Artillery, (4 batteries), Maj. George H. Stone.
Sappers and Miners, Lieut. Christian Lochbihler.

DISTRICT OF COLUMBUS, KY.‡

Brig. Gen. THOMAS A. DAVIES.

DISTRICT OF JACKSON, TENN.

Maj. Gen. STEPHEN A. HURLBUT.

*Infantry.**

18th Illinois, Lieut. Col. Daniel H. Brush.
29th Illinois, Col. Charles M. Ferrell.
43d Illinois, § Col. Adolph Engelmann.
48th Illinois, Col. Isham N. Haynie.
49th Illinois, Col. William R. Morrison.
54th Illinois, Lieut. Col. Greenville M. Mitchell.

61st Illinois, § Maj. Simon P. Ohr.
62d Illinois, Col. James M. True.
109th Illinois, § Col. Alexander J. Nimmo.
122d Illinois, Col. John I. Rinaker.
12th Michigan, § Lieut. Col. William H. Graves.
7th Tennessee, Lieut. Col. Isaac R. Hawkins.

---

* Brigade organization not indicated on original return.
† Afterward known as the Sixty-sixth Illinois Infantry.
‡ Troops not indicated on original. Brig. Gen. J. M. Tuttle, commanding Division of Cairo.
§ Post of Bolivar, Brig. Gen. M. Brayman commanding.

Artillery.

Maj. CHARLES J. STOLBRAND.

1st Illinois, Battery F,* Capt. John T. Cl eney.
1st Illinois, Battery D, Capt. Henry A. Rogers.
2d Illinois, Battery B, Capt. Relly Madison.
2d Illinois, Battery G, Capt. Frederick Sparrestrom.
Springfield (Illinois) battery,† Capt. Thomas F. Vaugh.1.
14th Indiana Battery, Capt. Meredith H. Kidd.
14th Ohio Battery, Lieut. Homer H. Stull.
15th Ohio Battery,‡ Capt. Edward Spear, jr.
7th Wisconsin Battery, Lieut. Galen E. Green

Cavalry.

2d Illinois, Company A, Capt. John R. Hotaling.
4th Illinois, Col. T. Lyle Dickey.
11th Illinois, Maj. Lucien H. Kerr.
12th Illinois, Company H, Capt. Franklin T. Gilbert.
4th Ohio Company, Capt. John S. Foster.
5th Ohio (nine companies),§ Col. W. H. Taylor.
6th Tennessee, Col. Fielding Hurst.
Hawkins' Horse.
Stewart's Independent Cavalry.§

LA GRANGE, TENN., *November* 11, 1862.

General HAMILTON:

Direct your troops to draw rations as soon as possible to include the 20th, and be prepared for an advance movement when ordered. To-morrow will be early enough to draw them.

U. S. GRANT,
Major-General.

HEADQUARTERS LEFT WING,
La Grange, November 11, [1862]—8.30 p. m.

General GRANT:

Colonel Lee is not out. He does not wish to start until the morning, and then to make his arrangements so as to enter Holly Springs just at daybreak. He is a little afraid his return may be embarrassed by a larger force of cavalry than he has.

I have directed Quinby to send a brigade with one battery as far as Lamar to-morrow for Lee to fall back upon if pressed. Lee has had his scouts in the front to-day.

C. S. HAMILTON,
Brigadier-General.

LA GRANGE, TENN., *November* 11, 1862.

General HAMILTON:

I have just directed five companies of cavalry to report to Colone Lee in the morning, and sent a communication for you to furnish a bri gade and battery, just as your dispatch states you have done.

U. S. GRANT,
Major-General.

---

* Also reported as in the District of Memphis.
† Post of Bolivar, Brig. Gen. M. Brayman commanding.
‡ Also reported as in McKean's division, right wing.
§ See District of Corinth.

LA GRANGE, TENN., *November* 11, 1862.

General HAMILTON:

Information just received from deserters proves that Lumpkin's Mill is evacuated and that Coldwater Bridge is still standing. If this is so the brigade going out should remain there, and the balance of Quinby's and one other division move up as soon as possible.

U. S. GRANT,
Major-General.

LA GRANGE, TENN., *November* 11, 1862.

General HAMILTON:

I only wanted the advance made to Holly Springs in the event that Coldwater Railroad Bridge is standing. If that is done, Quinby can return.

My dispatch to you was in consequence of the superintendent of telegraph reporting that all the troops had left Davis' Mill.

U. S. GRANT,
Major-General.

SPECIAL ORDERS, }   HDQRS. 13TH A. C., DEPT. OF THE TENN.,
No. 15.   }   *La Grange, Tenn., November* 11, 1862.

I. Brig. Gen. Thomas J. McKean is hereby assigned to the command of the Fourth Division, right wing of the army, and will immediately assume command.

II. Brig. Gen. Leonard F. Ross will relieve Brig. Gen. D. S. Stanley in the command of the division of the left wing of the army, now commanded by General Stanley.

III. In pursuance of orders from the general-in-chief of the Army, Brig. Gen. D. S. Stanley is relieved from duty in this department, and will report in person without delay to Major-General Rosecrans, commanding Department of the Cumberland.

*   *   *   *   *   *   *

By order of Maj. Gen. U. S. Grant:

JNO. A. RAWLINS,
Assistant Adjutant-General.

LA GRANGE, TENN., *November* 12, 1862.

General HAMILTON:

Have you sent forward more than one brigade? My instructions were that if Wolf River Railroad Bridge is still standing, and Holly Springs and Lumpkin's Mill deserted, as I understand they are, these two divisions were to be pushed forward. Answer if the two divisions have already gone. If so, I want telegraph office pushed forward and a brigade sent to Davis' Mill.

U. S. GRANT,
Major-General.

HEADQUARTERS LEFT WING,
November —, 1862—12 m.

Major-General GRANT:

GENERAL: Only one brigade has moved, and that as a support for Lee. The other brigade of Quinby's is ordered to supply itself with rations for the whole division and be ready to move. Stanley's division is ordered to be ready to move forward with Quinby's Second Brigade, but not to move until we get reports from Colonel Lee that Holly Springs and Lumpkin's Mill were evacuated. I don't expect that report from Lee before to-morrow a. m. Colonel Lee will establish couriers every 3 miles and send back word. Wolf River Railroad Bridge is not standing. The country around Holly Springs is used up for forage, and if a command goes there before the bridge over Wolf River is completed it will be difficult to supply it with forage. The movement you ordered will take place, however, as soon as we hear from Colonel Lee that the enemy is across the Tallahatchie.

C. S. HAMILTON.

HAMILTON'S HEADQUARTERS,
November 12, 1862.

Major-General GRANT:

No report from Lee as yet about the Coldwater Bridge. Quinby is at Davis' Mill with one brigade. I should like to have a telegraph station there. Can an operator be sent down ?

C. S. HAMILTON,
Brigadier-General.

GENERAL ORDERS, }   HEADQUARTERS DISTRICT OF MEMPHIS,
No. 93.   }   *Memphis, November* 12, 1862.

The troops now at Memphis and arriving will be arranged into five brigades :

First Brigade, Brig. Gen. M. L. Smith.—Eighth Missouri, Col. Giles A. Smith; Sixth Missouri, Col. Peter E. Bland; One hundred and thirteenth Illinois, Col. George B. Hoge; Fifty-fourth Ohio, Col. T. Kilby Smith ; One hundred and twentieth Illinois, Col. G. W. McKeaig.

Second Brigade, Col. J. Adair McDowell.—Sixth Iowa, Lieut. Col. J. M. Corse ; Fortieth Illinois, Lieut. Col. J. W. Boothe; Forty-sixth Ohio, Lieut. Col. C. C. Walcutt ; Thirteenth U. S. Infantry, Maj. D. Chase.

Third Brigade, Brig. Gen. J. W. Denver.—Forty-eighth Ohio, Col. P. J. Sullivan ; Fifty-third Ohio, Col. W. S. Jones ; Seventieth Ohio, Col. J. R. Cockerill.

Fourth Brigade, Col. David Stuart.—Fifty-fifth Illinois, Lieut. Col. O. Malmborg ; Fifty-seventh Ohio, Col. W. Mungen ; Eighty-third Indiana, Colonel Spooner ; One hundred and sixteenth Illinois, Colonel Tupper ; One hundred and twenty-seventh Illinois, Lieutenant-Colonel Eldridge.

Fifth Brigade, Col. R. P. Buckland.—Seventy-second Ohio, Lieut. Col. D. W. C. Loudon ; Thirty-second Wisconsin, Col. J. H. Howe ; Ninety-third Illinois, Maj. J. M. Fisher commanding ; Ninety-third Indiana, Colonel Thomas commanding.

These brigades will be arranged into two divisions :

First Division, Brigadier-General Denver commanding.—Second, Third, and Fifth Brigades.

General Denver will have his headquarters in Fort Pickering, and will be considered the commander thereof, and will give all necessary orders for its guard, police, &c.

Second Division, Brig. Gen. M. L. Smith commanding.—First and Fourth Brigades.

General Smith will be considered specially in command of the outer lines, and will give his attention to the location of camps, their police and discipline. Headquarters on Poplar street.

II. All the troops at Memphis will prepare at once for field service. Each regiment will reduce its baggage and transportation to the standard fixed in General Orders, No. 160, from the Headquarters of the Army, and will pay special attention to their arms, ammunition, and equipments.

III. The First Division will draw their supplies of provisions from Captain Morton, commissary of subsistence, in the warehouse at Fort Pickering.

The Second Division will draw their supplies from Captain Hinsdill, commissary of subsistence on board the wharf-boat. Quartermaster and ordnance supplies will as heretofore be drawn from Capt. J. Condit Smith, assistant quartermaster, and Captain Neely, ordnance officer, Fort Pickering. Capt. H. S. Fitch is announced as post quartermaster, specially charged with the administration of his department at Memphis, and Captain Swain, assistant quartermaster, charged with the transportation department and such other duties as may be assigned him.

IV. The regiments to arrive will be assigned to brigades to fill up the blanks in the brigades, and will at once report to their respective brigadiers, who will at once instruct them in their duties.

V. Commanders of divisions and brigades will at once fill their respective staffs and announce their names and office in orders. All such staff officers must be well mounted, and if they be not entitled by law to horses their commanders will make the necessary requisitions for approval and order at these headquarters. Officers acting as staff officers and mounted orderlies are entitled to forage drawn on returns, the same as officers and men of like rank in the cavalry service.

VI. The commanding general expects all officers now to vie with each other in the display of soldierly zeal, for all have now had most valuable experience under all the circumstances to which soldiers are usually exposed. Let all marches and military movements be conducted in compact, good order, in cheerfulness and silence, and honor and fame will be our certain reward.

By order of Maj. Gen. W. T. Sherman:

J. H. HAMMOND,
Assistant Adjutant-General.

SPRINGFIELD, ILL., *November* 13, 1862—10.30 a. m.

Hon. E. M. STANTON,
Secretary of War :

Five regiments Indiana infantry left yesterday for Memphis, and the Sixty-third Regiment Indiana Infantry will leave to-day. I infer that General Grant claims the right to change their destination, and to control all the troops sent to Columbus and Memphis.

JOHN A. McCLERNAND,
Major-General.

LA GRANGE, *November* 13, 1862.

Brig. Gen. J. S. HAMILTON,
    Commanding Left Wing, &c.:

Artillery firing was heard south from Moscow. I have no reconnaissance in that direction. Have you heard anything further from Lee? Direct him to return.

U. S. GRANT,
Major-General.

HEADQUARTERS LEFT WING,
November 13, 1862.

General GRANT:

Sullivan sends word that the Coldwater Bridge is some distance off his route, but the citizens say the road has not been molested.

C. S. HAMILTON,
Brigadier-General.

HEADQUARTERS LEFT WING,
November 13, 1862.

General GRANT:

I recalled Sullivan while you were here to-day. Have since learned that Sullivan went on to Holly Springs at Lee's request without orders. His orders were to go to Lamar, and in no event beyond Coldwater. Lee and Sullivan have both been recalled by courier from Holly Springs. Colonel Sanders, at Davis' Mill, reports five reports of cannon in the southwest at 3.30 p. m., apparently heavy caliber.

C. S. HAMILTON,
Brigadier-General.

HEADQUARTERS LEFT WING,
November 13, 1862.

General GRANT:

Sullivan reached Holly Springs at 12.30. I think he must have gone to Lee's support at Latham's Mill and fired a few shots at the cavalry engaged with Lee; but five shots were heard, and I do not doubt it was Sullivan's artillery. The couriers recalling him and Lee ought to have reached them by 4 p. m.

C. S. HAMILTON,
Brigadier-General.

WAR DEPARTMENT,
Washington, November 14, 1862.

Maj. Gen. U. S. GRANT, *La Grange*:

Some one signing himself John Riggin, superintendent of military telegraphs, is interfering with the management of telegraphs in Kentucky and Tennessee. This man is acting without the authority of Col. Anson Stager, general superintendent of military telegraphs (see General Orders, No. 38, April, 1862), and is an imposter. Arrest him and send him north of your department before he does mischief by his interference.

By order of the Secretary of War:

P. H. WATSON,
Assistant Secretary of War.

GENERAL GRANT'S HEADQUARTERS,
La Grange, November 14, 1862.

P. H. WATSON, ESQ.,
    Assistant Secretary of War :

John Riggin, referred to in your dispatch, is my aide. He has given but one order referring to telegraphing, and that was dictated by me. It was that private dispatches might be sent over the wire before 10 a. m., when they did not interfere with military dispatches. Colonel Riggin is assigned the duty of military superintendent of telegraphs within the department—a position which interferes with no present arrangement, but is intended solely for my relief. Misrepresentations have been made.

U. S. GRANT.

WAR DEPARTMENT,
Washington, November 14, 1862.

Major-General GRANT, *La Grange, Tenn.:*

Col. Anson Stager having been appointed by the Secretary of War superintendent of military telegraphs and of the construction and management of all military lines, Colonel Riggin must not interfere. Colonel Stager has appointed deputies believed to be competent, but if they fail in their duties a report of the fact to Colonel Stager will bring a prompt remedy.

P. H. WATSON,
Assistant Secretary of War.

HEADQUARTERS LEFT WING,
November 14, 1862.

General GRANT:

Sullivan camped at Hudsonville last night, and will reach Davis' Mill by noon to-day. He has 36 prisoners, including 7 officers.

C. S. HAMILTON,
Brigadier-General.

HEADQUARTERS DEPARTMENT OF THE TENNESSEE,
La Grange, Tenn., November 14, 1862.

Maj. Gen. WILLIAM T. SHERMAN, *Memphis, Tenn.:*

After writing to you by Colonel Grierson I received a dispatch from General Halleck stating that in addition to troops already ordered to this department some from Ohio and Kentucky were also ordered, all to be collected at Memphis, from which place a combined military and naval expedition would move on Vicksburg. This, taken in connection with the mysterious rumors of McClernand's command, left me in doubt as to what I should do. I therefore telegraphed Halleck to know if that movement was to be made independent of mine here—if I was to lie still where I am or to penetrate as far south as possible with the means at hand; he replied that all troops sent into the department would be under my control—fight the enemy my own way.*

From information brought in by spies sent from Corinth by General Rosecrans before he left there, the enemy are expecting re-enforcements from Bragg's army and also from Virginia. Have also been re-enforced by Holmes and Hindman. This latter I do not credit.

---

* See Part I, p. 469.

I think it advisable to move on the enemy as soon as you can leave Memphis with two full divisions of twelve regiments of infantry each and the proper proportion of other arms. If troops should come sufficiently rapidly to enable you to bring three divisions it would be more advisable. The country through which you would pass would no doubt afford supplies of forage. I will have provisions here to furnish you on arrival; also ordnance stores. Not less than 300 rounds per man should be brought from Memphis, however.

Our reconnaissances have driven the enemy to beyond the Tallahatchie. Yesterday our cavalry went 6 or 7 miles beyond Holly Springs, where they met five regiments of rebel cavalry and infantry and a battery. Colonel Lee, of the Seventh Kansas Cavalry, one of the best cavalry officers I ever saw, drove them back, capturing, killing, and wounding a large number. He has now taken since we have been here some 250 prisoners, killed perhaps 50, and wounded a large number, with a loss on his side of only 3 men wounded.

I am ready to move from here any day and only await your movements. You can inform me by messenger what day you will start, with what force and by what route, and I will make my calculations accordingly.

The route you should take will depend upon the force you can bring with you, the number of days' supplies you can transport, and whether the enemy is materially re-enforced.

If you can move with three divisions and so as to reach Oxford with three days' supplies, I would say go there; but I am not advised whether the new regiments joining you are supplied with transportation. I presume they are not. I will have here from 500 to 600 wagons for a supply and ordnance train, and the road in running order to beyond Holly Springs, probably to the Tallahatchie.

If you cannot move to Oxford, and I don't expect it, the next best place would be to move to Tallahatchie, or water some place 6 miles west or southwest from Holly Springs. I would then move to Holly Springs, so as to reach there at the same time. All future plans could be arranged after our arrival at these positions.

I have asked to have three locomotives purchased and sent to Memphis, with the view of having the Grenada and Memphis road used.

I have ordered Lauman and will send Hurlbut to report to you in a few days.

Let me hear from you by special messenger as soon as possible. Any suggestions you may have to make will be gladly received and duly considered.

I am exceedingly anxious to do something before the roads get bad and before the enemy can intrench and re-enforce.

U. S. GRANT,
Major-General.

P. S.—I inclose you summary of the information brought by General Rosecrans' spies.*

WAR DEPARTMENT,
November 15, 1862—1.40 p. m.

Major-General MCCLERNAND, *Springfield, Ill.:*

Your several telegrams have been received, and, so far as answer is required, will be answered by the general-in-chief, to whom they have

---

* Not found.

been referred. General Frank Blair will be attached to your expedition, and ordered to Helena, that being designated as one point of concentration. The troops sent to Helena are not to be withdrawn from your command, but are only sent there temporarily for organization, as at Memphis.

EDWIN M. STANTON,
Secretary of War.

WAR DEPARTMENT,
Washington, November 15, 1862.

Maj. Gen. JOHN A. McCLERNAND, *Springfield, Ill.:*

It is not important whether regiments go to Memphis or Helena. Detachments will be made from both places for the same object. General Curtis will send what he has to Helena. The Illinois regiments at Alton, if not guarding prisoners, will be sent down the Mississippi.

H. W. HALLECK,
General-in-Chief.

WASHINGTON, *November* 15, 1862.

Assistant Secretary FOX,
    Navy Department:

DEAR SIR: By what day will Rear-Admiral Porter be ready to operate down the river on Vicksburg, and with how many gunboats?

Yours, truly,

H. W. HALLECK,
General-in-Chief.

WASHINGTON, D. C.,
November 16, 1862—1.10 p. m.

Major-General McCLERNAND, *Springfield, Ill.:*

All the Indiana troops taken at Richmond have been exchanged. This will increase the force for your expedition about eight thousand.

EDWIN M. STANTON,
Secretary of War.

LA GRANGE, TENN., *November* 16, 1862.

Brig. Gen. C. S. HAMILTON,
    Commanding Left Wing:

Relieve Quinby's division with one of the others, and direct him to move to Moscow, 8 miles west of La Grange. I will send cavalry from McPherson's command for him.

If I do not get over to see you to-morrow I would like to have you come here the next day.

U. S. GRANT,
Major-General.

SPECIAL FIELD ORDERS, } HDQRS. THIRTEENTH ARMY CORPS,
                            }   DEPT. OF THE TENNESSEE,
    No. 6.   }   *La Grange, Tenn., November* 16, 1862.

I. Until further orders no passes will be granted to any civilian to pass south of Wolf River, nor will any civilian be permitted to come within our lines from south of said river.   All passes heretofore granted inconsistent with this order are hereby revoked.

II. The facts having been officially reported to the major-general commanding that a portion of the Twentieth Regiment Illinois Infantry Volunteers did on the night of the 7th of November instant, at Jackson, Tenn., break into the store of G. W. Graham & Co. and take therefrom goods to the amount of $841.40, the property of said Graham & Co., and did cut the tent of R. B. Kent and N. A. Bass and take therefrom goods to the value of $345, the property of said Kent and Bass, and burn and destroy the tent and poles, also the property of said Kent and Bass of the value of $56.25, all of which damages amount to the sum of $1,242.66; and it further appearing from said report that Capt. C. L. Paige, Company D; Capt. J. M. North, Company E; Capt. G. W. Kennard, Company I; Lieuts. Henry King, Company B; William S. Sears, Company C; John A. Edmiston, Company E; David D. Wadsworth, Company I; J. B. Bailey, Company F; Victor H. Stevens, Company H; R. N. Evans, Company I; Charles Taylor, Company I, of said regiment, were absent from their commands at the time of the perpetration of these outrages, in violation of orders and without proper cause, when they should have been present; and also that Capt. Orton Frisbie, of Company H, acting in capacity of major, and Capt. John Tunison, of Company G, the senior captain, immediately after the commission of these depredations did not exercise their authority to ferret out the men guilty of the offenses, but that on the contrary Captain Tunison interposed to prevent search and discovery of the parties really guilty, and that Captain Frisbie, after the commission of the said depredations, being in command of the regiment, remained behind twenty-four hours after the regiment marched; and the names of the individual parties guilty not having been disclosed, it is therefore ordered:

1st. That the said sum of $1,242.66 be assessed against said regiment and the officers hereinbefore named, excepting such enlisted men as were at the time sick in hospital or absent with proper authority; that the same be charged against them on the proper muster and pay rolls, and the amount each is to pay noted opposite his name thereon, the officers to be assessed pro rata with the men on the amount of their pay proper, and that the same so collected will be paid by the commanding officer of the regiment to the parties entitled to the same.

2d. That Capt. Orton Frisbie and Capt. John Tunison, of the Twentieth Regiment Illinois Volunteer Infantry, for willful neglect of duty and violation of orders, are hereby mustered out of the service of the United States, to take effect this day.

By order of Brig. Gen. U. S. Grant:

JNO. A. RAWLINS,
Assistant Adjutant-General.

———

EXECUTIVE MANSION,
Washington, November 17, 1862.

Hon. F. P. BLAIR:

Your brother says you are solicitous to be ordered to join General McClernand.   I suppose you are ordered to Saint Helena; this means that you are to form part of McClernand's expedition as it moves down the river; and General McClernand is so informed.   I will see General Halleck as to whether the additional force you mention can go with you.

A. LINCOLN.

HEADQUARTERS DISTRICT OF MEMPHIS,
Memphis, November 17, 1862.

Major-General HALLECK, *Commander-in-Chief:*

GENERAL: Of course I know that officially and privately you have more than your share of work. Though silent I have not been idle this summer. I think Memphis is now the best and most complete base of operations on the Mississippi. The fort is admirable; twenty-eight heavy guns in position with good magazines, shot, shell, and canister piled alongside and men instructed for the guns. My old infantry division now forms a good basis for the new levies, of which fourteen infantry regiments are already come and more *en route.* I shall form them into two divisions of twenty-four infantry regiments, with a reserve of five to be left here to occupy Fort Pickering. My field artillery, nine good batteries, are in good drill, horses in good order, and all well provided with ammunition. I have but one cavalry regiment, ten companies of the Sixth Illinois, and two of Thielemann's; but am advised that three more cavalry regiments will come to me. I am ready to move inland, down the river, or anywhere. At Memphis, troops can be raised, organized, fed, and equipped better than at any place I have ever seen. There is abundance of corn throughout the country, but all else has to come from above.

We have roused, also, the Union element, and our enemies, having burned cotton, taken corn, fodder, and supplies from the country people, have shaken their faith in the secession authorities; so that we have really a substantial beginning of the conversion of the people to our cause.

The new troops come full of the idea of a more vigorous prosecution of the war, meaning destruction and plunder.

I take brick from kilns, lumber from piles, wood, corn, &c., giving brigade quartermaster's receipts, to be settled at the termination of hostilities on proof of loyalty, claims not transferable; but I do not permit any one below the rank of brigadier to presume to take and appropriate private property.

The quartermaster's department here has possession of over 600 houses, some of which are used for public purposes and the balance are rented out, bringing over $12,000 a month income. I mention these facts to interest you in your future plans in this quarter of the world. I expect very soon to move inland to report to General Grant. The enemy is now behind the Tallahatchie, and West Tennessee is free of the enemy, save very small bands of guerrillas, whom the people will soon dispose of rather than feed and submit to. I have learned that the Confederate authorities have adopted a plan of fortification for the mouth of Yazoo, which if completed will embarrass us much. The country between Yazoo and Mississippi is of black vegetable mold, full of streams and bayous, and exceedingly impracticable in wet and wintry weather. With the Yazoo open to us, our land forces could disembark on its east bank on high, fine ground, the same ridge which forms the bluff of Walnut Hills at Vicksburg. If a fort is built on the bluff near mouth of Yazoo (Haines') it would have to be reduced before we could proceed against Jackson and Vicksburg, and would give time for concentration. One or two good iron-clads in Yazoo would prevent the construction of such a fort. I have notified Admiral Porter of this and he may act on such information.

I know your mind and attention are taken up with the East, but feel assured you will so order that a perfect concert of action will result from the ample force now on the Mississippi and its valley under Admiral Porter, Generals Grant and Curtis.

With great respect, your obedient servant,

W. T. SHERMAN,
Major-General, Commanding District.

P. S.—The old navy-yard here was used by the Confederate authorities for founding cannon, constructing gun-carriages, transportation wagons, and all sorts of military stores. Though donated by Congress to the city of Memphis, I think it is fairly liable to confiscation, but I have only taken certain parts of it for necessary workshops, taking accurate inventories of tools and materials. I am making a kind of pontoon train for General Hovey at Helena and another for myself. Indeed, these shops are admirably adapted to Government purposes.

HEADQUARTERS UNITED STATES FORCES,
Island No. 10, November 17, 1862.

Captain LOVELL,
Assistant Adjutant-General, Columbus, Ky. :

SIR : I have moved my command, with all the commissary stores and Government property, to the island, except the large guns, which the steamer Rob Roy cannot move, on account of her decks being insufficient to hold them. The guns have all been removed to the river bank, ready to be loaded and brought over as soon as we have any boat for that purpose. If the general will send down the O'Brien I think we can put them on to her without any difficulty.

A few matters have been brought to my attention in regard to which I desire some instructions. A number of the citizens here who have taken the oath have asked permission to bring down small quantities of powder and shot for fowling purposes; the same in regard to salt and quinine. They ask to be allowed to purchase, in small quantities only, enough for their individual use.

There are two prisoners at Mr. Milton Donaldson's, near this place, who were wounded in the affair with Falkner's cavalry. They have been in a very precarious condition and were too sick to be moved, but now are recovering, and some disposition will soon have to be made of them.

There are also two men who were taken prisoners when this place was occupied—by name Seale. They took the oath, were released, and have been living here since then. One of them is very ill, not expected to live; the other one is also in bad health. They reside in Dallas County, Arkansas, about 150 miles back of Helena, and desire, if possible, permission to return to their homes beyond our lines. Can it be granted? They belong to the Twelfth Arkansas Regiment.

I am, sir, your obedient servant,

JOHN A. GORDON,
Captain, Fifteenth Wisconsin Volunteers, Commanding Post.

HDQRS. THIRTEENTH ARMY CORPS, DEPT. OF THE TENN.,
La Grange, Tenn., November 17, 1862.

Col. L. B. PARSONS,
Assistant Quartermaster, Saint Louis, Mo. :

DEAR SIR : General Grant telegraphed you to-day that we needed 6 locomotives and 200 cars, and wished you to visit personally roads in Indiana, Michigan, and the Northwest and procure the engines. General Halleck telegraphs they cannot be procured at the East. The supposition is you can procure one or two engines from a road and have them changed at their shops to 5-feet gauge. These engines are needed at the shortest possible moment to open the road south of Memphis. Of the cars we will want 50 platform-cars, and the balance of the number box-cars. Seventy-five cars to be sent to Columbus and the rest to Memphis. Also please order us five good hand-cars for Memphis. The Northwest roads have not been called upon much for engines, and they must help. We hope you will within two weeks start a portion of above on the way, as our army cannot move without them. There are a number of cars in course of construction at Dayton, which might be taken. Keep us advised what can be depended upon.

Respectfully,

GEO. G. PRIDE,
Chief Engineer Military Railroads, Dept. of the Tennessee

SPECIAL ORDERS, } HDQRS. 13TH A. C., DEPT. OF THE TENN.,
No. 21.   }   *La Grange, Tenn., November* 17, 1862.

*   *   *   *   *   *   *

VIII. Brig. Gen. J. M. Tuttle will turn over the command of the post of Cairo and dependencies to the senior officer and repair without delay to Jackson, Tenn., and relieve Maj. Gen. S. A. Hurlbut in the command of the District of Jackson.

On being relieved Maj. Gen. S. A. Hurlbut will report in person to Major-General Sherman at Memphis, Tenn.

*   *   *   *   *   *   *

By order of Maj. Gen. U. S. Grant:

[JNO. A. RAWLINS,]
Assistant Adjutant-General.

LA GRANGE, TENN., *November* 18, 1862.

Brig. Gen. GRENVILLE M. DODGE, *Corinth, Miss.*:

Can you get information from the East, say as far as Florence? I want to hear from along the Tennessee from Tuscumbia eastward to know if any rebel troops are crossing there.

U. S. GRANT,
Major-General.

MOSCOW, *November* 18, 1862—4 p. m.

Major-General GRANT:

The Second Brigade of my division reached here just at dark last night. The First Brigade camped 5 miles back and came in at 7 o'clock this morning. I have occupied the day so far in examining my surroundings, establishing pickets, &c. There is a large amount of railroad property here, consisting of wheels and axles, together and detached, locomotive tires, &c.

The people are taking cotton in large quantities to Memphis and bringing back all sorts of commodities, contraband and otherwise. I have stopped it until further orders.

Have ordered all roads running south from Memphis and Charleston, except that from here, obstructed; all teams coming from Charleston to report here, and teams taking cotton turned back.

There is some cotton about here unpacked, but a large amount picked and ginned and unginned. I have directed it to be kept until I receive your orders about it.

I. F. QUINBY,
Brigadier-General.

LA GRANGE, TENN., *November* 18, 1862.

Brig. Gen. I. F. QUINBY, *Davis' Mill, Miss.:*

You may permit all persons living at home to save their cotton and bring it in for sale. Such persons as are known to be in the Southern Army, or have contributed, directly and voluntarily, to the support of the rebellion, their cotton may be taken, if they have any, and sent here to be sold for the benefit of the Government. Persons who prefer taking their cotton to Memphis may be permitted to do so. Persons whose negroes have run off and have cotton yet to pick will be allowed to hire the negroes in charge of Government here.

U. S. GRANT,
Major-General.

MOSCOW, *November* 18, 1862.

Col. JOHN A. RAWLINS:

I have directed the reduction of the transportation and public and private property of my division to conform to recent orders in view of the movements likely to take place. This is important. It is reported to me that the quartermaster at La Grange will not receipt for surplus public property. Some surplus teams will be sent in to-morrow. Will you call Major-General Grant's attention to this matter?

I. F. QUINBY,
Brigadier-General.

MOSCOW, *November* 19, 1862.

Major-General GRANT:

Major Nelson, Seventh Illinois Cavalry, reports the enemy's pickets on the two roads to the west of that running from this place to Holly Springs.

The Seventh Illinois Cavalry is mostly armed with Smith's carbines, and for these there are but 6 rounds of ammunition each. I will obstruct all of these roads for 15 miles running south from the wagon road to Memphis, except the first, unless you should otherwise order. May I ask you to order ammunition for Smith's carbine—an excellent arm? There is much work for my small cavalry force; could use two companies more to advantage.

I. F. QUINBY,
Brigadier-General.

SPECIAL ORDERS, ⎰   HDQRS. 13TH A. C., DEPT. OF THE TENN.,
    No. 23.   ⎱   *La Grange, Tenn., November* 19, 1862.

I. Brig. Gen. J. C. Sullivan will proceed without delay to Jackson, Tenn., and relieve Maj. Gen. S. A. Hurlbut in the command of the District of Jackson.

*   *   *   *   *   *   *

By order of Maj. Gen. U. S. Grant:

JNO. A. RAWLINS,
Assistant Adjutant-General.

SAINT LOUIS, MO., *November* 20, 1862—3.30 p. m.

Maj. Gen. H. W. HALLECK, *General-in-Chief:*

General Grant telegraphs that he requires 200 cars and 6 locomotives as soon as possible. Colonel Parsons goes to Chicago and Cincinnati to procure them, but thinks a military order may be necessary to insure dispatch, and that the order had best be for at least 300 cars and 8 locomotives, and then take them as fast as required. Please send such order by telegraph to Colonel Parsons, care Captain Potter, Chicago, Ill.

ROBT. ALLEN,
Chief Quartermaster.

WAR DEPARTMENT,
Washington, November 22, 1862.

General ROBERT ALLEN, *Saint Louis, Mo. :*

I have telegraphed to General Grant that it is not intended to use the railroads south of Memphis, and that only such cars and locomotives must be purchased as were necessary for the roads already in operation.

H. W. HALLECK,
General-in-Chief.

HDQRS. THIRTEENTH A. C., DEPT. OF THE TENN.,
La Grange, Tenn., November 22, 1862.

Brig. Gen. GRENVILLE M. DODGE, *Corinth, Miss. :*

A dispatch from General Rosecrans, of date Nashville, Tenn., November 21, 1862, just received, says there are some indications that the rebels are attempting to cross the Tennessee from the east; that signs to that effect reached him that night. You will send out spies and scouts east and obtain all the information possible.

By order of Maj. Gen. U. S. Grant:

JNO. A. RAWLINS,
Assistant Adjutant-General.

COLUMBUS, *November* 22, 1862.

Major-General GRANT:

Telegram from Chicago forwarded. I telegraphed General Grant from Saint Louis on Thursday, as follows to wit:

SAINT LOUIS, *November* 20.

Major-General GRANT, *La Grange:*

Your dispatch of the 19th instant is received. I shall not wait your requisitions, but go to Chicago at once, where I hope to get all you require. There are at least

10,000 cars on the railroads terminating there. Will you not be likely to want more?
Would it not be better to make requisitions on them for 500 cars and 10 locomotives,
and take at once what you now require, and others as needed. Answer at Chicago.

                                        L. B. PARSONS.

I get no reply. Please give it to him if with you, or send it forward
if he has left.

                                        L. B. PARSONS.

                                        CAIRO, *November* 22, 1862.
Maj. Gen. U. S. GRANT:
I have sent a large force to the mouth of the Yazoo River with some
light-draught vessels to prevent the enemy from erecting fortifications,
with orders to hold the position until we are ready to land the army
there with two iron-clads left at Helena.

The rivers are too shallow for our vessels. I have a few vessels here.
Where will you have them?

                                        PORTER,
                                        Rear-Admiral.

                                        SAINT LOUIS, *November* 23, 1862.
Col. J. C. KELTON,
     Assistant Adjutant-General:
On the 25th October General Grant telegraphed as follows:

Major-General CURTIS:

New Madrid being out of my department I would like to withdraw the detachments
of troops I have there as soon as they can be relieved. Will you send troops to relieve them?

I replied same day:

Dispatch received. Can't spare troops from New Madrid at present.

General Grant same day says:

The troops at New Madrid are detachments from other troops of my command. If
they cannot remain subject to my orders I must remove them.

On the 21st November, before I had opportunity to relieve the troops,
Brigadier-General Davies telegraphs:

In accordance with orders from Major-General Grant the troops from New Madrid
are being removed to Island No. 10. If you intend sending troops to New Madrid the
guns will be left; if not, they shall be removed.

On the 22d I answered as follows:

Troops and forts in my department are under my command, not General Grant's.

On the 22d, in reply, General Davies telegraphs:

The troops belonging to this command which were at New Madrid have been ordered away. Notice was given you that you might replace them if you so thought
necessary, and no answer was received until this morning. General Grant did not
think it safe to leave the guns there without anybody to guard them, so ordered a
boat to take them to Island No. 10.

I have stopped the Thirty-second Iowa to go and supply this vacuum,
and briefly reported the facts to headquarters, with a request that at
least General Grant should be ordered to return the guns. Please report to General Grant.

                                        SAML. R. CURTIS,
                                        Major-General.

LA GRANGE, *November* 23, 1862.

General SULLIVAN:

There is said to be in Jackson a cotton-buyer from Cincinnati by the name of Handy, who at home is known as a secessionist. He is re ported to have made overtures by which he would smuggle through our lines quinine. Arrest him.

U. S. GRANT,
Major-General.

BOLIVAR, *November* 23, 1862.

Brigadier-General SULLIVAN:

The rebel cavalry are a few miles from Somerville on the road to Jackson, about 200 strong. The rest below Somerville.

M. BRAYMAN,
Brigadier-General, Commanding.

HAMILTON'S HEADQUARTERS,
November 23, 1862.

Major-General GRANT:

I have intelligence from private sources that turnpike bridge, over Tallahatchie, is destroyed. The rebels use floating bridge.

Price is on this side of Tallahatchie and Pemberton at Abbeville.

C. S. HAMILTON,
Brigadier-General.

HDQRS. THIRTEENTH A. C., DEPT. OF THE TENN.,
La Grange, Tenn., November 23, 1862.

Brig. Gen. I. F. QUINBY:

General Brayman telegraphs that a man from Somerville, who knows Jackson, says that he is there with cavalry, three pieces of artillery, and several hundred infantry, waiting for re-enforcements from farther west of there and preparing to come in this direction. They probably intend to break both roads. Have you or can you obtain any information of the truth of same?

By order of Maj. Gen. U. S. Grant:

JNO. A. RAWLINS,
Assistant Adjutant-General.

MOSCOW, *November* 23, 1862.

Major-General GRANT:

I was informed just at dark that there was to-day a large rebel cavalry force at Hay's Bridge, about 6 miles west of this place. These, in connection with the report just received that Colonel Lee had already been sent toward Somerville, led me to believe that the rebel force has got south of the Wolf River. They could have been intercepted by sending out a force to guard Hay's Bridge. I will send out all of my disposable cavalry early to-morrow, hoping to catch them.

I. F. QUINBY,
Brigadier-General.

LA GRANGE, TENN., *November* 23, 1862.

Brig. Gen. I. F. QUINBY, *Moscow, Tenn.*:

You can fit out an expedition to go to Somerville.

U. S. GRANT,
Major-General.

LA GRANGE, *November* 23, 1862.

Generals SULLIVAN and BRAYMAN:

A considerable force of cavalry, from 5,000 to 10,000, crossed the Tennessee River and are now moving west. Look out for them on the railroad.

U. S. GRANT,
Major-General.

GENERAL ORDERS, }   HEADQUARTERS DISTRICT OF MEMPHIS,
No. 94.   *Memphis, November* 23, 1862.

I. Brigadier-General Lauman, having reported for duty, is assigned to the command of the Sixth Brigade. The Fifth and Sixth Brigades will constitute the Third Division, under command of Brigadier-General Lauman.

II. The commanders of each of the divisions will detail one regiment from their divisions to remain at Memphis to compose the garrison of Fort Pickering. The regiment from the First Division will occupy the right flank; that of the Second Division to occupy the left flank, and the Third Division the center within the cavalier. Each division commander will also cause all the sick in hospital to be transferred to the general hospital, and the sick in quarters to be organized into one or more companies, under command of invalid officers, to remain at Fort Pickering as a part of its garrison.

III. The post quartermaster will provide a suitable storehouse in which to receive all surplus baggage of all regiments about to march, and commanders of regiments will forthwith reduce their baggage to the minimum prescribed by General Orders, No. 3, Headquarters Department of the Tennessee, November 1, 1862, and be prepared to march on Wednesday morning, the 21st instant.

IV. Each regiment will provide itself with five days' rations and ammunition at the rate of 200 cartridges per man. The chief of artillery will assign three field batteries to each division, and the Sixth Illinois Cavalry will attach its train to that of the First Division, and will move under the immediate orders of the commanding general. The quartermaster will at once organize all army wagons not belonging to regiments on the march into three trains, about equal numbers to accompany the three army divisions. These will be loaded with provisions and be ready to move on Wednesday morning. The train for the First Division will be parked in front of the fort, prepared to move by Jackson street; that for the Second Division on Poplar street, near General Smith's headquarters, and that for the Third Division south of the fort near the camp of the Thirty-second Wisconsin, each being careful to leave the road clear.

V. The chief quartermaster may seize any wagon or carriage or other vehicle suitable for the transportation of stores for the sick, to be added to the train, and forage will be obtained in the same manner as during the march last summer, viz, brigade quartermasters or commissaries will take from the farmers and planters, giving a memorai da receipt, which receipt will be taken up by the chief quartermaster or commissary by loyalty vouchers. Pillage or robbery by the soldiers or subordinate officers must be promptly checked and punished. The route of march and destination will be confided to the commanders of divisions.

By order of Maj. Gen. W. T. Sherman:

J. H. HAMMOND,
Assistant Adjutant-General.

LA GRANGE, TENN., *November* 24, 1862.

Brig. Gen. C. S. HAMILTON,
Commanding Left Wing:

Your instructions for the move on Friday will be sent over in a short time. Lee need not go, as he could not ascertain if the enemy are evacuating Tallahatchie in time for an earlier move than we expect to make in any event.

U. S. GRANT,
Major-General.

LA GRANGE, TENN., *November* 24, 1862.

Brig. Gen. I. F. QUINBY, *Moscow, Tenn.:*

You may send out an expedition to break up Richardson's camp, near Somerville.

U. S. GRANT,
Major-General.

LA GRANGE, TENN., *November* 25, 1862.

Brig. Gen. C. S. HAMILTON,
Commanding Left Wing:

If the evacuation of Tallahatchie has taken place be prepared to follow with all your command.

U. S. GRANT,
Major-General.

BOLIVAR, TENN., *November* 25, 1862.

General SULLIVAN:

Colonel Haynie sends two couriers from Bethel. Henderson Station was taken by a large body of rebel cavalry this morning. His communication with Jackson cut off. He wants a regiment sent down from Jackson; says that General Dodge will send up a regiment from Corinth. He has sent a company to McNairy Station, and will send the Forty-eighth when General Dodge's regiment arrives. I think the rebels will try to strike this road near Medon to-night. I will strengthen our guards on railroad and be ready here.

M. BRAYMAN,
Brigadier-General, Commanding.

LA GRANGE, TENN., *November* 25, 1862.

Brig. Gen. M. BRAYMAN, *Bolivar, Tenn.*:

General Sullivan has sent troops after the guerrillas that took Henderson Station. Troops from here are after those that are west from Bolivar.

U. S. GRANT,
Major-General.

JACKSON, *November* 25, 1862.

Major-General GRANT:

I have just received the following dispatch:

The rebel cavalry, about 400 strong, came into Henderson, captured the post, killed 1 man, took the balance of the company prisoners, burned the station-house and Mount Pinson Station and tank, and burned 74 bales cotton. I have ordered out one regiment and all the cavalry to proceed to Henderson.

JER. C. SULLIVAN,
Brigadier-General, Commanding District.

LA GRANGE, *November* 25, 1862.

General SULLIVAN:

Pursue the rebels that captured Henderson until they are driven out of the State. Were any cars captured? Tell General Webster to place men on the road to repair it at once.

U. S. GRANT,
Major-General.

JACKSON, *November* 25, 1862.

Major-General GRANT:

The bridge at Henderson is safe. The rebels fired bridge after they left. The women of town put the fire out.

All my available cavalry and two regiments of infantry are in pursuit.

JER. C. SULLIVAN,
Brigadier-General.

HEADQUARTERS COMMANDANT OF DISTRICT,
Jackson, Tenn., November 25, 1862.

Col. M. K. LAWLER, *Commanding Post*:

You will immediately pursue the rebels that attacked Henderson this morning, driving them from the State. Your instructions are: If they prove to be guerrillas, to hang on the spot the prominent leaders.

JER. C. SULLIVAN,
Brigadier-General, Commanding District.

[HEADQUARTERS DISTRICT OF JACKSON,
Jackson, Tenn., November 25, 1862.]

Colonel KENT:

The cavalry, if not already with you, will reach you in the morning. Make a vigorous pursuit. Let the cavalry pursue with speed and the

infantry follow.   Make the enemy cross the Tennessee or capture them.
I will send rations to Henderson Station to meet you on your return,
and if you get out of rations draw on the country and give receipts.
  Keep your command together.   Allow no straggling.

M. K. LAWLER,
Colonel, Commanding Post.

HEADQUARTERS DISTRICT OF MEMPHIS,
Memphis, November 25, 1862.

General STEELE,
    Commanding United States Forces, Helena:

  DEAR SIR: Yours of yesterday is before me.* I wish I had met you
going down, but somehow we passed each other.
  The mode of attacking and threatening the flank of the enemy detailed by you is excellent.   Nothing better.
  I march to-morrow with my whole force toward Chulahoma, about 20
miles south of Holly Springs.   Grant will at same time be at Lumpkin's
Mill, south of Holly Springs.   If Hovey can reach the river near
Charleston about Sunday or Monday the effect will be good.   If the
cavalry force can break that road good anywhere between Coffeeville
and Grenada the enemy is forced to fight or retreat eastward.
  I know that General Hovey's heart is in it, and that he will succeed.
Nothing but heavy rains can prevent full success.   I will send your letter to General Grant.   My news from the enemy places them at Talla-
hatchie, near Abbeville, fortifying all crossing places.
  As ever, your friend,

W. T. SHERMAN,
Major-General, Commanding.

GENERAL ORDERS, }   HEADQUARTERS DISTRICT OF MEMPHIS,
    No. 97.   }   <i>Memphis, November 25,</i> 1862.

  First day's march.—General Denver moves by the Pigeon Roost road
out Vance street, crosses Nonconah, and camps 14 or 15 miles out.
General Smith marches out Poplar street and State Line road to Germantown.   General Lauman marches out Hernando road to the cross-
road beyond Anderson's, turns east and makes, say, 13 miles.
  Second day's march.—General Denver moves on the Pigeon Roost
road to Byhalia, 14 miles.   General Smith moves from Germantown to
Byhalia, camping on the left of Denver.   General Lauman moves up to
Pigeon Roost road and follows Denver, camping on his right rear.
  Third day's march.—General Denver leads on the Chulahoma road,
about 12 miles across Pigeon Roost Creek.   General Lauman follows
Denver and encamps to his right rear.   General Smith follows Lauman
and encamps to his left rear.
  Fourth day's march.—General Denver moves into Chulahoma.   General
Lauman follows and encamps on his right.   General Smith follows and
encamps on his left.
  Cavalry.—Four companies to accompany Lauman; eight companies
keep with the main center, and during the three days' march will file
to the left and communicate with Grant near Holly Springs or Lump-

---

* Not found.

kin's Mill, 7 miles south of Holly Springs. Each division will have a good advance guard and flankers when necessary ; also a good guard for the train.

By order of Maj. Gen. W. T. Sherman :

J. H. HAMMOND,
Assistant Adjutant-General.

Special Orders, } Headquarters District of Memphis,
    No. 332.   }   *Memphis, November 25, 1862.*

Maj. Gen. S. A. Hurlbut, having reported at these headquarters, is assigned to the command of the post of Memphis, and will enter on duty at once.

By order of Maj. Gen. W. T. Sherman :

J. H. HAMMOND,
Assistant Adjutant-General.

Hdqrs. Thirteenth A. C., Dept. of the Tenn.,
La Grange, Tenn., November 26, 1862.

Brig. Gen. C. S. Hamilton,
Commanding Left Wing, Army in the Field :

General : You will be prepared to move with your entire command, except one regiment of McArthur's division now in charge of contrabands, southward, making Coldwater the first day, by the most easterly roads found practicable for artillery. Ross' and McArthur's divisions are only embraced in the troops to march by this route. Quinby will march directly from Moscow, taking everything clean from that place, leaving no garrison. He will encamp the first night to the right of right wing ; second day from the rear, and come up and take his position with the left wing when he encamps in the evening. Three days' rations will be taken in haversacks and five in wagons. Two hundred thousand rations will be taken down the railroad on Monday morning next, as far as the road may then be practicable, from which point your teams will have to haul further supplies. No provision will be made for a reserve for the entire command, but each wing commander will provide for and have charge of his own reserve.

The order of march from each wing will be provided for by wing commanders.

Sherman leaves Memphis to-day, and is instructed to reach water to the southwest of Holly Springs on Sunday next. Our march must be so arranged as to reach water to the south, southeast, and southwest of Holly Springs on the same day.

Each commander will have with him 200 rounds of ammunition per man for the infantry and cavalry, and all the artillery ammunition their means of transportation will allow. Further supplies will be provided for by the ordnance officer, under instructions which he will receive direct from these headquarters.

Wing commanders will require all men to keep in ranks. At least one field officer should march in the rear of his regiments, and company officers should at all times be directly with their companies. On the first halt, regimental commanders, under supervision of division and brigade staff officers, should make an inspection of their entire commands, and take from every officer and soldier who is not entitled to forage from the United States that may be found mounted his horse and horse equipments, and send them back to the quartermaster at this place.

U. S. GRANT,
Major-General.

GENERAL ORDERS, }   HDQRS. 13TH A. C., DEPT. OF THE TENN.,
No 10.   }   *La Grange, Tenn., November 26, 1862.*

I. A district provost-marshal will be appointed from these headquarters for each district in this department, who will have general supervision of all local provost-marshals in his respective district, and to whom they will make weekly reports of all arrests, seizures, and dispositions of all persons arrested and property seized.

II. District provost-marshals will receive their instructions from the provost-marshal general, to whom they will make semi-monthly reports of all arrests in their respective districts, stating the name, offense, officer by whom arrested, and the disposition made of the arrested party; also all property seized, by whom, and why seized, and the disposition made of the same, accompanying said report with a receipt from the quartermaster to whom the property has been turned over.

III. Local provost-marshals are prohibited from selling or disposing of confiscated property. They will turn all such property over to the nearest post quartermaster, and if there is no post quartermaster convenient then to a division, brigade, or regimental quartermaster, taking triplicate receipts therefor, two to be forwarded with report to the district provost-marshal. If property seized is such as is properly embraced in the commissary or ordnance departments the provost-marshal may turn it over to the proper officers of these departments instead of to quartermasters, taking receipts therefor, as provided in cases of quartermasters.

By order of Maj. Gen. U. S. Grant:

[JNO. A. RAWLINS,]
Assistant Adjutant-General.

SPECIAL ORDERS, }   HDQRS. 13TH A. C., DEPT. OF THE TENN.,
No. 30.   }   *La Grange, Tenn., November 26, 1862.*

*   *   *   *   *   *   *

X. Second Lieut. Orlando H. Ross, of Company D, Twentieth Regiment Illinois Infantry Volunteers, is hereby appointed and announced as agent and general superintendent of military mails for this department, and he will be obeyed and respected accordingly. All military mail messengers will be detailed from the ranks and be subject to his orders.

*   *   *   *   *   *   *

By order of Maj. Gen. U. S. Grant:

JNO. A. RAWLINS,
Assistant Adjutant-General.

GENERAL ORDERS, }   HEADQUARTERS CAVALRY DIVISION,
                 }   U. S. FORCES, 13TH ARMY CORPS,
No. 1.   }   *La Grange, Tenn., November 26, 1862.*

I. In obedience to Special Orders, No. 30, Department of Tennessee,*

---

* Not found.

the undersigned hereby assumes command of the cavalry division, which embraces—

First Brigade: Seventh Kansas, Second Illinois, Fourth Illinois, Second Battalion Second Iowa, Col. A. L. Lee commanding.

Second Brigade: First and Third Battalions Second Iowa, Seventh Illinois, Fifth Ohio, Colonel Hatch commanding.

Third Brigade: Third Michigan, Sixth Illinois, and Thielemann's Battalion Illinois Cavalry, Col. B. H. Grierson commanding.

II. Commanders of regiments and detachments mentioned in this order will at once report for orders to their respective brigade commanders mentioned in this order, except the commander of the Third Michigan Cavalry Regiment, who will report for the time being to Major-General McPherson, commanding forces near La Grange.

III. The commanding officer of the First Brigade will report with his brigade for duty to Brigadier-General Hamilton, commanding the left wing of this army.

IV. The commander of the Second Brigade will report with his brigade for duty to Major-General McPherson, commanding United States forces at and near La Grange.

V. The Third Brigade (with the exception of the Third Michigan Cavalry) will remain until further ordered, doing duty under and reporting to Maj. Gen. W. T. Sherman, commanding the United States forces, District of Memphis.

VI. Until otherwise ordered the several brigades, regiments, and detachments will draw their supplies through the appropriate channels of the command with which they may be doing duty.

T. LYLE DICKEY,
Colonel and Chief of Cavalry, Commanding Division.

TRENTON, *November* 27, 1862—11 p. m.

General SULLIVAN:

My scouts report to-night from Cageville that 200 to 250 of Jackson's and Falkner's cavalry are at or near Bend's Ferry, on the Hatchie, enforcing the conscript act.

JACOB FRY,
Colonel, Commanding Post.

SPECIAL FIELD ORDERS,   HDQRS. 13TH ARMY CORPS,
                   DEPARTMENT OF THE TENNESSEE,
No. 7.   *La Grange, Tenn., November* 27, 1862.

Upon the forming of a junction between the forces now moving from here under Generals McPherson and Hamilton with those from Memphis under Major-General Sherman, the army in the field will be known and designated as follows:

Right wing, Maj. Gen. W. T. Sherman commanding, and will be composed of the troops now under his command and such as are transferred to it by Special Orders, No. 30.*

Center, commanded by Maj. Gen. J. B. McPherson, and left wing, Brig. Gen. C. S. Hamilton commanding.

By order of Maj. Gen. U. S. Grant:

JNO. A. RAWLINS,
Assistant Adjutant-General.

---

* Not found.

SPECIAL ORDERS,)   HDQRS. 13TH A. C., DEPT. OF THE TENN.,
      No. 31.   )   *La Grange, Tenn., November* 27, 1862.

* * * * * * *

II. On the advance of the army, La Grange, Grand Junction, and Davis' Bridge will constitute a military command. Major-General Mc-Pherson will designate two regiments of infantry and one battalion of cavalry from the right wing to form this garrison, one regiment of which and at least two companies of cavalry will be stationed at Davis' Mill.

The Fifteenth Michigan Volunteer Regiment, now at Grand Junction, will continue to occupy that place and will form a part of the garrison.

It will be the duty of the commanding officer to protect the railroad south of Grand Junction to Coldwater, and from La Grange to Grand Junction.

By order of Maj. Gen. U. S. Grant:

> JNO. A. RAWLINS,
> *Assistant Adjutant-General.*

HEADQUARTERS ARMY IN THE FIELD,
Old Lamar, November 28, 1862.

Brig. Gen. C. S. HAMILTON,
      Commanding Left Wing:

GENERAL : Move to-morrow at the earliest possible hour and reach the nearest water to the south or southeast of Holly Springs. I have no information of water nearer than Lumpkin's Mill, except directly east from Holly Springs. If I should not come up with you at Holly Springs to-morrow you can exercise your own judgment as to the ex-pediency of sending McArthur's division eastward to Chewalla Creek.

Detail four good companies of cavalry, well commanded, to remain at Holly Springs until they receive orders from me. I want to send them to communicate with Sherman.

> U. S. GRANT,
> *Major-General.*

P. S.—Holly Springs will be my headquarters after to-morrow until further orders.

UNION CITY, *November* 28, 1862.

Brigadier-General SULLIVAN :

I have reliable information that three of the most prominent Union citi-zens of this county were last night captured at or near Troy, in this county, a town noted for the treason of its inhabitants. They were captured by guerrillas, who infest the Obion Bottom, near that town, and are daily carrying off Union citizens and robbing them of their property, especially their horses.

Troy is a hot-bed of traitors ; not a Union man living in the town. The 3 men captured have been our main stand-by for five months past, one of whom is Colonel Bradford. I propose, if it meets with your ap-proval, to give the authorities of the town notice that if the 3 men cap-tured are not returned in five days that I will burn up the town. Gen-eral, as unwell as I am, if you will give me the command at Trenton,

which is a central point, I will have this country from the Memphis and
Ohio Railroad to the Hatchie cleared of the last guerrilla in it before
the return of my papers, as I know every district of the country. This
will be a pleasure to me, as I have done so once before.

THOS. W. HARRIS,
Colonel Fifty-fourth Illinois.

SPRINGFIELD, *November* 29, 1862.

Hon. E. M. STANTON,
Secretary of War:

I arrived here yesterday. General McClernand has favored me with
a copy of a dispatch to be sent by him to you showing that he has sent
all the available troops raised in this State into the field.

I hope he will be soon sent forward in command of the expedition
identified with his name.

RICHD. YATES,
Governor of Illinois.

HEADQUARTERS ARMY IN THE FIELD,
Holly Springs, Miss., November 29, 1862.

Brig. Gen. C. S. HAMILTON,
Commanding Left Wing:

GENERAL: Telegraph complete and working to this point. Move a
portion of your troops eastward from their present position if they can
obtain water and be in supporting distance of each other. They should
also move a few miles farther south. I want to get McPherson in between you and Sherman, to move southeast from his present position if
water and proper ground can be found. I shall send him word very
early in the morning to reconnoiter for these two conditions. Send back
to Coldwater on Monday all the teams you can spare, with instructions
to load up from the train and remain there until such time as you can
send for them or direct a proper escort should accompany the train.
Your train is not yet through passing this point, 7.50.

Your teams will be nearer forage at Coldwater than here, and be out
of the way of operations. One division from your wing will be detailed
to be selected by you to guard from Coldwater southward as far as it
will hold.

I have ordered up a regiment from Bolivar for Coldwater, which will
be added to the brigade sent back here; so that the smallest brigade
from the division selected will be sufficient to send back here, and Tuesday early enough to send it back.

U. S. GRANT,
Major-General.

HEADQUARTERS ARMY IN THE FIELD,
Holly Springs, Miss., Saturday, November 29, 1862—11.30 a. m.

Maj. Gen. WILLIAM T. SHERMAN,
Commanding Right Wing:

GENERAL: Your note to Lee I have just received. Your calendar is
just one day ahead of time, but by staying where you are to-day it just
brings you up to time.

Two divisions of Hamilton's column will encamp to-night at Lumpkin's Mill; the third on Spring Creek, and not move from there until his front is reconnoitered. The head of his column is now there. There was a little skirmishing with rebel cavalry at this place and some at Lumpkin's Mill. Reconnoiter your front as you propose to-day, and move to-morrow to a good position near Chulahoma. To-morrow telegraphic comunication I hope will be open with the rear. The railroad will also be open to Coldwater. I have directed that the cars come up that far on Monday with 200,000 rations. From that point they will have to be teamed. There are also 800,000 rations at La Grange, from which place they can be brought in case of accident. Two train-loads of grain are also directed to be brought up on Monday and Tuesday, or the earliest day thereafter practicable. You can make your calculations for rations and forage accordingly. It is not desirable that this forage should be used until it becomes necessary.

Your letter and Steele's were duly received. Steele's is quite encouraging.

I have no reliable information from the enemy. A contraband just in says he left the Tallahatchie on Tuesday, and that they were then cooking rations to retreat. Opposed to this, a spy who was taken last night, and who was pumped by one of Hamilton's scouts who was dressed in secesh uniform and put in prison with him, says that the enemy mean fight.

U. S. GRANT,
Major-General.

P. S.—Bragg's forces were anxiously looked for. The Third Michigan Cavalry will report to you to-morrow or the day following.

HOLLY SPRINGS, MISS.,
November 29, 1862—8 p. m.

Maj. Gen. WILLIAM T. SHERMAN,
Commanding Right Wing:

GENERAL: Your two dispatches just received. I inclose with this one just received from Hamilton, which will give you the latest news from the front. I have directed Hamilton to move to his south and east, so as to let McPherson, who is now here with one division, in between him and you. Mac's second division will be up by 10 a. m to-morrow, and could go on to Lumpkin's Mill, but I will retain it until Monday. If you can find water to your southeast, or rather to the southeast of Chulahoma, I would like you to move in that direction. At Chulahoma our front will be too extended. I will direct Hurlbut to send the cavalry of which you speak—sent as you desire. I do not know positively of any ford on the Tallahatchie west of the railroad except at Wyatt. To the east there are several, but I cannot now send you a sketch showing them. The crossings between Coil's Ferry and Wyatt I believe are all ferries. Between Wyatt and the railroad I think there is no ford.

U. S. GRANT,
Major-General.

[Inclosure.]

LUMPKIN'S MILL,
Sundown, November 29, 1862.

GENERAL: Lee has pushed the enemy to within 4 miles of Tallahatchie, and will hold his position for the present. His advance was a continual skirmish. He sends in 1 prisoner and finds 4 dead rebels on the road.

The enemy will fight on the Tallahatchie. Country in front of us stripped of forage.

Please notify me of the completion of telegraph, so that I can call in courier posts. My scout is in from Grenada. About 7,000 troops have come up to Van Dorn in last two weeks. Mouth of Tippah Creek thoroughly fortified.

Enemy has no idea of evacuating as yet. Scout heard nothing of movement of Steele.

O. S. HAMILTON,
Major-General.

HOLLY SPRINGS, MISS., *November* 29, 1862.

Col. A. STAGER,
    Superintendent Military Telegraph, Washington:

Your insolent dispatch to telegraph operators in this department just received.* My orders must be obeyed and Mr. Van Duzer removed and some one else appointed to fill his place. I send Van Duzer out immediately.

U. S. GRANT,
Major-General.

SPECIAL FIELD ORDERS, }   HDQRS. DISTRICT OF MEMPHIS,
    No. 2.   }   *Army in the Field, November* 29, 1862.

All citizens whatsoever, except those who are employed in the army, are hereby ordered to leave this command.

It is further ordered that all women, including the wives of officers and men, shall also leave.

The major-general commanding will send a train to Holly Springs, to which place the above persons and all unauthorized hangers-on must accompany it, and hereafter not be found in any camp under any pretext whatsoever. Letters and documents should go to Holly Springs at the same time.

By order of Maj. Gen. W. T. Sherman:

J. H. HAMMOND,
Assistant Adjutant-General.

LUMPKIN'S MILL, *November* 30, 1862—10 a. m.

General GRANT:

I send a little sketch of country in front. Lee camped with his cavalry at Ebenezer Church last night. I have supported him with a battery and four regiments infantry this morning and directed a reconnaissance to the river.

The infantry is under Deitzler. They will avoid any engagement except with Jackson's cavalry, and will make full report of country on main road.

I shall send out a strong reconnaissance under Quinby, taking a road from near Waterford to the southeast toward mouth of Tippah Creek.

---

* See Grant to Kelton, December 3, p. 377.

Each reconnaissance will require two days, but in the mean time I shall move my camp to the southeast if I can find water, and go some miles.

Lieutenant Webber, Fourth Illinois Cavalry, was seriously but not dangerously wounded in neck yesterday.

I can make room for McPherson here, but from here to Tallahatchie there is no water on the road.

Respectfully,

C. S. HAMILTON,
Brigadier-General.

LUMPKIN'S MILL, MISS., *November* 30, 1862—3 p. m.

General GRANT :

I have just heard from Lee. He has pushed the enemy to the river and is himself within 1 mile of the river. He reports this side of river protected by two circular field works, four to six embrasures each, and they are occupied in force. He will return this evening, leaving cavalry enough to mask our front.

I have a negro who left Abbeville last night at 11 o'clock. He is servant to private in General Lovell's force. Heard his master say that Price with his army had gone to Panola, on Grenada and Memphis road. Says bulk of rebel army is at Tallahatchie, mouth of Tippah, and at Rocky Ford. He says orders were given yesterday morning to strike tents and put three days' rations in haversacks, and thinks it is a preparation to leave, but knows nothing more to confirm it. Says the enemy was in line of battle yesterday at Tallahatchie. Thinks railroad bridge is not injured yet.

Lee says quite a force will be necessary to carry works on this side. He has shelled them, but his fire was returned with interest. I suppose he is now falling back, but will keep force enough to mask the ground gained and also to watch the enemy. The rebel pickets are within 4 miles of me on the southeast. I will clean out things in that direction to-morrow morning.

Yours,

C. S. HAMILTON,
Brigadier-General.

HDQRS. LEFT WING, ARMY OF THE TENNESSEE,
Lumpkin's, November 30, 1862—3 p. m.

Colonel LEE :

Your second dispatch just received. You have done well enough. In falling back leave force to watch and report if enemy fall back during the night. Things look something like evacuation, and if they do leave we want to know it at once. If they give up this side, leaving their works, it will be pretty good evidence of general move to the rear.

I sent you instructions about falling back by previous courier. Nothing further to add. If rebels hold on where they are you will have to make a dash at their rear with all the cavalry in a day or two, going to the eastward. I shall look for you this evening. Don't get out of ammunition. Save enough to use if it shall be necessary to cover your falling back.

Yours,

C. S. HAMILTON,
Brigadier-General.

HEADQUARTERS ARMY IN THE FIELD,
Holly Springs, Miss., November 30, 1862.

Brig. Gen. C. S. HAMILTON,
Commanding Left Wing :

Your dispatch just received Watch the enemy closely, as I know you are doing, but instruct the advance not to attempt to carry any intrenchments until we are prepared. I will be up in the morning, and we will prepare for a heavy reconnaissance to the southeast and the enemy's rear if practicable.

A number of sick are being returned here without rations and without a surgeon. Rations have been issued to the men, and regimental surgeons should attend to their own sick until preparations are made for them.

U. S. GRANT,
Major-General.

HOLLY SPRINGS, MISS., *November* 30, 1862.

Colonel NORTON,
Commanding Post, La Grange, Tenn. :

It is reported that a party of the enemy with flag of truce came into La Grange, exchanged prisoners, and returned without.

This should not have been permitted. You have no authority to exchange prisoners, and should have had pickets out. The enemy's real object was to learn your strength and position. You may look out for an attempt on their part to destroy our supplies at Grand Junction and La Grange. The One hundred and twenty-sixth Illinois Infantry has been ordered to report to you, which, with the infantry and cavalry designated as a garrison for those places, will be, with proper diligence on your part, sufficient to hold them and protect our stores.

Picket the several roads leading to Grand Junction and La Grange at once and keep a sharp lookout to the east and west of you.

By order of Maj. Gen. U. S. Grant:

JNO. A. RAWLINS,
Assistant Adjutant-General.

HEADQUARTERS ARMY IN THE FIELD,
Holly Springs, Miss., November 30, 1862.

Colonel NORTON,
Commanding, La Grange, Tenn. :

You will arrest at once Mr. J. C. Van Duzer, manager of the United States Military Telegraph in this department, for disobedience of orders and conduct prejudicial to the interest of the service, and keep him in close confinement, prohibiting communication between him and all telegraph operators. He is perhaps at Grand Junction; if so, send an officer there for him.

By order of Maj Gen. U. S. Grant:

JNO. A. RAWLINS,
Assistant Adjutant-General.

HOLLY SPRINGS, MISS., *November* 30, 1862.
Col. A. STAGER,
      Superintendent Military Telegraph, Washington:
I have arrested Van Duzer. Will send charges by mail.
                                        U. S. GRANT,
                                             Major-General.

———

HOLLY SPRINGS, MISS., *November* 30, 1862.
Maj. Gen. WILLIAM T. SHERMAN,
      Commanding Right Wing:
GENERAL: At as early a day as practicable I want to have made a cavalry reconnaissance to the enemy's right, taking with them three days' rations. Tuesday will probably be the day for starting this expedition, and all the cavalry except escort companies and just sufficient for cavalry picket duty will be required. I will try to see you to-morrow, and when relative positions are fixed between the different wings, will establish telegraph offices to each. If you are likely to have any important information within a few hours you can retain the messenger that takes this to bring it back. No news from Hamilton this morning.
                                        U. S. GRANT,
                                             Major-General.

———

LA GRANGE, *November* 30, 1862.
General SULLIVAN:
How many contrabands can you furnish for work on fortifications at Corinth? Answer at once.
By order of General Grant:
                                        JNO. A. RAWLINS,
                                        Assistant Adjutant-General.

———

WASHINGTON, D. C., *December* 1, 1862.
Major-General GRANT, *Holly Springs, Miss.:*
Report to this Department by telegraph the charges upon which Van Duzer is arrested.
By order of the Secretary of War:
                                        P. H. WATSON,
                                        Assistant Secretary of War.

———

HEADQUARTERS,
Springfield, Ill., December 1, 1862.
Hon. E. M. STANTON,
      Secretary of War:
When I entered upon the work of forwarding troops from Indiana, Illinois, and Iowa, preparatory to the Mississippi River expedition, in pursuance of your orders of the 21st ultimo, there were in Indiana twenty regiments of infantry, one regiment of cavalry, and five companies of artillery; in Illinois there were twenty regiments of infantry, three regiments of cavalry, and five companies of artillery, and in Iowa nineteen regiments of infantry, one regiment of cavalry, and one company of artillery. In the mean time I have forwarded from Indiana twelve regiments of infantry; from Illinois sixteen regiments of in-

fantry and two companies of artillery, and from Iowa twelve regiments of infantry. Leaving yet to be forwarded from Indiana eight regiments of infantry, one regiment of cavalry, and five companies of artillery; from Illinois four regiments of infantry, three regiments of cavalry, and three companies of artillery, and from Iowa seven regiments of infantry, one regiment of cavalry, and one company of artillery.

A member of my staff, just returned from the capital of Indiana, informs me that all proper arrangements are made for the earliest dispatch of the troops remaining in that State into the field. Another member of my staff, just returned from Iowa, reports the same in regard to the troops remaining in that State, and most all remaining in Illinois have gone or are going forward.

I think a mustering, pay, and ordnance officer for each of these States would amply suffice to close up the unfinished business in each of them. The rest of the officers detailed for those duties might be remanded to their commands.

Under these circumstances I trust it will meet with your views to order me forward to Memphis, or such other rendezvous as you may think preferable, in order that I may enter upon the more advanced work of organizing, drilling, and disciplining my command, preparatory to an early and successful movement, having for its object the important end of liberating the navigation of the Mississippi River.

Having worked early, assiduously, and zealously in this great enterprise, having it at heart, and the Governors and people of the Northwest having pronounced favorably upon it and, so far as I can hear, upon me as the executor of it, I trust that the honorable Secretary of War will continue to encourage me by his sympathy and support.

I would further add, by way of explanation, that the Eighty-seventh Illinois Regiment is retained at Shawneetown to guard that frontier. The One hundred and thirty-first Illinois had marching orders several days ago. The One hundred and eighteenth and One hundred and twenty-eighth Illinois will be started by the middle of this week, as will also two of the Illinois batteries. There is little prospect of filling up the cavalry regiments at present, except by consolidation, which I have recommended. From Indiana the Sixteenth, Fiftieth, Sixty-ninth, One hundred and first, and Sixty-seventh Regiments Infantry have gone forward, and the following will go one a day, beginning to-day, in the following order: Sixtieth, Sixty-eighth, Sixty-sixth, and Eighty-ninth, so that on Thursday next there will be left in this State only one regiment of infantry, one company of artillery, and three regiments of cavalry, raising; in Indiana eight regiments of infantry, one of cavalry, and five companies of artillery, and in Iowa seven regiments of infantry, one of cavalry, and one of artillery.

I await your orders in the premises.

Your obedient servant.

JOHN A. McCLERNAND,
Major-General and Superintendent Mustering Service.

HOLLY SPRINGS, MISS., *December* 1, 1862.

Brig. Gen. GRENVILLE M. DODGE, *Corinth, Miss.*:

Keep me informed of appearances around you. Should you be advanced upon by any considerable force I will re-enforce you.

U. S. GRANT,
Major-General.

HDQRS. LEFT WING, ARMY OF THE TENNESSEE,
December 1, 1862.

Colonel LEE:

Yours received. I will send forward a brigade this p. m., and hold two more brigades in readiness to move. It looks like evacuation in earnest, and in that case I want to follow up as rapidly as possible. The brigade sent forward to-day will be ready to cross the river in the morning, if rebels shall have gone.

I will try and have the reconnaissance to the southeast put off, for I want you with your whole force to pursue on the other side, where they shall have gone.

Yours,

C. S. HAMILTON,
Brigadier-General.

———

HDQRS. LEFT WING, ARMY OF THE TENNESSEE,
December 1, 1862.

Brigadier-General MCARTHUR:

Send Deitzler's brigade to the front with three days' rations and 60 rounds of ammunition per man as soon as possible. He will take a good battery of rifled guns. Enemy have evacuated this side and my cavalry is in possession of this bank of the river. I think they are evacuating, and if that shall prove true to-morrow morning then Deitzler will extemporize a bridge and be prepared to cross.

Hold the rest of your division in readiness to move at daylight. Deitzler will be careful not to expose his men to artillery fire from the other side.

C. S. HAMILTON,
Brigadier-General, Commanding.

———

HUDSONVILLE, *December* 1, 1862.

T. H. HARRIS:

An Indiana regiment of about 350 men are on guard from Davis' Mill to Coldwater, 17 miles. This is the only force on the line excepting the Engineer Regiment, a portion of which are not here at all. Those here will to-morrow be working from Coldwater south; their commanding officer, of Indiana regiment, is at Lamar. A dispatch for him sent to Junction to-night can be forwarded to him by train in the morning. There is no post at Coldwater, but is at Hudsonville, where we now unload stores. Guard there is but 25 men. A number of important bridges to guard between Lamar and Coldwater. An attack was this eve made on the guard here, but repulsed. We hear of a cavalry force east of us to-night about 10 miles. Guard should be increased if possible. Please answer.

GEO. G. PRIDE,
Chief Engineer.

———

GRAND JUNCTION, [*December*] 1, 1862.

General SULLIVAN:

Effective force of infantry at Grand Junction, 231 officers and men. No cavalry and no artillery.

T. E. MORRIS,
Major Fifteenth Michigan Infantry, Commanding Post.

HEADQUARTERS ARMY IN THE FIELD,
Abbeville, Miss., December 2, 1862.

Maj. Gen. WILLIAM T. SHERMAN:

McArthur's division is here. Quinby with his division, and McPherson with Logan's division, on the north side of the river, with instructions to camp there for the night and repair bridges. Our cavalry have gone to the front several hours since, and are probably now at Oxford. Artillery has been heard from the south, but as no messenger has returned I imagine it is nothing but an attempt on the part of the enemy to cover their retreat. I do not expect you to be able to do anything to-morrow with your artillery or infantry, but with the cavalry a reconnaissance can be made to your front and southwest.

If this rain continues the roads will become so impassable that the distance to haul supplies will be shortened as much as practicable. In that case you can move the forces with you to join those here, and instruct the remaining division to move up to the neighborhood of Lumpkin's Mill. I cannot tell until news is received from the advance cavalry whether I will pursue any farther for the present or not with infantry and artillery.

Let me hear from you by the messenger that will deliver this.

U. S. GRANT,
Major-General.

WYATT, *December* 2, 1862—p. m.

General GRANT:

DEAR SIR: I wrote you about two hours since, but Grierson met your messenger at the ferry and returned with it, and I send it with this.

The roads are cut up terribly. M. L. Smith is hard at work on a bridge. I have four boats in the river and a kind of raft made of the two halves of the ferry-boat, which was a good large one, cut in two. Grierson is now across with his cavalry, and my advance regiment is across.

I advise you to let me hold this ground till you resolve what action to take. I can make a good bridge and clear out the obstructions on the river. I will throw M. L. Smith's division across as soon as the bridge is done, and all my men and wagons will be up to-night. I will order Grierson to-night to look toward Oxford, cross to Abbeville, and come in to-morrow.

I sent a train of 100 wagons to Coldwater this morning for rations, and ordered it to come to Wyatt unless you ordered otherwise. There is a by-road, however, to Holly Springs, and this is one of the main traveled roads to Oxford; with a bridge it will be as good a route as by Lumpkin's Mill. To Holly Springs, 20 miles; to Oxford, 14 miles; to Abbeville, 6 miles.

This country is simply impracticable in rainy weather.

Rumor among citizens is that Federals have Panola. Can it be possible that Steele's expedition did not reach Grenada and turned to Panola? This would account for the retreat, but won't accomplish our purpose. I have a prisoner who says he went to Abbeville to get on the cars yesterday, but they were so crowded that he could not get in, and was picked up this a. m. by our men.

From a high hill here at 11 a. m. I saw a high smoke at Oxford. I think the enemy has gone to Grenada, back of the Yalabusha.

I will cross with two divisions; bring all transportation here; camp at the forks of the road, and report to you at Abbeville to-morrow evening unless you send me different orders by Grierson.

I am, &c.,

W. T. SHERMAN,
Major-General.

HEADQUARTERS,
Springfield, Ill., December 2, 1862.

Hon. E. M. STANTON,
Secretary of War:

In pursuance of the authority with which you were pleased to vest me, and agreeably to your expressed wish, I have diligently striven to provide for the adequate increase of the cavalry arm of the proposed Mississippi expedition; but in consequence of the large draft made upon the male population of military age for the prosecution of the war, and of impediments interposed by the great demand for labor to carry on industrial pursuits, have not succeeded to the desired extent.

In view of this fact I would respectfully suggest a different mode of accomplishing the same object. I would provide horses or mules with equipments complete to mount at least one-fifth of the whole infantry force of the expedition; or, if horses or mules cannot be purchased in time, I would seize such as might be found in the possession of disloyal citizens in the hostile districts through which the column might pass. Inferior animals of the description mentioned would answer, if the best could not be had, as they would only be used occasionally to meet an emergency requiring the rapid conveyance of infantry from one place to another. Of course the men would dismount in action.

In any event, however, saddle-blankets, bridles, rope for halters, nose-bags, and spurs would be required.

If it should be objected that such service would tend to demoralize the infantry (not so upon the plan I propose) I would not charge them with the care of the animals except when using them. At all other times they should be cared for by slaves seeking refuge in my camp, or who had been impressed for that purpose.

Thus mounted, the infantry would be prepared to perform the double duty of men on foot and on horseback. By rapid movements they could retard the advance of the foe, cut his communications, destroy his trains, and harass him at every step. In like manner they could rapidly pursue a retreating foe and continually annoy and distress him. To add to their efficiency I would also provide them with a suitable number of mountain howitzers to meet any demand for artillery service; and for the same purpose I would supply each battalion of cavalry with two pieces of the same character.

If an example was required to illustrate the soundness of these views I might refer to the success of the enemy in capturing our forces at Murfreesborough, in Tennessee; in overrunning Kentucky, and in signalizing these frequent raids by the spoils torn from peaceful citizens.

Another question of great importance relates to the means to be employed to transport army supplies. While it might not be advisable to curtail the complement of wagons and teams allowed to each regimental and other organization of the forces, yet it is deemed highly important that suitable provision should be made for converting the team animals into pack animals whenever occasion might require it. Indeed such provision is deemed indispensable to certainty and celerity of movement in the country in which it is supposed the column will operate during the rainy season. Without it the frequent construction of roads and bridges over low and marshy grounds must necessarily cause much delay and disappointment.

The pack animals, properly equipped, can carry a burden of 200, even 300, pounds 20 miles a day. The equipments should consist of pack-saddles, with straps or ropes for fastening the pack, and nose-bags—at least sixty to each regiment.

Your obedient servant,

JOHN A. McCLERNAND,
Major-General and Superintendent Mustering Service.

WAR DEPARTMENT,
Washington, December 2, 1862.

Major-General CURTIS, *Saint Louis, Mo.:*

Telegraph in round numbers the forces which can be detached from your department by the 15th instant, including Blair's brigade, for an expedition on the Mississippi River.

H. W. HALLECK,
General-in-Chief.

ABBEVILLE, MISS., *December* 2, 1862.

Col. T. LYLE DICKEY,
Commanding Cavalry Division:

In your pursuit to-morrow be cautious not to be led into ambush. Push them, however, as far as possible. When you discontinue the pursuit, if practicable, push off to the east and come back by some route off from the railroad, living upon the enemy, and examine their resources, especially as to forage.

Grierson I presume has not been able to cross the river to-day, and will not be able to join in the pursuit. I have instructed Sherman, however, to send out to the southwest from Wyatt.

I will send infantry and artillery to Oxford to-morrow.

U. S. GRANT,
Major-General.

HEADQUARTERS ARMY IN THE FIELD,
Abbeville, Miss., December 2, 1862.

Maj. Gen. J. B. McPHERSON,
Commanding Center:

If Brigadier-General Logan's division has two days' rations send it forward to Oxford early to-morrow morning.

By order of Maj. Gen. U. S. Grant:

JNO. A. RAWLINS,
Assistant Adjutant-General.

LA GRANGE, [*December*] 2, 1862.

T H. HARRIS,
Assistant Adjutant-General, Jackson:

A guerrilla force of about 200 were near Moscow yesterday afternoon. A small force entered Moscow and captured 6 convalescent sick of the

109 and paroled them. A force of 6 came within a half mile and captured four teams loaded with cotton and one cotton-speculator. I recovered all of the wagons, cotton, and 2 mules; they escaped with the other animals. The pickets, 3 miles below Lamar, were attacked yesterday about 5 p. m. by a small guerrilla force. The guerrillas were repulsed. No one hurt.

A. S. NORTON,
Colonel, Commanding.

———

HEADQUARTERS IN THE FIELD,
Abbeville, Miss., December 3, 1862—6.30 p. m.

Maj. Gen. H. W. HALLECK, <i>General-in-Chief:</i>

The following dispatch from General Dodge received:

One of our most reliable scouts has just arrived from Huntsville, Ala. Left that place last Tuesday. Says Bragg was at Tullahoma and along that railroad, but that a considerable force of his cavalry are on the road between Decatur, Eddytown, and Columbus, collecting large amounts of forage and subsistence at points from 10 to 15 miles apart. Gives the names of the persons. The citizens and the soldiers say that a portion of Bragg's army is ordered to Columbus by that road and a portion to Chattanooga, and that one other corps is ordered down to Columbus by a road farther east. He says that the cavalry are scattered along the road in squads for 60 miles, as far as he went, and very active in collecting supplies. He brought in with him several refugees who live in that section of country, who all tell the same story. Up to Tuesday no infantry or artillery had passed Huntsville or Decatur, but says the citizens at those places were looking for them every day.

U. S. GRANT,
Major-General.

———

ABBEVILLE, MISS., <i>December</i> 3, 1862.

Col. J. C. KELTON, <i>Washington, D. C.:</i>

I have been constrained to arrest and confine J. C. Van Duzer, superintendent of telegraphs in this department. I felt no disposition to restrain him of his liberty, but I was afraid that if allowed to leave the department unrestrained he would so tamper with the operators along the line as seriously to interfere with the working of the wires. In fact I was told that he made his boast that if discharged he would carry off the operators employed by him. I have ordered that he be sent out of the department immediately and escorted to Cairo, so as to prevent interference on his part.

The difficulty with him has been as follows: When I commenced the move from Corinth and Bolivar to La Grange, Mr. Van Duzer was in Cairo, and I had to superintend and direct the extension of telegraphs and establishment of offices in person. After getting Mr. Van Duzer up to attend to his business he was very obstinate and seemed evidently inclined to the belief that he could only receive directions from Colonel Stager. Any directions that I would give were immediately dispatched to Washington, and a wrong impression of the nature of the directions evidently conveyed.

On completing the line to La Grange I was a whole day prevented from sending a dispatch because the wires were being used from offices along the line sending paying dispatches. I immediately ordered that no private dispatches should be sent. This order was only continued in force, however, one day. I then directed Colonel Riggin, aide-de-camp, to write an order (the very wording of it dictated by myself) authorizing private dispatches to be sent over the wires until 10 a. m. when they did not interfere with the public service. The following dispatch was the result of this order:

WASHINGTON, *November* 14, 1862.

To Major-General GRANT:

Some one signing himself John Riggin, superintendent of military telegraphs, is interfering with the management of telegraphs in Kentucky and Tennessee. This man is acting without the authority of Col. Anson Stager, general superintendent of military telegraphs (see General Orders, 38, April, 1862), and is an impostor. Arrest him and send him north of your department before he does mischief by his interference.

By order of the Secretary of War:

P. H. WATSON,
Assistant Secretary of War.

The following was my reply:

LA GRANGE, TENN., *November* 14, 1862.

P. H. WATSON,
Assistant Secretary of War, Washington, D. C.:

John Riggin, referred to in your dispatch, is my aide. He has given but one order referring to telegraphing, and that was dictated by myself. It was that private dispatches might be sent over the wires before 10 o'clock a. m. when they did not interfere with military dispatches.

Colonel Riggin is assigned to the duty of military superintendent of telegraphs within this department, a position which interferes with no present arrangements, but is intended solely for my relief.

Misrepresentations must have been made.

U. S. GRANT,
Major-General.

Assistant Secretary Watson replied to this as follows:

Col. Anson Stager having been appointed by the Secretary of War superintendent of military telegraphs and of the construction and management of military lines, Colonel Riggin must not interfere. Colonel Stager has appointed deputies believed to be competent, but if they fail in their duty a report of the facts to Colonel Stager will bring a prompt removal.

P. H. WATSON,
Assistant Secretary of War.

It was not intended that Colonel Riggin should have any authority to interfere in any way with any arrangement made either by the Secretary of War or Colonel Stager, but simply that he should give my instructions to the department superintendent as to where wires should be run and where offices should be established and see that it was done and report the fact.

After these dispatches I saw nothing to complain of until the 26th of November. On that date dispatches sent into the office in the morning were not sent off until 10 o'clock at night. The wires were down about three hours of that time, but they were at work several hours in the morning and again in the evening, several hours before they could be got off. The operator on being asked the reason for this replied that the wires were being used from other offices sending cotton-dispatches. I reminded Van Duzer that my order of the 14th was still in force, in this language:

HDQRS. THIRTEENTH ARMY CORPS, DEPT. OF THE TENNESSEE,
La Grange, November 26, 1862.

J. C. VAN DUZER,
Assistant Superintendent Military Telegraphs, Grand Junction:

The order prohibiting the transmission of commercial or private dispatches over the telegraph lines between here and Cairo, except before the hour of 10 a. m., is still in force and must be enforced.

U. S. GRANT,
Major-General.

Mr. Van Duzer replied that my orders should be obeyed, but immediately removed the operator who had always been at my headquarters office and put in a new man, evidently because the first had done his duty in informing me why my dispatches had been detained. I sent for Mr. Van Duzer and warned him against making changes at my headquarters in the future without consulting me. I permitted the change to take place, however, notifying Mr. Van Duzer that I would have no person about the office who would not let me know when dispatches could not be sent and the reason why.

Some days after this I was astonished at receiving the following dispatch:

WASHINGTON, *November* 28, 1862.

All Operators in the Department of the Tennessee:

Mr. J. C. Van Duzer has been assigned to the management of the United States military telegraph lines in the Department of the Tennessee. You will obey instructions received from him. Orders from any other source will not be obeyed.

A. STAGER,
Colonel and General Superintendent Military Telegraphs.

I was indignant at this interference in my command and the implied charge of interference on my part. I have neither the time nor the inclination to take upon myself the duties of others, and neither proposed to curtail the prerogatives of either Colonel Stager or Mr. Van Duzer; but as commander of the department I see nothing in the order of the Secretary of War referred to in one of these dispatches that leaves the telegraph in this department a distinct institution, that cannot be controlled or directed by the department commander.

Colonel Stager sending this dispatch after my denial of any interference on the part of Colonel Riggin determined me to remove this man, who I had no doubt was the cause of the whole controversy, and who at any rate is entirely unfit for his position, at least in this department. There are some small matters, not mentioned here, against Van Duzer that convince me of his unfitness for the place.

You will oblige me by laying this matter before the Secretary of War as embracing the charges I have against Mr. Van Duzer. I have also to request that some other person be appointed to fill his place. I have so little confidence in the man that unless ordered by some one whose orders I am bound to respect I cannot let him stay in this department.

[U. S. GRANT,]
Major-General.

OXFORD, MISS., *December* 3, 1862.

Lieutenant-Colonel MCDERMOTT,
Commanding Post at Grand Junction:

Release Mr. Van Duzer on parole, as directed by the Secretary of War.

U. S. GRANT,
Major-General.

HEADQUARTERS ARMY IN THE FIELD,
Abbeville, Miss., December 3, 1862.

Col. T. LYLE DICKEY,
Commanding Cavalry Division:

Dispatch of 11 o'clock a. m. to-day is received. It was my intention to send the expedition east to strike the Mobile and Ohio Railroad, as you propose, but thought first to give the cavalry one day's rest. You will, however, send them, if you deem it practicable, immediately after driving the enemy beyond the Yockna River, moving slow, so as not to tire out the cavalry, and after reaching the railroad and accomplishing the object of the expedition they will return to the main body of our forces at or near this place.

U. S. GRANT,
Major-General.

ABBEVILLE, MISS., *December* 3, 1862.
Col. G. G. PRIDE,
    Chief Engineer Military Railroads, Hudsonville, Miss.:

COLONEL: Am glad to hear you are progressing so well with your work. Push on the repairs to the Tallahatchie. It is the intention to rebuild the Tallahatchie Bridge, and Quinby has been directed to commence getting out timber to that end.

U. S. GRANT,
Major-General.

ABBEVILLE, MISS., *December* 3, 1862.
Admiral PORTER, *Cairo, Ill.:*

Our move has been successful so far as compelling the evacuation of the Mississippi Central road as far as Grenada. A spy who left Corinth some weeks ago and just returned this evening, reports that it is the intention of the rebels to evacuate Arkansas and concentrate their whole force east of the Mississippi. In this event they will cross at Vicksburg. Please inform me of so much of your movements as you deem prudent to pass over the wires.

U. S. GRANT,
Major-General.

ABBEVILLE, MISS., *December* 3, 1862.
Lieut. Col. C. A. REYNOLDS,
    Chief Quartermaster, Holly Springs, Miss.:

COLONEL: You will make Holly Springs for the present your main depot for supplies and get forward there all the supplies of every kind needed, and issue from there as required. La Grange will no longer be made a depot. Any artillery horses that arrive send to the front.

By order of Maj. Gen. U. S. Grant:

JNO. A. RAWLINS,
Assistant Adjutant-General.

HEADQUARTERS DISTRICT OF JACKSON,
Jackson, Tenn., December 3, 1862.

Commanding Officers Union City, Troy, Crockett, Kenton, Rutherford, Dyer, Trenton, Humboldt, Carroll, Medon, Toone's, Bolivar, Middleburg, Hickory Valley, Grand Junction, La Grange, Davis' Mill, Coldwater:

Commanding officers are informed that guerrilla bands are moving with intention of burning railroad stations, tanks, and bridges. The general commanding orders that great vigilance be exercised. Guarding railroads and keeping communication open to the army is now the vitally important duty of troops in this district. Energy, courage, and daring are required of officers and men. The attacking party must be repulsed and annihilated. Disloyal persons are to understand that destruction of their property will follow a guerrilla raid. A surprise will always be attempted. The attack will be sudden but must be repelled. Disgrace will inevitably follow a defeat.

JER. C. SULLIVAN,
Brigadier-General, Commanding.

SPECIAL FIELD ORDERS,	HEADQUARTERS RIGHT WING,
	ARMY IN THE FIELD,
No. 6.	*Wyatt, Miss., December 3, 1862.*

The general commanding having observed with pain and regret the non-observance on the part of many of orders promulgated to this command before leaving Memphis, directs that the following instructions be issued for the government of all parties concerned, and the officers to whom they are directed are held rigidly responsible for their strict observance:

I. Division quartermasters will immediately obtain the exact number of ambulances in their respective divisions, and will thereupon meet and make an equitable division, one to each regiment, massing the remainder into division trains. The artillery and cavalry are alone excepted.

II. Hereafter every morning, when the army moves at any early hour, the division surgeons will inform themselves of the number of sick who of necessity must be transported, and will thereupon see to the placing of them in the division train, leaving the regimental ambulances empty for service during the day with their respective regiments. They will hold regimental surgeons to a strict accountability that none are permitted to ride who are improper cases for this indulgence. Men who are temporarily exhausted must, when rested, give place to others, as it is not intended to transport this army to the scene of action in ambulances. No knapsacks or muskets or forage must be put into the ambulances, which will be kept strictly for the uses declared by Army Regulations and general orders, viz, transportation of the sick and wounded. To secure a strict observance of these orders, division surgeons will make from time to time on the march personal inspection, and will detail an assistant surgeon to take charge, under their direction, of the division train of ambulances.

III. Ambulances, medicine wagons, pannier mules, and teamsters are in the charge of regimental and division quartermasters respectively, who are responsible for the condition of the vehicles, teams, and drivers, and they will be under the orders of the regimental and division surgeons respectively, who are responsible that they are made to subserve the interests of the service in the manner prescribed by regulations and general orders.

IV. It will not be practicable to send sick to the rear as a general rule, and none will be sent when opportunity occurs without a report of their number, their regiment, and the circumstances rendering it necessary. It is not intended that this command shall melt away and be permitted to stay behind to serve out their time in general hospitals without a record of their whereabouts and precise information at these headquarters as to the causes of their absence. Regimental surgeons are instructed that they are to treat the sick in their regiments, and none must be sent away merely to get rid of them. Any want of attention or dereliction of duty, if reported to these headquarters, will be promptly noticed, and officers so reported will be recommended for dismissal from the service. The success of our arms depending so largely upon the healthy condition of the troops it is expected that medical officers will use every effort to secure and maintain the highest possible state of health and efficiency in their respective commands.

Strict conformity to these instructions is enjoined upon all parties concerned.

By order of Maj. Gen. W. T. Sherman:

J. H. HAMMOND,
Assistant Adjutant-General.

WASHINGTON, D. C.,
December 4, 1862—7.05 p. m.

OFFICER COMDG. AT GRAND JUNCTION, MISS. [TENN.]:

You will immediately take the parole of J. C. Van Duzer, superintendent of telegraphs, and release him if he is in confinement and report to this Department.

EDWIN M. STANTON,
Secretary of War.

WAR DEPARTMENT,
Washington, December 4, 1862.

Major-General CURTIS, *Saint Louis, Mo. :*

I regret very much that you have moved General Steele into Mississippi without authority. It seriously interferes with operations ordered by the President. You will concentrate at Helena as early as possible all the available forces in your department, and telegraph me the numbers sent to that point and the time of sending them. There must be no further evasion of the orders for this concentration.

H. W. HALLECK,
General-in-Chief.

SAINT LOUIS, Mo., *December* 4, 1862—10 p. m.

Maj. Gen. H. W. HALLECK, *General-in-Chief:*

You suggested a move on Grenada by telegraph November 4 [3?]. On the 6th I telegraphed you, " Shall I destroy railroad at Grenada if I can?" I directed organization of an expedition on the 7th to wait further orders.* On the 8th you ordered me to put General Steele in command of forces at Helena,† which I have done. On December 2 General Steele informs me he has moved on Grenada, according to my plan, at the instance of General Grant, and I telegraphed this fact immediately to you. Why reproach me with evasions ? I will send copy of General Steele's explanation. I planned the movement; others have started it, and it was gone four days before I knew it.

SAML. R. CURTIS,
Major-General.

---

* See Curtis to Hovey, November 7, p. 323.
† See Series I, Vol. XIII, p. 782.

HEADQUARTERS DEPARTMENT OF THE MISSOURI,
Saint Louis, December 4, 1862.

Maj. Gen. H. W. HALLECK, *General-in-Chief:*

GENERAL: Your telegram inquiring how much force I can furnish for a down-river expedition was illegible until yesterday. I responded by telegraph, "20,000."

In this I propose to give all my available force to the primary object of opening the Mississippi, leaving at Helena only enough to hold that point, deferring any and all interior movements until the main down-river forces can be returned. Nothing of great importance can be done interior from Helena until we have boats to run and hold position on the White, Arkansas, Washita, and Red Rivers, and especially that we hold the mouths of these rivers. Up to a very recent period the rebels have had the constant or general possession of the mouths of all these great arteries of the Trans-Mississippi country. While the enemy can run gunboats on these rivers, wagon trains cannot support a military force beyond; and therefore Little Rock should not be taken until after the Mississippi is taken, and gunboats of proper draught can be used on the White and Arkansas.

With this view as to my department, I feel that the down-river movement is of the first importance, not only to your entire command in the West, but to this department especially.

Knowing also your views of the primary move as avowed a year ago I am ready to lend all my lines of operations to the river movement and put all available force in that column. But I do not wish to lose all control of the force; or rather I suppose it is to be immediately available in my department when the main trunk is opened or so much as may seem necessary and proper for my command.

I shall leave only about 5,000 at Helena, and strip all the eastern portion of my command to do this, leaving only what seems absolutely necessary to guard prisoners and keep the peace in the country.

I write this to explain my understanding of your wishes. I will send General Steele with the troops and place General Gorman in command at Helena, hoping he will make a better administrative officer than General Steele, and believing General Steele will prefer to go with the troops.

If I am to properly organize and equip my portion of down-river force I wish to be so instructed, and of course I would like to command them. I have earned a name in rebel lines which, without arrogance, I claim to have some influence against them. But I have never asked for specialties and will take any position assigned me without a murmur. All I ask is that I may not be prejudiced by *ex-parte* presentations of my acts and intentions.

I have the honor, general, to remain, your obedient servant,

SAML. R. CURTIS,
Major-General.

HEADQUARTERS DEPARTMENT OF THE MISSOURI,
Saint Louis, Mo., December 4, 1862.

Maj. Gen. H. W. HALLECK, *Washington, D. C.:*

GENERAL: Your dispatch of to-day expressing your regret that I have moved General Steele into Mississippi without authority, and saying, also, "there must be no further evasion of the orders for this concentration," is a surprise and most painful reproach. I carefully planned at your suggestion a move on Grenada, and sent General Washburn with careful instructions as to how it should be executed if you sent me permission; also writing General Hovey. This was about the 8th of November, and I informed you, asking if the blow should be struck. You did not respond, and so the matter rested. General Hovey got up an expedition on the Arkansas Post, but fearing he might get the forces out of reach I wrote him on the 11th November :*

In view of operations more immediately under the directions of the General-in-Chief I deem it inconsistent therewith to encourage the carrying out of your idea at this time.

But being assured that the matter would only occupy three or four days I did not fear its interference with a down move to which I referred. After such assurance of my desire to defer all matters to your orders I was surprised to see General Steele's letter of the 27th informing me that the Grenada matter had been undertaken. It was too late to countermand it, and the request of General Grant through General Sherman seemed to excuse it, as General Grant had over a month ago come to confer with me on such a move, which he said you and he were maturing. However this may be, the final move, although on my plan, was without my knowledge or consent. If my plan is adhered to the expedition should have returned to the river before this time, and I trust will not delay me in bringing my troops up to time in any move you may order.

I cannot imagine how you should suppose I try to evade a concentration of force to serve in the down-river column. I fully concurred with you and the President in the primary importance of this last fall. As soon as I came to Helena in July I came with Commodore Davis to Cairo and explained the necessity of taking complete possession of the Mississippi as a preliminary to taking Little Rock, as gunboats could go up the Arkansas and White Rivers and intercept my trains. My State and the whole West are deeply interested in opening the river, and I have deplored every diversion of troops away and rejoiced at every effort to concentrate on the Mississippi. I certainly do not know myself, or I have an awful way of misrepresenting myself to you, if I have induced you to suppose I am not devoted to the work of opening the Mississippi. I took and held the advance post on that line, and, in conjunction with the navy, made excursions far below Helena, destroying a battery in the Yazoo and the railroad leading west from Vicksburg, and I now send promptly every man I can spare, and as fast as I can organize and arm them, to join your downward movement. I am determined, general, to deserve the favorable consideration of my commanding general and my country, if my judgment and strength do not fail me. It has been more a source of trouble to me than to you that for some time General Steele has felt himself almost independent of my command. But I do not name this to reproach him for this last act of allowing the move on Grenada (he did not go himself), which I think was done in good faith, and I hope may result in no evil. I have thus demonstrated to you my entire innocence in regard to the Grenada move at this time, and I trust explained the circumstances which made others suppose they were doing right in attacking that place; and I respectfully ask you to withdraw the imputation of an "evasion" of your orders charged in your telegram of to-day.

I have the honor to be, general, your obedient servant,

          SAML. R. CURTIS,
            Major-General.

---

* See Series I, Vol. XIII, p. 788.

HEADQUARTERS ARMY IN THE FIELD,
Oxford, Miss., December 4, 1862.

Col. T. LYLE DICKEY,
  Commanding Cavalry Division:

Tilghman was left in command of troops at Rocky Ford and must now be working his way south some distance east of the railroad. He will be easily confused and routed. Look out for him, and if a chance occurs attack him with your full force. In striking eastward much will necessarily depend on the information you may be able to gather and your own discretion. If you learn, however, as I think is the fact, Columbus is only defended by conscripts it would be a great strike to get in there and destroy the enemy's armories, machine shops, &c.

Headquarters will be at Oxford at present, and this the point for you to return to.

U. S. GRANT,
Major-General.

———

OXFORD, MISS., *December* 4, 1862.

Brig. Gen. C. S. HAMILTON, *Abbeville, Miss.:*

As soon as practicable let McArthur's division move up here and one brigade of Quinby's move up to Abbeville. Ross and the remainder of Quinby's division had better remain where they are until the railroad is completed.

U. S. GRANT,
Major-General.

———

SPECIAL FIELD ORDERS, }   HEADQUARTERS RIGHT WING,
      No. 9.   }   *Wyatt, December* 4, 1862.

*   *   *   *   *   *   *

II. The Second Division, General Morgan L. Smith, will march to-morrow on the right-hand Oxford road to a good camp on the other side of the Hurricane Creek, near Bowles' Mill.

III. The First Division, General Denver, will follow, taking the left-hand road and proceeding to College Hill, and there select a good camp.

IV. General Denver's regimental train will then follow him.

V. General Morgan L. Smith's regimental train will then follow to his camp.

VI. General Lauman's division will remain at Wyatt till the day after to-morrow and then move to a camp on the left-hand Oxford road beyond and near Hurricane Creek, leaving one regiment at Wyatt to guard the division trains and the bridge.

VII. Maps will be furnished each division commander, and as the roads are very bad every soldier must carry his knapsack and as much provision as possible.

By order of Maj. Gen. W. T. Sherman:

J. H. HAMMOND,
Assistant Adjutant-General.

———

OXFORD, MISS., *December* 5, 1862.

Col. A. STAGER:

By order of General Grant we have extended line to this place. Work does not go smoothly. General Grant gives operators choice of obeying his orders or working on fortifications. Men all dissatisfied and want to leave.

SCHERMERHORN,
Chief Operator, Advance Telegraph Corps.

OXFORD, MISS., *December* 5, 1862.

COMMANDING OFFICER GRAND JUNCTION:

The release of Van Duzer does not entitle him to interfere with telegraph matter or to remain in this department. He must leave by first train.

U. S. GRANT,
Major-General.

HEADQUARTERS,
Grand Junction, Miss., December 5, 1862—5.50 p. m.

Maj. Gen. H. W. HALLECK, *General-in-Chief:*

SIR: I have the honor to report that J. C. Van Duzer arrived here under guard with a written order signed by General Grant for his removal to Cairo. I did not feel that I had the responsibility of him and declined to liberate him, as I receive my orders from General Grant and not from the War Department. I had good reason to suppose the dispatch bogus for the purpose of having Van Duzer released.

J. McDERMOTT,
Lieutenant-Colonel, Commanding Post.

WAR DEPARTMENT,
Washington, December 5, 1862.

Major-General GRANT, *Abbeville, Miss.:*

The Secretary of War has called my attention to your telegraphic dispatches in regard to operators and officers. Colonel Stager was charged by the President, under a law of Congress, with the entire management of military telegraph operations. He directs all purchases and appoints and removes all officers, under direction of the Secretary of War. If any operator fails in his duty report him for removal. In extreme cases he may be arrested, just as you can arrest an officer of the Navy or of the Treasury Department. Colonel Stager directs all telegraphic purchases. In case of deficiencies report the fact, but do not order purchases. They cannot be paid for out of the Quartermaster's Department. Any orders to that effect given by you will be immediately countermanded.

H. W. HALLECK,
General-in-Chief.

OXFORD, MISS., *December* 5, 1862.

Maj. Gen. H. W. HALLECK, *General-in-Chief:*

I have never ordered a purchase nor the disbursement of a dollar for telegraph purposes; never interfered with the prerogative of the superintendent; never ordered the establishment of an office or extension of a wire except through the assistant superintendent when he could be reached. The assistant superintendent of this department it is impossible for me to get along with. I arrested him and notified operators of the fact, and that his orders would not be obeyed. Colonel Stager was notified of his arrest.

U. S. GRANT,
Major-General.

OXFORD, MISS., *December* 5, 1862.
Brig. Gen. C. S. HAMILTON, *Abbeville, Miss.*:

Owing to the bad condition of the roads do not move McArthur's division any farther from their supplies.

U. S. GRANT,
Major-General.

OXFORD, MISS., *December* 5, 1862.
Brig. Gen. C. S. HAMILTON, *Abbeville, Miss.*:

I ordered up the remainder of Logan's division yesterday and one of yours to come to-day. Learning that Logan's supplies could not reach him to march yesterday, you were ordered to send a division as soon as practicable. The rain of last night making the roads so bad, you were then directed not to move any farther from your supplies. There has been system enough, but some failure in my dispatches reaching you.

U. S. GRANT,
Major-General.

BETHEL, TENN., [*December*] 5, 1862.
Major-General GRANT:

Courier came just now. Artillery heard in the direction of Pocahontas, and, I think, just east of that place. Possibly, if Hurlbut is out, it may be him; he has forces moving threatening the rebels. None of my scouts are in yet from that direction.

I. N. HAYNIE,
Colonel, &c.

LA GRANGE, TENN., *December* 5, 1862.
Capt. T. H. HARRIS, *Assistant Adjutant-General*:

The following information has just been received from below Davis' Mill:

Mitchell's band has made another raid upon the forces below us, killing one of the Twenty-ninth Illinois Volunteers. His band is increasing daily, and will have two pieces of artillery here within a few days. Now is the time to bag him. We could do it easily with the help of 40 or 50 more cavalry for a few days, and if we should neglect now his annoyance will be constant.

I will send communication to-morrow. Have asked several questions which remain unanswered.

A. S. NORTON,
Colonel, Commanding.

HUMBOLDT, TENN., *December 5, 1862.*

General SULLIVAN, *Jackson :*

I would again respectfully call your attention to the fact that these pretended deserters from the rebel army are coming here very thick. Two here in office of provost-marshal now. They think the oath is not binding on them when they are where the rebels have the power, and if the rebels should again have it here they would not be found. There is another class who have been with Dawson and have been taken. They prefer to have been paroled and exchanged, yet for the purpose of getting home they take the oath, expressing the same belief as to its obligations as above stated. It does look like they were attempting to get a band of guerrillas within our lines. These men profess no sort of friendship for the Government whatever. I would suggest that they should be sent North as prisoners, to be exchanged, and only let those take the oath who show unmistakable evidence of determination to become loyal citizens. I make the suggestion because it begins to look alarming to turn so many of these loose among us. I make the statement and suggestion because we are here where we see the facts and you ought to be informed of them. Please answer by covering the case suggested.

Yours, respectfully,

JOHN I. RINAKER,
Colonel, Commanding Post.

HDQRS. THIRTEENTH A. C., DEPT. OF THE TENN.,
Oxford, Miss., December 6, 1862.

Col. T. LYLE DICKEY,
Commanding Cavalry Division :

Rest your horses and men where you are, and when sufficiently recruited strike to the east and destroy the Mobile and Ohio Railroad as much as possible. As stated by me in a previous dispatch it would be a great strike to reach Columbus and destroy armories and machine-shops there.

The cavalry force you will have with you can subsist on the country through which you pass. The plundering propensity exhibited by some of the cavalry should be suppressed as far as practicable. This can be partially done by making a detail from each regiment and charging them with procuring rations and forage for their regiments and replacing broken-down animals.

There is no depot of supplies here or I would forward some to you. Let me know how soon you can start, and I will relieve you by making an infantry and artillery demonstration in the same direction.

U. S. GRANT,
Major-General.

OXFORD, MISS., *December 6, 1862.*

Brig. Gen. GRENVILLE M. DODGE, *Corinth, Miss. :*

The general commanding has communicated with the general commanding Confederate forces on the subject of army surgeons who are captured having the right to retain their horses and other private property, indicating his willingness to let them take with them when released everything that is necessary to enable them to perform their vocations in the field, but has not yet received a reply, and until he does their horses and surgical instruments will be held, they having set the example in depriving our surgeons when captured of such property.

By order of Maj. Gen. U. S. Grant:

JNO. A. RAWLINS,
Assistant Adjutant-General.

HEADQUARTERS ARMY IN THE FIELD,
Oxford, Miss., December 6, 1862.

Brig. Gen. C. S. HAMILTON,
Commanding Left Wing :

You will put the divisions of your command (the one at Waterford and the one at Abbeville) in the best possible condition for defense and the comfort of the men, and let each remain where it now is until further orders, instructing the commanding officers of the respective divisions to collect as much forage and supplies from the surrounding country as possible, and sending out as far as is practicable to obtain it.

By order of Maj. Gen. U. S. Grant:

JNO. A. RAWLINS,
Assistant Adjutant-General.

HEADQUARTERS ARMY IN THE FIELD,
Oxford, Miss., December 6, 1862.

Maj. Gen. J. B. McPHERSON,
Commanding Center :

You will put the division you have at Waterford in the best possible condition for defense and the comfort of the men, and leave it where it is for the present, instructing commanding officer to collect as much forage and supplies as possible from the surrounding country as far out as it is practicable to obtain it.

By order of Maj. Gen. U. S. Grant:

JNO. A. RAWLINS,
Assistant Adjutant-General.

CORINTH, MISS., *December* 6, 1862.

General SULLIVAN:

If that command works south inform me. Roddey's whole force is 10 miles east of me and on the move; it may be that the two intend to make a junction. My cavalry are all out east toward the river; am inclined to think they will be able to drive Roddey back.

G. M. DODGE,
Brigadier-General.

BETHEL, *December* 6, 1862.

General SULLIVAN:

I have to-day heard from Savannah and 20 miles above on the Tennessee. My scouts are also down nearly to Clifton; no movement of the enemy reaches me from these directions. Two scouts came in from Yellow Creek above Hamburg. No enemy there or in that direction. Maxwell also reports same from Savannah. This evening I heard from Pocahontas; nothing there. Can be ready to move in thirty minutes, and will await your orders at any hour to-night.

I. N. HAYNIE,
Colonel, Commanding Post.

LA GRANGE, TENN., *December* 6, 1862.

Capt. T. H. HARRIS, *Assistant Adjutant-General:*

It is reported the guerrillas will attack our pickets at Davis' Mill to-night. I have sent all my cavalry. Can you not send me a company? I have over a million and a half of ammunition which is exposed, besides large quantities of stores.

A. S. NORTON,
Colonel, Commanding.

GENERAL ORDERS,)   HEADQUARTERS RIGHT WING,
    No. 2.   )   *College Hill, Miss., December* 6, 1862.

I. The indiscriminate and extensive plundering by our men calls for a summary and speedy change. Our mission is to maintain, not to violate, all laws, human and divine. Plundering is hurtful to our cause and to the honorable tone which characterizes the army of a great nation.

The Government of the United States undertakes to pay, clothe, and feed her troops well, and is prepared to do it. The officers and soldiers have no right to look to any other quarter for compensation and subsistence. By existing orders the quartermasters and commissaries of brigades may take corn-fodder and any species of forage, and cattle, hogs, sheep, meal, or any species of subsistence stores, which property they account for to the Government (in the same manner as if purchased, leaving to the proper authorities of our Government) to pay for the same or not according to the loyalty of the owner. Fire-wood can be taken by the troops from the standing or fallen timber, or even rails, when such timber is not to be had; but the taking of chickens, turkeys, pigs, or anything by soldiers is as much pillage and stealing as though committed in our own country, as these articles in fact belong to the Government of the United States, whose agents are present prepared to take them and issue to the troops as a part of their regular rations.

II. Each brigadier will hold each colonel or commander of a regiment responsible that when any of his men leave their ranks and pillage not only shall the stolen articles be turned into the brigade quartermasters or commissary, but that the soldiers be punished by fine or otherwise by sentence of a field officer.

III. Each brigadier may detail an officer and a sufficient number of men to forage, who will collect cattle, hogs, sheep, or any kind of subsistence, and also forage, which shall in all instances be receipted for by the proper accounting officer and issued to troops as part of their regular supplies.

IV. On a march soldiers must never leave their ranks without the order of their brigadier. If found out of their ranks, unless in the ambulances by order of the surgeon, the colonel will see that they are tried by a field officer as stragglers or pillagers.

V. The firing of a gun is a false alarm, and will be punished as such, and if any man is a mile from his camp, unless sent for water or other duty, by the Articles of War he must be very severely punished. Patrols sent out may fire on such men, as they are as much enemies of their country as secesh.

VI. Colonels of regiments will cause the Articles of War to be read to their men now, and repeat it every month, and impress on them that they are employed to do the work of their Government and not their own will, and that we are in a hostile country where large armies, though unseen, are maneuvering for our destruction. To be ready we must act in concert, prepared to move in any direction at a moment's notice, and this would be impossible if men are allowed to roam about the country plundering at will.

By order of Maj. Gen. W. T. Sherman:

J. H. HAMMOND,
Assistant Adjutant-General.

War Department,
Washington, D. C., December 7, 1862.

Major-General McClernand, *Springfield, Ill.:*

Your letter of the 2d instant reached me yesterday. Your proposed change of organization and equipment requires careful consideration and consultation with the General-in-Chief and Quartermaster-General before it can be approved, and also information from other heads of bureaus. I will have the questions determined as speedily as possible; but you will take no action on the subject until you receive instructions.

EDWIN M. STANTON,
Secretary of War.

Corinth, *December 7, 1862.*

General Sullivan:

My cavalry are all on the move to the east, following Roddey. If it should become necessary I could send a sufficient force from here to the river to act in conjunction with you for all purposes; but I do not think any force except cavalry will venture this side of Tennessee north of Pittsburg, and of that I have already little.

G. M. DODGE,
Brigadier-General.

Headquarters Thirteenth Army Corps,
Oxford, Miss., December 7, 1862.

Colonel Mizner,
        Commanding Cavalry Division:

Major Rowley reports a reasonably good force on the Yockna River, at Springfield. Put a strong picket there; also send two companies to the crossing of the Yockna where Colonel Lee's brigade crossed as we went south. A flag of truce from the enemy will be in shortly, and it must not be allowed to pass the Yockna. Instruct your pickets to stop the flag and send courier to these headquarters.

By order of Maj. Gen. U. S. Grant:

T. LYLE DICKEY,
Colonel and Chief of Cavalry.

Oxford, Miss., *December 7, 1862.*

Colonel Mizner,
        Comdg. Cavalry Division, Thirteenth Army Corps:

You will hold the crossing of the Yockna and rest and recruit men and horses for another expedition. Forage and subsist upon the country around you to the north and west as far as practicable. Prohibit all straggling from their proper camps by either company officers or

soldiers. Do the foraging under written orders from brigade or regimental officers and always under personal charge of a reliable commissioned officer, who shall keep foraging party under his control.

By order of Maj. Gen. U. S. Grant:

T. LYLE DICKEY,
Colonel and Chief of Cavalry.

HDQRS. RIGHT WING, ARMY OF THE TENNESSEE,
Oxford, Tenn., December 8, 1862.

Rear-Admiral DAVID D. PORTER,
Commanding U. S. Naval Forces, Cairo, Ill.:

The movement thus far has been eminently successful. General
Grant's moving down directly upon the enemy's strong lines behind
Tallahatchie while the Helena force appeared unexpectedly on their
flank, utterly confounded them, and they are now in full retreat, and
we are at a loss where they will bring up. We hope they will halt and
reform behind the Yalabusha with Grenada as their center. If so,
General Grant can press their front, while I am ordered to take all the
spare troops from Memphis and Helena and proceed with all dispatch
to Vicksburg.

Time now is the great object. We must not give time for new combinations. I know you will promptly co-operate. It will not be necessary to engage their Vicksburg batteries until I have broken all their
inland communication. Then Vicksburg must be attacked by land and
water. In this I will defer much to you.

My purpose will be to cut the road to Monroe, La., to Jackson, Miss.,
and then appear up the Yazoo, threatening the Mississippi Central road
where it crosses the Big Black.

These movements will disconcert the enemy and throw them on to
Meridian, especially as General Grant presses them in front. All this
should be done before the winter rains make General Grant's roads impassable. I will leave for Memphis to-morrow (Tuesday) night, and
will reach Memphis with one of my old divisions Friday night. We
ought to leave Memphis before the 20th, and I do earnestly desire you
should meet me there at all events. Even if the larger gunboats cannot proceed at once, send those of light draught down with Captains
Phelps, Gwin, Shirk, or some officer to assist me in the preliminary
work. Of course Vicksburg cannot be reduced till you arrive with the
large gunboats.

General Grant's purpose is to take full advantage of the effects of
this Tallahatchie success.

I am, with great respect,

W. T. SHERMAN,
Major-General, Commanding.

HDQRS. THIRTEENTH A. C., DEPT. OF THE TENN.,
Oxford, Miss., December 8, 1862.

Brig. Gen. FRED. STEELE,
Commanding U. S. Forces, Helena, Ark.:

I have just received authority to retain all General Curtis' forces now
within my department until further orders. This is from the General-
in-Chief, and contemplates their being used in co-operative movements
to effect the capture of Vicksburg. If these troops have gone back to

Helena I wish you would return them to Friar's Point, or the most suitable place to march them directly upon Grenada, or embark them for Vicksburg, as I may decide upon. General Halleck's dispatch was only this moment received, and my mind is not fully made up as to the best method of capturing Vicksburg. I can, by the time our troops could reach there, have the railroad completed to Grenada and a supply of provisions thrown in there. From that point Jackson, Miss., could be reached without the use of the roads. Jackson once in our possession would soon insure the capitulation of Vicksburg.

I rather incline, however, to the plan of sending your forces, and all I can spare from Memphis and here, say 25,000 in addition to yours, down the Mississippi to effect a landing above Vicksburg, probably a short distance up the Yazoo, and have them co-operate with the gunboats, whilst I move south with the remainder of my forces from here.

Please inform me by return couriers all you know about the present condition of our gunboats. You having been so long on the Mississippi River looking toward Vicksburg are possessed of much information as to the best method of attacking that point that I am not possessed of. I would be very glad to have your views.

I shall send Sherman, if the Mississippi route is determined upon, and would be very glad if you could accompany him. I have no definite news of the result of Hovey's expedition. From the enemy evacuating Tallahatchie so suddenly I judged that it had proven successful. We followed up the evacuation with all dispatch, our cavalry pressing their rear all the way from the river to Coffeeville, killing and wounding many and capturing about 700. Besides this many deserted and are coming in every day.

Word was sent me to-day by a deserter who gave himself up that there were near 2,000 Southern soldiers east of this place, scattered through the country, desirous of coming in if we would send out cavalry to drive out the guerrillas that hover in that direction and make it unsafe for them to venture in this direction.

U. S. GRANT,
Major-General.

P. S.—Send me word what number of men you have river transportation for. I shall adopt the plan of sending a force down the Mississippi. I will send instructions to the commanding officer of the cavalry forces that will necessarily be left behind for their guidance.

HDQRS. THIRTEENTH A. C., DEPT. OF THE TENN.,
Oxford, Miss., December 8, 1862.

Commanding Officer U. S. Cavalry Forces, Friar's Point, Miss.:

By the authority of General-in-Chief of the Army I retain under my command, until otherwise directed, all the forces from General Curtis' command now east of the Mississippi River, or those who recently crossed to co-operate with me on this side.

All the cavalry, one regiment of infantry to be designated by Brigadier-General Hovey, and at least one section of artillery will rendezvous at Friar's Point or Delta, whichever may be the most defensible point and best landing. The infantry and artillery will form the permanent garrison of the post and will protect the stores for the entire command. The senior officer will command the whole and make all reports to these headquarters. All the forces except the cavalry and garrison for Friar's Point will receive instructions from Major-General Sherman.

It is desirable that the cavalry should be recruited as much as possible until about the 18th instant, after which it is expected of them to make an active campaign, instructions for which will be sent in due time. Supplies of provisions and forage will be obtained from chiefs of subsistence and quartermaster's departments in Saint Louis. As far as practicable, however, we should live off of the enemy. For this purpose you will appoint, if you have not already got, a quartermaster and commissary. All property taken should pass through their hands and be accounted for and go to the benefit of the Government. Receipts must be given for all property taken where proprietors are at home, and in no case should wanton destruction of property be tolerated.

No licensed trading will be tolerated for the present, and all passing of citizens to and fro should be prohibited. Where foraging parties are sent out they should always be under the direction of an efficient commissioned officer, who will be held responsible for the good conduct of the men.

No straggling should be allowed from camp nor parties while out. All information of the movements of the enemy will be sent here via river to Columbus and by telegraph from there. When it is of sufficient importance a cavalry force may be sent here direct.

U. S. GRANT,
Major-General.

P. S.—The cavalry, with the exception of one squadron to be left at Friar's Point, may be sent to Polkville, at the mouth of Coldwater, keeping on the west bank for security. All the ferries from Panola as far south as practicable should be collected and taken to Polkville without delay.

TRENTON, December 8, 1862.

General SULLIVAN:

I received a dispatch from Colonel Hawkins, Second Tennessee Cavalry, who is scouting with 150 men, the country near Huntingdon and Lexington, saying that no rebels in that neighborhood had been seen or heard of up to this morning 7 o'clock.

JACOB FRY,
Colonel, Commanding.

LOUISVILLE, KY., December 8, 1862.

Colonel STAGER:

See following message and advise me what to do in the case:

SAINT LOUIS, MO., [December] 7, 1862.

SAMUEL BRUCH:

I was sent out of department under guard, and General Tuttle informed me that he is ordered to arrest and confine me if I return. I do not understand that General Grant intends to give me any chance to show by an investigation that I am right. I desire to return to the department in preference to any other position in the service, but to do it must have safe-conduct of War Department or General Grant will shoot me.

J. C. VAN DUZER.

If General Grant has charges against Van D. he should make them at once, so Van could either be removed or reinstated.

SAM. BRUCH.

HEADQUARTERS DEPARTMENT OF THE MISSOURI,
Saint Louis, Mo., December 9, 1862.

Brigadier-General GORMAN, Helena, Ark.:

GENERAL: I am required to have most of the troops now at Helena ready for a down-river expedition. I am anxious to have Hovey's command back on the river bank, so there may be no delay. Do all you can to facilitate any orders I may receive from General Halleck in this regard. I am sorry to have to leave you with only force enough to hold Eastern Arkansas, but I have urged the necessity of an early return or the accommodation of the matter by the immediate supply of new forces.

Blunt and Herron have fought a battle and won a victory at Fayetteville over Hindman.

Truly, yours,

SAML. R. CURTIS,
Major-General.

HEADQUARTERS DEPARTMENT OF THE MISSOURI,
Saint Louis, Mo., December 9, 1862.

Brigadier-General STEELE, Helena, Ark.:

GENERAL: Your dispatches relating to the Grenada movement have been duly received and promptly reported to headquarters at Washington. I hope it will continue to prove a success. As General Halleck complains of it as a diversion of troops that may be needed for down river, I explained that it would be back on the river in time for you to move with other forces, which I hope you will have ready to move at a moment's notice. I want all except about 5,000 or thereabouts ready for a down-river expedition. How they are to move and who is to be commander-in-chief has not transpired, but I expect you and General Blair will be of the number.

Respectfully, yours,

SAML. R. CURTIS,
Major-General.

HDQRS. THIRTEENTH A. C., DEPT. OF THE TENN.,
Oxford, Miss., December 9, 1862.

Col. T. LYLE DICKEY,
Commanding Cavalry Division:

In making the detour east, concerning which you have received instructions from the general commanding, select such of your cavalry as you may deem most suitable for the expedition, leaving about half your cavalry force where they now are, for within the next forty-eight hours a strong infantry and artillery force will be moved from here to the place where you are now encamped, and it is the intention to push southward with cavalry in front.

By order of Maj. Gen. U. S. Grant:

JNO. A. RAWLINS,
Assistant Adjutant-General.

OXFORD, *December* 9, 1862.

General SULLIVAN:

The army now having penetrated far into Mississippi, trade may be resumed in Tennessee, subject only to Treasury restrictions and such other restrictions as local commanders may deem necessary to preserve good order and discipline.

U. S. GRANT,
Major-General.

———

HEADQUARTERS RIGHT WING,
College Hill, December 9, 1862.

General GRANT,
Commanding Thirteenth Army Corps, Oxford:

DEAR GENERAL: Colonel Grierson is about to start for Helena with your dispatches, and I also toward Memphis. When he returns he will report to you in person. Colonel Grierson has been with me all summer and I have repeatedly written to you and spoken in his praise. He is the best cavalry officer I have yet had. I commend him specially to your consideration. He has already had assigned to him a brigade, but the cavalry has been so busy that he has not yet had his command. I ask for him anything you can do for his benefit and the good of the service. I know that you will soon appreciate his merits.

Yours, truly,

W. T. SHERMAN,
Major-General.

———

SPECIAL FIELD ORDERS, }   HDQRS. ARMY IN THE FIELD,
No. 18.   }   *Oxford, Miss., December* 9, 1862.

*   *   *   *   *   *   *

II. The division commanded by Brigadier-General Denver, to be known as the First Division, is hereby assigned to the command of Major-General McPherson.

III. Brigadier-General Lauman will move one brigade of his present command to a point convenient for water on the line of the railroad, and from 4 to 6 miles south of Abbeville, to guard the road from that point south; the other brigade to Waterford, to report to Col. J. V. Du Bois for further orders.

These dispositions being made, General Lauman will relieve General McKean in command of the Fourth Division, and bring it to Oxford with as little delay as practicable.

*   *   *   *   *   *   *

V. Women and children are hereafter to be excluded from the army in the field. Wing commanders will see that all now with their respective commands are sent to Holly Springs or some point north of that place. Negro women and children and unemployed men will be sent to Chaplain J. Eaton, jr., superintendent of contrabands, Grand Junction, Tenn., who will provide for them. This is not intended to exclude authorized laundresses, hospital nurses, or officers' servants, of which wing and division commanders are empowered to judge of the expediency of retaining.

*   *   *   *   *   *   *

By order of Maj. Gen. U. S. Grant:

[JNO. A. RAWLINS,]
Assistant Adjutant-General.

GENERAL ORDERS,   }   HEADQUARTERS RIGHT WING,
     No. 3.   }   *College Hill, December* 9, 1862.

I. The battalion of regulars and a section of 20-pounder Parrott guns, commanded by Lieutenant Hart, are hereby attached to the Second Division, General M. L. Smith, and will proceed forthwith to join that division at its camp.

II. The Second Division, General M. L. Smith, will take up its line of march toward Memphis, crossing the Tallahatchie at Wyatt to-day and await the arrival of the commanding general. General Smith will turn over to General Lauman any surplus ammunition or stores, with their wagons.

III. The First and Third Divisions, Generals Denver and Lauman, will make their consolidated reports, each separate, to General Grant's headquarters, and the commander of each division will report by letter for orders to Col. J. A. Rawlins, assistant adjutant-general, Oxford, Miss.

By order of Maj. Gen. W. T. Sherman:

                     J. H. HAMMOND,
                     Assistant Adjutant-General.

GENERAL ORDERS,   }   HDQRS. RIGHT WING, ARMY IN FIELD,
     No. 5.   }   *College Hill, December* 9, 1862.

General Sherman in taking leave of officers and men of the First and Third Divisions of his command expresses his earnest regret that the necessities of war cause the temporary separation. We have now been together since the eventful expedition up the Tennessee River, and have slowly but surely and steadily advanced into the enemy's country till we have broken one of their last barriers to our progress. The general thanks officers and men for their courage and patriotism, and feels assured that we will soon meet again under most happy auspices. We are all embarked in the same cause, venerate the same Constitution and Government, and march toward the same destination. Our routes are for a short time different, and he will watch with a feeling heart for the familiar colors of the regiments from which he is thus temporarily separated. Until that time he bids all a heartfelt good-by. He assures the men and officers that their general studies by night and day the plan which leads to victorious results at the least cost of life and treasure, and they may go on with confidence and courage, assured that every step they take is on the certain road to success and glory.

With wise counsels and unity of action our country must in the end rise from this horrible war purified and ennobled by the struggles and labors of her patriotic soldiery.

                     W. T. SHERMAN,
                     Major-General.

                 SAINT LOUIS, *December* 10, 1862—4 p. m.
Hon. E. M. STANTON:

General Grant telegraphs for 1,000,000 bushels of coal without designating any particular point for delivery. I think half a million bushels should be sent to Memphis and another half million to Cairo, to be subject to orders on arrival there. From these two points the coal can be distributed as requested.

                     ROBT. ALLEN,
                     Chief Quartermaster.

OXFORD, MISS., *December* 10, 1862.
Col. T. LYLE DICKEY,
    Commanding Cavalry Division :
    Several infantry divisions will move up to Yockna to-morrow. On their arrival I want the cavalry moved forward to Water Valley and as many of the railroad bridges saved as possible.
                                                        U. S. GRANT,
                                                            Major-General.

HEADQUARTERS DEPARTMENT OF THE TENNESSEE,
                            Oxford, Miss., December 10, 1862.
Col. T. LYLE DICKEY,
    Commanding Cavalry Division :
    The detail to accompany Colonel McCullough's remains and effects may be made.
    The train for provisions for part of your forces is now here. They will have to go to Waterford and possibly Holly Springs.
    Three divisions are going to the front as far as the Yockna. On their approach I want the cavalry to proceed as far as Water Valley, especially if the bridges are standing to that point.
    You need not start on the other expedition until you receive further orders from here.
                                                        U. S. GRANT,
                                                            Major-General.

JACKSON, *December* 10, 1862.
Major-General GRANT:
    Scouts from Tennessee River report that Bragg is moving toward Florence. The rebels have large force, say between 6,000 and 8,000, on east side of Tennessee, from Duck River to Florence. My scouts have been sent to the river. I will report as soon as heard from.
                                                        JER. C. SULLIVAN,
                                                            Brigadier-General.

SPECIAL FIELD ORDERS, }   HDQRS. ARMY IN THE FIELD,
        No. 19.   }   *Oxford, Miss., December* 10, 1862.
    I. Colonel Buckland's brigade will be transferred to the division now commanded by Brigadier-General Ross. The latter will designate one regiment from his present command to be left on the railroad at a suitable point for water from 4 to 6 miles south of Abbeville.

    *   *   *   *   *   *   *

By order of Maj. Gen. U. S. Grant:

                            [JNO. A. RAWLINS,]
                            Assistant Adjutant-General.

WAR DEPARTMENT,
                        Washington, December 11, 1862.
Brigadier-General ELLET, *Cairo, Ill.:*
    General Grant has been ordered to assign Company K, Eighteenth Illinois, to the ram fleet. Communicate with him in regard to location of the company and when it will join the fleet.
                                                        H. W. HALLECK,
                                                            General-in-Chief.

SAINT LOUIS, MO., *December* 11, 1362
Major-General GRANT:

Your dispatch received. We will furnish the transportation you require as rapidly as possible. It cannot be done within the time you mention. Coal is very scarce—must depend principally upon obtaining it from points on the Ohio. I have telegraphed to all points. The river is low. I cannot tell how fast coal can be brought down. Steamboatmen inform me that with little delay wood can be chopped when coal cannot be supplied. I had, previous to your dispatch, informed the General-in-Chief and the Quartermaster-General that coal must be sent from the Ohio, and am informed that prompt attention will be given.

ROBT. ALLEN,
Chief Quartermaster.

OXFORD, MISS., *December* 11, 1862.
Col. T. LYLE DICKEY, *Springfield, Miss.*:

Lieutenant Wilson has gone to the front. You need not start east until Saturday. Strike the road as far south as possible and travel north along it, doing all the damage possible. I will instruct Dodge to move out a brigade from Corinth. Send your sick back here.

U. S. GRANT,
Major-General.

OXFORD, MISS., *December* 11, 1862.
Brig. Gen. GRENVILLE M. DODGE, *Corinth, Miss.*:

Cavalry will leave Springfield on Saturday to strike Mobile road. Send out a force from Corinth to co-operate, allowing them to go as far south as Tupelo if practicable. Keep a sharp lookout for Bragg's forces. Should he approach Corinth I will re-enforce you sufficiently. You have a much more important command than that of a division in the field.

It would probably be well to send toward Iuka at the same time you send south.

U. S. GRANT,
Major-General.

BETHEL, TENN., [*December*] 11, [1862].
Major General GRANT:

Your dispatch received, concerning which I learn to-day from the Tennessee River as follows: That rebel forces are making headquarters on Indian Creek, 20 miles east of Savannah—Biffle's and Cox's men. My scouts do not report re-enforcements, but say Forrest's forces are in and about Columbia. Roddey's men are said to have crossed the Alabama; not sure of it. I expect to get word from Biffle's camp to-night. I have scouts extending from Hamburg to Clifton, on the Tennessee. They are citizen scouts, but are reliable and active. I have furnished them arms. They are away from home and need subsistence. May I issue to them?

I. N. HAYNIE,
Colonel, Commanding Post.

BETHEL, TENN., *December* 11, 1862.

Major-General GRANT:

Scout Perkins, just in from Yellow Creek, 15 miles above Hamburg, reports Roddey's men, 800 strong, there.   Left there at daylight this a. m.; says there are several ferry-boats in river—one at State Line Ferry, one at Yellow Creek, and the other above Yellow Creek.   No report of forces crossing.   Perkins gathers from secesh that Roddey is said to be the advance of larger forces.   Southern scrip in good demand up there.   Returned Confederates say the army is destitute and is coming on this way after supplies.   Scouts start to-night to hunt main forces.

I. N. HAYNIE,
Colonel.

NASHVILLE, TENN., *December* 11, 1862.

Major-General GRANT:

Tell the authorities along the road to look out for Forrest.

W. S. ROSECRANS.

OXFORD, MISS., *December* 11, 1862.

Brig. Gen. GRENVILLE M. DODGE, *Corinth, Miss.:*

Look out for Forrest's cavalry on line of railroad.   Dispatch from General Rosecrans would indicate he is threatening it at some point, though he does not state where.

By order of Maj. Gen. U. S. Grant:

JNO. A. RAWLINS,
Assistant-Adjutant General.

(Same to General Sullivan.)

LA GRANGE, *December* 11, 1862.

Brigadier-General SULLIVAN:

One hundred of Forrest's (now Richardson's) cavalry left Moscow yesterday morning; supposed to be near Macon.   Batteries in position, breastworks built, and troops on their arms to-night.   All is prepared.

A. S. NORTON,
Colonel, Commanding.

SPECIAL ORDERS, }   HDQRS. 13TH A. C., DEPT. OF THE TENN.,
No. 44.   }   *Holly Springs, Miss., December* 11, 1862.

On and after Monday, December 15, 1862, trade and travel will be open to Oxford, Miss., which place will constitute the southern limit until further orders, and beyond which persons not connected with the army are prohibited from passing.

District and post commanders and provost-marshals are authorized to grant permits accordingly.

*   *   *   *   *   *   *

By order of Maj. Gen. U. S. Grant:

[JNO. A. RAWLINS,]
Assistant Adjutant-General.

HEADQUARTERS,
Springfield, Ill., December 12, 1862.

His Excellency ABRAHAM LINCOLN:

Since my return here on the 25th October last, and receipt of orders to assist the Governors of Illinois, Indiana, and Iowa in mustering and forwarding troops, I have forwarded to the rendezvous of the Mississippi expedition forty-nine regiments of infantry and two batteries, containing upward of 40,000 men. There are still a few infantry regiments and batteries nearly ready to march and a few others recruiting.

The work remaining to be done in those States may be satisfactorily performed by the mustering officers of the U. S. Army in those States, or by a member of my staff, and is not of importance enough in my judgment to detain me from the more advanced organization of the expedition and its movement upon Vicksburg. May I not ask therefore to be sent forward immediately?

Very respectfully, your obedient servant,

JOHN A. McCLERNAND,
Major-General.

HEADQUARTERS,
Springfield, Ill., December 12, 1862.

Hon. E. M. STANTON,
Secretary of War:

If the recent victory achieved by our arms at Prairie Grove, Ark., is as decisive as reported, why may not a considerable portion of our forces in that quarter, including also a portion of those south of Pilot Knob and Rolla in Missouri, be assigned to the Mississippi expedition or to some other field of service? I only ask the question suggestively.

I am anxiously awaiting your order sending me forward for duty in connection with the Mississippi expedition.*

Respectfully, your obedient servant,

JOHN A. McCLERNAND,
Major General.

WASHINGTON, *December* 12, 1862.

Maj. Gen. SAMUEL R. CURTIS, *Saint Louis:*

GENERAL: Your communication of the 4th, in regard to the Grenada expedition, is received and the explanations satisfactory.

In the numerous telegrams and dispatches sent from this office daily some errors will necessarily occur. The language of my telegram of November 3 is perhaps a little ambiguous, but was not intended to authorize the sending of troops from Helena to Grenada. The first object of sending troops to Saint Helena was stated to be the capture of Little Rock, which has been continuously urged on me for the last six months. If that could not be done then they would be used to co-operate with Grant's intended movement on Grenada. This was the idea intended to be conveyed. It was by no means intended that they should be sent to Grenada. The President had directed that all available troops on the Mississippi be sent to another place. I consequently ordered General Grant not to move on Grenada, but was informed by him that Steele had already moved from Helena on Grenada, and if he (Grant) did not co-operate Steele's forces might be cut off. This very much

* See p. 413.

surprised me, as your suggestion to send them had not yet been acted on. I was thus placed in a position where I could not carry out the President's wishes either by moving the Helena forces on Little Rock or down the Mississippi River. As I had neither ordered nor consented to the sending of these troops into the interior of Mississippi I was exceedingly annoyed at its being done at the very time when they were wanted elsewhere. On referring to my telegram of November 3 I find that its words are not fully expressive of my meaning.

The movements on the Western rivers are frequently determined on by the joint action of the War and Navy Departments, and it sometimes happens that I can give no answer to the proposed plans of our generals in the West.

In regard to the proposed expedition down the Mississippi and its commander I can give you no reply. I have been informed that the President has selected a special commander, and that instructions have been or will be given to him by the War Department. If so they have not been communicated to me, and until I receive them I shall consider the officer of the highest rank as the commander, whoever he may be. Probably the whole matter will be decided on in a few days, but how I do not know.

Very respectfully, your obedient servant,
H. W. HALLECK,
General-in-Chief.

SAINT LOUIS, MO., *December* 12, 1862.

Major-General HALLECK:

Every possible effort is being made to get the full requirements of General Grant. The only trouble is coal, and if we fail in a supply of this I am assured by steamboat captains that they can rely without fail upon wood, which they can chop and provide at a loss of not more than from two to four hours in the twenty-four. Still an extraordinary effort should be made to get coal down the Ohio, that it may follow up the enterprise. Can you not help my requisition, particularly Treasury notes, through the Treasury? If you have further instructions please let me know them without loss of time.

General Grant's requisition comes too late to be met within the time prescribed, but there will be no delay that can be possibly avoided.

ROBT. ALLEN,
Chief Quartermaster.

HEADQUARTERS RIGHT WING, GRANT'S ARMY,
Memphis, December 12, 1862.

Brigadier-General GORMAN,
Commanding, Helena, Ark.:

SIR: I left Oxford three days since. General Grant had a telegraphic dispatch from General Halleck, a copy of which I have in my baggage (not yet in), to the effect that all the troops detached for the movement on Grenada were to be retained by him and used by him in the contemplated move on Vicksburg. General Grant estimated that force at 2,000 cavalry and 12,000 infantry. I sent Colonel Grierson with his regiment (the Sixth Illinois Cavalry) over to Helena by land from Oxford to carry to General Steele a letter addressed to him on this subject. I brought in with me from the Tallahatchie one division, 7,000 men, and find here for service two divisions (A. J. Smith's and Morgan's), 7,000 each, making, say, 20,000 men. I want 10,000 at least from Helena, ready to embark for Vicksburg on the 18th instant. I wish that General Steele, if possible, go in command of these forces, organized into say three strong brigades, with a reasonable proportion of field artillery, cavalry only enough for scouts, pickets, and to keep up communications; transportation say three or four six-mule teams per regiment; camp equipage full, and at least twenty days' rations. There may be some irregularity in the manner of receiving these orders, but the importance of dispatch will suggest itself to your mind. The enemy was in full retreat before Grant, and it is all-important that we be ready by the 18th. The quartermaster was ordered to have transportation for 30,000 men here by the 18th. I will dispatch to Helena the due proportion for say 10,000. General Grant further requested the 2,000 cavalry to be posted on the Tallahatchie, near where General Hovey crossed, say near Polkville, west side, and one regiment of infantry and one section of artillery to be stationed at Delta or Friar's Point, as the most eligible point on the east side; but if Colonel Grierson got through to Helena you will be in free possession of all these points.

I send one of my aides down to bring me back a full answer on these points, and I trust you have already written to General Grant.

I am, &c.,

> W. T. SHERMAN,
> *Major-General.*

OXFORD, MISS., *December* 12, 1862.

Col. T. LYLE DICKEY, *Water Valley:*

Start on your eastward expedition early to-morrow morning. Lieut. Charles Dickey left here this morning to join you. Lieutenants Wilson and Goodell started for the front yesterday.

By order of Maj. Gen. U. S. Grant:

> JNO. A. RAWLINS,
> *Assistant Adjutant-General.*

OXFORD, MISS., *December* 12, 1862.

Brig. Gen. GRENVILLE M. DODGE, *Corinth, Miss.:*

Monday morning will be early enough for your troops to strike Saltillo.

> U. S. GRANT,
> *Major-General.*

HEADQUARTERS DISTRICT OF CORINTH,
Corinth, Miss., December 12, 1862.

Col. AUG. MERSY,
Commanding Second Brigade:

You will prepare to move two regiments (1,000 strong), in light marching order, blankets and overcoats, with five days' rations, at daylight to-morrow morning; 100 rounds of cartridges will be taken. The infantry will move in wagons. All the wagons of the Second Brigade will be taken and the balance from the Third Brigade. The pickets of one regiment will be relieved to-night by Col. M. M. Bane. The regiment left will picket the rest of the brigade front.

Colonel Mersy will report at these headquarters this evening for instructions.

By order of Brig. Gen. G. M. Dodge:

GEO. E. SPENCER,
Captain and Assistant Adjutant-General.

HEADQUARTERS DISTRICT OF CORINTH,
Corinth, Miss., December 12, 1862.

Col. AUG. MERSY,
Commanding Second Brigade :

You will proceed, in command of two regiments of infantry in wagons, one section of artillery, and cavalry, south, if practicable, as far as Tupelo. You will leave Corinth at daylight to-morrow (Saturday) morning; reach Saltillo at daylight Monday morning. A force of cavalry from Spring Dale, on Grand Junction and Grenada Railroad, will leave that place at same time you leave here, and cross the railroad some point near Tupelo. Your movement is made to co-operate with them. On your return you will strike east of Mobile and Ohio Railroad and wipe out any straggling bands of the enemy you may find coming to Corinth by way of Jacinto. You will keep me advised of all your movements by couriers, and take extra care that no unauthorized depredations are committed by the troops. All good stock mules and horses, belonging to rebels in arms, found fit for service will be taken and brought here. Any cotton found belonging to rebels in arms will also be taken on the return, and all the teams when near Corinth will be loaded with forage.

These instructions are given as the general outline, but full discretion is given the commanding officer to vary from them so far as march and attack are concerned should circumstances require it.

Great care must be taken in keeping the destination of the forces secret, and that it is not in any way surprised; and every endeavor will be taken to ascertain the force of the enemy at Saltillo to see that it has not been re-enforced.

By order of Brig. Gen. G. M. Dodge:

GEO. E. SPENCER,
Captain, Assistant Adjutant-General.

OXFORD, MISS., *December 12, 1862.*

Admiral PORTER, *Cairo, Ill. :*

A large force of rebel cavalry is moving west from Columbia, Tenn., toward Savannah, Tenn. Can a light-draught gunboat get up there at this time ?

U. S. GRANT,
Major-General.

CAIRO, ILL., *December 12, 1862.*

General GRANT:

Two gunboats are working their way up Tennessee River, but cannot get higher than Cuba Ford. One is ashore.

DAVID D. PORTER,
Acting Rear-Admiral.

JACKSON, *December* 12, 1862.
Major-General GRANT:

Scouts from Tennessee River report at Bethel that Forrest's cavalry are marching via Waynesborough from Columbia, striking the river at Savannah. I will order all the roads obstructed and try and force them south. Cannonading was heard in the direction of Yellow Creek to-day from Bethel. The people of this district are flocking in to take the oath. I allow them until Monday.

JER. C. SULLIVAN,
Brigadier-General.

SPECIAL FIELD ORDERS, }   HDQRS. ARMY IN THE FIELD,
No. 21.   }   *Oxford, Miss., December* 12, 1862.

I. Distress and almost famine having been brought on many of the inhabitants of Mississippi by the march of the two armies through the land, and humanity dictating that in a land of plenty no one should suffer the pangs of hunger, the general commanding directs that the following provision shall be made at all military posts within this State:

II. At each post one or more loyal persons will be authorized to keep for sale provisions and absolute necessaries for family use. Nothing will be sold except on permits granted by the commanding officers of posts, and no permits will be granted for a greater amount of any one article than the commander may believe is necessary for the family of the purchaser.

III. A fund may be created at each post to supply the necessaries of destitute families gratis, either by levying contributions upon those disloyal persons who are able to pay, taxing cotton brought to their posts for sale, or in any other equitable way.

IV. All contributions so collected will be expended by the post commissary on the order of the commanding officers, and the accounts will be kept separate from all other accounts.

V. The commanding officers of posts will require all accounts of these disbursements to be presented for their examination weekly, and they will be held responsible that these accounts are properly kept.

VI. All such accounts will be open for inspection to the inspector-general of the department at any time he may call for them.

*   *   *   *   *   *   *

By order of Maj. Gen. U. S. Grant:
[JNO. A. RAWLINS,]
Assistant-Adjutant-General.

CAIRO, *December* 12, 1862.
O. H. ROSS, Esq.,
In Charge of Mails for General Grant's Army:

You will without delay take possession of all mail-locks, keys, or other property belonging to the Post-Office Department found in the hands of any one in the lines of the army except the adjutant-general or other officer at headquarters. You will turn the same over to the postmaster at Cairo, taking his receipt for the same.

A. H. MARKLAND,
Special Agent Post-Office Department.

SAINT LOUIS, MO., *December* 13, 1862—10 a. m.

Maj. Gen. H. W. HALLECK, *General-in-Chief:*

I have the honor to report that recruiting for the Mississippi Marine Brigade progresses very slowly, and in view of the importance of its early foundation and of the great difficulty of subsisting men at this time, I would respectfully suggest that I be authorized to obtain men from commands already in the service. I would further suggest that these men be obtained from the convalescents in the hospitals. Many men who are utterly unfitted for the ordinary service in the field would make efficient soldiers for this service, which is so much lighter and less fatiguing. It is especially suggested that by this means the hospitals may be greatly relieved by the men rendered serviceable, who will otherwise continue to be a burden upon the country, or have to be discharged. Again, these men being disciplined soldiers will, as soon as formed into companies, be ready for service, while recruits will have to be kept out of service until drilled. The boats are purchased and being put in a condition to receive the men, and it is earnestly hoped, by the means proposed, the brigade may be ready as soon as the boats. Thus the value of the command from which the men are taken will not be impaired, while this service will be greatly promoted.

Very respectfully,

ALFRED W. ELLET,
Brigadier-General.

HDQRS. RIGHT WING, THIRTEENTH ARMY CORPS,
Memphis, December 13, 1862.

General DAVIES,
Commanding Columbus, Ky.:

SIR: If Captain Fitch be at Columbus hand him the inclosed letters, to be telegraphed to Generals Grant and Curtis and then remitted. I am anxious to get the one to Curtis promptly and get his answer to Helena with all dispatch or I foresee a mistake. I expect to hear from Helena to-night, but deem it important to get an order from General Curtis requiring this co-operating force. I will have here 5,000 less than Grant estimated, and if also the Helena force remain there I will have too small a body to accomplish the results expected at the time and in the manner required. Please use my name and power and send to Helena with all dispatch General Curtis' telegraphic orders and send me copies.

I will be all ready to embark at the date proposed by General Grant.

I am, &c.,

W. T. SHERMAN.
Major-General, Commanding.

[Inclosures.]

HEADQUARTERS DISTRICT OF EASTERN ARKANSAS,
Helena, Ark., December 13, 1862.

Maj. Gen. U. S. GRANT,
Comdg. Thirteenth Army Corps, Dept. of the Tenn.:

GENERAL: Yours dated at Oxford, Miss., December 8, 1862, and addressed to Brig. Gen. F. Steele, commanding United States forces at

Helena, has been received; also another letter of the same date addressed to the commanding officer of the United States cavalry forces at Friar's Point, Miss.

The expedition which left this point under the command of Brigadier-General Hovey, and which moved in the direction of Grenada, Miss., has returned and his forces are now all on this side of the river. As the General-in-Chief evidently intended these troops to be used in co-operation with others in the capture of Vicksburg I will return them and out of them garrison Friar's Point, as indicated by you.

You ask General Steele's opinion as to the best point to land troops below here with a view of attacking Vicksburg. General Steele says that the troops should be landed at the lower end of Milliken's Bend, opposite an island called My Wife's Island, say 2 or 3 miles above the Yazoo River. From that point operations could be directed as may be hereafter indicated by yourself and General Sherman. The above point is about 25 miles by water above Vicksburg and some less by land.

I inclose * the reply of Naval Officer Gwin to your inquiry as to the present position of our gunboats between this and Vicksburg, from which you will perceive there are six iron-clads, four light-draught wooden boats, and two rams.

The enemy have a battery on the Yazoo about 15 miles from the mouth of that river and about 12 miles by land from Vicksburg.

I have only about 12,000 infantry for duty, and about 4,700 cavalry and five efficient batteries.

You can rely upon 5,000 infantry, 2,000 cavalry, and two batteries to accompany General Sherman, which is a little more than the force sent in the Hovey expedition; but if when I meet General Sherman he desires me to send the whole force, except enough to garrison this post, as I may not have time to communicate with General Curtis, I will take the responsibility of sending all.

I am, general, very respectfully, your obedient servant,

W. A. GORMAN,
Brigadier-General, Comdg. Eastern District of Arkansas.

HDQRS. RIGHT WING, THIRTEENTH ARMY CORPS,
Memphis, December 13, 1862.

Major-General CURTIS,
Commanding Department of the Missouri :

SIR: When at Oxford, Miss., on Tuesday last, I saw a telegram from General Halleck to the effect that General Grant should retain the troops of your department which had moved on Grenada. The supposition was that this force was 12,000 infantry, 2,000 cavalry, and a due proportion of artillery. I learn that only 5,000 infantry composed that expedition. I am ordered against Vicksburg with a force composed of certain troops here and those from Helena, 12,000. Now, if that force be reduced to 5,000 my strength will be inadequate. Will you not order 12,000 infantry from Helena to act with me, and if not wanted for any other purpose they cannot be better employed. I am not ambitious of the command, but Grant's movements in interior depend on this. Send dispatch to Helena via commanding officer Columbus, Ky., who will forward with dispatch.

W. T. SHERMAN,
Major-General.

---

* Not found.

HDQRS. RIGHT WING, THIRTEENTH ARMY CORPS,
Memphis, Tenn., December 13, 1862.

Col JOHN A. RAWLINS,
Assistant Adjutant-General, Oxford:

COLONEL: I wrote at length last night and sent to Columbus by Captain Fitch to be telegraphed through to-day.

I have to report the arrival of Morgan L. Smith's division in the city, so that my Memphis forces, of Third Division, are now on hand. My aide has gone to Helena to see about that force, and will be back tomorrow. General Washburn is up from Helena. He commanded the cavalry force which accompanied Hovey. They made a floating bridge at mouth of Coldwater. Infantry force of 5,000 advanced to the Yockna whence the cavalry force of 2,000 proceeded to Oakland, Preston, and within 5 miles of Grenada, where he became satisfied he could not surprise the place, and his horses very fatigued by a ride of 55 miles in one night, he caused the road to be broken about 5 miles from Grenada and wires cut. He is satisfied now that he could have gone into Grenada, but General Hovey and he apprehended the enemy would move from Abbeville toward Panola and Coldwater and cut off their retreat.

Evidently the road was very slightly damaged. General Washburn broke a small bridge on the Memphis and Grenada road about 10 miles north of Grenada, with which exception he thinks the whole from Coldwater to Grenada is in good order. He wants to make a strike at Yazoo City from some point of the river coincident with a movement south. He also says that they have full 25,000 men at Helena, and could spare 15,000 easy, but there is some doubt about Gorman's permitting any to go unless Curtis orders it.

Being no longer in your department, and only 5,000 infantry having been there, there is a doubt whether Halleck's order embraces them. To make sure, get Halleck to order a specific number of men, say 12,000 infantry, 2,000 cavalry, and some three batteries, to be transferred to you.

I will have all things ready by the 18th, and expect, as a matter of course, the transportation.

I have ordered the quartermaster here to hold on to ten steamboats for our use.

I am, &c.,

W. T. SHERMAN,
Major-General.

HDQRS. RIGHT WING, THIRTEENTH ARMY CORPS,
Memphis, December 13, 1862—Midnight.

General WILLIS A. GORMAN,
Commanding District of East Arkansas, Helena:

DEAR SIR: Yours of December 12* was handed me to-night, and I thank you for the spirit in which you have met the proposed movement. General Washburn was here to-day, and explains that only 5,000 infantry and 2,000 cavalry had composed the expedition to Grenada and that all had returned to Helena. Anticipating the very conclusion to which you arrive I immediately sent to Columbus, Ky., by boat, a letter for General Curtis, to be telegraphed to him, to make telegraphic an-

---
* Not found.

swer to be sent you with all dispatch, so that I have little doubt you will receive full sanction and authority for anything you may do to accomplish the great end designed by General Halleck. At Oxford General Grant calculated that Smith's and Morgan's divisions, which were known to have passed Cairo for Memphis, were each about 7,000 strong, and also some eight new regiments had been reported as having passed for the same destination, and as I brought in from Oxford one of my divisions it was calculated I should get here 30,000 and 10,000 from Helena, so that he reported I would leave this point by the 18th with 40,000. Now, Morgan's and Smith's divisions were mere skeletons, and they absorbed the new regiments, so that embracing them they do not average 7,000 each, and instead of 30,000 here I do not count on over 20,000. The importance, therefore, of as large an accession from Helena as possible is counted on. General Robert Allen, chief quartermaster at Saint Louis, is ordered to send here transportation for 30,000 men, and I have ordered our quartermaster to hold on to ten good steamboats here, so that I expect ample transportation. A feeble demonstration on Vicksburg would do harm rather than good, and I beg you will endeavor to increase the force to about 10,000 infantry and artillery, and make the disposition of cavalry and a support at Delta such as General Grant asks for, as I know General Halleck will command it. You have now the dispatches by Grierson and have seen Captain McCoy. I will attend to all transportation and supplies, and would be obliged for all information, maps, and suggestions. Now is the appointed time for striking below, and all things should bend to it. Grant is ready and impatient, and the enemy is shaken by their being outwitted at the Tallahatchie. Before leaving Oxford I telegraphed to Quartermaster Allen, suggesting that all the chartered boats should come, half loaded with coal and half with forage and supplies. I expect to receive from the same quarter plenty of axes, so that if pushed we can cut fuel, and also picks and shovels for approaches, should we be compelled to counter ratter the works at Vicksburg. I will be all ready to embark the 18th if the boats arrive. I expected Admiral Porter here to-day, but he is not come. I sent you by General Washburn an authenticated copy of General Halleck's dispatch, but Grierson's arrival supplied you with all data. Of course General Curtis must conform to the orders of the commanding general, but even without that I feel certain he will heartily co-operate in so desirable an object. As soon as his answer is received I will send it to you with all possible dispatch, and in the mean time I hope you will prepare the command for embarkation by the date fixed. I will have here four 6-gun batteries (6s) and James' rifled guns; also six 10-pounder Parrott guns and ten 20-pounder Parrotts. I have also sent to Cairo for four 30-pounder Parrotts. I understand you have a supply of light batteries, and I would ask that the force to be made up at Helena have a full supply of field guns.

Grant has about 45,000 men, and can hold his own and pass down in front while we operate in flank and on the rear. Independent of the designed attack on the works at Vicksburg and the Yazoo he naturally wants the cavalry to watch the country between Delta or Friar's Point and the Tallahatchie.

I should be pleased to hear that you give to General Steele a command of the troops taken from your command. There is no objection to General Washburn making a simultaneous movement on Yazoo City and the fleet of boats. Hindman and Bragg are now too far off to go to the river, and therefore one great reason for some haste. If the boats come from Saint Louis I will proceed to the work, let my strength be what it may.

I am, with great respect, yours, truly,

W. T. SHERMAN,
Major-General, Commanding.

HELENA, ARK., *December* 13, 1862.

Maj. Gen. U. S. GRANT,
Commanding Thirteenth Army Corps:

DEAR GRANT: Curtis sent Gorman, the only brigadier-general in the department, to supersede me. He relieved me in the command here once before and sent me to Pilot Knob, for which he was severely rapped by Halleck and ordered to send me back. Halleck also mentioned this movement in his official report to the President as being most unfortunate.

Curtis will do everything in his power to injure me because I have denounced his d—d rascality.

I shall go in command of the troops to co-operate with you from this station, and shall have the satisfaction of knowing that with you and Sherman I shall be properly dealt with.

It is my opinion that if the movement down the river could be properly timed it would be best for the troops not to be back on the Mississippi at all, but in connection with the gunboats to take the battery on the bluff up Yazoo River and land the troops at that point under cover of the gunboats. This battery is 15 or 20 miles up the Yazoo and 12 miles from Vicksburg, on the road between the latter place and Yazoo City.

I am afraid Gorman will refuse to give me as large a force as I desire, as he may well imagine that I shall not come under his command again if I can avoid it. He is an old acquaintance of mine, and I like him socially, but would rather be commanded by a military man.

There is a movement by the army here as well as by the citizens to get me reinstated in this command.

Our troops under militia rule have torn this country all to pieces, and the citizens are alarmed at the change of commanders.

I will write to Sherman to-night.

Very truly, your friend,

FRED'K STEELE,
Brigadier-General.

OXFORD, MISS., *December* 13, 1862.

Col. T. LYLE DICKEY,
Commanding Cavalry Division:

I want you to strike the Mobile road as far south as possible and follow up north, destroying it all you can. Particular roads to pass over cannot be given. You may encounter difficulties that will defeat the object of the expedition. I do not want any great risk run, but leave this entirely to your judgment.

Dodge starts a force of probably 2,500 men from Corinth southward to-day, intended to co-operate with you. If practicable you might continue north until you meet them and return by Pontotoc to the front.

U. S. GRANT,
Major-General.

OXFORD, MISS., *December* 13, 1862.

Maj. Gen. GRENVILLE M. DODGE, *Corinth, Miss.*:

A cavalry force leaves our front to strike the Mobile road as far south as possible. They are instructed then to push north, destroying the road until they meet the force sent by you, if practicable.

Your troops should be instructed to be back within six days, and to run no risk of being cut off.

U. S. GRANT,
Major-General.

———

WATER VALLEY, MISS., *December* 13, 1862.

Maj. Gen. U. S. GRANT:

As directed by Colonel Dickey, chief of cavalry, I report myself in command of the cavalry division, with headquarters at this place. The information I get is that the mass of the rebel army is at Grenada. An outpost of cavalry at Torrance Station; strength about 1,200. The rest of the cavalry are at Stratham's, on Yalabusha. No infantry north of Grenada. Pickets 3 miles south of Coffeeville, with occasional patrols in Coffeeville. I am guarding railroad bridge at this place and the crossings of the Otuckalofa. Let the Sixth Illinois Cavalry come up, if possible.

J. K. MIZNER,
Colonel, Commanding Cavalry Division.

———

WATER VALLEY, *December* 13, 1862.

General GRANT:

A scout sent to Oakland captured a messenger with orders to Major Blythe to destroy all cotton between the Tallahatchie and Coldwater, and all other points accessible. He expected to find Major Blythe at Horn Lake, 14 miles from Memphis. We also learn from him that Price is camped 5 miles west of Grenada, and Van Dorn 3 miles east of Grenada. Force of each, 15,000. Six hundred re-enforcements arrived from below, on Thursday. Pemberton is at Grenada. Lovell left for Richmond on Tuesday. Enemy is throwing up earthworks north of Yalabusha; work is done by negroes. Pickets are 7 miles north of Grenada. I moved at daylight.

J. K. MIZNER,
Colonel, Commanding Cavalry Division.

———

OXFORD, MISS., *December* 13, 1862.

Colonel MIZNER, *Spring Dale*:

Move with your cavalry to the south or southeast slowly, to cover the movement of Colonel Dickey. You should remain out until Monday evening or Tuesday. Should you discover any movement of the enemy toward Colonel Dickey apprise him of the fact or go to his assistance, as may seem best.

U. S. GRANT,
Major-General.

WATER VALLEY, *December* 13, 1862.

Major-General GRANT, *Oxford* :

I am not advised as to Colonel Dickey's intended route. I will move as you direct. No infantry has yet arrived here. I will have to leave a guard over the bridges in this vicinity. Cannot move. Cavalry will be sent to the front to make a considerable demonstration, or is your desire that no advance be made farther than that indicated in your last dispatch ?

J. K. MIZNER,
Colonel, Commanding Cavalry.

OXFORD, MISS., *December* 14, 1862.

Maj. Gen. WILLIAM T. SHERMAN:

I have not had one word from Grierson since he left, and am getting uneasy about him. I hope General Gorman will give you no difficulty about returning the troops that were on this side of the river, and Steele to command them. The 21,000 men you have, with 12,000 from Helena, will make a good force. The enemy are as yet on the Yalabusha. I am pushing down on them slowly, but so as to keep up the impression of a continuous move. I feel particularly anxious to have the Helena cavalry on this side of the river, if not now, at least after you start. If Gorman will send them, instruct them where to go and how to communicate with me. My headquarters will probably be in Coffeeville one week hence ; in the mean time I will be at Spring Dale. It would be well if you could have two or three small boats suitable for navigating the Yazoo. It may become necessary for me to look to that base for supplies before we get through.

U. S. GRANT,
Major-General.

HEADQUARTERS DISTRICT OF EASTERN ARKANSAS,
Helena, December 14, 1862.

Brigadier-General STEELE,
Commanding First Division :

GENERAL : I am directed to say that the general commanding wishes you to get your division in complete readiness to embark on transports on the 18th instant at this place. You will take four teams to the regiment for their transportation by land. You will only allow such an amount of camp and garrison equipage, hospital stores, and officers' baggage as can be easily carried in the transportation allowed. You will have turned over all other camp and garrison equipage to the chief quartermaster and all excess of teams not allowed by this order. You will have the sick of your command left in proper care at this place. There must be no delay in getting on board transports when notified of their readiness. You will take twenty days' rations for 10,000 men with you, which will be put on board your transports, and forage for 500 cavalry and 100 artillery horses, with medical stores for all.

You will see that your command have 40 rounds of cartridges in their boxes. You will take an ammunition train sufficient to take all your reserve ammunition, say 80 additional rounds to the man to that in the men's cartridge-boxes.

Two batteries of artillery will also be sent with you and 500 or more cavalry.

I am, general, very respectfully, your obedient servant,

J. W. GORMAN,
Assistant Adjutant-General.

JACKSON, *December* 14, 1862.

Colonel RAWLINS,
  Assistant Adjutant-General:

COLONEL: The reported crossing of the Tennessee River by a large guerrilla force seems to be false. The country south of Hatchie is not in my command, but I propose to visit it with all my cavalry and three regiments of infantry during this week. I will have at La Grange and Grand Junction, as soon as I can procure arms and equipments, about 500 cavalry.

An advance made by Hurlbut toward the Hatchie and my troops marching on the south side toward Somerville will clear all the guerrillas from the haunts in that direction.

Commanders of posts and regiments are unable to make their monthly returns for November for want of blanks. I am without any for my own headquarters. Can you supply?

JER. C. SULLIVAN,
Brigadier-General.

WAR DEPARTMENT,
Washington, December 15, 1862.

Major-General McCLERNAND, *Springfield:*

I had supposed that you had received your orders from the General-in-Chief. I will see him and have the matter attended to without delay.

EDWIN M. STANTON,
Secretary of War.

CAIRO, ILL., *December* 15, 1862.

Maj. Gen. H. W. HALLECK, *Washington, D. C.:*

GENERAL: We did not get General Grant's orders, or have any intimation from any source when any river movement would be made or whether we should be called on for any boats, until noon of the 11th instant. Of course to get up sixty transports, most of which were abroad on trips, have them supplied with crews, stores (especially with coal), and go 450 miles, with extremely low water, in three and a half days was impossible. We have, however, done all that could be done. I have sent forward twenty large transports, and think I shall have twenty to thirty more on the way by Wednesday morning, and hope to be in Memphis Thursday night, Friday at farthest, with sixty boats and fuel enough to make the trip. I have taken on the boats all the coal we could get at Saint Louis and this place, and ordered the boats not to use any of it until they get to Memphis, but rely upon such wood as they can purchase or cut, and bring to Memphis at least fifty cords of wood by Thursday night. We hope to get 30,000 to 40,000 bushels of coal to-morrow; but this fuelmatter has given me much anxiety. At the present moment things look more favorable in all respects than I expected when we got General Grant's order. I leave for Memphis to-morrow night, to get there on Thursday and take charge of the transports myself. I need not assure you that no efforts on my part shall be spared to render the expedition a success and carry out your plans.

Very respectfully, your obedient servant,

L. B. PARSONS,
Colonel and Aide-de-Camp.

OXFORD, MISS., *December* 15, 1862.

Maj. Gen. WILLIAM T. SHERMAN, *Memphis, Tenn. :*
(Care of Captain Fitch, Columbus, Ky.)

If there is any difficulty about getting possession of the forces at Helena that were thrown to the east bank of the river, assume command of them, by General Halleck's order, and organize them and take them off. I hope Steele will be able to go with them.

It is to be hoped that you will have no trouble in getting possession of these troops; but be prepared to act positively if necessary.

U. S. GRANT,
Major-General.

[DECEMBER 15, 1862.—For Gorman to Curtis, in reference, among other things, to force from Helena, Ark., to co-operate in the Vicksburg expedition, see Series I, Vol. XXII.]

CORINTH, *December* 15, 1862.

Brig. Gen. J. C. SULLIVAN,
Commanding, Jackson :

No forces crossing the Tennessee from Savannah to Tuscumbia, except a force at latter place, is reported. We whipped out the force at Tuscumbia Thursday, and they may be getting a better re-enforcement.

Biffle's cavalry and a small part of Forrest's were at Waynesborough a few days ago; they may be crossing, but do not think Bragg has moved. I shall have cavalry at Savannah to-night. If you could push them to Clifton, on the Tennessee, we could ascertain. The Tennessee has raised 2 feet. Report if you get any track of them.

G. M. DODGE,
Brigadier-General.

TRENTON, TENN., *December* 15, 1862.

Brigadier-General SULLIVAN :

I sent yesterday a scouting party of 20 men toward Lexington, and shall send forthwith a company of 50 men of Second Tennessee Cavalry—men who were raised in the country and are excellent scouts—the same way.

As soon as I receive news will communicate it to you. A detachment of 300 of Fifth Ohio Cavalry, Colonel Taylor with them, passed here to-day and will probably reach Jackson to-morrow.

JACOB FRY,
Colonel, Commanding.

BETHEL, TENN., *December* 15, 1862.

General SULLIVAN:

I have just received the following letter from Captain Carter, First West Tennessee Cavalry, who is near Clifton:

Colonel HAYNIE: I inform you from a source believed to be reliable that a force is to cross the river at Clifton, supposed to be Forrest's cavalry, said to be 3,000 strong.

The above was brought to me by Mr. Craven, of Craven's Landing, who left home at 2 o'clock this a. m. I am under orders to report to General Grant immediately. I will turn over this command to Colonel Morrison this morning.

I. N. HAYNIE,
Brigadier-General, Commanding Post.

JACKSON, *December* 15, 1862—6.30 p. m.

Major-General GRANT:

Forrest is crossing Tennessee at Clifton. A large force of cavalry is crossing above. Bragg's army is reported by scouts to be moving this way, through Waynesborough. It has been raining hard all day.

JER. C. SULLIVAN,
Brigadier-General.

COLUMBUS, *December* 15, 1862.

Brigadier-General SULLIVAN:

At what point on the Tennessee River are the rebels crossing? I will try to push forward the regiment here to-night. If not, they will leave in the morning.

THOS. A. DAVIES,
Brigadier-General.

SPECIAL ORDERS, }   HDQRS. OF THE ARMY, ADJT. GEN.'S OFFICE,
No. 394.   }   *Washington, December* 15, 1862.

*   *   *   *   *   *   *

III. Brig. Gen. W. K. Strong, U. S. Volunteers, is relieved from duty in New York and will report to Maj. Gen. U. S. Grant, U. S. Volunteers, for duty with his command.

*   *   *   *   *   *   *

By command of Major-General Halleck:

E. D. TOWNSEND,
Assistant Adjutant-General.

SPRINGFIELD, ILL., *December* 16, 1862.

Maj. Gen. H. W. HALLECK, *General-in-Chief:*

Having substantially accomplished the purpose of the order sending me to the States of Indiana, Illinois, and Iowa, by forwarding upward of 40,000 troops, as more particularly explained in my letter of the 1st instant to the Secretary of War and referred by him to you, I beg to be sent forward, in accordance with the order of the Secretary of War of the 21st of October giving me command of the Mississippi expedition.

Very respectfully, your obedient servant,

JOHN A. McCLERNAND,
Major-General.

HOLLY SPRINGS, MISS., *December* 16, 1862.

Maj. Gen. U. S. GRANT,
   Commanding Department of the Tennessee:

GENERAL: I have the honor to acknowledge the receipt of your communication of the 14th instant, for which I beg leave to tender my sincere thanks.*

I shall not presume to address you again upon this subject, but in
my own justification send the inclosed statement, which, if satisfactory,
as I trust it will be, I am sure will afford you pleasure in my justification.

   I have the honor to be, respectfully, your obedient servant,
                                    A. S. NORTON,
                         Colonel Seventeenth Illinois Volunteers.

[Inclosure.]

HOLLY SPRINGS, MISS., *December* 16, 1862.

GENERAL: I was first charged with having permitted a flag of truce
to come to my headquarters without my knowledge. This is so far true
that the flag passed inside of where my pickets should have been and
was approaching town before it was known to any one on duty. They
were then met by the provost-marshal and sent to my quarters. The
prisoners alleged to have been exchanged were three men whom it was
said were arrested on the Somerville road when being in possession of
a flag of truce. I know nothing of the facts. I received a communication from Colonel Richardson, a copy of which is marked A. I also inclose a copy of my reply, marked B. I had previously closely examined all of the books and papers in the provost-marshal's office and could
find no charges alleged against them, and having learned you had ordered the release of others connected with the same party I thought I
was doing only what you would approve in ordering their release. I at
that time had no infantry pickets on the different roads through the
day, but had cavalry patrols out, and at night placed infantry pickets
on all of the roads and cavalry according to the inclosed instructions,
marked C.*

The second time the flag came in they were brought direct to my
headquarters, in charge of one non-commissioned officer and one private,
from the picket station about 1 mile from town. At each time an officer
accompanied the flag. The officer in charge of the station neglected
his duty in permitting the flag to come beyond the picket, but pleaded
a want of knowledge of his duty on such an occasion.

I also inclose copy of dispatch, marked D, and my reply, marked E.
They were immediately sent back in charge of the same escort.

The house occupied by the Confederate prisoners was vacated by sending the prisoners to Cairo. The provost-marshal informed me that the
house was closed up after the prisoners left and was not entered until
it was discovered to be on fire, and that the fire broke out near the roof,
and he was satisfied it proceeded from a defective flue. Mrs. Millington told me a small house or shed was burned near her house, but could
not inform me as to the origin of the fire. Those were the only fires
which came to my knowledge. I investigated the facts as far as I
could, but could learn nothing further.

At the time of the snow-storm the ordnance officer received ten car-

---

* Not found.

loads of ammunition, which he desired to have moved into buildings immediately. The medical purveyor also received at the same time a very large quantity of medical supplies, which it was necessary should be sheltered. I at the same time had about 1,200 convalescent soldiers in camp without rations or fuel; neither had any of the troops at La Grange (the Seventeenth, Ninetieth, and One hundred and twenty-sixth Regiments) any fuel. Many of those in camp had the measles, and the medical officer in charge of the camp said it was absolutely necessary they should have fire to save, perhaps, life. I had but three teams at the post to perform the labor which at that time required not less than thirty.

I gave directions to the officer in charge to send out his well men and procure rails sufficient for the emergency, and sent Captain Curtis with a detail to take any teams from citizens for that occasion. The depredations complained of were committed at that time.

The Ninetieth Illinois took a portion of the fence from the inclosure around your former headquarters. The One hundred and twenty-sixth also committed some depredations around the premises of Dr. Millington. The Seventeenth were quartered on Main street and were on duty nearly all of the time, and in justice to my officers I must award them great praise for their attention to duty and their exertions to prevent any depredations being committed by their men.

I do not deny having a few very bad men, whom I have long been trying to get drummed out of service; the most of them, however, are good men, and are generally obedient to orders. I am aware of a laxity of discipline on the part of some of the officers of my regiment; but with the exception of perhaps 10 or 12 men I think, general, they will compare favorably in point of discipline and correct deportment with any regiment in the Western Army. They once had the name of being one of the best.

On the 5th instant, at 10.20 p. m., I received your telegram that trade and travel were open to Holly Springs. About 7 o'clock the following morning I delivered the inclosed order, marked F,* to the provost-marshal; also posted one copy (the one inclosed) on the house near the door of my headquarters in a very conspicuous place, and told all applicants for passes to inform their friends who had applied for passes that they could be procured from the provost-marshal. These are facts which are susceptible of any proof which may be desired.

I trust you will pardon me, general, for being so lengthy in this communication. I have at various times been the recipient of your courtesy and kindness, and freely acknowledge there is no officer in the army whose good opinion I am more desirous to retain than your own.

I omitted to mention, relative to the monopoly referred to, that I arrested four teams loaded with cotton coming through my picket lines from the south, who exhibited a pass signed by Colonel Hillyer, permitting them to pass anywhere between Holly Springs and La Grange. (This was some time before I received your telegram.) I also telegraphed reporting several persons who had passed south in disobedience to orders. Citizens complained to me of a monopoly, which they said was permitted, but I carried out your orders in letter and spirit, I believe, in every instance.

I am, sir, very respectfully, your obedient servant,

A. S. NORTON,
Colonel Seventeenth Illinois Volunteer Infantry.

---

* Not found.

[Sub-inclosure A.]

NOVEMBER 29, 1862.

Major-General GRANT,
　　Commanding U. S. Army at La Grange :

G. W. Tatum, G. W. Clay, W. E. Ballard were part of escort of flag of truce with dispatch of 26th instant, proposing exchange of Thomas Boyle, J. H. Sinon, and Thomas Sinon for James F. Bell, E. W. Matthews, and Dr. Theodore Wilkenson.

The prisoners were left under flag of truce in custody of Tatum, Clay, and Ballard near Somerville, while Captain Bell proceeded to your headquarters with dispatches. Major Mudd captured Tatum, Clay, and Ballard, horses and equipments, besides three horses and a buggy used to convey the prisoners, Boyle and two Sinons.

This is a violation of the flag of truce, which is only necessary to bring to your notice to have corrected. Capt. W. Bell and J. E. Raney are bearers of flag of truce and this dispatch.

　　Very respectfully,
　　　　　　　　R. V. RICHARDSON,
　　Colonel, Comdg. Regiment Partisan Rangers, C. S. Army.

[Sub-inclosure B.]

HEADQUARTERS POST OF LA GRANGE,
　　　　La Grange, Tenn., November 30, 1862.
Col. R. V. RICHARDSON,
　　Commanding Regiment Partisan Rangers :

COLONEL: I am in receipt of your flag of truce and communication of the 29th instant disapproving the act of the officer making the arrest of Messrs. Tatum, Clay, and Ballard. I have unconditionally ordered their release and delivery to Captain Bell, the bearer of your flag. I am not aware of the name of the officer making the arrest.

　　I am, sir, respectfully, your obedient servant,
　　　　　　　　A. S. NORTON,
　　　　　　Colonel, Commanding Post.

[Sub-inclosure D.]

FAYETTE COUNTY, TENNESSEE,
　　　　　December 8, 1862.
COMMANDER U. S. ARMY AT LA GRANGE, TENN.:

SIR : On the 18th November Lieutenant-Colonel Dawson, of Confederate States Army, captured and paroled Capt. G. J. Shepardson, Company I, Fourth Illinois Cavalry, and E. B. Powers, private of Captain Shepardson's company; also M. S. Payone, private of Company D, Tenth Illinois Regiment; also, on the 28th November, the Confederate States forces under my command captured and paroled R. E. Ryan, Alonzo Baker, Charles Butler, Adam Steems, John Clon, Wilson Goodwin, Jesse Mintrow, and John A. Rutherford, of One hundred and twenty-seventh, One hundred and ninth, One hundred and thirtieth, and Seventh Illinois Regiments of United States forces. On the 26th of November the United States Army captured Capt. J. W. Marshall, Capt. P. W. Moore, Lieutenant Anderson, and 10 privates, all attached to Colonel Dawson's battalion of cavalry, Confederate States Army. Ten days have now elapsed, when, under the cartel, all should have been paroled ; but so far as I am advised only Captain Moore and Privates Reynolds and

Warren have been paroled.   I invariably parole prisoners in a very few days after capture, and had hoped that a like humane practice would prevail with the United States Army.   I now propose the exchange of Captain Shepardson for Captain Marshall and private for private, according to lists and paroles herewith inclosed.   Adjt. J. L. B. Barksdale, of Lieutenant-Colonel Dawson's battalion, and A. W. Montague are bearers of flag of truce and this dispatch, to make exchange, &c.

I **have** the honor to be, respectfully,

R. V. RICHARDSON,
Colonel, Comdg. Partisan Rangers in West Tennessee.

[Sub-inclosure E.]

HEADQUARTERS POST OF LA GRANGE,
La Grange, Tenn., December 10, 1862.

Col. R. V. RICHARDSON,
Commanding Partisan Rangers:

COLONEL: None of the prisoners referred to are in my possession, nor are they, so far as I know, in the department.   My instructions are to send all Confederate prisoners to Cairo, Ill., from whence they will be sent to Vicksburg, Miss., for the purpose of exchange.

I am, respectfully, yours, &c.,

A. S. NORTON,
Colonel, Commanding Post.

———

SPECIAL FIELD ORDERS, }   HDQRS. RIGHT WING, 13TH A. C.,
     No. 19.   }   *Memphis, December* 16, 1862.

The following directions are issued for the government of all parties concerned:

1st. *Ambulances.*—All ambulances will be immediately examined by the regimental and division quartermasters respectively, to the end that all may be put in complete repair.   One ambulance will be retained by each regiment, and all the surplus, comprising all now on hand at this post, will be equitably divided among the three divisions comprising this command, to be formed into division trains in the charge of the division quartermaster, and under the orders of the division surgeons. They will be so arranged in embarkation and transportation as to be with and under the control of the division to which they belong.

2d. *Hospital tents.*—Each regiment will have one hospital tent; all other hospital tents in the command, for whatever other purpose used, will be turned in to the division quartermaster.   If there are so many surplus tents as to afford it, each division quartermaster will take six, to be used as a field hospital for his division, as necessity may arise.   If there is not a sufficient number, whatever surplus there may be will be equally distributed.

3d. Sick men who must be left will be examined by a board of three medical officers in each division, who will pronounce upon their condition, and none will be left for the convalescent or general hospital without their descriptive lists.   Company commanders will on no account neglect this plain duty.   None will be left behind whose names are not on the record of the board of examiners, as it will not be permitted that this command shall melt away without cause and without the knowledge of the commanding general as to the whereabouts of the men.   Lists signed by the president and members of the board will be forwarded to the office of the medical director, who will give orders for the proper disposition of the cases.

4th. Sick and convalescents left behind on the movement of the 26th ultimo will be examined by a board of medical officers within the fort, and all who are able will rejoin their commands at once. Requisitions for immediate necessary supplies will be made in triplicate, according to Form 49, Quartermaster's Department, approved by the medical director.

By order of Maj. Gen. W. T. Sherman:

J. H. HAMMOND,
Assistant Adjutant-General.

SPRINGFIELD, ILL., *December* 17, 1862—9 a. m.
(Received 10.16 a. m.)

His Excellency ABRAHAM LINCOLN,
President of the United States:

I believe I am superseded. Please advise me.

JOHN A. McCLERNAND,
Major-General.

SPRINGFIELD, ILL., *December* 17, 1862—9 a. m.
(Received 10.16 a. m.

Hon. E. M. STANTON,
Secretary of War:

I believe I have been superseded. Please inquire and let me know whether it is and shall be so.

JOHN A. McCLERNAND,
Major-General.

WAR DEPARTMENT,
Washington City, D. C., December 17, 1862.

Major-General McCLERNAND, *Springfield, Ill.:*

Your telegram this moment received. It surprises me, but I will ascertain and let you know immediately.

EDWIN M. STANTON,
Secretary of War.

WAR DEPARTMENT,
Washington, D. C., December 17, 1862.

Major-General McCLERNAND, *Springfield, Ill.:*

There has been, as I am informed by General Halleck, no order superseding you. It was designed, as you know, to organize the troops for your expedition after they should reach Memphis or the place designated as their rendezvous. The troops having been sent forward they are now to be organized. The operations being in General Grant's department, it is designed to organize all the troops of that department in three army corps, the First Army Corps to be commanded by you, and assigned to the operations on the Mississippi under the general supervision of the general commanding the department. General Halleck is to issue the order immediately.

EDWIN M. STANTON,
Secretary of War

HEADQUARTERS DISTRICT OF EASTERN ARKANSAS,
Helena, December 17, 1862.

Maj. H. Z. CURTIS,
   Assistant Adjutant-General:

General Sherman informs me by letter to-day that he will be here to-morrow with 20,000 men, and wants 10,000 from this command. I have informed him that I will have this number ready to embark by the time he gets here. This force is over and above General Blair's brigade, who proposes to rest a few days, as one regiment is afflicted with measles and one or two cases of varioloid, or small-pox in a mild form, and the surgeon thinks it improper to send them into the field for a few days. But they shall all (four regiments) be sent forward at once if General Sherman wants them. I shall move the whole command to the mouth of the Arkansas, at Napoleon, if General Sherman desires it, unless I receive orders to the contrary from you before ten days. This move is so universally approved that I most respectfully ask your full concurrence. The gunboats will hold this place as easy as they do any other spot on the river above and below. If I leave I will destroy the fortification and take the guns below. The Arkansas River is up, and they can soon move on Little Rock, unless the whole of this army is needed to aid General Sherman.

Please reply.

I am, very truly, your obedient servant,
               W. A. GORMAN,
               Brigadier-General, Commanding.

SAINT LOUIS, MO., *December* 17, 1862.

Major-General HALLECK:

General Grant telegraphs for six locomotives. Shall they be purchased?

               ROBT. ALLEN,
               Chief Quartermaster.

SAINT LOUIS, MO., *December* 17, 1862.

Major-General HALLECK:

The body of the Memphis fleet will leave Cairo to-night. Colonel Parsons is along and reports everything right. There will be sixty-two steamers in all.

               ROBT. ALLEN,
               Chief Quartermaster.

HDQRS. THIRTEENTH A. C., DEPT. OF THE TENN.,
Oxford, Miss., December 17, 1862.

Hon. C. P. WOLCOTT,
   Assistant Secretary of War, Washington, D. C.:

I have long since believed that in spite of all the vigilance that can be infused into post commanders, the specie regulations of the Treasury Department have been violated, and that mostly by Jews and other unprincipled traders. So well satisfied have I been of this that I instructed the commanding officer at Columbus to refuse all permits to Jews to come South, and I have frequently had them expelled from the department, but they come in with their carpet-sacks in spite of all that can be done to prevent it. The Jews seem to be a privileged class that can travel everywhere. They will land at any wood-yard on the river and make their way through the country. If not permitted to buy cotton themselves they will act as agents for some one else, who will be at a military post with a Treasury permit to receive cotton and pay for it in Treasury notes which the Jew will buy up at an agreed rate, paying gold.

There is but one way that I know of to reach this case; that is, for Government to buy all the cotton at a fixed rate and send it to Cairo, Saint Louis, or some other point to be sold. Then all traders (they are a curse to the army) might be expelled.

U. S. GRANT,
Major-General.

WASHINGTON, *December* 17, 1862.

Assistant Secretary Fox, *Navy Department:*

SIR: It is reported that Bragg's army is moving down the Tennessee River with the probable intention of occupying some point or points on the east bank in order to interrupt navigation. Generals Grant and Rosecrans urge the importance of sending some gunboats up that river as early as possible to prevent the enemy from effecting a lodgment and from crossing to the west side.

Very respectfully, your obedient servant,
H. W. HALLECK,
General-in-Chief.

NAVY DEPARTMENT,
December 17, 1862.

Maj. Gen. H. W. HALLECK,
Commander-in-Chief U. S. Army, Washington:

SIR: In a dispatch, dated the 12th instant, received by this Department from Acting Rear-Admiral D. D. Porter, commanding the Mississippi Squadron, occurs the following:

Five light-draught steamers have been refitted and sent up the Tennessee and Cumberland Rivers and have entirely put a stop to the guerrillas in that direction, and vessels go up and down those streams without molestation.

Admiral Porter has been instructed to send gunboats up the Tennessee River, in accordance with your request of this morning.

Very respectfully,
G. V. FOX,
Assistant Secretary of the Navy.

HEADQUARTERS DEPARTMENT OF THE TENNESSEE,
Oxford, Miss., December 17, 1862.

Brig. Gen. C. S. HAMILTON,
Commanding Left Wing:

You may instruct McArthur to move up with his division, taking position to the east of Yockna Station. By starting to-morrow at 12 m. he will be able to make the march by next day evening.

McArthur's division will furnish a guard for the station and stores that will be there to-morrow, and for that purpose, if practicab.e, two companies should be sent forward with the cars.

U. S. GRANT,
Major-General.

HEADQUARTERS DEPARTMENT OF THE TENNESSEE,
Oxford, Miss., December 17, 1862.

Maj. Gen. J. B. McPHERSON,
Commanding Right Wing:

I wish you as soon as practicable to make a reconnaissance to the front as far as Otuckalofa Creek with the view of making an advance to that point. I will not move my headquarters until Saturday, and then probably to Spring Dale.

U. S. GRANT,
Major-General.

JACKSON, *December* 17, 1862.

Major-General GRANT:

Couriers sent by Captain Carter, Tennessee cavalry, report force of several thousand rebel cavalry with battery 7 miles this side of Clifton, near McCorkle's, estimated 10,000. I have had out since yesterday p. m. 600 cavalry with a section, with orders to proceed to Clifton. I have heard nothing from them.

JER. C. SULLIVAN,
Brigadier-General.

NASHVILLE, *December* 17, 1862—2 a. m.

General SULLIVAN, *Jackson:*

Bragg was in Murfreesborough yesterday morning. Withers, Cheatham, and Breckinridge there yesterday. Review there by Jeff. Davis Saturday. Hardee at Triune, 12 miles west, on same day. Scouts from Waynesborough two days ago; no troops moving that way then. Davis said Middle Tennessee must, could, and should be held. Forrest's cavalry may and probably will cross and make a raid on you. They have too many cavalry for my little force. I don't think any more will be done.

Jeff. Davis left on Sunday for Mobile.

W. S. ROSECRANS,
Major-General.

HDQRS. RIGHT WING, THIRTEENTH ARMY CORPS,
Memphis, December 17, 1862.

General GORMAN, *Commanding, Helena, Ark.:*

DEAR GENERAL: Yours of the 15th December was handed me last night. General Blair went down yesterday and will explain what regiments are to follow him. I think that Generals Halleck and Curtis will see that an adequate force is provided for the expedition to Vicksburg, and also for Helena or Napoleon, whichever may be selected for the movement into Arkansas.

I have understood from some quarter that Davidson's forces are moving from the Iron Mountain road toward Little Rock.

Herron and Blunt having defeated Hindman put that army in confusion for some time and relieved Southwest Missouri of the presence of a threatening force.

The Admiral is aground at Island 23. The river is very low above and may delay our fleet of transports, none of which are yet in from above. I count upon nine boats at Helena, ten here, and expect sixty from above; of these I have ordered my chief quartermaster (Eddy) to send transports enough to Helena for 12,000 men. If more than that force is to go you can hold on to the boats that bring down Blair's brigade. Nothing is now wanting but transports; my troops here are all ready and impatient.

A boat from above just in reports a rebel force crossing the Tennessee from the east toward the west at Clifton, which is on the Tennessee, 25 miles below and north of Savannah. It may be that Bragg is going to throw his forces in this district to interpose between Grant and Columbus; but Rosecrans ought to be at his heels and Grant can easily shift his reserve to Memphis, and he ought to gain advantage by any such desperate move. I rather suspect it is designed to draw us back from our purpose of going to Vicksburg. I shall disregard these signs unless orders come from Grant or Halleck.

Yours, truly,

W. T. SHERMAN,
Major-General, Commanding.

GENERAL ORDERS, ⎫   HDQRS. 13TH A. C., DEPT. OF THE TENN.,
No. 11.   ⎬   *Holly Springs, December* 17, 1862.

The Jews, as a class violating every regulation of trade established by the Treasury Department and also department orders, are hereby expelled from the department within twenty-four hours from the receipt of this order.

Post commanders will see that all of this class of people be furnished passes and required to leave, and any one returning after such notification will be arrested and held in confinement until an opportunity occurs of sending them out as prisoners, unless furnished with permit from headquarters.

No passes will be given these people to visit headquarters for the purpose of making personal application for trade permits.

By order of Maj. Gen. U. S. Grant:

JNO. A. RAWLINS,
Assistant Adjutant-General.

WAR DEPARTMENT,
Washington, December 18, 1862.

Major-General CURTIS, *Saint Louis, Mo.:*

It is the President's wish that the Mississippi expedition be made as effective as possible by re-enforcements from Helena; but it is not intended to weaken your forces there, so as to endanger any necessary operation in Arkansas. If the movement into Arkansas cannot wait for the result of the other it must be made; but it is inexpedient to undertake too much at once, if it can be avoided. Please state how many troops you propose to retain in Arkansas.

H. W. HALLECK,
General-in-Chief.

HEADQUARTERS DEPARTMENT OF THE TENNESSEE,
Oxford, Miss., December 18, 1862.

Maj. Gen. JOHN A. McCLERNAND:

GENERAL: I have been directed this moment by telegraph from the General-in-Chief of the Army to divide the forces of this department into four army corps, one of which is to be commanded by yourself, and that to form a part of the expedition on Vicksburg.*

I have draughted the order and will forward it to you as soon as printed. The divisions now commanded by Brig. Gen. George W. Morgan and Brig. Gen. A. J. Smith will compose all of it that will accompany you on the expedition, and the divisions of Brig. Gen. F. Steele and Brig. Gen. M. L. Smith will accompany you, and will be commanded directly by Maj. Gen. W. T. Sherman, who will command the army corps of which they are a part. Written and verbal instructions have been given General Sherman, which will be turned over to you on your arrival at Memphis.

I hope you will find all the preliminary preparations completed on your arrival and the expedition ready to move.

I will co-operate with the river expedition from here, commanding this portion of the army in person.

Major-General Hurlbut will have command of the Third Army Corps, most of which is here with me. He will therefore be directed to report immediately to these headquarters for orders.

The instructions now with General Sherman provide for the garrison of Memphis, and forms part of the Second Army Corps.

The District of Columbus is attached to your command, but for the present will report direct to these headquarters and will receive orders direct also.

It is desirable that there should be no delay in starting. If unforeseen obstacles should be in your way, however, inform me of it by messenger to Columbus and by telegraph from there. Also send me a field return of your entire command—that is, of the river expedition—before starting.

U. S. GRANT,
Major-General.

OXFORD, MISS., *December* 18, 1862.

Brig. Gen. THOMAS A. DAVIES, *Columbus, Ky.:*

Please send the following dispatch to General Sherman, at Memphis:

WASHINGTON, *December* 18, 1862—10.30 a. m.

Maj. Gen. U. S. GRANT:

The troops in your department, including those from Curtis' command which join down-river expedition, will be divided into four army corps. It is the wish of the President that General McClernand's corps shall constitute a part of the river expedition, and that he shall have the immediate command, under your direction.

H. W. HALLECK,
General-in-Chief.

Inform General Sherman that his army corps will be composed of Steele's forces and General Morgan L. Smith's division, and General McClernand's of the divisions of Generals A. J. Smith and Morgan, and that General McClernand and he will descend the river.

U. S. GRANT,
Major-General.

---

* See McClernand to Sherman, January 4, 1863, p. 534, and Part I, p. 476.

HDQRS. RIGHT WING, THIRTEENTH ARMY CORPS,
Memphis, December 18, 1862.
Col. JOHN A. RAWLINS,
    Assistant Adjutant-General, Oxford, Miss.:

SIR: Capt. H. S. Fitch arrived last night with your dispatches of December 15 and 16. All right. I am now in full receipt of letters from Colonel Parsons, General Allen's agent for chartering boats, who assures me plenty of boats will be here to-day. I am promised the names of some sixty boats. I have some fifteen here now loading, and have at Helena about ten, and am momentarily looking for the whole fleet. As soon as they arrive I will be aboard and off for Helena.

Admiral Porter is just in from above, having been detained four days by low water, but his letters are all we could ask. I am also informed that there is a rise in the water above, so that the fleet of boats ought not to be longer delayed. Every possible preparation has been made, so that no moment should be lost. If the fleet comes to-day all shall be on board to-morrow, and I hope to be at Helena the 20th and at Milliken's Bend, where we shall first begin to act, by the 23d or 24th. Nothing is wanting but the boats, and I feel every assurance they will be here to-day. I was all ready, so that even the loss of one day must not be charged to me. Generals Gorman and Steele both write me most satisfactorily from Helena, and indeed we must admit they have fulfilled their parts handsomely. I give Steele full command of the division at Helena, which, by the addition of Blair's brigade, part of which (three regiments) have passed and two more reported near at hand, will reach near 13,000 men, so that I hope to have 33,000 men. Such a force operating at Vicksburg in concert with the gunboats will make something yield and prepare your way. You will have heard that our iron-clad gunboat Cairo was sunk in the Yazoo by the explosion of one of the infernal machines.

The weather is fine, and I repeat that I only await the fleet of gunboats to be off.

Yours, truly,

W. T. SHERMAN,
Major-General.

OXFORD, MISS., *December* 18, 1862.
Admiral PORTER, *Cairo, Ill.:*

I am informed there is now four feet of water in the Tennessee. Gunboats there would be of immense value.

Forrest and Napier are now on this side of the river with from 5,000 to 10,000 men and have got near to Jackson.

I hope my force will be able to drive to the river. I have been concentrating troops all day to meet them.

U. S. GRANT,
Major-General.

CAIRO, *December* 18, 1862.
Major-General GRANT:

Five light-draught gunboats left Ohio River for Tennessee River on 15th instant. They draw about 3 feet and have orders to go up with the rise. They are only musket-proof.

A. M. PENNOCK,
Fleet Captain and Commandant of Station.

OXFORD, MISS., *December* 18, 1862.

Brig. Gen. GRENVILLE M. DODGE, *Corinth, Miss.*:

General Sullivan is directed to collect forces and attack the enemy, who are now west of the Tennessee River. Send forces from your command either to hold Bethel and relieve that garrison to join him or send direct to Jackson.

U. S. GRANT,
Major-General.

OXFORD, MISS., *December* 18, 1862.

Brig. Gen. GRENVILLE M. DODGE, *Corinth, Miss.*:

If safe, leave your post to a reliable officer and take such forces as can be spared and with the troops at Jackson attack Forrest and drive him east of the Tennessee.

U. S. GRANT,
Major-General.

OXFORD, MISS., *December* 18, 1862.

Brig. Gen. GRENVILLE M. DODGE, *Corinth, Miss.*:

Move to-night with all the forces you can spare from Corinth to Jackson, if you can get there; if not, strike them in the flank or rear. Be governed by your own judgment when you get near them.

U. S. GRANT,
Major-General.

CORINTH, *December* 18, 1862.

General SULLIVAN:

I shall leave here myself at daylight, go by cars to Bethel and join my command at Purdy. Keep me well posted of movements, so that I can judge when to strike. What road did they come on? My troops have just left.

G. M. DODGE,
Brigadier-General.

HDQRS. UNITED STATES FORCES ON THE TUSCUMBIA,
Camp Davies, December 18, 1862.

Col. AUG. MERSY, *Commanding Expedition:*

COLONEL: Inclosed please find telegram from General Dodge. I presume it is requisite you should move the cavalry to-night, and, if possible, your whole force. All my cavalry is ordered and gone out from Corinth. Each order and movement denotes present emergency. Bragg is reported crossing the Tennessee River, near Clifton or Chalk Bluff, and may march either on Jackson or Corinth.

I am, colonel, very respectfully, your obedient servant,

P. E. BURKE,
Colonel Fourteenth Missouri Volunteers, Commanding.

[Inclosure.]

CORINTH, *December* 18, 1862—5 p. m.
Col. P. E. BURKE:

Send a messenger to Colonel Mersy and tell him to hurry back with his column and to push his cavalry on immediately. He will return on road east of railroad.

G. M. DODGE,
Brigadier-General.

OXFORD, MISS., *December* 18, 1862.
Brigadier-General LOWE, *Fort Henry, Tenn.*:

The enemy are reported crossing the Tennessee River at Wright's Island; 3,000 already across. Make a demonstration with all the force you can possibly spare to harass and prevent him crossing any more troops.

U. S. GRANT,
Major-General.

OXFORD, MISS., *December* 18, 1862.
Colonel LOWE, *Fort Henry, Tenn.*:

Forrest is now west of the Tennessee. Take 1,500 of your command and attack him. You can take them from Henry and Heiman and order troops from Donelson to take their places. This should be done at once. Troops are now on the way from Jackson to attack.

U. S. GRANT,
Major-General.

OXFORD, MISS., *December* 18, 1862.
Maj. Gen. J. B. McPHERSON,
      Commanding Right Wing:

All the provisions yet arrived have been left here. The chief commissary reported that the facilities at Yockna Station were not sufficient for unloading there, except to be immediately issued.

If you are about out of rations send your trains back here to draw five days, and move forward after they reach you.

Forrest and Napier have crossed the Tennessee River and are now near Jackson. I have directed such a concentration of troops that I think not many of them will get back to the east bank of the Tennessee. They will probably succeed, however, in cutting the road and wires so as to interrupt communication north for a day or two.

U. S. GRANT,
Major-General.

HDQRS. RIGHT WING, THIRTEENTH ARMY CORPS,
      Camp Yocknapatalfa, December 18, 1862.
Major-General GRANT,
      Commanding Department of the Tennessee:

GENERAL: Your dispatch received. I was down to Water Valley and examined the roads and ground in the vicinity of the Otuckalofa Creek day before yesterday with a view to a forward movement. The ground along the banks of this creek is well adapted for camping, being high and rolling, with plenty of good water.

I have inclosed a sketch showing the relative positions of my troops and the routes by which they can march to the positions designated. Colonel Leggett's brigade is now encamped on the south side of the Yockna, the advance being within 3 miles of Water Valley. Lee's and Mizner's cavalry are encamped near this creek. Lee's headquarters being about 1 mile west of Water Valley, and Mizner's a short distance east of that place, I can move forward with Logan's division to-morrow to the Otuckalofa, leaving Denver's and Lauman's divisions to come up the next day, or I can move them all forward to-morrow, in either case leaving a regiment temporarily to guard the bridges across the Yockna.

Since writing this your dispatch in relation to train loaded with provisions has just been handed me. The first train load better be left at the Yockna Station and the remainder sent forward to Spring Dale or Water Valley, if the whole of my command moves forward to-morrow and the day following.

Very respectfully, your obedient servant,
JAS. B. McPHERSON,
Major-General.

JACKSON, *December* 18, 1862—2 a. m.

Maj. Gen. U. S. GRANT:

The following was received from our cavalry scout sent out yesterday:

Captain O'Hara, who went out at daylight yesterday, reports that the enemy are crossing the Tennessee at Wright's Island in considerable force. At noon yesterday 3,000 infantry, 800 cavalry, and six pieces had crossed and were still crossing. O'Hara had 70 men; fell back to where I now am, at Buck River, 5 miles southeast of Lexington.

When first seen the enemy were 10 miles from the Tennessee. Their pickets are now within 6 miles of me. I have sent out two companies of Colonel Hawkins' to reconnoiter. I will keep you as well informed as possible. Intend to push on in the morning. I believe they are going on the Bolivar and Clifton road.

I have now 450 men. Our pickets are now in sight of the enemy's.
R. G. INGERSOLL,
Colonel Eleventh Illinois Cavalry.

JER. C. SULLIVAN,
Brigadier-General.

OXFORD, *December* 18, 1862.

General SULLIVAN:

Get the position of the troops that have crossed the Tennessee and collect your forces, all that can be spared from the railroad, and attack them.

You can take one regiment and the Tennessee cavalry from Bolivar and get one regiment from Davies and probably two from Dodge. Let me know your plans. Telegraph through General Davies to General Lowe at Fort Henry movements of the enemy.

U. S. GRANT,
Major-General.

JACKSON, *December* 18, 1862.

Major-General GRANT:

As far as I can learn the rebels are near Mifflin. My force here is so small, numbering only 1,300, that until the troops I have ordered in arrive I cannot move. General Brayman will be here this afternoon with 700 men and one battery. The Thirty-ninth Iowa will be here this evening. I have ordered from Union City and Trenton all the available force, say 700 men. I will attack the rebels in the morning if they do not first attack me. My preparations for defense are good. I can hold Jackson against all their force if it numbers 10,000, and meet and whip them if they are 5,000 strong.

JER. C. SULLIVAN,
Brigadier-General.

OXFORD, *December* 18, 1862.

General SULLIVAN:

Have you made preparations to get forces from Corinth ? Don't fail to get up a force and attack the enemy. Never wait to have them attack you.

U. S. GRANT,
Major-General.

JACKSON, *December* 18, 1862—5 p. m.

General GRANT:

General Dodge telegraphs there are no cars at Corinth. I have to send train from here, and at present we have no spare engine. Will send train as soon as possible.

Want of information from Colonel Ingersoll as to direction the enemy are marching keeps me still. I have sent out another party to find their position and will move to attack them at once. A rumor is here that Ingersoll's cavalry has been whipped and dispersed; know nothing about it.

JER. C. SULLIVAN,
Brigadier-General.

JACKSON, *December* 18, 1862.

Major-General GRANT:

The enemy have attacked my cavalry. They have been fighting all day between Mifflin and Lexington. I will hold this post till the last.

JER. C. SULLIVAN.

JACKSON, *December* 18, 1862.

General GRANT:

The enemy are within 4 miles of this place. My infantry regiments have checked their advance, which seems to be cavalry.

General Dodge is moving against their flank and I will attack in front to-morrow morning.

JER. C. SULLIVAN,
Brigadier-General.

GRANT'S HEADQUARTERS, *December* 18, 1862.

General SULLIVAN:

Colonel Lowe is instructed to move from Fort Heiman with 1,000 to 1,200 to get in rear of the enemy. Dodge will also be up with a force.

There are now five light-draught gunboats in Tennessee, so that if you get enemy on retreat and push them I expect to hear a good account from Jackson to-morrow.

U. S. GRANT,
Major-General.

HEADQUARTERS DISTRICT OF JACKSON,
Jackson, Tenn., December 18, 1862.

Instructions to Colonel Lawler, commanding Post of Jackson, Tenn.

Place one section of artillery and 50 men at Mrs. Hays' house, near depot; 100 men in brick depot; 50 men in Tomlin's house; 50 men in G. N. Harris' house.

The officers in command of these parties will see that their men have 100 rounds of ammunition each on their persons, with an additional 100 rounds in boxes in the houses to be occupied; also four gallons of water to each man, with three days' rations of, at least, coffee and bread. Three crow-bars will be provided for each house.

The negroes in town will at daylight be pressed into the service, and be employed in carrying stores within the inner line. They will also be prepared, under charge of a competent officer, to level the fences from Tomlin's house out. There will be in the court-house at least four gallons of water per man; also water with buckets in cupola of court-house. The windows and doors in front will be removed; the rear blockaded and loop-holed. Officers' wives and loyal ladies in the city will be prepared to leave town at a moment's notice. They will be furnished transportation to Trenton, Tenn. Major Smith will see that these orders are executed.

By order of Brig. Gen. Jer. C. Sullivan:

A. S. BUCHANAN,
Acting Assistant Adjutant-General.

CORINTH, MISS., *December* 18, 1862.

General SULLIVAN:

One of my men arrived just now. Left Shelbyville Friday; Columbia Saturday; went to Tuscumbia; could not get through and returned to Waynesborough; left there yesterday at 2 o'clock.

Forrest, with 2,000 to 2,500 cavalry and five pieces of artillery, left Columbia Saturday, crossed the Tennessee at Clifton, or near there, Tuesday; Napier, with from 2,000 to 3,000 and four pieces of artillery, crossing at Carrollsville Monday to join Forrest. They reported that they were to strike Jackson first and Bethel next, the intention being to stop supplies to our army. No infantry had left Shelbyville west, but there was a movement of all forces taking place north. Some said they were to go west, but this could not be ascertained. No infantry accompanied Forrest to Columbia. The scout that brings this has never yet failed, and I believe his statement.   He saw Forrest's cavalry and artillery, but did not see Napier's command, but saw men from Carrollsville who did see it.

G. M. DODGE,
Brigadier-General.

———

CORINTH, MISS., *December* 18, 1862.

General SULLIVAN:

I move.   At what time will you move?   Where is the enemy?   A force is reported at Chalk Bluff.   Can you order a scout out from Bethel?   General Grant has ordered me to move and in conjunction with you to attack Forrest.

G. M. DODGE,
Brigadier-General.

———

BETHEL, *December* 18, 1862.

General SULLIVAN:

Colonel Hurst, just from that locality, reports rebels on White Oak Creek, 11 miles west of Clifton, and between the road leading from Clifton to Jackson and this place.   He don't think the force large.

WM. R. MORRISON,
Colonel, Commanding Post.

———

CORINTH, *December* 18, 1862.

General SULLIVAN:

I move immediately with my force.

Order Colonel Morrison to join me with one regiment or more, as can be spared.

G. M. DODGE,
Brigadier-General.

———

TRENTON, TENN., *December* 18, 1862.

General SULLIVAN:

Six men of Colonel Hawkins' Second West Tennessee Cavalry, just arrived from Lexington, report that they, with cavalry from Jackson, met the enemy at daybreak this morning near Lexington; that our troops, after a sharp fight, were repulsed and two pieces of artillery taken from us.

JACOB FRY,
Colonel, Commanding Post.

———

GENERAL ORDERS, ⎰ WAR DEPARTMENT, ADJT. GEN.'S OFFICE,
      No. 210.   ⎱   *Washington, December* 18, 1862.

By the direction of the President the troops in the Department of the Tennessee and those of the Department of the Missouri operating on the Mississippi River will be divided into four army corps, to be numbered the Thirteenth, Fifteenth, Sixteenth, and Seventeenth.

Maj. Gen. J. A. McClernand is assigned to the command of the Thirteenth Army Corps;

Maj. Gen. W. T. Sherman to the command of the Fifteenth Army Corps;

Maj. Gen. S. A. Hurlbut to the command of the Sixteenth Army Corps; and

Maj. Gen. J. B. McPherson to the command of the Seventeenth Army Corps.

By order of the Secretary of War:

E. D. TOWNSEND,
Assistant Adjutant-General.

SPECIAL FIELD ORDERS, }   HDQRS. 13TH A. C., DEPT. OF TENN.,
No. 27.   }   *Oxford, Miss., December* 18, 1862.

*   *   *   *   *   *   *

VI. Foraging for any troops of an organized division will be conducted and regulated under the authority of the division commanders. Each division commander will select a suitable officer, who will report as assistant to the division commissary, whose duty will be to use all exertions to collect subsistence from the surrounding country, wherever the troops may be, and for running any corn-mills that may be in the vicinity of his division.

By order of Maj. Gen. U. S. Grant:

JNO. A. RAWLINS,
Assistant Adjutant-General.

WAR DEPARTMENT,
Washington, December 19, 1862—3 p. m.
General ROBERT ALLEN, *Saint Louis, Mo.:*

Give General Grant the locomotives he requires.

H. W. HALLECK,
General-in-Chief.

SAINT LOUIS, MO., *December* 19, 1862—1 p. m.
(Received 7 p. m.)
Maj. Gen. H. W. HALLECK, *General-in-Chief:*

In answer to yours of yesterday I proposed to furnish all General Sherman calls for from Helena—12,000—leaving about 13,000 to operate in Arkansas. This last force I propose to move cautiously till the down-river move is accomplished. Blunt's force in Arkansas—about 18,000—is still at north base of Boston Mountains, scouts extending near to Arkansas River. I wish to draw these forces toward each other as fast as circumstances will permit. A move from Helena will prevent Holmes and Hindman massing forces against Blunt if nothing more, and it can go cautiously, awaiting the move and return of down-river force. Will this plan suit you?

SAML. R. CURTIS,
Major-General.

HEADQUARTERS DEPARTMENT OF THE MISSOURI,
Saint Louis, December 19, 1862.
Maj. Gen. WILLIAM T. SHERMAN:

GENERAL: I get orders and requests from everybody in relation to a down-river move and try to accommodate all. Your dispatch of the

13th was so long coming I send this reply by my chief of staff, Colonel Chipman, who goes to Helena to aid in organizing forces to accommodate demands. You speak of infantry only. I direct the arrangement of troops to sail as far as I can. Would like to be along. Have been in the advance, and do not think it just right to stand on the bank and present arms to a galley movement. But I am no grumbler. I despise fault-finding, bickering, whining affairs, and stand ready to lead or follow or fall back, just as circumstances seem to require or commanders arrange. I shall co-operate cordially with any one, you especially, having confidence in your zeal and fidelity.

I am detaining a boat to write this.

I am, general, your friend and fellow-soldier,

SAML. R. CURTIS,
Major-General.

[DECEMBER 19, 1862.—For Curtis to Gorman, in reference to Sherman's expedition, see Series I, Vol. XXII.]

HDQRS. THIRTEENTH A. C., DEPT. OF THE TENN.,
Oxford, Miss., December 19, 1862.

Col. G. G. PRIDE,
Superintendent Military Railroads east from Vicksburg :

COLONEL: You will proceed to Saint Louis and Chicago, if you find it necessary, and procure such material, machinery, tools, teams, and wagons as you think are required for a rapid construction and for running the railroad east from Vicksburg. You will also engage such employés as you may deem proper, and fix the rate of wages for same. All materials and men so procured will be forwarded at once to Cairo and be ready to be shipped south at short notice. Lieut. Col. C. A. Reynolds, chief quartermaster of this department, will detail a quartermaster to report to you for this duty, and will himself direct the shipping of the same, and all steamboats and barges necessary for shipment will be moved south under his direction. The chief quartermaster and chief commissary at Saint Louis are requested to furnish such supplies as may be required by you for this expedition.

You will report as frequently as possible to these headquarters.

U. S. GRANT,
Major-General.

GENERAL ORDERS, }   HDQRS. RIGHT WING, 13TH ARMY CORPS,
No. 9.   }   *Memphis, December* 19, 1862.

The First, Second, and Third Divisions of the right wing will em bark to-morrow, Saturday, December 20, according to previous notice, and in the manner before ordered, and proceed with all dispatch by divisions below Helena and lay to shore on the Mississippi side, the head of the column at Friar's Point and the other divisions well closed up, there to await further orders.

The quartermaster, Captain Eddy, will provide the necessary transportation and dispose the boats according to previous orders.

By order of Maj. Gen. W. T. Sherman:

J. H. HAMMOND,
Assistant Adjutant-General.

GENERAL ORDERS, }   HDQRS. RIGHT WING, 13TH ARMY CORPS,
    No. 10.   }   *Memphis, December* 19, 1862.

The following named officers are announced as the staff of Maj. Gen. W. T. Sherman:

Maj. J. H. Hammond, assistant adjutant-general and chief of staff.
Maj. Ezra Taylor, chief of artillery.
Maj. W. D. Sanger, acting inspector-general, aide-de-camp.
Maj. Charles McMillan, medical director.
Capt. John T. Taylor, aide-de-camp.
Capt. James C. McCoy, aide-de-camp.
Capt. Lewis M. Dayton, aide-de-camp.
Capt. J. Condit Smith, chief quartermaster.
Capt. Charles A. Morton, chief commissary of subsistence.
Capt. W. L. B. Jenney, Engineer Corps.
Capt. O. H. Howard, Signal Corps.
Capt. Julius Pitzman, Topographical Engineers.
Lieut. Kilian Frick, Topographical Engineers.
Headquarters for the present are on board the Forest Queen.
By order of Maj. Gen. W. T. Sherman:

J. H. HAMMOND,
Assistant Adjutant-General.

OXFORD, MISS., *December* 19, 1862.

Brig. Gen. C. S. HAMILTON,
    Commanding Left Wing:

You will detach two brigades from your command, one from Quinby's and one from Ross' division, to proceed to-morrow to Pontotoc, Miss., taking with them five days' rations. They will return to their present camp by the time their rations are out.

Each brigade will take with it one battery of artillery and one caisson to each battery. This will enable them to attach an additional pair of horses to each team. Brigadier-General Ross is assigned to the command of the whole.

Colonel Mizner has been directed to send a regiment of cavalry with the expedition.

Arriving at Pontotoc, the officer in command will cause reconnaissance to be made as far to the south and east as practicable, and should any farther advance be necessary to rescue Colonel Dickey or drive back an inferior force of the enemy it will be made.

It is desirable that on this march there should be no straggling from the ranks, and all pillaging should be prevented.

By order of Maj. Gen. U. S. Grant:

JNO. A. RAWLINS,
Assistant Adjutant-General.

HEADQUARTERS DEPARTMENT OF THE TENNESSEE,
Oxford, Miss., December 19, 1862.

Maj. Gen. J. B. MCPHERSON,
    Commanding Right Wing, &c.:

There will be no farther advance of our forces until further directions. The enemy under Forrest have crossed the Tennessee below Clifton and are now near to Jackson. Communication is cut off, so that I cannot hear from there.

Sullivan reports the strength of the enemy at from 5,000 to 10,000 and still crossing. Dodge, however, had a scout among them before they commenced crossing, who estimates their force at about 5,000.

Ingersoll's cavalry watched their movements for the last 25 miles, and yesterday had an engagement with them at Lexington, resulting in a defeat for us, Colonel Ingersoll and two pieces of artillery falling into the hands of the enemy. Last night Sullivan brought them to a halt about 6 miles from Jackson.

I have re-enforced Sullivan to the full extent of the capacity of the road to carry troops, partly from Columbus, partly from Corinth, one brigade from here, and by concentrating of the forces of the District of Jackson. Lowe is also moving from Heiman. I think the enemy must be annihilated, but it may trouble and possibly lead to the necessity of sending further forces from here.

A dispatch from General Halleck, received late last night, directs me to divide my forces in o four army corps, one of which is to be commanded by Major-General McClernand, he to have the chief command of the Vicksburg expedition, but under my direction. I was in hopes the expedition would be off by this time, and it may be that they are about starting.

We must be ready for any move. I think, however, it will not be a retrograde one.

U. S. GRANT,
Major-General.

OXFORD, MISS., *December* 19, 1862.

Maj. Gen. J. B. McPHERSON, *Water Valley:*

The report of the surgeon is untrue. Order his arrest for being an alarmist. The following dispatch just received from General Sullivan says:

I will move and attack in front this afternoon. The enemy are within 3 miles of this place. They have burned the bridges on the Corinth and Bolivar roads. I have force enough to drive what force they have here to the river. The river is falling very rapidly.

General Dodge moved last night from Corinth with a force of at least 2,000, and is probably within striking distance of their flank or rear.

Colonel Lowe was ordered to move with all his avaliable force against the enemy 2 o'clock yesterday afternoon from Fort Henry. The order reached him promptly. He is perhaps near them. One brigade (Colonel Fuller's) was sent from here last night, and it is to be hoped we will not only be able to whip the enemy but will prevent his recrossing the Tennessee.

By order of Maj. Gen. U. S. Grant:

JNO. A. RAWLINS,
Assistant Adjutant-General.

OXFORD, MISS., *December* 19, 1862.

Brig. Gen. GRENVILLE M. DODGE, *Corinth, Miss.:*

Jackson is now moving north with a cavalry force of about 3,000. He will probably be near the Tallahatchie to-night. I will have him followed with cavalry. Look out for him.

U. S. GRANT,
Major-General.

WATER VALLEY, *December* 19, 1862.

Major-General GRANT:

Scouts which returned last night bring information that a heavy cavalry force passed from Grenada to Graysport and toward Pontotoc on Tuesday morning, and it was rumored that it was to cut us off. News of Colonel Dickey's move had probably reached them.

The scout returning from Banner and Paris was fired on from ambush 9 miles east of here. One man was killed and Lieutenant McEntee and 2 men wounded, the lieutenant mortally, I fear. Captain Nugent, of another scout, brought in 9 prisoners and 12 horses. Lieutenant Corbyn and 1 man of his command were wounded. Jeff. Davis was at Grenada Sunday, and General J. E. Johnston is also said to be there.

There is a rumor of a heavy force at Pontotoc, spoken of as a portion of Bragg's army. Do you hear from Colonel Dickey? I am scouting well out and would like to be advised of any information you have, to act and plan accordingly.

J. K. MIZNER,
Colonel, Commanding Cavalry.

OXFORD, MISS., *December* 19, 1862.

Colonel MIZNER, *Water Valley, Miss.:*

I have no information from Colonel Dickey. The forces that went from Corinth to co-operate have returned to their post, having captured quite a number of prisoners.

I will send two brigades to Pontotoc, taking with them five days' rations. I want you to send at least one regiment of cavalry with the expedition, with instructions to reconnoiter as far to the east and south as practicable.

U. S. GRANT,
Major-General.

WATER VALLEY, *December* 19, 1862.

Major-General GRANT:

A scout employed by General Logan just in reports a column of four regiments of cavalry moving up the Pontotoc road this a. m. northeast; also that heavy artillery, convalescents, and commissary stores are being put south, and that the force at Grenada is preparing to fall back to Jackson; that the cavalry is sent out to cover this movement. I have scouts out south and southeast, and may have more news soon.

J. K. MIZNER,
Colonel, Commanding Cavalry Division.

HDQRS. RIGHT WING, THIRTEENTH ARMY CORPS,
Camp Yocknapatalfa, December 19, 1862.

Major-General GRANT,
Commanding Thirteenth Army Corps:

GENERAL: I inclose you copy of letter from Colonel Mizner, Water Valley.

In answer to Colonel Mizner's request I have sent Colonel Leggett's brigade of infantry to Water Valley, and directed Colonel Grierson to report to Mizner with his cavalry. I think the rebel cavalry he speaks of are after Colonel Dickey, and have suggested that it would be a good plan to assemble all his cavalry and go to Dickey's relief by pushing out after the rebels toward ———.

I have ordered another brigade across the Yocknapatalfa to take the place of Leggett's when he moves forward.

Very respectfully, your obedient servant,

JAS. B. McPHERSON,
Major-General.

[Inclosure.]

WATER VALLEY, *December* 19, 1862.

Major-General McPHERSON :

GENERAL : I inclose dispatches just received for you.

If you can possibly inform me where our different commands are I would be obliged to you. I have telegraphed to headquarters, but can obtain nothing. I have been there three days and have heard nothing except from the front. I do not know where to look for assistance should I require any.

A heavy column of cavalry left Grenada on Tuesday morning last, going toward Graysport to Pontotoc. A portion of Bragg's command is expected at Pontotoc. A scout just in reports a column of four regiments of cavalry moving up from Grenada on Pontotoc road from Coffeeville; that this move is to cover a retreat from Grenada. The heavy artillery, commissary stores, and convalescents, the scout says, are being moved to Jackson and the force at Grenada will fall back to Jackson. The column of cavalry coming up may turn toward this place. I have scouts out to watch them.

My cavalry force here is not large, and much of it being on duty as guards, pickets, and scouting I think an infantry support should be sent to this place to make my whole force available.

I have telegraphed all the news I have to General Grant, and will, I think, apply to him for a regiment or two of infantry as a sort of grand guard at this place.

Please let me hear from you.

Very respectfully, your obedient servant,

J. K. MIZNER,
Colonel, Commanding Cavalry.

P. S.—Is the Sixth Illinois Cavalry with you, and cannot they be ordered to this point? If they are and have no orders, send them down, as they belong to my brigade.

J. K. M.

———

WATER VALLEY, *December* 19, 1862.

Major-General GRANT:

Having so much of my cavalry force on guard, picket, and scouting I think it would be well to have some infantry sent here as a sort of grand guard and in order to make the whole cavalry force available should any of the heavy columns of rebel cavalry reported to be in motion make an attack here.

J. K. MIZNER,
Colonel, Commanding Cavalry.

OXFORD, MISS., *December* 19, 1862.

Colonel MIZNER, *Water Valley:*

I want you to take all of the available cavalry, including the Sixth Illinois, but excluding that just returned with Colonel Dickey, and take the most direct route to Rocky Ford. When you get on Jackson's trail follow him until he is caught or dispersed. Jackson must be prevented from getting to the railroad in our rear if possible. I have ordered Colonel Grierson to meet you with his command.

U. S. GRANT,
Major-General.

WATER VALLEY, *December* 19, 1862.

Major-General GRANT:

The Seventh Kansas, Fourth Illinois, and Third Michigan Cavalry Regiments are here; much of it is out scouting, &c. Probably a force of 1,200 in all could go. The Sixth Illinois, I have just learned, is with General Denver. Why it has not reported to me I do not know. If Jackson passed Pontotoc yesterday he is not less than 70 miles from here now. It is 50 miles from here to Pontotoc. Jackson's force that left Grenada was reported to be 7,000; probably, however, not half that number, or perhaps seven regiments Nearly the whole of the Third Michigan Cavalry is out, but I will collect all I can to-night if you desire me to do so.

J. K. MIZNER,
Commanding.

OXFORD, MISS., *December* 19, 1862.

Colonel MIZNER, *Water Valley:*

Send orders to the Sixth Illinois Cavalry to report to you at once. Collect all the forces possible and proceed without delay as per order.

U. S. GRANT,
Major-General.

OXFORD, MISS., *December* 19, 1862.

Col. R. C. MURPHY, *Holly Springs, Miss.:*

Jackson is moving north with a large force of cavalry; will probably be at Rocky Ford to-night. Send out all the cavalry you can to watch their movements. I am sending cavalry from the front to follow Jackson. Let the Second join them in the pursuit.

U. S. GRANT,
Major-General.

OXFORD, MISS., *December* 19, 1862.

Commanding Officers at Holly Springs, Davis' Mill, Grand Junction, La Grange, and Bolivar:

Jackson's cavalry has gone north with the intention, probably, of striking the railroad north of this place and cutting off our communication. Keep a sharp lookout and defend the road, if attacked, at all hazards. A heavy cavalry force will be in pursuit of him from here.

U. S. GRANT,
Major-General.

HOLLY SPRINGS, MISS., *December* 19, 1862.

General GRANT:

Have ordered out all my cavalry as you order. Where is Rocky Ford you speak of? I found no map here and have none but what I have made of surrounding country that are reliable. Shall have cavalry on the New Albany and Pontotoc road. Will that be the course?

R. C. MURPHY.

OXFORD, MISS., *December* 19, 1862.

Col. R. C. MURPHY, *Holly Springs, Miss.:*

Rocky Ford is on the Tallahatchie, about 20 miles above Abbeville, on railroad crossing. In the morning will be early enough for your cavalry to start, and then go due east from Holly Springs to watch the enemy. They must be on their guard not to be caught, and, if they can, retard the movements of Jackson until Mizner can get up.

U. S. GRANT,
Major-General.

BOLIVAR, *December* 19, 1862.

Major-General GRANT:

Two hundred and twenty-seven infantry, 24 cavalry, two 6-pounder James rifled cannon, and 29 artillerymen; this is all within 2 miles of these headquarters.

Your dispatch to Brigadier-General Dodge started all right.

W. L. BARNUM,
Acting Assistant Adjutant-General.

BOLIVAR, *December* 19, 1862.

Brigadier-General SULLIVAN:

The following just received from Oxford to Colonel Sprague:

Disembark your command at Bolivar and make such disposition of them as best to defend our line of communication to this place.
By order of Maj. Gen. U. S. Grant:

JNO. A. RAWLINS,
Assistant Adjutant-General.

W. L. BARNUM,
Acting Assistant Adjutant-General.

FORT HENRY, *December* 19, 1862.

General SULLIVAN:

Have started all my cavalry force up on west side of Tennessee. Will leave with infantry and artillery on boats in morning. Will try to get as high as Carrollsville. You are mistaken as to Napier's force; he has about 700 men and two pieces of artillery. Have you any news? Answer

W. W. LOWE,
Colonel, Commanding.

FORT HENRY, *December* 19, 1862.

General SULLIVAN:

The cavalry started yesterday morning up the west side of the Tennessee River. I leave this morning with the infantry and artillery on boats. Will try to get in the enemy's rear and communicate with your forces. Will go as far up the river as I think necessary.

W. W. LOWE,
Colonel, Commanding.

NASHVILLE *December* 19, 1862.

Brigadier-General SULLIVAN:

Your telegram received. General Rosecrans advises that you mount your infantry and chase Forrest out of the country.

J. P. GARESCHÉ,
Aide-de-Camp.

WAR DEPARTMENT,
Washington, December 20, 1862.

Major-General CURTIS, *Saint Louis, Mo.*:

You can use the forces at Helena as you propose. The troops which join the Mississippi expedition will be temporarily under the general direction of General Grant.

H. W. HALLECK.

MEMPHIS, *December* 20, 1862—8 p. m.

GENERAL: We commenced loading this morning, and the first division (General M. L. Smith's), ten boats, are just leaving port; the second (General Morgan's), thirteen boats, will follow in an hour, and the third (General A. J. Smith's), thirteen boats, will leave early in the morning. This last division is delayed by having a very bad place to load. General Gorman left to-day for Helena. We all rendezvous early to-morrow at Helena, when General Steele's division joins us with twelve or fifteen boats. I think we have nearly if not quite fuel enough to carry us to Vicksburg, and 66,000 bushels of coal is on the way from Cairo. We are also supplied with several hundred axes to use in an emergency. I think we have done well to load in a single day, especially as several of our boats only arrived during the day. Everything has gone well so far. We are two days behind the day fixed for starting, but General Grant's telegraph was two days reaching Colonel Allen, and we have been at least two days detained by extreme scarcity of fuel. I shall go down with the fleet, so as to discharge as many boats as possible, as we have left none to do our transportation from Saint Louis. General Sherman is a trump, and makes things move. I like his business mode of doing things, his promptness and decision.

Very respectfully,

L. B. PARSONS,
Colonel and Aide-de-Camp.

COLUMBUS, Ky., *December* 20, 1862.

Major-General HALLECK, *General-in-Chief*:

Communication with General Grant has been stopped by the cutting of the line, both railroad and telegraph, for the last two days. Forrest's cavalry crossed the Tennessee River at Clifton, and threatened Jackson, Tenn,, with a considerable force. Troops were withdrawn from Trenton, Kenton, and Union City to Jackson. The rebels made a feint on Jackson yesterday and took Trenton. This p. m. there were only 50 men left at Union City, and two companies between here and there. As the rebels are now marching on Kenton it will probably fall by to-morrow. I shall withdraw the small force at Union City and this side to Columbus to-night, not having troops enough here to warrant my sending re-enforcements. I shall hold Columbus. Have you any orders to communicate to General Grant or myself? We have information that Holly Springs, Miss., fell into the hands of the enemy yesterday. No reliable couriers.

THOS. A. DAVIES,
Brigadier-General.

———

OXFORD, MISS., *December* 20, 1862.
Col. C. C. MARSH, *Waterford, Miss.:*

Two regiments will be at Abbeville in one hour on the cars. If you require them, telegraph to them and they will go up at daylight. Mizner will join you to-night with 2,000 cavalry. I want those fellows caught, if possible, and any support you can give toward it with your infantry and artillery I want you to do it.

U. S. GRANT,
Major-General.

———

WATERFORD, *December* 20, 1862.
Maj. Gen. U. S. GRANT:

Enemy still at Holly Springs. Scout just in from their pickets. They are burning ammunition and stores. I start at daylight for Springs. Think I have all the force I need. Train can come here safely.

C. C. MARSH,
Colonel, Commanding District.

———

WATERFORD, *December* 20, 1862.
Major-General GRANT:

Colonel Buckland with two regiments close here. I left one of his regiments at the river. If you have one more to spare I can use it to advantage.

Shall be in Holly Springs or be whipped to-morrow morning.

C. C. MARSH,
Colonel, Commanding.

———

HEADQUARTERS THIRTEENTH ARMY CORPS,
Oxford, Miss., December 20, 1862—9 p. m.
Colonel HATCH,
Commanding Second Brigade, Cavalry Division:

You will at once break all the cavalry camps in the front and send the trains, camp and garrison equipage, and ambulances to this place. You will then take all the effective cavalry force south of the Yocknapatalfa River and make a demonstration as far toward Grenada as you can go without serious resistance and thence return to this place, destroying thoroughly on your return all bridges on railroad and wagon roads and all mills on the line of your march.

By order of Maj. Gen. U. S. Grant:

JNO. A. RAWLINS,
Assistant Adjutant-General.

ABBEVILLE, MISS., *December* 20, 1862.

Major-General GRANT:

Colonel Marsh is at Waterford. I could not overtake him, and am encamped near Colonel Buckland, at the Tallahatchie. I learn from the surgeon of Bissell's Engineer Regiment, who left Holly Springs at 11 a. m. to-day, that every man was taken, supplies of all kinds burned; also 3 locomotives and 40 cars. The rebel cavalry number 4,000. Jackson and Armstrong are with Van Dorn.

The doctor was a prisoner. The town was taken a little after daylight. It was a surprise; not above 40 shots were fired. The rebels took citizens, sutlers, and everybody. They are paroling them. They destroyed everything they could not carry away.

J. K. MIZNER,
Colonel, Commanding Cavalry.

OXFORD, MISS., *December* 20, 1862.

Colonel MIZNER, *Abbeville, Miss.:*

Go forward and join Colonel Marsh to-night as you were instructed. Don't allow him to be cut up by piece-meal.

U. S. GRANT,
Major-General.

OXFORD, MISS., *December* 20, 1862.

Col. C. C. MARSH, *Waterford, Miss.:*

Colonel Mizner was ordered to join you to-night. He is camped at the Tallahatchie. Has been ordered again to proceed to-night and join you. If in the morning he shows any reluctance in the pursuit, arrest him and turn over the command to next in rank.

U. S. GRANT,
Major-General.

HEADQUARTERS DISTRICT OF THE TALLAHATCHIE,
North side of River, December 20, 1862.

Maj. Gen. U. S. GRANT:

Lieutenant Carter informs me that the enemy are in possession of Holly Springs and Waterford; that Jackson and Forrest are united. They have some artillery. I think it prudent to return the train from here. Their advance has been within 2 miles of here this morning. I have formed line of battle, thrown out skirmishers, and will feel my way cautiously.

If you think necessary to send me re-enforcements and some cavalry do so by train.

Hastily,

C. C. MARSH,
Colonel, Twentieth Illinois Infantry, Comdg. District.

HOLLY SPRINGS, *December* 20, 1862.

Colonel RAWLINS:

Contraband just in reports Van Dorn only 14 miles from here with 5,000 cavalry, intending to destroy stores here, and then dash on Grand Junction. He is on the Ripley [road] and expected to reach here by daylight. Have ordered out my cavalry, but my force is only a handful.

R. C. MURPHY.

HOLLY SPRINGS, *December* 20, 1862.

Colonel RAWLINS:

Have ordered out my cavalry to the east. Have sent some trains on to bring up my troops on the north as far as Coldwater and the south as far as the tank. I have now here, exclusive of cavalry, less than 500 men. Van Dorn was informed of this fact by paroled prisoners on yesterday.

R. C. MURPHY.

BOLIVAR, TENN., *December* 20, 1862—1 a. m.

Brigadier-General SULLIVAN:

Lieutenant-Colonel Breckenridge, First West Tennessee Cavalry, from White Oak Ridge, Hardin County, sends courier that rebels under General Morgan are to join cavalry force at Trenton; are fortifying at Kelly's old road track, 8 miles from Clifton. Have considerable artillery and reserve at Clifton.

W. L. BARNUM,
Acting Assistant Adjutant-General.

TRENTON, *December* 20, 1862.

General SULLIVAN:

A negro just in reports 700 or 800 Confederate cavalry at Spring Creek last night. This position commands roads leading to Huntingdon, Trenton, and Jackson.

ISAAC R. HAWKINS,
Colonel, Second West Tennessee Cavalry.

LA GRANGE, *December* 20, 1862.

General SULLIVAN:

I am informed that a large force under Jackson and Van Dorn that attacked Holly Springs last night was at Coldwater this afternoon. Heavy cannonading has been distinctly heard. They evidently intend to strike this point or Grand Junction. We have but few troops here. Will you not re-enforce us to-night? We shall hold as long as possible.

J. RICHMOND,
Colonel, Commanding Post.

BOLIVAR, *December* 20, 1862.

J. C. SULLIVAN, *Brigadier-General:*

Holly Springs is reported in possession of the enemy, and heavy firing is reported as having been heard at Bethel. Can you re-enforce me?

JOHN W. SPRAGUE,
Colonel, Commanding.

HEADQUARTERS THIRTEENTH ARMY CORPS,
December 20, 1862.

Brigadier-General DENVER,
    Commanding First Division:

GENERAL: I am apprehensive that the cavalry dash into Holly Springs has been a pretty serious affair for us, though I have not heard anything definite as yet. I have not learned what route the rebels took after leaving Holly Springs, or in fact whether they have left that place, though quite a large force has been sent that way. I think you had better destroy the bridge (McFarland's) about 5 miles to the west of your position, as we may thus succeed in cutting off the rebels' retreat if they should attempt to return by a route to the west of us. Do not send out any forage trains to the west or northwest until we know what route the enemy has taken. Keep scouts well out to the right and rear of your position as well as in front. We must not allow ourselves to be caught napping.

Call a board of survey on Major Prophet's cotton, to examine and report upon all the facts in the case which can be brought to bear, and will constitute a claim to be settled after the war.

The cotton marked "C. S. A." which you have seized upon you can send to Oxford or the Yockna Station, whichever point you send your wagons to first.

An order will be sent to your command putting your troops on three-quarter rations. I shall do the same for the whole of my command, until we ascertain the extent of the damage.

As soon as I know what direction the rebels have gone I will notify you.

Very respectfully, your obedient servant,
JAS. B. McPHERSON,
Major-General.

OXFORD, MISS., *December* 20, 1862.

Maj. Gen. J. B. McPHERSON,
    Commanding Right Wing:

Fall back with your entire command to the north side of the Tallahatchie, the troops retiring by the same route they advanced on.

I will instruct the cavalry to advance toward Grenada to keep up the idea of an advance as much as possible. Keep your transportation as well to the front as much as possible and instruct your commissaries to collect all the cattle fit for beef they can and corn-meal from the mills. Destroy all the mills within reach of you and the bridges after you are done using them.

U. S. GRANT,
Major-General.

HDQRS. RIGHT WING, THIRTEENTH ARMY CORPS,
December 20, 1862.

Maj. Gen. U. S. GRANT,
    Commanding Thirteenth Army Corps:

GENERAL: I am just in receipt of your dispatch. Will order Leggett's brigade back to this point this afternoon, and will move for the north bank of the Tallahatchie with my whole command to-morrow evening at 6 o'clock. I am anxious to know something about the cavalry, as a portion of their train is at Water Valley, and if I destroy the bridges across the Yocknapatalfa which I have had built and repaired they cannot well get back. I do not wish to have a bridge left standing, and therefore desire to have an understanding with the officer in command of the cavalry as to what bridge or bridges I am to leave for him to cross on and then destroy.

I am, sir, very respectfully, your obedient servant,

JAS. B. McPHERSON,
Major-General.

HDQRS. RIGHT WING, THIRTEENTH ARMY CORPS,
Camp, Yocknapatalfa, December 20, 1862.

Major-General GRANT,
Commanding Thirteenth Army Corps:

GENERAL: General Logan's division will move to the position occupied by General McArthur's, near the Yockna Station, at 6 o'clock to-morrow morning.

I send you extract of a letter from Colonel Leggett,* giving some information brought in by a scout from his command whom we sent out. If this information is correct, and it seems to be confirmed, at least partially, from other sources, I am decidedly of the opinion that the rebels are concentrating their forces at Jackson and Vicksburg, with a view of throwing them all in Vicksburg, if necessary, and that our policy is to have as many or more men at that point than they can bring to bear.

In view of the fact that the railroad from Grenada to Memphis is so seriously damaged that it will take some weeks to open it, and that with our present long line of communication interrupted and liable to be so again when reopened we cannot well go beyond Grenada and form a junction with the forces moving down the river, I think it best to fall back to the north side of the Tallahatchie, hold that line, and then send as many as two divisions to Memphis, to be added to the forces collecting for the Vicksburg expedition; open the railroad from Memphis to Grand Junction, and establish an easy and rapid communication, which I think could be protected with our strong cavalry force and a body of infantry and artillery on the Tallahatchie, Holly Springs, Hernando, &c.

I have merely suggested these remarks in consequence of the note at the bottom of your letter; and I will also add that in consequence of orders from Washington placing General McClernand in charge of the expedition under you I would, if in your place, proceed to Memphis and take command of it myself. It is the great feature of the campaign, and its execution rightfully belongs to you.

In case you go I would like to accompany you with two divisions, Lauman's and Logan's; but am ready for any position to which you may assign me.

I am, sir, very respectfully, your obedient servant,

JAS. B. McPHERSON,
Major-General.

HDQRS. RIGHT WING, THIRTEENTH ARMY CORPS,
December 20, 1862.

Col. M. D. LEGGETT,
Commanding Second Brigade, Water Valley:

COLONEL: Your dispatch is received, and I have sent a copy to General Grant.

---

* Not found.

There has probably been a fight at or near Jackson, Tenn., as the rebels were near that place in considerable force, but Grant has concentrated a pretty heavy force to meet them and has no fears for the result. He thinks very few of them will get away. The rebel cavalry which your scout speaks of dashed into Holly Springs this morning early and inflicted considerable damage, cut the telegraph wires, &c. It is not known yet the amount of damage done, or whether they captured any of our soldiers.

As our cavalry, or nearly all of it, has been moved from your front you must be on your guard, vigilant, wide awake. Do not get surprised, and learn as much as you can about the movements and designs of the enemy. Keep me well informed.

Yours, truly,

JAS. B. McPHERSON,
Major-General.

WAR DEPARTMENT,
Washington, D. C., December 21, 1862.

Maj. Gen. SAMUEL R. CURTIS, *Saint Louis, Mo.*:

Re-enforce Columbus as quickly and strongly as you can.

H. W. HALLECK,
General-in-Chief.

WAR DEPARTMENT,
Washington, December 21, 1862.

COMMANDING OFFICER CAIRO, ILL.:

Send to Columbus all your available forces.

H. W. HALLECK,
General-in-Chief.

WAR DEPARTMENT,
Washington, December 21, 1862.

Brig. Gen. THOMAS A. DAVIES, *Columbus, Ky.*:

General Curtis and the commanding officer at Cairo have been directed to re-enforce you as quickly as possible. Do everything in your power to reopen and protect the railroad. Notify General Hurlbut and the commanding officer at Memphis of the condition of affairs. What is the enemy's force? Communicate with Admiral Porter, who will probably be able to prevent the enemy from recrossing the Tennessee.

H. W. HALLECK,
General-in-Chief.

WATERFORD, *December* 21, 1862.

General GRANT:

No signs of Mizner yet. Shall I move without him? Rations needed here to-day

C. C. MARSH,
Colonel, &c.

OXFORD, MISS., *December* 21, 1862.

Colonel MIZNER, *Waterford, Miss.*:

Turn your command over to the officer next in rank with the instructions you have received.*

U. S. GRANT,
Major-General.

WATERFORD, *December* 21, 1862.

Major-General GRANT :

GENERAL : I marched until 6.30 p. m. yesterday, and learning that Colonel Marsh was at Waterford, 9 miles farther on, my horses, I believed, would not stand a farther journey.

I started at 2 this morning, and would have been here an hour before day but for the difficulties attending crossing the Tallahatchie Bottom in the dark.

I reached here at broad daylight, and every officer must say that I made no unnecessary delay. I make this statement in justice to myself, for I believe circumstances demand it of one who has in good faith honestly endeavored to do his duty.

J. K. MIZNER,
Colonel Third Michigan Cavalry.

OXFORD, MISS., *December* 21, 1862.

Col. J. K. MIZNER, *Waterford, Miss.* :

Your apparent reluctance at starting from here and the want of alacrity in complying with my orders has so shaken my confidence in you that no matter how well qualified you may be to command such an expedition as the one you have started on, I should feel insecure with you in command. My instructions to turn over the command to the next in rank will therefore be obeyed.

U. S. GRANT.

HOLLY SPRINGS, *December* 21, 1862.

General GRANT :

Am here. Van Dorn left for north yesterday p. m. Have started messengers north and sent two companies of cavalry to hover in their rear for information. Mizner has turned over his command to Grierson. Lee is on one road, Grierson on the other. Will follow in pursuit if not ordered to the contrary.

C. C. MARSH,
Colonel Commanding.

OXFORD, MISS., *December* 21, 1862.

Col. C. C. MARSH, *Waterford, Miss.*:

Try to get messenger through north to all the stations where we have troops, and direct them to fall back to Bolivar, taking with them all they can and destroying the balance.

You will have to supply your troops from the country.

U. S. GRANT,
Major-General.

---

* Resumed command December 25. See Part I, p. 519.

HOLLY SPRINGS, *December* 21, 1862.

Major-General GRANT:

Cavalry here or close by. Your message forwarded.

C. C. MARSH,
Colonel, Commanding.

OXFORD, MISS., *December* 21, 1862.

Col. C. C. MARSH, *Holly Springs, Miss.* :

The enemy should be pursued. If they have gone north, pursuit may prevent them doing further damage, and by throwing infantry and artillery off in the direction they wish to return, they might be considerably damaged. There will be two divisions in Holly Springs to-morrow.

U. S. GRANT,
Major-General.

OXFORD, MISS., *December* 21, 1862.

Col. C. C. MARSH, *Holly Springs* :

Send a company of cavalry through to learn news from Jackson. The company can go to Grand Junction and call on commanding officer there for another company. If the wires are not at work to send by telegraph they can go until an office is found that has communication. Forward the inclosed for General Halleck.

U. S. GRANT,
Major-General.

HOLLY SPRINGS, *December* 21, 1862.

Major-General GRANT:

Scouts returned from Lamar. No enemy in that vicinity. All information leads to the belief that after going a short distance north they took a southeasterly course toward Rocky Ford.

C. C. MARSH,
Colonel, Commanding.

HOLLY SPRINGS, *December* 21, 1862.

Major-General GRANT:

Nothing yet from troops sent north. Information varies as to direction taken by enemy. It is certain that a portion, and that a large one, moved back on the road they came in on. Their numbers have been underrated by us.

C. C. MARSH.
Colonel, Commanding District.

HOLLY SPRINGS, *December* 21, 1862.

Major-General GRANT:

Shall I endeavor to countermand orders to fall back from Grand Junction and to destroy property?

C. C. MARSH,
Colonel, Commanding.

OXFORD, MISS., *December* 21, 1862.
Col. C. C. MARSH, *Holly Springs, Miss.:*

By all means, send orders countermanding any order for falling back from posts north of you.

U. S. GRANT,
Major-General.

GRAND JUNCTION, *December* 21, 1862.
General SULLIVAN, *Commanding Post:*

The enemy are rebuilding the bridge across Wolf River, on the Ball's Bluff road. If you could send a few re-enforcements immediately we shall drive them back to their haunts. Answer.

J. McDERMOTT,
Lieutenant-Colonel, Commanding.

GRAND JUNCTION, *December* 21, 1862.
General SULLIVAN:

The enemy, 10,000 strong, reported within 3 miles of here, on the Saulsbury road.

J. McDERMOTT,
Lieutenant-Colonel, Commanding.

GRAND JUNCTION, *December* 21, 1862.
OFFICER COMMANDING JACKSON:

Van Dorn, with eight regiments cavalry, is moving on and will attack either La Grange or Grand Junction. Coldwater and Hudsonville taken by the enemy.

Holly Springs retaken by General Ross. Our forces have driven the enemy from Davis' Mill.

J. McDERMOTT,
Lieutenant-Colonel, Commanding.

BETHEL, *December* 21, 1862—10 p. m.
General DODGE:

A courier who left Bolivar at 3 o'clock this p. m. arrived this moment. General Brayman writes me that he is all in the dark; that he is afraid to use the Jackson wire because there is, he thinks, a rebel officer on that line; that the wires are working to Grand Junction and that he had just received from Grand Junction the following:

The latest from Holly Springs reports that town burned with its contents. Colonel McNeil with 250 men prisoners. Van Dorn, advancing this way, reported to be within 3 miles of this place—Grand Junction.

General Brayman telegraphs me to look out for Jackson's cavalry, 6,000 strong. It is reported that they have passed Saulsbury on their way to Bethel; that he knows them to be in this direction.

Now, general, after looking at this position, don't you think I ought to have my regiment and artillery, and that you ought to get back at once and save your district and Corinth? General Sullivan has no men that are available to him. Humboldt and Trenton are both gobbled up, and unless we are on the lookout we shall go in the same way.

All quiet here. Wire working from Corinth to Jackson. It was cut above here last night. All quiet toward Savannah.

Keep me advised.

WM. R. MORRISON,
Colonel, Commanding Post.

LA GRANGE, TENN., *December* 21, 1862.

General SULLIVAN:

Send help to-night. Our forces repulsed them this afternoon at Davis' Mill. They are marching to attack this place. We will do the best we can.

J. RICHMOND,
Colonel, Commanding Post.

HEADQUARTERS DEPARTMENT OF THE TENNESSEE,
Oxford, Miss., December 21, 1862.

Brig. Gen. C. S. HAMILTON,
  Commanding Left Wing:

You will instruct the divisions of McArthur and Ross to move immediately upon Corinth by the most practicable routes. The troops should be instructed to be as careful as possible of their rations. Organized foraging parties should be formed to collect all the provender and food that may be required and see to its proper distribution.

In entering Corinth, if it is ascertained that communication is cut north, as large a supply of forage as possible should be carried in with the troops.

If it is learned that a move is being made on Corinth the troops should make a forced march to their destination.

All mills on the route should be destroyed and the means of supporting an army carried off as far as practicable or destroyed also.

U. S. GRANT,
Major-General.

HEADQUARTERS DEPARTMENT OF THE TENNESSEE,
Oxford, Miss., December 21, 1862.

Maj. Gen. J. B. McPHERSON,
  Commanding Right Wing:

I have ordered two divisions back to Corinth, and facts may develop through the day which will make it necessary to send much more force to that point. It is now reported that Bragg is in motion for Corinth. If so, our whole force will be required for its defense. You will fall back, therefore, to the north bank of the Tallahatchie, by which time facts enough will be developed to determine upon our further course.

My present plan is to send Quinby's and Logan's divisions to Memphis, and either you or Hamilton in command, and to go myself, if allowed, and send the other two divisions to Bolivar, from which position they can be made available for any point that may be threatened

If the rebels get such a check as to leave the road in a condition to be repaired in one week I shall hold the line of the Tallahatchie for the present.

If I go to Memphis I shall take either you or Hamilton, leaving the other in command of all the forces except those accompanying the river expedition.

U. S. GRANT,
Major-General.

HEADQUARTERS RIGHT WING,
Camp, Yocknapatalfa, December 21, 1862.

Major-General GRANT,
Commanding Thirteenth Army Corps:

GENERAL: I will commence my march for the Tallahatchie to-morrow morning.

I would like very much to see the officer who is to remain in charge of the cavalry, to have some definite understanding about destroying the wagon-road bridges as we retire. I propose to have a regiment of infantry move back along the line of the railroad and destroy every bridge and trestle-work from the Otuck north.

I sent over to General Denver yesterday afternoon to destroy the bridge (McFarland's) about 5 miles to the west of him, across the Yockna, thinking perhaps the rebel cavalry might return from their raid into Holly Springs by that route and we might thus be enabled to make some of them repent of their rashness.

I issued an order this morning putting my men on three-fourths rations, and by so doing have enough provisions on hand to last ten days.

Leggett is still at Water Valley, and I shall not make any move to the rear until the cavalry is ready to make the demonstration in front and screen our movements, unless I hear from you.

Very respectfully, your obedient servant,

JAS. B. McPHERSON,
Major-General.

HDQRS. RIGHT WING, THIRTEENTH ARMY CORPS,
December 21, 1862.

Brig. Gen. J. W. DENVER,
Commanding First Division:

GENERAL: You will move your command back to the north side of the Tallahatchie by the same route on which you advanced, camping to-morrow night on Clear Creek, west of Oxford, and the next night at Wyatt, on the north side of the Tallahatchie.

Your command will start at 6 o'clock a. m. to-morrow. You will as far as practicable have all your empty wagons filled with forage on the route, and will instruct your commissary to seize all provisions, cattle, &c., on the route and take along. You will keep your train well to the front, preceded by a strong advance guard, and will cause all the bridges on the route to be destroyed after your troops have crossed, except the bridge over the Tallahatchie.

Very respectfully, your obedient servant,

JAS. B. McPHERSON,
Major-General.

HDQRS. RIGHT WING, THIRTEENTH ARMY CORPS,
December 21, 1862.

Brig. Gen. J. G. LAUMAN,
Commanding Fourth Division :

GENERAL: You will move your whole command back to the north side of the Tallahatchie by the same route on which you advanced, camping on the creek about 5 miles north of Oxford to-morrow night. Your command will move at 6 o'clock a. m. to-morrow. You will before starting destroy the railroad bridge across the Yocknapatalfa, in your front, and will send a regiment of infantry along the line of the railroad to destroy all the bridges and trestle-work from the Yockna to Oxford. You will keep your train well in front, preceded by a strong advance guard, and keep the whole column well closed up to guard against any sudden dash of rebel cavalry. You will instruct your commissaries to seize all provisions, beef cattle, &c., and take along whenever practicable.

Very respectfully, your obedient servant,
JAS. B. McPHERSON,
Major-General.

HDQRS. RIGHT WING, THIRTEENTH ARMY CORPS,
December 21, 1862.

Brig. Gen. JOHN A. LOGAN,
Commanding Third Division :

GENERAL: You will move your command back to Oxford, starting at 7 o'clock to-morrow morning, by the same road on which you advanced. You will keep your train in front, preceded by a strong advance guard, and the whole column will be kept well closed up. I will give you definite instructions about the bridge across the Yocknapatalfa to-morrow morning. Instruct your commissary to seize all provisions, cattle, &c., and take along.

Very respectfully,

JAS. B. McPHERSON,
Major-General.

SPEC'L FIELD ORDERS, }   HDQRS. RIGHT WING, 13TH A. C.,
No. 30.   } *Steamer Forest Queen, Helena, Dec.* 21, 1862.

General Steele, with four brigades of cavalry, artillery, and infantry, having been assigned to this wing of the Army of the Tennessee, will embark his command on the boats provided and drop down to a point in the river on the Arkansas shore opposite Friar's Point. All boats should be there by sunrise to-morrow, December 22.

By order of Maj. Gen. W. T. Sherman:
J. H. HAMMOND,
Assistant Adjutant-General.

COLUMBUS, KY., *December* 22, 1862—11 p. m.
(Received December 23, 4 p. m.)

Maj. Gen. H. W. HALLECK,
General-in-Chief, U. S. Army :

Your dispatch received. Things are still unsettled. I had communicated them to General Hurlbut. No connection south. No intelli gence south of Trenton. General Sullivan has withdrawn force from Union City, Kenton, Trenton, &c., to Jackson. Trenton and the railroad to Union City in hands of the enemy. Troops at Trenton captured, say, 200; at Dyer, say, 50; at Rutherford, say, 50; and those at Kenton, say, 200; and at Union City, say, 60. By withdrawing them have sent a force, 1,500, to-day to Union City. Shall push down and repair railroad and fight. Ordered boats below Fort Henry to be taken out of the river to prevent rebels crossing. Heard from 700 of them near Dresden; presume they will try to cross near Paducah. Cannot judge of their force—estimated from 1,500 to 7,000; seven pieces of artillery. No gunboats at Cairo; all gone south. Colonel Lowe, from Henry, Heiman, and Donelson, in pursuit of enemy. Have taken every means to prevent their crossing Tennessee River. Think Columbus will be attacked, but am ready for any force they can bring. Public property here estimated at $13,000,000. Have sent couriers through to urge up the forces from south to join me. Think things will be right in a few days.

THOS. A. DAVIES.

OXFORD, MISS., *December* 22, 1862.

Brig. Gen. JOHN MCARTHUR,
  Waterford, Miss.:

If your entire division has moved let it continue to Waterford and camp for the night.

By command of Maj. Gen. U. S. Grant:

JNO. A. RAWLINS,
  Assistant Adjutant-General.

GRAND JUNCTION, *December* 22, [1862].

Major-General GRANT:

Bridges destroyed between La Grange and Moscow. Scouts sent out toward Somerville found all bridges destroyed. Courier from Major Moyers, Third Michigan Cavalry, reports that Twelfth Michigan Infantry were attacked this morning at Middleburg, and repulsed the enemy, taking some prisoners.

Major Saylor, of Third Michigan Cavalry, reports a prisoner taken who states that Van Dorn expected to make a junction with Price to-morrow morning and attack Bolivar. Major Moyers was moving toward Spring Hill.

C. C. MARSH,
  Colonel, Commanding.

HOLLY SPRINGS, *December* 22, [1862].

Maj. Gen. U. S. GRANT:

Send 50 men and tools, and road can be opened north in six hours after they reach here. Engine from Bolivar came below Coldwater last evening.

C. C. MARSH,
  Colonel, Commanding.

HOLLY SPRINGS, *December* 22, 1862.

Maj. Gen. U. S. GRANT:

Cavalry mostly here; they may as well be at the front. Leave me all you can spare of them.

C. C. MARSH,
Colonel, Commanding.

———

OXFORD, MISS., *December* 22, 1862.

Col. C. C. MARSH, *Holly Springs, Miss.:*

Send Colonel Mizner, with the Third Michigan Cavalry, through to Grand Junction and Bolivar, if necessary, to ascertain the condition of the road to our rear and to re-establish the garrisons, if they have been deserted. Send the balance back here.

U. S. GRANT,
Major-General.

———

HOLLY SPRINGS, *December* 22, [1862].

General GRANT:

I never saw your instructions to the cavalry, and was not informed that you had given such orders.

C. C. MARSH,
Colonel, Commanding.

———

OXFORD, MISS., *December* 22, 1862.

Brig. Gen. C. S. HAMILTON,
Abbeville or Holly Springs:

Concentrate one of your divisions at Holly Springs and one at Waterford. I will give Quinby directions here. They will not move on toward Corinth without further directions, unless you get information making it necessary.

U. S. GRANT,
Major-General.

———

WATERFORD, *December* 22, 1862.

General GRANT:

Two dispatches received. McArthur's division goes to Holly Springs to-night. Ross stops here. Will push cavalry to the north. If no cavalry at hand will send forward Marsh with brigade to-night.

Shall be in Holly in one hour.

C. S. HAMILTON,
Brigadier-General.

———

HOLLY SPRINGS, *December* 22, 1862.

General GRANT:

Marsh starts soon with four regiments. Grierson is here; also Lee. Can use both to great advantage in heading off Van Dorn. Shall I keep both?

HAMILTON.

OXFORD, MISS., *December* 22, 1862.

Brig. Gen. C. S. HAMILTON, *Holly Springs, Miss.*:

The cavalry need not start to-night, if not already started. Their camp equipage is all ordered to Abbeville, where they will remain until further orders.

You may retain Lee's cavalry with you. Open communication with the north, if possible, and get information from Corinth. I telegraphed you instructions to-day to send one division to Holly Springs and one to Waterford. I will give Quinby instructions here.

You need not move from positions indicated here without further directions.

U. S. GRANT,
Major-General.

HOLLY SPRINGS, *December* 22, 1862.

General GRANT:

Van Dorn went to Salem; then to Davis' Mill, where he was repulsed; then down south bank Wolf to Moscow. He pulled up some rails near Davis' Mill. He started north from Moscow at 3 o'clock this morning. All right at Corinth. I think I will send a brigade to Salem to head Van Dorn.

C. S. HAMILTON,
Brigadier-General.

HEADQUARTERS THIRTEENTH ARMY CORPS,
Oxford, Miss., December 22, 1862.

Brig. Gen. I. F. QUINBY,
Commanding Seventh Division:

You will move from here to-morrow with your command and encamp it in the neighborhood of Lumpkin's Mill. It is not necessary that this should be done in one day.

General Denver has been ordered to move to Abbeville and there encamp to-morrow night.

By order of Maj. Gen. U. S. Grant:

JNO. A. RAWLINS,
Assistant Adjutant-General.

JACKSON, *December* 22, 1862—7.45.

Major-General GRANT:

Jackson, Humboldt, and Bolivar all right. The rebels are in strong force all around us—entirely cavalry. I am busy repairing the road north, and will use all my force to keep it open. Trenton was taken by Forrest. Our loss, no one killed and but 2 or 3 wounded. All surrendered. The wires are not in order above here.

JER. C. SULLIVAN,
Brigadier-General.

[Indorsement.]

General HAMILTON:

Send word to Marsh to push on to Grand Junction to-night. There is a large force of cavalry in north of them. There are about 100,000 rations at Grand Junction.

U. S. GRANT,
Major-General.

HOLLY SPRINGS, *December* 22, 1862.

General GRANT:

Grierson impatient to pursue enemy; has been after me several times to telegraph to you on subject. He has been ready to pursue ever since yesterday noon.

WM. S. HILLYER,
Colonel and Aide-de-Camp.

[Indorsement.]

General HAMILTON:

Let Grierson, Lee, and Fifth Ohio Cavalry push after enemy until they find him. They may travel over West Tennessee in pursuit of the enemy until it will no longer support an army.

U. S. GRANT,
Major-General.

BOLIVAR, *December* 22, 1862.

General M. BRAYMAN:

Sent last night by courier, at request of Colonel Morrison, the latest news. Holly Springs reported burned with its contents. Colonel McNeil, supposed of Second Illinois Cavalry, with 250 men, prisoners. Van Dorn advancing this way; reported to be within 3 miles of Grand Junction. Rebels supposed to be on Saulsbury road in force. Keep good lookout. Wires working north to Jackson and south to Grand Junction. All quiet here.

W. L. BARNUM,
Acting Assistant Adjutant-General.

CORINTH, *December* 22, 1862.

General GRENVILLE M. DODGE:

I returned to Corinth Saturday at 11 a. m. Have taken every precaution to defend this place against any force.

I have assumed command of forces in and about Corinth.

AUG. MERSY,
Colonel, Commanding.

BOLIVAR, *December* 22, 1862.

General J. C. SULLIVAN:

General Dodge sends by courier to this post, addressed to Maj. Gen. U. S. Grant, the following:

LEXINGTON, [*December*] 21, [1862]—2 a. m.

I have moved 24 miles; all gone north. Four hundred men and two pieces of artillery joined Forrest to-day. I will push for him to-morrow. Expect to hear from General Sullivan to-night.

Later—LEXINGTON, [*December*] 21, [1862]—2 p. m.

I am pushing here toward Spring Creek, as Forrest, I learn, is there. It seems to me we should get the railroad clear first.

We are getting a long distance from Corinth. I may be wrong, but it appears to me all-important that we should open your communication north.

W. L. BARNUM,
Acting Assistant Adjutant-General.

BOLIVAR, TENN., *December* 22, 1862.

Brigadier-General SULLIVAN:

La Grange and Grand Junction not taken. The enemy passed west of them and are within 12 miles of here, supposed to be 4,000 strong—cavalry. Send down the Forty-third and Sixty-first if you can spare them. I don't, at any rate, fear the result.

M. BRAYMAN,
Brigadier-General, Commanding.

HENDERSON, *December* 22, 1862.

General SULLIVAN:

I hear that General Hamilton has sent scouts to Bethel, and that no force lies between Bolivar and Bethel. I shall send Hurst's cavalry to Bolivar to-morrow.

I must get my command to Corinth and ration them ready for another move. If it becomes necessary I will demonstrate in that direction.

G. M. DODGE,
Brigadier-General.

GRANT'S HEADQUARTERS,
December 22, 1862.

General SULLIVAN:

What news from Jackson? Are the road and wires right north of you?

U. S. GRANT,
Major-General.

HUMBOLDT, TENN., *December* 22, 1862.

General SULLIVAN:

I arrived here at dusk. Bridges all right this far; reported badly broken toward Trenton.

Strong rumor of an attack here to-night. I am making arrangements for them.

I. N. HAYNIE,
Brigadier-General.

HUMBOLDT, *December* 22, 1862.

General SULLIVAN:

A citizen from near Trenton reports the Confederate cavalry left for Union City; their plunder left this morning only for Tennessee River.

GEORGE P. IHRIE,
Colonel, Commanding.

GRAND JUNCTION, *December* 22, 1862.

General GRANT:

I received dispatch to-day for all troops north of Holly Springs and south of Bolivar to fall back to Bolivar, signed by General Grant.

I could not fall back, as the enemy was in our rear. Was the order genuine? Everything quiet, but the enemy in large force near.

J. McDERMOTT,
Lieutenant-Colonel, Commanding.

[Indorsement.]

JOHN MCDERMOTT, *Colonel, Commanding:*

Barricade with cotton-bales if you have them. A force is moving north from Holly Springs to your assistance; will reach you by morning.

U. S. GRANT.

GRAND JUNCTION, *December* 22, 1862.

General SULLIVAN:

The enemy expected every moment. I am good for Van Dorn and all his imps in way of cavalry. I have a good position and will hold it.

J. MCDERMOTT,
Lieutenant-Colonel, Commanding.

GRAND JUNCTION, *December* 22, 1862.

General SULLIVAN, *Commanding:*

By order of General Grant all troops south of Bolivar are ordered to fall back to that point and destroy all they cannot take along.

J. MCDERMOTT,
Lieutenant-Colonel, Commanding.

GRAND JUNCTION, *December* 22, 1862.

General SULLIVAN:

I cannot fall back; the enemy are in our rear. I will stand and hold my position if possible.

J. MCDERMOTT,
Lieutenant-Colonel, Commanding.

GRAND JUNCTION, *December* 22, 1862.

General SULLIVAN:

The order to fall back came through Colonel Marsh, commanding District of Tallahatchie. Do you think it genuine?

J. MCDERMOTT,
Lieutenant-Colonel, Commanding.

GRAND JUNCTION, [*December*] 22, [1862].

General GRANT:

We are now skirmishing with the enemy and will hold them in bay until morning.

J. MCDERMOTT,
Lieutenant-Colonel, Commanding.

BETHEL, *December* 22, 1862.

General SULLIVAN:

Captain Wooster and 20 men who scout for General Hamilton are here; left Pocahontas this morning; came 15 miles southwest from there yesterday; have been five days in country toward Pocahontas and Salem; they heard nothing. Jackson's cavalry force scouts from here; have scoured the country along Hatchie west of here and find all quiet.

I don't think General Brayman's information reliable as to Jackson passing Saulsbury in this direction. All quiet toward Savannah and eastward. Good many report 300 cavalry east of Tennessee River, opposite Saltillo, yesterday evening.

WM. R. MORRISON,
Colonel, Commanding Post.

La Grange, December 22, 1862.

General Sullivan:

The last information we have had is that they are at Ball's Bluff Bridge. Suppose are repairing bridge.

Have re-enforcements started?

J. RICHMOND,
Colonel, Commanding.

La Grange, December [22], 1862.

General Sullivan:

The enemy is right upon and between here and Bolivar. We cannot fall back, but will send them home.

J. RICHMOND,
Colonel, Commanding.

Bolivar, December 22, 1862.

Brigadier-General Sullivan:

Brig. Gen. Robert Looney, rebel cavalry officer, lately from Grenada, supposed to be organizing about 1,200 cavalry somewhere between Colliersville and Dancyville, and contemplates an attack upon this road; point not known. Thirty United States teams, 40 men, and 30 negroes captured at Raleigh, 9 miles from Memphis. Captain Burrow was in command of the rebel force that made the above capture.

JOHN W. SPRAGUE,
Colonel, Commanding.

Bolivar, December 22, 1862.

Brigadier-General Sullivan:

News from below confirms by note from Colonel Graves that a large force of rebels are marching on this way. Re-enforcements to be available must be hurried up.

JOHN W. SPRAGUE,
Colonel, Commanding.

Henderson, December 22, 1862.

General Sullivan:

I have just received a dispatch from General Dodge that he is at the Forked Deer Creek, 3 miles from here, and will take rail to-night for Bethel to re-enforce Colonel Morrison. I thought it well to advise you.

W. J. STEPHENSON,
Captain, Commanding Post.

GENERAL ORDERS, ⎰　　HDQRS. DEPARTMENT OF TENNESSEE,
　No. 14.　　⎱　　　*Holly Springs, Miss., December 22, 1862.*

By direction of the General-in-Chief of the Army the troops in this department, including those of the Department of the Missouri operating on the Mississippi River, are hereby divided into four army corps, as follows:

1st. The troops composing the Ninth Division, Brig. Gen. G. W. Morgan commanding; the Tenth Division, Brig. Gen. A. J. Smith commanding, and all other troops operating on the Mississippi River below Memphis not included in the Fifteenth Army Corps, will constitute the Thirteenth Army Corps, under the command of Maj. Gen. John A. McClernand.

2d. The Fifth Division, Brig. Gen. Morgan L. Smith commanding; the division from Helena, Ark., commanded by Brig. Gen. F. Steele, and the forces in the District of Memphis will constitute the Fifteenth Army Corps, and be commanded by Maj. Gen. W. T. Sherman.

3d. The Sixth Division, Brig. Gen. J. McArthur commanding; the Seventh Division, Brig. Gen. I. F. Quinby commanding; the Eighth Division, Brig. Gen. L. F. Ross commanding; Second Brigade Cavalry, Colonel Lee commanding, and the troops in the District of Columbus commanded by Brigadier-General Davies, and those in the District of Jackson commanded by Brigadier-General Sullivan, will constitute the Sixteenth Army Corps, and be commanded by Major-General Hurlbut.

4th. The First Division, Brig. Gen. J. W. Denver commanding; the Third Division, Brig. Gen. John A. Logan commanding; the Fourth Division, Brig. Gen. J. G. Lauman commanding; First Brigade of Cavalry, Col. B. H. Grierson commanding, and the forces in the District of Corinth commanded by Brig. Gen. G. M. Dodge, will constitute the Seventeenth Army Corps, and be commanded by Maj. Gen. J. B. McPherson.

District commanders will send consolidated returns of their forces to these headquarters, as well as to army corps headquarters, and will for the present receive orders from department headquarters.

By order of Maj. Gen. U. S. Grant:

　　　　　　　　　　JNO. A. RAWLINS,
　　　　　　　　　　Assistant Adjutant-General.

　　　　　　　SPRINGFIELD, ILL., *December* 23, 1862.
　　　　　　　　　　(Received 7.30 p. m.)

Hon. E. M. STANTON,
　　Secretary of War:

I received on yesterday the following dispatch from General Halleck, dated December 21:

The following telegram is forwarded for your information:

"Major-General GRANT, *Oxford, Miss.:*

"The troops in your department, including those from General Curtis' command which join the down-river expedition, will be divided into four army corps. It is the wish of the President that General McClernand's corps shall constitute a part of the river expedition, and that he shall have the immediate command, under your directions.

　　　　　　　　　　"J. C. KELTON,
　　　　　　　　　　"Assistant Adjutant-General."

Yet I am not relieved from duty here so that I may go forward and receive orders from General Grant. Please order me forward.

JOHN A. McCLERNAND,
Major-General.

WAR DEPARTMENT,
Washington City, D. C., December 23, 1862—8.45 p. m.

Major-General McCLERNAND, *Springfield, Ill.:*

It has not been my understanding that you should remain at Springfield a single hour beyond your own pleasure and judgment of the necessity of collecting and forwarding the troops. You are relieved of duty at Springfield, and will report to General Grant for the purpose specified in the order of the General-in-Chief.

EDWIN M. STANTON,
Secretary of War.

COLUMBUS, KY., *December* 23, 1862.
(Received 5.30 p. m.)

Major-General HALLECK,
General-in-Chief, U. S. Army:

The forces of the enemy, derived from a paroled officer, are: Russell's cavalry, 450; Gurley's cavalry, 120; Forrest's (old), 500; Woodward's mounted infantry, 400; Dibrell's, 400; Starnes', 500; Cox's battalion, 250; Little's body guard, 100; others, 500; eight pieces of artillery, 180 men; total, 3,400. From all information most of them are unreliable troops; some picked men.

In October last I applied to General Grant to mount the Second Division with such material as could be taken from the country in Mississippi. If you would allow me to make a suggestion, I think we require mounted infantry, and if the authority can be given for such a force it can be promptly done and these raids effectually prevented. The road will probably be in running order in a very few days.

THOS. A. DAVIES,
Brigadier-General.

WAR DEPARTMENT,
Washington, December 23, 1862.

Brig. Gen. THOMAS A. DAVIES, *Columbus, Ky.:*

Telegraph condition of affairs in West Tennessee. Have you any communication with General Grant?

H. W. HALLECK,
General-in-Chief.

COLUMBUS, KY., *December* 23, 1862—10.30 p. m.

Maj. Gen. H. W HALLECK, *General-in-Chief:*

Your dispatch of 11.35 received. The amount of the raid in round numbers is about 400 or 500 troops captured, as far as I can ascertain. Very little public property destroyed. The enemy left Rutherford yesterday at 8 a. m. Nothing heard from there since. I have a construction train. Leave here to-morrow morning. Have four bridges, 1,500 feet of trestle-work ready, and think in four or five days will clear out the enemy and restore communication. I have had no communication with any place south of Trenton which was captured, from which I think all is safe below that point. I have only received that from paroled officers and soldiers. Nothing from General Grant. Have sent dispatches to him by the way of Memphis.

THOS. A. DAVIES,
Brigadier-General.

HEADQUARTERS DEPARTMENT OF THE TENNESSEE,
Holly Springs, Miss., December 23, 1862.
COMMANDING OFFICER EXPEDITION DOWN MISSISSIPPI : *

Raids made upon the railroad to my rear by Forrest northward from Jackson, and by Van Dorn northward from the Tallahatchie, have cut me off from supplies, so that farther advance by this route is perfectly impracticable. The country does not afford supplies for troops, and but a limited supply of forage.

I have fallen back to the Tallahatchie, and will be only able to hold the enemy at Yalabusha by making a demonstration in that direction or toward Columbus and Meridian.

News received here from the south says that Vicksburg is now in our hands. Butler with Farragut's fleet are said to have ascended the river and to have been successful in their attack. This does not come, however, in sufficiently reliable a shape to have any order or change of plan upon it.

These raids have cut off communication, so that I have had nothing from the north for over a week. Telegraph will probably be working through by to-morrow and railroad within five days.

U. S. GRANT,
Major-General.

HEADQUARTERS DEPARTMENT OF THE MISSOURI,
Saint Louis, Mo., December 23, 1862.
Brig. Gen. F. P. BLAIR :

GENERAL : Yours of the 12th was duly received, and I have cordially done all I could to start your command as well and fast as possible. In this I only do my duty to a soldier who has in the commencement of the war done enough to deserve the position he holds and the special favors the honorable Secretary of War and His Excellency the President have sought to confer on him. I am sorry to be obliged to hurry forward your command or hold you for an interior move. I had to correspond with headquarters to procure permission to make certain prescribed moves and now work somewhat to an agreed programme. Prompt action is necessary to success at Vicksburg, for the enemy has railroad facilities for massing troops there which may be used to great advantage to the rebels. My hope is that Grant has diverted that force; if so, Vicksburg must be struck before it can be re-enforced, and the Jackson Railroad must be destroyed. Success must depend more on action than strength. Strategy is better than force, but not such strategy as confines evolutions to a single line of operation. If you do not arrive at Vicksburg before the rebels mass a great army there you

* See Rawlins to Commanding Officer Memphis, December 25 p 480.

should fall back and make a strike across the country at Yazoo City or do something else to draw off the rebel force from Vicksburg and again come to the charge.

I am, general, very truly, your obedient servant,

SAML. R. CURTIS,
Major-General.

HEADQUARTERS DISTRICT OF EASTERN ARKANSAS,
Helena, December 23, 1862.

Major-General GRANT:

I will start 2,000 cavalry to the Tallahatchie to-morrow; will be at mouth of Coldwater the 25th. If they can cross they will come to Oxford; if not, will wait a day or two to hear from you. But if it comes on rain we must return to the Mississippi River, as they cannot cross the river bottom and would be cut off by mire and overflow. General Sherman will be at the mouth of Yazoo on the 24th.

I have infantry at Friar's Point.

W. A. GORMAN,
Brigadier-General, Commanding.

[DECEMBER 23, 1862.—For Gorman to Curtis, see Series I, Vol. XXII, Part I, p. 858.]

HOLLY SPRINGS, *December* 23, 1862.

COMMANDING OFFICER GRAND JUNCTION, TENN:

Arrest and return to this place all officers and men who may find their way to your post claiming to be paroled, and permit no one connected with the army under any pretext to pass north without written authority from these headquarters, sending back under guard all who do not properly belong to your post.

By order of Maj. Gen. U. S. Grant:

JNO. A. RAWLINS,
Assistant Adjutant-General.

JACKSON, *December* 23, 1862—11 a. m.

Major-General GRANT:

An order was issued for the troops at Grand Junction and La Grange to fall back to Bolivar. They were unable to obey on account of the enemy being in their rear. Shall I reissue the order? No news of the rebels. I will be able to reach Trenton to-day with cars.

JER. C. SULLIVAN,
Brigadier-General.

HOLLY SPRINGS, *December* 23, 1862.

General SULLIVAN:

The order to fall back to Bolivar was countermanded. I now have three regiments of cavalry and four of infantry besides the old garrison there; think they will be able to take care of all the rebels this side of Bolivar.

U. S. GRANT,
Major-General.

JACKSON, *December* 23, 1862.

Major-General GRANT:

Colonel Ingersoll has just come in.   He thinks the rebels have gone to Columbus and then to cross over and destroy Rosecrans' line of railroad.   They number at least 7,500 men.   Their intention was to destroy stores at Jackson, having been informed of our exact force by a Tennessee officer in United States forces.   I am ordering my available force north and will try and have the road repaired in a week.

JER. C. SULLIVAN.

JACKSON, *December* 23, 1862—6.20 p. m.

Major-General GRANT:

I will occupy Trenton to-morrow.   I have sent a force toward Denmark and north side of Hatchie.   General Haynie is pushing north on railroad with a force strong enough to open the road.

JER. C. SULLIVAN,
Brigadier-General.

HOLLY SPRINGS, *December* 23, 1862.

General SULLIVAN:

Instruct all your post commanders to collect all the forage, beef cattle, and fat hogs in their vicinity belonging to secessionists, and have them issued by the commissary and quartermaster.   Send some forage and cattle to Corinth immediately, or as soon as possible; they are out of rations.

U. S. GRANT,
Major-General.

HOLLY SPRINGS, MISS., *December* 23, 1862.

Col. B. H. GRIERSON,
Grand Junction, Tenn.:

Pursue the enemy with all vigilance wherever they may go, reporting wherever you can reach a telegraph office.   Take the Third Michigan with you.

U. S. GRANT,
Major-General.

GRAND JUNCTION, *December* 23, 1862

General GRANT:

Just received the following from Bolivar:

Col. B. H. GRIERSON:

The enemy are going north.   Come here and I will put you on their track.
M. BRAYMAN.

Column moving northeast.   Have halted them.
Shall I act on the above?

B. H. GRIERSON,
Colonel, Commanding Cavalry.

HOLLY SPRINGS, MISS., *December 23, 1862.*
Col. B. H. GRIERSON,
    Grand Junction, Tenn. :

If you are on the track of the enemy follow him. Don't be turned off by directions from post commanders unless you think you will get after the enemy by a shorter route or in a more effective way by doing so.

                       U. S. GRANT
                           Major-General

                      GRAND JUNCTION, *December 23, 1862.*
General GRANT:

    I am moving as rapidly as possible north to Bolivar.

                       B. H. GRIERSON,
                 Colonel, Commanding Cavalry.

                         BOLIVAR, *December 23, 1862.*
Brigadier-General SULLIVAN:

    Our scouts just in. Thirteen of them met a force of 300, 7 miles out toward Whiteville; killed 2, and came in without injury, except clothes by buckshot. They learn that eight regiments are coming here on the Whiteville, Somerville, and Brownsville roads. Colonel Richmond, at La Grange, says the enemy encamped 2 miles north of Somerville; also that four regiments of our cavalry are coming this way in pursuit of them. Our scouts say the rebels are dressed in our clothing, probably captured at Holly Springs. Our cavalry will probably arrive during the night, but I have no fear of them as we are.

                       M. BRAYMAN,
                    Brigadier-General.

                         BOLIVAR, *December 23, 1862.*
General SULLIVAN:

    The force that threatened Bolivar yesterday have passed Somerville and apparently approaching the mouth of Clover Creek, where the Hatchie River is fordable. From that crossing a blind road leads to Medon Station.

    I now think they intend to attack Medon, as they did before from the same direction. Their vedettes will probably occupy the main roads and their main force the secret road. Had you not better strengthen Medon while I re-enforce Toone's Station? I have no fear for Bolivar, but for the road between us.

                       M. BRAYMAN,
              Brigadier-General, Commanding.

                       NEAR OXFORD, *December 23, 1862.*
General U. S. GRANT:

    GENERAL: My command found the enemy's pickets about 2 miles north of Coffeeville on the morning of the 22d; drove them south of Coffeeville 3 miles, where I found the enemy in force; destroyed the railroad trestle-work south of Coffeeville and between that point and the Yocknapatalfa.

                    EDWARD HATCH,
         Colonel, Commanding Second Brigade of Cavalry.

HUMBOLDT, TENN., [*December*] 23, [1862].
General GRANT:

I left Oxford the next morning after I saw you; came to Jackson same day; found forces concentrated there and trouble generally. I declined to proceed farther; reported to General Sullivan for duty, and after the rebels fell back from Jackson I was directed to take command of the forces ordered toward Columbus and re-establish communications. I am now trying to do so. Came here last night; will go to Trenton to-morrow, and rebels are on ahead, so reported. When I shall go through I do not know. I sent a courier to General Davies this morning requesting him to move down this way and check Forrest so that we can drive him off of railroad or whip him. I want to get home, and before I get there my furlough will expire. I would like to have it so changed as to allow me to have a leave that won't expire before it begins. I am progressing well, and will lend all energies to get road through to Columbus and send stores down.

I. N. HAYNIE,
Brigadier-General.

HUMBOLDT, *December* 23, 1862.
General SULLIVAN:

I have taken command here for the present; am pushing forward repairs on road. Rations are running short; I will forage on the country if possible to supply us. Will open road to Trenton I think to-day. It is said the road is badly torn up beyond there. I came away without definite instructions, and have been acting as judgment decided to be best. What is your pleasure with reference to my command and myself?

I. N. HAYNIE,
Brigadier-General.

GRAND JUNCTION, *December* 23, 1862.
Major-General GRANT:

Five regiments cavalry here and moving on in pursuit of enemy. It is absolutely necessary to leave one company here. I have no cavalry.

J. McDERMOTT,
Lieutenant-Colonel, Commanding.

HOLLY SPRINGS, MISS., *December* 23, 1862.
Colonel McDERMOTT, *Grand Junction, Tenn.* :

Has Colonel Marsh joined you? I wish him to remain at Grand Junction, La Grange, and Davis' Mill until otherwise ordered, unless he sees an opportunity to operate against enemy advantageously.
Show this to Colonel Marsh.

U. S. GRANT,
Major-General.

GRAND JUNCTION, *December* 23, 1862.
General SULLIVAN:

Rebels in force a few miles northwest of La Grange toward Moscow.

Small squads hovering around. We drove back their scouts this morning. Four regiments of our cavalry have arrived from Holly Springs. We are after them.

> J. McDERMOTT,
> *Lieutenant-Colonel, Commanding.*

GRAND JUNCTION, *December* 23, 1862.

Major-General GRANT:

Arrived here at 2 o'clock with four regiments of infantry. Cavalry just leaving here for the north.

> C. C. MARSH,
> *Colonel Twentieth Illinois, Commanding.*

GRAND JUNCTION, *December* 23, 1862.

General U. S. GRANT:

Colonel Richmond telegraphs that his pickets have been fired on to-night. He calls for re-enforcements.

> C. C. MARSH,
> *Colonel.*

GRAND JUNCTION, *December* 23, 1862.

General SULLIVAN:

I am here with cavalry. Telegraph me any information as to movements of the enemy.

> B. H. GRIERSON,
> *Colonel, Commanding Cavalry.*

OXFORD, *December* 23, 1862.

General GRANT:

GENERAL: Having learned that a strong cavalry force was 5 miles east of Waterford at 3 o'clock, I have ordered Colonel Hatch, with his entire command, to move immediately toward Pontotoc and see if he cannot get on track of the rebels. Have also sent orders to General Lauman, General Denver, and the officers in command of guards for trains to be on the alert, and guard especially against any cavalry dash.

> JAS. B. McPHERSON,
> *Major-General.*

HOLLY SPRINGS, MISS., *December* 23, 1862.

Maj. Gen. J. B. McPHERSON, *Oxford, Miss.*:

A force of rebel cavalry are now encamped at the mouth of Tippah Creek, going south with a large number of led horses and mules, probably those captured here. The main body of the rebels went north from here. Send this word to Hatch. By properly directing his course he may recover much that was lost here.

> U. S. GRANT,
> *Major-General.*

OXFORD, *December 23, 1862*—10 p. m.
General GRANT:

I have already given directions to Colonel Hatch, and his whole command will be here to start in a few minutes in an east-northeasterly direction until he strikes the road running from the mouth of Tippah Creek to Pontotoc, and try, if possible, to head the rebels off. I think he will reach this road before daylight and have instructed him to use all efforts to ascertain the whereabouts of the enemy and ambush them.

JAS. B. McPHERSON,
Major-General.

OXFORD, MISS., *December 23, 1862.*
Col. JOHN M. LOOMIS,
Commanding Oxford, Miss.:

Upon General McPherson moving his division from here you will break up this post and proceed with your command to Holly Springs, Miss., keeping with General McPherson's division as far as it moves on the same road.

U. S. GRANT,
Major-General.

[DECEMBER 23, 1862.—For Curtis to Davies and Curtis to Gorman, see Series I, Vol. XXII.]

SPECIAL FIELD ORDERS, ⎫ HDQRS. 13TH A. C., DEPT. OF TENN.,
No. 32. ⎬ *Holly Springs, Miss., Dec. 23, 1862.*

It having come to the knowledge of the commanding general that officers are in the habit of quartering in houses, boarding in families, and living in towns in the vicinity of their commands, in violation of General Orders, No. 23, Headquarters District of West Tennessee, dated Savannah, March 18, 1862, it is therefore ordered:

I. That all officers of the army, except generals commanding divisions, are required to occupy tents with their respective commands.

II. All officers found occupying houses or boarding in families will be arrested by their immediate commanders and reported through the proper military channels to these headquarters for dismissal from the service, with forfeiture of pay and allowances, or such other penalty as the nature of the case may require.

III. Sick officers form no exception to this order. They must enter general hospitals.

IV. Commanding generals are prohibited from quartering troops in houses unless by consent of the general commanding army corps to which they belong.

V. Generals commanding divisions will occupy quarters contiguous to their respective commands.

VI. Division commanders will report at once to these headquarters the receipt of this order and its promulgation to their respective commands.

By order of Maj. Gen. U. S. Grant:

JNO. A. RAWLINS,
Assistant Adjutant-General.

COLUMBUS, KY.,
Via Cairo, Ill., December 24, 1862—8 a. m.

Major-General HALLECK, *General-in-Chief:*

I am informed General Cheatham has crossed the Tennessee with 40,000 men and is marching north. I cannot hold Columbus against that force. The information had reached me before that he had crossed but I did not credit it till now.

THOS. A. DAVIES,
Brigadier-General.

———

WAR DEPARTMENT,
Washington, December 24, 1862.

Brig. Gen. THOMAS A. DAVIES, *Columbus, Ky.:*

Columbus must be held at all hazards. You will be immediately re-enforced. Communicate by river with General Grant and Memphis.

H. W. HALLECK,
General-in-Chief.

———

COLUMBUS, KY., *December* 24, 1862—11.30 a. m.

Maj. Gen. H. W. HALLECK,
General-in-Chief, U. S. Army:

I have suspended the repairs on the road south till I learn more definitely the position of things. My small picket at Union City was captured last night just before sundown; the force reported at 7,000. The information that Cheatham, with 40,000 men, had crossed Tennessee River has induced me to place Columbus in a condition to hold it at all hazards. I shall load the commissary stores and all other property here (which only costs labor, which we have) on boats, and then I can hold the place with the forces I have here now—5,000 men all told. I shall probably get some more re-enforcements. I take these precautions because of the risk I may run of leaving the place without, as I telegraphed you I could not hold the place with the property in its present position. I do not know that the circumstances warrant the movement, but from all I can learn after consultation I deem this course prudent.

THOS. A. DAVIES,
Brigadier-General.

———

MEMPHIS, TENN., *December* 24, 1862.

Maj. Gen. H. W. HALLECK, *General-in-Chief:*

The railroad having been cut at Holly Springs and points between Jackson and Columbus deprives me of communication with General Grant until he opens his way to General Sherman, on the Mississippi. The fort at this point was constructed for garrison of 8,000 men. I have four regiments raw infantry, 200 cavalry, and 27 artillerists. No gunboats on this station. I require four more regiments of infantry, one cavalry, armed with carbines, in order to hold city and patrol adjoining country. The Partisan Rangers are within 5 miles, on northeast and south, about 1,300 in all, as far as I can learn. Van Dorn reported at Somerville, 45 miles. There are heavy stores here of ordnance and supplies. I hold city by terror of heavy guns bearing upon it and the belief that an attack would cause its destruction. I should request that the Second Missouri Artillery, Saint Louis, be sent here to man the heavy guns on the forts, now manned by inexperienced infantry, and that gunboats be ordered here at once.

S. A. HURLBUT,
Major-General, Commanding.

WAR DEPARTMENT,
Washington, December 24, 1862.

Major-General CURTIS, *Saint Louis, Mo.:*

Columbus is reported as in danger of an attack. Re-enforce it with all your available forces. The movement must be prompt.

H. W. HALLECK,
General-in-Chief.

MEMPHIS, *December* 24, 1862.

Major-General CURTIS, *Saint Louis:*

GENERAL: You perceive by the date hereof that we drag along slowly. I have succeeded, however, in getting an express-boat from General Hurlbut, who is here in command, and will start in half an hour. Grant's line of communication is completely severed and cannot be repaired for weeks. Holly Springs was surrounded by rebel cavalry and surrendered without resistance; over a million rations burned, several hundred bales of cotton destroyed, sutlers' stores, goods on speculation, &c., to a large amount; and 2,000 troops [captured], who were paroled and will arrive here soon (this I learn from General Asboth). This rebel cavalry force then proceeded along the Mobile and Ohio Railroad toward Columbus, Ky., and destroyed the road and stations, and were within 20 miles of Columbus, as I telegraphed you when we passed there. There is a general stampede here; several hundred cavalry hover around the city, threatening to enter. They saucily sent in flag of truce yesterday to reconnoiter position of things. Great fear among foreign traders and loyal citizens and equally strong hope among rebels prevail, making the excitement intense. General Asboth has command of the fortifications, but his force is entirely inadequate. He has some 10,000 feet of works to defend with 1,000 men, but little artillery, and not one artillerist. From his garrison he furnishes the usual guards, patrols, pickets, &c., leaving him very weak. Columbus was left with like inadequate force. This policy is very questionable, and is a matter of much surprise to officers. The moral effect of taking Memphis or Columbus would be disheartening to us, dangerous to our armies in the advance, and inspiriting to our foes; such risks are perilous. These things are outside of my mission, and I only write as of interest to you.

Asboth sends regards to yourself and staff. He showed the major and myself every consideration and went with us to General Hurlbut's headquarters.

The Thirty-sixth Iowa is detained here and the transports also. Your messenger, Lieutenant Dickenson, Bowen's battalion, just arrived in time to go aboard my boat. Hurlbut thinks Sherman left yesterday with his entire expedition. I think not. The news is conflicting on that point and nothing official yet received. He certainly has not received a reply to his dispatch asking troops of you.

As I am on the first boat going down, slow as we have come I could not have gone faster had I come via Cairo on cars.

I would be remembered to Mrs. C., Madame Julia, and Sadie. A Merry Christmas to yourself and staff.

I fear General Fisk will be too late for operations in this quarter.

I am, general, very respectfully, your obedient servant,

N. P. CHIPMAN.

HOLLY SPRINGS, MISS., *December* 24, 1862.

Col. C. C. MARSH, *Grand Junction, Tenn.*:

Notify troops at Davis' Mill to be in readiness to repel any attack that may be made.

By order of Maj. Gen. U. S. Grant:

JNO. A. RAWLINS,
Assistant Adjutant-General.

GRAND JUNCTION, *December* 24, 1862.

Col. JOHN A. RAWLINS,
Assistant Adjutant-General:

Dispatch received. I notified Colonel Morgan at 6 o'clock to be prepared for attack, and that if attacked I would go to his assistance. I send dispatch to Colonel Grierson to Saulsbury.

C. C. MARSH,
Colonel, Commanding.

GRAND JUNCTION, *December* 24, 1862.

Col. JOHN A. RAWLINS:

I have re-enforced Colonel Morgan and Colonel Richmond to the extent of my ability, and am prepared to co-operate with either of them in case of attack at Davis' Mill or La Grange.

C. C. MARSH,
Colonel, Commanding.

GRAND JUNCTION, *December* 24, 1862.

Major-General GRANT:

I have read your dispatch to Colonel Grierson. I will leave at once to join the command at Saulsbury. I hope as much cavalry as possible will be thrown out east to intercept the enemy's retreat, that they may be effectually used up. I will keep you advised, reporting as often as practicable.

J. K. MIZNER,
Colonel, Commanding Cavalry.

HEADQUARTERS,
Camp on Tallahatchie, December 24, 1862.

Major-General GRANT:

GENERAL: I have been examining into the ration question this morning. General Denver has only enough, on three-quarter rations, to include the 28th instant; General Logan to include the 31st; General Lauman to include the 30th.

JAS. B. McPHERSON,
Major-General.

HDQRS. RIGHT WING, THIRTEENTH ARMY CORPS,
CAMP IN FIELD, NORTH SIDE OF TALLAHATCHIE,
December 24, 1862—8.30 p. m.

Major-General GRANT,
Commanding, &c., Holly Springs:

My command is in camp on the north side of the Tallahatchie, with the exception of Colonel Leggett's brigade, which I left at Abbeville, with one battery of artillery, to assist in guarding the cotton, &c., until it can be removed. Left Oxford at 12 o'clock m. Everything in that vicinity quiet. Colonel Hatch left Oxford at 12 o'clock last night, in an east-northeast direction to try and intercept the rebels. Have not heard from him yet. Your dispatch, inclosing one from Colonel Grierson, just received. Will immediately send 30 of my escort with it to Colonel Hatch, if he can be found.

Very respectfully, your obedient servant,
JAS. B. McPHERSON,
Major-General.

HOLLY SPRINGS, MISS., *December* 24, 1862.

Brig. Gen. I. F. QUINBY, *Waterford, Miss.:*

If I go to Memphis your division goes also. It is reported, however, from the south that Vicksburg is now in our possession.

Your division will all be concentrated at Lumpkin's Mill until further orders.

U. S. GRANT,
Major-General.

HDQRS. THIRTEENTH A. C., DEPT. OF THE TENN.,
Holly Springs, Miss., December 24, 1862.

Brig. Gen. C. S. HAMILTON,
Commanding, &c., Holly Springs, Miss.:

You will please move Ross' division of your command to-morrow morning, the 25th instant, to Davis' Mill, Grand Junction, and La Grange.

By order of Maj. Gen. U. S. Grant:

JNO. A. RAWLINS,
Assistant Adjutant-General.

HEADQUARTERS DEPARTMENT OF THE TENNESSEE,
Holly Springs, Miss., December 24, 1862.

Brig. Gen. C. S. HAMILTON,
Commanding Left Wing:

Inclosed I herewith send you a copy of dispatch just received from Colonel Grierson. One a little later from Grand Junction says fighting is now going on north of that place. It is probable therefore that the enemy are now turning their course south:

VAN BUREN, *December* 24—4 p. m.

Major-General GRANT:

The rebels have just passed through this place and are going directly south. Van Dorn is in command. They are moving toward Saulsbury, 5½ miles from here. We are still in close pursuit and constantly skirmishing with their rear. They broke the telegraph, set fire to the culverts and trestle-work, and destroyed dwellings and barns. The garrison at Middleburg killed, wounded, and captured a number, giving them a hot reception and fighting nobly. I dispatched you from Middleburg.

B. H. GRIERSON,
Colonel, Commanding Cavalry.

The force at Salem should be informed of this, and be on the lookout for them to give them a salute as they pass.

U. S. GRANT,
Major-General.

HOLLY SPRINGS, MISS., *December* 24, 1862.

Maj. Gen. J. B. McPHERSON, *Oxford, Miss.:*

The following dispatch is just received. Send it to Colonel Hatch by to-morrow morning if possible:

NEAR BOLIVAR, *December* 24, 1862.

Major-General GRANT:

I arrived in Bolivar 11 o'clock last night. Pickets at that place were driven in last night. Our presence no doubt saved the place, as it is evident they did not know of our presence until this morning.

We struck their trail on Middleburg road this morning, evidently a large force. 7,000 or 8,000. My column is now moving. Have been skirmishing all the morning; a number of the enemy killed and wounded; no loss on our side.

Later—MIDDLEBURG, *December* 24.

The enemy repulsed from this place by our infantry. We came up with their rear; they struck off to the left toward the Van Buren road; we are in close pursuit; their number from 5,000 to 7,000. I have but 1,400 men. Cannot the Seventh Illinois, Third Iowa, and balance of the Third Michigan be sent after me. From latest information they appear to be going southeast.

Will keep you advised as well as possible.

B. H. GRIERSON,
Commanding.

U. S. GRANT,
Major-General.

BOLIVAR, TENN., *December* 24, 1862—a. m.

General GRANT:

Arrived at 11 o'clock last night; pickets driven in here this morning; think only a feint; think they have gone north to join Forrest.

My column now moving east of north; will keep you advised as far as possible.

B. H. GRIERSON,
Colonel, Commanding Cavalry.

HOLLY SPRINGS, MISS., *December* 24, 1862.

Col. B. H. GRIERSON,
In pursuit of Van Dorn, near Van Buren:

Your dispatches from near Middleburg and Van Buren have been sent to the commanding officer at Salem, whose forces consist of infantry and artillery and are about 15 miles east of here; also to Colonel Hatch, who started last evening with his cavalry force to the mouth of Tippah Creek, on the Tallahatchie, in pursuit of a portion of the enemy near there. He may be able to join you after you cross the Tallahatchie, and may intercept the enemy's retreat.   Make every possible exertion to harass and destroy the enemy.

Take Hatch with you in the pursuit if you meet with him.

By order of Maj. Gen. U. S. Grant:

JNO. A. RAWLINS,
Assistant Adjutant-General.

SAULSBURY, *December* 24, 1862—after dark.

Major-General GRANT:

GENERAL: Have just arrived at this place; enemy still going southward, their rear only a mile ahead.   We are constantly picking up their stragglers.   Have just learned that they talk of turning to the left a short distance.   Shall throw out scouts and observe their movements, and camp to-night without camp-fires.   I sent you dispatch from Middleburg and also from Van Buren.

B. H. GRIERSON,
Colonel, Commanding Cavalry.

SAULSBURY, *December* 24, 1862.

Major-General GRANT:

GENERAL: Your dispatch received this evening.   I am camped within 2½ miles of the enemy.   I sent out scouts, who reported to me an hour ago that they had left, still going south.   I start in pursuit in one hour and will follow them to their den.

B. H. GRIERSON,
Colonel, Commanding.

BOLIVAR, *December* 24, 1862.

General SULLIVAN:

The enemy have appeared in our front, and Colonel Grierson has gone out with his entire command and I am with him, but shall return soon.

M. BRAYMAN,
Brigadier-General, Commanding.

BOLIVAR, *December* 24, 1862.

Brig. Gen. J. C. SULLIVAN:

Just returned from outside lines.   The enemy followed and drove in our pickets and are firing on infantry pickets.   I have no fear of harm; it is probably the rear guard covering their movement north to join Forrest.

Colonels Grierson and Lee are here with 1,500 calvary and will pursue until they overtake the enemy.   I join the pursuit.

M. BRAYMAN,
Brigadier-General, Commanding.

BOLIVAR, *December* 24, 1862.
(Received Jackson, Dec. 24, 1862.)

Brig. Gen. J. C. SULLIVAN:

After my last the rebels advanced in line of battle. Grierson, Lee, and the Jayhawkers [Seventh Kansas Cavalry] are now after them. I had but a dissolving view of them. If you have any information or any guides send out and intercept Grierson. They may get across the railroad, but I have no fear they will do mischief.

M. BRAYMAN,
Brigadier-General, Commanding.

BOLIVAR, *December* 24, 1862.

Brig. Gen. J. C. SULLIVAN:

Rebels occupying a threatening position on the Bethel road. I will shell them in a few minutes; you will probably hear it.

M. BRAYMAN,
Brigadier-General.

BOLIVAR, *December* 24, 1862.

General J. C. SULLIVAN:

The shelling had good effect; the rebels ran out of sight. Every point is guarded well. They cannot get at us. They cut the wire twice at Middleburg. They fired the track in four places, but our men and a number of faithful negroes saved it. Please call Colonel Webster's attention to the damage.

M. BRAYMAN,
Brigadier-General, Commanding.

BOLIVAR, *December* 24, 1862.

General J. C. SULLIVAN:

Glad to find line open again. After my last the whole rebel force turned back; 3,000 went direct to Middleburg and attacked the Twelfth Michigan. I immediately sent the whole body of cavalry after them. Colonel Graves held out gallantly till past noon, when the Jayhawkers arrived. I have not the result, but think all is safe. They cut the wire and set the track on fire, but it was extinguished with little damage.

A messenger is in from Colonel Graves. The party that went above are in flight and will soon be attacked; no fears for the result, but you will not need a regiment from here until they get through with us. We expect to fight them to-night.

M. BRAYMAN,
Brigadier-General.

BOLIVAR, *December* 24, 1862.

Brig. Gen. J. C. SULLIVAN:

Better still The Twelfth Michigan beat them off before the cavalry arrived, killing a dozen and wounding more. The rebels fled toward Saulsbury and the Jayhawkers are after them. We are about shelling those that remain in sight.

M. BRAYMAN,
Brigadier-General, Commanding.

BOLIVAR, *December* 24, 1862.

Brig. Gen. J. C. SULLIVAN:

Colonel Graves has sent up 13 prisoners, including 1 lieutenant. He reports 6 rebels dead, besides a number buried by the rebels; 13 other prisoners wounded. We had but 3 wounded. Our cavalry went south. The rebels supposed to have turned back this way.

M. BRAYMAN,
Brigadier-General.

[DECEMBER 24,? 1862.]

General SULLIVAN:

What steps are you taking to drive out the enemy? Are you collecting forage and supplies?

U. S. GRANT,
Major-General.

HUMBOLDT, *December* 24, 1862.

General J. C. SULLIVAN:

Captain Burbridge sent from Trenton, reports that our forces met Forrest at Obion River and whipped them; that Forrest is falling back this way, and is 6 miles northeast of Trenton. I learned from a scout sent out east of here that the rebels say that they will attack this place soon. I do not know whether to credit it or not. Railroad is reported to be not so badly torn up as was expected. The long trestle-work beyond Trenton not much hurt. Foraging parties to-day met with fine success.

I. N. HAYNIE,
Brigadier-General.

MEDON STATION, *December* 24, 1862.

General SULLIVAN, *Jackson:*

I hear from two sources that the rebels occupy Denmark in force, and that they have 700 3 miles this side of Denmark, the advance of their force marching on us. If they do not come to see us to-night I will go and meet them in the morning.

M. K. LAWLER,
Colonel, Commanding.

HEADQUARTERS DISTRICT OF EASTERN ARKANSAS,
Helena, December 25, 1862.

Major-General SHERMAN:

GENERAL: I am ordered to move on Little Rock up the Arkansas, first striking Post Arkansas. General Curtis has ordered movements from the east by Blunt, Herron, Schofield, and Davidson, and by myself as above indicated. I am powerless with my force without some good gunboats.

I have asked Admiral Porter to aid me if possible. Will you do me the favor to write me a note, or, if perfectly convenient, to see him on the subject? I will be in Napoleon in ten days from this date. I am ordered to attract the attention of General Holmes that he may not be able to send forces to aid General Hindman at Van Buren, against which Blunt, Herron, &c., are moving. I am utterly powerless without gunboats with my force, 5,000 infantry and 2,000 cavalry.

I have 2,000 cavalry scouting toward the Tallahatchie and 1,000 infantry and a section of artillery at Friar's Point.

I am, your obedient servant,

W. A. GORMAN,
Brigadier-General, Commanding.

HOLLY SPRINGS, *December* 25, 1862.

Maj. Gen. J. B. McPHERSON, *Abbeville :*

Send one brigade of your command to Lumpkin's Mill and keep it running. Both divisions that were there have been removed, one to Davis' Mill the other as escort to wagon train.

Relieve General Smith from command of his brigade and order him to report to me. Ross is in arrest, and I want Smith to take his division.

U. S. GRANT,
Major-General.

HOLLY SPRINGS, MISS., *December* 25, 1862.

Maj. Gen. J. B. McPHERSON, *Abbeville, Miss. :*

The office at Abbeville can be moved back to your headquarters or another established. No news from Grierson to-day. Parties in from the east report hearing artillery off toward Rocky Ford for several hours this forenoon.

Communication will be opened with Columbus to-morrow. Sullivan reports road much less damaged than he expected. Will be in order by Monday or Tuesday. All in order now to Jackson. Dodge reports Roddey at Guntown with 1,500 cavalry and some artillery moving west.

If our cavalry get Van Dorn under good headway toward Pontotoc I would like them to give Mr. Roddey a dash.

U. S. GRANT,
Major-General.

CAMP NEAR TALLAHATCHIE,
December 25, 1862—2.30 p. m.

Lieut. Col. JOHN A. RAWLINS,
Assistant Adjutant-General :

Dispatch received. Division trains will be at Tallaloosa at 12 m. to-morrow, 26th instant. Orders for Colonel Hatch, inclosing copy of dispatches from Colonel Grierson, sent to Colonel Hatch and received by him at 1 this morning. His command would start immediately in the direction of Rocky Ford and Ripley. All our cavalry have left Oxford and I presume a small force of rebel cavalry are in the place, as the cavalry pickets were fired on early this morning. I have notified Colonel Leggett at Abbeville that all our cavalry has been removed from his front in the direction of Oxford and that his sentinels and outposts must be on the alert to guard against surprise. I shall order Colonel Leggett's brigade from Abbeville to this side of the river as soon as the cotton, &c., is removed. I have given orders to have the rebel works on the south side of the Tallahatchie silenced.

JAS. B. McPHERSON,
Major-General.

COLUMBUS, KY., *December* 25, 1862—noon.

Major-General HALLECK:

Island No. 10 is safe. There was but a small force there, and the country open to the enemy; but twenty-five heavy guns mounted and in order, with large quantities of ammunition, which was captured. I shall run the risk no longer, and sent down yesterday to have the ammunition and gun-carriages destroyed and guns spiked, being of no use, and so cripple the armament as not to be dangerous in case of capture. I shall send a second messenger to-day. Everything, including sick, will be loaded probably to-day on boats, which very much aids my defenses, and shall soon be out of danger. The enemy are in force—about 7,000 cavalry and artillery—near Union City, probably waiting a train load of troops or hoping to draw me out. I shall soon be in a position to go. I hear nothing more of Cheatham.

THOS. A. DAVIES,
Brigadier-General.

COLUMBUS, KY., *December* 25, 1862—2.20 p. m.

Major-General HALLECK, *General-in-Chief:*

The following received from General Hurlbut, Memphis, as the report of fugitive men and officers of the Second Illinois Cavalry, who were at Holly Springs. It appears from their statement that the One hundred and first Illinois and Seventy-eighth Ohio Infantry were surprised in their tents and are unquestionably captured. McNeil, lieutenant-colonel Second Illinois Cavalry, charged repeatedly, but fruitlessly, the force being too strong. Murphy, of Iuka fame, was in command. Heavy stores of all kinds were captured and destroyed. We had 700 head of cattle and 1,000,000 of rations, which are gone. The ammunition was blown up. One officer said the Sixty-second Illinois were also in garrison.

THOS. A. DAVIES,
Brigadier-General.

COLUMBUS, KY., *December* 25, 1862—7 p. m.

Maj. Gen. H. W. HALLECK, *General-in-Chief:*

Things are easing up every way. I shall hold the place against any force. I hear no more from infantry, but a heavy cavalry force is hovering close. A flag of truce sent in to-day asking rations and train to bring over paroled prisoners from Moscow. I shall make good use of it to gain time. Everything in the shape of public property, except some forage, is nearly out of the way. I shall send three boat loads of supplies to Memphis to-night. I have a light gunboat and one coming from Cairo. Have got a lot of howitzers from navy, and shall make them available. No news except a cavalry fight at Fort Pillow. The notorious Gus Smith, your old guide, turned traitor, was killed, and several others. None of our men hurt. No news from any point south except what I telegraphed to you this morning from Memphis. I understand from deserters that the road is not much damaged, except bridges and trestle-work burned.

THOS. A. DAVIES,
Brigadier-General, Commanding.

CAIRO, ILL., *December* 25, 1862.

Maj. Gen. H. W. HALLECK, *General-in-Chief:*

By direction of Major-General Sherman I telegraph you the fact that his expedition embarked from Memphis, December 20, in sixty transports, 22,000 strong; 12,000 more to be taken on at Helena with cavalry. Arrangements were already made for the cavalry to operate between Helena and the Tallahatchie. The general expects to be at Gaines' Landing on 23d, Milliken's Bend on 24th, and in all probability at mouth of Yazoo to-day. This dispatch should have been forwarded two days ago, but accident and unavoidable delay on steamboat in which I came up rendered it impossible. Passed Island No. 10 and Hickman last night. All quiet and very different from what they seemed to think at Columbus since General Grant's communication has been cut off. It may not be unimportant to know that General Sherman took with him 1,600,000 rations, or 600,000 more than originally intended, anticipating, as I understood, the possibility of General Grant being compelled to draw supplies from him for a short time in case of accident to his railroad communication.

HENRY S. FITCH,
Captain and Assistant Quartermaster.

HDQRS. THIRTEENTH A. C., DEPT. OF THE TENN.,
Holly Springs, Miss., December 25, 1862.

COMMANDING OFFICER MEMPHIS, TENN.:

Inclosed find communication for General J. A. McClernand,* which you will deliver to him if he be at Memphis. If he has gone down the river you will please forward it to him. The original letter was sent to the commanding officer at Cairo, with instructions to deliver it to General McClernand if he had not already passed that point going south, and if he had to send it to him at Memphis. Communication was cut off north and it did not probably reach him.

By order of Maj. Gen. U. S. Grant:

JNO. S. RAWLINS,
Assistant Adjutant-General.

HEADQUARTERS DEPARTMENT OF THE TENNESSEE,
Holly Springs, Miss., December 25, 1862.

Maj. Gen. STEPHEN A. HURLBUT, *Memphis, Tenn.:*

Just as Forrest's raid upon our railroad was commenced I received a dispatch from the General-in-Chief of the Army to divide my command into four army corps, giving one to General McClernand and placing him in chief command, under my direction, of the expedition on Vicksburg

I immediately wrote the order giving you command of the Third Army Corps, and directed General McClernand to order you here to take command of it. Before this got off all communication was cut off with the north, and has not yet been resumed. General McClernand consequently has not yet received my directions and orders.

Communication now being cut off and the probabilities being that Vicksburg is already in our hands a change of plans will probably be

---

* Probably Grant to Commanding Officer Expedition down the Mississippi, December 23, p. 463.

adopted and also a change of organization of army corps. I would direct therefore that you retain command of the District of Memphis until receipt of orders arranging army corps in accordance with the instructions referred to.

I will be glad to hear from you and to learn when the river expedition sailed and any other news you may have to communicate.

U. S. GRANT,
Major-General.

DECEMBER 25, 1862.

Major JONES, *Commanding at Island No.* 10:

The order I sent you last evening to "destroy ammunition and burn gun-carriages and spike" I hope you have carried out. Send up by the O'Brien 500 rounds of canister, 8-inch, if you have it.

The object I have in view is to so cripple the armament there that it will not be available to the enemy as a point of defense in case they should capture it.

You can save such of the guns as will be serviceable for your own defense, but be careful not to retain too much ammunition.

THOS. A. DAVIES,
Brigadier-General.

HEADQUARTERS DISTRICT OF COLUMBUS,
December 25, 1862.

Col. JOHN A. RAWLINS,
Assistant Adjutant-General :

SIR: I have sent communications to you by the way of Jackson by courier, and do not know whether you have received them or not. I have been in the hope of receiving some directions from you. As you have been apprised, Trenton was taken on the 20th. The troops having been removed up as far as Union City by General Sullivan there were left at Trenton about 200, under Colonel Fry, who were captured. A few, say 25, at Humboldt, captured. They captured the troops at Dyer and Rutherford. I withdrew the force at Trenton, about 200 men, and those at Union City, about 50.

We have been threatened here by what was reported to be 6,000 or 7,000, with eight pieces of artillery. I have been re-enforced by General Curtis, so that I have here now a little over 5,000 men, and I can hold the place against any force that they can bring against me. I have a small gunboat here, and the navy has furnished me with four 8-inch howitzers. To protect the stores from being burned I have been compelled to divide my force about equally between the plain and the forts on the hill.

I received information of a large infantry force moving in the rear of this cavalry, said to be under the command of Cheatham. Being unable to get any more re-enforcements I determined upon loading all the public property upon steamboats that were here, so as to relieve force on the plain to aid in holding the forts against any force which might come. Everything excepting some forage will, I think, be loaded by to-morrow noon.

I communicated with General Halleck, who ordered me to hold Columbus at all hazards.

Two boat loads of supplies will go down to Memphis in the morning. I shall send another boat load to Helena to-morrow.

As near as I can learn the rebels have taken about 500 prisoners and destroyed most of the bridges and trestle-works on the road where they have gone. I have 1,500 feet of trestle-work and four bridges ready to proceed with the construction as soon as it can be done with safety to this place. I hope to get some additional re-enforcements to drive them off and commence the reconstruction. I have withdrawn the force from Hickman, Moscow, and Little Obion.

They have destroyed nothing this side of Union City as yet, but presume they will. I cannot give you an idea of the exact position of their forces. All I know from the south is that they have a heavy cavalry force hovering about Clinton and Moscow. The cavalry at Fort Pillow have had a fight, in which the famous Gus Smith was killed and several others; no loss on our side.

As the enemy can have possession of the bank of the Mississippi to Island No. 10 I have ordered the armament there to be so thoroughly crippled by the destruction of the powder, spiking the guns, and burning the gun-carriages which are of no use to us, that if the island should fall into their hands they could not close the navigation of the river.

In the absence of orders from you I keep open communication with General Halleck, and have informed him of all my movements.

No damage has yet been done by the rebels in my district. I shall continue to press things and do all that can be done under the circumstances. I think that nothing very serious will come out of the whole matter.

I am, very respectfully,

THOS. A. DAVIES,
Brigadier-General.

HOLLY SPRINGS, MISS, *December* 25, 1862.

Brig. Gen. GRENVILLE M. DODGE, *Corinth, Miss.*:

Parole the prisoners you have and turn them loose. Send a complete roll of them to the Adjutant-General of the Army and retain a copy.

Van Dorn was at Saulsbury last night; our cavalry close on him. He was repulsed at every place except here. It is possible that Van Dorn turned east from Saulsbury.

Have you any news from Rosecrans or Bragg?

U. S. GRANT,
Major-General.

CORINTH, *December* 25, 1862.

Lieut. Col. JOHN A. RAWLINS:

Morgan has tried a raid in the rear of Rosecrans at same time it was tried on us; do not know what success he had. I heard from Bragg's army; scout seven days on the road; everything was in same position as I last reported, except one brigade at Shelbyville has been mounted. I expect more news to-morrow. Roddey left Tuscumbia last Saturday with his whole command; camped Monday night at Bay Springs; was out at Guntown Tuesday, and going west. He had about 1,500 mounted men; five pieces artillery. I have scouts on his track.

I have some Texans of Withers' brigade, who were dismounted when they left Arkansas. Since they fell back from Holly Springs the whole brigade has been remounted; the horses came from Texas. I have 200 prisoners, taken in the last week. Cannot I send them through the lines? Where is Van Dorn's cavalry?

G. M. DODGE,
Brigadier-General.

HOLLY SPRINGS, MISS., *December* 25, 1862.

Col. A. S. NORTON, *Abbeville, Miss.*:

Have your advance guards on railroad to Oxford drawn in? If they have not, draw them in at once.

The railroad is to be abandoned from Abbeville to Oxford. Keep out guards for defense of Abbeville only.

By order of Maj. Gen. U. S. Grant:

JNO. A. RAWLINS,
Assistant Adjutant-General.

JACKSON, *December* 25, 1862—4 p. m.

Major-General GRANT:

The road to Columbus is not so badly hurt as supposed. I hold Trenton. My forces whipped Forrest yesterday at Obion. General Brayman beat him off at Bolivar. I think the road will be in running order by the first of next week. I will send a large force in that direction to protect Colonel Webster and his repairs. I have secured Jackson in such a manner that all the rebels cannot take it. The surrender of Trenton mortifies me, but the damage to road is not worth grieving about.

JER. C. SULLIVAN,
Brigadier-General.

HOLLY SPRINGS, *December* 25, 1862.

General SULLIVAN:

Three miles north of Toone's Station are three bridges unguarded. You will at once protect them.

U. S. GRANT,
Major-General.

GRAND JUNCTION, *December* 25, 1862.

General HAMILTON and General GRANT:

Mistake about rebels being near La Grange. Colonel Richmond says they were 3 miles below Somerville at 3 p. m. yesterday, giving the impression that they were going to unite with Johnston at Jackson. I will move northward, striking between Bolivar and Somerville. Third Michigan has arrived.

B. H. GRIERSON,
Colonel, Commanding Cavalry.

HUMBOLDT, *December* 25, 1862.

General SULLIVAN:

I have just received the following report from my scouts out toward Brownsville:

Van Dorn crossed at Estanaula yesterday, supposed to attack Jackson. Colonel Dawson has passed through Dyer County to join Forrest at Union City or above. My scout says he will go toward Brownsville and look out toward Jackson.

I. N. HAYNIE,
Brigadier-General.

GRAND JUNCTION, *December* 25, 1862.

General GRANT:

An escaped prisoner reports that Van Dorn encamped last night at Jonesburg, on Corinth road, heading toward Corinth.

C. C. MARSH,
Colonel, Commanding.

RIPLEY, *December* 25, 1862—3.30 p. m.

Maj. Gen. U. S. GRANT,
Commanding Thirteenth Army Corps, Holly Springs:

We have followed the enemy all day, but have not been able to come up close enough to engage him. Van Dorn left his camp, 2 miles south of Saulsbury, at 8 p. m. yesterday and moved 10 miles south on Ripley road, where he remained till daylight. They are now on the Pontotoc road and probably 6 miles south of here. I shall move on, and if I do not succeed in coming up with them to-night will camp 5 miles south, on Pontotoc road.

I joined the command at 8 a. m. this morning. I have been joined here by a portion of the Second Illinois. Colonel Deitzler came into the Ripley road 10 miles north of here, I am informed, after we passed.

If Hatch can get south of Van Dorn and block the roads we may get a fight out of them. I will continue on early in the morning. Van Dorn is making his way back to Grenada or below as fast as he can travel.

I have several prisoners, but have had no fight.

Very respectfully, your obedient servant,

J. K. MIZNER,
Colonel, Commanding Cavalry.

TALLAHATCHIE RIVER, MISS., *December* 25, 1862.

Hon. E. M. STANTON,
Secretary of War, Washington, D. C.:

DEAR SIR: The necessity which has compelled us to fall back to this place it seems to me makes it obvious that some plan of operations other than that of keeping up long lines of railroads should be adopted. I have not time to write in full, but would merely suggest that at least 20,000 of our troops (infantry) should be mounted and made to scour the whole country, while those on foot could take and hold possession. Such a force could soon break up the enemy's lines of communication in every direction and would soon confine them to very narrow limits. From all I have been able to learn the rebels have adopted this plan in the late movements they have made in our rear.

The most effective cavalry we now have are those armed with the revolving rifle, and dismount when going into action. Ordinary infantry if mounted would be just about as good. They could subsist on the country, and, carrying their shelter-tents, would require no baggage train.

Yours, in haste,

J. W. DENVER.

SPECIAL FIELD ORDERS, }   HDQRS. RIGHT WING, 13TH A. C.,
No. 32.   }   *Milliken's Bend, December 25, 1862.*

General A. J. Smith will detach a brigade at this point to march to the southwest and destroy effectually a section of the Vicksburg and Shreveport Railroad near the Tensas, at or near a place called Joe's Bayou. Each regiment will carry about ten axes and materials for firing the wood-work. Railroad trestles, ties, and iron for a reach of about a mile will be piled up and burned. If any railroad bridges are encountered they will be burned, and telegraph lines pulled down and hidden in some deep water. Men will be provided two days' rations. The officer in command will press any number of guides, white or black, and may take any provisions, wagons, or carriages needed by his command. He will start as early as possible, march in silence, and having accomplished his purpose will return and re-embark his command.

By order of Maj. Gen. W. T. Sherman:

J. H. HAMMOND,
Assistant Adjutant-General.

SPECIAL FIELD ORDERS, }   HDQRS. THIRTEENTH ARMY CORPS,
                       }   DEPARTMENT OF THE TENNESSEE,
No. 34.   }   *Holly Springs, Miss., December 25, 1862.*

The Seventh Division, left wing, Army in the Field, Brig. Gen. Quinby commanding, will proceed without delay to Memphis, Tenn., as escort to train for supplies for the army. A train of 50 wagons will be detached from each division for this purpose, besides the regimental train of the Seventh Division. The train of the right wing will be collected at Tallaloosa by 12 o'clock m. on the 26th instant, escorted by details from their respective commands to that place, details to return as soon as the train is taken charge of by General Quinby. The train from the Sixth Division will move immediately west to the same point and be there at the same time. The Seventh and Eighth Divisions will receive their directions from General Quinby where they are.

The route to be taken to Memphis will be the Pigeon Roost road, leading from Tallaloosa to Memphis. The chief commissary of subsistence will detail a commissary of subsistence to accompany the train, and will give the proportions of each component part of the rations to be drawn.

By order of Maj. Gen. U. S. Grant:

JNO. A. RAWLINS,
Assistant Adjutant-General.

WAR DEPARTMENT,
Washington, December 26, 1862.

Brigadier-General DAVIES, *Columbus, Ky.:*

I beg leave to repeat that Columbus must be held at all hazards. No movements which will endanger that position must now be made.

H. W. HALLECK,
General-in-Chief.

COLUMBUS, KY., *December* 26, 1862.

Major-General CURTIS, *Saint Louis, Mo.:*

Safely arrived. We can hold the post against the entire Confederacy, but not strong enough to go out and whip the rascals. Can you spare the Twenty-ninth Iowa? Send Colonel Cornyn's regiment to report to me here.

CLINTON B. FISK,
Brigadier-General.

COLUMBUS, KY., *December* 26, 1862.

Colonel LEWIS,
    Commanding Twenty-eighth Wisconsin:

SIR: You will proceed with your regiment on board the steamer Black Hawk down the river to Hickman. You will meet the gunboat New Era on the way up or find her at Hickman. If you do not, you must land your regiment above Hickman, out of range of artillery if any is there, and capture and totally destroy two large guns, which I am informed the rebels are mounting at that point on the bank of the river. They are two large pieces of ordnance left there by the navy as condemned. They are mounting them on the river bank. Burn all the gun-carriages you can find on the river bank or in the town, and utterly destroy the guns if you can or roll them into the river if you cannot get them away by any other means. Take good care that while you are doing this by a detail that you are not surprised by a charge of cavalry. I hope you will use every precaution to resist an attack if one is made. I do not fear that you will be so attacked; but if you are do the best you can. You will know the gunboat when you meet her by her color being brown.

I send with you Captain Hutchens, who has been in command of Hickman, and a guide who will tell you where you can land above Hickman.

Have your steamboat while you are ashore lay off a little way in the stream, say 20 or 30 feet, so that she may not be surprised during your absence. The remainder I leave to your discretion.

THOS. A. DAVIES,
Brigadier-General.

If you can ascertain any one who has been engaged in this operation arrest them and bring them up here. When you have accomplished the work you will return to this place.

THOS. A. DAVIES,
Brigadier-General.

COLUMBUS, *December* 26, 1862.
COMMANDING OFFICER GUNBOAT NEW ERA:

SIR: I send a regiment of infantry to assist in landing at Hickman. I am informed that they are mounting two large guns at that place, which were thrown off there by the navy as condemned. It is very heavy ordnance, and if they are not destroyed will give some trouble. I wish you would take such steps, with the aid of the infantry, as to prevent their use by totally destroying them. If they have fired on any boat or made such preparations you know what to do. You probably have your orders from Admiral Porter. I leave the rest to your discretion.

Look through the town and see if there is anything else that can be used and destroy that also.

THOS. A. DAVIES,
Brigadier-General.

———

CAMP NEAR TALLAHATCHIE, *December* 26, 1862.
Major-General GRANT:

GENERAL: I have selected a place on this side of the river near one of the new rebel batteries for the cars to stop at when they run down with supplies, &c. The mills which General Sherman had in operation where Colonel Buckland's brigade was are on the south side of the Tallahatchie, on Hurricane Creek, and about 12 miles from here. By moving Denver's division to Wyatt and rebuilding the bridge across the river I could place a brigade at the mills and set them to running again. Colonel Leggett has a small mill in operation near Abbeville, and will, I think, have another started soon.

JAS. B. McPHERSON,
Major-General.

———

HOLLY SPRINGS, *December* 26, 1862.
Maj. Gen. J. B. McPHERSON, *Abbeville, Miss.*:

I hardly think it would pay to detach a division so far from the main body, but if you think it would you can send Denver to Wyatt.

No news from Van Dorn or our cavalry. The rebels are encamped up near Trenton. I expect they will do serious damage to the road near Union City.

U. S. GRANT,
Major-General.

———

CAMP ON TALLAHATCHIE, *December* 26, 1862.
Major-General GRANT:

Dispatch received. Every means will be taken to secure everything in the [way] of provisions which this section will supply. I have directed my command to be placed on half rations until it is definitely known how soon we will get a supply over the railroad. Colonel Leggett's command will remain at Abbeville to-day and possibly to-morrow, depending somewhat upon the weather and news of the enemy's movements.

No word as yet from Colonel Hatch.

JAS. B. McPHERSON,
Major-General.

HOLLY SPRINGS, MISS., *December* 26, 1862.

Maj. Gen. J. B. McPHERSON,
Commanding Right Wing:

Van Dorn passed Ripley yesterday going south. Our cavalry was after him, but from 6 to 10 miles in the rear. Van Dorn got the start by making a march after he had apparently encamped for the night. The hope now is that Hatch may have succeeded in heading him south until other troops come up. I think by foraging liberally we can give the men more than half rations, but would not give more from the supply on hand. The road north of Trenton is worse than at first reported. I have directed work to progress toward Memphis. I ordered Sullivan to mount infantry to follow those fellows up north. He reports that he can mount 1,500 at once.

U. S. GRANT,
Major-General.

HOLLY SPRINGS, MISS., *December* 26, 1862.

Maj. Gen. J. B. McPHERSON, *Abbeville, Miss:*

Send Denver's division to Moscow and La Fayette. I will commence opening that road.

U. S. GRANT,
Major-General.

CORINTH, *December* 26, 1862.

Maj. Gen. U. S. GRANT, *Holly Springs:*

My scouts are in from east of Tennessee River; left Waynesborough and Clifton yesterday. At former place are about 500 Mississippi cavalry; at Clifton, about 100. At Old Town a large lot of hogs are collected in charge of Robertson's cavalry. Yesterday the citizens at Savannah had a fight with some of Robertson's company; wounded 2 and took 6 prisoners, which the scouts brought here. Some of my cavalry crossed to-night to help them through. In Wayne County are some 200 armed Union men, whom the Mississippi cavalry have been sent to put down. At Old Carrollsville Forrest has his trains and what he has captured. A good regiment of cavalry could capture the lot, or a force up the river from Fort Henry could catch them. Men from Clifton who saw Forrest cross say he did not cross over 3,500 men. I think he will return farther down the river. River is very low. No movement of Bragg that I can discover. Jeff. Davis in Chattanooga last Sunday; Johnston with him.

G. M. DODGE,
Brigadier-General.

CORINTH, *December* 26, 1862.

Brig. Gen. J. C. SULLIVAN:

There must be some mistake about Van Dorn being at Brownsville, as he was in Ripley yesterday. My cavalry just in from there bring prisoners from his column going south.

G. M. DODGE.

CORINTH, MISS., *December* 26, 1862.

Major-General GRANT:

One of our men arrived yesterday from Tullahoma, Tenn.; ten days on the road. The main body of Bragg's army was there. They were retreating to Chattanooga. All the stores were being sent there and they were collecting all the corn and stock and forage, taking it to Chattanooga. On his road he met fifteen droves of hogs, cattle, and sheep, in Lincoln and Giles Counties, all being driven to the same place. They saw men from Bragg's army in three counties to the Tennessee River, collecting produce and stock and taking it all that way. He brings same report as sent two days ago of force south of Tennessee River.

G. M. DODGE,
Brigadier-General.

HOLLY SPRINGS, *December* 26, 1862.

General SULLIVAN, *Jackson, Tenn.*:

Van Dorn went to Bolivar pursued by our cavalry, then struck southeast through Saulsbury and Ripley. Our cavalry was still in pursuit at that point, and have not since been heard from. This was yesterday. They are now near Grenada. Two deserters came in from Van Dorn to-day; they left him 10 miles north of New Albany at 10 o'clock last night, still going south. If there is any cavalry north of the Hatchie it must be some small irregular band.

Send cars to Davis' Mill and I will order four regiments more up to you. Collect all the bacon, beef, hogs, sheep, and grain you can from planters. Mount all the infantry you can and drive Forrest east of the Tennessee.

U. S. GRANT,
Major-General.

HOLLY SPRINGS, MISS., *December* 26, 1862.

General SULLIVAN:

How are your forces now located?

U. S. GRANT,
Major-General.

JACKSON, *December* 26, 1862—11.20 a. m.

Major-General GRANT:

I have one-third of my force opening road to Union City, under command of General Haynie. I have under Colonel Lawler 1,000 men who have been after the rebs, and will to-day be at Toone's Station or on their return. I will send immediately that force north on railroad. I am unable to get nearer the enemy than within sight, when they immediately retreat.

My cavalry was entirely broken up, and it is difficult to reorganize it. All my officers telegraph that they are collecting forage and cattle, but have received no statement of amount. Van Dorn is reported to have escaped our cavalry, and, crossing the Hatchie, has made his way to join Forrest. Reports from Obion are less favorable, but as they are merely rumors I do not place much reliance on them.

JER. C. SULLIVAN,
Brigadier-General.

DECEMBER 26, 1862.

SULLIVAN:

What success did you have in collecting forage and subsistence? You had better collect all the bacon and meat from the secessionists in town to use in case of emergency. If they don't like the association of Yankees, let them move south among their friends.

U. S. GRANT,
Major-General.

HOLLY SPRINGS, *December* 26, 1862.

General SULLIVAN:

Can you collect enough to mount three or four regiments of infantry to pursue Forrest? If you can, do it.

U. S. GRANT,
Major-General.

HOLLY SPRINGS, MISS., *December* 26, 1862.

General SULLIVAN:

Have you a force moving north sufficient to drive out the rebels from the road? Those fellows should be kept off the road at least.

U. S. GRANT,
Major-General.

[DECEMBER 26, 1862.]

General S.:

It is important that the road between you and Corinth and the Junction should be secure beyond a peradventure. Have you made arrangements to send for four regiments at Davis' Mill?

U. S. GRANT,
Major-General.

DECEMBER 26, 1862.

SULLIVAN:

My cavalry is now in pursuit of Van Dorn, and must be near Grenada. They will be well tired out by the time they return. Do you hear anything of the force ordered from Fort Henry to co-operate with you?

U. S. GRANT,
Major-General.

DECEMBER 26, 1862.

SULLIVAN:

Make the best disposition you can to drive Forrest out, and communicate with me often what you are doing. Good-night.

U. S. GRANT,
Major-General.

HOLLY SPRINGS, *December* 26, 1862.

General SULLIVAN, *Jackson:*

Dodge learns from persons who saw Forrest cross the Tennessee River that he has but 3,500 men at the furthest. Act on the theory that he has no more.

U. S. GRANT,
Major-General.

JACKSON, *December* 26, 1862—3.30 p. m.

Major-General GRANT:

The following dispatches I have this moment received from General Haynie, dated at Trenton at noon to-day:

GENERAL: We arrived here at noon. I met one of my scouts who went up toward Columbus day before yesterday. He reported to me that all I have heard of the favorable condition of the road and bridges is untrue; says that Union City was taken and all or nearly all the bridges and trestles are burned that high up, and that it will take a long while to repair them. The rebel force is large. I can move after Forrest, but then I leave points unguarded; and a force of several hundred are threatening the road between Humboldt and this point north of Brownsville.

Colonel Dawson has a regiment, and John Irwin, brother-in-law of Cheeny, of Savannah, reports another force of cavalry or mounted infantry as crossing the Tennessee. I can possibly mount 1,500 men. I will do so and attack if I can.

JER. C. SULLIVAN,
Brigadier-General, Commanding.

JACKSON, *December* 26, 1862—7.30 p. m.

Major-General GRANT:

Van Dorn seems to be in north of Hatchie with a large force. Forrest is near Union City. Mr. Spears brings me information that Van Dorn is planning an attack on Jackson. I think now, general, that a sufficient force should be speedily sent here to capture the whole of this force. I am not able with my small force to assume the offensive and guard what we yet hold.

JER. C. SULLIVAN,
Brigadier General.

JACKSON, *December* 26, 1862—8.30 p. m.

Major-General GRANT:

Every available man is now north. I will send this evening troops that have just returned from a fatiguing march. I have no doubt that the design of the rebels is to weaken this post by making me send off my men, and then, marching rapidly to the rear, capture and destroy the stores. What can be done shall be done.

JER. C. SULLIVAN,
Brigadier-General.

JACKSON, *December* 26, 1862.

U. S. GRANT:

Colonel Webster will furnish the cars to-morrow. The cars will probably follow the mail train in the morning. I can secure the road as you wish. I have organized my forces to meet Forrest. I have made every attempt to mount infantry but cannot succeed in procuring more than 1,000 horses. I believe by moving toward Dresden and Paris Forrest will be compelled to pass behind Bolivar and Jackson to escape. Unless he has arrangements for crossing the Tennessee lower than Clifton, your cavalry can meet him.

JER. C. SULLIVAN.

JACKSON, *December* 26, 1862.

General GRANT:

General Haynie has at Trenton about 1,000 men at Humboldt 475; Colonel Lawler has 1,000 men just returning from pursuits. General Brayman has two regiments Fuller's brigade, Forty-third Illinois, Twelfth Michigan, Fiftieth Indiana. I have two regiments of Fuller's brigade and scattering forces at Bethel, Forty-eighth and Forty-ninth Illinois and one battery at Bolivar, one section with Haynie, one with Lawler; balance here.

JER. C. SULLIVAN.

SPECIAL ORDERS, }   HDQRS. 13TH A. C., DEPT. OF THE TENN.,
    No. 53.   }   *Holly Springs, Miss., December* 26, 1862.

I. Brig. Gen. John E. Smith is hereby assigned to the command of the Eighth Division, left wing, Army of the Tennessee, and will report at once to Brig. Gen. C. S. Hamilton.

*   *   *   *   *   *   *

By order of Maj. Gen. U. S. Grant:

[JNO. A. RAWLINS,]
Assistant Adjutant-General.

HOLLY SPRINGS, MISS., *December* 26, 1862.

Brig. Gen. J. E. SMITH, *Davis' Mill:*

Sullivan is calling for more troops to drive the rebels out of the north part of Tennessee.

I have notified him that I will send four regiments if he will send cars. You may hold them in readiness from your command to embark on arrival of cars.

U. S. GRANT,
Major-General.

HOLLY SPRINGS, MISS., *December* 26, 1862.

Brig. Gen. J. E. SMITH, *Davis' Mill:*

Send one brigade of your command to Moscow, leaving one regiment between La Grange and Moscow. Instructions will be sent for the repairs to the road. They should start the mill at Moscow and gather all the forage and supplies possible. Send with this brigade such portion of the pioneer corps formed by General Ross as you have with you.

U. S. GRANT,
Major-General.

HOLLY SPRINGS, MISS., *December* 26, 1862.

Brig. Gen. J. E. SMITH, *Davis' Mill:*

Assume command of all the forces at La Grange, Grand Junction, and Davis' Mill, and you will retain command of them at any other point to which they may be sent for duty. The balance of the division will be returned as soon as Forrest is driven out of West Tennessee.

The regiment ordered to occupy the road between La Grange and Moscow may go on to Moscow to hold the bridge at that place until

Denver's division arrives, when it will return and guard the road indicated in the first order. You can place your artillery at the different posts within your command according to your judgment. At all bridges the men should build block-houses.

U. S. GRANT,
Major-General.

HUMBOLDT, *December 26, 1862.*
General SULLIVAN:

I am now ready to start north. Cannot say how far I shall go to-day. Whenever I stop I will at once telegraph, if communication be not broken. In case it is I desire that you send me re-enforcements, for it may be that after we get away near the Obion the rebels will seek to cut communications and attack on both sides. To provide against this, if communication be cut, send some old troops, and if not needed I will send them back. No news this a. m. Have you any?

I. N. HAYNIE,
Brigadier-General.

NINETEEN MILES SOUTH OF RIPLEY, MISS.,
December 26, 1862.
Major-General GRANT:

Van Dorn is making his way back to Pemberton as fast as he can go. I have followed him as closely as possible. I am 19 miles from Pontotoc, but may go there. Unless I can learn that a force of ours is south of Van Dorn farther pursuit will be useless, and to-morrow I shall turn back toward Oxford. If I can make him fight I will do so.
I have taken many prisoners.

J. K. MIZNER,
Colonel, Commanding Cavalry.

WAR DEPARTMENT,
Washington, December 27, 1862.
Major-General CURTIS, *Saint Louis, Mo.:*

General Davies reports Columbus as now entirely safe, but General Hurlbut reports Memphis as not sufficiently strong. Can you not give him re-enforcements for a few days till he can open communication with General Grant? These raids are probably intended to draw back our troops from Vicksburg. This must be avoided.

H. W. HALLECK,
General-in-Chief.

COLUMBUS, KY., *December 27, 1862—noon.*
(Received 4 p. m.)
Major-General HALLECK,
General-in-Chief, U. S. Army:

From the best information from persons from Trenton and other points I find the road is greatly damaged, not so much in the woodwork as in the rails. They built fires upon the rails on one side, which expands the rails and throws the track, ties, and all out of place, and when the iron gets so hot that it can push no farther the rail knuckles, and when it cools breaks the rails. I understand miles of the road are thus destroyed.

The enemy, from all accounts, have left, going south. The reports are contradictory, however. I am now in a position to send a construction train out and hold the place against any force which they can bring. I shall, however, do nothing in that way until I am sure of the position of the enemy and their strength, which must soon be developed. I have about 6,000 troops and will be assisted by Brigadier-Generals Tuttle and Fisk. I shall await your orders or those of General Grant as to the commencement of repairs on this road. My impression is that the damage is so extensive that it may involve a change of base to Memphis or below.

THOS. A. DAVIES,
Brigadier-General.

COLUMBUS, KY., *December* 27, 1862.

Maj. Gen. H. W. HALLECK, *General-in-Chief:*

One of my couriers sent to Jackson has returned, but could not penetrate nearer than 27 miles of that place. Heard cannonading in that direction. Colonel of Forrest's cavalry informed him that Buckner was attacking Jackson and would have it before night; that Corinth had fallen, also Bolivar; that they were going to take Paducah, and would move on Columbus as soon as Forrest was re-enforced. This is rumor and must be taken for what it is worth. They have two cordons of pickets extending from Jackson to the Tennessee River, 15 miles apart. Van Dorn is at Brownsville, just back of Fort Pillow. This is reliable. One of our own men marched three days with him. I shall re-enforce Fort Pillow by troops from New Madrid by daylight to-morrow morning.

THOS. A. DAVIES,
Brigadier-General.

HEADQUARTERS FISK'S BRIGADE,
Columbus, Ky., December 27, 1862.

Maj. Gen. SAMUEL R. CURTIS,
Commanding Department of Missouri:

MY DEAR GENERAL: I reached Columbus yesterday and proceeded directly to business. Found General Davies very much alarmed and quite nervous. A large force of rebels was reported as very near and approaching. I was immediately put in command of the left wing of the forces here, including all the forts on the heights. General Tuttle commands the right wing and holds the low grounds near the railroad. We have now about 7,000 troops. Your prompt re-enforcement of this point saved it, with its $13,000,000 of Government stores, beyond any doubt; General Davies has so telegraphed General Halleck. General Davies was inclined to evacuate the position; had placed much of the Government stores on transports ready for departure. General Tuttle and myself have resisted any such conclusion. I told General Davies I had come to Columbus by your order with your forces to aid in saving the post, and I should obey orders. If he left, I should stay and fight it out. General Tuttle, true to his Iowa grit, said "amen." I fear

General Davies is easily frightened. He has withdrawn his force from Hickman; has destroyed all the guns and ammunition at Island No. 10; has ordered Colonel Scott, of the Thirty-second Iowa, to roll his guns into the river at New Madrid, burn carriages, blow up magazines, abandon his post, and remove his forces to Fort Pillow. You will hardly indorse all this. Colonel Scott was advised by me of your wishes to hold New Madrid at all hazards. I fear that he has carried out the orders of General Davies. The Thirty-sixth Iowa did not remain here—was gone when I arrived. The general thinks they behaved badly to leave him in trouble.

Forces from your department on duty here are as follows: Twenty-ninth and Thirty-third Iowa, Thirty-third and Thirty-fifth Missouri, Schofield's battery, Colonel Bowen, with three companies and four howitzers, cavalry all excellent, vigilant troops. I forgot to name the Twenty-first Missouri, Colonel Moore. It was very fortunate that you were able to respond so quickly and in such force.

I have been busy day and night organizing my forces, planting guns, and scouting. Cheatham and Forrest have a force of about 15,000 very near us. I don't believe they will advance. They cannot take us if they do. They may make a dash on Paducah. If so, I fear they will capture it. I am quite convinced that your plan of giving up the long line of railroads and opening and holding the river is the true one.

The gunboat has not yet arrived; all are anxiously waiting for it. We have one small one, which has run down to Fort Pillow, where an attack is also expected. All the gunboats and most of General Grant's army have gone southward, leaving Cairo, Paducah, Columbus, and vicinity as a prey to the marauding chieftains, Forrest and Cheatham. I am using for my headquarters the best secesh house in town, formerly occupied by the Right Rev. Maj. Gen. Bishop Polk, C. S. Army.

I am, general, very respectfully, your obedient servant,

CLINTON B. FISK,
Brigadier-General.

COLUMBUS, KY., *December* 27, 1862.

ADJUTANT-GENERAL U. S. ARMY,
Washington, D. C.:

GENERAL: I have the honor to inform you that a rebel force of mounted infantry (having some ten cannons) have for the last eight or ten days held possession of the United States military (Mobile and Ohio) railroad. Said rebel force is variously estimated at from 2,000 to 6,000 or even 8,000 men, under command of General Forrest. Parties who were taken prisoners, held two days, and then paroled assure me that the force is fully 6,000. They have injured the road very much, and it must of necessity take some time to repair it after said force has been driven away.

My object in writing this is to bring to your knowledge the fact that the rebel general in command has taken as prisoners not only the troops along the road, but all the civilian employés, even to laborers and wood-choppers. The civilians have to a great extent been paroled, being sworn first not to enter Tennessee or Kentucky again during the war, &c.

I am, very respectfully, your obedient servant,

CARLOS DUTTON,
Captain and Assistant Quartermaster.

HEADQUARTERS DISTRICT OF EASTERN ARKANSAS,
Helena, December 27, 1862.
Major-General HURLBUT:

GENERAL: If you have a chance to send a dispatch safely through to General Grant I respectfully ask that he may be informed that agreeably to his request I send General Washburn with 2,000 cavalry and four pieces of artillery to Coldwater and with orders to make his way to General Grant if possible; that I have garrisoned Friar's Point with infantry, artillery, and cavalry.

General Washburn found the bottom lands so utterly impassable that he was compelled to return, and when the least rain falls at this season of the year the bottoms are impassable at all points between the Mississippi and Tallahatchie; that every effort has been made to get a communication with Oxford, but it is impossible from the causes stated.

There is no enemy in force this side the Tallahatchie.

I am, general, your obedient servant,

W. A. GORMAN,
Brigadier-General, Commanding.

WAR DEPARTMENT,
Washington, December 27, 1862.
Maj. Gen. STEPHEN A. HURLBUT, *Memphis, Tenn.*:

Memphis must be held at all hazards. I have asked General Curtis to re-enforce you. Endeavor to communicate with General Grant; also with gunboats down the river. There are none above.

H. W. HALLECK,
General-in-Chief.

JOHNSON'S LANDING,
Yazoo River, 8 *miles from its mouth, December* 27, 1862.
Major-General HALLECK, *Washington, D. C.*:

GENERAL: We all arrived at Milliken's Bend, 12 miles above the mouth of the Yazoo, on Christmas eve, in good order and condition. We were detained a little at Helena, but have not been delayed at all from lack of fuel, as I feared we should be. Most of the boats had an abundance, and those which had not we supplied while lying at shore for other purposes. I am satisfied that if an order was issued requiring boats in all cases to pay in money for wood there would soon be an abundance of it. Policy requires this without any reference to loyalty or disloyalty. I have examined carefully and am confident I am right.

I am glad to be able to say that notwithstanding the very brief notice given for so large transportation of troops and stores (sixty-seven boats), and the great difficulties in getting coal, the expedition was not delayed beyond a day for lack of transportation, if at all. General Sherman sent out a brigade of General A. J. Smith's division, from Milliken's Bend, some 30 miles and destroyed the Vicksburg and Shreveport Railroad, as also some 1,000 bales of cotton belonging to the Confederate States.

Steele's, Morgan's, and M. L. Smith's divisions landed here yesterday and A. J. Smith's to-day, and all are pushing out. Some skirmishing has been going on this afternoon, and the prospect of a severe conflict soon seems decided. We are hopeful and sanguine, but on this point you will no doubt hear fully from General Sherman.

A. J. Smith is assigned to the right; Morgan L. Smith, next; Steele, next, and Morgan the left. There is a strong battery some 12 miles above here, and believed to be supported by some 10.000 or 12,000 troops. It is also believed there are about the same number in Vicksburg with strong fortifications and guns of heavy caliber. Re-enforcements are also arriving from Jackson.

The news came yesterday that General McClernand was soon to arrive and take command. Of course General Sherman must have felt unpleasantly, but he does not show it in the least and bears it like the true soldier he is.

General Sherman thinks it best to detain the transports a few days; until he discharges them I shall venture to remain. As there is said to be a plan on foot to intercept the boats on their return, a gunboat will probably escort us.

Very respectfully,

L. B. PARSONS,
Colonel and Aide-de-Camp.

ABBEVILLE, *December* 27, 1862.
Major-General GRANT:

GENERAL: Fifty teams from General Denver's division went out on a forage expedition under Colonel Stevenson and have not yet returned, so that he could not start to-day. He will take the road via Holly Springs and Hudsonville, and his orders, given after the receipt of your first dispatch, were to start as soon as possible. He will see you in Holly Springs. Two companies of cavalry will report to you to-morrow by 9 o'clock. From information gathered from citizens it appears that a large force of rebels under General Holmes are moving northeast from Grenada. I shall not place much reliance upon it unless confirmed from other sources.

To-morrow morning the telegraph office will be at my headquarters, and I can then communicate immediately; now it takes fully three hours.

JAS. B. McPHERSON,
Major-General.

HOLLY SPRINGS, MISS., *December* 27, 1862.
Brig. Gen. GRENVILLE. M. DODGE, *Corinth, Miss.*:

There are now five light-draught gunboats in the Tennessee River waiting to run up on the first rise. They will naturally destroy all means of crossing the river. I wish, however, to make sure you would send a request for them to do so.

If you can get a messenger through to Lowe instruct him to destroy Forrest's train.

U. S. GRANT,
Major-General.

TRENTON, *December* 27, 1862.
General J. C. SULLIVAN:

Forrest, as I am informed, was in Dresden last night. You can reach Huntingdon better from there than from Jackson. I have ordered the advance to be made.

I. N. HAYNIE,
Brigadie--General.

TRENTON, *December* 27, 1862.

General SULLIVAN:

The third train is here with troops.   One regiment of Colonel Fuller's brigade not yet arrived.

I have positive information that Forrest, with 2,000 men and six guns, passed to and stopped in Dresden last night on his way to Reynoldsburg or some other point on the river.   They left Middleburg yesterday evening, where I had hoped to catch them.   I will start a brigade up toward Kenton, if you think it best; but there are, I am pretty sure, no rebels there.   Now, I am informed that the road to Dresden is good except one bridge, and that by going the Huntingdon road we may get on the enemy's flank and thus prevent his escape.   Give me orders which way to start.   I delayed this long hoping you would be up on this last train.

I. N. HAYNIE,
Brigadier-General.

TRENTON, *December* 27, 1862.

General SULLIVAN:

I sent Captain Silence yesterday to Brownsville.   He has just come to me here and makes report as follows:

I arrived at Humboldt at 5 o'clock this evening.   I went within 5 miles of Brownsville.   Union men direct from there report no rebel forces at Brownsville.   I spent the night on Forked Deer; had guards at Cherryville and Sheron's Ferry.   Twelve mounted men with double-barreled guns crossed this way at 12 o'clock last night.   I found the neighborhood filled with rebels, apparently on leave.   I heard no definite, concerted move except that sent you last night.

NED R. SILENCE,
Captain, Commanding Cavalry.

The captain also tells me that a report reached him that Van Dorn was expecting to hear of Bragg's forces moving on to Jackson and he was to act in concert with him.   He perhaps means the late move of Forrest on Jackson.   Re-enforcement question all right.

I. N. HAYNIE,
Brigadier-General.

TRENTON, *December* 27, 1862—11 a. m.

Major-General GRANT:

Forrest has left for Tennessee River, supposed crossing at Reynoldsburg.   I am pursuing on Huntingdon road.   The Tennessee River has risen 2 feet since Sunday.   I will not leave him until he is out of the district.

JER. C. SULLIVAN,
Brigadier-General.

HEADQUARTERS, POTTS' FARM,
Fifteen miles southwest from Holly Springs, Miss.,
December 27, 1862—4 p. m.

Maj. Gen. U. S. GRANT,
Commanding Thirteenth Army Corps:

GENERAL: Colonel Hatch with his command arrived at New Albany four hours after I had passed.   I continued the pursuit 9 miles south of that place, when, being convinced that farther pursuit would be fruitless and having gone to a point farther south than our lines extended, I turned west and camped at King's Bridge, 7 miles west of New Albany.

Last night Colonel Hatch reported to me by letter at 6 p. m.   He was at New Albany.   I directed him to proceed by the most practicable route to our advance post.   He will go via Waterford to Abbeville.

My command is exhausted from fatigue and were drenched by the rain last night.   I shall camp here to-night, finding an abundance of forage, and will proceed to Holly Springs in the morning.

Some ambulances and wagons belonging to the command were left at Bolivar and were ordered to Grand Junction.   Will you have them ordered to meet us?   Our train should also be ordered to join us at Holly Springs, as the command is without a change of clothing and in such a condition as to require rest.

I am, sir, very respectfully, your obedient servant,

J. K. MIZNER,
Colonel, Commanding Cavalry.

I sent a line to you by Major Mudd.   We pressed the enemy hard and took many prisoners.

HOLLY SPRINGS, *December* 27, 1862.

Major-General MCPHERSON, *Abbeville :*

As soon as the cavalry returns I want two companies (the freshest that can be got) to send through to Memphis.   From what I understand the road can be put in order in a few days.   I want in that case to order Quinby to return by the State Line road, guarding the road from Germantown until he meets the cars with his division, and send his supplies through by rail.

U. S. GRANT,
Major-General.

CAIRO, ILL., *December* 27, 1862—8 p. m.

Col. A. STAGER.

James W. Forbes, operator from Jackson, just arrived from Humboldt; brought dispatches through safely, but was prisoner twenty-four hours at Union City.   Says Jackson, Bolivar, and Grand Junction safe late as morning of 24th, but Van Dorn had surrounded Grand Junction, and Forrest, with 8,000 men, said would have Jackson in twenty-four hours.   Railroad and telegraph destroyed for 20 miles between Trenton and Union City.   Our men repairing northward from Humboldt.   Nothing late from Memphis.

SAM. BRUCH,
Capt. and A. Q. M. and Asst. Manager U. S. M. T.

HEADQUARTERS DEPARTMENT OF THE MISSOURI,
Saint Louis, December 28, 1862.

Major-General HURLBUT, *Memphis, Tenn.:*

GENERAL : I am sending some force to re-enforce your point, regarding it as rather weak and of utmost importance to the whole country.

I shall expect such force to be returned to my side of the Mississippi the moment General Grant gets his own force in an available position. I must also assure you that I am exposing my department and weakening all my efforts by thus sending forces to sustain the east side, and I trust the officers of the Department of the Tennessee will appreciate the necessity of an early co-operation with me, if danger appears on my side of the common artery of the West.

I am, general, very truly, yours,

SAML. R. CURTIS,
Major-General.

SAINT LOUIS, *December* 28, 1862.

General DAVIES, *Columbus* :

General Halleck wants me to strengthen Memphis. If you can spare my last shipment of troops let them go to Memphis. I trust you will not move the troops interior so as to get them away from the river. They may be needed on this side, and the river is my whole dependence to supply Helena.

SAML. R. CURTIS,
Major-General.

COLUMBUS, KY., *December* 28, 1862—10 a. m.
(Received 5 p. m.)

Maj. Gen. H. W. HALLECK, *General-in-Chief* :

I have just received a telegram from Fort Henry that Col. William W. Lowe, who was sent by General Grant to attack Forrest, has just returned. Reports that he went up as far as Lexington, and finding that General Dodge was following Forrest he returned to Fort Henry, dispersing on his way back Napier's band and destroying some property. With his return to Fort Henry I consider Forts Donelson, Henry, and Heiman, which were assigned to my command, measurably secure. Paducah is still weak for the want of a regiment or two. I telegraphed to Paducah to stop a regiment if any came down the Ohio. Columbus I consider out of all danger. Hickman has been evacuated, there having been only 150 men there. Island No. 10 has been rendered useless in case of capture. New Madrid will be evacuated to-night and the useless heavy armament there destroyed. The troops will re-enforce Fort Pillow. I hope Fort Pillow will be strong enough to stand with the re-enforcements. I have learned from reliable sources that their plans of operations have not been so much directed toward the railroad as to gain possession of Island No. 10 and then New Madrid. To this end they had arranged to take Hickman, haul-to some steamboats. and proceed down to Island No. 10. They fired upon the Duke at Hickman yesterday morning, but the gunboat New Era, which I sent there in anticipation of the movement, hove in sight just as they fired, and the rebels ran fast as she came up. They endeavored yesterday to mount two 64-pounders, condemned guns, at Hickman, but I sent down a regiment just as they got one of the carriages in position to throw the guns into the river and burn the carriages, which they did, and returned immediately here. There is no communication with General Grant.

THOS. A. DAVIES,
Brigadier-General.

HEADQUARTERS DISTRICT OF MEMPHIS,
December 28, 1862.

Brig. Gen. THOMAS A. DAVIES,
Commanding at Columbus, Ky.:

SIR: I inclose herewith copy of a dispatch just received from Brigadier-General Gorman:*

Unless you have orders from Washington or from Major-General Curtis requiring or authorizing the detention of troops destined for Helena I would advise you to forward them at once. I will not at this distance, and on the vague reports we have, put this advice into the shape of an order.

My best information is that the force which has broken your road did not exceed 3,500, and those mainly cavalry. It is my opinion that Columbus is perfectly defensible with 2,000 men. I am holding Memphis with 2,500, and no advantages of natural position or strong works. Such regiments as are under orders to join me here will report as soon as practicable, as this point has now become the basis of supply.

General Grant is at Holly Springs, with one division at Abbeville, and Quinby is coming in with his division and a wagon train. Forward as soon as practicable the medicine supplies.

I sincerely hope your order for the destruction of the armament at Island No. 10 has not been fulfilled. The order is premature. The armament can be destroyed when defense is impossible. If not carried into effect the order will be countermanded and the island held, with instructions not to destroy the armament until capture becomes imminent.

Very respectfully, your obedient servant,

S. A. HURLBUT,
Major-General.

COLUMBUS, KY., *December* 28, 1862.

Maj. Gen. SAMUEL R. CURTIS:

General Halleck telegraphed to me to hold Columbus at all hazards and make no movements of troops till Columbus is perfectly secure. I have barely troops enough, with these you sent me, to secure this object. Van Dorn is in the rear of Fort Earnest by last account; from this I judge he has threatened Memphis and intends to try Fort Earnest; from this fact I think Memphis is in no danger. On consultation with Fisk yesterday I ordered the evacuation of New Madrid, in your command, and destroyed the siege guns and ammunition there, which are of no use to us and of great danger if they fall into the hands of the enemy. The place can be reoccupied at any time by your troops under the exigencies existing. I hope this will meet with your approval. The troops at New Madrid were sent to re-enforce Fort Earnest.

THOS. A. DAVIES,
Brigadier-General, Commanding.

MEMPHIS, TENN., *December* 28, 1862.

Maj. Gen. U. S. GRANT,
Commanding, &c., Holly Springs:

I avail myself of the first moment to communicate the accompanying papers.

---

* Not found.

No. 1 is the order of the Secretary of War recognizing the Mississippi expedition and assigning me to the command of it. The President's indorsement thereon manifests the interest he feels in the expedition.

No. 2 is the copy of an order issued by the General-in-Chief to you, which I send lest the original has failed to reach you. This order. while giving to me the immediate command of the expedition, makes it a part of your general command.

No. 3 is an extract from an order, issued by the Secretary of War, relieving me from duty at Springfield, Ill., and instructing me to report to you for the purpose specified in No. 2.

No. 4 is an extract from a communication from the Secretary of War.

I have the honor to ask your instructions in the premises, and that you will be kind enough to afford me every proper facility in reaching my command.

I found the reports that the Mississippi River between Cairo and this place was invested by guerrillas unfounded. At the expiration of twenty four hours after leaving Cairo I reached here, without hinderance or interruption.

General Hurlbut informs me that General Sherman left Helena last Tuesday, and that a steamer coming up last night brings the report that the enemy have planted a battery at Bolivar, nearly opposite the mouth of the Arkansas River. With a gunboat and detachment from Helena I could test the truth of the report.

I regret that the expectation that I would find you here is disappointed. I have much that I would like to communicate to you. Much valuable information could be obtained by you at once here respecting the operations of your command, not only in General Davies' district, but on the Lower Mississippi. At this time access can be obtained without difficulty to all parts of your command from this place, at least above Bolivar.

I shall anxiously watch events upon the river until I hear from you.

Very respectfully, your obedient servant,

JOHN A. McCLERNAND,
Major-General.

[Inclosure No. 1.]

Ordered, That Major-General McClernand be, and he is, directed to proceed to the States of Indiana, Illinois, and Iowa to organize the troops remaining in those States and to be raised by volunteering or draft, and forward them with all dispatch to Memphis, Cairo, or such other points as may hereafter be designated by the General-in-Chief, to the end that when a sufficient force, not required by the operations of General Grant's command, shall be raised an expedition may be organized under General McClernand's command against Vicksburg and to clear the Mississippi River and open navigation to New Orleans.

[Indorsement.]

OCTOBER 20, 1862.

This order, though marked confidential, may be shown by General McClernand to Governors, and even others, when in his discretion he believes so doing to be indispensable to the progress of the expedition.

I add that I feel deep interest in the success of the expedition and desire it to be pushed forward with all possible dispatch consistently with the other parts of the military service.

A. LINCOLN.

[Inclosure No. 2.]

The following telegram is forwarded for your information:

WASHINGTON, *December* 18, 1862.

Major-General GRANT, *Oxford, Miss.*:

The troops in your department, including those from General Curtis' command which join the down-river expedition, will be divided into four army corps.

It is the wish of the President that General McClernand's corps shall constitute a part of the river expedition, and that he shall have the immediate command under your directions.

[Inclosure No. 3.]

You are relieved of duty at Springfield, and will report to General Grant for the purpose specified in the order of the General-in-Chief.

[Inclosure No. 4.]

GENERAL: The importance of the expedition on the Mississippi is every day becoming more manifest, and there will be the utmost endeavor on the part of the Government to give it aid and strength.

In conversing with you I indicated the importance of a coastwise expedition against Texas to aid you and create a diversion of the enemy's force.   Major-General Banks is now organizing an expedition for that purpose, which will be in condition to co-operate with any movements that may be made after you have succeeded in clearing the Mississippi River.

———

HOLLY SPRINGS, MISS., *December* 28, 1862.

Maj. Gen. STEPHEN A. HURLBUT,
    Commanding District of Memphis:

Please forward the following letter to its address by the first opportunity.

General Halleck's instructions to me were that I could retain that portion of the Helena forces sent to this side of the river under General Hovey.   Immediately on receiving his dispatch to this effect I sent orders for one regiment of infantry and one battery to remain at Friar's Point and garrison that place, and the cavalry to take a station about the mouth of Coldwater.   When this order reached Friar's Point these troops had gone back to Helena, and I have not since learned whether they have been returned.

If you are aware of the fact that they have not been returned please destroy the letter addressed to the commanding officer Friar's Point.

U. S. GRANT,
Major-General.

[Inclosure.]

HEADQUARTERS DEPARTMENT OF THE TENNESSEE,
    Holly Springs, Miss., December 28, 1862.

COMMANDING OFFICER FRIAR'S POINT, MISS.:

The falling back of my forces from the Yockna to the Tallahatchie River renders it unnecessary longer to keep a force at Friar's Point. You will therefore order the entire cavalry force at Friar's Point to proceed by the most practicable route to Holly Springs, Miss., keeping north of the Tallahatchie River, where it can be used to great advantage in clearing out the country of rebel cavalry.   The infantry and artillery you will send to Memphis, Tenn.; the quartermaster's department at Memphis will furnish you the necessary transportation. The cavalry should report here as soon as practicable.

U. S. GRANT,
Major-General.

HOLLY SPRINGS, MISS., *December* 28, 1862.

Brig. Gen. I. F. QUINBY,
Commanding Seventh Division:

Fearing that damages to the railroad north to Columbus will take several weeks to repair, I have directed the opening of the Memphis road. Investigation shows that but little damage has been done it at Moscow, and consequently cars can be run in a day or two at least as far as La Fayette, 21 miles west of Grand Junction. The roads from Memphis to that point are good. I have directed, therefore, that cars be got as far west as practicable to meet you on your return, and have also sent troops to guard the road to La Fayette, and I think for some miles farther west. You will then return by the State Line road until you meet the cars, and then in the absence of further orders dispose of your troops to guard the road westward as the work progresses. We may find it necessary to send the wagons back to get a second load of supplies. This will depend, however, on the extent of damages to be repaired, both on the road north and the Memphis road. I have no idea of keeping open the Memphis road except for temporary purposes. It may become necessary, however, to send more troops to Vicksburg. In that event the road will be very convenient.

U. S. GRANT,
Major-General.

HEADQUARTERS SECOND BRIGADE, U. S. VOLUNTEERS,
Columbus, Ky., December 29, 1862.

Maj. Gen. SAMUEL R. CURTIS,
Commanding Department Missouri:

GENERAL: I have the honor to report the forces from your department now on duty temporarily at this post as in good fighting condition and ready for action at the tap of the drum. Your prompt response to the call for aid from threatened Columbus must ever be regarded by the War Department as a very commendable instance of military courtesy.

From all the reports I can gather from deserters, intelligent contrabands, and reliable gentlemen I conclude that the brigand Forrest, with about 8,000 mounted rebels with eight pieces of artillery, undertook a raid on a large scale upon the Mobile and Ohio Railroad, his intention being the destruction of the railroad and the immense stock of supplies on hand here, together with cars, engines, public buildings, steamers, &c., and then fall back toward Memphis and La Grange. He was rapidly accomplishing his purpose when re-enforcements began to arrive from Saint Louis. His bands are now scattering, he in the mean time holding his headquarters at a point about 10 miles distant, where he is throwing up fortifications. I have been begging General Davies to let me take 4,000 men and go out there and whip him (Forrest), but the general will not allow the movement, is quite nervous about the post, but I am fully convinced we could defeat or skedaddle the entire rebel horde. I know I am a young general, but I believe I am old enough to see through a mill-stone with so large a hole in it. Unless I am much mistaken the entire line of railroad could be put in order in ten days, and your forces be relieved and sent on down to Helena, but General Grant cannot keep this line open and running with his present force in this district. I trust that in no event your forces here and myself will be retained on this side of the river. I am not yet advised whether or not Colonel Scott, of the Thirty-second Iowa, executed General Davies' order respecting the destruction of our works at New Madrid and the evacuation of that post. It is rumored here to-day that Jeff. Thompson and [W. L.] Jeffers are marching toward New Madrid, with quite a large force. I believe Colonel Scott could make a successful resistance.

Gunboat has not yet arrived.

Your boys are all in fine spirits and very desirous to get back under your immediate direction.

I am, general, very respectfully, your obedient servant,

CLINTON B. FISK,
Brigadier-General.

COLUMBUS, KY., *December* 29, 1862—10 a. m.

Maj. Gen. H. W. HALLECK, *General-in-Chief:*

Colonel Ihrie, of General Grant's staff, came through last night from Trenton. Officers are arriving by land. Report no forces west of railroad. Road reported complete to Dyer, and telegraph communication and trains running all the way down, as before. From best information the enemy have left or are concentrating. I think the former most probable.

THOS. A. DAVIES,
Brigadier-General.

ABBEVILLE, *December* 29, 1862.

Major-General GRANT:

Colonel Hatch returned with his cavalry last evening without having met the enemy. He went within 10 miles of Pontotoc, to Rocky Ford, and New Albany.

JAS. B. McPHERSON,
Major-General.

HUNTINGDON, TENN., *December* 29, 1862—8.06 p. m.

Major-General GRANT,
Headquarters Thirteenth Army Corps:

I reached Huntingdon before the rebels knew I had left Trenton. I have Forrest in a tight place, but he may escape by my not having cavalry. The gunboats are up the river as far as Clifton, and have destroyed all the boats and ferries. To escape, Forrest must pass as far south as Savannah. My troops are moving on him in three directions, and I hope for success.

JER. C. SULLIVAN,
Brigadier-General.

SPECIAL FIELD ORDERS, ⎱ HDQRS. THIRTEENTH ARMY CORPS,
⎰ DEPARTMENT OF THE TENNESSEE,
No. 35. ⎰ *Holly Springs, Miss., December* 29, 1862.

I. Foraging parties will leave for the use of families and their servants a sufficient supply of provisions for sixty days, and when families have a less supply beyond this if found in the country within reach of the army. This order is not, however, to be construed to deprive the soldier of his rations whilst the country affords it. If suffering must fall on one or the other, the citizen must bear it.

II. Hereafter no houses will be taken for any purposes except by order of post or chief quartermasters, and no buildings will be assigned except for storage purposes, hospitals, and to officers entitled to quarters under existing orders or those having special permits from district commanders or higher authority to occupy houses.

III. The exception in Paragraph I of Special Orders, No. 32, is hereby extended to include commanders of army corps, wings, districts, and posts, surgeons of posts and general hospitals, and such staff officers as have no immediate connection with troops. Regimental surgeons must remain in camp with their regiments.

IV. Chief of staff department will see that all officers of their respective departments remain with their stores, prepared to issue the same at all times when called upon.

By order of Maj. Gen. U. S. Grant:

JNO. A. RAWLINS,
Assistant Adjutant-General.

PADUCAH, KY., *December* 29, 1862.

Hon. ABRAHAM LINCOLN,
President of the United States:

General Orders, No. 11, issued by General Grant at Oxford, Miss., December the 17th, commands all post commanders to expel all Jews, without distinction, within twenty-four hours, from his entire department. The undersigned, good and loyal citizens of the United States and residents of this town for many years, engaged in legitimate business as merchants, feel greatly insulted and outraged by this inhuman order, the carrying out of which would be the grossest violation of the Constitution and our rights as good citizens under it, and would place us, besides a large number of other Jewish families of this town, as outlaws before the whole world. We respectfully ask your immediate attention to this enormous outrage on all law and humanity, and pray for your effectual and immediate interposition. We would respectfully refer you to the post commander and post adjutant as to our loyalty, and to all respectable citizens of this community as to our standing as citizens and merchants. We respectfully ask for immediate instructions to be sent to the commander of this post.

D. WOLFF & BROS.
C. F. KASKELL.
J. W. KASWELL.

HEADQUARTERS,
Memphis, Tenn., December 30, 1862.

Lieutenant-Colonel RAWLINS,
Assistant Adjutant-General, Holly Springs:

COLONEL: I desire to report to the major-general commanding department that General Quinby, with his division, escorting a heavy supply train, arrived at this post yesterday. Every preparation had been made in advance to facilitate the loading, but the teams were fatigued, and General Quinby deferred commencing until this morning. We have an abundance of rations, and the commissary of subsistence has been notified by Colonel Haines to keep always 4,000,000 on hand.

I have obtained 700,000 feet of lumber, and propose to erect within the fort a storehouse for 2,000,000, which, with our other accommodations, will give abundant storage. It will also be necessary to erect a barrack hospital within the ramparts.

The ground in front of the fort is now being cleared of houses, &c., to a distance of about 250 yards, and Captain Prime proposes to erect a flank work at the north end to cover the quartermaster's and commissary's depots and flank the heavy guns.

The garrison is all within the fort except one regiment on provost duty at the square in the city.

The strength of the command is shown by the returns herewith.*

I stopped the Thirty-sixth Iowa for a few days, but have sent them on.

The city is restless, but cowed. I have not hesitated to announce that an attack would involve the destruction of Memphis. I am enrolling the Union Club as Home Guards and propose to arm them.

Since General Sherman took away the force from here smuggling has been unlimited. I occasionally catch them with cavalry patrols and certificate. [?]

I have ordered General Davies to send down all forces destined originally for Memphis and Helena and stopped by him, and have forwarded to-day the order of Major-General Grant to the same effect.

I regret to say that it is my opinion, from all I can learn, that the good of the service demands inquiry into the conduct of General Davies. The destruction and abandonment of Island No. 10, the unnecessary accumulation of troops, the keeping these troops so accumulated under arms night after night, and the neglect to push out forces into the country are strongly reported to me by rumor. These rumors may be unjust, but I fear they are not altogether so.

I regret to report that the paroled prisoners arrived here in the wildest disorder. Colonel Ferrell, of the Twenty-ninth Illinois, who commanded after the major-general relieved Colonel Murphy from duty, exercised no authority over his officers and men, and when the command arrived at the Nonconah, 7 miles out, abandoned them and rode in an ambulance with his wife. The example spread, and officers and men came in squads and parties and spread all over the city. I was compelled to order the provost-guard to arrest all officers and men and force them to the fort. Colonel Ferrell is under arrest, and I have no doubt, when you receive the report of General Quinby, will be mustered out of service for disobedience of orders and desertion of his men. I shall be able to get them off to Saint Louis to-morrow. Colonel Murphy has been arrested and awaits orders.

Colonel Howe's Third Regular Cavalry, about 200 strong, is here, a fine body of men, but armed only with pistol and saber. They are all by education mounted riflemen. If the major-general will send me Grierson's regiment I would be glad to send Howe's in exchange. Two companies of Third United States are at Corinth. My reason for asking for Grierson is that he is thoroughly acquainted with this country— will be more useful than any other.

I am of opinion that General Gorman has withdrawn most of his forces from this side of the river, and I learn from him that the cavalry made an ineffectual attempt to cross from Friar's Point to Oxford, but

---

* Not found.

were prevented by mud. He is ordered both by Generals Curtis and Halleck to move by the 3d January toward Little Rock in a combined movement with Blunt, Herron, and Schofield. A fleet of light-draught boats are now passing down to him, so that I suppose he will proceed up Arkansas or White River, both now full.

I have no report from Sherman except stories brought up to different persons that Sherman was at Vicksburg; landed within 6 miles of the town, moving on, and Banks below the city.

I do not think that any troops will come to this place from Helena, but hope for a regiment or more from Columbus when Davies lets them go.

I have been compelled to postpone the election for member of Congress from the 29th December to 20th January on account of this raid; by that time I hope the country will be quiet.

I beg you will state to the general that Maj. Gen. John A. McClernand went down the river this morning on the Express. He will need convoy to get through below.

I am sorry that my health, hitherto good, is failing me. I am unfit for the field on account of an obstinate erysipelas, which annoys me exceedingly about the face and eyes, that prevented my riding for two weeks. I am, however, fit for office work and to hold Memphis, especially as Halleck will not let me go home.

I am, very respectfully, your obedient servant,

S. A. HURLBUT,
Major-General.

HOLLY SPRINGS, MISS., *December* 30, 1862.

Maj. Gen. STEPHEN A. HURLBUT,
Commanding District of Memphis, Tenn. :

Your communication, inclosing dispatch from Washington, was duly received.

As you are not in sufficient health to take the field I will be very glad to retain you in command of Memphis for the present. In fact I have been somewhat troubled to know who I could send there to relieve you.

General Davies has a force of 5,000 at Columbus, when one regiment is the greatest abundance to hold the place, and has been during all of the late scare. I have directed him to reduce his garrison to what it was before, sending all the spare troops to Memphis. My cavalry force is very weak, but if the 2,000 cavalry belonging to Hovey's command are still on this side of the river I will be able to send you one regiment of it. I have ordered this cavalry to report here. I am now opening the Memphis and Charleston road, and have placed a large force on the road to protect it. With the additional forces you will receive from Columbus you will be able to hold the road to Germantown. The balance will be provided for from here.

No special news here. An unofficial dispatch received last evening from Humboldt says that our troops now have Forrest in a tight place. The Tennessee has risen, and our troops, I believe, have destroyed all the flats on the river. With a sufficient cavalry force Forrest's fate would be sealed. Infantry, however, he may succeed in evading.

U. S. GRANT,
Major-General.

HEADQUARTERS COMMANDER POST,
Jackson, December 30, 1862—7 p. m.

General GRANT:

Major Funke, Eleventh Illinois Cavalry, reports a ferry-boat at Lowrey's Ferry, on the Hatchie. He was followed from there through Brownsville on his return by 300 cavalry; their number on both sides of the river is reported at 1,000. If you send me a regiment of infantry I will drive the rebels across the river.

M. K. LAWLER,
Colonel, Commanding Post.

LA GRANGE, *December* 30, 1862.

General GRANT:

Two of McArthur's brigades are at Moscow; the other (Crocker's) will reach La Fayette to-morrow. I will recall Smith's regiments from those places. McArthur reports large numbers of guerrillas along the road west. I hope the cavalry will reach Moscow to-morrow

C. S. HAMILTON,
Brigadier-General.

HOLLY SPRINGS, MISS., *December* 30, 1862.

Maj. Gen. J. B. MCPHERSON, *Abbeville, Miss.:*

I have detained Denver's division here and sent McArthur to La Fayette and Moscow, thus keeping the two commands more together. I have rebrigaded the cavalry, making two brigades, the one commanded by Grierson to be assigned to you. For the present they are encamped east of Holly Springs, a few miles out. They had better remain where they are, but be ready for an expedition in any direction. Do you hear anything from the front? I have had 2,000 cavalry at Friar's Point that made an unsuccessful attempt to reach me at Oxford. I have now ordered them to get here by the most practicable route. They may have gone back to Helena, however.

U. S. GRANT,
Major-General.

MCPHERSON'S, *December* 30, 1862.

Major-General GRANT:

Colonel Hatch's cavalry went into Oxford to-day; captured 2 prisoners belonging to Colonel Slemons' regiment. They scouted country 2 miles south of Oxford; encountered and chased about 60 rebel cavalry. Failed to find out anything about movements of enemy.

JAS. B. MCPHERSON,
Major-General

SPECIAL ORDERS, }   HDQRS. RIGHT WING, 13TH ARMY CORPS,
No. 38.   }   *December* 30, 1862.

I. The three divisions will occupy the ground now held, keeping the front picket line close up to the bayou and toward Vicksburg. All but the pickets and supports will retire to near the effective range of canister and form line parallel to the county road from Vicksburg to Haines'

Bluff, stack arms, and rest. Men may make fires in hollows 500 yards back of picket line.

II. General Morgan's left is on the bayou and the other divisions and their pickets will connect with him. General Steele's division will be held in reserve along Chickasaw Bayou, with pickets on its east side. The enemy will doubtless shell our positions, but our artillery must not reply unless with a certainty of execution. The ammunition must not be wasted, as they will fire at our whole camp instead of a distinct object. Our artillery should be covered by earthworks, and commanders of infantry brigades will, on application of any artillery officer lying near him, furnish details for this work.

The First and Second Divisions will furnish working parties of a regiment each, who will report to Captain Jenney, of the Engineers, with all the axes to be had, to corduroy the road from the landing to camp. The regiments at the steamboat landings will furnish 100 men each, with due proportion of officers, to work the road along the levee. They must corduroy all the boggy ground. Rations can be had at Lake's; artillery ammunition at headquarters and on board the boat General Anderson. Musket ammunition should be carefully husbanded and distributed in each division. All musket ammunition not now in the boxes of men or in regimental wagons will forthwith be sent on board the General Anderson and delivered to Lieutenant Neely, ordnance officer, who will receipt for the same and reissue to regimental commanders, so that each man has on his person 60 rounds. This should be attended to at once.

All absentees not wounded must be collected and reports made to respective headquarters of the killed, wounded, and missing.

By order of Maj. Gen. W. T. Sherman:

J. H. HAMMOND,
Assistant Adjutant-General.

LA FAYETTE, *December* 31, 1862.

Col. JOHN. A. RAWLINS:

Arrived here this evening from Memphis. Will get to Holly Springs by noon to-morrow. No late news at Memphis. All reports confirm the taking of Vicksburg by Sherman, but no particulars can be obtained.

General McClernand and his 49 staff officers chartered the steamer Tigress and started for Vicksburg yesterday. Hurlbut thinks the enemy have erected batteries on the river that will prevent Mack from getting down. Holmes is moving against Helena, but there is sufficient force there to protect the place. General Gorman is moving upon Little Rock by steamers. No damage has been done the railroad between Memphis and this point. The country is full of guerrillas, who will destroy the trestle-work and small bridges unless they are protected. A regiment could protect the road from here to Memphis and no time ought to be lost in sending it forward. Hurlbut has no troops that he can possibly spare.

I examined the telegraph closely. There is but little wire missing; the line can be repaired in a day.

There is no wood for railroad at Memphis, but there is an abundance of dry wood along the road.

T. S. BOWERS,
Aide-de-Camp.

HOLLY SPRINGS, MISS., *December* 31, 1862.

Brig. Gen. J. B. MCPHERSON, *Abbeville, Miss.:*

At Memphis all reports confirm the taking of Vicksburg by Sherman, but no particulars can be obtained. General McClernand and 49 staff officers chartered the Tigress and started for Vicksburg yesterday. Hurlbut thinks the enemy have erected batteries on the river that will prevent him from getting down. Holmes is moving against Helena, but there is sufficient force there to protect the place. General Gorman is moving on Little Rock by steamers. No damage has been done railroad between La Fayette and Memphis.

There has been a great deal of cannonading to-day east of Henderson Station. Hope Sullivan has Forrest in a tight place.

I will try and get down to see you on the 2d.

U. S. GRANT,
Major-General.

SPECIAL ORDERS, }   HDQRS. 13TH A. C., DEPT. OF THE TENN.,
No. 58.   }   *Holly Springs, Miss., December* 31, 1862.

*   *   *   *   *   *   *

IV. 1st. It having been alleged that the One hundred and ninth Regiment Illinois Infantry Volunteers has shown indications of disloyalty, and many members of the regiment having voluntarily hunted up citizens in the neighborhood of their camp to surrender and obtain paroles from, is hereby placed in arrest.

2d. The regiment will be disarmed by the commander of the brigade to which the regiment is temporarily attached, and the arms and ammunition of the regiment turned over to the ordnance officer, Lieutenant Carter, to be disposed of as may hereafter be ordered.

3d. Officers and men will be confined within camp limits until otherwise ordered.

The conduct of Company K of said regiment being in honorable contrast to the balance of the regiment, is exempt from the effect of the above order, and will be placed on duty with the brigade to which said regiment is attached.

*   *   *   *   *   *   *

By order of Maj. Gen. U. S. Grant:

[JOHN A. RAWLINS,]
Assistant Adjutant-General.

Abstract from Return of the Department of the Tennessee, Maj. Gen. U. S. Grant commanding, for December, 1862.

Command.	Present for duty.		Aggregate present.	Aggregate present and absent.	Aggregate present and absent last monthly return.	Pieces of artillery.	
	Officers.	Men.				Heavy.	Field.
RIGHT WING, THIRTEENTH ARMY CORPS.							
(Headquarters north side Tallahatchie River, Miss.)							
Maj. Gen. JAMES B. McPHERSON.							
Staff	11		11	11	11		
First Division.							
(Headquarters Holly Springs, Miss.)							
Brig. Gen. J. W. DENVER.							
Staff	7		7	7	6		
Infantry	229	4,372	5,118	6,685	6,764		
Artillery	11	392	425	465	467		16
Total First Division	247	4,764	5,550	7,157	7,237		16
Third Division.							
(Headquarters Tallahatchie River.)							
Brig. Gen. JOHN A. LOGAN.							
Staff	3		5	3	3		
Infantry	324	5,998	7,228	8,970	9,027		
Artillery	14	491	524	602	553	4	20
Total Third Division	341	6,489	7,755	9,575	9,583	4	20
Fourth Division.							
Headquarters Tallahatchie River, or Waterford, Miss.)							
Brig. Gen. J. G. LAUMAN.							
Staff	3		3	3	2		
Infantry	299	5,791	6,625	8,193	8,255		
Artillery	12	552	602	668	538		24
Total Fourth Division	314	6,343	7,230	8,864	8,795		24
First Cavalry Brigade.							
Col. B. H. GRIERSON.							
Staff	3	4	7	7			
1st Cavalry Brigade	81	1,912	2,152	2,959			7
4th company Ohio Independent Cavalry, Capt. J. S. Foster.	3	79	107	116			
Total cavalry	87	1,995	2,266	3,082	3,075		7
Total right wing, Thirteenth Army Corps	1,000	19,591	22,812	28,689	28,701	4	67
SIXTH DIVISION, LEFT WING, ARMY OF THE TENNESSEE.							
(Headquarters La Fayette, Tenn.)							
Brig. Gen. JOHN McARTHUR.							
Staff	3		3	3	2		
Infantry	273	4,731	5,652	7,339	6,817		
Cavalry	2	57	64	69	69		
Artillery	11	314	347	395	399		16
Total Sixth Division	289	5,102	6,066	7,806	7,287		16

Abstract from Return of the Department of the Tennessee, &c.—Continued.

Command	Present for duty.		Aggregate present.	Aggregate present and absent.	Aggregate present and absent last monthly return.	Pieces of artillery.	
	Officers.	Men.				Heavy.	Field.
SEVENTH DIVISION, THIRTEENTH ARMY CORPS.							
(Headquarters near Memphis, Tenn.)							
Brig. Gen. I. F. QUINBY.							
Staff	8	....	8	8	8	......	......
Infantry	304	5, 614	6, 750	9, 257	9, 372	......	......
Cavalry	1	27	38	71	70	......	......
Artillery	8	367	413	643	653	......	20
Total Seventh Division	321	6, 008	7, 209	9, 979	10, 103	......	20
TENTH DIVISION, THIRTEENTH ARMY CORPS, ARMY OF THE MISSISSIPPI.							
(Headquarters Young's Point, La., opposite Vicksburg.)							
Second Brigade.							
Col. W. J. LANDRAM.							
Staff	5	....	5	5	4	......	......
Infantry	155	2, 970	3, 572	4, 736	4, 776	......	......
Total Second Brigade	160	2, 970	3, 577	4, 741	4, 780	......	......
DISTRICT OF CORINTH.							
(Headquarters Corinth, Miss.)							
Brig. Gen. GRENVILLE M. DODGE.							
Infantry	313	5, 363	6, 951	8, 313	7, 898	......	......
Cavalry	8	218	287	352	355	......	......
Artillery	10	305	376	411	454	......	......
Sappers and Miners	1	60	61	69	69	......	......
Total District of Corinth	332	5, 946	7, 675	9, 145	8, 776	......	......
DISTRICT OF COLUMBUS.*							
(Headquarters Columbus, Ky.)							
Brig. Gen. THOMAS A. DAVIES.							
Staff	9	....	9	10	10	......	......
Columbus, Ky.: Maj. John R. Edie	36	867	1, 186	1, 429	1, 361	11	......
Cairo, Ill.: Brig. Gen. T. M. Tuttle	41	776	853	946	947	......	......
Paducah, Ky.: Col. Silas Noble	10	249	426	679	685	......	3
Forts Henry, Heiman, and Donelson: Col. W. W. Lowe	104	2, 079	2, 735	2, 973	2, 957	4	9
Hickman, Ky.: Capt. E. W. Blake	2	131	162	166	166	2	2
Island No. 10, Tenn.: Maj. R. B. Jones	4	69	115	124	223	61	2
Fort Pillow, Tenn.: Maj. W. T. Strickland	22	474	617	694	714	......	......
En route to Fort Pillow: Capt. Frank Moore	....	....	98	98	......	......	......
Total District of Columbus	228	4, 645	6, 201	7, 119	7, 063	78	16
Grand total†	2, 330	44, 262	53, 540	67, 479	66, 710	82	119

* Taken from return of December 10.

† Cavalry division not reported as reorganized. Grierson's brigade reported in right wing.

Organization of troops in the Department of the Tennessee, commanded by Maj. Gen. U. S. Grant, December, 1862.

(Incomplete.)

RIGHT WING, THIRTEENTH ARMY CORPS.

Maj. Gen. JAMES B. McPHERSON.

FIRST DIVISION.

Brig. Gen. JAMES W. DENVER.

Second Brigade.	*Third Brigade.*
Col. J. ADAIR McDOWELL.	Col. JOSEPH R. COCKERILL.
40th Illinois, Maj. Rigdon S. Barnhill. 12th Indiana, Lieut. Col. Solomon D. Kempton. 100th Indiana, Lieut. Col. Albert Heath. 6th Iowa, Lieut. Col. John M. Corse. 46th Ohio, Lieut. Col. Chas. C. Walcutt.	97th Indiana, Col. Robert F. Catterson. 99th Indiana, Col. Alexander Fowler. 53d Ohio, Col. Wells S. Jones. 70th Ohio, Lieut. Col. De Witt C. Loudon.

Artillery.

Capt. WILLIAM COGSWELL.

1st Illinois, Battery F, Capt. John T. Cheney.
1st Illinois, Battery I, Capt. Edward Bouton.
1st Illinois, Battery M,* Capt. William Cogswell.
6th Indiana Battery, Capt. Michael Mueller.

THIRD DIVISION.

Brig. Gen. JOHN A. LOGAN.

First Brigade.	*Fourth Brigade.*
Col. C. CARROLL MARSH.	Col. JOHN D. STEVENSON.
20th Illinois, Capt. George W. Kennard. 31st Illinois, Col. Lyndorf Ozburn. 45th Illinois, Lieut. Col. Jasper A. Maltby. 124th Illinois, Col. Thomas J. Sloan. 23d Indiana, Maj. William P. Davis.	8th Illinois, Lieut. Col. Robert H. Sturgess. 63d Illinois, Col. Joseph B. McCown. 81st Illinois, Col. James J. Dollins. 7th Missouri, Lieut. Col. Wm. S. Oliver.
Second Brigade.	*Artillery.*
Col. MORTIMER D. LEGGETT.	Maj. CHARLES J. STOLBRAND.
30th Illinois, Col. Elias S. Dennis. 20th Ohio, Col. Manning F. Force. 68th Ohio, Col. Robert K. Scott. 78th Ohio, Lieut. Col. Zach. M. Chandler.	1st Illinois, Battery D, Capt. Henry A. Rogers. 2d Illinois, Battery G, Capt. Frederick Sparrestrom. 2d Illinois, Battery L, Capt. William H. Bolton. 8th Michigan Battery, Cap. Samuel De Golyer. 3d Ohio Battery, Capt. Wm. S. Williams.

* So borne on returns.   Officially known as Cogswell's Independent Battery.

FOURTH DIVISION.

Brig. Gen. Jacob G. Lauman.

First Brigade.

Col. Isaac C. Pugh.

41st Illinois, Lieut. Col. John H. Nale.
53d Illinois, Col. Daniel F. Hitt.
3d Iowa, Maj. Aaron Brown.
33d Wisconsin, Col. Jonathan B. Moore.

Second Brigade.

Col. Cyrus Hall.

14th Illinois, Lieut. Col. William Cam.
15th Illinois, Col. George C. Rogers.
46th Illinois, Col. Benjamin Dornblaser.
76th Illinois, Col. Alonzo W. Mack.

Third Brigade.

Col. Amory K. Johnson.

28th Illinois, Lieut. Col. Richard Ritter.
32d Illinois, Lieut. Col. William Hunter.
53d Indiana, Col. Walter Q. Gresham.
12th Wisconsin, Col. George E. Bryant.

Artillery.

Capt. George C. Gumbart.

2d Illinois, Baty. E, Sergt. Martin Mann.
2d Illinois, Battery K, Capt. Benjamin F. Rodgers.
9th Indiana Baty., Capt. Geo. R. Brown.
5th Ohio Battery, First Lieut. Anthony B. Burton.
7th Ohio Battery, Capt. Silas A. Burnap.
15th Ohio Battery, Capt. Edward Spear, jr.

Escort.

4th company Ohio Independent Cavalry, Capt. John S. Foster.

SIXTH DIVISION, LEFT WING, ARMY OF THE TENNESSEE.

Brig. Gen. John McArthur.

First Brigade.

Col. George W. Deitzler.

17th Illinois, Col. Addison S. Norton.
95th Illinois, Lieut. Col. Thomas W. Humphrey.
1st Kansas, Lieut. Col. Otto M. Tennison.
16th Wisconsin, Maj. Thomas Reynolds.
2d Illinois Artillery, Battery F, Lieut. Joseph W. Mitchell.

Second Brigade.

Col. T. E. G. Ransom.

11th Illinois, Lieut. Col. Garrett Nevins.
14th Wisconsin, Lieut. Col. Lyman M. Ward.
17th Wisconsin, Maj. Thomas McMahon.
18th Wisconsin, Col. Gabriel Bouck.
1st Missouri Artillery, Battery C, Lieut. Edward Brotzmann.

Third Brigade.

Col. Marcellus M. Crocker.

11th Iowa, Lieut. Col. John C. Abercrombie.
13th Iowa, Lieut. Col. John Shane.
15th Iowa, Col. Hugh T. Reid.
16th Iowa, Maj. William Purcell.
10th Ohio Battery, Capt. Hamilton B. White.

Unattached.

11th Illinois Cavalry, Company G, Capt. John R. Coykendall.
1st Minnesota Battery, First Lieut. William Z. Clayton.

TENTH DIVISION, THIRTEENTH ARMY CORPS.*

Second Brigade.

Col. WILLIAM J. LANDRAM.

77th Illinois, Col. David P. Grier.
97th Illinois, Col. Friend S. Rutherford.
108th Illinois, Col. John Warner.
131st Illinois, Col. George W. Neeley.
19th Kentucky, Lieut. Col. John Cowan.
48th Ohio, Capt. S. G. W. Peterson.

CAVALRY DIVISION, DEPARTMENT OF THE TENNESSEE.†

Col. T. LYLE DICKEY.

First Brigade.

Col. BENJAMIN H. GRIERSON.

6th Illinois, Maj. Reuben Loomis.
7th Illinois, Lieut. Col. Edward Prince.
2d Iowa, Col. Edward Hatch.

Second Brigade.

Col. ALBERT L. LEE.

2d Illinois (7 cos.), Maj. John J. Mudd.
4th Illinois (10 cos.), Lieut. Col. M. R. M. Wallace.
7th Kansas, Lieut. Col. Thos. P. Herrick.
5th Ohio (8 cos.), Capt. Phineas R. Miner.

SEVENTH DIVISION, THIRTEENTH ARMY CORPS.

Brig. Gen. ISAAC F. QUINBY.

First Brigade.

Col. JESSE I. ALEXANDER.

72d Illinois, Col. Frederick A. Starring.
48th Indiana, Col. Norman Eddy.
59th Indiana, Lieut. Col. Jefferson K. Scott.
4th Minnesota, Lieut. Col. John E. Tourtellotte.

Second Brigade.

Col. EPHRAIM R. ECKLEY.

56th Illinois, Col. Green B. Raum.
17th Iowa, Lieut. Col. Clark R. Wever.
10th Missouri, Col. Samuel A. Holmes.
24th Missouri, Company F, Lieut. William W. McCammon.
80th Ohio, Capt. Charles H. Mathews.

Third Brigade.

Col. GEORGE B. BOOMER.

93d Illinois, Col. Holden Putnam.
5th Iowa, Col. Charles L. Matthies.
10th Iowa, Lieut. Col. William E. Small.
26th Missouri, Lieut. Col. John H. Holman.

Artillery.

Lieut. Col. ALBERT M. POWELL.

1st Missouri, Battery M, Capt. Junius W. MacMurray.
11th Ohio Battery, Capt. Frank C. Sands.
6th Wisconsin Battery, Capt. Henry Dillon.
12th Wisconsin Battery, Capt. William Zickerick.

Cavalry.

5th Missouri, Company C, Lieut. Russel W. Maryhugh.

DISTRICT OF CORINTH.

Brig. Gen. GRENVILLE M. DODGE.

First Brigade.

Col. THOMAS W. SWEENY.

52d Illinois, Maj. Edwin A. Bowen.
66th Indiana, Capt. John F. Baird.
2d Iowa, Col. James B. Weaver.
7th Iowa, Col. Elliott W. Rice.

Second Brigade.

Col. AUGUST MERSY.

9th Illinois, Lieut. Col. Jesse J. Phillips
12th Illinois, Maj. James R. Hugunin.
22d Ohio, Lieut. Col. Homer Thrall.
81st Ohio, Lieut. Col. Robert N. Adams

---

* Incomplete.
† As reorganized by Special Orders, No. 57, Headquarters Thirteenth Army Corps, Department of the Tennessee, December 30, 1862.

Third Brigade.

Col. MOSES M. BANE.

7th Illinois, Lieut. Col. Richard Rowett.
50th Illinois, Maj. Thomas W. Gaines.
57th Illinois, Col. Silas D. Baldwin.
18th Missouri, Lieut. Col. Charles S. Sheldon.

Tuscumbia.	*Glendale.*
Col. PATRICK E. BURKE.	Lieut. Col. JOHN MORRILL.
14th Missouri, Col. Patrick E. Burke.*	64th Illinois, Lieut. Col. John Morrill.
5th Ohio Cavalry (3d battalion), Capt. Joseph C. Smith.	Independent Company Illinois Cavalry, Capt. William Ford.

Corinth.

1st U. S. Infantry (battalion of), Capt. E. D. Phillips.
Stewart's Illinois Battalion Cavalry, Capt. Eagleton Carmichael.
1st Missouri Light Artillery, Maj. George H. Stone.
Sappers and Miners, Lieut. Christian Lochbihler.

DISTRICT OF COLUMBUS.†

Brig. Gen. THOMAS A. DAVIES.

Columbus, Ky.	*Cairo, Ill.*
Maj. JOHN R. EDIE.	Brig. Gen. JAMES M. TUTTLE.
18th Illinois (detachment of), and U. S. Infantry, Lieut. Col. Daniel H. Brush.	35th Iowa, Col. Sylvester G. Hill.
111th Illinois, Col. James S. Martin. 2d Illinois Cavalry (one company). 4th Illinois Cavalry (one company). Detachm't 15th and 16th U. S. Infantry.	*Forts Henry, Heiman, and Donelson.*
	Col. WILLIAM W. LOWE.
Paducah, Ky.	83d Illinois, Col. Abner C. Harding. 71st Ohio, Maj. James H. Hart. 13th Wisconsin, Col. William P. Lyon. 5th Iowa Cavalry, Lieut. Col. Matthewson T. Patrick.
Col. SILAS NOBLE.	
2d Illinois Cavalry, Company L, Capt. Francis T. Moore. 15th Kentucky Cavalry Battalion. 1st Illinois Artillery, Battery K, Capt. Jason B. Smith.	2d Illinois Artillery (two companies).
	Island No. 10., Tenn.
Hickman, Ky.	Maj. R. B. JONES.
Capt. EDGAR W. BLAKE.	15th Wisconsin (two companies).
13th Wisconsin (one company). Stewart's cavalry (one company).	*En route to Fort Pillow.*
Fort Pillow, Tenn.	Capt. FRANK MOORE.
Maj. WILLIAM T. STRICKLAND.	2d Illinois Cavalry, Company D.
52d Indiana, Lieut. Col. Zalmon S. Main.	

---

* Afterward known as the Sixty-sixth Illinois.
† According to return for December 10, 1862.

LA GRANGE, TENN., *January* 1, 1863.
General GRANT:

There were indications of a rebel force a few miles north of this place last night, and confirmed this morning. We are all right here. In ordering me here last night I intended to clean out this force. It may be a part of Forrest's force, but think it is only a congregation of guerrillas to the number of perhaps 1,500. No fear of Grand Junction or this place. Your dispatch of last night received. I have sent Lee his instructions at Moscow.

C. S. HAMILTON,
Brigadier-General.

LA GRANGE, *January* 1, 1863.
General GRANT:

Richardson's guerrillas are hovering about Somerville, 800 to 1,200 strong. Is it best for Lee to forage in the neighborhood, so that the scoundrels can't subsist there? To do that it may be necessary to burn the mills. I want to see them cleaned out.

I propose to send a couple of infantry regiments to Somerville in a few days on a foraging expedition, and see if Somerville bacon is good. Quinby is at La Fayette. Train of cars goes there in the morning.

C. S. HAMILTON,
Brigadier-General.

HOLLY SPRINGS, MISS., *January* 1, 1863.
Brig. Gen. C. S. HAMILTON, *La Grange, Tenn.*:

I would forage off the neighborhood of Somerville, but destroy nothing, not even the mills. We can use all they have.

Sullivan caught up with Forrest and gave him a tremendous thrashing; captured six pieces of his artillery, killed and wounded a great many, took his baggage and several hundred prisoners. The gunboats got up and destroyed all his ferries. Dodge says that a scout brings in the news that Rosecrans has had a fight and whipped the enemy badly.

Vicksburg is not taken. Kirby Smith is re-enforcing that place with his army corps, 30,000 strong.

U. S. GRANT,
Major-General.

MCPHERSON'S, *January* 1, 1863.
General GRANT:

The defeat of Johnston [Bragg] is good news for New Year's day. I have nothing definite from Grenada or the southeast. The scout whom I expected back from Grenada has not returned. I have sent three more, one southeast, one in south of Panola, and one toward Grenada, but it is very difficult to get good scouts here. The citizens generally don't know anything, and when they do are not to be trusted, unless corroborated from other sources. The cavalry are out every day, but thus far have got no news of the enemy's movements.

JAS. B. MCPHERSON,
Major-General.

McPHERSON'S, *January* 1, 1863.
Major-General GRANT:

Would it not be well to move Colonel Leggett's brigade to this side of the Tallahatchie ?   There is nothing left at Abbeville, and the rebel fortifications on the south side have been leveled down by the contrabands.   The bridges can be guarded from this side and I can keep a good force of cavalry at Abbeville to scour the country.   The road across the bottom is very bad, making communication somewhat difficult.

JAS. B. McPHERSON,
Major-General.

———

McPHERSON'S, *January* 1, 1863.
Major-General GRANT:

Cavalry scouts just in and confirm report that Van Dorn is this side of Coffeeville with part of his cavalry force.
I will come up to-morrow, leaving here at 7 o'clock.

JAS. B. McPHERSON,
Major-General.

———

HOLLY SPRINGS, MISS., *January* 1, 1863.
Maj. Gen. J. B. McPHERSON, *Abbeville, Miss.*:

I have just heard most reliably from all south of us.   There are but about 8,000 troops at Grenada.   Van Dorn is about Coffeeville with the cavalry.   Very few troops at Jackson; all have gone to Vicksburg.   Kirby Smith's forces have gone and are on the road.   Banks has superseded Butler.   I wish you could come here to-morrow.   I will not be able to go down.

U. S. GRANT,
Major-General.

———

ORDERS.]   HEADQUARTERS FIRST AND SECOND DIVISIONS,
RIGHT WING, ARMY OF THE TENNESSEE,
January 1, 1863.

You will at once stop all fortifying and intrenching of your present positions, and without noise have everything pertaining to your brigade loaded, packed, and moved back to the boats.   Each regiment will embark, if practicable, upon the same boats upon which they came.

Let one regiment do picket duty until 4 a. m. to-morrow, when they also will return to the landing.   Let wagons gather up all the tools.   You will please notify the Chicago batteries, A and B, also Hart's battery and the 30-pounder Parrotts, that they may be in in time.   All this must be done without noise or sign.

By order of Brig. Gen. A. J. Smith:

J. HOUGH,
Acting Assistant Adjutant-General.

———

JANUARY 1, 1863.
Major-General HURLBUT:

SIR: Your communication of 28th December is received.   The troops of General Curtis' command which are detained here are so detained by order of General Halleck, to hold Columbus at all hazards and make no movement of troops that would endanger it from any force.

I have not been able to gain any reliable information south of this place, all my scouts having been turned back or arrested until within a few days, say two. This fact has compelled me to act as against a maximum at all points in my command.

With your information I presume you regard (as you say you do) my order to destroy the ammunition at Island No. 10 premature. I was well informed of the intentions of the enemy to turn my right and occupy Hickman, which I had evacuated (having only 133 men there for duty), or some other point on the river, haul-to a transport and proceed to Island No. 10, probably in the night-time, and take the 71 men which are there for duty, and with the armament and ammunition there close the Mississippi River. This was a risk in the present state of our fleets and gunboats that should not be run, even if there was one chance in fifty that Island No. 10 might be surprised and fall an easy prey to 200 men in flats and skiffs.

The thing was in progress of execution, as the steamer Duke was fired into at Hickman, and she was about rounding-to when the gunboat New Era hove in sight (having sent her down there anticipating it), and the rebels ran. The armament is not destroyed; it is only rendered useless in case of capture.

The consequences resulting from capture of Island No. 10, or New Madrid, in our present state, would almost be fatal, and consequently there should be no risk run where there is no real loss to us. The armament at both these points is of no earthly use to us.

I think you would, with the same information before you, acted as I have done; at least I have done that which my best judgment at the time dictated.

I am, very respectfully, your obedient servant,

THOS. A. DAVIES,
Brigadier-General.

COLUMBUS, KY., *January* 1, 1863—2 p. m.

Maj. Gen. H. W. HALLECK, *General-in-Chief:*

I have received the following order from General Grant:

Forward to Memphis immediately all the forces you have detained at Columbus. The force you had before Forrest's raid is abundant to garrison that place.

I had here, before the raid, 811 men for duty to the entire post. As you have been so very positive in your orders about this place I deem it my duty to report the order to you first, as I can get answer before I could make the arrangements. I can get no reliable information about the position of the enemy, though all agree, from having seen them only in small squads, that they have left. The rivers are all rising. General Grant is at Holly Springs. He has returned to the north bank of the Tallahatchie, General McPherson holding the advance. The Memphis and Grenada road will be running, it is said, to-morrow. General Quinby came into Memphis, with his division and train, for supplies. General Sherman within 12 miles of Vicksburg, and our two construction trains are within 15 miles of each other, and the Ohio bottom and bridge lies between them. Accounts vary so much that it is hard to tell how long it will take to get through. Shall I carry out General Grant's orders?

THOS. A. DAVIES,
Brigadier-General.

WAR DEPARTMENT,
Washington, January 2, 1863.

Brig. Gen. THOMAS A. DAVIES, *Columbus, Ky.:*

You must use your best discretion about the number of troops to be retained at Columbus, until you can communicate further with General Grant. Columbus and its stores must be well guarded.

H. W. HALLECK,
General-in-Chief.

HDQRS. DIST. OF COLUMBUS, DEPT. OF THE TENNESSEE,
Columbus, Ky., January 2, 1863.

Lieutenant-Colonel RAWLINS:

SIR: The order received from Major-General Grant, as regards sending troops to Memphis, shall be complied with as soon as transportation can be furnished.

Very respectfully,

THOS. A. DAVIES,
Brigadier-General.

MCPHERSON'S, *January 2, 1863.*

Major-General GRANT:

Scout just in from Grenada and confirms report that a considerable portion of the force there has gone south, though those remaining are still fortifying. No attempts have been made to repair the railroad this side of Grenada, and only sufficient repairs on the dirt roads to facilitate the passage of cavalry. Van Dorn is very popular since his return, and the report is that his forces are concentrating near Pontotoc for another movement. Hatch says there has been a regiment of rebel cavalry near Rocky Ford, but nothing more, he thinks. He has sent out four companies of cavalry to reconnoiter. The whole country is full of small parties hovering near our lines to pick up stragglers and watch our movements. I sent scouts in the direction of Panola yesterday morning, but they have not returned.

JAS. B. MCPHERSON,
Major-General.

BOLIVAR, *January 2, 1863.*

Lieutenant-Colonel RAWLINS,
Assistant Adjutant-General:

All possible vigilance will be used. I have only 45 mounted men, not enough for pickets, and will rely on infantry.

Colonel Mizner, with the Third Michigan Cavalry, passed toward Jackson this morning. Richardson's band of guerrillas is west of here, 300 strong. I want cavalry very much; our defenses are strong, and Bolivar is safe, but I wish to clear the neighborhood.

M. BRAYMAN,
Brigadier-General.

MEMPHIS, *January* 2, 1863.

General GRANT:

GENERAL : I send this by an express scout, and will send a copy on the other road. Affairs do not look well; it is reported, but not, I think, reliable, that a force of cavalry from the Grenada army is working up between your line and the river, indicating toward Panola and Sena-tobia. No news here ; have heard nothing from Quinby since he left. Great activity and a new impetus to guerrillas below, burning cotton and wood-piles to hinder navigation. Kirby Smith and Morgan are in Kentucky—Morgan at Glasgow. Rosecrans still stationary; in God's name, why does he not move? We have 4,000,000 rations due here and to be kept on hand at that amount. Gorman moves from Helena, leav-ing only a garrison in fort; this move is in conjunction with Curtis' force toward Little Rock. Gorman's dispatch within will explain more fully matters below.

Your obedient servant,

S. A. HURLBUT.

[Inclosure.]

HEADQUARTERS DISTRICT OF ARKANSAS,
Helena, January 1, 1863.

General HURLBUT, *Memphis :*

GENERAL : The Minnehaha has been returned with the rebel prison-ers sent down from Cairo a few days since, owing to progress of fight at Vicksburg. Captain White, of this steamer, informs me that our fleets and gunboats are in great need of coal. I send the steamer Ken-ton to report to you. See if it is possible for you to send two barges of coal to General Sherman and the fleet. The Blue Wing was cap-tured at Napoleon, or near there, with a mail, some artillery ammuni-tion, and two barges of coal, by the enemy, and I think the steamer Home has also been captured, with two barges of forage. The fighting on Monday was terrific; our loss perhaps 2,000 or 3,000 or more. The dead body of Colonel Wyman, of Thirteenth Illinois, is here on board the flag-of-truce boat. We had taken on Monday one fortification with nine guns. We also took three rifle-pits and their big work, but it had to be given up again. Captain White will give you further particulars of General Sherman's fight. I learn that General Sherman needs re-enforcements, but have no word from the general or from the admiral on the subject, officially or otherwise.

I am, general, very respectfully,

W. A. GORMAN.

HOLLY SPRINGS, MISS., *January* 2, 1863.

Maj. Gen. STEPHEN A. HURLBUT, *Memphis, Tenn. :*

Some of the rebel cavalry captured between here and Memphis were armed with perfectly new carbines, which evidently were procured in Memphis. These marauders are probably also getting all other con-traband supplies from there.

I know it is impossible, with your present small force, to prevent smuggling in contraband articles entirely, but I would suggest that the provost-marshal be directed to make a descent upon all business houses, and if any are found to be carrying on an illegal traffic confiscate their stock in trade and ship the offenders south of our lines.

Have you heard from Davies, whether he is sending you re-enforce-ments, or from Gorman, whether the cavalry of Hovey's command is coming here? I require them very much. I am taking measures to clean out the country from here to Memphis of all guerrillas. If it cannot be done in any other way I will be compelled to take and destroy the last bushel of grain between the Hatchie and the Tallahatchie, and all the stock. I will make it the interest of the citizens to leave our lines of communications unmolested.

Sullivan has whipped Forrest and entirely broken up his band. He has killed and wounded great numbers; captured over 400 prisoners, all their train, several wagon loads of small-arms, six pieces of artillery, over 500 horses, and recaptured much of the clothing and other property taken from our posts that surrendered.

By order of Maj. Gen. U. S. Grant:

JNO. A. RAWLINS,
Assistant Adjutant-General.

CIRCULAR.*]   HOLLY SPRINGS, *January* 2, 1863.

Stockades must be built at every military post or station. A cavalry raid under Van Dorn may be looked for any day and must be resisted. He is now concentrating his force of cavalry at Pontotoc. Notify every officer of your command to be ready and on the alert.

Acknowledge receipt of this order.

U. S. GRANT.

SPECIAL ORDERS, ｝ HDQRS. 13TH A. C., DEPT. OF THE TENN.,
    No. 2.   ｝   *Holly Springs, Miss., January* 2, 1863.

*　　*　　*　　*　　*　　*　　*

VI. A court of inquiry is hereby appointed, to meet in Holly Springs, Miss., on Monday, the 5th day of January, A. D. 1863, or as soon thereafter as practicable, to inquire into and investigate the allegations and charges against the One hundred and ninth Regiment Illinois Infantry Volunteers mentioned in Paragraph IV of Special Orders, No. 58, of date December 31, 1862, from these headquarters.†

Detail for the court.

Lieut. Col. De Witt C. Loudon, Seventieth Regiment Ohio Infantry Volunteers.

Lieut. Col. Albert Heath, One hundredth Regiment Indiana Infantry Volunteers.

Lieut. Col. Solomon D. Kempton, Twelfth Regiment Indiana Infantry Volunteers.

Maj. Henry H. Giesy, Forty-sixth Regiment Ohio Infantry Volunteers.

Maj. John M. Berkey, Ninety-ninth Regiment Indiana Infantry Volunteers.

No other officers than these can be assembled without manifest injury to the service.

The court will sit without regard to hours.

*　　*　　*　　*　　*　　*　　*

By order of Maj. Gen. U. S. Grant:

[JNO. A. RAWLINS,]
Assistant Adjutant-General.

---

* To every commander at all military posts at every station between Grand Junction and Memphis.

†See p. 511 and General Orders, No. 12, Hdqrs. Dept. of the Tenn., Feb'y 1, 1863, *post.*

LA GRANGE, *January* 3, 1863.
General GRANT:

Is it not probable that Van Dorn is preparing to go to Forrest's aid rather than to make another attack on the railroad? There is no point now where he can cross Wolf River. If he goes to Forrest he must go by Chewalla, and Dodge may head him on the Tuscumbia.

HAMILTON.

HOLLY SPRINGS, *January* 3, 1863.
General DODGE:

The enemy's cavalry and mounted infantry have been crossing at Pontotoc with design no doubt of getting into our rear or possibly to re-enforce Forrest. Keep a sharp lookout for him and don't let him get across the Tuscumbia if it can be helped.

U. S. GRANT,
Major-General.

HEADQUARTERS SEVENTH DIVISION, LEFT WING,
THIRTEENTH ARMY CORPS, DEPT. OF THE TENNESSEE,
January 3, 1863—12 m.
Brig. Gen. C. S. HAMILTON,
Commanding Left Wing, La Grange, Tenn.:

GENERAL: I have the honor to report that pursuant to your instructions my division is now posted on the Memphis and Charleston Railroad from Colliersville, within 3 miles of Memphis. The Second Brigade, Colonel Eckley, guards the road from Colliersville to Germantown; the Third Brigade, Colonel Boomer, from Germantown to White's Station, and the First Brigade, Colonel Alexander, from the latter point to crossing of the Pigeon Roost road with the railroad, 3 miles from Memphis, where I have established my headquarters for the present.

I am, very respectfully, your obedient servant,
I. F. QUINBY,
Brigadier-General, Commanding.

General CROCKER:

General Hamilton orders the inclosed to be forwarded immediately to General Quinby by courier.

Yours,

OPERATOR.

[Inclosure.]

HOLLY SPRINGS, *January* 3, 1863.
General QUINBY:

(In charge of commanding officer at La Fayette, to be forwarded to him at once.)

Give notice to the citizens on the road to Memphis that if necessary to secure the railroad every family and every vestige of property, except land itself, between the Hatchie and the Coldwater will be removed out of these limits or confiscated.

Arrest and parole all citizens between eighteen and fifty years of age. Collect forage as far as practicable from south side of the road.

U. S. GRANT,
Major-General, Commanding.

LA GRANGE, *January* 3, 1863.
General McARTHUR:

Van Dorn is concentrating at Pontotoc for another raid. Have stockades put up at points occupied by troops along the railroad, and let every command be on the alert. No officer or man will be allowed to accept a parole from any cavalry force. The raid must be repulsed while there is a musket or a cartridge.

                              C. S. HAMILTON,
                                   Brigadier-General.

LA GRANGE, *January* 3, 1863.
General GRANT:

Lee has returned to near Moscow. Richardson ran off. Lee got 8 prisoners and 170 horses and mules. Shall begin moving infantry. Sullivan is here.

                              C. S. HAMILTON,
                                   Brigadier-General.

MCPHERSON'S HEADQUARTERS,
                              January 3, 1863.
General GRANT:

The river is rising so fast there is danger of its carrying bridges away, and I think of ordering Colonel Leggett's brigade over to this side. What is to be done with Captain Font's company and the contrabands? I did not exactly understand yesterday whether it was understood between Captain Prince and yourself that I was to order them to Holly Springs.

                              JAS. B. McPHERSON,
                                   Major-General.

HEADQUARTERS DEPARTMENT OF THE TENNESSEE,
          Holly Springs, Miss., January 3, 1863.
Maj. Gen. STEPHEN A. HURLBUT,
     Commanding District of Memphis:

Some citizens of Memphis were overheard to say that there was a determination that we should not run the Memphis and Charleston Railroad; that it will be easier to interrupt that and force us to move the army to Memphis for supplies than to come here to fight the main army.

It is my determination to run the road as long as we require it, and if necessary I will remove every family and every species of personal property between the Hatchie and Coldwater Rivers. I will also move south every family in Memphis of doubtful loyalty, whether they have taken the oath of allegiance or not, if it is necessary for our security, and you can so notify them. For every raid or attempted raid by guerrillas upon the road I want ten families of the most noted secessionists sent south. If the enemy, with his regularly-organized forces, attack us I do not propose to punish non-combatant citizens for it; but these guerrillas receive support and countenance from this class of citizens, and by their acts will bring punishment upon them.

In this matter I wish to give this letter all the force of an order.

                              U. S. GRANT,
                                   Major-General.

MEMPHIS, *January* 3, 1863.

General GRANT:

I have received dispatches from Gorman. Sherman has had a bitter fight; forced the first line of intrenchments, captured and holds one 9-gun battery; captured their main fort on Walnut Hills at point or bayonet, but supports did not come up, and our men were driven out with great slaughter. Morgan Smith is wounded; Giles Smith, colonel Eighth Missouri, and Wyman, Thirteenth Illinois, killed. Loss about 3,000, killed and wounded. No official report from Sherman. Price and Joe Johnston are at Vicksburg. Steamers from below are seen bringing up troops. I fear Sherman is overmatched. He has sent for ammunition. I sent him to-day all I have, 230,000 rounds. Have sent his order forward to be telegraphed from Cairo. He wants 4,000,000 rounds. The Blue Wing, with ammunition, was taken below Helena and has gone up the Arkansas. I this day send three barges of coal for the fleet, which they greatly need. Davies still holds the troops above and says he does it by order of General Halleck. Sherman ought to be re-enforced. I think they outnumber him, besides the advantage of position.

Nothing heard from Banks. I have suggested to Gorman propriety of throwing his whole available force, except fort garrison, to Vicksburg.

The messenger Schultz, who was bringing your reply, was captured, but destroyed his dispatches. The road from here to Germantown is full of guerrillas and some regular cavalry. I trust the railroad may be forced through rapidly. It must be strongly guarded down to the depot, as we can't spare any guard. Sherman's wounded will be here before long, I suppose. I am preparing hospital buildings in case they arrive. I require more force than for ordinary guards, and especially cavalry, to beat up these guerrillas. Major Blythe is within 14 miles, on the Hernando road. Richardson near Wolf River, about Germantown.

S. A. HURLBUT,
Major-General.

HEADQUARTERS DISTRICT OF MEMPHIS,
Memphis, Tenn., January 3, 1863.

Brigadier-General GORMAN:

I have sent your dispatches to General Grant. I do not like the look of things at Vicksburg. It is impossible for Grant to send re-enforcements, at all events in time. I have serious doubts as to Sherman maintaining his advance unless Banks comes up. Vicksburg is a place of such vast consequence that it may be well to consider whether it will not be your duty to throw your whole force to that point if it will assure success. I have but four regiments here. Davies has not yet sent the troops down from Columbus.

Grant's army will connect with me by railroad to-day or to-morrow.

I shall send coal down in barges by the Kenton to Helena. The Rattler (Mosquito Fleet) will follow to-night and will convoy the Kenton and her barges down. It will not do to permit valuable boats to go below without convoy.

The Blue Wing was probably purposely surrendered; her captain has a bad reputation among loyal river men.

I send by the Rattler all the ammunition I have—about 230,000 rounds—and have telegraphed from Cairo to fill Sherman's call.

Things appear dark, for there is no question Sherman has to meet more than his own force. I am assured that a large part of Pemberton's army is there, moving in that direction as soon as Grant fell back.

We have an abundance of commissary supplies here, but nothing of ordnance. It would be a most wretched casualty if Sherman's force should run out of ammunition.

I have here now 2,400 sick, and the best I can do for the prisoners on the Minnehaha is to ship them up to Cairo.

Let me constantly have the last news.

Your obedient servant,

[S. A. HURLBUT,]
Major-General.

HEADQUARTERS POST OF BOLIVAR,
Bolivar, Tenn., January 3, 1863.

Col. JOHN A. RAWLINS,
Assistant Adjutant-General:

SIR : For information of Major-General Grant I inclose on next page a statement of my forces.

Of the Forty-third Illinois, Sixty-first Illinois, and Forty-third Ohio (at least 380), and all of the Twelfth Michigan are on special duty, leaving only about 460 for sudden call.

The absence of the First West Tennessee with General Dodge leaves me about 45 mounted men; they inexperienced.

I wish it understood that with my present force, small as it is, I can retire within the fortifications and repel any attack. But to do this it might be necessary to compromise the safety of the town, and as now circumscribed as to cavalry I cannot pursue or drive away the hostile forces that hover around and annoy us in a provoking manner.

Yours, &c.,

M. BRAYMAN,
Brigadier-General, Commanding.

[Inclosure.]

Return of the effective force of the Post of Bolivar, Tenn., District of Jackson, for Saturday, January 3, 1863.

Regiment, corps, or detachment.	Commanding officer.	Post or station.	Commissioned officers.	Enlisted men.	Aggregate.
43d Illinois Infantry	Colonel Engelmann	Bolivar	29	371	400
61st Illinois Infantry	Captain Mann	do	3	60	63
12th Michigan Infantry	Colonel Graves	Middleburg	20	326	346
43d Ohio Infantry	Colonel Swayne	Bolivar	20	409	429
Total			72	1,166	1,238
1st West Tennessee Cavalry	Lieutenant Smith	Bolivar	9	168	177
Vaughn's Battery	Capt. T. F. Vaughn	do	5	101	106
Grand total			86	1,435	1,521

HEADQUARTERS MISSISSIPPI RIVER EXPEDITION,
Steamer Tigress, Milliken's Bend, Mississippi River, Jan. 3, 1863.

Hon. E. M. STANTON,
Secretary of War:

SIR : Notwithstanding your order of October 21, 1862, authorizing the Mississippi River Expedition and assigning me to the command of the same, I have reason to suppose that prior to my dispatch of the 16th [17th] of December, 1862, informing you that I believed I had been superseded, Major-General Halleck, General-in-Chief, had assigned Major-General Grant to the same command.

On the 21st ultimo Major-General Halleck's assistant adjutant-general communicated to me a copy of a telegram to Major-General Grant, dated December 18, 1862, assigning the latter to the general command of the expedition and me to the immediate command of the land forces composing the same. This, as far as I can recollect, was the first and only recognition, and that an indirect one, which the General-in-Chief had ever made of my connection with the expedition, and I attribute that to your interference as a consequence of my telegram of the 16th [17th] to you and the President, touching my supersedure.

A portion of the forces designed for the expedition having been detached from General Grant's army and marched to Memphis by General Sherman, preparatory to embarkation for Vicksburg, prior to the 16th ultimo, it would appear conclusively that Generals Grant and Sherman had received orders in the premises prior to that date. Moreover, it is worthy of especial notice that General Sherman started with the expedition from Memphis on the 20th ultimo, and that not until the second day after—the 22d—did I receive notice of Major-General Halleck's telegram to General Grant.

On the 23d I was relieved from duty at Springfield, Ill., and immediately started south to find and receive orders from General Grant, according to your instructions. Arriving at Memphis on Sunday, the 28th, I immediately dispatched Major Schwartz and Captain Freeman, of my staff, across the country, which was infested by guerrilla bands, to communicate with General Grant at Holly Springs, 45 miles from Memphis. Reaching there the same night these officers were informed that orders assigning me to the immediate command of the expedition had been forwarded on the same day. These orders reached me on Monday, the 29th, one day after the repulse of our forces near Vicksburg, and before I had had time to leave Memphis. This explanation is made for the purpose of establishing the fact that either through the intention of the General-in-Chief or a strange occurrence of accidents, the authority of the President and yourself, as evidenced by your acts, has been set at naught, and I have been deprived of the command that had been committed to me.

I will not say that in consequence of this circumstance the Mississippi River Expedition has so far failed, for that would do injustice to General Sherman, whom I deem, indeed know, to be a brave and meritorious officer. He has probably done all in the present case that any one could have done, and I would not detract anything from him, but give him all credit for good purposes, which unfortunately failed in execution.

The explanation of the failure is simply this :

1st. Much valuable time was lost in setting the expedition on foot, and thus ample opportunity was furnished to the enemy to prepare himself and strongly fortify against attack.

2d. The movement to Vicksburg lacked every kind of co-operation. General Grant's cessation of his advance toward Grenada and Jackson, Miss., afforded the enemy's forces at those points and at Port Hudson opportunity to concentrate a considerable army for the defense of Vicksburg. Nor is it altogether improbable that troops from Bragg's army and even from Virginia had been brought to this neighborhood, not being needed in Tennessee or in Virginia on account of the seeming cessation of hostilities in those quarters.

3d. The organization of the different arms composing the expeditionary army was essentially defective. In my communication of October 16, 1862, to you and to the Commander-in-Chief the estimate of troops required for the reduction of Vicksburg was as follows: Twenty-four thousand infantry, 1,000 sharpshooters, 400 sappers and miners, 3,000 cavalry, 1,500 light artillery, and 100 heavy artillery. The number of batteries to be assigned to the artillery arm was ten, of six guns each, consisting of fourteen 10-pounder Parrott guns, twenty-eight 12-pounder Napoleon guns, six 24-pounder howitzers (brass), four 12-pounder howitzers, eight 6-pounder smooth-bore guns; also eight 30-pounder Parrott guns and four 10-inch mortars.

Instead of with these proportions the expedition was constructed without the least harmony in its elements, and with no regard to that effectiveness which is alone to be obtained by giving to each arm its proper proportion.

Since the attack of our forces on Sunday, according to reports, the enemy's forces at Vicksburg have been increased to 50,000 or 60,000.

The attack on Monday, notwithstanding signal instances of courage and heroism on the part of the officers and the display of much endurance and bravery among the men, entirely failed of success. I am informed that the position of the enemy at Vicksburg is of unusual strength. A continual series of bluffs extends, as will be seen from the accompanying drawings, from the city to Haines' Bluff, on the Yazoo River, a distance of from 12 to 14 miles. Haines' Bluff has been strongly fortified and is defended by batteries of heavy caliber. It is reported to be a fortress in itself; besides seven field works are said to be located in front of it and near the river. The Yazoo is blocked up, and lakes and bayous in the low and swamp lands between the Mississippi and Yazoo Rivers are lined with rifle-pits, while the rear of the position, from the Yazoo to the Black River, is reported as being defended by rifle-pits and other field works. Moreover, the heavy rain pouring down at the moment of writing this hasty report will strengthen the enemy's position, and the lands between the Mississippi and the Yazoo Rivers will become impassable.

The gunboats being unable to reduce the fortifications at Haines' Bluff, General Sherman proposed a night attack to carry them with the bayonet; but Rear-Admiral Porter declined to co-operate in such an undertaking, regarding it as too hazardous. The troops under General Sherman therefore descended the Yazoo and landed at Milliken's Bend, in Louisiana.

If I am asked for a plan by which Vicksburg might yet be taken I would suggest that General Grant immediately make Memphis his base of operations, put the Mississippi and Tennessee Railroad from Memphis toward Grenada in running order, and push forward his column to the latter place and to Jackson, marching upon the rear of Vicksburg, while the forces here and those below Port Hudson co-operate by such demonstrations as may be found practicable.

So soon as I shall have verified the condition of the army—perhaps to-day—I will assume command of it.

Very respectfully, your obedient servant,

JOHN A. McCLERNAND,
Major-General, Commanding.

WAR DEPARTMENT,
Washington, January 4, 1863.

Major-General GRANT,
    Holly Springs, Miss.:

A paper purporting to be General Orders, No. 11, issued by you December 17, has been presented here. By its terms it expels all Jews from your department. If such an order has been issued, it will be immediately revoked.

H. W. HALLECK,
General-in-Chief.

HOLLY SPRINGS, MISS., *January* 4, 1863.

NAVAL COMMANDER CAIRO, ILL.:

Some light-draught gunboats now in the Tennessee River would be of great value. Forrest has gone to the east bank, but there are strong signs of him recrossing in the vicinity of Savannah. Can any be sent?

U. S. GRANT,
Major-General.

HEADQUARTERS DEPARTMENT OF THE TENNESSEE,
Holly Springs, Miss., January 4, 1863.

Brig. Gen. GRENVILLE M. DODGE, *Corinth, Miss.:*

I am not informed that the force at Pontotoc is yet moving; think it is not. If I ascertain there is a combined movement of Roddey's forces and the force said to be at Pontotoc I will send a division to you. If I learn, as it is now reported, that Vicksburg is ours, I can send you a division any way. My latest advices from Vicksburg direct are of the 29th. There had then been desperate fighting. Sherman had lost about 3,000 men, killed and wounded, but had carried the enemy's rifle-pits, and one fort of nine guns. I hear from a citizen that the Grenada Appeal of the 31st says that the Yankees had possession of Vicksburg.

U. S. GRANT,
Major-General.

LA GRANGE, *January* 4, 1863.

General GRANT:

I am told to-day that Morgan, of Kentucky, had united his cavalry with Van Dorn, and was with him at Holly Springs. I have no doubt it was so, and that he is with him again.

C S. HAMILTON.

HOLLY SPRINGS, MISS., *January* 4, 1863.

Brig. Gen. C. S. HAMILTON, *La Grange, Tenn.*:

There is no doubt of a concentration of troops for the purpose of attacking Corinth. It will be necessary to strengthen that place with at least a division.

If Fuller's brigade has not yet returned, instruct them to go there, and I will send the balance of the division as soon as they can be replaced by troops from here.

U. S. GRANT,
Major-General.

HOLLY SPRINGS, MISS., *January* 4, 1863.

Brig. Gen. J. B. McPHERSON, *Abbeville, Miss.*:

If the report of Vicksburg being in our possession proves true I will fall back to the line of Memphis and Corinth at once. There is no objection to your falling back now to the Waterford and Chulahoma road, leaving a small force on the road near the river.

A long dispatch from Vicksburg on the 29th is just received. Sherman had had a desperate fight, in which he had lost 3,000 men, killed and wounded; he had carried enemy's rifle-pits and one fort of nine guns, and also their principal fort, but from the latter he had been forced to fall back, owing to support not coming up in time. Morgan Smith and his brother were both wounded, the former probably dead.

When the boat left a fleet was coming up the river, probably Banks'. I have news overland of his arrival in New Orleans, and a dispatch to-day from General Halleck says that he is to push up the river.

U. S. GRANT,
Major-General.

HOLLY SPRINGS, MISS., *January* 4, 1863.

Col. W. S. HILLYER, *La Fayette, Tenn.*:

A dispatch just received from General Halleck says that Banks is pushing up the Mississippi to Vicksburg. This with the news from Vicksburg that a fleet is seen coming up the river is satisfactory that Sherman is re-enforced before this. It would take me four days to get re-enforcements for him to Memphis, unless I should abandon the railroad.

Inform Hurlbut of these facts.

U. S. GRANT,
Major-General.

LA GRANGE, *January* 4, 1863.

General GRANT:

Fuller's brigade yesterday had gone to Clifton. All the troops from my command sent to Sullivan have pushed far to the east and north. I have telegraphed Sullivan to send Fuller immediately.

C. S. HAMILTON.

HOLLY SPRINGS, MISS., *January* 4, 1863.

Brig. Gen. C. S. HAMILTON, *La Grange, Tenn.*:

A scout just in reports that there are but few troops at Pontotoc.
Van Dorn is said to have gone east, and is collecting all the cavalry
and Partisan Rangers he can.

Dodge says also that he understands a division of rebels will be at
Jacinto to-morrow night. Roddey is at Tuscumbia. Probably they will
join in a raid. Have your cavalry ready for a pursuit if necessary.

U. S. GRANT,
Major-General.

HOLLY SPRINGS, MISS., *January* 4, 1863.

Brig. Gen. GRENVILLE M. DODGE, *Corinth, Miss.*:

Scout just in from Pontotoc. Found out nothing reliable, but report
said Van Dorn had gone east; was getting up all the cavalry and
Partisan Rangers he could. He evidently means mischief. I will direct
rations to be sent to you as fast as possible, and order Sullivan to send
you forage.

U. S. GRANT,
Major-General.

HOLLY SPRINGS, MISS., *January* 4, 1863.

Brig. Gen. J. C. SULLIVAN, *Jackson, Tenn.*:

Van Dorn has gone east from Pontotoc, and is gathering all the cavalry and Partisan Rangers he can. Roddey is about Tuscumbia. The
probabilities are that he will be heard from about Corinth, Bethel, or
Bolivar. Have the two latter on their guard. If possible, send Dodge
forage promptly.

U. S. GRANT,
Major-General.

HOLLY SPRINGS, MISS., *January* 4, 1863.

Maj. Gen. J. B. McPHERSON, *Abbeville, Miss.*:

It looks evident that Van Dorn, Forrest, and Roddey are going to
unite their forces and attack Corinth, or make a general raid upon the
roads. Van Dorn is now marching toward Jacinto. Roddey is at
Tuscumbia and Forrest back of Savannah. There is no special object
longer in holding the Tallahatchie. You may therefore fall back as far
as you can to-morrow.

U. S. GRANT,
Major-General.

McPHERSON'S, *January* 4, 1863.

General GRANT:

General Sherman has had a severe time of it. I hope Banks got
there in time with his re-enforcements, so that the place is ours, so the
war can be carried into the heart of Mississippi. I will move my command back, as directed, to-morrow, leaving Colonel Leggett's brigade
and one battery at this place.

JAS. B. McPHERSON,
Major-General.

MCPHERSON'S, *January* 4, 1863.

Major-General GRANT:

My command will march to the vicinity of Holly Springs to-morrow. Shall I destroy the railroad bridge over the Tallahatchie? I understand that I cannot leave a force of infantry here, but have Colonel Leggett's brigade march back as far as Lumpkin's Mill at least, and then follow on after everything there and at Waterford has been removed.

JAS. B. McPHERSON,
Major-General.

HOLLY SPRINGS, MISS., *January* 4, 1863.

Maj. Gen. J. B. McPHERSON, *Abbeville, Miss.* :

I think it is not necessary to destroy the Tallahatchie Bridge. The road is destroyed so far south that the enemy cannot use it for some time, and we may want it; at least we will keep up the appearance of wanting it. Move your whole force back, however, leaving one brigade at Lumpkin's Mill.

U. S. GRANT,
Major-General.

MCPHERSON'S, *January* 4, 1863.

Major-General GRANT:

The battalion of cavalry sent out day before yesterday to Rocky Ford has not returned. They were instructed to push on until they met the enemy or learned something of his movements, and as they have not returned or sent any word back I think they have gone beyond Rocky Ford.

JAS. B. McPHERSON,
Major-General.

MCPHERSON'S, *January* 4, 1863.

Major-General GRANT:

Scout just returned from Pontotoc. Only a few cavalry there; he could not learn anything of Van Dorn's movements that was definite, though reports said he had gone east toward the Mobile and Ohio Railroad, and was collecting all the cavalry, Partisan Rangers, &c., that he could.

The battalion of cavalry has just returned from Rocky Ford; found no enemy except few straggling guerrillas on this side of the Tallahatchie, and only heard of a small force being on the other side.

Lieutenant Gile has not returned yet with flag of truce.

JAS. B. McPHERSON,
Major-General.

MCPHERSON'S, *January* 4, 1863.

General GRANT:

I have sent to Colonel Grierson at Waterford to move with two battalions of cavalry immediately toward Tallaloosa.

Colonel Hatch has three companies of cavalry at Chulahoma, and I have directed him to send two companies more to the same point, and then to move from there up to the south and west of Chulahoma.

JAS. B. McPHERSON,
Major-General.

HEADQUARTERS MISSISSIPPI RIVER EXPEDITION,
Steamer Tigress, January 4, 1863—11 a. m.

Maj. Gen. WILLIAM T. SHERMAN,
Comdg. Second Army Corps, Dept. of West Tennessee:

GENERAL : I have the honor to inclose the copy of a communication from Maj. Gen. U. S. Grant, bearing date of the 18th December, 1862,* but only received by me at Memphis on the 29th.

The communication, as you will perceive, requires me to take command of all the land forces of every kind forming the Mississippi River Expedition, and to receive from you all written and verbal instructions given by him in that connection, which he accordingly directs to be turned over to me.

General Orders, No. 1, a copy whereof is also herewith inclosed, is based upon the same communication, as well as others received direct from Washington, and explains itself.

May I ask of you the favor that you will communicate the instructions called for, and all useful and desirable information respecting the present organization and strength of the forces with you ?

Respectfully, your obedient servant,

JOHN A. McCLERNAND,
Major-General, Commanding Mississippi River Expedition.

[Inclosure.]

GENERAL ORDERS,   HDQRS. ARMY OF THE MISSISSIPPI,
                       Steamer Tigress, Milliken's Bend, La.,
No. 1.   *January* 4, 1863—11 a. m.

I. Maj. Gen. John A. McClernand, in pursuance of an order to that effect by the General-in-Chief of the Army of the United States, communicated to him by Maj. Gen. U. S. Grant, commanding the Department of the Tennessee, this day assumes command of such troops of the First and Second Army Corps of the said department as constitute the " Mississippi River Expedition " to be designated the "Army of the Mississippi."

II. Maj. Gen. W. T. Sherman will continue in the command of the Second Army Corps, which will form the right wing of the Army of the Mississippi, and Brig. Gen. G. W. Morgan, the senior officer in the First Army Corps, will assume command of the latter, which will form the left wing of the army.

III. All unauthorized interference with private property is prohibited, and offenders must be immediately punished.

IV. All firing of arms, except under competent orders, is prohibited, and offenders must be punished.

V. Straggling from the ranks upon the march or in battle must be prevented, and force must be employed for that purpose if it should become necessary.

---

*See p. 425.

VI. The infantry will carry 40 rounds of ammunition in their cartridge-boxes and 20 more, when going into action, on their persons; and the men of all arms will keep on hand at least two days' cooked rations while on the move in the presence of or near the enemy.

VII. No transports will be allowed to leave the fleet except with the permission of the general commanding the army.

VIII. Neither officers nor soldiers will be permitted during an engagement to fall out of the ranks and to care for the wounded. Musicians, and, if necessary, details made for that purpose, will be assigned for that duty, such persons to wear a white badge on the left arm above the elbow as a distinction.

IX. Commanders of army corps will forward to these headquarters without delay full and complete statements of the forces composing their commands; also of the means of land transportation, the number of intrenching tools, quantity of ammunition, and all other information relating to the condition and efficiency of their commands.

Commanders of army corps will see that these orders are fully and faithfully executed.

By order of Maj. Gen. John A. McClernand, commanding Army of the Mississippi.

A. SCHWARTZ,
Major and Acting Assistant Adjutant-General.

COLUMBUS, *January* 4, 186 .

Col. JOHN A. RAWLINS, *Holly Springs:*

The trouble is transportation. Have telegraphed to Saint Louis; none to be had. One regiment will leave in the morning on the Swallow. I am stopping all boats, up and down, as fast as they arrive to send troops as ordered. They will go as soon as boats can be had.

One battery left this morning.

THOS. A. DAVIES,
Brigadier-General.

GENERAL ORDERS, } HDQRS. RIGHT WING, 13TH ARMY CORPS,
No. 12.   }   *Milliken's Bend, La., January* 4, 1863.

Pursuant to the terms of General Orders, No. 1, made this day by Major-General McClernand, the title of our army ceases to exist, and constitutes in the future the "Army of the Mississippi," composed of two army corps, one to be commanded by Brig. Gen. G. W. Morgan and the other by myself.

In relinquishing command of the right wing of the Army of the Tennessee, and restricting my authority to my own corps, I desire to express to all commanders, to the soldiers and officers recently operating before Vicksburg, my hearty thanks for the zeal, alacrity, and courage manifested by them on all occasions. We failed in accomplishing one great purpose of our movement—the capture of Vicksburg—but we were but a part of a whole. Ours was but one part of a combined movement, in which others were to assist. We were on time; unforeseen contingencies must have delayed the others.

We have destroyed the Shreveport road; we have attacked the defenses of Vicksburg, and pushed the attack as far as prudence would justify; and having found it too strong for our single column, we have drawn off in good order and in good spirits, ready for any new move.

A new commander is now here to lead you. He is chosen by the

President of the United States, who is charged by our Constitution to maintain and defend it, and he has the undoubted right to select his own agents. I know that all good officers and soldiers will give him the same hearty support and cheerful obedience they have hitherto given me. There are honors enough in reserve for all, and work enough, too. Let each do his appropriate part, and our nation must in the end emerge from this dire conflict purified and ennobled by the fires which now test its strength and purity.

All officers of the general staff not attached to my person will hereafter report in person and by letter to Major-General McClernand, commanding Army of the Mississippi, on board the steamer Tigress, at our rendezvous at Gaines' Landing and Montgomery Point.

By order of Maj. Gen. W. T. Sherman:

> J. H. HAMMOND,
> *Assistant Adjutant-General.*

SPECIAL ORDERS, }   HDQRS. RIGHT WING, 13TH ARMY CORPS,
No. 3.   }   *Milliken's Bend, January* 4, 1863.

I. The troops will not disembark at Milliken's Bend, but will proceed on another important military expedition.

The first rendezvous will be the wood-pile opposite Gaines' Landing.

The second rendezvous will be mouth of White River or Montgomery Point.

II. Colonel Parsons, quartermaster, will see that his transports have enough fuel to reach some known wood-pile, and division commanders may lie by to gather wood and rails at convenient points, of which there is a supply known to be 10 miles above Milliken's, near Greenville, opposite Gaines' and near Napoleon. Whenever boats stop for wood there should be a good picket kept beyond the working party.

The fleet will move in the reverse order of coming, viz, fourth, third, second, and first, but all must be at each rendezvous before another move is made. All possible fuel should be collected before we reach White River.

III. Colonel Parsons will forthwith detail eight good, strong transport boats, best supplied with fuel, to proceed to the mouth of the Yazoo and report to Admiral Porter by 10 a. m. to-day, for the purpose of towing the slow gunboats up-stream; and that the troops on board such tugs may not suffer, one of these boats must be a supply boat.

IV. The commanding general will give the signal to move from rendezvous, but between the rendezvous division commanders may control their boats and lie by whenever they choose to collect wood. On arrival at Montgomery Point boats should have full two days' fuel, and the whole time consumed in reaching Montgomery Point should not exceed sixty hours.

By order of Maj. Gen. W. T. Sherman:

> J. H. HAMMOND,
> *Assistant Adjutant-General.*

HOLLY SPRINGS, *January* 4, 1863.

Col. F. D. CALLENDER,
        Chief of Ordnance, Saint Louis, Mo.:

Have you sent ordnance stores to Vicksburg? Sherman requires 400,000 rounds assorted small-arm ammunition immediately.

> U. S. GRANT,
> *Major-General.*

SAINT LOUIS, *January* 5, 1863.
Major-General GRANT:

Dispatch received. Shipping to-day a large quantity of small-arm ammunition to Memphis for General Sherman, and ammunition for field-guns, including a large supply for 10 and 20-pounder Parrotts, to replace that captured on the steamer Blue Wing.

F. D. CALLENDER.

HEADQUARTERS ARMY OF THE MISSISSIPPI,
Steamer Tigress, January 5, 1863.

Maj. Gen. WILLIAM T. SHERMAN, *Commanding, &c.*:

GENERAL: The following instructions are transmitted for your information. They only give an outline of the movement contemplated against Post Arkansas, Ark., and are based in part upon information respecting the nature and condition of the ground in the vicinity of the Post. This information has been hastily obtained, and in some instances from sources not authentic. Commanders of army corps will therefore be indulged in the exercise of a discretion as to the best modifications of the method proposed for the accomplishment of the object in contemplation. This method is set forth in the following instructions:

1st. Having arrived at the mouth of the White River the commanders of the army corps of the Army of the Mississippi will lose no time in moving their commands upon their transports up that river to the cut-off, and through it into and up the Arkansas River to a suitable point on the left or east bank of the same near and below Post Arkansas for disembarkation.

2d. The army corps will move from the mouth of the White River in the following order: The Second Army Corps, Major-General Sherman commanding, forming the right wing, right in front, first; the First Army Corps, Brigadier-General Morgan commanding, following the left wing in the same order, next.

3d. Arrived at the proposed point for debarkation the two corps will immediately debark, being careful to preserve their distinctness, protect their landing by skirmishers and advanced detachments, leaving all the means of land transportation and other incumbrances on board the steamers until otherwise ordered by the general commanding the army, and rapidly march as follows:

The Second Corps by the rear of the Post until its right has reached the river above it. In executing this movement the commander may find it expedient to make the Brownsville road a *point d'appui* on or from which to deploy his column for the purpose of investing the enemy's works and preparatory to attacking him. The First Corps, following the Second to or near the Lawrenceville road, may also find it expedient to make the latter road a *point d'appui* for the deployment of its column for the purpose aforesaid.

4th. Each army corps should extend its lines so as to complete the investment of the enemy's works, and if in order to do so the left wing has to move so far to the right as to leave too great a space between its left and the river, the same will be secured by a detachment of infantry and artillery from the First Corps, posted in a commanding position for that purpose.

5th. Notwithstanding what precedes, the commander of the First Army Corps will debark two regiments of infantry, one company of cavalry, and three pieces of artillery at a suitable point on the right or west bank of the river and near and below the Post, under instructions to ascend the right bank (beyond the reach of the enemy's guns on the opposite shore) to a point on the river above the Post, giving control of the river.

6th. Skirmishers should in all cases precede the movements herein ordered. Cavalry detachments should be sent out in different directions to reconnoiter the country. Reserves should be kept to the rear of the investing line ready to be moved to any point in case the enemy should venture to make a sortie, and to every battery of light artillery a company of infantry should be detailed for the purpose of protecting it and assisting in its advance.

7th. Having completed the investment according to the plan indicated, the enemy will be equally cut off from re-enforcements and escape, and must, together with his works and all his munitions of war, become a capture to our arms.

By order of John A. McClernand, major-general commanding :

A. SCHWARTZ,
Major and Acting Assistant Adjutant-General.

JACKSON, *January* 5, 1863.

Major-General GRANT :

Six of my regiments are now returning from pursuit of Forrest across the river. Colonel Fuller's brigade is ordered to report to Corinth. Three regiments will be at Trenton to-day that will also be forwarded to Corinth. My line of road has been guarded all the time, but when I send the regiments belonging to Ross' division away I will be very short. There are plenty of men at Columbus that can be ordered here. The six regiments mentioned above have been ordered to Bethel; from there to Corinth.

JER. C. SULLIVAN,
Brigadier-General.

GENERAL ORDERS, } HDQRS. SECOND CORPS, ARMY OF THE MISS.,
No. 1.   }   *Steamer Forest Queen, January* 5, 1863.

I. The undersigned hereby assumes command of the Second Army Corps, Army of the Mississippi, and announces its organization as follows :

W. T. SHERMAN, major-general, commanding.
J. H. HAMMOND, assistant adjutant-general and chief of staff.
EZRA TAYLOR, major and chief of artillery.
W. D. SANGER, major and inspector-general.
CHARLES MCMILLAN, medical director.
JAMES C. MCCOY, captain and aide-de-camp.
JOHN T. TAYLOR, captain and aide-de-camp.
LEWIS M. DAYTON, captain and aide-de-camp.
J. CONDIT SMITH, captain and chief quartermaster.
CHARLES A. MORTON, captain and chief commissary of subsistence.
W. L. B. JENNEY, captain, Engineer Corps.
O. H. HOWARD, captain, Signal Corps.
JULIUS PITZMAN, captain, Topographical Engineers.
KILIAN FRICK, lieutenant, Topographical Engineers.
J. C. NEELY, captain, and ordnance officer.

FIRST DIVISION.

Brig. Gen. FREDERICK STEELE commanding.

First Brigade.

Brig. Gen. F. P. BLAIR commanding.

13th Illinois, Lieut. Col. A. B. Gorgas.
29th Missouri, Col. John S. Cavender.
30th Missouri, Lieut. Col. Otto Schadt.
31st Missouri, Lieut. Col. Samuel P. Simpson.
32d Missouri, Col. F. H. Manter.
58th Ohio, Capt. B. Benkler.

Second Brigade.

Brig. Gen. C. E. HOVEY commanding.

17th Missouri, Col. F. Hassendeubel.
25th Iowa, Col. George A. Stone.
3d Missouri, Col. Isaac F. Shepard.
76th Ohio, Col. Charles R. Woods.
31st Iowa, Col. William Smyth.
12th Missouri, Col. Hugo Wangelin.

Third Brigade.

Brig. Gen. J. M. THAYER commanding.

4th Iowa, Col. J. A. Williamson.
9th Iowa, Lieut. Col. W. H. Coyl.
26th Iowa, Col. Milo Smith.
30th Iowa, Col. Charles H. Abbott.
34th Iowa, Col. George W. Clark.

Artillery.

1st Iowa Battery, Capt. H. H. Griffiths.
4th Ohio Battery, Capt. Louis Hoffmann.
1st Missouri Horse Artillery, Capt. C. Landgraeber.

Cavalry.

3d Illinois, Col. L. F. McCrillis.
Blair's escort, First Lieut. D. W. Ballou.
Steele's escort, Capt. W. C. Wilder.

SECOND DIVISION.

Brig. Gen. DAVID STUART commanding.

First Brigade.

Col. G. A. SMITH commanding.

6th Missouri, Lieut. Col. J. H. Blood.
13th U. S., 1st Battalion, Maj. D. Chase.
8th Missouri, Lieut. Col. D. C. Coleman.
113th Illinois, Col. G. B. Hoge.
116th Illinois, Col. N. W. Tupper.

Second Brigade.

Col. T. KILBY SMITH commanding.

55th Illinois, Lieut. Col. O. Malmborg.
57th Ohio, Col. William Mungen.
83d Indiana, Col. B. J. Spooner.
127th Illinois, Col. J. Van Arman.
54th Ohio, Capt. S. B. Yoeman.

Cavalry.

Thielemann's Battalion, Capt. Berthold Marschner.

Artillery.

1st Illinois, Battery A, Capt. P. P. Wood.
1st Illinois, Battery B, Capt. S. E. Barrett.
1st Illinois, Battery H, Lieut. Levi W. Hart.
8th Ohio Battery, Lieut. J. F. Putnam.
Four siege 30-pounder rifles, unattached.

II. Each division and brigade commander will at once enter upon the discharge of his duty, and will select and announce his staff to his own command, a copy of the order to be sent to these headquarters. Provision returns should be approved at division headquarters, and requisitions for quartermaster's and ordnance stores at these general headquarters.

Morning reports should be made to division headquarters; and consolidated morning reports, prepared in great detail and accuracy, made to these headquarters tri-monthly.

All orders heretofore issued by General Sherman at Memphis or in the field will be considered binding on his present command, unless they conflict with those of our common superiors.

III. The title of this *corps d'armée* will be the Second Army Corps of the Army of the Mississippi until it is constituted one of the series for the whole army of the United States. When such is announced in General Orders from the Adjutant-General's Office, Washington, D. C., then it will take its new title without other changes.

By order of Maj. Gen. W. T. Sherman:

J. H. HAMMOND,
Assistant Adjutant-General.

SPECIAL ORDERS, }   HDQRS. RIGHT WING, 13TH ARMY CORPS,
No. 2.   }   *Holly Springs, Miss., January 5, 1863.*

I. The Fourth Division, Brigadier-General Lauman commanding, will remain to garrison the post of Holly Springs until further orders.

The Third Brigade of the Fourth Division, Col. A. K. Johnson commanding, will be stationed at Waterford until all the Government stores are removed, when it will rejoin the division at Holly Springs.

By order of Major-General McPherson:

WM. T. CLARK,
Assistant Adjutant-General.

MOSCOW, *January 6, 1863.*

General MCARTHUR:

Rebel cavalry force of 2,000 or 3,000 is reported camped last night at Tallaloosa, 10 miles west of Holly Springs. They are reported to be on the way to strike this road between this point and Memphis, probably near Colliersville or Germantown. If at all, attack will probably be made to-morrow morning. Some artillery is reported. Will you send messengers immediately with the intelligence to all points? Answer.

A. L. LEE,
Colonel, &c.

JACKSON, *January 6, 1863.*

JOHN A. RAWLINS,
Colonel and Assistant Adjutant-General:

I have had Colonel Mizner out in that direction for three days, and intend to keep him there.

I am so completely enveloped with roaming squads of rebel cavalry that it is almost impossible to get courier through. Colonel Lawler has orders to watch movements closely, and in case the force is too large to fall back slowly until I can re-enforce him.

JER. C. SULLIVAN,
Brigadier-General.

JACKSON, *January 6, 1863.*

General GRANT:

Lieutenant Hart, of the Tennessee Cavalry, reports to me that Buckner and Cheatham are crossing the river at Saltillo and Shannonville. The report of General Rosecrans whipping Bragg is received from same source and that this portion of the rebels made their way to the river. Had I not better hold my troops here and re-enforce Corinth, if it should be attacked? I sent off to General Dodge to-day one regiment.

JER. C. SULLIVAN,
Brigadier-General.

HOLLY SPRINGS, MISS., *January* 6, 1863.

Col. W. W. LOWE, *Fort Henry, Tenn.*:

There are said to be large numbers of flat-boats and other craft for crossing the Tennessee River hid away at the mouth of streams emptying into the Tennessee. You will therefore please request the gunboats, which are reported to be up the river, to use every means for their destruction, that the enemy may be prevented from crossing into West Tennessee and Kentucky. They should proceed up the river as far as the water will permit.

Answer if you are in communication with the gunboats and their whereabouts.

By order of Maj. Gen. U. S. Grant:

JNO. A. RAWLINS,
Assistant Adjutant-General.

CAIRO, [ILL., *January* 6, 1863]—6 p. m.

General GRANT:

Two light-draught gunboats have gone up Cumberland River as convoys for supplies for Rosecrans. Two have orders to ascend Tennessee River with rise. The fifth is disabled and now undergoing repair. I have no others to send. They are only bullet-proof.

A. M. PENNOCK,
Fleet Captain of Station.

HOLLY SPRINGS, MISS., *January* 6, 1863.

Brig. Gen. C. S. HAMILTON, *La Grange, Tenn.*:

Nothing from Corinth to-day. Rosecrans has whipped Bragg badly at Murfreesborough and forced him to fall back. Probably Van Dorn is going there. Sullivan telegraphs that rebels are crossing the Tennessee again. I can hardly think it. The Tennessee is now up and the naval commander at Cairo says there are several gunboats up the river.

I do not know what day I will be going to Memphis. You can go there, or as soon as other troops arrive to replace Ross' division, which will be to-morrow. Let Lee clear Richardson out if he can.

U. S. GRANT,
Major-General.

HEADQUARTERS ARMY OF THE MISSISSIPPI,
Steamer Tigress, January 6, 1863.

Rear-Admiral PORTER,
Commanding Mississippi River Flotilla:

ADMIRAL: I have the honor to transmit for your information a copy of the instructions* communicated to the general commanding the two army corps of the Army of the Mississippi.

I am, admiral, very respectfully, your obedient servant,

A. SCHWARTZ,
Major and Acting Assistant Adjutant-General.

---

*Not found. Probably copy of instructions on p. 537.

CROSSING OF THE PIGEON ROOST AND M. AND C. R. R.,
January 6, 1863.

Maj. Gen. U. S. GRANT, *Holly Springs, Miss.:*

GENERAL: There is a continuous stream of wagons loaded with cotton coming from Mississippi over the Pigeon Roost road, taking out on their return all sorts of supplies, the owners acknowledging themselves to be disloyal. This thing is so manifestly wrong that I have taken the responsibility of stopping and sending back all cotton in the hands of the original owners who cannot produce satisfactory proofs of loyalty.

It is reported to me that buyers in Memphis are paying specie for cotton.

I hope you will sustain me in this course, which to me seems vital to our cause.

> I. F. QUINBY,
> *Brigadier-General.*

SPECIAL ORDERS, }   HDQRS. 13TH A. C., DEPT. OF THE TENN.,
    No. 6. - }   *Holly Springs, Miss., January 6, 1863.*

*   *   *   *   *   *   *

XI. Maj. Gen. S. A. Hurlbut is relieved from duty at Memphis, Tenn., and will assume command of the Sixteenth Army Corps.

XII. Brig. Gen. James C. Veatch is hereby assigned to the command of the District of Memphis, and will immediately proceed to Memphis, Tenn., and assume command accordingly.

XIII. Brig. Gen. A. Asboth is hereby relieved from duty at Memphis, Tenn., and will report in person without delay to these headquarters for orders.

By order of Maj. Gen. U. S. Grant:

> [JNO. A. RAWLINS,]
> *Assistant Adjutant-General.*

WAR DEPARTMENT,
Washington, January 7, 1863.

Major-General GRANT, *Holly Springs, Miss.:*

Give us the earliest possible information of affairs at Vicksburg, as movement of troops here depends upon the capture of that place.

> H. W. HALLECK,
> *General-in-Chief.*

WAR DEPARTMENT,
Washington, January 7, 1863.

Major-General GRANT, *Holly Springs, Miss.:*

Richmond papers of the 5th and 6th say that Sherman has been defeated and repulsed from Vicksburg. Every possible effort must be made to re-enforce him. We cannot communicate with Banks, but he has been urged to lose no time in co-operating. Curtis has been directed to give you all he can spare. Take everything you can dispense with in Tennessee and Mississippi. We must not fail in this if within human power to accomplish it.

> H. W. HALLECK,
> *General-in-Chief.*

HOLLY SPRINGS, MISS., *January* 7, 1863—6 p. m.

Maj. Gen. H. W. HALLECK, *General-in-Chief:*

All supplies not taken from the country are now brought from Memphis. Think it advisable to complete railroad to Columbus to get rolling-stock on this side and possibly to hold it for short time. Am throwing large supply of subsistence into Corinth. With use of two or three light-draught gunboats the Tennessee can be used. Nothing from Sherman since last dispatch. Will be ready to re-enforce him from Memphis if necessary. Will move heavy artillery from east bank of river. Is Helena, Ark., in my department? Can have troops at Corinth to operate from there soon as supplies can possibly be got there.

U. S. GRANT,
Major-General.

HOLLY SPRINGS, MISS., *January* 7, 1863.

Brig. Gen. GRENVILLE M. DODGE, *Corinth, Miss.:*

I am now sending re-enforcements to you. Will it not be practicable for you when you get them to drive Roddey to the north bank of the river and destroy his boats?

U. S. GRANT,
Major-General.

JACKSON, *January* 7, 1863.

Colonel RAWLINS:

The following dispatch just received from commanding officer at Bethel:

A man just from Florence, Ala., reports that Roddey has raised the steamboat Dunbar, sunk by our gunboats last winter, and is trying to fix up her engines; also that Kirby Smith's command crossed the river about there last week, going to re-enforce Price. He is vouched for as a Union man and one that is reliable.

W. W. SANFORD,
Colonel, Commanding Post.

JER. C. SULLIVAN,
Brigadier-General.

HEADQUARTERS SEVENTEENTH ARMY CORPS,
Camp, Holly Springs, Miss., January 7, 1863.

Colonel GRIERSON,
Commanding Cavalry Brigade:

COLONEL: It is reported that there is a force of rebel cavalry on the Pigeon Roost road, from 7 to 15 miles from here, estimated at several hundred. I do not really believe the report, but there is undoubtedly some cavalry in that direction, and I think it would be well for a portion of your force, say two battalions, to make a scout in that direction as soon as possible, striking the Pigeon Roost road west of Tallaloosa and then coming in to this place. The balance of your command, with the exception of scouts and patrols necessary to watch the country north of the Tallahatchie, will move back here with Colonel Johnson's brigade. Send one of your staff officers in advance and I will show him where you will camp.

Very respectfully, your obedient servant,

JAS. B. McPHERSON,
Major-General.

HDQRS. LEFT WING, ARMY OF THE TENNESSEE,
La Grange, Tenn., January 7, 1863.
Brig. Gen. JOHN E. SMITH,
Commanding Division :

By direction of the major-general commanding army, on being relieved by the division of General Logan, you will move to Corinth via
Bolivar, with all the regiments of your command now in this vicinity,
taking with you six days' rations. The troops which have been detached to General Sullivan will for the present remain under his orders.
On arriving at Corinth you will report to Brig. Gen. G. M. Dodge.
The baggage belonging to the detached regiments should be sent to
them on your arrival at Bolivar. The march will be conducted with
good order, allowing no straggling or depredations.

By order of Brig. Gen. C. S. Hamilton:

R. M. SAWYER,
Assistant Adjutant-General.

CIRCULAR.]   HDQRS. 13TH ARMY CORPS, DEPT. OF THE TENN.,
Holly Springs, Miss., January 7, 1863.

By direction of General-in-Chief of the Army, at Washington, the
general order from these headquarters expelling Jews from the department is hereby revoked.

By order of Maj. Gen. U. S. Grant:

JNO. A. RAWLINS,
Assistant Adjutant-General.

HOLLY SPRINGS, *January 8, 1863*—3 a. m.
General H. W. HALLECK, *Washington, D. C.:*

I will get off re-enforcements to Sherman without delay. I have had
no reports to confirm statements of the Richmond papers.

U. S. GRANT,
Major-General.

HOLLY SPRINGS, MISS., *January 8, 1863*—9.35 p. m.
Maj. Gen. H. W. HALLECK, *General-in-Chief :*

Scouts just into Corinth from south and east report enemy moving
east from Jackson and north on Mobile road, fortifying near Meridian.
Have been moving several days. This is not confirmatory of Richmond report. Some of Bragg's forces are passing south on line of Athens
and Nashville road.

U. S. GRANT,
Major-General.

HOLLY SPRINGS, MISS., *January 8, 1863.*
Captain PENNOCK, U. S. Navy, *Cairo, Ill.:*

Can I have gunboats at Memphis to convoy re-enforcements to Vicksburg? I will want them by the 11th.

U. S. GRANT,
Major-General.

HOLLY SPRINGS, MISS., *January* 8, 1863.

Maj. Gen. J. B. McPHERSON, *Holly Springs, Miss.*:

Order Denver to move immediately to take Logan's place, Logan to move west and relieve McArthur until Lauman can be pushed to Moscow and La Fayette.

A dispatch from General Halleck just received says that Richmond papers of the 5th say that Sherman has been repulsed, and to re-enforce him with all troops possible to spare.

U. S. GRANT,
Major-General.

HOLLY SPRINGS, MISS., *January* 8, 1863.

Brig. Gen. J. B. McPHERSON, *Holly Springs, Miss.*:

As soon as all public stores, sick, &c., are removed from Holly Springs fall back with the troops now occupying the place to the vicinity of La Grange, Grand Junction, or Davis' Mill.

When you arrive there, examine the railroad to the east and ascertain the practicability of supplying troops to Pocahontas by rail and teams. If practicable, and you think it advisable, Denver's division may be moved to that place.

The Twenty-fifth Iowa and Ninetieth Illinois, now doing railroad duty, will be added to General Denver's division, giving him twelve regiments. By taking two regiments from the old brigade a new one can be formed.

U. S. GRANT.
Major-General.

WAR DEPARTMENT,
Washington, January 8, 1863.

Major-General WRIGHT, *Cincinnati, Ohio:*

Send Ewing's brigade down the Mississippi, reporting to General Grant, at Memphis.

H. W. HALLECK,
General-in-Chief.

CINCINNATI, OHIO, *January* 8, 1863—1 p. m.

Maj. Gen. H. W. HALLECK, *General-in-Chief:*

Ewing's brigade (2,600 strong) is about leaving Louisville, by river, for Nashville. Have you any information from Vicksburg which makes it important to send this force there rather than to General Rosecrans? Ewing is instructed to stop at Smithland for orders. Please answer at once.

H. G. WRIGHT,
Major-General, Commanding.

HEADQUARTERS ARMY OF THE MISSISSIPPI,
Steamer Tigress, January 8, 1863.

Maj. Gen. SAMUEL R. CURTIS,
Commanding Department of the Frontier, Saint Louis, Mo.:

GENERAL: Upon the retirement of the forces under Major-General Sherman's command from the vicinity of Vicksburg to Milliken's Bend I assumed command of them on the 4th instant.

Learning from the instructions and other papers turned over to me by General Sherman that you had promptly and generously co-operated to insure the success of the Mississippi River Expedition, and would be pleased, under favorable circumstances, to have his co-operation in turn, I immediately determined to sail with my whole army to the Post of Arkansas via the mouth of the White River, the cut-off, and the Arkansas River, for the purpose of reducing it.

The reduction of that place will free the navigation of the Mississippi River in the vicinity of the mouths of the White and Arkansas Rivers from the molestation inflicted by hostile parties sent from the Post.

Whether I will advance beyond the Post to Brownsville and Little Rock, or to either, will depend upon circumstances yet undeveloped.

If, as I understand, your columns are moving in the direction of the last-named places, a favorable conjuncture may conspire to give our arms early, if not immediate, control of the State of Arkansas.

Hoping to hear from you fully and frankly upon all matters of public interest, I have the honor to conclude by assuring you of my high regard for you, both personally and officially.

Your obedient servant,

JOHN A. McCLERNAND,
Major-General, Commanding.

HEADQUARTERS ARMY OF THE MISSISSIPPI,
Steamer Tigress, January 8, 1863.

Maj. Gen. U. S. GRANT,
Commanding Department of the Tennessee:

When I arrived at the mouth of the Yazoo River I found that our army, having been repulsed near Vicksburg, was re-embarked under General Sherman's order for conveyance to Milliken's Bend, on the Mississippi River.

On the next day, the 4th, while the troops were still on the transports, I assumed command of the land forces of the Mississippi River Expedition and immediately determined, with the co-operation of Admiral Porter, to sail with my whole command for the Post of Arkansas via the mouth of White River, the cut-off, and the Arkansas River, for the reduction of that Post.

I am now here and will immediately resume my voyage to the appointed destination. The reasons justifying and requiring this movement may be stated as follows:

1st. The failure of the Mississippi River Expedition in the object of reducing Vicksburg and the present impracticability of reducing that place with the force under my command by a front attack unsupported by a co-operative movement in the rear of the place.

2d. The importance, nay duty, of actively and usefully employing our arms not only for the purpose of subduing the rebellion but to secure some compensation for previous expense and loss attending the expedition.

3d. The importance of reducing the Post as a means of freeing the navigation of the Mississippi River in the vicinity of the mouths of White and Arkansas Rivers from molestation by the enemy.

4th. The importance of making a diversion of the enemy, who are alleged to be marching to certain points in Missouri, and of co-operating with General Curtis' column in Arkansas.

5th. The counteraction of the moral effect of the failure of the attack near Vicksburg and the reinspiration of the forces repulsed by making them the champions of new, important, and successful enterprises.

6th. The intense desire of all worthy officers and men to be usefully employed.

I will dispatch officers on transports from this place for additional supplies of quartermaster's, commissary, and ordnance stores. The same transports will bear all who were wounded near Vicksburg in our hands to the hospitals above.

I expect, after completing any operations undertaken in Arkansas, unless otherwise directed, to return with my command to a point on the Mississippi River near Vicksburg, and direct my attention to the following objects: The seizure of Monroe, on the Vicksburg and Shreveport Railroad, and, if possible, New Carthage, on the Mississippi, below Vicksburg, and some point on the Red River; also to the practicability of isolating Vicksburg by opening another channel for the Mississippi.

Having been *en route* on their transports since starting from Milliken's Bend, and my taking command, I have been unable to obtain, and consequently am unable to furnish, reports of the strength and condition of my forces. I will do this at the earliest practicable moment.

Very respectfully, your obedient servant,

JOHN A. McCLERNAND,
Major-General, Commanding.

HEADQUARTERS ARMY OF THE MISSISSIPPI,
Steamer Tigress, January 8, 1863.

Admiral DAVID D. PORTER,
Commanding Mississippi River Flotilla:

ADMIRAL: Will you please inform me when you are ready to move? I will also inform you when the transports will move.

By order of Maj. Gen. J. A. McClernand:

W. STEWART,
Colonel and Chief of Staff.

HEADQUARTERS ARMY OF THE MISSISSIPPI,
Steamer Tigress, January 8, 1863.

Admiral DAVID D. PORTER,
Commanding Mississippi Squadron:

ADMIRAL: The signal officer to whom you refer has left. I will first send you word when my command is ready to move and afterward fire a signal gun; upon the doing of which, you leading off, I will follow with the transports, convoyed by your gunboats, according to the arrangement indicated by your General Orders, No. 30.

If you think it unsafe for the fleet to run all night I will stop with you at the cut-off; otherwise I would prefer to run to-night and arrive at the Post in the morning.

I will follow your example and proceed or stop, as you may deem it best.

Your obedient servant,

JOHN A. McCLERNAND,
Major-General, Commanding.

HEADQUARTERS ARMY OF THE MISSISSIPPI,
Steamer Tigress, January 8, 1863.

Admiral DAVID D. PORTER,
Commanding Mississippi Squadron:

ADMIRAL: The signal officer to whom you refer has left. In view of your suggestion of the unsafeness of running at night, and of the necessity of delaying longer for some of my transports, I propose to start in the morning at 8 o'clock, and have accordingly so ordered in regard to my command. [You] leading off in the morning at the hour named I will follow.

I learn this evening from an officer of General Morgan L. Smith's staff that the gunboats might find a favorable landing for the protection of the disembarkation of the land forces at Notrib's farm, 3 miles below the Post.

JOHN A. McCLERNAND,
Major-General, Commanding.

———

LA GRANGE, TENN., *January 8, 1863.*

Brig. Gen. I. F. QUINBY,
Commanding Seventh Division:

GENERAL: Hold your command ready to move to Memphis, and move them along as rapidly as troops arrive to relieve them.

C. S. HAMILTON,
Brigadier-General, Commanding.

———

HEADQUARTERS DISTRICT OF MEMPHIS,
Memphis, Tenn., January 8, 1863.

Brigadier-General GORMAN:

GENERAL: The major-general commanding directs me to give you a copy of Major-General Grant's dispatch, received this p. m. If you can, send it to Major-General Sherman:

What number of troops have you transportation for in Memphis? I will send at least 15,000 more down the river, and want transportation ready for them. Send word, if you can send down the river, that re-enforcements are going to them.

U. S. GRANT,
Major-General.

We have no transportation here, but shall stop all boats coming down that can convey them. If you have any boats that can be spared from your fleet send them here immediately.

I have the honor to be, very respectfully, your obedient servant,

——— ———,

Acting Assistant Adjutant-General.

———

HEADQUARTERS SEVENTEENTH ARMY CORPS,
Holly Springs, Miss., January 8, 1863.

Brig. Gen. J. W. DENVER,
Commanding First Division:

GENERAL: You will immediately move your command to Davis' Mill, Grand Junction, and La Grange, and relieve Brigadier-General Logan's division.

The brigade going to La Grange will have to guard the railroad **west** to Moscow.

Very respectfully, your obedient servant,

[JAS. B. McPHERSON,]
Major-General.

HEADQUARTERS SEVENTEENTH ARMY CORPS,
Holly Springs, Miss., January 8, 1863.

Brig. Gen. JOHN A. LOGAN,
Commanding Third Division, La Grange:

GENERAL: As soon as your division is relieved by General Denver's you will move your command west, relieving General McArthur's division. Orders have been sent to General Denver to move his division immediately to relieve yours. But for fear there may be some difficulty in sending the order from here via Salem I have inclosed a copy which I wish you to send him from Grand Junction. His command is stationed on the north side of Wolf River, between Spring Hill and naan.

Very respectfully, your obedient servant,

[JAS. B. McPHERSON,]
Major-General.

SPECIAL ORDERS, } HDQRS. SECOND CORPS, ARMY OF THE MISS.,
    No. 5.   }   *Montgomery Point, January 8,* 1863.

I. The corps will start to-morrow at 8 a. m. The boats must keep in their exact order, about 100 yards apart:

First, Forest Queen; second, Continental, followed by boats of the First, Second, and Third Brigades of Steele's division; third, the Westmoreland, followed by boats of the First and Second Brigades of Stuart's division.

II. Two companies on each boat must be armed and equipped ready to return a fire if a boat is fired on from shore. In case of the firing a volley or anything indicating a force the boat fired at will run by and land above, while the succeeding boats will land below, and promptly attack the party, unless a gunboat be near, when it will shell the place from which the firing comes.

III. On reaching the place of disembarkation each division commander will send a brigade out to cover the landing, and will immediately proceed to disembark men, arms, horses, wagons, &c., for a five days' operation similar to our move at Yazoo. A small guard of the sick will remain at each boat, but any man remaining with the boat without the written detail of the colonel will be treated as deserting his colors in action.

By order of Maj. Gen. W. T. Sherman:

·   J. H. HAMMOND,
Assistant Adjutant-General.

LA GRANGE, TENN., *January 9,* 1863—1 p. m.

Maj. Gen. H. W. HALLECK, *General-in-Chief:*

Sherman has returned to Napoleon. His loss was small. Will send you the particulars as soon as learned. I will start for Memphis immediately, and will do everything possible for the capture of Vicksburg.

U. S. GRANT,
Major-General, Commanding.

WAR DEPARTMENT,
Washington, January 9, 1863.

Major-General GRANT, *Holly Springs, Miss.:*

Ewing's brigade has been sent by General Wright to report to you at Memphis. How many troops has Sherman, and how many more can you send him, and when?

H. W. HALLECK,
General-in-Chief.

———

LA GRANGE, TENN., *January* 9, 1863—9 p. m.

Maj. Gen. H. W. HALLECK, *General-in-Chief:*

General Sherman has 32,000 men, less casualties. I can send from 12,000 to 15,000 more. I am on my way to Memphis to attend to all wants of the expedition.

U. S. GRANT,
Major-General.

———

LA GRANGE, *January* 9, 1863.

Major-General GRANT:

Lee had cavalry all over the country yesterday for 20 miles south of railroad, and reports only about 400 guerrillas under Blythe not far from Hernando. There is no danger of attack.

C. S. HAMILTON,
Brigadier-General.

———

CAIRO, *January* 9, 1863—1 p. m.

General GRANT:

Will send one light-draught gunboat, bullet-proof, one-fourth manned. I can do no more. Can't you place under the command of her captain soldiers enough to work her guns?

A. M. PENNOCK,
Fleet Captain.

———

SPECIAL ORDERS, } HDQRS. DISTRICT OF WESTERN KENTUCKY,
No. 8.   }   *Louisville, January* 9, 1863.

*   *   *   *   *   *   *

IV. Brig. Gen. Hugh Ewing, commanding brigade, will proceed with-out delay with his command by river to Memphis, Tenn., and will re-port on his arrival at that place to Maj. Gen. U. S. Grant.

*   *   *   *   *   *   *

By command of Brig. Gen. J. T. Boyle:

A. C. SEMPLE,
Assistant Adjutant-General.

———

WAR DEPARTMENT,
Washington, January 10, 1863.

Major-General WRIGHT,
Cincinnati, Ohio:

Are there not fractional regiments organized in Ohio, Indiana, and Illinois which can be consolidated by the Governors and immediately sent down the Mississippi? It is of vital importance that the army against Vicksburg be re-enforced as rapidly as possible. It is expected that you will use every exertion to accomplish that object. All our paroled prisoners taken prior to December 10 are declared exchanged. Get them back to their regiments in the field as rapidly as possible.

H. W. HALLECK,
General-in-Chief.

HEADQUARTERS DEPARTMENT OF THE TENNESSEE,
Memphis, Tenn., January 10, 1863.

Maj. Gen. JOHN A. McCLERNAND,
Commanding Expedition on Vicksburg:

GENERAL: Since General Sherman left here I have been unable to learn anything official from the expedition which you now command. Your wants and requirements all have to be guessed at. I am prepared to re-enforce you immediately with one division from my old command, one brigade from General Curtis, and one brigade coming from General Wright's command. I can also further re-enforce you with one more division from my old command besides sending all other troops that come to me from elsewhere.

This expedition must not fail. If there is force enough within the limits of my control to secure a certain victory at Vicksburg they will be sent there. But I want to be advised of what has been done, what there is to contend against, and an estimate of what is required. I take it for granted that ordnance stores, rations, &c., will be required for the command now with you in addition to what they now have, and to a full supply for all re-enforcements.

I would like to have a full report immediately for my guidance as to what is to be done.

Troops are assembling here and all transports coming into port are being detained. If you have any not required for the troops with you release them and let them come up here.

I am, general, very respectfully, &c.,

U. S. GRANT,
Major-General.

MEMPHIS, TENN., *January* 10, 1863.

Maj. Gen. JOHN A. McCLERNAND,
Commanding Vicksburg Expedition:

In sending re-enforcements to you, gunboats will be required to convoy them. They cannot be obtained at Cairo. Please request Admiral Porter, if practicable, to detach boats from his fleet for that purpose.

U. S. GRANT,
Major-General.

MEMPHIS, TENN., *January* 10, 1863.

Rear-Admiral DAVID D. PORTER,
Commanding Mississippi Fleet:

I send Colonel Bissell, of the Engineer Regiment of the West, to report to you for the purpose of surveying the ground and determining the practicability of reopening the canal across the tongue of land opposite Vicksburg. Any suggestions from you I would be most happy to receive. I have not had one word officially from the expedition which left Helena on the 22d December since that time, and am consequently very much at a loss to know how to proceed. I am, however, preparing to re-enforce General McClernand, and can do it to the extent of 20,000 men certainly, and possibly more.

By the same boat that takes this I am writing to General McClernand, and expect to get such reply as will enable me to act more understandingly.

U. S. GRANT,
Major-General.

SAINT LOUIS, *January* 10, 1863.
Major-General GRANT:

Some twenty steamboats are idle at Helena. Send for them. This river is almost destitute of boats. I have ordered all the boats coming up to be turned back, and have sent an officer expressly on this service. I hope to have the requisite number of boats, but you must crowd them if necessary. All the boats on the Ohio have been sent to General Rosecrans.

ROBT. ALLEN,
Chief Quartermaster.

HEADQUARTERS ARMY OF THE MISSISSIPPI,
January 10, 1863.
Maj. Gen. U. S. GRANT, *Commanding, &c.:*

GENERAL : I am landed within 3 miles of the Post of Arkansas, and am marching a corps by a detour upon the enemy's works. General Morgan's corps will follow with the artillery as rapidly as possible.

A brigade with a section of artillery is landed on the right bank and is marching across a neck to take position on the river, above the fort commanding the river. The enemy's force is variously estimated at from 7,000 to 12,000 men.

General Gorman sends word that he is moving with 12,000 men from Helena toward Devall's Bluff, on the White River, and Brownsville.

More anon.
Yours, most respectfully,

JOHN A. McCLERNAND,
Major-General, Commanding.

HEADQUARTERS DISTRICT OF EASTERN ARKANSAS,
Helena, January 10, 1863.
Major-General CURTIS:

GENERAL : Colonel Colburn leaves in a few moments for Saint Louis. I send by him, to be disposed of at Memphis or Cairo, a few prisoners of war.

My transports will begin to leave to-morrow morning at daylight.

General McClernand has assumed command of all of General Sherman's forces at Vicksburg, and has come back to the mouth of the Arkansas and gone up with part of the naval force under Admiral Porter in person to attack Old Post.

I went down and had a personal conference with General Sherman,

&c. It is agreed that they proceed up the Arkansas, and that I proceed up the White River, each having some naval forces.

General McClernand designs to go entirely up to Little Rock, and I shall go to Devall's Bluff, and perhaps send some force as high as Jacksonport, on White River. If the fog does not prevent I will enter White River day after to-morrow (the 12th), at daylight.

McClernand will have 32,000 infantry, 1,000 cavalry, and forty or more pieces of artillery. I will have 10,000 infantry, 2,000 cavalry, and 30 pieces of artillery.

I will send of the cavalry force 1,500 by land from Helena to Saint Charles and Clarendon if it is possible for them to get through, but they will have to go without transportation. They will take five days' rations for the men in their haversacks and rely upon the country for forage for their horses. It is utterly impracticable to send teams.

Colonel Colburn will give you further detailed particulars. I shall try to communicate with Schofield.

I am, general, very respectfully, your obedient servant,

W. A. GORMAN,
Brigadier-General, Commanding.

SPECIAL ORDERS, ⎱   HDQRS. DEPARTMENT OF THE TENNESSEE,
No. 10.   ⎰   *Memphis, Tenn., January* 10, 1863.

*   *   *   *   *   *   *

II. Brig. Gen. C. S. Hamilton is hereby assigned to the command of the Sixteenth Army Corps, Department of the Tennessee, and will relieve Maj. Gen. S. A. Hurlbut, to enable him to take the benefit of a leave of absence this day granted him.

*   *   *   *   *   *   *

By order of Maj. Gen. U. S. Grant:

[JNO. A. RAWLINS,]
Assistant Adjutant-General.

MEMPHIS, TENN., *January* 11, 1863—3.30 p. m.

Maj. Gen. H. W. HALLECK, *General-in-Chief:*

General McClernand has fallen back to White River, and gone on a wild-goose chase to the Post of Arkansas. I am ready to re-enforce, but must await further information before knowing what to do.

U. S. GRANT,
Major-General, Commanding.

HEADQUARTERS DEPARTMENT OF THE TENNESSEE,
Memphis, Tenn., January 11, 1863.

Major-General McCLERNAND,
Commanding Expedition on Vicksburg:

GENERAL: Unless absolutely necessary for the object of your expedition you will abstain from all moves not connected with it.

I do not approve of your move on the Post of Arkansas while the other is in abeyance. It will lead to the loss of men without a result. So long as Arkansas cannot re-enforce the enemy east of the river we have no present interest in troubling them. It might answer for some of the purposes you suggest, but certainly not as a military movement looking to the accomplishment of the one great result, the capture of Vicksburg.

Unless you are acting under authority not derived from me keep your command where it can soonest be assembled for the renewal of the attack on Vicksburg.

Major-General Banks has orders from Washington to co-operate in the reduction of Vicksburg, and if not already off that place may be daily expected. You will therefore keep your forces well in hand at some point on the Mississippi River, where you can communicate with General Banks on his arrival. Should you learn, before you have an opportunity of communicating with him, that he is making an attack on Vicksburg, move at once to his support. Every effort must be directed to the reduction of that place.

From the best information I have, Milliken's Bend is the proper place for you to be, and unless there is some great reason of which I am not advised you will immediately proceed to that point and await the arrival of re-enforcements and General Banks' expedition, keeping me fully advised of your movements.

I am, general, very respectfully, your obedient servant,

U. S. GRANT,
Major-General.

HEADQUARTERS SEVENTEENTH ARMY CORPS,
La Grange, January 11, 1863.

Major-General GRANT:

The head of General Lauman's division entered Moscow 6 p. m., and the advance of the ammunition and quartermaster train reached this place at 6.30.

I directed the train-master at Grand Junction yesterday to send train to Hudsonville and Lamar Station to bring away the cotton, &c. I sent orders to the troops and guards along the road to fall back and join their commands as soon as all the property was removed. Everything worked well to-day, and no delay except from the heaviness of the roads. There were no houses burned in Holly Springs that were occupied and only two or three of any importance, though a good many small frames and stables were destroyed.

JAS. B. McPHERSON,
Major-General.

SPECIAL ORDERS, } HDQRS. DEPARTMENT OF THE TENNESSEE,
No. 11.   }   *Memphis, Tenn, January* 11, 1863.

I. Brig. Gen. A. Asboth is hereby relieved from duty at Memphis, Tenn., and will proceed without delay to Columbus, Ky., and relieve Brig. Gen. T. A. Davies in the command of the District of Columbus.

II. Brig. Gen. T. A. Davies is hereby relieved from duty in the District of Columbus and will turn over the command of the same to Brig Gen. A. Asboth and report in writing to the Headquarters of the Army, Washington, D. C., for orders.

   *   *   *   *   *   *

By order of Maj. Gen. U. S. Grant:

[JNO. A. RAWLINS,]
Assistant Adjutant-General.

WAR DEPARTMENT,
Washington, January 12, 1863.

Major-General GRANT, *Memphis, Tenn.:*

You are hereby authorized to relieve General McClernand from command of the expedition against Vicksburg, giving it to the next in rank or taking it yourself.

H. W. HALLECK,
General-in-Chief.

MEMPHIS, TENN., *January 12, 1863.*

Brigadier-General GORMAN
Commanding Helena, Ark.:

The following dispatch is just received:

SAINT LOUIS, *January 11, 1863.*

Major-General GRANT:

Please use the following dispatch at your discretion:

"Brig. Gen. W. A. GORMAN, *Helena, Ark.:*

"Continue to regard the Vicksburg move of primary importance. Let all other moves delay if deemed necessary. Send boats and men for that object, but do not weaken Helena so as to endanger the position.

"SAML. R. CURTIS,
" Major-General."

You will therefore, in accordance with the spirit of the above dispatch, please send forward to report to the commanding officer of the expedition against Vicksburg every available man that can be spared from your command, keeping in view the safety of Helena. General Banks has been ordered from Washington to co-operate in the reduction of Vicksburg, and I have sent orders to the expedition from here to repair to a point on the Mississippi River where communication can most likely be had with General Banks on his arrival.

U. S. GRANT,
Major-General.

JACKSON, *January 12, 1863.*

Major-General GRANT:

I have driven Richardson across the Hatchie, taking a number of prisoners. A regiment of cavalry sent toward Somerville can head him off.

JER. C. SULLIVAN,
Brigadier-General.

JACKSON, *January 12, 1863.*

General DODGE:

Colonel Wood is in command at Benton. He is so good an officer that I cannot fill his place, and it is absolutely necessary to have a good man at that place for a short time. I have three regiments here that I hold by order of General Grant that will be forwarded you if necessary.

I whipped Richardson yesterday, destroyed his ferry, and have a number of prisoners. I can hear of no band of guerrillas in my district. Sherman was compelled to fall back from Vicksburg; our loss, 1,100 killed and wounded.

JER. C. SULLIVAN,
Brigadier-General.

SAINT LOUIS, MO., *January* 12, 1863.

Maj. Gen. H. W. HALLECK, *General-in-Chief:*

General Grant has made requisitions upon me for transportation for 16,000 men to embark from Memphis. I have sent down an express boat with an officer on board instructed to turn back all boats bound upward. This will take all boats from this river. Have also telegraphed to Colonel Swords to send all the boats he can procure from the Ohio. I feel confident that there will be transportation sufficient for all the troops at General Grant's disposal. General Curtis has advised General Gorman to send all the troops he can spare from Helena. At least 5,000 men could be sent from that point.

ROBT. ALLEN.

GENERAL ORDERS, } HEADQUARTERS FIFTEENTH ARMY CORPS,
No. 2.   }   *Post of Arkansas, January* 12, 1863.

Pursuant to General Orders, No. 210, dated December 18, 1862, Adjutant-General's Office, Washington, D. C., the corps now commanded by Maj. Gen. W. T. Sherman will be known as the Fifteenth Army Corps. Its organization will remain unchanged.

By order of Maj. Gen. W. T. Sherman:

J. H. HAMMOND,
Assistant Adjutant-General.

SPECIAL ORDERS, } HDQRS. DEPARTMENT OF THE TENNESSEE,
No. 12.   }   *Memphis, Tenn., January* 12, 1863.

*   *   *   *   *   *   *

IX. Brigadier-General Ewing's brigade, now under orders to join the Mississippi expedition, is hereby assigned to Brig. Gen. Morgan L. Smith's division of the Fifteenth Army Corps, and will report accordingly.

By order of Maj. Gen. U. S. Grant:

[JNO. A. RAWLINS,]
Assistant Adjutant-General.

GENERAL ORDERS, } HEADQUARTERS FIFTEENTH ARMY CORPS,
No. 3.   }   *Post of Arkansas, January* 12, 1863.

I. Ignorance of the rules of war as to pillage and plunder can no longer be pleaded. Laws of Congress, orders of the President, and my own have again and again been published.

A thorough inspection of every regiment and boat will be made within twenty-four hours of the publication of this order, and the colonel of any regiment or commander of any company who allows any officer or soldier in his command to keep or use a horse, mule, gun, pistol, saddle, or any property not his own will be arrested, and the offender will at once be put in irons or tried and confined in the hold of some steamboat, in charge of the provost guard.

Colonel Hoge, of the One hundred and thirteenth Illinois, is charged with the execution of this order, and his regiment is assigned to duty as provost guard. Colonel Hoge by himself, or any officer of his regiment with a written order, may search for stolen property, take it away by violence—even to killing—and will deliver the same to the chief quartermaster of the corps, Capt. J. Condit Smith. If the officer or soldier, camp-follower or steamboat hand, passenger, or any person with this army violate the laws of Congress and orders of the President it is the duty of everybody to seize him and deliver him forcibly and sternly to this provost guard.

That Colonel Hoge may execute this order thoroughly he will camp near these headquarters, and use some steamboat-hold or house in which to confine prisoners.

Prisoners found in possession of stolen horses, mules, saddles, muskets, rifles, shot-guns, or any species of property captured by the United States forces will, while awaiting trial, be confined to bread and water, unless the chief surgeon of one or other of the divisions certifies that the health of the prisoner is endangered thereby.

The commanding general appeals to the good officers and soldiers, of whom he is proud to know his corps is mostly composed, to aid him in bringing to condign punishment the cowardly rascals who hang back when danger threatens, but are foremost in stealing, robbing, and plundering.

Twenty-four hours' notice is given that those in doubt may turn in property not their own; after that this order must be rigorously enforced.

II. Each division commander will early to-morrow detail a sufficient party to bury the dead of the enemy and the horses that lie in their immediate front. Accounts of the dead buried will be kept and reported along with the events of the recent battle.

III. Officers and soldiers found on steamboats or in houses who have not a disabling wound or who are not in a regularly appointed hospital of their own regiment and brigade will be arrested and turned over to the provost guard as deserters and confined on bread and water.

IV. The general enjoins on all in authority to spare no pains to encourage and provide for the good, honest soldier; but not to spare the shirks who avail themselves of every plea, even sickness, to avoid the honorable duties of the good and brave.

The men who in times like these will not do their full share of fighting and labor cannot be allowed to eat our rations and enjoy the shelter of boats and houses. These must be reserved to those who do their whole duty.

By order of Maj. Gen. W. T. Sherman:

J. H. HAMMOND,
Assistant Adjutant-General.

MEMPHIS, TENN., *January* 13, 1863.

Maj. Gen. J. B. McPHERSON, *La Grange, Tenn.*:

It is my present intention to command the expedition down the river in person. I will take two divisions with me, Logan's and McArthur's, I think. It will not be necessary for Logan to move, however, until further orders. I do not know where McClernand is, but have sent orders for him to proceed to Milliken's Bend and remain there or co-operate with Banks, should he be coming up the river.

Was Holly Springs destroyed? Report here says so.

U. S. GRANT,
Major-General.

LA GRANGE, *January* 13, 1863.
General GRANT:

GENERAL: In accordance with instructions received from Colonel Rawlins last night, I sent orders to General Logan to move to Memphis with his entire command as soon as relieved by General Lauman. I have now sent orders for them to remain as they were until further orders from you. Holly Springs was not burned, only a few houses, comparatively, burned; all frame buildings except the Magnolia Hotel, and none of them occupied. I have had cavalry scouts out south and southeast, and they report no movement of enemy. I will endeavor to be prepared for them if they come.

JAS. B. McPHERSON.

GLENDALE, *January* 13, 1863.
Major-General BLAIR:

No further information received than already reported. S. D. Lee is said to have reached Tuscumbia last Friday night with three brigades and five or six guns. A citizen of Franklin County reports that he is on his way to assist Forrest and Wheeler in cutting off Rosecrans' communication. Jeff. Forrest with 600 men at Cherokee, Ala. Colonel Spencer has started a man to Tuscumbia; will take four days to get back.

I will be in Corinth by next train.

JOHN E. SMITH,
Brigadier-General.

PRAIRIE LANDING,
On Steamer Ruth, January 13, 1863.
Maj. Gen. JOHN A. McCLERNAND,
   Comdg. Expedition against Vicksburg and Little Rock:

GENERAL: On the 10th instant, at Memphis, I received from General Grant * the inclosed communication to yourself with instructions to myself to "proceed with all possible dispatch to Vicksburg, Miss., or until you can communicate in person with Maj. Gen. John A. McClernand or the officer commanding the Mississippi expedition."

On my arrival at Helena on the 11th instant I was advised by General Gorman that you had retired from Vicksburg with your command and gone up the Arkansas to operate against Old Post, and that he (General Gorman) was then organizing an expedition for the White River; that my command was to be a portion of said expedition, and that we were to co-operate with you.

I was not advised yesterday that a dispatch boat was to leave the mouth of White River for your fleet or I should have forwarded the dispatch. I have made an effort to get communication with you from this point across the country, distance 12 miles, but my superiors have thought it not advisable.

I now send the dispatches to the hospital fleet at the mouth of this river with instructions that they be immediately forwarded to you.

Very respectfully, your obedient servant,
CLINTON B. FISK,
Brigadier-General.

---

* Probably Grant to McClernand, January 10, p. 551.

MEMPHIS, TENN., *January* 13, 1863.

Maj. Gen. JOHN A. McCLERNAND,
   Commanding Expedition on Vicksburg :

On the 11th instant I wrote to you disapproving of the diversion of your expedition from the main object, but owing to the difficulty of getting a convoy the dispatch has not yet got off. I am in receipt of yours of same date and have forwarded it to Washington. I cannot tell positively what is best for you to do; but unless there is some object not visible at this distance your forces should return to Milliken's Bend, or some point convenient for operating on Vicksburg, and where they can co-operate with Banks should he come up the river. Banks was in New Orleans on the 16th December, and under orders to push up the river with all possible dispatch. What difficulties he may have had to encounter below I do not know, but understand that Port Hudson has been made very strong. Should he get past that place, however, it is our duty to be prepared to co-operate.

One brigade assigned to the division of Morgan L. Smith goes down to join you at the same time with this. I understand also that there are still other forces coming down the river with the same destination, but of this I am not officially informed. I will still further re-enforce with two divisions from here unless the next few days prove it to be unnecessary.

The transports in the river available for moving troops are becoming very limited in consequence of the great number now with you. You will therefore discharge any that are not absolutely necessary for your purposes and order them to report here without delay.

U. S. GRANT,
Major-General.

HEADQUARTERS SEVENTEENTH ARMY CORPS,
   La Grange, Tenn., January 13, 1863.

Brig. Gen. JOHN A. LOGAN, *La Fayette :*

GENERAL: As soon as relieved by General Lauman's division you will move with your command to Memphis, taking all your camp and garrison equipage, and report to Major-General Grant for orders.

Very respectfully, your obedient servant,
[JAS. B. McPHERSON,]
Major-General.

HEADQUARTERS SEVENTEENTH ARMY CORPS,
   La Grange, Tenn., January 13, 1863.

Brigadier-General LAUMAN, *Moscow :*

GENERAL: You will immediately move a portion of your command west on the line of the railroad and relieve General Logan's division, which is ordered to Memphis. Moscow being one of the most important points to be guarded, you will retain at that place your best brigade, two batteries, and two regiments from one of the other brigades. The remaining six regiments and batteries you can station at La Fayette and Colliersville, as you may think best, in order to cover the railroad and keep the communication between here and Memphis secure. At all the points to be guarded defensive stockades must be constructed to render the command safe against a sudden cavalry dash.

Very respectfully, your obedient servant,
[JAS. B. McPHERSON,]
Major-General.

HEADQUARTERS ARMY OF THE MISSISSIPPI.
Post Arkansas, January 13, 1863.

Maj. J. H. HAMMOND,
   A. A. G., Second Army Corps, Army of the Mississippi:

MAJOR: General McClernand directs me to inquire of you by what
authority you call the Second Army Corps of the Army of the Mississippi the "Fifteenth Army Corps," and he wishes also to be informed
why you make a distinction between General Sherman's army corps and
General McClernand's, well knowing that General Morgan is in command of the First Army Corps.

You will confer a favor upon me by immediately stating your authority.

   Respectfully, your obedient servant,
                              A. SCHWARTZ,
             Major and Acting Assistant Adjutant-General.

GENERAL ORDERS, } HEADQUARTERS FIFTEENTH ARMY CORPS,
   No. 4.   }   Post Arkansas, January 13, 1863.

This corps will make preparation to re-embark on the transports as
near as possible at the place where we landed, viz, just below Notrib's
farm.

General Steele will move his command back to that point by the route
he came, leaving one regiment on picket to destroy the cantonment
now held by him when he received written orders from General Sherman to that effect; he will also leave a regiment to destroy the enemy's
rifle-pits from our extreme right toward our left.

General Stuart will move his division back along the river bank, leaving one regiment as a picket and working party, to report to Captain
Jenney, of the Engineers, who is charged with the destruction of the
rifle-pits carried by our corps. This work should be done by night and
all details called in and assembled at the point of embarkation. The
boats will be ordered to drop down to their places as soon as the new
assignment is complete.

Wagons, horses, and all camp equipage will be put on board to-night,
and the men embarked at daylight to-morrow ready to make a new
move.

   By order of Maj. Gen. W. T. Sherman:
                              J. H. HAMMOND,
                       Assistant Adjutant-General.

MEMPHIS, TENN., January 14, 1863—12.30 a. m.

Maj. Gen. H. W. HALLECK, General-in-Chief:

I learn by special messenger sent to the fleet in Arkansas that it will
be fifteen days before they can act efficiently again. I had hoped to
get off early next week, but will have to defer until all things are ready.
I will go down to the fleet in a day or two, and by consultation with
McClernand, Sherman, and Porter will have a better understanding of
matters than I now have. McClernand is now, I believe, moving on
Devall's Bluff. Orders have been sent him to assemble his forces on
the Mississippi, convenient to co-operate with any force that may be
coming up the river.
                              U. S. GRANT,
                                  Major-General.

HEADQUARTERS ARMY OF THE MISSISSIPPI,
Post Arkansas, January 14, **1863.**

Maj. Gen. U. S. GRANT,
Commanding Department of the Tennessee:

GENERAL : I have all the prisoners embarked for Saint Louis, Mo.

My reasons for sending them are these : 1st, I have received no orders to exchange them ; 2d, the headquarters of the commissioner for the exchange of prisoners is there ; 3d, it would seem to me criminal to send the prisoners to Vicksburg if they may be properly sent elsewhere. To send them there would be to re-enforce a place with several thousand prisoners at the moment we are trying to reduce it.

I would sail from here to Little Rock and reduce that place but for want of sufficient water in the channel of the Arkansas River.

This being the case I will proceed, as soon as I have completed the demolition of the enemy's works here, to Napoleon, by which time I I hope to hear from you.

Your obedient servant,

JOHN A. McCLERNAND,
Major-General, Commanding.

HEADQUARTERS ARMY OF THE MISSISSIPPI,
Post of Arkansas, January 14, 1863.

Maj. Gen. U. S. GRANT,
Commanding Department of the Tennessee:

GENERAL : I have the honor to acknowledge the receipt this moment of your dispatch of the 10th instant, and hasten to say that in former dispatches I informed you of the repulse of the Mississippi River Expedition, under General Sherman, near Vicksburg ; of my assuming command on the 4th instant at Milliken's Bend ; of my departure from that place on the same day ; of my arrival at the mouth of White River, and subsequently at Notrib's Landing, near this place ; and of my attack upon and reduction of the Post of Arkansas, on the 11th instant. I am left to infer that these dispatches had not reached you on the 10th instant, but doubtless some if not all of them have reached you since that date.

I have only to add now, in view of your dispatch, that although I had hoped to be able to push my successes farther in this direction I will immediately return with my command to Napoleon, on the Mississippi River, and, unless otherwise ordered, after such brief delay as may be necessary, will return from there to Milliken's Bend or some other point near Vicksburg, where I will await the arrival of the re-enforcements mentioned by you unless sooner joined by them.

In compliance with your instructions I have requested Rear-Admiral Porter to send a gunboat to Memphis to convoy the transports upon which will be borne the re-enforcements on their way to join me.

General Fisk's brigade, sent by you under orders to join me, was diverted by General Gorman, as I am informed to-day, up the White River. If I can get a gunboat I will immediately send an order for the brigade to join me at Napoleon or wheresoever it may find me.

I am glad to be informed by you that you have anticipated the wants of my command by ordering commissary, ordnance, and other stores to be sent to it. I may say, however, that before leaving the Mississippi River for this place I had dispatched officers connected with each of these departments for such stores.

Having previously communicated my opinion as to the most feasible plan for the reduction of Vicksburg I will not enlarge upon that subject now.

I find that our success here is more extensive than I at first supposed. So soon as the corps commanders send in their reports, which will probably be soon, I will forward to you a formal report of our operations in advancing upon and reducing the Post. Herewith you will find an approximate estimate of the strength of my command, based upon the reports of corps commanders, which, as the troops are most of the time moving upon the transports, cannot be correct. I will send an accurate statement as soon as it can be obtained.

On December 31, 1862, the number of enlisted men was 27,480; the aggregate, 31,753; deduct from this our loss at Vicksburg and Post of Arkansas, say about 2,000, and there remains an aggregate of about 29,753.

Admiral Porter informs me this very moment that there are two gunboats at Memphis, one of which is ready to convoy the troops down here when you are ready to send them.

JOHN A. McCLERNAND,
Major-General, Commanding.

HEADQUARTERS ARMY OF THE MISSISSIPPI,
Old Post Arkansas, January 14, 1863.

Brig. Gen. W. A. GORMAN, *Commanding:*

GENERAL: I ascended White River on the 9th instant and on the 11th carried this Post. The results are that about 5,000 prisoners, 17 guns (some of very large caliber), quartermaster's, commissary, and ordnance stores in large quantities have fallen into our hands. The forces that were at Saint Charles were captured here.

My orders from Major-General Grant require me at once to go to Napoleon, but I shall delay a day or two in order to threaten Little Rock and Pine Bluff as a diversion in your favor.

I sent out yesterday my cavalry toward Saint Charles, under Colonel Stewart.

[The road] at Prairie Landing is quite passable and also that to Saint Charles. I send this by express up White River, and ask you to immediately send to Napoleon, or wherever I may be, General Fisk, with his command, as it is of vital importance that he join me at once.

I am, dear general, your obedient servant,

JOHN A. McCLERNAND,
Commanding.

HEADQUARTERS ARMY OF THE MISSISSIPPI,
January 14, 1863—9.45 a. m.

Maj. Gen. WILLIAM. T. SHERMAN,
Commanding Fifteenth Army Corps:

GENERAL: Your favor of this date* is this moment received. The numbers given to the two army corps composing my present command were given pursuantly to information which I communicated to you verbally in advance. That information was a letter of instruction from Major-General Grant, commanding Department of the Tennessee, of

---

* Not found.

which a copy was communicated to you, and of which the following are extracts:

The divisions now commanded by Brig. Gen. George W. Morgan and Brig. Gen. A. J. Smith will compose all of it (*i. e.*, my corps) that will accompany you (*i. e.*, myself) on the expedition, and the divisions of Brig. Gen. F. Steele and Brig. Gen. M. L. Smith will accompany you and be commanded directly by Maj. Gen. W. T. Sherman, who will command the army corps, of which they are a part.

Major-General Hurlbut will have command of the Third Army Corps, &c.

The instructions now with General Sherman provide for the garrison of Memphis, and forms part of the Second Army Corps.

This authority, in my judgment, not only justifies but requires the order made by me numbering the corps of my command First and Second, as above mentioned. The order, I believe, also met with your approbation.

The order made by the Secretary of War numbering my corps (at present commanded by General Morgan) the Thirteenth and yours the Fifteeenth never reached me until this morning, and that only through your courtesy. I learn that you had received it some three or four days since. I have not yet received one through any regular military channel.

It only remains, however, for me to number the corps conformably to the order of the Secretary of War, which will be immediately done.

Respectfully, your obedient servant,

JOHN A. McCLERNAND.

HEADQUARTERS ARMY OF THE MISSISSIPPI,
Post Arkansas, January 14, 1863.

Maj. Gen. WILLIAM T. SHERMAN:
Commanding Second Army Corps:

GENERAL: Your favor* containing various valuable suggestions is thankfully received.

The night after the reduction of the Post I addressed a communication to Rear-Admiral Porter respecting the practicability of ascending with our transports to Little Rock. His answer was not encouraging. I have since the battle closely watched the fluctuations of the river. If it had been practicable I would have been at or near Little Rock with my whole command by this time. It is still my purpose not only to ascend and reduce that place, but to march from there on the enemy at Brownsville if within a short time I should find that the stage of water will permit our transports to ascend and descend the river in safety. All turns on this vital point. It would be a disaster more than counterbalancing our victory here, and for which I could not bring defense, should all or even the larger and more valuable of our transports be locked up in the river. In that event the commerce and business of the upper rivers would fail for want of means of transportion.

I have already written to Generals Curtis and Gorman informing them of our success here. Both of them will doubtless take advantage of it as a diversion in favor of the military movements now being executed under their orders. General Gorman is already taking advantage of it. His transports bearing his troops and convoyed by two gunboats passed up the White River yesterday. The Blue Wing, bearing the hostile garrison of Saint Charles, some 200 strong, was not far ahead of him. This information was brought to me last night by Colonel Stewart, of my staff and chief of cavalry, who made a reconnaissance yesterday to the White River.

---

* Not found.

It is not improbable that orders from General Grant will control the movements of our forces when we reach the Mississippi River. I may say, however, that I advised General Grant, upon my taking command, that I would return from this place to a point near Vicksburg unless he should otherwise order, and that one of my objects in so doing would be to cut the enemy's communications by the Red River.

    Your obedient servant,

JOHN A. McCLERNAND,

Major-General, Commanding.

GENERAL ORDERS, }   HDQRS ARMY OF THE MISSISSIPPI,
    No. 9.   }   *Post Arkansas, January* 14, 1863.

    In accordance with General Orders, No. 210, issued by order of the Secretary of War, from the Adjutant-General's Office, Washington, December 18, 1862, the army corps of Major-General McClernand, at present commanded by Brig. Gen. George W. Morgan, will constitute and be known as the Thirteenth Army Corps of United States forces, and the army corps commanded by Maj. Gen. W. T. Sherman will constitute and be known as the Fifteenth Army Corps.

    By order of Maj. Gen. John A. McClernand:

A. SCHWARTZ,

Major and Acting Assistant Adjutant-General.

MEMPHIS, TENN., *January* 15, 1863—2.30 a. m.

Maj. Gen. H. W. HALLECK, *General-in-Chief:*

    I will send McArthur's division (all I have transports for) immediately to join the expedition on Vicksburg; send Logan's in a few days, and hold Quinby ready to embark when called for; abandon the railroad north from Jackson at once, and move the machine-shop and public stores from that place here, and hold all the troops from Grand Junction around the railroad to Corinth in readiness to be placed on the line from here east. I will go down and take McPherson, leaving Hamilton to command and carry out instructions for those changes in the old District of West Tennessee.

U. S. GRANT,

Major-General.

ADAMSVILLE, *January* 15, 1863.

General DODGE, *Corinth, Miss.:*

    SIR: The river raised 4 feet last night; that leaves it now about 12 feet above low-water mark. No boats as yet, on account of the bad weather, and having no tents or no houses to put up in I was compelled to fall back to Adamsville, where I could get house-room and forage. I will move back to Pittsburg Landing as soon as the tents come or the weather gets favorable. I am informed that there are about 200 guerrillas back of Savannah and about 800 at the Red Sulphur Springs; the latter I don't credit. Have you ever heard from General Grant in regard to the balance of those four companies that are with me? I am informed that the greater part of the troops across the river are ordered to meet Bragg at Chattanooga.

    Yours, truly,

W. K. M. BRECKENRIDGE,

Lieutenant-Colonel, First West Tennessee Cavalry.

SPECIAL ORDERS, ⎱   HDQRS. DEPARTMENT OF THE TENNESSEE,
    No. 15.   ⎰   *Memphis, Tenn., January* 15, 1863.

I. Lieut. Col. C. A. Reynolds, chief quartermaster of the department, is hereby ordered to stop all steamboats at Memphis that may be required to transport troops and stores for the expedition down the Mississippi River, and recharter the same.

II. Brig. Gen. C. S. Hamilton is hereby assigned to the command of the Districts of Columbus, Jackson, Corinth, and Memphis, headquarters at Memphis for the present, but subject to be removed to any other part of the command required by the exigencies of the service.

III. It is regarded of primary importance the line east from Memphis to Corinth should be maintained; and, so long as practicable, the line from Grand Junction to Corinth, via Jackson, Tenn.

IV. So soon as all public stores can be removed the road north from Jackson will be abandoned, the troops guarding it returning to their proper commands.

V. All public stores and property at Jackson and Bolivar not required for the immediate use of the troops will be removed to Corinth or Memphis immediately, and the troops within the District of Jackson be held in readiness to be used wherever required.

VI. The divisions of Brigadier-General McArthur, Brigadier-General Logan, and Brigadier-General Quinby are detached from the command of Brigadier-General Hamilton, and all dispositions made for the maintenance of his positions will be made without reference to them.

VII. General Quinby's, now guarding a portion of the road, will be the last division to move, and while on such duty will be governed by instructions received from General Hamilton.

VIII. The whole command of General Hamilton will be known as the District of West Tennessee.

*   *   *   *   *   *   *

IX. The chiefs of artillery and of ordnance will immediately procure and ship ordnance stores for 50,000 infantry, 26 batteries of artillery, and 2,000 cavalry, at the rate of 500 rounds per man for the infantry and cavalry, and refill caissons for the artillery twice. This supply is required in addition to the amount to be kept on hand by the troops at all times, but embracing all other stores for issue.

*   *   *   *   *   *   *

XI. The divisions now commanded, respectively, by Brigadier-Generals Quinby, Logan, and McArthur are designated to re-enforce the expedition operating down the Mississippi River, Maj. Gen. J. B. McPherson to command the whole.

XII. Brigadier-General McArthur's division will at once embark on transports and proceed down the river to report to Major-General McClernand for orders until the arrival of Major-General McPherson with the remainder of his command.

XIII. Brigadier-General Logan will embark and proceed to the same destination as soon as transports can be supplied, and General Quinby will hold himself in readiness to move at the shortest notice.

XIV. Troops on this expedition will want immediately in their own hands all the ammunition required by previous orders. They will move with three days' cooked rations in haversacks and seven days' additional on hand.

XV. Division commanders will take thirty days' rations for future use.

XVI. All axes, spades, and other tools in the hands of troops must be carefully preserved and taken along for such exigencies as may occur.

XVII. Troops designated to go south will take with them five wagons to each regiment and one to each company of artillery, one wagon in addition for each brigade and division commander. Two ambulances will be allowed to each regiment. The balance of trains will be turned over to such quartermaster as Colonel Reynolds, chief quartermaster, may designate to receive them.

*   *   *   *   *   *   *

By order of Maj. Gen. U. S. Grant:

JNO. A. RAWLINS,
Assistant Adjutant-General.

MEMPHIS, TENN., *January* 16, 1863.

Maj. Gen. SAMUEL R. CURTIS,
    Comdg. Department of the Missouri, Saint Louis, Mo.:

I was just starting down the river to join the Mississippi expedition when I met some steamers loaded with prisoners, ordered by Major-General Sherman to Saint Louis. I find no dispatches to myself, and do not know what there may be directed to yourself. As I am leaving Memphis and can make no orders for the disposal of these prisoners I hope you will have the kindness to take charge of them and communicate with the General-in-Chief as to their final disposition. You can state that the last prisoners sent to Vicksburg were refused by the Southern commander there. I have received instructions from Washington that no more commissioned officers are to be paroled. This, I presume, is in retaliation for a course pursued by Southern authorities toward our prisoners.

U. S. GRANT.
Major-General.

P. S.—The probable reason the last prisoners were not received at Vicksburg was in consequence of the attack having commenced before their arrival. I am opposed to sending any more troops to Vicksburg just at this time, however, if I knew they would be received, because they would go at once to re-enforce the very point we wish to reduce.

HEADQUARTERS ARMY OF THE MISSISSIPPI,
Post Arkansas, January 16, 1863.

His Excellency ABRAHAM LINCOLN,
    President of the United States:

SIR: Herewith I have taken the liberty to transmit a copy of a communication to General Grant.

I believe my success here is gall and wormwood to the clique of West Pointers who have been persecuting me for months. How can you expect success when men controlling the military destinies of the country are more chagrined at the success of your volunteer officers than the very enemy beaten by the latter in battle? Something must be done to take the hand of oppression off citizen soldiers whose zeal for their country has prompted them to take up arms, or all will be lost.

Do not let me be clandestinely destroyed, or, what is worse, dishonored, without a hearing. The very moment you think I am an impediment to the public service, upon the slightest intimation of it my resignation will be forwarded. Until then you may count upon my best endeavors, at whatever peril, to sustain the sacred cause for which we are contending.

In addition to the reasons set forth in the copy of the dispatch inclosed for the Arkansas River expedition I might assign the order of the Secretary of War, indorsed by you, to open the Mississippi River.

The Mississippi River being the only channel of communication, and that being infested with guerrillas, how can General Grant at a distance of 400 miles intelligently command the army with me? He cannot do it. It should be made an independent command, as both you and the Secretary of War, as I believe, originally intended.

Very respectfully, your obedient servant,

JOHN A. McCLERNAND.

[Inclosure.]

HEADQUARTERS ARMY OF THE MISSISSIPPI,
Post Arkansas, January 16, 1863.

Maj. Gen. U. S. GRANT,
Commanding Department of the Tennessee:

GENERAL : Your dispatch of the 16th [13th] instant came to hand at 6 o'clock p. m. this day, and I hasten at the same moment to answer it.

I take the responsibility of the expedition against Post Arkansas, and had anticipated your approval of the complete and signal success which crowned it rather than your condemnation.

In saying that I could not have effected the reduction of Vicksburg with the limited force under my command, after its repulse near that place under General Sherman, I only repeat what was contained in a previous dispatch to you. From the moment you fell back from Oxford, and the purpose of a front attack upon the enemy's works near Vicksburg was thus deprived of co-operation, the Mississippi River Expedition was doomed to eventuate in a failure.

I had heard nothing of General Banks when I left Milliken's Bend on the 4th instant, and if, as you say, Port Hudson has been made "very strong," it will be some time before he will be in a situation to receive the co-operation of the Mississippi River Expedition, unless he should prove more successful than the latter.

Had I remained idle and inactive at Milliken's Bend with the army under my command until now I should have felt myself guilty of a great crime. Rather had I accept the consequences of the imputed guilt of using it profitably and successfully upon my own responsibility.

The officer who, in the present strait of the country, will not assume a proper responsibility to save it is unworthy of public trust.

Having successfully accomplished the object of this expedition I will return to Milliken's Bend, according to my intention communicated to you in a previous dispatch, unless otherwise ordered by you.

Respectfully, your obedient servant,

JOHN A. McCLERNAND,
Major-General, Commanding.

HEADQUARTERS FIFTEENTH ARMY CORPS,
Napoleon, Ark., January 16, 1863.

Maj. A. SCHWARTZ,
Assistant Adjutant-General to General McClernand:

SIR : My corps is now all assembled here with the exception of one boat, the Spread Eagle, which I heard of at the mouth of White River, but which must learn there of their mistake easily by coming down the main river; also the Omaha with the Fifty-seventh Ohio, Colonel Mungen, which I detached yesterday morning to report to General McClernand, according to your orders.

Five boats arrived from Memphis this afternoon containing a small brigade commanded by Brigadier-General Ewing, which was detached from Western Virginia for General Rosecrans but sent to us on receipt of the intelligence that Rosecrans had repulsed Bragg and that we on the Mississippi needed re-enforcements. Brigadier-General Ewing brings orders, of which the following is a copy:

SPECIAL ORDERS, }   HEADQUARTERS DEPARTMENT OF THE TENNESSEE,
    No. 12.   }   *Memphis, January 12, 1863.*

*   *   *   *   *   *   *

X. Brigadier-General Ewing's brigade, now under orders to join the Mississippi expedition, is hereby assigned to Brig. Gen. Morgan L. Smith's division, of the Fifteenth Army Corps, and will report accordingly.

By order of Major-General Grant:

JNO. A. RAWLINS,
Assistant Adjutant-General.

This gives three brigades to each of my two divisions and gives me an effective force of 15,909 men.

Three of A. J. Smith's boats are here, who have reported they were ordered to follow certain boats, one of which had been dispatched down.

My orders state " Morgan's corps will follow to some point (Napoleon) as soon as practicable." I have not ordered in case of these boats, but merely mentioned to the commanders that I believed Morgan would follow. If you want them up at the Post send me word and I will dispatch them. On your way down you will find wood and rails near the cut-off and some fine cribs of corn a short distance above. I send for the general some late papers and invite his attention to the Memphis Bulletin of the 10th instant. He will see our success at Post Arkansas recorded, and also the fact that the rebels are investing Springfield, Mo., and threatening Lexington. The report I received of acting Brigadier-General Garland that Herron and Blunt had retreated from Van Buren must be correct, and this may be additional reason why we should make some move up the Arkansas. The Mississippi River is reported to have fallen slightly, but it looks to me full and high here; but we had not a particle of difficulty in descending.

Napoleon is a hard-looking place, and I can see no place where I could form a brigade. I doubt if we can do much in the way of drill or discipline anywhere whilst we are afloat, but I will continue to try.

My chief object in sending a boat up to the general is to send him the newspapers, which give full accounts of Rosecrans' battle. Bragg retreats in the direction of Chattanooga. Grant is in Memphis. Nothing doing on the Rappahannock, and accounts from rebel sources that Banks approaches Port Hudson.

I am, with great respect, your obedient servant,

W. T. SHERMAN,
Major-General, Commanding Corps.

HEADQUARTERS SEVENTEENTH ARMY CORPS,
La Grange, Tenn., January 16, 1863.
Maj. Gen. U. S. GRANT,
Commanding Department of the Tennessee, Memphis :

GENERAL : I am just in receipt of orders assigning me to the command of a portion of the forces to operate against Vicksburg. I cannot express to you the gratification it gives me, and I shall most assuredly do my utmost to merit your confidence.

I shall leave here as soon as General Logan's division is on the march, probably to-morrow, as General Lauman was ordered last night to move forthwith. The roads, however, are in a horrible condition and the movements will necessarily be slow. But as Logan and his whole division are keen to go they will move to Memphis as rapidly as circumstances will admit.

I intend to send out a cavalry expedition this morning to try and break up the guerrillas in north and west of Somerville, as they could be tracked to their place of rendezvous, but the roads are so very bad and the horses ball up so badly with snow that they cannot travel. I was forced to abandon it for the present.

Very respectfully, your obedient servant,
JAS. B. McPHERSON,
Major-General.

GENERAL ORDERS, } HDQRS. DEPARTMENT OF THE TENNESSEE,
No. 5.   }   *Memphis, Tenn., January* 16, 1863.

Hereafter there shall be collected by provost-marshals for secret-service and hospital fund the following fees :

For each permit to buy cotton at any military post, whether as principal or agent, $100.

For each permit to trade at any military post where trade is not regulated by the civil authorities, $100.

The amount thus collected shall be reported and paid over by each local provost-marshal to the provost-marshal of his district at the time of making his weekly report, and by district provost-marshals reported and paid over to the provost-marshal-general at the time of making their semi-monthly report.

The provost-marshal-general will pay over said fund to the chief quartermaster of the department, who will hold the same subject to the order of the general commanding the department.

Each local provost-marshal will keep a duplicate of all permits granted under this order, and will state in his report the name and residence of the party obtaining the permit and the date thereof.

All permits heretofore granted will be considered revoked and the parties required to comply with the terms of this order.

This order is not to be construed to remove any restrictions imposed by previous orders.

By order of Maj. Gen. U. S. Grant:

JNO. A. RAWLINS,
Assistant Adjutant-General.

GENERAL ORDERS, } HDQRS. DISTRICT OF WEST TENNESSEE,
No. 1.   }   *Memphis, Tenn., January* 16, 1863.

I. In pursuance of Special Orders, No. 15, Headquarters Department of the Tennessee, January 15, 1863, the undersigned hereby assumes command of the District of West Tennessee.

II. The returns and reports required by existing orders will be made direct to these headquarters by the commanders of divisions, and the Districts of Corinth, Jackson, Columbus, and Memphis.

C. S. HAMILTON,
Brigadier-General, Commanding.

MEMPHIS, TENN., *January* 17, 1863—4.30 p. m.
Maj. Gen. H. W. HALLECK, *General-in-Chief:*

I start immediately to the fleet. My design is to get such information from them as I find impossible to get here. I will return here in a few days, and in the mean time re-enforcements will be forwarded with all dispatch.

U. S. GRANT,
Major-General.

NAPOLEON, *January* 17, 1863.
Rear-Admiral DAVID D. PORTER, *Commanding, &c.:*

ADMIRAL: The fleet is ordered to leave this point at 12 o'clock m. to-morrow and proceed directly to Milliken's Bend. Will you please advise me what disposition you think proper to make of your squadron in convoy of the transports?

Very respectfully, your obedient servant,
JOHN A. McCLERNAND,
Major-General, Commanding.

P. S.—JANUARY 18, 1863—11 A. M.—Not having been able to ascertain the position of your boat till this morning the above was not sent to you. The order for leaving is suspended until I know your pleasure relative to furnishing a convoy, for which we are waiting.

HEADQUARTERS FIFTEENTH ARMY CORPS,
On board Forest Queen, Napoleon, Ark., January 17, 1863.
Maj. Gen. U. S. GRANT,
Commanding Department of Tennessee:

DEAR GENERAL: I take a liberty of writing you direct semi-officially. Official reports will convey to you a pretty clear idea of our success at the Post of Arkansas.

I infer from a remark made by General McClernand that you have disapproved the step. If I could believe that Banks had reduced Port Hudson and appeared at Vicksburg during our absence I would feel the force of your disapproval, but I feel so assured that we will again be at Vicksburg before Banks is there that I cannot think any bad result of this kind can occur. As long as the Post of Arkansas existed on our flank, with boats to ship cannon and men to the mouth of the Arkansas, we would be annoyed beyond measure whilst operating below. The capture of the Blue Wing was a mere sample. We were compelled to reduce it. Its importance to the enemy cannot be doubted by one who has seen their preparations and heard the assertions of its garrison that it was deemed impregnable. The fort proper was constructed with great care and its armament as good as it could be made. The Post of Arkansas could only have been taken by a strong force, both by land and water, as we took it, and had we given any previous notice it would have been strongly re-enforced. They had huts built for full 10,000 men, and with 15,000 they could have held the levee as far down as the Notrib house, and our landing would have been resisted. Could we have followed up, the capture of Little Rock would have been easy; but even as it is the enemy up the Arkansas can be held in check by a single wooden gunboat. I assure you when next at Vicksburg I will feel much less uneasiness about our communications.

We leave here to-morrow, and will be at Milliken's Bend or Young's Point by the next day, and if Banks has taken Port Hudson and appeared below Vicksburg we can easily communicate across; but I do not expect he will be there for some time.

It may be we can put some guns in position along the shore of the Mississippi at a point where I had my pickets, which might occupy the attention of one set of batteries, and if the gunboats will assail the city in front we might possibly land right under the guns, or we may try Haines' Bluff; but as to forcing a passage at any point along the Yazoo from its mouth to Haines' I doubt it. I wish you would come down and see. I only fear McClernand may attempt impossibilities.

Again, if Banks does come up it may be the approach from the south may be better; but all their old defenses of last year look to the south. I saw enough to convince me they have about ten field batteries, and I should estimate their siege guns at fifty; I saw about thirty.

The importance of Vicksburg cannot be overestimated, and if possible a larger force should somehow reach the ridge between the Black and Yazoo, so as to approach from the rear.

Please give much attention to the quantity of ammunition and tools. I carried down with me 1,200 axes, picks, and spades but in spite of all efforts many are lost. We built batteries at Yazoo and up at the Post, and you know how details of our careless men neglect tools.

We have a good deal of real sickness and still more of that sort which develops on the approach of danger.

An attack on Vicksburg will surely draw thither the Grenada force, so that I think you might safely join us and direct our movements.

I am, with great respect, your obedient servant,

W. T. SHERMAN,
Major-General, Commanding.

HEADQUARTERS ARMY OF THE MISSISSIPPI,
Steamer Tigress, January 11, 1863.

Maj. Gen. WILLIAM T. SHERMAN,
Commanding Fifteenth Army Corps:

GENERAL: Take measures immediately to extinguish the flames which are consuming Napoleon, and find if possible the incendiaries and punish them.

Place guards to stop the scandals which are being perpetrated by worthless men.

By order of Maj. Gen. John A. McClernand:

WALTER B. SCATES,
Lieutenant Colonel and Assistant Adjutant-General.

HEADQUARTERS FIFTEENTH ARMY CORPS,
On board Forest Queen, January 17, 1863.

Lieut. Col. WALTER B. SCATES,
Assistant Adjutant-General:

SIR : Pursuant to your orders, this 4 p. m. I went in person to direct the extinguishment of the fire in Napoleon. It was impossible to extinguish it. I first tried to limit it to the middle of the block but failed, but by the destruction of a store and barn at the end of the block limited the fire to one block.

It is impossible to find out the incendiary ; not a clue can now be found. In some future time the actor will boast of it, when it can be fixed on him. In the mean time the only way to apply a remedy will be to assess the damages upon the whole army, officers included. No man in the army has labored harder than I have to check this spirit in our soldiers, and am free to admit we all deserve to be killed unless we can produce a state of discipline when such disgraceful acts cannot be committed unpunished.

In consequence of the order to start at 12 m. I had called in my provost guard and pickets, and most of my boats are below gathering wood, but I have ordered a guard to patrol the town.

I am, with respect, your obedient servant,

W. T. SHERMAN,
Major-General, Commanding Corps.

GENERAL ORDERS, }   HDQRS. ARMY OF THE MISSISSIPPI,
No. 11.   }   *Steamer Tigress, January* 17, 1863.

I. The entire fleet will be in readiness to start from Napoleon by 12 o'clock m. to-morrow, January 18, and will not land until arrival at Milliken's Bend, except for necessary fuel or other imperative cause.

II. Each transport of the fleet will, by the hour named, provide itself with sufficient fuel to run it to Milliken's Bend.

III. If transports cannot get sufficient fuel at or near Napoleon they may drop down the river by divisions to any point not exceeding 25 miles from that place, but every boat will be in readiness to fall into line in its assigned place immediately on the passing of the flag boat Tigress.

IV. Officers in command of troops on each transport will promptly furnish details and give all required assistance in procuring fuel.

V. The fleet will move conformably to the inclosed order.

VI. Divisions must be kept together and transports must be kept in their assigned places unless prevented by imperative necessity, and in no case pass the transports bearing their divisions or corps commanders.

VII. In case any transport is disabled or requires assistance, on blowing the whistle five times, the transports nearest in line following will go to its assistance and take it in tow, if necessary, until other orders are issued by the division commanders.

VIII. Upon starting, one gun will be fired from the flag-boat Tigress and will be promptly responded to by one gun from each boat bearing a division commander, when all will at once fall into line.

IX. Corps, division, and brigade commanders will be held responsible for a strict compliance with this order.

By command of Maj. Gen. John A. McClernand, commanding.

A. SCHWARTZ,
Major and Acting Assistant Adjutant-General.

[Inclosure.]

Tigress, flag-boat, headquarters of General McClernand, command-ing Army of the Mississippi.

Empress, headquarters corps commanded by General Morgan.

Des Arc, headquarters division, General A. J. Smith.

J. C. Snow, Citizen, Metropolitan, J. S. Pringle, J. W. Cheeseman, R. Campbell, jr., Duke of Argyle, Iowa, City of Alton, City of Louisi-ana, J. H. Dickey, Ohio Belle.

Fannie Bullitt, headquarters division commanded by General Oster-haus.

Lady Jackson, War Eagle, Pembina, Des Moines, Jesse K. Bell, Northerner, Key West, Belle Peoria, Crescent City, General Anderson, ordnance boat; Lavinia Logan, ordnance boat; Adriatic, commissary boat; Warsaw, quartermaster's department; Isabella, quartermaster's department; Luzerne, quartermaster's department, sent to Memphis; Madison, commissary.

Forest Queen, headquarters commanded by General Sherman.

Continental, headquarters division commanded by General Steele.

Dacotah, Tecumseh, Gladiator, Emma, Meteor, Fanny Ogden, Sucker State, Ella, Decatur, Polar Star, Thomas E. Tutt, Kennett, John War-ner, D. G. Taylor, J. R. Williams, Wisconsin and barges, Champion, Von Phul, Hiawatha.

Westmoreland, headquarters division commanded by General D. Stuart.

Spread Eagle, Universe, Sunny South, Chancellor, Omaha, Sioux City, Southwester, R. Allen, E. Walsh, Planet.

Prima Donna, headquarters General Ewing, commanding brigade.

Mariner, Aurora, F. Loring, West Wind.

By order of Maj. Gen. John A. McClernand:

WALTER B. SCATES,
Lieutenant-Colonel and Assistant Adjutant-General.

NAPOLEON, ARK., *January* 18, 1863,
Via Memphis, Tenn., January 20, 1863—10.30 a. m.

Maj. Gen. H. W. HALLECK, *General-in-Chief:*

McClernand's command is at this place; will move down the river to-day. Should Banks pass Port Hudson this force will be ready to co-operate on Vicksburg at any time. What may be necessary to reduce the place I do not yet know, but since the late rains think our troops must get below the city to be used effectively.

U. S. GRANT,
Major-General.

COLUMBUS, *January* 18, 1863.

Maj. Gen. U. S. GRANT,
Commanding Department of the Tennessee:

Six 8-inch howitzers are mounted at Fort Halleck, Columbus. They will be brought to the river at daybreak to-morrow and shipped with the ammunition as soon as possible. During the snow-storm yesterday Colonel Lowe, commanding Fort Henry, sent out an expedition to Waverly, which captured 1 major, 2 captains, 1 quartermaster, 1 sergeant, and 7 privates, belonging to different regiments of the Confederate Army, together with horses, arms, &c.

ASBOTH,
Brigadier-General, Commanding District.

HEADQUARTERS ARMY OF THE MISSISSIPPI,
Steamer Tigress, January 18, 1863.

Maj. Gen. U. S. GRANT,
Commanding Department of the Tennessee :

GENERAL : General Ewing's brigade has been attached to General Sherman's corps in pursuance of your order. This addition gives General Sherman's corps thirty-one regiments, and, according to his last official returns, 25,042 men to twenty-three regiments and 18,000 men in General Morgan's corps. I wish to call your attention to this disparity, not doubting in the absence of any good reason to the contrary you will at once equalize the strength of the corps.

It would be agreeable to General Morgan that General Osterhaus' old brigade, consisting of the Third, Twelfth, and Seventeenth Missouri, the Fourth Ohio Battery, and Seventy-sixth Ohio, Colonel Woods, should be transferred to the Second Division, commanded by General Osterhaus, of General Morgan's corps. The same division was formerly commanded by General Morgan himself. Nor would this arrangement be disagreeable to any one so far as I know.

With this arrangement, General Sherman would have twenty-seven regiments to General Morgan's twenty-seven.

Neither the supplies of ordnance, commissary, and quartermaster stores sent for by me, or referred to in your dispatch of the 13th instant as ordered by you, having arrived, although sufficient time has elapsed, I have to urge that you will cause such supplies to be forwarded without delay.

To be caught without such stores, particularly ordnance stores, at so remote a point as the vicinity of Vicksburg, with the river infested by guerrillas, would indeed be a dilemma.

Your obedient servant,

JOHN A. McCLERNAND,
Major-General, Commanding.

MEMPHIS, TENN., *January 19, 1863.*

Major-General HALLECK, *General-in-Chief:*

Scouts here to-day from Central Mississippi and Northern Alabama both report re-enforcements to Bragg and Pemberton from Virginia. To latter, 15,000; to former, 30,000.

C. S. HAMILTON.
Brigadier-General, Commanding.

JACKSON, *January 19, 1863.*

JOHN A. RAWLINS,
Lieutenant-Colonel and Assistant Adjutant-General :

After the rebel raid, by which Henderson Station depot-buildings, &c., were destroyed, I assessed the secession sympathizers living near the place a sum sufficient to pay all damages. I have in my possession about $8,000. What shall be done with it? I need money as secret-service fund, having employed several citizens as scouts.

JER. C. SULLIVAN,
Brigadier-General, Commanding.

SPECIAL ORDERS, } HDQRS. OF THE ARMY, ADJT. GEN.'S OFFICE,
No. 30.   }   *Washington, January 19, 1863.*

I. Brig. Gen. N. B. Buford, U S. Volunteers, is assigned to the command of Cairo, Ill., and will report to Major-General Grant, U. S. Volunteers, commanding the Department of the Tennessee.

*   *   *   *   *   *   *

By command of Major-General Halleck:

L. THOMAS,
Adjutant-General.

HEADQUARTERS DEPARTMENT OF THE TENNESSEE,
Memphis, Tenn., January 20, 1863.

Brig. Gen. C. S. HAMILTON,
Commanding District of West Tennessee:

GENERAL: Complaints have come in from Somerville from the few Union men of the outrageous conduct of the Seventh Kansas, and in one case of Colonel Lee's conduct where he was informed of the status of the party. This was the case of Mr. Rivers, who called on Colonel Lee to try and get him to restrain his men, and was replied to by being made to dismount and give up the animal he was riding.

If there are any further complaints, well substantiated, I wish you to arrest Colonel Lee and have him tried for incompetency and his regiment dismounted and disarmed.

The conduct of this regiment at New Albany, in their pursuit of Van Dorn, stopping to plunder the citizens instead of pursuing the enemy when they were so near them, and again when after Richardson, about the 8th of this month, they passed near where they knew or at least were informed he was and went on to the town for the purpose of plunder—all the laurels won by the regiment and their commander on the pursuit of the enemy from Holly Springs to Coffeeville have been more than counterbalanced by their bad conduct since.

Their present course may serve to frighten women and children and helpless old men, but will never drive out an armed enemy.

I am, general, with great respect, yours, &c.,

U. S. GRANT,
Major-General.

GENERAL ORDERS, } HDQRS. DEPARTMENT OF THE TENNESSEE,
No. 7.   }   *Memphis, Tenn., January 20, 1863.*

I. All trading, trafficking, or the landing of boats at points south of Memphis other than at military posts or points guarded by the navy is positively prohibited.

II. All officers of boats violating this order will be arrested and placed in close confinement. The boats and cargoes, unless the property of the Government, will be turned over to the quartermaster's department for the benefit of the Government.

III. All officers of the army passing up and down the river are directed to report all violations of this order, together with the names of the boats, place, and date, to the first military post on their route and to the commanding officer at the end of their route.

IV. The navy is respectfully requested to co-operate in the enforcement of this order.

By order of Maj. Gen. U. S. Grant:

JNO. A. RAWLINS,
Assistant Adjutant-General.

Abstract from Return of the Department of the Tennessee, Maj. Gen. U. S. Grant commanding, for the 20th January, 1863 *(headquarters Young's Point, La).*

[Incomplete.]

Command.	Present for duty.		Aggregate present.	Aggregate present and absent.	Aggregate present and absent last monthly return.	Pieces of artillery.	
	Officers.	Men.				Heavy.	Field.
THIRTEENTH ARMY CORPS.							
Brig. Gen. GEO. W. MORGAN.							
Total *	427	8,669	14,325	19,359	19,589	6	18
FIFTEENTH ARMY CORPS.							
Major-General SHERMAN.							
Eleventh Division.							
Brigadier-General STEELE.							
Infantry	317	5,652	8,937	11,725	....	....	......
Artillery	9	236	289	337	....	....	16
Cavalry	22	277	520	698	....	....	......
Total Eleventh Division.................	348	6,165	9,746	12,760	....	....	16
Fifth Division.							
Brigadier-General STUART.							
Infantry	269	6,056	7,586	10,269	....	....	......
Artillery	7	338	365	447	....	....	16
Cavalry	4	80	93	125	....	....	......
Total Fifth Division....................	280	6,474	8,044	10,841	....	....	16
District of Memphis.							
Brigadier-General VEATCH.							
Infantry.................................	141	2,589	5,400	5,853	....	....	......
Artillery	3	54	80	84	....	....	......
Cavalry	35	592	748	1,028	....	....	......
Total District of Memphis	179	3,235	6,228	6,965	....	....	......
Total forces Fifteenth Army Corps.....	807	15,874	24,018	30,566	....	....	33

* Not reported in detail on original.

Abstract from Return of the Department of the Tennessee, &c.—Continued.

Command.	Present for duty.		Aggregate present.	Aggregate present and absent.	Aggregate present and absent last monthly return.	Pieces of artillery.	
	Officers.	Men.				Heavy.	Field.
SIXTEENTH ARMY CORPS.							
Brigadier-General HAMILTON.							
Sixth Division.							
Brigadier-General McARTHUR.							
Infantry	273	4,731	5,652	7,339	6,317		
Artillery	11	314	347	395	178		16
Cavalry	5	103	116	153	153		
Total Sixth Division	289	5,148	6,115	7,887	6,648		16
Seventh Division.							
Brigadier-General QUINBY.							
Infantry	304	5,614	6,749	9,255	9,369		
Artillery	8	367	413	643	653		20
Cavalry	1	27	38	71	70		
Total Seventh Division	313	6,008	7,200	9,969	10,092		20
District of Jackson.							
Brigadier-General SULLIVAN.							
Infantry	344	5,886	8,151	10,506			
Artillery	9	343	387	428			
Cavalry	53	1,130	1,388	2,023			
Total District of Jackson	406	7,359	9,926	12,957			
Second Brigade, Cavalry Division.							
Col. A. L. LEE.							
Total *	39	914	1,151	1,696	1,703		
Total forces Sixteenth Army Corps	1,047	19,429	24,392	32,509			36
SEVENTEENTH ARMY CORPS.							
Major-General McPHERSON.							
First Division.							
Brigadier-General DENVER.							
Infantry	229	4,372	5,118	6,685	6,764		
Artillery	11	392	425	465	467		16
Total First Division	240	4,764	5,543	7,150	7,231		16
Third Division.							
Brigadier-General LOGAN.							
Infantry	324	5,998	7,228	8,970	9,027		
Artillery	14	491	524	602	553	4	20
Total Third Division	338	6,489	7,752	9,572	9,580	4	20
Fourth Division.							
Brigadier-General LAUMAN.							
Infantry	299	5,791	6,625	8,193	8,255		
Artillery	12	552	602	668	538		24
Total Fourth Division	311	6,343	7,227	8,861	8,793		24

* Not reported in detail on original.

Abstract from Return of the Department of the Tennessee, &c.—Continued.

Command.	Present for duty.		Aggregate present.	Aggregate present and absent.	Aggregate present and absent last monthly return.	Pieces of artillery.	
	Officers.	Men.				Heavy.	Field.
District of Corinth.							
Brigadier-General DODGE.							
Infantry	314	5,423	7,012	8,382	7,967		
Artillery	10	305	376	411	454		
Cavalry	8	218	287	352	355		
Total District of Corinth	332	5,946	7,675	9,145	8,776		
First Brigade, Cavalry Division.							
Col. B. H. GRIERSON.							
Total*	84	1,991	2,259	3,075	†3,075		7
Total forces Seventeenth Army Corps	1,305	25,533	30,456	37,803	37,455	4	67
Engineer Regiment of the West.							
Colonel BISSELL.							
Total*				625	814	814		
Grand total Department of Tennessee	3,586	69,505	93,816	121,051		10	153

HEADQUARTERS DEPARTMENT OF THE MISSOURI,
Saint Louis, January 23, 1863.

Maj. Gen. U. S. GRANT,
Comdg. Department of the Tennessee, Memphis, Tenn.:

GENERAL : The prisoners are arriving here, and what to do with them is a difficult question. I have them on Arsenal Island, without shelter. I am obliged to put them where a small guard will do, for I have sent everything down to help you in the down-river matters.

I telegraphed General Gorman through you at Memphis on the 11th instant to—

Continue to regard the Vicksburg movement of primary importance. Let all other moves delay if deemed necessary. Send boats and men for that object, but do not weaken Helena so as to endanger the position.

Now, I receive orders extending your command over—

All troops in Arkansas which may be within reach of his orders; that portion of Arkansas occupied by such troops will be temporarily attached to the Department of the Tennessee.

You will please inform me at your earliest convenience what troops and what territory you will assume, as I must arrange my supervision of affairs to your orders. I suppose you will include Helena in the enlargement of your command.

If Holmes and Hindman mass all their forces this side of the Arkansas River they may give me trouble, but I hope you will close out

---

* Not reported in detail on original.
‡ To balance aggregates, being the first report.

Vicksburg before they can do much and return to my command all the force necessary to clean out Arkansas.

With my best wishes for your success, I remain, general, very truly, yours,

SAM'L R. CURTIS,
Major-General.

HEADQUARTERS DISTRICT OF EASTERN ARKANSAS,
Helena, January 24, 1863.

Maj. Gen. U. S. GRANT,
Commanding Department of the Tennessee, Memphis :

GENERAL : I have returned from my White River expedition and am actively engaged in sending off troops to join your forces at Vicksburg. I am also sending forward to Memphis as rapidly as possible all surplus transportation for your use.

I ascended the White River as high as Des Arc, 217 miles from the mouth.

At Saint Charles I captured a considerable quantity of forage and some prisoners. I blew up their magazine and destroyed their fortifications, which were somewhat formidable.

At Clarendon I captured a few more prisoners. At Devall's Bluff I captured two 8-inch columbiads and carriages in complete order, one company of infantry, and about 100 new Enfield rifles. I destroyed one railroad bridge 200 feet long and one 90 feet long, and 3 platform cars, and burnt up the railroad depot.

At Des Arc I captured 100 prisoners, a large rebel mail, over 100 stand of arms, several hundred rounds of fixed 6-pounder ammunition, and destroyed the Little Rock telegraph.

The entire Arkansas force of the enemy retreated rapidly across to the west side of the Arkansas River.

I learn that Jeff. Thompson, Jeffers, and Marmaduke, and also Cabell and Anderson's commands, and part of Hawes' forces are concentrating on Crowley's Ridge and are moving in the direction of this place. I do not know their strength, and will not until I hear from General Curtis, unless my scouts bring me information.

I am, general, very respectfully, your obedient servant,

W. A. GORMAN,
Brigadier-General, Commanding.

WAR DEPARTMENT,
Washington City, January 24, 1863.

Major-General McCLERNAND :

GENERAL : Your communication of the 3d instant in relation to the Vicksburg operations has received my earnest attention. I think you need no new assurance of the sincere desire of the President and myself to oblige you in every particular consistent with the general interest of the service, and I trust that the course of events will be such as will enable the Government to derive the utmost advantage from your patriotism and military skill.

I shall be happy to hear from you fully whenever it is convenient for you to write, and shall be glad to contribute to your success.

Yours. truly.

EDWIN M. STANTON,
Secretary of War.

IN SIGHT OF VICKSBURG, *February* 1, 1863.

Major-General SHERMAN:

DEAR SIR: On the 20th December last I arrived in Memphis from above, and with but two or three hours' delay came to Helena on one of the boats of your expedition. Arriving there I went on board the steamer Continental, which shortly after moved down the stream in the direction of Vicksburg. On the way down I was told that you had issued some order relative to civilians accompanying the expedition, but I was unable to learn its substance or procure a copy until after your forces had landed on the banks of the Yazoo.

During the operations on the Yazoo and on Chickasaw Bayou my sources of information were exceedingly limited. I had been informed that an order was in existence requiring my arrest and detention; accordingly I remained very quietly on board the boat where I was staying, going but twice to the battle-field during the entire time. I am now informed by yourself and your adjutant-general that no such order ever existed.

In my account of the battle published in the Herald of the 18th ultimo I gave what I supposed was the correct history of the affair, depending as I did upon narrow channels of information.

Yesterday I had the opportunity of listening to the reading of many orders, plans, and reports connected with those operations. For the first time I have the correct history of the proceedings. I find to my regret that I labored under repeated errors, and made in consequence several misstatements, which I now take pleasure in correcting.

From listening to and examining your plans and orders concerning those operations I find that nothing could have been more full and complete. I have several times during this war been afforded the use of plans after the termination of the results for which they were designed, and in no instance have I found them so minute in detail and so admirably calculated to cover every contingency as in your own case. I am now satisfied that neither to yourself nor any officer of your command can be attributed the failure to accomplish the object of your expedition.

I find that in my then imperfect knowledge of affairs I did not give proper credit to several officers of your command; among these I may mention Generals Morgan, A. J. Smith, and Burbridge, Colonel De Courcy, and other brigade and regimental commanders. From a perusal of the official reports of the operations on Chickasaw Bayou I learn with pleasure that all these officers did their part promptly, gallantly, and well. Particularly I find this the case concerning General Morgan and the officers under him in the assault of the hill.

In regard to Colonel De Courcy and his brigade, in which were the Sixteenth Ohio and Twenty-second Kentucky Infantry, my published statements are not supported by the facts as I find them in the official reports. From these documents I ascertain that this brigade is deserving especial honor. Even were other proof wanting, the heavy loss of which I was not before aware would be ample testimony to its gallantry.

In conclusion let me say that from recent conversations with officers of this and other portions of General Grant's army, and especially from examination of the maps, plans, orders, and reports of the campaign, I am fully convinced of your prompt, efficient, and judicious management of the troops under your control from its commencement to its close.

Deeply deploring the existence of the above errors in the history of operations on the Yazoo, and trusting that neither myself nor any other journalist may again be so unfortunate in the collection of data for a published record, I remain, respectfully, yours.

THOS. W. KNOX,
Correspondent New York Herald.

HEADQUARTERS FIFTEENTH ARMY CORPS,
February 1, 1863.

General F. P. BLAIR :

SIR : Knox, the correspondent of the New York Herald, was brought into my presence last night, and in the presence of Dr. McMillan, Col. T. Kilby Smith, Major Hammond, and Captain Dayton, and no others I had his printed assertions of matters on the Yazoo read to him, and invariably he gave you as authority for most of his general and specific assertions. Though I cannot believe him after your specific denial to me in the presence of Generals Steele and Stuart, yet his reiterated assertions and reference to you as his authority for a statement of facts warrant me in calling on you for answers to specific questions.

Did you not know that I was ordered to leave Memphis December 18, in concert with other large armies and the fleet of gunboats ?

Was there any delay in embarking or reaching the point of attack that I could have prevented ?

Did I not on December 23 furnish division commanders general instructions as specific as the case then admitted ?

Did I not daily during the movement make an order of the day and send it to division commanders explaining the movements of the day ?

Was it not difficult, if not impossible, on our reaching the place of disembarkation to get information of the exact condition of the country lying between it and Vicksburg, and had we not to reconnoiter the bayou under very close fire ?

Did you or do you know anything of the ground in front of A. J. Smith's division ?

Did you or do you know anything of the ground in front of Morgan L. Smith's position ?

Do you not know that the best point of assault was at Morgan's position ?

Was not Morgan there with his three brigades at the time of the assault ?

Were not your brigade and Thayer's on the spot with orders and prepared to support Morgan in the assault ?

Was not General Hovey's brigade known to be close at hand ?

Did not these six brigades, or two divisions, compose more than half of my command ?

Did you at any time before, at the time, or after advise any other mode or plan of attacks ?

Did you not and do you not approve the withdrawal of my forces from Yazoo Island ?

Were not my orders specific that nothing should be left behind except a few barrels of pork and some hard bread, which your commissary reported to me in person could not be moved back ?

Do you know of a gun, a cartridge, ax, spade, wagon, or anything left behind but the pork and bread referred to, and what was its quantity ?

Do you not know that I personally remained in our camp at the bayou till every particle of ordnance, wagons, &c., and all the troops but the rear guard had reached the river?

Do you not know that I communicated with General McClernand before leaving the Yazoo? Do you not know that I remained at Yazoo Landing till every transport was off?

Was there any haste or confusion in re-embarking our command other than what is incident to large fleets and masses of men?

Have you not reason to know the enemy did not regard it as a retreat, but advised the people to look out for us in some other quarters?

Do you believe my force, independent of Grant's and Banks', could have taken and held Vicksburg?

Do you not know that the attack on Haines' Bluff was not attempted because Admiral Porter declared it to be too hazardous?

I ask this of you as an officer and a gentleman, because Knox quotes you all through. I do not design it for publication, but purpose to send your answer to my brother, John Sherman, that he may partially protect me from the effect of the base accusations and slanders published to the world and dated on the Continental (Blair's headquarters boat).

Yours, truly,

W. T. SHERMAN,
Major-General.

CAMP BEFORE VICKSBURG, *February* 1, 1863.

Maj. Gen. WILLIAM T. SHERMAN:

GENERAL: I have this moment received your letter in regard to the statement made by Mr. Knox, correspondent of the New York Herald, in your presence and in the presence of a number of other officers named by you in your letter, and have to request that you will read my answer to the same gentlemen.

It is a matter of mortification to me to receive such a letter from you after the conversation which occurred between yourself, Generals Steele and Stuart, and myself, and to which you refer in your letter.

I made no statement to Mr. Knox at any time which would serve as the foundation of his criticism upon you. All the conversation which occurred was in the presence of General Steele and his staff, and I recollect of saying nothing which could have wounded your feelings had you been present. I remarked on one or two occasions that I had understood that General Steele advised the first attack to be made on Haines' Bluff, and I thought that, as at this point we should have had the help of the gunboats, it was a great error to go where they could not assist us. I did not make the remark with a view of furnishing a text for criticism upon you, but simply in course of discussions such as often arise under such circumstances.

I will also say candidly that upon the application of Mr. Knox I allowed him to read a copy of my official report of the transactions upon the Yazoo, which had been sent to you through my immediate commander, with authority to make use of any statement of facts contained in it.

And now, after the preliminary statement, I proceed, in compliance with your request, to answer your specific questions; and inasmuch as from the tenor of your letter it would appear that these questions grow out of the attacks made on you, and for which I am quoted as authority, therefore I shall take the liberty, in addition to my general denial of having instigated attacks on you, to say in reference to each specific question whether I made any remarks to any one touching the matters involved in it that could have given ground for any assault on you.

First question. Did I not know that you were ordered to leave Memphis December 18, in concert with other large armies and the fleet of gunboats?

Answer. I knew that you had been so ordered, and the only comment I ever made on it was in commendation of the promptitude with which the movement was made.

Second question. Was there any delay in embarking or reaching the point of attack that you could have avoided?

Answer. My answer to the first question answers this, and I have never made any statement to any one which contradicts it.

Third question. Did you not on December 23 furnish division commanders general instructions as specific as the case then admitted?

Answer. You furnished instructions at the time mentioned to the division commanders, which were in turn furnished to brigade commanders, which I presume gave all the information you thought necessary or important. I have never made any comment complaining of you to Mr. Knox or any one.

Fourth question. Did you not daily during the movement make an order of the day and send it to division commanders explaining the movements of the day?

Answer. You did; and I never said anything to the contrary.

Fifth question. Was it not difficult, if not impossible, on our reaching the place of debarkation to get information of the exact condition of the country lying between it and Vicksburg, and had we not to reconnoiter the bayou under very close fire?

Answer. I answer both questions in the affirmative. I have never myself nor did I ever hear any one deny either of the propositions.

Sixth question. Did I or do I know anything of the ground in front of General A. J. Smith's division?

Answer. I did not and do not, and never made any pretense of knowing.

Seventh question. Did I or do I know anything of the ground in front of General M. L. Smith's division?

Answer. I saw what could be seen of it by looking at it with a glass across the bayou during the 28th. I thought it very formidable, and I have since been informed that it was defended by works which had not been discovered when I left that point. In speaking of this position I have always held this language.

Eighth question. Do I not know that the best point of assault was at Morgan's position?

Answer. From what I know, and have ascertained from others, I am of the opinion that, with the exception of Haines' Bluff, Morgan's position was the best for the assault; but with the aid of the gunboats I think that Haines' Bluff would have been our best point. I confess, however, that I knew nothing of the ground at Haines' Bluff except from conversation with others, and my opinion is grounded upon my faith in the heavy guns of the navy, strengthened by witnessing the execution done by them at Arkansas Post. I think it unfortunate that a point of attack should have been selected for assault which made it impossible to move with the co-operation of the navy.

Ninth question. Was not Morgan there with his three brigades at the time of the assault?

Answer. I presume such to be the fact. I think only two regiments of his whole division ever got into the enemy's works. I saw no more, and have said so very often.

Tenth question. Were not my brigade and Thayer's on the spot with orders and prepared to support Morgan in the assault?

Answer. My brigade and Thayer's were on the spot with orders and prepared to support Morgan in the assault. I have stated to many persons that instead of supporting Morgan's division Thayer's brigade and my own went in advance of him. My whole brigade was in the works before a single regiment of Morgan's appeared, and General Thayer stated to me that when he entered the enemy's works he found two regiments of Morgan's lying down in the first line of rifle-pits. When we were repulsed I came out of the works at the same time with General Thayer, and we both saw Colonel De Courcy, commanding one of Morgan's brigades, outside of the works with a large body of troops formed in column under the bluff upon which the first line of rifle-pits was built. He refused to take or order his men into the enemy's works. I have often made these statements, and I have also stated that General Morgan ordered me to assault without giving me a particle of information as to the nature of the ground over which I was to assault or giving me time to reconnoiter and obtain it, and that he did this against my earnest and repeated protest.

Eleventh question. Was not General Hovey's brigade close at hand?

Answer. It was.

Twelfth question. Did these six brigades, or two divisions, compose more than one-half your command.

Answer. I believe so.

Thirteenth question. Did I at any time before, at the time, or after advise any other mode or plan of attack?

Answer. I did not, and never made a suggestion to any one that I had been guilty of such presumption.

Fourteenth question. Did I not and do I not approve the withdrawal of your forces from Yazoo Island?

Answer. I do not recollect to have expressed any opinion on the subject, but I have no hesitation in saying that I approved and still approve the withdrawal of the forces from the Yazoo. I have no doubt the enemy had been largely re-enforced and greatly exceeded us in number.

Fifteenth question. Were not your orders specific that nothing should be left behind except a few barrels of pork and some hard bread, which my commissary reported to you in person could not be moved back?

Answer. I answer the whole of the above in the affirmative, and add that when my commissary reported to me that he had left some barrels of pork and hard bread by your orders, I sent him and my quartermaster back to bring it up, and told the commissary he had no business to go to the general-in-chief at such a moment to inform him that he could get no transportation; that it was not to be supposed that at such a moment you could give attention to such a matter; that his business was to impress all transportation that he could find unemployed and bring in the supplies. The quartermaster and commissary went back with a regiment, furnished by General Hovey, and brought in all the provisions except sixteen barrels of pork, which had been rolled into the bayou and was not considered of sufficient value to wet the men in the effort to get it. I believe a small amount of damaged bread was also left behind.

Sixteenth question. Do I know of a gun, cartridge, ax, spade, wagon, or anything left behind but the pork and bread referred to, and what was its quantity?

Answer. I know of nothing left behind except as stated in my last answer, which is as accurate as to quantity as I am able to state.

Seventeenth question. Do I not know that you personally remained in our camp at the bayou till every particle of ordnance, wagons, &c., and all the troops but the rear guard had reached the river?

Answer. I believe such to be the fact.

Eighteenth question. Do I not know that you communicated with General Mc-Clernand before leaving the Yazoo? Do I not know that you remained at the Yazoo Landing until every transport was off?

Answer. I answer that it is my impression that such was the case, although I know nothing except what I heard.

Nineteenth question. Was there any haste or confusion in re-embarking our command other than what is incident to large fleets and masses of men?

Answer. I observed no haste or confusion in the re-embarkation. The feeling was that the enemy would confer a great favor on us by leaving his works and giving us battle on equal terms.

Twentieth question. Have I not reason to know the enemy did not regard it as a retreat, but advised the people to look out for us in some other quarter?

Answer. I have reason to believe this. Such advice I believe was given in the public prints, and their conduct was in accordance with the advice.

Twenty-first question. Do I believe your force, independent of Grant's and Banks', could have taken and held Vicksburg?

Answer. My opinion has been that our whole force, aided by the gunboats, would have taken Haines' Bluff and held it if we had attacked it immediately upon our arrival in the Yazoo, and that we could thence not only have communicated with Grant but we could also by means of the Yazoo have united his force to ours, and with our combined forces we could have operated on the enemy's communications with Vicksburg and forced them to give us battle on our own ground or evacuate the place.

Twenty-second question. Do I not know that the attack on Haines' Bluff was not attempted because Admiral Porter declared it too hazardous?

Answer. I understand that such was Admiral Porter's opinion after it was ascertained that Grant had fallen back to Memphis. It could not have been his opinion on the evening of December 30 last, because he advised the attack that night, and we all agreed to it, and had prepared to make it. But for the dense fog it would have been made, and I have heard you since express the opinion that it would have been successful; Steele had no doubt of it. We all thought then that we could have intrenched ourselves, and, with the gunboats to protect our flanks, held it.

I have given you candid and specific answers to all of your questions. I confess myself greatly mortified and annoyed in being called on to answer such interrogatories under such circumstances.

Some days since, in the presence of Generals Steele and Stuart, you called my attention to a letter in the Missouri Republican and stated positively that it was written by some one in my brigade. I told you it was not so; but you were evidently unconvinced. I have since ascertained who wrote the letter to the Republican by a letter written from Saint Louis to Lieutenant-Colonel Peckham, who showed the paragraph to Capt. Charles McDonald, assistant adjutant-general to General Stuart, and I have taken other steps to advise you in regard to it. I now give you the means by referring to General Steele and his staff, who were on the Continental and heard my conversations, of ascertaining whether this letter is not in strict consonance with what I said in their hearing, and whether I have not invariably expressed myself in the kindest manner toward you, and in a manner entirely becoming in a brother officer engaged in a common object.

I am well aware, also, that you planned and in a great measure executed the movement against Arkansas Post, and have not failed to say what I knew of it on proper occasions.

I hope to receive no more letters of the same character from you and shall not answer them in the same spirit if I do. I have forborne something I thought was due to myself in making this response after the very explicit declarations I made to you some days since in the presence of Generals Steele and Stuart.

Very respectfully, your obedient servant,

FRANK P. BLAIR,
Brigadier-General.

P. S.—I repeat that I desire this letter may be made known to the officers present at the examination of Mr. Knox, and then you can make any use you please of it. I do not place the restrictions on its use which you impose on yourself in your letter.

GENERAL ORDERS, }   HDQRS. DEPT. OF THE TENNESSEE,
      No. 12.   }   *Young's Point, La., February* 1, 1863.

The proceedings of the court of inquiry convened at Holly Springs, Miss., by Special Orders, No. 2, of date January 2, 1863, from these headquarters, and of which Lieut. Col. De Witt C. Loudon, of the Seventieth Ohio Volunteers Infantry, was president, to inquire into and investigate the allegations and charges of disloyalty against the One hundred and ninth Illinois Infantry Volunteers, exonerates said regiment, as a regiment, from all suspicion of disloyalty, satisfactorily vindicates its innocence, and places it where the general commanding hoped to find it—among the pure and patriotic in their country's defense. That whatever cause for suspicion or charges of disloyalty there were arose from the conduct and declarations of the following-named officers, who are hereby dismissed the service of the United States, with forfeiture of pay and allowances, to take effect from this date, for the offenses of which they are severally shown to be guilty:

Lieut. Col. Elijah A. Willard, for disobedience of orders, and deserting his command in the face of an enemy, that he might be taken prisoner.

Capt. John M. Rich, for disobedience of orders, encouraging his men to desert, and discouraging his men from fighting in the face of the enemy.

Capt. Thomas Boswell, for encouraging his men to desert, that they might be captured and paroled, and advising them to apply for discharges for slight causes; also for trying to impress upon the minds of the officers and men of his regiment that they were embraced in the surrender of Holly Springs by Colonel Murphy, on the 20th day of December, 1862, well knowing the same to be false.

Capt. John J. McIntosh, for declaring in the hearing of his men and in the presence of the enemy that he would not fight if attacked near Holly Springs, Miss., on the 20th day of December, 1862.

Captain Penninger, of Company G, for proposing a plan by which the regiment could be surrendered to the enemy, and attempting to induce others of the regiment to aid in carrying it into execution during the raid of the enemy's cavalry on Holly Springs, on the 20th day of December, 1862.

Second Lieut. John Stokes, for straggling from his command and procuring for himself and a number of his men fraudulent paroles from a rebel citizen.

Second Lieut. Daniel Kimmel, for advising the colonel of his regiment if attacked by the enemy to surrender, and on feigned sickness procuring a surgeon's certificate to go to the hospital at Holly Springs, Miss., by reason of which he was captured and paroled by the enemy during the raid on that place.

First Lieut. and Adjt. James Evans, for inciting dissatisfaction among the men of his regiment, and speaking in an improper manner of the war and the President, in violation of the fifth article of war.

Commissary Sergt. Joshua Misenheimer is reduced to the ranks for declaring that he would never fire a gun upon the enemy, and on hearing a camp rumor that Major-General Burnside was defeated with a loss of 20,000 men, wishing it was so.

By order of Maj. Gen. U. S. Grant:

JNO. A. RAWLINS,
Assistant Adjutant-General.

CAMP NEAR VICKSBURG, *February* 2, 1863.

Brig. Gen. F. P. BLAIR:

DEAR SIR: Yours of last evening, handed me in person at your headquarters, was carefully perused on my reaching my room, and I express my satisfaction at the full and frank answers you have made to my interrogatories. Whether under similar circumstances a next time you will answer in an equally friendly spirit need not now arrest my thoughts, as I do not expect there will be a next time; or, if so, should I ask you fair, plain, direct questions again under similar circumstances, I believe you will give equally fair and plain answers.

I am willing to admit that I do owe you an explanation of the reason why after your full and frank disclaimers in the presence of Generals Steele and Stuart I should renew the subject. I could hardly believe that a white man could be so false as this fellow Knox. He certainly came down in the Continental, on which for a month you and Steele had your headquarters. He dated his paper there and eulogized every officer and man of that division and did not even attempt to approach the truth as to anybody else; did not know or care to know that Burbridge commanded the expedition from Milliken's Bend, ignoring General A. J. Smith, or spoke of him as "frittering away his time," &c., and indeed abused everybody but the officers of the Fourth Division. Officers of the other three divisions could and had come to but one conclusion, that he was in your pay or favor. I now know otherwise, and am glad that your letter enables me to put the fellow where he really belongs, as a spy and infamous dog. I shall show and read your letter to Dr. McMillan, Colonel Smith, and others, that their minds may be disabused on the same point

At a very early period I took ground that such men were spies. Take this case of Knox. He published in New York the first account of our attempt on Vicksburg, and now to my face tells me if he (Knox) cannot get at the truth he must publish falsehood. In other words, a commander, in addition to his already manifold labors, must unfold to every correspondent (for a distinction would surely be unfair) his orders, plans, and the developments. Knox has published his article as coming from a division headquarters. This publication is now in Vicksburg, and its commander can tell within 1,000 men our present force; but worse yet for our cause—Van Dorn now is at Holly Springs *en route* northward, knows our force and the chances of Vicksburg are against us, and in full confidence goes on his work of regaining ground we have fought for several times. I do know that the day will come when every officer will demand the execution of this class of spies; and without further hesitation I declare that if I am forced to look to the New York Herald as my law and master instead of the constituted authorities of the United States my military career is at an end.

If it be so that the people of the United States demand and must have news, true, if possible, but still news, their condition is likened to that of the drunkard, whose natural tastes have become so vitiated that nought but brandy will satisfy them, and they must pay the penalty. I for one am willing no longer to tamely bear their misrepresentations and infamies, and shall treat Knox and all others of his type as spies and defamers.

I am, with respect, your friend,

W. T. SHERMAN,
Major-General.

HEADQUARTERS FIFTEENTH ARMY CORPS,
Near Vicksburg, February 3, 1863.

Brig. Gen. F. P. BLAIR:

DEAR SIR: As it is now proper I will explain to you certain things which I think you ought to know to enable you to understand the history of recent events in connection with the attack on Vicksburg.

General Steele never reported to me his belief that Haines' Bluff was the true point of attack first to be made. He wrote to General Grant to that effect from Helena by Colonel Grierson, who crossed over to General Grant at Oxford after I had taken my departure; but I know it was the general conviction of all military men who studied the maps that an attack on Vicksburg should be made by way of the Yazoo, landing at the first bluff or hard land above its mouth. This was usually styled Haines' Bluff, but in fact the first high ground touches the Yazoo 2 or 3 miles lower down, at Snyder's house, and is now known as Drumgould's Bluff, the same on which the enemy had made his fortifications. I also was of the same impression, and the moment our fleet reached the mouth of Yazoo I repaired on board the flag-ship and there met Captain Gwin and many most intelligent navy officers, who had been repeatedly up the Yazoo last summer, fall, and winter, up to the hour of our arrival. They described Drumgould's Bluff as very strongly fortified; that not only were heavy guns there in position, but earth forts and rifle-pits and a strong force of infantry camped immediately behind, at Milldale. The Yazoo, also, was obstructed by a raft; and for 3 miles below by a system of torpedoes, one of which had exploded and sunk the Cairo. Even the gunboats could not approach Snyder's Bluff, much less our frail transports. All agreed that a landing of the troops must be made lower down, and there was no difference of opinion but that Johnson's plantation was the best if not only place to disembark the troops, even if Haines' Bluff were to be the point of real attack.

From the levee above Chickasaw Bayou where Steele landed all the way up to Snyder's is an impracticable swamp, passable at only two points, one near Benson Blake's and the other which Steele attempted, and which he pronounced officially as more difficult than the Bridge of Lodi. There is one small bayou close up to Snyder's, another a short distance below, and about a mile below is the large creek called Skillet Goliah, and all along the foot of the hills is a swamp and bayou similar to the one we had so much trouble with. At first the enemy expected us there, but when we landed at Johnson's they of course changed to the points accessible from Johnson's. They were familiar with every foot of ground, and we had to study it under extreme difficulties.

I think that the chances against Snyder's were better after we had drawn the enemy to the head of Chickasaw Bayou than before. More over in the interim; Admiral Porter had constructed a prow to one of the rams with which to take up or explode in advance the torpedoes that filled the Yazoo. The moment he was willing to attack the batteries at Snyder's I was ready to co-operate, and, as you say, we made prompt and secret preparations for the attack. General Steele was confident and so was I, and we did not abandon the attempt till the admiral declared it "too hazardous." But an essential feature in the proposed attack on the morning of January 1, 1863, at Snyder's was a simultaneous attack at Morgan's front and that of A. J. Smith. At great labor we had brought up four 30-pounder Parrott guns, and had all our field batteries placed according to our then more perfect knowledge of the ground and the enemy's position. I held all ready to begin the moment I heard you engaged at Snyder's, and I contend we at Chickasaw Bayou could and would have held the infantry force there, leaving the gunboats and Steele's forces to fight the batteries above at Snyder's. It is for this reason that I say the military chances were better on the early morning of January 1 than if we had gone with our fleet direct up to Haines' Bluff on the morning of December 27. We do know the difficulties we encountered, and it may be, as is always the case, that we cannot do as well on the ground as we can figure on paper, but in my mind I know I studied night and day to acquire the most accurate information; that I acted in perfect harmony with the naval squadron, and that I communicated frankly and fully to all division commanders all facts that reached me. I do know that Morgan's advance was on the true line of attack; that his attack was the signal for all others; that he was full of confidence; that he knew early on the morning of December 29 of the road by which you returned from the assault; that his entire division was ordered to carry the road and up the hill to the first summit; that your brigade and Steele's whole division were ordered to support Morgan; that the pontoon bridge was designed only as auxiliary, so as to enable Morgan to cross a part of his troops by a route where the enemy had made no seeming preparations for resistance.

I know that the Second Division did commence when Morgan opened fire, and I know it occupied large masses of the enemy who otherwise would have encountered Morgan. I know the same of the First Division, and that the ground to its front was absolutely impassable to any army except skirmishers; but still Colonel Landram, commanding that brigade, did push his skirmishers through the tangled mass of timber, which I have examined personally, and he did occupy the attention of the batteries and troops in Vicksburg. I have observed an impression that the road on which A. J. Smith advanced might have been made a line of attack. I tell you no; and I defy any one who saw and examined the obstructions placed there by the enemy to say otherwise.

My calculations were that Morgan's whole division, supported by Steele's, could at some considerable loss carry the county road and first hills at Chickasaw, and then a gunboat attack on Snyder's would be certain of success. We could not have secured a footing at Snyder's easier than by way of Chickasaw Bayou.

I may be and am too reckless of public opinion, but I am not of my officers and men. I would not have them think or feel that I am reckless of their safety and honor or that I neglect to take every possible precaution against danger or fail to study every means to attain success. I am very careful to obey orders and instructions of my superiors, because I know the importance of it in large combined operations, and I may expect too much of volunteers, who think for themselves and don't feel the implicit confidence of regulars in their officers. I am fully aware that General Morgan did not carry to the assault all his division as I expected. I have his official reports, and all are now in the hands of our Government. I know General Morgan's enthusiasm and devotion to the cause and will not question these, and assume to myself the consequences of failure rather than throw it off on any generous and brave man or set of men.

Failures result from many causes, without a necessity for that bitter vituperation that pulls down rather than builds up. As you remark, we are all engaged in the same cause, which calls for the united action of all, and I think I am in mind as willing to bear and suffer as any one if such forbearance adds one atom to the chances of success in the great national struggle. If at one time I did think you had incautiously dropped expressions which gave a newspaper spy the grounds of accusations against all save those in your brigade and division, I now retract that and assure you of my confidence and respect.

Yours, truly,

W. T. SHERMAN,
Major-General.

SPECIAL ORDERS, }   LAKE PROVIDENCE, LA.,
No. 6.   }   *April* 10, 1863.

The officers of the One hundred and ninth Regiment Illinois Volunteers, except those of Company K, having been reported as utterly incompetent to perform the duties of their respective commissions, and evincing no disposition to improve themselves, are hereby discharged from the service of the United States.

This is the regiment which was within a few miles of Holly Springs when attacked by the rebels and failed to march to the support of their comrades, but drew in their pickets and stood ready to surrender. From nine companies 347 men deserted, principally at Memphis, and but 1 from Company K.

To render the men efficient it is necessary to transfer them to a disciplined regiment, and they are accordingly transferred to the Eleventh Regiment Illinois Volunteers, Company K to make the tenth company.

The officers thus discharged are Col. A. J. Nimmo, Maj. T. M. Perrine, First Lieut. C. B. Dishon, regimental quartermaster; Capts. J. C.

Hunsaker, Hugh Andrews, Samuel M. P. McClure, S. O. Lewis; First Lieuts. James P. McLane, Morgan Stokes, Jacob A. Milikin, Charles Barringer, B. F. Hartline, Josiah Toler, Abram L. Misenheimer, R. B. Bartleson; Second Lieuts. M. A. Goodman, Squire Crabtree, T. T. Robinson, Henry Gassaway, Charles Klutts, Andrew Colvin. -

Chaplain P. H. Kroh will, as the regiment has been consolidated, be mustered out of the service.

Surg. John L. Dewey, Asst. Surgs. John W. Henley and George H. Dewey will be assigned by Major-General Grant to other Illinois regiments to fill vacancies.

By order of the Secretary of War:

L. THOMAS,
Adjutant-General.

CONFEDERATE CORRESPONDENCE. ETC.

HEADQUARTERS WESTERN DEPARTMENT,
Tupelo, Miss., June 10, 1862.

Maj. Gen. MANSFIELD LOVELL,
  Commanding Department No. 1, Jackson, Miss.:

GENERAL: * * * You ask what are my future plans. They will depend somewhat on the movements of the enemy. I intend to fight him here if he advances upon me and my force be strong enough to meet him with a chance of success; otherwise, I will fall back toward my true base, via Columbus and the Meridian and Selma Railroad. But should circumstances favor it I shall march from here to Oxford via Pontotoc. The first movement would necessarily cause the withdrawal of all my troops west of this place to concentrate them here. What would then become of you and your command must be left for you to decide. I would advise you, if my advice were asked, to concentrate them here also, in order to enable me to take the offensive, if practicable. The only thing left to us now is to endeavor to divide the enemy's forces, if possible, and then to unite ours rapidly for a sudden blow on any one of his fractional commands.*

*   *   *   *   *   *   *

Respectfully, your obedient servant,

G. T. BEAUREGARD,
General, Commanding.

ADJUTANT AND INSPECTOR GENERAL'S OFFICE,
Richmond, Va., June 11, 1862.

Maj. Gen. EARL VAN DORN,
  (Through General Beauregard), Baldwyn, Miss.:

GENERAL: Your telegraphic dispatch to the President recommending Major Cabell and Lieutenants Phifer and Armstrong for appointment of brigadier-generals to your command has induced the President to call on this office for information respecting the organization of your command into divisions and brigades. The information has been furnished in your return of May 4 last. In that return you exhibit three divisions, each consisting of three brigades, viz: The First Division, under Maj. Gen. S. Jones, with the brigades commanded by Brigadier-

---

* Portions of letter here omitted printed in Series I, Vol. XV, p. 752.

Generals Rust, Maury, and Roane; the Second Division, under Major-General Price, with the brigade commanded by Brigadier-General Little and two other brigades not represented by brigadiers; and the Third Division, under Major-General McCown, with two brigades commanded each by Brigadier-Generals Hogg and Churchill and one other brigade not represented by a brigadier, this last brigade, with the exception of one regiment, not having yet joined your command, according to the remarks on the return.

It is the wish of the President that the spirit of the law in relation to organization should be conformed to by placing as far as practicable the regiments from the several States in the same brigades, so that each brigade shall be composed of regiments from the same State. This he has observed is strictly the case in respect to General Rust's brigade, of the First Division, but is not followed out in the organization of some of the other brigades. He has therefore instructed me to call your attention to these discrepancies, and to request that you will cause the following changes to be made, viz: First, that the Arkansas regiment and battalion under Colonel McRae and Lieutenant-Colonel Adams, respectively, in the Second Brigade, First Division, be exchanged with the Texas regiments under the command, respectively, of Colonels Stone and Sims, in the Third Brigade of that division, and that the Arkansas regiment under Colonel Embry, in the Second Brigade, Third Division, be added to the Second Brigade, Second Division, in place of the regiment under Colonel ———, not named and not enumerated in that brigade. Second, that the Arkansas regiment under Colonel Hill, in the First Brigade, Second Division, be transferred to the Second Brigade, Third Division, in place of Embry's regiment, transferred to the Second Brigade, First Division. Third, that Lieutenant-Colonel McCray's (Arkansas) battalion, of the First Brigade, Third Division, and Colonel Harper's (Arkansas) regiment, of the Second Brigade, same division, exchange places.

The above changes will complete the organization of your command by arranging the troops from the same States into the same brigades, with the single exception of the Second Brigade, Second Division, where the troops, being from different States, must remain as at present brigaded.

The President further suggests, in respect to brigade commanders, the following changes, viz: That Brig. Gen. J. C. Moore be assigned to the Second Brigade, First Division, in place of Brigadier-General Maury, to be assigned to the Third Brigade, Second Division, and that Brigadier-General Hébert be assigned to the Second Brigade, Second Division. This will give you eight brigadiers, leaving the ninth brigadier (Third Brigade, Third Division) to be appointed and assigned when that brigade (now absent) shall have joined your command.

Very respectfully,

S. COOPER,
Adjutant and Inspector General.

———

HEADQUARTERS ARMY OF THE WEST,
Priceville, Miss., June 11, 1862.

General BEAUREGARD, *Tupelo, Miss.:*

GENERAL: Is it your wish that the causeway across the Old Town Creek should be doubled, or that a new road should be constructed at some other point? I crossed the creek this morning near the lake. The road comes out about 2 miles north of Verona, and a very good road could be made there with plank. The swamp is not bad. From the lake to Verona is about 3 miles. Columns of infantry and cavalry can cross the swamp anywhere in the vicinity I speak of—I mean now; after a rain it would be doubtful.

Do you desire that I should continue to call at 10 o'clock? I have thought that it was not now necessary; will do so, however, cheerfully if you desire it. I perceive that the district I commanded across the Mississippi has been increased and is now a department (Trans-Mississippi Department). Have you any orders in regard to it? Have I been relieved of the command?

Respectfully, general, I am, your obedient servant,

EARL VAN DORN,
Major-General.

TOWN OF FULTON, MISS., *June* 11, 1862.

[General BEAUREGARD:]

GENERAL: On the 10th a member of my company was in Jacinto among the Federals. He reports that Nelson's division encamped at Jacinto on Monday night last; that they moved east in the direction of Tuscumbia, or on the Tuscumbia road.

On the 10th, at 3 o'clock, General Crittenden's division passed Jacinto, going east, on the same road taken by General Nelson. It is estimated that Nelson's and Crittenden's divisions number about 25,000 (say 15,000). In addition to these two divisions it is estimated that 15,000 or 20,000 troops have gone in the same direction—some think as many as 30,000—previous to Crittenden's and Nelson's forces. I am satisfied all the above is correct. My scout is sensible and reliable. I send you Northern papers; I have not had time to read them.

Respectfully,

L. E. HILL,
Captain, Commanding Dixie Cavalry.

P. S.—I want, if it is consistent with the service, general scouting orders. I am sure I can be of more service in that way than any other. I sent a scout to Rienzi to-day; will send his report when made. I could have taken General Crittenden and staff, but did not feel authorized to send out my men, or rather take them.

Respectfully,

L. E. H.

P. S.—I have just looked over a Louisville paper of the 4th, and would send it up, but the owner refuses to give it up. The enemy carried some eighty or one hundred pieces of artillery with Crittenden's and Nelson's divisions.

[Indorsement.]

————, —— —, 1862.

If the above be true we must be prepared to take the offensive at once against those in our front, and our cavalry must be pushed forward to ascertain where they are, and one regiment toward the Jacinto road.

G. T. B.

TUPELO, MISS., *June* 12, 1862.

Maj. Gen. EARL VAN DORN, *Present:*

DEAR GENERAL: The information you sent me this morning is con-firmed; but it would seem the enemy is coming toward Fulton or Columbia. If that be the case we must attack at once those in our front, and then take the others in the rear. Will you commence making the necessary preparations for such a move, which, however, you will keep secret? Provisions need not be cooked yet (three days' and two or three in wagons), but have them all ready. Send a strong force of cavalry to observe the movements of the enemy toward Jacinto. We will leave one or two brigades to guard our right and rear. God and liberty!

Yours, truly,

G. T. BEAUREGARD.

P. S.—See that all our officers and men are provided with haversacks.

JUNE 12, 1862—2 p. m.

GENERAL: I return you the papers sent, and fully agree we should be ready to strike as soon as we can verify the reports; but we must not conceal from ourselves the great difficulty of operating to the front. Water, forage, and food will be scarce, and it is almost disheartening to look at our scanty resources; still we are gaining nothing on that score by lying still. I will put Chalmers in motion to try and develop the enemy in front.

Yours, truly,

BRAXTON BRAGG.

HEADQUARTERS ARMY OF THE MISSISSIPPI,
Tupelo, Miss., June 12, 1862.

Brigadier-General CHALMERS,
       Commanding Cavalry, &c.:

GENERAL: We have information that is considered reliable by the commanding general indicating movements of large bodies of the en-emy to the east via Jacinto. Others are reported moving west, leav-ing him very weak in front. Can you use your cavalry—especially such companies as Roddey's—to feel and develop him? We must not lose an opportunity to strike whenever he presents it. It is reported that two divisions passed through Jacinto to the east on the 9th and 10th.

Respectfully, general, your obedient servant,

GEO. G. GARNER,
Assistant Adjutant-General.

RICHMOND, VA., *June* 12, 1862.

General G. T. BEAUREGARD, *Baldwyn, Miss.:*

The President has been expecting a communication explaining your last movement. It has not yet arrived.

S. COOPER,
Adjutant and Inspector General.

TUPELO, MISS., *June* 12, 1862.
General S. COOPER:

Have had no time to write report; busy organizing and preparing for battle, if pursued. Will write soon, however. Halleck's dispatch nearly all false; retreat was a most brilliant and successful one.

G. T. BEAUREGARD.

GRENADA, MISS., *June* 12, 1862.
General THOMAS JORDAN, *Tupelo, Miss.*:

I have some 1,500 men armed and about 2,000 unarmed; also Colonel Jackson's regiment of cavalry and Colonel Stewart's twelve guns. I am in want of the Fourth and Eleventh Regiments of Louisiana troops, and three regiments more of good troops for partisan service along our northern border. I am in want of arms and I will send full particulars tonight by Colonel Augustin. General Villepigue is here commanding post. Answer.

DANIEL RUGGLES,
Brigadier-General, C. S. Army.

TUPELO, *June* 12, 1862.
Lieut. Col. R. B. LEE, *Chief of Subsistence Department*:

COLONEL: The general commanding directs that you will remove all supplies from along the Mississippi Central Railroad to the following depots, as follows:

1. Tupelo	10 days', always on hand.
2. Columbus	20 days', always on hand.
3. Macon	15 days', always on hand.
4. Gainesville	30 days', always on hand.
5. Demopolis	5 days', always on hand.
6. Meridian	3 days', always on hand.
7. Enterprise	2 days', always on hand.
8. Selma	5 days', always on hand.
9. Montgomery	20 days', always on hand.
Total	110

For 75,000 or 80,000 men.

He also directs that you have constantly on hand at Grenada ten days' supplies for 5,000 men, until the place shall have been abandoned by General Ruggles' command.

Very respectfully, &c.,

GEORGE WM. BRENT,
Acting Chief of Staff.

SPECIAL ORDERS, }   HEADQUARTERS WESTERN DEPARTMENT,
No. 80.   {   *Tupelo, Miss., June* 12, 1862.

I. Col. W. H. Jackson, of the cavalry, will remain at or near Holly Springs with his regiment as long as practicable, or until otherwise ordered.

II. It having been represented by responsible persons that an efficient and considerable force may be raised in North Mississippi and the southern counties of West Tennessee for special service—the defense of that region from the inroads and ravages of marauding parties of the enemy—Colonel Jackson is authorized to muster into service, under the act of Congress approved August 21, 1861, providing for local defense and special service. These troops will remain in service for ninety days, unless sooner discharged; must be armed and equipped by themselves, and not liable to service under the conscript act approved April 16, 1862.

III. When the requisite number of these troops shall have been mustered into service they may be employed, under the orders of the department, either in West Tennessee or in Mississippi, according to the exigencies of the service.

By command of General Beauregard:

GEORGE WM. BRENT,
Acting Chief of Staff.

SPECIAL ORDERS, } HEADQUARTERS ARMY OF THE WEST,
No. 112.   } *Priceville, June* 12, 1862.

*   *   *   *   *   *   *

IV. Brigadier-General Little, having reported for duty, is assigned temporarily to the command of Price's division, Army of the West. Brig. Gen. M. M. Parsons, Missouri State Guard, will turn over all orders, &c., pertaining to the headquarters Price's division, Army of the West.

By order of Maj. Gen. Earl Van Dorn:

M. M. KIMMEL,
Major and Assistant Adjutant-General.

Abstract from Weekly Return of the First Corps, Army of the Mississippi, commanded by Maj. Gen. Leonidas Polk, June 12, 1862.

[Headquarters near Tupelo, Miss.]

| Troops. | Present for duty. | | | | Effective total. | Aggregate present. | Aggregate present and absent. |
| | Infantry. | | Artillery. | | | | |
	Officers.	Men.	Officers.	Men.			
First Division	343	3,206	5	213	3,659	4,791	9,824
Second Division	302	3,381	8	144	3,745	4,532	7,526
Grand total	645	6,587	13	357	7,404	9,306	17,350

RICHMOND, *June* 13, 1862.

General EARL VAN DORN, *Tupelo, Miss.*:

Your dispatch of yesterday received. General Price has not arrived. The department is large and will be important. Regret the necessity which has kept you so long absent. Wrote to you about affairs in Arkansas.

JEFFERSON DAVIS.

HEADQUARTERS WESTERN DEPARTMENT,
Tupelo, Miss., June 13, 1862.
Brig. Gen. DANIEL RUGGLES,
Commanding, &c., Grenada, Miss.:

GENERAL: I am instructed to acquaint you with the following wishes of the commander of the forces: Grenada will be evacuated as a depot for this army with the least delay practicable, to which end you will have all the ordnance, ordnance stores and supplies, and other public property there sent with all practicable dispatch to Gainesville, Ala., via Jackson and Meridian, Miss., reserving only subsistence for your command while at Grenada and ten days' rations for the movement. Meanwhile, if practicable, or as soon as practicable, all unarmed troops under your command will be sent to Columbus by means of the railroads. This, however, must not interfere with the rapid removal of the ordnance supplies in store at Grenada. Hold your effective force ready to march hither at short notice via Coffeeville, Sarepta, Pontotoc, and Harrisburg, or by any better route should you be able to find one by a careful reconnaissance, especially with regard to water, of the routes in this direction, which the general desires you to have made at once by judicious and fully competent persons. At the same time it is particularly desirable that the subsistence resources of the country through which you will march shall be ascertained, and, if practical, subsistence should be purchased and collected at points on your line of march, so that you may move if possible with less than ten days' rations or, indeed, with only the small rations. You will thus save means of transportation, which you will be expected to collect in your vicinity, stipulating, if necessary, with the owners that their wagons and teams shall be returned to them without delay from this place, if not from points on the march. The command will bivouac and move with only cooking equipment and the proper changes of clothing. All other baggage will be sent off by the railroad.

Respectfully, general, your obedient servant,
GEORGE WM. BRENT,
Acting Chief of Staff.

CAMP NEAR TOMBIGBEE RIVER,
June 13, 1862.
Colonel KIMMEL,
Adjutant-General, Army of the West:

SIR: I have just heard through one of my spies that the whole Federal army is moving in the direction of Tuscumbia by way of Iuka. General Buell passed through Burnsville yesterday. The soldiers of the Federal army report that 60,000 are going to Virginia as rapidly as they can march. They also report our forces at Cumberland Gap have cut their army to pieces, and that a portion of their army will march to that point. It is a universal report among the citizens that the enemy have vacated the following points: Baldwyn, Booneville, Rienzi, and Corinth. They have left 5,000 cavalry to bring up the rear. I leave with my command at daylight in the morning, and will send a messenger from the nearest point to the enemy where reliable information can be obtained.

I am, colonel, very respectfully, your obedient servant,
W. R. BRADFUTE,
Commanding Outpost Cavalry.

GRENADA, MISS., *June* 13, 1862.

General BEAUREGARD, *Tupelo, Miss.*:

I send you extract of dispatch just received from Col. W. H. Jackson, commanding in the advance:

Enemy moving a very heavy force, under Wallace and McClernand, toward Memphis.

DANIEL RUGGLES,
Brigadier-General.

GRENADA, MISS., *June* 13, 1862.

Colonel HARMAN, or COMMANDING OFFICER,
Holly Springs, Miss.:

You will prohibit the destruction or burning of buildings of every description unless positive orders are sent for that purpose from these headquarters. You will communicate this order immediately to all military and civil authorities in the surrounding district.

DANIEL RUGGLES,
Commanding.

TUPELO, MISS., *June* 14, 1862.

Brig. Gen. DANIEL RUGGLES:

Continue to have everything removed from Grenada to Gainesville, except twenty days' supply for 5,000 men, which I suppose will be the forces under your order. See to their proper drilling and organization.

G. T. BEAUREGARD.

RICHMOND, VA., *June* 14, 1862.

General G. T. BEAUREGARD, *Tupelo, Miss.*:

The president of the Mississippi Central Railroad telegraphs, date yesterday, that the station-house and work-sheds at Holly Springs depot are being burned. Is this by your orders; if so, for what purpose?

S. COOPER,
Adjutant and Inspector General.

RICHMOND, VA., *June* 14, 1862.

General BEAUREGARD,
Baldwyn, Mobile and Ohio Railroad:

We learn that Asst. Surgs. T. S. Foster and Newton Vowles, of the Missouri State Guard, have been captured and one of them condemned to death by General Halleck as a bridge-burner. We have executed private individuals for burning bridges, but we deny the right to punish an officer acting under orders. Ascertain the facts and inform General Halleck that we shall retaliate on the prisoners in our hands for any execution in violation of the rules of civilized warfare, and that we shall consider ourselves at liberty to examine into the regularity of the proceedings under which any citizen of Missouri shall be executed, and to retaliate if we find that a fair trial was not granted.

G. W. RANDOLPH,
Secretary of War.

RICHMOND, VA., June 14, 1862.
General BRAXTON BRAGG, Tupelo, Miss. :

You will immediately proceed to Jackson, Miss., and temporarily assume command of the department now commanded by General Lovell. After General Magruder joins, your further services there may be dispensed with. The necessity is urgent and absolute.

JEFFERSON DAVIS.

TUPELO, MISS., June 14, 1862.
(Received at Richmond, Va., June 15, 1862.)
General S. COOPER:

General Bragg has just communicated to me a telegram sending him to relieve temporarily General Lovell. His presence here I consider indispensable at this moment, especially as I am leaving for a while on surgeon's certificate. For four months I have delayed obeying their urgent recommendation in that respect. I desire to be back here in time to take the offensive as soon as our forces shall have been sufficiently organized. I must have a short rest.

G. T. BEAUREGARD.

[JUNE 14, 1862.—For Davis to W. P. Johnston, directing an inspection of Beauregard's army, see Series I, Vol. X, Part I, p. 786.]

SPECIAL ORDERS, }   HDQRS. MISSISSIPPI STATE TROOPS,
No. 5.   }   Major-General's Office, Canton, Miss., June 14, 1862.

The commanders of regiments and separate battalions in the First Brigade, division composed of the counties of De Soto, Marshall, Tippah, Tishomingo, Itawamba, Pontotoc, La Fayette, Panola, Tunica, and Coahoma, will direct their respective commands of organized minutemen to obey such orders as may hereafter emanate from Brigadier-General Ruggles, of the Confederate States Army, for the destruction of cotton, for the preservation or removal of other property, and for the protection of laborers engaged in the service of the Confederate States. It is further ordered that such minute-men, while engaged in obedience to orders of Brigadier-General Ruggles, shall be considered as in active service. Brig. Gen. M. T. Berry, and, in his absence, the commanders of regiments and battalions of his brigade, are charged with the execution of this order.

T. C. TUPPER,
Major-General.

GENERAL ORDERS, } HEADQUARTERS WESTERN DEPARTMENT,
No. 72.   }   Tupelo, Miss., June 14, 1862.

I. General Orders, No. 30, from these headquarters, dated Corinth, Miss., May 19, 1862, are modified to read as follows: From this date, until otherwise ordered by the War Department the component parts of rations issued to the army will be as follows:

Pork or bacon to the ration ....ounces.. 8
Salt or fresh beef..pounds.. 1
Flour or corn-meal..ounces.. 24
Flour or hard bread ....pounds.. 1
Beans or pease to 100 rations ....quarts.. 8

Rice, in lieu of beans or pease..pounds.. 10
Coffee to 100 rations..do.... 3
Rye to 100 rations...do.... 3
Sugar to 100 rations...do.... 12
Molasses to 100 rations..quarts.. 12
Vinegar to 100 rations..do.... 4
Soap to 100 rations ....pounds.. 4
Salt to 100 rations ....quarts.. 2
Sperm candles to 100 rations ....pounds.. 1
Star candles to 100 rations ....do.... 1¼
Tallow candles to 100 rations...do.... 1¼

Eight ounces of lard may be issued in lieu of one ration of bacon or pork. Extra issues of fresh vegetables when practicable. Pork and bacon two days in seven, and fresh and salt beef five days in seven. The commutation price of rations until further orders will be twenty-five cents.

II. Under existing circumstances no officer's wife or family shall be permitted to remain with the troops in the field when within two days' march or 50 miles of the enemy.

By command of General Beauregard:

GEORGE WM. BRENT,
Acting Chief of Staff.

SPECIAL ORDERS, }   HEADQUARTERS WESTERN DEPARTMENT,
No. 82.   }   *Tupelo, Miss., June 14, 1862.*

*   *   *   *   *   *   *

IV. Col. St. John R. Liddell, Provisional Army of the Confederate States, will assume command of the First Brigade, Third Army Corps, and report at once to Major-General Hardee.

*   *   *   *   *   *   *

By command of General Beauregard:

[GEORGE WM. BRENT,]
Acting Chief of Staff.

Abstract from Statement of Troops at and about Grenada, Miss., Brig. Gen. John B. Villepigue, C. S. Army, commanding, June 14, 1862.

Commands.	Totals.			
	Present.	Absent.	Present and absent.	Unarmed.
1st Alabama..	111	58	169	......
12th Louisiana...	849	217	1,066	275
20th Mississippi.......................................	45	....	45	45
33d Mississippi..	669	310	979	979
Harman's Mississippi regiment.....................	102	92	194	194
Missouri Volunteers..................................	247	127	374	209
1st Confederate Battalion...........................	320	111	431	......
Ford's cavalry company..............................	58	17	75	75
Morehead's Partisan Rangers.......................	42	42	84	......
Point Coupée Light Artillery........................	165	9	174	......
Ward's Artillery Battalion...........................	202	49	251	174
Gallimard's Sappers and Miners....................	50	....	50	......
Total..	2,860	1,032	3,892	1,951

HEADQUARTERS WESTERN DEPARTMENT,
Tupelo, Miss., June 15, 1862.

GENERAL : After delaying as long as possible to obey the oft-repeated recommendations of my physicians to take some rest for the restoration of my health, I have concluded to take advantage of the present lull in the operations of this army, due to the necessity of attending to its organization and discipline and to the uncertain movements of the enemy, for absenting myself a short while from here, hoping to be back in time to assume the offensive at the earliest moment practicable. Meanwhile I will transfer the command of the forces of this department to the next officer in rank—General B. Bragg—furnishing him with such instructions as will enable him to give all orders required during my absence.

I propose leaving here to-morrow at 12 p. m. for Mobile, where I will remain a day or two inspecting the condition of its defenses, and will offer to Brigadier-General Forney such advice as, in my judgment, may be necessary and he may be willing to accept. I will then repair to Bladon's Springs, on the Tombigbee River, about 75 miles north of Mobile, where I will remain about one week or ten days, or long enough to restore my shattered health.

Very respectfully, your obedient servant,

G. T. BEAUREGARD,
General, Commanding.

General S. COOPER, C. S. Army,
Adjutant-General, Richmond, Va.

[Inclosure.]

HEADQUARTERS WESTERN DEPARTMENT,
Tupelo, Miss., June 14, 1862.

We hereby certify that, after attendance upon General Beauregard for the past four months and treatment of his case, in our professional opinion, he is incapacitated physically for the arduous duties of his present command, and we urgently recommend rest and recreation.

R. L. BRODIE,
Surgeon, Provisional Army, Confederate States.
SAML. CHOPPIN,
Surgeon, Provisional Army, Confederate States.

GRENADA, MISS., *June* 15, 1862.

General JORDAN, *Tupelo, Miss.* :

Mr. Proctor has arrived with his dispatch. Shall I burn the cotton throughout the interior ?

DANIEL RUGGLES,
Brigadier-General, Commanding.

TUPELO, MISS., *June* 15, 1862.
(Received June 16, 1862, 11 p. m.)

Brig. Gen. DANIEL RUGGLES :

Yes; burn all cotton in danger of falling into the hands of the enemy. Where is Villepigue ?

G. T. BEAUREGARD.

[GRENADA, MISS., *June* 15, 1862.]

General BEAUREGARD, *Tupelo, Miss.* :

Villepigue is here commanding troops.

DANIEL RUGGLES,
Brigadier-General.

TUPELO, MISS., *June* 15, 1862.
(Received 5 p. m.)

General DANIEL RUGGLES, *Commanding* :

It is reported enemy intend moving on Grenada. Send away at once everything from there and elsewhere as already instructed. Send also unarmed troops to Jackson, Miss., with ample provisions, and when compelled to evacuate Grenada repair to same place, reporting for the present to General Lovell or officer in command there. Keep only twenty days' provisions at Grenada for your armed troops.

G. T. BEAUREGARD.

GRENADA, MISS., *June* 15, 1862.

Colonel JACKSON, *Commanding Advance* :

You will assume command of all troops serving in the counties of Tunica, De Soto, Marshall, and Tippah, on our northern border. You will destroy the railroad tracks and bridges, the telegraph, and all cotton exposed to the depredations of the enemy. Unnecessary destruction of buildings and other property is positively prohibited. Take measures to impede the advance of the enemy at all points.

DANIEL RUGGLES,
Brigadier-General, C. S. Army, Commanding.

HERNANDO, MISS, *June* 15, 1862.

Brigadier-General RUGGLES, *Grenada, Miss.* :

GENERAL : Your orders for the past few days have been received, and as far as was in my power have been fully complied with. I do not fully understand your order to tear up railroad above this point. If it is your wish that the iron shall all be taken up you will have to order some one of the railroad men now in your town up here to superintend it, and I will try and get a force of negroes from the planters in this region to do the work. There is not a man here to whom I can intrust the management of this work, and as all the men who are and have been connected with our railroads are in and around Grenada I shall have to trust you to supply this necessity. If you only wish the bridges and trestle-work on the road burned I can have this done from my own resources. The roads as far down as Horn Lake Depot will be destroyed to-day by my order. I await an answer from you explanatory before doing more.

With regard to burning cotton I have been doing all I could with the means at my disposal, but the order you sent me embraces a very extensive area of country and will require, to be certainly and promptly done, an additional force of from 50 to 100 cavalry. Please let me know if I can rely upon getting this additional force.

The market for supplies is rather bare at this place, but at the different depots between this and Grenada I am told a great many supplies could be procured if proper effort be made at an early day. I have a man here whom I intend sending out through the country adjoining, but I would respectfully suggest that the most efficient plan by which this work can be done is for you to send some good quartermaster to this place for that purpose, and I will post him and aid him in his task.

I have information again from Memphis this morning. The force of the enemy is being increased daily, and as they now have a great many cavalry I think that any work we have to do in or near this region should be done speedily.

Respectfully,

J. H. EDMONDSON,
Captain, C. S. Army.

Organization of the First Corps, Army of the Mississippi, commanded by Maj. Gen. Leonidas Polk, June 15, 1862.

FIRST DIVISION.

Brig. Gen. CHARLES CLARK commanding.

First Brigade.	*Second Brigade.*
Brig. Gen. P. SMITH commanding.	Brig. Gen. A. P. STEWART commanding.
12th Tennessee, Colonel Bell. 13th Tennessee, Col. [A. J.] Vaughan. 22d Tennessee, Col. L. P. McMurry. 47th Tennessee, Major Shearon. Bankhead's battery, Lieutenant Scott.	13th Arkansas, Lieut. Col. Brown. 4th Tennessee, Col. O. F. Strahl. 5th Tennessee, Col. C. D. Venable. 31st Tennessee, Col. [W. M.] Bradford. 33d Tennessee, Col. [W. P.] Jones. Battery, Capt. T. J. Stanford.

SECOND DIVISION.

Maj. Gen. B. F. CHEATHAM commanding.

First Brigade.	*Second Brigade.*
Col. A. S. FULTON commanding.	Brig. Gen. GEORGE MANEY commanding.
8th Tennessee, Maj. C. C. McKinney. 15th Tennessee, Col. R. C. Tyler. 16th Tennessee, Col. J. H. Savage. 51st Tennessee, Col. John Chester. 154th Senior Tennessee, Col. E. Fitzgerald. Carnes' battery, Capt. W. W. Carnes.	1st Tennessee, Col. H. R. Feild. 6th Tennessee, Lieut. Col. W. M. R. Johns. 9th Tennessee, Lieut. Col. J. W. Buford. 27th Tennessee, Col. A. W. Caldwell. Smith's battery, Capt. M. Smith.

DETACHED BRIGADE.

Brig. Gen. S. B. MAXEY commanding.

41st Georgia, Col. C. A. McDaniel.
24th Mississippi, Lieutenant-Colonel McKelvaine.
9th Texas, Col. [W. H.] Young.
Battery, Captain Eldridge.

GRENADA, MISS., *June* 17, 1862.

General BEAUREGARD, *Tupelo, Miss.:*

Col. W. B. Shelby reports the enemy, 5,000 infantry and 300 cavalry, advancing rapidly on Holly Springs at 2 a. m. He has fallen back of Tallahatchie.

DANIEL RUGGLES,
Brigadier-General, Commanding.

[JUNE 17, 1862.]

Col. W. B. SHELBY, *Oxford, Miss.*:

You will hold the Tallahatchie Bridge, and also break up the railroad track as near to Holly Springs as practicable, moving the iron in this direction. Impress negro labor. Call on Colonel Goodman for special instructions as to the manner of breaking up the track. You will burn the cotton as near Holly Springs as practicable in the event of the enemy having reached there. Remove the telegraphic apparatus from there; take down wire as far as practicable.

Communicate your present position to Colonel Jackson.

> DANIEL RUGGLES,
> *Brigadier-General, Commanding.*

GRENADA, *June* 17, 1862.

Colonel SHELBY, *Tallahatchie Bridge*:

Break up the track, if you can, beyond the bridge and cut off the telegraph and save the apparatus. Bring all rolling stock this side of the bridge and prevent its falling into the hands of the enemy. Prepare to destroy the railroad track over the bridge, and call on President Goodman, at Oxford, for an agent to assist in effecting it.

Communicate with Colonel Jackson your position. Send here all useless men and baggage from your regiment, and retain cars enough to prevent surprise. Burn cotton toward Holly Springs in the vicinity of the enemy. Keep couriers observing his movements.

> DANIEL RUGGLES,
> *Brigadier-General, C. S. Army.*

TISHOMINGO CITY, MISS., *June* 17, 1862.

Captain RODDEY:

DEAR SIR: We have been happily successful in obtaining important information of the enemy's movements. There have been four brigades at Iuka, viz, McCook's, Crittenden's, Wood's, and Nelson's. They are all gone—Wood's toward Decatur, Ala., the others across the river at Eastport, with a large cavalry force, except part of Nelson's brigade, which is to leave to-morrow; the other part left this morning. The enemy has drawn in his pickets near town to-day. The enemy has a very large amount of stores at Iuka and Eastport. He has 400 wagons running between those points without any guard over them. There are two acres of ground covered with stores at Eastport. We learn there are to be 100 men left at Iuka to guard the stores.

We do not know how many men are at Bear Creek Bridge. It was finished yesterday. There is but one engine and about fifteen cars yet, but they say they will have a lot of rolling stock from above. There is reported to be two cavalry regiments between Jacinto and Cartersville. I will get more information to-morrow. I would give more now, but it is getting too dark. The above is from what I consider unquestionable authority.

Respectfully,

> J. T. WILLIAMS.

[Indorsement.]

T. T. Herridge will forward this to General Chalmers immediately, and if he is absent carry it to General Bragg, as the information is all fully reliable and may be of some importance at headquarters.

Very respectfully,

P. D. RODDEY,
Captain, &c.

P. S.—I think that General Pope's division is on the Mobile and Ohio Railroad, or probably now moving in the direction of Iuka.

Very respectfully,

P. D. R.

———

GRENADA, MISS., *June* 17, 1862.

ASSISTANT ADJUTANT-GENERAL,
Headquarters Department, Grenada, Miss.:

MAJOR: In conformity with instructions from the general commanding I have the honor to submit the following information relative to the character of the country lying north of the Tallahatchie River:

By personal observation and by reliable information gathered from various sources the stretch of country alluded to as a theater of defensive military operations is untenable. It is an open and wide-settled country. The plantations are numerous and extensive. Excellent and well-established roads at short intervals intersect each other throughout the country and merge either with the roads leading to Memphis or to the points on the railroads suited to the shipment of the common staple. There is no position of which I am informed that does not admit of a number of approaches, a fact that renders a small force operating against a larger one unavailable. Doubtless large quantities of cotton still remain in the hands of the planters, and with the advantages which the enemy possess will be secured. There may be positions at the forks of creeks and at remote and small farms which will be overlooked by the enemy, but the necessities of some and the lukewarmness of others in the cause may possibly induce them to dispose of their staples to the enemy rather than resort to the course which both law and patriotism direct. It may not be improper to remark here that Captain Thomasson's company (unattached Arkansas volunteers) is guarding the railroad bridge over the Tallahatchie River under my instructions. It will be for the general commanding to decide whether its services in that direction are any longer required.

I have the honor to be, major, your obedient servant,

B. D. HARMAN,
Colonel, Commanding Harman's Confederate Regiment.

———

HEADQUARTERS WESTERN DEPARTMENT,
Tupelo, Miss., June 17, 1862.

Col. J. D. MARTIN,
Colonel Commanding Post, Meridian:

COLONEL: Your several communications of the 16th instant have been received. The general commanding instructs me to reply that he approves of your proceedings in the collection of stragglers, &c. Also in the appointment of Capt. R. Y. Rew as provost-marshal. Should you lose his services, as you anticipate, it is not deemed necessary to sup ply his place by the appointment of a citizen. Some officer can be selected, who will be ordered to report to you for that purpose.

He also instructs me to say that there is no general order on the subject of impressment of negro labor. In some special cases, where the public exigencies demanded it, negro labor has been impressed, discriminating, however, against all hands employed in the production of cotton. Should an extreme case occur you are authorized to exercise this power. The exercise of such a power, however, should be abstained from if possible.

I am, colonel, very respectfully, your obedient servant,

GEORGE WM. BRENT.

GENERAL ORDERS, }   HEADQUARTERS WESTERN DEPARTMENT,
No. 74.   }   Tupelo, June 17, 1862.

The general commanding takes pleasure in calling the attention of the armies of this department to the gallant conduct of Capt. B. B. McCaa, and his command of Brewer's cavalry regiment on the morning of the 14th instant, when by a bold and dashing charge he put to flight a superior force of the enemy's cavalry. In this affair Private John Graham was especially distinguished, and will be rewarded with the badge of honor on some suitable occasion.

This success should teach our cavalry forces what they can accomplish by bravery and daring, and should incite them to like deeds of valor.

By command of General Beauregard:

GEORGE WM. BRENT,
Acting Chief of Staff.

GENERAL ORDERS, }   HEADQUARTERS WESTERN DEPARTMENT,
No. 75.   }   Tupelo, Miss., June 17, 1862.

For the benefit of his health the commander of the forces has found it necessary to take a short respite from the arduous duties of the command of this army and department, and hereby relinquishes the chief command during his absence from the limits of the Western Department to General Braxton Bragg.

By command of General Beauregard:

GEORGE WM. BRENT,
Acting Chief of Staff.

GENERAL ORDERS, }   HEADQUARTERS WESTERN DEPARTMENT,
No. 76.   }   Tupelo, Miss., June 17, 1862.

During the absence from the department of General Beauregard the undersigned assumes chief command of the forces of the department.

BRAXTON BRAGG,
General, C. S. Army.

SPECIAL ORDERS, }   HEADQUARTERS WESTERN DEPARTMENT,
No. 85.   }   Tupelo, Miss., June 17, 1862.

*   *   *   *   *   *   *

IX. The Fourth and Seventeenth Regiments Louisiana Volunteers and all unarmed troops at Jackson and Grenada, Miss., belonging to the forces of this department are temporarily assigned to duty in Department No. 1, under command of Major-General Lovell, C. S. Army, who is also authorized, in case of a military exigency, to call on General Ruggles for troops.

*   *   *   *   *   *   *

By command of General Beauregard:

[GEORGE WM. BRENT,]
Acting Chief of Staff.

FULTON, MISS., *June* 18, 1862.

Colonel KIMMEL:

I send you a note received at 2 o'clock last night from Captain Hill. He is near Pleasant Site, Ala.   Will have another messenger some time to-night from him.

W. R. BRADFUTE,
Colonel, Commanding.

[Inclosure.]

NEAR PLEASANT SITE, ALA., *June* 17, 1862.

[Colonel BRADFUTE:]

The Federals are going east, at least 40,000 strong, carrying heavy trains.

L. E. HILL.

P. S.—The enemy say they are going to Chattanooga.

L. E. H.

P. S.—I am in a dangerous place, but am still going forward.

L. E. H.

P. S.—The Yankees say they would as soon be in hell as Corinth.

L. E. H.

FULTON, MISS., *June* 18, 1862.

Colonel KIMMEL:

Inclosed you will find another note * from Captain Hill. He is at the point to gather information.   Send me all the army news.   I am at a loss to know something about the movements of the army.   I want 2,000 cavalry very badly, and think that I am entitled to the command of such force.   With that number I can turn over the whole Federal army.   It is scattered all over the route they are moving.   This command that I now have is not worth a cent.   You cannot get more than 40 good fighting men from it.

W. R. BRADFUTE,
Colonel, Commanding Post.

GRENADA, MISS., *June* 18, 1862.

His Excellency Governor PETTUS, *Jackson, Miss.*:

The enemy's cavalry, some 300 strong, attacked our advance at Tallahatchie Bridge, Central Railroad, this morning.   I am sending re-

---

* Not found.

enforcements to that point.   Can you add materially to my strength b.
calling out the minute-men and militia of the State of Mississippi?

DANIEL RUGGLES,
Brigadier-General, Commanding.

TUPELO, MISS., *June* 18, 1862.

General DANIEL RUGGLES, *Commanding:*

Detach at once Fort Pillow command under General Villepigue to
defend crossing on Tallahatchie River.   He will destroy bridges and
do all possible to check advance of enemy until re-enforcements reach
him there, which will march at once.   Cars, &c., wanted, ordered.

Report departure of General Villepigue and answer this.

By command of General Bragg:

THOMAS JORDAN,
Assistant Adjutant-General.

GRENADA, MISS., *June* 18, 1862.

General BRAGG, *Tupelo, Miss.:*

Colonel Shelby reports enemy's cavalry (300) at Tallahatchie Bridge.
Skirmishing this morning.   He fears that he cannot hold the bridge
until night.   I ordered Captain Isbell, with his battalion, to proceed to
that point night before last, and he is about leaving.

Colonel Jackson's cavalry has not been heard of for some days.

I have ordered the Tallahatchie Bridge burned if necessary.   I have
just ordered General Villepigue, with his Fort Pillow command, to proceed to Tallahatchie Bridge.

DANIEL RUGGLES,
Brigadier-General, Commanding.

HEADQUARTERS WESTERN DEPARTMENT,
Tupelo, June 18 1862.

Brig. Gen. WILLIAM PRESTON,
    Commanding Reserve Division, Army of the Mississippi:

GENERAL: I am instructed to communicate the following instructions for your guidance:

You will proceed with the division under your command with the
least delay to Oxford, Miss., or to the headquarters of Brigadier-General Villepigue, in that vicinity, and form a junction with the command
of that officer for the purpose of repelling an invasion of that region by
a detachment of the enemy.

In the movement all usual military precautions will be taken, and as
you approach the line of the Mississippi Central Railroad especial care
should be observed to guard against the possibility of surprise.   Moreover, every precaution should be used to prevent news of your movements from reaching the enemy.   It might be well, indeed, to give out
Grenada as the point of your destination.

Communicate through an officer with General Villepigue so that you
may be accurately informed of his movements and purposes, and also
when precisely your junction with him shal' take place.

An officer of the Engineer Corps will report to you in order that you may employ him in advance of your command in the selection of the best routes of march and the proper camp grounds. Efficient staff officers should accompany him, with orders to procure and collect forage at the halting places; also subsistence as far as practicable—fresh meat especially.

Should it be necessary you are authorized to avail yourself of the resources of the country, in the way of transportation, but will do so with the understanding that all teams shall only be temporarily retained and returned to their owners from Oxford and that vicinity.

The commander of the forces hopes that you will be fortunate enough to meet with the enemy, and wishes the officers and men of your command particularly impressed with the fact that our soldiers have always been victorious over our present adversaries, despite odds, when they have resolutely dashed at them. Advancing with a stern and inflexible will to drive the invader back success will surely follow.

Respectfully, general, your obedient servant,

THOMAS JORDAN,
Assistant Adjutant-General.

HEADQUARTERS WESTERN DEPARTMENT,
Tupelo, June 18, 1862.

Officer in Charge Military Railroad Transportation :

SIR : One hundred freight cars and five effective locomotives must be sent as soon as practicable to Grenada, Miss., to be reported to General Ruggles, commanding at that point.

The commander of the forces desires that these cars and locomotives, as far as practicable, should be taken from the rolling stock of the Memphis and Charleston Railroad now on the Mobile and Ohio Railroad, and expects that timely measures will be taken to secure their rapid transit over the railroad from Meridian to Jackson with as little interruption as possible at the same time to the transportation of public stores over same road from Jackson eastward. He thinks with the exercise of proper energy and judgment these trains can be dispatched through without material delay.

Report to this office the dispatch of these trains and their arrival at Meridian, Jackson, and Grenada.

Respectfully, your obedient servant,

THOMAS JORDAN.

HEADQUARTERS WESTERN DEPARTMENT,
Tupelo, Miss., June 18, 1862.

Col. R. W. SMITH and
Lieutenant-Colonel POLIGNAC:

COLONEL : The troops that have been discharged from the army of Major-General Van Dorn are not in the service of the Confederate States Army, but Missouri State Guard. All such troops may be allowed to go hence.

I am, colonel, very respectfully, your obedient servant,

GEORGE WM. BRENT.

TUPELO, MISS., *June* 18, 1862.
(Received June 19, 1862.)

General E. KIRBY SMITH, *Chattanooga, Tenn.*:

Re-enforcements requested are held ready, depending, however, upon movements of enemy in our front, which are not yet sufficiently developed for our action.*

BRAXTON BRAGG.

SPECIAL ORDERS, }   HEADQUARTERS WESTERN DEPARTMENT,
No. 86.   }   *Tupelo, Miss., June* 18, 1862.

I. Breckinridge's corps, Army of the Mississippi, will be prepared to move in light marching order with all possible celerity, with six days' subsistence and 100 rounds of ammunition for small-arms and the current supply for field batteries. Brigadier-General Preston will report at once to the commander of the forces for special instructions.

II. Pinson's (late Lindsay's) cavalry will march without delay, and by the nearest practicable route, to Oxford, or to the headquarters of General Villepigue, in that vicinity, to whom it will be reported for further orders. The regiment will be provided with five days' subsistence and a proper supply of ammunition. Celerity is important. Forage will be procured by the wayside, to which end proper staff officers will be sent ahead.

III. In consequence of the necessary division of the cavalry forces of this army with the several army corps, Brigadier-General Beall is relieved from the chief command of the cavalry and will report to Major-General Van Dorn for duty in the Army of the West.

IV. The supplies for the forces under Major-General Van Dorn will hereafter be delivered at Verona, where General Van Dorn will establish the depots for his command, with the necessary staff officers.

By command of General Bragg:

GEORGE WM. BRENT,
Acting Chief of Staff.

SPECIAL ORDERS, }   HEADQUARTERS ARMY OF THE WEST,
No. 117.   }   *Priceville, Miss., June* 18, 1862.

*   *   *   *   *   *   *

II. The troops under the command of General M. M. Parsons, known as the Missouri State Guard, are relieved from duty with this army and will prepare to march to-morrow with eight days' rations. The Confederate troops under General Parsons will, if artillery, report to the commanding officer of the artillery brigade; if infantry or cavalry, will report to the commanding officer of their division (General Little). A battery of four pieces of artillery will march with him. The rest of the artillery of Parsons' brigade will be turned over to the chief of artillery, or such officers as he may order to receive it, who will give the necessary receipts for the same. General Parsons will cause descriptive lists to be furnished to the Confederate troops under his command.

By order of Maj. Gen. Earl Van Dorn:

M. M. KIMMEL,
Assistant Adjutant-General.

---

* See Smith to Taylor, June 21, 1862, Series I, Vol. XVI, Part II, p. 696.

GRENADA, MISS., *June* 19, 1862.

General BRAGG, *Tupelo, Miss.*:

Brigadier-General Villepigue, with his command, left at 4 o'clock this morning for the Tallahatchie Bridge.

Colonel Jackson has fallen back near Coldwater Depot, Mississippi and Tennessee Railroad.

DANIEL RUGGLES,
Brigadier-General, Commanding Department, C. S. Army.

GRENADA, MISS., *June* 19, 1862.

Brigadier-General VILLEPIGUE,
Tallahatchie, Central Railroad:

Is the report that the enemy is falling back from Holly Springs confirmed? Take prompt and vigorous measures to burn all cotton in advance of your position. If you need more force inform me.

DANIEL RUGGLES,
Brigadier-General, Commanding.

IN THE WOODS,
Two-and-a-half miles from Buzzard Roost, June 19, 1862.

Colonel BRADFUTE:

Yesterday General Smith's division went east to Cherokee Station From some cause it turned back, and is now encamped between Big Bear Creek and Iuka. The enemy are running the train east. The train went up yesterday loaded with provisions and ammunition. No box-cars—all flat cars. The enemy have built a floating bridge at Florence, Ala., across the Tennessee River.

Smith's division passed back from Cherokee about 10 o'clock yesterday, since which time no Yankees have been seen going east except those on the railroad train, which went up at 3 o'clock on the 18th. The enemy say they are going to release their prisoners, and a part are going to Chattanooga and some to take Richmond. They have sent on wagons without number, a great many cannon, and some few siege guns. They take all their sick with them. They leave nothing at depots.

Yours, truly,

L. E. HILL.

FULTON, MISS., *June* 19, 1862.

Colonel KIMMEL:

Captain Hill sends me another note. Generals Buell's, Nelson's, and Crittenden's divisions have gone east under a forced march, and the whole army is leaving. They cannot stand the climate. General Smith's brigade, or division, was marching east, but was suddenly ordered back to guard their ammunition and stores. Captain Hill is of the opinion that the entire Federal army is moving east, leaving only a few men to guard and keep up appearances. I have heard from citizens that there are no troops west of Jacinto except scouting parties, and only 1,000 cavalry at Jacinto. Captain Davenport was in my office this morning and reported that he was just from the vicinity where he had been gathering up his company—recruited before the Federals came in the country—and says that the people, who are reliable, told him that all the Federals had left Booneville, Rienzi, and Corinth. It comes from reliable authority that the enemy have their property scattered from Iuka to Eastport. Captain Roddey reports 250 Federals at Frankfort, Franklin County, Alabama, raising a flag. I will have men in from Jacinto and Booneville to-night or early in the morning.

W. R. BRADFUTE,
Colonel, Commanding.

TUPELO, MISS., June 19, 1862.

Hon. GEORGE W. RANDOLPH,
Secretary of War :

The completion of the Mississippi and Alabama Railroad from Meridian to Selma is a military necessity. The appropriation made by Congress will effect it in a short time. Can the money be had, or may I use military funds ?

BRAXTON BRAGG.

RICHMOND, VA., June 19, 1862.

Gov. JOHN J. PETTUS, Jackson, Miss. :

My efforts to provide for the military wants of your section have been sadly frustrated. General Bragg was ordered to go immediately to Jackson, and I did not doubt would reach there by Monday last; but after he received the order General Beauregard turned over the command of the retreating army to him and left on surgeon's certificate for the benefit of his health. Last evening this became known to me, and I sent a telegram directing General Van Dorn to proceed with all possible dispatch to assume the command of the Department of Southern Mississippi and East Louisiana. I hope he will answer the popular desire. The arms referred to in a former dispatch were 1,000 Enfield rifles. By some misunderstanding it is supposed they were sent from Mobile to Corinth. To repair the evil a like number of muskets were sent to you two days since. A special agent is to leave to-morrow evening with 1,300 muskets and about 175 long-range rifles, to be delivered to General M. L. Smith, Vicksburg, route by Mobile and Jackson. Some arms (said to be on their way from Grenada to Gainesville) have been directed to be stopped at Jackson. I wish you would give any aid which may be required in repairing and cleaning them. The heroic determination of my neighbors gives assurance that you will use effectively all the means you possess. I would they were larger, and earnestly wish it were consistent for me to be with you in the struggle.

JEFFERSON DAVIS.

GRENADA, MISS., June 19, 1862.

Governor PETTUS:

It is reported that the enemy is retreating from Holly Springs. You will please suspend the movement of troops until we get further information.

DANIEL RUGGLES,
Brigadier-General.

GRENADA, *June* 19, 1862.

Capt. J. H. EDMONDSON, *Senatobia, Miss.*:

Do not burn the bridge over the Coldwater until compelled to do so by a large force of the enemy. General Thompson will communicate my orders. Destroy cotton in advance endangered by the enemy. Consult General Thompson about bridges on common roads. Answer.

DANIEL RUGGLES,
Brigadier-General, Commanding.

HEADQUARTERS WESTERN DEPARTMENT,
Tupelo, June 19, 1862.

Maj. Gen. EARL VAN DORN,
Commanding Army of the West, near Tupelo:

GENERAL: I am instructed to convey to you the orders of the President that you shall repair, "with all possible dispatch, to assume command of the Department of South Mississippi and East Louisiana." You will be regarded, the President further directs, as "temporarily detached" from your present command.

Respectfully, general, your obedient servant,

THOMAS JORDAN,
Assistant Adjutant-General.

JUNE 19, 1862.

Captain RODDEY:

DEAR SIR: I have ascertained that Wood, McCook, Crittenden, and Nelson command divisions instead of brigades. Wood's division came to Iuka June 4, remained a few days, and then went in the direction of Decatur, Ala. McCook's division came to Iuka June 11, then went across the river at Eastport. Crittenden's division came to Iuka on the 13th and crossed the river at Eastport. Nelson's division came on the 14th; part left on the 17th in the same direction. They drew in their pickets and were to remove entire on the 18th, but the order was countermanded, and the pickets posted out farther on the 18th than they had been before, and that part of Nelson's division which had left was ordered back, and Wood's division was also ordered back. There was considerable stir and bustle among the officers on the 18th; could not learn the cause. The enemy is getting large amounts of stores at Iuka. He is hiring citizens to haul, paying $5 per day for two-horse wagons and $10 per day for four-horse wagons and teams. He is buying cotton, paying 15 cents per pound. The enemy is doing us great harm in that part of the country by making friends of nearly all the citizens. Numbers have taken the oath of allegiance. Conscript soldiers are released on parole of honor. One or two men of Iuka are going to Paducah to get stocks of groceries, &c., in a few days. There were no soldiers stationed at Burnsville June 18.

Respectfully,

J. T. WILLIAMS.

SPECIAL ORDERS, } HEADQUARTERS ARMY OF THE WEST,
No. 118. } *Priceville, June* 19, 1862.

I. Forrest's cavalry command will prepare to march immediately with ten days' rations. The commanding officer will report in person at these headquarters for orders.

II. Brig. Gen. W. N. R. Beall, having reported for duty with the Army of the West, will report for duty to General D. H. Maury, commanding division.

*   *   *   *   *   *   *

By order of Maj. Gen. Earl Van Dorn :

M. M. KIMMEL,
Major and Assistant Adjutant-General.

GRENADA, *June* 20, 1862.

Brigadier-General VILLEPIGUE, *Tallahatchie Bridge:*

You will retain your present advanced position. Colonel Jackson has been ordered to report to you for orders.

When shall you want rations ?

DANIEL RUGGLES,
Brigadier-General, Commanding.

RICHMOND, VA., *June* 20, 1862.

General BRAXTON BRAGG, *Tupelo, Miss.:*

Your dispatch informing me that General Beauregard had turned over the command to you and left for Mobile on surgeon's certificate was duly received. You are assigned permanently to the command of the department, as will be more formally notified to you by the Secretary of War. You will correspond directly and receive orders and instructions from the Government in relation to your future operations.

JEFFERSON DAVIS.

GRENADA, MISS., *June* 20, 1862.

General BRAGG, *Tupelo, Miss. :*

Shall I hold the line of the Tallahatchie ? I have directed General Villepigue to remain at Tallahatchie. I shall send additional force to cover Panola. Government stores and many millions of property are involved in the protection of this line. Governor Pettus will give me minute-men and militia—some 3,000. Answer.

DANIEL RUGGLES,
Brigadier-General, Commanding.

TUPELO, MISS., *June* 20, 1862.
(Received 5.30 p. m.)

General RUGGLES :

Not only hold line but take offensive. General Villepigue will have force enough to take Memphis; and, if he can, ought to do it. Canton is in General Lovell's department (now General Van Dorn's), who is authorized to call upon you at his discretion for troops. Defend with all available means at all hazards. Inform and confer with General Van Dorn, now *en route* for Jackson.

BRAXTON BRAGG.

YAZOO CITY, MISS., *June* 20, 1862.

Brig. Gen. DANIEL RUGGLES, C. S. Army,
Commanding Grenada, &c. :

SIR : May I, with reference to the common defense, venture to call your attention to that portion of the Mississippi River from Helena toward Vicksburg, on the left bank, as suitable for the operations of light guns against the contemplated commerce of the enemy? There are many deep bends on this portion of the river, across which light batteries might pass and compel an enemy's boat to sustain double attacks from the same guns. The roads from now until December will be good along the river, and the country between the Mississippi, Sunflower, and Yazoo Rivers impenetrable to pursuit, offers safe asylum to small parties should the enemy land in force. A company of mounted men, to act in conjunction with a light battery, would, I think, make the portion of the river referred to very unsafe to any vessels except ships of war.

I am, very respectfully, yours.

ISAAC N. BROWN,
Lieutenant, C. S. Navy.

———

TUPELO, *June* 20, 1862.

Brig. Gen. D. W. ADAMS,
Commanding Columbus, Miss. :

GENERAL : Your communication of the 15th instant has been laid before the commander of the forces, who instructs me to reply as follows :

Railroad agents, conductors, and other employés must not be arrested or taken away from their offices or trains under the circumstances you report. In all such instances the name of the delinquent will be reported to these headquarters with specific allegations and a brief of the evidence that can unquestionably be adduced against him. Any other course is deemed prejudicial to the effective administration of the road at this time.

In the matter of the character of works with which Columbus is to be covered, the general telegraphed you, but I am instructed to say he wishes constructed a line of detached redoubts, properly placed. Captain Harris will from his experience be able to give the best locations practicable. He also knows General Beauregard's views as to the best character of detached works for the purposes in view.

The garrison for the defense of your works will not be less than that now under your command.

Respectfully, your obedient servant,

THOMAS JORDAN.

———

SPECIAL ORDERS, ⎰ HEADQUARTERS WESTERN DEPARTMENT,
No. 88. ⎱ *Tupelo, Miss, June* 20, 1862.

* * * * * * *

III. Major-General Van Dorn, commanding Department of Southern Mississippi and East Louisiana, is authorized, at his discretion, to order for service within the limits of his department the troops of this department on or near the line of the Mississippi Central Railroad.

IV. Brig. Gen. W. N. R. Beall is hereby relieved from duty in the Army of the West, and will report to Major-General Van Dorn, at Jackson, Miss.

    *   *   *   *   *   *   *

By command of General Bragg:

[GEORGE WM. BRENT,]
Acting Chief of Staff.

GENERAL ORDERS, }   HEADQUARTERS ARMY OF THE WEST,
No. 47.   }   *Priceville, Miss., June 20, 1862.*

Having been ordered by the President to assume command of the Department of Southern Mississippi and East Louisiana the under-signed relinquishes command temporarily of the Army of the West.

EARL VAN DORN,
Major-General.

GENERAL ORDERS, }   HEADQUARTERS ARMY OF THE WEST,
No. 1.   }   *Priceville, Miss., June 20, 1862.*

As senior officer present I assume command of the Army of the West.

J. P. McCOWN,
Major-General.

GENERAL ORDERS, } HEADQUARTERS WESTERN DEPARTMENT,
No. 78.   }   *Tupelo, June 20, 1862.*

I. The commander of the forces desires to call the attention of the army to the worthy conduct of Private E. J. Kinney, Company —, Fourth Kentucky Volunteers, in the preservation of public property and army stores at Booneville Station during an attack upon our transportation train at that place by a cavalry force of the enemy on the 30th ultimo. A suitable badge of distinction will be awarded him at some future day, to be announced in orders.

By command of General Bragg:

GEORGE WM. BRENT,
Acting Chief of Staff.

HEADQUARTERS ARMY OF THE MISSISSIPPI,
Tupelo, Miss., June 21, 1862.

Brigadier-General PRESTON,
   Commanding Reserve Corps, Army of the Mississippi:

GENERAL: From information received and considered reliable, the general commanding deems it imprudent for you to advance beyond the Tallahatchie River, as the enemy is in considerable force with large re-enforcements at Grand Junction and Memphis. You will therefore extend your line to and hold that river.

The general further directs that you will hold your command in readiness to execute any orders received from Major-General Van Dorn, who has succeeded Major-General Lovell in command. It is reported that the enemy will soon make a demonstration in force either against Vicksburg or Canton, and all available troops will be needed.

Respectfully, general, your obedient servant,

GEO. G. GARNER,
Assistant Adjutant-General.

GRENADA, *June* 21, 1862.

General VILLEPIGUE, *Abbeville, Miss.*:

Hold 2,000 men with four guns at Oxford ready to march to-night to Panola, if ordered. Send two companies of cavalry under a field officer to Panola, without delay, to co operate with General Thompson at Senatobia. Answer.

DANIEL RUGGLES,
Brigadier-General, C. S. Army.

GENERAL ORDERS,) HEADQUARTERS ARMY OF THE WEST,
No. 2.   (*Priceville, Miss., June* 21, 1862.

The major-general commanding temporarily the Army of the West announces the following staff to the command :

Adjutant-General's Department.—Maj. H. S. Bradford, assistant adjutant-general; Capt. B. N. Mathes, acting assistant adjutant-general.

Aides-de-Camp.—Capts. Henry S. Foote, jr., C. S. Army, and George T. Smoote.

Inspector-General's Department.—Capt. Batt Barrow, inspector.

Ordnance Department.—Capt. J. A. Allison, ordnance officer.

Quartermaster's and Commissary Departments.—Maj. W. E. Dyer, assistant quartermaster.

Medical Department.—Maj. Gus. B. Thornton, surgeon.

Artillery.—Col. George W. McCown, chief of artillery.

J. P. McCOWN,
Major-General.

GENERAL ORDERS,) HEADQUARTERS SPECIAL DEPARTMENT,
No. 9.   (*Grenada, Miss., June* 22, 1862.

I. In conformity with Special Orders, No. 5, dated at Headquarters Mississippi State Troops, Major-General's Office, Canton, June 14, 1862, Brig. Gen. M. T. Berry, or, in his absence, the commanders of regiments and battalions of his brigade will call out the minute-men of his brigade for immediate service in the field.

II. These minute-men will meet on twenty-four hours' notice at their respective county seats, or at such other more convenient points as may be designated by their commanders, having in view concentration in advance of the Tallahatchie River, on the great railroad thoroughfare, to resist and impede the progress of the enemy.

III. These troops will supply their own arms and make requisition on the adjutant-general of the State for ammunition to the extent of 50 rounds per man, and their subsistence will be purchased in their respective districts by competent officers belonging to the respective battalions.

IV. Commanders of battalions and companies will report immediately their organization, strength, station, and outfit to their brigadier-general or other commander, and send a copy of each report to the assistant adjutant-general at these headquarters.

V. The general commanding this special department is sensible that no appeal is necessary to the Mississippians in the defense of their families and their firesides, their Household Gods and their native land against insolent invaders engaged in a barbarous and fanatical crusade.

By command of Brigadier-General Ruggles :

L. D. SANDIDGE,
Actg. Asst. Adjt. and Insp. Gen., C. S. Army.

Abstract from Weekly Return of the Army of the Mississippi, General Braxton Bragg commanding, June 22, 1862.

Command.	Present.		Total present and absent.	Remarks.
	Effective total.	Total.		
First (Polk's) Corps:				Five batteries.
First (Clark's) Division	3,200	3,831	6,936	
Second (Cheatham's) Division	4,730	5,490	8,538	
Cavalry	43	46	69	
Second (Bragg's) Corps:				Seven batteries.
First (Withers') Division	7,995	9,992	16,936	
Second (Anderson's) Division	7,316	8,393	13,052	
Third (Hardee's) Corps	8,606	10,625	16,025	Five batteries.
Reserve (Breckinridge's) Corps				Not reported.
Grand total	31,890	38,397	61,556	

Organization of the Army of the Mississippi, commanded by General Braxton Bragg, June 22, 1862.

FIRST CORPS.

Maj. Gen. LEONIDAS POLK commanding.

First Division.

Brig. Gen. CHARLES CLARK commanding.

First Brigade, Colonel Russell commanding.

Second Brigade, Brig. Gen. A. P. Stewart commanding.

Second Division.

Maj. Gen. B. F. CHEATHAM commanding.

First Brigade, Brig. Gen. D. S. Donelson commanding.

Second Brigade, Brig. Gen. George Maney commanding.

Maxey's brigade, Brig. Gen. S. B. Maxey commanding.

ATTACHED.

One company of cavalry.

SECOND CORPS.

General BRAXTON BRAGG commanding.

First Division.

Brig. Gen. J. M. WITHERS commanding.

First Brigade, Brig. Gen. Frank Gardner commanding.

Second Brigade, Brig. Gen. J. R. Chalmers commanding.

Third Brigade, Brig. Gen. John K. Jackson commanding.

Fourth Brigade, Col. A. M. Manigault commanding.

Second Division.

Brig. Gen. J. P. ANDERSON commanding.

First Brigade, Col. R. A. Smith commanding.

Second Brigade, Col. A. Reichard commanding.

Third Brigade, Brig. Gen. W. H. T. Walker commanding.

DETACHED SERVICE.

1st Regiment Louisiana Infantry.

THIRD CORPS.

Maj. Gen. W. J. HARDEE commanding.

First Brigade, Col. St. John R. Liddell commanding.
Second Brigade, Brig. Gen. P. R. Cleburne commanding.
Third Brigade, Brig. Gen. S. A. M. Wood commanding.
Fourth Brigade, Brig. Gen. J. S. Marmaduke commanding.
Fifth Brigade, Col. A. T. Hawthorn commanding.

RESERVE CORPS.

Maj. Gen. J. C. BRECKINRIDGE commanding.

(Not reported.)

Number of batteries in First Corps 5
Number of batteries in Second Corps 7
Number of batteries in Third Corps 5

Total number of batteries in the Army of the Mississippi 17

[JUNE 22–23, 1862.—For Bragg to Cooper, and Randolph's reply, see Series I, Vol. XVI, Part II, pp. 701, 702.]

TUPELO, MISS., *June* 23, 1862.
(Received at Richmond, Va., June 24, 1862.)

General S. COOPER:

Please define the limits of my command. Is it the Western Department or Department No. 2, as defined in General Orders, No. 39, Paragraph III?

BRAXTON BRAGG.

(Copies sent to the President, Secretary of War, and General Lee June 25.)

GRENADA, MISS., *June* 23, 1862.

General BRAGG, *Tupelo, Miss.:*

Troops all forwarded on requisition of General Van Dorn. Sherman has 25,000 at Grand Junction. General Thompson busy with enemy at Coldwater. Can you send me 5,000 men to defend Tallahatchie?

DANIEL RUGGLES,
Brigadier-General.

GRENADA, MISS., *June* 23, 1862.

General VAN DORN, *Vicksburg, Miss.:*

Colonel Jackson's cavalry and Colonel Stewart's field artillery are indispensable here. Can you do without them?

DANIEL RUGGLES,
Brigadier-General.

June 23, 1862.

General M. Jeff. Thompson, *Panola:*

General: Withdraw most of your force to Panola. Let the trains bring down freight at once. Let the freight cars and passenger cars, excepting one or two, remain under the orders of Colonel Hurt, military superintendent of transportation. It is a case of urgency.

DANIEL RUGGLES,
Brigadier-General, C. S. Army.

HEADQUARTERS WESTERN DEPARTMENT,
Tupelo, June 23, 1862.

And. W. McKee, *Agent Subsistence Department:*

Sir: Your communication of the 15th instant to Lieutenant-Colonel Lee has been submitted to the general commanding, who directs me to say that he has found your suggestions in most respects practicable and promising valuable military results, but the region in which the operations are proposed is not in his command, and therefore he is unable to give the proper orders in the case.

Major-General Van Dorn, whose headquarters are at Jackson, is the proper officer to address in all matters affecting military operations in Louisiana.

General Hindman will be instructed not to permit his agents to interfere with the bacon or beef cattle you are collecting.

Your action touching the transmission of food for the suffering poor in New Orleans is approved, but great vigilance must be observed to prevent our people in West Louisiana from being the dupes in this connection of the present Federal commander at New Orleans, whose character and recent conduct must lead us to distrust his honorable performance of any promise or stipulation. However, this matter really comes within the province of the Governor of the State (who should be freely consulted) and of General Van Dorn.

The general is pleased to hear of your successful ferriage across the Mississippi of so many beef cattle.

Respectfully, your obedient servant,

THOMAS JORDAN,
Chief of Staff and Assistant Adjutant-General.

HEADQUARTERS WESTERN DEPARTMENT,
Tupelo, June 23, 1862.

General C. G. Dahlgren, *La Fayette, Miss.:*

General: As your recent command was exercised within limits now embraced within the department under command at present of Major-General Van Dorn, I have been instructed to transmit your valuable report of the 3d instant to him for his information on many points therein.

As to any expenses incurred by you in the discharge of duties intrusted to you in orders from these headquarters, I am directed to say that if the proper accounts are made out in duplicate and forwarded here, duly certified to that the property was purchased or the expenses incurred as required by the Treasury regulations, they will be promptly approved and orders given for their immediate payment. It may be well to say that in these accounts care should be taken not to blend expenditures of the subsistence and quartermaster's departments in the same voucher.

The general is heartily sorry to hear such unpromising accounts of the behavior of the people of Adams County, but trusts the panic will pass by speedily, and the inspirations of patriotism, loyalty, and of the manhood of our fathers will resume full sway, sweeping aside the despicable and cheating promptings of selfishness.

Respectfully, your obedient servant,

THOMAS JORDAN,
Chief of Staff.

HEADQUARTERS WESTERN DEPARTMENT,
Tupelo, June 23, 1862.

Capt. E. E. PORTER,
Commanding Partisan Rangers :

CAPTAIN: Your letter of the 17th instant, addressed to General Beauregard, has been read with great satisfaction by the general commanding, who instructs me to say that he entirely approves what you have done in the destruction of cotton and the removal of Government stores and bank assets. Indeed, all your movements appear to have been conducted with energy and judgment.

Send a statement of your expenditures, including subsistence and forage. Immediate attention will be given to it and early arrangements made for reimbursing you. State number and kind of arms you want, and direct your quartermaster to make an estimate of forage and subsistence needed by your command and forward same to this office.

It is the desire of the general commanding that you continue burning cotton as near Grand Junction as possible without too much hazard. There are a number of persons in that neighborhood whose cotton should be burned, among whom is Colonel Leake.

In the matter of medicines, your suggestions are very considerate, and you are hereby authorized to make such arrangements to procure them as you may deem proper. A list of the articles most needed will be furnished you by the medical director as soon as practicable.

It would be well to establish communication with these headquarters by means of an occasional courier.

You are instructed not to destroy any railroad bridges, as the road may be rendered useless to the enemy by frequently firing into trains from places of concealment by small parties of your command or by citizens.

Please forward an early return of the strength of your company to these headquarters, and also a copy of any correspondence with General Beauregard in relation to its organization and duties.

Respectfully, your obedient servant,

THOMAS JORDAN,
Assistant Adjutant-General.

HDQRS. RESERVE CORPS, ARMY OF THE MISSISSIPPI,
Near Abbeville, Miss., June 23, 1862.

Brig. Gen. DANIEL RUGGLES:

GENERAL: Note of yesterday received. The corps under my command is in readiness to move at such time as General Van Dorn may order. It is presumed from your note that the transportation will be by rail. The division quartermaster will proceed at once to ascertain at Abbeville what trains may be had. Transportation for five brigades will be needed, with six or seven days' subsistence, ammunition in boxes, twenty-one field pieces, and the usual camp equipage. I have about 250 wagons and 2,000 animals. If by wagon train, I am now ready to move; if by rail, as soon as the trains arrive. Let your quartermaster report to Maj. A. Boyd, division quartermaster, at these headquarters, as to what transportation can be had.

W. PRESTON,
Brig. Gen., Comdg. Reserve Corps, Army of the Miss.

SPECIAL ORDERS, } HDQRS. FIRST CORPS, ARMY OF THE MISS.,
No. 75.   }   *Camp near Tupelo, Miss., June 23, 1862.*

*   *   *   *   *   *   *

V. Capt. John L. Saffarans, acting commissary of subsistence, is hereby authorized to burn cotton that is in danger of falling into the hands of the enemy and to give certificates to that effect to the owners of the cotton. The certificate must state as briefly as possible the imminence of the danger of the cotton being seized by the enemy, and must state the number of bales, the mark, and weight in pounds, if practicable.

By command of Major-General Polk:

GEORGE WILLIAMSON,
Assistant Adjutant-General.

JUNE 23, 1862.
General WILLIAM PRESTON, *Abbeville:*

General Van Dorn has ordered that your troops proceed with least possible delay to Vicksburg. Copy of last telegram will be furnished. Transportation by rail has been sent you to-night for at least two brigades. Rations have been ordered for ten days. Your mule teams will be disposed of by orders to-morrow morning. Prompt action is necessary.

DANIEL RUGGLES,
Brigadier-General, C. S. Army.

RICHMOND, VA., *June 24, 1862.*
Gov. JOHN J. PETTUS, *Jackson, Miss.:*

Your letter of 11th received. Your request for arms and buck-shot had been complied with to the extent of our power. Have just received some long-range rifles, from which a further supply will be sent. Buck-shot might be supplied from Columbus; to be made if not on hand.

JEFFERSON DAVIS.

TUPELO, *June 24, 1862.*
General VILLEPIGUE:

The commander of the forces directs that as General Ruggles has left the limits of the department you are assigned to the command of the sub-department along the Mississippi Central Railroad and to the last from the Tallahatchie River to the thirty-third parallel of latitude.

THOMAS JORDAN,
Chief of Staff and Assistant Adjutant-General.

MOBILE, ALA., *June* 25, 1862.

General S. COOPER,
  Adjutant-General, C. S. Army, Richmond, Va.:

GENERAL: Inclosed please find the certificate of my physicians, members of my general staff as inspectors, recommending that I should withdraw for awhile from the command of Department No. 2.

This is the third certificate to the same effect I have received from them since my arrival at Jackson, Tenn., but finding or believing that my presence until now was absolutely necessary with the forces under my command I persistently refused to avail myself of their recommendation until the present moment, when I feel that in justice to myself and to the cause I am endeavoring to defend I must take a little rest and retire for awhile from the active scenes of life to which I have been accustomed for the last sixteen months. I will for the present repair to Bladon Springs, Ala., where I will always be ready to obey any orders of the department (regardless of my health) to resume the active duties of the field whenever circumstances will require that I should be so ordered.

Respectfully, your obedient servant,

G. T. BEAUREGARD.
  General, C. S. Army.

———

GENERAL ORDERS, }   HDQRS. ARMY OF THE MISSISSIPPI,
  No. 19.   }   *Tupelo, Miss., June* 25, 1862.

I. Withers' division, Second Corps, is transferred and will constitute the Reserve Corps, Army of the Mississippi.

II. Jones' division will be known as Second Corps, Army of the Missisipi.

By command of General Bragg:

GEO. G. GARNER,
  Assistant Adjutant-General.

———

GENERAL ORDERS, }   HEADQUARTERS DEPARTMENT No. 2,
  No. 80.   }   *Tupelo, Miss., June* 25, 1862.

I. Lieut. Col. R. B. Lee, of subsistence department, at his own request, is relieved from duty as the chief of his department with these headquarters. He will carry with him the thanks of the commander of the forces for his labors as chief of his department of the staff, a position environed by uncommon difficulties and embarrassments. A veteran of forty years, he leaves behind him a justly grateful remembrance of services rendered with that zeal that springs from a long-trained sense of duty, quickened by an ardent patriotism. Colonel Lee will report in person to the Adjutant-General of the Army in Richmond.

II. Maj. John J. Walker, subsistence department, will relieve Lieutenant-Colonel Lee and at once enter upon the duties of the chief of subsistence of this department. He will be obeyed and respected accordingly.

By command of General Bragg:

THOMAS JORDAN,
  Chief of Staff.

SPECIAL ORDERS, } ADJT. AND INSPECTOR-GENERAL'S OFFICE,
No. 146.   }   *Richmond, Va., June 25, 1862.*

*   *   *   *   *   *   *

XVI. Paragraphs II and III, General Orders, No. 39, current series, are so modified that Department No. 2 shall now embrace that portion of its former limits which is east of the Mississippi River, and in addition thereto shall comprise Department No. 1, and have its eastern boundary extended to the line of railroad from Chattanooga via Atlanta to West Point, on the Chattahoochee River, and thence down the Chattahoochee and Apalachicola Rivers to the Gulf of Mexico.*

*   *   *   *   *   *   *

By command of the Secretary of War:

JNO. WITHERS,
Assistant Adjutant-General.

—

GENERAL ORDERS, } WAR DEPT., ADJT. AND INSP. GEN.'S OFFICE,
No. 39.   }   *Richmond, Va., May 26, 1862.*

*   *   *   *   *   *   *

II. The limits of Department No. 1, under command of Major-General Lovell, will hereafter embrace that portion of the State of Mississippi south of the thirty-third parallel and west of Pascagoula and Chickasawha Rivers, including also that part of the State of Louisiana east of the Mississippi River.

III. Department No. 2, under command of General Beauregard, is extended south to the thirty-third parallel east of the Mississippi River, and extending on that parallel to the eastern boundary of Alabama.

*   *   *   *   *   *   *

By command of the Secretary of War:

S. COOPER,
Adjutant and Inspector General.

——

HEADQUARTERS DEPARTMENT No. 2,
Tupelo, June 26, 1862.

General S. COOPER,
Adjutant and Inspector General:

GENERAL: I have to acknowledge the receipt of a telegraph dispatch from the Secretary of War, dated the 21st instant, touching the completion of the railroad connection between Meridian, Miss., and Selma, Ala. That connection is one of such vital military necessity, and so immediately affecting military operations in the department intrusted to me, that I feel it my duty to communicate frankly my views for the information and consideration of the department.

The papers accompanying,† marked A, B, and C, will show conclusively how little the company, unfortunately invested with the privilege of completing this all-important work, have done toward the execution of their contract. Since the passage of the act there has been ample time, under a vigorous management, for the construction of the railroad

---

*See General Orders, No. 50, Adjutant and Inspector General's Office, July 18, 1862, p. 649.

† Not found.

as far as represented practicable at present by the eminent engineer sent by me to carry out what I regarded as the spirit of the act, the intention of Congress, and what I knew to be required for the public defense.

At a time when the Memphis and Charleston Railroad is in possession of the enemy a rail connection of this character is pregnant with too many advantages in military operations to be left to the mortgaged means of a small and unreliable railroad corporation. To trust the work to such feeble, inefficient hands may result in incalculable mischief. And in view of impending military conditions, I earnestly protest against the inevitable delay that must and the irreparable injury that may ensue if they are relied on.

I would appeal to the spirit of the act of Congress recognizing the military necessity for the immediate completion of this unfinished link in our interior line of railroads. Congress assuredly aimed to have that completion made as soon as possible; but, misinformed and misled, doubtless gave the work to a railroad company as the means best calculated to that end, for certainly the legislature of the country could never be brought to such prostitution as that of intentionally giving a job to a corporation.

I would therefore carry out the spirit of the act in question. I would have no more precious days, weeks, or months wasted with this incapable company—would wait not a moment longer for the execution of mortgage contracts; for meantime it may be too late for all practical purposes. Mobile may fall after the manner of water-approached places. Our lines of communication with the east would then be cut off, and the true expectations of Congress be frustrated.

I cannot present in too strong language the mischief that must result from further reliance on this company. By their past failure they ought to be judged, and the work should at once be carried on by the Government, under military control from these headquarters, by engineers knowing the resources of the country and by none other.

Respectfully, your obedient servant,

[BRAXTON BRAGG.]

TUPELO, MISS., *June* 26, 1862.
(Received at Richmond, Va., June 28, 1862.)

Hon. GEORGE W. RANDOLPH,
Secretary of War:

The following dispatch just received from the president of Alabama and Mississippi River Railroad:

DEMOPOLIS, ALA., *June* 26, 1862.

General BRAXTON BRAGG:

To finish our road we must have military and pecuniary assistance. The board will render your officers all the aid in their power, and we are much pleased with the judicious arrangements of Major Fleming, whose return to the road would give great satisfaction. Major Goodwin is also favorably known in this country. Our contract with the War Department is for the faithful application of money loaned and its repayment.

G. G. GRIFFIN,
President Alabama and Mississippi River Railroad.

BRAXTON BRAGG,
General, &c.

HEADQUARTERS DEPARTMENT No. 2,
Tupelo, Miss., June 27, 1862.

Pursuant to the orders of the President I assume the permanent command of the forces in this department.

The weighty duties, the grave responsibilities of the place, the momentous issues impending, and my high sense of the eminent capacities of the distinguished leader and soldier whom I have succeeded make me accept the position with unfeigned reluctance. Relying, however, on the justice of the cause of an invaded people, in the zeal and skill of subordinate officers of all ranks, and confidently depending on the unswerving bravery, devotion, and individual intelligence of a soldiery fighting on their own soil, at the very doors of their own homes, in defense of all worth living for or that has ever inspired men to heroism, I enter hopefully on my duties.

But, soldiers, to secure the legitimate results of all your heavy sacrifices, which have brought this army together, to infuse that unity and cohesion essential for a resolute resistance to the wicked invasion of our country, and to give to serried ranks force, impetus, and direction for driving the invader beyond our borders, be assured discipline at all times and obedience to the orders of your officers on all points, as a sacred duty, an act of patriotism, is of absolute necessity. Without this spirit the bravest army must sink soon into an armed rabble, as impotent for defense as of offense. I shall proudly hope to see this spirit in the brave men of Shiloh and of Elkhorn; hope to see them as soldierly and obedient to necessary authority as becomes brave men called to arms to battle for the right to live in independence.

Soldiers, great events are impending; an insolent but wary foe has invested the seat of your Government. Your brethren of the Armies of the Potomac and of the Peninsula stand steadfastly to their posts to meet the desperate conflict which must soon come. I doubt not victory will be with them. Others of your countrymen, under the lead of Jackson and Ewell, in the Valley of Virginia, have recently shed imperishable renown on our arms, and shown what a small, obedient, disciplined volunteer army can do.

A few more days of needful preparation and organization and I shall give your banners to the breeze—shall lead you to emulate the soldiers of the Confederacy in the East, and with the confident trust that you will gain additional honors to those you have already won on other fields. But be prepared to undergo privation and labor with cheerfulness and alacrity.

BRAXTON BRAGG,
General, Commanding.

SPECIAL ORDERS, }   HEADQUARTERS DEPARTMENT No. 2,
      No. 96.   }   *Tupelo, Miss., June* 27, 1862.

*   *   *   *   *   *   *

II. Major-General McCown will repair with all practicable dispatch with his division of the Army of the West to Chattanooga and report for duty to Maj. Gen. E. Kirby Smith.

III. The quartermaster's department will make arrangements for the speedy movement of these troops hence to Mobile, and thence by the most expeditious route.

*   *   *   *   *   *   *

By command of General Bragg:

THOMAS JORDAN,
Assistant Adjutant-General.

HEADQUARTERS WESTERN ARMY,
Near Tupelo, Miss., June 28, 1862.
Maj. GEORGE G. GARNER,
 Assistant Adjutant-General:

MAJOR : I have the honor to transmit to you (herewith inclosed) the consolidated statement* of ordnance and ordnance stores at Confederate States Arsenal at Columbus and at ordnance depots at Tupelo, Verona, and Okolona, Miss.

The arsenal at Columbus being in its infancy the work necessary for public service is not at present prosecuted with the result adequate to emergency. At armory shop is employed 32 gunsmiths, 16 stockers, and 8 machinists for boring barrels and making and repairing tools; with this force, 50 arms a day can be repaired fit for service. At saddlery, 40 saddlers and harness-makers are employed; they are occupied in repairing artillery harness and in making new. At laboratory, 70 hands are employed; with this force can be manufactured about 20,000 cartridges for small-arms and 500 rounds of ammunition, fixed, in one day. The machinery for making percussion-caps was at the time of my inspection in bad order, undergoing repairs, and in a short time the making of caps will be satisfactory, if only a supply of nitric acid can be procured. I was informed that the operatives employed are quitting work for reason of enormous prices charged for their boarding. I represented the case to General Adams, but he gave me no encouragement to remedy the evil, only to replace them by details from the army. If the views of the commanding general are favorable I should respectfully request that as many as can be found in the army—such as blacksmiths, turners, saddlers, and carpenters—be detailed from the army and ordered for duty at arsenal.

H. OLADOWSKI.

RICHMOND, VA., June 29, 1862.

General BRAGG, *Tupelo, Miss.:*

Your department is extended so as to embrace that part of Louisiana east of the Mississippi, the entire States of Mississippi and Alabama, and the portion of Georgia and Florida west of the Chattahoochee and Apalachicola Rivers.† You can take charge of the Selma and Meridian connection, but the only funds appropriated to the work are the $400,000 authorized by Congress to be loaned to the Alabama and Mississippi Railroad Company. They can disburse it under your directions. After two days' fighting McClellan is in a critical position. Large re-enforcements are expected from the West. Strike the moment an opportunity offers.

G. W. RANDOLPH,
Secretary of War.

HEADQUARTERS DEPARTMENT No. 2,
Tupelo, Miss., June 29, 1862.
General S. COOPER,
 Adjutant and Inspector General, Richmond, Va.:

GENERAL : Several embarrassing questions meet me at the outset in assuming the command which has so unexpectedly devolved upon me.

---

* Not found.

† See Special Orders, No. 146, Adjutant and Inspector General's Office, June 25, 1862, p. 624, and General Orders, No. 50, July 18, 1862, p. 649.

First is the vital matter of subsistence.   Were supplies ample in our rear their transportation as wanted would be a most difficult affair with but the facilities of a single-track railway, but added to that is the fact that we have only about sixty days' rations of salt meat available, with no prospect of any addition.   The supply of fresh meat is very limited and precarious, having to be drawn from a country with little or no surplus.   The resources of Texas having been cut off before we received what was promised from there, nothing remains but to look to the grazing-grounds of Southern Alabama, Georgia, and Florida.   An agent dispatched thither to procure beef cattle it is ascertained has been superseded by one sent by the Commissary-General.   If we are to depend on the new agent I must suggest as prudent that he should take early means of gaining accurate knowledge of our wants and where those wants exist.   Under every aspect I can but look to the future with concern.

Transportation is another matter of the gravest moment.   So long as our operations were confined to the lines of the railroads in our possession we could dispense with large supply trains; but to make a forward movement now (and I hope no other will again be necessary) roads and wagons must be substituted.   Our present supply of these means of mobility is only adequate for the baggage of the troops.   Every effort is, however, being made to increase our means of transportation, and I shall trust that the sacrificing, intelligent patriotism of our people will soon and in time make up the deficiency.   No movements, however favorable the opportunity, can be made without it.   The country, I may add, between us and the Tennessee River is entirely destitute of any supplies.   What our own troops had left has been seized by the enemy. We must, therefore, move full-handed until we can reach his depots, which we know to be well supplied.

The next great want of this army is that of proper commanders for its sub-divisions.   Since the battle of Shiloh (where we lost many of our best officers) the elective feature of the conscript law has driven from the service the best who remained, and to a great extent has demoralized the troops.   So many of our general officers have been absent, wounded or sick, that it has been quite difficult to keep up any organization, especially as the whole number attached was short of the real wants of the service.   Many recommendations made were not ratified, and some general officers appointed or promoted without recommendations from this quarter are only incumbrances and would be better out of the way.   Of all the major-generals, indeed, in this army now present, since the transfer of Van Dorn, Breckinridge, and Hindman, but one (Hardee) can now be regarded as a suitable commander of that grade.   Among the junior brigadiers we have some excellent material, but it is comparatively useless, being overshadowed.   Could the Department by any wholesome exercise of power or policy relieve this army from a part of this dead-weight it would surely give confidence to the troops and add much to our efficiency.   I acknowledge the difficulties in the way and the delicacy of the measure, but the safety of our cause may depend on it.

Recommendations for promotions and appointments are inclosed,* to which the speedy attention of the Department is invited.

Respectfully, your obedient servant,

BRAXTON BRAGG,
General, Commanding.

---

* Not found.

RICHMOND, VA., *June* 30, 1862.

General BRAGG, *Tupelo, Miss., via Mobile, Ala.*:

In looking at my dispatch to you of yesterday I find that I stated the appropriation to the Selma and Meridian connection to be $400,000. I should have said $150,000. The act of Congress requires it to be advanced to the Alabama and Mississippi Railroad Company, who are to give security for its faithful application. It will be necessary, therefore, for me to pay it to them, and they must disburse it under your directions. I have so informed them, and requested them to send on their mortgage and an agent to draw the money.

G. W. RANDOLPH,
Secretary of War.

———

TUPELO, MISS., *June* 30, 1862.

Hon. GEORGE W. RANDOLPH,
Secretary of War:

No troops going east from here but Buell's command. Twenty-five thousand crossing the Tennessee at Tuscumbia and moving by Huntsville toward Chattanooga. Want of transportation holds me in check. Am sending a small division to East Tennessee.

BRAXTON BRAGG.

———

HEADQUARTERS ARMY OF THE MISSISSIPPI,
Tupelo, Miss., June 30, 1862.

Brigadier-General CHALMERS, *Commanding Cavalry:*

GENERAL: In accordance with your suggestion the general commanding has directed the Reserve Corps to move early to-morrow by the most direct route via Ellistown. It will take three days for infantry to make the march—about 45 miles from here. He wishes you to make a corresponding move with the cavalry, say 1,200 or 1,500, via Blackland, striking any enemy there and brushing him away, and by a feint create the impression that you are after Rienzi; then suddenly make for Ripley, but in rear of the enemy, so that he cannot retreat on Rienzi; and should he attempt to reach Grand Junction you must push him with great vigor, and compel him if possible to give us battle. Should he entirely escape us you may possibly convert the expedition into something useful by pushing on to the Memphis and Charleston Railroad and breaking it up, as well as destroying bridges. You will receive further instructions from Brigadier-General Withers, who will command the expedition, but much is expected from your known intelligence and zeal in the conducting of the cavalry operations.

Respectfully, general, your obedient servant,

GEO. G. GARNER,
Assistant Adjutant-General.

———

GENERAL ORDERS, }   HDQRS. SECOND BRIG., RESERVE CORPS,
No. 61.   }   *In Camp near Tupelo, Miss., June* 30, 1862.

Col. R. A. Smith relieves Col. T. W. White, and hereby assumes command of this brigade. The various staff officers will continue to discharge the duties of their respective positions.

R. A. SMITH,
Colonel.

TUPELO, MISS., *June* 30, 1862.

General GEORGE W. RANDOLPH,
          Secretary of War:

Your dispatch about General Preston's staff was received and sent to him for information, as I replied. He is with Breckinridge's division. Was at Vicksburg. Will inform you as soon as he replies. Bombardment at Vicksburg for three days. No harm done our batteries. About forty vessels are below; if they land, Van Dorn will defeat them. Your news is most exciting. I will start immediately to threaten, and, if possible, will attack. A part of Buell's force is still this side of Tennessee.

BRAXTON BRAGG,
General, Commanding.

Field Return of the Confederate forces commanded by General Braxton Bragg, July 1, 1862.*

Command	Present											Absent								Present and absent	
	For duty		Sick		Extra duty		In arrest		Effective total	Total	Aggregate	Detached duty		With leave		Without leave		Sick		Total	Aggregate
	Officers	Enlisted men	Officers	Enlisted men	Officers	Enlisted men	Officers	Enlisted men				Officers	Enlisted men	Officers	Enlisted men	Officers	Enlisted men	Officers	Enlisted men		
INFANTRY.																					
Army of the Mississippi	2,375	27,935	442	7,417	79	2,457	24	144	30,536	37,953	40,873	189	2,828	305	6,247	37	1,948	307	9,300	62,776	66,484
Army of the West	823	8,867	125	2,637	25	774	2	31	9,672	12,909	13,284	46	1,110	122	4,505	6	359			18,283	19,432
At Columbus	152	1,905	53	1,438	3	209	1	13	2,127	3,565	3,774	26	404	43	1,267	1	80		4	5,820	5,599
Total	3,350	38,707	620	11,492	107	3,440	27	188	42,335	53,827	57,931	211	3,842	470	12,019	44	2,387	307	9,304	86,879	91,515
ARTILLERY.																					
Army of the Mississippi	58	1,551		195		37		2	1,590	1,785	1,843	12	75	11	251		99		201	2,411	2,500
Army of the West	38	675	3	65	2	41		2	718	783	824	8	64	10	113	1	16	8		976	1,036
At Columbus	28	469		118		11	1		480	598	629		25	4	107		5			735	770
Total	124	2,695	3	378	2	89	1	4	2,788	3,166	3,296	20	164	25	471	1	120	8	201	4,122	4,306
Cavalry	19	265	1	44		4	1	1	270	314	334	18	171	2	165		31		7	688	728
Grand total	3,493	41,667	624	11,914	109	3,533	28	193	45,393	57,307	61,561	249	4,177	497	12,655	45	2,538	315	9,512	91,189	96,549

* Original was inclosure to Col. W. P. Johnston's report of July 15, 1862. See siege of Corinth, &c.

NOTE.—Differences in totals and aggregates are accounted for thus: Army of the Mississippi, arrival of new regiments; Army of the West, McCown's division leave for Chattanooga. This return shows force at Columbus, Miss. Returns from cavalry not handed in owing to the distance they picket from department headquarters.

Respectfully submitted.

BRAXTON BRAGG,
General, Commanding.

Confederate States forces, General Braxton Bragg, commanding Army of the Mississippi, June 30, 1862.

FIRST ARMY CORPS.

Maj. Gen. L. POLK commanding.

FIRST DIVISION.

Brig. Gen. C. CLARK.

First Brigade.	Second Brigade.
Col. R. M. RUSSELL.	Brig. Gen. A. P. STEWART.
12th Tennessee.	13th Arkansas.
13th Tennessee.	4th Tennessee.
47th Tennessee.	5th Tennessee.
154th Tennessee.	31st Tennessee.
Bankhead's battery.	33d Tennessee.
	Stanford's battery.

SECOND DIVISION.

Maj. Gen. B. F. CHEATHAM.

First Brigade.	Second Brigade.
Brig. Gen. D. S. DONELSON.	Brig. Gen. GEORGE MANEY.
8th Tennessee.	1st Tennessee.
15th Tennessee.	6th Tennessee.
16th Tennessee.	9th Tennessee.
51st Tennessee.	27th Tennessee.
Carnes' battery.	Smith's battery.

DETACHED BRIGADE.

Brig. Gen. S. B. MAXEY.

41st Georgia.
24th Mississippi.
9th Texas.
Eldridge's battery.

SECOND ARMY CORPS.

Maj. Gen. SAMUEL JONES commanding.

First Brigade.	Second Brigade.
Brigadier-General ANDERSON.	Col. A. REICHARD.
25th Louisiana.	45th Alabama.
30th Mississippi.	11th Louisiana.
37th Mississippi.	16th Louisiana.
41st Mississippi.	18th Louisiana.
Florida and Confederate Battalion [Battalion 1st Florida and Confederate Guards Response Battalion].	19th Louisiana.
	20th Louisiana.
Slocomb's battery.	Burnet's battery.

Third Brigade.

Brigadier-General WALKER.

1st Arkansas.
13th Louisiana.
21st Louisiana.
Crescent, Louisiana.
Independent Tennessee.
38th Tennessee.
Lumsden's battery.
Barret's battery.

THIRD ARMY CORPS.

Maj. Gen. W. J. HARDEE commanding.

First Brigade.

Col. ST. J. R. LIDDELL.

2d Arkansas.
5th Arkansas.
6th Arkansas.
7th Arkansas.
8th Arkansas.
Pioneer Company.
Roberts' battery.

Third Brigade.

Brig. Gen. S. A. M. WOOD.

16th Alabama.
32d Mississippi.
33d Mississippi.
44th Tennessee.
Baxter's battery.

Second Brigade.

Brig. Gen. P. R. CLEBURNE.

15th Arkansas.
2d Tennessee.
5th [35th] Tennessee.
24th Tennessee.
48th Tennessee.
Calvert's battery.

Fourth Brigade.

Brig. Gen. J. S. MARMADUKE.

3d Confederate.
25th Tennessee.
29th Tennessee.
37th Tennessee.
Swett's battery.

Fifth Brigade.

Col. A. T. HAWTHORN.

33d Alabama.
17th Tennessee.
21st Tennessee.
23d Tennessee.
Austin's battery.

RESERVE CORPS.

Brig. Gen. J. M. WITHERS commanding.

First Brigade.

Brig. Gen. FRANK GARDNER.

19th Alabama.
22d Alabama.
25th Alabama.
26th Alabama.
39th Alabama.
Sharpshooters.
Robertson's battery.

Third Brigade.

Brig. Gen. J. K. JACKSON.

17th Alabama.
18th Alabama.
21st Alabama.
24th Alabama.
5th Georgia.
Burtwell's battery.

Second Brigade.

Brig. Gen. J. R. CHALMERS.

5th Mississippi.
7th Mississippi.
9th Mississippi.
10th Mississippi.
29th Mississippi.
Blythe's Mississippi.
Ketchum's battery.

Fourth Brigade.

Col. A. M. MANIGAULT.

28th Alabama
34th Alabama.
1st Louisiana, Lieutenant-Colonel Farrar.
10th South Carolina.
19th South Carolina.
Waters' battery.

ARMY OF THE WEST.

Maj. Gen. J. P. McCown commanding.

FIRST DIVISION.

Brig. Gen. HENRY LITTLE.

First Brigade.

Col. ELIJAH GATES.

16th Arkansas.
1st Missouri Cavalry (dismounted).
2d Missouri.
3d Missouri.
Missouri Battalion.
Wade's battery.

Second Brigade.

Brig. Gen. LOUIS HÉBERT.

3d Louisiana.
14th Arkansas.
17th Arkansas.
Whitfield's Texas Legion Cavalry (dismounted).
Greer's regiment Texas cavalry (dismounted).
MacDonald's battery.

Third Brigade.

Brig. Gen. M. E. GREEN.

4th Missouri.
Missouri Battalion.
Missouri Battalion Cavalry (dismounted).
Confederate Rangers (dismounted).
King's battery.

SECOND DIVISION.

Maj. Gen. J. P. McCown.

First Brigade.

Brig. Gen. W. L. CABELL.

McCray's Arkansas.
10th Texas Cavalry (dismounted).
11th Texas Cavalry (dismounted).
14th Texas Cavalry (dismounted).
Andrews' Texas regiment.
Good's battery.

Second Brigade.

Brig. Gen. T. J. CHURCHILL.

1st Arkansas Riflemen (dismounted).
2d Arkansas Riflemen (dismounted).
4th Arkansas Regiment.
4th Arkansas Battalion.
Turnbull's Arkansas battalion.
Humphreys' battery.
Reves' Missouri Scouts.

THIRD DIVISION.

Brig. Gen. D. H. MAURY.

First Brigade.

Col. T. P. DOCKERY.

18th Arkansas.
19th Arkansas.
20th Arkansas.
McCarver's Arkansas battalion.
Jones' Arkansas battalion.
—— Battery.

Second Brigade.

Brig. Gen. J. C. MOORE.

35th Mississippi.
2d Texas.
Hobbs' Arkansas regiment.
Adams' Arkansas regiment.
Bledsoe's battery.

Third Brigade.

Brig. Gen. C. W. PHIFER.

3d Arkansas Cavalry (dismounted).
6th Texas Cavalry (dismounted).
9th Texas Cavalry (dismounted).
Brooks' battalion.
McNally's battery.

RESERVED BATTERIES.—Captains Hoxton's, Landis', Guibor's, and Brown's.
CAVALRY.—Forrest's regiment, Webb's squadron, Savery's company, McCulloch's regiment, and Price's body guard.

Abstract from Field Return of the Confederate forces commanded by General Braxton Bragg July 1, 1862.

Command.	Present for duty.						Total effective.	Aggregate present.	Aggregate present and absent.
	Infantry.		Cavalry.		Artillery.				
	Officers.	Enlisted men.	Officers.	Enlisted men.	Officers.	Enlisted men.			
Army of the Mississippi	2,375	27,935			58	1,551	32,126	42,716	63,984
Army of the West	823	8,867			38	675	10,390	14,108	20,468
Columbus	152	1,905			28	469	2,607	4,403	6,369
Cavalry			19	265			270	334	728
Grand total	3,350	38,707	19	265	124	2,695	45,393	61,561	91,549

HEADQUARTERS ARMY OF THE MISSISSIPPI,
Tupelo, Miss., July 1, 1862.

Brigadier-General CHALMERS,
Commanding Cavalry, Booneville, Miss.:

GENERAL: The general commanding directs me to acknowledge the receipt of a dispatch from your adjutant-general, and to inclose to you a copy of instructions already forwarded to you.* It is of the utmost importance that you should co-operate with General Withers in the movement upon Ripley. He further directs me to state that he has information that an empty train is now on the road from Ripley to Rienzi, to which a little attention might profitably be directed.

Very respectfully, your obedient servant,
P. H. THOMSON,
Assistant Adjutant-General.

GENERAL ORDERS, } HEADQUARTERS DEPARTMENT NO. 2,
No. 86. } *Tupelo, Miss., July* 1, 1862.

*　　*　　*　　*　　*　　*　　*

II. Major-General Hardee will assume the general command of the Department at Tupelo and environs.

*　　*　　*　　*　　*　　*

By command of General Bragg:

THOMAS JORDAN,
Chief of Staff.

---

* See Garner to Chalmers, June 30, 1862, p. 629.

GENERAL ORDERS, }   HEADQUARTERS DEPARTMENT NO. 2,
     No. 87.   }   *Tupelo, Miss., July* 2, 1862.

The commander of the forces is pleased to have occasion to commend to the emulation of the cavalry officers of this army the intelligently con ducted and enterprising expedition recently led by Capt. W. C. Bacot (Forrest's cavalry), sent to reconnoiter the enemy's movements on the right flank. Captain Bacot penetrated his lines, surprised a strong picket post, and killed and captured almost the whole detachment. It is hoped that frequent instances of similar enterprise will have to be noticed.

By command of General Bragg:

THOMAS JORDAN,
Chief of Staff.

GENERAL ORDERS, }   HEADQUARTERS DEPARTMENT NO. 2,
     No. 89.   }   *Tupelo, Miss., July* 2, 1862.

I. In compliance with orders from the War Department, dated the 24th and 25th ultimo, the commander of the forces assumes command of Department No. 2, as extended by the President, and embracing, in addition to the limits already announced, all of Department No. 1, the entire State of Alabama, and eastward to the line of railroad from Chattanooga via Atlanta to West Point, Ga., on the Chattahoochee River, and thence down that stream and the Apalachicola to the Gulf of Mexico.

II. The department is subdivided as follows:

1st. District of the Mississippi, embracing all the country west of Pearl River from its mouth to Jackson, Miss., and the line of the Mississippi Central Railroad to Grand Junction, Maj. Gen. Earl Van Dorn commanding.

2d. District of the Gulf, which will include all the country east of Pearl River to the Apalachicola, and as far north as the thirty-second parallel of latitude, Brig. Gen. John H. Forney commanding.

III. The following rearrangement of the forces near these headquarters will have immediate effect:

1st. Major-General Polk, relieved from the command of a corps, is announced to the army as second in command of the forces.

2d. Maj. Gen. W. J. Hardee is assigned to the command of the Army of the Mississippi, the several corps of which hereafter will be designated as divisions.

IV. District commanders will render as early as practicable returns of their forces and posts.

By command of General Bragg:

THOMAS JORDAN,
Chief of Staff.

GENERAL ORDERS, }   HEADQUARTERS ARMY OF THE WEST,
     No. 6.   }   *Priceville, Miss., July* 3, 1862.

The undersigned, as senior officer present, hereby assumes command of the Army of the West.

STERLING PRICE,
Major-General.

GENERAL ORDERS,   HEADQUARTERS ARMY OF THE WEST,
No. 7.   *Priceville, Miss., July 3*, 1862.

The major-general commanding announces the following as the staff of the Army of the West:

Adjutant-General's Department.—Maj. Thomas L. Snead and Capt. James M. Loughborough, assistant adjutants-general.

Quartermaster's Department.—Maj. Randolph H. Dyer, chief quarter-master.

Subsistence Department.—Maj. John Reid, chief commissary of subsistence.

Medical Department.—Surg. T. D. Wooten, medical director.

Ordnance Department.—Capt. Thomas H. Price, chief of ordnance.

Inspector-General's Department.—Capt. Henry M. Clark, inspector general.

Engineer's Department.—Lieut. John G. Kelly, chief engineer.

Aides-de-Camp.—Lieuts. Robert C. Wood and Clay Taylor.

By order of Major-General Price:

         JAMES M. LOUGHBOROUGH,
              Assistant Adjutant-General.

         HEADQUARTERS DEPARTMENT No. 2,
            Tupelo, Miss., July 4, 1862.

Col. SAMUEL TATE,
     President Memphis and Charleston Railroad:

COLONEL: As you have kindly consented to take the general superintendence of the work of completing the Meridian and Selma Railroad the commanding general instructs me to request you to repair to Demopolis, Ala., at your earliest convenience and relieve Capt. P. H. Thomson, C. S. Army.

The principal object of taking military control of this important work is to give such aid to the company that it may be completed in the shortest time possible and render it available for military purposes. You will therefore please confer freely with the officers of the company in question, who have at their disposition a loan of $150,000. You will doubtless be able so to arrange matters that while the interests of the company should be properly secured all possible expedition may be given to the completion of the work. You are fully authorized to employ all necessary engineers, agents, overseers, &c. Labor will be obtained by hire, material by purchase, when practicable; but military necessity and the high public interest depending on the most vigorous prosecution of the work will justify impressment whensoever obstacles are interposed. It is hoped, however, this may be avoided; but if not, you will promptly resort to it. It is anticipated especially that you may find it difficult to secure all the iron, spikes, &c., for the road without impressment. In all such cases impress promptly and firmly, taking the needful articles from available sources where the least damage will be done or burden imposed.

Pleased to secure your services at this time, the general intrusts the work to you with every confidence in your known energy and long experience, well assured of an early and successful completion of the work. Please inform the general of the condition in which you may find the work, and from time to time of the progress made under your direction.

Respectfully, your obedient servant,

              THOMAS JORDAN.

GENERAL ORDERS, } HDQRS. FIRST DIST., DEPARTMENT NO. 1,
    No. 4.   }   Tangipahoa, La., July 4, 1862.

I. The passing of negroes, slaves or free, toward or into the enemy's lines is positively prohibited without a pass from the master (if a slave), countersigned and approved by the provost-marshal or highest military authority of the parish to which he belongs; if free, in addition to the permission of the local authorities, the approval of the provost-marshal-general at these headquarters will be required. Every negro, slave or free, who shall violate this order will be shot in the attempt unless he or she shall immediately submit to arrest when making the attempt to pass the lines or beyond the prescribed limits indicated by our advanced pickets or guards. All negroes, slave or free, who come from the enemy within our lines will be taken immediately under charge by our pickets and guards and delivered to the nearest provost-marshal for examination and detention, who will report each case without delay to these headquarters.

By command of Brigadier-General Ruggles:

L. D. SANDIDGE,
Actg. Asst. Adjt. and Insp. Gen., C. S. Army.

GENERAL ORDERS, } HEADQUARTERS DEPARTMENT NO. 2,
    No. 92.   }   Tupelo, Miss., July 4, 1862.

I. Maj. L. W. O'Bannon, C. S. Army, is announced as chief quartermaster of the department. He will be obeyed and respected accordingly.

II. Until otherwise ordered the salt ration for this army will be three quarts for every 100 rations issued.

By command of General Bragg:

THOMAS JORDAN,
Chief of Staff.

SPECIAL ORDERS, } HEADQUARTERS DEPARTMENT NO. 2,
    No. 105.   }   Tupelo, Miss., July 4, 1862.

*   *   *   *   *   *   *

XII. Withers' division, of the Army of the Mississippi, will take position without delay at Saltillo, on the Mobile and Ohio Railroad. The brigade of that division near these headquarters will be moved forward as soon as practicable.

*   *   *   *   *   *   *

By command of General Bragg:

THOMAS JORDAN,
Chief of Staff.

GENERAL ORDERS, } HEADQUARTERS DEPARTMENT NO. 2,
    No. 93.   }   Tupelo, Miss., July 5, 1862.

The commander of the forces has to announce to the army a well-planned and soldierly-executed expedition within the enemy's lines, led by Col. W. H. Jackson, First Tennessee Cavalry, with a portion of his regiment, resulting in the capture of a Federal colonel and some 56 non-commissioned officers and privates and the destruction of a locomotive and train of cars near La Fayette Station, Memphis and Charleston Railroad, on the 25th ultimo.

On the 30th ultimo another detachment, under command of Major Duckworth, in the same vicinity, dashed upon the enemy's pickets and killed 6 and captured 8, with slight casualty to his own command. These affairs are happy presages of the spirit with which this army is prepared to enter upon the impending campaign in emulation of the heroic deeds of our brothers in arms and in blood in Virginia.

By command of General Bragg:

THOMAS JORDAN,
Chief of Staff.

GENERAL ORDERS, }   HEADQUARTERS ARMY OF THE MISSISSIPPI,
No. 22.   }   *Tupelo, Miss., July 5, 1862.*

In compliance with General Orders, No. 89, Paragraph III, dated Headquarters Department No. 2, Tupelo, Miss., July 2, 1862, General Bragg relinquishes the command of the Army of the Mississippi to Major-General Hardee.

By command of General Bragg:

GEO. G. GARNER,
Assistant Adjutant-General.

GENERAL ORDERS, }   HEADQUARTERS ARMY OF THE MISSISSIPPI,
No. 23.   }   *Tupelo, Miss., July 5, 1862.*

In obedience to General Orders, No. 89, from Headquarters of Department No. 2, the undersigned hereby assumes command of the Army of the Mississippi.

The following officers are announced as the staff: Capt. T. B. Roy, assistant adjutant-general; Lieut. D. H. Poole, acting assistant adjutant-general; Lieut. D. G. White and Capt. T. S. Hardee, aides-de-camp; Lieut. Col. E. D. Blake, inspector-general; Maj. W. D. Pickett, Lieut. Col. S. L. Black, and Lieut. T. W. Hunt, assistant inspectors-general; Col. John C. Moore, judge-advocate; Lieut. W. W. Wilkins, assistant judge-advocate; Capt. L. Hoxton, chief of artillery; Surg. D. W. Yandell, medical director; Surg. A. L. Breysacher, medical inspector; Maj. L. O. Bridewell, chief quartermaster; Maj. M. J. Wicks, chief commissary; Col. S. H. Perkins and Capt. Henry Flash, volunteer aides-de-camp.

W. J. HARDEE,
Major-General.

HEADQUARTERS DEPARTMENT NO. 2,
Tupelo, Miss., July 6, 1862.

Capt. W. C. BACOT,
Commanding Alabama Cavalry:

CAPTAIN: You will effect a crossing of the Tennessee River at the most practicable point with your command, and thence watch as closely as practicable the movements of the enemy. You will hang upon his rear, intercept his communications, cut off his forage parties and supply trains, capture his couriers and mails, and do all in your power to harass and annoy him.

An officer of the quartermaster's department has been directed to re-port to you for duty with your expedition. You will see that he makes proper requisitions for funds, both on quartermaster's and subsistence departments. Make as frequent report of any operations as may be practicable.

Respectfully, your obedient servant,

THOMAS JORDAN,
Chief of Staff.

TUPELO, MISS., *July* 7, 1862.

General G. T. BEAUREGARD:

MY DEAR GENERAL: I have tried several times [to write to] you, and I had a letter partly written for more than ten days, but before I finished it tore it up because I got mad as I wrote. We were all greatly startled by the orders placing General Bragg in permanent command. I knew well the President was watching his opportunity with a lynx eye to do you a disservice, and I had some vague apprehensions that he would attempt some injury when you left here; but I must confess I was little prepared for the boldness of the measure. As you perceive from a copy of the telegram inclosed there is a *suggestio falsi* in a sort of rea-son given for the act; that is, that you had quit the department on a surgeon's certificate. At the same time I learn that a rumor was set afloat in Richmond that you had applied for a leave of absence for four months, all of which looks very much like guarding somebody's rear. As soon as you feel rested I hope you will report for duty and orders to the War Department. I hope that you will be able to do so soon, and thus force your arch enemy to show his hand decisively at an early day if he dare do it. I have a fancy as to the line of policy that will be resorted to when you do report. It will be attempted to exile you to some small and inactive command, the Department of South Caro-lina for example, and the defense of Charleston and Savannah at a season when the climate will be a better defense than casemated forts. In that event I hope you will decline as incommensurate with your rank at this juncture, and then claim firmly either restoration to the command of this army, present and embodied as you should say at the call of your own voice, and organized and shaped by you, or a command in Virginia with that portion of the army there that you had also molded and or-ganized.

General Bragg, before he received your note about your general staff, had at once requested me to remain with him as his chief of staff. I assented, knowing that you would wish it, and feeling it my duty to the cause, as I could of course be useful to him with my experience in the duties of the office, and my endurance under long-continued hours of labor such as such a place must involve. I should have preferred to go to Virginia at this time, but felt my duty was to stay and assist the general who has so little help in his officers of high rank. The glorious events in Virginia have, however, unsettled me greatly, and I begin to look that way with longing eyes and heart, especially as the signs of an advance of this army do not look as promising as I had expected by this time, especially when the spirit and temper of this army has so greatly improved. I do not think I can remain quiet if we are to remain here much longer, but I shall not move in the matter without consulting you; and be assured further, I shall be at your service whenever you take the field, a day near at hand I earnestly hope.

I have my eyes on an officer, high in rank, of this army, who, I think, is disposed to give aid and comfort to your enemies for the sake of his own selfish ends and gain. I may be wrong, and therefore will not name him until I feel better assured. Meantime I inclose a newspaper slip* which was written by that man Alexander, whom you expelled as a letter-writer, and who, I feel sure, got his notion about the "lost opportunity" from the officer in question, for I heard a Senator say the same thing one day, who had come to my office with that same officer, at whose quarters the Senator was staying, and the officer rather assented; besides Alexander was well acquainted with the officer whom I suspect of starting the under-current.

Now, Prentiss repeatedly said to me on the evening of the 6th that Buell would be up that night, and doubtless he said as much to you. He certainly did not attempt to deceive me, but boasted of the defeat that must ensue to us from the coming of Buell, and in the morning when the firing began he remarked, "Ah! did I not tell you so? They are at it." As for the intrenchment matter, abundant evidence was given to show none existed and none was feared, and I do not believe Prentiss said what is stated, but the main matter is the alleged order from you to withdraw (not so).   •

I was in advance when the troops began the retrograde, Sunday. It must have been after 6 p. m., and so weary and scattered were the troops that no combined advance seemed practicable. At the time I saw no officer of rank present, and I feel sure General Bragg was in my rear. I have never understood from you that you actually gave any order to cease the pursuit; but that when it had ceased, simply because of the exhaustion of the men after meager meals for twenty-four hours and twelve hours of continuous fighting, you then gave orders to have the straggling, scattered fragments of regiments, brigades, and corps collected together and posted in advance of Shiloh. It was sundown when I joined you from the front near Shiloh Church.

Now, permit me to suggest to you to address a note to Generals Bragg and Hardee, both of whom are referred to in the scrap inclosed, and call their attention to the matter and inquire for a statement of events of the last hour of the battle of April 6. I have particular reasons for urging this, for I see a ramified plot to make it appear that had General Johnston lived the advantage would have been pressed on Sunday so effectually as to have made Buell halt on the east bank of the river. I hear around me murmurs of the smaller conspirators, and can trace the leaders too, I think; the cue came from Richmond.

Excuse this long letter, so long deferred. I will write again soon, and will keep you advised of all matters of interest. I have the papers you sent me, and will watch carefully, be assured, for your record. I have shown your answers to the feeble interrogatories. I have no means of printing them just yet, but I shall give them circulation. I shall try to write you oftener and shorter notes. This I shall send (July 10) by Dr. Choppin. Excuse this illegible hand, which I have come to write from writing so much and so fast.

Your nephew is still with me (young Proctor), and has become very useful to me. I shall take care of him.

As I can, I shall overhaul all the records to see what properly belongs to your military history since June, 1861.

Yours, sincerely,

THOMAS JORDAN.

P. S.—What fate or fortune could be harder than that of General Joe

---

* Not found.

Johnston to have commanded such an army up to the very eve of such a campaign, and when his army was ripe for great deeds, to lose the command in a petty affair; and how fortunate of the most fortunates is General Lee?

SPECIAL ORDERS, }   HEADQUARTERS ARMY OF THE WEST,
No. 8.   }   *Priceville, Miss., July 7, 1862.*

I. The cavalry of this army will be, until further orders, under the immediate command of acting Brig. Gen. Frank C. Armstrong, to whom the commanding officers of all regiments, battalions, unattached companies, and squads of cavalry in the Army of the West will report forthwith.

*   *   *   *   *   *   *

By command of Major-General Price:

THOS. L. SNEAD,
Assistant Adjutant-General.

SPECIAL ORDERS, } HEADQUARTERS ARMY OF THE MISSISSIPPI,
No. 59.   }   *Tupelo, Miss., July 7, 1862.*
*   *   *   *   *   *   *

V. Brig. Gen. S. A. M. Wood will relieve Brig. Gen. B. R. Johnson in command of the Third Division, Army of the Mississippi.

VI. Brig. Gen. B. R. Johnson is assigned to the command of the Third Brigade, Third Division, Army of the Mississippi.

*   *   *   *   *   *   *

By command of Major-General Hardee:

T. B. ROY,
Assistant Adjutant-General.

HEADQUARTERS DEPARTMENT No. 2,
Tupelo, Miss., July 8, 1862.

General CHALMERS,
      Commanding Cavalry Brigade:

GENERAL: Your communication* of the 8th instant has been laid before the general commanding, and he directs me to express his approbation of the energy, celerity, and skill exhibited in your late movements, and his satisfaction at the results accomplished. The duty to which you are assigned is one of great importance, and the services you are now rendering of more value than any you could possibly perform in any other on which you could be employed. You will therefore continue to harass the enemy as much as possible, striking whenever an opportunity occurs, burn all cotton liable to fall into his hands, and gain whatever information you can of his whereabouts and intentions. He further directs me to inform you that he has learned that citizens who burn their cotton are maltreated by the enemy and their property destroyed. A letter has been sent to General Halleck under a flag of truce, informing him that any one committing such depredations will, if caught, suffer the most summary penalty. You are directed to use every exertion to arrest such offenders, that they may be brought to judgment.

Respectfully, your obedient servant,

GEO. G. GARNER,
Assistant Adjutant-General.

---

* Not found.

HDQRS. DEPARTMENT NO. 2, ORDNANCE OFFICE,
Near Tupelo, Miss., July 8, 1862.

Maj. J. T. CHAMPNEYS,
Commanding Ordnance Depot, Okolona, Miss. :

MAJOR: By order of the commanding general of the department you will please to have in ordnance depots at Tupelo and Verona, as far as the storage in each of those places will permit, 50 rounds of ammunition (fixed) for each and every piece of artillery now in the field, independent of 200 rounds of ammunition now in caissons. The artillery in the Army of the Mississippi consists of forty-one 6-pounders, six 12-pounder guns, thirty-six 12-pounder howitzers, and fourteen rifled guns, the caliber of which last (rifled), as also of number of guns and their caliber in the Army of the West, you will please to ascertain from the chief of artillery of Department No. 2. The balance of ammunition (fixed) now at Okolona will be retained at that depot. The strapped projectiles not necessary in field service, materials for ordnance stores, damaged ammunition, powder obtained from broken cartridges (unfit for service by reason of its low range and being too soft), and edged tools unfit for service in field, if any, artillery equipments and implements unserviceable, &c., will be sent to Columbus, Miss., and turned over to Maj. W. R. Hunt, commanding Confederate States Arsenal at that place. As there is no intention to fabricate at your post any other articles than blank cartridges for field rifled pieces, you will please to exercise your own judgment as to which stores and articles you may need besides ammunition (fixed) for field artillery service in prosecution of the war.

Permit me to mention to you that we have in our service the following (not rifled) guns, viz, 6-pounder, 3.3-inch and 3-inch for field service.

Please order to be prepared an inventory of all ordnance and ordnance stores which you may judge proper to retain under your charge, and make requisition for necessary articles you may require at your depot and send to me to enable us to procure them.

Lieut. W. M. Levy is ordered to report to you for duty. I cannot say he is entirely posted in ordnance manual, but permit me to introduce him as an intelligent and energetic young officer, and I hope, with your instructions and teachings, he will be efficient.

Very respectfully,

H. OLADOWSKI.

GENERAL ORDERS, ⎰   HDQRS. FIRST DIV., ARMY OF THE MISS.,
No. 1.   ⎱   *Camp near Tupelo, Miss., July* 8, 1862.

Hereafter the different brigades of this command will report directly to these headquarters, and will be denominated First, Second, Third, Fourth, and Fifth Brigades, as follows:

First Brigade, Brig. Gen. Daniel S. Donelson, composed of Sixteenth, Fifteenth, Fifty-first, and Eighth Regiments Tennessee Volunteers and Captain Carnes' battery of light artillery.

Second Brigade, Brig. Gen. A. P. Stewart, composed of Fourth, Fifth, Twenty-fourth, Thirty-first, and Thirty-third Regiments Tennessee Volunteers and Captain Stanford's battery of light artillery.

Third Brigade, Brig. Gen. S. B. Maxey, composed of Forty-first Regiment Georgia Volunteers, Ninth Regiment Texas Volunteers, Twenty-fourth Regiment Mississippi Volunteers, and Captain Eldridge's battery of light artillery.

Fourth Brigade, Brig. Gen. George Maney, composed of Ninth, Sixth, and Twenty-seventh Regiments Tennessee Volunteers and Capt. M. Smith's battery of light artillery.

Fifth Brigade, Brig. Gen. Preston Smith, composed of One hundred and fifty-fourth, Twelfth, Thirteenth, and Forty-seventh Regiments Tennessee Volunteers, Captain Edmondson's company of sharpshooters, and Capt. S. P. Bankhead's battery of artillery.

By command of Major-General Cheatham:

MARCUS J. WRIGHT,
Acting Assistant Adjutant-General.

TUPELO, MISS., *July* 10, 1862.

General S. COOPER:

Bombardment Vicksburg ceased. Enemy now endeavoring to make cut-off across neck of land west and direct channel river from under our batteries. A long and disastrous drought, threatening destruction to the grain crop, continues here, and renders any move impracticable for want of water.

BRAXTON BRAGG.

ADJUTANT AND INSPECTOR GENERAL'S OFFICE,
Richmond, Va., July 10, 1862.

General BRAXTON BRAGG,
Commanding, &c., Tupelo, Miss.:

GENERAL: The Secretary of War instructs me to say, in reply to your communication of 26th ultimo, relating to the railroad connection between Meridian, Miss., and Selma, Ala., that the department fully appreciates the importance of this road and is most desirous of completing it. Accordingly, with the consent of the company, it has already authorized you to take possession of and complete it. Until Congress meets in August the only appropriation applicable to the purpose is the $150,000 authorized to be advanced to the company. The department proposes to execute the law by making this advance, taking security for its application, and by permitting the company to make the necessary disbursements under your order. To complete this work by seizing the road and the material required for its completion will be not only illegal, but will run the Government to enormous cost, irritate the people, and leave open a question between the Government and the company concerning transportation, &c.

Very respectfully, &c.,

S. COOPER,
Adjutant and Inspector General.

HEADQUARTERS DEPARTMENT NO. 2,
Tupelo, Miss., July 12, 1862.

The ADJUTANT AND INSPECTOR GENERAL,
Richmond, Va.:

SIR: Since my communication of June — last nothing requiring special report has occurred in this command. The time since that has been diligently applied to organization, discipline, and instruction, with a very marked improvement. The health and general tone of the troops, too, exhibit results no less gratifying. Our condition for service is good and has reached a culminating point under the defective skeleton organization. My suggestion for improving this by a consolidation of regiments has already been submitted.

No move in force against the enemy's main body has been practicable by reason of want of transportation until within a few days, but we have kept him constantly in alarm by small expeditions against his outposts, in all of which we have been successful. Especially have our cavalry and Partisan Rangers damaged him in the region between Memphis, Grand Junction, and the Tallahatchie River, where several valuable trains and about 100 prisoners have fallen into our hands. All of these expeditions, successful in themselves, have developed the impracticability of any move in force from here against the enemy's present position at and near Corinth. A drought almost unprecedented has left the country, naturally dry, without water sufficient for the inhabitants. The enemy in their strongly-fortified positions, garnished with heavy artillery, rely entirely on wells, as we do here. The forces detached from here to support Vicksburg and Chattanooga, amounting to about 12,000, leaves us less than 40,000 of all arms and conditions with which to face an enemy of not less than 60,000, strongly intrenched. Could I have foreseen the barrier to operations which is now between us a considerable portion of this force would have been thrown into East Tennessee, where successful operations might have been carried on directly into and behind the enemy's lines; but the means of transportation here then rendered such a move slow and tedious. It is unfortunate that our railroad connection across by Meridian and Selma was not sooner opened. With the force which the enemy has sent in that direction he will be enabled, I fear, unless we are strengthened, to force our lines and do us very great damage. Without putting myself purely on the defensive and exposing the whole of Mississippi and South Alabama, no further assistance can be sent from here unless more arms can be furnished. A number of new regiments just passing through the diseases of camp will soon be fit for service if arms can be supplied them.

By the latest advices from Vicksburg it seems the enemy has given up the reduction of that place by water. The cut-off is a failure, and it is now said they are constructing a railroad across the neck of land that we can easily render useless by putting up batteries opposite the termini.

The determined defense of Vicksburg, which I directed General Van Dorn to make at every hazard and to the last extremity, has been highly creditable to him and to his troops, and has disappointed the enemy and disconcerted his plans. He is suffering much, too, from the frequent and unexpected attacks of our troops in ambush on the bank of the river.

So far the navigation of the Lower Mississippi has not been attended with any beneficent results to them, unless it may be in the sugar regions. Though out of my department, I would suggest the appointment of an active, energetic, and determined commander in that section of Louisiana, who might do much good in preventing illicit traffic and checking the spirit of disloyalty now springing up there. In this connection I would mention that I have recently sent some arms and ammunition to Major-General Hindman, commanding the Trans-Mississippi Department, with which I have no doubt he will do fine service.

Major-General Price has exhibited to me the authority of the War Department to allow his command, at my direction, to return to the west of the Mississippi River. Were it at all prudent for me to spare them, I do not see how it it practicable to cross such a force over the river.

I am, sir, very respectfully, your obedient servant,

BRAXTON BRAGG,
General, Commanding.

[JULY 13, 1862.—The Missouri State Guard, under command of Brig. Gen. Moseby M. Parsons, relieved from duty east of the Mississippi and ordered to Arkansas. See Series I, Vol. XIII, p. 855.]

HDQRS. CAVALRY BRIGADE, ARMY OF THE WEST,
Plantersville, Ala., July 13, 1862.

Maj. THOMAS L. SNEAD,
Assistant Adjutant-General, Army of the West:

MAJOR: In obedience to circular from department headquarters I have the honor to report the following commands in this brigade: Forrest's cavalry, Lieut. Col. D. C. Kelley commanding, stationed near Priceville—four companies detached on special service from headquarters department; McCulloch's battalion, nine companies, Lieutenant-Colonel McCulloch commanding, near Plantersville; Louisiana Squadron, Captain Webb, near Plantersville; Hill's company of Mississippi cavalry, at Fulton; Second Tennessee Battalion, seven companies, Lieut. Col. C. R. Barteau commanding, near Bay Springs. The pickets occupy a line extending from near Baldwyn to Marietta, Bay Springs, and Fulton. There are also two detachments—one at General Little's headquarters and one at General Green's—which I propose to form into a company and put into McCulloch's battalion, making it a regiment. I would suggest that the squadron of Louisiana cavalry be merged into one company, as there are not sufficient men to justify the number of officers required in a squadron. The best officers might be selected and an efficient company formed. Captain Sanders' company encamped near Verona, but is now scouting northward from Marietta.

Very respectfully, your obedient servant.

FRANK C. ARMSTRONG,
Brigadier-General, Commanding.

GENERAL ORDERS, }   HEADQUARTERS DEPARTMENT No. 2,
No. 98.   }   *Tupelo, Miss., July* 13, 1862.

Suitable cavalry detachments from each army will be kept constantly patroling in the vicinity of the several encampments occupied by the forces and in the neighborhood. These detachments will arrest all stragglers and persons improperly absent from their regiments, and will rigidly suppress depredations on the gardens, corn fields, and property of our citizens, which, the commanding general learns with extreme mortification, are carried on to a disgraceful extent. Soldiers, your enemy is represented as more regardful of the private property of our people than you have been of late. This must not continue; it will lead to your shame and demoralization. A demoralized army can never shed honor on our arms or give lasting success to any cause.

By command of General Bragg:

THOMAS JORDAN,
Chief of Staff.

[JULY 15, 1862.—For Col. W. P. Johnston's report of inspection in Department No. 2, see Series 1, Vol. X, Part I, pp. 780–793.]

HEADQUARTERS DEPARTMENT NO. 2,
Tupelo, Miss., July 16, 1862.

General S. COOPER,
Adjutant and Inspector General, Richmond, Va.:

GENERAL: I have the honor to submit herewith, for the consideration of the War Department, the inclosed papers*, which exhibit in part the endless perplexities and difficulties growing out of the existing laws and regulations touching army organization when enforced. I can see indeed no hope of completing the organization of the regiments of this army under the requirements of present laws and orders. As yet not half the vacancies created have been filled. Elections are followed often by rejections by boards, rejections by new elections, and in many instances persons elected have declined, while in some companies and regiments there is a want of adequate and proper material for officers. In the mean time confusion and demoralization have resulted, which would appear farcical in some instances were it not for the serious consequences impending. All acting appointments made by my predecessor and myself, as you are aware, have been directed to be vacated as soon as the places can be filled by election or promotion; with what effects may be seen too clearly and truly in the clamor of division, brigade, and regimental commands. Unless some material relaxation of these orders is soon authorized much that had been done to restore the tone of this army and fit it for a reputable campaign will have been utterly in vain.

Respectfully, your obedient servant,

BRAXTON BRAGG.

GENERAL ORDERS, } HEADQUARTERS ARMY OF THE MISSISSIPPI,
No. 31.   }   *Tupelo, Miss., July* 16, 1862.

All vacancies now existing or that may hereafter occur among company or regimental officers of this army will be filled by promotion according to seniority, according to rank, except a vacancy in the lowest grade of commissioned rank, which will be filled by election. When a vacancy occurs the brigade commanders will announce in orders the promotion of the officer next in rank, and forward a copy of the order for the approval of the Secretary of War, except when there are reasonable grounds to doubt the qualification or fitness for commission of the officer elected or to be promoted, when his brigade commander, if there be one, or if not, then his division commander, will assemble a board of not less than three commissioned officers of equal or superior rank to the officer elected or promoted, who shall inquire into his qualifications and fitness for commission, and shall report for the information of the War Department the facts of the case and their own opinion of the qualification and fitness of the officer. In such case the vacancy will not be filled pending the decision of the Department. All positions held by appointed officers will be considered vacancies, and the officers holding such will be returned to their former positions as soon as these vacancies can be regularly filled. But appointed officers accounted for on the muster-rolls as officers shall be entitled while acting as such to

———————————————————
* Not found.

the pay of their respective grades. When elections have been held at reorganization and the officers elected have been rejected by the examining board that regiment or company, as the case may be, is considered to have exhausted the elective franchise, and the old officers will retain their places.

By command of Major-General Hardee:

T. B. ROY.

Abstract from Field Return of the Confederate forces commanded by General Braxton Bragg, July, 16, 1862.

Troops.	Present for duty.				Aggregate present and absent.
	Officers.	Men.	Effective total.	Aggregate present.	
Army of the Mississippi (Hardee)	2,560	28,633	31,638	44,130	66,035
Army of the West (Price)	944	9,932	11,057	15,016	20,383
At Columbus (Adams)	195	3,065	3,280	4,790	6,344
Near Abbeville (Villepigue)	235	3,138	3,331	4,187	6,436
Grand total	3,934	44,768	49,306	68,123	99,198

GENERAL ORDERS, }   HEADQUARTERS DEPARTMENT No. 2,
　　No. 100. 　 }   *Tupelo, Miss., July* 17, 1862.

The personal and general staff of the commander of the forces are announced as follows:

Personal Staff.—First Lieuts. Towson Ellis and F. S. Parker, jr., aides-de-camp; Lieut. Col. D. Urquhart and Majs. L. M. Conner and John M. Huger, volunteer aides-de-camp.

General Staff.—Brig. Gen. Thomas Jordan, chief of staff; Lieut. Col. George G. Garner and Capts. F. H. Jordan and John M. Otey, assistant adjutants-general; Brig. Gen. J. E. Slaughter, inspector-general; Lieut. Cols. C. J. Polignac and W. K. Beard and Capts. J. P. Jones and G. B. Cooke, assistant inspectors-general; Lieut. Col. H. W. Walter, judge-advocate; Lieut. Col. L. W. O'Bannon, chief quartermaster; Maj. M. B. McMicken, assistant to chief quartermaster; Maj. A. J. Smith, chief quartermaster in the department of pay; Maj. J. J. Walker, chief of subsistence; Maj. F. Malloy, assistant to chief of subsistence; Surg. A. J. Foard, medical director; Surgs. J. C. Nott and S. E. Chaillé, medical inspectors; Col. John Pegram, chief of engineers; Lieut. Col. H. Oladowski, chief of ordnance; Col. M. L. Clark, chief of artillery; Lieut. Col. J. H. Hallonquist, inspector of artillery; Maj. J. W. Goodwin, quartermaster's department, military superintendent of railroads.

By command of General Bragg:

THOMAS JORDAN,
Chief of Staff.

SPECIAL ORDERS, }   HEADQUARTERS DEPARTMENT No. 2,
　　No. 123. 　 }   *Tupelo, Miss., July* 17, 1862.

The following operations will take place without delay:

I. Brigadier-General Chalmers will advance with the disposable cavalry of his command, including Wirt Adams' regiment, and endeavor to get behind Grand Junction and cut off and obstruct the railroad thence to Jackson, Tenn., and also destroy all cotton within the region of his operations. At the same time General Villepigue will detach any infantry and artillery force that General Chalmers may require, and also Jackson's and Pinson's regiments of Tennessee [and Mississippi] cavalry, to co-operate with the movement of General Chalmers, to which end the two generals will communicate with each other and arrange as early as practicable for the most efficient and prompt execution of this order. It is further expected that opportunities may occur in the course of this expedition for striking at considerable detachments of the enemy, to which end all due preparation will be made for a signal success.

II. The available cavalry force of the Army of the West, under acting Brigadier-General Armstrong, will move at once toward the Tennessee River, as near as practicable to Decatur. General Armstrong will communicate with Captain Roddey, commanding cavalry scouts in that quarter, after which he will operate at his own discretion, doing all practicable things to harass the enemy and cut off any detachments or supply trains. General Armstrong will likewise destroy all cotton within the district of his operations.

By command of General Bragg:

THOMAS JORDAN,
Chief of Staff.

TUPELO, MISS., *July* 17, 1862.

General S. COOPER:

Will General Magruder pass by these headquarters? Have important information for him.

BRAXTON BRAGG.

HEADQUARTERS DEPARTMENT No. 2,
Tupelo, Miss., July 17, 1862.

Brig. Gen. JAMES R. CHALMERS, *Commanding, &c.*:
(Through Major-General Hardee.)

GENERAL: The order directing you to withdraw your command on this point is revoked, and instead the commander of the forces directs me to say he wishes you to prosecute any expedition in which you are engaged, and to push and harass the enemy with the utmost vigor compatible with due military precaution, prudence, and the strength and composition of your command.

Respectfully, your obedient servant,

THOMAS JORDAN,
Chief of Staff.

GENERAL ORDERS, }   WAR DEPT., ADJT. & INSP. GEN.'S OFFICE,
No. 50.   }   *Richmond, Va., July* 18, 1862.

*   *   *   *   *   *   *

II. Military Department No. 2 will embrace the States of Mississippi, Alabama, East Louisiana, and part of Florida which is west of the Chattahoochee and Apalachicola Rivers.

*   *   *   *   *   *   *

By command of the Secretary of War:

S. COOPER,
Adjutant and Inspector General.

GENERAL ORDERS, }   HEADQUARTERS DEPARTMENT No. 2,
    No. 101.   }   *Tupelo, Miss., July* 18, 1862.

It is necessary that the military service should have all the disposable forage, breadstuffs, and meat along the line of the Mobile and Ohio Railroad without competition with speculators or dealers in produce, and all such persons, or persons not purchasing for their own actual consumption, are ordered to make their purchases in other districts. The rich districts of the Alabama River and the railroads in Alabama are open to their operations, and competition with Government agents, so highly obstructive and injurious, will not be any longer permitted.

By command of General Bragg:

THOMAS JORDAN,
Chief of Staff.

SPECIAL ORDERS, }   HEADQUARTERS DEPARTMENT No. 2,
    No. 125.   }   *Tupelo, Miss., July* 18, 1862.

In consequence of his health, Brig. Gen. James R. Chalmers having asked to be relieved from the command of the cavalry of the Army of the Mississippi and of the outposts, he will turn over the command to Col. Joseph Wheeler, Alabama Volunteers, and rejoin his brigade of infantry.

The general commanding is pleased to bear testimony to the energy, enterprise, and intelligence which have characterized Brigadier-General Chalmers as the commander of the outposts of the forces and his successful efforts to introduce discipline and good order into the cavalry, as well as the gallantry with which he has handled his troops in several affairs with the enemy.

By command of General Bragg:

THOMAS JORDAN,
Chief of Staff.

HDQRS. CAVALRY BRIGADE, ARMY OF THE WEST,
Near Fulton, Miss., July 19, 1862.

Maj. THOMAS L. SNEAD,
Acting Assistant Adjutant-General:

MAJOR: In pursuance to verbal instructions from the general commanding department I marched on the 18th to Fulton with the available force of my brigade, after leaving several companies for picket duty at Bay Springs and Marietta. I inclose report* of my command present. In order to deceive the Union men, who infest the direct route toward Russellville, I have deemed it best to make a detour, passing near Pikeville and getting into the Bull Mountain road, then moving rapidly northward toward Decatur. I can obtain some forage by that route. In case the picket left at Bay Springs and Marietta are forced to fall back (and I have ordered the officer in command to do it only before an overwhelming force), to do so in the direction of Mooreville, reporting to you and the pickets at Baldwyn. If a battalion or regiment could be placed 30 miles from Fulton on the road to Russellville they could obtain forage and clear the country of a number of Union men, who inform the enemy of every movement of our army. At present I

---

* The report inclosed shows that his command consisted of Forrest's regiment, McCulloch's and Savery's battalions, Sanders' and Hill's companies, and the Second Tennessee; aggregate present for duty, 651.

cannot spare the command to do it. It would draw a portion of their cavalry from Lawrence and Morgan Counties, Alabama, and give me an opportunity to operate completely in their rear and on the Memphis and Charleston road with more effect. I only make this suggestion in case there should be any cavalry in the Army of the Mississippi that the major-general could get temporarily attached to this brigade. I intend to move slowly until I can get near enough to act vigorously before the enemy can gain much knowledge of my approach.

I have the honor to be, with respect, your obedient servant,

FRANK C. ARMSTRONG,
Brigadier-General, Commanding.

HEADQUARTERS ARMY OF THE MISSISSIPPI,
Tupelo, Miss., July 20, 1862.

Col. JOSEPH WHEELER,
Comdg. Cavalry Brigade, Army of the Mississippi:

COLONEL: I am instructed by Major-General Hardee to say that the regiments of your command have been ordered to rendezvous at Ripley immediately. He desires that you will use the utmost possible dispatch to set on foot the movement in contemplation.

Respectfully, colonel, your obedient servant,

T. B. ROY,
Assistant Adjutant-General.

HEADQUARTERS DEPARTMENT No. 2,
Tupelo, Miss, July 20, 1862.

Maj. Gen. E. KIRBY SMITH,
Commanding, &c., Knoxville, Tenn.:

GENERAL: Your dispatch announcing General Buell's arrival opposite Chattanooga was received and answered yesterday.* Confronted here by a largely superior force strongly intrenched, it will be impossible for me to do more than menace and harass the enemy from this quarter, as we constantly do with our cavalry by driving in his outposts and capturing his foraging parties and all stragglers from his lines. The fact is we are fearfully outnumbered in this department, the enemy having at least two to our one in the field, with a comparatively short line, upon which he may concentrate. With the division from here, the new levies from Alabama and Georgia, and the 4,000 from among which I authorized General McCown to stop and appropriate, I have hoped you would be able to cope with General Buell's force, especially as he would have to cross a broad and deep river in your immediate presence. That hope still exists; but I must urge on you the propriety of assuming command in person at Chattanooga. The officer I sent you, I regret to say, cannot be trusted with such a command, and I implore you not to intrust him indeed with any important position. New Madrid fell by his errors and want of decision and firmness, as is supposed, while other prominent instances and evidences of his want of capacity and nerve for a separate, responsible command have just been brought to my notice. His high rank constraining me to send him with his division, I had no alternative at the time.

---

* See Series I, Vol. XVI, Part II, p. 730.

I am left in doubt, from what I can learn, whether yours is a sepa-rate command, or still, as formerly, a part of General Johnston's old de-partment and hence embraced within my command. Can you enlighten me by copies of any orders or instructions you may have? My only desire is to know the precise limits of my responsibilities, not to inter-fere in the least with your operations and command, as you must know best when and how to act, and have my fullest confidence.

That was a gallant, brilliant operation of Forrest's, and has given us one of the most obnoxious of the enemy's leaders. Such successful efforts deserve immediate reward, and I will cheerfully meet with you in recommending Colonel Forrest. This affair, added to his gallantry at Shiloh, where he was severely wounded, mark him as a valuable soldier.

We have driven off the enemy, badly crippled, from Vicksburg, but they are probably organizing for a land attack in force. Curtis has escaped from Arkansas and reached the Mississippi in safety. He will now be enabled to unite against us.

Respectfully, general, your obedient servant,

BRAXTON BRAGG.

General Braxton Bragg's Command.—(*About July* 20, 1862.)

ARMY OF THE MISSISSIPPI.

(General Braxton Bragg.)

First Corps, Maj. Gen. L. Polk commanding.

First Division.—First Brigade, Col. R. M. Russell; Second Brigade, Brig. Gen. A. P. Stewart.

Second Division.—First Brigade, Brig. Gen. D. S. Donelson; Second Brigade, Brig. Gen. George Maney; detached brigade, Brig. Gen. S. B. Maxey.

Second Corps, Maj. Gen. Samuel Jones commanding.

First Brigade, Brigadier-General Anderson; Second Brigade, Col. A. Reichard; Third Brigade, Brigadier-General Walker.

Third Corps, Maj. Gen. W. J. Hardee commanding.

First Brigade, Col. St. J. R. Liddell; Second Brigade, Brig. Gen. P. R. Cleburne; Third Brigade, Brig. Gen. S. A. M. Wood; Fourth Bri-gade, Brig. Gen. J. S. Marmaduke; Fifth Brigade, Col. A. T. Hawthorn.

Reserve Corps, Brig. Gen. J. M. Withers commanding.

First Brigade, Brig. Gen. Frank Gardner; Second Brigade, Brig. Gen. J. R. Chalmers; Third Brigade, Brig. Gen. J. K. Jackson; Fourth Brigade, Col. A. M. Manigault; First Louisiana Infantry (detached), Lieutenant-Colonel Farrar.

ARMY OF THE WEST.

(Maj. Gen. J. P. McCown.)

First Division (Brig. Gen. Henry Little).—First Brigade, Col. Elijah Gates; Second Brigade, Brig. Gen. Louis Hébert; Third Brigade, Brig. Gen. M. E Green.

Second Division (Maj. Gen. J. P. McCown).—First Brigade, Brig. Gen. W. L. Cabell; Second Brigade, Brig. Gen. T. J. Churchill.

Third Division (Brig. Gen. D. H. Maury).—First Brigade, Col. T. P. Dockery; Second Brigade, Brig. Gen. J. C. Moore; Third Brigade, Brig. Gen. C. W. Phifer.

Reserved Batteries.—Captains Hoxton's, Landis', Guibor's, and Brown's.

Cavalry.—Forrest's regiment, Webb's squadron, Savery's company, McCulloch's regiment, and Price's body guard.

HEADQUARTERS DEPARTMENT OF THE FORCES,
Tupelo, Miss., July 21, 1862.

Col. M. L. CLARK, *Chief of Artillery:*

COLONEL: The field artillery of the Army of the Mississippi has been ordered to move by land on Chattanooga via Aberdeen, Columbus, Tuscaloosa, Talladega, and Rome, Ga., with the least delay practicable. It is the wish of the general that this move should be made in the most efficient manner possible, and he thinks it best that you should accompany and assume immediate command of the artillery while in movement. It is the wish of the general as you pass Columbus that you should exchange inferior horses for the best that are in the batteries there.

Respectfully, your obedient servant,
THOMAS JORDAN,
Chief of Staff.

RICHMOND, VA., *July* 21, 1862.

General BRAXTON BRAGG, *Tupelo, Miss.:*

General Magruder has been relieved by General Holmes in command of the Trans-Mississippi Department. It is presumed the latter will pass by Tupelo. Have telegraphed General Holmes that you have important information to communicate.

S. COOPER,
Adjutant and Inspector General.

TUPELO, MISS., *July* 21, 1862.
(Received at Richmond, Va., July 22, 1862.)

General S. COOPER,
Adjutant and Inspector General:

Communications and orders continue to reach me to and from the Trans-Mississippi Department. Is it not a separate command, independent of this?

BRAXTON BRAGG.

RICHMOND, VA., *July* 21, 1862.

General BRAXTON BRAGG, *Tupelo, Miss.:*

Your dispatch about Selma and Meridian Railroad referred. Agent was here and received money; is probably by this time at Selma.

JEFFERSON DAVIS.

GENERAL ORDERS, } HEADQUARTERS DISTRICT OF TENNESSEE,
      No. 1.   {   *Tupelo, Miss., July* 21, 1862.

I. The undersigned, by order of the general commanding the department, assumes command of the District of the Tennessee, which comprises Northwestern Alabama and all that portion of the State of Mississippi which is north of the thirty-second parallel latitude and east of
the Pearl River, and of the line of the Mississippi Central Railroad from
Jackson to Grand Junction.   Headquarters have been established until
further orders at Tupelo.

*   *   *   *   *   *   *

IV. The following officers are announced as constituting the staff of
the major-general commanding: Maj. Thomas L. Snead, chief of staff
and assistant adjutant-general; Capts. James M. Loughborough and L.
A. Maclean, assistant adjutants-general; Capt. Henry M. Clarke, inspec-
tor-[general]; Maj. John Reid, chief commissary; Maj. Randolph H.
Dyer, chief quartermaster; Surg. Thomas D. Wooten, medical director;
Surg. Joseph T. Scott, medical inspector; Capt. Thomas H. Price, chief
of ordnance; Capt. L. Fremaux, acting chief of engineers; Lieuts. Robert
C. Wood and H. Clay Taylor, aides-de-camp.

STERLING PRICE,
Major-General, Commanding.

SPECIAL ORDERS, }   HEADQUARTERS OF THE FORCES,
      No. 3.   {   *Tupelo, Miss., July* 21, 1862.
*   *   *   *   *   *   *

IV. Adams', Slemons', and Wheeler's regiments of cavalry are transferred for duty to the Army of the West.   Colonel Wheeler's will report accordingly to Major-General Price.

*   *   *   *   *   *   *

By command of General Bragg:

THOMAS JORDAN,
Chief of Staff.

ADJUTANT AND INSPECTOR GENERAL'S OFFICE,
Richmond, Va., July 22, 1862.
General BRAXTON BRAGG,
    Commanding, &c., Tupelo, Miss.:

Your letter of June 29th was duly received and submitted to the President.   In reply to that part of it which relates to the appointment of
additional general officers of your command, I am instructed by the
President to say that he feels himself not a little embarrassed in carrying out your wishes on account of the restrictions of law.   By the act
of Congress of March 6, 1861, "to provide for the public defense," the
President is authorized to organize regiments into brigades and brigades into divisions, and to appoint the commanding officers of such
brigades and divisions, subject to the confirmation of Congress, who
are to hold their offices only while such brigades and divisions are in
service.   To this extent and no further has the President the power to
appoint general officers.

In examining your return showing the organization of your command
he finds that you have 29 brigades and 7 divisions, including the command of Brigadier-General Breckinridge, while the records of appoint-

ment show that 9 major-generals and 34 brigadier-generals have already been appointed for that command, making a surplus of 2 major-generals and 5 brigadiers.   True, he finds that some of these general officers are not under assignment or with their proper commands on account of sickness or other causes ; but they still hold their appointments, and the President has not the power to remove them from office.   It is for this reason he is prevented from making additional appointments of general officers for your command.

You remark that many recommendations made are not ratified, and some general officers, appointed or promoted without recommendation from this quarter, are only incumbrances and would be better out of the way.   The President had been under the impression that all the appointments of general officers for your command, or nearly all, had been made by him on the recommendations of the commanding general, and he would be glad to be furnished with the names of the individual officers to whom your objections apply.   He is aware that many recommendations that were made were not ratified by him, and for reasons which he considered good and sufficient and for the interest of the service.

Those portions of your letter which relate to subsistence and transportation have been referred to the chiefs of the staff department having charge of those branches, and will receive due attention.

I have the honor to be, very respectfully, your obedient servant,

S. COOPER,
Adjutant and Inspector General.

RICHMOND, VA., *July* 22, 1862.

BRAXTON BRAGG, *Tupelo, Miss.* :

GENERAL : The Trans-Mississippi Department is a separate command, independent of your command, and to which Major-General Holmes has been assigned as its commanding general.

S. COOPER,
Adjutant and Inspector General.

RICHMOND, VA., *July* 22, 1862.

Gov. JOHN J. PETTUS, *Jackson, Miss.* :

Captain Brown, of the Arkansas, requires boatmen, and reports himself doomed to inactivity by the inability to get them.   We have a large class of river boatmen and some ordinary seamen on our Gulf coast who must be now unemployed.   Can you not help Captain Brown to get an adequate crew ?

JEFFERSON DAVIS.

HEADQUARTERS,
Tupelo, Miss., July 23, 1862.

General COOPER :

GENERAL : The great importance of the line of connection through East Tennessee, now seriously threatened by a heavy column under General Buell, forces upon me the necessity of still further strengthening the position held by Maj. Gen. E. K. Smith.   To do this necessarily places me on the defensive here so long as the enemy keeps up the heavy force in our front, numbering not less than 10,000. I have concluded thus to reduce this position, infinitely less important, to the defensive, move my spare force rapidly to East Tennessee, and there endeavor to frustrate his lines and assail him in the rear. Copies of my orders will indicate the dispositions made. Major-General Van Dorn, with about 16,000 effectives, will hold the line of the Mississippi. Major-General Price, with a similar force, will face the enemy on this frontier, and a sufficient garrison will be left for Mobile and the Gulf. With the balance of the forces, some 35,000 effectives, I hope, in conjunction with Major-General Smith, to strike an effective blow through Middle Tennessee, gaining the enemy's rear, cutting off his supplies and dividing his forces, so as to encounter him in detail. In any event much will be accomplished in simply preserving our line and preventing a descent into Georgia, than which no greater disaster could befall us My forces commenced the move yesterday, those in and about Mobile proceeding first, so as to re-enforce General Smith at the earliest moment. As long as we are passing, Mobile is safe, and at the close a sufficient force will be left there. I shall move to-morrow with department headquarters to Chattanooga.

I am, sir,

BRAXTON BRAGG,
General, Commanding.

HEADQUARTERS DEPARTMENT No. 2,
Tupelo, Miss., July 23, 1862.

Maj. Gen. EARL VAN DORN,
Commanding District of Mississippi, Jackson, Miss.:

GENERAL: Special Orders, No. 4, Headquarters of the Forces, dated Tupelo, July 21, 1862, is transmitted herewith for your information, touching the important movement therein directed. The headquarters of the department, I am instructed to say, after to-morrow will be transferred to Chattanooga, Tenn.

Generals Sherman and Hurlbut, of the Federal Army, have hastily abandoned their positions in vicinity of Grand Junction and retired on Memphis, destroying, it is reported, the bridges behind them. Their troops are represented to be much demoralized, in consequence of a wide division of sentiment concerning the negro question. A cavalry force from this army to co-operate with General Villepigue's cavalry is now moving on and to the rear of Grand Junction to menace and harass the enemy. It is the wish of the commanding general that you should consult freely and co-operate with Major-General Price. It is expected that you will do all things deemed needful without awaiting instructions from these headquarters. General Price will be instructed to the same effect.

Respectfully, general, your obedient servant,

THOMAS JORDAN,
Chief of Staff.

[Inclosure.]

SPECIAL ORDERS, } HEADQUARTERS OF THE FORCES,
No. 4. } *Tupelo, Miss., July 21, 1862.*

I. The Army of the Mississippi, Major-General Hardee commanding, will be transferred with the least delay practicable to Chattanooga, Tenn., in the following order and manner:

1st. The artillery, cavalry, engineer, pioneer, and wagon trains will move via Aberdeen, Columbus, Miss., Tuscaloosa, through Will's Valley to Gadsden, Ala., and Rome, Ga. The batteries may be sent by rail from Randolph via Talladega, the horses by the ordinary roads, meeting the batteries at the terminus of the railroad.

2d. The regiment of Louisiana infantry will march with the trains as an escort.

3d. Cheatham's, Withers', and Jones' divisions will be dispatched by rail via Mobile in the order named. Wood's division will move in accordance with instructions to be hereafter given; meantime it will be held in readiness.

4th. The several chiefs of staff departments of the forces will take measures to carry out these movements.

5th. Commanders especially and officers of all grades are earnestly called on to enforce discipline, secure good order, and prevent straggling. No delays must occur by the wayside from tardiness on the part of the troops. The high reputation this army has made for itself must not be sacrificed for petty personal gratifications; its efficiency must be preserved in order that it may strike the enemy effectively and decisively in the impending campaign.

II. Major-General Price, commanding Army of the West, will assume command of all troops in the State of Mississippi not included in the Districts of the Mississippi and of the Gulf. He will be charged with all operations within the prescribed limits and Northwest Alabama. This command will be known as the District of the Tennessee.

III. The available infantry force now at Mobile and Pollard will be thrown forward to Chattanooga with all possible dispatch. They will be replaced by a part of Jones' division, Army of the Mississippi.

By command of General Bragg:

THOMAS JORDAN,
Chief of Staff.

SPECIAL ORDERS, }　　　HEADQUARTERS OF THE FORCES,
No. 6. 　　　 }　　　　　　　*Tupelo, Miss., July 23, 1862.*

*　　*　　*　　*　　*　　*　　*

So much of Paragraph III, Special Orders, No. 4, Headquarters of the Forces, July 21, 1862, as relates to Jones' division is revoked, and Major-General Hardee will detach from his command the Seventeenth and Eighteenth Regiments Alabama and the Eighteenth and Nineteenth Regiments Louisiana Volunteers, to form part of the garrison of the defenses of Mobile, and to report to the commanding general of the District of the Gulf.

*　　*　　*　　*　　*　　*　　*

By command of General Bragg:

JNO. M. OTEY,
Assistant Adjutant-General.

HEADQUARTERS DEPARTMENT NO. 2,
Tupelo, Miss., July 24, 1862.

Maj. Gen. STERLING PRICE,
Commanding Army of the West, &c.:

GENERAL: I am instructed by the commander of the forces to inform you that Captain Roddey is detached with a squadron of cavalry on special service in Northwest Alabama, where he has shown himself to be an officer of rare energy, enterprise, and skill in harassing the enemy and procuring information of his movements. Captain Roddey has the entire confidence of the commanding general, who wishes to commend him to you as one eminently worthy of trust. He wishes Captain Roddey to remain detached as now and to continue, as at present, invested with the widest discretion as to his movements and operations. The general has always directed Captain Roddey to be furnished with money and supplies on his requisition.

Respectfully, your obedient servant,

THOMAS JORDAN,
Chief of Staff.

GENERAL ORDERS, }   HEADQUARTERS DEPARTMENT No. 2,
    No. 103.   }   *Tupelo, Miss., July* 24, 1862.

By direction of the President of the Confederate States a court of inquiry is appointed to assemble at such time and place as may hereafter be determined by Major-General Van Dorn to examine into the conduct of Maj. Gen. G. B. Crittenden, Provisional Army of the Confederate States, under the provisions of the "act to punish drunkenness in the army," approved April 21, 1862.

Detail for the Court: Maj. Gen. Earl Van Dorn, Provisional Army of the Confederate States; Maj. Gen. John C. Breckinridge, Provisional Army of the Confederate States; Brig. Gen. Daniel Ruggles, Provisional Army of the Confederate States. Lieut. Col. G. W. Brent is appointed judge-advocate, and is authorized to issue summons or subpœnas to all the necessary witnesses within the limits of the department, which all persons will be required to obey promptly.

By command of General Bragg:

THOMAS JORDAN,
Chief of Staff.

SPECIAL ORDERS, }   HEADQUARTERS DEPARTMENT No. 2,
    No. 131.   }   *Tupelo, Miss., July* 24, 1862.

I. The headquarters of the department are transferred to Chattanooga, Tenn., where all the required reports will be made as usual.

II. The different chiefs of staff departments will take early measures to reduce the depots of supplies in their respective departments in the District of Tennessee to a proper supply basis.

III The medical director will arrange for the early reduction of the general hospitals, and all convalescents of the Army of the Mississippi will be sent after their regiments as soon as practicable.

*   *   *   *   *   *   *

By command of General Bragg:

THOMAS JORDAN,
Chief of Staff.

RICHMOND, VA., *July* 26, 1862.

General BRAGG, *Mobile, Ala* :

Adjutant-general informs me that he has written to you at Tupelo in relation to additional generals, pointing out limitation of authority in laws. Have you received the letter? I wish to aid and sustain you in every practicable manner. Only generals for brigades and divisions can be appointed by me, as legally authorized.

JEFFERSON DAVIS.

Special Orders, }   Headquarters Department No. 2,
   No. 133.   }   Mobile, Ala., July 26, 1862.

I. Maj. Gen. Samuel Jones is relieved from duty with the Army of the Mississippi, and will assume command of the District of the Gulf, relieving Brigadier-General Forney, who will then report to Major-General Hardee, commanding Army of the Mississippi.

II. Captain Semple will proceed to Chattanooga with his battery and report for duty to Major-General Hardee.

III. The commanding officer at Columbus, Miss., will detach and send to Mobile the best organized, equipped, and instructed of the reserve batteries at that point.

*   *   *   *   *   *   *

V. The Twenty-first Alabama Volunteers will be detached from the Army of the Mississippi and assigned to duty as a part of the garrison of Mobile. Forsyth's battalion Alabama artillery will be relieved from duty in the District of the Gulf, and will report to Major-General Hardee, at Chattanooga.

By command of General Bragg:

THOMAS JORDAN,
Chief of Staff.

RICHMOND, VA., July 26, 1862.

General BRAXTON BRAGG, Mobile, Ala.:

The confidence felt in General Forney, at Mobile, and the knowledge he has acquired as the successor of General Jones, render the propriety of withdrawing him very doubtful. Please reconsider your purpose in that regard. There are other reasons which I would communicate, if time permitted me to do so, by mail.

JEFFERSON DAVIS.

Special Orders, }   Headquarters Department No. 2,
   No. 134.   }   Mobile, Ala., July 27, 1862.

Paragraph I, Special Orders, No. 133, Headquarters Department No. 2, Mobile, Ala., July 26, 1862, is revoked, and General Forney will remain in command of the District of the Gulf.

By command of General Bragg:

THOMAS JORDAN,
Chief of Staff.

HEADQUARTERS ARMY OF THE WEST,
Tupelo, Miss., July 27, 1862.

Capt. SOL. G. KITCHEN:

CAPTAIN: You will, by order of the major-general commanding, proceed at once to Fulton with all the efficient men of McCulloch's battalion. You will there select from the detachment of the Second Tennessee Cavalry, commanded by Major Morton, as many non-commissioned officers and men, not exceeding 50, as you may choose. These, with three commissioned officers, will be detailed by Major Morton and placed under your command. Major Morton will also deliver to you the instructions, written and verbal, which were given to him by Brig. Gen. Frank Armstrong on or about the 19th instant, and you are directed to carry out these instructions carefully. Having gotten your command together you will proceed without delay to Bay Springs and establish your headquarters in that immediate vicinity, and take command of all the cavalry which may be there and at Marietta and in the neighborhood of these places.

You will, as far as the instructions of General Armstrong to Major Morton permit, extend your operations in the direction of Tennessee River, between Jacinto and Iuka, and gain all the information that you can as to the position, strength, and movements of the enemy. You will send daily information to these headquarters of your movements.

Lieutenant Wells, commanding a detachment of scouts, will report to you with 14 men as part of your command. He is a very reliable officer. You will, if possible, arm his men efficiently for the expedition. The arms will be returned immediately. The commissary of the cavalry brigade will be ordered to provide subsistence for you at Bay Springs after the expiration of five days, and you are authorized to purchase such subsistence and forage as you may require, and to give orders for the payment of the same on the proper officers of the brigade.

The major-general commanding reposes trust in the intelligence, prudence, and courage with which you will conduct this expedition.

You will upon leaving Fulton report the fact to these headquarters, with the number of your officers and men.

I am, very respectfully, your obedient servant,

THOS. L. SNEAD,
Assistant Adjutant-General.

[JULY 28, 1862.—For Beauregard to Bragg, in reference to military operations, see Series I, Vol. XVI, Part I, p. 711.]

HEADQUARTERS ARMY OF THE MISSISSIPPI,
Tupelo, Miss., July 29, 1862.

Maj. Gen. SAMUEL JONES,
Comdg. Second Division, Army of the Mississippi:

GENERAL: I am instructed by the major-general commanding to acquaint you that he will leave Tupelo on to-day's train. The general will expect division commanders to exert every energy to forward promptly the troops of their respective commands. A regimental supply of ammunition will in all cases be kept on hand and be transported with the regiment. The troops will be provided with seven days' rations of bacon and two days' rations of bread. Fresh supplies of bread will be obtained at Mobile, Montgomery, and Atlanta. Division commanders are authorized to order the discharge of non-conscripts whose names shall be reported for discharge by the examining boards appointed under General Orders, No. 28, current series.

Respectfully, your obedient servant,

T. B. ROY,
Assistant Adjutant-General.

HEADQUARTERS ARMY OF THE WEST,
Tupelo, Miss., July 29, 1862.

Brigadier-General LITTLE,
Commanding Division:

GENERAL: You will at once take position at Saltillo with two brigades of your division, ordering General Green's brigade forward instantly, as that place and Guntown are threatened by the enemy. Colonel Wheeler, commanding a regiment of cavalry near Guntown, will report to you there. The major-general commanding instructs m(to request you to cause General Green's brigade with one battery to move forward without delay.

I am, very respectfully, your obedient servant,

THOS. L. SNEAD.

Abstract from Return of the District of the Mississippi, commanded by Maj. Gen. Earl Van Dorn, July, 1862 *(headquarters Vicksburg, Miss.).*

Troops.	Present for duty.		Aggregate present.	Aggregate present and absent.
	Officers.	Men.		
FIRST SUB-DISTRICT.				
Sumter Regiment (30th Louisiana)	22	271	382	592
Detachment Stewart's Legion	8	211	273	293
1st Regiment Partisan Rangers	35	817	852	852
Miles' Legion	22	320	573	599
Magruder Partisans	2	33	35	64
Lewis' Partisans	4	36	41	69
Terrell Dragoons	3	66	76	81
Norman's cavalry	2	34	41	75
Jones' cavalry	4	65	74	78
Semmes' battery	5	91	101	104
Connor Battery	4	50	86	92
Boone's battery	5	118	123	123
Brookhaven Artillery	3	95	105	118
Seven Stars Artillery	4	130	135	146
SECOND SUB-DISTRICT.				
4th Louisiana	32	371	719	775
17th Louisiana	27	373	540	637
26th Louisiana	29	389	721	805
27th Louisiana	26	249	917	973
28th Louisiana	25	278	496	658
3d Mississippi	35	476	709	886
6th Mississippi Battalion	17	161	555	818
28th Mississippi Cavalry	20	285	448	527
English's battery	2	29	32	32
1st Battalion Louisiana Artillery	17	214	398	465
8th Battalion Louisiana Artillery	9	77	133	259
1st Mississippi Light Artillery	24	399	625	877
Regiment heavy artillery	16	153	284	330
Sappers and Miners	2	12	18	23
THIRD SUB-DISTRICT.				
1st Alabama	9	91	137	193
Confederate regiment	32	422	604	791
12th Louisiana	41	546	662	1,043
20th Mississippi	3	37	46	74
33d Mississippi	31	475	640	984
39th Mississippi (Company I)			76	105
39th Mississippi	29	541	683	846
Stewart's Legion	6	169	190	256
Falkner Partisans				115
Carroll Dragoons		26	42	71
Jackson's cavalry	39	581	696	1,087
Pinson's cavalry	22	220	299	801
Ward's Battalion Artillery	10	96	137	172
Sappers and Miners	1	41	48	53
FOURTH SUB-DISTRICT.				
Porter's Partisans	3	96	109	127
Battalion Zouaves	4	102	114	165
Escort cavalry	3	33	55	58
Grand total	637	9,279	14,030	18,292

Abstract from Morning Reports of Ruggles' division, July 31, 1862.

Commands.	Present for duty.		Presen sick.	
	Officers.	Men.	Officers.	Men.
First Brigade	78	933	3	139
Second Brigade	71	930	1	99
Total	149	1,863	4	238

[AUGUST 1, 1862.—For Bragg to Cooper, from Chattanooga, see Series I, Vol. XVI, Part II, p. 741.]

CHATTANOOGA, TENN., *August 2*, 1862.

General STERLING PRICE:

Rosecrans commands Pope's army. Nearly the whole force at Corinth should be moved this way. The road is open for you into Western Tennessee. Captain Roddey must ascertain and report if he crosses river.

BRAXTON BRAGG.

HEADQUARTERS ARMY OF THE WEST,
August 3, 1862.

General ARMSTRONG:

GENERAL: The major-general commanding desires you to make a descent, if practicable, upon Iuka and Eastport. It is said that they are feebly garrisoned, and that the public stores at the latter place are very valuable. He does not wish you to incur any risk, nor to make attack unless you shall be fully satisfied of your ability to withdraw your command, the presence of which and also yourself is very important to this army. He also instructs me to impress upon you the absolute importance of not delaying an hour in the vicinity of any place where you may strike a blow, and of moving your command rapidly to some distant point.

Captain Kitchen is at Bay Springs with about 100 good men. He is a perfectly reliable man and excellent officer. He will be instructed to hold himself in readiness to obey your orders. Major-General Little is at Saltillo with his command.

The bearer, Lieutenant Trezevant, of Forrest's cavalry, will explain the omissions and give you much valuable information. You will please hasten to return with your command to camp, as there is important work to be done.

General Bragg has sent the following dispatch to the major-general commanding:

Convey to General Armstrong my cordial congatulations at his successes. The conduct of himself and his gallant command shall be made the subject of a special dispatch to the Government.

You will please notify me of the receipt of this communication.

I am, very respectfully, your obedient servant,

THOS. L. SNEAD,
Assistant Adjutant-General.

GENERAL ORDERS, }   HEADQUARTERS DEPARTMENT NO. 2,
No. 104.   }   *Chattanooga, Tenn., August* 3, 1862.

At the request of Brig. Gen. W. H. Carroll, Provisional Army of the Confederate States, the allegations against that officer will be laid before and investigated by the officers appointed in General Orders, No. 103, Department No. 2, Tupelo, Miss., July 24, 1862, as a court of inquiry to inquire into the conduct of Major-General Crittenden.

In the matter of Brigadier-General Carroll, these officers will constitute and sit as a court of inquiry within the purview of the ninety-first article of war, and will take up the investigation at such time or times and place or places as Major-General Van Dorn may direct.

By command of General Bragg:

THOMAS JORDAN,
Chief of Staff.

HEADQUARTERS DISTRICT OF THE TENNESSEE,
Tupelo, Miss., August 4, 1862.
Brig. Gen. THOMAS JORDAN,
Chief of Staff, Chattanooga, Tenn.:

GENERAL: I have the honor to inclose, for the information of the general commanding, copies of two letters which I have addressed to General Van Dorn and Governor Pettus, respectively [A and B]. I addressed similar communications to them on the 31st ultimo [C and D], but have not yet received any reply.

I am extremely impatient to begin a forward movement, and am bending every energy to do so without any unnecessary delay. I am ordering forward the entire disposable force in the district. I expect to begin my march within a week or ten days.

The enemy are still moving eastward rapidly. I do not think that they have at this time more than 15,000 men in the vicinity of Corinth, and probably about the same number at Memphis, Bolivar, and Jackson. General Armstrong has not returned yet. Colonel Wheeler got here to-day. His command will arrive to-morrow, and Hagan's and Wade's regiments will leave at once *en route* for Chattanooga.

I have the honor to be, with the greatest respect, your obedient servant,

STERLING PRICE,
Major-General, Commanding.

[Inclosure A.]

HEADQUARTERS DISTRICT OF THE TENNESSEE,
Tupelo, Miss., August 4, 1862.
Maj. Gen. EARL VAN DORN,
Commanding District of the Mississippi:

GENERAL: I telegraphed you yesterday that dispatches from General Bragg make it almost impossible for me to re-enforce General Breckinridge. He says very pointedly that West Tennessee is now open to my army, intimating that he expects me to enter it. I do not feel at liberty to disregard such an intimation, especially when I consider the very important relations which this army bears to that in East Tennessee. I cannot get possession of the railroad before Thursday. It will then take at least a week to transport to this point the troops, &c., **which** must be brought hither preparatory to a forward movement. I regret very much that I have to submit to even this unavoidable delay. I cannot think of protracting it, except under compulsion of the gravest necessity. To attempt to re-enforce General Breckinridge would protract it indefinitely. The success of the campaign depends now upon the promptness and boldness of our movements and the ability which we may manifest to avail ourselves of our present advantages. The enemy are still transferring their troops from Corinth and its vicinity eastward. They will by the end of this week have reduced their force to its minimum. We should be quick to take advantage of this, for they will soon begin to get in re-enforcements under the late call for volunteers. The present obstructed condition of the railroads is another reason for instant action. In fact every consideration makes it important that I shall move forward without a day's unnecessary delay. I earnestly desire your co-operation in such a movement, and will, as I have before said, be glad to place my army and myself under your command in that contingency. The very names of yourself and General Breckinridge would bring thousands to our ranks and carry dismay to those of the enemy.

You speak in your dispatch of the frightful amount of sickness in General Breckinridge's division. I fear the sweltering heats of this latitude will soon begin to tell fearfully upon my own ranks, and am for that reason the more anxious to take them northward, where we hope to gain accessions from those Tennesseeans and Kentuckians who have seen and felt the wretchedness of northern domination.

Captain Loughborough will deliver this communication to you and explain more particularly the condition of things in this vicinity.

Please inform me by telegraph of your determination, so that in the event of its being favorable we may concert a plan of operations.

I am, general, with the profoundest respect, your obedient servant,

STERLING PRICE,
Major-General, Commanding.

[Inclosure B.]

HEADQUARTERS DISTRICT OF THE TENNESSEE,
Tupelo, Miss., August 4, 1862.

Gov. JOHN J. PETTUS,
    Jackson County, Mississippi:

GOVERNOR: The events of each day impress me more deeply with the importance of prompt action on the part of this army, and you will therefore pardon me for again invoking your assistance. You can strengthen my army several thousand by calling out about 2,000 of the militia to garrison Meridian, Columbus, Okolona, and Verona, and to protect the railroad bridges and trestle-work. This will enable me to withdraw all the Confederate troops from that duty and put them in the field. I must beg you in the event of your being willing to comply with this request to act promptly, as I intend to order all the disposable troops forward to Tupelo within the present week, preparatory to an immediate forward movement. I would suggest to Your Excellency the propriety of preserving absolute secrecy as to the proposed movement, as the enemy are doubtless impressed with the idea that the whole army is being moved eastward and as they seem to be acting upon that belief. You may also aid me very greatly by sending forward recruits, and in this connection I may say that Captain Gholson proposes, with your concurrence, to raise a battalion of sharpshooters for service with the Army of the West. I hope that you will give him your assistance in this work. The necessity of immediate action must be my apology for again addressing Your Excellency upon this subject without awaiting your reply to my preceding communication.

I have the honor to be, with the greatest respect, your obedient servant,

STERLING PRICE,
Major-General.

[Inclosure C.]

HEADQUARTERS DISTRICT OF THE TENNESSEE,
Tupelo, Miss., July 31, 1862.

Maj. Gen. EARL VAN DORN,
Comdg. District of the Mississippi, Vicksburg, Miss. :

GENERAL : Official dispatches from General Armstrong and the reports of scouts and others all confirm the fact that General Halleck's army is being rapidly transferred eastward, and that Buell's, Thomas', and Rosecrans' divisions have already passed Tuscumbia, Rosecrans passing Tuscumbia on Saturday. I do not think that General Grant, who remains in command at Corinth, can have more than 15,000 troops there, though Colonel Wheeler, commanding a cavalry brigade in North Mississippi, reports that the enemy have recently concentrated about 10,000 at Bolivar. This must, however, be an overestimate. It at all events seems to me unquestionable that they must, in order to meet General Bragg, continue to remove troops eastward, and that they cannot leave more than 20,000 under General Grant. This will be our opportunity, and I am extremely anxious that we shall avail ourselves of it. I therefore send a gentleman to Governor Pettus to ask his cooperation, and another, Dr. Luke P. Blackburn, volunteer aide-de-camp, to you to submit the matter to your consideration. It is my opinion that, if we will advance our armies rapidly and concurrently toward Grand Junction or some other point on or near the Tennessee line at the same time obstructing the railroads, we can move irresistibly through Western or Central Tennessee into Kentucky. The enemy can only confront us by weakening the army opposed to General Bragg. The result will be the same in either case—a victory to the Confederate arms either through our forces or through those under the immediate command of General Bragg. It seems to me that in view of the great results that would flow from the reoccupation of Tennessee we ought not to hesitate to endanger every minor one; that the true way, in other words, of completing the work of regaining complete possession of the Mississippi, which you have so gloriously begun at Vicksburg, is to advance with our armies into Kentucky. I can put 15,000 effective men in the field. I am getting them in readiness for instant service. I will gladly place them under your command if you will co-operate with me in the proposed movement, and be proud to serve under the defender of Vicksburg. The Governor of Mississippi can surely increase our forces several thousand, and can garrison the posts and continue the defense of Vicksburg with the State Militia.

I am, general, with the greatest respect, your obedient servant,

STERLING PRICE,
Major-General, Commanding.

[Inclosure D.]

HEADQUARTERS DISTRICT OF THE TENNESSEE,
Tupelo, Miss., July 31, 1862.

Governor PETTUS,
  Governor of Mississippi :

GOVERNOR : I have sent a gentleman to General Van Dorn asking his co-operation in a proposed movement of our combined forces. My proposition presupposes your co-operation. I therefore send a gentleman, the Rev. Mr. Gladney, to lay the matter before you and to ascertain your views. I inclose a copy of the letter [see Inclosure C] which I have addressed to General Van Dorn. I shall immediately order forward every efficient man who can be spared for the protection of the depots and arsenals within the district. I would like to order every one of them who is in the Confederate service forward, and by supplying their places with militia you can enable me to do so. I also respectfully urge upon you the importance of immediately sending to my army as many recruits, by conscription or otherwise, as you possibly can. We can quickly relieve your State of the presence of the foe if we will only be prompt, energetic, and bold.

I have the honor to be, with the greatest respect, your obedient servant,

STERLING PRICE,
Major-General, Commanding.

TUPELO, MISS., *August 4, 1862.*

General BRAGG, *Chattanooga, Tenn. :*

Colonel Wheeler has returned. Can you not leave Hagan's and Wade's cavalry here? I shall move forward immediately and need more cavalry. I have asked General Van Dorn to co-operate with me.

Respectfully,

STERLING PRICE,
Major-General.

HEADQUARTERS ARMY OF THE WEST,
Tupelo, Miss., August 4, 1862.

Brigadier-General ARMSTRONG :

GENERAL : Dispatches from Captain Kitchen are to the effect that some 4,000 of the enemy have just been moved to Iuka. This, if true and if they remain there, must change the plan proposed. In that event you will return to these headquarters without delay. The major-general commanding instructs me to caution you again not to incur any risk.

I am, very respectfully, your obedient servant,

THOS. L. SNEAD,
Assistant Adjutant-General.

HEADQUARTERS DISTRICT OF THE TENNESSEE,
Tupelo, Miss., August 5, 1862.

Col. JOHN ADAMS,
  Commanding Post, Columbus, Miss. :

COLONEL : The major-general commanding wishes all the troops at Columbus that can be possibly spared from garrison duty to be moved instantly to this place. The first train for their transportation will be at Columbus on Thursday, the 7th instant, and the general, relying upon your well-known energy and experience, charges you with the duty of causing them to be transported without delay. Measures must be promptly taken to bring into camp all those who are well enough. The whereabouts and condition of those not well enough will be carefully ascertained and reported. No more furloughs or leaves of absence will be granted until further orders, except under peculiar circumstances. You will please communicate these orders to the commanders of the troops at Columbus, and designate which troops are to remain there on garrison duty. Retain only so many as are absolutely necessary, and hold them in readiness to be moved at any moment, for it is hoped that they will soon be relieved by the State Militia. The general suggests for your consideration the propriety of removing the prisoners of war from Columbus to a point where the public property is less valuable and where the facilities for escape are not so great. Their removal would obviate the necessity of keeping so large a garrison at Columbus, and might be beneficial otherwise. You will please consider the subject and report the facts and your opinion to the general. You will please telegraph whether you will be able to begin the shipment of the troops on Thursday.

I am, very respectfully, your obedient servant,

THOS. L. SNEAD,
Chief of Staff.

CHATTANOOGA, TENN., *August* 5, 1862.
(Received at Tupelo, Miss., August 6, 1862.)

General STERLING PRICE:

Impossible to spare you more cavalry than already given. None here now, and our movements much retarded for want of it. Your movement will accord finely with ours.

BRAXTON BRAGG.

HEADQUARTERS ARMY OF THE WEST,
Tupelo, Miss., August 6, 1862.

Capt. GEORGE L. BAXTER:

CAPTAIN: The major-general commanding directs me to say that he submits it altogether to your discretion whether you make the attempt to capture General Grant or not. While the exploit would be very brilliant if successful, you must remember that failure might be disastrous to you and your men. The general commends your activity and energy, and expects you to continue to show these qualities.

I am, very respectfully, your obedient servant,

THOS. L. SNEAD,
Assistant Adjutant-General.

HEADQUARTERS DEPARTMENT NO. 2,
Chattanooga, Tenn., August 6, 1862.

General S. COOPER,
Adjutant and Inspector General, Richmond, Va.:

GENERAL: I have the honor to inclose herewith a list* of the general officers serving with the troops in this department, and a statement* of

---

* Not found.

the organization, by which it may be seen at a glance how deficient these forces are in commanders. These papers are submitted in view of the objections made to appointments recommended. No allowance has been made for sickness or other disability and none for the men absent from the ranks. Were the men borne on the muster-rolls present for duty, as they should be, our brigades would be largely increased in numbers. I do not hesitate to assert that a fourth of our efficiency is lost for want of suitable brigade and division commanders. Scarcely a disaster has befallen our arms that cannot be traced to this cause. It is, in my judgment, a pernicious rule to rely for commanders on established rank. No appointing power can avoid errors through which in time each grade must become incumbered with some incapable and inefficient officers, who cannot be employed without material prejudice to the service. For this reason alone our division commanders should be selected from the best brigadiers available, which cannot be done unless the rank of major-general is conferred upon them. It will add nothing to their pay and emoluments or increase the expense to the Government, while all experience convinces me of the advantages that may be anticipated.

Respectfully, general, your obedient servant,
BRAXTON BRAGG.

HEADQUARTERS DISTRICT OF THE TENNESSEE,
Tupelo, Miss., August 6, 1862.

Hon. GEORGE W. RANDOLPH, *Secretary of War:*

I have the honor to inform you that when I assumed command of the Army of the West I found that a large portion of the troops had never been paid, though they had been in service for from six to eight months. I immediately caused statements to be made of the pay in arrears and forwarded them to the general commanding the department, and received in reply the inclosed communication,* signed by Maj. Albert J. Smith, chief paymaster of the department. This reply encouraged me to hope that the funds might yet be obtained in a reasonable time; but General Bragg, when he left for Chattanooga, directed me to send to Richmond for them and not to expect them to be forwarded through his headquarters. I therefore send Major Williams, quartermaster of one of the divisions of this army, to Richmond with the proper estimates, and I beg you to order him to be facilitated in this business as far as possible. Many of my officers and men are in very great need of money, and the chiefs of the several departments also. As we are about to begin an active campaign it is very important that we should not be crippled by a want of funds.

I am, sir, with the greatest respect, your obedient servant,
STERLING PRICE,
Major-General, Commanding.

HEADQUARTERS DISTRICT OF THE TENNESSEE,
August 7, 1862.

Colonel FALKNER, *Commanding Partisan Rangers:*

COLONEL: The major-general commanding directs me to say in reply to your questions that—

1st. You will send all prisoners to headquarters without unnecessary delay.

---
* Not found.

2d. You will pursue a kind and conciliatory policy toward all Union men who are not suspected of giving aid and comfort to the enemy. These you will arrest and keep under guard and notify the general of the fact. Private property must not be impressed.

3d. You will promptly arrest all men who sell cotton to the enemy and send them to these headquarters.

4th. You will make your requisitions for quartermaster's and commissary supplies upon any post quartermaster or commissary, and such officer is hereby authorized and required to fill such requisitions when practicable.

It is utterly impossible to furnish you transportation from this point. The chief quartermaster of the army will be directed to give you instructions as to that and as to the purchase of forage.

I am, very respectfully, your obedient servant,

THOS. L. SNEAD,
Assistant Adjutant-General.

TUPELO, MISS., *August* 7, 1862.

Col. JOHN ADAMS, *Columbus, Miss.:*

Only two regiments can be left at Columbus, and they must be in readiness to move.

THOS. L. SNEAD,
Assistant Adjutant-General.

HEADQUARTERS DISTRICT OF THE TENNESSEE,
Tupelo, Miss., August 7, 1862.

Col. W. H. MOORE,
Comdg. Forty-third Mississippi Regiment, Gainesville, Miss.:

COLONEL: You will move your regiment at once to Tupelo. The trains will be put at your disposal for that purpose within the next three or four days. One company may, if absolutely required, be left to garrison the post for a few days. General Price expects you to move promptly.

I am, colonel, very respectfully, &c.,

THOS. L. SNEAD,
Assistant Adjutant-General.

CHATTANOOGA, TENN., *August* 7, 1862.

General G. T. BEAUREGARD:

MY DEAR GENERAL: I did not write you about the movement here or during the course of it because General Bragg said he would, and he of course could write more intelligibly than I could of the plans and views with which the movement was undertaken. To me, as matters stood—at a dead-lock—at Tupelo, the transfer of the Army of the Mississippi to this place and change of base were most acceptable, though really, in view of past events, I am not so hopeful as I used to be of seeing a mobilized army, and I shall not count too strongly on results until I see this army on the other bank of the Tennessee. McLean has been changed, but not for the better I fear, and I fear much the present incumbent of the chief quartermaster's chair is a complete obstruction, who might do very well to administer in peace times the duties of a post quartermaster at a two-company post on the Texas frontier. Hence, I have no hopeful anticipations about transportation or an effective administration of the quartermaster's department, which is the vital force of such an army in the campaign proposed.

Meantime, however, Kirby Smith has a fine opportunity to strike a blow at General Morgan before Cumberland Gap. The proper force has been furnished, and if he does not effect something so great it will be truly unfortunate. The enemy in our front, unless we are grossly deceived by all appearances and a large amount of concurrent testimony, are disposed in a manner astonishingly favorable for our attack, being very much scattered and separate; if in a line, by no means favorable for rapid concentration if requisite; indeed, it looks as if they want to give as little trouble as possible; but it remains to be seen how efficiently, that is, how speedily, we shall be able to take advantage of their kindness. Buell of course can have no serious notion of attempting to cross the Tennessee now, at Bridgeport, with this army to contest the passage; therefore I am at a loss to comprehend his movements, especially his concentration of so many men at Bridgeport and thereabouts, and his division of his forces at points that can be struck from here like Murfreesborough was.

I hope you are now about ready to report for duty and that you will hasten to do so. The rest, quiet, and respite from duty you have enjoyed must have placed you all right on your feet again, and re-entrance in the legitimate sphere for you in times like these may now be better for you than the quietude of so warm a place as Bladon Springs must be at this season. I shall hope to hear that you have indeed already made application for orders. I sometimes hope that Mr. Davis may make certain amends and order you to Virginia for duty. He gave Governor Harris, however, to understand that you were not permanently taken away from this army—did not say so expressly, but, the Governor says, left the distinct impression on his mind that you would resume command of this department when well again. Your criticisms on the Richmond combats are certainly sound, and the more I hear of that field the more I am amazed at the paucity of results.

Dick Taylor was here yesterday *en route* for West Louisiana, where he is to command as a major-general. General Bragg asked for him in that grade with this army. He was appointed, but sent to West Louisiana. He says Huger has been assigned to duty with only his rank of colonel in the Confederate Army, his provisional grade of major-general having been abated. Magruder is charged with incompetency and loss of head, and much blame attached both to his and Huger's slowness.

D. H. Hill told Toombs on the field either to move up or resign his brigade into hands that had the nerve to lead it. Toombs challenged Hill; he declined on religious grounds. Toombs has a divided judgment as to his course, and halts, as an ass between two bundles of hay, whether to resign and cowhide Hill, or resign, make some facile Georgia member of Congress resign, take his place and overturn the Government from the floor of Congress. I had but little chance to talk with Taylor, and did not have a chance to hear more Richmond news.

The war is rapidly drifting to the black-flag phase. We cannot escape it if the new system prescribed in Pope's orders, and already inaugurated in my native county (Page) and village (Luray) is not stopped. We must accept the gauntlet thrown to us—accept the war as tendered to us, and the sooner the better. The letter of the President and the orders are in the right direction, but not radical enough. Private soldiers, as well as officers, must not go with impunity. Already officers urge that acts are done despite their efforts to repress disorder.

Even if you don't choose to report for duty, don't you think it were well for you to make your way up into this mountain region? It is a more bracing atmosphere.

The London Post (Palmerston's organ) has a most significant article, indicating our early recognition in plain terms as inevitable. Lyndsay's resolution of recognition was withdrawn from the House of Parliament at the request of Lord Palmerston, who begged that the matter should be left to the Government. All the signs indicate, I think unmistakably, an early action on the part of England and France, but you will remember that I have always said the same—yes, I have always held that it was inevitable and the only way that this war could be ended. Europe, be assured, will not permit it to be carried on much longer, especially on the destructive, savage basis inaugurated by Pope—a modern imitation of the course of Attila, the Hun.

Excuse this long letter, which I presume you would have preferred in installments. Captain Deslonde was here to-day; said he would write to you soon.

Hoping that you have now recovered and feel ready for duty, I remain, truly, your friend,

THOMAS JORDAN.

HEADQUARTERS DEPARTMENT No. 2,
Chattanooga, Tenn., August 8, 1862.

General S. COOPER,
    Adjutant and Inspector General, C. S. Army:

GENERAL: I regard it my duty to submit the following for the consideration of the War Department:

Many of the regiments of this army are mere skeletons, but with complete regimental organization, which makes them costly without corresponding benefits to such a degree as to call for a speedy and radical remedy. There are two methods by which the evil may be cured: The weaker regiments may be broken up; the men, with a limited or restricted choice between regiments and companies, may be permanently distributed among the troops of the same State and the officers discharged; or such regiments may be temporarily broken up, the men assigned for the time to such other regiments as may most require them, and the supernumerary officers detached to assist in collecting and enrolling conscripts and establishing and conducting camps of instruction, from which men shall be drawn to fill up the regiments in the service, and to reorganize the old regiments, in which case all the old soldiers scattered in other regiments shall be restored.

To the first plan, which has been partially authorized in this department, there are some patent objections in operation. By it very many incapable, inefficient officers are retained and some of the best officers in the army are necessarily discharged. Injustice is done to some worthy, zealous officers, and material injury wrought to the service, which can ill afford to lose one capable officer at this juncture. In several instances, in view of an existing deleterious condition, I have recommended resort to this plan, but am satisfied some better one must be sought. That, I think, will be found in the second remedy proposed, namely, the temporary breaking up of all these skeleton regiments, the dispersion of the men among the several regiments from the same State, and the retention and employment of all effective, competent officers, with a view to the ultimate restoration of men and officers to their reg-iments when recruited from conscripts and volunteers. This method appears to be in harmony with the spirit of the act approved April 16, and I feel assured will have all the advantages with none of the defects of the other plan, while it will be more satisfactory to officers and men. To continue these costly skeleton organizations in the field I trust will not be thought of, and I cannot hesitate to ask that I may at once be invested with authority to inaugurate the proposed system of reform.

In connection with this I must suggest another and much-needed re-form measure: The rolls of every regiment are encumbered with officers absent sick, many of whom have been absent for months. Men thus absent unfit for duty would be discharged on surgeon's certificate, and there can be no good reason why the same rule should not apply to officers, and a regulation established requiring the discharge of all field and company officers who remain unfit for duty (except from wounds in battle) for the period of ninety days. Such a regulation would work no hardship to the officers, and be fruitful of benefits to the service and a great contribution to the efficiency of our arms in the field.

Respectfully, general, your obedient servant,

BRAXTON BRAGG.

GENERAL ORDERS, }   HEADQUARTERS DEPARTMENT No. 2,
No. 109.   }   *Chattanooga, Tenn., August* 8, 1862.

I. Until otherwise ordered the forces in this department, when taking the field, will be provided with the following :

Means of transportation.—One wagon for cooking utensils, &c., for 100 men ; one wagon for extra ammunition, &c., for 400 men ; one wagon for each regimental headquarters ; one ambulance (or light two-horse wagon) for 300 men ; one wagon each for brigade and division head-quarters ; two wagons for headquarters Army Corps.

Camp equipage.—One tent to each regiment for medical department ; one tent to regimental headquarters ; two tents to brigade headquarters ; two tents to division headquarters ; six tent-flies for every 100 men.

Ammunition.—One hundred rounds ammunition of proper description for small-arms ; a full supply for artillery, and 100 rounds for infantry and 50 rounds for the artillery (extra), to be transported by the ordnance train.

II. All surplus wagons and teams and other means of transportation not prescribed in the first paragraph of these orders will be turned in immediately to the quartermaster's department.

III. All surplus tents will be transferred to the division quartermas-ters, to be turned into the nearest depot quartermaster, or for disposi-tion by the chief quartermaster of the forces.

IV. Division and brigade commanders will be held responsible for the prompt and faithful execution of the foregoing orders. They will have a thorough inspection made before taking the field of every regi-ment, company, and man to see that these and previous orders fixing the marching outfit of officers and soldiers are complied with.

V. All quartermasters will be required on the march to remain habit-ually with the rear of their trains, unless specially detached, moving promptly along to the front whenever the train is interrupted, to ascer-tain and correct the difficulty if in their trains.

By command of General Bragg :

THOMAS JORDAN,
Chief of Staff.

HEADQUARTERS DEPARTMENT No. 2,
Chattanooga, Tenn., August 9 1862.

Hon. GEORGE W. RANDOLPH,
Secretary of War :

SIR : Your letter of July 22 has just been received, having been to Tupelo and returned. My reply to a telegram from the President must have removed an erroneous impression in regard to the proportion between troops and generals in this command. In your letter you entirely ignore one-half of Van Dorn's, the whole of Forney's, and a large portion of Price's commands, not organized into brigades or divisions for want of commanders. I inclose a tabular statement* of the whole command, showing what its organization should be and the number of general officers we have and the number required.

The fact that some of the generals are absent from sickness and other causes does not remove the difficulty, for a greater proportion of the troops are also absent from similar causes. The presence of both would compel a large increase in the number of brigades and divisions.

In reference to the want of qualifications in some general officers I alluded particularly to Major-Generals Crittenden, McCown, and Cheatham, and Brigadiers Carroll, Trapier, and Hawes, as, in my judgment, unsuited for their responsible positions, and, as far as I can learn, not recommended from here.

The practice of giving command of divisions and brigades to senior brigadiers and colonels does not work well, and at times is fraught with great danger.

The recent exchange of prisoners will restore some of our generals and remove to that extent my embarrassments.

Very respectfully, your obedient servant,
BRAXTON BRAGG,
General, Commanding.

———

HEADQUARTERS DEPARTMENT No. 2,
Chattanooga, Tenn., August 9, 1862.

ADJUTANT-GENERAL C. S. ARMY, *Richmond, Va. :*

SIR : I have the honor to acknowledge receipt of your favor of the 21st ultimo, inclosing copy of communication from the acting Postmaster-General to you. In reply I will state that the Post-Office Department is misinformed. No military possession or control of the telegraph lines in my department has been assumed by me. General Johnston and afterwards General Beauregard, my predecessors, had a telegraph operator of honesty and skill as superintendent for the regulation of such matters. The same officer and the same system have been continued by me. The operator is regarded as any other member of my staff—as an agent simply to see to the faithful discharge of the duties of his department. He requires the revenues of the lines erected by military funds to be properly collected and accounted for. He also audits the accounts of telegraph companies against the Government, and by his action in this particular a large number of fraudulent charges against the Government have been detected and rejected. Had the Postmaster-General, under the recent act of Congress, applied for the control of the lines in my department he would have encountered no opposition from me. The extent of the department and the importance of military operations in it, in my opinion, made it his duty to assume

---

* Not found.

control of these lines. Having failed to discharge this duty it is not graceful in him to withhold necessary supplies for me to do it for him.

It is but justice that I should be furnished with the name of the man who makes this false report to the Post-Office Department. If my suspicions are correct it will be found that a certain telegraph operator or agent of that department—a notorious Dr. Morris, the corrupt tool and representative of a Yankee corporation—will figure in the result. I am credibly informed by an operator on the line that my official dispatches from Tupelo were never permitted to pass until inspected by this man Morris and approved by him. This may account for the non-reception by General Smith at this point of some important dispatches from Tupelo, by which our very important operations here are very much retarded. Had I really assumed the control of the lines to the extent imputed by the Postmaster-General it might have been unsafe for this tool of the Yankees to have played the spy—if not traitor—as to my military dispatches.

I would respectfully suggest that an imaginary error of mine would not justify the suspension of telegraph operations in this department, by which our cause might be greatly jeopardized if not lost. It may be important for the Post-Office Department to get control of the telegraph, but it is equally important for us to keep up communications with our troops and defeat the enemy.

I am, sir, very respectfully, your obedient servant,

BRAXTON BRAGG,
General, Commanding.

HEADQUARTERS DISTRICT OF THE TENNESSEE,
Tupelo, Miss., August 9, 1862.

GOVERNOR OF ALABAMA:

GOVERNOR: I have the honor to state that I have been compelled, in view of resuming offensive operations, immediately to withdraw the regiment which has been guarding the valuable public stores and workshops at Gainesville, in your State, and to request you to order out a sufficient number of the militia to take its place. I cannot wait for the regiment to be relieved by the State troops, but must withdraw it on Monday, the 11th instant, and orders to that effect have been already issued. I hope that Your Excellency will act without delay. Col. Thomas H. Rosser, commanding the post, can inform Your Excellency as to the number of troops that will be required. I presume 500 will suffice. Governor Pettus has promptly responded to a similar call by ordering 2,000 of the militia to garrison the several posts in this State, from which I am withdrawing the garrisons. I most respectfully beg Your Excellency to organize a sufficient militia force to garrison such other posts as it may become necessary for us to establish in Alabama as we advance northward.

Relying confidently upon your desire to co-operate with me vigorously in the effort which I am about to make—to drive the Federal armies from this State and Alabama—and upon the patriotism of the people of your State, I shall myself move steadily forward.

Major John Tyler, one of my staff officers, will present this letter to you and explain my views more fully to Your Excellency.

I am, very truly, your obedient servant,

STERLING PRICE,
Major-General.

HEADQUARTERS CAVALRY BRIGADE,
Guntown, Miss., August 10, 1862.

Maj. THOMAS L. SNEAD,
Assistant Adjutant-General, District of the Tennessee:

MAJOR: Pursuant to instructions I have established my headquarters at this place, and have nearly all of my brigade encamped in advance of me. Wirt Adams' cavalry nor the Arkansas regiment have yet arrived. The Fourth Mississippi Cavalry reported five companies present last evening, but not more than three of them armed. Their horses are in good condition, but the officers have seen no service. Will it be possible to have the ordnance officer at Columbus directed to have all cavalry arms sent to Verona or Tupelo, where I can draw them to arm these companies? The train came up yesterday, but the quartermaster failed to send any forage. My whole brigade is to-day without any. A train of corn every day might be sent up. It is impossible to obtain it in any other way. I hope, major, that some exertion on the part of the quartermaster's department will be made to furnish what I ask for, as it will be useless to keep my brigade together without it. I respectfully request that the telegraph line be put in working order to this place, as it would save much riding and express duty.

I have the honor to be, major, with much respect, your obedient servant,

FRANK C. ARMSTRONG,
Brigadier-General.

CHATTANOOGA, TENN., *August* 10, 1862.
(Received at Tupelo, Miss., August 11, 1862.)

General STERLING PRICE:

General Van Dorn directed to move as suggested by you and co oper ate. General Smith in motion from Knoxville; we will follow soon Are you advised as to Rosecrans crossing to join Buell? We have such report.

BRAXTON BRAGG.

JACKSON, MISS., *August* 11, 1862.

General STERLING PRICE:

Am directed to take offensive toward Grand Junction and Memphis. Breckinridge is near Baton Rouge; enemy been re-enforced from New Orleans; am afraid Breckinridge is too feeble to make decisive result. It will be two weeks before I can do anything. Very important to secure mouth of Red River. Can you not, therefore, send Breckinridge a brigade to make sure? They can then go with me to Grand Junction and rejoin you there. Answer. If yes, when will be here? Bragg can not move, I think, in three weeks yet.

EARL VAN DORN.

HEADQUARTERS DEPARTMENT No. 2,
Chattanooga, Tenn., August 11, 1862.

Maj. Gen. EARL VAN DORN,
Commanding Army of the Mississippi:

GENERAL: In view of the operations from here it is very desirable to press the enemy closely in West Tennessee. We learn their forces there are being rapidly reduced, and when our movements become known it is certain they must throw more forces into Middle Tennessee and Kentucky or lose those regions. If you hold them in check we are sure of success here; but should they re-enforce here so as to defy us then you may redeem West Tennessee and probably aid us by crossing to the enemy's rear.

I cannot give you specific instructions, as circumstances and military conditions in your front may vary materially from day to day. To move your available force to Holly Springs by railroad, thence into West Tennessee, co-operating with General Price (who will move soon toward Corinth), or to move to Tupelo by rail and join Price, are suggestions only. Positive instructions, except to strike at the most assailable point, cannot be given when so little is known and when circumstances may change daily. Of course when you join Price your rank gives you the command of the whole force.

I inclose a copy of Captain Jones' inspection report.* Many of the points in it require your immediate attention. First and most important is the prompt reduction of your light artillery. You have enough for an army of 100,000 men. It is impossible to keep it all up and be effective. To keep it all ineffective must be avoided. Eight batteries of four guns each is ample for your present force. As you cannot discharge the companies without authority from the War Department I suggest that you dismount them, giving such horses and material as they have to make other corps effective and transfer the officers and men to your heavy batteries, relieving infantry; or you could arm them as infantry and put them in the field. Some companies, I see, are still being equipped. Put a stop to it immediately. Other parts of the report, too, require your prompt consideration, especially in the staff departments.

The reports from the medical inspector coming in are equally unsatisfactory. Your short time in command and close engagement at Vicksburg have allowed you but little time for these matters, but I trust you will be able, through intelligent and effective staff officers, in correcting some of the evils soon.

It is with deep regret I see you lose General Villepigue, as I consider him equal to any officer in our service.

Brigadier-General Duncan, and perhaps others, exchanged, will soon be with us, when you shall be attended to.

I am, general, most respectfully and truly, yours,

BRAXTON BRAGG,
General, Commanding.

HEADQUARTERS DISTRICT OF THE TENNESSEE,
Tupelo, Miss., August 11, 1862.

Hon. GEORGE W. RANDOLPH,
Secretary of War, Richmond, Va.:

SIR: I have instructed one of my staff, Dr. Luke P. Blackburn, to wait upon you for the purpose of endeavoring to obtain from the Department for the troops of the Army of the West a portion of the improved small-arms which have lately come into the possession of the Government by capture and otherwise. Many of my troops are very badly armed, and some of the new regiments have no arms at all. I

---

* Not found.

expect, however, to arm these with inferior arms from the arsenal at Columbus. Governor Pettus has also ordered 2,000 of the militia to report to me to relieve the troops which I am withdrawing from the posts within the district, and which are guarding the railroad. These will need arms. General Van Dorn also telegraphs to me that about 15,000 of the exchanged prisoners will soon be at Vicksburg, and that many of them may be ordered to his army and this, and he asks whether I can supply them with arms. I hope, too, that as we advance into Tennessee accessions to our ranks will also occasion a want of arms.

For all these reasons I respectfully ask that you will be pleased to furnish me for the use of these troops such portion of the arms in your possession as may not be more wanted elsewhere.

I am, with the greatest respect, your obedient servant,

STERLING PRICE,
Major-General, Commanding.

HEADQUARTERS DEPARTMENT No. 2,
Chattanooga, Tenn., August 12, 1862.

Maj. Gen. STERLING PRICE,
Commanding District of Tennessee:

GENERAL: I have received copy of your letter to General Van Dorn asking co-operation in your advance upon the enemy, and have instructed him by telegraph to-day. I write and herewith inclose you a copy of my letter.* The details of your movements I must leave to your own judgment and intelligence, relying on your patriotism for a cordial co-operation. General E. K. Smith is now on march to turn the Cumberland Gap, and we hope to destroy General Morgan, who holds that with about 10,000. As soon as my transportation comes up we shall move into Middle Tennessee, and, taking the enemy's rear, strike Nashville, or perhaps, leaving that to the left, strike for Lexington and Cincinnati, both of which are entirely unprotected. The fortifications the enemy are throwing up at Huntsville, Stevenson, &c., then give us but little concern. In this move you can see how important it is for us to be sustained in West Tennessee, even with a division. I hope the enemy will so weaken himself as to enable you to do more; but you must be cautious and not allow him to strike you a fatal blow. I regret to learn General Parsons has failed to cross the Mississippi. Now that our navy is entirely defunct in the loss of the Arkansas I fear the prospect of getting him over at all is but slim. Yet let us trust we may open some other route to Missouri.

We are getting prisoners and deserters daily from the enemy, and a captured letter from Nelson to Buell of the 8th says if something is not done to prevent our sending paroled men back to his lines it will demoralize his whole command. "Fortunately," he says, "they do not parole the officers." In future let us do it, except in exceptional cases. This has been a favorite scheme with me, and it seems is bearing good fruit. Our prospects are bright.

Wishing you all success, I am, general, most respectfully and truly yours,

BRAXTON BRAGG,
General, Commanding.

---

* See Bragg to Van Dorn, August 11, 1862.

HEADQUARTERS, *August* 12, 1862.

ADJUTANT-GENERAL C. S. ARMY, *Richmond, Va.*:

SIR: In inclosing copies of the inspection reports of Lieutenant-Colonel Hallonquist and Captain Jones for the information of the War Department, I beg to call attention to the absence of proper organization and to the great disparity of numbers in the arms of the service in General Van Dorn's command. The enormous amount of field artillery—ninety-four guns—for an effective infantry of 16,000 is a palpable absurdity and evil I shall proceed to abate by all legal means in my power. No treasury could long stand such expenditures, and the resources of no country could supply material for guns, ammunition, harness, horses, and forage; besides, it would effectually destroy the efficiency of any force to be thus encumbered by the most unwieldy of arms. As this organization was in existence before Major-General Van Dorn took the command he is probably not responsible for it, though his recent requisitions call for means to keep up and even increase the artillery. The commands of Major-General Breckinridge and Brigadier-Generals Ruggles and Villepigue appear to be homogeneous and in proportion, but those of Brigadiers Smith and Beall are worse than incumbrances. A very large portion of this artillery I recommend be at once converted into infantry.

Attention is especially called to the very comprehensive and thorough report of Captain Jones. It shows great industry, zeal, and professional ability, and proves the author worthy of a higher position in the service. Many points relating to the staff departments and officers are worthy of the early attention of the War Department.

I am, sir, very respectfully, your obedient servant,

[BRAXTON BRAGG,]
General, Commanding.

TUPELO, MISS., *August* 12, 1862.

General BRAGG, *Chattanooga, Tenn.*:

The reports from Rosecrans are conflicting; he is probably on this side of the Tennessee.

STERLING PRICE,
Major-General.

HEADQUARTERS DISTRICT OF THE TENNESSEE,
Tupelo, Miss., August 12, 1862.

General BRAGG:

Rosecrans, with his command, is at Corinth and Rienzi. All reports confirm this, and I believe it to be reliable.

STERLING PRICE,
Major-General, Commanding.

HEADQUARTERS DEPARTMENT No. 2,
Chattanooga, Tenn., August 14, 1862.

Col. J. GORGAS,
Chief of Ordnance, Richmond, Va.:

SIR: I beg to call your attention to the arsenal at Columbus, Miss., and suggest a thorough inspection and overhauling. It is being expanded into proportions too gigantic for my notions of its importance, and thus far the results from the labors there have been insignificant compared with the means furnished. I am certainly indisposed to make any additions to the very large number of operatives now detailed from my command unless some results are to follow.

I am, colonel, very respectfully, your obedient servant,

BRAXTON BRAGG,
General, Commanding.

CHATTANOOGA, TENN., *August* 14, 1862.

General G. T. BEAUREGARD:

MY DEAR GENERAL: I had written you some days ago a long letter, which I hope has reached you before this, explaining why I had not written sooner. Until I reached here I was without my usual office assistance, and hence so much occupied that I could not write as satisfactorily to the Savannah Republican as I wished; and as the matter in question is one purely of history now I thought time of no moment compared with the effect I desire to make when I do write. I have written a paper on the points suggested in your notes, with some points (which I know you will approve) added. I have been calm, avoided epithets, and stated facts as I knew them, in simple language, without assailing P. W. A., if for no other reason than that there is higher game to fly at some day, as I will explain when we meet. I prefer to deal gently with P. W. A. as a dupe, which I know to be the case, while I see clear traces of the intrigues of others. The fact is, there was a hard-working party in the Army of the Mississippi engaged in underrating you—men in various ways connected with the Army of Pensacola. These are the men to be watched, tracked, and, in due time, uncovered; not mere newspaper men like Alexander, who can be taken away from them. These fellows—I have my eye on them—are toadeaters, sycophants, who think they do service to another high officer by intimating detraction of you, and some of them are staff officers. I see exactly the secret springs at work, and some others help me to see what my own powers of vision cannot reach. Be assured we are not mistaken. One of the first steps was to get rid of your staff after you left. It was partially done, and those who have been retained are objects of incessant petty jealousy—so much so that I should only remain a little while longer. I shall wait, hoping that you may obtain service. If not, I shall seek command of a brigade of Virginia troops in Virginia.

By the way, have you seen an article in a Montgomery paper based on a letter from Slaughter to the editor, with the reply of the editor, T. G. Reid, addressed to General Bragg? The letter of Slaughter, to say the least, is weak and unfortunate; that of the editor unmerciful and as cold as an avalanche of ice. It is a great pity that such matters should get into our papers or be in any way provoked. This is the second time Slaughter has written injudicious, vulnerable letters for General Bragg. He means well, but has neither the education nor natural ability for the important place he holds.

It is possible I may go to Vicksburg to arrange the final exchange of our prisoners, in which event I shall try to see you, as I do not desire to resume my duties on my return.

I shall have the copies made of the papers which you want and hand them to you.

I will write directly to Pollard, the writer or compiler of "The First Year of the War," and let him know in a private note the facts, besides which I will reach him through a friend in Richmond. You know he is an editor of the Examiner, a paper become quite friendly to you of late out of opposition to Mr. Davis.

Possibly our troops may begin to cross on Saturday. They have noble opportunities—or, as you say, "ten strikes"—before them, but I fear some advantages have been lost by delay.

Since the foregoing was written General Bragg has assigned to me the special service of going to Vicksburg to supervise the reorganization of the paroled and exchanged men into regiments and to assign them to army corps at my discretion, hence I shall be able to see you before you enter on duty. As the commissioner who will represent the Government is not here yet, I shall not leave at once; besides I am not well enough to travel, having rheumatism.

Truly, your friend,

THOMAS JORDAN.

GENERAL ORDERS, ⎰   HEADQUARTERS DEPARTMENT No. 2,
No. 114.   ⎱   Chattanooga, Tenn., August 14, 1862.

I. Lieut. G. W. Brent, adjutant and inspector general's department, is assigned to duty in the inspector-general's department, and will report to Brigadier-General Slaughter.

II. Capt. E. H. Cummins is announced as the chief signal officer of the department, and will be obeyed and respected accordingly. He will proceed to organize his corps on the most effective basis and in accordance with the provision and requirements of General Orders, No. 40, War Department, Adjutant and Inspector General's Office, Richmond, Va., May 29, 1862.

III. Maj. George Williamson, adjutant-general's department, is placed on temporary duty in the office of the chief of staff.

By command of General Bragg:

THOMAS JORDAN,
Chief of Staff.

TUPELO, MISS., August 15, 1862.

Major-General VAN DORN, Jackson, Miss.:

I can arm most of the returned prisoners.

STERLING PRICE,
Major-General.

GENERAL ORDERS, ⎰   HEADQUARTERS DEPARTMENT No. 2,
No. 117.   ⎱   Chattanooga, Tenn., August 16, 1862.

I. The following modification is made in Paragraph I, General Orders, No. 109, Headquarters Department No. 2, Chattanooga, August 8, 1862: One wagon for the extra ammunition for every 300 instead of 400 men.

II. In addition to the allowance indicated in Paragraph I, general orders specified above, there shall be provided for the medical department one two-horse wagon for each wing, division, and brigade of the forces in the field.

III. No officer or soldier will be permitted to take a trunk into the field ; soldiers shall be restricted to a knapsack and officers to a carpet-sack or small valise.

IV. Whenever prisoners are captured by our troops the ranking officer of the capturing detachment will immediately forward to these head-quarters a descriptive list of the prisoners, giving their names, rank, ages, regiments, and companies.

V. Whenever prisoners are paroled the paroles will be forwarded to these headquarters and a duplicate copy (compared and certified) retained by the officer who may grant the parole. In taking paroles, officers will be careful to have them signed if practicable ; but if not signed by the prisoners paroled, a certified list stating their names, rank, ages, regiments, and companies should be attested by an Abolition officer if one be present. In the absence of an Abolition officer the list must be certified by the Confederate officer who grants the parole. These lists must be made in duplicate if practicable, one copy to be retained by the officer taking the parole and the other to be forwarded to these headquarters without delay.

By command of General Bragg :

THOMAS JORDAN,
Chief of Staff.

GENERAL ORDERS, }   HDQRS. DISTRICT OF THE MISSISSIPPI,
No. 38.   }   *Jackson, August 17, 1862.*

All authority heretofore granted to raise Partisan Rangers in this district is revoked, and no further authority will be granted. All Partisan Rangers who are now in readiness to be mustered into service will be mustered in at once under the direction of the commanding officers of sub-districts, and at once organized into regiments and battalions.

The sub-district commanders will recommend the field officers for appointment.

By order of Maj. Gen. Earl Van Dorn :

M. M. KIMMEL,
Major and Assistant Adjutant-General.

RICHMOND, VA., *August 18, 1862.*

Major-General VAN DORN, *Vicksburg, Miss.* :

The conscript law requires all conscripts and volunteers to enter companies in service on the 16th of April, and the President has prohibited persons subject to enrollment from joining Partisan Rangers. I have so instructed the enrolling officers of Mississippi, and must request that you will bring to their notice all violations of the law and of the President's order that come to your knowledge, and that you will instruct your subordinate officers to do the same.

The officers charged with the enrollment of conscripts receive their orders from the Department, and have been instructed to distribute the conscripts of each State among the regiments of the State in proportion to their deficiencies. If you wish any departure from this rule in reference to the Mississippi regiments under your command it will be allowed

G. W. RANDOLPH,
Secretary of War.

HEADQUARTERS ARMY OF THE WEST,
Tupelo, Miss., August 19, 1862.

Colonel ROSSER:

The Governor of Alabama will order several companies of militia to garrison Gainesville. The general hopes that you will find them a sufficient force for the protection of the public stores at that post.

I am, very respectfully, your obedient servant,

THOS. L. SNEAD,
Assistant Adjutant-General.

CHATTANOOGA, TENN., *August 19, 1862.*

General STERLING PRICE:

Send the guns, if General Van Dorn desires. Have ordered 5,000 exchanged prisoners sent to you. Columbus has arms when repaired. General Smith is in motion for Kentucky. We are crossing river for Middle Tennessee. Morgan has given first blow at Gallatin. They must soon weaken [on] your front, so as to open West Tennessee, but do not depend much on Van Dorn; he has his hands full.

BRAXTON BRAGG.

AUGUST 21, 1862.

Messrs. J. W. HARRIS AND OTHERS,
Columbus, Miss.:

The difficulty of getting engines and iron for armor would render the prompt completion very difficult. Any aid that I could give would be freely rendered.

JEFFERSON DAVIS.

HEADQUARTERS CAVALRY BRIGADE,
August 22, 1862.

Maj. THOMAS L. SNEAD,
Chief of Staff, District of the Tennessee:

MAJOR: I have the honor to report that I have started with about 1,600 men of my brigade, and encamp to-night 3 miles south of Birmingham. I will move to-morrow in the direction of Holly Springs. After reaching that vicinity I shall push rapidly forward toward Grand Junction and northward. I shall move rapidly through that country and strike at any point that may be assailable. I send a strong scout north from Ellistown toward Ripley, thence in toward Booneville and back to Guntown, where they will report to Lieutenant-Colonel Lewis, whom I have left in command of about 1,200 effective men, with instructions to keep the pickets on the same line from Ellistown to Bay Springs. Captains Sanders and Mann are at the latter place. Lieutenant-Colonel Lewis, commanding cavalry at Guntown, has been ordered to report until my return to Brigadier-General Little. My quartermaster and commissary of subsistence remain at Guntown.

I wrote to Colonel Falkner to push in toward Chewalla. He will have about 400 men. An express can reach me via Holly Springs.

I have the honor to be, major, your obedient servant,

FRANK C. ARMSTRONG,
Brigadier-General.

AUGUST 25, 1862.

ADJUTANT-GENERAL :

SIR : I inclose you a copy of a dispatch from Major-General Price, indicating that the enemy are about to fall back from West Tennessee. They are already on the move back from the Memphis and Charleston Railroad toward Nashville. Large bodies have moved toward McMinnville in the last two days, and my impression is they are concentrating at or near Nashville. General Buell is certainly there now.

The latter part of General Price's dispatch requires prompt attention. The agent of the Post-Office Department is making an effort, it seems, to work our telegraph lines in that section, and the execution of my order to discharge operators employed by military authority must work serious inconvenience. We are very fearful that competent operators in sufficient numbers cannot be had by the present post-office agent, who is specially obnoxious to all of the best known to me, and they refuse to work under him. Only three lines which pay good dividends have yet been taken possession of by him, and the general impression prevails that we are in the hands of the " money-changers." If the object of the agent of the Post-Office Department was to embarrass commanders and military operations in this department he could not more successfully accomplish it.

I am, &c.,

BRAXTON BRAGG.

[Inclosure.]

TUPELO, MISS., *August 24, 1862.*

General BRAGG :

A gentleman just from Tuscumbia says it is well understood there that a strong body of troops (30,000) are to be moved eastward immediately. He knows that they are making large preparations for a movement. Have sent my cavalry to annoy them, and will continue to do it as much as possible with my force. Will the order discharging all telegraph operators in Government employ leave me without any on this line?

STERLING PRICE,
Major-General.

HEADQUARTERS DISTRICT OF THE TENNESSEE,
Tupelo, Miss., August 25, 1862.

Hon. GEORGE W. RANDOLPH,
Secretary of War:

SIR : I feel that it is not necessary for me to apologize to you for the frequency with which I request you to do such acts as seem to me calculated to promote the efficiency of the army under my command, but that it is my duty to make such requests as often as the occasion arrives. I therefore call your attention to the deficiency of general officers in the Army of the West, and to the unfortunate consequences which necessarily result from this fact.

My troops are distributed into two divisions and a cavalry brigade, commanded, respectively, by Brigadier-Generals Little and Maury and acting Brigadier-General Armstrong. Little's division (which is much the larger at present by reason of the recent addition of six regiments of Mississippi troops) consists of four brigades, commanded by Brigadier-Generals Hébert and Green and Colonels Gates and Martin; Maury's division consists of three brigades, under the command of Brigadier-General Moore and Majors Cabell and Phifer, the last two having been assigned by General Van Dorn months ago to the command of their respective brigades as acting brigadier-generals. Colonel Armstrong, who is an acting brigadier-general by appointment of General Bragg, commands the cavalry brigade, which consists of five regiments and three battalions. I do not think it will be advisable to lessen the number of these brigades, especially in view of the fact that General Bragg has informed me of his purpose to strengthen my army by ordering to it several thousand of the exchanged troops.

You will perceive from this statement that the two divisions are each commanded by brigadier-generals, while five of the eight brigades are commanded by colonels and majors. This anomalous condition of things not only deprives regiments of their proper commanders and brigades of their appropriate staff officers, but gives rise to rivalry and jealousy, which are extremely prejudicial to the harmony and discipline of the army, and which would not otherwise exist. The existence of these within this army has been brought to my knowledge for the first time since the decision of the department in the cases of Majors Cabell and Phifer has been made known. That decision disclosed the fact that there were five vacant brigadierships in this army, and the knowledge of that fact has given rise to efforts which are tending to disturb the good feeling which has hitherto characterized it. I hope that it may be your pleasure to put a summary end to all this by assigning brigadier-generals to the command of the several brigades. I do not feel that I ought, nor do I desire, to express any opinion as to the filling of these vacancies, though I will do so if such is your wish or the will of the President.

I may, however, be permitted to say that I hope that Generals Little and Maury will not be superseded in the command of their respective divisions, except by officers of acknowledged ability, and I very respectfully submit to you the impolicy of placing either of them under the command of any officer who was their junior in the United States Army, unless he has particularly distinguished himself. I may also express the wish that General Little be appointed major-general. He happened to be in Missouri when the war broke out. He at once resigned his position in the United States Army and tendered his services to me. I placed him upon my staff as assistant adjutant-general, in which capacity he continued to serve until I began, some nine months ago, to organize a brigade of Missouri troops for the Confederate service. I assigned him to the command of these. He organized, drilled, and disciplined them, and has remained in command of them ever since. They constitute the First Brigade of his division, and are as well disciplined and as efficient as any troops in the Confederate service. General Little commanded this brigade during my retreat from Springfield and at the battle of Elkhorn, and on both occasions displayed distinguished coolness, courage, and skill, and military ability of a very high character, thus demonstrating his ability not only as an organizer and disciplinarian but as a commander upon the field. His officers and men place the greatest confidence in him, and every one from Missouri has appeared willing to yield precedence to him, though he is not and has never been a resident of that State. I cannot commend him too highly nor urge the President too strongly to appoint him major-general. I would regret very much to see him superseded by any less distinguished officer, particularly if he be totally unknown to the troops.

Brigadier-General Maury, who commands the other division, has been with this army ever since the battle at Elkhorn, and was placed in his present position by General Van Dorn during the retreat from Corinth. He is a brave, gallant, intelligent, and skillful officer, attentive to all his duties, devoted to the well-being of his troops, and in every way worthy of promotion and of retention in his present command.

I repeat that I have no suggestions to make with reference to the vacant brigadierships, and that it is my only, as it is my very earnest, wish that the President will be pleased to assign able and efficient officers to them without delay, so that the troops may be at once placed under those who are to command them in the impending campaign, and that all causes which tend to the disturbance of its harmony and discipline may be removed from my army.

Brigadier-General Bowen has not yet reported for duty. I fear that he ranks both Generals Little and Maury, neither of whom ought to be superseded by him. I shall be glad to obtain the assistance of so excellent an officer, if it can be done without injury to the service or manifest injustice to those gentlemen who have been so long associated with and who are so favorably known to the army.

I have the honor to be, very respectfully, your obedient servant,
STERLING PRICE.
Major-General.

CHATTANOOGA, TENN., *August 25, 1862.*

General STERLING PRICE:

Watch your front and strike whenever it is weakened. In the mean time harass your opponent by all your cavalry. Buell is falling back toward Nashville. We must keep them moving. The Post-Office Department is required to keep up the telegraph, and its agent reports me for refusing to give up to him; hence my order. (See Paragraph III, General Orders, No. 44.) Discharge all military operators and communicate by mail.

BRAXTON BRAGG,
General, Commanding.

[Inclosure.]

GENERAL ORDERS, }   WAR DEPT., ADJT. & INSP. GEN.'S OFFICE,
No. 44.   }   *Richmond, Va., June 17, 1862.*

*   *   *   *   *   *   *

III. Congress having conferred on the President the right, during the existing war, " to take such control of the lines of telegraph in the Confederate States, and of such offices connected therewith, as will enable him effectually to supervise the communications passing through the same," and to exercise other powers in reference to telegraph lines, and the President having charged the Postmaster-General with the discharge of these duties, requisitions for building lines, the establishment and discontinuance of offices, the appointment of operators and agents, the disposition of material, &c., must be addressed to the Postmaster-General, and officers are prohibited from exercising these powers.

*   *   *   *   *   *   *

By command of the Secretary of War:

S. COOPER,
Adjutant and Inspector General.

RICHMOND, VA., *August 26*, 1862.

Gov. JOHN J. PETTUS, *Jackson, Miss.:*

I learn that the arms sent, except 1,000, were not marked for you. The chief of ordnance has been instructed to send to your address the 2,000 you request.

JEFFERSON DAVIS.

RICHMOND, VA., *August 26*, 1862.

General EARL VAN DORN, *Jackson, Miss.:*

The chief of ordnance will send you some heavy guns, and I hope they may serve the purpose proposed. Why were the arms sent to Milliken's Bend? If the railroad has not been repaired they should have been hauled from De Soto rather than exposed.

JEFFERSON DAVIS.

HEADQUARTERS,
Near Bay Springs, Miss., August 26, 1862.

Col. J. H. LEWIS:

SIR: I have to report that on yesterday the enemy came down to Paden's Mill, 10 miles north of Bay Springs, on an incendiary excursion. Paden's, Robinson's, and Vauter's Mill and eight dwelling-houses and all their contents were burned, with all the corn and meal. The vandals would not permit the women to even save their bedding. The force consisted of 60 cavalry, and after destroying the property and arresting all the men they could find returned in the direction of Iuka.

It was 10 o'clock in the morning when I first heard that the Federals were at Robinson's Mill. My first information was that they were in strong force, with infantry and artillery. I immediately dispatched the news to Captain Mann, and sent Lieutenant Coffey, of my command, with a small scout to the mill to ascertain the actual strength of the enemy. They had finished burning and started back before Lieutenant Coffey reached them. The lieutenant followed them until he ascertained their strength and that they had returned to Iuka.

My first information was received from some men who were acting as scouts, with passes approved by General Price. These fellows, in nine cases out of ten, run when they hear of the enemy, and never stay to learn the number or character of their forces, and I want to know what I must do with them when they run in here making false reports. The fact is some of them have been lying around doing nothing ever since I have been here, and I gave it out that if they did not go to work I would arrest them and send them to headquarters. Since that time they keep outside my pickets and pretend to be at work scouting.

There was one Yankee killed and another wounded on Thursday last at or near Robinson's Mill, and that is the reason assigned by the Federals for the depredations committed yesterday. The Yankee that was killed and his partner were out "guerrillaing," and were shot by two of our scouts. These are the facts as I have them. If you can relieve me of picket duty and let me remain here I will take the contract to put a stop to all such little excursions as that of the enemy on yesterday.

My scout from Iuka last night still report the enemy moving east and crossing the river at Eastport.

Yours, respectfully,

T. C. FLOURNOY,
Lieut., Comdg. Confederate Rangers at Bay Springs, Miss.

HOLLY SPRINGS, MISS., *August* 27, 1862.

Major SNEAD:

I arrived here yesterday. Have consulted General Villepigue. His cavalry do operate with me. I leave my train within his pickets. I send you dispatches by Dr. Webb. I will move from here to-night. A telegram will overtake me.

FRANK C. ARMSTRONG,
Brigadier-General, Commanding.

HEADQUARTERS DISTRICT OF THE TENNESSEE,
Tupelo, Miss., August 27, 1862.

Maj. Gen. EARL VAN DORN,
Comdg. District of the Mississippi, Jackson, Miss. :

GENERAL : I acknowledge with a great deal of pleasure the receipt of your letter of the 24th instant, and am glad that you agree to my proposition to unite our forces for an aggressive campaign. I fully concur in the opinion that we should move our combined armies through Western Tennessee toward Paducah, and thence wherever circumstances may dictate. It seems to me that we should first drive the enemy from his position at and near Corinth, so as to retain control of the railroad. I fear that my own forces are hardly sufficient to accomplish this, as the enemy are equal to them in numbers and strongly intrenched, and I am not willing to risk a doubtful engagement under present circumstances. I therefore think that it is decidedly better that we should concentrate our forces at or near this point for the purpose of attacking the enemy at Corinth. This ought to be done straightway, so as to hinder and delay the re-enforcements of Buell as much as possible, and also to anticipate any re-enforcements which may be on their way to Corinth. In both of these views speedy action is very important. Having driven the enemy from Corinth we may then decide upon the future conduct of the campaign. I have sent General Frank C. Armstrong, with almost 2,000 cavalry, upon an intended reconnaissance. He has probably reached Grand Junction. He will make the circuit of Corinth, striking at whatever points may appear most available. I will be able to advise you more particularly as to the enemy's strength and position after hearing from him. Let us meanwhile hasten our preparations to move. I can have my army ready within five days. Our success must depend in a great measure, and may depend altogether, upon the rapidity of our movements. We must attack the enemy before they begin to receive their new levies and while they are still discouraged by their late reverses. We ought to avail ourselves, too, of the moral force which we would gain by participating in the great forward movement which our armies are now making everywhere. An advance on our part would put the whole line in movement from the Atlantic to the Territories, for we alone are stationary. The dispatches this afternoon announce that the enemy are falling back from the line of the Tennessee. Let us keep them moving.

I am, general, with the greatest respect, your friend and servant,

STERLING PRICE,
Major-General.

HEADQUARTERS DEPARTMENT No. 2,
Chattanooga, Tenn., August 27, 1862.

Maj. Gen. STERLING PRICE,
Comdg. District of the Tennessee, Tupelo, Miss.:

GENERAL: We move from here immediately, later by some days than expected, but in time, we hope, for a successful campaign. Buell has certainly fallen back from the Memphis and Charleston Railroad, and will probably not make a stand this side of Nashville, if there. He is now fortifying at that place. General E. K. Smith, re-enforced by two brigades from this army, has turned Cumberland Gap and is now marching on Lexington, Ky. General Morgan (Yankee) is thus cut off from all supplies. General Humphrey Marshall is to enter Eastern Kentucky from Western Virginia. We shall thus have Buell pretty well disposed of. Sherman and Rosecrans we leave to you and Van Dorn, satisfied that you can dispose of them, and we shall confidently expect to meet you on the Ohio and there open the way to Missouri.

Respectfully, your obedient servant,

BRAXTON BRAGG,
General, Commanding.

(Similar letter of same date to Van Dorn at Tupelo.)

HEADQUARTERS CAVALRY BRIGADE,
Holly Springs, Miss., August 27, 1862.

Maj. THOMAS L. SNEAD,
Chief of Staff, District of the Tennessee:

MAJOR: I arrived here yesterday. By my request General Villepigue met me here, and after consulting with him I am satisfied there are not more than 4,000 of the enemy at Bolivar, still a smaller force at Jackson, and about 1,500 at Somerville. The enemy have repaired the road from Bolivar to Fort Pillow, and are moving everything in that direction. We are both of the opinion that they will in a day or two evacuate Bolivar completely. The force at Somerville is only to cover their movements west. Our cars run above this place. I shall move with my command and about 1,100 men, under Colonel Jackson, threaten Bolivar, and, if possible, take Jackson and destroy the Mobile and Ohio Railroad. General Villepigue has positive information that the enemy are moving their supplies and troops to Fort Pillow, and have also strengthened Memphis from Bolivar and Jackson. The cotton they had gathered in Bolivar and Jackson has all been shipped, and they refuse to receive any more after to-day. If the cavalry at Guntown could be pushed forward above Booneville and Rienzi threatened I think I can do the balance in Tennessee. It would prevent depredations and I am confident hasten their departure.

I am, major, with respect, your obedient servant,

FRANK C. ARMSTRONG,
Brigadier-General.

P. S.—General Villepigue will, I hope, get orders to move forward in a few days. He has orders to hold himself in readiness to advance.

LA GRANGE, TENN., *August* 28, 1862.
Received at Tupelo (via Holly Springs), Aug. 29, 1862.

Maj. THOMAS L. SNEAD, *Chief of Staff:*

Your dispatch received. I will spare no efforts to make a dash on them. Nothing between here and Bolivar. I was right in my surmises about that place. Push the other cavalry after them. I will co-operate rapidly.

ARMSTRONG.

HEADQUARTERS ARMY OF THE WEST,
Tupelo, Miss., August 28, 1862.

Brig. Gen. HENRY LITTLE, *Commanding Division:*

GENERAL: You will order Capt. E. J. Sanders to move northward immediately with his company and Captain Mann's Partisan Rangers for the purpose of ascertaining the position and movements of the enemy between the Mobile and Ohio Railroad and Tuscumbia. These companies are now at Bay Springs. You may attach Lieutenant Wells' scouts to the command if you see fit to do so. Captain Sanders will report daily to these headquarters through you.

I am, very respectfully, your obedient servant,

THOS. L. SNEAD,
Chief of Staff.

VAN BUREN, TENN.,
Eight miles from Holly Springs, south of Bolivar, Tenn.,
August 29, 1862.

Major SNEAD, *Chief of Staff:*

All right up here. The Federals have concentrated everything at Bolivar. My command is getting on finely. My plan is succeeding finely.

ARMSTRONG.

HEADQUARTERS ARMY OF THE WEST,
Tupelo, Miss., August 30, 1862.

Brig. Gen. FRANK C. ARMSTRONG,
Commanding Cavalry Brigade:

GENERAL: Your dispatches from Holly Springs by Dr. Webb and from La Grange by telegraph have been received, and the major-general commanding instructs me to say that measures will be promptly taken to give an efficient support to the movement suggested in his dispatch of the 27th to you, and adopted in yours of the 28th instant. He is confirmed in the opinion that that is the proper movement, but he does not make his instructions imperative. He expects you, however, to keep him fully advised of your whereabouts. Colonel Falkner reports that he inflicted a severe loss upon the enemy in his late operations, with the loss of only one man captured.

I am, very respectfully, your obedient servant,

THOS. L. SNEAD,
Chief of Staff.

TUPELO, MISS., *August* 30, 1862.

[General LITTLE:]

GENERAL: I am directed by General Price to instruct you to assume command in the absence of General Armstrong, or until further orders, of all the cavalry of this army, including Partisan Rangers. Colonel Falkner, commanding a battalion of them at Orizaba, has been ordered to report to you. You will take care that General Armstrong's instructions to him be not so modified as to endanger the success of the cavalry expedition.

General Armstrong was at La Grange, Tenn., on the 28th instant. He expected to go there and as far north as Jackson, and then to return by way of the roads which run to the east of Corinth. You will, in order to support him, move one of your brigades to Baldwyn, and push the cavalry to, or as near as practicable to, Booneville, making such disposition of your other brigades as may in your opinion be proper. You are expected to keep a vigilant watch for General Armstrong and to render him prompt and efficient support whenever and wherever it may be required.

I am, very respectfully, your obedient servant,

THOS. L. SNEAD,
Assistant Adjutant-General.

TUPELO, MISS., *September* 2, 1862.

Major-General VAN DORN,
Commanding District of the Mississippi, Jackson, Miss.:

GENERAL: I received last night a dispatch, of which the following is a copy:

SEQUATCHIE VALLEY, TENN., *August* 29, 1862.

General STERLING PRICE:

Buell's whole force in full retreat upon Nashville, destroying their stores. Watch Rosecrans and prevent a junction; or if he escapes you follow him closely.

BRAXTON BRAGG.

I feel that this order requires me to advance immediately, and I shall have my whole command ready to move in three days. That portion of my cavalry which did not accompany General Armstrong has been ordered forward to Booneville, and General Little is moving his division to Guntown and Baldwyn. I hope nothing will prevent you from coming forward without delay with all your disposable troops. Be pleased to telegraph your determination, in such way, however, that it will not be understood by others, and to write to me fully by my aide-de-camp, Lieutenant Wood, who will hand this to you.

I inclose for your information copies of a letter from General Bragg, dated August 27, and of a dispatch* from General Armstrong, announcing the result of an engagement in front of Bolivar.

I am, general, with the greatest respect, your obedient servant,

STERLING PRICE.

[SEPTEMBER 2, 1862.—For Beauregard to Bragg, see Series I, Vol. XVI, Part II, p. 790.

---

* See Part I, p. 51.

SPECIAL ORDERS, }   HDQRS. ARMY OF THE MISSISSIPPI,
No. 58.   }   *Jackson, Miss., September 2, 1862.*

*   *   *   *   *   *   *

II. Semmes' and Fenner's batteries of light artillery will proceed to Opelousas, La., and report to Maj. Gen. Richard Taylor, commanding West Louisiana. Brigadier-General Beall will direct them to cross the river at the most practicable and safe point. An officer will be sent to Opelousas at once to report with a copy of this order.

*   *   *   *   *   *   *

IV. Maj. Gen. Gideon J. Pillow will proceed to Richmond, Va., and report to the Adjutant and Inspector General C. S. Army.

By order of Maj. Gen. Earl Van Dorn:

M. M. KIMMEL,
Major and Assistant Adjutant-General.

HEADQUARTERS DISTRICT OF THE MISSISSIPPI,
Jackson, Miss., September 3, 1862.

General STERLING PRICE,
Commanding Army of the West:

GENERAL: Your dispatches by the hands of Captain Wood, aide-de-camp, have been received. I shall move all the troops I have to Holly Springs on Saturday, and will probably be ready to march on the 12th. If Rosecrans remains at Corinth we had better join forces west of him and maneuver him out of that strong place, and at the same time prevent Grant and Sherman from joining him. I think it would be well even to turn your column as far as Grand Junction to join me, and then march in a northeast direction across the Tennessee and Cumberland Rivers, if Rosecrans does not move at once. If, however, he moves off you will have to follow him to the river and bring him at bay until I can join you, which I will do with all possible dispatch. Separated we can do but little; joined we may do much. Let us join between the forces of the enemy, somewhere between Grand Junction and Corinth; then bearing off toward his line of supplies we will compel him to fly toward Nashville or north of that city without being able to receive forces of Sherman or Grant. These will then fall back up the river and we will follow Rosecrans. Keep me advised, will you not, of your movements? I will go to Holly Springs Sunday; will join you as soon as possible. Do not leave me and go east if you can avoid it; we can do more together west of the Tennessee, for awhile at least. We should try and shake them loose from all points in West Tennessee; then march to join Bragg, if necessary. We will have 10,000 more men, too, in a short time; these would join by way of Grand Junction or Corinth.

I am not very well to-day and will beg you to pardon this poorly written paper. Will write again in a day or two.

Very respectfully, general, I am, your obedient servant,

EARL VAN DORN,
Major-General.

JACKSON, MISS., *September 3, 1862.*

General STERLING PRICE:

I had proposed to meet you at Holly Springs, but if the enemy at Corinth are leaving better fall on him at river. I go to Grand Junction or

Holly Springs in a few days. Will join you, or you me, according to circumstances. I think we can maneuver enemy out of his position without fight. Some returned prisoners at Vicksburg. How many arms have you? If enemy remain at Corinth better join me west of that place.

EARL VAN DORN,
Major-General.

HEADQUARTERS DISTRICT OF THE TENNESSEE,
Tupelo, Miss., September 4, 1862.

Maj. Gen. EARL VAN DORN,
  Commanding District of the Mississippi :

GENERAL : One of your staff officers (Colonel Lomax) having requested me to do so, I state for your information that I can put in the field 13,000 infantry, 3,000 cavalry, and 800 artillery, effective total; that they are supplied with transportation and ammunition, as prescribed in General Bragg's last general orders; that subsistence has been provided to October 1; that the commissary trains will transport seven days' provisions, and that I will have arms for all my troops, including those exchanged prisoners that General Bragg has ordered to be sent to me.

I am, general, very respectfully, your obedient servant,

STERLING PRICE,
Major-General, Commanding.

CHATTANOOGA, TENN., September 4, 1862.

General STERLING PRICE, *Tupelo, Miss.:*

Governor Shorter, of Alabama, telegraphs me that the enemy is ravaging the country on the railroad south of the Tennessee River, in Alabama, and calls on me to send troops to relief of country. He must mean country from Decatur west, in your jurisdiction. I have no force to send. Cannot you organize expedition by way of Russellville and co-operate with Roddey, understood to be about Moulton, and let your scouts on the right communicate with mine on my left?

SAM. JONES,
Major-General.

SPECIAL ORDERS, }   HDQRS. DEPARTMENT OF THE MISSISSIPPI,
  No. 59.   }   *Jackson, Miss., September* 4, 1862.

I. General Breckinridge will move his division by railroad to Holly Springs, commencing the movement Saturday, the 6th instant. The quartermaster's department will see that the necessary trains are prepared, so that the movement may be made with the least delay possible.

By order of Maj. Gen. Earl Van Dorn :

M. M. KIMMEL,
Major and Assistant Adjutant-General.

HEADQUARTERS DISTRICT OF THE TENNESSEE,
Tupelo, Miss., September 5, 1862.

Maj. Gen. EARL VAN DORN,
  Comdg. District of the Mississippi, Jackson, Miss.:

GENERAL : I have received your reply to my letter of the 2d instant, and regret very much that you cannot move in this direction at once.

I feel that General Bragg's instructions and the situation of affairs within my district alike compel me to keep near the line of this road. If I move toward Holly Springs, as you suggest, I not only endanger the safety of the road, which is essential to the supply of my army, but I expose my supplies of every kind and the valuable workshops and public property at Columbus and Gainesville to destruction by the enemy. I learn that a cavalry force of theirs, 1,700 strong, is even now within forty-eight hours' march of Columbus. General Bragg's orders also compel me to keep a close watch upon Rosecrans, and I hear that he is now at Iuka and crossing his army at Eastport. I am therefore pushing my army slowly forward, and shall remove my own headquarters to Guntown on Sunday. I shall then determine by what route to advance. I shall keep you fully advised of my movements, so that we may co-operate or unite our forces, as may be most advisable.

I am, general, very sincerely, your friend and obedient servant,

STERLING PRICE,
Major-General.

HEADQUARTERS CAVALRY BRIGADE,
La Grange, Tenn., September 5, 1862.

[Maj. THOMAS L. SNEAD:]

MAJOR: I send this by Captain Pryor, who has been serving with me during a part of my expedition. He was on leave, and knowing the country well, I took the liberty of keeping him over his time. My command is at this place and on the railroad, 7 miles south of Grand Junction. I am ready for any service. General Villepigue's command is at Holly Springs. General Van Dorn is to be here on Tuesday; General Breckinridge on Sunday. He has selected an encampment 16 miles north of Holly Springs. The Federals keep close in to Bolivar. I think of moving over toward Salem and Ripley, and will communicate with you from there. I will send a full report of my expedition in a day or two. It has been all that I could have desired. Excuse my delay in making report.

I am, yours, with respect,

FRANK C. ARMSTRONG,
Brigadier-General.

P. S.—Can you not send Captain Sanders' company to report to me at Ripley?

TUPELO, MISS., *September 5, 1862.*

Brig. Gen. FRANK C. ARMSTRONG,
Via Holly Springs, Miss.:

The major-general commanding directs me to acknowledge the reception of your dispatches of the 3d* and 5th instant. He congratulates you and the brave men under you for successes due to your and their gallantry. He directs that you move as speedily as possible to Guntown with your command.

JAMES M. LOUGHBOROUGH,
Assistant Adjutant-General.

---

* Not found.

GENERAL ORDERS, }   HDQRS. DISTRICT OF THE MISSISSIPPI,
     No. 46.   }   *Jackson, Miss., September* 5, 1862.

During the absence in the field of the major-general commanding, the affairs of the district will be under the supervision of Brig. Gen. Daniel Ruggles, second in command, who will establish his headquarters at Jackson, Miss. He will assume command and announce his staff to-morrow, the 6th instant.

By order of Maj. Gen. Earl Van Dorn:

M. M. KIMMEL,
Major and Assistant Adjutant-General.

GENERAL ORDERS, }   HDQRS. DISTRICT OF THE MISSISSIPPI,
     No. 47.   }   *Jackson, Miss., September* 5, 1862.

The honorable Secretary of War having announced to the general commanding the district that martial law can only be declared by the President, and that it has not been declared by him in Mississippi, General Orders, No. 9,* from these headquarters, dated Vicksburg, July 4, 1862, and all other orders arising under the declaration of martial law in this district, are hereby revoked. All provost-marshals will be discharged, and all prisoners, other than soldiers, will be turned over to the proper civil authorities. The general commanding in declaring martial law was influenced to do so only by what he considered the best interests of the country, and not by any desire to accumulate power. A soldier of more than twenty years in their service, he had no ambition to play the tyrant over the citizens of his own State, whom he was sent to defend. The exigencies of the times seemed to him to call for the interposition of a stronger and more prompt hand than the civil authorities were able to hold out against the abuses incident to the times, and with numerous precedents for doing so, he declared martial law. The general commanding hopes that throughout his district the efficiency of the civil authority will demonstrate that his judgment has been at fault and that there exists no necessity for martial law. He takes this occasion to say, however, that he fears this will not be the case, at least in some parts of the district, and to inform the civil authorities that he will cheerfully co-operate with them, and will come to their aid with the forces under his command whenever legally called upon to do so.

By order of Maj. Gen. Earl Van Dorn:

M. M. KIMMEL,
Assistant Adjutant-General.

CHATTANOOGA, TENN., *September* 6, 1862.

General STERLING PRICE:

General Bragg directs me to telegraph you that the enemy has evacuated Alabama and rapidly falling back from all points in Middle Tennessee to Nashville. Rosecrans must follow; and that you should move rapidly for Nashville. Our army fairly down the mountain September 4 and would immediately move toward enemy.

SAM. JONES,
Major-General.

---

*See Series I, Vol. XV, p. 771.

TUPELO, MISS., *September* 6, 1862.

General LLOYD TILGHMAN, *Jackson, Miss.*:

I received 4,000 small-arms last night. When will I get exchanged prisoners and how many?

STERLING PRICE,
Major-General.

TUPELO, MISS., *September* 6, 1862.

General LITTLE, *Guntown, Miss.*:

Send immediately for enough percussion muskets to supply your division. Turn in your surplus arms.

THOS. L. SNEAD,
Assistant Adjutant-General.

TUPELO, MISS., *September* 7, 1862.

General SAMUEL JONES:

Inform General Bragg that my army is marching. My advance guard is at Booneville, and I move my headquarters to Guntown to-morrow. Will push forward.

STERLING PRICE,
Major-General.

JACKSON, MISS, *September* 8, 1862.

General STERLING PRICE:

Are the enemy crossing the Tennessee? I hear so. I am moving to Holly Springs. Will write to-day.

EARL VAN DORN,
Major-General.

HEADQUARTERS DISTRICT OF THE TENNESSEE,
Tupelo, Miss., September 8, 1862.

Col. JOHN ADAMS,
Commanding Post, Columbus, Miss.:

COLONEL: I am directed by General Price to instruct you to put the troops which are still at Columbus in readiness to move at once. Let all the absentees be called in and the men be put in as good condition as possible. When the enemy abandon the country south of the Tennessee there will be no further occasion for these troops at Columbus, while they will be greatly needed in Kentucky. Please order all convalescents and stragglers forward. The general moved his headquarters to Guntown to-day.

I am, yours, very truly,

THOS. L. SNEAD,
Assistant Adjutant General.

HEADQUARTERS ARMY OF THE WEST,
Tupelo, Miss., September 8, 1862.

Maj. M. M. KIMMEL,
Asst. Adjt. Gen., District of the Miss., Holly Springs, Miss.:

MAJOR: General Price left this morning for Guntown, directing me to inform General Van Dorn that he had done so, and that he expected to move immediately against Iuka in accordance with orders just received from General Bragg, who again instructs him to follow Rosecrans. He also directs me to say that he will be able to furnish General Van Dorn, if he needs them, with 1,000 stand of arms as soon as they can be repaired at Columbus, whither they have been sent from Richmond.

I am, major, very truly, your obedient servant,

THOS. L. SNEAD,
Assistant Adjutant-General.

HEADQUARTERS DISTRICT OF MISSISSIPPI,
Jackson, Miss., September 8, 1862.

Maj. Gen. STERLING PRICE, *Commanding Army of the West:*

GENERAL: Your letter of September 5 has been received. I have requested Major Wright to go and confer with you in regard to the matter now claiming our attention.

If Rosecrans has crossed the Tennessee and got beyond your reach do you not think it would be better for us to join forces at Jackson, Tenn., clear Western Tennessee of the enemy, and then push on together into Kentucky, along the Ohio River? We together would have a force to oppose any one there. If Rosecrans is much ahead of you he could join Buell and meet Bragg before you could aid him. On the other hand Bragg could form a junction with Smith and Marshall southwest of Lexington and defeat Buell and Rosecrans combined. You would not be in the contest. We, joined on the Ohio, would be between Buell's army and the forces from the west and prevent junction, or by crossing eastward from the Ohio behind Buell could join Bragg and aid him in case of need.

This is suggested in the event that Rosecrans is over the river and out of reach. If he is still on this side and standing I will join you from Holly Springs and attack him with you; push him hard with our left and force him back on the river, and prevent junction with Sherman and McClernand, who would then retire on and up the Mississippi. Rosecrans would be disposed of. I presume, however, he is gone. At all events, general, I will be in a short distance of Grand Junction in a few days, and we will confer by couriers. I will join you if needed. If you go off at once after Rosecrans can I not take your 5,000 returned prisoners with me? There will be no necessity for them behind you. With them I can put an army in the field to cope with the Western troops of the enemy, and will push on and upward with the great line of advance with the same colors that wave over you and the brave troops of the Army of the West.

However all this may turn out, I shall always be happy to be found associated with you in this noble struggle, and I pray God you may be victorious wherever you may go.

Very truly and sincerely, general, your friend and obedient servant,

EARL VAN DORN,
Major General.

HEADQUARTERS ARMY OF THE WEST,
Tupelo, Miss., September 8, 1862.

Brigadier-General JORDAN, *Chief of Staff, Department No.* 2 :

GENERAL: General Price left this morning and will go as far as Guntown to-night. His cavalry advance is at Booneville; Little's division at and near Baldwyn; Maury's at Saltillo. The general expects to move with his whole army in the direction of Iuka within forty-eight hours. Nothing is delaying him but the want of transportation. He will lose no time in carrying out the instructions of General Bragg as conveyed to him through General Jones by dispatch dated at Chattanooga on the 6th instant.

I am, general, very respectfully, your obedient servant,

THOS. L. SNEAD.

HEADQUARTERS DISTRICT OF THE TENNESSEE,
Guntown, Miss., September 8, 1862.

Brig. Gen. FRANK C. ARMSTRONG:

The major-general commanding directs that you will join him with your command at this place without delay. A similar order to this was sent you by courier and by telegraph; but not having heard anything from you it is again sent, as it is of the greatest importance that you should reach here.

I am, general, very respectfully, your obedient servant,

[THOS. L. SNEAD,
Assistant Adjutant-General.]

SPECIAL ORDERS, }   HDQRS. DISTRICT OF THE MISSISSIPPI,
No. 61.   }   *Jackson, Miss., September* 8, 1862.

I. Maj. Gen. M. Lovell having reported for duty with this army is assigned to the command of a division composed of the brigade of Brig. Gen. J. B. Villepigue and other brigades to be organized.

II. Brigadier-General Rust having reported for duty in this command will report to Maj. Gen. J. C. Breckinridge.

By order of Maj. Gen. Earl Van Dorn:

M. M. KIMMEL,
Major and Assistant Adjutant-General.

JACKSON, MISS., *September* 9, 1862.

Hon. SECRETARY OF WAR:

Enemy concentrating at Bolivar and Jackson, West Tenn., leaving Memphis. My force is too small. Will you let me have the returned prisoners? I can make a successful campaign in West Tennessee with them; little without them.

I ought to have command of the movements of Price, that there may be concert of action. Want some arms to take into Tennessee and Kentucky; expect accessions. Bragg is out of reach; I refer to you. Will be near Grand Junction in a few days with what force I have. Give me orders for what conscripts may now be in camp. General Tilghman anxious about his arms. None have arrived up to this date at Columbus. He will need all of the 15,000 asked for.

EARL VAN DORN,
Major-General.

[Indorsements.]

Respectfully referred to the President.

I supposed these matters would be regulated by General Bragg, and feel some hesitation in giving directions which might conflict with his plans. Something, however, should be done. Shall I order him to take command of the prisoners, subject to General Bragg's orders, and to reorganize them?

G. W. RANDOLPH,
Secretary of War.

The exchanged prisoners should join the headquarters of their regiments. The regiments received let General Van Dorn retain without reference to former brigade or division organization. Conscripts should be distributed as the necessity of the service may indicate. The chief of ordnance will make all possible effort to arm the exchanged prisoners belonging to the regiments of General Van Dorn's command. The rank of General Van Dorn secures to him the command of all the troops with whom he will be operating. Brigades should, as far as may be, be of regiments of the several States.

J. D.

HEADQUARTERS ARMY OF THE WEST,
Guntown, Miss., September 9, 1862.

Maj. Gen. EARL VAN DORN,
Commanding District of Mississippi:

GENERAL: Major Wright has handed me your letter of the 8th instant. I am sorry to say that I feel General Bragg's repeated instructions compel me to move without any further delay toward Nashville. I was very anxious to place myself and my army under your command, so that we might together liberate West Tennessee, and regain control of the Mississippi. General Bragg has, however, just ordered me to "move rapidly for Nashville," and I must obey his orders. I shall therefore move hence for Iuka Thursday morning, the 11th instant. I am sure that you will do what you can to facilitate the movement. It will give you an opportunity to strike the enemy heavily. I have just learned that they are evacuating Corinth and Rienzi, destroying the former place by fire.

I regret that this change of plan also forces me to refuse your request to give you the exchanged prisoners that were ordered to report to me. Moving as I will across the Tennessee in pursuit of Rosecrans, I shall need every man that I can get. General Bragg, too, who ordered them to report to me, will unquestionably count upon their addition to the army which I am taking to him. The War Department has also just sent me 4,000 stand of arms with which to arm them. Under all these circumstances I cannot accede to your request, but must ask you to urge General Tilghman to rapidly forward my share of the exchanged prisoners to Tupelo, where they will be armed and equipped.

Of course nothing could please me more than that you should unite your army to mine and move in command of the combined armies for Nashville.

I am, very truly, your obedient servant,

STERLING PRICE.

HEADQUARTERS ARMY OF THE WEST,
Guntown, Miss., September 10, 1862.

GENERAL: You will move your command to Marietta by to-morrow **night** with at least seven days' rations. General Armstrong has been ordered to take such position with the cavalry brigade as to protect the left flank of the army.

I am, very respectfully, your obedient servant,

THOS. L. SNEAD,
Assistant-Adjutant General.

HEADQUARTERS DISTRICT OF THE TENNESSEE,
Guntown, Miss., September 10, 1862—12 m.

Brigadier-General ARMSTRONG,
Commanding Cavalry Brigade:

GENERAL: It is reported that the enemy have sent a force toward Bay Springs. If you find such to be the fact, and you have a sufficient force to do so successfully, make a dash upon them.

I am, very respectfully, your obedient servant,

THOS. L. SNEAD,
Assistant Adjutant-General.

Abstract from Return of Third Sub-district, District of the Mississippi, Brig. Gen. M. L. Smith, C. S. Army, commanding, for September 10, 1862 *(headquarters Vicksburg, Miss.).*

Troops.	Aggregate present for duty.	Aggregate present.	Aggregate present and absent.
Field and staff	12	12	12
17th Louisiana, Colonel Richardson	351	495	603
26th Louisiana, Colonel De Clouet	406	716	775
27th Louisiana, Colonel Marks	371	894	941
28th Louisiana, Colonel Thomas	264	531	631
3d Mississippi, Colonel Mellon	507	770	916
6th Mississippi Battalion, Lieutenant-Colonel Balfour	176	596	777
1st Mississippi Light Artillery, Colonel Withers	695	925	1,456
Heavy artillery, Colonel Beltzhoover	653	959	1,160
28th Mississippi Cavalry, Colonel Starke	436	662	865
Partisan Rangers (three companies)	202	263	383
Sappers and Miners, Capt. D. Wintter	11	19	22
Total	3,884	6,822	8,544

WAR DEPARTMENT, *September* 11, 1862.

Major-General VAN DORN, *Jackson, Miss.:*

The exchanged prisoners must be sent to their respective regiments. Where the headquarters of the regiment is with you it will remain under your command, and brigades and divisions may be formed without reference to former brigades and divisions, but troops of the same State must be brigaded together as far as practicable. Conscripts must be distributed to all the regiments of the State. Every effort will be made to arm and equip the troops. Your rank necessarily gives you the right to command General Price when you are acting together. Nothing in these instructions must be considered as rescinding the orders or interfering with the arrangements of General Bragg.

G. W. RANDOLPH,
Secretary of War.

RICHMOND, VA., *September* 11, 1862.

Maj. Gen. EARL VAN DORN,
  Grand Junction, Tenn.:

The troops must co-operate, and can only do so by having one head. Your rank makes you the commander, and such I supposed were the instructions of General Bragg given in his orders to you. The exchanged prisoners will join their proper regiments. You can keep the regiments which have their headquarters in your district instead of sending them to their former army corps. You will have due care to the safety of Vicksburg, Port Hudson, &c.

                                                    JEFFERSON DAVIS.

JACKSON, MISS., *September* 11, 1862.

Hon. SECRETARY OF WAR, *Richmond, Va.:*

Your dispatches about arms received. Chief of ordnance of Van Dorn's command believes, as I do, that a conflict of orders exists about arms. Gorgas says he sent 7,000 to Price and 2,000 to Pettus. There are no arms at Columbus or elsewhere for exchanged prisoners arriving rapidly and anxious to go forward. Please see ordnance officer at Richmond and direct arms to be sent to Colonel Stockton, at Jackson.

                                                    LLOYD TILGHMAN.

[Indorsements.]

Chief of Ordnance, for immediate attention.

                                                    G. W. RANDOLPH.

The above arms were sent by special messengers with Capt. Clay Taylor.

                                                    J. GORGAS.

RICHMOND, VA., *September* 11, 1862.

His Excellency Governor PETTUS, *Jackson, Miss.:*

The action taken was on suggestion of telegraph companies, and is designed to protect the Confederate States and to secure the receipts to the true and loyal owners. The president of the company is with the enemy, and the company is not in condition to fulfill its purpose.

                                                    JEFFERSON DAVIS.

HEADQUARTERS DISTRICT OF TENNESSEE,
  Guntown, Miss., September 11, 1862.

COLONEL COMMANDING FORTY-SECOND ALABAMA REGT.:

COLONEL: You will put your regiment in marching order to-morrow, so that it may move thoroughly armed and with three days' cooked rations on the morning of the 13th instant. The officers at the post have been ordered to fill your requisitions promptly. You will send your wagons forward with your baggage to or near the point at which the Tupelo and Saltillo road intersects the Saltillo and Bay Springs road, and move your men by railway to Saltillo as early as possible the next morning, so that you may overtake your wagons and make a full day's march upon the 13th. From Saltillo you will follow the road taken by Maury's division, which you will join without any unnecessary delay and report your command to General Maury, who will assign it to Moore's brigade. If the militia do not arrive in time to permit you to leave on the 13th, or if any other unforeseen circumstance shall prevent you from leaving Tupelo that day, you will leave as soon thereafter as possible, sending forward meanwhile a courier to General Maury to advise him of the detention. You will also, if the quartermaster can provide transportation, take at least two days' uncooked rations in your wagons. The cooked rations may be carried either on the person or in the wagons. The general directs me to call your attention to the great importance of your overtaking his army at the earliest possible moment. The two companies of artillery from Columbus will march with you as attached to your regiment until you join the army, when they will report to the major-general commanding.

I am, very respectfully, your obedient servant,

THOS. L. SNEAD,
Assistant Adjutant-General

HOLLY SPRINGS, MISS., *September* 11, 1862.
(Received at Guntown September 12, 1862.)

General STERLING PRICE:

Enemy evacuating Memphis. Seventeen transports from Curtis' army passed, going up, Sunday. Enemy reported evacuating also Bolivar and Jackson, going toward Fort Pillow. I will write you by courier when I see Major Wright, who will be here in the morning. I cannot march until I get my wagons. They will come up on railroad.

Answer.

EARL VAN DORN,
Major-General.

HOLLY SPRINGS, MISS., *September* 12, 1862.

Hon. SECRETARY OF WAR:

Your dispatches received. I know nothing of Mississippi regiments at Gainesville not in my command. In regard to Partisan Rangers I respectfully recommend that they be disbanded and that all of conscripts enrolled be turned over to regiments in the field. Curtis' army at Helena, going up river. Seventeen transports passed Memphis. Memphis being evacuated, as reported this morning by scouts. I have a regiment of cavalry between the Mississippi River and the Yazoo. No particular necessity for troops there, but if the company is composed of men not liable to conscription, may answer purpose proposed. Isolated companies of Partisan Rangers have no discipline and cannot be depended upon. I am near Grand Junction with Breckinridge and Villepigue; Price near Corinth. He proposes to follow Rosecrans toward Nashville. I propose to clean out West Tennessee, now occupied by enemy in some force, and then go across Tennessee and Cumberland into Kentucky; therefore there can be no co-operation. If you decide I shall join him I will do so, but I think it best to clear the west. Give me the returned prisoners and I can do so without Price. I hope soon to occupy Memphis. I shall be active, but hope you will give me more means.

EARL VAN DORN,
Major-General.

HEADQUARTERS ARMY OF THE WEST,
Bay Springs, Miss., September 12, 1862.

General ARMSTRONG, *Commanding Cavalry:*

GENERAL: Little's division will move to-morrow on the road leading by Peyton's Mill. Maury will probably move by the old Natchez Trace road. General Price will leave at sunrise and stop at Peyton's Mill or beyond.

Yours, respectfully,

THOS. L. SNEAD,
Assistant Adjutant-General.

———

HEADQUARTERS ARMY OF THE WEST,
Bay Springs, Miss., September 12, 1862.

Brigadier-General LITTLE, *Commanding Division:*

GENERAL: You will move your division at sunrise to-morrow, or immediately after the major-general shall have passed, upon the left-hand or most western road to Iuka. They fork about 1½ miles northeast of this place. Please order all wagons to be kept out of the road until you begin to move. Send your forage agents ahead to purchase forage and make the neighbors haul it to your encampment, which will be a little beyond Peyton's Mill. Allow General Armstrong's wagons to pass you on the right-hand road before sunrise, if they can do so without delaying your march. Send your pioneers ahead early enough to repair the road.

I am, yours, very respectfully,

THOS. L. SNEAD,
Assistant Adjutant-General.

———

HEADQUARTERS ARMY OF THE WEST,
Camp No. 4, Peyton's Mill, Miss., September 13, 1862.

Brigadier-General MAURY, *Commanding Division:*

GENERAL: Armstrong is at Iuka. He drove in the enemy's pickets at about 11 a. m., but had to retire when the enemy opened their artillery. He thinks that they have only one brigade. General Price will advance to-night as soon as the moon rises. You will push forward with two brigades of your infantry, bringing one day's rations on the person and leaving a detail behind to bring on two days' rations in the wagons. The distance is about 13 miles from here.

Very respectfully,

THOS. L. SNEAD,
Assistant Adjutant-General.

———

IUKA, MISS., *September* 14, 1862.

General VAN DORN, *Holly Springs, Miss.:*

Rosecrans has gone westward with about 10,000 men. I am ready to co-operate with you in an attack upon Corinth. My courier awaits your answer.

STERLING PRICE,
Major-General.

IUKA, MISS., *September* 14, 1862.

General THOMAS JORDAN, *Chattanooga, Tenn.:*

Inform General Bragg and the War Department that, having ascertained that Rosecrans was here with about 10,000 men, I left Guntown last Thursday to attack him. He, however, retreated westward Friday night leaving a rear guard of about 1,500 men, who evacuated the place last night, abandoning several hundred thousand dollars' worth of army stores. My cavalry entered the town at daybreak.

STERLING PRICE,
Major-General.

HOLLY SPRINGS, MISS., *September* 15, 1862.

Hon. GEORGE W. RANDOLPH,
Secretary of War:

I now propose to send Breckinridge, with force equal to that assigned to Bragg of exchanged prisoners, to join Price, who moves to join Bragg, and retain Bragg's assignment of prisoners here. Will you allow this? I think Breckinridge should go into Kentucky, and this is the only way he can be spared.

EARL VAN DORN,
Major-General.

HDQRS. ARMY OF THE DISTRICT OF THE MISSISSIPPI,
Holly Springs, Miss., September 16, 1862.

Maj. Gen. STERLING PRICE,
Commanding Army of the West in the Field:

GENERAL: I sent you a telegram in reply to yours of the 14th instant from Iuka, in which you stated that you were ready to co-operate with me in an attack on Corinth. I am ignorant of your exact position, but presume that your troops are near Iuka. I propose that you march to Rienzi and from thence toward Pocahontas, so that we may join our forces and attack without loss of time. There is now at Bolivar a force of about 12,000 or 15,000 men, evidently preparing to move. It may be impossible to form a junction at Pocahontas or that vicinity before these Bolivar troops join Rosecrans. At all events, the move I propose seems to me to be the best. It may be that Rosecrans will move and join the Bolivar troops at Jackson and make a stand there. If they form a junction at Corinth we must attack from the west and southwest, and the position I have proposed is right; if they move toward Jackson it is still right; and if they leave a force at Corinth it is still right. When you get to the line of wires telegraph me and I will reply by couriers across the country. Send a courier to telegraph when you will reach Rienzi, and when you may be expected to reach the vicinity of Pocahontas. I have but about 35 miles to march, and can reach you with 10,000 men in three days. I will be ready to march by the time that I should do so. My wagons are coming up. Rosecrans is a quick, skillful fellow, and we must be rapid also. You can't reach Rienzi too soon. If he were to move this way rapidly and order down the Bolivar forces on me I would be in a bad way just at this time. I have been acting under the impression that he had crossed the Tennessee and had evacuated Corinth. You see my position—close to Grand Junction, with only 9,000 or 10,000 men; my depot at this place; my wagons not up. I have ordered out scouts to Ripley and in the direction of Corinth, and shall watch closely.

Sherman received nine transports of troops (new levies) day before yesterday at Memphis, and now has about 6,000 men (probably a little more); Hurlbut, at Bolivar, has 12,000 or 15,000; 2,000 at Jackson; and then there are garrisons at Fort Pillow and Columbus. Rosecrans has probably 15,000. All that combined will give them about 35,000 men in West Tennessee. Curtis is within short time of Memphis, at Fort Pillow, with about 15,000; and so you see we must be quick in our movements when we start the campaign; take them in detail and strike rapidly. Rosecrans and Hurlbut have about our force. We must whip them combined. We may take them in detail if they are not wary; but once combined we will make a successful campaign, clear out West Tennessee, and then——

I have directed the exchanged prisoners assigned to you to be sent off as fast as they arrive. Can you not spare some arms for mine? I have none yet; none have been sent to me that I have heard of.

General, I think you had better send forward quite a cavalry force in the direction northeast of Ripley from Rienzi in advance of you, or as soon as possible. I do not feel secure here by any means. My depot here might be destroyed by a cavalry dash from Corinth. Villepigue's brigade and most of my cavalry are now toward Memphis. They have been ordered in, but still I am not secure. I have also to observe toward Memphis.

Congratulating myself, general, that I shall be once more thrown with you in the glorious struggle for our country, and with assurances of my esteem and friendship, I am, your obedient and humble servant,

EARL VAN DORN,
Major-General.

P. S.—Send forward courier to communicate as often as possible.

RICHMOND, VA., *September* 16, 1862.

Maj. Gen. EARL VAN DORN, *Jackson, Miss.:*

Exchanged prisoners must join their regiments; must be brigaded, as far as practicable, by States. Subject to these requirements and to General Bragg's instructions, you may distribute them as you think best. It is obviously proper for Breckinridge to have the Kentucky regiments. It is impossible for the Department to instruct you as to your line of operations, but co-operation between Price and yourself is indispensable to success, and was contemplated by General Bragg. Refer to the President's dispatch of September 11 and you will find such instructions as we consider it practicable to give. You are the senior officer, and, subject to General Bragg's instructions, can exercise your own discretion.

G. W. RANDOLPH,
Secretary of War.

JACKSON, MISS., *September* 16, 1862.

General STERLING PRICE, *Iuka, Miss.:*

Not under twenty days. The exchange must be ratified first. I shall thoroughly equip, except arming, and if I had your arms could drill the raw men. How many arms have you, and where are they?

LLOYD TILGHMAN,
Brigadier-General.

GENERAL ORDERS, }   HDQRS. DISTRICT OF THE TENNESSEE,
    No. 35.   }   *Camp No. 5, Iuka, Miss., September* 16, 1862.

I. Brig. Gen. John C. Moore will assume command of all troops in that part of the District of the Tennessee which is south of a line drawn east and west through Booneville. He will establish his headquarters at Tupelo. All officers commanding posts or troops within the limits above defined will report to him and obey his orders.

*   *   *   *   *   *   *

By command of Major-General Price:

L. A. MACLEAN,
Assistant Adjutant-General.

CHATTANOOGA, TENN., *September* 16, 1862.
General S. COOPER,
    Adjutant and Inspector General, Richmond, Va.:

General Price, telegraphing from Iuka 14th, desires me to inform you that he marched from Guntown on 11th to attack Rosecrans, who was understood to be at Iuka with about 10,000 men. Rosecrans retreated westward on 12th, leaving rear guard of about 1,500 men, who evacuated the place Saturday night, abandoning several hundred thousand dollars' worth of army stores. Our cavalry entered Iuka daylight Sunday. From General Bragg on 12th, near Glasgow, Ky., I learn that Rosecrans and part of his army was at Nashville.

SAM. JONES,
Major-General.

HOLLY SPRINGS, MISS., *September* 17, 1862.
General STERLING PRICE:

From telegram, don't know exactly where you are. I propose that you move toward Rienzi and send cavalry out to meet my scouts. I will move in that direction in a few days, or as soon as my wagons are up. With scouts out we will make junction west of Corinth not far from Pocahontas. Enemy at Bolivar 12,000 or 15,000. Must try and prevent junction with Rosecrans. Enemy receiving re-enforcements at Memphis (new levies). Campaign in West Tennessee imperative and necessary to Bragg. Send reply at once and let us understand. Will write.

EARL VAN DORN,
Major-General.

HEADQUARTERS DISTRICT OF THE TENNESSEE,
    Iuka, Miss., September 17, 1862.
Maj. Gen. EARL VAN DORN,
    Commanding District of the Mississippi:

GENERAL: I entered this town with my army on last Sunday morning, the rear guard of Rosecrans' army evacuating it at my approach and retreating westward. I telegraphed you immediately, proposing a combined movement upon Corinth, and sent the dispatch by special messenger to Guntown, with instructions to forward it to you immediately and to await your reply. This has not been received yet. I hope the you will answer me at once, for General Bragg has just sent me another dispatch in these words:

> EN ROUTE TO KENTUCKY, *September* 12, 1862.
>
> By the proceedings of a council of war in Nashville, captured by us, it seems Rosecrans with a part of his army is there. I have anxiously expected your advance, and trust it will not longer be delayed.
>
> BRAXTON BRAGG.

I cannot remain inactive any longer, and must move either with you against Rosecrans or toward Kentucky. The courier who takes this to you will bring your reply.

I am, very respectfully, your obedient servant,

STERLING PRICE,
Major-General.

HOLLY SPRINGS, MISS., *September* 18, 1862.

General STERLING PRICE, *Iuka, Miss.*:

Enemy evacuating Bolivar; many going north. Breckinridge, with Kentucky regiments, has been ordered to Chattanooga to follow Bragg. I retain exchanged prisoners to take their place, so will have about 8,000. You will get 5,000. Can you not send me arms for them? I have equipage, &c. Will start to meet you as soon as I get your telegram that you have reached neighborhood of Rienzi. Nine [trains?] of troops passed through Jackson, Tenn., from the direction of Corinth Saturday and Sunday. Enemy say they cannot hold West Tennessee now. Telegram from President says we must co-operate to succeed. Send me all the arms you can spare; I have 8,000 men to arm. These will be added to our strength. Answer.

EARL VAN DORN,
Major-General.

JACKSON, MISS., *September* 18, 1862.
(Received at Baldwyn, Miss., September 19, 1862.)

General STERLING PRICE, *Iuka, Miss.*:

I am ordered to organize here when exchange is concluded. I shall need all the arms heretofore sent to you for exchanged prisoners. I shall equip fully and splendidly, then move up the whole division. How many arms have you, and where can I get them?

TILGHMAN,
General.

HEADQUARTERS ARMY OF THE WEST,
September 18, 1862.

Brigadier-General MAURY:

GENERAL: General Armstrong reports that the enemy seem to be advancing in considerable force by the Burnsville road, and that his pickets have fallen back before them. General Little has been ordered to take position in line of battle upon your right. Please make the necessary dispositions.

By order of the major-general commanding:

THOS. L. SNEAD,
Assistant Adjutant-General.

HEADQUARTERS ARMY OF THE WEST,
September 18, 1862—7.45 p. m.

Brigadier-General LITTLE:

GENERAL: General Armstrong reports that his pickets have been driven in by the enemy, who seem to be advancing in force by the Burnsville road. A deserter, who has just come in, confirms the fact of their advance in considerable force. The major-general commanding directs you to take a good position in line of battle as soon as your men have supped. You will form upon General Maury's right. As you are familiar with the ground the general intrusts to you the selecting of your position.

I am, &c.,

THOS. L. SNEAD,
Assistant Adjutant-General.

RICHMOND, VA., *September 19, 1862.*

General BRAGG,
(Care of General McCown), Knoxville, Tenn.:

Telegrams from Tennessee and Mississippi indicate a want of co-intelligence and co-operation among the generals of the several columns. No copy of your instructions in regard to operations in Tennessee has been received, and I am at a loss to know how to remedy evils without damaging your plans. If Van Dorn, Price, and Breckinridge each act for himself disaster to all must be the probable result. The return prisoners have not been formally exchanged and are, therefore, not available. Van Dorn, with three divisions, might perform valuable service. If to act alone, he had better have remained in Jackson.

JEFFERSON DAVIS.

RICHMOND, VA., *September 19, 1862.*

Major-General VAN DORN,
Grand Junction, Tenn.:

We fear that a serious misunderstanding exists with reference to the movements of Price, Breckinridge, and yourself. General Bragg, we are informed, expected Breckinridge to follow Kirby Smith with 7,000 men, and that Price and yourself should act in concert. This co-operation seems to us essential to success, and nothing should be allowed to obstruct it. If Breckinridge cannot go to Smith without endangering the success of your operations he must be retained. When in company with Price you will, by virtue of seniority, direct the movements of the embodied forces.

G. W. RANDOLPH,
Secretary of War.

IUKA, MISS., *September 19, 1862.*

General VAN DORN:

I will make the movement proposed in your dispatch of the 17th instant. Enemy concentrating against me. Please make demonstration toward Rienzi. Have written by courier. Send your telegrams to Tupelo.

STERLING PRICE,
Major-General, Commanding.

HEADQUARTERS ARMY OF THE WEST,
Iuka, Miss., September 19. 1862.

Major-General VAN DORN, *Commanding, &c.:*

GENERAL : Your couriers have both arrived, bringing your dispatches of the 16th instant.

I will move my army as quickly as I can in the direction proposed by you. I am, however, expecting an attack to-day, as it seems, from the most reliable information which I can procure, that they are concentrating their forces against me. Ross' division is said to have gotten here yesterday from Bolivar. General Ord, commanding the left wing of Grant's army, is in front of me. A demonstration by you upon Rienzi would greatly facilitate the execution of the movement which you suggest. I have ordered a cavalry regiment to keep our line of communication open. It left yesterday for Baldwyn.

I am, &c.,

STERLING PRICE,
Major-General.

HEADQUARTERS ARMY OF THE WEST,
Iuka, Miss., September 19, 1862.

Brigdier-General LITTLE :

GENERAL : The enemy are driving in our pickets upon the Iuka and Bay Springs road, the one by which the army approached Iuka. You will please order Brigadier-General Hébert to move forthwith upon that road with his brigade and to prevent their further advance. General Armstrong will detail two or three squadrons of cavalry to report to him. The order is inclosed.

I am, &c.,

THOS. L. SNEAD,
Assistant Adjutant-General.

[Inclosure.]

HEADQUARTERS ARMY OF THE WEST,
Iuka, Miss., September 19, 1862.

General ARMSTRONG:

GENERAL : General Hébert has been ordered to move with his brigade upon Iuka and Bay Springs road (the one by which we entered Iuka), upon which the enemy are advancing and driving in our pickets. The major-general commanding directs you to detail two or three squadrons, to report forthwith to General Hébert as part of his command, and he suggests that you detail for that purpose Roddey's and Sanders' commands, though this merely a suggestion and not an order.

I am, &c.,

THOS. L. SNEAD,
Assistant Adjutant-General.

HEADQUARTERS ARMY OF THE WEST,
Iuka, Miss., September 19, 1862.

General LITTLE :

GENERAL : You will, by direction of the major-general commanding, send another brigade to the support of General Hébert, and if the latter is not already marching, direct him to move with all haste.

I am, &c.,

THOS. L. SNEAD.

JACKSON, MISS., *September* 22, 1862.

Brig. Gen. MARTIN L. SMITH,
   Commanding at Vicksburg :

First. Lay out a battery of four guns at the bend of the river above Vicksburg. Commence work upon it.

Second. Send an engineer officer to construct a boom at Haines' Bluff; also to establish a battery of guns there.

Third. Send the light-draught steamers from the Yazoo to the Red River as soon as possible with safety.

Fourth. Then repair the raft thoroughly at Liverpool.

Fifth. Occupy Haines' Bluff with a sufficient force to protect the position, and repair the road leading thence to Vicksburg.

Sixth. Employ a sufficient force of negro labor to prosecute the work indicated rapidly.

                         DANIEL RUGGLES,
                    Brigadier-General, Commanding.

HEADQUARTERS ARMY OF THE WEST,
   Near Baldwyn, Miss., September 22, 1862.

Maj. Gen. EARL VAN DORN, *Holly Springs, Miss. :*

GENERAL: The army will get here to-morrow. Will be ready to move in two days, as suggested by you. Surplus arms will be sent at once to Jackson. Movement from Iuka made in perfect order, without the loss of a wagon.

The battle on Friday afternoon between the enemy's right, under Rosecrans, and two brigades, under Hébert and Martin, was very bloody. General Little was killed; Colonels Whitfield, Mabry, and Gilmore wounded. We drove them back about 600 yards, capturing nine pieces of artillery and about 50 prisoners, and slept on the field. Our loss was nearly 300 in killed, wounded, and missing; the enemy's greater. Finding that the enemy were receiving heavy re-enforcements from Bolivar, Corinth, and Jacinto, and that our position was very bad, General Price determined to carry out the marching orders which he had previously published, and we left the town after sunrise, bringing away everything but the badly wounded. Colonels Whitfield and Gilmore are with us. General Price will get here to-day.

Respectfully,

                         THOS. L. SNEAD,
                    Assistant Adjutant-General.

HEADQUARTERS ARMY OF THE WEST,
   Baldwyn, Miss., September 22, 1862.

General TILGHMAN, *Jackson, Miss. :*

General Price will direct all disposable arms to be sent to Jackson for exchanged prisoners. His army will get here to-night. The movement from Iuka was effected without loss of any kind.

Respectfully,

                         THOS. L. SNEAD,
                    Assistant Adjutant-General.

DAVIS' MILL, MISS., *September* 23, 1862.

Maj. Gen. STERLING PRICE:

I march to-morrow morning toward Rienzi; will reach there in three days, on the 26th or 27th. I will send cavalry in front. If you send out they will meet. Send me all the information you have. I came within one hour day before yesterday of cutting off Hurlbut's division from Bolivar. They came as near as Grand Junction. I shall send cavalry to attempt to cut railroad from Corinth to Jackson, Tenn. Telegraph me the strength of the enemy in your front and where they are. Watch them closely with your cavalry.

EARL VAN DORN,
Major-General.

HEADQUARTERS ARMY OF THE WEST,
Camp Little, Miss., September 23, 1862.

General VAN DORN:

GENERAL: I have received your letter of the 20th instant, indicating your readiness to move. I will leave here in two days to form a junction with you, and I desire to know at what point we will meet. It is important that we should get together soon, as, by a telegram received this morning from Governor Pettus, and other sources, I fear the enemy are in possession of our proposed movements and some dispatches have fallen into their hands. Indeed it would be better if you could come some portion of the way to meet me, as proposed in yours of the 17th. From the information I have I deem it prudent that we meet somewhere at or near Ripley, through which I propose to pass, and which point I can easily reach in two days' march. Our scouts can communicate before then.

I have the honor to be, &c.,

STERLING PRICE,
Major-General, Commanding.

BALDWYN, MISS., *September* 23, 1862.

General EARL VAN DORN:

I will leave here on Friday morning, 26th. Wrote you this morning, stating that I would meet you at Ripley. As you know more of the country, if any point be better name it and I will meet you there. A few days ago the enemy's strength was 35,000. I learn that they are leaving in the direction of Jackson, and whether we attack them or not before receiving our exchanged prisoners it is important that we should unite.

STERLING PRICE,
Major-General.

SPECIAL ORDERS, }   HDQRS. ARMY OF THE DIST. OF THE MISS.,
No. 74.   }   *Camp, Davis' Mill, Miss., September* 23, 1862.

*   *   *   *   *   *   *

XII. Brigadier-General Pillow having reported for duty with this army, and there being no division or brigade to which he can at present be assigned, he will await the ratification of exchange and reorganization of the returned prisoners of war at Jackson. In the mean time he will be considered as awaiting orders, and will report weekly by letter his address.

*   *   *   *   *   *   *

By order of General Earl Van Dorn :

M. M. KIMMEL,
Major and Assistant Adjutant-General.

GENERAL ORDERS, ⟩ HDQRS. OF THE ARMY, DIST. OF THE MISS,
    No. 50.   ⟩   *Camp at Davis' Mill, Miss., Sept. 23, 1862.*

The brigades of Brigadier-Generals Rust, Bowen, Villepigue, W. H. Jackson (cavalry), and Waul's Texas Legion will compose a division, to be commanded by Major-General Mansfield Lovell. The troops of this command will be in readiness to march to-morrow morning at 6 o'clock with fifteen days' rations.

*   *   *   *   *   *   *

By order of General Earl Van Dorn :

M. M. KIMMEL,
Major and Assistant Adjutant-General.

DAVIS' MILL, MISS., *September* 24, 1862.
General STERLING PRICE:

Your dispatch received. I commenced march to Ripley this morning; will move slowly and meet you. Ross' division returned from Corinth to Bolivar on Monday last. Troops arriving Tuesday morning. They are preparing for some moves; can't learn yet what intention. This move was made in consequence of my advance toward that point. I send Jackson with 1,100 cavalry to-day to cut railroad between Corinth and Jackson, Tenn. He may thus take them in detail. One of my scouts reports quite a large force at Rienzi. Would you have transportation for the 5,000 returned prisoners if they should join you at Baldwyn or Guntown? Have you their arms with you? Waul's Texas Legion will soon join me—2,000 men. I get 8,000 prisoners, but no arms yet. I will write. I have sent out scouts to meet your cavalry.

EARL VAN DORN,
Major-General.

[Indorsement.]

Tell Van Dorn the arms have been ordered to Jackson, Miss.

STERLING PRICE.

HDQRS. ARMY OF THE DISTRICT OF THE MISSISSIPPI,
Camp near Grand Junction, Miss., September 24, 1862.
Maj. Gen. STERLING PRICE,
    Commanding Army of the West, Baldwyn :

GENERAL : One of my brigades has marched and will encamp to-night at Salem, on the Ripley road; the others will march to-morrow morning. I will probably reach Ripley a day or two before you. As you suggest, it is important that we should unite our forces. No better place than Ripley. The enemy are stronger than I had supposed, and it may be necessary for us to await the arrival of some of the exchanged prisoners.

I made a demonstration on Bolivar pending the arrival of my trains, and have succeeded in withdrawing Ross' division from Corinth. I send Jackson now to cut the railroad between Jackson and Corinth. After doing this he will join me on the enemy's right flank.

Your courier reaches me as I now write. Your telegraph came this morning. I meet you at Ripley on the 28th.

Have you transportation for your exchanged prisoners should they arrive at Baldwyn? I will receive 8,000; you 5,000. I get also Waul's Texas Legion, which will arrive at Holly Springs in a few days. I must send a regiment or two to Port Hudson. We will have accession therefore of about 14,000 men. I now have 7,000. If it becomes necessary to wait it will not be unfortunate, as we are holding a large force in check; later we will defeat them, free West Tennessee, and penetrate Kentucky or cross the Ohio. I do not think it necessary to act hurriedly. On the contrary, a little delay, attacking, as it were, *en échelon* from Maryland to West Tennessee and Arkansas, seems to me advisable.

If Bragg and Smith are successful the enemy in our front will withdraw. We will follow and re-enforce Bragg. However, it is not necessary here to discuss this. I will meet you at Ripley on the 28th.

In regard to the Governor's dispatch I know of no lost dispatches between us. I am satisfied the enemy know nothing of our intentions, or they would not have re-enforced Bolivar from Corinth. We are in fine spirits and in good health.

Very truly, general, I am, your friend and obedient servant,

EARL VAN DORN,
Major-General.

SPECIAL ORDERS, }   ADJT. AND INSPECTOR GENERAL'S OFFICE,
No. 223.   }   *Richmond, Va., September 24, 1862.*

*   *   *   *   *   *   *

II. Military commanders of Confederate States forces, as soon as they approach or enter the territory of the United States bordering upon the Mississippi River or the tributaries thereof, will publish proclamations assuring the people of those States, as well as all others interested, of the free navigation of the Mississippi River, in accordance with a resolution adopted by the Confederate States Senate September 12.

*   *   *   *   *   *   *

By command of the Secretary of War:

JNO. WITHERS,
Assistant Adjutant-General.

Resolution of the Confederate States Senate, passed September 12, 1862.

Resolved, That the President be and is hereby respectfully requested to direct such of our military commanders as may at the time be in command of the respective columns of our forces as soon as they approach or enter the territory of the United States bordering upon the Mississippi River or the tributaries thereof, to publish proclamations assuring the people of those States, as well as all others interested, of the free navigation of the Mississippi River, according to the provisions of an act of the Provisional Congress, entitled "An act to declare and establish the free navigation of the Mississippi River," approved February 25, 1861; and that said commanders cause to be published copies of said act with such proclamations.

Official.

JNO. WITHERS,
Assistant Adjutant-General.

HEADQUARTERS DEPARTMENT No. 2,
Bardstown, Ky., September 25, 1862.

Major-General VAN DORN:

GENERAL: We have driven and drawn the enemy clear back to the Ohio. Push your columns to our support, and arouse the people to re-enforce us. We have thousands of arms without people to handle them. Nashville is defended by only a weak division; Bowling Green by only a regiment. Sweep them off and push up to the Ohio. Secure the heavy guns at these places and we will secure the Tennessee and Cumberland Rivers. All depends on rapid movements. Trusting to your energy and zeal we shall confidently expect a diversion in our favor against the overwhelming force now concentrating in our front.

Respectfully and truly, yours,

BRAXTON BRAGG,
General, Commanding.

[Indorsement.]

HEADQUARTERS ARMY OF WEST TENNESSEE,
Holly Springs, Miss., November 2, 1862.

The above dispatch was this day received and forwarded. I cannot account for the detention in transmittal.

EARL VAN DORN,
Major-General.

———

DAVIS' MILL, MISS., *September* 25, 1862.

GEORGE W. RANDOLPH,
Secretary of War:

For the three brigades of returned prisoners (8,000 men), Second Division, have no major-general, and but one brigadier (Tilghman) for the three brigades; and [for] First Division (7,000 men) I have but two brigadiers; General Lovell commands division. General officers present: Lovell, Ruggles, Tilghman, Smith, Beall, Villepigue, and Rust; Ruggles in charge of district; Smith in command of brigade at Vicksburg; Beall in command at Port Hudson; Pillow absent, but may return. I shall want therefore five general officers, or six if I put Lovell in command of corps. All I ask is that some of the officers sent me may not be the doubtful cases awaiting orders. I will venture to recommend Cols. J. P. Major and W. H. Jackson as two of the brigadiers and General D. H. Maury as major-general. Price will require two major-generals also and several brigadiers. Little killed; Phifer and Cabell rejected by President.

EARL VAN DORN,
Major-General.

———

RICHMOND, VA., *September* 25, 1862.

Gov. JOHN J. PETTUS, *Jackson, Miss.:*

Commissary-general has directed one of his officers to get consent of owner of salt mine and open a shaft for supply of his department. General Taylor has been instructed to give the requisite protection, and, if necessary, to exercise authority to promote the working of the mine. I hope this will answer the purpose sought by you.

JEFFERSON DAVIS.

HEADQUARTERS ARMY OF THE WEST,
Ripley, Miss., September 28, 1862.

His Excellency ISHAM G. HARRIS,
Governor of Tennessee:

GOVERNOR: I have just received your communication of the 20th instant, dated from Lebanon.*

In obedience to instructions from General Bragg I started with my army for Nashville, intending to cross the Tennessee River at or near Eastport. I proceeded without interruption to Iuka, where I captured a large quantity of stores, the enemy's force there having evacuated and gone in the direction of Corinth. At Iuka I found myself threatened by a force of the enemy more than double my own and was unable to proceed farther. I was attacked in the evening by the enemy, with heavy loss on both sides. The numbers and positions of the enemy were such that the preservation of my army, as well as that under Major-General Van Dorn, required that the two armies should be joined together, and I accordingly moved my forces to this place by way of Baldwyn.

I will add—as the Northern account so grossly misrepresents the matter—that in the battle of the 19th the enemy was driven from the field, leaving in my hands nine pieces of artillery, which we carried into Iuka and there destroyed, not having any means of bringing them away. We were not attacked on the following day, and I moved off with my whole army and stores, including those captured at Iuka, without any loss.

General Van Dorn's forces met me here to-day, and with the combined armies we will at once proceed northward, endeavoring to overcome the enemy in front of us; with what success I cannot, of course, tell, but we have every confidence in our ability to defeat him.

Your Excellency may rest assured that I most earnestly desire the liberation of your State, and shall leave nothing undone to secure it. The enemy having much larger force in the vicinity of Corinth than was anticipated by us has alone prevented me from carrying out General Bragg's orders.

With sentiments of highest esteem, I remain, Your Excellency's obedient servant,

STERLING PRICE,
Major-General.

HEADQUARTERS COMBINED FORCES WEST TENNESSEE,
Ripley, Miss., September 28, 1862.

Major-General PRICE,
Commanding Army of the West:

GENERAL: Will you please direct three days' rations to be cooked; as many wagons emptied as possible, and send them to Holly Springs to be loaded with bacon, flour, and salt. Please send two armed convalescents or weakly men with each wagon as an escort, with one officer from each division. General Lovell will do the same, and the wagons will start back to-morrow via Salem. The chief quartermaster has been directed to hire as many wagons between this place and Holly Springs as he can find. General Lovell will move his division up on the Ruck-

---

ersville road about 5 or 6 miles to-morrow morning. Please hold your army in readiness to move in same direction. They may move to-morrow if the preparations above desired can be made in time.

Very truly and sincerely, sir, I am, your obedient servant,

EARL VAN DORN,
Major-General.

RICHMOND, VA., *September 29, 1862.*

Major-General VAN DORN,
Davis' Mill (via Holly Springs), Miss.:

Assume forthwith the command of all the troops left in Mississippi, including General Price's column. Concentrate them without loss of time; reorganize and arm the exchanged prisoners; make proper disposition for the defense of the Mississippi River, and also for an advance into Tennessee, and acknowledge the receipt of this order by telegraph.

G. W. RANDOLPH,
Secretary of War.

RICHMOND, VA., *September 29, 1862.*

General VAN DORN, *Holly Springs, Miss.:*

Have you received my telegram of September 11, addressed to you at Grand Junction? If so, what action have you taken on it?

JEFFERSON DAVIS.

OXFORD, MISS., *September 30, 1862.*

Maj. M. M. KIMMEL, *Assistant Adjutant-General:*

In compliance with Special Orders, No. 74,* of Major-General Van Dorn, I report myself at this place, where I shall await his orders. On my return from his headquarters I addressed a dispatch to the Secretary of War, of which I inclose you a copy. The object of this dispatch was, without loss of time, to take ten of the skeleton Tennessee regiments and proceed at once to some portion of Tennessee and by volunteer recruits to fill them up. I sent the dispatch to the Secretary, understanding from my interview with General Van Dorn that he did not feel authorized to make any order in regard to the return prisoners until General Tilghman had reported the whole of them organized. I inclose the Secretary's reply. The construction I place upon the reply is that the Secretary approves of the suggestion, but leaves the whole matter to General Van Dorn's judgment.

By order of General Albert Sidney Johnston I was placed in command of a division of ten regiments, and was in command of that division when suspended. General Buckner, having arrived at Chattanooga on the eve of General Bragg's advance, was placed in command of my division, and when I was ordered by General Bragg to report to General Van Dorn I supposed it was that I should take command of his division; but, inasmuch as some of General Buckner's regiments were Kentuckians, which could be more promptly filled by a Kentucky general, I proposed to take Tennessee regiments only, believing I could promptly fill them by volunteer recruits. If the suggestion in my dispatch to the Secretary of War meets with General Van Dorn's approval I make the

---

* Of September 23.

application to him. Inasmuch as the Secretary of War has (that being the construction I place on his reply) referred the whole matter to him I respectfully submit it to his judgment. By detailing an officer from each company of each regiment to proceed to different portions of Tennessee, and with a knowledge of the fact that the recruits would be united with Tennessee regiments, and would come under my command, I am confident I could fill the regiments in a very short time. If General Van Dorn should grant the application I would be gratified if he would assign Captain Humes' company of artillery to my command, so that I might, while filling the regiments, procure horses, &c., so as to fit a battery of light artillery for the field.

With great respect,

GID. J. PILLOW,
Brigadier-General, C. S. Army.

[Inclosures.]

OXFORD, MISS., *September* 25, 1862.

GEORGE W. RANDOLPH, *Secretary of War:*

Reported to General Van Dorn as ordered by General Bragg. No command for me until returned prisoners are organized. Among these are thirteen skeleton Tennessee regiments. If ten of these are placed under me I can proceed to Middle Tennessee and fill them by volunteers in thirty days. They aggregate about 4,000. Organization proceeding very slowly. If all 15,000 remain at Jackson until organized and armed much time will be lost. General Van Dorn thinks he can make no order about it; Bragg out of reach. I [have] nothing to do. Please answer.

GID. J. PILLOW,
Brigadier-General, C. S. Army.

RICHMOND, VA., [*September*] 27, 1862.

Brigadier-General PILLOW:

General Van Dorn has telegraphed that he is expecting you and will assign you to a command.

G. W. RANDOLPH,
Secretary of War.

———

RICHMOND, VA., *September* 30, 1862.

Gov. JOHN J. PETTUS, *Jackson, Miss.:*

Your dispatches of 28th and 29th* received. Orders have been sent to General Van Dorn, and will no doubt receive his attention. Major-General Pemberton goes directly to Jackson to command in your section. He is an officer of great merit, and I commend him to your kind consideration. His department will be Mississippi and Louisiana, east of the river. I have directed more arms to be sent.

JEFFERSON DAVIS.

———

WAR DEPARTMENT, C. S. A.,
Richmond, Va., September 30, 1862.†

Maj. Gen. J. C. PEMBERTON:

GENERAL: You will proceed to Jackson and relieve General Van Dorn from the command of the district assigned to him by General

---

* Not found.

† Recorded in War Department books as of October 4, 1862. Original dated as above.

Bragg, for the purpose of permitting him to command the forces ordered to advance into West Tennessee. You will turn your attention immediately to the defense of the States of Mississippi and Louisiana east of the Mississippi River, and consider the successful defense of those States as the first and chief object of your command.

You will also organize the troops in your department and prepare them for the field, and give such assistance to the officers charged with the enrollment of conscripts as they may require. The commandants of the camps of conscripts are charged with the duty of enrolling and assigning them. They act under general orders and report directly to this Department; but it will be in your power to assist them in the discharge of their duties.

If a favorable opportunity offer for an attack on New Orleans you will avail yourself of it, and act in concert with Maj. Gen. Richard Taylor, who commands the District of Louisiana west of the Mississippi. You will communicate with him as speedily as possible and concert with him a joint plan of operations for the defense of the river and the capture of New Orleans.

Your military department will comprise the State of Mississippi and so much of Louisiana as lies east of the Mississippi River. Until further orders you will report directly to this Department.

Very respectfully, your obedient servant,

G. W. RANDOLPH,
Secretary of War.

HOLLY SPRINGS, MISS., *October* 1, 1862.

Hon. GEORGE W. RANDOLPH,
Secretary of War :

Dispatch received October 1 (to-day) at Pocahontas, Tenn. I have made union with General Price and am now before Corinth. Joined forces at Ripley, Miss., on September 28. Expect some of the returned prisoners at Holly Springs within ten days; probably all of them. Will send two regiments to Port Hudson, commanded sufficiently. Force now at Vicksburg. Expect to take Corinth; move to [Chewalla] division in the morning to feel position and strength, and to cut, with cavalry, the railroad to Jackson, Tenn.

One division of the Corinth command and some artillery left on the 25th for the north, Rosecrans, in command, with it. Is said two divisions are left at Corinth.

EARL VAN DORN,
Major-General.

HEADQUARTERS COMBINED FORCES,
Pocahontas, Tenn., October 1, 1862.

Major-General PRICE,
Commanding Army of the West :

GENERAL: I had intended to call and see you this evening, but have not been able to do so. I have ordered General Lovell to move his division in the morning toward Chewalla and the cavalry to meet Armstrong near there, and to move forward and feel the condition of affairs about Corinth—that is, the cavalry—also to cut the Jackson Railroad. I have ordered General Lovell to leave you 12,000 rations. Please hold yourself in readiness with your army corps to march at short notice. It may be that we shall march some time to-morrow; it will depend upon

Lovell's report. Fifteen regiments have left Corinth since the 23d; three trains also of artillery and a large quantity of ammunition. Please order the bridge over the Hatchie at Pocahontas made, if possible, by to-morrow night. I send a courier in the morning to Holly Springs. You have an opportunity to write. Send to-night.

Very truly and respectfully, sir, your obedient servant,

EARL VAN DORN,
Major-General.

HEADQUARTERS,
Camp near Pocahontas, October 1, 1862.

General PRICE:

The major-general commanding directs that you at once send heavy details to repair the bridge at Pocahontas over the Hatchie. They will work night and day until completed. The lumber is in the town and quartermaster will furnish all necessary material.

I am, very respectfully, your obedient servant,

M. M. KIMMEL,
Major and Assistant Adjutant-General.

GENERAL ORDERS, } ADJT. AND INSPECTOR GENERAL'S OFFICE,
No. 73. } *Richmond, Va., October 1, 1862.*

I. The State of Mississippi and that part of Louisiana east of the Mississippi River is constituted a separate military department, the command of which is assigned to Maj. Gen. John C. Pemberton.

* * * * * * *

By order:

S. COOPER,
Adjutant and Inspector General.

HEADQUARTERS ARMY OF THE WEST,
Near Pocahontas, October 1, 1862.

Maj. M. M. KIMMEL, *Assistant Adjutant-General:*

MAJOR: I have the honor to submit the following statement of the effective men of my command, enlisted, as reported by Generals Hébert and Armstrong, at Ripley, and General Maury, at this place:

	Effective.	Pieces of artillery.				
		6-pounders.	12-pounders.	12-pounder howitzers.	24-pounder howitzers.	3½ rifles.
Hébert:						
Infantry	6,602					
Cavalry	61					
Artillery	477	10	2	10	2	
Maury:						
Infantry	3,896					
Cavalry	858					
Artillery	451	6		10		4
Armstrong's cavalry	1,428					
Falkner's cavalry (approximated)	500					
General Price's escort	90					
Total	14,363	16	2	20	2	4

Two regiments of cavalry are absent, one at Baldwyn and the other east of there. One of these has been ordered here, and will probably be up in three or four days.

I am, major, very respectfully, your obedient servant,

STERLING PRICE,
Major-General, Commanding.

HDQRS. DISTRICT OF THE MISSISSIPPI,
Jackson, Miss., October 3, 1862.

Major-General VAN DORN,
Commanding Army in the Field :

GENERAL : I have the honor to state for your information that so far as we have received advices of the enemy's strength and intentions we are bound to consider Vicksburg and Port Hudson both threatened by land as well as by water. The defenses at Vicksburg are of course well known to you, and I need only send you the copy of a letter just received from Brigadier-General Smith* to insure your consideration of the necessity of retaining an adequate force there to meet probable contingencies. It is the current opinion that the enemy has at Helena, Ark., at the least 15,000, and some say 20,000 men. It is reported, however, since writing the above, that General Curtis' army is moving up the Mississippi and that only one division remains. I doubt its correctness. The defenses at Port Hudson are far from completion for the want of guns and ammunition.

There is also difficulty in obtaining the requisite negro labor there as well as at Vicksburg. The 10-inch columbiad from Richmond has reached here without the ammunition, which has been left behind at Mobile. The movements of the enemy along the river border in the vicinity of Helena have, I doubt not, come within your knowledge, and the influence resulting fully appreciated by you. I have found it necessary to call on the Governor of Mississippi for militia, as follows, viz : A battalion of 200 for service as guards, patrols, &c., at Jackson, Miss.; a regiment at Haines' Bluff, on the Yazoo, to replace other troops allowed by the Governor to return home. A battalion will also concentrate at Woodville, Miss., available at Port Hudson and Natchez.

A regiment is already concentrated at Panola with the prospective increase of a battalion. It is questionable whether the Governor can supply a sufficient militia force to afford substantial aid for defensive operations.

I send this letter by Colonel Sandidge, a member of my staff, to insure its prompt and safe delivery, especially as General Smith's letter ought not to be committed to the mail.

Very respectfully, your obedient servant,

DANIEL RUGGLES,
Brigadier-General, Commanding District.

HEADQUARTERS, *October* 4, 1862—1 a. m.

General PRICE:

General Van Dorn still hears of the enemy leaving Corinth. The general will open with twelve or fourteen guns on the town as soon as

---

* Not found.

he gets them in position. General Maury has been notified. If you are attacked, repel the attack, but do not advance until further orders.

By order of General Van Dorn:

M. M. KIMMEL,
Major and Assistant Adjutant-General.

[Indorsement.]

Sent for General Hébert, who will conform to it.

By order of General Price:

JAMES M. LOUGHBOROUGH,
Assistant Adjutant-General.

2.15 O'CLOCK.

Maj. Gen. STERLING PRICE,
Commanding Army of the West:

GENERAL: If we are compelled to fall back take the Oxford road—the one you are now encamped upon—your wagons to go about 6 miles from their present position. Lovell will take the Pontotoc road and go as far as Orizaba. You will the next day march at 3 a. m. and go to Hickory Flat, where Lovell will again join you. Your wagons should be hitched up ready to move at an order. Move up as rapidly as possible. Lovell is formed on the Pocahontas road; you will form on his left on the Middletown road. Nothing as yet reported on our right. In haste.

Yours, &c.,

EARL VAN DORN.

HEADQUARTERS, *October* 4, 1862.

General PRICE:

GENERAL: The general commanding directs that you send a battery in the best condition to move on the road to Rienzi, to report to General Armstrong. They will pass these headquarters and the general will give them the necessary directions as to the road, &c. You will move with your command at 5 a. m. on the Rienzi road, right in front. Wagons and ambulances will follow their brigades.

By order of General Van Dorn:

M. M. KIMMEL,
Major and Assistant Adjutant-General.

[Indorsement.]

The battery will be at the bridge at 4 a. m. to-morrow.

HDQRS. ARMY OF THE DISTRICT OF THE MISSISSIPPI,
October 4, 1862.

Maj. Gen. STERLING PRICE:

GENERAL: Please detail from each of your divisions 100 men, with 1 captain and 1 lieutenant from each division, and a field officer of intelligence and good address, to go to Corinth to bury our dead. The detail from each division will take a wagon and the necessary picks and spades, and will report at these headquarters before the command moves in the morning.

By order of General Van Dorn:

M. M. KIMMEL,
Assistant-Adjutant-General.

———, ———, 1862.

General PRICE:

Please direct your brigade commanders to hold their troops well in hand, to keep up the line, and to sleep on their arms. You can send some of the cavalry to the rear with canteens for water and to water horses. If we straggle off we may yet lose all.

EARL VAN DORN.

HEADQUARTERS, *October* 5, 1862—night.

General STERLING PRICE:

GENERAL: The Army of the West will march to-morrow, right in front; batteries with their brigades. General Lovell's division will march in rear.

By order of General Van Dorn:

M. M. KIMMEL,
Major and Assistant Adjutant-General.

P. S.—The troops will be in readiness to move as soon as the train is closed up.

HEADQUARTERS, *October* 6, 1862—midnight.
(Received at 4 a. m.)

General PRICE:

General Van Dorn directs that you move immediately with your whole command and encamp 4 miles south of Ripley, on the Oxford road. Allow no one to stop in Ripley. Leave a guard at Ripley to prevent stragglers from stopping in town. All of your wagons will take Oxford road. General Lovell moves on the Pontotoc road.

By order of General Van Dorn:

M. M. KIMMEL,
Major and Assistant Adjutant-General.

HDQRS. DISTRICT OF THE MISSISSIPPI,
Jackson, Miss., October 6, 1862.

General S. COOPER,
Adjutant and Inspector General, Richmond, Va.:

GENERAL: I have the honor to forward, for the information of the War Department, a communication from Brig. Gen. M. L. Smith respecting the defenses at Vicksburg, under his immediate command, a subject which I recommend to special consideration. There is reason to believe, however, that Curtis' army has been withdrawn, in part at least, from Helena, reputed to have gone northward, though some plundering expeditions have landed in Mississippi opposite to Helena, penetrating as far as Swan Lake, and at Gaines' Landing, on the Arkansas side, below. The withdrawal of the Federal forces, it is believed, is temporary, and that, in conjunction with the gunboat fleet still remaining, and which it is represented will be soon strengthened by the addition of light-draught iron-clad gunboats now being constructed on the Ohio, a formidable demonstration against Vicksburg will be made at no distant day. The magnitude of the interest which impels the Federal Government to persevere in the endeavor to break through this barrier to the commerce of the Northwest has been apprehended by many—has not been fully appreciated by the Confederate Government. I have felt it my duty to direct a careful examination and report of the existing defenses of Vicksburg, with the view of strengthening them by the addition of such auxiliary works as it might be expedient to establish.

The report of the chief engineer, herewith transmitted, indicates that it is scarcely expedient to establish a battery at the bend of the river above, in consequence of the labor involved, the additional force necessary to protect it, and the long reach of the arm of the river above the bend. It is well understood, as a military principle, that the protection of the town is of minor importance in comparison with the obstruction of the navigation of the river, on which point the report is not entirely explicit. There is reason to believe that a field work of considerable magnitude placed at the neck of the bend opposite Vicksburg, with two detached batteries flanking the river above and below, would prove of very great service as an auxiliary to the defense. The establishment of these works, however, would involve the necessity of having a land force of from 5,000 to 10,000 men to man them and defend that bank of the river, especially the canal, which has been in part already opened by the enemy. It is to be hoped that the importance which the enemy attaches to the question of the unobstructed navigation of the Mississippi has received due consideration, and that early measures will be taken to perfect the details connected with the defense. The defense of the Yazoo River and the extensive fertile region embraced between it and the Mississippi River is a matter of great importance, requiring prompt action and consideration. Details connected with this district will be forwarded at an early moment. The defensive position assumed at Port Hudson, La., has been fortified as rapidly as possible with the means provided. Some fifteen heavy guns are already in position on the east bank of the river, and other guns with ammunition are being forwarded as rapidly as possible. The position is naturally strong, and easily defended from attacks by water and favorable for defensive disposition by land. I respectfully recommend that an auxiliary force of 1,000 infantry, one battery of field guns, and 100 cavalry be placed on the right bank to co-operate with the defenses on the left, especially at any period when an immediate attack of the enemy is anticipated. The accompanying map will show the outline of the position. The accompanying requisition for guns and munitions is recommended to favorable consideration. The intervening portion of the Mississippi River between Vicksburg and Port Hudson, as well as the Red River remaining in our uninterrupted possession, will prove of the greatest importance to the Confederate Government connected with the transit of supplies, especially subsistence from the west.

Before leaving the District of East Louisiana I directed Colonel Marigny to establish a temporary camp in Ascension Parish, some 35 miles bel w Baton Rouge, with the view of overcoming the reputed demoralization of the people controlling intercourse with the enemy, filling up our ranks with conscripts and volunteers, and as a preliminary measure in any plan connected with operations having in view the recovery of New Orleans. The present campaign on the Northern Mississippi border involves so many important considerations coming under the special jurisdiction of the commanding general of the army in the field that I will merely say that every effort has been made here to second his plans and enable him to carry them into a successful execution.

Very respectfully, your most obedient servant,

DANIEL RUGGLES,
Brigadier-General, Commanding District.

[Indorsement.]

To Secretary of War, October 16, 1862. Received back Adjutant and Inspector General's Office, October 24, 1862. Four inclosures missing.

HDQRS. CHIEF OF ORDNANCE, DIST. OF THE TENN.,
Tupelo, Miss., October 7, 1862.

Maj. Gen. STERLING PRICE,
Commanding Army of the West:

GENERAL: I have the honor to report that in pursuance of your orders I have delivered over 8,000 stand of arms to Brigadier-General Tilghman's ordnance officer at Jackson, Miss. Out of the whole lot on hand at present I think I can assort 500 or 1,000 stand of serviceable arms, mostly flint-lock muskets, which I will retain for the present, having heard of your late desperate battle and fearing that you may need them to replace such arms as may have been lost on the field. I will proceed to Crawford to-morrow to stop any further shipment from that place until I can hear from you. In the mean time I will have bayonets fitted on the guns, as many as possible, and have them prepared for shipment as rapidly as possible. I know you must need ammunition after so much fighting, especially for your cannon. I have a tolerable supply of small-arm ammunition on hand and some for cannon, but I will telegraph to Columbus to have a large lot of assorted ammunition for cannon and small-arms in readiness immediately. I have been trying to get all the musket-caps I could to supply the deficiency in that particular, and have succeeded in getting several lots from Richmond and other places. Captain Kennerly will be in readiness to issue what stores we have on hand at Tupelo. I will leave nothing undone that can be done to refit the army with stores from my department. I am informed by the commandant of this post that there are now in this place about 1,200 convalescents who are without arms; and had I known this fact sooner I should have stopped the last shipment of 1,400 stand of arms to Jackson, although my orders are to ship all the serviceable arms within the district to that place. I hope the ordnance officers of divisions will be sent forward immediately with their requisitions, so that I may be informed more particularly what is needed at the earliest day possible.

Believe me, very respectfully, your obedient servant,

THOS. H. PRICE,
Chief of Ordnance, District of the Tennessee.

OCTOBER 8, 1862.

General PRICE:

I learn from General Armstrong that the enemy have been firing on his rear pickets, 5 miles back. You will have to put a thousand men and a battery of artillery into position in rear on the road at a strong place and check his advance. I think it can be nothing but cavalry or a small force. You must be on your guard.

EARL VAN DORN,
Major-General.

JACKSON, MISS., *October* 9, 1862.

Major-General HOLMES, *Monroe, La.:*

(Care of General Blanchard, who is desired to forward immediately.)

General Van Dorn has fallen back from Corinth to Holly Springs, the enemy concentrating in pursuit. Curtis' army is reported to have abandoned Helena and marched toward Holly Springs. With what force can you cross the river to re-enforce Van Dorn, and in what time? We are in want of supplies. Allow bacon and flour to cross at Vicksburg. Answer immediately.

> DANIEL RUGGLES,
> *Brigadier-General.*

JACKSON, *October* 9, 1862.

General S. COOPER:

The circumstances under which I was ordered to the command of this department have been so much changed by movements of the enemy in the State of Mississippi that it is now impossible to carry out instructions given me, Generals Van Dorn and Lovell being both my seniors. I therefore ask further instructions.

> J. C. PEMBERTON,
> *Major-General.*

[Indorsement.]

OCTOBER 10, 1862.

Your nomination to higher grade now before the Senate and confirmation expected in a day or so, when you will be advised. Meantime the President desires that you use your energies to obtain additional force, and give attention to defense of Port Hudson.

> S. C.

COMMANDANT'S OFFICE, NAVAL STATION,
Jackson, October 10, 1862.

Major-General PEMBERTON,
    Comdg. Military District of Mississippi and East Louisiana:

GENERAL: I have the honor to inclose for your consideration a copy of a letter I addressed to your predecessor in command on the 9th instant.

The crews of the gunboat Mobile and of the late ram Arkansas are at Yazoo City in readiness to man any batteries that may be constructed for the defense of the raft and the protection of the vast amount of public and private property upon the river Yazoo and its adjacent banks. Great and increasing difficulties are encountered in the purchase of food for those men, about 200 in number, and I respectfully ask that you will authorize your chief commissary of subsistence to fill requisitions, approved by the commanding naval officer of the station, bills for which will be liquidated on presentation to Paymaster Nixon, of the Confederate Navy, whose office is in this city.

I am, very respectfully, your obedient servant,

> W. F. LYNCH,
> *Flag-Officer, Commanding Naval Forces of the West.*

[Inclosure.]

COMMANDANT'S OFFICE, NAVAL STATION,
Jackson, October 9, 1862.

Brigadier-General RUGGLES,
Commanding Military District of the Mississippi :

GENERAL : In the expectation of being relieved from this station I beg leave to submit the fruits of my observation as to the protection of the naval works on the Yazoo, participating in which protection are twenty-three large river steamers and an immense amount of cotton upon the river and its adjacent banks.

Apart from its position as commanding the right flank of the defenses of Vicksburg, Haines' Bluff, if properly fortified, would control the mouths of the Yazoo and its tributaries, the Great and Little Sunflower Rivers.

Besides a battery of heavy guns, with a protecting force therefor, an efficient barricade in the channel of the river abreast is indispensable; otherwise the battery will prove but a slight impediment to the upward passage of iron-clad vessels.

There is a barricade formed of sunken vessels and a raft of logs at Liverpool, on the Yazoo River, above which lies the vast amount of property to which I have alluded.

It would be unwise to open that barricade even after the river is obstructed below, but perfect madness to attempt to open it under present circumstances. On the contrary, a sluice worn upon the right bank should be blocked up by sinking one of the steamers now in the Upper Sunflower River, which can be brought around on the first temporary rise of water. I take the liberty of speaking earnestly on this point because during my late visit to the banks of the Yazoo some parties, claiming to act by your authority, professed the intention of opening the barricade at Liverpool, professedly for the egress of some of the steamers lying above. They could exhibit no authority and I ordered the commander of the gunboat Mobile to sink any vessel attempting to pass, until I received official notification of the sanction of such an attempt.

I have ordered the officers and crew of the late ram Arkansas to the Yazoo, and if you can divert a few heavy guns from other points and allow them to be placed in position at Liverpool, those officers and men, if a force be at hand to prevent the battery from being flanked, will protect the barricade against any force that may assail it.

There are but two light smooth-bore 32-pounders mounted at Liverpool in the place of the four heavy guns taken away by General Van Dorn, and subsequently destroyed by the enemy. As soon as intelligence of their destruction reached me I applied to the Naval Ordnance Bureau for other guns of like caliber, but the reply then, as well as to a subsequent application, was that the bureau had not one such gun at its disposal.

Once within the barrier of the Yazoo the enemy would control 150 miles of inland navigation, and after destroying a vast amount of public and private property be enabled to strike the Great Northern Railroad at various accessible points.

If you knew how deeply I feel the importance of preparation and how much I grieve for the loss of every moment I am sure that you would excuse the liberty I take in addressing you.

I am, very respectfully, your obedient servant,

W. F. LYNCH,
Flag-Officer, Commanding Naval Forces of the West.

JACKSON, MISS., *October* 11, 1862.

General S. COOPER,
　　　Adjutant and Inspector General, Richmond, Va. :

General Van Dorn with 12,000 men is at Holly Springs. General Price with about 12,000 men, demoralized, is some 10 miles distant. The enemy is concentrating in their front. General Tilghman is about joining Van Dorn with the few remaining exchanged prisoners. I have called on the Governor of Mississippi for the militia. I have called on General Blanchard to prepare to re-enforce Van Dorn. He needs strong re-enforcements at once. General Forney has sent a regiment to Columbus. Musket-caps, cartridges, lead, and cannon ammunition are needed.

　　　　　　　　　　　DANIEL RUGGLES,
　　　　　　　　　　　　Brigadier-General.

JACKSON, MISS., *October* 11, 1862.

Major-General VAN DORN, *Holly Springs :*

Your telegram received. One of our prisoners of war, a colonel, informs General Beall that an expedition of 5,000 infantry, three companies of cavalry, and two batteries is about to leave New Orleans, supposed for Camp Moore, as troops are moved by night by railroad to Lake Pontchartrain. This news and your telegram received at the same time. Steedman's regiment, not armed, at Port Hudson; Drake's at Ponchatoula. Have ordered troops at Vicksburg in readiness. Have telegraphed Blanchard for re-enforcements. General Tilghman will join you to-morrow with his last men. I have called on the Governor for militia to concentrate on the Tallahatchie for your orders. General Forney has sent one regiment to Columbus. We trust in God that you will whip the enemy.

　　　　　　　　　　　DANIEL RUGGLES,
　　　　　　　　　　　　Brigadier-General.

JACKSON, MISS., *October* 11, 1862.

Hon. GEORGE W. RANDOLPH :

I am directed by General Van Dorn to say that he will give battle at Holly Springs, or this side the Tallahatchie, as circumstances may determine.

　　　　　　　　　　　CLEMENT SULLIVANE,
　　　　　　　　　　　　Aide-de-Camp.

EXECUTIVE OFFICE,
Richmond, Va., October 11, 1862.

Hon. J. PHELAN, *Confederate States Senate :*

MY DEAR SIR : I have read and return the telegram inclosed. My attention was given to the subject in anticipation of disaster, which the want of co-intelligence and co-operation suggested. Major-General Pemberton was sent to Jackson, and as soon as the repulse of our forces at Corinth was known I submitted, for the advice and consent of the Senate, the nomination of General Pemberton to be lieutenant-general, having confidence in his ability to make the most of the means for the protection of Mississippi, &c. If he is confirmed he will be able to secure unity of action among the different parts of our forces in that region. In the mean time he has been directed to give all the aid in his power to the army at Ripley, now under the command of General Van Dorn; and General Jones, commanding in East Tennessee, has been directed to sustain Forrest, whose movement may make a diversion and relieve Van Dorn.

Very respectfully and truly, yours,

JEFFERSON DAVIS.

———

HOLLY SPRINGS, MISS., *October* 12, 1862.
(Received at Richmond, Va., October 13, 1862.)

Hon. GEORGE W. RANDOLPH,
    Secretary of War:

Order of General Pemberton just received. Enemy 40,000 in West Tennessee. I attacked Corinth and took it, but could not hold it. Am at Holly Springs. I depend on the railroad for supplies until I can repair my strength, including Price's 22,000. The Department has not considered the difficulties before me. Pemberton's order mentions that I take the field for East Tennessee; does it not mean West Tennessee? I have never received instructions of any kind. I shall act for the best, but I am now an isolated body in the field in Mississippi, relieved of command of my department. I hope this will be corrected.

EARL VAN DORN,
Major-General.

———

GENERAL ORDERS, }   HDQRS. ARMY OF WEST TENNESSEE,
    No. 52.   }   *Holly Springs, Miss., October* 12, 1862.

By direction of the Secretary of War, Major-General Van Dorn assumes command of all the troops in the State of Mississippi, including all exchanged prisoners. They will render the returns and reports required by regulations and existing orders to this office. In addition a field return will be made on the 15th of each month giving effective strength.

By order of General Van Dorn:

M. M. KIMMEL,
Major and Assistant Adjutant-General.

———

RICHMOND, VA., *October* 13, 1862.

A. M. CLAYTON, *Holly Springs, Miss.:*

General Johnston is still unable to go on duty. Lieutenant-General Pemberton is assigned to command, and will, I am sure, do all that is practicable.

JEFFERSON DAVIS.

———

RICHMOND, *October* 14, 1862.

Lieut. Gen. J. C. PEMBERTON:

Your nomination as lieutenant-general has been confirmed by the Senate. You will immediately assume the command of the forces intended to operate in Southwestern Tennessee in addition to the command heretofore assigned to you. The Adjutant-General will send you written orders, but you must not wait for them. Acknowledge by telegraph the receipt of this order. Answer.

G. W. RANDOLPH,
Secretary of War.

SPECIAL ORDERS, } ADJT. AND INSPECTOR GENERAL'S OFFICE,
No. 240. } *Richmond, Va., October* 14, 1862.

*   *   *   *   *   *   *

XXIV. Maj. Gen. John C. Pemberton having been appointed lieutenant-general by the President, by and with the advice and consent of the Senate, will assume command of the forces intended to operate in Southern Tennessee in addition to the command assigned to him in Paragraph I, General Orders, No. 73, current series.

*   *   *   *   *   *   *

By command of Secretary of War :

JNO. WITHERS,
Assistant Adjutant-General.

GENERAL ORDERS, } HDQRS. DEPT. OF MISS. AND EAST LA.,
No. 1. } *Jackson, Miss., October* 14, 1862.

I. In compliance with instructions received from the War Department, at Richmond, Va., the undersigned this day assumes command of the Department of Mississippi and East Louisiana, including the forces intended to operate in Southwestern Tennessee. For the present headquarters of the department will be at Jackson, Miss.

II. Maj. J. R. Waddy, adjutant-general's department, is announced as chief of staff and adjutant-general of the department, to whom all official communications intended for these headquarters will be addressed.

J. C. PEMBERTON,
Lieutenant-General, P. A. C. S., Commanding Department.

HOLLY SPRINGS, *October* 16, 1862.

Lieut. Gen. J. C. PEMBERTON:

It is advisable that you should come here as soon as possible. Events are gathering near. You cannot be here too soon to prepare for action under whatever policy you may see fit to adopt. If you cannot come at once will you inform me if you desire that I should resist the occupation and fortifying of La Grange or Grand Junction? It is probable this will be done by the enemy in a few days, unless I resist it. The enemy in West Tennessee is about 45,000 strong, and re-enforcements daily arriving. You had better get some of Holmes' troops, if you would save Mississippi.

EARL VAN DORN,
Major-General.

SPECIAL ORDERS, } HDQRS. ARMY OF WEST TENNESSEE,
No. 53. } *Holly Springs, October* 16, 1862.

I. Acting Brigadier-Generals Cabell, Phifer, and Armstrong are relieved from duty with their brigades, and will report for special duty at these headquarters. The senior officer present will assume command of their respective brigades.

II. The following assignments of exchanged prisoners are made to the divisions of Major-Generals Price and Lovell, and will report immediately to Major-General Price, viz:

Col. J. E. Bailey's consolidated regiment; Col. J. M. Simonton's consolidated regiment; Colonel Quarles' consolidated regiment; Captain Humes' consolidated battalion.

To Major-General Lovell: Col. A. E. Reynolds' consolidated regiment; Col. H. B. Lyon's consolidated regiment; Col. D. R. Russell's consolidated regiment; Col. A. Heiman's consolidated regiment; Col. W. E. Baldwin's Fourteenth Mississippi Regiment; Col. C. A. Sugg's consolidated regiment; Col. C. H. Walker's consolidated regiment.

III. Brigadier-General Bowen is relieved from the command of the Second Brigade, Lovell's division, and will report to Major-General Price.

IV. The First Missouri Regiment, Lovell's division, is hereby transferred to the army corps of Major-General Price.

V. Brigadier-General Tilghman will report to Major-General Lovell.

VI. The divisions and brigades in the two army corps will be equalized as near as may be, and brigades will be composed of troops from the same States as far as practicable.

VII. All officers and soldiers belonging to the different regiments and battalions, &c., of exchanged prisoners, and now doing duty by order, or having joined other commands by enlistment or otherwise, will at once join their proper commands.

By order of General Van Dorn:

M. M. KIMMEL,
Major and Assistant Adjutant-General.

GENERAL ORDERS, }   HDQRS. ARMY OF WEST TENNESSEE,
No. 54.   }   *Holly Springs, Miss., October* 16, 1862.

I. All the cavalry of this army, both regular and partisan, will report immediately to Col. W. H. Jackson, who is hereby announced as chief of cavalry. He will make his reports direct to the headquarters of the army.

II. This army will hereafter be known as Army of West Tennessee, and will be divided into two army corps, to be commanded respectively by Major-Generals Lovell and Price. The commanding officers of army corps will arrange their commands into brigades and divisions.

III. The general commanding has repeatedly called the attention of officers to the irregularities existing in the army, especially in regard to straggling from the various camps, and depredations committed on property of citizens living in the vicinity of the camps. He has often appealed to the commanding officers of brigades, regiments, and companies to aid him in keeping good order among the troops; but still complaints are daily made—property is destroyed, fences torn down and burnt, gardens robbed, corn fields laid waste, and even thefts committed with impunity by worthless stragglers, who openly bring their plunder into camp. These things bring disgrace to the good soldiers as well as to those who commit them, and it is somewhat surprising that the good soldier allows such things to be done by men who are associated with him. Should the army be a terror to our own country?

Generals commanding corps will at once organize proper guards and patrols to prevent such irregularities, and the troops nearest the property of any citizen who may suffer loss will be held responsible for it, and the brigade commanders will cause the amount of damage to be stopped on the first pay-rolls of his troops, whenever the offender or offenders cannot be discovered.

IV. The articles of war, under the direction of brigadier-generals commanding brigades, will be read to all the troops of this army at 9 o'clock a. m. on the 19th instant, and it is hoped that all officers will be made to feel the responsibility of their positions, and that they will properly appreciate their duties and faithfully discharge them.

By order of General Van Dorn:

M. M. KIMMEL,
Major and Assistant Adjutant-General.

CLARKSVILLE, TENN., October 17, 1862.

His Excellency JEFFERSON DAVIS, Richmond :

DEAR SIR : Permit me to make known to you the Rev. Mr. Taylor and his young friend Mr. William Hume, both among the most respectable of our citizens. They have been commissioned to deliver you a memorial adopted at a town meeting to-day, asking the protection of the Confederate Government against marauders from the Northwest, who are daily committing the most gross outrages upon our citizens, briefly set forth in the memorial, and will be more fully explained by the Rev. Mr. Taylor, who is conversant with the facts, and who is a gentleman of undoubted integrity and possesses the entire confidence of this community and a thorough knowledge of the operations of our armies in this section, embracing the valleys of the Cumberland and Tennessee Rivers, which can and will furnish an immense quantity of provisions for the Confederate armies if they can be made secure from the depredations of these jayhawkers from Iowa and Northern Illinois. I am confident there are not less than 50,000 or 60,000 barrels of flour in the mills in this immediate neighborhood, and immense crops of corn ready for gathering. Two or three regiments of these thieves and robbers are stationed at Forts Henry, on the Tennessee, and Donelson, on the Cumberland, who are daily visiting and destroying everything that comes in their way and seem likely to lay waste the whole section. Our immediate neighborhood has furnished three regiments for the Confederate service—the Fourteenth, Forty-ninth, and Fiftieth—who have taken most of the arms in the country and left us entirely without the means of defense. Unless some protection can be afforded before the winter freshets in our rivers take place most of the citizens will be compelled to abandon their homes and seek protection in other sections not within the reach of their gunboats.

There is but little difference among our citizens, indeed I may say none, upon the great questions now in contest between the North and the South, and therefore the Federals more willingly harass and oppress us than in other sections less united.

I have the honor to be, most respectfully, your friend and servant,

C. JOHNSON.

[Inclosure.]

CLARKSVILLE, TENN., October 17, 1862.

At a meeting of some of the citizens of Clarksville, held this day for the purpose of apprising the War Department of the Confederate States of America of the manner in which the people of this portion of the country have been treated by Col. [W. W.] Lowe, and Col. A. C. Harding, of the Eighty-third Illinois Regiment, and other Federal officers commanding at Fort Donelson, on motion the Hon. Cave Johnson was called to the chair and Rev. Dr. McMullan was appointed secretary.

The following statement of facts was then made and unanimously adopted by the meeting as an expression of a part of the outrages that have been committed as above mentioned:

The commanders above named and others have been and still are engaged in arresting many of the citizens of this portion of country and placing them in a loathsome dungeon and keeping them there unless they take the oath of allegiance, these citizens being in no way connected with the Confederate Army. They have gone to the premises of many citizens, seizing them, and destroying or carrying away all their property of every description. In some cases they burn everything before them. They have taken away many hundreds of negroes. They have visited houses, insulting ladies, and threatening to shoot, stab, bayonet, or even burn them. They have robbed them of their wardrobes, not only those of men, but even those of women and children. They are in the habit of taking all the negroes wherever they go and also all the horses. They have burned the rolling-mill of Woods, Lewis & Co., destroying everything, and taking away 240 negroes. They have also broken up or destroyed the various iron mills and furnaces in this region of country, so that this interest, so important to the Government, is now, and until we can be protected must remain, wholly inoperative. We in this city have been visited by these men and treated in a savage and brutal manner, and they daily threaten that they will return and utterly destroy the city and imprison all the citizens who do not take the oath of allegiance to the Federal Government. The aforesaid Harding visited a church in the country and arrested two ministers of the Gospel and placed them in prison, where they still are. He also took the horses and carriages from the congregation, and required the persons present, both male and female, to take the oath or go to prison, and he proclaims that every man in the country shall be arrested and either take the oath or go to the dungeon. This is our present condition. Now, we are wholly unprepared to repel these insults and oppressions. It is true there are still many men here who are willing to meet them, but we are wholly destitute of both arms and ammunition, nor is there any military force in this vicinity that is able to repel them.

We think it will appear to the Department, as it is perfectly manifest to ourselves here, that unless these marauders can be driven from this region of country this whole region will soon be devastated by them.

We earnestly call the attention of the War Department to this subject in the hope that whatever can be done for the suppression and prevention of these evils will soon be accomplished.

In order that the whole matter may certainly and speedily be laid before the Department we send this paper by William Hume, as our special agent and messenger.

C. JOHNSON,
Chairman.

B. B. McMULLAN, *Secretary.*

[Indorsements.]

OCTOBER 25, 1862.

Respectfully submitted to the President.

This information, coming from reliable sources, seems to justify the outlawry that has been denounced against Pope and others. The messenger returns on Monday and wishes to carry some assurance that the Government will act in the matter. I therefore recommend that he be authorized to say that the Government will exert itself to redress the wrongs of the people of Clarksville, and will immediately declare Colonels Harding and Lowe not to be entitled to the treatment of prisoners of war, and that if captured they will be treated as felons.

G. W. RANDOLPH,
Secretary of War.

To the SECRETARY OF WAR:

The outrages set forth in this paper and the inclosed letter of the Hon. C. Johnson call for the most strenuous efforts to redress the wrongs suffered. It would be well to bring the matter to the special notice of General Bragg and to give him a copy of these communications; also to declare, for the reasons set forth, that the officers named would not be (unless exculpated by evidence) regarded as entitled to the consideration accorded to soldiers and treatment of prisoners of war, who are by stipulation of cartel to be released if captured, upon parole.

JEFFERSON DAVIS.

NOVEMBER 1, 1862.

ADJUTANT-GENERAL:

Furnish copies to General Bragg, and prepare and submit for consideration a general order carrying out the President's instructions; also a general order rescinding the order against Pope in consideration of his having left the army operating in Virginia and of an assurance from the Adjutant-General of the United States Army that his obnoxious orders were not considered to be in force.

G. W. RANDOLPH.

HOLLY SPRINGS, *October* 20, 1862.

Lieutenant-General PEMBERTON:

I have just learned through Colonel Barteau, at Guntown, that the bridge between Rienzi and Booneville is repaired, and that the enemy are re-enforcing at Rienzi. There is no indication of the enemy's cavalry moving on Columbus.

EARL VAN DORN,
Major-General.

HOLLY SPRINGS, *October* 20, 1862.

General PEMBERTON:

Flag of truce turned back by meeting one from Corinth and arrival at Colonel Barry's force. Enemy have not left Corinth. Reported that a force from there has taken position at Chewalla. Reported that a number of general officers assembled at Jackson, at General Grant's headquarters. Another conflicting report that troops are moving from Corinth by railroad toward Jackson, Tenn. Have sent a squadron of cavalry to find out definitely the truth and to burn bridges on railroad.

EARL VAN DORN,
Major-General.

*Organization of the Army of the West, Maj. Gen. Sterling Price, C. S.
Army, commanding, October 20, 1862.**

BOWEN'S DIVISION.

Brig. GEN. JOHN S. BOWEN.

First Brigade.	Second Brigade.
Brig. Gen. LOUIS HÉBERT.	Brig. Gen. MARTIN E. GREEN.
14th Arkansas.	1st Missouri.
17th Arkansas.	2d Missouri.
3d Arkansas Cavalry (dismounted).	3d Missouri.
Rapley's Arkansas Sharpshooters.	4th Missouri.
Stirman's Arkansas Sharpshooters.	5th Missouri.
3d Louisiana.	6th Missouri.
1st Missouri Cavalry (dismounted).	
3d Missouri Cavalry (dismounted).	

Third Brigade.

Col. J. E. CRAVENS.

16th Arkansas.
18th Arkansas.
19th Arkansas.
20th Arkansas.
21st Arkansas.
Adams' Arkansas battalion.
Hobbs' Arkansas battalion.
Jones' Arkansas battalion.

MAURY'S DIVISION.†

Brig. Gen. DABNEY H. MAURY.

37th Alabama.	Bailey's regiment.‡
42d Alabama.	Quarles' regiment.‡
35th Mississippi.	Simonton's regiment.‡
36th Mississippi.	Humes' battalion.‡
37th Mississippi.	2d Texas.
38th Mississippi.	3d Texas Cavalry.
40th Mississippi.	6th Texas Cavalry.
43d Mississippi.	9th Texas Cavalry.
7th Mississippi Battalion.	Whitfield's Texas Legion.

RICHMOND, *October* 21, 1862.

Major-General VAN DORN, *Holly Springs, Miss.:*

I did not mean that Pemberton would not command, but that you would
not be deprived of your division nor Price of his by the order issued here.
How did Lovell get your corps? Why will you have no command? I
think to remove you now would be injurious to you. To what other field
would you be transferred? Will write by Captain Schaumburg.

JEFFERSON DAVIS.

---

* As announced in General Orders, No. 41, Headquarters Army of the West, October
19, and General Orders, No. 2, Bowen's division, October 20, 1862. Assignments of
artillery and cavalry not given in the orders. See also General Orders, No. 4, October 22, p. 736.

† Brigade organization not indicated in original orders. Brigadier-General Moore
assigned to the division October 19, 1862.

‡ See Special Orders, No. 53, October 16. 1862, p. 728, and Price to Kimmel, October
26, 1862, p. 737.

HOLLY SPRINGS, *October* 21, 1862.

General PEMBERTON:

Enemy have not left Corinth. There seems to be, as far as I can yet learn, no indication of evacuation; on contrary, there are indications of preparations for advance. Have sent 1,000 cavalry to force information. Disarrangement of subsistence department at Jackson grows out of leave of absence given to Captain Colby, who had all instructions from my chief where arrangements had been made and who was responsible for the supply; he was relieved, and now the responsibility must rest at Jackson. My chief has been directed to communicate our wants to the chief subsistence officer at Jackson, acting under your order. I advise that a supply of at least ten days' subsistence be kept continually on hand here.

EARL VAN DORN,
Major-General.

JACKSON, MISS., *October* 21, 1862.

Maj. Gen. EARL VAN DORN,
Commanding, Holly Springs:

Give General Samuel Jones, at Knoxville, Tenn., the earliest reliable information you obtain of movements of the enemy. He desires now to know whether the enemy is evacuating Corinth, Bolivar, and Jackson, and, if so, what route they are taking. Tell him at once all you know.

J. C. PEMBERTON,
Lieutenant-General, Commanding.

JACKSON, MISS., *October* 21, 1862.

General SAMUEL JONES, *Knoxville, Tenn.*:

There are contradictory reports from General Van Dorn as to enemy's movements. I have no reliable information that he has abandoned Corinth or is doing so. I have directed General Van Dorn to give you the earliest information.

J. C. PEMBERTON,
Lieutenant-General, Commanding.

[OCTOBER 21, 1862.—For General Orders, No. 3, Headquarters Department of Mississippi and East Louisiana, see Series I, Vol. XV, p. 840.]

SPECIAL ORDERS, } HDQRS. BOWEN'S DIV., ARMY OF THE WEST,
    No. 1.   }   *Camp near Lumpkin's Mill, October* 21, 1862.

I. The following details of troops will be made from this division to report as soon as practicable at Waterford Station, on the railroad. They will be provided with three days' cooked rations; will take all their baggage, tents, &c., with them. The senior officer present will take command of each detail. Brigade commanders will notify these headquarters when the detail from their respective commands will reach Waterford. The transportation of the detailed corps will be turned over to Major Haines, division quartermaster.

First Brigade.—Fourteenth Arkansas Regiment; Seventeenth Arkansas Regiment.

Second Brigade.—Sixteeenth Arkansas Regiment; Eighteenth Arkansas Regiment; Adams' Arkansas infantry; Jones' Arkansas infantry. Immediate attention must be paid to this detail.

II. Rapley's battalion of Arkansas Sharpshooters is transferred from the First to the Third Brigade.

By order of Brig. Gen. John S. Bowen:

R. R. HUTCHINSON,
Captain and Assistant Adjutant-General.

HOLLY SPRINGS, *October* 22, 1862.

General PEMBERTON:

Scouts have just returned from Rienzi and report three regiments of Federal infantry at Rienzi; one regiment infantry and some cavalry near Ruckersville; Corinth being largely re-enforced.

EARL VAN DORN,
Major-General.

HOLLY SPRINGS, *October* 22, 1862.

General PEMBERTON:

Bragg is falling back; so reported. We may now expect a large force to land at Columbus and Memphis very shortly. Do you think it advisable to send off the troops ordered to Meridian now? They are ready and only await transportation. Reported eleven regiments at Bone Yard; ten regiments at Chewalla; large force at Rienzi; cavalry at Jumpertown.

EARL VAN DORN,
Major-General.

HOLLY SPRINGS, MISS., *October* 22, 1862.

SECRETARY OF WAR:

Bragg is reported to be falling back toward Cumberland Gap. It may be presumed that large re-enforcements of the enemy will soon be thrown into West Tennessee at Columbus and Memphis. Already several thousand men have arrived. If we are not strengthened here we shall lose this State. There are indications of preparations for an advance. Can any part of Bragg's force be thrown here?

EARL VAN DORN,
Major-General.

JACKSON, MISS., *October* 22, 1862.

Maj. Gen. EARL VAN DORN, *Holly Springs:*

If the enemy increases in strength and there is evidence of his intention to advance you will take position behind the Tallahatchie.

J. C. PEMBERTON,
Lieutenant-General, Commanding.

HOLLY SPRINGS, *October* 22, 1862.

General PEMBERTON:

Have sent officer to Tallahatchie to examine bridges, fords, and forest, and to see that the forces there guard them properly. The enemy are watched. Will obey your orders if indications take a more decisive character.

EARL VAN DORN,
Major-General.

JACKSON, MISS., *October* 22, 1862.

Maj. Gen. EARL VAN DORN:

It is necessary that the troops ordered should proceed to this point. They will probably be needed for the defense of Port Hudson.

J. C. PEMBERTON,
Lieutenant-General, Commanding.

GENERAL ORDERS, }   HDQRS. BOWEN'S DIV., ARMY OF WEST,
No. 4.   } *Camp near Lumpkin's Mill, October* 22, 1862.

I. On account of the transfer of Brigadier-General Hébert and the Third Louisiana Regiment to Maury's division the Missouri troops of the First Brigade will report to Brigadier-General Green for orders and the Arkansas troops to Colonel Cravens. The division organization will then be as follows:

First Brigade.	*Second Brigade.*
Brigadier-General GREEN.	Colonel CRAVENS.
1st Missouri.	14th Arkansas.
1st Missouri Cavalry (dismounted).	16th Arkansas.
2d Missouri.	17th Arkansas.
3d Missouri.	18th Arkansas.
3d Missouri Cavalry (dismounted).	19th Arkansas.
4th Missouri.	20th Arkansas.
5th Missouri.	21st Arkansas.
6th Missouri.	3d Arkansas Cavalry (dismounted)
	Stirman's Arkansas Sharpshooters.
	Rapley's Arkansas Sharpshooters.
	Adams' Arkansas battalion.
	Hobbs' Arkansas battalion.
	Jones' Arkansas battalion.

By command of Brig. Gen. J. S. Bowen:

R. R. HUTCHINSON,
Captain and Assistant Adjutant-General.

HDQRS. DEPT. OF MISSISSIPPI AND EAST LOUISIANA,
Jackson, October 24, 1862.

Col. W. S. LOVELL,
Assistant Adjutant and Inspector General:

COLONEL: I am instructed by the lieutenant-general commanding to say to you that you will proceed at once to Haines' Bluff, on Yazoo River, and examine the road between that place and Vicksburg; the condition of obstruction of said river; state the best point to establish a battery near the obstructions; number of troops (Confederate and State); should there be any Confederate troops, name the regiments and a roster of officers. You will make a similar inspection at Vicksburg, and carry out the instructions concerning troops, giving as far as practicable their positions, &c.

Respectfully, &c.,

J. R. WADDY,
Assistant Adjutant-General.

JACKSON, MISS., *October* 25, 1862.

Hon. GEORGE W. RANDOLPH,
Secretary of War:

I request that all conscripts from Mississippi and Louisiana be assigned to regiments in this department. More troops are greatly needed. Cannot some of Holmes' be spared?

J. C. PEMBERTON,
Lieutenant-General, Commanding.

HEADQUARTERS ARMY OF THE WEST,
October 26, 1862.

Major KIMMEL:

MAJOR: The following regiments were ordered to report for duty at Meridian:

From General Bowen's division:

Fourteenth Arkansas, Captain Fowler; Sixteenth Arkansas, Colonel Provence; Seventeenth Arkansas, Captain Dotson; Eighteenth Arkansas, Captain Barnett; Adams' Arkansas, Colonel Adams; Jones' Arkansas battalion, Major Wilson.

From General Maury's division:

Forty-ninth and Fifty-fifth Tennessee, Colonel Bailey; Forty-second Tennessee, Colonel Quarles; First Mississippi, Fifty-third Tennessee, Ninth Tennessee, Forty-sixth Tennessee, and Twenty-seventh Alabama, Colonel Simonton.

Respectfully submitted.

STERLING PRICE,
Major-General, Commanding.

HDQRS. DEPT. OF MISSISSIPPI AND EAST LOUISIANA,
Jackson, October 28, 1862.

Maj. Gen. EARL VAN DORN,
Commanding, Holly Springs:

GENERAL: You will cause all men between the ages of eighteen and thirty-five years now attached to corps of Partisan Rangers, who have been enrolled in those corps since July 31, 1862, to be enrolled as conscripts, their connection with partisan organizations after that date being in positive violation of the orders of the President of the Confederate States. Col. T. W. White, Ninth Mississippi Volunteers, has been duly authorized to enroll the men referred to under your command. You are requested to afford every facility for the accomplishment of this purpose, and in the event of any officer attempting to impede or interfere with the enrollment you will take prompt measure to bring him to trial. I request that you inform me what measures have been taken in relation to the disbanding corps of partisans raised without competent authority, if any such there be in your command.

Very respectfully, &c.,

J. C. PEMBERTON,
Lieutenant-General, Commanding.

HDQRS. DEPT. OF MISSISSIPPI AND EAST LOUISIANA,
Jackson, October 29, 1862.

General MARTIN L. SMITH, *Commanding, Vicksburg :*

I am instructed by Lieutenant-General Pemberton to say to you that if negro labor is not furnished upon the call to obstruct the Yazoo River you are directed and authorized to impress such labor as you may require for its speedy completion. The general also directs that you cause all the railroad bridges in your district to be well guarded rather than risk their destruction.

Very respectfully, &c.,

J. R. WADDY,
Assistant Adjutant-General.

HDQRS. DEPT. OF MISSISSIPPI AND EAST LOUISIANA,
Jackson, October 30, 1862.

Maj. Gen. EARL VAN DORN, *Holly Springs:*

I have been notified by the Secretary of War at Richmond, by telegram under date October 28, that seven regiments have been ordered from General Holmes' army for General Lee in Virginia, but that I am authorized to detain them. The regiments are stated to be unarmed, but I am notified that arms are being sent from Richmond for them. I propose to place them under your command. With this increase, of infantry strength I think it will be well to allow the Texas regiments to be remounted. The cavalry brigade organization you can continue. If you have more cavalry than you need I have other points where their services are greatly wanted. Let me hear from you on the subject.

Respectfully, &c.,

J. C. PEMBERTON,
Lieutenant-General, Commanding.

HDQRS. DEPT. OF MISSISSIPPI AND EAST LOUISIANA,
Jackson, October 30, 1862.

Col. P. B. STARKE,
Twenty-eighth Mississippi Volunteers, Panola, Miss. :

COLONEL : Upon the information afforded by your report of the position of a part of the enemy (about 250) at a point opposite Helena, the lieutenant-general commanding directs that you attempt a surprise and capture of said party, to effect which end you will proceed with your regiment (taking every man who can endure the journey, and calling upon Major Blythe with his command to co-operate with you, together with such State troops as may be available) with great caution, arriving within about 1 mile of the enemy at dusk in the evening, dismounting and making proper disposition of your troops between that time and daylight, about which time it would be best to make the attack. You will proceed as cautiously as possible, endeavoring by such means to capture or destroy the enemy. Capt. James E. Mathews, under Major Blythe, is suggested as a good guide, being well acquainted with the country.

Unless certain of accomplishing the object by surprise you are not expected to undertake the expedition. It is not intended you should attack the enemy if you should discover them to be intrenched with artillery, for by so doing you endanger your command to too great an extent.

Respectfully, &c.,

R. W. MEMMINGER,
Assistant Adjutant-General.

JACKSON, MISS., *October* 31, 1862.

GEORGE W. RANDOLPH,
Secretary of War :

I respectfully advise that General Price's Missouri and Arkansas troops be ordered to the Trans-Mississippi Department and their places supplied by an equal number of other troops from General Holmes' command. Will communicate further by mail.

J. C. PEMBERTON,
Lieutenant-General, Commanding.

HDQRS. DEPT. OF MISSISSIPPI AND EAST LOUISIANA,
Jackson, October 31, 1862.

Maj. Gen. EARL VAN DORN, *Commanding, &c. :*

Scouts on the Mobile and Ohio Railroad report the enemy leaving Corinth and suppose him to be moving toward Buell. I desire you to ascertain as far as possible the truth of this statement and to inform me.

Respectfully, &c.,

J. C. PEMBERTON,
Lieutenant-General, Commanding.

GENERAL ORDERS, } HDQRS. BOWEN'S DIV., ARMY OF THE WEST,
    No. 10.   }   *Lumpkin's Mill, October* 31, 1862.

The sum of $279 has been assessed upon this division to pay for pillage committed by troops composing it, and ordered to be paid from army headquarters. The First Brigade will pay $179; the Second Brigade will pay $100. The amounts will be collected by brigade commanders at the next pay-day, in accordance with General Orders, No. 54, current series, Headquarters Army of West Tennessee, and handed over to Major Haines, assistant quartermaster, at these headquarter

By command of Brig. Gen. John S. Bowen:

R. R. HUTCHINSON,
Captain and Assistant Adjutant-General.

HDQRS. DEPT. OF MISSISSIPPI AND EAST LOUISIANA,
Jackson, November 1, 1862.

Col. JOHN ADAMS,
Commanding, &c., Columbus :

COLONEL : The lieutenant-general commanding directs that you push forward along the Mobile and Ohio Railroad as far as possible the whole cavalry force under your command, reserving only so many as may be required as couriers and to keep up your communications in the city. You are desired if possible to push forward as far as Baldwyn. You will make a reconnaissance previous to pushing forward your whole cavalry and ascertain as much information as possible concerning the movements and situation of the enemy. You will scout the country thoroughly and establish a police over the negroes, restraining them and preventing their running about the country. You are desired to report all information received to these headquarters.

Respectfully, &c.,

R. W. MEMMINGER,
Assistant Adjutant-General.

———

JACKSON, *November 3, 1862.*

Lieutenant-General PEMBERTON,
Holly Springs, Miss. :

I learn from reliable sources that the enemy is re-enforcing heavily at Corinth and strengthening fortifications; also moving buildings from Burnsville and re-erecting them in Corinth, getting large quantities of lumber from neighboring mills.

C. R. BARTEAU,
Lieutenant-Colonel, Commanding Post.

———

HOLLY SPRINGS, MISS., *November 3, 1862.*

General S. COOPER,
Adjutant and Inspector General, Richmond :

I desire to withdraw my recommendations as to exchange of General Price's troops. I have just witnessed a review and am much pleased with them.

J. C. PEMBERTON,
Lieutenant-General, Commanding.

———

HOLLY SPRINGS, *November 4, 1862.*

General PEMBERTON :

Corinth force moving on State Line road toward Saulsbury. I move to-morrow across Tallahatchie, or one corps will get across no doubt. I think of general movement you had better telegraph to Bragg. I do not know where to send to him.

EARL VAN DORN,
Major-General.

———

HOLLY SPRINGS, *November 4, 1862.*

General PEMBERTON :

The enemy are advancing. Have driven in my pickets at Grand Junction and La Grange. Said to be thirty regiments infantry and four of cavalry. Nothing yet from the direction of Corinth; may have to-night. Will keep you advised.

EARL VAN DORN,
Major-General.

———

HOLLY SPRINGS, MISS., *November* 4, 1862.
Major-General PRICE,
Commanding Second Corps :

GENERAL : The enemy are advancing and have driven in our pickets at La Grange and Grand Junction.

Have your command placed in readiness to move at once. Cook three days' rations.

Reported thirty regiments infantry and four cavalry. Have no report yet from direction of Corinth ; may have to-night.

Have sick in readiness to be sent to the rear by cars.

Respectfully,

EARL VAN DORN,
Major-General.

———

HOLLY SPRINGS, MISS., *November* 4, 1862.
(Received 11.30 p. m.)
Maj. Gen. STERLING PRICE,
Commanding Second Corps :

GENERAL : I have ordered the bridge across the Tallahatchie repaired to-night and well guarded, but you had better send a discreet officer there to-night to see that it is in condition for your train to pass to-morrow morning. I desire that you will please move your train to-morrow morning across the Tallahatchie, but hold your troops where they are until further orders, of course with their three days' cooked rations.

Have your train parked just beyond the river, near Abbeville.

General Lovell will move his train back to where your camp now is and across the river, if possible. The enemy are moving from Corinth toward Saulsbury on the State Line road.

Respectfully,

EARL VAN DORN,
Major-General.

———

HDQRS. DEPT. OF THE MISSISSIPPI,
Jackson, Miss., November 4, 1862.
Maj. Gen. STERLING PRICE,
Commanding, &c., near Holly Springs :

GENERAL : I am directed by the lieutenant-general commanding to say he does not desire that you should order more horses for that portion of your cavalry force which is now dismounted, the proportion of cavalry in relation to the infantry of the army being already too great. Such horses as you may have already obtained you will use in mounting additional men but it is not desired that you should increase your present cavalry force to any extent.

I am, respectfully, your obedient servant,

R. W. MEMMINGER,
Assistant Adjutant-General.

RICHMOND, *November* 4, 1862.

Lieut. Gen. J. C. PEMBERTON, *Holly Springs* :

Corps may be raised within the enemy's lines in Tennessee with Governor Harris' approval, who will indicate the counties where this may be accomplished, the raising to be limited to the 1st December by law.

S. COOPER,
Adjutant and Inspector General.

HOLLY SPRINGS, *November* 5, 1862.

General PEMBERTON:

Enemy encamped 3 miles south of Saulsbury, La Grange, and Grand Junction at 4 o'clock this morning. No farther advancement reported this morning. Our wagons on the road to cross Tallahatchie. Troops will not move unless enemy advance. Not being in command and having to refer to Jackson you should be here to assume control. Don't you think so? Will keep you advised.

EARL VAN DORN,
Major-General.

JACKSON, *November* 5, 1862.

Maj Gen. EARL VAN DORN,
Commanding, Holly Springs :

Unless it is positively certain that the enemy is advancing on you in full force do not change your position yet. I doubt his intention to do so. I want you to keep all your available cavalry threatening him. I have a train ready if you think it advisable for me to go up.

J. C. PEMBERTON,
Lieutenant-General, Commanding.

NOVEMBER 5, 1862.

Major-General VAN DORN:

With your infantry and artillery take position behind the Tallahatchie if the enemy advance in force against you. Feel the enemy with your cavalry; take measures at once to strengthen the position we may be compelled to occupy at the ford by intrenchments. I shall have a train ready to move up if necessary. Make every effort to learn whether the enemy is moving his whole force. Am anxious to hear from Corinth. Advise General Bragg of this movement if found to be correct.

J. C. PEMBERTON.

JACKSON, *November* 5, 1862.

General SAMUEL JONES, *Knoxville, Tenn.* :

General Van Dorn reports apparent move of the enemy's entire force in Southwestern Tennessee and Northwestern Mississippi in the direction of Holly Springs. Will you inform the commanding officer of General Bragg's army of it?

J. C. PEMBERTON.

HOLLY SPRINGS, *November* 5, 1862.

Lieutenant-General PEMBERTON:

Enemy have not advanced to-day. Jackson drove in their pickets at 10 o'clock. Think probable that they only intend to hold and fortify La Grange. Shall I drive them off?

EARL VAN DORN,
Major-General.

HDQRS. DEPT. OF MISSISSIPPI AND EAST LOUISIANA,
Jackson, November 5, 1862.

Col. R. F. LOONEY, *Holly Springs:*

In answer to your dispatch of this date I am directed by Lieutenant-General Pemberton to inform you that Partisan Rangers can be raised within the enemy's lines in Tennessee, with Governor Harris' approval, who will indicate the counties. After this has been accomplished you can refer the subject to this office for final action; the raising of the company to be limited to the 1st day of December by law.

Very respectfully, &c.,

J. R. WADDY,
Assistant Adjutant-General.

KNOXVILLE, *November* 6, 1862.
(Forwarded from Jackson.)

Lieutenant-General PEMBERTON:

Our forces all in motion, which may create a diversion in your favor. My cavalry in North Alabama ordered to observe the enemy and harass his rear. Wrote you to-day.

BRAXTON BRAGG.

HEADQUARTERS ARMY OF THE WEST,
Holly Springs, Miss., November 6, 1862.

Major-General PRICE, *Commanding Corps:*

GENERAL: Send for your provision wagons at once. We will not fall back unless the enemy advance in force. We will bivouac for a day or so to see what will be done. Send in requisition for provisions, using a few wagons to haul them. The main part keep for the present at Price's camp.

The enemy do not seem to be advancing: on the contrary, have fallen back to original line on Wolf River. Keep out infantry pickets on road in front and right flank.

Yours, &c.,

EARL VAN DORN,
Major-General.

HOLLY SPRINGS, MISS., *November* 7, 1862.

General BRAXTON BRAGG, *Knoxville, Tenn.:*

The enemy is in front of Wolf River; not advancing. If I knew your plans I might perhaps assist them.

J. C. PEMBERTON,
Lieutenant-General, Commanding.

HOLLY SPRINGS, *November* 7, 1862.

Major-Generals LOVELL, PRICE, and VAN DORN:

The lieutenant-general commanding directs me that you will suspend the publication of Paragraph II, Special Orders, No. —, November 7, 1862, from these headquarters, relieving Maj. Gen. E. Van Dorn from the command of the army of operations until further orders.

J. C. PEMBERTON,
Lieutenant-General, Commanding.

HEADQUARTERS DEPARTMENT No. 2,
Knoxville, November 7, 1862.

Lieut. Gen. J. C. PEMBERTON:

MY DEAR GENERAL: I have your dispatch notifying me of the reported movement of the enemy on your position at Holly Springs. I immediately ordered a force of cavalry, in North Alabama, near Tuscumbia, to examine the enemy at Corinth, and, if he moved, to harass his rear and destroy his trains. This was all that we could do directly for your aid. We are moving our available forces, as rapidly as possible, into Middle Tennessee, to resume the offensive against the enemy there. This throws us in the rear of your opponents, and ought to create some diversion. I would prefer striking the enemy in rear, at Corinth, were it practicable, but the Tennessee is a barrier we cannot overcome. It has occurred to me that you are exposing your important depot at Columbus, Miss., to great danger by removing your whole force, if I am correctly informed, to Holly Springs. The depot containing machinery and stores we cannot replace; so that its loss would be great and irreparable. The position, too, at Holly Springs is not as strong and defensible as one farther to the rear, behind the Tallahatchie River; but of all this of course you have informed yourself. I only throw out the suggestions as having occurred to my mind when in that country.

I am, general, very truly, yours,

BRAXTON BRAGG,
General, C. S. Army.

HEADQUARTERS ARMY OF THE WEST,
Holly Springs, Miss., November 8, 1862.

Major-General PRICE,
Commanding Second Corps:

GENERAL: Order your corps in readiness to move to-morrow morning.

Send all wagons, baggage, &c., to Abbeville, at early daylight.

Keep your troops in position awaiting orders.

Lovell's corps will move back to-night; his baggage train, &c., will move immediately.

Enemy are advancing in force and are near Rust's division.

Let your train park near Abbeville.

Respectfully,

EARL VAN DORN,
Major-General.

ABBEVILLE, MISS., *November* 9, 1862.

General S. COOPER,
Adjutant and Inspector General, Richmond:

The enemy placed himself in very strong force at Grand Junction, La Grange, and Davis' Mill, with every indication of an immediate and general advance. I deemed it advisable to withdraw from the unde-fensible position at Holly Springs and take a strong one behind Talla-hatchie, and am fortifying.

Very respectfully,

J. C. PEMBERTON,
Lieutenant-General, Commanding.

ABBEVILLE, MISS., *November* 9, 1862.

Colonel STARKE, *Panola:*

This army has retired from Holly Springs behind the Tallahatchie. Inform Major Blythe, of Mississippi forces, of this fact.

Respectfully,

J. C. PEMBERTON,
Lieutenant-General, Commanding.

HEADQUARTERS FIRST ARMY CORPS,
Army of West Tennessee, November 9, 1862.

[General STERLING PRICE:]

GENERAL: I understood that orders had been sent you last evening early by General Van Dorn. In the absence of such I think it better that as soon as the wagons can be got well out of the way your com-mand should start, to be followed by the First Corps at an hour's interval.

Respectfully, your obedient servant,

M. LOVELL,
Major-General.

SPECIAL ORDERS, }   HDQRS. ARMY OF WEST TENNESSEE,
No. 99.   }   *Abbeville, Miss., November* 10, 1862.

I. The Army of the West will be posted on the most suitable ground between Abbeville and the bridge over the Tallahatchie. The army corps of Major-General Lovell will be posted at or near the ford at the mouth of Tippah.

II. General George, with the State troops under his command at and near Abbeville, will take post at Oxford, Miss., to guard the public property at that place. General George will assume command of that post, but will give no orders to post quartermaster and commissary except so far as to supply his own command.

III. Commanding officers of army corps will furnish such details as may be called for by Capt. S. H. Lockett, chief engineer.

IV. Commanding officers of army corps will take stringent measures to prevent straggling from the army, and will arrest deserters and have them properly tried. Attention is again called to all officers to prevent destruction of private property in the vicinity of their camps, as they will be held strictly responsible for all such damages.

V. The enemy will be fought on this line and corps commanders will arrange matters to that end.

VI. Capt. H. L. Boone, assistant quartermaster, is assigned to duty as post quartermaster, and Captain Payne as post commissary.

VII. Corps commanders will remain as near as possible at the most convenient position to their corps; division and brigade commanders will remain immediately with their commands.

  *   *   *   *   *   *   *

By order of General Van Dorn:

M. M. KIMMEL,
Major and Assistant Adjutant-General.

JACKSON, MISS., *November* 11, 1862.

Maj. Gen. EARL VAN DORN, *Abbeville, Miss.:*

I have just received the following telegram, viz:

I have pretty direct information that Federal forces are crossing Tennessee River and going toward Nashville. The force left at Corinth is exceedingly small.

C. R. BARTEAU.

Send at once reliable persons to ascertain any movement of enemy from Grand Junction, Davis' Mill, &c.; also from Corinth. Direct the scouts to be as prompt as possible and report only what is reliable.

J. C. PEMBERTON,
Lieutenant-General, Commanding.

ABBEVILLE, *November* 11, 1862.

Lieutenant-General PEMBERTON:

Scouts report that the enemy have fallen back from Coldwater to Wolf River, and our cavalry still in possession of Holly Springs.

EARL VAN DORN,
Major-General.

ABBEVILLE, *November* 11, 1862.

Lieutenant-General PEMBERTON:

Dispatch from Colonel Starke informs me that 2,000 infantry, 500 cavalry, and 4 pieces artillery encamped last night 12 miles north of Hernando. I have ordered Jackson to send out scouts in their rear to ascertain definitely what force is in that road. Heard yesterday that Memphis had been re-enforced. Will send a brigade mounted Texans and battery to-morrow morning to crossings above Panola unless you order me to the contrary. All quiet in front. Holly Springs in our possession.

EARL VAN DORN,
Major-General.

JACKSON, MISS., *November* 11, 1862.

Lieutenant-Colonel BARTEAU:

Send reliable scouts, citizens or soldiers, to ascertain certainly the movements of the enemy about Corinth; also whether any movement is being made from Grand Junction, Bolivar, &c. Report by telegraph as well as by mail.

J. C. PEMBERTON,
Lieutenant-General, Commanding.

GUNTOWN, *November* 11, 1862.

General PEMBERTON :

I have pretty direct information that Federal forces are crossing Tennessee River and going toward Nashville. The force left at Corinth is exceedingly small.

C. R. BARTEAU,
Colonel, Commanding Post.

HEADQUARTERS ARMY OF WEST TENNESSEE,
Abbeville, Miss., November 11, 1862.

[General PRICE :]

GENERAL : Maury has just left my quarters. I gave him orders to have his mounted Texas brigade gotten in readiness to march to-morrow morning to Tobytubby Ferry, below here. The enemy are moving out from Memphis, 2,000 infantry, 500 cavalry, and battery of artillery. May be only advance guard. They encamped last night 12 miles from Hernando. The mounted infantry will best come in play on this occasion.

Respectfully,

EARL VAN DORN,
Major-General.

PANOLA, *November* 12, 1862.

Lieutenant-General PEMBERTON :

My scouts just in ; report the enemy 12 miles this side of Memphis, with 2,000 infantry, 500 cavalry, and 4 pieces of artillery ; have advanced no farther. Major Blythe's command is between them and Hernando.

P. B. STARKE,
Colonel, Commanding.

PANOLA, *November* 12, 1862.

Lieutenant-General PEMBERTON :

I am just in receipt of dispatch from Lieutenant Hurt, State troops, to the effect that 3,000 Federals are on east side of the river, opposite Helena, and still crossing. My scouts will be in to-day with further intelligence, of which you will be advised. Am scouting toward Memphis, watching approach of the enemy, and obstructing fords across Tallahatchie, under orders of General Van Dorn. You shall be advised at the earliest moment of anything important that occurs.

P. B. STARKE,
Colonel, Commanding.

[Indorsement.]

General Holmes notified. General Van Dorn directed to move a brigade toward Panola.

HDQRS. DEPT. OF MISSISSIPPI AND EAST LOUISIANA,
Jackson, Miss., November 12, 1862.

Maj. Gen. EARL VAN DORN,
Commanding, Abbeville, Miss. :

Colonel Starke, at Panola, informs me by telegraph that his scouts report 3,000 Federals on the east side of the river, opposite Helena, and still crossing. This may be in consequence of an advance against Helena in large force by Holmes, or an advance on our left. I wish you to have a full brigade, with a field battery, put in motion toward Panola unless you should receive later information rendering it unnecessary.

J. C. PEMBERTON,
Lieutenant-General, Commanding.

JACKSON, *November* 12, 1862.
Brigadier-General SMITH,
Commanding, Vicksburg :

Send a courier rapidly to General Holmes with this telegram :

The commanding officer at Panola, on Mississippi Central Railroad, informs me by telegraph that his scouts report 3,000 Federals on the east side of the river and still crossing. If General Holmes will indicate his movements to me I will endeavor to co-operate with him. At present I am entirely in the dark. All my troops except cavalry are behind the Tallahatchie.

J. C. PEMBERTON,
Lieutenant-General, Commanding.

JACKSON, MISS., *November* 12, 1862.
Col. J. GORGAS, *Richmond, Va.:*

Neither the Parrott guns, siege guns, 24-pounder howitzers, or 12-pounder bronze guns have been received yet. Have any been sent? I am terribly in want of arms.

J. C. PEMBERTON,
Lieutenant-General, Commanding.

JACKSON, MISS., *November* 12, 1862.
Brig. Gen. MARTIN L. SMITH, *Vicksburg, Miss.:*

Soldiers between eighteen and thirty-five are conscripts, and must be retained.

J. C. PEMBERTON,
Lieutenant-General, Commanding.

HDQRS. DEPT. OF MISSISSIPPI AND EAST LOUISIANA,
Jackson, Miss., November 12, 1862.
Brig. Gen. MARTIN L. SMITH,
Commanding, &c., Vicksburg, Miss.:

GENERAL: I am directed by the lieutenant-general commanding to say that until further orders your military districts will extend from Big Black River to the line of the Mississippi Central Railroad; thence to 1 mile south of Grenada; thence due west to the Mississippi River. Panola and all points north of that line to be under the command of the commanding general of the Army of West Tennessee.

I am, respectfully, your obedient servant,

R. W. MEMMINGER,
Assistant Adjutant-General.

HDQRS. DEPT. OF MISSISSIPPI AND EAST LOUISIANA,
Jackson, Miss., November 13, 1862.

General S. COOPER,
Adjutant and Inspector General:

GENERAL: The honorable Secretary of War informed me by telegraph under date 28th October that I was authorized to detain seven regiments unarmed Texans which had been ordered to General Lee, and also that arms were being sent me. Up to this date I have heard nothing further of either the troops or arms. I am greatly in need of both. In fact, I have now nearly 5,000 unarmed men. About this number of muskets needing repairs (at present unserviceable) are at Briarsfield Arsenal, Columbus, Miss. I have sent some fifty gunsmiths to expedite their repair, but it will be a long time before they will be available to any considerable extent. Ammunition for small-arms as well as for field artillery is also much needed. I shall be very glad to receive the two 30-pounder Parrott guns and all other heavy guns that can be sent me. Neither Vicksburg nor Port Hudson is as strong as I desire to make them.

It is very important also that some heavy artillery be placed in position at Snyder's Mill, on the Yazoo, where an obstruction is now being arranged. Soon after my arrival here I applied to Chief of Ordnance for twenty siege guns from 12 to 24 pounders for the land defenses of Vicksburg and Port Hudson. In answer Colonel Rhett, Ordnance Department, inquired whether 24-pounder howitzers and 12-pounder bronze guns would answer my purpose; but as I have heard nothing further from him I do not know whether to expect them or not.

This army generally is very deficient in clothing, shoes, and blankets. I am using every exertion to provide them. The process is slow, and in the mean time the men suffer greatly. I should be very glad if some assistance could be rendered from other points in that way.

The ordinary source of supplies for the medical purveyor's department having been interrupted by the execution of my instructions to prevent trade with points in possession of the enemy renders it necessary that other means be employed to provide the medical department. Surgeon Potts, purveyor, proposes to obtain supplies by contract by way of Texas from Mexico, and is confident of his ability to do so. I have approved plan and shall authorize him to carry it out, but in the mean time the small stock in his hands will be inadequate to the demands of this department, and I hope the Purveyor-General may be able to supply deficiencies.

Very respectfully, your obedient servant,

J. C. PEMBERTON,
Lieutenant-General, Commanding.

[Indorsements.]

Respectfully referred to Colonel Gorgas, Chief of Ordnance, who, after noting the contents for such action as may be necessary, will please refer it to the Surgeon-General.

By command of the Secretary of War:

JASPER S. WHITING,
Major and Assistant Adjutant-General.

Respectfully returned to the Secretary of War. Attended to.

J. GORGAS,
Colonel, Chief of Ordnance.

JACKSON, *November* 13, 1863.

Major-General VAN DORN:

Have the works directed to be thrown up at Wyatt Ferry, on the opposite side of the river, pushed forward as rapidly as possible; also an abatis constructed on the south side of the river at the ferry.

J. R. WADDY,
Assistant Adjutant-General.

HEADQUARTERS ARMY OF WEST TENNESSEE,
Abbeville, Miss., November 13, 1862.

Lieutenant-General PEMBERTON,
Commanding Department, Jackson, Miss.:

GENERAL: Reports from citizens say that quite a large number of troops have been moving down the river in the last five or six days. I have a report also, which confirms the report sent me by Colonel Starke, that the enemy are concentrating a force opposite Helena, with the intention of marching toward Grenada. We must have more troops.

Holly Springs was taken by the enemy to-day, having driven off our cavalry pickets at that place. Re-enforcements are reported coming down from Columbus to Jackson and Bolivar. The column of the enemy that marched out of Memphis, in the direction of Hernando, has returned.

I am getting in negroes as fast as possible, and doing what I can with the means at my disposal. Send me all the intrenching tools you can. I think if you can spare Lockett he had better be here to take charge of works, &c.

Very respectfully, your obedient servant,

EARL VAN DORN,
Major-General.

SALTILLO, *November* 13, 1862.

General PEMBERTON:

It was mistake about Federals crossing river toward Nashville. None went that way; only sick men sent by rail back to Columbus. Troops went from Corinth to Grand Junction and Bolivar. Federal force at Corinth, 3,000; at Rienzi, 600 infantry and 200 cavalry; at Kossuth, 1,600; at Jumpertown, near Blackland, 400.

C. R. BARTEAU,
Lieutenant-Colonel.

HEADQUARTERS,
Magnolia, Miss., November 14, 1862.

General VAN DORN, *Abbeville, Miss.:*

Do you think there is any prospect of the enemy advancing on you? If so, I will join you at once; if not, I am very anxious to go to Port Hudson. Very important for me to go there.

I await your answer here. It will take me three days.

J. C. PEMBERTON,
Lieutenant-General, Commanding.

ABBEVILLE, *November* 14, 1862.

Lieutenant-General PEMBERTON:

Enemy gone back to Coldwater.

EARL VAN DORN,
Major-General.

————

JACKSON, *November* 18, 1862.

Maj. Gen. MARTIN L. SMITH, *Vicksburg, Miss.*:

Following dispatch received from Shufordsville, November 17:

Twelve transports with three gunboats loaded with troops passed Friar's Point this evening, I suppose for Vicksburg.*

Acknowledge receipt of this.

J. C. PEMBERTON.

————

JACKSON, MISS., *November* 18, 1862.

GEORGE W. RANDOLPH,
Secretary of War, Richmond, Va.:

A telegram received this morning states:

Twelve transports with three gunboats loaded with troops passed Friar's Point this evening.

Large numbers of troops are reported to have left Helena by transports, and artillery and cavalry moving down river by land. Have sent courier to General Holmes. Should not General Bragg move directly to threaten the rear of large force in front of us? I should be re-enforced at once.

J. C. PEMBERTON.

————

ABBEVILLE, *November* 19, 1862.

General PEMBERTON:

Dispatch from Friar's Point, 16th, states enemy moving down the river. Thirteen transports, one tug, and one gunboat passed at 2 p. m.

EARL VAN DORN,
Major-General.

————

SALTILLO, MISS., *November* 19, 1862.

General PEMBERTON:

Old troops left Rienzi and raw troops have taken their place. The same seems to be the case at Corinth. The enemy's picket lines are down in close to the above places and no passing allowed. Do not think that any new troops are now arriving at Corinth. Cavalry picket force at Rienzi and infantry at Glendale lately increased to a strength greater than formerly. Pickets on north and northeast sides of Corinth drawn in to less than a mile of the place.

C. R. BARTEAU,
Colonel.

————

* November 16–21, 1862. Expedition from Helena against Arkansas Post, Ark. See Series I, Vol. XIII, pp. 358–360.

ADJUTANT AND INSPECTOR GENERAL'S OFFICE,
Richmond, November 19, 1862.

General BRAXTON BRAGG, *Tullahoma, Tenn.:*

General Pemberton telegraphed on the 19th that twelve transports with three gunboats loaded with troops passed Friar's Point on the 17th, supposed for Vicksburg. Large numbers of troops are reported to have left Helena by transports, and artillery and cavalry moving down the river by land. He asks for re-enforcements at once. General Pemberton is under your command, and you must do what in your judgment is necessary to save Vicksburg from capture.

General Holmes has been requested to send 10,000 men to Vicksburg if they can be spared for that purpose.

S. COOPER,
Adjutant and Inspector General.

OFFICE CHIEF OF SUB., DEPT. OF MISS. AND EAST LA.,
Jackson, Miss., November 19, 1862.

Maj. T. B. REED, *Vicksburg, Miss.:*

SIR: As the season of the year is approaching rapidly when we can but expect a rise in the waters of the Mississippi River, and with it the approach of the enemy, I deem it a matter of the greatest importance to purchase all the stores that can be had in that section of country most likely to be subject to the raids of the enemy. In view of this fact I now have my agents purchasing corn, meal, pease, and potatoes in the parishes west of and lying on the west bank of the Mississippi River. But pressed as I am with the duties of my office I am unable to give to this matter that personal attention which its importance justly entitles it to. Hence I have to ask your aid and assistance to enable me to fully carry out my object. You are therefore hereby fully authorized to take the full supervising control of the matter, subject to such orders and instructions as you may from time to time receive from me. I will direct all my agents to report to you, that you may be fully advised of their acts, &c.

I am informed that a number of mills can be procured in that section. I wish them to be immediately put to work; that the meal obtained from them be shipped to Port Hudson and Vicksburg for immediate use, so as to enable us to retain the corn for future use; from these mills an abundant supply of meal can be obtained. The command at Port Hudson requires about 8,000 bushels per month, which you will cause to be shipped to them by steamboats. You will see that ample transportation is had both to get these stores up the river to Vicksburg, and when it arrives see that they are at once unloaded. To facilitate this matter you had better call on the quartermaster to have wagons, &c., ready, as I am informed that he is not properly supplied, and that drays are employed at very high rates. I will send to Vicksburg an agent to aid you in the shipment of these stores. I also deem it advisable that all stores that can be procured from North Louisiana be also purchased before our communication with that section is interrupted. To accomplish this I will send an agent or agents to that section of which I will advise you.

You can but see, major, the greatest importance in obtaining stores from the west bank of the river before it is too late; hence it is needless in me to urge upon you great exertions to obtain them. I therefore trust that you will give me your full co-operation and that you will give the matter your personal attention, as I intrust it to you. It is not with an intention that all these stores remain at Vicksburg, but that they be shipped to this place, at least a large proportion of them. You will keep me by reports duly advised of your acts in the premises.

I am, major, respectfully, your obedient servant,

R. H. CUNEY,
Major and Chief of Subsistence.

RICHMOND, *November* 19, 1862.

Lieut. Gen. T. H. HOLMES,
Little Rock, Ark., via Vicksburg, Miss.:

Vicksburg is threatened and requires to be re-enforced. Can you send troops from your command—say 10,000—to operate either opposite to Vicksburg or to cross the river? It is conceded here that this movement will greatly add to the defense of Arkansas.

S. COOPER,
Adjutant and Inspector General.

RICHMOND, *November* 19, 1862.

General PEMBERTON:

General Holmes has been ordered by telegraph to send 10,000 men to Vicksburg, and General Bragg telegraphed to do what in his judgment is necessary to save Vicksburg from capture. General Bragg by virtue of his rank commands all that section of country.

S. COOPER,
Adjutant and Inspector General.

OFFICE CHIEF OF SUB., DEPT. OF MISS. AND EAST LA.,
Jackson, Miss., November 20, 1862.

Maj. T. B. REED, *Vicksburg, Miss.:*

SIR: Since writing you on yesterday it has occurred to me that perhaps my letter of instructions was not as full as I intended that it should be; hence I again write.

I wish you to take all necessary measures to obtain and accumulate at Vicksburg all army stores that can be procured, and that you obtain them from any points where they can be procured. I also deem it a matter of the greatest importance to secure mills within the lines of defenses at Vicksburg, to grind meal in case the enemy cut off the supply from other points. You are therefore particularly charged to attend this matter and secure the mills. I deem it most advisable to contract for the grinding of the meal; but if this cannot be done, then you must secure a Government mill.

Respectfully, your obedient servant,

R. H. CUNEY,
Major and Chief of Subsistence.

JACKSON, MISS., *November* 20, 1862.

General BRAXTON BRAGG, *Tullahoma, Tenn.:*

The enemy is concentrating from Memphis, Jackson, Bolivar, and other points about Grand Junction. He has now three corps in and near La Grange. I am behind Tallahatchie, and hear nothing from Holmes. Can you not more seriously threaten his rear?

> J. C. PEMBERTON,
> *Lieutenant-General, Commanding.*

JACKSON, *November* 20, 1862.

Major-General VAN DORN,
     Commanding, Abbeville:

Keep strong pickets as near Memphis as they can be got, and watch any movement from Memphis. Have you a brigade toward Panola? Have you intrenched there yet, and at or near Pontotoc? They must both be fortified. I must go to Vicksburg this evening; return to-morrow.

> J. C. PEMBERTON,
> *Lieutenant-General, Commanding.*

JACKSON, MISS., *November* 20, 1862.

Maj. Gen. EARL VAN DORN, *Abbeville, Miss.:*

Dispatch from Panola reports enemy is largely increasing his force at Memphis, with indications of a forward movement.

> J. C. PEMBERTON,
> *Lieutenant-General, Commanding.*

JACKSON, MISS., *November* 20, 1862.

Maj. Gen. MARTIN L. SMITH, *Vicksburg, Miss.:*

It is reported to me there is a large accumulation of force at Memphis and evidence of movement by the enemy.

> J. C. PEMBERTON,
> *Lieutenant-General, Commanding.*

PANOLA, MISS., *November* 20, 1862.

Lieutenant-General PEMBERTON:

Major Blythe dispatches me that from the accumulation of forces and the actions of the enemy in the neighborhood of Memphis he thinks a movement south will commence this week. Colonel Starke is still very ill with pneumonia.

> J. T. McBEE,
> *Captain, Commanding Twenty-eighth Regiment.*

SALTILLO, MISS., *November* 20, 1862.

General PEMBERTON, *Jackson, Miss.:*

There is at Corinth a portion of Davies' division, namely, Logan's brigade, and a skeleton brigade, commanded by Colonel Burke; at Danville, two regiments; at Rienzi, Western Sharpshooters, 350; Seventh Kansas Cavalry, 275; part of Second Iowa, 360; Sixth Illinois, 500; Major Fight[?] or Colonel Mercer commanding. On Sunday one regiment of cavalry went from Rienzi to join the forces on outpost toward Holly Springs.

C. R. BARTEAU,
Colonel.

(Telegraphed to Van Dorn same day.)

HEADQUARTERS MISSISSIPPI AND EAST LOUISIANA,
Jackson, Miss., November 20, 1862.

Maj. R. H. CUNEY,
 Chief Commissary of Subsistence, Jackson:

MAJOR: I am instructed by Lieutenant-General Pemberton to inform you that you will keep on hand at Vicksburg, Miss., a supply of rations for 10,000 men for five months.

I am, respectfully,

J. R. WADDY.

[Indorsement.]

Respectfully referred to Major Reed, who will please return this letter. The 10,000 men are additional to those now here.

JNO. G. DEVEREUX,
Assistant Adjutant-General.

TULLAHOMA, November 21, 1862.

General S. COOPER:

To send re-enforcements from here to General Pemberton would require the evacuation of Middle Tennessee. The enemy in our front is now largely superior in numbers. Immense supplies of subsistence would be sacrificed. General Pemberton telegraphs to-day the enemy concentrating on his front at Grand Junction. I send a large cavalry force under Forrest to create a diversion by assailing their rear and communications in West Tennessee. Have sent 3,000 muskets to General Pemberton. Have received no orders extending my command.

BRAXTON BRAGG.

TULLAHOMA, November 21, 1862.

Lieutenant-General PEMBERTON:

A large cavalry force under Forrest starts to operate in the enemy's rear and create a diversion in your favor. Cannot move infantry across the Tennessee.

BRAXTON BRAGG.

VICKSBURG, MISS., November 21, 1862.

Major-General VAN DORN:

I have but one regiment available; that is at Jackson, about 400 strong. I only wish the brigade referred to to be in position to move at once to Panola, and get there before the enemy if he should move a column in that direction. I will go up at any time you think advisable—to-morrow, if necessary.

J. C. PEMBERTON,
Lieutenant-General, Commanding.

JACKSON, MISS., *November* 21, 1862.

Maj. Gen. EARL VAN DORN, *Abbeville, Miss.:*

Send cavalry out in the adjoining country and seize as many negroes as may be necessary for work on Pontotoc.

J. C. PEMBERTON,
Lieutenant-General, Commanding

ABBEVILLE, *November* 21, 1862.

General PEMBERTON:

Forces here cannot be spared yet to send to Pontotoc. I think I am getting all the negroes I can. We have not enough troops here to defend this line. There is represented to be a good road leading from Friar's Point, on Mississippi River, to Charleston and Coffeeville. I have a brigade of mounted Texans at Tobytubby Ferry. The most cavalry force can be concentrated at Panola if necessary, should enemy advance in that direction. Report from Colonel Jackson does not confirm the report that Sherman's corps is near La Grange, but that one of the army corps has moved westward to Moscow. No advance from Memphis. Heavy works required at Wyatt if put on opposite side. Have works on this side.

EARL VAN DORN,
Major-General.

ABBEVILLE, *November* 21, 1862.

General PEMBERTON:

Cavalry brigade at Tobytubby. Brigade can reach there before enemy. No movements yet from Memphis. Enemy going down river, as well as re-enforcing Memphis; supposed destination White River, to get in rear of Holmes; may be Yazoo River. Reported strength at Grand Junction, &c., about 60,000; probably about 45,000; from reports, will be soon on the march. If you fight the battle here you should be here now to learn position, &c. You must have more men.

EARL VAN DORN,
Major-General.

ABBEVILLE, *November* 22, 1862.

General PEMBERTON:

It is my opinion that if Holmes does not send troops to this side river soon the opportunity will be lost. The troops at Memphis may take position at Milliken's Bend to prepare for operations against Vicksburg.

EARL VAN DORN,
Major-General.

JACKSON, MISS., *November* 22, 1862.

Major-General VAN DORN:

I have telegraphed to Holmes to know what he is going to do. I am promised 10,000 men from him. I leave here for you to-morrow evening.

J. C. PEMBERTON,
Lieutenant-General, Commanding.

LITTLE ROCK, *November* 22, 1862.
(Received November 26, 1862.)

General S. COOPER:

I could not get to Vicksburg in less than two weeks. There is nothing to subsist on between here and there, and the army at Helena would come to Little Rock before I reached Vicksburg.

TH. H. HOLMES,
Lieutenant-General.

JACKSON, MISS., *November* 22, 1862.

General S. COOPER, *Richmond, Va.*:

Is it the desire of the Department that the designations now used by Generals Van Dorn and Price, "Army of West Tennessee" and "Army of the West," should be continued to be used? Should it not be styled "Army of North Mississippi"? Please answer. It is important that this be settled.

R. W. MEMMINGER,
Assistant Adjutant-General.

JACKSON, MISS., *November* 23, 1862.

General VAN DORN, *Abbeville*:

It is very necessary that strong works should be put on opposite side of Wyatt Ferry.

J. C. PEMBERTON,
Lieutenant-General, Commanding.

RICHMOND, VA., *November* 24, 1862.

General PEMBERTON:

The designations given to Generals Van Dorn's and Price's commands are improper. They should properly be styled "First and Second Army Corps of the Department of the Mississippi," under your command. In your personal absence both should be under the command of the senior officer present for duty.

S. COOPER,
Adjutant and Inspector General.

SPECIAL ORDERS, } ADJT. AND INSPECTOR GENERAL'S OFFICE,
No. 275.   } Richmond, *November* 24, 1862.

*   *   *   *   *   *   *

III. General J. E. Johnston, C. S. Army, is hereby assigned to the following geographical command, to wit: Commencing with the Blue

Ridge range of mountains running through the western part of North Carolina, and following the line of said mountains through the northern part of Georgia to the railroad south from Chattanooga; thence by that road to West Point, and down the west or right bank of the Chattahoochee River to the boundary of Alabama and Florida; following that boundary west to the Choctawhatchee River, and down that river to Choctawhatchee Bay (including the waters of that bay) to the Gulf of Mexico.

All that portion of country west of said line to the Mississippi River is included in the above command.

General Johnston will, for the purpose of correspondence and reports, establish his headquarters at Chattanooga, or such other place as in his judgment will best secure facilities for ready communication with the troops within the limits of his command, and will repair in person to any part of said command whenever his presence may for the time be necessary or desirable.

*   *   *   *   *   *   *   *

By command of the Secretary of War:

JNO. WITHERS,
Assistant Adjutant-General.

RICHMOND, VA., *November 24, 1862.*

General S. COOPER,
    Adjutant and Inspector General:

SIR: I had the honor this afternoon to receive Special Orders, No. 275, of this date.

If I have been correctly informed the forces which it places under my command are greatly inferior in number to those of the enemy opposed to them, while in the Trans-Mississippi Department our army is very much larger than that of the United States. Our two armies on this side of the Mississippi have the further disadvantage of being separated by the Tennessee River, and a Federal army (that of Major-General Grant) larger probably than either of them. Under such circumstances it seems to me that our best course would be to fall upon Major-General Grant with the troops of Lieutenant-Generals Holmes and Pemberton, united for the purpose, those of General Bragg co-operating if practicable.

The defeat of Major-General Grant would enable us to hold the Mississippi and permit Lieutenant-General Holmes to move into Missouri. As our troops are now distributed Vicksburg is in danger.

Most respectfully, your obedient servant,

J. E. JOHNSTON,
General.

COLUMBUS, MISS., *November 25, 1862.*
(Received November 26, 1862.)

Major WADDY:

Sixty cavalry, entire number effective, go immediately with wagons to join 50 on patrol duty at Cotton Port. All take post between Guntown and Abbeville. All Confederate infantry and 375 State Militia go by rail to-morrow, leaving 300 militia, 1 battery, and 80 heavy artillery entire force here.

JOHN ADAMS,
Colonel, &c.

WAR DEPARTMENT, C. S. A.,
Richmond, Va., November 26, 1862.

Lieut. Gen. J. C. PEMBERTON:

GENERAL: Herewith you will receive the copy of a letter from Maj. Gen. Sterling Price, which has been addressed direct to this Department. From it you will perceive General Price is urgent to be transferred with his command to the Trans-Mississippi Department, and sustains his request by reference to the past engagements of this Department. The only specific engagement known to me is that contained in the passage from a letter of my predecessor, cited by General Price, and is expressly limited and guarded. The Department now as then would be pleased to gratify the wish of General Price, but must have primary reference to the exigencies of the service and the public safety. You will therefore report whether, consistently with the safety of your command and the success of your proposed operations, General Price with his command can be spared to the Trans-Mississippi Department. Should such be your conclusion, without further instructions from this Department you will order him to cross the river with his command and report to General Holmes, commanding that military department. Should you conclude that the command of General Price cannot now be spared you will consider and report the practicability and expediency of effecting an exchange with General Holmes of a like command, and thus, without weakening your own force, gratify the wish of General Price to be transferred with his command. The attention of General Holmes will be invited to such exchange, and it is hoped such an arrangement may be effected to the satisfaction of all interested and without detriment to either command. Whenever, in your opinion, feasible and judicious, such arrangement, if made with General Holmes, may be accomplished by you without further reference to this Department.

Very respectfully,

J. A. SEDDON,
Secretary of War.

[Inclosure.]

HEADQUARTERS ARMY OF THE WEST,
Abbeville, Miss., November 15, 1862.

Hon. GEORGE W. RANDOLPH,
Secretary of War:

SIR: In a communication which you addressed to me on the 24th June you said:

Your division has been already retained longer than the President contemplated when it was ordered across the Mississippi, and General Bragg will order it to be transferred to the Trans-Mississippi Department so soon as it can be safely spared. The time of transfer will of course depend on the possibility of throwing troops across the river in its present stage or on the military operations now in progress, in which you have expressed a wish to co-operate.

Nearly five months have passed since that promise was made. The military operations then in progress have been completed. The troops can be spared with as much safety at this as at any time in the immediate future, and the possibility of throwing them across the river is likely to diminish daily, and the officers and men (I speak of the Missouri troops constituting the division referred to) are clamorous for the fulfillment of your promise. I do hope that you will not delay its fulfillment any longer.

I have been informed that a law has been recently passed which authorizes the President to commission general, field, and other officers to recruit and organize troops in Missouri, and that he is urged to make a great many appointments under that law. He will pardon me for suggesting that he could not better execute that law than by sending the officers of my old division with the remnants of their commands upon that duty.

Those officers have shown themselves upon many battle-fields to be able, brave, and fit to command. They are experienced and tried gentlemen, deserving and enjoying the confidence of their troops. They have won their commands by hard service, in which they have demonstrated their merit. Whom could the President more fitly or more justly send to Missouri to recruit and organize troops than these very officers? Their presence there with their war-worn veterans would not excite the prejudice and feeling which are likely to be aroused against those who, owing their commissions to presidential favor, shall present themselves in Missouri to supersede the gentlemen who have been raising troops there and who have not made themselves known to His Excellency or his advisors by pressing their claims to office. Every one knows, too, that these old regiments and batteries would if recruited be far more efficient than twice the number of new regiments. I am, moreover, of opinion that no officers could recruit troops in Missouri as rapidly as these would. I am sure that the people of that State would more gladly enlist in these old regiments, which have won immortal renown by their prowess on many fields and which are commanded by known and experienced officers, than in any new regiment whatever.

These facts are too plain to require elucidation. The President must admit the desirableness of executing the law referred to in this mode, provided these troops can be safely spared from this point. I do not feel at liberty to discuss that question. I am certain that they can be spared as safely now as at any time within my prospect, and that the President ought not to hesitate any longer to order them across the river, in fulfillment of his and your promises. A statement of their numbers is the best argument on this point. The Missouri troops consist of six regiments of infantry, one regiment and one battalion of dismounted cavalry, one battalion of cavalry, and seven light batteries.

The present effective total of the infantry and dismounted cavalry is only 2,662; the aggregate present only 3,283, or less than 350 men to the regiment. There are about 500 men in the batteries and about 250 men in the cavalry battalion. These are the remnants of a force of nearly 10,000 men which have been fighting the battles of the Confederacy for the last eleven months. Their comrades have fallen in the many bloody battles which their courage has prominently illustrated, or have been consigned to their graves or the hospitals by the casualties of war and the pestilential atmosphere of the Mississippi swamps. I cannot believe that the safety of this point can be endangered materially by the withdrawal of so insignificant a force; but this is a matter upon which I ought not to express my opinion to the President, who is of course better informed as to the position of affairs here than I can possibly be.

There are, however, Mr. Secretary, several points to which I desire to very respectfully call the particular attention of yourself and His Excellency. The Missouri troops were enlisted in the Confederate service upon my assurance to them that the President had declared to the commissioners who negotiated the militia treaty between Missouri and the Confederate Government in October, 1861, that while he would not stipulate to that effect in the treaty it was neither his wish nor expectation even to take away the Missouri troops from their own State. They enlisted under that assurance, and were instantly ordered to this side of the Mississippi River.   When I called the President's attention to that fact last June he expressed his regret that they had been withdrawn and promised to send them back, as was subsequently more explicitly stated in your communication.

When I returned to the army those promises were made known to my officers and men. They have relied upon those promises and are anxiously awaiting the fulfillment of them.   I have been told that the President expresses his astonishment that troops professing to be patriotic and obedient should insist as these troops do upon being sent to a particular point.

The position of Missouri is peculiar, and that peculiarity ought to be recognized. It explains the conduct of her people and troops.   The State is and has been for nearly a year in the actual military possession of the enemy, and it is but natural that her people should begin to fear that a treaty of peace will leave her in the Union and drive such of them as take up arms into exile. It is that belief which prevents them from entering the Confederate service. To do so is only to devote themselves and theirs to ruin. They believe, however, that if the Government would make an earnest effort to achieve the independence of Missouri it would succeed and bind it to the Confederacy in any contingency. Those of them who are in the army are therefore anxious that such an effort should be made. They insist that they at least may be permitted by the Government to make it. Is there anything unreasonable in this request? In other words, the Missourians insist upon fighting in Missouri not only because their ruined home is there and their unprotected and oppressed families, but because they believe, and with too much cause, that unless they go there, and that right speedily, to fight for her independence her doom is sealed, and that all their sufferings and the blood of their comrades will have only brought ruin on their wives and children and desolation on their homes. It is not just to say that the soldiers from other States have as much right to ask to be sent to their own States. The case is entirely different.   The Mississippian, wherever he fights, knows that he is fighting for his own home and his own liberty, for his State must necessarily form part of the Confederacy ; but this is not the case with the Missourian ; he cannot fight under any such cheering belief except upon his own soil. These are facts the Government ought to recognize. The troops here feel them so acutely that they are, as I have said, clamoring to be led back to Missouri ; their terms of service begin to expire next month ; they do not admit the right of the Government to conscript them ; they will claim their discharges. The Government may choose to force them to continue in the service. I confide in its wisdom not to do so. It will be far better to act justly, and in a spirit of conciliation to order myself and the troops under my command back to Missouri in accordance with your and the President's promises.

I have the honor to be, very respectfully, your obedient servant,

STERLING PRICE,
Major-General.

JACKSON, *November* 26, 1862.

Maj. J. R. WADDY:

Twenty-one thousand Federal troops in Memphis under marching orders. They move to-morrow morning at 5 a. m. toward Hernando, Miss.

JNO. B. MORRIS,
Manager.

PANOLA, MISS., *November* 26, 1862.

Lieutenant-General PEMBERTON :

The following just received from Major Blythe, November 25, 1862 :

The whole Federal force in Memphis are under marching orders and will move to-morrow morning at 5 a. m. They move in the direction of Hernando.

E. P. JONES,
Major, Commanding.

JACKSON, MISS., *November* 26, 1862.

Lieutenant-General PEMBERTON :

General Smith reports that the gunboats have left on their way back; did not descend below Ashton, near Grand Lake.

Colonel Adams has sent the men ordered, leaving at Columbus 300 militia, 1 battery, and 80 heavy artillerists. I ordered Captain Landis this morning to proceed with his battery to Abbeville; it came from that post here to be fixed up.

J. R. WADDY,
Assistant Adjutant-General.

PANOLA, *November* 26, 1862.

Major-General VAN DORN :

Federal fleet of transports, gunboats, mortars, and rams passed yesterday below Helena. Enemy re-enforcing and have 15,000 on this bank, opposite Helena. This information believed reliable.

E. P. JONES,
Major, Commanding.

ABBEVILLE, *November* 26, 1862—11 p. m.
(Received November 27, 1862.)

Maj. J. R. WADDY :

Generals Pemberton and Van Dorn are not here. The enemy reported moving down from Memphis and in front, and gunboats, transports, mortar-boats, and rams are said to have gone down yesterday. I believe the attack is to be on Vicksburg. The generals are expected to-morrow. Your dispatches received. I suggest that the Holmes matter needs your attention, as the general may not return until late to-morrow.

EDW'D DILLON,
Major, C. S. Army.

JACKSON, *November* 27, 1862.

General S. COOPER, *Richmond:*

Major-General Smith, at Vicksburg, telegraphs me as follows :

Inform General Pemberton that General Holmes is understood as objecting to troops going from his command to Vicksburg. Another order from the War Department is necessary.

General Pemberton is with the army at Abbeville, Miss.

J. R. WADDY,
Assistant Adjutant-General.

ABBEVILLE, *November* 27, 1862.
General S. COOPER,
 Adjutant and Inspector General :
 The enemy is advancing in force; crossed a considerable force from Helena; is also moving down the river in boats. I am told General Holmes objects to sending 10,000 men ordered to Vicksburg; it is essential to its safety. I hope the order will be reiterated at once. I have no doubt we shall soon be attacked by greatly superior force. A strong demonstration also against Port Hudson.

J. C. PEMBERTON,
Lieutenant-General, Commanding.

JACKSON, *November* 27, 1862.
Major-General SMITH, *Vicksburg :*
 The enemy reported as moving down from Memphis and in front, and gunboats, transports, mortar-boats, and rams are said to have gone down yesterday.

J. R. WADDY,
Assistant Adjutant-General.

ABBEVILLE, *November* 27, 1862.
J. R. WADDY, *Assistant Adjutant-General:*
 Turn all troops ordered from Columbus, Ponchatoula, and Jackson to this place to Vicksburg at once.

J. C. PEMBERTON,
Lieutenant-General.

PANOLA, *November* 27, 1862.
Lieutenant-General PEMBERTON :
 The following dispatch has just been received :

SENATOBIA, November 27, 1862.

Colonel STARKE:
 Enemy advancing. They are near my pickets.

G. L. BLYTHE.

C. B. BUCKNER,
Captain, Comdg. Twenty-eighth Mississippi Volunteers.

PANOLA, *November* 27, 1862.
Lieutenant-General PEMBERTON :
 Enemy advancing in three columns of 10,000 each on State Line, Pigeon Roost, and Hernando roads; had not reached Coldwater at latest advices from our pickets. Large number of troops reported on this side the Mississippi River, but no advance this way indicated yet. I have 60 pickets in that direction and a scouting party toward Helena. This command guarding approaches north of Tallahatchie. Obstructions and fortifications here progressing rapidly.

E. P. JONES,
Major, Commanding.

VICKSBURG, *November* 27, 1862.

Lieutenant-General PEMBERTON :

Some of the enemy's boats are above Lake Providence this afternoon and reported descending. No land movement heard of.

M. L. SMITH.

ABBEVILLE, *November* 27, 1862.

General S. COOPER,
     Adjutant and Inspector General :

Cannot General Forney send me some troops? If Vicksburg falls Mobile goes also. My force here is very much less than the enemy's in my front.

J. C. PEMBERTON,
Lieutenant-General, Commanding.

HDQRS. SUBSIST. DEPT., 2D DIST., DEPT. MISS. AND E. LA.,
Vicksburg, November 27, 1862.

Capt. W. O. KEY,
     Post Quartermaster, Vicksburg :

SIR : As you seem to have misunderstood the nature of my letter of the 24th instant, I beg leave to call your attention especially to the following points :

Under instructions from Lieutenant-General Pemberton, commanding department, communicated to me through Major-General Smith, commanding this district, I am required to collect very large amounts of commissary stores at this point, and as I am dependent for corn, meal, pease, &c., on the river above and below this point, it is absolutely necessary that I should have at least two steamboats, which will be kept running constantly, in order to secure all I can in places which are likely to be cut off by the raids of the enemy. I applied for the steamboat Louis D'Or some days ago, and on ascertaining that she was needed temporarily for special service elsewhere, I stated I must have another. You will therefore please turn over to me for immediate use the steamboats Louis D'Or and Home, which will be immediately sent for corn and meal already engaged and awaiting transportation.

I am also ordered to construct houses in which to secure supplies, and as it is important to furnish them without delay I must urge you to use all dispatch in securing lumber and nails necessary. I will need about 70,000 feet of lumber and six or eight kegs of nails.

Very respectfully, your obedient servant,

T. B. REED,
Major and Commissary of Subsistence.

List of general officers in the armies under General Johnston's command, November 27, 1862.

LIEUTENANT-GENERALS.

E. Kirby Smith.
Leonidas Polk.
W. J. Hardee.
John C. Pemberton.

MAJOR-GENERALS.

1. Earl Van Dorn.
2. Mansfield Lovell.
3. Sterling Price.
4. B. F. Cheatham.
5. J. P. McCown.
6. J. C. Breckinridge.
7. Richard Taylor.
8. S. B. Buckner.
9. Jones M. Withers.
10. C. L. Stevenson.
11. D. H. Maury.
12. M. L. Smith.

BRIGADIER-GENERALS

1. Charles Clark.
2. D. S. Donelson.
3. Daniel Ruggles.
4. A. G. Blanchard.
5. W. H. Carroll.
6. A. P. Stewart.
7. Henry Heth.
8. S. A. M. Wood.
9. Johnson K. Duncan.
10. J. K. Jackson.
11. B. R. Johnson.
12. J. P. Anderson.
13. J. R. Chalmers.
14. W. W. Mackall.
15. Albert Rust.
16. P. R. Cleburne.
17. Samuel B. Maxey.
18. J. E. Slaughter.
19. Seth M. Barton.
20. John S. Bowen.
21. B. H. Helm.
22. Franklin Gardner.
23. W. N. R. Beall.
24. William Preston.
25. D. W. Adams.
26. J. C. Moore.
27. St. J. R. Liddell.
28. N. B. Forrest.
29. M. E. Green.
30. E. D. Tracy.
31. M. D. Ector.
32. John Gregg.
33. J. C. Brown.
34. W. E. Baldwin.
35. J. C. Vaughn.
36. William B. Bate.
37. Preston Smith.
38. Joseph Wheeler.
39. James E. Rains.
40. E. McNair.
41. T. H. Taylor.
42. W. G. M. Davis.
43. A. Gracie, jr.
44. W. R. Boggs.
45. S. D. Lee.
46. John Pegram.
47. John A. Wharton.

ED. A. PALFREY,
Major and Assistant Adjutant-General.

RICHMOND, *November* 28, 1862.
Lieutenant-General HOLMES,
  Little Rock, via Vicksburg:

General Pemberton on 27th reports a considerable force from Helena is moving down the river in boats, and an enemy advancing in his front. Other information is that an attack on Vicksburg is threatened.*

---

*This paragraph telegraphed also to General Bragg at Tullahoma.

The reduction of force at Helena must make it impossible for the enemy to move upon Little Rock, but rather exposes Helena to capture by your forces, the importance of which is even greater now than before. You will perceive the necessity for successful defense at Vicksburg.

Is not your force sufficient under these circumstances to make a detachment, as heretofore proposed, to re-enforce General Pemberton before a rise in the Arkansas and White Rivers? That detachment might again return to west side of river. Whatever can be done should be executed with the utmost rapidity.

By the President:

S. COOPER,
Adjutant and Inspector General.

LITTLE ROCK, *November* 28, 1862.
(Received Jackson, Miss., November 29, 1862.)

Brigadier-General BLANCHARD, *Monroe, La.* :
(To be forwarded to General Pemberton, Jackson.)

Telegraph General Pemberton a large number of troops on transports at Helena; destination supposed to be Arkansas Post or Vicksburg.

TH. H. HOLMES,
Lieutenant-General.

ABBEVILLE, *November* 28, 1862.
(Received November 29, 1862.)

General S. COOPER, *Richmond* :

Reliable information derived from many sources represents the enemy in my front at not less than 60,000, preparing to advance on my front and right under Grant and Sherman; while Steele with 12,000 or 15,000 from Delta and Friar's Point march by Charleston and Coffeeville; while an expedition by the river is preparing under McClernand directly against Vicksburg. It is evident also that another expedition is preparing against Port Hudson. This army does not exceed 24,000 effectives of all arms. Have sent to Vicksburg every man I can. The force there will not be over 4,500; Port Hudson about the same. Unless Holmes' army gets to Vicksburg at once I shall be compelled to withdraw this army to defend it. My forces are entirely inadequate.

J. C. PEMBERTON,
Lieutenant-General, Commanding.

SALTILLO, *November* 28, 1862.

General PEMBERTON :

The Federals evacuated Rienzi yesterday evening at 3 o'clock. They went back to Corinth, and I think they are leaving that place also.

C. R. BARTEAU.

WATERFORD, *November* 28, 1862.

General VAN DORN:

Heard of no more from La Grange. Enemy reported in force on Coldwater. Advance reached Holly Springs. They will advance to Lumpkin's Mill to-morrow.

W. H. JACKSON,
Chief of Cavalry.

VICKSBURG, *November* 28, 1862.

Lieutenant-General PEMBERTON:

Two gunboats, one steam-tug, and two transports passed Lake Providence at 8 o'clock this morning down river.

M. L. SMITH.

ABBEVILLE, *November* 28, 1862.

Maj. J. R. WADDY, *Assistant Adjutant-General:*

I do not wish any cavalry to go from Columbus. If any has gone to New Albany let it return to the front of Columbus on the line of the railroad.

J. C. PEMBERTON,
Lieutenant-General, Commanding.

ABBEVILLE, *November* 28, 1862.

General PEMBERTON:

Enemy advancing from Mississippi River fired with artillery at pickets near mouth of Coldwater. Cavalry had better return. Reported crossing Tallahatchie with cavalry at sundown this evening. I will send the Tobytubby cavalry to that point.

EARL VAN DORN,
Major-General.

YOCONA, *November* 28, 1862.
(Received November 29, 1862.)

JEFFERSON DAVIS, *President:*

General Holmes informs me he cannot send a man from his army, but will send Sibley's cavalry brigade from Texas. That will help Vicksburg but little; to save it I shall be compelled to withdraw from Tallahatchie unless General Bragg co-operates at once with me.

J. C. PEMBERTON,
Lieutenant-General, Commanding.

[Indorsement.]

General COOPER:

Has General Holmes replied to your dispatch? I am disappointed by a renewed attempt to withdraw Sibley's brigade from the special service for which it was designed, and a refusal to send a man when he asks for an addition of 20,000 muskets to his previous supply.

Please attend to this dispatch, as connected with yours to Generals Holmes and Bragg.

J. D.

NOVEMBER 29, 1862.

The PRESIDENT:

I have received no reply to my dispatch to General Holmes in respect to re-enforcements from his command for defense of Vicksburg.

In respect to General Sibley's brigade, which he had some time since ordered to Virginia in answer to my early telegraph to send five Texas regiments to Virginia on the suggestion of Senator Wigfall, but which

I countermanded by telegraph two days after, I infer from a telegram received by General Sibley at Mobile, announcing that his order to come to Washington was countermanded, that General Holmes had revoked the order for the movement of Sibley's brigade to Virginia.

It is too early to receive an answer to my telegraph to General Holmes sent to him on yesterday; that telegraph reiterated a call on him to send re-enforcements to Vicksburg.

I will attend at once to the dispatch of General Pemberton which you send me.

  With great respect,

            S. COOPER.

         RICHMOND, *November* 29, 1862.*

General PEMBERTON:

Send the following by most expeditious route to General Holmes, Little Rock:

Sibley's brigade is not wanted at Vicksburg. Order it to report to General Taylor in West Louisiana. Send to Vicksburg without delay the infantry force which you have been twice telegraphed for. The case is urgent and will not admit of delay.

          S. COOPER,
        Adjutant and Inspector General.

        MOBILE, *November* 29, 1862.

Lieutenant-General PEMBERTON:

I am ordered to station a brigade at Meridian subject to your orders, but to be recalled when threatened here. This brigade is at Montgomery. If urgent, I will send the one at this place.

Will you have commissary stores at Meridian for them?

         JNO. H. FORNEY,
       Major-General, Commanding.

       ABBEVILLE, *November* 29, 1862.

General PEMBERTON:

Sherman encamped last night 8 miles north of Chulahoma, marching this morning toward Chulahoma. Grant encamped in force on Coldwater last night, advancing this morning rapidly, all toward our front.

Nothing more from Charleston. Large number of troops reported moving down the river from Memphis.

        EARL VAN DORN,
         Major-General.

       ABBEVILLE, *November* 29, 1862.

General PEMBERTON:

Enemy reported advancing rapidly this morning toward our front. No flank movement reported this morning yet. Large re-enforcements also reported moving down the river by Memphis.

  Truly and respectfully,

        EARL VAN DORN,
         Major-General.

---

* Repeated November 30, 1862. Received by Pemberton December 1, 1862.

VICKSBURG, *November* 29, 1862.

Capt. W. O. KEY,
    Post Quartermaster, Vicksburg:

SIR : I will be compelled to have wagons and trains for the transportation of stores now accumulating here on the river bank to the warehouses prepared for them in the rear, and will have to urge upon you the importance of giving me all the aid you can at once, and also suggest that you procure teams and harness for the wagons now idle, so that they can be made available. This is a matter of great moment to the Government, and as I cannot move a thing from the river until I get transportation you will please give it your immediate attention. I have no doubt that if a proper man of activity and energy were sent into the country from 10 to 50 miles from here a sufficient number of plantation wagons might be had here in a very short time.

    Very respectfully,

                                        T. B. REED,
                            Major and Commissary of Subsistence.

ABBEVILLE, *November* 29, 1862.

Maj. J. R. WADDY,
    Assistant Adjutant-General:

Enemy 5 miles north of river; encamped for the night. Skirmishing all day with our cavalry. All have concentrated at Waterford. May attack in the morning. Reported that only about 12,000 or 15,000 of the enemy in our front.

                                        M. M. KIMMEL,
                            Major and Assistant Adjutant-General.

MURFREESBOROUGH, *November* 29, 1862.
                        (Received December 1, 1862.)

General PEMBERTON:

Have sent a strong brigade to Meridian subject to your orders. It will support both Vicksburg and Mobile when necessary. One thousand men on way from here to join you. Please let me know your forces and how disposed.

                                        BRAXTON BRAGG,
                                    General, Commanding.

SALTILLO, *November* 29, 1862.

General PEMBERTON:

No enemy at Rienzi and Danville, and force much smaller at Corinth than at any time before. Information from beyond Corinth indefinite; citizens there say 12,000 or 15,000 went on Humboldt and Ohio road to State Line and thence on Edgefield and Kentucky road to Nashville.
                                        C. R. BARTEAU.

JACKSON, *November* 29, 1862.

Maj. Gen. STERLING PRICE, *Abbeville, Miss.* :

Telegraph me immediately how much small-arm ammunition and the caliber you need to make 100 rounds per man; also what amount of field ammunition you require.

> J. C. PEMBERTON,
> *Lieutenant-General, Commanding.*

JACKSON, *November* 29, 1862.

General VAN DORN, *Abbeville :*

General Holmes tells General Blanchard to "Telegraph General Pemberton a large number of troops on transports at Helena; destination supposed to be Arkansas Post or Vicksburg." Undoubtedly Vicksburg.

> J. C. PEMBERTON,
> *Lieutenant-General, Commanding.*

JACKSON, *November* 29, 1862.

Col. J. GORGAS,
  Chief of Ordnance, Richmond, Va. :

It is my opinion that the machinery and ordnance stores at the Briarfield Arsenal, Columbus, should be removed to the interior, as I have no force to meet the enemy on my right.

> J. C. PEMBERTON,
> *Lieutenant-General, Commanding.*

JACKSON, *November* 29, 1862.

General MARTIN L. SMITH, *Vicksburg :*

Headquarters of department are temporarily removed to Oxford, Miss. Will leave for that place this evening.

> J. R. WADDY,
> *Assistant Adjutant-General.*

RICHMOND, *November* 29, 1862.

Lieutenant-General PEMBERTON, *Jackson, Miss.* :

Edward D. Frost, superintendent of railroad, telegraphs from Yocona that he has your orders to military officers to seize the trains and run them with no notice to him. It is not expedient to take military possession of the road. Assurances are given to employ the whole power of the road for military purposes. Fulfill the Ruggles contract, and act in the view indicated in your letter of 19th.

> S. COOPER,
> *Adjutant and Inspector General.*

VICKSBURG, MISS., *November* 30, 1862.

General PEMBERTON:

Five gunboats and a steam-tug at the mouth of the Yazoo attempted to land with small party at Milliken's Bend; were attacked and an officer killed. No other news.

M. L. SMITH,
Major-General.

ABBEVILLE, MISS., *November* 30, 1862.

General BRAXTON BRAGG, *Tullahoma, Tenn.*:

I am compelled to fall back for the defense of Vicksburg. The effective force there does not exceed 4,000. General Holmes is doing nothing to assist me. The enemy is moving from 10,000 to 15,000 from Delta by mouth of Coldwater toward Grenada. Sherman with 20,000 is at Lumpkin's Mill, 12 miles in my front. Grant is moving also with the whole or part of his army, from 35,000 to 40,000, and will doubtless cross a large force at New Albany. Columbus, Miss., is not fortified. Within a few days a large expedition by the Mississippi River will move direct for Vicksburg for a combined land and water attack. You see my situation; it is for you to decide how far you can help me. I am now moving my baggage to Yalabusha.

J. C. PEMBERTON,
Lieutenant-General, Commanding.

My effective force for battle will not exceed 20,000 at this or any other point south.

J. C. PEMBERTON,
Lieutenant-General, Commanding.

HDQRS. MAURY'S DIVISION, ARMY OF THE WEST,
November 30, 1862.

Maj. M. M. KIMMEL,
Assistant Adjutant-General:

MAJOR: I am directed by Major-General Maury to say that all the pieces in this division are fully supplied with ammunition except the 3-inch rifle guns, and that he is advised that the post ordnance officer has none of that kind of ammunition on hand. I am also directed to say that there is as much ammunition for small-arms on hand as can be transported.

Very respectfully, your obedient servant,

JOHN W. GILLESPIE,
Ordnance Officer, Maury's Division.

JACKSON, MISS., *November* 30, 1862.

General COOPER,
Adjutant-General, Richmond:

Lieutenant-General Pemberton joined the army in advance yesterday. The enemy's cavalry to-day cut off communication at Grenada with him and his army.

The enemy are pressing our army in great force.

Am I authorized to call on Lieutenant-General Holmes for re-enforcements?

> DANIEL RUGGLES,
> *Brigadier-General.*

GENERAL ORDERS, }   HDQRS. ARMY OF WEST TENNESSEE,
      No. 67.   }   *Abbeville, November* 30, 1862.

All trains, with the exception of the ordnance wagons, will be sent immediately behind the Yocona. Those of the First Corps will march by the nearest practicable road from the various positions occupied by the corps to the point on the Yocona near where the Oxford and Dallas road (leading southeast) crosses that stream. Those of the Second Corps will take the roads leading from the present positions of the troops to Oxford, thence south to the point where the road crosses the Yocona. All the trains will be parked behind that stream and await further orders. Cavalry trains will follow the trains belonging to the troops nearest which they are encamped. No time will be lost in getting off these trains. Colonel Jackson will detach one company of cavalry on each road leading south from Tobytubby, Wyatt, Abbeville, and Tippah, with orders to prevent straggling from the army and to apprehend and send back to their commands all men not authorized to accompany the trains. Quartermasters will accompany their trains.

By order of General Van Dorn:

> M. M. KIMMEL,
> *Major and Assistant Adjutant-General.*

SPECIAL ORDERS, }   HDQRS. DEPT. OF MISS. AND EAST LA.,
      No. —.   }   *Abbeville, Miss., November* 30, 1862.

All the troops of this army will march at daylight in the morning and concentrate at Oxford. What cannot be transported will be destroyed. There must be no failure in carrying out this order. The squadrons of cavalry left at Tobytubby Ford, Wyatt Ford, railroad bridge, and Tippah Ford will remain at those points to watch the enemy left in our rear. They will fall back only when compelled to do so and keep these headquarters informed of all movements. Each column will have a regiment and a section of artillery as rear guard. A column of the enemy has crossed the Tallahatchie and are in our rear. The rain to-night will cut it off. They are to be fought, and there must be no failure to concentrate our forces at Oxford as indicated.

> J. C. PEMBERTON,
> *Lieutenant-General, Commanding.*

OXFORD, *December* 1, 1862.

JEFFERSON DAVIS,
     President, Richmond, Va.:

I am endeavoring to place myself behind the Yalabusha River, but am strongly threatened both in front and rear. Am now at Oxford, but shall move to-morrow morning.

> J. C. PEMBERTON,
> *Lieutenant-General, Commanding.*

JACKSON, MISS., *December* 1, 1862.

General S. COOPER,
    Adjutant and Inspector General:

Information just received from General Pemberton's army, which is said to be falling back toward Grenada. Railroad communication open with him; telegraph interrupted. Enemy still threatens Grenada in large force.

DANIEL RUGGLES,
Brigadier-General.

HEADQUARTERS DISTRICT OF THE GULF,
Mobile, December 1, 1862.

Lieut. Gen. J. C. PEMBERTON:

GENERAL: I am directed by General Bragg so soon as the Tennessee regiments (Brigadier-General Vaughn's command) arrive to send a strong brigade of infantry to Meridian subject to your orders, but to be recalled whenever we are threatened here. I have directed General Vaughn to proceed, without stopping, to Meridian with his command, agreeably to these instructions.

His command consists of three regiments of infantry. If cavalry will be of any service to you I think I can furnish you with one regiment. I might also spare you a few independent cavalry companies. Please advise me on this point.

I am, general, very respectfully, your obedient servant,

JNO. H. FORNEY,
Major-General, Commanding.

SPECIAL ORDERS, }   HDQRS. DEPT. OF MISS. AND EAST LA.,
    No. —. }   *Oxford, December* 1, 1862.

I. In the event of the approach of the enemy in such force that they cannot be resisted by the force left here, all public property at this point will be destroyed upon the order of the officer left in command.

II. All sick men left at this point who can travel will be allowed twenty days to proceed eastward, and will report to the surgeon in charge of the nearest hospital on the line of the Mobile and Ohio Railroad, reporting as early as practicable, through the hospital surgeon, to their regimental or company commanders.

By order of Lieut. Gen. J. C. Pemberton:

J. R. WADDY,
Assistant Adjutant-General.

SPECIAL ORDERS, }   HDQRS. ARMY OF WEST TENNESSEE,
    No. —. }   *Oxford, December* 1, 1862.

I. All troops encamped on the Yocona River will move by the most practicable and direct routes at 7 a. m. to-morrow to Coffeeville and encamp on the mouth of stream north of the town. The two army corps will encamp under the direction of their respective corps commanders. Maury's division, Scott's brigade, and Waul's Legion will move by the most direct route to the same point.

II. Chief of cavalry will detail McCulloch's brigade to remain in Oxford until Colonel Slemons' brigade arrives, when they will form junction and remain in rear until the stores are removed from this place or until forced away by the enemy, in which case he will destroy all Government stores at this place.

III. Wagons will move in rear of the column with a strong rear guard.

By order of General Van Dorn:

W. C. SCHAUMBURG,
Assistant Adjutant-General.

DECEMBER 2, 1862.

General PEMBERTON, *Oxford, Miss.:*

It is the desire of the President that you control the telegraphic and other communications of General Ruggles made direct to the authorities here. Being under your command, all his communications must pass through your headquarters.

S. COOPER.

HDQRS. DEPT. OF MISSISSIPPI AND EAST LOUISIANA,
Water Valley, December 2, 1862.

Maj. Gen. STERLING PRICE:

GENERAL: The lieutenant-general commanding directs that you hold your command in readiness to move in either direction. Skirmishing reported in front.

I am, respectfully, your obedient servant,

R. W. MEMMINGER,
Assistant Adjutant-General.

HDQRS. DEPT. OF MISSISSIPPI AND EAST LOUISIANA,
Water Valley, December 2, 1862.

Maj. Gen. STERLING PRICE:

GENERAL: The lieutenant-general commanding directs that you collect all your men and hold them in readiness; prepare your batteries and ammunition for action; put out pickets at all points for observation. Skirmishing reported in rear; will inform you further. Push on your wagon trains and the cavalry brigade in advance to assist Colonel Griffith. Keep infantry regiment with train in advance.

I am, respectfully, your obedient servant,

R. W. MEMMINGER,
Assistant Adjutant-General.

JACKSON, MISS., *December* 2, [1862]—10.30 a. m.

Major-General FORNEY, *Mobile:*

Communications with General Pemberton are now open.

Please carry your original plan into effect and send your troops to Meridian.

DANIEL RUGGLES,
Brigadier-General.

OXFORD, MISS., *December* 2, 1862.

Maj. Gen. MARTIN L. SMITH, *Vicksburg:*

All the steamboats that would certainly fall into the enemy's hands must be burned.

J. C. PEMBERTON

ORDNANCE BUREAU, *Richmond, December* 2, 1862.

Hon. JAMES A. SEDDON,
    Secretary of War :

SIR : I respectfully return herewith telegram from Maj. G. U. Mayo, chief of ordnance for General Pemberton, to His Excellency the President, with your indorsement thereon.   I send you memorandum showing arms, &c., sent to General Pemberton since 29th of October, by special messengers.   I sent a messenger from here some time since to hasten forward all arms on any of the railroads, and on Sunday, at my request, the Quartermaster-General telegraphed to his officers controlling transportation to urge forward all arms and munition for General Pemberton.   I have ordered Major Childs, at Charleston, to send to him all small-arms that could be spared from that arsenal.

There is a large number of arms at Columbus, Miss., needing repairs, and some time since I directed the commanding officer there to repair these as rapidly as possible and send them.   This morning I have a telegram from him in which he says, "Am sending about 600 arms per week to General Pemberton."

In a letter just received from Lieutenant-Colonel Oladowski, chief of ordnance for General Bragg's army (dated November 23, 1862), he says:

To Atlanta, in addition to 2,220 arms sent previously, I forwarded 800 more, and by order of General Bragg I instructed Major Wright as soon as these will be repaired to issue them to General Pemberton, 500 of which are already forwarded.

I have authorized Colonel Stockton, commanding arsenal at Jackson, Miss., to call upon all contiguous arsenals for ammunition, &c., to supply General Pemberton.

    Very respectfully, your obedient servant,
                        J. GORGAS,
                    Colonel, Chief of Ordnance.

[Inclosures.]

                        RICHMOND, *November* 30, 1862.
His Excellency JEFFERSON DAVIS :

Only 1,700 arms received yet from Richmond.   General Pemberton joined army last night.   Arms seem to be continually delayed on the road.

                    GEORGE UPSHUR MAYO,
                    Major and Chief of Ordnance.

Ordnance and ordnance stores ordered to Lieut. Gen. J. C. Pemberton's command.

October 29, Richmond : One thousand seven hundred small-arms.

October 29, Richmond : Four 4.62 rifled and banded guns, with carriages and ammunition complete ; four 12-pounder bronze guns ; four 24-pounder howitzers, with carriages, caissons, and ammunition complete.

November 9, Richmond : Four thousand rounds ammunition for 6-pounder gun and 12-pounder howitzer (three-fifths gun and two-fifths howitzer) ; 80 rounds 20-pounder Parrott ammunition ; 200 rounds 3-pounder Parrott ammunition.

November 10, Charleston : Eight hundred arms to General Smith, Vicksburg.

November 10, Atlanta: Five hundred 3-inch rifle shot and shell.

November 11, Richmond: Seventy rounds 20-pounder ammunition

November 18, Richmond and Lynchburg: One thousand five hundred arms and ammunition.

November 18, Knoxville: One thousand five hundred arms and ammunition.

November 18, Atlanta: Five hundred arms and ammunition.

November 24, Richmond: Three 10-inch columbiads.

Copy of this with names of messengers was sent to General Pemberton about a week since.

HDQRS. SUBSIST. DEPT., 2D DIST., DEPT. OF MISS. AND E. LA.,
Vicksburg, Miss., December 2, 1862.

Maj. R. H. CUNEY,
Commissary of Subsistence, Jackson, Miss. :

SIR: I must again call your attention to the importance of shipping supplies of salt, bacon, flour, coffee, and candles to this place. The last three articles I am aware can only be sent in limited quantities for the use of hospitals and filling of requisitions in special cases, but it is important for me to secure the amount of same necessary for the time fixed in the order of the lieutenant-general commanding the department, viz, five months. The major-general commanding the district has again called upon me in regard to these things, and is urging me to get them here so that they will be on hand whenever the necessity should arise of being independent of outside supplies. He especially urges me to see to the beeves intended for this command, and wishes to know what you intend to do in order to keep up the supplies necessary for our subsistence during the five months, say six months, from this time. It will require 8,000 beeves, averaging 400 pounds each, to supply us, and they should be within our own lines, so that in case we are cut off we can be independent. We ought also to get our salt here without delay, and as the time has about arrived when we may expect the commencement of hostilities at this place I need only lay the facts before you to let you see how great is the necessity for exertion and activity in order to put everything here that is needed, a list of which I send at foot. We will want the following supplies: Eight thousand beeves, 250 casks bacon, 1,200 boxes soap, 1,000 sacks salt, 300 tierces rice, 675 barrels of vinegar, 1,500 barrels of flour, 70 sacks coffee, 100 boxes candles, and such an amount of whisky as will be necessary for men at batteries and where they are exposed on special service to extra duty. Corn, meal, pease, sugar, and molasses I will make every effort to get in sufficient quantities here and from the river above and below here; but the other rations enumerated above I must call on you to supply and urge you to commence shipping at once. Please send orders in regard to the rations of beef and meal, fixing it at 125 pounds per 100 rations per day. Please also send funds. I have had to borrow, and not having them is a drawback in procuring supplies. The $10,000 special, written about previously, is particularly needed. Your agents, contractors, and vendors should report to me in person and not to a non-commissioned agent, so that I may keep advised of the entire business of the district.

Very respectfully, your obedient servant,

T. B. REED,
Major and Commissary of Subsistence.

HDQRS. SUBSIST. DEPT., 2D DIST., DEPT. MISS. AND E. LA.,
Vicksburg, December 2, 1862.
Maj. L. MIMS,
 Chief Quartermaster, Jackson, Miss. :

DEAR SIR : I have been instructed by the major-general commanding to accumulate large amounts of commissary stores here, and in order to preserve them properly it will be necessary to construct rough houses in which to store them. The corn, pease, and meal are now arriving here, and it is very important to have them hauled from the river bank and put under shelter as rapidly as possible. I have applied to the quartermaster here frequently, but can get no lumber nor nails, and must call your attention to the necessities of the department and urge upon you the great importance of sending these things on speedily as possible. A telegram from Major-General Smith went this morning to you requesting shipment of sixty mules and harness complete in order to move the stores from the river bank. I inclose approved requisition for same, and hope they will come to hand immediately, as the transportation question is a very serious one at this time and is becoming more important every day. Please see to getting lumber and nails immediately.

Very respectfully, your obedient servant,
T. B. REED
Major and Commissary of Subsistence.

RICHMOND, *December* 3, 1862.
General JOSEPH E. JOHNSTON, *Chattanooga, Tenn.* :

General Pemberton has fallen back from his positions by advance of very superior force of the enemy. General Holmes has been peremptorily ordered to re-enforce him, but his troops may arrive too late. The President urges on you the importance of sending a sufficient force from General Bragg's command to the aid of General Pemberton.
S. COOPER,
Adjutant and Inspector General.

HEADQUARTERS,
Water Valley, December 3, 1862—8 o'clock.

Lieutenant-General PEMBERTON, *Commanding:*

GENERAL : All of Lovell's train on this road are over the river; those going by Lawsher's are now passing. Gregg is halted where the Spring Dale road comes into this. Lovell's corps is yet 5 miles in rear coming up. Maury is in rear yet. Lovell goes to Lawsher's; Maury comes here. I shall remain until he comes up.

I shall send back for a company of cavalry, but it will be late before it gets up. No cavalry here.

Respectfully, &c.,
EARL VAN DORN,
Major-General.

Nothing reported from the rear. All quiet.

HEADQUARTERS,
Water Valley, December 3, 1862--3.15 o'clock.

Lieutenant-General PEMBERTON, *Commanding:*

GENERAL: I inclose you a dispatch from Colonel Griffith, just received.* Maury's division has just arrived at this point. Lovell's troops are on the road to Lawsher's, and will be across the river, he says, about 10 o'clock p. m. Gregg is marching upon Spring Dale road; will be up soon. Maury will bivouac just behind the town. Gregg will bivouac in front of town. All will move in the morning at 4 o'clock.

Maury says there has been no heavy skirmishing in rear to-day. No artillery firing. Thinks there has been nothing but cavalry. All will march at 4 o'clock in morning.

Respectfully,

EARL VAN DORN,
Major-General.

SPECIAL ORDERS, }   HDQRS. 2D DIST., DEPT. MISS. AND E. LA.,
No. 33.   }   *Vicksburg, December* 3, 1862.

*   *   *   *   *   *   *

II. Mr. W. H. Johnson having been made a special agent for the accumulation of Government supplies in this district as well as in this department, and instructed to establish his office at this point, the following directions are issued relative thereto:

1st. The district and depot commissaries and the depot quartermaster will report to him the names of all agents appointed by them for the purchase of supplies; also direct such agents to report to him for instructions.

2d. Arrangements for the transportation of all such supplies, either up or down the river by boats, will be under his control.

3d. As far as practicable all Government and other stores needing transportation will be taken by the boats employed by him, for which purpose information of their movements will always be given to the depot quartermaster.

4th. All disbursements connected with purchases and freights controlled by Mr. Johnson will be made by him.

By command of Maj. Gen. M. L. Smith:

JNO. G. DEVEREUX,
Assistant Adjutant-General.

GRENADA, *December* 4, 1862.

General BRAXTON BRAGG,
     Murfreesborough, Tenn.:

I shall be in position on the Yalabusha with part of my forces to-night; the remainder to-morrow; probably in all about 21,000 effectives. My rear guard has been skirmishing with the enemy since leaving Tallahatchie. They have been skirmishing also on my right flank with troops from the Mississippi River.

We have about 6,000 effective men for the defense of Vicksburg and Yazoo; about 4,500 effective at Port Hudson; have no troops of any moment elsewhere. The brigade you send me will be held for the present at Jackson.

J. C. PEMBERTON.

---

* Not found.

GRENADA, *December* 4, 1862.

ADJUTANT-GENERAL C. S. ARMY, *Richmond :*

I expect my army to be in position on the Yalabusha, part to-night and part to-morrow night—about 21,000 effectives. Brigade sent by Bragg will for the present be retained at Jackson. The enemy is in strong force from our rear to Wolf River. Daily skirmishing with the rear guard and with troops on the Mississippi River on our right. I left the army at Water Valley at 1 o'clock this morning. It was in fine spirits and condition. No important losses in stores of any kind. I shall endeavor to maintain this position. I have not overestimated the enemy's strength.

J. C. PEMBERTON,
Lieutenant-General, Commanding.

———

DECEMBER 4, 1862—8 a. m.

General [VAN DORN]:

The enemy fell back to Oakland last night and are not progressing this way this morning. I shall move on them to Oakland immediately and get after and harass them. Don't fear for our train in this quarter; the danger is lower down. I can and will keep them back from Oakland and Preston east. A cavalry force thrown out by you west of Torrance Depot would be prudent.

Yours, truly,

JOHN S. GRIFFITH,
Colonel, Commanding Brigade Texas Cavalry.

Col. Robert McCulloch has arrived. He will move on to Oakland via Preston road.

GRIFFITH.

———

COFFEEVILLE, *December* 4, 1862.

Lieutenant-General PEMBERTON:

Enemy fallen back from Oakland; reported by Colonel Griffith. Cavalry still following. Have ordered all our cavalry to Harding Station to fall on their flank. Maury and Lovell will march to-morrow at 8 o'clock; will get to Grenada about sundown. Train of cars with sick and property will be in soon.

EARL VAN DORN,
Major-General.

———

HEADQUARTERS ARMY OF THE WEST,
At Mr. Harrison's, 3½ *miles from Grenada, Dec.* 4, 1862.

Capt. R. W. MEMMINGER,
   Assistant Adjutant-General :

CAPTAIN: Be pleased to inform the general commanding that my command is encamped at this place. The rain of to-day has made the roads so bad that my train would not be able to get farther to-night. I have heard no report of the enemy to-day.

I am, captain, very respectfully, your obedient servant,

STERLING PRICE,
Major-General.

JACKSON, *December* 4, 1862.

Major-General SMITH, *Vicksburg:*

Headquarters department re-established at this point.

J. R. WADDY,
Assistant Adjutant-General.

———

CHATTANOOGA, TENN., *December* 4, 1862.

General S. COOPER, *Adjutant-General, Richmond, Va.:*

Can you give me General Pemberton's force and that of the enemy; the direction in which he is moving and where he is? Use the President's cipher of last spring.

J. E. JOHNSTON,
General.

———

CHATTANOOGA, TENN., *December* 4, 1862.

General S. COOPER, *Adjutant and Inspector General:*

SIR: I have received this morning your telegram of yesterday informing me that Lieutenant-General Pemberton is falling back before a very superior force; that Lieutenant-General Holmes has been peremptorily ordered to re-enforce him, but that as General Holmes' troops may be too late the President urges on me the importance of sending a sufficient force from General Bragg's command to the aid of Lieutenant-General Pemberton.

Three railroad accidents delayed my journey so much that I did not reach this place until after 12 last night; consequently your dispatch was delivered to-day too late for communication with General Bragg before to-morrow, when I shall visit his headquarters.

I do not know General Pemberton's late positions. His march, I suppose, will be toward Vicksburg, where General Holmes' troops must cross the river. His movements therefore are facilitating the junction, while they daily render that of General Bragg with him more difficult. The enemy, too, is exactly between the latter and himself. It seems to me consequently that the aid of General Holmes can better be relied on than that of General Bragg. I therefore respectfully suggest that that officer be urged to the utmost expedition. Should the enemy get possession of Vicksburg we cannot dislodge him. The Tennessee River is a formidable obstacle to the expeditious march of General Bragg's troops into Mississippi. He may, besides, be compelled to take a circuitous route; of this, however, I am not fully informed, nor have I learned the enemy's attitude in Tennessee. It is to be presumed that all such information can be acquired at General Bragg's headquarters, which I shall reach to-morrow.

Most respectfully, your obedient servant,

J. E. JOHNSTON,
General.

———

CHATTANOOGA, *December* 4, 1862.

Lieutenant-General PEMBERTON:

Let me know by express which way you are moving and what your plans are. Urge General Holmes to quick movement. I am without the necessary information. Give it.

J. E. JOHNSTON.

GRENADA, *December* 4, 1862.

General JOSEPH E. JOHNSTON, *Chattanooga:*

I shall be in position behind the Yalabusha to-morrow. The advance is 3 miles off.

Will write by courier at large.

J. C. PEMBERTON,
Lieutenant-General, Commanding.

CHATTANOOGA, TENN., *December* 4, 1862.

Col. J. GORGAS,
Chief of Ordnance, Richmond:

From a dispatch just received from the Adjutant-General I think General Pemberton's suggestion should be adopted. I do not know the condition of things so well as the President.

J. E. JOHNSTON,
General.

CHATTANOOGA, TENN., *December* 4, 1862.

General BRAGG, *Tullahoma:*

The enemy is advancing on General Pemberton, who is falling back. Can you delay the advance by throwing cavalry on enemy's rear? I will join you to-morrow.

J. E. JOHNSTON.

[Indorsement.]

This dispatch was not received by General Bragg, who took the measure suggested upon intelligence given him by Lieutenant-General Pemberton.

J. E. J.

CHATTANOOGA, TENN., *December* 4, 1862.

General COOPER, *Richmond:*

The map convinces me that General Holmes' troops can re-enforce sooner than General Bragg's. Urge him again to press his troops forward. I shall be with Bragg as soon as possible, which will be to-morrow.

J. E. JOHNSTON.

CHATTANOOGA, TENN., *December* 4, 1862.

General S. COOPER, *Richmond:*

I have only the cipher the President established with me last spring. I have no signal officer; shall know to-morrow if General Bragg has. I telegraphed General Pemberton this morning via Jackson, but have no reply. The march of Bragg's troops to Pemberton's present position would require several weeks.

J. E. JOHNSTON.

HDQRS. SUBSIST. DEPT., 2D DIST., DEPT. MISS. AND E. LA.,
Vicksburg, Miss., December 4, 1862.

Maj. R. H. CUNEY,
  Commissary of Subsistence, Jackson, Miss.:

DEAR SIR: Referring you to my letter of the 2d, the major-general commanding this district says that we will require a larger quantity of supplies than I wrote for. As we may have a long siege it is important to have a plenty of supplies. You will forward immediately the following articles: Eight thousand beeves, 400 casks bacon, 1,800 boxes of soap, 1,500 sacks salt, 500 tierces of rice, 1,000 barrels of vinegar, 2,500 barrels flour, 125 sacks coffee, 150 boxes candles.

Very respectfully, your obedient servant,
                              T. B. REED,
                    Major and Commissary of Subsistence.

GENERAL ORDERS, }   DEPARTMENT HEADQUARTERS,
    No. 1.   }   *Chattanooga, December 4, 1862.*

The undersigned assumes the command to which he is assigned in Special Orders, No. 225, dated Richmond, November 24, 1862. The following officers constitute his staff:

Col. B. S. Ewell, adjutant-general.
Lieut. Col. T. B. Lamar, assistant adjutant-general.
Maj. A. P. Mason, assistant adjutant-general.
Col. Charles M. Fauntleroy, inspector-general.
Lieut. Col. Edwin J. Harvie, assistant inspector-general.
Maj. Alfred M. Barbour, chief quartermaster.
Lieut. J. Barroll Washington, aide-de-camp.
Lieut. Wade Hampton, jr., aide-de-camp.
                              J. E. JOHNSTON,
                                      General.

                         RICHMOND, VA., *December 5, 1862.*

General JOSEPH E. JOHNSTON, *Chattanooga, Tenn.:*

Pemberton telegraphs yesterday from Grenada. His force, 21,000, at Yalabusha River. Near by enemy, 60,000, extending from his rear to Wolf River. Daily skirmishing with rear guard and with troops on Mississippi River on his right.

The word in cipher can be explained by one of General Bragg's signal officers. The President has not the cipher you refer to. If it is a dictionary cipher, please let me know the particular edition of the dictionary you have, that copies of the same may be obtained here, if possible, to work by.

                              S. COOPER,
                    Adjutant and Inspector General.

              LITTLE ROCK, *December 5, 1862.*
        (Received Richmond, December 8, 1862.)

General S. COOPER:

Two-thirds of my force is in Northwest Arkansas to meet a heavy advance there from Springfield, Mo. I expect a fight daily. Not a soldier has left Helena, but it has been re-enforced by two divisions. There are now there 25,000 men.

Except the regiment for the defense on the fortifications on the Lower Arkansas and White Rivers I have but 6,000 infantry to defend this valley. The distance to Vicksburg is 300 miles, with no supplies on the road. I could not get there in twenty-five days, and all would be lost here before I could return.

I beseech you to answer this at once.

> TH. H. HOLMES,
> *Lieutenant-General.*

HEADQUARTERS TRANS-MISSISSIPPI DEPARTMENT,
Little Rock, Ark., December 5, 1862.
(Received December 23, 1862.)

General S. COOPER,
Adjt. and Insp. Gen., C. S. Army, Richmond, Va.:

GENERAL: Since the receipt of your first dispatch, desiring me to send 10,000 men to Vicksburg, the enemy have made two strong demonstrations on this frontier—one from the northwest, in which General Hindman's cavalry division were driven back 14 miles from Cane Hill, Ark., leaving the enemy in possession of that part of the State and half the Cherokee Nation, to reclaim which General Hindman is now advancing with his entire force; the other, from Helena, with 9,000 men, on the Post of Arkansas, was made by land and water. It failed because the low water prevented concert of action between the two intended attacks. This expedition is the force that General Pemberton supposed had left Helena. It returned there three days after, and since then Generals Steele's and Osterhaus' divisions have been added to the garrison, where there are now not less than 25,000 men, with sixty pieces of artillery. To oppose this force I have 2,500 to defend the fortifications at the Post of Arkansas and at Saint Charles, on White River, and twelve infantry regiments, numbering about 6,000 fighting men, near Brownsville, with three regiments of cavalry at Devall's Bluff, on White River.

This was the precise state of affairs when your telegrams of the 28th and 29th reached me this evening. If I withdraw the infantry as directed there will be nothing to prevent the enemy's coming to Little Rock. The whole valley of the Arkansas will be stampeded, and the political party which has constantly cried out that the country is deserted by the Government will pave the way to dangerous disloyalty and disgust. Besides this, if this river goes, the entire trans-Mississippi region goes with it, for the country between this and Red River is denuded of supplies, and the valley of the Red River is so crowded with slaves, carried there from Mississippi, Louisiana, and Arkansas, that it is doubtful whether its abundant crops will more than feed its population for another year.

Under these circumstances, and with the greatest reluctance, I hesitate to obey your last order, because it presupposes the safety of this river; besides this, I could not reach Vicksburg in less than thirty days, as I should have to carry my supplies, and the streams, now much swollen, would cause delay that could not be avoided, the distance being over 300 miles and the troops unaccustomed to marching. I believe my information is certain that it will not be attacked until the army in Mississippi is destroyed. For this purpose they have landed immense forces at Memphis, coming from the Ohio River, and except at Helena there is not a Federal soldier below there. If I had left here when first directed to do so this valley would now have been in their possession. If I leave here now it will be so in less than thirty days.

I expect General Hindman to attack Schofield at Cane Hill to-morrow morning at daylight. If he succeeds, that part of Arkansas and the Indian country will be free. If he fails, it must be abandoned, as the supplies for an army there would have to come—the breadstuffs from here and the beef from Texas. If I erred in not moving at once to Vicksburg it was because all your telegrams presupposed the safety of Arkansas. Sibley's brigade was to have gone as infantry and had been strengthened by two regiments. General Taylor had not informed me of his urgent necessity in Louisiana, and I supposed they could be spared. I have no other infantry troops than those above disposed of.

I am, general, very respectfully, your most obedient servant,

TH. H. HOLMES,
Major-General, Commanding.

HDQRS. DEPT. OF MISSISSIPPI AND EAST LOUISIANA,
Grenada, Miss., December 5, 1862.

General JOSEPH E. JOHNSTON,
Commanding, &c., Chattanooga, Tenn. :

GENERAL: Your telegram of the 4th instant reached me at a late hour last night, and a brief message was forwarded in reply, indicating my present position.

The large re-enforcements received by the enemy in West Tennessee within the last few weeks, and his concentration of forces to the amount, I believe, of not less than 60,000 at La Grange, Grand Junction, and other points between my position on Tallahatchie and his base, rendered it more than doubtful whether I should be able to hold so long a line with the very small force at my disposal. I was aware also that a considerable force (not much less than my own) had been landed on the east bank of the Mississippi River, at Friar's Point and Delta. About the 27th November the enemy commenced a simultaneous movement of his armies in my front and from the Mississippi River, threatening my rear. Gunboats and transports loaded with troops were also reported descending the river toward Vicksburg, and a demonstration from below was made at the same time against Port Hudson, on the successful holding of which point, together with Vicksburg's defenses, depends the navigation of the Mississippi River.

Port Hudson is an isolated position, not naturally strong by its land approaches, and at any time open to attack from below. It is by this time strongly intrenched and garrisoned by about 5,500 effectives. Port Hudson is distant 58 miles from the railroad depot at Tangipahoa. These troops are not available on a sudden emergency for any other point nor can it be readily re-enforced. Vicksburg is strongly intrenched, and about 6,000 of all arms are held in immediate vicinity for its defense. My army on the Tallahatchie, including artillery and cavalry, num bered about 22,000 effectives, most of the cavalry being in advance and covering both flanks.

Under the circumstances narrated above, I determined to withdraw from the Tallahatchie and to establish my line behind the Yalabusha River. The movement was commenced on the morning of the 1st of December, the advance guard as a reconnoitering party of the enemy consisting of five regiments of infantry, two of cavalry, and two field batteries having advanced to skirmishing distance from our advanced works.

By the gross misconduct of the authorities of the Mississippi Central Railroad, and the positive disobedience by them of my orders, a small amount of public property, say 300 rounds field ammunition, a few tents, &c., were burned before leaving.

The enemy's cavalry and some mounted infantry have followed up our movement, occasionally skirmishing with our rear guard, without, however, delaying our march, which has progressed without the loss of a wagon or any description of property.

General Price's corps is now being established between this point and the Tuscahoma Ferry. Van Dorn will occupy the ground on his right.

The heavy rains which have fallen will, I believe, enable me to hold this position with my small force unless a movement is made by the enemy to turn my right by the Mobile and Ohio Railroad.

I am, general, very respectfully, your obedient servant,

J. C. PEMBERTON,
Lieutenant-General, Commanding.

P. S.—The re-enforcements ordered by General Bragg will be retained for the present at Jackson. I have no hope of any assistance from General Holmes, and have telegraphed fully on that subject to Richmond some days since.

Respectfully,

J. C. PEMBERTON,
Lieutenant-General.

GRENADA, *December* 5, 1862.

Maj. J. R. WADDY:

Have all troops ready to move at moment's notice. Are they provided with ammunition? Direct three days' rations to be kept cooked. Tell General Ruggles to enforce strict police and order in and about Jackson, keeping guards and patrols night and day. Tell Major Mayo to have small-arm ammunition ready if needed, particularly ball, and ball and buck, caliber .69.

J. C. PEMBERTON,
Lieutenant-General, Commanding.

GRENADA, *December* 5, 1862.

Major-General VAN DORN, *Coffeeville:*

I wish you to start at an early hour in the morning, so as to arrive this side the river to-morrow evening. A regiment of cavalry, under a good officer, must be sent as quickly as possible to Greenwood, where the roads and crossing are said to be good.

J. C. PEMBERTON,
Lieutenant-General, Commanding.

COFFEEVILLE, *December* 5, 1862.

Lieutenant-General PEMBERTON:

I will start the wagons in the morning. Will start the troops soon after they get off. Doubt if we can reach Grenada by dark with the

artillery. The roads are horrible. I may reach Tatum's Station.
Maury's division will get in; Lovell's corps doubtful. In the fight this
evening we lost about 40 killed and wounded; took about 30 prisoners;
killed and wounded quite a number.

EARL VAN DORN.

RICHMOND, December 6, 1862.

General HOLMES,
    Little Rock, Ark., via Vicksburg:

The President reiterates his orders that you send without delay sufficient force from your command to General Pemberton.

S. COOPER,
Adjutant and Inspector-General.

GRENADA, December 6, 1862.

General S. COOPER:

General Lovell being senior to General Price, what disposition shall
be made of him?

J. C. PEMBERTON,
Lieutenant-General, Commanding.

GRENADA, December 6, 1862.

General S. COOPER:

I have taken position behind the Yalabusha River. My left cannot
easily be turned, and if attacked in front shall endeavor to hold the position. Yesterday had sharp and successful skirmishing. We had
about 40 killed and wounded; the enemy more, and 45 prisoners. All
prisoners taken from us have been sick and wounded.

J. C. PEMBERTON,
Lieutenant-General, Commanding.

HDQRS., FIRST CORPS, ARMY OF WEST TENNESSEE,
Torrance Station, December 6, 1862.

Maj. J. R. WADDY,
    Assistant Adjutant-General, Grenada:

MAJOR: When I left the Tallahatchie, the Fourth Alabama, having
the small-pox among it, was ordered to take a route east of that taken
by the army, to avoid the towns, and proceed south of the Yalabusha
River. If it is near Sarepta it is making its way south. I have had
no report from it.

    Respectfully, your obedient servant,

M. LOVELL,
Major-General, &c.

RICHMOND, December 7, 1862.

General J. C. PEMBERTON:

Are you in communication with General J. E. Johnston? Hope you
will be re-enforced in time.

JEFFERSON DAVIS.

GENERAL ORDERS, }   HDQRS. DEPT. OF MISS. AND EAST LA.,
    No. 17.   }   *Grenada, December* 7, 1862.

I. By direction of the Secretary of War, hereafter this army will be denominated Army of the Department of Mississippi and East Louisiana, to consist of two corps, designated First and Second Corps, and will be commanded respectively by Maj. Gen. Earl Van Dorn and Maj. Gen. S. Price.

The above designations will be used in all official communications emanating from the headquarters of said corps. In the absence of the lieutenant-general commanding the senior officer present will exercise the immediate command of the army.

II. Each corps will consist of two divisions, to be denominated the First and Second Divisions; and each division to consist of two brigades, First and Second Brigades of such division of such corps.

III. Commanders of corps will organize the divisions at once in accordance with the above, observing so to arrange the brigades that there shall be at least one brigadier-general by commission to each division.

IV. All officers who may be relieved from command of brigades by this order and all acting staff officers attached to their headquarters will immediately rejoin their respective regiments and companies.

V. Major-General Van Dorn resuming command of the First Corps of this army, Maj. Gen. Mansfield Lovell is relieved thereby, and not having been assigned to duty by the War Department will await further orders.

*   *   *   *   *   *   *

By order of Lieutenant-General Pemberton :
                    R. W. MEMMINGER,
                        Assistant Adjutant-General.

LITTLE ROCK, *December* 8, 1862.
(Received Richmond, December 9, 1862.)
General S. COOPER:

The movement from Helena reported by General Pemberton October 27 was no doubt a part of a force that about that time made a strong demonstration against the Post of Arkansas. It was to have been combined with a land force that actually reached White River, within 12 miles of the Post. The water movement failed and the whole withdrew. Helena has been re-enforced and is now occupied by 25,000 of the enemy. Hindman reported he would be engaged by dawn to-day near Cane Hill. McCulloch has but 6,000 effectives, and these are the only troops that can possibly be sent away. Withdraw him (McCulloch) and the country is open from Helena, unless we occupy it by General Hindman's forces, in which case Fort Smith and the Indian country will be open to the forces now in front of Hindman.

It will take thirty days for McCulloch to reach Vicksburg, as much to return, and so long as may be required to be of effect there for two months and a half. Then the enemy has us at his discretion.

With the above information before him, does the President insist on the order of the 29th ultimo. McCulloch is now engaged in preparations to march, and will be ready by the time I get your reply. Solemnly, under the circumstances, I regard the movement ordered as equivalent to abandoning Arkansas.

The above is unanimously concurred in by the general and staff officers whom I have had in consultation with me, and this dispatch is intended to take the place of the one I forwarded to you last night.

TH. H. HOLMES,
Lieutenant-General, Commanding.

YAZOO CITY, MISS., *December* 9, 1862.

Lieutenant-General PEMBERTON, C. S. A.,
Commanding Department of the Mississippi:

GENERAL: The Navy Department having instructed me to discontinue work on the gunboats at this place unless the defenses of the Yazoo River should, in my opinion, be sufficient to keep the enemy from ascending that stream, I beg leave respectfully to submit a note on these defenses for your consideration:

They now consist of batteries mounting one light 8-inch gun, one heavy 8-inch, rifled, and a 24-pounder; one smooth-bore 32-pounder, one rifled 32-pounder, two heavy 12-pounders, rifled, and two siege 24-pounders, besides field artillery.

Of these guns I do not think more than two would be available against the enemy's armor-plated vessels. The raft is a strong barrier, impassable, in my opinion, to ships, so long as the enemy can be kept from landing on it to destroy it, and this may be prevented if firm men are placed at the howitzers and with rifles in the rifle-pits overlooking this important work. But I consider necessary to the completion of the whole defenses at least one 10-inch gun, so that when the enemy's progress shall be arrested at the raft he may be there destroyed. Without such addition to our batteries there I fear the enemy might lay under them with but little risk.

I beg leave to add that this note will be handed to you by Mr. John McFarland, a citizen of Yazoo City, a gentleman who has been long, zealously, and efficiently engaged in pushing on our public defenses, and one, permit me to add, who is every way worthy of a patient hearing from you regarding the defenses of the Yazoo Valley.

I have the honor to be, very respectfully,

ISAAC N. BROWN,
Commander, C. S. Navy, &c.

ABERDEEN, *December* 9, 1862.

Hon. JEFFERSON DAVIS:

DEAR SIR: I doubt not you have ascertained from more authentic sources the unhappy condition of affairs in this State. The army, if I am correctly informed, is in a most deplorable state as to its *morale* and organization; bad enough before, its retreat from Abbeville, where so much labor has been done and which was supposed to be so strong a position, has, I fear, put the finishing touch to its inefficiency. Pemberton has not impressed himself either upon the people or the army; while the flank movement from Friar's Point, by which his retreat was forced, and which, it is declared, might have been prevented, has dealt a staggering blow upon those who desired to brace him with the public confidence. It seems that but few even know that General Pemberton is at the head of the army, and his want of prominence of itself at such a crisis depresses the spirit of the people. It is yet called "Van Dorn's Army;" and the universal opprobrium which covers that officer, and the "lower than the lowest deep" to which he has fallen in the estimation of the community of all classes, you cannot be aware of. He may be but an illustration of the truth of the proverb, "Give a dog a bad name," &c.; but so it is, and the fact, not its justice or its truth, must be confronted. He is regarded as the source of all our woes, and disaster, it is prophesied, will attend us so long as he is connected with this army. The atmosphere is dense with horrid narratives of his negligence, whoring, and drunkenness, for the truth of which I cannot vouch; but it is so fastened in the public belief that an acquittal by a court-martial of angels would not relieve him of the charge. I know you have confidence in him—you believe he has merit—high merit, I heard you so declare, and it may be true; but, not to criticise his actions with reference to the foundation of your good opinion, that opinion is not held, far from it, by those whose estimation of his character more immediately affects our common welfare. I know I hazard nothing in saying that Van Dorn's removal from the army with which he is now associated would benefit it. The army, I believe, have no respect for him—have lost confidence in themselves, and will not fight under him. A gentleman from the West stated yesterday that the country between Houston and Oxford was full of straggling troops, who openly declared that they had abandoned the army and never designed to return until they were placed under officers fit to command them.

The present alarming crisis in this State, so far from arousing the people, seems to have sunk them in listless despondency. The spirit of enlistment is thrice dead. Enthusiasm has expired to a cold pile of damp ashes. Defeats, retreats, sufferings, dangers, magnified by spiritless helplessness and an unchangeable conviction that our army is in the hands of ignorant and feeble commanders, are rapidly producing a sense of settled despair, from which, if not speedily dissipated by some "bright event or happy change," the most disastrous consequences may be apprehended.

I imagine but one event that could awaken from its waning spark the enthusiastic hopes and energy of Mississippians. Plant your own foot upon our soil, unfurl your banner at the head of the army, tell your own people that you have come to share with them the perils of this dark hour, and appeal to every Mississippian who is not "so base that would be a bondman" to rally to your side in rolling back the insolent foe who invades our homes, and I believe a shout would welcome your presence and a multitude respond to your appeal that would make the invader quail before the uproar of such a popular tempest. If ever your presence was needed as a last refuge from an "Iliad of woes" this is the hour. It is not a point to be argued. It may be you would admit Pemberton to be even an abler general than yourself. All such suggestions may be truth, but it does not then change the fiction, as available as fact to the popular sentiment, that you can save us or help us save ourselves from the dread evils now so imminently pending.

If those evils, so threateningly near, can be averted by your presence I need not pause to imagine and reply to objections based upon your required presence at Richmond as President of the Republic. That can, may, must be obviated. There is a multitude of thoughts which arise in my mind by which I could enforce the step I suggest, but they will be more than compassed by your own reflections give them but ample range. Its contemplation makes me feel eloquent, but I am conscious my ardor and fervency would appear but "dribbled chilliness reflected through the inky portraiture of cold white paper." "Think on these things."

A vast amount of commissary stores are reported to have been destroyed at Abbeville. If so, God only knows where the sustenance of the army is to be obtained. Our State is now barely able to feed itself. In fact, want is now severely felt in certain portions. Even in this rich and usually abundant section everything is scarce; small, lean pork is 20 cents, and but little to sell at that.

Why is it the conscript acts are so inefficiently enforced? So far as I could learn in the course of my travels, conscription is a mere farce. Two months had elapsed since the enemy evacuated Northern Alabama and yet no enrolling officer had been there. Crowds of men subject to duty are everywhere—on cars, boats, in the streets, stores, &c.; but the subject of their conscription seems not to have entered their heads. The enrolling officers, now as important as President, so far as I see or hear, are young men utterly unfit for that sacred, stern duty, whom nobody fears, for whom nobody cares, and who exercise their discretion as to exemptions with unblushing partiality and indifference. I believe the enforcement of the act in this State and Alabama, where I have been, to be an utter failure. Instead of being, as it ought to be, a measure that saved the country, it threatens to be the cause of its subjugation. It arrested all volunteering, &c., and assumed by force the augmentation of the army, and now failing to do so our "last end is worse than the first." I had a talk with Governor Shorter, of Alabama, upon the subject. He gives an account of the correspondence between Mr. Randolph and himself, which left the matter in confusion, and he admits the enforcement of the act in Alabama is a humbug and farce. Surely the most stern, sober, substantial men should be selected for enrolling officers. If not enforced, as they ought to be, with iron and unrelenting firmness, our cause is lost. You cannot imagine the open, bold, unblushing attempts to avoid getting in and to keep out of the army. All shame has fled and no subterfuge is pretended, but a reckless confession of an unwillingness to go or to remain. All that gave attractive coloring to the soldier's life has now faded into "cold, gray shadow" with nine tenths of the army, and if permitted, in my opinion, would dissolve tomorrow, heedless of the future. Let an iron band be welded around it; for the pressure, take my word for it, is nearly overwhelming. There are many plausible reasons for this desire to get away which I need not detail. A rigorous enforcement of the conscription would tend to allay this spirit of discontent. Reorganize the whole system, and let popular attention be started and attracted by the prominent, rich, and influential men being swept into the ranks.

Never did a law meet with more universal odium than the exemption of slave-owners. Its injustice, gross injustice, is denounced even by men whose position enables them to take advantage of its privileges. Its influence upon the poor is most calamitous, and has awakened a spirit and elicited a discussion of which we may safely predicate the most unfortunate results. I believe such a provision to be unnecessary, inexpedient, and unjust. I labored to defeat it and predicted the consequences of its enactment. It has aroused a spirit of rebellion in some places, I am informed, and bodies of men have banded together to resist; whilst in the army it is said it only needs some daring man to raise the standard to develop a revolt. As I opposed the provision violently, predicted the consequences, and believe they have occurred, I hope you will satisfy yourself of the truth with reference to the recommendations of your message. I shall offer a bill to repeal it the first day of the session.

I am satisfied that the whole policy of admitting substitutes is wrong.

The reasons I need not detail. Let me, however, suggest one. In case of large pay it causes a certain class of men to seek exemption on their own account, straining to reach beyond the age, to be regarded as mechanics, &c. Again, it causes men who are liable to be ever on the search to find some man to take their place, and therefore never become imbued with the spirit of the soldier nor buckle on the harness for regular duty. A bill nearly abolishing the whole system did pass the Senate but was lost in the House by having been foolishly and unconstitutionally linked with another measure. I shall offer to abolish it *in toto*, and wish you could give it the benefit of your recommendation.

How is it that such numbers of paroled men are traveling all over the country, to their homes and otherwise? Not a tithe of them will ever again be heard of. Mere general orders that they shall report at some place amount to nothing. If permitted to scatter at all, orders never reach them; if published in a few smutted lines in small type in the corner of a newspaper, a reading man may read the sheet and never see the order. But not even the paper ever falls into the hands of one in a thousand for whom it was intended; and when once sheltered in the coves and mountains of the country or lost in the general population they are gone forever. A man has but to say he is a paroled soldier and the question is settled. Paroled men ought never to be permitted to go at large, if I may use the term. Each army ought to have a camp or place where they are required to report, and no such soldier be permitted to travel without arrest, except in going to such camp. I don't know exactly how the remedy is to be applied, but I assure you the evil is a great one. Give it your attention.

There was a most important financial measure passed unanimously by the Senate last session, which I had supposed also passed the House, but certain facts have suggested a doubt. It proposed to the States to issue their bonds, sell them for Confederate notes, and to invest the notes so obtained in Confederate bonds. It is the most safe, certain, and prompt means of retiring a portion of our circulation that has been suggested. I have never heard it submitted to an intelligent mind that did not at once heartily approve it. If properly pressed upon and explained to the respective Legislatures I am satisfied the scheme would be adopted. The Legislature was in session in Montgomery, and I inquired whether the measure had been brought to its attention by the members from Alabama. I was informed that it had not nor was any member advised of the existence of such a law. Governor Shorter informed me he had received no communication from yourself on the subject. The Governors of Georgia and North Carolina make no reference to such a law, and I must therefore suppose the act did not pass. Did it or not? Advise me by telegraph at Jackson. The Assembly convenes on the 17th, and I desire to be there.

The Alabama Legislature passed an act declaring militia officers liable to conscription under the Confederate laws. I urged the passage of a similar act in relation to justices of the peace, &c. Several leading men agreed to try and do so, but I am not informed as to the result. Ought not every State to pass such an act?

The number and character of men scattered through the country and army, and in some way connected with it, but without guns in their hands, is a subject of severe criticism and of loud complaint. Young men in groups are "hangers-on" around every officer of any rank, doing nothing but exciting discontent among the working soldiery, whilst every sort of office, great and small, is filled with such vermin. It seems as if nine tenths of the youngsters of the land whose relatives are conspicuous in society, wealthy, or influential obtain some safe perch where they can doze with their heads under their wings. Partiality, favoritism, perhaps bribery and corruption, sustain this acknowledged evil. It exists at least to an enormous extent, and should be dug up and cast out by the roots.

Again, why cannot men over forty-five act as teamsters, wagon guard, &c., and other details, instead of taking hundreds of younger soldiers from the ranks and thus weakening the line?

But I am extending this letter too far. May God have you in his holy keeping.

Your friend,

JAMES PHELAN.

P. S.—I wrote you from Montgomery asking the appointment of Judge Sale as an army judge. I hope you received it and will appoint him.

SPECIAL ORDERS, }   HDQRS. DEPT. OF MISS. AND EAST LA.,
No. —.   *Grenada, December 9,* 1862.

I. During the temporary absence of the lieutenant-general command-ing the immediate command of the Army of Mississippi devolves upon Maj. Gen. Earl Van Dorn, who will also retain that of the First Corps.

II. Capt. R. W. Memminger, assistant adjutant-general, will remain in charge of the duties of the assistant adjutant-general's office con-nected with the army, and all official communications will be addressed accordingly.

By order of Lieutenant-General Pemberton:

R. W. MEMMINGER,
Assistant Adjutant-General.

VICKSBURG, MISS., *December* 10, 1862.

Maj. Gen. MARTIN L. SMITH,
    Commanding, &c., Vicksburg:

DEAR SIR: In accordance with your instructions I proceeded yester-day to the headquarters of the forces on the Yazoo to make arrange-ments for the establishment of a depot for commissary stores there for the troops, and to appoint a post commissary for the accumulation of a sufficient amount to prevent suffering in case the communications be-tween here and there were cut off by the enemy.

I consulted with Col. Edward Higgins, senior officer in command, and also with Colonel Withers, of the First Mississippi Artillery, and we have agreed it would be best to appoint a commissary at once and to have a sufficient supply of provisions to last the command there thirty days in advance. In order to secure all the corn, pease, and such other necessary articles of subsistence as can be had from the country above there, and satisfy planters that they will not only find a market for their produce by bringing it there but that they will be safe in doing so, I ordered the construction of a flat-boat and purchased one other already completed for the establishment of a Government ferry at a point on the Yazoo River very near or at Haines' Bluff, where it will be entirely out of the range of fire in the event of an engagement on the river below the raft. I also ordered the construction of such rough log houses as may be necessary, convenient to the command, for storage of heavy articles, such as sugar, bacon, rice, and molasses, and have secured the use of such houses on the place of Mr. Ben. Roach as are necessary for storage of such articles as will be better to have kept there. I also made arrangements with him to grind corn and furnish a sufficient amount of meal for all the troops. He also agrees to furnish pasturage for 150 to 200 head of beeves. He will act as a Government agent under the post commissary to assist in purchasing and storing such supplies as can be had near and above the Yazoo forces, and thus avoid the necessity for transporting them by land from this place.

Very respectfully, your obedient servant,

T. B. REED,
Major and Commissary of Subsistence.

JACKSON, *December 10, 1862.*
Major-General VAN DORN, *Grenada :*

Send a courier to Major Blythe and tell him to destroy all the cotton between the Tallahatchie and Coldwater and all other points accessible.

J. R. WADDY,
Assistant Adjutant-General.

RICHMOND, *December 11, 1862.*
General T. H. HOLMES, *Little Rock, Ark. :*

Your second dispatch of 8th received. You were telegraphed yesterday, in answer to your dispatch of 5th, in which you were told you must exercise your judgment in the matter; that it is impossible at this distance to judge of your necessities, but that if you could give aid it was hoped you would do so.

S. COOPER,
Adjutant and Inspector-General

JACKSON, *December 11, 1862.*
Maj. Gen. MARTIN L. SMITH, *Vicksburg :*

I have .3,000 to re-enforce Vicksburg, if necessary, but prefer keeping them here until you are seriously threatened.

J. C. PEMBERTON,
Lieutenant-General, Commanding.

VICKSBURG, *December 11, 1862.*
Lieutenant-General PEMBERTON :

I do not seriously apprehend an attack, but, having re-enforced the position at Snyder's Mill, would like another regiment.

M. L. SMITH,
Major-General.

HDQRS. DEPT. OF MISSISSIPPI AND EAST LOUISIANA,
Jackson, December 11, 1862.
Maj. Gen. MARTIN L. SMITH,
  Commanding Second Military District:

GENERAL: In answer to inquiry of this date I am instructed by the lieutenant-general commanding to inform you that there is a brigade of troops at this point which will be sent you in an emergency.

I am, general, very respectfully,

J. R. WADDY,
Assistant Adjutant-General.

CIRCULAR.]   HDQRS. DEPT. OF MISS. AND E. LA.,
                          Jackson, Miss., December 12, 1862.

The necessities of this army and the abuses occasioned by speculators render it necessary that no corn or fodder shall be taken by private parties beyond the limits of this department.

The necessity for prompt and ample transportation to move the large quantity of Government forage now being purchased requires that no corn or fodder belonging to private parties be transported over any of the railroads in this department until otherwise ordered from these headquarters.

By order of Lieut. Gen. J. C. Pemberton:

J. R. WADDY,
Assistant Adjutant-General.

SPECIAL ORDERS, } HDQRS. 2D CORPS, DEPT. OF MISS. AND E. LA.,
  No. 82.   }   *Grenada, Miss., December* 14, 1862.

I. The major-general commanding has learned with very profound regret that the troops of Green's brigade are greatly disaffected by reason of their being kept upon this side of the Mississippi River, and particularly by the detention in the service beyond their original term of enlistment. He has been informed that there is danger that some of them may under the impulse of this disaffection (which has been artfully intensified by designing men) do acts which will not only bring disgrace upon themselves and their families but upon their comrades and their State, and which may bring disaster and ruin upon the cause for which they have done and suffered so much. He therefore asks them to listen to a few words of counsel and advice.

He admits they have much seeming cause to be discontented. They were, most of them, enlisted under his assurance that they would not be brought away from Missouri, but would be permitted to fight there for the independence of their own State and for the defense or the recovery of their own homes. He believes that without that assurance they would have preferred to fight, as they had theretofore fought, an unpaid soldiery under that flag of Missouri, beneath whose folds they had never suffered defeat, but under which they had won victories which will never be forgotten so long as valor and patriotism shall be honored among men. He gave that assurance in perfect good faith, believing then, as he believes now, that he was authorized to give it. The men who had enlisted under that assurance were nevertheless immediately transferred to this side of the Mississippi River, far away from their invaded homes and their hapless families, and they had hardly been brought hither before they were impressed as it were into the service beyond the period of their original and voluntary enlistment.

He admits that these facts have given them too much seeming cause to believe that the Government has designedly entrapped them into its service: and artful men have, he has been told, used these facts to convince them that they have been wronged and outraged by it, and that they ought to resist its attempts to hold them in its service.

If the major-general commanding believed this, and that the Government had acted thus basely, he would place himself at your head and lead you back to the State of your devotion and his love, and no obstacle should prevent him. But, soldiers, he does not believe it. The Government may have erred; it has not willfully or intentionally wronged you.

The major-general commanding has never ceased to urge your transfer back to the Trans-Mississippi Department. He has never since this war begun lost sight of the smoke of your camps but once, and then he left you reluctantly to go to Richmond in order to entreat the President to send you and him back to Missouri to battle there for the Confederacy. He has recently forwarded other urgent entreaties to the same effect and one of his staff is even now in Richmond awaiting the President's answer to them, and he has been informed that the President says that you shall be sent back to Missouri as soon as you can be spared from this place. Await his answer with that patient forbearance which becomes the good citizen as well as the brave soldier.

The major-general commanding has carefully examined the laws relating to this subject, and he thinks that there can be no doubt that the terms of enlistment of all the Missouri troops in this corps between the ages of eighteen and forty years have been extended by the provisions of those acts to three years from their date of enlistment in the Confederate service, if the war shall last so long.

The law of April 16 says in so many words that " all the persons aforesaid (that is to say, all white men who are residents of the Confederate States between the ages of eighteen and thirty-five years) who are now in the armies of the Confederacy, and whose term of service will expire before the end of the war, shall be continued in the service for three years from the date of their original enlistment, unless the war shall have been sooner ended," and no subsequent act in his opinion changes that provision except to extend the age to forty years.

This may and doubtless does seem hard to you, but it is a hardship which bears upon the citizens of every State alike, and surely you, who have shown yourselves to be so brave and patriotic, will not claim exemption from a law which has been manfully submitted to by the citizens of every State in the Confederacy.

Soldiers of Missouri! be patient; be, as you have heretofore been, long-suffering and obedient. Remember what you owe, not only to yourselves and to your families but to the memory of the brave comrades who have already fallen in this death struggle. Remember that they have died that you may be free.

You have by your exalted patriotism and your glorious services not only won for yourselves the respect of the world and the love of the Southern people, but you have made the name of Missouri honored wherever the history of your deeds has been told. Throw not away by an act of cowardly desertion all that you have so hardly and so gloriously won, and bring not disgrace upon the name which you have made so honored just at the day and perhaps at the hour when you may be reaching the wished-for goal of all your struggles and all your hopes.

Remember that you are the inheritors and should be the defenders of the honors and glories which cluster about the old State Guard. Hold the old banner still aloft and trail it not home in disgrace.

No past services, however glorious, can save from dishonor him who meanly deserts his country and his comrades in the hour of danger nor shield his wife and children from the shame and ignominy which cling ever after to the deserter's family. But if there be among you one cowardly enough to desert let him consider the difficulties which obstruct his path and remember the fate which awaits him. From that fate the major-general commanding cannot save him if he would.

Be then patient for awhile. Every effort is being made to accomplish your wishes and to take you back to your homes. Thwart not those efforts by mutinous behavior or dastardly desertion.

The major-general commanding claims the right to speak to you plainly. He has never deceived you. He has never hesitated to share your every discomfort and your every danger. He might at any time have gone back to Missouri to command a new army had he been willing to part from you. He might go there to-morrow if he would consent to leave you; but he will never abandon the brave soldiers and long-suffering men whom he has led from the beginning, who have always followed him so nobly, and who have won for him all the honor and glory which a partial people has lavished upon him. He asks that you will continue to stand by him as he has stood by you and as he will stand by you to the end.

By order of Major-General Price:

THOS. L. SNEAD,
Assistant Adjutant-General.

SPECIAL ORDERS, }   HEADQUARTERS DEPARTMENT No. 2,
No. 62.   }   *Murfreesborough, Tenn., December* 14, 1862.

*   *   *   *   *   *   *

II. Maj. Gen. Franklin Gardner is relieved from duty with Army of the Tennessee, and will proceed to Jackson, Miss., and report to Lieutenant-General Pemberton for duty.

III. Brigadier-General Maxey is relieved from duty with Army of the Tennessee, and will proceed to Jackson, Miss., and report to Lieutenant-General Pemberton for duty.

*   *   *   *   *   *   *

By command of General Bragg:

GEO. G. GARNER,
Assistant Adjutant-General.

COLUMBUS, *December* 15, 1862.

Captain HOOE:
Copy of dispatch received:

OKOLONA, *December* 15, 1862.

To Colonel ADAMS:

I will retire as I am forced back, destroying the railroad and telegraph. A portion of my cavalry is now arriving at Verona. The Federal force immediately in front of us is 2,500, infantry, cavalry, and artillery. Colonel Roddey will watch any movement upon Columbus eastward of railroad.

C. R. BARTEAU,
Colonel.

JOHN ADAMS.

List of stores in Vicksburg, Miss., December 15, 1862.

	Rations.
Bacon	7,570
Lard	1,560
Flour	1,098
Meal	133,301
Corn	168,660
Rice	281,000
Pease	2,033,906
Sugar	485,833
Molasses	166,000
Vinegar	12,000
Soap	3,750
Salt	1,108,608

DECEMBER 16, 1862—3.30 p. m.

Lieutenant-General PEMBERTON, *Grenada:*

The following telegram just received:

COLUMBUS, *December 16, 1862.*

Captain HOOE:

Enemy fired on railroad train 5 miles above Okolona. Part of Barteau's command is perhaps cut off at Verona, 2 miles above Okolona. Enemy reported in two columns, one from Corinth, other from Oxford; column from Corinth 3,000 strong. No ammunition here at arsenal; must have 20,000 rounds musket and shot-gun ammunition; also an additional force from Jackson or some point; cannot hold this place against 5,000 of enemy. My effective force only about 600 strong. All machinery is still at arsenal. Large amount of quartermaster and commissary stores here.

JOHN ADAMS,
Colonel, C. S. Army, Commanding.

I am about commencing a movement of troops from this point.

DANIEL RUGGLES,
Brigadier-General.

JACKSON, *December 16, 1862.*

Lieutenant-General PEMBERTON, *Grenada:*

General Smith says does not think there is danger of an immediate attack there. Have ordered Vaughn's brigade to you and Colonel Coleman's regiment to Columbus. They will leave early in the morning.

J. R. WADDY,
Assistant Adjutant-General.

GENERAL ORDERS, }   HDQRS. DEPT. OF MISS. AND EAST LA.,
     No. 19.   }   *Jackson, Miss., December 16, 1862.*

Maj. T. Johnson, Provisional Army of the Confederate States, is hereby assigned to duty as chief commissary of Department of Mississippi and East Louisiana, relieving Maj. R. H. Cuney, commanding, of said duty. Maj. R. H. Cuney will turn over to Maj. T. Johnson all funds, orders, both written and verbal, and papers belonging to said department, also giving him all necessary information relating to the department. Major Johnson will take most active measures in supplying the army at Grenada and troops of this department with the necessary commissary stores and in carrying out such instructions as have been given to Maj. R. H. Cuney as to collecting, both at Vicksburg and Port Hudson, subsistence stores for 10,000 men for five months. Maj. R. H. Cuney will report to Maj. T. Johnson how far this has been done and what measures have been taken to accomplish it. Maj. T. Johnson will make requisition on Colonel Broadwell for funds for commissary department, to whom the funds have been turned over, instead of the chief commissary of department. Maj. T. Johnson will learn from Colonel Broadwell and Major Dameron what supplies they have for the department and the measures taken to further provide for the same.

By order of Lieutenant-General Pemberton:

J. R. WADDY,
Assistant Adjutant-General.

MONTGOMERY, ALA., *December* 17, 1862.

General BRAGG, *Murfreesborough:*

General Pemberton reports enemy on railroad to Columbus. Hurry your cavalry operations and hasten the troops this way.

J. E. JOHNSTON.

GRENADA, MISS., *December* 17, 1862.

Brigadier-General RUGGLES:

Have all sick removed off line of railroad above Meridian and all stores brought down that transportation can be got for. It is certain that the enemy move with infantry in considerable force; railroad bridges must be destroyed.

J. C. PEMBERTON,
Lieutenant-General, Commanding.

COLUMBUS, *December* 17, 1862.

General RUGGLES:

Enemy's cavalry destroyed depot at Okolona; fear Barteau's cavalry are not resisting their advance. Federal cavalry reported about 400; Barteau has perhaps 800. Please order Barteau to oppose enemy, or there is nothing to prevent his reaching Meridian. Roddey would be of service on Mobile and Ohio Railroad if he could be ordered there.

JOHN ADAMS,
Colonel, Commanding.

COLUMBUS, *December* 17, 1862.

General RUGGLES:

Engine Mobile and Ohio Railroad stolen from West Point 8 o'clock to-night. Barteau continues to fall back; is near West Point now. Cannot you send the brigade to save Artesia? Otherwise we cannot get off the stores.

JOHN ADAMS.

JACKSON, *December* 17, 1862.

General PEMBERTON, *Grenada:*
  The following telegram just received:

COLUMBUS, *December* 17, 1862.

Captain HOOE:
  Copy of dispatch:

" EGYPT, 16*th*.

"Colonel ADAMS:
  "Force of 300 which burned Shannon Depot was from Oxford and has returned. Force stationary at Tupelo, 2,500 infantry, nine pieces of artillery, and some cavalry; force at Pontotoc probably 1,000 cavalry, with artillery, not advancing, but ravaging country. I do not think their demonstration is now threatening to Columbus, though such may have been their original intention. I retreated to this place last night, the better to counteract any possible movement by way of Fulton and Aberdeen, and also apprehending attack from Pontotoc. I need more cavalry.
                "BARTEAU,
                      "*Colonel, &c.*"

                    JOHN ADAMS,
                        Colonel, &c.

                DANIEL RUGGLES.

COLUMBUS, *December* 17, 1862.

Captain HOOE:
  Copy of dispatch from Barteau forwarded; consider Barteau more reliable; hope to hear from him to-morrow. Arsenal machinery taken down and work stopped. Enemy not nearer than Okolona. All prepared for defense.

                JOHN ADAMS,
                    Colonel, &c.

JACKSON, MISS., *December* 17, 1862.

Brigadier-General MACKALL, *Mobile, Ala.:*
  I send you copy of telegram just received:

COLUMBUS, *December* 17, 1862.

Enemy have burned Okolona; their cavalry reported near West Point. Enemy advancing in direction of Aberdeen.

                JOHN ADAMS.

  I have sent Colonel Coleman's regiment to Columbus; no more troops to send. Can you send a force to protect the railroad above Columbus?

                DANIEL RUGGLES,
                    Brigadier-General.

SPECIAL ORDERS, }   HDQRS. ARMY OF THE MISSISSIPPI,
  No. 7.   }   *Grenada, December* 17, 1862.
  I. The brigade of Brigadier-General Vaughn, just arrived at this point, is assigned to the command of Major-General Maury, Second Corps, and will report accordingly.

  *   *   *   *   *   *   *

  By order of Lieutenant-General Pemberton:

                R. W. MEMMINGER,
                    Assistant Adjutant-General.

HDQRS. SUB. DEPT., 2D DIST., DEPT. OF MISS. AND E. LA.,
Vicksburg, Miss., December 19, 1862.

Maj. R. H. CUNEY,
  Chief of Subsistence, Jackson, Miss. :

DEAR SIR : It is impossible for me to carry out the orders of the generals commanding the department and district to lay in supplies for six months, according to my letters to you of the 2d and 4th instant, without assistance from you, as I must rely on your post for some of the stores needed. I must again call your attention to the necessity of sending them forward as soon as possible. Of the stores named that will be required here, in my letters alluded to, I have only received notice of shipments of some 500 small sacks salt and 200 tierces rice, only a small portion of which have yet been received. Keep me fully advised of the stores to be sent here and what I can rely on. This matter is very important, and if there is to be any failure to comply with orders the responsibility must attach where it properly belongs.

I telegraphed for funds this morning. Please forward at once.

Very respectfully,

T. B. REED,
Major and Commissary of Subsistence.

VICKSBURG, *December* 21, 1862.

Major-General LORING, *Grenada, Miss. :*

Direct General Price to put himself and corps in readiness to move at once to the defense of Vicksburg. You will be notified by telegram when to move.

J. C. PEMBERTON,
Lieutenant-General, Commanding.

SPECIAL ORDERS, }   HEADQUARTERS DEPARTMENT No. 2,
  No. 66.   }   *Murfreesborough, Tenn., December* 18, 1862.

I. Stevenson's division, Smith's corps, will immediately move to Chattanooga, thence to Mississippi, via Mobile, and report to Lieutenant-General Pemberton.

*   *   *   *   *   *   *

By command of General Bragg :

GEO. G. GARNER,
Assistant Adjutant-General.

JACKSON, MISS., *December* 19, 1862.

Maj. Gen. MARTIN L. SMITH, *Vicksburg :*

President Davis and myself leave here by train this evening for Vicksburg with six staff officers.

J. E. JOHNSTON.

VICKSBURG, MISS., *December* 22, 1862.

Mr. PRESIDENT: From such information as I have been able to obtain I think that we shall require, to hold this department and the Mississippi River, an active army of about 40,000 men to oppose the troops of Grant and Banks, and garrisons at Vicksburg and Port Hudson capable of holding those places against combined attacks until succored by the active army.

Major-General Smith has about 5,900 artillery and infantry for duty to defend a line of 10 miles, exclusive of the position of Snyder's Mill, which requires three of his eight regiments. Should the enemy attack by land as well as by water, which is highly probable—almost certain—we would require at least eight more regiments of 500 or 600 men each.

I have not seen Port Hudson, but a map of the ground gives me the opinion that it requires a garrison as strong as that necessary here. It now amounts to about 5,500 of all arms, so that an addition of as many more will be required there, in all 11,000 or 12,000 men.

For the active force we have now 21,000 men near the Yalabusha. About 9,000 have been ordered to this department from Lieutenant-General Smith, and it is supposed that an equal force is on its way from Arkansas.

No more troops can be taken from General Bragg without the danger of enabling Rosecrans to move into Virginia or to re-enforce Grant. Our great object is to hold the Mississippi. The country beyond the river is as much interested in that object as this, and the loss to us of the Mississippi involves that of the country beyond it. The 8,000 or 10,000 men which are essential to safety ought therefore, I respectfully suggest, to be taken from Arkansas, to return after the crisis in this department.

I firmly believe, however, that our true system of warfare would be to concentrate the forces of the two departments on this side of the Mississippi, beat the enemy here, and then reconquer the country beyond it which he might have gained in the mean time.

I respectfully ask Your Excellency's attention to the accompanying letter* of Major-General Smith, in relation to the inadequacy of the garrison of Vicksburg, begging you to take his estimate of the force needed instead of mine, as his is based upon accurate calculation.†

Most respectfully, your obedient servant,

J. E. JOHNSTON,
General.

GENERAL ORDERS, }   HDQRS. ARMY OF THE MISSISSIPPI,
No. 7.   }   *Grenada, Miss., December 22, 1862.*

Hereafter the corps commanders will give their special attention to the protection of all private property from any injury or depredation by their commands, and they will charge their inspectors-general with and see to their making daily investigation for such cases, and on their occurrence they will promptly report the commanding officer of the offenders to this office, and will notify the proper paymaster that such company, battalion, squadron, or regiment as the said offenders may belong to will not be paid until the cost of the injury inflicted be subtracted from the amount due the same.

Great responsibility rests with the commanders of troops of this army in their co-operation in carrying out the intent of the above, lest disgrace be brought upon this command.

By order of Lieutenant-General Pemberton:

J. C. TAYLOR,
Aide-de-Camp and Acting Assistant Adjutant-General.

---

* Not found.
† Copy was referred by Mr. Davis to General Holmes. See Holmes to Johnston December 29, 1862, p. 810.

JACKSON, MISS., *December* 23, 1862.

Hon. JAMES A. SEDDON:

There is immediate and urgent necessity for heavy guns and long-range field pieces at Vicksburg.

JEFFERSON DAVIS.

VICKSBURG, MISS., *December* 23, 1862.

Major-General SMITH,
   Commanding, &c., Vicksburg:

DEAR SIR: Maj. Theodore Johnson, commissary of subsistence at Jackson, has called on me to ship him 20,000 bushels corn as soon as possible, for the use of the troops above and below that place; he desires as much of this as can be spared in meal. He says he can have the corn ground at Jackson if the meal cannot be sent. Under your order I am now using every effort to accumulate five months' supplies at this post. which I construe to mean that five months' supplies must be stored here to rely upon and render the troops independent entirely of any outside resources after hostilities shall have commenced, and that there must be a sufficient supply for the daily current demands of the troops independent of the amount stored.

Under date of November 20, 1862, Lieutenant-General Pemberton orders that rations be kept on hand for 10,000 men for five months; this order was sent me through Maj. John G. Devereux, who indorsed on it, "The 10,000 men are additional to those now here," as the number of men at that time was about 7,500. I at once made an estimate of the rations that would be required for 10,000 more men, allowing for one month's supplies additional, which would be consumed from day to day previous to commencement of hostilities; thus I estimate for at least 15,000 men for six months. Major Johnson informs me that the orders are to provide for 10,000 men for five months, and for that reason wants to get any surplus we may have now or may yet receive. Another difficulty in the way of answering his demand is the scarcity of sacks. We now need 10,000 more than we have, and if the few we have are sent away from the post it may be several weeks before we can again secure the use of them. He sent a telegram on yesterday morning ordering 200 bushels of salt to be shipped to the commissary at Port Hudson. We have not much more than two months' supply on hand, and as we will need much of this article in order to put up beef and pork I will wait orders from you before doing anything in the premises. We have secured by extreme exertion a small amount of bacon and flour, and as these articles (as well as salt) are scarce, and if sent from here I might not be able to replace them, I would like to receive your instructions in regard to my course when I may be called on to ship them to other places. Please inform me on all these points, and what answer I shall make to Major Johnson especially in regard to the corn and salt.

I inclose statement of stores on hand, besides which we have about 30,000 bushels of corn, which are now on the levee and in machine-shops. You can see by comparing these items with inclosed estimate of stores required what our condition is, and what can be sent away.

Very respectfully, your obedient servant,

T. B. REED.

Please return inclosed statements, as I need them for reference.

SPECIAL ORDERS }   HDQRS. ARMY OF THE MISSISSIPPI,
    No. 12.   }   *Grenada, Miss., December 23, 1862.*

I. Brigadier-General Vaughn's brigade is relieved from duty with General Maury's division, and will proceed with all dispatch to Vicksburg, Miss., and report to Major-General Smith. Quartermasters will furnish the necessary transportation.

 * * * * * * *

By order of Lieutenant-General Pemberton:
        R. W. MEMMINGER,
         Assistant Adjutant-General.

    HEADQUARTERS ARMY OF THE MISSISSIPPI,
       Grenada, December 24, 1862.
Maj. Gen. STERLING PRICE,
 Commanding Second Corps:

GENERAL: The lieutenant-general commanding directs that you immediately order your command to take position by divisions at points most convenient along the line of fortifications.

I am, respectfully, your obedient servant,
        R. W. MEMMINGER,
         Assistant Adjutant-General.

      HEADQUARTERS REGIMENT,
     Deer Creek, December 24, 1862.
Lieut. Gen. J. C. PEMBERTON,
 Comdg. Dept. of Mississippi and East Louisiana, Grenada:

GENERAL: Forty-five of the enemy's transports, with troops, and ten gunboats passed Friar's Point on the 22d instant. Of this number twenty-four transports and two gunboats had passed Melrose Landing, 5 miles below Prentiss, at 12 m. yesterday, 23d instant. They have not yet reached Greenville, but may be expected early this morning.

I have sent this information to Major-General Smith, at Vicksburg, and he should be in possession of it to-day.

In obedience to your order I have stationed a picket guard at Skipwith's Landing, with orders to report to you promptly any landing of the enemy at that point.

Under the orders of General Smith, of 20th November, I shall march my command in the direction of Vicksburg without delay. Should the enemy attempt to pass across from Skipwith's Landing to the Yazoo I will harass him as much as I can.

Your order of 22d in reference to conscripts in this district was received last evening.

I remain, general, most respectfully, your obedient servant,
        WIRT ADAMS,
      Colonel, Commanding Cavalry.

      VICKSBURG, *December 25, 1862—2. a. m.*
General PEMBERTON:

Sixty-four of enemy's boats have passed Lake Providence to-night. Send at once what re-enforcements you intend.
         M. L. SMITH.

DE SOTO, *December* 25, 1862.

General PEMBERTON:

Sixty-four boats passed Transylvania, which is 65 miles above here, at 11 o'clock last night. They ran with lights, at a rate of 18 miles an hour. There are now eighty-one boats between this and Lake Providence.

PHILLIP FALL,
Operator.

TALLULAH, *December* 25, 1862.

General SMITH:

I have about 550 men. The pickets report 6,000 on shore between Milliken's Bend and Morancy's. They came down at 12 o'clock last night, a moment after I had left the pickets.

PARGOUD,
Colonel.

GRENADA, MISS., *December* 25, 1862.

Maj. Gen. MARTIN L. SMITH:

A brigade left here night before last. Another will be sent as soon as transportation can be had.

J. E. JOHNSTON,
General.

VICKSBURG, *December* 25, 1862.

Major-General MAURY, *Vaughan's Station, Miss.:*

Leave the regiments of Hébert's brigade, now at Vaughan's, there. Come on to Vicksburg with the rest of your division as quickly as possible.

J. C. PEMBERTON,
Lieutenant-General, Commanding.

HEADQUARTERS CAVALRY OUTPOST,
December 25, 1862.

Maj. Gen. W. W. LORING, *Commanding First Corps, &c.:*

GENERAL: My scouts have just returned, and report the enemy as having crossed Yocona River with their whole force. They are moving off on all the roads leading north and quite a large force moving west. The scouts passed through all their encampments on this side of the river and represent them as being very extensive. Their route was up through Paris and returned through Water Valley.

I am, general, very respectfully, your obedient servant,

H. R. WITHERS,
Lieutenant-Colonel, Commanding Cavalry.

[Indorsement.]

HEADQUARTERS,
Grenada, December 25, 1862.

Respectfully forwarded. Statement of Colonel Withers that the enemy are still falling back. Scouts report that the enemy have burned the railroad bridge across the Yocona.

W. W. LORING,
Major-General, Commanding.

VICKSBURG, MISS., *December* 25, 1862.

Maj. T. B. REED,
  Commissary of Subsistence, Second District:

MAJOR: I am informed by Mr. G. Messinger, who is interested in that section of country, that on the Sunflower River there is an immense quantity of corn which the planters are anxious to dispose of to the Government. They say that if encouraged they will haul it to the landings during this dry spell of weather, which is not certain to last long, and then as the rise of the river must occur soon it can be boated away. Please give this matter early and special attention.

I am, major, yours, respectfully,

JNO. G. DEVEREUX,
  Major and Assistant Adjutant-General.

VICKSBURG, *December* 26, 1862.

Maj. L. MIMS,
  Chief Quartermaster, Jackson, Miss.:

I have ordered Maury's division to Vaughan's Station. Send transportation for 4,000 troops to Grenada at once; also, if possible, for four field batteries; but do not interfere with transportation from Jackson or Meridian for Vicksburg. Acknowledge.

J. C. PEMBERTON,
  Lieutenant-General, Commanding.

GRENADA, *December* 26, 1862.

Lieutenant-General PEMBERTON:

Aggregate effective strength of General Maury's division as follows: Infantry, 3,726; artillery, 409. Aggregate, 4,135.

W. W. LORING,
  Major-General, Commanding.

VICKSBURG, *December* 26, 1862.

General JOSEPH E. JOHNSTON, *Jackson, Miss.:*

Brig. Gen. S. D. Lee reports enemy landing at Mrs. Lake's, 8 miles above; two regiments, infantry and cavalry.

I have ordered Maury's division at once to Vaughan's Station.

J. C. PEMBERTON,
  Lieutenant-General, Commanding.

VICKSBURG, *December* 26, 1862

Maj. J. R. WADDY,
  Assistant Adjutant-General, Jackson:

Push forward the troops as rapidly as possible. The enemy is landing.

J. C. PEMBERTON,
  Lieutenant-General, Commanding.

JACKSON, MISS., *December* 26, 1862.

Lieutenant-General PEMBERTON, *Vicksburg:*

Would not Canton be a better place than Vaughan's Station?   What force do you report landing?

J. E. JOHNSTON,
General.

VICKSBURG, MISS., *December* 26, 1862.

General JOSEPH E. JOHNSTON, *Jackson:*

I prefer Canton. It has reference to fortifications at Yazoo City to prevent passage of river force at that point. Landed about 3,000 above mouth of river.

J. C. PEMBERTON,
Lieutenant-General, Commanding.

JACKSON, *December* 27, 1862.

Lieutenant-General PEMBERTON:

General Loring reports that enemy burnt Yocona Bridge and has crossed the Tallahatchie.

Memphis papers say seventy transports with troops left Memphis and Helena Sunday and Monday, 12,000 troops to follow from Helena. Where is Adams' regiment? Loring expects to hear more of Grant to-day. If of the same sort we must bring troops southward. Any news from Arkansas?

J. E. JOHNSTON,
General.

VICKSBURG, *December* 27, 1862.

Major WADDY, *Assistant Adjutant-General:*

Seventy-ninth, Eightieth, Eighty-first Tennessee Regiments constitute Vaughn's brigade. Third and Thirtieth consolidated; Tenth and Forty-first consolidated; Fiftieth and Fifty-first Tennessee Regiments and First Battalion constitute Gregg's brigade. Fortieth, Forty-second, Forty-third Georgia Regiments, of Barton's brigade, have arrived; Forty-first and Fifty-first Regiments *en route.*

J. C. PEMBERTON,
Lieutenant-General, Commanding.

VICKSBURG, *December* 27, 1862.
(Received December 27.)

Major WADDY, *Assistant Adjutant-General:*

Send forward all the troops that arrive to-night with full supply of ammunition. They will be wanted in the morning.

J. C. PEMBERTON,
Lieutenant-General, Commanding.

GRENADA, *December* 27 1862.

General PEMBERTON :

The latest scouts inform me that Grant had crossed the Tallahatchie and was thought to be moving to Memphis. The accounts of yesterday said he was going to Corinth. He is no doubt moving away. I expect to hear to-morrow definitely. Our scouts report that the Federals say that Memphis was attacked on the 22d at three different points by cavalry, supposed to be Van Dorn's. No result given except that a large quantity of supplies was destroyed. Seventy transports with troops left Helena and Memphis on Sunday and Monday, 12,000 remaining to follow. Memphis papers say Forrest broke up the track between Humboldt and Carroll Station on the 19th, cutting off Grant's supplies and preventing the trains passing between Jackson and Columbus.

W. W. LORING,
Major-General.

HEADQUARTERS, &C.,
Grenada, December 27, 1862.

Lieut. Gen. J. C. PEMBERTON, *Commanding :*

GENERAL : The most of one brigade of Maury's division, including artillery, left this morning for Vaughan's Station; the remainder will leave to-morrow. Immediately on the receipt of your telegram ordering the division, instructions were at once given for it to leave as soon as transportation could be furnished, with a full supply of ammunition and three days' cooked rations, taking their cooking utensils and leaving their heavy baggage. Their transportation was also ordered by the road, and in order that we might proceed in accordance with your wishes you were telegraphed to know if it was so desired.

Respectfully, your obedient servant,

W. W. LORING,
Major-General, Commanding.

GRENADA, *December* 27, 1862.

Lieutenant-General PEMBERTON :

Two scouts, Lieutenant Coleburn and Captain Forrest, report that a considerable force of the enemy—cavalry, artillery, and infantry—landed at Friar's Point and were last seen near General Alcorn's, on the Yazoo Pass, on the 25th.

W. W. LORING,
Major-General.

HEADQUARTERS, &C.,
Grenada, December 28, 1862.

General STERLING PRICE, *Commanding, &c.:*

GENERAL : I this moment received the inclosed telegram. Be kind enough to give the necessary instructions for the movement when the notification comes.

Very respectfully, your obedient servant,

W. W. LORING,
Major-General, Commanding.

[Inclosure.]

VICKSBURG, *December* 27, 1862.

Major-General LORING:

Direct General Price to put himself and corps in readiness at once to move to the defense of Vicksburg. You will be notified by telegraph when to move.

J. C. PEMBERTON,
Lieutenant-General, Commanding.

VICKSBURG, *December* 28, 1862.

General JOSEPH E. JOHNSTON:

Will you send a special messenger at once for ammunition wherever it can be had; also caps; a great deficiency of both. The men will want Enfield shot.

J. C. PEMBERTON.

JACKSON, MISS., *December* 28, 1862.

Major-General VAN DORN, *Grenada :*

I wish to see you at this place as soon as possible with regard to future cavalry operations.

J. E. JOHNSTON,
General.

JACKSON, *December* 28, 1862.

Lieutenant-General PEMBERTON:

General Van Dorn and command arrived here 4 o'clock this afternoon.

W. W. LORING,
Major-General.

VICKSBURG, *December* 28, 1862.

Maj. L. MIMS,
Chief Quartermaster, Jackson, Miss.:

I have ordered one brigade of Maury's division to move direct to Vicksburg. Make arrangements accordingly. The brigade at Vaughan's Station will remain there for the present.

J. C. PEMBERTON,
Lieutenant-General, Commanding.

PEACH CREEK, PANOLA COUNTY, MISSISSIPPI,
December 29, 1862—9 p. m.

Lieutenant-General PEMBERTON:

Helena and Memphis expedition left for Vicksburg Sunday night and Monday. From 30,000 to 40,000 troops gone down the river. About 12,000 at Helena still, and General Alcorn says they are going to march by mouth of Coldwater. No troops on this side of the river. From good authority I learn that Helena is soon to be evacuated and Fort Curtis dismantled. Yankees report Memphis attacked from three directions on Monday last, 22d instant, by rebel cavalry. They state that we captured a large amount of supplies. Sixteen pickets killed west of Helena yesterday morning, and 25 or 30 wounded and captured.

Expedition down the river took about seventy transports. Yankees from all quarters report a great loss at Fredericksburg—greater than in any former battle. Report reached me this evening that General Grant was falling back toward Memphis. Can't vouch for its truth, for I have not been to see; will go to-morrow.

General Alcorn ought to know the destination of the 12,000 troops, though I doubt their going by mouth of Coldwater on account of bad roads.

Report would have been sent earlier, but those sent on to Helena were arrested and not released until late yesterday evening.

Very respectfully, &c.,

W. M. M. CONNELL,
Second Lieutenant, Henderson's Scouts.

JACKSON, MISS., *December* 29, 1862.

Lieutenant-General PEMBERTON, *Vicksburg:*

Do you want any troops in addition to those ordered? Say in cipher. Write cipher in capital letters.

J. E. JOHNSTON,
General.

JACKSON, MISS., *December* 29, 1862.

Lieutenant-General PEMBERTON, *Vicksburg:*

Did you order General Stevenson to Vicksburg? I intended his troops, except what you have, for reserve. I'll send all you want, however.

J. E. JOHNSTON,
General.

VICKSBURG, *December* 29, 1862.

General JOSEPH E. JOHNSTON, *Jackson, Miss.:*

Yes; I want all the troops I can get. The service in the trenches is exceedingly exhausting to the men. I wish to send some from here to Port Hudson.

J. C. PEMBERTON,
Lieutenant-General, Commanding.

JACKSON, MISS., *December* 29, 1862.

Lieutenant-General PEMBERTON, *Vicksburg:*

Your dispatch just received. It is necessary to send to Vicksburg just the troops you want, not all we have. Can you not estimate the number necessary?

A man just from New Orleans, known to the President, reports Banks' force 3,000; others give it at 8,000. Neither number endangers the place you mention. It is necessary that we act together.

J. E. JOHNSTON,
General.

VICKSBURG, *December* 29, 1862.

General JOSEPH E. JOHNSTON:

The enemy are endeavoring to throw two pontoon bridges across the lake.

J. C. PEMBERTON,
Lieutenant-General, Commanding.

HEADQUARTERS TRANS-MISSISSIPPI DEPARTMENT,
Little Rock, Ark., December 29. 1862.

General JOSEPH E. JOHNSTON,
Commanding Department of the West:

GENERAL: The President has referred to me your letter to him dated at Vicksburg, December 22; also Maj. Gen. M. L. Smith's letter to you of the same date; both in reference to the defenses of Vicksburg. These communications are accompanied by one from the President on the same subject, and expressing the hope that the condition of affairs in this State would justify me in detaching some portion of my forces for the purpose of re-enforcing the garrison of that city.

Fully concurring with all that has been urged as to the great importance of holding Vicksburg, which can scarcely be exaggerated, you can understand how inexpressibly painful it has been to me to have failed, from whatever cause, to render the desired assistance, and how imperative I considered it to retain all my small force for the defense of the valley of the Arkansas. The belief as to my ability to render such assistance I must believe has grown out of very erroneous impressions of my strength, which my repeated reports to the War Department it seems have not been able to correct. At no time have I had more than 22,000 effective men in this State, and several regiments of these were Indians, upon whom no reliance can be placed. This small force, now reduced by an alarming amount of sickness, by desertions and the casualties of battle, to but little over 16,000 men, not including the troops in the fortifications, is my entire dependence to resist largely superior forces of the enemy threatening us in the north, west, and east.

At the time the demand was first made upon me for troops to re-enforce Vicksburg the enemy was moving with a heavy force upon Van Buren and Fort Smith. General Hindman, taking the initiative, had crossed the Boston Mountains to attack him. The forces of the enemy were so superior that it seemed too much to expect a favorable result, and I could not think it justifiable in me to send General McCulloch's division, my only reserve, toward Vicksburg, which it would require nearly a month in reaching, during which time the enemy might be quietly taking possession of the valley of the Arkansas, the key of the department.

Under such circumstances I do not believe that either the President or yourself would have desired me to send away nearly one-half of my entire effective strength could you have known all the circumstances.

General Hindman met the enemy at Prairie Grove and fought them with very favorable results; and I had hoped and confidently expected that, in consequence of his losses in battle and the utter destitution of the northwestern counties of this State of all supplies for supporting his army, the enemy would not make an attempt to advance again this winter. Yesterday, however, I received information from General Hindman that the enemy were advancing in force upon Van Buren, and at noon were within 20 miles of the Arkansas River. General Hindman's whole force, reduced by sickness and casualties to about 10,000 men, is on the south side of the Arkansas River and is therefore safe, but is too weak to make any successful resistance to the enemy, whose forces number about 20,000, and the crisis which I hoped had been deferred at least two months is thus unexpectedly upon us. Under these embarrassing circumstances would it be justifiable to strip this country of its only means of defense, thereby allowing the enemy to overrun the State and win a wavering people from their loyalty to us by the seductive promises of peace and protection, while at the same time it is a matter of extreme doubt whether the troops thus sent away could reach Vicksburg in time, or rather with the almost certainty that they would not do so?

My information from Helena is to the effect that a heavy force of the enemy has passed down the Mississippi on transports, doubtless for the demonstration upon Vicksburg. Corroboratory of this I received a telegram last night from General Blanchard at Monroe, La., informing me of the landing of a large force of the enemy at Milliken's Bend and the destruction of the railroad depot at Delhi and the bridge over Bayou Macon. Thus it seems very certain that any force I can now send from here would not be able to reach Vicksburg, and if at all not before such a re-enforcement would be useless, while such a diversion would enable the enemy to penetrate those portions of the Arkansas Valley where the existence of supplies of subsistence and forage would afford them leisure to overrun the entire State and gradually reduce the people to a dependence upon the Federal Government.

I am, general, very respectfully, your obedient servant,

TH. H. HOLMES,
Lieutenant-General, Commanding Department.

VICKSBURG, MISS., *December* 30, 1862.

General JOSEPH E. JOHNSTON, *Jackson, Miss.:*

In saying, "want all the troops I can get," I mean that if the enemy continues to increase his force, and I have no doubt he will, that all the troops ordered to re-enforce me will be absolutely necessary to insure the safety of Vicksburg and Port Hudson. I cannot entirely abandon Grenada. The heavy rain will relieve the approach from Skipwith's Landing. Have accordingly ordered troops from Vaughan's to Snyder's Mill via Yazoo River, an important position. Relief for men in trenches is necessary; they have been now three days in them. So far we have held all advanced points with very considerable loss to enemy and small to ourselves.

The enemy will strengthen at Baton Rouge. Their strength is 8,000. If necessary, troops can be returned from there. This is the vital point. The enemy is persevering. I desire to work with you.

J. C. PEMBERTON,
Lieutenant-General, Commanding.

JACKSON, MISS., *December* 30, 1862.

General BRAGG, *Murfreesborough, Tenn.:*

Van Dorn has destroyed the depot at Holly Springs. Grant has recrossed the Tallahatchie. I wish to unite Forrest and Roddey with Van Dorn for further operations. Please inform them and tell where they are.

J. E. JOHNSTON,
General.

JACKSON, *December* 30, 1862.

JEFFERSON DAVIS,
    President Confederate States, Mobile :

General Van Dorn thinks the immediate appointment of Cols. W. H. Jackson and F. C. Armstrong as brigadier-generals very important. Brigades are now commanded by incompetent officers. May they be put on duty as such ? About 6,000 muskets were destroyed at Holly Springs with the large depot of ammunition and provision of Grant's army. Prisoners, about 2,000; 1,000 revolvers.

J. E. JOHNSTON,
General.

VAUGHAN'S STATION, *December* 30, 1862.

Lieutenant-General PEMBERTON :

Have just received telegram of this date. Will move on Yazoo City as soon as possible. Have no transportation. Have sent to Captain Brown for wagons. Will telegraph my departure from this place.

LOUIS HÉBERT,
Brigadier-General.

HEADQUARTERS, &C.,
Grenada, December 30, 1862.

Lieut. Gen. J. C. PEMBERTON,
    Commanding, &c. :

GENERAL : I send you the recent reports of scouts. The enemy are at this time on the Tallahatchie ; they do not seem to be moving beyond that river; their scouts are on this side. In addition to the statements heretofore forwarded of scouts from the vicinity of Yazoo Pass, I have the following statement from a Mr. Pearce, who resides 14 miles east of Friar's Point and 18 miles south of General Alcorn's, and vouched for as a reliable man.

He states that he left home on Sunday morning, the 28th; that there were 3,000 of the enemy's cavalry encamped opposite Alcorn's, thence to Barron's place. There were also twelve pieces of artillery, between 500 to 1,000 infantry, at Friar's Point. The Coldwater road is not all blockaded, nor is there any timber felled in the Yazoo Pass. The cavalry and artillery have been camped at Alcorn's since Thursday, 25th. Said they were waiting for the infantry to join them, to move in force.

Respectfully, your obedient servant,

W. W. LORING,
Major-General, Commanding.

VICKSBURG, *December* 31, 1862.

Major-General VAN DORN, *Grenada, Miss. :*

Want 2,000 cavalry to move immediately in the direction of Snyder's Mill. Unless you have information of the enemy's movement toward Grenada, which I do not suppose to be the case, move as rapidly as possible.

J. C. PEMBERTON,
Lieutenant-General, Commanding.

JACKSON, *December* 31, 1862—10.45 a. m.

Lieutenant-General PEMBERTON:

General Johnston thinks I may go home for a few days. Will give directions for expedition at once.

EARL VAN DORN,
Major-General.

JACKSON, *December* 31, 1862.

Lieutenant-General PEMBERTON, *Vicksburg:*

The movement you direct General Van Dorn to make will require, he says, a week, and prevent the use to which you applied it. I intended to add to his command Forrest and Roddey. Would not infantry from Grenada serve your purpose better?

J. E. JOHNSTON,
General.

JACKSON, *December* 31, 1862.

Lieutenant-General PEMBERTON, *Vicksburg:*

I wish Van Dorn, with his cavalry, Forrest's and Roddey's, to prevent Grant's advance. Your order will make that impossible. Will not infantry from Grenada be better? They can join you sooner, and cannot keep back Grant. They are too far for that. Reply quick.

J. E. JOHNSTON,
General.

JACKSON, *December* 31, 1862.

Lieutenant-General PEMBERTON, *Vicksburg:*

A dispatch was sent before the one in cipher. Cavalry will be more valuable in the northern part of the State; infantry more useful about Snyder's Mill. Infantry from Grenada can get there before cavalry.

J. E. JOHNSTON,
General.

JACKSON, MISS., *December* 31, 1862.

Lieutenant-General PEMBERTON, *Vicksburg:*

The following just received from General Loring:

Scouts report enemy repairing road and bridge, 3 miles west of Pontotoc, on the Tobytubby Creek. Please inform me whether you know of any movement in force eastward of Tallahatchie.

C. R. BARTEAU,
Lieutenant-Colonel.

Our information is that the enemy is on the Tallahatchie; one brigade at Abbeville, 3 miles this side: others at Rocky Ford. Have scouts at Pontotoc.

W. W. LORING,
Major-General

The enemy may be attempting Van Dorn's movements.

J. E. JOHNSTON,
General.

HDQRS. DEPT. OF MISSISSIPPI AND EAST LOUISIANA,
Vicksburg, December 31, 1862.

Colonel WHITFIELD, *Yazoo City:*

COLONEL: The lieutenant-general commanding directs that you move your cavalry across the Yazoo and march with caution and celerity to Haines' Bluff, opposite Snyder's Mill, at which point, or just below, it is supposed the enemy is constructing mortar or other batteries. If this party be small and you think it can be accomplished you will attack and break up this work, taking the precaution to dismount before bringing your men into action. You will procure the best guide the country affords. You will have to make your own way if there be no good road. Move rapidly, but with caution.

I am, colonel,

J. H. MORRISON,
Aide-de-Camp.

HEADQUARTERS FORCES IN THE TRENCHES,
December 31, 1862.

Colonel MORRISON, *Aide-de-Camp:*

COLONEL: I have granted the enemy a truce of four hours, commencing at 1 p. m., to enable them to bury their dead.

I am, respectfully, your obedient servant,

C. L. STEVENSON,
Major-General, Commanding.

Abstract from Monthly Return of the troops in the Department of Mississippi and East Louisiana, commanded by Lieut. Gen. J. C. Pemberton, for December, 1862.

| Troops. | Present for duty. | | | | | | Aggregate present. | Aggregate present and absent. |
| | Infantry. | | Cavalry. | | Artillery. | | | |
	Officers.	Men.	Officers.	Men.	Officers.	Men.		
First Corps, Army North Mississippi ...	798	9,671	.....	.....	.....	.....	12,284	17,980
Second Corps, Army North Mississippi..	714	9,187	.....	.....	.....	.....	11,726	20,731
Cavalry corps	.....	.....	246	3,607	.....	.....	4,432	4,432
Cavalry escort....................	.....	.....	2	27	.....	.....	51	53
Vaughn's (Tennessee) brigade...........	110	1,508	.....	.....	.....	.....	1,730	2,734
First Military District................	.....	.....	14	140	10	161	476	849
Second Military District..............	258	3,173	45	563	46	863	6,757	8,426
Third Military District...............	570	6,939	31	208	34	545	10,685	14,950
Grand total.................	2,450	30,478	338	4,545	90	1,569	48,141	70,155

Organization of the troops in the Department of Mississippi and East Louisiana, commanded by Lieut. Gen. J. C. Pemberton, December, 1862.

ARMY NORTH MISSISSIPPI.

1st Corps, Maj. Gen. M. Lovell.
2d Corps, Maj. Gen. S. Price.
Cavalry corps, Colonel Jackson.
Cavalry escort, Capt. John Bradley.
Vaughn's (Tennessee) brigade, composed of—
 79th Tennessee.
 80th Tennessee.
 81st Tennessee.

FIRST MILITARY DISTRICT.

Columbus, troops at—
 White's cavalry company.
 Hewlett's Battalion Partisan Rangers.
 Owens' light artillery.
 Rice's heavy artillery.
 Thrall's heavy artillery.
Squadron of cavalry at Jackson, Miss.

SECOND MILITARY DISTRICT.

First Brigade State Troops.
17th Louisiana.
22d Louisiana.
26th Louisiana.
27th Louisiana.
28th Louisiana.
3d Mississippi.

46th Mississippi.
Adams' cavalry.
28th Mississippi Cavalry (Company I).
Partisan Rangers (one company).
Ogden's command (artillery).
1st Mississippi Light Artillery.
Clinch's command (light battery).
Sterling's command (heavy artillery).
Sappers and Miners (one company).
Signal Corps.

THIRD MILITARY DISTRICT.

First Brigade.
Second Brigade.
Third Brigade.
Fourth Brigade.
Fifth Brigade.
1st Alabama Regiment.
Daigre's cavalry (one company).
Hughes' cavalry (battalion).
Jones' cavalry (one company).
Garland's Partisan Rangers (battalion)
12th Louisiana Battalion (artillery).
English's company (artillery).
Boone's battery (light artillery).
Fenner's battery (light artillery).
Withers' battery (light artillery).
Baton Rouge forces.
Camp Moore forces.
Ponchatoula forces.

HEADQUARTERS FORCES IN THE TRENCHES,
January 1, 1863.

Col. J. H. MORRISON,
 Actg. Asst. Adjt. Gen., Dept. of the Mississippi, &c.:

COLONEL: All quiet in front. The enemy are engaged in constructing rifle-pits near the lake in front of Barton's position.

All quiet at Snyder's Mill at 5 p. m. on yesterday. The enemy had advanced his pickets in front of Wofford's battery.

 Respectfully,

    C. L. STEVENSON,
    Major-General, Commanding.

JACKSON, *January* —, 1863.
[Lieut. Gen. J. C. PEMBERTON:]

GENERAL: I respectfully request you to communicate to me the substance of all the orders you may give for movement of troops, and as much as practicable to confer with me before giving them. The telegraph will prevent loss of time. Your position at Vicksburg is most important, however it interferes with the supervision of other parts of the department. You are aware, I believe, that I was brought here by the President to assist you. My great object is to do so.

Colonel Marigny reports that Banks brought about 8,000 men to

New Orleans from Ship Island, and that ten transports and, I think, fourteen gunboats are at Baton Rouge. E. Hiriart, to whom you gave permission to trade for Josephs and ———, reports the number brought from Ship Island at 3,000—8,000 being left on the island, destined for other service.

A letter forwarded by General Buckner from Mobile gives 35,000 as Banks' force. It seems to me that it would be safest to send troops to Port Hudson from here. I have informally authorized Major-General Van Dorn to visit his family. You will oblige me by directing Major Armstrong to report to Major-General Van Dorn.

Most respectfully, your obedient servant,

J. E. JOHNSTON,
General.

The President has appointed W. H. Jackson brigadier-general. A sister-in-law of General Beauregard reported Banks' force at 8,000.

VICKSBURG, *January* 1, 1863.

General JOSEPH E. JOHNSTON, *Jackson, Miss.:*

When my telegram was sent I had not received your letter. Will reply by mail; am about leaving for Snyder's Mill. I want to re-enforce Port Hudson.

J. C. PEMBERTON,
Lieutenant-General, Commanding.

JACKSON, *January* 1, 1863.

General W. W. LORING, *Grenada:*

Direct all of the Texas regiments of cavalry to march at once to Snyder's Mill, on the Yazoo River. Let the movement be as rapid as possible.

J. R. WADDY,
Assistant Adjutant-General.

JACKSON, MISS., *January* 1, 1863.

Lieutenant-General PEMBERTON, *Vicksburg:*

General Van Dorn received your dispatch yesterday. He thinks cavalry could not operate at the place you name. You have been three times asked by telegraph if infantry from Grenada would not be better. General Van Dorn says it could get there much sooner. No reply has been received. Please answer.

J. E. JOHNSTON,
General.

VICKSBURG, *January* 1, 1863.

General JOSEPH E. JOHNSTON, *Jackson:*

I considered it necessary to understand your telegram in cipher before answering. Your last did not reach me until 10 p. m. If enemy reaches the hills he cuts off Snyder's Mill. The only force which could operate against his flanks or rear would be mounted Texans, armed and fighting as infantry and cavalry. I have only Wirt Adams' regiment here. I am endeavoring to provide against what I expect—an army vastly outnumbering mine. Unless circumstances compel I do not wish to withdraw more infantry from Grenada. These are my views. With the Texas cavalry I can do. Forrest, Roddey's, and remainder at Grenada I think sufficient for movements north. I am prepared to direct them, with my respects, at once.

J. C. PEMBERTON,
Lieutenant-General, Commanding.

JACKSON, MISS., *January* 1, 1863.

Lieutenant-General PEMBERTON, *Vicksburg:*

The Texas cavalry is ordered. Forrest and Roddey are not in this department. They belong to General Bragg's. I am trying to find them.

J. E. JOHNSTON,
General.

HDQRS. DEPT. OF MISSISSIPPI AND EAST LOUISIANA,
Vicksburg, January 1, 1863.

Major-General Smith will send forthwith a reliable person across the river to communicate with our army in Arkansas, to ascertain whether there be any movements of our army there connected with ours on this side.

By order of Lieutenant-General Pemberton:

J. THOMPSON,
Assistant Adjutant-General.

HDQRS. SUBSIST. DEPT., 2D DIST., DEPT. OF MISS. AND E. LA.,
Vicksburg, Miss., January 1, 1863.

Maj. THEO. JOHNSTON,
Commissary of Subsistence, &c.:

DEAR SIR: In accordance with the order from Lieutenant-General Pemberton I have made an estimate of the stores required for 10,000 men for five months, and find that I am well supplied with (or ample arrangements have been made to get supplies of) everything except the following articles: Bacon, soap, salt, rice, vinegar, coffee, candles, and flour. These articles are much needed, and I have made every effort to procure the required amounts, but have not yet succeeded. I will make out and remit to you as soon as possible a statement of the amounts on hand and the amounts wanting to fill the estimate, and I do hope you will try to supply the wants of this post at once.

Very respectfully, your obedient servant,

T. B. REED,
Major and Commissary of Subsistence.

JACKSON [COLUMBUS], MISS., *January* 1, 1863.

The inclosed is a report of all the troops at this post, except the Mississippi State troops. Of these there are here the Fifth Regiment, aggregate, 384; for duty, 178; the Third Battalion, aggregate, 399; for duty, 197 (at the time they were detached from this post). They were sent to Vicksburg by order of Lieutenant-General Pemberton of date November 28, 1862, and are now there in the actual service of the Confederate States. These troops never were mustered into the service of the Confederate States, but have been and still are performing guard and other duties at this post. In obedience to Special Orders, No. 33, from General Price's headquarters, dated Headquarters District of Tennessee, Tupelo, September 5, 1862, I have furnished to these troops subsistence, camp and garrison equipage, arms, and ammunition, upon the receipts of Brigadier-General Harris, commanding.

The State troops are styled by the Governor Minute-Men; have officers detailed to drill and instruct them; have consequently arrived at a certain degree of proficiency, and will compare favorably with Confederate States troops of the same length of service.

Colonel Burgin, who left this post in command of the battalion of Minute-Men, is stationed at Snyder's Bluff, and, I learn, in command of a brigade. These troops are armed with muskets, caliber .69, most of them altered percussion-lock.

The Fifth Regiment is stationed 1½ miles north of Columbus, on the military road near the fortifications.

Captain Rice's company of heavy artillery is stationed 1¼ miles north of Columbus, on the Aberdeen road. They have no battery; they have 30 percussion muskets, 10 Enfield rifles, 4,000 buck-and-ball cartridges, 5,000 musket-caps and all necessary accouterments; 2 horses, 2 mules, and 1 wagon; all in good condition. This company is to serve the guns on the fortifications.

Captain Thrall's company of heavy artillery is stationed 1½ miles north of Columbus, on the Aberdeen road. They have one 32-pounder siege gun, one 3-inch rifle gun, and one 6-pounder smooth-bore gun, with equipments; 103 rounds 12-pounder blank cartridges, 30 rounds 12-pounder Read shot, 40 rounds 12-pounder canister, 51 percussion muskets and accouterments, 4,000 musket-cartridges, and 4,000 percussion caps; all in good condition. This company is also to serve guns on the fortifications.

Captain Owens' company of light artillery is stationed 1½ miles north of Columbus, on the military road. They have five 6-pounder guns (bronze), limbers and caissons for same; one 3.3-inch rifle (bronze), limber and caisson; one battery wagon and limber, one battery forge and limber, 500 solid shot, fixed; 400 spherical-case, fixed; 80 canister, fixed (all for 6-pounders); 100 3.3-inch rifle Read shot, 100 3.3-inch rifle shell, 240 blank cartridges; equipments nearly complete; all in good condition. They also have 100 horses, 16 mules, and 3 baggage wagons. The men are all in good condition, well clothed, &c.

Maj. W. A. Hewlett's battalion Partisan Rangers is stationed at Buttahatchee Bridge, 12 miles north of Columbus, on the Aberdeen road. They have 307 double-barrel guns and accouterments, 320 sabers and belts, 45 flint-lock pistols, 8,320 rounds of cartridges, 4,320 percussion caps; all in good condition.

Captain White's cavalry company is stationed 4½ miles northwest of Columbus, on the road to Buttahatchee Bridge. They have 113 double-barrel guns (some of them inferior), 60 holster-pistols, 113 cavalry sabers, with necessary accouterments for guns, pistols, and sabers, camp equipage, &c.; one wagon and 6 mules; all in good condition. This company is engaged particularly in outpost and scouting duty.

The battalion of heavy artillery, composed of the companies commanded by Captains Lynch, Johnson, and Bains, was sent to Vicksburg by order of Lieutenant-General Pemberton, dated November 28, 1862, and are now on detached service at that place. Their aggregate when they left this post was 304.

The ordnance officer of this post reports on hand the following: Five hundred friction-primers, 11,000 buck-and-ball cartridges, 7,000 buck-shot cartridges, 24,000 musket-ball cartridges, 36,000 musket-caps, 1,000 sporting-caps, and 5 kegs of powder; 97 sabers and belts, 29 shoulder-straps, 2 cartridge boxes and belts, 4 bayonet scabbards, 21 haver-sacks, 28 canteens, and 74 gun-slings.

The arsenal, with all its machinery, works, stores, &c., is being re-moved from this post by direction of authorities at Richmond.

As to the fortifications, defenses, &c., at this post I beg leave to re port: The city of Columbus is inclosed on the west by the Tombigbee River, on the east and south by the Looxapalila, on the north and west by a chain of breastworks and rifle-pits over 5 miles in length.

On the Looxapalila there are three bridges and four fords, upon all of which I have placed heavy works. The Tombigbee is a natural de-fense, except at two points, at which there are defenses.

There is now in process of construction an entire line of defenses for the northern approaches about 4 miles from the city, running from the Looxapalila across the military and Aberdeen roads to the Tombigbee River. These works are a series of bastions and redoubts, with breast-works to command the ravines. The outer works, commanding the approaches by the Aberdeen and military roads, are constructed on eminences which give an uninterrupted view north and northeast of some 3 or 4 miles, the intervening distance between these roads being about 4 miles.

There is also being constructed on the outer spurs which command the plains in front a series of works which command all approaches, roads, ravines, &c. One-fifth of these is already completed. The number of hands that have been employed is between 950 and 960. The num-ber of guns mounted is thirteen, viz: One 32-pounder, one 12-pounder, (siege), nine 6-pounders (field), and two 3-inch rifle (field). The officers engaged in the department are Lieuts. A. B. De Saulles, Topp, Law, and Labor.

For the better understanding of this report, the localities referred to, &c., you are referred to the accompanying map of Columbus and its surroundings. It is respectfully requested that this map be forwarded to General Johnston.

The quartermaster and commissary stores are being removed from this post to Jackson, Miss., by direction of Lieutenant-General Pem berton. Their reports, together with the report of the post surgeon, are attached hereto.

JOHN ADAMS,
Colonel, C. S. Army, Commanding.

[Inclosure.]

TROOPS AT JACKSON.

There are at this post the following troops, viz: Captain Marsh's company (E), detached from the Fortieth Regiment Alabama Volun-teers, serving as a provost-guard with Captain Bolen's company of dis-mounted cavalry, exchanged prisoners, numbering 20 men, and the Crescent Artillery, exchanged prisoners, Capt. T. H. Hutton commanding, which latter company is unorganized and is under orders (temporarily suspended) to report to His Excellency Thomas O. Moore, Governor of Louisiana.

Captain Marsh reports the following ordnance on hand: Fifty-six muskets (2 unserviceable); 6 musket-bayonets, 20 Enfield rifles, 20 Enfield-rifle bayonets, 2,240 rounds musket-cartridges, 2,300 musket-caps, 780 Enfield-rifle caps, 800 Enfield-rifle cartridges, 70 knapsacks, and 70 canteens.

Captains Hutton's and Bolen's companies have been furnished with muskets to use while acting as guards at this post.

DANIEL RUGGLES,
Brigadier-General, Commanding District.

JACKSON, MISS., January 2, 1863.

Major-General LORING, <i>Grenada</i>:

Recall the Texan cavalry, if you can, and order all cavalry to get ready to march. The enemy has re-embarked in the Yazoo near Vicksburg.

J. E. JOHNSTON,
General.

VICKSBURG, January 2, 1863.

General JOSEPH E. JOHNSTON, <i>Jackson</i>:

The pikes and revolvers on special service not for Vicksburg. If permitted I shall immediately direct a strong cavalry force movement toward and in rear of mouth of Coldwater; shall include Texas cavalry. Information just received indicates re-embarkation of enemy from my front. Shall, however, wait certainty of such movement.

J. C. PEMBERTON,
Lieutenant General, Commanding.

JACKSON, MISS., January 2, 1863.

Lieutenant-General PEMBERTON, <i>Vicksburg</i>:

Make the cavalry movement. W. H. Jackson is brigadier-general. I telegraphed Major-General Loring to get the troops in readiness, and desire Major Waddy to turn back the Texans.

J. E. JOHNSTON,
General.

VICKSBURG, January 2, 1863.

General JOSEPH E. JOHNSTON, <i>Jackson</i>:

Before receiving your letters I had countermanded orders to Texas cavalry; also directed Lieutenant-Colonel Waddy not to send forward any more troops until further orders. A brigade at least should go, I think, to Port Hudson; if you prefer, one of Stevenson's from Jackson; also a good field battery with rifle guns in it. The fleet may bombard us to-morrow, but if all is quiet I shall probably go to Jackson.

J. C. PEMBERTON.

HEADQUARTERS FORCES IN FRONT,
Chickasaw Bluffs, Miss., January 2, 1863.
Col. J. H. MORRISON, *Aide-de-Camp:*

COLONEL: To retain the organization of brigades, thoroughly occupy our lines, and give relief to the men in the trenches, I respectfully ask authority to make the following assignment of the troops under my command:

Right—Major-General Maury commanding right, including Snyder's Bluff. Force—Maury's division, Lee's and Vaughn's brigades.

Center—Brigadier-General Barton commanding: Barton's and Taylor's brigades.

Left—Brigadier-General Tracy commanding: Tracy's and Gregg's brigades.

Reserve for inner works—Col. A. W. Reynolds' brigade.

I am, sir, respectfully, your obedient servant,
C. L. STEVENSON,
Major-General, Commanding.

7.30 A. M.—All quiet in our immediate front. No apparent change since yesterday.

VICKSBURG, *January 2,* 1863—7.10 a. m.
General TRACY:

GENERAL: The lieutenant-general commanding directs that you move immediately to the front with all the troops of your command and report to Major-General Stevenson, commanding forces in front. The utmost dispatch is requisite. You may be needed now. Inform all commanding officers of regiments that arrived yesterday and last night, and who are encamped in your vicinity to move immediately with you and report to General Stevenson.

J. H. MORRISON,
Aide-de-Camp.

ON THE RIGHT, *January 2,* 1863.
Colonel MORRISON,
Acting Assistant Adjutant-General, &c.:

COLONEL: I am satisfied that the enemy have left our front. Most of them have re-embarked, and the transports are moving down the river. Have sent forces to feel them. Will watch the movements of the transports and report from time to time.

Respectfully,
C. L. STEVENSON,
Major-General, Commanding.

VICKSBURG, *January 2,* 1863.
Brig. Gen. W. H. JACKSON,
Chief of Cavalry, Grenada, Miss.:

The enemy is represented on Yazoo Pass, opposite to Colonel Alcorn's. His strength is supposed to be about 3,000, with artillery. I wish you to take all the cavalry (leaving only a sufficiency to do picket and scouting duty in front of Grenada), move to the rear of the enemy, drive him from his position, capture his artillery, and do him all the damage otherwise in your power. You had better move by the edge of the bottom until you can pass Coldwater north of the mouth of the Pass; but this route I leave to your discretion. You can extend your operations as circumstances in your judgment admit. If you leave the Pass return to the river, move to the north of Grant's position, cutting off his communications and destroying his wagon trains.

> J. C. PEMBERTON,
> *Lieutenant-General, Commanding.*

JACKSON, MISS., *January 2,* 1863.

Major-General VAN DORN, *Mobile:*

General Pemberton telegraphs that the enemy is re-embarking. It will be necessary to make another cavalry dash. Come in time to overtake him.

> J. E. JOHNSTON,
> *General.*

VICKSBURG, *January 2,* 1863.

Maj. GEORGE WHITFIELD,
    Assistant Quartermaster, Jackson:

Send no more troops here until further orders.

> J. C. PEMBERTON,
> *Lieutenant-General, Commanding*

VICKSBURG, *January 2,* 1863.

Major-General LORING, *Grenada:*

Countermand the order for movement of Texas cavalry. The enemy has re-embarked and gone down the Yazoo, leaving large quantity of intrenching tools and other property.

> J. C. PEMBERTON,
> *Lieutenant-General, Commanding.*

JACKSON, MISS., *January 2,* 1863.

Lieutenant-General PEMBERTON, *Vicksburg:*

In directing the cavalry movement we must consider that Grant is on the Central road. I have directed the scouts on the river to be on the alert. I shall stop the troops which come from the east until I hear from you. Can the enemy intend another attempt to approach Vicksburg?

> J. E. JOHNSTON,
> *General.*

JACKSON, MISS., *January 2,* 1863.

Lieutenant-General PEMBERTON, *Vicksburg:*

The President telegraphs twelve frigates, two brigs, two schooners, and two transports at Pensacola. General Loring, in reply to a question, reports 10,000 men gone from Holly Springs to Memphis. General

Bragg reports the enemy has yielded this strong point and is falling back. We shall follow him. General Wheeler, with his cavalry, is behind him. If you have not heard from Major-General Gardner it would be well to do so before sending troops. I am told that he is confident, with his present force. I had rather keep Stevenson's troops together as they don't belong to the department.

J. E. JOHNSTON,
General.

JACKSON, *January* 2, 1863.

Lieutenant-General PEMBERTON, *Vicksburg:*

General Loring telegraphs that two scouts report that 10,000 enemy have gone to Memphis. Prisoners say that a part of Grant's army is going to Corinth. About 7,000 at Tobytubby Ferry, on the Tallahatchie.

J. E. JOHNSTON,
General.

JACKSON, *January* 2, 1863.

Mr. PRESIDENT: General Pemberton continues to command at Vicksburg; he has asked for all the troops here, after being re-enforced by Maury's division, in addition to those brigades agreed upon between us. The line of 12 miles to Snyder's Mill probably requires them all; I fear difficulty of subsisting them, however. A report just handed in by the inspecting officers shows that the supply of provision is much smaller than General Pemberton supposed. The place may be reduced I fear in consequence of this; or should it be invested we shall not have a sufficient force to break the investment.

Grant is still on the Tallahatchie, so that the remainder of Loring's and Price's troops cannot be withdrawn from Grenada. From his halting I suppose he is repairing the railroad. The force at Grenada (about 11,000 effective) is too weak to do more than delay the passage of the river by the enemy. My hope of keeping him back is in Van Dorn, under whom I propose to unite all the available cavalry when Forrest and Roddey can be found.

Should Grant join Sherman at Vicksburg it would be very embarrassing; for as he could reach the place from Memphis as soon as we could learn whether he was embarking or moving along the railroad to Grenada it could be invested by the combined armies. We could not break the investment with 11,000 men, but it would be necessary to try.

The necessity of holding the Yazoo as well as Vicksburg employs a large force too widely distributed to be in condition for the offensive.

We have no news from Arkansas, which proves I think that we are to get no help from that side of the Mississippi. The Legislature has done nothing yet.

We require about 20,000 men, the number you have asked for from Arkansas, to make headway against both Grant and Sherman. Will the great victory at Fredericksburg enable General Lee to spare a part of his force?

Should the enemy's forces be respectably handled the task you have set me will be above my ability. But the hand of Almighty God has delivered us in times of as great danger. Believing that He is with us I will not lose hope.

J. E. JOHNSTON.

GENERAL ORDERS, }   HDQRS. DEPT. OF MISS. AND EAST LA.,
     No. 5 [21].   }   *Grenada, January 2, 1863.*

Hereafter the organization of the army, Department of Mississippi and East Louisiana, will be as follows, viz:

The army will consist of two divisions, to be known as First and Second Divisions, and commanded, respectively, by Maj. Gen. W. W. Loring and Maj. Gen. Sterling Price. Each division will consist of two brigades.

First Division comprises Tilghman's brigade, Rust's brigade, and Waul's Texas Legion, Colonel Waul commanding.

General Tilghman will take command of the brigade hitherto under command of Brigadier-General Baldwin.

The command hitherto known as Rust's division is merged into one brigade, to be known as Rust's brigade.

Second Division comprises Bowen's brigade and Green's brigade.

The command hitherto known as Bowen's division is resolved into two brigades, Brigadier-General Bowen taking command of one, Brigadier-General Green having command of the other.

The light batteries will remain as at present organized, with the exception of being attached to division in place of corps.

  *   *   *   *   *   *   *

By order of Lieutenant-General Pemberton:
                              R. W. MEMMINGER,
                                   Assistant-Adjutant-General.

                    HEADQUARTERS FORCES IN FRONT,
                         Chickasaw Bluffs, January 2, 1863.

Col. J. H. MORRISON, *Aide-de-Camp, Dept. of Miss. and E. La.*:

COLONEL: I send herewith the nearest approximation that can be made to the strength of my command. Under the existing circumstances, most of the troops being in the trenches, it is impossible to make a field return:

Vaughn	1,678
Gregg	1,290
Barton	2,100
Tracy	1,850
Maury	6,600
	13,518

Two brigades (nine regiments) are now absent and are not included; about 4,000 strong.

I am, colonel, very respectfully, your obedient servant,
                              C. L. STEVENSON,
                                   Major-General, Commanding.

Return of a part of First Brigade, First Division, commanded by Brig. Gen. S. M. Barton, January 2, 1863.

40th Georgia, Colonel Johnson	365
42d Georgia, Colonel Henderson	450
43d Georgia, Colonel Harris	404
52d Georgia, Colonel Philips	377
Anderson's battery	46
Aggregate present	1,642

                              S. M. BARTON,
                                   Brigadier-General.

Field report of Second Brigade, First Division, Smith's corps, commanded by Brig. Gen.
E. D. Tracy.

20th Alabama	630	
30th Alabama	400	
31st Alabama	260	Eight companies only arrived.
23d Alabama	100	Two companies only reported.
46th Alabama	...	Forty-sixth not reported.
Grand aggregate	1,390	

Station, Chickasaw Bluffs, near Vicksburg.
Date, January 3, 1863.

E. D. TRACY,
Brigadier-General.

Return of effective troops in Major-General Smith's command, January 3, 1863.

Commands.	Officers.	Rank and file.	Aggregate.
Brig. Gen. S. D. Lee	6	.....	6
3d Mississippi	38	600	638
4th Mississippi	34	470	504
46th Mississippi	32	471	503
17th Louisiana	40	433	473
22d Louisiana	20	156	176
26th Louisiana	36	526	562
28th Louisiana	30	448	478
31st Louisiana	23	519	542
3d Battalion Mississippi State troops	24	250	274
Withers' light artillery	37	757	794
Hill's Partisan Ranger company	3	86	89
Johnson's company (I) Mississippi Cavalry	4	83	87
Brigadier-General Gregg			
10th Tennessee	.....	.....	349
50th, 51st, and 1st Tennessee	.....	.....	512
3d and 30th Tennessee	.....	.....	851
41st Tennessee	.....	.....	526
Wirt Adams' cavalry	35	539	574
Post of Vicksburg	37	530	567
40th Alabama (in Vicksburg)	18	314	332
Upper batteries, Vicksburg	48	465	513
Lower batteries, Vicksburg	35	383	418
Sapper and Miner company	4	21	2?
Signal Corps	1	13	14
Total	.....	.....	9,807

NOTE.—General Gregg has a four-gun battery attached to his brigade, but it is broken up among other commands, and hence is not reported.

JNO. G. DEVEREUX,
Major and Assistant Adjutant-General.

HDQRS. SECOND DIST., DEPT. MISS. AND E. LA.,
Vicksburg, Miss., January 3, 1863.

JACKSON, *January 3, 1863.*

Lieutenant-General PEMBERTON, *Vicksburg:*

Have the transports moved? We must confer about the cavalry's movement so as not to derange the general one.

J. E. JOHNSTON,
General.

HEADQUARTERS FORCES IN FRONT,
January 3, 1863.

Col. J. H. MORRISON, *Aide-de-Camp :*

COLONEL : The troops are suffering very much in the trenches from the rain.   If there is no appearance of the enemy in front can they be drawn back within the lines to their tents, leaving a sufficient picket force in front?

Respectfully, your obedient servant,

C. L. STEVENSON,
Major-General, Commanding.

HEADQUARTERS DEPARTMENT,
Jackson, January 3, 1863.

Maj. Gen. C. L. STEVENSON, *Vicksburg :*

Have General Gregg's brigade got ready to move to Port Hudson at once.   It will be replaced by other troops of your division.

J. C. PEMBERTON,
Lieutenant-General, Commanding.

HEADQUARTERS DEPARTMENT,
Jackson, January 3, 1863.

Colonel WADDY :

Order the troops of Stevenson's division now here, exclusive of artillery, to proceed at once to Vicksburg and report to General Stevenson.

J. C. PEMBERTON,
Lieutenant-General, Commanding.

JACKSON, *January 4, 1863.*

Lieut. Col. C. R. BARTEAU, *Okolona :*

Send to Colonel Roddey, in North Alabama, this order :

Go with your cavalry into northeast part of Mississippi, where you will receive other orders.   Report by bearer where those orders can reach you.

J. E. JOHNSTON,
General.

JACKSON, *January 5, 1863.*

General S. COOPER

The enemy made several attacks upon the line between Vicksburg and Snyder's Mill, in which he was repulsed with a loss of about 1,100 ; ours 150.   The transports and troops at last accounts were at Milliken's Bend.   Lieutenant-General Pemberton deserves high credit.

J. E. JOHNSTON,
General.

JACKSON, *January 5, 1863.*

Brig. Gen. JOHN ADAMS, *Columbus :*

You will proceed to this point to assume command of this post, relieving Brigadier-General Ruggles.

By order of Lieutenant-General Pemberton :

J. R. WADDY,
Assistant Adjutant-General.

JACKSON, *January* 5, 1863.

Major-General LORING, *Grenada, Miss.*:

Return of enemy's force from mouth of Coldwater renders the movement of cavalry heretofore ordered unnecessary.   You will direct Brigadier-General Jackson to follow up the rear of the enemy immediately, harass him in his retreat, and cut off his wagon train and supplies as far as possible.

By order of Lieutenant-General Pemberton:

J. THOMPSON,
Assistant Adjutant-General.

———

JACKSON, *January* 5, 1863.

General GREGG, *Vicksburg* :

In descending the river with your brigade do so with great care.   If you learn that the enemy's gunboats can prevent you from landing at Port Hudson you will land your command at Bayou Sara and march by land to Port Hudson.   You will take measures before reaching Port Hudson to find out the position of their gunboats by sending a boat-light in advance of you or by other communication with General Gardner.

J. R. WADDY,
Assistant Adjutant-General.

———

ACKSON, *January* 6, 1863.

Lieutenant-General PEMBERTON, *Vicksburg:*

Please have a messenger sent across the river to learn if there are any movements from Arkansas connected with ours.

J. E. JOHNSTON,
General.

———

JACKSON, *January* 6, 1863.

The PRESIDENT, *Richmond :*

Your dispatch of yesterday received.*   Enemy's troops and transports reported gone up the river from Milliken's Bend.   We hear of no movements in this direction by General Holmes.

Grant's forces are reported distributed at Memphis, Holly Springs, and Corinth.   The country said to be impracticable.   General Bragg reports he has been checked.   I hear indirectly that he has withdrawn from Murfreesborough.   Should he need help, and appear no danger in Mississippi except by the river, could E. K. Smith's men return ?

The impossibility of my knowing condition of things in Tennessee shows that I cannot direct both parts of my command at once.   I am hoping to hear from General Bragg.

J. E. JOHNSTON,
General.

———

SPECIAL ORDERS, ⎱ HDQRS. FIRST DIST., DEPT. MISS. AND E. LA.,
No. 1.   ⎰   *Jackson, Miss., January* 6, 1863.

I. Paragraph I, Special Orders, No. 24, dated December 22, 1862, from these headquarters, reading as follows—

In conformity with Special Orders, No. 62, Headquarters Department of Mississippi and East Louisiana, December 20, 1862, all Louisiana State troops now serving in the

———

* Not found

First Military Distric; of this department, taken prisoners at New Orleans and now exchanged, will report without unnecessary delay to His Excellency Thomas O. Moore, Governor of the State of Louisiana—

having been suspended, is hereby revived and will be carried into immediate execution, excepting in the cases of the following-named officers, who will continue to exercise the duties to which they have been assigned until further orders, viz:

(1.) Col. Ig. Szymanski, Chalmette Regiment.
(2.) Capt. William Chapman, Chalmette Regiment.
(3.) First Lieut. Thomas H. Marshall, Chalmette Regiment.
(4.) Second Lieut. J. A. Chambers, Chalmette Regiment.
(5.) Lieut. F. J. Ames, Beauregard Regiment.

By order of Brigadier-General Ruggles:

R. M. HOOE,
Assistant Adjutant-General.

JACKSON, MISS., *January 7, 1863.*

The PRESIDENT, *Richmond:*

The following dispatch was received by Gen. M. L. Smith:

I am returning from Little Rock.   No troops will be sent.

J. E. JOHNSTON,
General.

HEADQUARTERS FORCES IN FRONT OF VICKSBURG,
January 7, 1863.

Lieut. Col. J. THOMPSON,
Asst. Adjt. Gen., Dept. of Miss. and East La.:

COLONEL: I have the honor to acknowledge the receipt to-day of Special Orders, No. 4, Headquarters Department of Mississippi and East Louisiana, dated Jackson, January 4, 1863.

I have to report that General Gregg's brigade left for Port Hudson yesterday and the day before. I would further state that the battery of Parrott guns which I was ordered by the lieutenant-general commanding to send to Port Hudson left on the steamer Hodges yesterday.

I am, colonel, respectfully, your obedient servant,

C. L. STEVENSON,
Major-General, Commanding.

VICKSBURG, *January 8, 1863.*

Hon. JAMES A. SEDDON,
Secretary of War, Richmond, Va.:

From latest information I am satisfied the enemy's transports have gone up the river. Only seven gunboats between the mouth of the Yazoo River and Milliken's Bend.

Vicksburg is daily growing stronger. We intend to hold it.

J. C. PEMBERTON,
Lieutenant-General, Commanding.

GRENADA, *January* 8, 1863.

Colonel J. R. WADDY:

Aggregate present for duty, First Corps, 8,153; aggregate present for duty, Second Corps, 4,681; Jackson's cavalry, 2,500; aggregate present for duty, Grenada, 15,334. Will send Gregg's brigade and Maury's division, absent at Vicksburg. Aggregate present and absent, 29,083.

W. W. LORING,
Major-General.

JACKSON, *January* 8, 1863.

Lieutenant-General PEMBERTON, *Vicksburg:*

Following just received from Grenada:

Scouts report that the enemy has left the Tallahatchie, and the general impression is that they will soon leave Holly Springs. They are moving to Memphis and to the Charleston Railroad. Cars reported as running to Grand Junction. Stockades are being constructed along it. No enemy near the Grenada and Memphis road. Aggregate of Maury's division for duty by the last report, 3,661; Gregg's brigade, 2,485.

W. W. LORING.

J. R. WADDY,
Assistant Adjutant-General.

JACKSON, *January* 9, 1863.

Maj. M. R. CLARK, *Brookhaven:*

The Sixth, Fifteenth, and Twenty-second Mississippi Regiments are at Grenada. The Forty-sixth Mississippi is at Vicksburg.

J. R. WADDY,
Assistant Adjutant-General.

JACKSON, *January* 9, 1863.

Major-General STEVENSON, *Vicksburg:*

Let me know the effective and aggregate force in Second Military District. The information has been delayed for three days. It is desired at Richmond at once.

J. R. WADDY,
Assistant Adjutant-General.

VICKSBURG, *January* 9, 1863.

Col. J. R. WADDY,
    Assistant Adjutant-General:

I referred your request for returns to senior officer in district. My command reports effective 6,765; aggregate, 9,929.

M. L. SMITH,
Major-General.

HEADQUARTERS FORCES IN FRONT OF VICKSBURG,
January 9, 1863.

Col. J. THOMPSON,
    Asst. Adjt. Gen., Dept. of Miss. and East Louisiana:

COLONEL: I reconnoitered the country in the vicinity of Warrenton on yesterday, and I am of the opinion that with the force here we cannot prevent the enemy from landing at that distance from the city, as the country above Warrenton for a short distance and below it for many miles affords easy landings. A single battery at any one point would therefore be of no effect.

I shall not commence the work directed on yesterday until I receive further instructions from the lieutenant-general commanding.

The left of our line is decidedly the weak point, and I respectfully suggest that works be thrown up there as rapidly as possible, that the intrenchments to surround the city be completed on the left, and a suitable line selected in advance of them for rifle-pits from which to meet the enemy, should they land below. Will you please instruct General Smith to give his attention at once to that part of the line. As many negroes as can be obtained should be kept constantly at work.

If it is intended to hold Vicksburg to the last extremity I respectfully ask to be permitted to prepare for any emergency by collecting forage for animals and packing beef for subsistence. This cannot be done in a few days, and I apprehend that the quartermaster and subsistence departments are moving too slowly therein. Please give me authority to purchase and boat corn on the Yazoo to Snyder's Bluff, to be transported therefrom by our wagon trains, and to purchase salt and pack beef for sixty days' rations for this command.

I am, sir, your obedient servant,

C. L. STEVENSON,
Major-General, Commanding.

VICKSBURG, MISS., *January 9, 1863.*

Maj. THEO. JOHNSTON,
Chief of Subsistence, Jackson:

DEAR SIR: I inclose statement of stores on hand by the post commissary. Besides these we have in the Government warehouse at the machine-shop about 160,000 rations salt, 589,000 rations corn, 3,500,000 rations pease, 38,000 rations flour, 20 sacks of coffee, 17 boxes of wine, besides a considerable quantity of corn in slip-shuck and on the ear, of which I have not the means of ascertaining the exact amount, as it is on the levee.

Very respectfully,

T. B. REED,
Major and Commissary of Subsistence.

JACKSON, *January 10, 1863.*

Lieut. Gen. J. C. PEMBERTON,
Port Hudson, La.:

Scouts report that ninety boats have passed the mouth of White River going up the Mississippi, on the 6th and 7th. Some of them stop along the way, apparently to bury the dead.

Many negroes and other property taken and destroyed. Stragglers report that treason and rebellion are rife among the troops, and that the attack upon Vicksburg failed because Grant and Banks neglected to discharge the duties assigned them.

W. W. LORING,
Major-General.

HEADQUARTERS FORCES IN FRONT OF VICKSBURG,
January 10, 1863.

Lieutenant-Colonel WADDY,
    Asst. Adjt. Gen., Dept. of Miss. and East La., Jackson:

COLONEL: Your telegram dated the 9th, the first addressed to me on the subject, calling for the effective and aggregate force in the Second District, I received this morning. In my reply to it there was a slight inaccuracy, which you will find corrected below. The following is the aggregate present of effective troops of this district:

STEVENSON'S DIVISION.

First Brigade, Barton	1,905	
Second Brigade, Tracy	1,945	
Third Brigade, Taylor (temporarily at Jackson)	1,883	
Fourth Brigade, Reynolds	1,960	
		7,693

SMITH'S DIVISION.

Lee's brigade	2,737	
Vaughn's brigade	1,427	
Twenty-seventh Louisiana (on police duty)	561	
Stationary batteries	931	
Ward's Battalion Artillery	122	
Sappers and Miners and Signal Corps	39	
Adams' regiment (cavalry)	433	
		6,250

MAURY'S DIVISION.

Moore's brigade	2,436	
Hébert's brigade	2,819	
Artillery	700	
		5,955
		19,898
In and around Vicksburg (less Taylor's brigade)	1,883	
		18,015

I am, colonel, respectfully, your obedient servant,
                  C. L. STEVENSON,
                    Major-General, Commanding.

VICKSBURG, *January* 10, 1863.

Capt. W. M. JONES, *Assistant Quartermaster:*

SIR: There are large lots of corn and some small lots of fodder and pease lying on the bank belonging to the Government. Waterproof, Saint Joseph, and Ashwood are the chief points. It is highly important that these stores should be brought to this point as soon as possible, as they are from exposure to the late rains in damaging condition. If you will order the steamer Charm to go for and bring up these stores they will be pointed out to her by Zenas Preston, at Waterproof, and George Williams, at Saint Joseph, both Government agents. If the Charm is not prepared to bring corn in the shuck she can take on board at Natchez enough lumber there belonging to this post to make the necessary pens, &c.

Very respectfully,
                  W. H. JOHNSON,
                  Special Government Agent.

At Diamond Bend Landing there is probably a lot of fodder also belonging to this post.

JACKSON, MISS., *January* 11, 1863.

Lieutenant-General PEMBERTON, *Port Hudson:*

I want to combine a cavalry expedition in the two departments Please assign General Van Dorn to the same cavalry, with instructions to report to me.

J. E. JOHNSTON,
General.

JACKSON, MISS., *January* 11, 1863.

Lieutenant-General PEMBERTON, *Port Hudson:*

The object of the expedition under Van Dorn will be to interrupt any movement into Mississippi or Middle Tennessee.

J. E. JOHNSTON,
General.

JACKSON, MISS., *January* 11, 1863.

General BRAGG, *Tullahoma:*

One of Van Dorn's great objects will be to cover your left by preventing Federal troops from going from West to Middle Tennessee. Roddey will contribute far more to this object under Van Dorn than separate. This is the only pressure possible by the troops in Mississippi. Please order Roddey to report to Van Dorn. Grant is reported to intend to repair the railroad to Corinth.

J. E. JOHNSTON,
General.

JACKSON, *January* 11, 1863.

Major-General BUCKNER, *Mobile:*

Can you without inconvenience lend Van Dorn 1,000 or 1,500 cavalry immediately? If so, order them.

J. E. JOHNSTON,
General.

JACKSON, *January* 11, 1863.

Colonel BARTEAU, *Okolona:*

Send your most reliable scouts immediately toward Corinth to ascertain movements and strength of enemy there and in neighborhood. Let him report to me from nearest point by telegraph the result.

J. C. PEMBERTON,
Lieutenant-General, Commanding.

JACKSON, *January* 11, 1863.

Major-General LORING, *Grenada:*

Send the most reliable of Henderson's scouts immediately to ascertain the movements of the enemy about Corinth, his strength, &c. Report without delay.

J. C. PEMBERTON,
Lieutenant-General, Commanding.

PORT HUDSON, LA., *January* 11 1863.
General JOHNSTON:

All quiet here. I think everything will be in good condition in one week.

J. C. PEMBERTON,
Lieutenant-General, Commanding.

JACKSON, *January* 11, 1863.
(Received January 12, 1863.)

General S. COOPER:

Aggregate present for duty at Grenada, 15,000 effective; at Vicksburg, 18,000; at Port Hudson, La., 10,000; reserve at Jackson, 1,800; at Columbus, 1,800, including those on line of Mobile and Ohio Railroad. General Pemberton absent.

J. R. WADDY,
Assistant Adjutant-General.

JACKSON, MISS., *January* 12, 1863.

Major-General BUCKNER, *Mobile:*

Has the cavalry regiment at Montgomery no arms? I can furnish about 500 muskets. When ordered, they should go to Columbus.

J. E. JOHNSTON,
General.

JACKSON, *January* 13, 1863.

Major-General VAN DORN, *Grenada:*

Colonel Roddey is ordered to report to you; also the regiment at Montgomery, which has no arms; it goes to Columbus. Muskets and about 300 sabers can be furnished. Will you have the latter?

J. E. JOHNSTON.

VICKSBURG, *January* 13, 1863.

General VAN DORN, *Jackson:*

You are assigned to command of all the cavalry in this department except that in the Second Military District. You will report to General Johnston for operation in connection with Bragg's cavalry.

J. C. PEMBERTON,
Lieutenant-General, Commanding.

GRENADA, *January* 13, 1863.

Lieutenant-General PEMBERTON:

You place me in command of all the cavalry in your department except in District No. 2. Please inform me as to your wishes in regard to force to be left as cavalry pickets. I desire to put a cavalry force command in the field for active operations. Adams, for instance, is on the river. Do you need him there?

EARL VAN DORN,
Major-General.

JACKSON, *January* 13, 1863.

Major-General VAN DORN, *Grenada:*

I need Adams' regiment. Leave about 800 effectives for picket duty.

J. C. PEMBERTON,
Lieutenant-General, Commanding.

JACKSON, *January* 13, 1863.

Maj. Gen. EARL VAN DORN, *Grenada:*

Am sorry, but cannot spare Wirt Adams from his present service; have no other cavalry to supply his place. Bledsoe's horses and men are in Vicksburg. When do you expect to leave?

J. C. PEMBERTON,
Lieutenant-General, Commanding.

HDQRS. DEPT. OF MISSISSIPPI AND EAST LOUISIANA,
Jackson, January 13, 1863.

Lieut. Col. THOMAS SHIELDS, *Tangipahoa:*

COLONEL: I am directed by Lieutenant-General Pemberton to say to you that for the present he can make no change in the position of troops. As soon, however, as the interest of the service will admit of it, changes will be made to meet the emergency.

I am, colonel, very respectfully, &c.,

J. R. WADDY,
Lieutenant-Colonel and Assistant Adjutant-General.

MOBILE, *January* 13, 1863.

General JOSEPH E. JOHNSTON:

GENERAL: On arriving at Columbus I found that Lieutenant Topp, of the Engineer Corps, and Major Hewlett, of the cavalry, had within a few days past made the trip over the country between that point and Decatur. I concluded not to make the journey overland, but to send you their reports, with tracings of the route, which Mr. Topp was kind enough to furnish.

The commissary at Columbus, Major Guy, has quite a good supply of provisions on hand, and with two or three days' notice can readily collect whatever supplies may be necessary to sustain an army in its march over the country. The same may be said of Major Anderson, the quartermaster, who informs me that with two or three days' notice he can readily establish depots on the line of traval for foraging the animals. I am now on my way to Decatur to see what facilities can be had for crossing the river, and have been laid over here to-day by missing the connection.

I sent you this afternoon by express a whole venison and a can of very fine oysters. I telegraphed Barbour to look out for them, and told him to take a portion of the venison for his mess. I expect to be able to reach Jackson Saturday.

Very faithfully,

A. D. BANKS.

JACKSON, *January* 13, 1863.

Major-General VAN DORN, *Grenada:*

General Bragg considers Forrest essential to him in Middle Tennessee. I'll try to find Colonel Cosby.

J. E. JOHNSTON.

GENERAL ORDERS, }   HEADQUARTERS CAVALRY DIVISION,
No. 1.   }   *Grenada, Miss., January* 13, 1863.

By order of the lieutenant-general commanding the Department of Mississippi and East Louisiana the undersigned assumes command of all the cavalry in his department, with the exception of that in District No. 2. Complete reports, exhibiting the strength and organization of each cavalry command, will therefore be made without delay to the adjutant-general at my headquarters (Maj. M. M. Kimmel); also the number and condition of horses, equipments, arms, and accouterments, and, in a word, of everything necessary to give me a perfect knowledge of the condition of the cavalry assigned to my command. Active measures will be taken at once to put the cavalry in condition to take the field.

By order of Major-General Van Dorn:

M. M. KIMMEL,
Major and Assistant Adjutant-General.

Abstract from Field Return of the Cavalry Brigade, Army of the Mississippi, Brig. Gen. John A. Wharton commanding, for January 14, 1863 (headquarters Shelbyville).

Command.	Present for duty.		Effective total present.	Aggregate present.	Aggregate present and absent.	Horses serviceable.	Effective aggregate December 30, 1862.
	Officers.	Men.					
14th Alabama Battalion	13	197	195	273	420	43	204
1st Confederate Regiment	19	156	156	263	476	140	131
3d Confederate Regiment	32	459	457	616	821	606	329
2d Georgia Regiment	19	283	283	438	655	292	135
4th Tennessee Regiment	27	352	352	420	690	304	344
Colonel Murray's regiment	15	193	193	269	535	205	170
Texas Rangers	29	385	385	501	684	325	350
Escort company	3	29	29	34	58	20	41
Captain White's battery	2	52	52	59	73	35	63
Grand total	159	2,106	2,102	2,873	4,412	1,970	1,767

NOTE.—In the aggregate present and absent, the wounded and missing are included.

HDQRS. DEPT. OF MISSISSIPPI AND EAST LOUISIANA,
Jackson, January 15, 1863.

Maj. Gen. W. W. LORING, *Grenada, Miss.:*

GENERAL: I am instructed by the lieutenant-general commanding to say to you that you will at once prepare the Army of Mississippi for a forward movement on the line of the Mississippi Central Railroad.

You will move with light wagons, repairing all roads as you advance, getting your supplies from the country through which the army is moving, sending back to Grenada what supplies you may be able to collect. You will communicate with these headquarters by telegraph as you move forward.

I am, general, very respectfully,

J. R. WADDY,
Assistant Adjutant-General.

CAMP ON DEER CREEK, *January* 15, 1863.

Brigadier-General HÉBERT,
   Commanding at Snyder's Bluff:

We have had thirty-six hours of constant rain, and this morning the snow and sleet has commenced falling rapidly. Our march has been temporarily arrested by this weather and the almost impassable condition of the roads.

From a reliable source I learned yesterday that the Yankee fleet was seriously troubled for fuel on its upward passage. It was delayed two days chopping wood and packing off fence rails. I had, when here before, fortunately burned about 10,000 cords of wood on the river bank near Greenville. They stopped at that point and gathered every stray stick remaining. It was whilst engaged in this work for two days near Greenville that General Reynolds, of the Federal Army (who is from Missouri, I think), restored to Mrs. Polk, wife of Dr. Thomas Polk, a pair of carriage horses, stolen from her as the expedition against Vicksburg was descending. He denounced in the strongest terms those acts of pillage of private [property], and discussed with much freedom and force the present war and the objects of its promotion. He states that the people of the West had engaged in this contest solely for the preservation of the Union and the unrestricted navigation of the Mississippi River. That Lincoln's emancipation proclamation of 1st of January had converted the war into an abolition crusade, which would not be approved by the people of the West, and would entirely estrange them from the Lincoln Government. The recent attack upon Vicksburg had resulted in a bloody repulse and they were fully convinced of the utter impossibility of reducing the place; that the men had refused to renew the attack and were prepared to throw down their arms if it had been insisted on. He went on further to say that a union of New England with the West was impossible; that the natural and proper allies of his section were the Southern States, and to them they would cling.

These are strange utterances for a Federal general and may indicate a radical change of Western sentiment and action. To be sure it may be they were the inspirations of the Vicksburg reverse, but still he would scarcely have ventured upon such declarations without the conviction of strong support among his own people.

After Lieutenant Bradford's visit to Milliken's Bend he proceeded by my instructions directly up the river as far as Greenville. He has not yet returned to the command. I will write you fully the result of his observations.

The roads above the Rolling Fork of Deer Creek, leading in the direction of the Yazoo, are utterly impassable. In addition to their recent obstruction I learn that the rain-water has accumulated so rapidly that it is now swimming to a horse.

A returned prisoner observed on a map of this river district, hanging in the commanding general's office at Memphis, a mark on Greenville with a corresponding foot-note to the effect that this region abounded in corn and large amounts of Government cotton. So they do not lack information.

Yours, very truly,

WIRT ADAMS.

Statement of subsistence stores on hand at the post commissary, Vicksburg, Miss., January 15, 1863.

Articles.	Quantity.	Rations.	Remarks.
Pork .... pounds..	800	1,066$\frac{2}{3}$	$\frac{3}{4}$ pound to the ration.
Bacon .... do....	5,600	7,466$\frac{2}{3}$	$\frac{3}{4}$ pound to the ration.
Flour .... do....	53,031	47,138$\frac{2}{3}$	1$\frac{1}{8}$ pounds to the ration.
Meal .... do....	29,340	23,472	1$\frac{1}{4}$ pounds to the ration.
Pease .... do....	103,595	690,633$\frac{1}{3}$	15 pounds to the 100 rations.
Rice .... do....	6,200	62,000	10 pounds to the 100 rations.
Coffee .... do....	630	10,500	6 pounds to the 100 rations.
Sugar .... do....	28,230	235,250	12 pounds to the 100 rations.
Candles .... do....	140	9,333$\frac{1}{3}$	1$\frac{1}{2}$ pounds to the 100 rations.
Soap .... do....	506	12,650	4 pounds to the 100 rations.
Salt .... do....	14,635	325,222$\frac{2}{9}$	4$\frac{1}{2}$ pounds to the 100 rations.
Lard .... do....	2,275	3,033$\frac{1}{3}$	$\frac{3}{4}$ pound to the 100 rations.
Rice flour .... do....	500		
Molasses .... gallons..	3,223	161,150	2 gallons to the 100 rations.
Wine .... do....	180		
Brandy .... do....	120		
Corn .... bushels..	161$\frac{33}{56}$		

I have received no money from the department, having made no estimate for funds. I have been waiting to form something near an exact estimate of amount as near as possible I shall need.

Very respectfully, your obedient servant,

JOS. B. SMITH,
Captain and Assistant Commissary of Subsistence.

JACKSON, *January* 16, 1863.

Major-General GARDNER,
Port Hudson, La.:

You cannot send troops across the river to General Sibley.

J. C. PEMBERTON,
Lieutenant-General, Commanding.

JACKSON, *January* 16, 1863.

Maj. Gen. C. L. STEVENSON,
Commanding, Vicksburg:

This telegram received this evening:

> Fifteen transports, loaded with troops, and two gunboats passed Delta on their way down Mississippi 9 o'clock a. m., 12th January.
>
> W. W. LORING,
> *Commanding General.*

May probably attempt Snyder's Mill.

J. C. PEMBERTON,
Lieutenant-General, Commanding.

COMO, MISS., *January* 16, 1863 [1864].*

Major-General FORREST, *Panola:*

Henderson's scouts from Memphis report Sixteenth Army Corps under marching orders to drive you from North Mississippi. Rumored they will start from Memphis, La Grange, Corinth, and Yazoo City simultaneously.

JAMES R. CHALMERS.

———

SPECIAL ORDERS, }   HEADQUARTERS CAVALRY CORPS,
No. 3.   }   *Grenada, January* 16, 1863.

The following-named commands of cavalry are detailed for duty with the Army of the Department of Mississippi and East Louisiana, and will at once report to the commanding officer of that army, viz: Jackson's (Tennessee) cavalry, Second Regiment Arkansas Cavalry, Willis' battalion cavalry, Wilbourn's cavalry, Falkner's cavalry, and two companies of Second Missouri Cavalry, now serving in Second Corps. All the cavalry serving in this corps will report without delay to Brig. Gen. W. H. Jackson at Grenada, Miss.

By order of General Van Dorn:

M. M. KIMMEL,
Major and Assistant Adjutant-General.

———

JACKSON, MISS., *January* 17, 1863.

His Excellency the PRESIDENT, *Richmond:*

I have four brigades of cavalry and but one brigadier-general; senior colonels incompetent. An important expedition about to move under General Van Dorn. Do give me by telegraph Armstrong, Cosby, and R. A. Howard for brigadier-generals. They are strongly recommended by Major-Generals Van Dorn and Buckner, and are, I am confident, fully competent.

General Buckner requires a brigadier-general of cavalry.

J. E. JOHNSTON.

———

JACKSON, MISS., *January* 17, 1863.

His Excellency the PRESIDENT, *Richmond:*

I am preparing to send about 6,000 cavalry under Van Dorn to Bragg's aid to operate upon the enemy's communications. I think it of great importance. These brigades will be under utterly incompetent commanders unless you appoint brigadier-generals.

When Martin arrives one of the four can take command of Buckner's cavalry—a large brigade.

J. E. JOHNSTON.

———

JACKSON, MISS., *January* 17, 1863.

General BRAGG, *Tullahoma, Tenn.:*

Colonel Barteau, at Okolona, telegraphs to-day:

A scout, who is reliable, just from the vicinity of Corinth, reports enemy there 5,000, on half rations. A regiment 7 miles this side. All roads obstructed and bridges guarded.

Two prisoners taken day before yesterday say they are in great want.

J. E. JOHNSTON.

———

* Misplaced.

GRENADA, *January* 17, 1863.

Col. J. R. WADDY:

Scout Bonner, now at Lamar, reports on the 11th that they are running the railroad from Memphis to the Junction, making no use of it to Corinth. Reliable accounts say that troops of Grant are in Memphis, along the Charleston road, at La Grange, and at and near Holly Springs. One division reported gone to Jackson. Steamers are being stopped at Memphis to take troops below. Sent scout to Corinth; expect several from there to-day.

W. W. LORING,
Major-General.

———

JACKSON, MISS., *January* 17, 1863.

General W. W. LORING,
Commanding, &c., Grenada :

Send the Texas brigade to La Fayette, if the horses are shod; if not, send another brigade of cavalry under the general control of General Jackson. The brigade will scour the county of La Fayette by company or squadron as circumstances may require; this on the supposition that the reports are correct and not exaggerated. Occupy Coffeeville with an infantry brigade and one of the lightest field batteries you have. Let them take a full supply of axes. The cavalry will hold itself in readiness to join Van Dorn when he moves. The infantry brigade will remain at Coffeeville while you are collecting supplies to send to the rear.

Very respectfully, your obedient servant,

J. R. WADDY,
Assistant Adjutant-General.

———

VICKSBURG, *January* 17, 1863.

Capt. W. M. JONES, *Assistant Quartermaster :*

DEAR SIR: I have large quantities of corn, mostly in the shuck, lying on the banks of the river at Ship's Bayou, Ashwood, Upton's Landing, Gibson's Landing, King's Landing, Saint Joseph, and Waterproof. All of this—enough to load four steamboats—is liable to damage from exposure to the weather, and should be brought away to this point as soon as possible. Please furnish transportation for it.

Respectfully,

W. H. JOHNSON,
Special Government Agent.

———

WAR DEPARTMENT, C. S. A.,
Richmond, Va., January 18, 1863.

Lieut. Gen. J. C. PEMBERTON,
General commanding, &c. :

SIR: The President, since his return from his recent visit to the armies south, has communicated to me the apprehension entertained by you that recent contracts made by this Department with certain parties, expecting to fulfill them by supplies illicitly drawn from within the Federal lines, had caused already some and tended to produce much unlawful trading with the enemy and a consequent demoralization of the people of your department. I feel it, therefore, due to inform you of the motives inducing such contracts and the views entertained by the Department in relation to them.   The contracts were of course made reluctantly, but under a strong conviction of the necessity of resorting to such means of obtaining adequate supplies, especially of shoes and blankets, for the army.

When I assumed direction of this Department I found that internal resources of supplies for these articles had either not been judiciously managed or were deficient; that of late exports from abroad had been so interrupted by several captures by the enemy as to render that mode of supply too precarious for reliance, and that actual suffering was being experienced by the Army of Northern Virginia, in Tennessee, and I was informed by an officer of General Price's staff, then visiting Richmond, in the Southwestern Army likewise, from the want of adequate supplies of such articles.   Resolving that the armies were to be maintained in comfort and efficiency at any cost or sacrifice, I embraced their irregular modes of supply as the only resource.   Since, greater success in running the blockade has diminished the imperative need existing and apprehended at the time; but still supplies without the aid expected from these contracts must prove scant and precarious.   They must, therefore, if practicable, be carried out to the extent made, both from the want they supply and from the faith of the engagements made by the Department; but since hearing of the mischievous effects you suppose to have followed from them, I have abstained from making any more.   I very much fear, however, it will be absolutely necessary for the subsistence of the army that contracts for the supply of meat (bacon and pork) of a similar character must be entered into if they can still be made available, to a considerable amount.   In deference to your views, I shall forbear from them as long and make them as small as necessity will allow; but should they be made shall expect from you such co-operation and countenance as will make them effective.

I may add that, in your laudable desire to prevent all illicit trade, especially in cotton, with the enemy, you may have given an exaggerated influence to the effect of these contracts.   In truth, in a country where cotton is almost the sole product for sale, and is habitually looked to as the means of supply of all comforts and necessaries, it is impossible to expect that trading in it with the enemy will not be indulged in to a considerable extent.   Even the most loyal people are apt to yield to the pressure of want, to the extent at least of supplying their families and plantations.   To this cause, and not to the influence of a few contracts made by the Government for army supplies, with all deference, I think the trade so deprecated by you is ascribable.   It would have equally occurred without them.

I learn, however, that you fear the privilege accorded of passing the cotton, to be paid for by the receiver, will be abused and made the cover for carrying into the enemy's lines much larger quantities.   I cannot see how this can well occur, as the parties contracting are known; do not purchase the cotton at all, but only receive it when delivered in payment by the officers of the Government, and then are allowed to remove only that quantity under special permit which may even limit the quantity at such transmission.   The moral influence may be injurious, but surely due precaution will effectually guard against abuse or extension of the permit.   I shall be pleased, however, to have your views fully on this subject, and any suggestions you deem advisable to guard against abuse, in case further contracts for meat become indispensable.

With high consideration and esteem, very respectfully,

J. A. SEDDON,
Secretary of War.

JACKSON, MISS., *January* 18, 1863.

Major-General LORING, *Grenada, Miss.:*

Send cavalry to La Fayette County as you first intended, unless later information renders it in your opinion unnecessary. Send infantry brigade as heretofore directed.

J. C. PEMBERTON,
Lieutenant-General, Commanding.

JACKSON, *January* 18, 1863.

Major-General LORING, *Grenada, Miss.:*

It is desirable to bring your corps west of the Beton Bayou, unless the bridge across it can be at once made serviceable and kept so. Send one strong regiment of infantry and a battery of four to Vaiden from Rust's division; a squadron of cavalry to Greensborough. Send the brigade and field battery to Coffeeville, and as soon as practicable a brigade and field battery to Panola. Let me hear from you at once.

J. C. PEMBERTON,
Lieutenant-General, Commanding.

INSPECTOR-GENERAL'S OFFICE,
Jackson, Miss., January 18, 1863.

Col. CHARLES M. FAUNTLEROY,
Inspector-General, Jackson, Miss.:

COLONEL: I have the honor to submit the following report of my inspection of the Army of Mississippi, stationed at and near Grenada, Miss.:

In consequence of the weather and the high water generally I was induced to put off an inspection of the troops; but from conversations with corps and division commanders and an inspection of their papers I am enabled to give a tolerable account of the condition of the army.

With regard to the departments I gave them a minute examination and find their condition as follows, viz:

QUARTERMASTER'S DEPARTMENT.

This department is under the charge of Maj. E. A. Banks, who appears to be an active, efficient, and business-like man. The department has evidently been in a state of great chaos and confusion, but it is now being administered in a systematic manner under its present head.

Maj. George A. Turner is quartermaster at the post, having just been assigned to this duty. He has three assistants, all active and apparently efficient officers.

Major Banks has also established agencies at Coffeeville, Vaiden, Oakland, and other depots on the Mississippi and Tennessee Railroad. Officers of judgment have been selected for these points with instructions to throw out all their agents in the country adjacent and commence at once the purchase and collection of commissary and other stores at convenient points accessible to the Central road, in order that they may be shipped to Grenada.

The disbursements of money for this army are, I am informed, always made by regularly commissioned and bonded officers, the money intended for this army being turned over to Major Banks and distributed by him to quartermasters throughout the command.

CONDITION OF THE POST.

There is no property on hand for distribution at the post, with the exception of a few supplies now being transferred to the different commands.   Every demand of the hospital and commissariat is readily met, and every effort made to work harmoniously with these departments.

GENERAL CONDITION OF THE COMMAND.

The quartermasters of the army are said to be efficient and good executive officers, and, from the examination I was enabled to make, have rendered regular returns of their accountability to Richmond.

MEANS OF OBTAINING SUPPLIES.

Agents are scattered throughout the country purchasing, collecting, and shipping grain, while for other quartermasters' property the army is dependent upon Jackson, where three armies have to be supplied with their wants.   It is in my opinion impossible for one post, situated at Jackson and dependent simply upon the resources of the Mississippi, to meet such demands.   The grain in the section of country around Grenada is rapidly diminishing, and the quartermaster and commissary appear to be apprehensive lest they fail to sustain themselves there much longer.   The building of the bridges across the two railroads which branch at this point is earnestly recommended.

MEANS OF TRANSPORTATION.

First Corps.

Number of six-horse wagons	50
Number of four-horse wagons	223
Number of two-horse wagons	46
Ambulances	4
Total	323

Second Corps.

Number of six-horse wagons	243
Number of four-horse wagons	191
Number of two-horse wagons	26
Ambulances	26
Total	486

Jackson's Cavalry Brigade.

Number of six-horse wagons	12
Number of four-horse wagons	96
Number of two-horse wagons	22
Ambulances	8
Total	138

COMMISSARY DEPARTMENT.

This department is under the control of Maj. William M. Strickland, who appears to be well fitted for the post he fills. This department is well arranged and the officers under Major Fickland properly assigned. The difficulty of procuring supplies is great in a country abounding in but few of the articles needed to subsist an army. Agents are selected and sent through the country, and by their energy and industry they have thus far been enabled to meet the necessary current supply.

There is here storage for the lighter articles sufficient to secure rations of forty days for an army of 25,000 troops, and two large Government pork-houses, capable, if floored, of containing a large amount of more bulky articles.

The commissaries are generally bonded, and have rendered their papers up to date.

I counted the moneys of all at the post—some seven or eight in number; looked into their accounts; found them all right. Candles, coffee, and soap are much needed. Major Fickland reports that at the suggestion of General Johnston an application was made by him to Major Mason, assistant adjutant-general, for the stores at Gainesville, Ala., in charge of Maj. F. F. Jackson, assistant commissary of subsistence. Nothing has ever been heard of this application, and he begs to refer it again to the consideration of the general commanding.

ORDNANCE DEPARTMENT.

This department is under the charge of Capt. L. R Evans, an intelligent young officer, under whose direction system and order in this branch of the army seem to have been well established.

The total number of field guns in this army is fifty-six, as follows: One James rifled gun, caliber 3.70 inches; one Parrott rifled gun, caliber, 3.67 inches; nine Parrott rifled guns, caliber 3 inches; two 24-pounder howitzers (bronze), sixteen 12-pounder howitzers (bronze), two 12-pounder guns (bronze), twenty-five 6-pounder guns (bronze).

Thirty of the above-named guns are in the First Army Corps; twenty-six in the Second. The gun designated as Parrott rifled, caliber 3.67 inches, is of Yankee origin. It was captured in the outer intrenchments before Corinth on the 3d October, 1862, by the brigades of Brigadier-Generals Rust and Bowen. Its caliber has been named above. Its weight is 1,695 pounds. The gun with its carriage is in perfect condition. A caisson has been remodeled to convey ammunition for the piece, and horses and harness have been recently procured to transport it. All the guns are reported in serviceable condition, a limited amount of implements and equipments being required. The supply of ammunition is ample for the guns of smooth-bore, consisting of over 200 rounds for each piece. The small-arms, all of which are in the hands of the troops, number 11,438; bayonets for same, 5,854. You will observe the great deficiency in bayonets. There is also a limited deficiency in the various commands occasioned by the recent arrival of troops and return of convalescents. The arms in use are of various calibers, embracing the Mississippi rifle, caliber .54; Enfield, caliber .57; Minie, caliber .58; the musket, caliber .69, and the Belgian rifle and British musket, caliber .70.

Of wagons for the composition of ordnance trains there are 26 in the Second Corps, 21 in the Second Division, First Corps, and 2 in the First Division, First Corps.

It is designed to keep all reserved ordnance stores for this army at Duck Hill, 12 miles south of Grenada, on the railroad, where a depot has been established. At that point and at Grenada there are now on hand 5,200 rounds fixed cannon ammunition, 430,000 cartridges for small-arms, and 1,800 sets infantry accouterments. Captain Evans has no assistant ordnance officer, and consequently the duty of depot ordnance officer is imposed upon him. I recommend that an assistant be given him as soon as practicable.

MEDICAL DEPARTMENT.

This department appears to be well regulated, and is under the charge of Dr. G. A. Moses. He reports the sanitary condition of the army as better than it has been during the past year. In hospital at the post there are 450 sick, many of whom are the wounded of pickets in some of the late skirmishes at Coffeeville. In camp, 1,002 are reported sick. Of these, 8 are affected with small-pox. The whole army, excepting the cavalry, have been vaccinated during the past month. Ambulances are much needed, there being only 38 in the entire army. The commands are generally well supplied with medicines, but in case of a great increase of disease the present quantity will be insufficient. Dr. Moses says any quantity of medical stores could be obtained from Memphis in return for cotton, and warmly recommends that it be done. I think it would be unwise to do so myself. Many medical officers are employed either by the assignment of colonels of regiments or contract. These are being relieved of duty as rapidly as commissioned surgeons and assistants arrive. Men are not allowed to leave the army on surgeon's certificate without the approval of the medical inspector, and at the post a board of surgeons decides upon discharges and leaves of absence for those in hospital. The hospitals—two in number—are kept neat and clean and appear to be well regulated generally. Surgical instruments are much needed in this army; but ambulances, particularly, are required, and ought if possible to be supplied.

I inclose herewith a list of divisions, brigades, and regiments attached to the two corps of the army.* It will be observed that out of a paper force of 20,517, 12,058 are present, making number of absentees 8,459.

Division and brigade commanders unite in saying the condition of their several commands is good, and the commanding general reports the army generally in good fighting order.

A large proportion of these troops are from the adjacent counties; hence the number of absentees.

The following is a list of cavalry to go with General Van Dorn, and the number in each regiment and battalion, as obtained from him:

First Mississippi	275
Fourth Mississippi	390
Twenty-eighth Mississippi	625
Sanders' battalion	92
Balch's battalion	234
Second Mississippi Battalion (eight companies) [Second Missiouri?]	246
First Tennessee	430
Third Arkansas	354
Ballentine's battalion	259
One company of Jackson's regiment	80
Baxter's battalion	120
Third, Sixth, and Ninth Texas and Whitfield's Legion	1,500
Body guard	50
Total	4,655
Roddey's command	1,400
Regiment from Montgomery	700
Adams' regiment (on Mississippi River)	700
Total to go with General Van Dorn	7,455

* Not found.

LIST OF REGIMENTS TO REMAIN WITH THE ARMY.

Second Arkansas	207
Wilbourn's Partisan Battalion	39
Willis' Texas regiment	297
Jackson's regiment (nine companies)	250
Falkner's Partisans	75
Two companies Second Missouri	150
	1,018
Barteau's battalion, to remain on Mobile and Ohio Railroad	300

RECAPITULATION.

Van Dorn's corps	7,455
Cavalry with Mississippi Army	1,018
Cavalry on Mobile and Ohio Railroad	300
Total amount of cavalry	8,773

This, General Van Dorn informs me, was the present strength of the cavalry, as near as he could come to it.

Nothing remains to be said except that the 20-pounder Parrott gun, caliber 3.97, has been applied for at Vicksburg, and as it is unnecessary at Grenada I respectfully recommend that it be sent there.

I am, colonel, with much respect, your obedient servant,

E. J. HARVIE,
Lieutenant-Colonel, Assistant Inspector-General.

HEADQUARTERS SECOND CORPS,
Grenada, Miss., January 19, 1863.

Major-General LORING,
Commanding Army of the Mississippi, Grenada:

GENERAL: I have, in compliance with your orders, directed the Second Brigade of Bowen's division to hold themselves in readiness to move to Panola. The effective total of this brigade is 1,309. The effective total of Green's brigade (the only other troops of my corps now here) is 2,891.

I communicate these facts so that a different disposition may be made if the brigade ordered to Panola is too weak for the duties of that position.

I am, very respectfully, your obedient servant,

STERLING PRICE,
Major-General, Commanding Second Corps.

VICKSBURG, January 19, 1863.

Col. J. R. WADDY,
Assistant Adjutant-General:

One hundred and eight six-mule teams, 43 four-mule teams, 11 two-mule teams belong to this division. There are 300 tents in use by the division, besides 150 borrowed here from General Smith. The division aggregate strength, leaving out troops attached, over 7,000.

DABNEY H. MAURY,
Major-General.

SPECIAL ORDERS, ⎱ HDQRS. 1ST DIST., DEPT. OF MISS. AND E. LA.,
No. 3.   ⎰   *Columbus, Miss., January* 19, 1863.

I. Brigadier-General Harris, commanding State troops, will remove his brigade, consisting of Fifth Regiment and Third Battalion, from its present encampment to a suitable position about 1½ miles north of this post, on the Aberdeen road, where they will be temporarily encamped. He will maintain strict discipline and establish a thorough police system.

II. The Thirteenth Battalion Alabama Partisan Rangers, commanded by Maj. W. A. Hewlett, will remove from its present encampment without delay to a suitable position about 1½ miles in advance of Mrs. Cox's plantation, on the Aberdeen road, from which point Major Hewlett will picket 10 miles in advance on all avenues of approach, and scout to a distance of 20 miles at least beyond the most advanced picket; all pickets and scouting parties to be under the direction of commissioned officers.

*   *   *   *   *   *   *

By order of Brigadier-General Ruggles:

R. M. HOOE,
Assistant Adjutant-General.

SPECIAL ORDERS, ⎱ HDQRS. ARMY OF NORTHERN VIRGINIA,
No. 19.   ⎰   *January* 19, 1863.

*   *   *   *   *   *   *

VII. Agreeably to instructions from the Secretary of War, Brig. Gen. W. S. Featherston is relieved from duty with this army and will proceed to Jackson, Miss., and report for duty to General J. E. Johnston, commanding Army of the West, or, should he be absent, to Lieut. Gen. J. C. Pemberton, commanding in Mississippi.

*   *   *   *   *   *   *

By order of General Lee:

W. H. TAYLOR,
Assistant Adjutant-General.

Organization of the Cavalry Corps, Department of Mississippi and East Louisiana, Maj. Gen. Earl Van Dorn commanding, January 20, 1863.*

FIRST DIVISION.

Brig. Gen. W. H. JACKSON.

First Brigade.	*Second Brigade.*
1st Mississippi.	3d Arkansas.
4th Mississippi.	Ballentine's Mississippi regiment.
28th Mississippi.	2d Missouri.
Balch's Tennessee battalion.	1st Tennessee.

---

* As announced in General Orders, No. 3, Headquarters Cavalry Corps, Grenada, Miss., of th is date.

SECOND DIVISION.

_Third Brigade._*	_Fourth Brigade._
3d Texas. 6th Texas. 9th Texas. Whitfield's Texas Legion.	Colonel Roddey's command.†

RESERVE AT GENERAL HEADQUARTERS.

Baxter's scouts.
Sanders' battalion.
Company of regulars.

GENERAL ORDERS, }   HDQRS. DEPT. OF MISS. AND EAST LA.,
No. 33.   }   _Vicksburg, February_ 1, 1863.

I. A court of inquiry having assembled at Grenada, Miss., pursuant to Special Orders, No. 21, current series, Headquarters Army of Mississippi, for the purpose of investigating the circumstances attending the burning of tents in General Tilghman's division at the time of the retreat of the army from Abbeville, Miss., &c., and having found as follows—

That there was not sufficient transportation belonging to Brigadier-General Tilghman's division to haul said tents, and that they were burned and destroyed in compliance with and in obedience to an order issued by Lieutenant-General Pemberton, dated "Headquarters Department of Mississippi and East Louisiana, Abbeville, Miss., November 30, 1862;" and those that were destroyed on the march in compliance with and in obedience to a verbal order issued by Major-General Lovell to Brigadier-General Tilghman to throw out sufficient tents, as they were wet and heavy, to enable the wagons to pass over the bad roads and keep up with the train; and in the opinion of the court Brig. Gen. L. Tilghman is fully exonerated from all censure in relation to the burning and destroying of said tents, and we recommend that no further proceedings be had in relation thereto against him—

the decision of the lieutenant-general commanding the department is as follows:

That the order dated "Headquarters DepartmentMississippi and East Louisiana, Abbeville, Miss., November 30, 1862," required the stores that could not be transported to be destroyed, and it does not clearly appear to him that the transportation of the stores was impracticable, and their destruction consequently necessary.

II. The court of inquiry appointed by Special Orders, No. 21, Headquarters Army Mississippi, "for the purpose of investigating the circumstances attending the burning of tents in General Tilghman's division," is hereby dissolved.

By order of Lieutenant-General Pemberton:

J. R. WADDY,
Assistant Adjutant-General.

---

* Temporarily attached to First Division.
† Regiments not indicated n the order.

APPENDIX.

Embracing documents received too late for insertion in proper sequence.

UNION CORRESPONDENCE, ETC.

WASHINGTON CITY, *September* 28, 1862.

The PRESIDENT:

My apology for addressing you this communication is in the fact that you were pleased to invite it. Conscious of my inability to impart any information upon a subject with which you are already familiar, all I can hope to do is to quicken the interest and action of the military authorities upon a matter of acknowledged and urgent importance.

How the rebellion may be most speedily and effectually put down involves an inquiry as to the methods best adapted to that end. Originating, as it did, in the Cotton States, and believing that the sentiment which still sustains it more inveterate in those States than in any others, I would carry the war into their heart, not only for the purpose of crushing the rebellion itself, but as the quickest and surest way to reopen the Mississippi River; indeed, the reopening of that river is one of the first steps I would take in subduing the rebellion. Both in a military and commercial aspect this step is eminently important. It is important in a military view, first, because it would afford the means of cheap and easy communication between our troops disposed at different points on the Mississippi River and its navigable tributaries, and because it would facilitate the concentration of them at any one or more of those points; secondly, because it would cheapen the cost of supplying our men and animals at or near New Orleans with provisions and forage. It would do that by substituting the overflowing granaries of the Northwest for the remoter sources of such supplies in the East, and, thirdly, because, in securing to us the command of the Mississippi River, it would enable us to stop the communication between the revolted States and their armies east and west of that river, thus isolating each section as to the other, destroying the unity of their plans and combinations, and cutting off the rebel forces east of the river from their wonted source of supplies in Texas.

Commercially, the whole nation is deeply interested in the measure, and particularly so the people inhabiting the Mississippi Valley. They are painfully anxious upon the subject. They have not yet complained that the hostile obstacles, shutting them and their commerce out from New Orleans and the Gulf, and so the commerce of Europe by the same channel from that valley, and virtually turning the Mississippi into a dry bed, have not yet been removed. They have appreciated the difficulties surrounding the National Government, and, while emulating the most zealous and liberal in supporting it, have patiently waited for the auspicious period when their great interests would be liberated. Nay, they are grateful for what the Government has done, rather than complaining for what it has not done. Yet it is none the less true that the Mississippi River and its tributaries, affording an inland navigation of 10,000 miles in extent, and floating an annual commerce of the value of $150,000,000 in time of peace, is now locked against all egress or ingress to or from the ocean by a small, indeed comparatively insignificant garrison at Vicksburg, or that the products of agriculture meantime have been accumulating in the hands of producers until they have become well-nigh worthless.

Foreseeing that the continuance of this evil must ultimate in individual bankruptcy and the enervation of the Government itself, by withholding from the people the means of supplying its wants, it is not surprising that large assemblages should be now earnestly calling upon the Government for relief—the relief which would be afforded by the reopening of the Mississippi River. Such relief would be hailed as a benefaction at home and abroad. Without it, must we not fear an ultimate reaction of feeling and opinion in the Mississippi Valley unfavorable to the success of our army and the cause which they are upholding?

In order, then, to liberate the navigation of the Mississippi, I would have a force of at least 60,000 men to descend the river in transports convoyed by gunboats to the mouth of the Yazoo River, and ascend it to the first eligible landing on its south bank, perhaps to Drumgould's Bluff.

Both geographers and river pilots bear testimony to the remarkable character of this river. It is said that it is hardly " surpassed in navigable waters by any river of its size in the world, as steamboats can ascend it from its mouth to its origin in all stages of water and in all seasons of the year." If any impediment exists, it is in the bar at the mouth of the river, a passage through which could be readily made by a dredging machine or even by a steam propeller directing the action of its screw against it. This obstacle, only existing in a low stage of water, having been overcome, gunboats might ascend and cover the debarkation of troops at the bluffs named.

The Gulf column having thus disembarked, should, in whole or in part, march upon Vicksburg, and, aided by the gunboats, seize that place, and, after fortifying and garrisoning it, hasten to Jackson, the capital of the State of Mississippi, only 45 miles distant, and having in like manner fortified and garrisoned Jackson and reopened the railroad to Vicksburg, an armed force might be detached to reopen the railroad from Jackson to New Orleans, if it should be deemed expedient. In the accomplishment of the latter object, our forces at New Orleans might lend assistance, or, if the enemy should concentrate in any considerable force on that road, it would only remain to attack and defeat him there, instead of another place. It is believed, however, that he would not do so while Jackson, New Orleans, and the Mississippi River remained under our control, thus surrounding him on three sides, and leaving him no other chance of obtaining re-enforcements or escaping, except by a long march, obstructed by the numerous streams traversing the extensive district west of the Mobile and Ohio Railroad.

Securing Jackson, as already mentioned, the column should next push forward to the junction of the Southern Mississippi and the Mobile and Ohio Railroad, at the town of Meridian, 75 miles east of Jackson. Arrived at that place, the column would be within threatening distance both of Mobile and Montgomery, the capital of the State of Alabama, and would be guided in its movement, whether first to the one or the other of those places, by circumstances. If the enemy had concentrated at Mobile, the column should march upon him there, and, conjointly with our fleet, attack and destroy him, or, if he had concentrated at Montgomery, he should be attacked and destroyed there; but in either case Mobile should be secured as a new and more favorable base for operations farther eastward.

Having secured Meridian, Montgomery, and Mobile, and reopened the railroads connecting these places with each other, a depot of military stores should be established at Mobile, which is only 165 miles by rail from Montgomery, and from which our forces at or east of Montgomery could readily obtain supplies, while the garrisons in the rear could obtain them either from the same place or from Vicksburg. At Montgomery the advancing column would only be 75 miles by rail from Opelika, near the western boundary of Georgia. In a military view, this is a most important place. Here the whole railroad system of the Southern Atlantic States, including Georgia, converge into the Montgomery and West Point Railroad, which forms one of the two links connecting that system by rail with the Gulf system of railroads. Hence, seizing that place, the Atlantic communication by rail between the revolted States east and west would be severed.

As a measure tending to the success of the enterprise, I would also recommend that a Federal force be advanced from Port Royal, on the coast, in an interior direction, and that naval demonstrations should be made at the principal points along the Southern Atlantic and Gulf coasts; but I must forbear to dwell upon those matters.

In combination with the movement from Vicksburg, the noticeable railroad triangle, of which Boyce and Dalton, on the Memphis and Charleston Railroad, are the base, and Cleveland, on the Tennessee and Georgia Railroad, is the apex, should be seized. This should be done by advancing the forces now in West Tennessee or a portion of those in Kentucky, or conjunctively by both.

This co-operative movement is indispensable, unless the Gulf column be increased to more than 60,000 men. In executing it, the left flank of that column during its advance would be protected against any formidable attack from the north. The seizure of the triangle mentioned would not only give us possession of the remaining or interior link, connecting by rail the Southern Atlantic and Gulf States, but place a Federal army in a favorable position to march south upon Rome, in Georgia, the site of one of the principal arsenals and manufactories of arms in the revolted States, and to Atlanta, in the same State, one of the principal railroad centers in those States; or northeast to and beyond Knoxville, in Tennessee, in co-operation with any more easterly Federal movement directed against the Virginia and Tennessee Railroad or the enemy on or near it. The absence of any railroad south of Vicksburg, running east and west, would secure the right flank of the column against any serious danger from the south.

Incidentally, the two great railroad systems of the revolted States have been noticed. By reference to the map of those States, a more complete and satisfactory idea of those systems may be formed. The one, which may be called the eastern system, ramifies itself along the eastern coast; the other, which may be called the western system, radiates from the Gulf of Mexico or the Mississippi River, and runs in great uniform lines at wide intervals, either parallel or at right angles with that river.

These two systems, as I have already said, are only connected by two links, one being the road leading from Montgomery to Opelika, and the other being the more extended road leading from Lynchburg, in Virginia, southwest to Knoxville, and connecting with the railroad triangle before mentioned. These two roads are the umbilical cords of the two systems, and form their only bond of unity; cutting them, a serious and disastrous blow is struck at the rebellion, the effect of which must be greatly aggravated by the fact of the comparative destitution of work animals and wagons, and the want of skill and experience in working iron and wood in the South. A separation of the eastern and western revolted States would result, depriving each of the means of succoring the other.

Experience has proven that a border warfare will not serve to extinguish the rebellion, and that the dispersion of our troops along exterior lines must continue to invite guerrilla raids and attacks by the enemy in overwhelming numbers. Five hundred thousand armed rebels now in the field, and inspired by confidence, cannot be conquered by such a mode of warfare. It must and can only be done by destroying the enemy's railroad communications, cutting him off from his sources of supplies, and by invasive war and interior attacks upon his vital parts.

Where those parts are is well understood. They are in the Gulf States, the home and first love of the arch traitors who initiated our present national afflictions. Strike home a deadly blow in those States, and the rebellion will have been virtually subdued. This is what I propose by the plan thus hastily and imperfectly delineated. If, however, it should be the determination of the Government to give the movement from Vicksburg a westerly, rather than an easterly, direction, that could be easily done, and with good effect. Arkansas has already been entered overland by a column marching from Missouri, and might also be penetrated by a co-operating force ascending the Arkansas and other rivers. Northern Louisiana may be penetrated by the railroad leading west from Vicksburg, and to Western Louisiana and Northeastern Texas by the Red River.

Texas has some 300 miles of railroad concentrating at Houston, on the Buffalo Bayou, which empties into Galveston Bay; hence the capture of Galveston would give us control of all those roads; also of the Trinity River, which is navigable for some distance. But it is thought the principal movement upon Texas should be up the Red River, and from Indianola, on Matagorda Bay. With the Mississippi under our control, and the advance of the Federal column from Missouri into the heart of Arkansas, no hostile force capable of offering serious resistance would be left to oppose the advance up the Red River, and Indianola being unfortified, might be easily taken. Moving a column from Indianola to Austin, the capital of Texas, the disaffected portion of the State in the southeast would be separated from the western portion, inhabited by friendly Mexicans and Germans, while, if the loyal population in Northwestern Texas should rise, as it is said they would do, the State would be delivered, and soon after Louisiana and Arkansas would fall for want of intrinsic ability to sustain themselves in their isolated condition. In short, as a consequence of the plan proposed—

1st. The Mississippi River would again be liberated, and the interests of commerce, at home and abroad, promoted.

2d. The extensive railroad system and numerous rivers of the Gulf States would be reopened to lawful and peaceful uses.

3d. An extensive district, fruitful of cotton, sugar, and corn, would be opened to accustomed markets and the wants of our armies.

4th. The ax would be laid at the root of the rebellion by dividing and distracting the enemy's forces, and striking a blow at the very heart of the rebellion, or, if this plan should exceed the present capabilities of the Government, then, as a limited alternative, I propose a smaller force, whose immediate purpose, in conjunction with the Mississippi fleet, should be to capture Vicksburg and Baton Rouge, and simply reopen the Mississippi River, waiting for a more favorable period for the execution of the more extensive plan.

Accompanying this communication is a map illustrating the views it embodies,* all of which is here deferentially submitted.

Your obedient servant,

JOHN A. McCLERNAND,
Major-General.

WASHINGTON CITY, *October* 16, 1862.

The GENERAL-IN-CHIEF:

At the instance of the Secretary of War, with whom I have conversed upon the subject, I address you this communication.

Advised that an expedition of land and naval forces will be immediately set on foot, for the purpose of opening the Mississippi River, and that the land force will, presently, consist of 30,000 men, I would, in view of the character of the service contemplated, organize it into the different arms as follows: 24,000 infantry, 1,000 sharpshooters, 400 sappers and miners, 3,000 cavalry, 1,500 light artillery, and 100 heavy artillery.

I think ten batteries of six guns each might be very properly assigned to the artillery arm, these batteries to consist of guns of different caliber, as follows: fourteen 10-pounder Parrott guns, twenty-eight Napoleon guns, six 24-pounder howitzers (brass), eight 6-pounder smoothbore guns (brass), and four 12-pounder howitzers (brass). I would also add twelve siege pieces, as follows: eight 30-pounder Parrott guns and four 10-inch mortars.

Your obedient servant,

JOHN A. McCLERNAND,
Major-General.

HDQRS. FIRST DIVISION, ARMY OF THE TENNESSEE,
Memphis, October 25, 1862.

Col. D. C. ANTHONY, *Provost-Marshal, Memphis:*

SIR: The publication of my General Orders, No. 90, imposing on you new and additional labor and responsibility, makes the occasion proper for me to express my high appreciation of the manner you have hitherto performed the delicate and important duties of your office. Memphis is, in my judgment, a most important point in a military sense, designed as a base for operating on the Mississippi River and in the interior of Mississippi and Arkansas. It should be made as secure as Cincinnati, Louisville, or Saint Louis. To this end the quiet and good order of the city itself is necessary. This has been admirably accomplished by you, with as little interference with the people as possible. I have observed always that, however severe your measures were, all persons conceded to you generous and courteous treatment, and the suspicion of fraud and peculation, as connected with the handling of large amounts of confiscated property and custody of prisoners, has never been imputed to you or officers under your charge. You possess my undivided confidence, and in the discharge of your new duties you may feel assured that I will sustain you with my whole power. Your regiment is not stationed here,

---

* Not found.

nor is it under my command, and I have feared you would be called away.

General Orders, No. 140, from the War Department, provides for the organization of a special department for provost-marshals, with a head in Washington to supervise and control the acts of all. This is doubtless intended to render uniform the practice of all such officers throughout the United States, and will doubtless embrace the district of Memphis. If you are willing to accept such an office, in preference to the commission you now hold in the volunteer service, it will afford me pleasure to urge your appointment with all the influence I or my friends possess. You are already familiar with the past history of Memphis, and well acquainted with its prominent citizens, and with an established reputation for firmness, courtesy, and decision of character that entitles you to the office if you wish it.

Please examine General Orders, 140, and advise me what you prefer to do. A lieutenant-colonel of an active regiment, you will sooner or later be called away, and I think the interests of the Government require you to remain here at your present post.

I am, with great respect, your obedient servant,

W. T. SHERMAN,
Major-General, Commanding.

HDQRS. FIRST DIVISION, DEPARTMENT OF THE TENNESSEE,
Memphis, October 29, 1862.

Maj. Gen. W. S. ROSECRANS:

MY DEAR GENERAL: I have been intending to write you, conveying my hearty congratulations at the magnificent victory at Corinth. I know it to have been one of the most important achievements of the war. Its effect was felt by rebels over the whole valley of the Mississippi, and completely disconcerted their plans in Tennessee and Kentucky. A man named Keagg came here yesterday, bearing your letter of October 20, and I have ordered a horse, saddle, &c., to be given him that he may pursue his journey to the south. I have pretty accurate information from that quarter all the time through people who come to Memphis. Holly Springs is, of course, their headquarters. Pemberton arrived, but found Van Dorn and Lovell his seniors. His orders to the Department of Mississippi and Louisiana contemplated Van Dorn and Lovell in Tennessee, but you disappointed them in this, so there is a row in that family. Report has said that to obviate this difficulty Van Dorn and Lovell are to be ordered to Richmond; but last Friday Van Dorn and Lovell were at Holly Springs, and Pemberton had gone back to Jackson, Miss. All hands at Holly Springs are busy reorganizing. A large force of cavalry is near Holly Springs; as near as I can make out, fifteen regiments, under General [W. H.] Jackson. The infantry are so scattered that it is hard to estimate them, but they have the same force that attacked you, re-enforced by conscripts, also Waul's brigade of Texans, about 4,000; but, on the other hand, Villepigue's brigade has been sent to Meridian. All their dispositions are defensive. They would like to have Memphis, but you taught them to respect heavy batteries, and I have here a pretty line, with twenty-five heavy guns in position and about fifty small guns. My division is now in good drill, and I would like them to attempt my position. I occasionally send my cavalry into their lines, and it makes them very angry.

The evening papers just announced your appointment to the Army of Kentucky. I congratulate you, and assure you of my best wishes for your success in every sphere of action. The importance of the command cannot be exaggerated; I do not like departments; each line of operations should be intrusted to one mind, but the problem will work itself out. I hope you will soon be down to this latitude again.

As ever, your friend,

W. T. SHERMAN,
Major-General, Commanding.

HDQRS. FIRST DIV., DEPARTMENT OF THE TENNESSEE,
Memphis, Tenn., October 29, 1862.

Maj. JOHN A. RAWLINS,
Assistant Adjutant-General:

SIR: Inclosed please find a report of all the troops in this division of my own corps,* as well as companies attached, called for in your dispatch of the 24th, received yesterday. I have sent to Vicksburg my prisoners of war and exchanged them, but at various times prisoners have been paroled. I will make up a list of such and send you as soon as I can get the data from the provost-marshal. I have had several persons in from the interior who report that Pemberton reached Holly Springs, but finding Van Dorn and Lovell there, his seniors, he has returned to Jackson, Miss. The supposition is that he was ordered to the command in Mississippi on the supposition that Van Dorn's command would be on its way to Nashville. Rumor says now that Van Dorn and Lovell are to be ordered to Richmond, to make way for Pemberton.

Waul's brigade, from Texas, is reported to have passed Jackson to join the army at Holly Springs, said to be 4,000 strong. Detachments of drafted men are represented to be arriving at Holly Springs daily, who are assigned to the old regiments. The army is being reorganized and extensive changes made. Villepigue's brigade is said to be ordered to Meridian. Whole force at Holly Springs estimated at 40,000 men, of which 15,000 are cavalry, surplus of artillery.

Colonel Grierson's expedition toward the Hatchie was perfectly successful; he moved by night to Colliersville, coming upon a party of guerrillas, whom he dispersed. He then turned to the north, to Shelby Depot, where he met Stuart's regiment of infantry; then he crossed the Loosahatchee, and scoured the country all the way to Randolph, killing 7 guerrillas, wounding 14, and bringing in 17 prisoners. He captured 20 horses and destroyed a great number of shot-guns; he returned to Memphis in steamboats I had placed at Randolph, having lost not a single horse or man on the trip.

Stuart's regiment also destroyed the Shelby Depot and several buildings used as rendezvous and haunts of the guerrillas. The enemy, hoping to intercept Grierson on his return, interposed a heavy cavalry force at Germantown, their scouts coming in as far as White's Station, and was duly astonished to hear all had safely returned by the river.

The enemy is busy in preventing cotton coming to market, and I hear the people are getting very tired of them, and threaten to fight their way in. They cannot get supplies here unless they bring in cotton and other produce. Troops in fine health and everything doing well. No new attacks on steamboats.

W. T. SHERMAN,
Major-General.

---

* Omitted.

HDQRS. FIRST DIV., DEPARTMENT OF THE TENNESSEE,
Memphis, October 29, 1862.

Brigadier-General HOVEY,
　　Commanding United States Forces, Helena :

DEAR SIR: I was pleased to hear that you had succeeded to the command at Helena. We should keep up a correspondence of ideas, for although we are in different departments, we are near together.

An officer of your command has come up for some lumber. There is none here. My own regiments have made requisitions on requisitions for tent floors, cook sheds, &c., but I have made them get along with make-shift bricks and puncheons. Bricks are abundant here; laid in mud, they answer for walls and chimneys, and some of the soldiers have made tasteful huts; but boards are very scarce, except coarse stuff 3 inches thick, most of which we have used for gun platforms.

I wish you could come and see us. Our fort is very well advanced, and I think it is a good piece of work. We have about 6,000 negroes here, of which 2,000 are men—800 on the fort, 240 in the quartermaster's department, and about 1,000 as cooks, teamsters, and servants in the regiments. I have enlarged the Overton Hospital so as to accommodate about 1,000 patients; most of those are from your command, and I discharge all the surgeon in charge recommends. My notion is that when a soldier gets into a general hospital, unless he is wounded, he is lost to the service. Two new regiments have passed down to Helena, and I suppose you will have quite a force there. They all seem to think I have plenty of men here to make all sorts of detachments, but my present strength is less than yours; but they are well provided, and in good discipline as to drill. They do rob and steal occasionally, to my mortification, but on the whole behave pretty well.

I am now living in a house on Tennessee street, near the fort, and have all the departments inside, with a shop to repair arms, and will gradually enlarge so as to have it quite a depot. If you should be threatened, I could send a force across to Madison, which would divert attention, but I must be careful, as our enemy has a large force at Holly Springs, estimated at 40,000. I cannot hear that any have come over from Arkansas, but I hear of the arrival of Waul's brigade, from Texas. The reaction in favor of the civil over the military rule, in the whole South, will strip the people of the terror that has held them down so hard, but still we know the people are generally united in spirit and feeling against us, and must not count on any reaction until the safety of property changes their feeling, their political opinions, and Southern prejudices.

Many military changes are indicated north of us, but none in our immediate neighborhood. I shall always be pleased to hear from you, and to see you when I can.

　　　　I am, truly, your friend,

　　　　　　　　W. T. SHERMAN,
　　　　　　　　Major-General, Commanding.

────────

HEADQUARTERS FIRST DIVISION,
Memphis, October 30, 1862.

To commanders of regiments and companies in the service of the United States :

Generosity and benevolence to the poor and distressed are characteristics of good soldiers. I tell you that there are many poor families in and about Memphis, who, unless aided, will suffer for wood, clothing, and provisions. Government provides all these to our soldiers bounteously, and I know that, by the exercise of reasonable economy, every company can and does save a proportion of their allowance. What better disposition can be made of a part of this surplus than by giving it to the poor? I recommend to all who have spare bread, flour, meat, rice, coffee, sugar, or anything needed by poor and sick families, that they send it to the officers of the Central Relief Committee, in Jefferson Block, Second street, where it will be receipted for by an agent, and by him distributed to the worthy. By this process charity is done to the best advantage. I know that all our soldiers want is to know how to dispense their charity, and the above method, in my judgment, will accomplish the greatest amount of good.

W. T. SHERMAN,
Major-General, Commanding.

HEADQUARTERS DISTRICT OF MEMPHIS,
Memphis, November 1, 1862.

Maj. JOHN A. RAWLINS,
Assistant Adjutant-General, Jackson, Tenn. :

DEAR SIR : I received last night, at the hands of Colonel Hillyer, the general's communication of October 29.

I think the attitude of things with our enemy has changed since the writing of that letter. I have seen several persons who were in Holly Springs up to Wednesday afternoon at 4 o'clock. At that time both Van Dorn and Price were in Holly Springs, and their troops camped all round about in such a way that an estimate of numbers was out of the question. There were no signs by which one could judge of their intentions. They have, like ourselves, all sorts of camp rumors, most of which are to the effect that Kentucky is their destination. Doubtless Kentucky was their destination, if they could have passed Iuka or Corinth. A woman, whose accounts agree with those of others, insists that the railroad cars from Holly Springs south are all engaged in carrying artillery. She persists in her assertions that she saw for two days the cars loaded with guns, carriages, and horses, and the rumors from the south are that Holly Springs is being evacuated. There is no doubt in my mind that the Confederate Government mistrusts Van Dorn, and that there is some conflict of authority between him and Pemberton, who has been specifically assigned to the Department of Mississippi and Louisiana. Villepigue's brigade has gone to Meridian, but the great bulk of the force collected at Holly Springs is there, or was there on Wednesday. I hardly think they would move to the Mississippi or Memphis, or any point above, as they and their communications would be at your mercy. They would hardly venture to attack you or Corinth if it be true they sent off their artillery. I have a man of high intelligence who started yesterday for Grenada and thence to Holly Springs, who has promised to send me an account of what he sees. We can better judge of their intentions from facts than from their say so. It is barely possible they are sending surplus artillery to Mobile and their field artillery round to Chattanooga, intending to make a junction with Bragg's forces. I confess myself at a loss to divine their plans from any reliable facts in my possession.

Colonels Hillyer and Lagow, of your staff, now here, will better describe things than I can do by letter. I have requested the former to look to our forts, warehouses, &c., and they can tell you all about them. Memphis is admirably adapted as a point for assembling, forming, and organizing a force of operations on the Mississippi River, as well as for invading the States of Arkansas and Mississippi, and I will undertake to put in good order any number of troops you may send here. Of course I would much prefer to have recruits to fill up our present regiments to having new regiments, but we must take what we can get.

The collection of rents proceeds favorably. Some appeals have been taken, and I send with this one case—that of Wickersham, a neutral, native of Ohio, whose post-office was used by the Confederates, and the theater, which was vacant. The papers I send you give a full history of the case, and I hope the Secretary of War will sanction our acts. I certainly do have less sympathy for this class of middle men than for the out and out secessionist. I do not know but that I should send my answer to the Secretary through you, but he referred the case to me direct, calling for a full and prompt report. If the copy of my report herewith does not accord fully with your views, please write to the Secretary. My project for taking care of the destitute has met a ready response. Ward committees and a central board have been organized composed very fairly of representatives of all interests. I have given them the use of a vacant building, an order for 25 cords of wood a month (cut by contrabands and hauled by our teams), an order for prescriptions of medicines out of confiscated drugs, and $1,000 in money out of the collection of rents; also have made a recommendation to companies to send to the depot a part of their company savings in kind. This is liberal, and, with the contributions of merchants in kind, by theaters, and families, will enable the central board to provide for all the destitute and distressed. A special tax on secessionists would accomplish the end less effectually, for indeed all the public contributions above indicated come exclusively out of our enemies.

I shall enforce the banishment of the proscribed families, because if we must fight for the river we cannot afford to do it for the benefit of the families of men in open hostility. I have thrown the onus on them.

I note the general's allusion to Rosecrans, and was somewhat surprised, though convinced. I hope Hurlbut and McPherson will be retained in the department.

With great respect,

W. T. SHERMAN,
Major-General.

HEADQUARTERS DISTRICT OF MEMPHIS,
Memphis, November 1, 1862.

GEORGE D. PRENTICE, Esq.:

DEAR SIR: I have just placed your note in the hands of one of my staff, to make inquiries into the affairs and condition of that railroad in which you unfortunately own stock. As to incomes from such property during the war, I know you have made up your mind, but I believe the railroad is substantially uninjured, and in time will be valuable, but of this I will write when I am better posted on the "collaterals." Of course, I will ever do my best to save your interests and fulfill your wishes.

I still see no clear, well-defined issue to this war. We are groping in a mist, and, in spite of the teachings of history, we seem to mistrust our only compass of safety, viz, the written compact of Government—our Constitution. Our people, impatient, find fault with individuals, and think by displacing leaders they can produce results. This is natural, but, I fear, will do no real good. I hope the people of Kentucky have had enough of secesh rule to judge which is best, the old government of laws or the orders of irresponsible captains and colonels.

In discussing the arbitrary acts of our enemies and selves, I have frequently asserted that the Southern military leaders were the first to take the slaves of loyal masters and wagons and horses of our people. It was so represented to me in Kentucky that long before we permitted a slave to come into our military camps, the secession leaders pressed slaves to work on the forts at Columbus and Bowling Green, and that in many instances loyal masters did not get their slaves back. Also that Buckner, Johnston (Albert Sidney), Polk, and Pillow all helped themselves to wagons and horses, corn, wheat, &c., of farmers, without asking their consent. Am I not right in this? My opinion is that the adherents of the Southern cause have instituted principles of warfare that, when applied to themselves, will be destructive of material interests, and that if we retaliate they are estopped by their own practice.

Always with respect, your friend,

W. T. SHERMAN,
Major-General.

HEADQUARTERS DISTRICT OF MEMPHIS,
Memphis, November 6, 1862.

Maj. Gen. SAMUEL R. CURTIS,
Comdg. Department of the Missouri, Saint Louis, Mo.:

GENERAL : Brooks has gone to Helena, and thence, I suppose, to the interior. Of course, I do not suppose Joe Johnston to be in Arkansas ; Holmes commands there. I can, and will, send a man to White River and Little Rock, and advise you of any authentic facts. I have pretty good evidence that a part of the rebel army, formerly in Arkansas, has been sent down to Vicksburg, and thence a part has come to Holly Springs and balance gone to Port Hudson, Miss.

I also have reason to believe that a movement of our forces has been made from New Orleans to Bayou Manchac, mouth of Pontchartrain, but what for, or what its destination, I cannot make out. To counteract it, the rebels are assembling a force at Port Hudson ; also they design to fortify the mouth of Yazoo River. This will seriously interfere with a movement on Vicksburg. I do really think that your forces under Schofield and Steele could reach Fort Smith and Little Rock without serious opposition. If, then, Rosecrans' army should regain the latitude of Huntsville, the expedition down the Mississippi could easily go down.

I have here only my own division, but think my defenses are good against any force that can be brought against us. The force of the enemy at Holly Springs must be about 30,000, with a large proportion of cavalry. Of course, the secessionists continue to talk of taking Memphis, but their time has passed.

I do not understand you want me to supply affidavits that Uriel Wright, Senator [Trusten] Polk, [D. M.] Frost, Brown, [Bowen (?)] and others, of Missouri, are at Holly Springs. I can do it, if you cannot make proof there. It would be profitable if you could get the courts to accept other evidence, which you can procure on the spot.

I am, &c.,

W. T. SHERMAN,
Major-General.

HEADQUARTERS DISTRICT OF MEMPHIS,
Memphis, November 7, 1862.

Mrs. VALERIA HURLBUT, *Memphis:*

DEAR MADAM: Your letter of October — was duly received. I did not answer it at that time, as I had already instructed Colonel Anthony, provost-marshal, to suspend the execution of the order expelling certain families from Memphis, for fifteen days, to enable them to confer with the Confederate authorities upon the cause of that order, viz, the firing from ambush on our boats carrying passengers and merchandise by bands of guerrillas in the service of our enemies.

In war it is impossible to hunt up the actual perpetrators of a crime. Those who are banded together in any cause are held responsible for all the acts of their associates. The Confederate Government, in resisting what we claim to be the rightful prerogative and authority of our Government, by armies in the field and bands of armed men called guerrillas or partisan rangers, claims for these latter all the rights of war, which means that the Confederate Government assumes the full responsibility of the acts of these Partisan Rangers. These men have, as you know, fired on steamboats navigating the Mississippi River, taking the lives and endangering the safety of peaceful citizens who travel in an accustomed way, in no wise engaged in the operations of war. We regard this as inhuman and barbarous, and if the Confederate authorities do not disavow them, it amounts to a sanction and encouragement of the practice. We must stop this, and no measures would be too severe. The absolute destruction of Memphis, New Orleans, and every city, town, and hamlet of the South would not be too severe a punishment to a people for attempting to interfere with the navigation of the Mississippi. I have commenced mildly by requiring the families of men engaged in this barbarous practice to leave and go to their own people. Certainly there can be no hardship for the wife and children going to their own husbands and families. They ought to be glad of the opportunity, and the measure, instead of being severe, is very mild. How would they like it if we were to fire through the houses of their wives and families, as they do through the boats carrying our wives and families? If any person will look at this question who feels for our people, he or she will perceive that the measure of retaliation is mild, and I do not promise by any means that in future cases I will be so easy. Misplaced kindness to these guerrillas, their families, and adherents is cruelty to our people. Were you to travel on a boat and have the bullets whistle and hear the demon yells of these Confederate partisans, you would not feel so kindly disposed to those who approve the act.

I have given them time to disavow the attack on the Gladiator; they have not done it. They therefore approve, and I say not only shall the families go away, but all the Confederate allies and adherents shall feel the power of an indignant Government.

I am, &c.,

W. T. SHERMAN,
Major-General.

————

HEADQUARTERS DISTRICT OF MEMPHIS,
Memphis, November 8, 1862.

Maj. Gen. U. S. GRANT,
Comdg. Department of West Tennessee, La Grange, Tenn. :

DEAR GENERAL : Yours of November 6, from La Grange, was brought to me by Captain Newell, Third Michigan Cavalry, last night, he having ridden by circuitous routes and reached me without serious opposition; yet I fear his return might be hazardous, and I have ordered Colonel Grierson, Sixth Illinois Cavalry, to escort him back with about 300 select cavalry, and in going and returning to do certain things that will be of advantage to the service. He will show you his instructions.

I have not yet received the instructions via Columbus, referred to in yours of November 6, but am prepared on short notice to do anything you may require.

As yet but one regiment has reported to me, the Thirty-second Wisconsin, Colonel Howe, a strong regiment, of good material, well armed and equipped.

By the reduction of transportation under recent orders, I will have enough wagons for double my force, and since the incursions of Morgan and Kirby Smith into Kentucky and Stuart's raid into Pennsylvania, in which they took horses of private owners, we should no longer hesitate to replenish our stock in the country we operate in, giving owners simple receipts, to be settled for at the conclusion of hostilities, according to the circumstances.

I deem it good policy now to encourage the non-combatant population to trade with Memphis their cotton and corn for such articles of groceries and clothing as they need for their families and servants. Many of them are justly indignant at their own armies and partisans for burning their cotton, by the sales of which alone they can realize the means of purchase of the articles they absolutely need to maintain their suffering families, and I would like some expression of opinion from you on this policy. Of course, a part of these supplies will fall into improper hands, but the time must come when the inhabitants must choose their rulers, and even now I do not fear their choice if protected from their Confederate armies and bandits. Some of them, of course, make loud complaints against our troops burning rails and stealing potatoes, &c., but I tell them plainly these are the inevitable accompaniments of armies, for which those who provoke war and appealed to it are responsible, and not we. I am satisfied a change of opinion is rapidly growing here, which I endeavor to foster and encourage. On Monday next a Union club will come out in public; will decorate their houses with our flag, and have a public procession, speeches, &c. I will attend, of course, and aid them with every means to produce effect. The advance of your army to La Grange will have an admirable effect.

All my information goes to the belief that the force at Holly Springs is reduced by detachments to the south, so that it no longer threatens West Tennessee. Some farmers just in report Holly Springs evacuated, but I am not satisfied on that point. I have out two good men, who ought to be back in a day or two, whose report I will get through to you by some safe means.

I will keep my force well in hand, but will make a demonstration toward Coldwater to-morrow, &c., to gain information and withdraw attention from you. I do not believe that there is in Arkansas a force to justify the armies of Schofield, Steele, and Hovey (at Helena) remaining quiet, and would advise the latter to threaten Grenada and Yazoo by all means.

I will rapidly organize brigades, and equip all regiments coming to me, and be prepared to act with promptness the moment I learn the part you design me to play. Colonel McDowell, Sixth Iowa, Stuart, Fifty-fifth Illinois, and Buckland, Seventy-second Ohio, are fully competent to take brigades, and I will so dispose of them, unless you send me brigadiers duly commissioned.

Colonels Hillyer and Lagow, of your staff, recently here, will tell you fully of all figures, numbers, and facts that I deem imprudent to trust by this route.

I have already ordered one officer of every Ohio regiment to proceed with dispatch to Columbus, Ohio, to bring back the drafted men for the Ohio regiments, seven in number.

Health of troops good, and everything as well as I could wish. I will write to General Hovey, at Helena, telling him of your movements, and asking him to gather all information he can of the country toward Grenada.

Deserters come in constantly; one just now from Coldwater, where he was on picket. He did not know you were at La Grange, and said he deserted because he did not wish to go farther south. Heard that Price was to go to Jackson, but had not been to Holly Springs for five days.

I am, &c.,

W. T. SHERMAN,
Major-General.

[P. S.]—I send you our morning papers; one of Mobile, November 3, and Grenada, November 5.

HEADQUARTERS DISTRICT OF MEMPHIS,
Memphis, November 12, 1862.

Admiral DAVID D. PORTER,
Commanding United States Naval Forces, Cairo:

DEAR SIR: Yours of the 7th instant was duly received.

I regret that we cannot prevent the erection of a fort at the mouth of Yazoo, as it will force us to fight across the Yazoo above its mouth, unless we can land troops on its east bank. Still, as you say, we must fight it out, and we must take the Mississippi and Yazoo this winter. I have been studying the condition of things hence to Grenada. Now, the roads are good and practicable, but as soon as rain falls the black alluvion is terrible with heavy trains of wagons. General Grant is at La Grange and Grand Junction, 50 or 53 miles due east of Memphis. The Coldwater and Tallahatchie form the Yazoo, and both must be crossed by us in an advance. The enemy now lies behind the Coldwater, but every indication is that he will fall behind the Tallahatchie, and possibly behind the Yalabusha, near Grenada, before he fights. A demonstration on the Yazoo, opposite the railroad below Grenada, would have a magnificent effect, which I know you are fully aware, and that when you make it, it will be well done. Now, my information is that eleven large, fine steamboats are in the Yazoo below Honey Island; nine in one group and two a little farther down. All there are the large elegant packets formerly used as the New Orleans, Mobile, and Vicksburg lines—Magenta, Natchez, General Quitman, &c. I will send you a full list of their names and location as soon as I can inquire of a person not now present. A person living on the Yazoo tells me there are 4 feet of water on the bars below Yazoo City, and that several of the smaller Red River packets have been got out and are now running in a regular line from Vicksburg to the mouth of Red River and back, bringing sugar, cattle, and produce from Louisiana. My informant, whose name I withhold for the present, assures me that many planters along Yazoo are tired of war, and are actually praying for the coming of your fleet, but of this I do not profess to have much faith. At the same time it is not impossible, for their deprivation of the usual necessities of families is felt all over the country, and they are getting tired of the burning of their cotton and the consumption of their corn, potatoes, cattle, &c.

My fort here is well constructed, and I have twenty-eight heavy guns well mounted, besides nine good field batteries; but, as I will soon take the field, I will leave the heavy guns—24-pounders, 32-pounders, and 8-inch columbiads—with a garrison to hold it. I expect to have here some twenty-four regiments of infantry, three or four of cavalry, and about ten batteries of field guns. In going, I would probably leave five regiments of infantry and one field battery.

I hope you are in correspondence with General Grant, and that you will be able to be at the Yazoo by the time he approaches Grenada. Of course, we must expect heavy blows before we can reach Jackson and appear behind Vicksburg. The Helena affairs are doubtless well reported to you. I will in a day or two give you the names of the boats in the Yazoo, with a sketch of their positions. We could easily reach them by a march across from the main river, but I suppose the destruction of this fleet is reserved to you.

I am, with great respect, your obedient servant,
W. T. SHERMAN,
Major-General.

HEADQUARTERS DISTRICT OF MEMPHIS,
Memphis, November 12, 1862—11 p. m.

Hon. JUDGE SWAYNE, *Memphis:*

SIR: You expressed yourself hurt this morning at the severe terms in which I indulged in commenting on the charge you made the grand jury. It is now late at night, and I am worn out with writing purely official matter, and now, hastily and candidly, wish to convey to you my serious thoughts.

I concede to you the highest order of personal character, talents, and education, and will not pretend to argue with you constitutional or legal questions. I have repeatedly asserted, and now repeat my belief, that you are honest in your opinions and practice, but must say that, in my judgment, you are unintentionally drifting your country and people to ruin, misery, and death. In the first place, I regret that, in preparing your opinion or charge to the jury, the main part was omitted, and only that part published to the world which treats of the sworn duty of the grand jury to find bills under the enumerated laws of Tennessee touching slaves, utterly ignoring the laws of Congress and the state of war.

Thus take the statutes you quote, Nos. 26, 58, 59, 60, 61, 63, 64, 82, &c. How can any one of them be executed here without an absolute relinquishment of all that has been done in this war? Will the United States stultify herself by allowing a criminal court of a county to nullify the acts of the Congress and of armies raised at the expense of the blood and treasure of the nation? What is the law of Congress on this point?

ACT No. 160.—AN ACT to suppress insurrection, to punish treason and rebellion, to seize and confiscate the property of rebels, and for other purposes.

*   *   *   *   *   *   *

SEC. 9. *And be it further enacted,* That all slaves of persons who shall, after proclamation giving sixty days' notice, be engaged in rebellion against the Government of the United States, or who shall in any way give aid or comfort thereto, escaping from such persons and taking refuge within the lines of the army, and all slaves captured from such persons, or deserted by them and coming under the control of the Government of the United States, and all slaves of such persons found or being in any place occupied by rebel forces and afterward occupied by the forces of the United States, shall be deemed captives of war, and shall be for ever free of their servitude, and not again held as slaves.

SEC. 10. * * * And no person engaged in the military or naval service of the United States shall, under any pretense whatever, assume to decide on the validity of the claim of any person to the service or labor of any other person, or surrender up any such person to the claimant, on pain of being dismissed from the service.

Approved July 17, 1862.

Such is the law of the Congress of the United States, which I caused to be published many successive days in all the newspapers of Memphis as soon as received; and yet you made no mention of it in your charge to the jury. Certainly you must admit a state of war; that Memphis was a place held by the Confederate troops in June last and now in our military possession, and that during the pendency of war I am held by our Government as responsible for all that occurs in this district, and as much accountable for acts done by persons subordinate to my authority, as though done by myself. Therefore, in charging the jury, you could not but have foreseen it would raise a direct conflict. I admit that in our conversation you contended that your high sense of the character of a judge demanded you should announce the law, but that in doing so you qualified it by the expression—

If in regard to the slavery laws of the State, or any of the recited or other statutory or common law offenses, the jury should find themselves physically prevented by the circumstances about them—in other words, by the insufficiency of the power of the county—from the performance of their high duties as defined by the law, in that case their failure to perform these duties will be no dereliction on their part.

Now I hold, and so will every reader of your charge infer, that the jury is bound to hear and, on their oath, find bills against every person who has received, harbored, or employed a fugitive slave. No physical power will hinder them from finding such bills any more than it did you in making your charge; on the contrary, I would look for discreet action and a full and comprehensive laying down of the law to the learned and intelligent judge rather than the jury who are bound to receive the law as he gives it to them to apply to the cases that may come to their hearing.

I say the grand jury are bound to indict every man, woman, or child in the county of Shelby who has been governed by the laws of the Congress of the United States, instead of those of the State of Tennessee, late in open rebellion to the mild and generous sovereign of the whole country. Thus I contend that, when your community is already bound down by the afflictions of stern war, you have insisted, from what I deem a too delicate sense of your official obligations, in bringing a direct conflict between the State and National authority. I had in my former conversations with you expressed an earnest desire that, while armed thousands of strong men were arrayed against each other, ready at any moment to engage in deadly struggle, the common machinery of Government might be preserved, to protect the old and young, feeble and helpless, against the murderous robbers, thieves, and villains that are sure to take advantage of the complications of war to do their hellish work. I wanted of all things the criminal court of Shelby County to meet and punish crime—that class of crime known all the world over as *malum in se*, common to the codes of all civilized people—and reserve this question of slavery, this dire conflict between National and State authority, to be fought out by the armies now arrayed for that purpose. Personally, I have no hostility to slavery or any of your local laws. I would they had never been disturbed; that Federal and State authority had been mutually respected by the parties to this strife; but this event almost convinces me that they are utterly irreconcilable, when Judge Swayne, with the din of arms in his ears, with bayonets glistening at each street corner, with messengers coming and going with the cruel news of the mangling of hundreds and thousands of our common citizens in deadly strife, charges a grand jury under the old law of Tennessee as though there was no war, and utterly ignores the laws made by the Congress of the United States. I wanted, and still want, you to hold your court and punish the many malefactors that infest the country, but you must respect the laws of our common Government.

I do not want to dictate to you; I appeal to your reason. You cannot administer the laws you quote, but there is plenty you can do, and, to make the matter emphatic, I have instructed my provost-marshal and officers that if the criminal court of Shelby or any other county attempts by writs or otherwise to enforce those State laws, in contradiction with the plain laws of the United States, they must treat the sheriff or constable as in "contempt." I admit there is a direct issue between the United States and the State of Tennessee in this matter; but a county criminal court is not the place to adjudicate it. There is a tribunal provided by our fundamental law—our Constitution—viz, the Supreme Court of the United States, fit and proper to pass on such momentous issues. Until that tribunal makes its decision, I shall obey the plain law of Congress and the order of the President of the United States under it, and my army shall be used to enforce it.

I wish I had seen your charge before it was delivered, as I believe you would have modified it; at all events, that you would not have given such prominence to the impracticable statutes you quote. I wish to repeat that I appreciate the sense of duty that actuated you to assert what you believed to be the *only* law, and I hope you will award to me similar zeal when you allow for the sudden and stern conclusions to which military minds sometimes attain by a rapid intuition or judgment.

I also repeat that I am still anxious you should continue your court, and constitutionally and judiciously enforce the law against the many mischievous persons that infest your community. For God's sake, don't let this accursed question of slavery blind your mind to the thousand other duties and interests that concern you and the people among whom you live.

As you can perceive, I throw off these ideas, leaving you to fill up the logical picture. In my seeming leaning toward men of your character, I have risked my reputation and ability for good. Do not force me to conclude the conflict to be "irreconcilable," as you surely will if you or your grand jury or the officers of your court insist on enforcing the statutes of Tennessee touching negroes at this terrible crisis of our history.

With much respect, your obedient servant,

W. T. SHERMAN,
Major-General.

———

HEADQUARTERS DISTRICT OF MEMPHIS,
Memphis, November 14, 1862.

B. W. SHARP, Esq.,
    United States Commissioner, Memphis:

SIR: Yours of yesterday is received. The military authorities of the United States have other business to attend to besides administering the criminal law of Shelby County. I find it difficult to spare competent officers to try even the offenses against the military law.

Let the gabbling fools of Memphis draw their own conclusions as to our seeming concessions to the people. Our minds are operating in other points at this time.

When the Confederate armies in the field are defeated, then we can give the stay-at-home people a chance to choose between their lawful government and banishment. In the mean time, if any tribunal will fairly try criminals and dispose of them, let it do so; but Judge Swayne knows if he uses his court for political purposes, so as to nullify the laws of the Congress of the United States, he will himself change places with the criminal at the bar. If, however, he will confine himself and court to the punishment of the murderers, thieves, and scoundrels that infest the country, I will not be very critical as to the means by which such an end is to be attained.

The points you make are easily answered. Applicants for naturalization papers can easily be accommodated by enlisting in any one of our regiments. Criminals can easily be transported to the penitentiary at Nashville.

Appeals may come to us, and I will certify them, to await the future, sending the criminal in the mean time to a safe place of custody, viz, the penitentiary. No law of Tennessee, in conflict with the law of the United States, is the law, and if any lawyer or judge thinks different, the quicker he gets out of the United States the safer his neck will be.

We have confidence enough in our power to allow a little blowing off of surplus steam. Things are progressing fast enough, and those who think Tennessee is a sovereign power on earth will change their minds in time.

Your friend,

W. T. SHERMAN,
Major-General.

HEADQUARTERS,
Springfield, Ill., November 15, 1862.

Hon. E. M. STANTON,
Secretary of War, Washington City, D. C.:

Mr. Montgomery, late editor of the Vicksburg Whig, informs me, upon the authority of his mother, just arrived from Vicksburg, that Pemberton, Smith, and Villepigue, with only 5,000 men, are at that place, and that they are repairing the portion of the railroad, 18 miles in length, leading from a point opposite Vicksburg across the Mississippi bottom, particularly for the purpose of facilitating the introduction of supplies from the Washita country.

He also says the enemy are fortifying Haines' Bluff, on the Yazoo River, 12 miles from Vicksburg, and communicating with that place by a ridge road; also that the enemy are fortifying Port Hudson, below Bayou Sara, declaring that they will make that point more difficult to pass than Vicksburg. Would it not be advisable that the gunboats below that point should be ordered to frustrate this design, if practicable?

The way cleared from New Orleans to Vicksburg, it would be expedient that transports, under convoy of gunboats, should be sent up the Mississippi to a point as near Vicksburg as might be found safe to meet the contingency of a determination to cross our troops over the river below it, after having disembarked them above and marched them around.

Having already given my views as to the importance of dispatch in setting the proposed expedition for opening the Mississippi in motion, I will not consume your valuable time by adding anything more on that subject.

Yours, truly,

JOHN A. McCLERNAND,
Major-General.

HEADQUARTERS DISTRICT OF MEMPHIS,
Memphis, November 16, 1862.

Admiral DAVID D. PORTER,
Commanding United States Naval Forces, Cairo:

SIR: Yours of November 12 is just received, and though very busy receiving and disposing of troops, I hasten to answer as well as to fill my former promise to send you a sketch of the Yazoo country. Inclosed is a map* compiled by my engineers of the best data at hand. I have another map not well scaled, which makes the mouth of Yazoo somewhat different from the one inclosed. Somewhat thus:

DISTANCES FROM VICKSBURG.

	Miles.
To mouth of Old River	10
To mouth of Yazoo	8
Haines' Bluff	15
Mouth of Little Sunflower	15
Mouth of Big Sunflower	16
Satartia	9
Liverpool	5
Yazoo City	20
Honey Island	60
	158

To where bulk of boats are grouped.

Names of boats up Yazoo: Natchez, Magnolia, E. J. Gay, Mary Keane, R. J. Lockland, Magenta, Ferd. Kennett, Alonzo Child, Peytona, Holmes, Argo, Louisville, Samuel Hill, Cotton Plant, Paul Jones, and John Walsh.

I am not sure on this point, as at times I hear of eleven, and again some say as many as forty, but all agree as to the large boats, Natchez, Magnolia, Peytona, Magenta, &c.

My opinion is that a perfect concert of action should exist between all the forces of the United States operating down the valley; and I apprehend some difficulty may arise from the fact that you control on the river, Curtis on the west bank, and Grant on the east bank. Were either one of you in absolute command, all, of course, would act in concert. Our enemies are now also disconcerted by divided counsels; Van Dorn and Lovell are superior in lineal rank to Pemberton, and yet the latter is in command of the Department of Mississippi and Louisiana.

I think the forces now under Grant are able to handle anything in Mississippi; and our men are now confident and pretty well drilled. We can advance southward, striking Grenada and interposing between Vicksburg and Jackson, but your fleet should be abreast or ahead of

---

* Omitted, as unimportant.

the army.   You invite these suggestions, and I think General Halleck would order a concert of action any time you are prepared.

The possession of the river, with an army capable of disembarking and striking inland, would have a mighty influence.

I know that the people, though full of Southern ardor, are getting tired of the devastations of war.   Our new troops came with ideas of making vigorous war, which means universal destruction, and it requires hard handling to repress excesses.

I take freely of corn, horses, wood and lumber, brick, everything for the Government, but allow no individual plunder.

I was very anxious to see you before departing for the interior, but now expect soon to be off, acting under Grant, but hope we may meet below.   I have admirable maps of Memphis and country round about, of which I could give you copies; but as your operations are by water, these would be of little service.

I am, with great respect, yours,

W. T. SHERMAN,
Major-General, Commanding.

HEADQUARTERS DISTRICT OF MEMPHIS,
Memphis, November 17, 1862.

F. G. PRATT, Esq.,
Memphis, Tenn.:

DEAR SIR : Yours of November 14 has been before me some days. I have thought of the subject-matter, and appreciate what you say, but for the present think best not to tamper with the subject.   Money is a thing that cannot be disposed of by an order.   Were I to declare that Tennessee money should not be quoted higher than greenbacks, my order would do no good, for any person having cotton to sell has a right to barter it for anything he pleases; thus he might trade it for Tennessee money at 50 cents per pound, and for greenbacks at 52 cents, thereby making the discount.   Money will seek its value, and no king or president can fix value by a decree or order.   It has been tried a thousand times, always without success ; but let money alone and it finds its true value.

The reason why Tennessee money has been above greenbacks was, and is, because that kind of money was in demand for cotton. Now, is it our interest to encourage the bringing in of cotton ?   If so, must we not let the owner barter it for what he pleases ?   When we answer these questions in the affirmative, we must let the owner of the cotton sell it as he pleases.   Those who own cotton do not insult our Government by preferring Tennessee money to greenbacks.   Tennessee money suits their individual purposes better than greenbacks, and it pleases me, as I see they want their money for local home use, and not to send abroad for munitions of war.

Let these things regulate themselves.   War, and war alone, can inspire our enemy with respect, and they will have their belly full of that very soon.   I rather think they will in time cry, "Hold, enough!"   Till then, let Union men feel confident in their real strength, and determination of our Government, and despise the street talk of Jews and secessionists.

Yours

W. T. SHERMAN,
Major-General, Commanding.

HEADQUARTERS DISTRICT OF MEMPHIS,
Memphis, November 17, 1862.

JOSEPH TAGG, Esq.,
     President Washington Union Club:

DEAR SIR: The resolutions of November 16 are before me. I heard them read at the time, and the debate on them, but then did not make known what was in progress, nor can I now tell all, but the Union men may rest assured that no insult shall be made to our Government by Judge Swayne or anybody else, and stand unrebuked. Secessionists, when in power, may be tyrants and villains, but we must be men. We must heed the lessons of history and counsels of wise men, who have gone before us. They in rebellion use terror and force; we can afford to do right. They keep up clamors and rumors, boasts and arrogance; we, knowing ourselves to be right, can pursue "the even tenor of our way," calm and conscious of ultimate success.

Now, finding ourselves (the military) in Memphis firmly established, I naturally wanted to see order established among the people of your town. Among all nations, murder, arson, burglary, robbery, and personal violence are deemed crimes against human nature, and there is always a tribunal speedily appointed to try all such cases. These tribunals have no political power, and therefore in war remain unimpaired, and pursue their business, although all the rest of government might be in wreck and confusion. We all know that in Memphis you have a good deal of crime, too much, and somebody must punish it. The military is here to vindicate the right and dignity of the General Government, not to take care of the people. We have enough to do if we mind our own business, so that somebody else must punish murder, &c., among citizens. Finding a criminal court here, I conferred with Judge Swayne, and explained to him that whilst we were determined the flag of our country and the just authority of the Government should be respected all over the world, we wanted the people of Memphis protected against the criminals in their midst, and that he might hold his court.

He has organized it, and appointed his grand jury, and has let off some secession and State's rights nonsense. When a man makes big professions and falls far short in practice, what is the judgment of men? So when a judge makes a magnificent manifesto, and then tries a few pickpockets and loafers, what may we infer? Instead of being a subject of dread and fear, he becomes an object of ridicule. A criminal court is rather a small affair to make trouble among honest men, and this criminal court, what can it do? It may indict criminals that every Union man would like to see punished, but can they hurt any honest man? No; they must punish crime, but dare not attempt to execute any law of Tennessee in opposition to the laws of Congress. Let them attempt to indict a Union man for his opinion, or attempt to punish others for hiring a runaway slave, or let the court attempt the exercise of any foolish or despotic power, and Judge Swayne and that grand jury would learn a lesson in politics that would last them to their dying day. If this court minds its own business, and punishes crime, I will help them; but if they attempt to convert a petty criminal court into a political machine, I will promptly interfere.

Judge Swayne and the grand jury know my opinions, and I think the Union Club will have no reason to fear evil consequences. The Union people are not yet able to compose the necessary courts and machinery of Government. Who are your judges? Who are your lawyers? These you must have, before you can make county courts, district and supreme courts, and it behooves Union men to think of these things, for it is far more easy to destroy than build up a government, and you must be prepared, as the military goes on, to build up your own government. You are not now prepared, but I have no doubt that, by patience, prudence, and forbearance, you will in t.me be enabled to overcome the secesh, not only in arms, but law. Reason, justice, and all the attributes of a good and great Government are on your side of the question.

    I am, with respect,

W. T. SHERMAN,
Major-General.

HEADQUARTERS DISTRICT OF MEMPHIS,
Memphis, November 19, 1862.

Maj. JOHN A. RAWLINS,
    Assistant Adjutant-General, La Grange:

SIR : Inclosed is a communication of Lieut. Gen. J. C. Pemberton, Confederate Army, dated Jackson, Miss., November 12, 1862, received by me at the hands of a flag of truce night before last. I replied yesterday, and send you herewith a copy. I ought not to have answered, but the time to be consumed in referring it to you would have endangered the safety of the four men enumerated by General Pemberton. It seems he acts on orders from the Government at Richmond, and I thought proper to show him how certain retaliation by them would entail on their own prisoners certain destruction. To enable you to answer fully and conclusively, I subjoin a short history of the case.

On the 4th of September last, I sent Colonel Grierson, with a detachment of the Sixth Illinois Cavalry, toward Hernando, to break up a rendezvous of guerrillas, after accomplishing which his orders were to proceed over to the Pigeon Roost road, and break up certain other parties there forming near Coldwater. He accomplished the first-named purpose, taking 10 prisoners, whom he dispatched back toward Memphis, with an escort of 15 of his men, commanded by Lieut. Nathaniel B. Cunningham. This party returned along the main road, and, when near White's, about three-fourths of a mile south of the State line, and distant from Memphis about 13 miles, the party was fired on from ambush, and Lieutenant Cunningham and a Confederate prisoner were killed. The party was scattered, and, as soon as intelligence reached the camp of the Sixth Illinois Cavalry, Captain Boicourt took a small party of 25 men and hastened to the spot. Before reaching White's, they met a wagon coming into Memphis with the body of Lieutenant Cunningham, and learned the names of five men of the country who were engaged in the attack on this party. I subsequently sent Major Stacy, of the Sixth Illinois Cavalry, with 100 men, to punish the actors. They met Captain Boicourt near White's, and all the mention he made of the killing of White is that " one man was killed while running from the advance guard." Subsequently, the mother and wife of Mr. White came to see me, and reported that, hearing the firing near their house, they went to the road, and assisted in burying the dead Confederate, and saw the body of Lieutenant Cunningham taken up by a passing wagon and carried toward Memphis ; that soon after, Captain Boicourt and party of cavalry came to the house, arrested Mr. White, represented as twenty-three years old, delicate in health, and never a guerrilla, but, on the contrary, peacefully disposed and of Union sentiments ; but Captain Boicourt represented that he was concerned in the killing of Cunningham, mutilating his person and stripping it of money and clothing, the sight of which exasperated the men. When White was taken in custody, he was taken out through the yard, and, when near the gate, resisted, and finally attempted to escape, when he was killed, partly with blows and shots. The house of White was burned down.

Of course, I cannot approve the killing of any citizen on mere suspicion, but the firing from ambush near White's house, and the fact that Lieutenant Cunningham was mutilated and stripped of money and clothing, were circumstances calculated to inflame the minds of soldiers. The neighborhood, too, was, and is, infamous, so that I charge the whole on the system of guerrilla warfare adopted, approved, and encouraged by the Confederate authorities. Whatever claims the family and friends of White may have on the magnanimity of our Government I would recognize, but would make no concessions to the authorities of that Government which has turned loose bands of men without uniforms—without any marks of a soldier's calling—to do their will.

The killing of White was the natural consequence of the shooting of Lieutenant Cunningham, of which General Pemberton makes no mention. White was a citizen—not a Confederate soldier or a partisan. On what rule General Pemberton or his associates propose to retaliate on the persons of four of our soldiers, I do not understand. Of course, it is not for me to say what we should do should these four men suffer death, but we should demand their exchange promptly, under the cartel, and, if not accorded to, and they carry out their threats, we should make them feel our power and vengeance. Shall I not withhold all their prisoners for exchange until this threat is withdrawn? Strange that these partisans hang, kill, and shoot on any and all occasions, and yet we are threatened with retaliation for such a case as White's. I await your instructions.

Yours,

W. T. SHERMAN,
Major-General, Commanding.

[Inclosure No. 1.]

HEADQUARTERS DEPARTMENT OF MISSISSIPPI,
Jackson, Miss., November 12, 1862.

The General Officer Commanding United States Forces, Memphis, Tenn.:

SIR: I am credibly informed that on or about the 11th day of September, 1862, Mr. William H. White, a citizen of De Soto County, Mississippi, was inhumanly murdered in the presence of his mother and his wife near his residence on the Hernando and Memphis plank road, about 13 miles from Memphis; I am also informed that this murder was perpetrated by a party of Illinois cavalry (said to be the Sixth), in the service of the United States Government, and under the immediate command of one Captain Boicourt. It is further stated that Boicourt himself inflicted the first wound upon the murdered man.

In view of the reported facts, I have the honor to inform you that, by direction of my Government, I have taken by lot from the United States prisoners of war captured by our forces the four whose names follow: James E. Gaddy, Company E, Sixth Illinois Cavalry; Bernard Collins, Company E, Thirty-ninth Ohio Infantry; A. W. Shipman, Company D, Forty-third Ohio Infantry, and Michael Hart, Company C, Seventh Iowa Infantry.

I am also directed to inform you that if the account of the murder be true, retaliation will be made on prisoners, unless the murderers are punished.

The case, sir, is very plainly before you; there is not a shadow of doubt that the account of the murder is true, and I await your decision as to who shall suffer the penalty.

I have directed Maj. Gen. Earl Van Dorn to forward this communication through flag of truce.

Very respectfully, your obedient servant,

J. C. PEMBERTON,
Lieutenant-General, Commanding.

[Inclosure No. 2.]

HEADQUARTERS DISTRICT OF MEMPHIS,
Memphis, Tenn., November 18, 1862.

Lieut. Gen. J. C. PEMBERTON,
Commanding Confederate Forces, Jackson, Miss.:

SIR: Your letter of November 12, dated Jackson, Miss., is before me. General Grant commands the department which embraces Memphis, and I will send him your letter, that he may answer it according to the interests and honor of the Government of the United States.

You recite the more aggravated parts of the story of Mrs. White, concerning the killing of her husband by a party of the Sixth Illinois Cavalry, but you do not recite the attending circumstances.

In the early part of September last the public highway hence to Hernando was infested by a parcel of men who burned the cotton of the people and depredated on their property. A party of the Sixth Illinois Cavalry was sent to capture them, but on approach they fled and only 10 prisoners were taken. They were dispatched back toward Memphis, in charge of a lieutenant and 10 men. As this party was on the road near White's, they were fired on from ambush. The lieutenant and the Confederate soldier at his side were killed, one or more wounded, and the party scattered. As soon as the intelligence reached the camp of the Sixth Illinois Cavalry, in Memphis, Captain Boicourt started to the rescue, with a small detachment of his men. On the way out they met the dead body of the lieutenant being brought in, punctured by six balls, from which the story was started of barbarous treatment, viz, his being shot while lying on the ground. They also heard enough to connect the people of the neighborhood with this firing from ambush and mutilating their dead lieutenant, the taking of White, the accusation of his being concerned, his resistance, his attempt to escape, and all matters asserted and denied; and no one deplores more than I do that you have torn to pieces the fabric of our Government, so that such acts should ever occur, or, if they did, that they should not be promptly punished. White's house is almost on the line between Mississippi and Tennessee, but this affair occurred on the Mississippi side of the line. If the State of Mississippi was in a condition and should make due inquiry, and demand the parties for a fair trial, there would be some appearance of law and justice; but what shadow of right you have to inquire into the matter, I don't see.

White was not a Confederate soldier, not even a guerrilla, and some contend that he was a good Union man. I assert that his killing was unfortunate, but was the legitimate and logical sequence of the mode of warfare chosen by the Confederate Government—by means of guerrillas or partisan rangers.

Captain Boicourt has answered for his conduct to the Government of the United States, and, it may be, will to the civil authorities of Missis sippi, when peace is restored to her, but not to the Confederate Government or its officers. You now hold for retaliation four United States soldiers, whose names you say were ascertained by lot. We hold here thirty-odd wounded Confederate soldiers, left by your companions on the field of Corinth. They receive kind treatment at the hands of our surgeon. I expect a boat-load of other prisoners in a day or so from above, *en route* for Vicksburg, to be exchanged according to the solemn cartel made between the two contracting parties. Under the terms of that cartel, we shall expect at Vicksburg the four men you have named, and should they not be at Vicksburg, the officer in charge of your prisoners will have his orders. Our armies now occupy many Southern States; even Northern Mississippi is in our possession. Your guerrillas and partisan rangers have done deeds that I know you do not sanction. Do not make this war more vindictive and bloody than it has been, and will be, in spite of the most moderate counsels. If you think a moment, you will admit that retaliation is not the remedy for such acts as the killing of White; but the same end will be attained by regulating your guerrillas. This I know you are doing, and for it you have the thanks of your Southern Rights people, who were plundered and abused by them. General Grant commands this department, and you had better await his answer before proceeding to extremities. All I can now do is to see that the terms for the exchange of prisoners of war be faithfully executed, by your exchanging the four men you have in custody before we will send to Vicksburg any more.

I am, with great respect, your obedient servant,

W. T. SHERMAN,
Major-General.

HEADQUARTERS DISTRICT OF MEMPHIS,
Memphis, November 23, 1862.

The Officer Commanding Guard on Board Steamer Metropolitan:

SIR: I am officially advised by Lieut. Gen. J. C. Pemberton, commanding Confederate forces at Jackson, Tenn., that he holds four of our prisoners of war, viz, James E. Gaddy, Company E, Sixth Illinois Cavalry; Bernard Collins, Company E, Thirty-ninth Ohio Infantry; A. W. Shipman, Company D, Forty-third Ohio Infantry, and Michael Hart, Company C, Seventh Iowa Infantry, on whom he proposes, by order of the Confederate Government, to make retaliation for the killing of a citizen named White, of De Soto County, Mississippi, in September last. I have answered him at length by a flag of truce, and now inform you that it is not a case for retaliation, and have the honor to request that, on arrival at Vicksburg, you make specific demand for these prisoners, and, if they be not forthcoming, that you withhold from exchange four of like rank privates, to be ascertained by lot, and that you bring them to Memphis to await the action of our Government. I regard this as a fair breach of the cartel. White was not a Confederate soldier, or even guerrilla, and if the Confederate authorities want to offset the killing of White, you can quote plenty of private murders committed by their adherents.

I have the honor to be, your obedient servant,

W. T. SHERMAN,
Major-General, Commanding.

[P. S.]—Don't make known what you propose until you know whether these four men are ready to be exchanged, and then await an answer by telegraph from General Pemberton.

HEADQUARTERS DISTRICT OF MEMPHIS,
Memphis, November 23, 1862.

Major-General GRANT, *Comdg. Department of West Tennessee:*

DEAR GENERAL: As soon as I arrived here I dispatched an aide to Helena, who brings me back an answer perfectly satisfactory from General Steele, who has reached Helena with Osterhaus' division, which, added to the force there, makes a heavy command. I send you his letter, which assures us that he will send Hovey, with a large force, on Grenada, from Friar's Point, reaching the Tallahatchie about Charleston on next Monday; from that point they attack or threaten Grenada about Monday, Tuesday, and Wednesday.

I will march to-morrow (Wednesday), according to orders, Denver's division (two brigades—nine regiments of infantry and three batteries of artillery), on Pigeon Roost road, to Byhalia, and thence south to Chulahoma, reaching Byhalia Thursday and Chulahoma Sunday; Smith's division to Germantown, Byhalia, and Chulahoma (same force as Denver's). Lauman's division (eight regiments of infantry, three batteries, and four companies of cavalry) will take the Hernando road, and turn east and join Denver at Byhalia. I will accompany the center column, keeping with me Grierson, with eight companies of cavalry. Hurlbut has joined; has been assigned command of the post, garrisoned by four regiments, one battery, and Thielemann's two companies of cavalry. I will instruct him to organize into brigades and divisions all troops arriving ready to move inland, if called for. I leave as a part of the garrison the sick and helpless of the moving column, may be 1,000 men in all; better behind a parapet than in a general hospital. I have a very intelligent man in from Jackson, who has been to Abbeville, Grenada, Mobile, Vicksburg, everywhere; no doubt of the fact; some little doubt of his sincerity, but I believe he has large interests on the Yazoo which he is anxious to cover up. He wants to get his cotton out safe. He brings me late papers, which I send you. He says a court of inquiry acquitted Van Dorn, and that he commands the Army of the Tallahatchie, Pemberton commanding department at Jackson, Miss.; Van Dorn over Price, Tilghman, Bowen, and Jackson. Not a word of any of Bragg's or Holmes' forces. He describes much feeling against Van Dorn, for bad management or bad luck. They are fortifying all fords and ferries of the Tallahatchie, especially about the railroad crossing, and to-day they are ordered to commence at Panola; but all this will cease when they hear of Hovey coming across from Helena. His strength and purpose will be magnified. Mr. H. thinks that the aggregate force of Van Dorn does not reach 30,000, although he admits they are so scattered that it is hard to estimate. Van Dorn's headquarters are at Abbeville, and the Tallahatchie is their line.

I send this and inclosures by a special bearer of dispatches. I hear of a rebel cavalry regiment at Somerville, but suppose they will fall back as we advance. I have only Grierson's cavalry with me.

I am, &c.,

W. T. SHERMAN,
Major-General.

_____

HEADQUARTERS DISTRICT OF MEMPHIS,
Memphis, November 25, 1862.

The Mayor and Council, City of Memphis:

GENTLEMEN: I regret to notice that you propose to issue a species of currency of denomination as low as 10 cents (" shinplasters") to swell the amount of bad money with which your community is already sufficiently afflicted.

The issuing of bills of credit by way of money is, in my judgment, in direct violation of the Constitution of the United States, and I think Congress at the last session passed a bill prohibiting all issues below $1, and provided a species of currency called the "post-office currency," which will soon gradually supplant the worthless trash which now is a disgrace to the name of money. As soon as possible, enough of this post-office money will come here and suffice for the wants of the people.

Inasmuch as we seem to be imitating the example of Mexico, rather than those high models of ancient and modern times that we were wont to do in times past, I would suggest a simpler and better currency for the times. In Mexico soap is money, and the people do their marketing through the medium of cakes of soap.

Why can you not use cotton for money? It has a very convenient price—50 cents a pound. Put it up in pounds and fractions and it will form a far better currency than the miserable shinplasters you propose to issue. If cotton is king, it has the genuine stamp and makes money, is money; therefore I suggest that, instead of little bits of paper, you set to work and put up cotton in little parcels of 5, 10, 25, and 50 cents.

If it be my last act, I wish to spare the people of Memphis from the curse of any more bad money.

I am, &c.,

W. T. SHERMAN,
Major-General.

HEADQUARTERS DISTRICT OF MEMPHIS,
Memphis, November 25, 1862.

General STEELE,
Commanding United States Forces, Helena:

DEAR SIR: Yours of yesterday is before me. I wish I had met you going down, but somehow we passed each other. The mode of attacking and threatening the flank of the enemy, detailed by you, is excellent; nothing better. I march to-morrow with my whole force toward Chulahoma, about 20 miles southwest of Holly Springs. Grant will at same time be at Lumpkin's Mills, south of Holly Springs. If Hovey can reach the river, near Charleston, about Sunday or Monday, the effect will be good. If the cavalry force can break that road good, anywhere between Coffeeville or Grenada, the enemy is forced to fight or retreat eastward. I know that General Hovey's heart is in it, and that he will succeed; nothing but heavy rains can prevent full success. I will send your letter to General Grant.

My news from the enemy places them at Tallahatchie, near Abbeville, fortifying all the crossing places.

I am, &c.,

W. T. SHERMAN,
Major-General.

HEADQUARTERS RIGHT WING,
Memphis, December 15, 1862.

General GORMAN, *Helena:*

DEAR SIR: Captain McCoy arrived this morning with your letter of the 13th, and I thank you truly for the interest you manifest in the proposed expedition down the river. As usual, we have all overestimated our real force, but doubtless the enemy will also, and we can use the idea.

I will endeavor to embark here on the 18th, with 20,000, and send in advance ten or twelve good boats, which, in addition to those you have, will carry the troops you designate. I will carry about a million of rations, and as much fuel, coal and wood, as can possibly be obtained. I suggest that you keep afloat all provisions and ammunition designed for this expedition. General Steele can easily regulate details; five wagons per regiment will be sufficient, as it is not proposed to operate far from our boats.

I have a letter from Admiral Porter, perfectly satisfactory. I expect him every moment from above, and feel assured we will co-operate most cordially.

General Frank P. Blair is here, and will be with you as soon as this letter. Three of his regiments have already passed down, and two more will be at Helena before the 18th. I have also written to General Curtis a letter that will be telegraphed him from Columbus, telling him everything essential, so that I feel assured you will receive from him full official sanction for all you may do. Indeed, we have every reason to feel satisfied at the hearty and cordial concurrence of all minds in this expedition. Should Generals Grant and Halleck deem the force with which I start insufficient, they can easily re-enforce from the rear in time to take part in case we come to heavy blows.

I take it for granted that Hindman will not expose the west of Arkansas and the Indian Territory by withdrawing his forces eastward, and I am informed another column is moving from Iron Mountain road toward Little Rock. Your force at Helena will exceed that left with Major-General Hurlbut at Memphis, but I admit you are more exposed there, because Memphis is substantially covered by Grant's army at Oxford.

As soon as I learn that the fleets of boats from above are coming, I will send you ten or twelve good boats, and would like to know if you will need provisions and ammunition to complete the required quantities, viz, thirty days' rations and forage, 200 rounds of small-arm ammunition, and 500 per gun.

Blair brings with him two good field batteries. Can you not give Steele three batteries instead of two?

Thanking you again for the prompt and handsome manner in which you have met all offers, I am, with great respect, your friend and servant,

W. T. SHERMAN,
Major-General, Commanding.

GENERAL ORDERS, }   HDQRS. PROVISIONAL BRIGADE,
No. 1.   } *In the Field, near Humboldt, Tenn., Dec.* 20, 1862.

At the urgent and repeated solicitations of civilians and officers on board this regular passenger and mail train *en route* for Columbus, Ky., the undersigned, a staff officer of General Grant's staff, hereby assumes command of all the United States troops on and about this railroad until further orders.

Capt. George A. Williams, First U. S. Infantry, will perform the duties of adjutant, and First Lieut. Henry C. Whittemore, Second Illinois Artillery, the duties of aide-de-camp.

GEORGE P. IHRIE,
Colonel and Additional Aide-de-Camp, Commanding.

HDQRS. RIGHT WING, THIRTEENTH ARMY CORPS,
Steamer Forest Queen, Helena, December 21, 1862.

General GORMAN, *Commanding District of Eastern Arkansas, Helena:*

DEAR SIR: Knowing the plans and purposes of General Grant, I have the honor to express my entire satisfaction with the force you have assigned to compose part of the present expedition.

One thing more only is suggested. General Grant wants a diverting force connecting the Mississippi River at or near Delta or Friar's Point with him between Oxford and Grenada. He suggested that a regiment of infantry and a section of artillery should be posted at Delta or Friar's Point, covering their camp with a breastwork of earth or fallen timber. This is for the base of operations for the cavalry, which should have a perfect roving commission. If the roads become impassable to us, they will be also to the enemy. This cavalry can study the roads, creeks, farms, and country generally, making their appearance at unexpected times at the Coldwater, Tallahatchie, or even the Yazoo, down as far as Honey Island. The object of such a force will suggest itself to the mind of any intelligent commander, who could so mystify his movements as to disconcert all the calculations of an enemy. For the present I would not advise any such force to go below Honey Island, but as soon as intelligence reaches them that Grant is below Grenada, they might threaten Yazoo City. But the general plan of our enemy has been to operate with their cavalry on our communications, and it is to guard against this that a cavalry force is necessary to cover our rear and flanks. This cavalry force should communicate by any chance to any of our forces whom they approach or hear of. The sooner this is done the better.

I will be down as far as Gaines' Landing to-morrow, and by or before Christmas will be at the mouth of Yazoo. You know about my present strength. As to moving your whole command to Napoleon, I admit it strikes me forcibly, but think General Curtis should be consulted, as he may base some plan for other forces on the fact that you are at Helena. I would be obliged if you would write to the commanding officer at Columbus, Ky. (General Davies), the moment you make these dispositions, with a request that he telegraph the same to General Grant, wherever he may be.

I am, with great respect, your friend and servant,

W. T. SHERMAN,
Major-General, Commanding.

P. S.—I addressed a note to Admiral Porter this morning, asking his opinion as to the dispositions to be made of any boats that the cavalry force on the other side might find in the Tallahatchie, Sunflower, or Yazoo. His answer is, "I would advise the capture of all boats up the Yazoo, but not their destruction. The steam pipes can be taken off and the cylinder-heads also, which will render them useless. We may want them. Still, if the force is not going to stay there, it is better to destroy them." Therefore, if the cavalry should find a boat hid away, instruct them to cripple the boat in such a way as to render it useless to them, yet valuable to us. In case we get complete possession of the Yazoo, all flats and ferries should be destroyed, but steamers only disabled.

GENERAL ORDERS, ⎰　　　HDQRS. PROVISIONAL BRIGADE,
No. 2. ⎱　*Humboldt, Tenn., December 22, 1862—10 p. m.*

The undersigned having been relieved by Brig. Gen. Isham N. Haynie from the command of the United States troops now at this place, desires to officially express his thanks to the officers and men of Companies B, C, G, H, and I, of the One hundred and twenty-sixth Illinois Infantry, Lieut. Col. E. M. Beardsley commanding; Companies H, I, and K, of the One hundred and sixth Illinois Infantry, Capt. P. W. Harts commanding; "about 600 men" of the Seventh Tennessee Infantry, Col. John A. Rogers commanding, and Companies A and B (dismounted), of the Second Tennessee Cavalry, Captain Thompson commanding, for the alacrity, cheerfulness, and fearlessness with which all his orders, with one exception, were obeyed, in the trying situation in which we were placed.

To Col. A. G. Malloy, Seventeenth Wisconsin Infantry; Reverend Father [Napolean] Mignault, of the same regiment, and Mr. Miles Sells, of Saint Louis, Mo. (passengers), he tenders his appreciation of their proffered services.

To Capt. George A. Williams, First U. S. Infantry, adjutant; First Lieut. Henry C. Whittemore, Second Illinois Artillery, aide-de-camp, and Dr. S. L. Hamlen, of Cincinnati, Ohio, subsistence officer (passengers), he acknowledges with gratification their faithful and prompt discharge of onerous duties.

The facts of having saved two large railroad trains, and all and everything on board, from capture and probable destruction by the enemy, and having then driven them out and recaptured the town of Humboldt, Tenn., under very adverse circumstances, is glory enough for one day, and conclusively proves the absolute necessity, for military success, that colonels of regiments should be men selected and appointed for their military knowledge, and not for political and social reasons.

GEORGE P. IHRIE,
Colonel and Additional Aide-de-Camp on General Grant's Staff.

HDQRS. RIGHT WING, THIRTEENTH ARMY CORPS,
Forest Queen, December 27, 1862.

Admiral DAVID D. PORTER, *Flag-Ship Black Hawk:*

DEAR SIR: The commencement of rain and non-arrival of General A. J. Smith's division makes a modification of my plan necessary. I will move the three columns as before indicated, but will send Steele, with two brigades, to Blake's levee, at the mouth of Chickasaw Creek—

1st. To enfilade and threaten the levee along the Yazoo, behind which the enemy works his torpedoes.

2d. To follow the levee along Chickasaw Bayou, back to the hills, to secure a lodgment.

The gunboats could then threaten Haines' Bluff battery. It may become necessary for us to use Chickasaw Bayou to boat up stores to its head. Please cause an examination of its mouth when our forces are in possession of both shores.

I am, &c.,

W. T. SHERMAN,
Major-General, Commanding.

HDQRS. RIGHT WING, THIRTEENTH ARMY CORPS,
Forest Queen, December 27, 1862.

General STEELE, *Commanding Fourth Division:*

DEAR SIR: The commencement of rain and appearance of a great fall of water, and the non-arrival of General A. J. Smith's division, makes

self and all those about me, and we predicted the best results at Vicks-burg from seeing things commence so auspiciously. The landing at Johnson's place, and the taking position under the hills of Vicksburg, are all matters you will find mentioned in my report, and as it was all written previous to any attack on you by the press, and merely in ac-cordance with my duties, no one can suppose me influenced by what has since taken place.

As to the Arkansas Post affair, it originated with yourself entirely, and you proposed it to me on the night you embarked the troops, and before it was known you had been relieved and that General McCler-nand had arrived. Whatever disposition was made of the troops after landing, your plans, at least, were carried out, as far as the state of the woods and country would admit of, and the position you took so promptly, under adverse circumstances, and without any knowledge of the country, would have enabled you to cut off five times the number of the enemy had they been there.

In conclusion, general, permit me to say that I feel as indignant as you can be at the attacks made on you. They would hardly be worth notice, except for the satisfaction of your friends. As I am sure you have no political aspirations, you can well afford to pass without notice what is said by the press, which is not in all cases the most loyal. You possess in an eminent degree the confidence and love of your soldiers, who will follow you anywhere, and in saying that, I pay you the highest compliment that can be paid a general.

I have the honor to remain, very respectfully, your obedient servant,

DAVID D. PORTER,
Acting Rear-Admiral.

[Inclosure No. 1.]

UNITED STATES MISSISSIPPI SQUADRON,
Yazoo River, December 27, 1862.

Hon. GIDEON WELLES,
Secretary of the Navy, Washington, D. C.:

SIR: This morning we commenced early the work of removing the torpedoes. The boats worked under a brisk fire from the concealed riflemen in pits, but the enemy gradually receded before our vessels, and by 3 o'clock in the evening we had worked up to within half or three-quarters of a mile of the batteries, the strength of which it was desirable to feel. The army, in the mean time, advanced toward the heights. My object was to draw off a large portion of the troops from Vicksburg, to prevent our ascent of the Yazoo, by which we could throw troops on the Milldale road. At 2.30 the forts commenced firing briskly at our boats with eight heavy guns, without driving them in. The way being apparently clear of torpedoes, the channel having been thoroughly dragged with all sorts of contrivances, Lieutenant-Com-mander Gwin, at 3 o'clock, advanced to the farthest point where the boats had finished their work, which was about 1,200 yards from the forts, and opened his batteries. The other vessels were also ordered up, all of which were lying close behind. The river was, however, too narrow at that point to get even two vessels abreast, and the Benton bore the brunt of the fight. It lasted two hours, during which time the Benton was much cut up, but nothing happened to impair her efficiency. Her armor was shot-proof when it was struck, except on deck, but still, I regret to say, there were some serious casualties. Lieutenant-Com-mander Gwin was most seriously wounded by a rifle-shot striking him on the right breast and carrying away the muscle of the right arm. He refused to enter the shot-proof pilot-house, saying that a captain's place was on the quarter-deck. While there is life there is hope, and I trust the life of this gallant officer may be spared to us. The country can ill afford to lose his services. Mr. Lord, the executive officer of the vessel, was wounded severely in the foot, but fought the vessel gallantly after the captain had been carried below, and retired when the batteries were all unmasked, and when the object was accomplished for which the vessels went up. I had three of the iron-clads, and the Lexington, the Marmora, and the ram Queen of the West lying as a reserve, but none of them were struck, though in action, except the Cincinnati (Lieutenant [George M.] Bache), by which no material damage occurred to the vessel.

The army advanced at the same time we were attacking the forts, making the enemy believe we were going to force the river forts. This induced them to draw off a large part of their forces from Vicksburg, and their cavalry were kept employed driving the men back to their guns.

I send you a sketch of the present position of affairs. The fighting is going on now, but with what success I know not. Our troops, though, are gaining at every step, and I am in hopes that by morning General Sherman will cut the communication between Vicksburg and Milldale, which should, by rights, end the affair. The railroads have all been cut leading into Texas, and there will be no hope of supplies, even if Vicksburg can hold out for a short time.

The enemy cannot approach the left wing of our army until they reach the heights without coming in range of our gunboats. At that point the army will have all the fighting to do themselves.

The following is a list of the killed and wounded: Lieut. Commander William Gwin, severely wounded on the right breast, lacerating the pectoral muscles extensively, and also tearing away a portion of the muscles of the right forearm; George P. Lord, executive officer, severe contusion of the foot; Elias Reese, executive officer of the Marmora, slightly wounded; N. B. Willetts, gunner, severely wounded; Robert Rhoyal, master-at-arms, killed; Thomas Smith, seaman, mortally wounded; Alexander W. Lynch, seaman, severe contusion of the head; Alexander Campbell, seaman, severely wounded; Stephen Moss, slightly wounded, and George Collender (boy), slightly wounded.

I have the honor to be, very respectfully, your obedient servant,

DAVID D. PORTER,
Acting Rear-Admiral, Commanding Mississippi Squadron.

[Inclosure No. 2.]

UNITED STATES MISSISSIPPI SQUADRON,
Yazoo River, December 31, 1862.

Hon. GIDEON WELLES,
Secretary of the Navy, Washington, D. C.:

SIR: I have already written you a hurried report of the attack on the Yazoo batteries by the Benton, and have the honor to relate occurrences up to this date.

On the 27th instant, Lieutenant-Commander [John G.] Walker, of the Baron De Kalb, had cleared the river Yazoo of torpedoes nearly to the place where the Cairo was sunk, and had obtained possession of two landings. The enemy, to the number of 2,000, were contesting every inch of ground from rifle-pits and from behind levees, where, from high overhanging banks, they could fire on our vessels almost with impunity. The light-draught iron-clads Signal, Juliet, and Romeo were very serviceable in performing this duty, being perfectly bullet-proof all over, except in their upper cabins, which were pretty badly cut up.

I did not deem the landings already secured sufficiently good, and, on the 23d instant, Lieutenant-Commander Gwin, according to order, proceeded up the river in the Benton, accompanied by the Tyler, Lieutenant-Commander [James M.] Pritchett; Lexington, Lieutenant-Commander [James W.] Shirk; ram Queen of the West, Capt. E. W. Sutherland; ram Lioness, Master T. O'Reilly; Signal, Acting Master Scott; Romeo, Acting Ensign [Robert P.] Smith, and the Juliet, Acting Volunteer Lieutenant [Edward] Shaw.

The 24th, 25th, and 26th were occupied in getting up the torpedoes, of which there were a great many; but, as the water had risen in the river, our vessels were enabled to keep off the sharpshooters, and the boats, being well covered, drove them back when they came in small numbers. Thus the work continued until the boats turned the bend in the river, where a series of forts, dotted all around the hills, and a heavy raft, covered with railroad iron, seemed to forbid all further progress. I directed the work to go on in the boats as near to the forts as possible, and they proceeded until the forts opened on them at a distance of 1,200 yards.

Though much annoyed by the fire, on the 27th the boats continued their work, and the Benton closed up to cover them. It was blowing very hard at the time, and the current being checked by the wind, the Benton, at all times an unmanageable ship, had a tendency to turn head or broadside to wind, in consequence of which she had to be tied to the bank. Then the enemy opened fire on her, almost every shot hitting her somewhere. Seven or eight heavy guns were firing from the different forts—50-pounder rifles and 64-pounder solid. After she made fast to the bank she was hit thirty times. Whenever the shots hit the pilot-house or the defense on her sides they did but little harm, in some places scarcely leaving a mark; but whenever they struck her deck, they went through everything, killing and wounding 10 persons; among the latter Lieutenant-Commander Gwin. The wind blew so hard that the other iron-clads were unmanageable, and, though they brought their batteries to bear (as did the Lexington and Tyler) as well as the very narrow stream would permit, they could not fire very effectually. Two of the guns in the forts were silenced, and the boats being unable to work any longer, the vessels dropped back around the point out of fire. The object of the firing was only to cover the boats, as the forts can only be taken by a landing party, and a very strong one at that.

The Benton was not rendered inefficient in the least, though two of her guns were damaged so that they are no longer serviceable, having been hit with shot.

On the 28th, General Sherman had advanced his forces within skirmishing distance of the enemy, and I sent up a strong force to make a feint on the forts, and to fire across on the Milldale road, to prevent reenforcements from being sent that way from the Yazoo forts to Vicksburg. Owing to late heavy rains, General Sherman found the ground almost impassable, and was headed off at every step by innumerable bayous. On the 29th, the assault was to commence on the hills behind Vicksburg, provided the army could find an opening through the abatis, which was piled up before them in all directions, and thousands of sharpshooters, in rifle-pits, picking off the officers at every step. I brought up the only two mortars I had been able to get down here, and placed them in position (backed by the gunboats) to shell the woods on the right and left of our army, to prevent the enemy from doubling on

either wing; also placing a portion of them at different points, to protect the transports. The battle commenced early in the day on the
29th, and our troops, with great heroism, went to the assault. One
division succeeded in getting into the batteries on the hill, and drove
the enemy out; but one of the two divisions that were to assault being
behind time, the assault was unsuccessful. The men had to retire
again, and lay on their arms that night in a cold, heavy rain, that must
have decimated the army.

My opinion is that the present rain, which is heavy, will render any
attempts of our army to enter Vicksburg in that way useless. They
could scarcely move the artillery at first; it will be doubly troublesome
now. In the mean time the rebels are receiving re-enforcements by
every train, and are almost, if not quite, as numerous as our troops.
Our army will have to intrench themselves until the ground will enable
them to move. We have a good position, and the gunboats cover the
army in a semicircle of 8 miles. Since I came below, the commanders
of the different posts have all urgently demanded gunboats, many of
them holding positions where they could drive off three or four times
their number. At Island No. 10 I have been notified that the commander had been ordered to abandon that post and spike his guns. I
have ordered the Pittsburg up there to hold it, and to break up the
guns, as they are old ones and fit for nothing; still, the rebels might
get them in some of these stampedes. The commanding officer at Columbus hears that 40,000 men are advancing on him, and wants a gunboat. I sent him the New Era, and ordered Commander Pennock to
fit 32-pounders on the old mortar rafts, and plant them in front of Columbus and Hickman. General Curtis calls for a large force of gunboats,
to meet General Gorman on the 5th of January, 1863. General Curtis
has ordered movements from the east up the Arkansas, on Little Rock.
General Gorman wants two gunboats at Helena. He says he is utterly
powerless, with 5,000 infantry and 2,000 cavalry. I suppose I must
raise them. The General Bragg is stationed at Memphis to protect
that place and repair her machinery. I have sent the Conestoga to the
mouth of Arkansas River, to protect the troops about to be stationed
there, and to prevent any intercourse up or down the Arkansas. As
the light-draughts are finished they will be stationed at different points
on the river.

What our future operations will be here I cannot yet tell. We expected that General Grant would have been in the rear of Vicksburg
by this time, and that General Banks would have been at Port Hudson,
both of which movements were, I believe, part of the plan of operations.
We hear nothing of either of these generals.

The rebels are going to throw a powerful force in Vicksburg, to hold
it at all hazards, and the heavy rains at this time will cause a change
in the military operations. General Sherman is quite equal to the emergency, and nothing daunted by his want of success. Part of the programme of the rebels is to threaten our river ports, to make us draw
off our troops from here, but with the position held by the commanders
of these ports they can defy any force brought against them if they do
their duty and keep dispatch boats ready to notify the gunboats that
will soon be stationed on the river. If there is a delay it will enable
us to get down our iron-clads from above, of which I see no prospect at
present.

Five light-draught steamers, under Lieutenant-Commander Fitch, are
up the Tennessee River, and will be able to operate there, now that the
water is rising. We will soon have two others on the Ohio. Everything

in the squadron in the shape of a steamer has a gun of some kind mounted on her, and our vessels pass up and down without molestation.

The vessels now here are the Black Hawk, Benton, Baron de Kalb, Carondelet, Louisville, Cincinnati, Mound City, Lexington, Tyler, Signal, Romeo, Juliet, Forest Rose, Rattler, Marmora; rams Monarch, Queen of the West, Switzerland, Lioness; storeship Sovereign; ordnance vessels Judge Torrence and Great Western; floating smithery Samson; tug-boat Champion, and six small tugs and two mortars, water-logged.

The health of the squadron is improving. The hospital ship is on her way down here.

I have the honor to be, very respectfully, your most obedient servant,

DAVID D. PORTER,
Acting Rear-Admiral, Commanding Mississippi Squadron.

[Inclosure No. 3.]

UNITED STATES MISSISSIPPI SQUADRON,
Yazoo River, January 3, 1863.

Hon. GIDEON WELLES,
Secretary of the Navy, Washington, D. C.:

SIR: The army has changed its position, which it was obliged to do, owing to the heavy rains. The men have been without shelter for five days, the rain at times coming down in torrents. It was impossible for any army to work under the circumstances. They failed in the first assault only because the supporting division did not come up to its work, and the reserve fired (it is said) into our own men. Could the first division have held the batteries which they took for three minutes longer, our army could have commanded the hills back of Vicksburg. So desperate were the rebels that they fired grape and canister into and through their own retreating men, and mowed them down by the dozens. The point of attack, at one time practicable, was no longer so after the assault of our army. It was rendered impassable by abatis and stockades. It was then determined by General Sherman and myself to attempt the forts on the Yazoo, at Drumgould's Bluff, by a night attack. Ten thousand men were to have been thrown right at the foot of the cliffs, risking the loss of the transports, while all the iron-clads were to open fire on the batteries and try and silence them temporarily. The ram Lioness, under Colonel Ellet, was fitted with an apparatus for breaking torpedo wires, and was to go ahead and clear the way. Colonel Ellet was also provided with fifteen torpedoes, to blow up the raft and enable the vessels to get by, if possible. This desperate duty he took upon himself cheerfully, and no doubt would have performed it well had the opportunity occurred.

The details of the expedition were left to me, and it was all ready to start at 3.30 a. m. A dense fog unfortunately set in at midnight and lasted until morning, when it was too late to start. It was so thick that vessels could not move; men could not see each other at 10 paces. The river is too narrow for operations in clear weather, much less in a fog. After the fog, there was, in the afternoon, every indication of a long and heavy rain. The general very wisely embarked his whole army, without being disturbed by the enemy, and is now lying 5 miles above Vicksburg, waiting for good weather and for McClernand to take command. The latter arrived before the army left its position, and approved the change. As we left, the rain poured down in torrents, and will continue to do so for some time longer, rendering land operations perfectly impracticable. While the army leaders are deciding what to do, I have enough employment for the vessels here to patrol the river and occupy those posts which have been partially deserted, or where apprehension of invasion is felt.

I have the honor to be, very respectfully your obedient servant,

DAVID D. PORTER,
Acting Rear-Admiral, Commanding Mississippi Squadron.

[Inclosure No. 4.]

UNITED STATES MISSISSIPPI SQUADRON,
White River, January 18, 1863.

Hon. GIDEON WELLES, *Secretary of the Navy.*

SIR : The army will move to-morrow on Vicksburg, with re-enforcements furnished by General Grant, who, I believe, will accompany the expedition as commander-in-chief. Had the combinations been carried out in our last expedition, General Grant advancing by Grenada, General Banks up the river, and General Sherman down the river, the whole matter would have assumed a different aspect; but General Sherman was the only one on the ground. The army of General Grant had been cut off from its supplies ; General Banks never came up the river; and General Sherman, having attempted to take the enemy by surprise, lost about 700 wounded, 300 killed, and about 400 prisoners. All this was owing to Colonel De Courcy (who has since resigned) not following General Blair, who had no difficulty in getting into the works of the enemy. Had our troops been able to hold these works for three minutes, Vicksburg would have been ours; but that chance was lost and will not offer again. The enemy crowded in 20,000 men from Grenada and 10,000 from Jackson, and outnumbered us two to one. The rain forced General Sherman to embark, and we did so without the enemy being aware of it until everything was on board. Not a thing of consequence was left behind. When the enemy did discover it, they sent down three regiments, with field pieces, to attack the line of transports, which was covered at every point by the gunboats and light-draughts. The Lexington, Marmora, Queen of the West, and Monarch opened on the enemy with shrapnel, and cut them up very severely, causing them to fly in all directions, and not losing a man on our side. This is a short history of this affair. The operations to come will be of a different character. It will be a tedious siege—the first step, in my opinion, toward a successful attack on Vicksburg, which has been made very strong by land and water. I have always thought the late attempt was premature, but sometimes these dashes succeed, and certain it is that, but for the want of nerve in the leader of a brigade, the army would have succeeded.

The operations of the Navy in the Yazoo are worthy to be ranked amongst the brightest events of the war. The officers in charge of getting up the torpedoes and clearing 8 miles of the river distinguished themselves by their patient endurance and cool courage under a galling fire of musketry from well-protected and unseen riflemen, and the crews of the boats exhibited a courage and coolness seldom equaled. The Navy will scarcely ever get credit for these events. They are not brilliant enough to satisfy our impatient people at the North, who know little of the difficulties attending an expedition like the one mentioned, or how much officers and men are exposing themselves, while they wonder why we do not demolish mountains of granite.

The Department may rest assured that the navy here is never idle. The army depends on us to take entire charge of them on the water, and it employs every vessel I have. I have none too many. The light-draught vessels have only half crews. I am making up deficiencies with contrabands as fast as I can. We expect to disembark the troops opposite Vicksburg in four or five days. In the mean time I want to gather up the fleet which are operating at different points with the army. My opinion is that Vicksburg is the main point. When that falls, all subordinate posts will fall with it. Arkansas is, or will be, quiet for the present, and all smaller expeditions should be attached to the large one at Vicksburg. This will enable me to employ the gunboats to better advantage, which I cannot do now. The commander of every post requires a gunboat, but I do not encourage them always in their expectations, as it makes them very careless about defending themselves.

Very respectfully, your obedient servant,

DAVID D. PORTER,
Acting Rear-Admiral, Commanding Mississippi Squadron.

HEADQUARTERS FIFTEENTH ARMY CORPS,
Before Vicksburg, February 4, 1863.

Admiral DAVID D. PORTER, *Commanding Mississippi Squadron :*

DEAR SIR : I thank you most heartily for your kind and considerate letter, February 3, received this day, and am more obliged than you can understand, as it covers many points I had neglected to guard against. Before Vicksburg, my mind was more intent on the enemy intrenched behind those hills than on the spies and intriguers in my own camp and " at home."

The spirit of anarchy seems deep at work at the North, more alarming than the batteries that shell at us from the opposite shore. I am going to have the correspondent of the New York Herald tried by a court-martial as a spy, not that I want the fellow shot, but because I want to establish the principle that such people cannot attend our armies, in violation of orders, and defy us, publishing their garbled statements and defaming officers who are doing their best. You of the Navy can control all who sail under your flag, whilst we are almost compelled to carry along in our midst a class of men who on Government transports usurp the best state-rooms and accommodations of the boats, pick up the drop conversations of officers, and report their limited and tainted observations as the history of events they neither see nor comprehend. This should not be, and must not be. We cannot prosper in military operations if we submit to it, and, as some one must begin the attack, I must assume the ungracious task. I shall always account myself fortunate to be near the officers of the old Navy, and would be most happy if I could think it possible the Navy and the Army of our country could ever again enjoy the high tone of honor and honesty that characterized them in the days of our youth.

With sentiments of profound respect for you and the officers of your fleet, I am, truly, yours,

W. T. SHERMAN,
Major-General of Volunteers.

GENERAL ORDERS, }   HDQRS. DEPT. OF THE TENNESSEE,
No. 13.   }   *Young's Point, La., February 19, 1863.*

I. Before a general court-martial, which convened at Young's Point, La., February 5, 1863, pursuant to Special Orders, No. 34, dated Headquarters Department of the Tennessee, February 3, 1863, and of which Brig. Gen. J. M. Thayer, U. S. Volunteers, is president, was arraigned and tried Thomas W. Knox.

CHARGE 1ST.—Giving intelligence to the enemy, directly or indirectly.

Specification 1st.—In this, that Thomas W. Knox, citizen and camp-follower, did, while following and attending the Army of the United States, on board a chartered transport in the service of the United States, write for publication, and cause to be published in the New York Herald, of date January 18, 1863, a certain article purporting to be a history of the operations of the army before Vicksburg, dated Steamer Continental, Right Wing, Thirteenth Army Corps, Milliken's Bend, January 3, 1863, in which he gives the names of commanders of corps, divisions, and brigades comprising said army, with the number and description of the regiments composing one of said divisions, thereby indirectly conveying to the enemy an approximate estimate of its strength, in direct violation of the Fifty-seventh Article of War.

Specification 2d.—In this, that the said Thomas W. Knox, citizen and camp-follower, did publish or cause to be published in the New York Herald, under date of January 18, 1863, a certain article purporting to be a history of the operations of the army before Vicksburg, dated Steamer Continental, Right Wing, Thirteenth Army Corps, Milliken's Bend, January 3, 1863, in direct violation of General Orders, No. 67, dated War Department, Adjutant-General's Office, Washington, August 26, 1861.

CHARGE 2D.—Being a spy.

Specification 1st.—That said Thomas W. Knox, being a citizen and camp follower, and having no authority, leave, or consent to attend the army, did, at Helena, Ark., on or about the 21st day of December, 1862, get on board the transport Continental, and did remain on board said transport until about the 3d day of January, 1863, acting as a spy, in direct violation of General Orders, No. 8, dated Headquarters Right Wing, Thirteenth Army Corps, Memphis, Tenn., December 18, 1862, Paragraph VI, as follows:

Any person whatever, whether in the service of the United States or transports, found making reports for publication which might reach the enemy giving them information and comfort, will be arrested and treated as spies.

Which orders were published in the public newspapers of Memphis, and their purport known to the said Knox, on or about the 3d day of January, 1863, about which time he wrote for publication a letter of January 3, 1863, which was published in the New York Herald of January 18, 1863, containing all he pretended to know of the organization and strength of said army, and detracting from the merits of many officers high in command of said army, thereby giving information and comfort to the enemy.

Specification 2d.—That said Thomas W. Knox did, whilst so acting as a spy, publish or cause to be published in the New York Herald, under date of January 18, 1863, sundry and various false allegations and accusations against the officers of the Army of the United States, to the great detriment of the interest of the National Government and comfort of our enemies, to wit:

To his right was General Stuart, busy erecting a bridge over the bayou, and on the extreme right was General A. J. Smith, within 1¼ miles of Vicksburg, frittering away his time in preparing to throw a bridge across a place where his troops could readily march through. This was the situation up to the latter part of the forenoon of the

29th. With General Sherman's permission, rather than by his order, General Morgan made preparations for assaulting the hill. General Sherman had issued no order appointing a certain time for the assault upon the batteries, and there was no common understanding among the various generals of divisions and brigades. Colonel Williamson's regiment was fast falling before the concentrated fire of the rebels, and, with an anxious heart, General Thayer looked around for aid. Down the hill, crouched in the line of rifle-pits near the base, lay the Twenty-second Kentucky and the Sixteenth Ohio, the only regiments of Morgan that had attempted to make the assault. General Thayer rushed down to where these two regiments lay. In vain he implored, urged, ordered, and entreated them to go to his assistance. Move they would not, alleging as an excuse that the brigade commander (Colonel De Courcy) was not there to command. While General Thayer was begging them to go to his assistance, he was joined by General Blair on the same errand, the latter going to Colonel De Courcy in person. Their conjoined efforts were alike fruitless to move Colonel De Courcy or his men.

By some criminal oversight, there had been little preparation for battle on the part of Sherman's medical director, and the hospitals were but poorly supplied with many needed stores. Since the battle, General Sherman has persistently refused to allow a hospital boat to go above, though their detention in this region is daily fatal to many lives. The only known reason for his refusal is his fear that a knowledge of his mismanagement will reach the papers of the North.

As soon as the assault of the 29th had been concluded, General Sherman decided to make another attack on the same day. General Blair's brigade was moved from the north side of the bayou, and its place taken by the brigade of General Hovey. The latter officer was to attack the hill in his front, and was to be supported by General Thayer, General Blair, and General Morgan. Twice the order was given to advance up the hill, when it was countermanded by General Sherman. Once General Hovey had given the command "Forward!" but before he uttered the word "march!" a messenger came from General Sherman, ordering him to postpone his advance.

Finding that his own plan of attack had proved a failure, General Sherman now gave attention to the suggestions of his subordinates. General Steele had from the first advocated the ascent of the Yazoo as near as possible to Haines' Bluff. The troops were to be landed just out of the range of the guns of the forts, and as soon as they could be thrown on shore they were to storm and carry the position, said to be defended by but a few hundred men. The plan was approved by all the other officers of the army, and finally obtained the sanction of the commander-in-chief. For some unaccountable reason General Sherman issued an order that no whistle should be blown or bell rung on any of the boats for twenty-four hours under pain of death. General Sherman issued orders for the erection of batteries along the bayou in front of the enemy's works, and, from the moment of the repulse, he appeared anxious to change his tactics, and act on the defensive.

At the time we entered the Yazoo, it is certain that there were not more than 10,000 or 12,000 men in and around Vicksburg. Had we struck promptly at the batteries, it is probable that we could have taken possession of the high ground, and had an open road into Vicksburg. One of the commissaries had recently taken 50,000 rations to a depot in rear of the battle-field, only 1¼ miles from the landing. General Sherman ordered these destroyed, by rolling them into the bayou, as there was no time for their removal. A part of the supplies was tumbled into the bayou in obedience to instructions. Captain Smith, brigade commissary to General Blair, went out with a wagon train as the troops were being withdrawn, and brought in what had not already been destroyed. General Sherman also ordered commissary stores destroyed by General A. J. Smith's division, and there was much waste in consequence. All these stores might have been saved, and would have been, had General Sherman's orders been less peremptory. The embarkation was covered by the gunboats, so that the enemy would not be able to get to the bank before we could get away. Everything was hurry.

And many and other similar false, malicious imputations and charges against officers in the service of the United States, calculated to weaken their authority and to give aid and comfort to the enemy.

CHARGE 3D.—Disobedience of orders.

Specification 1st.—In this, that Thomas W. Knox did, knowingly and willfully, disobey the lawful command of the proper authority, as contained in General Orders, No. 8, dated Headquarters Right Wing, Thirteenth Army Corps, Memphis, Tenn., December 18, 1862, by accompanying the expedition down the Mississippi from Helena, Ark., about December 21, 1862

Specification 2d.—In this, that said Thomas W. Knox did, knowingly and willfully, disobey and directly violate General Orders, No. 67, dated War Department, Adjutant-General's Office, Washington, August 26, 1861, by writing, printing, or causing to be printed in the New York Herald, under date of January 18, 1863, correspondence and communication respecting operations of the army or military movements of the army near Vicksburg, Miss., without the authority and sanction of the general in command.

To all of which charges and specifications, except the second specification to second charge, which was, on motion of the prisoner, stricken out by the court, the prisoner pleaded as follows:

To 1*st specification* of 1st CHARGE, " Not guilty."
To 2*d specification* of 1st CHARGE, " Not guilty."
To 1st CHARGE, " Not guilty."
To 1*st specification* of 2d CHARGE, " Not guilty."
To 2d CHARGE, " Not guilty."
To 1*st specification* of 3d CHARGE, " Not guilty."
To 2*d specification* of 3d CHARGE, " Not guilty."
To 3d CHARGE, " Not guilty."

The court, after mature deliberation upon the testimony adduced, finds the accused as follows:

Of 1*st specification* of 1st CHARGE, " Guilty, except the words, ' thereby conveying to the enemy an approximate estimate of its strength, in direct violation of the Fifty-seventh Article of War.'"
Of the 2*d specification* of 1st CHARGE, " Guilty."
Of the 1st CHARGE, " Not guilty."
Of 1*st specification* of 2d CHARGE, " Not guilty."
Of 2d CHARGE, " Not guilty."
Of 1*st specification* of 3d CHARGE, the court finds the facts proven, but attaches no criminality thereto.
Of the 2*d specification* of 3d CHARGE, " Guilty."
Of 3d CHARGE, " Guilty."

And the court does therefore sentence him, Thomas W. Knox, to be sent without the lines of the army, and not to return under penalty of imprisonment.

Findings and sentence approved, and will be carried into effect.

The general court-martial, of which Brig. Gen. J. M. Thayer is president, is hereby dissolved.

By order of Maj. Gen. U. S. Grant:

[JNO. A. RAWLINS,]
Assistant Adjutant-General.

HEADQUARTERS FIFTEENTH ARMY CORPS,
Camp near Vicksburg, February 23, 1863

Col. JOHN A. RAWLINS,
Assistant Adjutant-General, Department of the Tennessee:

COLONEL : General Orders, No. 13, from your headquarters, of date February 19, 1863, involves certain principles that I think should be settled by the highest authority of our Government, and I beg most respectfully their reference, through the Judge Advocate-General, to the Commander-in-Chief.

The findings on the third charge, first specification, are, "the facts proven as stated, but attaches no criminality thereto," viz, that the accused knowingly and willfully disobeyed the lawful command of the proper authority by accompanying the expedition down the Mississippi below Helena. The inference is that a commanding officer has no right to prohibit citizens from accompanying a military expedition, or, if he does, such citizens incur no criminality by disregarding such command. The finding of the first specification, first charge, "Guilty, except the words 'thereby conveying to the enemy an approximate estimate of its strength, in direct violation of the Fifty-seventh Article of War,'" involves the principle that publication of army organization and strength in a paper having the circulation South and North of the New York Herald does not amount to an indirect conveyance of intelligence to an enemy.

I regard these two points as vital to our success as an army contending against an enemy who has every advantage of us in position and means of intelligence. I do not expect that any court-martial or any officer should do, or attempt to do, an unlawful act, but I do believe the laws of Congress and of war clearly cover both these points, and believing that the true interest of the Government and of our people demand a radical change in this respect, I avail myself of this means to invite their earnest consideration of the issues involved.

If a commanding officer cannot exclude from his camp the very class of men which an enemy would select as spies and informers, and if to prove the conveyance of indirect information to the enemy it be necessary to follow that information from its source to the very armies arrayed against us, whose country thus far our hundreds of thousands of men have been unable to invade, and yet whose newspapers are made up of extracts from these very Northern papers, then it is fruitless to attempt to conceal from them all the data they could need to make successful resistance to our plans, and to attack our detached parties and lines of communication. To this cause may well be attributed the past reverses to our armies and the failure of almost every plan devised by our generals. I believe this cause has lost us millions of money, thousands of lives, and will continue to defeat us to the end of time, unless some remedy be devised.

I am, with great respect,

W. T. SHERMAN,
Major-General, Commanding.

STEAMER CONTINENTAL,
Milliken's Bend, La., April 6, 1863.

Major-General SHERMAN:

Inclosed please find copy of the order of the President authorizing me to return to this department, and to remain, with General Grant's approval. General Grant has expressed his willingness to give such approval, provided there is no objection from yourself.

Without referring in detail to past occurrences, permit me to express my regret at the want of harmony between portions of the army and the press, and the hope that there may be a better feeling in future.

I should be pleased to receive your assent in the present subject-matter. The eyes of the whole North are now turned upon Vicksburg, and the history of the events soon to culminate in its fall will be watched with great eagerness.

Your favor in the matter will be duly appreciated by the journal I represent, as well as by—

Respectfully, yours,

THOS. W. KNOX,
Correspondent New York Herald.

[P. S.]—An answer addressed on board this boat will reach me.

[Inclosure.]

EXECUTIVE MANSION,
Washington, March 20, 1863.

Whom it may concern:

Whereas it appears to my satisfaction that Thomas W. Knox, a correspondent of the New York Herald, has been, by the sentence of a court-martial, excluded from the military department under command of Major-General Grant, and also that General Thayer, president of the court-martial which rendered the sentence, and Major-General McClernand, in command of a corps of that department, and many other respectable persons, are of opinion that Mr. Knox's offense was technical rather than willfully wrong, and that the sentence should be revoked; now, therefore, said sentence is hereby so far revoked as to allow Mr. Knox to return to General Grant's headquarters, and to remain if General Grant shall give his express assent, and to again leave the department if General Grant shall refuse such assent.

A. LINCOLN.

BEFORE VICKSBURG, *April* 6, 1863.

THOMAS W. KNOX,
Correspondent New York Herald:

The letter of the President of the United States authorizing you to return to these headquarters, and to remain with my consent, or leave if such consent is withheld, has been shown me.

You came here first in positive violation of an order from General Sherman. Because you were not pleased with his treatment of army followers, who had violated his order, you attempted to break down his influence with his command, and to blast his reputation with the public. You made insinuations against his sanity, and said many things which were untrue, and, so far as your letter had influence, calculated to affect the public service unfavorably.

General Sherman is one of the ablest soldiers and purest men in the country. You have attacked him and been sentenced to expulsion from this department for the offense. Whilst I would conform to the slightest wish of the President, where it is formed upon a fair representation of both sides of any question, my respect for General Sherman is such that in this case I must decline, unless General Sherman first gives his consent to your remaining.

U. S. GRANT,
Major-General.

HEADQUARTERS FIFTEENTH ARMY CORPS,
Camp before Vicksburg, April 7, 1863.

THOMAS W. KNOX, Esq.,
Correspondent New York Herald, Steamer Continental:

SIR: Yours of April 6, inclosing a copy of President Lincoln's informal decision in your case, is received.

I certainly do regret that Generals McClernand and Thayer regard the disobedience of orders emanating from the highest military source and the publication of willful and malicious slanders against their brother officers as mere technical offenses, and notwithstanding the President's indorsement of that conclusion, I cannot so regard it.   After having enunciated to me the fact that newspaper correspondents were a fraternity bound together by a common interest that must write down all who stood in their way, and that you had to supply the public demand for news, true if possible, but false if your interest demanded it, I cannot be privy to a tacit acknowledgment of the principle.

Come with a sword or musket in your hand, prepared to share with us our fate in sunshine and storm, in prosperity and adversity, in plenty and scarcity, and I will welcome you as a brother and associate; but come as you now do, expecting me to ally the reputation and honor of my country and my fellow-soldiers with you, as the representative of the press, which you yourself say makes so slight a difference between truth and falsehood, and my answer is, Never.

W. T. SHERMAN,
Major-General of Volunteers.

HEADQUARTERS FIFTEENTH ARMY CORPS,
Camp near Vicksburg, April 8, 1863.

Major-General GRANT:

DEAR SIR: I received last night the copy of your answer to Mr. Knox's application to return and reside near your headquarters. I thank you for the manner and substance of that reply. Many regard Knox as unworthy the notice he has received. This is true; but I send you his letter to me and my answer. Observe in his letter to me, sent long before I could have heard the result of his application to you, he makes the assertion that you had no objection, but rather wanted him back, and only as a matter of form required my assent. He regretted a difference between a "portion of the army and the press." The insolence of these fellows is insupportable. I know they are encouraged, but I know human nature well enough, and that they will be the first to turn against their patrons. Mr. Lincoln, of course, fears to incur the enmity of the Herald, but he must rule the Herald or the Herald will rule him; he can take his choice.

I have been foolish and unskillful in drawing on me the shafts of the press. By opposing mob law in California, I once before drew down the press; but after the smoke cleared off, and the people saw where they were drifting to, they admitted I was right. If the press be allowed to run riot, and write up and write down at their pleasure, there is an end to a constitutional government in America, and anarchy must result. Even now the real people of our country begin to fear and tremble at it, and look to our armies as the anchor of safety, of order, submission to authority, bound together by a real Government, and not by the clamor of a demoralized press and crowd of demagogues.

As ever, your friend,

W. T. SHERMAN.

CAMP NEAR VICKSBURG, April 8, 1863.

Mr. HALSTED, Cincinnati:

SIR: As, unhappily, I am singled out of a great mass of men who think as I do, but who have either bowed to the storm or been more lucky in steering their barks clear of the rock of danger, I take the liberty of sending, through Mrs. Sherman, copies of a short correspondence which involves a high moral and political principle. The whole will be plain to you at a glance, and I now propose to call your attention to one phase of it, and trace the logical sequence.

Knox, a citizen, entitled to all the rights of a citizen of any and every kind, a strong, stalwart man, capable of handling a musket, comes into the camp of a major-general whom he never saw in person, conversed with, or knew anything about, in open and known violation of his orders, and, dating his matter from the headquarters of a part of this very command, publishes a string of falsehood, abusive of every servant of the Government, except a small knot of "cunning and knowing ones bred in the same litter." These were heroes; all else were knaves, fools, cowards, everything, and the major-general in command, with commissions from a cadet all the way up to major-general, tested by twenty years' service in every part of this continent, who has managed all manner of business without a stain heretofore, is declared by this youngster and stranger as a mere ass, yea, insane. When called on in person to explain his motive—"Of course, General Sherman, I had no feeling against you personally, but you are regarded the enemy of our set, and we must in self-defense write you down."

When a court-martial banishes him, the President of the United States, upon the personal application of this man, fortified by "respectable persons," sends him back, subject to a condition not dependent on me. Does Knox exhibit any sign of appreciating the real issue? He "regrets" the unhappy difference between a portion of the army and himself. The whole "press" and the sheet, the New York Herald, which he represents will appreciate the fact of my humbling myself to its agent, to my tamely submitting to its insults.

When Mr. Calhoun announced to General Jackson the doctrine of secession, did he bow to the opinion of that respectable source and the vast array of people whom he represented? No. He answered, Secession is treason, death. Had he yielded an inch, the storm would then have swept over this country.

Had Mr. Buchanan met the seizure of our mints and arsenals in the same spirit, he would have kept this war within the limits of actual traitors; but, by temporizing, he gave the time and opportunity for the organization of a rebellion of half the nation. So in this case. The assertion of the principle that the "press" has a right to keep paid agents in our camps, independent of the properly accredited commanders appointed by law, would, if successful, destroy any army, and the certain result would be not only an open, bold, and determined rebellion, but dissension, discord, and mutiny throughout the land and in our very camps. In this point I may be in error, but, for the time being, I am the best judge. I am no enemy to freedom of thought, freedom of the "press" and speech, but in all controversies there is a time when discussion must cease and action begin. That time has not only come, but has been in plain, palpable existence for two years. No amount of argument will move the rebellious. They have thrown aside the pen and taken the sword. Though slow to realize this fact, though vacillating in preparation and act, the North must do the same or perish and become the contempt of all mankind. Persons at a distance, who can look back upon the North, see, with pain and sorrow, the dissensions and vain discussions which are kept alive by a free press. In it they see the exercise of an undoubted right—the same that a man has in his own household to burn his books, destroy his furniture, abuse his family, offend his neighbor—and fear lest he continue in the exercise of the same glorious privilege to maintain his right to personal freedom by burning his house with all its contents.

All I propose to say is that Mr. Lincoln and the press may, in the exercise of their glorious prerogative, tear our country and armies to tatters; but they shall not insult me with impunity in my own camp.

With respect, &c.,

W. T. SHERMAN.

CONFEDERATE CORRESPONDENCE, ETC.

RICHMOND, *June* 19, 1862.
(Received Tupelo, June 19.)

General BRAGG:

I am disappointed at the failure to execute my order, and fear the loss of time which has occurred may produce irreparable injury. Send General Van Dorn, with all possible dispatch, to assume command of the Department of South Mississippi and East Louisiana. He will be regarded as temporarily detached from his division.

JEFFERSON DAVIS.

MERIDIAN, *July* 25, 1862.

General VAN DORN:

Your dispatch received. Congratulate you and your command. All is well in our front. We are moving rapidly—a change of base. Act in conjunction with Price, who remains. You have the fullest confidence of all.

BRAXTON BRAGG.

JACKSON, MISS., *August* 25, 1862.

General BRECKINRIDGE:

GENERAL: The inclosed dispatch* from General Bragg explains itself. You will not have time to reach him. Organize your division as soon as possible, and let us push on with Price. A brilliant field is before us yet. Let us start as soon as possible. Set your officers to work. We have transportation sufficient and everything necessary. I go to Vicksburg for a few days. Give any orders in my absence you may deem necessary. I have directed my staff officers to observe them.

Yours, truly,

EARL VAN DORN,
Major-General.

CHATTANOOGA, *August* 25, 1862.

General VAN DORN:

Move as soon as practicable. Buell is falling back. Is now in Nashville. Price reports movement from Corinth to re-enforce Buell. Destroy them as they cross the river. Kirby Smith is in Kentucky, moving on Lexington. We move in a few days to sustain him or fight Buell if he stands. Morgan (Yankee) closed in at Cumberland Gap and cut off from supplies.

BRAXTON BRAGG,
General.

* See Bragg to Van Dorn, following.

SPECIAL ORDERS, }   HDQRS. BRECKINRIDGE'S DIVISION,
    No. 13.   }   *Jackson, Miss., September* 5, 1862.

In obedience to instructions from district headquarters, the First Brigade (Bowen's) will move by train to Abbeville, Miss., at 2 p. m. to-morrow.

*   *   *   *   *   *   *

By command of Brig. Gen. J. S. Bowen:
                              R. R. HUTCHINSON,
                    Captain and Assistant Adjutant-General.

GENERAL ORDERS, }   HDQRS. BRECKINRIDGE'S DIVISION,
    No. 8.   }   *Jackson, September* 7, 1862.

The remaining brigades of this division will be ready to move as soon as possible northward by rail. The transportation will be left to follow after, but a suitable number of quartermasters, wagon-masters, and teamsters will be left to attend to them. In moving, there must be perfect order, and especially no straggling or wandering from the cars, and a commissioned officer will go in each car to enforce discipline and order. Canteens will be filled with water before starting, and, as far as possible, buckets of water will be provided for each car. Each brigade commander will report to these headquarters the earliest moment at which his brigade will be ready to move; also about the number of men, horses, and guns to be transported; and as soon as an order to move is received, two days' cooked rations will be prepared to be taken with the troops. Everything necessary to a movement in the field will be taken with the troops, except the wagons and teams and one-half of the tents. A portion of the tents will be taken to shelter the sick and feeble until the transportation reaches the command.

By order of Major-General Breckinridge:
                              J. L. ROBERTSON,
                    Captain and Assistant Adjutant-General.

            HDQRS. SECOND BRIGADE, BRECKINRIDGE'S DIVISION,
                                        September 7, 1862.

Major-General BRECKINRIDGE:

GENERAL: The colonel commanding the brigade directs me to say that every arrangement can be perfected and the brigade ready to move by 3 o'clock on Tuesday morning, September 9.

Very respectfully, your obedient servant,
                              JNO. B. PIRTLE,
                    Acting Assistant Adjutant-General.

SPECIAL ORDERS, }   HDQRS. BRECKINRIDGE'S DIVISION,
    No. 16.   }   *Jackson, Miss., September* 8, 1862.

*   *   *   *   *   *   *

Brig. Gen. Albert Rust, having reported to these headquarters for duty, by order of the major-general commanding this district, is assigned to the command of the Fourth Brigade of this division   He will be obeyed and respected accordingly.

    *   *   *   *   *

By command of Major-General Breckinridge:
> J. L. ROBERTSON,
> *Captain and Assistant Adjutant-General.*

SPECIAL ORDERS, }   HDQRS. BRECKINRIDGE'S DIVISION,
No. 17.   }   *Jackson, Miss., September 9, 1862.*

    *   *   *   *   *   *

III. The Second Brigade of this division will be at the railroad station in Jackson to-morrow morning at 8 o'clock, and will take the cars for the north. The commanding officer will report to Brigadier-General Villepigue, at Holly Springs (or beyond, if he has moved), until the arrival of the major-general commanding this division.

    *   *   *   *   *   *

By order of Major-General Breckinridge:
> J. L. ROBERTSON,
> *Captain and Assistant Adjutant-General.*

SPECIAL ORDERS, }   HDQRS. BRECKINRIDGE'S DIVISION,
No. 18.   }   *Jackson, Miss., September 10, 1862.*

I. The Third Brigade of this division will be at the railroad station in Jackson to-morrow morning, one hour after sunrise. The battery attached to this brigade will be there at sunrise, and will take the cars for the north. The commanding officers will report to Brigadier-General Villepigue, at Holly Springs (or beyond, if he has moved), until the arrival of the major-general commanding this division.

    *   *   *   *   *   *

By command of Major-General Breckinridge:
> JOHN A. BUCKNER,
> *Major and Assistant Adjutant-General.*

SPECIAL ORDERS, }   HDQRS. BRECKINRIDGE'S DIVISION,
No. 20.   }   *Jackson, Miss., September 12, 1862.*

    *   *   *   *   *   *

II. The Fourth Brigade of this division will be at the railroad station in Jackson to-morrow morning (the 13th), at 9 o'clock, and will take the cars for the north. The commanding officer will report to Brigadier-General Villepigue at Holly Springs (or beyond, if he has moved), until the arrival of the major-general commanding this division. McClung's battery, now on the cars at the depot, is attached to this brigade, and will move with it.

    *   *   *   *   *   *

By order of Major-General Breckinridge:
> JOHN A. BUCKNER,
> *Major and Assistant Adjutant-General.*

SPECIAL ORDERS, }   HDQRS. BRECKINRIDGE'S DIVISION,
     No. 21.   }   *Jackson, Miss., September* 13, 1862.

    *   *   *   *   *   *

IV. The cavalry companies attached to this command will be at the railroad depot at Jackson to-morrow morning at 9 o'clock, prepared to take the cars for the north.

    *   *   *   *   *   *   *

By order of Major-General Breckinridge:
                              JOHN A. BUCKNER,
                         Major and Assistant Adjutant-General.

SPECIAL ORDERS, }   HDQRS. BRECKINRIDGE'S DIVISION,
     No. 23.   }   *Parham's House, September* 18, 1862.

    *   *   *   *   *   *   *

II. The Fourth, Fifth, and Sixth Kentucky Regiments and Cobb's battery, will for the present constitute a brigade, under the command of Col. R. P. Trabue, called the First Brigade. The Nineteenth, Twentieth, Twenty-eighth, and Forty-fifth Tennessee Regiments and Mc-Clung's battery will form another, to be called the Second Brigade, under command of Colonel [F. M.] Walker.*

    *   *   *   *   *   *   *

By command of Major-General Breckinridge:
                              JOHN A. BUCKNER,
                         Major and Assistant Adjutant-General.

SPECIAL ORDERS, }   HDQRS. BRECKINRIDGE'S DIVISION,
     No. 27.   }   *Meridian, Miss., September* 24, 1862.

I. Colonel Walker will move with the Second Brigade by rail to Mobile, thence to Montgomery and Chattanooga, taking his tents, ammunition, and fifteen days' rations.†

    *   *   *   *   *   *   *

By command of Major-General Breckinridge:
                              JOHN A. BUCKNER,
                         Major and Assistant Adjutant-General.

                              HEADQUARTERS,
                    Vicksburg, September 30, 1862.
[General VAN DORN:]

GENERAL: In the excitement and absorbing interest of events at a distance, I am seriously apprehensive that the safety of this important point may be, and actually is, overlooked. My conviction is that this command is to-day at the mercy of the army at Helena, provided such an attack is made against it as their abundant means of transportation enables them to make. Their unaccountable inertness has saved

---

     * Details of movement omitted.
     † The second paragraph directed same movement for Colonel Trabue's (First) brigade. Details of movement omitted.

Vicksburg from succumbing, for, since the departure of General Breckinridge's division, there has never been a day on which a successful land attack might not have been made by the force at Helena; but it is not right to calculate that they will continue inactive, nor fair to the interests involved to hold the place by sufferance.

The case is as follows: Above us, and within thirty hours' easy run of this place, are encamped 15,000 men, commanded by an experienced officer of the Regular Army, with a naval force at his control of some seven shot-proof rams and fourteen to eighteen gunboats positively known to be present, and doubtless more that could be obtained.   According to information, there could be spared from New Orleans at this present time 8,000 men for any expedition undertaken, and this force might reach here in four days from the time known to have started. Suppose either of these expeditions start for this point, what is there to oppose them here?   I have about 1,800 infantry, 200 cavalry, and six light batteries (two of these under orders to march), all partially drilled, but none ever under fire on the field.   If attacked, this force could be increased in five or six days by 400 cavalry of like discipline, and about the same number of State Minute-men.   If not threatened from New Orleans, a small increase might be expected from the direction of Lake Pontchartrain, say 500 men; in a word, if I can keep seven times my number at bay for nearly a week, a re-enforcement of 1,500 may be expected—making 3,500 against 15,000.

Now, I am willing to run any risk with my command the times demand, and, if it is necessary to guard this exposed point with a handful of men, there is nothing more to be said; but I repeat that, in my opinion, the interests involved here are too great to be left to chance, and it is felt as a duty to represent in decided terms that this point is in danger, and that we can be literally overwhelmed by the enemy at any moment.   Should there be a combined attack from above and below, there is not a possibility of saving it, and but a faint probability if attacked only from above.

It will be perceived that the foregoing statement leaves no infantry force to cover the heavy batteries, if attacked by the gunboat fleet and a landing attempted.

I am, very respectfully, your obedient servant,

M. L. SMITH,
Brigadier-General, Commanding.

HEADQUARTERS ARMY OF WEST TENNESSEE,
Holly Springs, October 23, 1862.

Maj. Gen. EARL VAN DORN:

SIR: I have the honor to report that the sanitary condition of the army under your command is now rapidly improving.   The exposure incidental to the late exhausting marches and terrific battles did in great measure produce considerable sickness.   Most of the sick have been removed to the general hospitals in the rear, on and convenient to the railroads.   The conduct of the medical department has not been such as I would altogether desire, but allowance must be made for the great confusion incidental to the rapid organization of your command, its celerity of movement to the attack, and the disorganization which ensued from the engagements of the 3d, 4th, and 5th of the present month.   Proper returns are now completed, and will be forwarded to the Surgeon-General's Office at the earliest practicable moment.   Notwithstanding the great numbers of wounded, it affords me unalloyed pleasure to state that the majority of the wounds are slight, and the recipients thereof will in a very short period of time be able to report for duty. The destructiveness of the enemy's artillery was very great; hence the apparent increase in the proportion of the killed, which is usually about one eighth or ninth. The total number killed and wounded was 2,655, of which number 512 were killed and 2,143 wounded.

The loss in officers was absolutely frightful, being more than one-sixth of the whole number, which speaks in thunder-tones of the heroism and self-devotion of a band of brothers worthy of imitation, and always to be remembered by a grateful country. Many of them now sleep the sleep of the brave, and as the silent tear of regret starts from its grief-bed, the memories of their deeds will stand forth entwined with the recollections of their soldier companions in arms who fell, as they followed through the storm of death, as monuments of Southern valor and devotedness more durable than marble and more brilliant than polished gold.

I have the honor to be, yours, most respectfully,
M. A. PALLEN,
Medical Director.

MR. ROBERTS' HOUSE,
One Mile from Coldwater, November 6, 1862—6.15 p. m.

General EARL VAN DORN,
Commanding Army:

GENERAL: I am sorry that the reports sent you by myself have not reached you. While I am in command of all the cavalry, it is impossible for me to be with all at the same time. I directed Colonel [J. T.] Wheeler, commanding on the Salem road, to report to you regularly, and then send the dispatch to me. Colonel [W. F.] Slemons has been commanding on La Grange road, and to hear from both commands I took a position at Hudsonville. It is unfortunate for me that I have to deal with rather inferior officers, and by virtue of their rank have to place them in command.

I have forwarded several dispatches to you to-day, general, which may not have reached you. I sent my adjutant this afternoon to order Colonel Wheeler to discover the enemy's exact position, and make them show their hands. I was going to attend to it in person, when I heard the firing on La Grange road, and turned back. The enemy occupy Lamar to-night. The force at La Grange and Junction is about 15,000 infantry and two regiments of cavalry. The force from Corinth, which is now about Saulsbury, from all I can learn, is between 20,000 and 25,000. I think 40,000 will cover their entire force.

Respectfully, general,

W. H. JACKSON,
Chief of Cavalry.

(Read by General Tilghman on the road.)

HDQRS. DEPT. OF MISSISSIPPI AND EAST LOUISIANA,
Holly Springs, November 8, 1862.

Maj. Gen. STERLING PRICE,
Commanding Second Corps, &c.:

GENERAL: The lieutenant-general commanding directs that you will suspend the publication of Paragraph I, Special Orders, No. —, November 7, 1862, from these headquarters, relieving Maj. Gen. E. Van Dorn from the command of the army of operation, until further orders.

I am, general, very respectfully, &c., your obedient servant,

J. C. TAYLOR,
Aide-de-Camp.

HEADQUARTERS FIRST CORPS,
Seven and a half miles from Water Valley, Dec. 2, [1862]—11.30 p. m.

General VAN DORN:

The enemy is reported skirmishing with our cavalry about 4 miles from here, on the Coffeeville road from Oxford, and Jackson sends word, at 9.40 p. m., that they are " advancing in force " on the Sarepta road, and are this side of Oxford, and moving.   General Price's train is just in front of me, and the rear of it has not attempted to move since noon to-day.   If you can't get him along, we must stand still with our train, exposed to be lost.   Part of Maury's force is in our rear, on Coffeeville road, and part on Sarepta road.   The rear of my train has not crossed the Yocony, on the Sarepta road.   Price's train (its rear) is not 3 miles from where it camped last night.   No one appeared to push it along. If I could get to the Spring Dale road, I would turn my column to the right.   General Pemberton will understand the road I mean.   I sketch the position.

Yours, respectfully,

M. LOVELL,
Major-General.

[P. S.]—The roads are horrible.   I cannot get on at all, except by daylight, with trains and artillery.

THOMAS' HOUSE, NEAR TRUMBULL'S CREEK,
December 9, 1862.

Maj. Gen. EARL VAN DORN:

MY DEAR GENERAL : I am encamped on this creek, about 9 miles from Grenada.   Some of Bowen's division are 4 miles below me.   Between me and Grenada (2 miles above me) the Troy road crosses the river, and has a practicable ford.   There is another ford near here.   The Troy road, leading direct from Charleston, should be well guarded, and I am about to ride up and look for an encampment there.

In my opinion, we should all be concentrated about Grenada with our "staves in our hand and our loins girt about," and ready for a quick exodus.   Why should we scatter our division in this way when no one division is strong enough to fight, and when it is not intended to fight?

If the engineer in charge of the works will have the railroad iron taken up, and will make his parapets of them, he will make quicker and better work of it.   Those we have on the Potomac would resist a 10-inch shell, and they give a great sweep to the gun, being so thin.

My family, including Dr. Holland, arrived safely at Aberdeen on Thursday.   Don't forget to order the payment of that claim.   I am the more anxious about it because, with a small amount she has besides, it will enable her to purchase three or four Confederate bonds, which will be for the present her sole means of support.

Can't I get [S. W.] Ferguson to command this Texas cavalry?   Suggest him to General Pemberton.

Sincerely, yours,

DABNEY H. MAURY.

ALTERNATE DESIGNATIONS OF ORGANIZATIONS MENTIONED IN THIS VOLUME.*

Abbott's (A. R.) **Artillery.** See *Illinois Troops*, 1st *Regiment, Battery* **E.**
Abbott's (Charles H.) **Infantry.** See *Iowa Troops*, 30th *Regiment.*
Abercrombie's (John C.) **Infantry.** See *Iowa Troops*, 11th *Regiment.*
Adams' (C. W.) **Infantry.** See *Arkansas Troops.*
Adams' (Robert N.) **Infantry.** See *Ohio Troops*, 81st *Regiment.*
Adams' (Wirt) **Cavalry.** See *Mississippi Troops.*
Alexander's (Jesse I.) **Infantry.** See *Indiana Troops*, 59th *Regiment.*
Alexander's (John W. S.) **Infantry.** See *Illinois Troops*, 21st *Regiment.*
Anderson's (J. W.) **Artillery.** See *Botetourt Artillery.*
Andrews' (J. A.) **Cavalry.** See *Texas Troops.*
Ault's (Jacob R.) **Infantry.** See *Missouri Troops, Union*, 18th *Regiment.*
Austin's Artillery. See *Arkansas Troops.*
Babcock's (A. C.) **Infantry.** See *Illinois Troops*, 103d *Regiment.*
Babcock's (Andrew J.) **Infantry.** See *Illinois Troops*, 7th *Regiment.*
Bacon's (George A.) **Infantry.** See *Illinois Troops*, 30th *Regiment.*
Bacot's (W. C.) **Cavalry.** See *Forrest's Cavalry.*
Bailey's Consolidated Regiment. See *J. E. Bailey.*
Bain's (S. C.) **Artillery.** *See Mississippi Troops*, 1st *Regiment, Battery* **L.**
Baird's (John F.) **Infantry.** See *Indiana Troops*, 66th *Regiment.*
Baker's (James) **Infantry.** See *Iowa Troops*, 2d *Regiment.*
Baker's (Samuel R.) **Infantry.** See *Illinois Troops*, 47th *Regiment.*
Balch's (R. M.) **Cavalry.** See *Tennessee Troops, Confederate*, 18th *Battalion.*
Baldwin's (Silas D.) **Infantry.** See *Illinois Troops*, 57th *Regiment.*
Baldwin's (W. E.) **Infantry.** See *Mississippi Troops*, 14th *Regiment.*
Balfour's (John W.) **Infantry.** See *Mississippi Troops*, 6th *Battalion.*
Ballentine's (John G.) **Cavalry.** See *Mississippi Troops.*
Ballou's (D. W.) **Cavalry.** See *Missouri Troops, Union*, 10th *Regiment.*
Bane's (Moses M.) **Infantry.** See *Illinois Troops*, 50th *Regiment.*
Bankhead's (Smith P.) **Artillery.** See *Tennessee Troops, Confederate.*
Bardwell's (F. W.) **Artillery.** See *Ohio Troops*, 10th *Battery.*
Barnett's (Charles M.) **Artillery.** See *Illinois Troops*, 2d *Regiment, Battery* **I.**
Barnett's (J. W.) **Infantry.** See *Arkansas Troops*, 18th *Regiment.*
Barnhill's (Rigdon S.) **Infantry.** See *Illinois Troops*, 40th *Regiment.*
Barret's (O. W.) **Artillery.** See *Missouri Troops, Confederate.*
Barrett's (Samuel E.) **Artillery.** See *Illinois Troops*, 1st *Regiment, Battery* **B.**
Barry's (William S.) **Infantry.** See *Mississippi Troops*, 35th *Regiment.*
Barteau's (C. R.) **Cavalry.** See *Tennessee Troops, Confederate.*
Baxter's (E.) **Artillery.** See *Tennessee Troops, Confederate.*
Baxter's (G. L.) **Cavalry.** See *Mississippi Troops.*
Beardsley's (Ezra M.) **Infantry.** See *Illinois Troops*, 126th *Regiment.*
Beebe's (Yates V.) **Artillery.** See *Wisconsin Troops*, 10th *Battery.*
Bell's (T. H.) **Infantry.** See *Tennessee Troops, Confederate*, 12th *Regiment.*
Beltzhoover's (D.) **Heavy Artillery.** See *Louisiana Troops*, 1st *Regiment.*
Benkler's (B.) **Infantry.** See *Ohio Troops*, 58th *Regiment.*
Biffle's (Jacob B.) **Cavalry.** See *Tennessee Troops, Confederate.*
Bishop's (William W.) **Infantry.** See *Illinois Troops*, 49th *Regiment.*
Bissell's (Josiah W.) **Engineers.** See *Missouri Troops, Union.*
Blair's (F. P., jr.) **Cavalry Escort.** See *D. W. Ballou's Cavalry.*
Bland's (Peter E.) **Infantry.** See *Missouri Troops, Union*, 6th *Regiment.*
Bledsoe's (H. M.) **Artillery.** See *Missouri Troops, Confederate.*
Blood's (J. H.) **Infantry.** See *Missouri Troops, Union*, 6th *Regiment.*

---

* References are to index following.

Blythe's (A. K.) Infantry. See *Mississippi Troops, 44th Regiment.*
Blythe's (G. L.) Cavalry. See *Mississippi Troops. State.*
Bolen's (James N.) Cavalry. *See Kentucky Troops, Confederate.*
Bolton's (William H.) Artillery. See *Illinois Troops, 2d Regiment, Battery L.*
Boomer's (George B.) Infantry. See *Missouri Troops, Union, 26th Regiment.*
Boone's (R. M.) Artillery. See *Louisiana Troops.*
Boothe's (James W.) Infantry. See *Illinois Troops, 40th Regiment.*
Borcherdt's (Albert) Cavalry. See *Missouri Troops, Union, 5th Regiment.*
Borgersode's (Rudolph von) Infantry. See *Minnesota Troops, 5th Regiment.*
Borland's (James A.) Artillery. See *Illinois Troops, 1st Regiment, Battery D.*
Botetourt Artillery. See *Virginia Troops.*
Bouck's (Gabriel) Infantry. See *Wisconsin Troops, 18th Regiment.*
Bouton's (Edward) Artillery. See *Illinois Troops, 1st Regiment, Battery I.*
Bowen's (Edwin A.) Infantry. See *Illinois Troops, 52d Regiment.*
Bowen's (William D.) Cavalry. See *Missouri Troops, Union, 10th Regiment.*
Bradford's (W. M.) Infantry. See *Tennessee Troops, Confederate, 31st Regiment.*
Bradley's (J.) Cavalry. See *Confederate Troops.*
Bradley's (Luther P.) Infantry. See *Illinois Troops, 51st Regiment.*
Breckenridge's (W. K. M.) Cavalry. See *Tennessee Troops, Union, 6th Regiment.*
Brewer's (R. H.) Cavalry.* See *Alabama Troops.*
Brookhaven Artillery. See *Mississippi Troops.*
Brooks' Cavalry. See *Kentucky Troops, Union, 15th Battalion.*
Brooks' (W. H.) Cavalry. See *Arkansas Troops.*
Brotzmann's (Edward) Artillery. See *Charles Mann's Artillery.*
Brown's (Aaron) Infantry. See *Iowa Troops, 3d Regiment.*
Brown's (A. R.) Infantry. See *Arkansas Troops, 13th Regiment.*
Brown's (Charles E.) Infantry. See *Ohio Troops, 63d Regiment.*
Brown's (George R.) Artillery. See *Indiana Troops, 9th Battery.*
Brown's (M.) Artillery. See *Louisiana Troops.*
Brown's (William R.) Infantry. See *Illinois Troops, 56th Regiment.*
Brush's (Daniel H.) Infantry. See *Illinois Troops, 18th Regiment.*
Bryant's (George E.) Infantry. See *Wisconsin Troops, 12th Regiment.*
Bryner (John) Infantry. See *Illinois Troops, 47th Regiment.*
Buckland's (Ralph P.) Infantry. See *Ohio Troops, 72d Regiment.*
Buford's (J. W.) Infantry. See *Tennessee Troops, Confederate, 9th Regiment.*
Burke's (Patrick E.) Sharpshooters. See *Missouri Troops, Union, 14th Regiment.*
Burnap's (Silas A.) Artillery. See *Ohio Troops, 7th Battery.*
Burnet's (William E.) Artillery. See *Alabama Troops.*
Burton's (Anthony B.) Artillery. See *Ohio Troops, 5th Battery.*
Burton's (Josiah H.) Artillery. See *Illinois Troops, 1st Regiment, Battery F.*
Burtwell's (J. R. B.) Artillery. See *Alabama Troops.*
Caldwell's (A. W.) Infantry. See *Tennessee Troops, Confederate, 27th Regiment.*
Caldwell's (William L.) Cavalry. See *Illinois Troops, 6th Regiment.*
Calvert's (J. H.) Artillery. See *Helena Artillery.*
Cameron's (James C.) Infantry. See *Yates Sharpshooters.*
Cam's (William) Infantry. See *Illinois Troops, 14th Regiment.*
Carmichael's (Eagleton) Cavalry. See *W. Stewart's Cavalry.*
Carnes' (W. W.) Artillery. See *Tennessee Troops, Confederate.*
Carpenter's (Stephen J.) Artillery. See *Wisconsin Troops, 8th Battery.*
Carroll Dragoons Cavalry. See *Louisiana Troops.*
Catterson's (Robert F.) Infantry. See *Indiana Troops, 97th Regiment.*
Cavender's (John S.) Infantry. See *Missouri Troops, Union, 29th Regiment.*
Chambers' (Alexander) Infantry. See *Iowa Troops, 16th Regiment.*
Chandler's (William P.) Infantry. See *Illinois Troops, 35th Regiment.*

---

* Also claimed by Mississippi

Chandler's (Zach. M.) Infantry.　See *Ohio Troops, 78th Regiment.*
Chapman's (Fletcher H.) Artillery.　See *Illinois Troops, 2d Regiment, Battery B.*
Chapman's (James F.) Infantry.　See *Wisconsin Troops, 13th Regiment.*
Chase's (Daniel) Infantry.　See *Union Troops, Regulars, 13th Regiment.*
Cheny's (John T.) Artillery.　See *Illinois Troops, 1st Regiment, Battery F.*
Chester's (John) Infantry.　See *Tennessee Troops, Confederate, 51st Regiment.*
Chetlain's (Aug. L.) Infantry.　See *Illinois Troops, 12th Regiment.*
Chicago Light Artillery, Company A.　See *Illinois Troops, 1st Regiment, Battery A.*
Chicago Light Artillery, Company B.　See *Illinois Troops, 1st Regiment, Battery B.*
Church's (Lawrence S.) Infantry.　See *Illinois Troops, 95th Regiment.*
Clanton's (James H.) Cavalry.　See *Alabama Troops, 1st Regiment.*
Clark Artillery.　See *Missouri Troops, Confederate.*
Clark's (George W.) Infantry.　See *Iowa Troops, 34th Regiment.*
Clayton's (William Z.) Artillery.　See *Minnesota Troops, 1st Battery.*
Clifford's (James) Cavalry.　See *Missouri Troops, Union, 1st Regiment.*
Clinch's (Henry A.) Artillery.　See *Louisiana Troops, 1st Regiment.*
Cobb's (R.) Artillery.　See *Kentucky Troops, Confederate.*
Cockerill's (Joseph R.) Infantry.　See *Ohio Troops, 70th Regiment.*
Cogswell's (William) Artillery.　See *Illinois Troops.*
Coleman's (A. A.) Infantry.　See *Alabama Troops, 40th Regiment.*
Coleman's (David C.) Infantry.　See *Missouri Troops, Union, 8th Regiment.*
Confederate Guards Response.　See *Louisiana Troops.*
Confederate Rangers.　See *Mississippi Troops.*
Connor Artillery.　See *Mississippi Troops, 1st Regiment, Battery H.*
Cooke's (G. Frederick) Artillery.　See *Minnesota Troops, 1st Battery.*
Cooley's (Charles G.) Artillery.　See *Illinois Troops.*
Coon's (D. E.) Cavalry.　See *Iowa Troops, 2d Regiment.*
Cornyn's (Florence M.) Cavalry.　See *Missouri Troops, Union, 10th Regiment.*
Corse's (John M.) Infantry.　See *Iowa Troops, 6th Regiment.*
Coulter's (John P.) Infantry.　See *Iowa Troops, 12th Regiment.*
Cowan's (John) Infantry.　See *Kentucky Troops, Union, 19th Regiment.*
Cox's (N. N.) Cavalry.　See *Tennessee Troops, Confederate.*
Coykendall's (John R.) Cavalry.　See *Illinois Troops, 11th Regiment.*
Coyl's (W. H.) Infantry.　See *Iowa Troops, 9th Regiment.*
Crescent Artillery.　See *Louisiana Troops.*
Crescent Infantry.　See *Louisiana Troops.*
Crocker's (Marcellus M.) Infantry.　See *Iowa Troops, 13th Regiment.*
Cunningham's (William T.) Infantry.　See *Iowa Troops, 15th Regiment.*
Curtis Horse Cavalry.　See *Iowa Troops, 5th Regiment.*
Curtis' (Isaac W.) Artillery.　See *Illinois Troops, 1st Regiment, Battery K.*
Curtis' (John G.) Cavalry.　See *Ohio Troops, 5th Regiment.*
Cushman's (William H. W.) Infantry.　See *Illinois Troops, 53d Regiment.*
Daigre's (H. L.) Cavalry.　See *Louisiana Troops.*
Davis' (John A.) Infantry.　See *Illinois Troops, 46th Regiment.*
Davis' (William P.) Infantry.　See *Indiana Troops, 23d Regiment.*
Dawson's (W. A.) Cavalry.　See *F. M. Stewart's Cavalry.*
De Clouet's (Alexander) Infantry.　See *Louisiana Troops, 26th Regiment.*
Dees' (Alexander W.) Artillery.　See *Michigan Troops, 3d Battery.*
De Golyer's (Samuel) Artillery.　See *Michigan Troops, 8th Battery.*
Deitzler's (George W.) Infantry.　See *Kansas Troops, 1st Regiment.*
Dennis' (Elias S.) Infantry.　See *Illinois Troops, 30th Regiment.*
Dibrell's (George G.) Cavalry.　See *Tennessee Troops, Confederate.*
Dickerman's (Willard A.) Infantry.　See *Illinois Troops, 103d Regiment.*
Dickey's (T. L.) Cavalry.　See *Illinois Troops, 4th Regiment.*
Dillon's (Henry) Artillery.　See *Wisconsin Troops, 6th Battery.*

Dollins' (James J.) **Cavalry.** See *W. Stewart's Cavalry.*
Dollins' (James J.) **Infantry.** See *Illinois Troops, 81st Regiment.*
Doran's (John L.) **Infantry.** See *Wisconsin Troops, 17th Regiment.*
Dornblaser's (Benjamin) **Infantry.** See *Illinois Troops, 46th Regiment.*
Dotson's (Josephus) **Infantry.** See *Arkansas Troops, 17th Regiment.*
Drake's (Joseph) **Infantry.** See *Mississippi Troops, 4th Regiment.*
Duckworth's (W. L.) **Cavalry.** See *W. H. Jackson's Cavalry.*
Dupeire's **Zouaves.** See *Louisiana Troops.*
Earl's (Seth C.) **Infantry.** See *Illinois Troops, 53d Regiment.*
Eaton's (Charles G.) **Infantry.** See *Ohio Troops, 72d Regiment.*
Eckley's (Ephraim R.) **Infantry.** See *Ohio Troops, 80th Regiment.*
Eddy's (Norman) **Infantry.** See *Indiana Troops, 48th Regiment.*
Edie's (John R.) **Infantry.*** See *Union Troops.*
Edmondson's (J. H.) **Sharpshooters.** See *Tennessee Troops, Confederate.*
Edson's (James C.) **Infantry.** See *Minnesota Troops, 4th Regiment.*
Eldridge's (Hamilton N.) **Infantry.** See *Illinois Troops, 127th Regiment.*
Eldridge's (J. W.) **Artillery.** See *Tennessee Troops, Confederate.*
Elwood's (Isaac) **Cavalry.** See *Illinois Troops, 11th Regiment.*
Embry's (B. T.) **Mounted Rifles.** See *Arkansas Troops, 2d Rifles.*
Engelmann's (A.) **Infantry.** See *Illinois Troops, 43d Regiment.*
Engineer Regiment of the West. See *Josiah W. Bissell's Engineers.*
English's (R. T.) **Artillery.** See *Mississippi Troops.*
Falkner's (W. C.) **Cavalry.** See *Mississippi Troops, 1st Regiment, Partisan Rangers.*
Farrand's (Charles E.) **Cavalry.** See *Union Troops, 2d Regiment.*
Farrar's (F. H., jr.) **Infantry.** See *Louisiana Troops, 1st Regiment.*
Faulkner's (W. W.) **Cavalry.** See *Kentucky Troops, Confederate.*
Feild's (H. R.) **Infantry.** See *Tennessee Troops, Confederate, 1st Regiment.*
Fenner's (C. E.) **Artillery.** See *Louisiana Troops.*
Ferrell's (Charles M.) **Infantry.** See *Illinois Troops, 29th Regiment.*
Fisher's (J. M.) **Infantry.** See *Illinois Troops, 93d Regiment.*
Fitzgerald's (E.) **Infantry.** See *Tennessee Troops, Confederate, 154th Senior Regiment.*
Flood's (James P.) **Artillery.** See *Illinois Troops, 2d Regiment, Battery C.*
Font's Company. Official designation unknown. See *Captain Font.*
Force's (Manning F.) **Infantry.** See *Ohio Troops, 20th Regiment.*
Ford's (William) **Cavalry.** See *Illinois Troops.*
Ford's (William H.) **Cavalry.** See *John G. Ballentine's Cavalry.*
Forrest Guards Cavalry. See *Tennessee Troops, Confederate.*
Forrest's (N. B.) **Cavalry Regiment.** See *Tennessee Troops, Confederate.*
Forsse's (Eric) **Infantry.** See *Illinois Troops, 57th Regiment.*
Forsyth's (R. C.) **Artillery.** See *Alabama Troops, 1st Battalion.*
Foster's (John S.) **Cavalry.** See *Ohio Troops, 4th Company.*
Fowler's (Alexander) **Infantry.** See *Indiana Troops, 99th Regiment.*
Fowler's (Pleasant) **Infantry.** See *Arkansas Troops, 14th Regiment.*
Frisbie's (Orton) **Infantry.** See *Illinois Troops, 20th Regiment.*
Fry's (Jacob) **Infantry.** See *Illinois Troops, 61st Regiment.*
Gaines' (Thomas W.) **Infantry.** See *Illinois Troops, 50th Regiment.*
Gallimard's Sappers and Miners. See *Louisiana Troops.*
Garland's (W. H.) **Partisans.** See *Mississippi Troops.*
Gibson's (William L.) **Cavalry.** See *Illinois Troops, 4th Regiment.*
Gilbert's (Alfred W.) **Infantry.** See *Ohio Troops, 39th Regiment.*
Gilbert's (Franklin T.) **Cavalry.** See *Illinois Troops, 12th Regiment.*
Gilbert's (Othniel) **Infantry.** See *Illinois Troops, 71st Regiment.*
Gillam's (Barclay C.) **Infantry.** See *Illinois Troops, 28th Regiment.*
Gillmore's (Robert A.) **Infantry.** See *Illinois Troops, 26th Regiment.*

---

*Commanded detachments of 15th and 16th Infantry.

Gooding's (Michael) Infantry. See *Indiana Troops, 22d Regiment.*
Good's (John J.) Artillery. See *Texas Troops.*
Gordon's (John A.) Infantry. See *Wisconsin Troops, 15th Regiment.*
Gorgas' (Adam B.) Infantry. See *Illinois Troops, 13th Regiment.*
Graves' (William H.) Infantry. See *Michigan Troops, 12th Regiment.*
Green's (Galen E.) Artillery. See *Wisconsin Troops, 7th Battery.*
Greer's (E.) Cavalry. See *Texas Troops, 3d Regiment.*
Gresham's (Walter Q.) Infantry. See *Indiana Troops, 53d Regiment.*
Greusel's (N.) Infantry. See *Illinois Troops, 36th Regiment.*
Grier's (D. P.) Infantry. See *Illinois Troops, 77th Regiment.*
Grierson's (B. H.) Cavalry. See *Illinois Troops, 6th Regiment.*
Griffiths' (Henry H.) Artillery. See *Iowa Troops, 1st Battery.*
Griffith's (Richard R.) Artillery. See *Wisconsin Troops, 7th Battery.*
Grosskopff's (Edward) Artillery. See *Ohio Troops, 10th Battery.*
Guibor's (Henry) Artillery. See *Missouri Troops, Confederate.*
Gumbart's (George C.) Artillery. See *Illinois Troops, 2d Regiment, Battery E.*
Gurley's (F. B.) Cavalry. See *Alabama Troops, 4th Regiment.*
Hagan's (James) Cavalry. See *Alabama Troops, 3d Regiment.*
Hall's (Cyrus) Infantry. See *Illinois Troops, 14th Regiment.*
Hall's (William) Infantry. See *Iowa Troops, 11th Regiment.*
Hancock's (John) Infantry. See *Wisconsin Troops, 14th Regiment.*
Harding's (Abner C.) Infantry. See *Illinois Troops, 83d Regiment.*
Harding's (Chester, jr.) Infantry. See *Missouri Troops, Union, 25th Regiment.*
Hare's (Abraham M.) Infantry. See *Iowa Troops, 11th Regiment.*
Harman's (B. D.) Infantry. See *Mississippi Troops.*
Harper's (R. W.) Mounted Rifles. See *Arkansas Troops, 1st Rifles.*
Harris' (S.) Infantry. See *Georgia Troops, 43d Regiment.*
Harris' (Thomas W.) Infantry. See *Illinois Troops, 54th Regiment.*
Hart's (James H.) Infantry. See *Ohio Troops, 71st Regiment.*
Hart's (Levi W.) Artillery. See *Illinois Troops, 1st Regiment, Battery H.*
Hart's (P. W.) Infantry. See *Illinois Troops, 106th Regiment.*
Hassendeubel's (F.) Infantry. See *Missouri Troops, Union, 17th Regiment.*
Hatch's (Edward) Cavalry. See *Iowa Troops, 2d Regiment.*
Hawkins' (Isaac R.) Cavalry. See *Tennessee Troops, Union, 7th Regiment.*
Hayes' (Charles S.) Cavalry. See *Ohio Troops, 5th Regiment.*
Haynie's (Isham N.) Infantry. See *Illinois Troops, 48th Regiment.*
Haywood's (R. W.) Rangers, Cavalry. See *Tennessee Troops, Confederate.*
Heath's (Albert) Infantry. See *Indiana Troops, 100th Regiment.*
Hecker's (Frederick) Infantry. See *Illinois Troops, 82d Regiment.*
Heg's (Hans C.) Infantry. See *Wisconsin Troops, 15th Regiment.*
Heiman's Consolidated Regiment. See *A. Heiman.*
Helena Artillery. See *Arkansas Troops.*
Henderson's (R. J.) Infantry. See *Georgia Troops, 42d Regiment.*
Henderson's (Thomas) Scouts. *See Mississippi Troops.*
Henning's (Henry R.*) Artillery. See *Illinois Troops, 2d Regiment.*
Hensler's (John E.) Infantry. See *Missouri Troops, Union, 5th Regiment.*
Herriok's (Thomas P.) Cavalry. See *Kansas Troops, 7th Regiment.*
Herrick's (Walter F.) Infantry. See *Ohio Troops, 43d Regiment.*
Hescock's (Henry) Artillery. See *Missouri Troops, Union, 1st Regiment, Battery G.*
Hewlett's (W. A.) Partisans. See *Alabama Troops, 13th Battalion.*
Hildebrand's (Jesse) Infantry. See *Ohio Troops, 77th Regiment.*
Hillis' (David B.) Infantry. See *Iowa Troops, 17th Regiment.*
Hill's (A. P.) Cavalry. See *Mississippi Troops.*
Hill's (J. F.) Infantry. See *Arkansas Troops, 16th Regiment.*

---

* In command of Batteries E and F.

Hill's (L. E.) **Cavalry.** See *Mississippi Troops.*
Hill's (Sylvester G.) **Infantry.** See *Iowa Troops, 35th Regiment*
Hill's (W.) **Engineers.** See *Josiah W. Bissell's Engineers.*
Hitt's (Daniel F.) **Infantry.** See *Illinois Troops, 53d Regiment*
Hobbs' (James H.) **Infantry.** See *Arkansas Troops,* 21*st Regiment,* and *Hobbs' Battalion.*
Hoffmann's (Louis) **Artillery.** See *Ohio Troops, 4th Battery.*
Hoge's (G. B.) **Infantry.** See *Illinois Troops, 113th Regiment.*
Hogg's (Harvey) **Cavalry.** See *Illinois Troops, 2d Regiment.*
Holman's (John H.) **Infantry.** See *Missouri Troops, Union,* 26*th Regiment.*
Holmes' (Samuel A.) **Infantry.** See *Missouri Troops, Union,* 10*th Regiment.*
Hopkins' (Henry) **Artillery.** See *Kansas Troops.*
Horney's (Leonidas) **Infantry.** See *Missouri Troops, Union,* 10*th Regiment.*
Hotaling's (John R.) **Cavalry.** See *Illinois Troops, 2d Regiment.*
Hotchkiss' (William A.) **Artillery.** See *Minnesota Troops,* 2*d Battery.*
Houghtaling's (Charles) **Artillery.** See *Illinois Troops,* 1*st Regiment, Battery C.*
Howe's (James H.) **Infantry.** See *Wisconsin Troops, 32d Regiment.*
Howe's (John H.) **Infantry.** See *Illinois Troops, 124th Regiment.*
Howe's (Marshall S.) **Cavalry.** See *Union Troops, 3d Regiment.*
Hoxton's (L.) **Artillery.** See *Tennessee Troops, Confederate.*
Hubbard's (Lucius F.) **Infantry.** See *Minnesota Troops, 5th Regiment.*
Hughes' **Cavalry.** See *Mississippi Troops.*
Hugunin's (James R.) **Infantry.** See *Illinois Troops, 12th Regiment.*
Humes' (W. Y. C.) **Artillery.** *See Tennessee Troops, Confederate.*
Humes' **Consolidated Battalion.** *See W. Y. C. Humes.*
Humphreys' (John T.) **Artillery.** See *Arkansas Troops.*
Humphrey's (Thomas W.) **Infantry.** See *Illinois Troops, 95th Regiment.*
Hunter's (William) **Infantry.** See *Illinois Troops, 32d Regiment.*
Hurlbut's (Frederick J.) **Infantry.** See *Illinois Troops, 57th Regiment.*
Hurst's (Fielding) **Cavalry.** See *Tennessee Troops, Union, 6th Regiment.*
Hutchens' (William D.) **Cavalry.** See *W. Stewart's Cavalry.*
Hutton's (T. H.) **Artillery.** See *Crescent Artillery.*
Immell's (Lorenzo D.) **Artillery.** See *Wisconsin Troops, 12th Battery.*
Ingersoll's (Robert G.) **Cavalry.** See *Illinois Troops, 11th Regiment.*
Isbell's (R. H.) **Infantry.** See *Alabama Troops, 1st Regiment.*
Jackson's (W. H.) **Cavalry Regiment.** See *Tennessee Troops.*
Jayhawkers **Cavalry.** See *Kansas Troops,* 7*th Regiment.*
Jefferson's (John W.) **Infantry.** See *Wisconsin Troops,* 8*th Regiment.*
Jenks' (Albert) **Cavalry.** See *Illinois Troops.*
Jennison's (C. R.) **Cavalry.** See *Kansas Troops, 7th Regiment.*
Johns' (W. M. R.) **Infantry.** See *Tennessee Troops, Confederate, 6th Regiment.*
Johnson's (Abda) **Infantry.** See *Georgia Troops, 40th Regiment.*
Johnson's (Amory K.) **Infantry.** See *Illinois Troops, 28th Regiment.*
Johnson's (William H.) **Cavalry.** See *Mississippi Troops, 28th Regiment.*
Johnston's (T. N.) **Artillery.** See *Tennessee Troops, Confederate.*
Joliat's (Francis J.) **Infantry.** See *Missouri Troops, Union, 15th Regiment.*
Jones' (Bart.) **Infantry.** See *Arkansas Troops.*
Jones' (J. W.) **Cavalry.** See *Louisiana Troops.*
Jones' (Robert B.) **Infantry.** See *Indiana Troops, 34th Regiment.*
Jones' (Wells S.) **Infantry.** See *Ohio Troops, 53d Regiment.*
Jones' (W. P.) **Infantry.** See *Tennessee Troops, Confederate, 33d Regiment.*
Judy's (James W.) **Infantry.** See *Illinois Troops, 114th Regiment.*
Kane County **Cavalry.** See *Illinois Troops.*
Kean's (Mortimer O.) **Infantry.** See *Illinois Troops, 38th Regiment.*
Keith's (Stephen) **Artillery.** See *Ohio Troops, 3d Battery.*

Kelley's (D. C.) **Cavalry.** See *N. B. Forrest's Regiment.*
Kempton's (Solomon D.) **Infantry.** See *Indiana Troops, 12th Regiment.*
Kennard's (George W.) **Infantry.** See *Illinois Troops, 20th Regiment.*
Kerr's (Lucien H.) **Cavalry.** See *Illinois Troops, 11th Regiment.*
Ketchum's (William H.) **Artillery.** See *Alabama Troops.*
Kidd's (Meredith H.) **Artillery.** See *Indiana Troops, 14th Battery.*
King's (Ezra) **Cavalry.** See *W. Stewart's Cavalry.*
King's (Houston) **Artillery.** See *Clark Artillery.*
Knobelsdorff's (Charles) **Infantry.** See *Illinois Troops, 44th Regiment.*
Lamberg's (Carl A.) **Artillery.** See *Michigan Troops, 3d Battery.*
Landgraeber's (Clemens) **Artillery.** See *Missouri Troops, Union.*
Landis' (John C.) **Artillery.** See *Missouri Troops, Confederate.*
Larison's (Thomas J.) **Cavalry.** See *Illinois Troops, 2d Regiment.*
Lawler's (Michael K.) **Infantry.** See *Illinois Troops, 18th Regiment.*
Lee's (Albert L.) **Cavalry.** See *Kansas Troops, 7th Regiment.*
Leggett's (Mortimer D.) **Infantry.** See *Ohio Troops, 78th Regiment.*
Lewis' (A. J.) **Partisans.** See *Mississippi Troops.*
Little's (Montgomery) **Cavalry.** See *Forrest Guards.*
Lochbihler's (Christian) **Sappers and Miners.** See *Josiah W. Bissell's Engineers.*
Lockwood's (Theodorus W.) **Artillery.** See *Michigan Troops, 8th Battery.*
Logan's (John) **Infantry.** See *Illinois Troops, 32d Regiment.*
Loomis' (John M.) **Infantry.** See *Illinois Troops, 26th Regiment.*
Loomis' (Reuben) **Cavalry.** See *Illinois Troops, 6th Regiment.*
Loudon's (De Witt C.) **Infantry.** See *Ohio Troops, 70th Regiment.*
Loudon's (De Witt C.) **Infantry.** See *Ohio Troops, 72d Regiment.**
Lowe's (William W.) **Cavalry.** See *Iowa Troops, 5th Regiment.*
Lum's (Charles M.) **Infantry.** See *Michigan Troops, 10th Regiment.*
Lumsden's (C. L.) **Artillery.** See *Alabama Troops.*
Lynch's (J. P.) **Artillery.** See *Tennessee Troops, Confederate.*
Lyon's Consolidated Regiment. See *H. B. Lyon.*
Lyon's (William P.) **Infantry.** See *Wisconsin Troops, 13th Regiment.*
McCaa's (B. B.) **Cavalry.** See *R. H. Brewer's Cavalry.*
McCammon's (William W.) **Infantry.** See *Missouri Troops, Union, 24th Regiment.*
McCarver's (J. S.) **Infantry.** See *Arkansas Troops.*
McClung's (H. L. W.) **Artillery.** See *Tennessee Troops, Confederate.*
McCook's (Edwin S.) **Infantry.** See *Illinois Troops, 31st Regiment.*
McCown's (Joseph B.) **Infantry.** See *Illinois Troops, 63d Regiment.*
McCray's (T. H.) **Infantry.** See *Arkansas Troops.*
McCrillis' (L. F.) **Cavalry.** See *Illinois Troops, 3d Regiment.*
McCulloch's (Robert) **Cavalry.** See *Missouri Troops, Confederate.*
McCullough's (William) **Cavalry.** See *Illinois Troops, 4th Regiment.*
McDaniel's (C. A.) **Infantry.** See *Georgia Troops, 41st Regiment.*
McDermott's (John) **Infantry.** See *Michigan Troops, 15th Regiment.*
MacDonald's (Emmett) **Artillery.** See *Saint Louis Artillery.*
McKeaig's (George W.) **Infantry.** See *Illinois Troops, 120th Regiment.*
McKelvaine's (R. P.) **Infantry.** See *Mississippi Troops, 24th Regiment.*
McKinney's (C. C.) **Infantry.** See *Tennessee Troops, Confederate, 8th Regiment.*
Mack's (Alonzo W.) **Infantry.** See *Illinois Troops, 76th Regiment.*
McMahon's (Thomas) **Infantry.** See *Wisconsin Troops, 17th Regiment.*
MacMurray's (Junius W.) **Artillery.** See *Missouri Troops, Union, 1st Regt., Batt. M.*
McMurry's (L. P.) **Infantry.** See *Tennessee Troops, Confederate, 22d Regiment.*
McNally's (Francis) **Artillery.** See *Arkansas Troops.*
McNeil's (Quincy) **Cavalry.** See *Illinois Troops, 2d Regiment.*
McRae's (D.) **Infantry.** See *Arkansas Troops, 21st Regiment.*

---

* Temporarily commanding.

Madison's (Relly) **Artillery.** See *Illinois Troops, 2d Regiment, Battery B.*
Magruder Partisans. See *Mississippi Troops.*
Main's (Zalmon S.) **Infantry.** See *Indiana Troops, 52d Regiment.*
Malmborg's (Oscar) **Infantry.** See *Illinois Troops, 55th Regiment.*
Maloney's (Maurice) **Infantry.** See *Wisconsin Troops, 13th Regiment.*
Maltby's (Jasper A.) **Infantry.** See *Illinois Troops, 45th Regiment.*
Mann's (Charles) **Artillery.** See *Missouri Troops, Union, 1st Regiment, Battery C.*
Mann's (Martin) **Artillery.** See *Illinois Troops, 2d Regiment, Battery E.*
Mann's (Martin J.) **Infantry.** See *Illinois Troops, 61st Regiment.*
Mann's (P. A.) **Cavalry.** See *Tennessee Troops, Confederate.*
Manter's (F. H.) **Infantry.** See *Missouri Troops, Union, 32d Regiment.*
Marks' (L. D.) **Infantry.** See *Louisiana Troops, 27th Regiment.*
Marschner's (Berthold) **Cavalry.** See *Christian Thielemann's Cavalry.*
Marsh's (C. Carroll) **Infantry.** See *Illinois Troops, 20th Regiment.*
Marsh's (Charles J.) **Artillery.** See *Ohio Troops, 5th Battery.*
Martin's (James S.) **Infantry.** See *Illinois Troops, 111th Regiment.*
Martin's (John A.) **Infantry.** See *Kansas Troops, 8th Regiment.*
Maryhugh's (Russel W.) **Cavalry.** See *Missouri Troops, Union, 5th Regiment.*
Mason's (Rodney) **Infantry.** See *Ohio Troops, 71st Regiment.*
Mathews' (Charles H.) **Infantry.** See *Ohio Troops, 80th Regiment.*
Matson's (Bellamy S.) **Artillery.** See *Ohio Troops, 5th Battery.*
Matteson's (Frederick W.) **Infantry.** See *Yates Sharpshooters.*
Matthies' (Charles L.) **Infantry.** See *Iowa Troops, 5th Regiment.*
Maurice's (Thomas D.) **Artillery.** See *Union Troops, Regulars, 2d Regiment, Battery F.*
Mayfield's (Manning *) **Infantry.** See *Illinois Troops, 48th Regiment.*
Mellon's (T. A.) **Infantry.** See *Mississippi Troops, 3d Regiment.*
Mercantile Artillery. See *Charles G. Cooley's Artillery.*
Mersy's (August) **Infantry.** See *Illinois Troops, 9th Regiment.*
Miles' (Jonathan R.) **Infantry.** See *Illinois Troops, 27th Regiment.*
Miles' (W. R.) **Legion.** See *Louisiana Troops.*
Miner's (Phineas R.) **Cavalry** See *Ohio Troops, 5th Regiment.*
Mitchell's (Greenville M.) **Infantry.** See *Illinois Troops, 54th Regiment.*
Mitchell's (J. W.) **Artillery.** See *Illinois Troops, 2d Regiment, Battery F.*
Mitchell's (W. R.) **Cavalry.** See *Mississippi Troops.*
Mizner's (J. K.) **Cavalry.** See *Michigan Troops, 3d Regiment.*
Mohrstadt's (John C.) **Cavalry.** See *Missouri Troops, Union, 5th Regiment.*
Molinard's (A. S.) **Artillery.** See *Union Troops, Regulars, 2d Regiment, Battery F.*
Moore's (David) **Infantry.** See *Missouri Troops, Union, 21st Regiment.*
Moore's (Francis T.) **Cavalry.** See *Illinois Troops, 2d Regiment.*
Moore's (Frank) **Cavalry.** See *Illinois Troops, 2d Regiment.*
Moore's (Jonathan B.) **Infantry.** See *Wisconsin Troops, 33d Regiment.*
Moore's (Risdon M.) **Infantry.** See *Illinois Troops, 117th Regiment.*
Moore's (W. H.) **Infantry.** See *Mississippi Troops, 43d Regiment.*
Morehead's (J. C.) **Partisans.** See *Kentucky Troops, Confederate.*
Morgan's (William H.) **Infantry.** See *Indiana Troops, 25th Regiment.*
Moro's (Francis) **Infantry.** See *Illinois Troops, 63d Regiment.*
Morray's (James B.) **Cavalry.** See *Illinois Troops, 6th Regiment.*
Morrill's (John) **Infantry.** See *Illinois Troops, 64th Regiment.*
Morrison's (William R.) **Infantry.** See *Illinois Troops, 49th Regiment.*
Morton's (George H.) **Cavalry.** See *C. R. Barteau's Cavalry.*
Morton's (Thomas) **Infantry.** See *Ohio Troops, 81st Regiment.*
Mower's (Joseph A.) **Infantry.** See *Missouri Troops, Union, 11th Regiment.*
Moyers' (G.) **Cavalry.** See *Michigan Troops, 3d Regiment.*
Mudd's (John J.) **Cavalry.** See *Illinois Troops, 2d Regiment.*

---

* Temporarily commanding.

Mueller's (Alexander L.) **Cavalry.** See *Missouri Troops, Union, 5th Regiment.*
Mueller's (Michael) **Artillery.** See *Indiana Troops, 6th Battery.*
Mungen's (William) **Infantry.** See *Ohio Troops, 57th Regiment.*
Murray's (J. P.) **Cavalry.** See *Tennessee Troops, Confederate, 4th Regiment.*
Nale's (John H.) **Infantry.** See *Illinois Troops, 41st Regiment.*
Napier's (T. A.) **Cavalry.** See *Tennessee Troops, Confederate.*
Neeley's (George W.) **Infantry.** See *Illinois Troops, 131st Regiment.*
Neil's (Henry M.) **Artillery.** See *Ohio Troops, 11th Battery.*
Nelson's (Horatio C.) **Cavalry.** See *Illinois Troops, 7th Regiment.*
Nevin's (Garrett) **Infantry.** See *Illinois Troops, 11th Regiment.*
Niles' (Nathaniel) **Infantry.** See *Illinois Troops, 130th Regiment.*
Nimmo's (Alexander J.) **Infantry.** See *Illinois Troops, 109th Regiment.*
Noble's (Silas) **Cavalry.** See *Illinois Troops, 2d Regiment.*
Nodine's (Richard H.) **Infantry.** See *Illinois Troops, 25th Regiment.*
Norman's (J. M.) **Cavalry.** See *Mississippi Troops.*
Northrop's (Charles) **Infantry.** See *Illinois Troops, 42d Regiment.*
Norton's (Addison S.) **Infantry.** See *Illinois Troops, 17th Regiment.*
Noyes' (Edward F.) **Infantry.** See *Ohio Troops, 39th Regiment.*
Ogden's (F. N.) **Artillery.** See *Louisiana Troops, 8th Battalion.*
O'Harnett's (M. J.) **Cavalry.** See *W. Stewart's Cavalry.*
Ohr's (S. P.) **Infantry.** See *Illinois Troops, 61st Regiment.*
Oliver's (W. S.) **Infantry.** See *Missouri Troops, Union, 7th Regiment.*
Owens' (J. A.) **Artillery.** See *Arkansas Troops.*
Ozburn's (Lyndorf) **Infantry.** See *Illinois Troops, 31st Regiment.*
Patrick's (Matthewson T.) **Cavalry.** See *Iowa Troops, 5th Regiment.*
Pease's (Phineas) **Infantry.** See *Illinois Troops, 49th Regiment.*
Perczel's (Nicholas) **Infantry.** See *Iowa Troops, 10th Regiment.*
Peterson's (S. G. W.) **Infantry.** See *Ohio Troops, 48th Regiment.*
Petri's (Charles) **Infantry.** See *Illinois Troops, 16th Regiment.*
Pfaender's (William) **Artillery.** See *Minnesota Troops, 1st Battery.*
Phillips' (C. D.) **Infantry.** See *Georgia Troops, 52d Regiment.*
Phillips' (E. D.) **Infantry.** See *Union Troops, Regulars, 1st Regiment.*
Phillips (J. J.) **Infantry.** See *Illinois Troops, 9th Regiment.*
Pile's (William A.) **Artillery.** See *Missouri Troops, Union, 1st Regiment, Battery I.*
Pinney's (Oscar F.) **Artillery.** See *Wisconsin Troops, 5th Battery.*
Pinson's (R. A.) **Cavalry.** See *Mississippi Troops, 1st Regiment.*
Pipe's (George) **Infantry.** See *Missouri Troops, Union, 14th Regiment.*
Pointe Coupée **Artillery.** See *Louisiana Troops.*
Porter's (Daniel A.) **Artillery.** See *Indiana Troops, 9th Battery.*
Porter's (Ed. E.) **Cavalry.** See *John G. Ballentine's Cavalry.*
Porter's (Jacob M.) **Artillery.** See *Ohio Troops, 8th Battery.*
Post's (P. Sidney) **Infantry.** See *Illinois Troops, 59th Regiment.*
Powell's (John W.) **Artillery.** See *Illinois Troops, 2d Regiment, Battery F.*
Price's Escort and Body Guard. See *E. M. Smith's Cavalry.*
Prince's (Edward) **Cavalry.** See *Illinois Troops, 7th Regiment.*
Provence's (David) **Infantry.** See *Arkansas Troops, 16th Regiment.*
Pugh's (Isaac C.) **Infantry.** See *Illinois Troops, 41st Regiment.*
Purcell's (William) **Infantry.** See *Iowa Troops, 16th Regiment.*
Putnam's (Holden) **Infantry.** See *Illinois Troops, 93d Regiment.*
Putnam's (J. F.) **Artillery.** See *Ohio Troops, 8th Battery.*
Quarles' Consolidated Regiment. See *W. A. Quarles.*
Quinn's (Francis) **Infantry.** See *Michigan Troops, 12th Regiment.*
Railroad Regiment **Infantry.** See *Indiana Troops, 52d Regiment.*
Rankin's (John W.) **Infantry.** See *Iowa Troops, 17th Regiment.*
Ransom's (T. E. G.) **Infantry.** See *Illinois Troops, 11th Regiment.*

Rapley's (W. F.) Sharpshooters. See *Arkansas Troops.*
Raum's (Green B.) Infantry. See *Illinois Troops, 56th Regiment.*
Reid's (Hugh T.) Infantry. See *Iowa Troops, 15th Regiment.*
Reves' (T.) Cavalry. See *Missouri Troops, Confederate.*
Reynolds' Consolidated Regiment. See *A. E. Reynolds.*
Reynolds' (Thomas) Infantry. See *Wisconsin Troops, 16th Regiment.*
Rhoads' (Frank L.) Infantry. See *Illinois Troops, 8th Regiment.*
Rice's (Elliott W.) Infantry. See *Iowa Troops, 7th Regiment.*
Rice's (Lafayette M.) Infantry. See *Missouri Troops, Union, 24th Regiment.*
Rice's (T. W.) Artillery. See *Tennessee Troops, Confederate.*
Richardson's (Robert) Infantry. See *Louisiana Troops, 17th Regiment.*
Richardson's (R. V.) Cavalry. See *Tennessee Troops, Confederate.*
Rinaker's (John I.) Infantry. See *Illinois Troops, 122d Regiment.*
Ritter's (Richard) Infantry. See *Illinois Troops, 28th Regiment.*
Robbins' (George W.) Infantry. See *Wisconsin Troops, 8th Regiment.*
Roberts' (F.) Artillery. See *Arkansas Troops.*
Robertson's Cavalry. Official designation unknown. *See Captain Robertson.*
Robertson's (F. H.) Artillery. See *Alabama Troops.* *
Roddey's (P. D.) Cavalry. See *Mississippi Troops.*
Rodgers' (Benjamin F.) Artillery. See *Illinois Troops, 2d Regiment, Battery K*
Rogers' (George C.) Infantry. See *Illinois Troops, 15th Regiment.*
Rogers' (Henry A.) Artillery. See *Illinois Troops, 1st Regiment, Battery D.*
Rogers' (John A.) Infantry. See *Tennessee Troops, Union, 7th Regiment.*
Rowett's (Richard) Infantry. See *Illinois Troops, 7th Regiment.*
Russell's Consolidated Regiment. See *D. R. Russell.*
Russell's (A. A.) Cavalry. See *Alabama Troops, 4th Regiment.*
Rutherford's (Friend S.) Infantry. See *Illinois Troops, 97th Regiment.*
Saint Louis Artillery. See *Missouri Troops, Confederate.*
Sampson's (Ezekiel S.) Infantry. See *Iowa Troops, 5th Regiment.*
Sanborn's (J. B.) Infantry. See *Minnesota Troops, 4th Regiment.*
Sanders' (E. J.) Cavalry. See *Tennessee Troops, Confederate.*
Sanderson's (W. L.) Infantry. See *Indiana Troops, 23d Regiment.*
Sands' (Frank C.) Artillery. See *Ohio Troops, 11th Battery.*
Sanford's (William W.) Infantry. See *Illinois Troops, 48th Regiment.*
Savage's (J. H.) Infantry. See *Tennessee Troops, Confederate, 16th Regiment.*
Savery's (P. M.) Cavalry. See *Missouri Troops, Confederate.*
Schadt's (Otto) Infantry. See *Missouri Troops, Union, 30th Regiment.*
Schaefer's (Frederick) Infantry. See *Missouri Troops, Union, 2d Regiment.*
Schmidt's (Charles H.) Artillery. See *Ohio Troops, 8th Battery.*
Schofield's (George W.) Artillery. See *Missouri Troops, Union, 1st Regiment, Battery A.*
Scott's (Jefferson K.) Infantry. See *Indiana Troops, 48th Regiment.*†
Scott's (Jefferson K.) Infantry. See *Indiana Troops, 59th Regiment.*
Scott's (Robert K.) Infantry. See *Ohio Troops, 68th Regiment.*
Scott's (W. L.) Artillery. See *Smith P. Bankhead's Artillery.*
Semmes' (O. J.) Artillery. See *Confederate Troops.*
Semple's (H. C.) Artillery. See *Alabama Troops.*
Seven Stars Artillery. See *Mississippi Troops.*
Shane's (John) Infantry. See *Iowa Troops, 13th Regiment.*
Shearon's (Thomas R.) Infantry. See *Tennessee Troops, Confederate, 47th Regiment.*
Sheldon's (Charles S.) Infantry. See *Missouri Troops, Union, 18th Regiment.*
Shepard's (Isaac F.) Infantry. See *Missouri Troops, Union, 3d Regiment.*
Sheridan's (Philip H.) Cavalry. See *Michigan Troops, 2d Regiment.*
Silfversparre's (Axel) Artillery. See *Illinois Troops, 1st Regiment, Battery H.*

---

* Claimed also for Florida.   † Temporarily commanding.

Simonton's Consolidated Regiment. See *J. M. Simonton.*

Simpson's (Samuel P.) **Infantry.** See *Missouri Troops, Union, 31st Regiment.*

Sims' (W. B.) **Cavalry.** See *Texas Troops, 9th Regiment.*

Sinclair (Robert P.) **Infantry.** See *Michigan Troops, 14th Regiment.*

Slack's (James R.) **Infantry.** See *Indiana Troops, 47th Regiment.*

Slemons' (W. F.) **Cavalry.** See *Arkansas Troops, 2d Regiment.*

Sloan's (Thomas J.) **Infantry.** See *Illinois Troops, 124th Regiment.*

Slocomb's (C. H.) **Artillery.** See *Washington Artillery, 5th Company.*

Small's (William E.) **Infantry.** See *Iowa Troops, 10th Regiment.*

Smith's Cavalry. See *Tennessee Troops, Union, 6th Regiment.*

Smith's (Baxter) **Cavalry.** See *Tennessee Troops, Confederate.*

Smith's (E. M) **Cavalry.** See *Missouri Troops, Confederate.*

Smith's (Francis M.) **Infantry.** See *Illinois Troops, 17th Regiment.*

Smith's (Giles A.) **Infantry.** See *Missouri Troops, Union, 8th Regiment.*

Smith's (James M.) **Infantry.** See *Indiana Troops, 52d Regiment.*

Smith's (Jason B.) **Artillery.** See *Illinois Troops, 1st Regiment, Battery K.*

Smith's (John B.) **Infantry.** See *Iowa Troops, 3d Regiment.*

Smith's (John E.) **Infantry.** See *Illinois Troops, 45th Regiment.*

Smith's (Joseph C.) **Cavalry.** See *Ohio Troops, 5th Regiment.*

Smith's (Melancthon) **Artillery.** See *Mississippi Troops.*

Smith's (Milo) **Infantry.** See *Iowa Troops, 26th Regiment.*

Smith's (T. Kilby) **Infantry.** See *Ohio Troops, 54th Regiment.*

Smyth's (William) **Infantry.** See *Iowa Troops, 31st Regiment.*

Snook's (John S.) **Infantry.** See *Ohio Troops, 68th Regiment.*

Sparrestrom's (Frederick) **Artillery.** See *Illinois Troops, 2d Regiment, Battery G*

Spaulding's (Z. S.) **Infantry.** See *Ohio Troops, 27th Regiment.*

Spear's (Edward, jr.) **Artillery.** See *Ohio Troops, 15th Battery.*

Sperry's (Isaiah M.) **Cavalry.** See *Illinois Troops, 6th Regiment.*

Spooner's (B. J.) **Infantry.** See *Indiana Troops, 83d Regiment.*

Spoor's (Nelson T.) **Artillery.** See *Iowa Troops, 2d Battery.*

Sprague's (John W.) **Infantry.** See *Ohio Troops, 63d Regiment.*

Springfield Artillery. See *Thomas F. Vaughn's Artillery.*

Stanford's (T. J.) **Artillery.** See *Mississippi Troops.*

Starke's (Peter B.) **Cavalry.** See *Mississippi Troops, 28th Regiment.*

Starnes' (J. W.) **Cavalry.** See *Tennessee Troops, Confederate.*

Starring's (Frederick A.) **Infantry.** See *Illinois Troops, 72d Regiment.*

Steedman's (I. G. W.) **Infantry.** See *Alabama Troops, 1st Regiment.*

Steele's (Frederick) **Escort.** See *Kane County Cavalry.*

Stenbeck's (Andrew) **Artillery.** See *Illinois Troops, 2d Regiment, Battery H.*

Sterling's (R.) **Artillery.** See *Tennessee Troops, Confederate, 1st Regiment.*

Stevenson's (John D.) **Infantry.** See *Missouri Troops, Union, 7th Regiment.*

Stewart's (F. M.) **Cavalry.** See *Tennessee Troops, Confederate.*

Stewart's Legion. See *Louisiana Troops.*

Stewart's (R. A.) **Artillery.** See *Louisiana Troops, Pointe Coupée Artillery.*

Stewart's (W.) **Cavalry.** See *Illinois Troops.*

Stirman's (Ras.) **Sharpshooters.** See *Arkansas Troops.*

Stone's (B. W.) **Cavalry.** See *Texas Troops, 6th Regiment.*

Stone's (George A.) **Infantry.** See *Iowa Troops, 25th Regiment.*

Stone's (George H.) **Artillery.** See *Missouri Troops, Union, 1st Regiment.*

Strahl's (O. F.) **Infantry.** See *Tennessee Troops, Confederate, 4th Regiment.*

Stuart's (David) **Infantry.** See *Illinois Troops, 55th Regiment.*

Stull's (Homer H.) **Artillery.** See *Ohio Troops, 14th Battery.*

Sturgess' (Robert H.) **Infantry.** See *Illinois Troops, 8th Regiment.*

Sugg's Consolidated Regiment. See *C. A. Sugg.*

Sullivan's (Peter J.) **Infantry.** See *Ohio Troops, 48th Regiment.*

Sumter Infantry. See *Louisiana Troops, 30th Regiment.*
Swanwick's (Francis) Infantry. See *Illinois Troops, 22d Regiment.*
Swarthout's (William) Infantry. See *Illinois Troops, 50th Regiment.*
Swayne's (Wager) Infantry. See *Ohio Troops, 43d Regiment.*
Sweeny's (Thomas W.) Infantry. See *Illinois Troops, 52d Regiment.*
Swett's (Charles) Artillery. See *Warren Light Artillery.*
Taylor's (W. H. H.) Cavalry. See *Ohio Troops, 5th Regiment.*
Tennison's (Otto M.) Infantry. See *Kansas Troops, 1st Regiment.*
Terrell's (V. L.) Dragoons. See *Mississippi Troops.*
Thielemann's (Christian) Cavalry. See *Illinois Troops.*
Thielemann's (Milo) Cavalry. See *Christian Thielemann's Cavalry.*
Thomas' (Allen) Infantry. See *Louisiana Troops, 29th Regiment.*
Thomas' (Dewitt C.) Infantry. See *Indiana Troops, 93d Regiment.*
Thomasson's (S. B.) Infantry. See *Arkansas Troops.*
Thompson's Cavalry. See *Tennessee Troops, Union, 7th Regiment.*
Thompson's (Noah S.) Artillery. See *Indiana Troops, 9th Battery.*
Thrall's (Homer) Infantry. See *Ohio Troops, 22d Regiment.*
Thrall's (J. C.) Heavy Artillery. See *Arkansas Troops.*
Tillson's (John) Infantry. See *Illinois Troops, 10th Regiment.*
Toler's (Silas C.) Infantry. See *Illinois Troops, 60th Regiment.*
Tourtellotte's (John E.) Infantry. See *Minnesota Troops, 4th Regiment.*
Tripp's (Stephen S.) Cavalry. See *Illinois Troops, 11th Regiment.*
True's (James M.) Infantry. See *Illinois Troops, 62d Regiment.*
Tupper's (N. W.) Infantry. See *Illinois Troops, 116th Regiment.*
Turnbull's (C. J.) Infantry. See *Arkansas Troops.*
Turner's (Thomas J.) Infantry. See *Illinois Troops, 15th Regiment.*
Tyler's (R. C.) Infantry. See *Tennessee Troops, Confederate, 15th Regiment.*
Union Brigade. Improvised. See *George W. Kittel.*
Van Arman's (John) Infantry. See *Illinois Troops, 127th Regiment.*
Van Dorn's (Earl) Body Guard. See *J. Bradley's Cavalry.*
Vaughan's (A. J., jr.) Infantry. See *Tennessee Troops, Confederate, 13th Regiment.*
Vaughn's (Thomas F.) Artillery. See *Illinois Troops.*
Venable's (C. D.) Infantry. See *Tennessee Troops, Confederate, 5th Regiment.*
Wade's (W. B.) Cavalry. See *Confederate Troops, Regulars, 8th Regiment.*
Wade's (William) Artillery. See *Missouri Troops, Confederate.*
Walcutt's (Charles C.) Infantry. See *Ohio Troops, 46th Regiment.*
Walker's Consolidated Regiment. See *C. H. Walker.*
Wallace's (M. R. M.) Cavalry. See *Illinois Troops, 4th Regiment.*
Walling's (Daniel P.) Artillery. See *Iowa Troops, 2d Battery.*
Wangelin's (Hugo) Infantry. See *Missouri Troops, Union, 12th Regiment.*
Ward's (Lyman M.) Infantry. See *Wisconsin Troops, 14th Regiment.*
Ward's (M. S.) Artillery. See *Mississippi Troops, 14th Battalion.*
Warner's (Col. John) Infantry. See *Illinois Troops, 108th Regiment.*
Warner's (Lieut. Col. John) Infantry. See *Illinois Troops, 41st Regiment.*
Warren Light Artillery. See *Mississippi Troops.*
Washington Artillery. See *Louisiana Troops.*
Waterhouse's (Allen C.) Artillery. See *Illinois Troops, 1st Regiment, Battery E.*
Waters' (D. D.) Artillery. See *Alabama Troops.*
Waul's (T. N.) Legion. See *Texas Troops.*
Weaver's (James B.) Infantry. See *Iowa Troops, 2d Regiment.*
Webb's (Junius Y.) Cavalry. See *Louisiana Troops.*
Weber's (Andrew J.) Infantry. See *Missouri Troops, Union, 11th Regiment.*
Wells' Cavalry. Official designation unknown. See *Lieutenant Wells.*
Western Sharpshooters, Infantry. See *Missouri Troops, Union, 14th Regiment*
Wever's (Clark R.) Infantry. See *Iowa Troops, 17th Regiment.*

Wharton's (John A.) **Escort.**　See *Baxter Smith's Cavalry.*
Wheeler's (J. T.) **Cavalry.**　See *Tennessee Troops, Confederate.*
White's (B. F.) **Artillery.**　See *Tennessee Troops, Confederate.*
White's (H. B.) **Artillery.**　See *Ohio Troops,* 10th *Battery.*
White's (J. F.) **Cavalry.**　See *Mississippi Troops,* 4th *Regiment.*
Whitfield's (J. W.) **Legion.**　See *Texas Troops,* 27th *Regiment* **Cavalry.**
Wilbourn's (C. C.) **Cavalry.**　See *Hughes' Cavalry.*
Wilcox's (John S.) **Infantry.**　See *Illinois Troops,* 52d *Regiment.*
Wilder's (W. C.) **Cavalry.**　See *Kane County Cavalry.*
Willcox (Lyman G.) **Cavalry.**　See *Michigan Troops,* 3d *Regiment.*
Williams' (George A.) **Infantry.**　See *Union Troops,* 1st *Regiment.*
Williams' (George A.*) **Infantry.**　See *Illinois Troops,* 47th *Regiment.*
Williams' (George C.) **Infantry.**　See *Wisconsin Troops,* 16th *Regiment.*
Williams' (Nelson G.) **Infantry.**　See *Iowa Troops,* 3d *Regiment.*
Williams' (W. S.) **Artillery.**　See *Ohio Troops,* 3d *Battery.*
Williamson's (James A.) **Infantry.**　See *Iowa Troops,* 4th *Regiment.*
Willis' (Leonidas) **Cavalry.**　See *T. N. Waul's Legion.*
Wilson's (M. R.) **Infantry.**　See *Bart. Jones' Infantry.*
Wintter's (D.) **Engineers.**　See *Confederate Troops, Regulars.*
Withers' (W. T.) **Artillery.**　See *Mississippi Troops,* 1st *Regiment, Light.*
Wofford's (Jeff. L.) **Artillery.**　See *Mississippi Troops,* 1st *Regiment, Battery D.*
Wolfe's (Edward H.) **Infantry.**　See *Indiana Troops,* 52d *Regiment.*
Woods' (Charles R.) **Infantry.**　See *Ohio Troops,* 76th *Regiment.*
Woods' (Oliver) **Infantry.**　See *Ohio Troops,* 22d *Regiment.*
Woods' (Peter P.) **Artillery.**　See *Illinois Troops,* 1st *Regiment, Battery A.*
Woodward's (T. G.) **Cavalry.**　See *Kentucky Troops, Confederate,* 1st *Regiment.*
Worthington's (Thomas) **Infantry.**　See *Ohio Troops,* 46th *Regiment.*
Wright's (Benjamin T.) **Infantry.**　See *Ohio Troops,* 22d *Regiment.*
Yates Sharpshooters, Infantry.　See *Illinois Troops,* 64th *Regiment.*
Yoeman's (S. B.) **Infantry.**　See *Ohio Troops,* 54th *Regiment.*
Young's (W. H.) **Infantry.**　See *Texas Troops,* 9th *Regiment.*
Zakrzewski's (Herman) **Infantry.**　See *Missouri Troops, Union,* 2d *Regiment U. S. R. C.*
Zickerick's (William) **Artillery.**　See *Wisconsin Troops,* 12th *Battery.*

*Temporarily commanding.

INDEX.

Brigades, Divisions, Corps, Armies, and improvised organizations are "Mentioned" under name of commanding officer; State and other organizations under their official designation. (See Alternate Designations, pp. 904–916.)

Page.

Abandoned and Captured Property. Communications from
Grant, U. S... 156
Sherman, W. T.. 106, 112, 156, 158, 219
    See also *Sherman to Rawlins*, pp. 121, 140, 169.
Abbott, Abial R. Mentioned.. 247
Abbott, Charles H. Mentioned... 539
Abercrombie, John C. Mentioned.. 515
Absentees. Communications from
Adjutant-General's Office, U. S. A... 165
Army Headquarters... 308
Beauregard, G. T.. 605
Grant, U. S... 303
Sherman, W. T.. 165
    See also *Sherman to Rawlins*, p. 169; *Sherman to Grant*, p. 178.
Adams, C. W. Mentioned... 592, 737
Adams, D. W.
Correspondence with Braxton Bragg.. 615
Mentioned.. 765
Adams, John.
Assignments to command.. 826
Correspondence with
    Barteau, C. R... 796, 799
    Pemberton, John C.. 740, 758, 826
    Price, Sterling.. 666, 669, 695
    Ruggles, Daniel... 796–799
Mentioned.. 627, 648, 762
Report of Confederate troops at Columbus, Miss., Jan. 1, 1863............... 817
Adams, Robert N. Mentioned.. 516
Adams, Wirt.
Correspondence with
    Hébert, Louis... 836
    Pemberton, John C.. 803
Mentioned.. 833, 834
Adjutant-General's Office, U. S. A.
Correspondence with
    Army Headquarters... 262
    Dutton, Carlos.. 495
    Grant, U. S... 155
    War Department, U. S.. 91
Orders, General, series 1862: **No. 159**, 278; **No. 168**, 292; **No. 210**, 432.
Orders, Special, series 1862: **No. 320**, 308.
Orders, Special, "special" series 1863 (*Thomas*): No. 6, 590.

(917)

Page.

Adjutant and Inspector General's Office, C. S. A.
 Correspondence with
  Beauregard, G. T 594, 595, 598, 599, 601, 623
  Bragg, Braxton 619,
      624, 627, 644, 647, 649, 653-655, 662, 667, 671, 673, 678, 683, 752, 755, 765
  Davis, Jefferson 767
  Holmes, Theophilus H 753, 757, 765, 768, 782, 783, 786, 787, 793
  Johnston, Joseph E 758, 777, 780-782, 826
  Jones, Samuel 705
  Ordnance Department, C. S. A 749
  Pemberton, John C 724,
      740, 742, 745, 749, 753, 757, 762-764, 766, 768, 770, 774, 779, 786, 833
  Ruggles, Daniel... .... 721, 726, 771, 773
  Van Dorn, Earl 591
  War Department, C. S 732
 Orders, General, series 1862: **No. 39,** 624; **No. 44,** 685; **No. 50,** 649; **No.
      73,** 718.
 Orders, Special, series 1862: **No. 146,** 624; **No. 223,** 712; **No. 240,** 728;
      No. 275, 757.
Adriatic, Steamer. Mentioned 573
Alabama.
 Conscription act. Enforcement of, in 790
 Militia.. 674, 682
 Military departments embracing 101, 624, 627, 649
 Operations in. See *Northern Alabama.*
Alabama, Governor of. Correspondence with Sterling Price 674
Alabama Troops. Mentioned.
 Artillery, Light—*Battalions:* 1st, 659. *Batteries:* Burnet's, 632; Burt-
      well's, 633; Ketchum's, 633; Lumsden's, 632; Robertson's,* 633;
      Semple's, 658; Waters', 633.
 Cavalry—*Battalions:* 1st, 66; 13th, 815, 818, 846; 14th, 835. *Regiments:*
      Brewer's,† 63, 66, 606; 1st, 63, 66; 3d, 663, 666; 4th, 462.
 Infantry—Yancey's Sharpshooters, 633. *Regiments:* 1st, 600, 608, 661,
      726, 815; 4th, 786; 16th, 633; 17th, 18th, 633, 657; 19th, 633; 20th, 825;
      21st, 633, 659; 22d, 633; 23d, 825; 24th, 25th, 633; 26th, 132, 633;
      27th, 737; 28th, 633; 30th, 31st, 825; 33d, 34th, 633; 37th, 733; 38th,
      310; 39th, 633; 40th, 797, 799, 819, 825; 42d, 267, 700, 733; 45th, 632;
      46th, 825.
Alcorn, J. L. Mentioned 808, 809
Alexander, Jesse I. Mentioned 147, 208, 248, 339, 516, 524
Alexander, John W. S. Mentioned 147
Alexander, P. W. Mentioned 641, 679
Alger, Russell A. Mentioned 203
Allen, Benjamin. Mentioned... 249
Allen, H. W. Mentioned 662
Allen R., Steamer. Mentioned....................................... 573
Allen, Robert.
 Correspondence with
  Army Headquarters.............................. 189, 190, 355, 402, 421, 433, 556
  Grant, U. S 399, 552
  Halleck, H. W 61
  War Department, U. S.. 397
  Mentioned... .... 61, 304, 409, 441

---

* Claimed also for Florida.   † Composed of Alabama and Mississippi companies.

Page.

Allison, J. A. Mentioned 617
Alonzo Child, Steamer. Mentioned 867
Alton, City of, Steamer. Mentioned 573
Ames, F. J. Mentioned 828
Anderson, ———. Mentioned 579
Anderson, General, Steamer. Mentioned 510, 573
Anderson, Patton. Mentioned 618, 632, 652, 765
Anderson, R. Y. Mentioned 418
Anderson, W. J. Mentioned 834
Andrews, Hugh. Mentioned 591
Anthony, Daniel R. Mentioned 54, 77
Anthony, D. C.
    Appointed and announced as provost-marshal of Memphis, Tenn 31, 294
    Correspondence with W. T. Sherman 853
    Mentioned 30, 31, 173, 179, 294, 860
Argo, Steamer. Mentioned 867
Argyle, Duke of, Steamer. Mentioned 573
Arkansas, C. S. S.
    Construction, etc. Communications from Jefferson Davis 655
    Mentioned 163, 175, 241, 242, 655, 677, 724, 725
Arkansas.
    Operations in, Nov. 20, 1862–Dec. 31, 1863. Communications from
        Army Headquarters 441
        Curtis, Samuel R 433
        Gorman, W. A 477
        Sherman, W. T 859
    See also
        June 10–July 14, 1862. *White River. Operations on the.*
        Nov. 16–21, 1862. *Arkansas Post. Expedition against.*
                28, 1862. *Cane Hill. Engagement at.*
        Dec. 4– 6, 1862. *Cane Hill. Operations about.*
        Jan. 4–17, 1863. *Arkansas Post. Expedition against.*
            13–19, 1863. *White River. Expedition up the.*
    Re-enforcements for. Communications from
        Army Headquarters 298
        Sherman, W. T 111
        Wright, H. G 299
        (See also *Halleck to Grant*, pp. 26, 67, 82; *Grant to Halleck*, pp. 29, 36, 54;
            Halleck to Stanton, pp. 59, 97; *Halleck to Lincoln*, p. 98; *Order of Hal-
            leck*, p. 99; *Halleck to Sherman*, p. 100; *Sherman to Rawlins*, p. 121.
Arkansas Post, Ark. Expeditions against.
    Nov. 16–21, 1862. Communications from
        Adjutant and Inspector General's Office, C. S. A 752
        Pemberton, John C 751
        Van Dorn, Earl 751
                See also *Holmes to Cooper*, p. 783.
    Jan. 4–17, 1863.
        Communications from
            Grant, U. S 553
            McClernand, John A.................. 537, 541, 545–548, 552, 561, 562
            Sherman, W. T 536, 538, 549
        See also *Gorman to Curtis*, p. 552; *McClernand to Lincoln*, p. 566; *Mc-
            Clernand to Grant*, p. 567; *Sherman to Grant*, p. 570.
        Co-operation, Navy, U. S., with Army........................... 536, 546–548

Page.

Arkansas Troops. Mentioned.

Artillery, Heavy—*Companies:* Thrall's, 815, 818.

Artillery, Light—*Batteries:* Austin's, 633; **Helena**, 633; **Humphreys'**, 634; **McNally's**, 635; **Owens'**, 815, 818; Roberts', 633.

Cavalry—*Battalions:* Brooks', 635. *Regiments:* 1st Rifles, 592, 634; 2d Rifles, 592, 634; 2d, 137, 509, 654, 838, 845; 3d, 635, 733, 736, 844, 846.

Infantry—*Battalions:* Adams', 592, 634, 733, 735–737; Hobbs', 733, 736; Jones', 634, 733, 735–737; McCarver's, 634; McCray's, 592; Rapley's, 733, 735, 736; Turnbull's, 634; 4th, 634. *Companies:* Thomasson's, 605. *Regiments:* 1st, 632; 2d, 267, 633; 4th, 634; 5th, 6th, 7th, 8th, 633; 12th, 352; 13th, 603, 632; 14th, 634, 733, 735–737; 15th, 633; 16th, 592, 634, 733, 735–737; 17th, 18th, 634, 733, 735–737; 19th, 20th, 634, 733, 736; 21st, 592, 634, 733, 736; 31st, 634; Stirman's Sharpshooters, 733, 736.

Arms, Ammunition, etc. Supplies of. See *Munitions of War.*

Armstrong, Major. Mentioned... 816

Armstrong, Frank C.

Assignments to command... 642, 728

Correspondence with Sterling Price..................................... 646, 650, 662, 666, 675, 682, 687–689, 693, 697, 699, 702, 708

Mentioned................. 140, 205, 218, 224, 229, 443, 591, 642, 649, 659, 660, 662, 663, 665, 683, 684, 687, 690, 698, 702, 706–708, 717, 718, 720, 723, 728, 812, 838

Army Corps, 1st, Army of the Mississippi.* (Confederate.)

Constituted... 787

Designation changed to "division"....................................... 824

Van Dorn, Earl, assigned to command.................................. 787

Army Corps, 1st, Army of the Mississippi.† (Union.)

Constituted... 534

Morgan, George W., assigned to command............................ 534

Army Corps, 1st, Army of the Mississippi.‡ (Confederate.) **Designation** changed to "division"... 636

Army Corps, 2d, Army of the Mississippi.‡ (Confederate.)

Constituted... 623

Designation changed to "division"....................................... 636

Army Corps, 2d, Army of the Mississippi.* (Confederate.)

Constituted... 787

Designation changed to "division"....................................... 824

Price, Sterling, assigned to command.................................. 787

Army Corps, 2d, Army of the Mississippi.† (Union.)

Constituted... 534

Orders, General and Special. See *Army of the Mississippi.*

Organization of, announced... 538–540

Sherman, W. T., assigned to, and assumes command........ 534, 538

Army Corps, 3d, Army of the Mississippi.‡ (Confederate.) **Designation** changed to "division"... 636

Army Corps, 13th, Department of the Tennessee.

Constituted.. 292, 432, 461, 564

Grant, U. S., assigned to command..................................... 292

McClernand, John A., assigned to command.................. 432, 461

Morgan, George W., assigned to command........................... 564

See also *1st Corps, Army of the Mississippi* (so styled).

---

* Of the Department of Mississippi and East Louisiana.

† So styled by McClernand.

‡ Of Western Department.

Page.

Army Corps, 14th, Department of the Cumberland.
Constituted...... 292
Rosecrans, W. S., assigned to command 292

Army Corps, 15th, Department of the Tennessee.
Constituted...... 432, 461, 556, 564
Sherman, W. T., assigned to command 433, 461, 564
    See also *2d Corps, Army of the Mississippi* (so styled).

Army Corps, 16th, Department of the Tennessee.
Constituted...... 432, 461
Hamilton, C. S., assigned to command 553
Hurlbut, Stephen A.
    Assigned to command 433, 461, 542
    Relieved from command...... 553

Army Corps, 17th, Department of the Tennessee.
Constituted...... 432, 461
McPherson, James B., assigned to command 433, 461

Army Corps, Reserve, Army of the Mississippi.‡ (Confederate.)
Constituted...... 623
Designation changed to "division" 636

Army Headquarters.
Correspondence with
    Adjutant-General's Office, U. S. A 262
    Allen, Robert...... 189, 190, 355, 402, 421, 433, 556
    Asboth, A...... 139
    Buell, Don Carlos...... 185
    Cairo, Ill., Commanding Officer at 447
    Curtis, Samuel R...... 185,
            320-322, 327, 356, 376, 382, 383, 401, 424, 433, 441, 447, 471, 493, 578
    Davies, Thomas A.. 441, 447, 453, 462, 470, 479, 486, 493, 494, 500, 505, 520, 521
    Ellet, Alfred W 149, 398, 406
    Elliott, W. L 139
    Fitch, Henry S 480
    Granger, Gordon...... 139
    Grant, U. S 136, 142,
            148, 150, 151, 160, 164, 168, 175, 176, 179, 182, 183, 185-189, 191, 194, 197-
            199, 202, 206, 209, 213, 214, 220, 222, 225, 227, 228, 232-235, 238, 240, 243,
            250, 262, 267, 268, 270, 274, 276, 279-281, 283, 290, 296, 298, 302, 303, 308,
            318, 377, 386, 425, 461, 503, 530, 542-544, 549, 550, 553, 555, 560, 564, 570, 573
    Hamilton, C. S...... 574
    Hurlbut, Stephen A 470, 496
    Illinois, Governor of...... 298, 303, 309
    McClernand, John A 334, 349, 415, 461, 853
    McDermott, J 386
    McPherson, James B...... 184
    Navy Department, U. S...... 349, 422
    Parsons, L. B 413, 441, 496
    Quinby, Isaac F 196, 198
    Rosecrans, W. S 139, 154, 175, 187, 239, 251, 286, 287, 290
    Sherman, W. T...... 186, 200, 351
    Sullivan, J. C 139
    Tuttle, J. M 269
    Wright, H. G...... 298, 299, 309, 335, 545, 550
Orders, Special, series 1862: **No. 225,** 205; **No. 394,** 415.
Orders, Special, series 1863: **No. 30,** 575.

Page.

Army Transportation. See *Munitions of War.*

Asboth, A.
  Assignments to command 542, 554
  Correspondence with
      Army Headquarters 139
      Grant, U. S 573
      Pope, John 5
      Rosecrans, W. S 27, 35, 62, 63, 74, 104
      Sheridan, Philip H 61, 62, 65
  Mentioned 9, 24, 39, 43, 44, 61, 62, 65, 66, 75, 86, 139, 471, 542, 554, 570

Assessments, etc. Confederates and sympathizers. Communications from
      J. C. Sullivan 574
Attila. Mentioned 671
Augustin, Numa. Mentioned 595
Ault, Jacob R. Mentioned 145, 249, 340
Aurora, Steamer. Mentioned 573
Austin, Guide. Mentioned 14
Babcock, Amos C. Mentioned 300
Babcock, Andrew J. Mentioned 145, 249, 341
Bache, George M. Mentioned 884
Bacon, George A. Mentioned 247
Bacot, W. C.
  Correspondence with Braxton Bragg 639
  Mentioned 636
Bailey, J. B. Mentioned 350
Bailey, J. E. Mentioned 729, 733, 737
Bains, S. C. Mentioned 819
Baird, John F. Mentioned 516
Baker, Alonzo. Mentioned 418
Baker, Conrad. Mentioned 324
Baker, James. Mentioned 145
Baker, Samuel R. Mentioned 248
Baldwin, Silas D. Mentioned 341, 517
Baldwin, William E. Mentioned 765, 824
Balfour, John W. Mentioned 699
Ballard, W. E. Mentioned 418
Ballentine, J. G. Mentioned 273
Ballou, Daniel W. Mentioned 539
Bane, Moses M. Mentioned 145, 341, 404, 517
Banks, A. D. Correspondence with Joseph E. Johnston 834
Banks, E. A. Mentioned 841, 842
Banks, Nathaniel P. Mentioned 302, 503, 508, 519, 526, 531, 532, 542, 554, 555, 557,
      559, 567, 568, 570, 571, 573, 582, 800, 809, 815, 816, 830, 880, 882, 886, 888
Barbour, Alfred M. Mentioned 782, 834
Bardwell, F. W. Mentioned 145
Barksdale, J. L. B. Mentioned 419
Barnett, Charles M. Mentioned 148
Barnett, J. W. Mentioned 737
Barnhill, Rigdon S. Mentioned 514
Barnum, William L. Correspondence with M. Brayman 457
      For correspondence as A. A. A. G., see *M. Brayman.*
Baron De Kalb, U. S. S. Mentioned 884, 887
Barrett, Samuel E. Mentioned 146, 212, 247, 341, 539
Barringer, Charles. Mentioned 591

Page.

Barrow, Batt. Mentioned.. 617
Barry, William S. Mentioned.. 732
Barteau, C. R.
    Correspondence with
        Adams, John.. 796, 799
        Johnston, Joseph E.. 826, 838
        Loring, W. W... 813
        Pemberton, John C................. 740, 746, 747, 750, 751, 754, 766, 769, 832
    Mentioned.. 646, 732, 798, 799, 838
Bartleson, R. B. Mentioned 591
Barton, Seth M. Mentioned 765, 806, 815, 821, 824, 831
Bass, N. A. Mentioned 350
Bate, William B. Mentioned 765
Baxter, George L. Correspondence with Sterling Price..................... 667
Beall, W. N. R.
    Assignments to command 610, 614, 616, 734
    Mentioned........................... 610, 614, 616, 678, 691, 713, 726, 765
Beard, W. K. Mentioned 648
Beardsley, E. M. Mentioned 878
Beauregard, G. T.
    Correspondence with
        Adjutant and Inspector-General's Office, C. S. A 594, 595, 598, 599, 601, 623
        Bragg, Braxton.. 594, 660, 690
        Hill, L. E... 593
        Jordan, Thomas 640, 669, 679
        Lee, R. B... 595
        Lovell, Mansfield 591
        Martin, J. D 605
        Ruggles, Daniel 595, 597, 598, 601–603
        Van Dorn, Earl.. 592, 594
        War Department, C. S.................................... 598
    Mentioned 5, 6, 18, 20,
        23, 29, 47, 57, 64, 162, 213, 599, 601, 606, 612, 614, 615, 621, 624, 660, 673, 690
    Orders, Congratulatory. Capt. B. B. McCaa............................ 606
    Relinquishes command of Western Department 601, 606
Beebe, Yates V. Mentioned.. 147
Bell, James F. Mentioned 418
Bell, Jesse K., Steamer. Mentioned... 573
Bell, T. H. Mentioned 603
Bell, W. A. Mentioned 418
Belle, Peoria, Steamer. Mentioned... 573
Beltzhoover, D. Mentioned 699
Benkler, B. Mentioned 539
Benton, U. S. S. Mentioned................................... 879, 883–885, 887
Benton Barracks, Mo. Thomas J. McKean assigned to command of paroled
        prisoners, and relieved from duty at........................... 101, 205
Berkey, John M. Mentioned 523
Berry, M. T. Mentioned 599, 617
Bigney, Thomas O. Mentioned... 203, 246
Bills, Deall. Mentioned 297
Binmore, Henry. For correspondence as A. A. G., see Stephen A. Hurlbut.
Bishop, William W. Mentioned... 144
Bissell, Josiah W. Mentioned............. 146, 201, 205, 211, 237, 244, 246, 551, 578
Black, S. L. Mentioned.. 639

Page.

Blackburn, Luke P. Mentioned................ .... 665, 676
Black Hawk, Steamer. Mentioned.. 468, 887
Blair, Frank P., jr.
    Correspondence with
        Curtis, Samuel R 463
        Lincoln, Abraham 350
        Sherman, W. T... 581, 582, 587, 588
        Smith, John E... 558
    Mentioned 349, 376, 395, 421, 423, 424, 426, 539, 549, 876, 879, 888, 891
Blake, E. D. Mentioned 639
Blake, Edgar W. Mentioned.. 246, 513, 517
Blanchard, Albert G.
    Correspondence with Theophilus H. Holmes................................. 766
    Mentioned 724, 726, 765, 770, 811
Bland, Peter E. Mentioned 212, 340, 344
Blood, James H. Mentioned 146, 246, 539
Blue Wing, Steamer. Mentioned.......................... 522, 526, 537, 563, 570
Blunt, James G. tineoned.......................... 395, 424, 433, 477, 478, 508, 568
Blythe, G. L.
    Correspondence with
        Jones, E. P.. 762
        Starke, P. B 763
    Mentioned................... 285, 286, 289, 411, 526, 550, 738, 739, 745, 754, 762, 793
Boggs, W. R. Mentioned 765
Boicourt, John M. Mentioned...................................... 870–872
Bolivar, Tenn.
    Expedition to, July 25–Aug. 1, 1862. See Holly Springs, Miss. Expedition
        from, July 25–Aug. 1, 1862.
    Expedition from, Sept. 20–22, 1862. Communications from
        Grant, U. S.. 228
        Hurlbut, Stephen A 226, 228, 231, 232
    Union troops at post of. Organization, strength, &c., Jan. 3, 1863 527
Bolivar, Tenn., Commanding Officer at. Correspondence with
    Grant, U. S.. 439
    Sullivan, J. C.. 380
Bollard, G. R. Mentioned.. 43
Bolton, William H. Mentioned 145, 247, 339, 514
Bonner, R. H. Mentioned... 839
Boomer, George B. Mentioned................................. 147, 339, 516, 524
Boone, H. L. Mentioned 746
Booneville, Miss.
    Action near, July 1, 1862. Communications from
        Asboth, A 62, 63
        Halleck, H. W.. 76
        Rosecrans, W. S... 62, 65
        Sheridan, Philip H 61–63, 65
        See also Halleck to Lincoln, p. 64.
    Expedition to and capture of, May 30, 1862. Congratulatory orders.
        (Bragg) 616
Boothe, James W. Mentioned 146, 212, 246, 340, 344
Borcherdt, Albert. Mentioned.. 148
Borgersode, Rudolph von. Mentioned 147
Borland, James A. Mentioned 338
Boston Mountains, Ark. Engagement at, Nov. 28, 1862. See Cane Hill, Ark.

Page.

Boswell, Thomas. Mentioned 586
Bouck, Gabriel. Mentioned 145 249, 340, 515
Bouton, Edward. Mentioned 146, 212, 247, 341, 514
Bowen, Edwin A. Mentioned.. 145, 516
Bowen, John S.
   Assignments to command.. 729, 824
   Mentioned 231, 233, 285,
      286, 305–307, 336, 685, 711, 729, 733, 737, 765, 824, 843, 859, 874, 898, 903
Bowen, William D. Mentioned 495
Bowers, T. S. Correspondence with U. S. Grant 510
Boyd, A. Mentioned... 622
Boyle, Jeremiah T. Mentioned.. 199
Boyle, Thomas. Mentioned 418
Brackett, A. B. Mentioned.. 137
Bradford, Colonel. Mentioned 365
Bradford, Lieutenant. Mentioned 836
Bradford, H. S. Mentioned 617
Bradford, W. M. Mentioned... 603
Bradfute, W. R.
   Correspondence with
      Hill, L. E... 607, 611
      Van Dorn, Earl..................................... 597, 607, 611
   Mentioned.. 107
Bradley, J. Mentioned 815
Bradley, Luther P. Mentioned.. 147
Bragg, General, U. S. S. Mentioned 886
Bragg, Braxton.
   Addresses to soldiers of Western Department.............................. 626
   Assignments to command 606, 626, 636, 639
   Congratulatory orders.
      Bacot, W. C., Capt 636
      Booneville, Miss. Expedition to, and capture of, May 30, 1862 616
      La Fayette Station, Tenn. Affair near, June 25, 1862................ 638
      Rising Sun, Tenn. Skirmish at, June 30, 1862..................... 639
   Correspondence with
      Adams, D. W 615
      Adjutant and Inspector General's Office, C. S. A...................... 619,
        624, 627, 644, 647, 649, 653–655, 662, 667, 671, 673, 678, 683, 752, 755, 765
      Bacot, W. C 639
      Beauregard, G. T 594, 660, 690
      Chalmers, James R 594, 629, 635, 642, 649
      Clark, M. L.. 653
      Dahlgren, C. G... 620
      Davis, Jefferson 599, 614, 619, 653, 658, 659, 707, 897
      Griffin, G. G 625
      Johnston, Joseph E....................... 781, 798, 811, 832, 838
      Lee, Robert E 619
      McKee, And. W 620
      Military Railroad Transportation, Officer in charge.................... 609
      Oladowski, H.. 627
      Ordnance Department, C. S. A 678
      Pemberton, John C 743, 744, 754, 755, 769, 771, 778
      Polignac, C. J 609
      Porter, E. E 621

Page.

Bragg, Braxton—Continued.

Correspondence with

Preston, William.. 608, 616

Price, Sterling... 657,

662, 663, 666, 667, 675, 677, 678, 682, 683, 685, 688, 690, 696, 703, 706

Ruggles, Daniel.. 608, 611, 614, 619

Smith, E. Kirby 610, 651

Smith, R. W... 609

Tate, Samuel 637

Van Dorn, Earl.. 613, 656, 675, 688, 713, 897

Villepigue, John B.. 622

War Department, C. S................... 612, 619, 625, 627, 629, 630, 673

Mentioned 18, 59, 64, 107, 132, 136, 139, 141, 153,
181, 192, 213, 216, 222, 235, 258, 261, 286, 289–291, 306, 347, 367, 377, 398,
399, 409, 414, 415, 422–424, 427, 437, 438, 451, 482, 488, 489, 498, 518, 529,
540, 541, 544, 564, 568, 574, 599, 601, 605, 606, 612, 618, 619, 631, 632, 635,
639–641, 648, 652, 660, 662, 663, 665, 668–670, 675, 677, 679, 680, 684, 690–
700, 703–707, 712, 714–717, 732, 735, 740, 742, 751, 753, 758, 759, 765, 767,
773, 775, 777, 779–781, 785, 801, 817, 823, 827, 833, 835, 838, 857, 874, 897

Staff. Announcements of 648

Brayman, Mason.

Correspondence with

Barnum, William L... 457

Grant, U. S.. 358, 360, 440, 521, 527

Grierson, Benjamin H.. 465

Sullivan, J. C 357, 359, 440, 444, 457, 458, 466, 475–477

Mentioned...................... 317, 337, 341, 342, 357, 430, 450, 460, 483, 492

Breckenridge, W. K. M.

Correspondence with G. M. Dodge................................... 564

Mentioned... 444

Breckinridge, John C.

Correspondence with

Van Dorn, Earl... 897

Walker, F. M... 898

Mentioned.............. 29, 34, 37, 43, 44, 47–49, 57, 58, 163, 175, 181, 208, 216, 220,
222–224, 229, 233–236, 238, 243, 244, 250, 251, 253, 261, 423, 610, 618, 619, 628,
630, 654, 658, 663, 664, 675, 678, 692, 693, 697, 701, 703, 704, 706, 707, 765, 901

Orders, General, series 1862: **No. 8,** 898.

Orders, Special, series 1862: **Nos. 13, 16,** 898; **Nos. 17, 18, 19, 20,** 899;
Nos. 21, 23, 27, 900.

Brent, George William. Mentioned.......................... 658, 680

For correspondence as Acting Chief of Staff, see *G. T. Beauregard* and *Braxton Bragg.*

Breysacher, A. L. Mentioned................................... 639

Bridewell, L. O. Mentioned................................... 639

Broadwell, W. A. Mentioned................................... 798

Brooks, ——. Mentioned...................................... 859

Brooks, James.

Correspondence with Alfred W. Ellet.............................. 148

Mentioned... 9

Brotzmann, Edward. Mentioned........................... 339, 515

Brown, ——. Mentioned.. 9

Brown, Aaron. Mentioned..................................... 515

Brown, A. R. Mentioned...................................... 603

Brown, Charles E. Mentioned.............................. 248, 339

Page.

Brown, George R. Mentioned 339, 515

Brown, Isaac N.
   Correspondence with
      Pemberton, John C 788
      Ruggles, Daniel 615
   Mentioned 655

Brown, J. C. Mentioned 765

Brown, Joseph E. Mentioned 791

Brown, William R. Mentioned 147

Browne, W. R. Mentioned 812

Bruch, Samuel. Correspondence with
   Stager, Anson 394, 499
   Van Duzer, J. C 394

Brush, Daniel H. Mentioned 212, 341, 517

Bryant, George E.
   Correspondence with
      Dodge, Grenville M 105
      Logan, John A 137, 141, 142, 203
      McClernand, John A 168, 174
   Mentioned 104, 107, 128–131, 146, 247, 339, 515

Bryner, John. Mentioned 148

Buchanan, A. S. For correspondence as A. A. A. G., see *J. C. Sullivan.*

Buchanan, James. Mentioned 896

Buckland, Ralph P. Mentioned 146,
     169, 212, 246, 329, 336, 340, 344, 358, 398, 442, 443, 487, 861

Buckner, C. B. Correspondence with John C. Pemberton 763

Buckner, Simon B.
   Correspondence with Joseph E. Johnston 832, 833
   Mentioned 494, 540, 715, 765, 816, 838, 859

Buell, Don Carlos.
   Assignments to command 3
   Correspondence with
      Army Headquarters 185
      Grant, U. S 168, 174, 177
   Mentioned 3, 22, 23, 26, 46,
     59, 67, 75, 83, 97, 98, 100, 101, 142, 148, 160, 166, 168, 173–179, 186, 189,
    191, 195, 203, 208, 210, 213, 238, 239, 261, 262, 286, 289, 291, 597, 611, 629,
    630, 641, 651, 655, 665, 670, 675, 677, 683, 685, 687, 688, 690, 696, 739, 897

Buford, J. W. Mentioned 603

Buford, N. B.
   Assignments to command 575
   Mentioned 74, 147, 203, 575

Bullitt, Fannie, Steamer. Mentioned 573

Burbridge, Simon C. Mentioned 15, 21, 477

Burbridge, Stephen G. Mentioned 580, 587

Burchfield, ——. Mentioned 257

Burgin, T. A. Mentioned 818

Burke, Patrick E.
   Correspondence with
      Dodge, Grenville M 428
      Grant, U. S 270
      Mersy, August 427
   Mentioned 145, 265, 266, 341, 517, 754

Burnap, Silas A. Mentioned 145, 247, 339, 515

Page.

Burnside, A. E. Mentioned 186, 230, 587
Burnt Bridge, Tenn. Skirmish at, Sept. 5, 1862. Communications from
    Bryant, G. E 203
    Dodge, Grenville M 203
Burrow, Reuben. Mentioned 460
Burton, Anthony B. Mentioned 515
Burton, Josiah H. Mentioned 247
Butler, Benjamin F. Mentioned 26, 150, 186, 225, 463, 519, 620
Butler, Charles. Mentioned 418
Buttles, Lucian. Mentioned 7
Cabell, William L.
    Assignments to command 728
    Mentioned 210, 579, 591, 634, 653, 684, 713, 728
Cadwalader, George.
    Assignments to command 153, 167
    Mentioned 151, 153, 167
Cairo, U. S. S. Mentioned 426, 884
Cairo, Ill.
    Buford, N. B., assigned to command 575
    Embraced in Department of the Tennessee 278
    Tuttle, J. M., relieved of command of the post of 353
Cairo, Ill., Commanding Officer at. Correspondence with Army Headquarters. 447
Cairo, Ill., Naval Commander at. For correspondence, etc., see A. M. Pennock.
Cairo, District of. (Union.)
    Embraced in the District of West Tennessee 101, 102
    Merged in the District of Mississippi 211
    Tuttle, J. M., assigned to command 166
Caldwell, A. W. Mentioned 603
Caldwell, D. M.
    Mentioned 76
    Report of skirmish on the Hatchie River, Miss., July 5, 1862 73
Caldwell, William L. Mentioned 146
Calhoun, John C. Mentioned 896
Callender, Franklin D.
    Correspondence with
        Grant, U. S 536, 537
        Rosecrans, W. S 105
    Mentioned 187, 282
Callie, Steamer. Mentioned 202
Cam, William. Mentioned 515
Cameron, James C. Mentioned 249
Campbell, A. B. Mentioned 225
Campbell, Alexander. Mentioned 884
Campbell, R., jr., Steamer. Mentioned 573
Cane Hill, Ark.
    Engagement at, Nov. 28, 1862. See Holmes to Cooper, p. 788.
    Operations about, Dec. 4–6, 1862. See Holmes to Cooper, p. 783.
Captured Property. See Abandoned and Captured Property.
Carmichael, Eagleton. Mentioned 144, 517
Carnes, W. W. Mentioned 603
Carondelet, U. S. S. Mentioned 140, 887
Carpenter, Stephen J. Mentioned 147
Carr, Eugene A. Mentioned 273, 280
Carroll, Tenn., Commanding Officer at. Correspondence with J. C. Sullivan. 380

Carroll, W. H. Page.
Court of Inquiry in case of, appointed... 663
Mentioned.. 663, 673, 765
Carter, James M.
Correspondence with Isham N. Haynie... 415
Mentioned.. 415, 423
Carter, Julien. Mentioned 443, 511
Catahoula, Steamer. Mentioned 281, 285, 288
Cates, O. G. Correspondence with
Halleck, H. W... 91, 92
Missouri, Governor of... 92
War Department, U. S... 93
Catterson, Robert F. Mentioned... 340, 514
Cavender, John S. Mentioned 539
Chaillé, S. E. Mentioned... 648
Chalmers, James R.
Assignments to command... 650
Correspondence with
Bragg, Braxton... 594, 629, 635, 642, 649
Forrest, N. B... 838
Mentioned 14, 61, 63, 66, 110, 594, 605, 618, 633, 635, 648–650, 652, 765
Chambers, Alexander.
Correspondence with M. M. Crocker... 190
Mentioned... 145
Chambers, J. A. Mentioned... 828
Champion, Steamer. Mentioned 184, 573
Champion, Tug. Mentioned... 887
Champneys, J. T. Correspondence with H. Oladowski... 643
Chancellor, Steamer. Mentioned... 573
Chandler, William P. Mentioned... 147
Chandler, Zachariah M. Mentioned... 338, 514
Chapman, Fletcher H. Mentioned... 247
Chapman, James F. Mentioned 250
Chapman, William. Mentioned... 828
Charm, Steamer. Mentioned 831
Chase, Daniel. Mentioned... 340, 344, 539
Chase, Salmon P. Mentioned 141
Cheatham, B. F. Mentioned... 131,
136, 423, 470, 479, 481, 495, 540, 596, 603, 618, 632, 652, 657, 673, 765
Cheeseman, J. W. Steamer. Mentioned... 573
Cheney, John T. Mentioned 146, 212, 341, 342, 514
Chenowith, B. P.
Correspondence with H. W. Halleck... 53
Mentioned... 77
Chester, John. Mentioned... 603
Chetlain, Augustus L. Mentioned... 145, 249, 341
Child, Alonzo, Steamer. Mentioned... 867
Childs, F. L. Mentioned... 775
Chipman, Norton P.
Correspondence with Samuel R. Curtis... 471
Mentioned... 434
Choppin, S. Mentioned... 641
Church, Lawrence S. Mentioned... 300
Church Services. Communications from U. S. Grant... 30
Churchill, T. J. Mentioned... 592, 634, 653

                                                                                    Page.
Cincinnati, U. S. S. Mentioned 884, 887
Citizen, Steamer. Mentioned 573
City of Alton, Steamer. Mentioned 573
City of Louisiana, Steamer. Mentioned 573
Clark, Charles. Mentioned......................... 181, 596, 603, 618, 632, 652, 765
Clark, George W. Mentioned... 539
Clark, Henry M. Mentioned... 637, 654
Clark, M. L.
    Correspondence with Braxton Bragg... 653
    Mentioned 648
Clark, M. R. Correspondence with John C. Pemberton 829
Clarksville, Tenn.
    Re-enforcements for. Communications from
        Army Headquarters 270
        Grant, U. S 274
    Statement of citizens of 730
    Surrender of, Aug. 18, 1862. Communications from
        Grant, U. S 186
        Hart, James H... 183
Clay, G. W. Mentioned.. 418
Clayton, A. M. Correspondence with Jefferson Davis...................... 727
Clayton, William Z. Mentioned... 340, 515
Cleburne, P. R. Mentioned............................... 619, 633, 652, 765
Clifford, James. Mentioned.. 148
Clon, John. Mentioned ....: 418
Clothing, Camp and Garrison Equipage. Supplies of, etc. See *Munitions
        of War.*
Cockerill, Joseph R. Mentioned.................... 146, 169, 212, 246, 340, 344, 514
Coffeeville, Miss. Engagement at, Dec. 5, 1862. See *Van Dorn to Pemberton,*
        p. 785; *Pemberton to Cooper,* p. 786.
Coffey, A. B. Mentioned 686
Cogswell, William. Mentioned 146, 212, 247, 341, 514
Colburn, Albert V. Mentioned.. 552, 553
Colby, P. T. Mentioned.. 734
Coldwater, Miss. Expedition to the, Sept. 8–13, 1862. See *Memphis, Tenn.
        Expedition from,* Sept. 8–13, 1862.
Coldwater, Miss., Comdg. Officer at. Correspondence with J. C. Sullivan.. 380
Coleburn, John C. Mentioned... 807
Coleman, D. C. Mentioned 539
Collender, George. Mentioned.. 884
Colliersville, Tenn. Scout to, Oct. 21, 1862. See *Memphis, Tenn. Scout from,*
        Oct. 21–24, 1862.
Collins, Bernard. Mentioned 871, 873
Columbus, Ky.
    Operations at and about.* Communications from
        Army Headquarters.. 470, 493, 521
        Davies, Thomas A 441, 453, 470, 479, 481, 486, 487, 500, 501, 519–521
        Fisk, Clinton B 494, 504
        Grant, U. S 520
        Hurlbut, Stephen A 501
                See also *Grant to Hurlbut,* p. 508.
    Re-enforcements for. Communications from
        Army Headquarters.. 447, 471
        Curtis, Samuel R.. 469

Page.

Columbus, Miss. Confederate troops at, Jan. 1, 1863. Report of John Adams. 817
Columbus, Ky., Commanding Officer at. Correspondence with U. S. Grant. 293
Columbus, District of. (Union.)
    Asboth, A., assigned to command... 554
    Constituted.. 297
    Davies, Thomas A.
        Assigned to command 297
        Relieved of command 554
    Embraced in District of West Tennessee 565
Colvin, Andrew. Mentioned.. 591
Commanding Officer 42d Alabama. Correspondence with Sterling Price.. 700
Conduct of the War. Communications from
    Army Headquarters 150, 283
    Davis, Jefferson... 732
    Dodge, Grenville M 164
    Grant, U. S....................... 51, 69, 88, 230, 280, 281, 370, 524, 525
    Halleck, H. W 88, 90
    Harris, Thomas W 365
    Hovey, Alvin P 98, 99
    Johnson, C... 730
    Leggett, M. D 229
    Norton, A. S 416, 418, 419
    Ord, E. O. C 229
    Pemberton, John C 871
    Price, Sterling 230
    Quinby, Isaac F 184
    Richardson, R. V.. 418
    Rosecrans, W. S 154, 291
    Sherman, W. T 90, 96, 114, 240, 280, 287, 289, 860, 870, 872, 873
    Thompson, M. Jeff 98
    Van Duser, J. C 230
    War Department, C. S 598, 731, 732
    See also *Randolph, Tenn. Burning of, Sept.* 25, 1862; *Halleck to McClernand,*
        p. 5; *McClernand to Logan,* p. 6; *Sherman to Rawlins,* pp. 121,
        279, 285, 857; *Sherman to Grant,* pp. 259, 272; *Rawlins to Hurlbut,*
        p. 522; *Garner to Chalmers,* p. 642; *Snead to Falkner,* p. 668.
Conestoga, U. S. S. Mentioned 30, 886
Confederate Troops.
    Mentioned. (Regulars.)
        Artillery, Light—*Batteries :* **Semmes',** 661, 691.
        Cavalry—*Companies :* **Bradley's,*** 661, 814, 815, 844, 847. *Regiments :*
            1st, 3d, 835; **8th,** 663, 666.
        Engineers—*Companies :* **Wintter's,** 661, 699, 815, 825, 831.
        Infantry—*Battalions :* **1st,** 600, 661. *Regiments :* **3d,** 633.
            For Volunteers, see respective States.
    Organization, strength, etc.
        Columbus, Miss... 817–819
        Grenada, Miss 600, 829
        Jackson, Miss... 819, 820
        Mississippi, Army of the.† See *Mississippi and East Louisiana, Department of.*
        Mississippi, Army of the‡ 596, 603, 618, 619, 631–633, 635, 648, 652, 835

---

* Company A, 1st Regiment.
† Of the Department of Mississippi and East Louisiana.
‡ Of the Western Department.

Page.

Confederate Troops—Continued.

Organization, strength, etc.

Mississippi, District of the 661, 662, 699

Mississippi and East Louisiana, Dept. of .. 814, 815, 824, 825, 831, 833, 846, 847

Vicksburg, Miss., Jan. 2–3, 1863 .... 824, 825, 829, 831

West, Army of the 631, 634, 635, 648, 652, 653, 718, 733, 736

Western Department................................ 631–635, 648, 652, 653

Recruitment, organization, etc. Communications from

Adjutant and Inspector General's Office, C. S. A............. 591, 654, 742, 757

Armstrong, Frank C 646

Beauregard, G. T 595, 607

Bowen, John S.. 736

Bragg, Braxton 609, 623, 627, 647, 648, 654, 667, 671, 673, 678, 680

Breckinridge, John C 900

Cheatham, B. F 643

Davis, Jefferson 658, 698, 700

Hardee, W. J 642, 647

Pemberton, John C 737, 743, 748, 757, 786, 787, 824

Pillow, G. J 715, 716

Price, Sterling.. 668, 683

Smith, R. A 629

Van Dorn, Earl.................... 610, 681, 697, 711, 713, 728, 729

War Department, C. S 681, 699, 704, 716

See also *Bragg to Van Dorn*, p. 675; *Johnston to Davis*, p. 812.

Congress, Confederate. Resolution of C. S. Senate. Free navigation of
Mississippi River and tributaries 712

Connell, W. M. M. Correspondence with John C. Pemberton................ 808

Conner, L. M. Mentioned.. 648

Conscription Act. Enforcement of, in

Alabama.. 790

Mississippi.................................... 681, 737, 738, 748, 790

Continental, Steamer. Mentioned.................... 549, 573, 580, 582, 586, 587, 890

Cooke, G. B. Mentioned 648

Cooke, G. Frederick. Mentioned 249

Cooley, Charles G. Mentioned 341

Coon, Datus E. Mentioned 248, 340

Cooper, Samuel. Mentioned.................... 619, 623, 662, 691, 728, 781

For correspondence, etc., see *Adjutant and Inspector General's Office, C. S. A.*

Corbyn, Frank. Mentioned 437

Corinth, Miss.

Advance upon and siege of, April 29–June 10, 1862. See

May 30, 1862. *Boonevills, Miss. Expedition to and capture of.*

30–June 10, 1862. *Corinth, Miss. Evacuation of, and pursuit of Confederate by Union forces.*

Battle of, Oct. 3–4, 1862. Communications from

Burke, P. E.. 270

Grant, U. S 250, 257

Haynie, Isham N.. 353, 257–259

Hurlbut, Stephen A 250, 251, 253, 255, 256, 259

Price, Sterling.. 718, 720

Rosecrans, W. S.................................... 251, 252, 254–257

Stanley, David S.. 251

Van Dorn, Earl.. 717–721

Cadwalader, George.

Assigned to command at 153

Relieved from command of 167

Page.

Corinth, Miss.—Continued.

Evacuation of, and pursuit of Confederates by Union forces, May 30- June
10, 1862. Communications from

    Adjutant and Inspector General's Office, C. S. A 594

    Beauregard, G. T.. 595

    Davis, Jefferson 599

Mail facilities.. 207

Ord, E. O. C.

    Assigned to command at 167

    Relieved temporarily of command of 153

Pursuit of Confederates from, Oct. 5–12, 1862. Communications from

    Haynie, Isham N.. 267

    Hurlbut, Stephen A... 263, 267–271, 274

    Rosecrans, W. S.. 263–265, 269, 271, 276

    Van Dorn, Earl... 721, 723, 726

Corinth, District of. (Union.)

Constituted... 297

Embraced in District of West Tennessee.................................... 565

Hamilton, C. S., assigned to, and assumes command..................... 297, 298

Orders, General and Special. See *Tennessee. Army of the. (Union.)*

Corse, John M. Mentioned.............................. 146, 212, 246, 340, 344, 514

Cosby, George B. Mentioned.. 835, 838

Cotton.

Burning of, by Confederates. See *Private Property.*

Trade in. See *Trade and Intercourse.*

Cotton Plant, Steamer. Mentioned 867

Coulter, John P. Mentioned.. 145

Courtland and Trinity, Ala. Operations at and in vicinity of, July 25, 1862.
Communications from

    Armstrong, Frank C 650

    Bragg, Braxton.. 648, 662

Courts-Martial. Case of Thomas W. Knox.

Charges and specifications 890–892

Proceedings, findings, and sentence..................................... 889–892

Courts of Inquiry. Cases of.

Carroll, W. H., appointed 663

Crittenden, George B., appointed 658

Destruction of tents, Tilghman's division. Findings, etc 847

One hundred and ninth Regiment Illinois.

    Appointed 523

    Order of Grant announcing results 586

Cowan, John. Mentioned... 516

Cox, Jacob D. Mentioned 299

Coykendall, John R. Mentioned 515

Coyl, W. H. Mentioned.. 539

Crabtree, Squire. Mentioned.. 591

Craven, A. M. Mentioned 415

Cravens, J. E. Mentioned 733, 735, 736, 739

Crescent City, Steamer. Mentioned 13, 573

Crittenden, General. Mentioned 171

Crittenden, George B.

Court of Inquiry appointed in case of...................................... 658

Mentioned... 658, 663, 673

Crittenden, Thomas L. Mentioned.................... 239, 593, 604, 611, 613

Page.

Crocker, Marcellus M.

Assignments to command.. 218

Correspondence with

Chambers, Alexander 190

Grant, U. S. 190

Telegraph operator 524

Mentioned.............................. 145, 197, 218, 219, 249, 252, 266, 275, 509, 515

Crockett, Tenn., Commanding Officer at. Correspondence with J. C. Sullivan 380

Cumberland, Department of the.

Constituted, and limits defined 292

Rosecrans, W. S., assigned to command 292

Stanley, David S., assigned to duty in 343

Cummins, E. H. Mentioned 680

Cuney, R. H.

Correspondence with

Pemberton, John C 755

Reed, T. B 752, 753, 776, 782, 800

Mentioned 797, 798

Cunningham, Nathaniel B. Mentioned............................ 205, 870, 871

Cunningham, William T. Mentioned... 340

Curtis, Captain. Mentioned.. 417

Curtis, H. Z. For correspondence as A. A. G., see *Samuel R. Curtis.*

Curtis, Isaac W. Mentioned.. 250

Curtis, John G. Mentioned.. 144

Curtis, Samuel R.

Co-operation with Grant. See

June 10, 1862–Jan. 20, 1863. *Northern Mississippi. Operations in.*

Oct. 31, 1862–Jan. 10, 1863. *Mississippi Central R. R. Operations on the.*

Dec. 20, 1862–Jan. 3, 1863. *Vicksburg, Miss. Operations against.*

Jan. 20–July 4, 1863. *Vicksburg, Miss. Operations against.*

Correspondence with

Army Headquarters.. 185,

320–322, 327, 356, 376, 382, 383, 401, 424, 433, 441, 447, 471, 493, 578

Blair, Frank P., jr 463

Chipman, Norton P 471

Davies, Thomas A 356, 469, 500, 501

Fisk, Clinton B 486, 494, 504

Gorman, Willis A 395, 414, 421, 434, 464, 469, 552, 555, 578

Grant, U. S 356, 555, 566, 578

Hovey, Alvin P 323, 384

Hurlbut, Stephen A 499

McClernand, John A 545

Sherman, W. T 407, 433, 859

Steele, Frederick... 395

Mentioned 26, 30, 34, 36, 37, 54, 55, 59, 67,

82, 86, 97, 98, 100, 101, 111, 121, 140–142, 166, 172, 175, 178, 179, 182, 188, 234,

235, 262, 269, 279, 280, 296–298, 303, 307, 308, 320, 336, 349, 352, 382, 392, 393,

406–410, 414, 423, 425, 434, 447, 461, 464, 469, 477, 481, 496, 501, 503, 508, 519,

522, 542, 546, 551, 556, 563, 579, 652, 701, 704, 719, 721, 724, 867, 876, 877, 886

Cushman, William H. W.

Correspondence with Stephen A. Hurlbut............................. 32

Mentioned... 145

Dacotah, Steamer Mentioned 573

Page.

Dahlgren, C. G. Correspondence with Braxton Bragg............................ 620

Dameron, W. H. Mentioned.. 798

Davenport, S. Mentioned.. 611

Davidson, John W. Mentioned 424, 477

Davies, Thomas A.

Assignments to command.. 297, 554

Correspondence with

    Army Headquarters... 441, 447, 453, 462, 470, 479, 486, 493, 494, 500, 505, 520, 521

    Curtis, Samuel R.. 356, 469, 500, 501

    Gordon, John A... 352

    Grant, U. S 303, 309–311, 319, 425, 481, 520, 521, 535

    Hurlbut, Stephen A.. 501, 519

    Jones, R. B 481, 880, 881

    Lewis, James M 486

    Lowe, W. W... 303

    New Era, U. S. S., Commanding Officer of 487

    Ransom, T. E. G.. 304

    Rosecrans, W. S 264

    Sherman, W. T 406

    Sullivan, J. C... 415

Mentioned.. 168, 177,

    206, 249, 252, 257, 264–266, 292, 297, 300, 310, 318, 341, 356, 429, 461, 467,

    469, 493–495, 502, 504, 505, 507, 508, 513, 517, 522, 526, 554, 754, 877, 880

Davis, Mr. Mentioned 54

Davis, Charles H. Mentioned 9, 187, 237, 384

Davis, Cressa K. Correspondence with Grenville M. Dodge................. 164

Davis, Jefferson.

Correspondence with

    Adjutant and Inspector General's Office, C. S. A....................... 767

    Bragg, Braxton............................. 599, 614, 619, 653, 658, 659, 707, 897

    Clayton, A. M 727

    Harris, J. W., et al.. 682

    Johnson, C 730

    Johnston, Joseph E 800, 812, 823, 827, 828, 838

    Johnston, William Preston... 599

    Mayo, George Upshur 775

    Mississippi, Governor of.................... 612, 622, 655, 686, 700, 713, 716

    Pemberton, John C.. 767, 772, 786

    Phelan, James... 726, 788

    Van Dorn, Earl 596, 686, 700, 715, 733

    War Department, C. S.................................. 697, 698, 731, 732, 802

Mentioned 423, 437, 488,

    591, 592, 594, 599, 613, 616, 619, 626, 636, 640, 654, 655, 658, 670, 673, 680,

    681, 684, 685, 694, 697, 704, 706, 712, 713, 724, 728, 731, 732, 737, 759–761,

    774, 775, 777, 780–782, 786, 787, 795, 800, 801, 809, 810, 815, 816, 822, 839

Davis, Jefferson C.

Correspondence with W. S. Rosecrans 36, 152

Mentioned 24, 27,

    35, 39, 74, 86, 105, 108, 111, 112, 144, 147, 151, 152, 167, 168, 174, 177, 179, 261

Davis, John A. Mentioned 145, 247

Davis, W. G. M. Mentioned... 765

Davis, William P. Mentioned.. 338, 514

Davis' Bridge, Hatchie River, Tenn. Skirmish at, Sept. 25, 1862. Communications from E. O. C. Ord.. 235

Page.

Davis' Mill, Miss., Commanding Officer at. Correspondence with

Grant, U. S.. 439

Sullivan, J. C. 380

Dawson, W. A. Mentioned 388, 418, 484, 491

Dayton, Lewis M. Mentioned.......................... 435, 538, 581

For correspondence as Aide-de-Camp, see *W. T. Sherman.*

Decatur, Steamer. Mentioned.. 573

De Clouet, Alexander. Mentioned 699

De Courcy, John F. Mentioned................... 580, 584, 888, 891

Dees, Alexander W. Mentioned................................ 248, 340

De Golyer, Samuel. Mentioned....................... 146, 338, 514

Deitzler, George W.

Correspondence with Isaac F. Quinby 34

Mentioned........................ 53, 77, 146, 249, 368, 373, 484, 515

De Kalb, Baron, U. S. S. Mentioned................... 884, 887

Denmark, Tenn. Affair near, July 29, 1862. See *Hatchie Bottom, Tenn.*

Dennis, Elias S.

Correspondence with

Lawler, Michael K... 192

Logan, John A... 180

Mentioned......................... 144, 197, 212, 338, 514

Denver, James W.

Correspondence with

McPherson, James B 445, 452, 548

Sherman, W. T.. 10, 13, 19

War Department, U. S 484

Mentioned 7, 8, 10, 11, 23, 27, 33, 50, 51, 81, 84, 85, 102,
109, 116, 118, 204, 212, 221, 242, 260, 340, 344, 345, 358, 361, 385, 396, 397, 429,
439, 452, 456, 461, 468, 472, 487, 488, 493, 497, 509, 512, 514, 545, 549, 577, 874

Department No. 1. (Confederate.)

Limits defined and extended 624

Merged into Western Department............................ 624, 636

Department No. 2. (Confederate.) See *Western Department.*

Derby, Nelson R. Mentioned................................... 188

Des Arc, Steamer. Mentioned................................. 573

De Saulles, A. B. Mentioned 819

Deslonde, E. A. Mentioned................................... 671

Des Moines, Steamer. Mentioned.......................... 573

Devereux, John G. Mentioned 802

For correspondence as A. A. G., see *Martin L. Smith.*

Dewey, George H. Mentioned............................... 591

Dewey, John L. Mentioned.................................. 591

De Wolff & Bros. Correspondence with Abraham Lincoln 506

D. G. Taylor, Steamer. Mentioned.......................... 573

Dickenson, Edward S. Mentioned........................ 471

Dickerman, Willard A. Mentioned....................... 339

Dickey, Charles. Mentioned 403

Dickey, J. H., Steamer. Mentioned........................ 573

Dickey, Theophilus Lyle.

Assignments to command........................ 4, 20, 30, 363

Correspondence with

Grant, U. S 376, 379, 385, 388, 395, 398, 399, 403, 410

Mizner, John K.. 391

Mentioned 4, 11, 12, 20, 30, 187, 282, 284, 342, 411, 412, 435, 437-439, 516

Page.
Dillon, Edward. Correspondence with John C. Pemberton................. 762
Dillon, Henry. Mentioned 148, 248, 340, 516
Dishon, C. B. Mentioned... 590
Dismukes, W. H. Mentioned.. 845
Dockery, T. P. Mentioned 634, 653
Dodge, Grenville M.
  Assignments to command 242, 310
  Correspondence with
    Breckenridge, W. K. M.. 564
    Bryant, George E 105
    Burke, Patrick E 428
    Davis, Cressa K.. 164
    Grant, U. S... 184, 194, 235, 327, 353, 355, 372,
      377, 388, 399, 400, 403, 411, 427, 436, 457, 482, 488, 489, 497, 524, 530, 532, 543
    Logan, John A 130, 137, 203
    McClernand, John A.. 161, 183
    Mersy, August 403, 404, 457
    Morrison, William R... 450
    Quinby, Isaac F .. 66, 81, 104, 107, 109, 110, 123, 131, 180, 192, 194, 195, 199, 206
    Ross, Leonard F 198
    Sullivan, J. C............................. 389, 391, 414, 431, 432, 458, 488, 555
  Mentioned 77, 202,
      242, 246, 250, 292, 310, 311, 319, 337, 341, 359, 377, 399, 410, 427, 429–431, 436,
      440, 457, 460, 461, 478, 490, 500, 513, 516, 518, 524, 527, 532, 540, 544, 570, 578
Dollins, James J.
  Correspondence with John A. Logan..................................... 125
  Mentioned 125, 144, 250, 338, 514
Donelson, Daniel S. Mentioned................................ 618, 632, 643, 652, 765
Donelson, Fort, Tenn. Embraced in
  Department of the Tennessee.. 278
  District of West Tennessee... 7
D'Or, Louis, Steamer. Mentioned... 764
Doran, John L. Mentioned.................................... 145, 249, 340
Dornblaser, Benjamin. Mentioned 339, 515
Dotson, Josephus. Mentioned... 737
Duble, J. A. Mentioned 30
Du Bois, John V. Mentioned 214, 215, 218–223, 252, 396
Duckworth, W. L. Mentioned.. 639
Duke, Steamer. Mentioned 500, 520
Duke of Argyle, Steamer. Mentioned 573
Dunbar, Steamer. Mentioned 543
Duncan, Johnson K. Mentioned 676, 765
Dutton, Carlos. Correspondence with Adjutant-General's Office, U. S. A..... 495
Dyer, Tenn., Commanding Officer at. Correspondence with J. C. Sullivan. 380
Dyer, Randolph H. Mentioned.. 637, 654
Dyer, W. E. Mentioned 617
Earl, Seth C. Mentioned 339
East Louisiana. Operations in, May 12, 1862–May 14, 1863. Communications
      from John C. Pemberton 834
Eastport, U. S. S. Mentioned.. 200
East Tennessee. Advance upon, and operations in. Communications from
  Bradfute, W. R 597, 607, 611
  Bragg, Braxton 610, 619, 626, 629, 639, 651
  Hill, L. E 593, 607, 611

Page.

East Tennessee. Advance upon, and operations in—Continued. Communications from

War Department, U. S 619

Williams, J. T 604, 613

See also *Halleck to Stanton*, pp. 45, 52, 59; *Stanton to Halleck*, p. 52; *Lincoln to Halleck*, pp. 53, 63.

Also *Courtland and Trinity, Ala. Operations at, etc., July* 25, 1862.

Eaton, Charles G. Mentioned 340

Eaton, John, jr. Mentioned 396

Eckley, Ephraim R. Mentioned........................ 147, 248, 339, 516, 524

Ector, M. D. Mentioned... 765

Eddy, A. R. Mentioned 424, 434

Eddy, Norman. Mentioned.................................... 147, 339, 516

Edie, John R. Mentioned.................................... 146, 513, 517

Edmoistn, John A. Mentioned.. 350

Edmondson, J. H. Correspondence with Daniel Ruggles................. 602, 613

Edson, James C. Mentioned 248

Edwards, Eugene E. Mentioned... 294

E. J. Gay, Steamer. Mentioned 867

Eldridge, Hamilton N. Mentioned....................................... 344

Eldridge, J. W. Mentioned.. 603

Ella, Steamer. Mentioned.. 573

Ellet, Alfred W.

Correspondence with

Army Headquarters............................... 149, 398, 406

Brooks, James 148

War Department, U. S 241, 277, 282

Directed to report to Admiral Porter............... 323

Mentioned...................................... 323

Ellet, Charles, jr.

Correspondence with War Department, U. S................ 8, 9

Mentioned....................................... 40

Ellet, Charles Rivers. Mentioned..................... 277, 887

Elliott, W. L.

Assignments to command 163

Correspondence with

Army Headquarters.................................. 139

Rosecrans, W. S 62

Mentioned.............................. 14, 47, 126, 162, 163

For correspondence as Chief of Staff, see *W. S. Rosecrans.*

Ellis, Towson. Mentioned 648

Elwood, Isaac. Mentioned........................... 144

Embry, B. T. Mentioned 592

Emelin, Steamer. Mentioned 211

Emma, Steamer. Mentioned 573

Empress, Steamer. Mentioned........................ 573

Engelmann, Adolph. Mentioned............ 144, 247, 341, 527

Essex, U. S. S. Mentioned......................... 175

Eugene, Steamer. Mentioned 235, 236

Evans, James. Mentioned 587

Evans, L. R. Mentioned......................... 843, 844

Evans, R. N. Mentioned 350

E. Walsh, Steamer. Mentioned 573

Ewell, Benjamin S. Mentioned 782

Page.

Ewell, Richard S. Mentioned 626
Ewing, Hugh. Mentioned 545,550,556,568,573,574
Express, Steamer. Mentioned.. 508
Falkner, W. C.
    Correspondence with Sterling Price... 668
    Mentioned.. 218,682,689,690
Fall, Phillip. Correspondence with John C. Pemberton 804
Fannie Bullitt, Steamer. Mentioned... 573
Fanny Ogden, Steamer. Mentioned.. 573
Farmington, James. Mentioned 104
Farragut, David G. Mentioned 43,97,463
Farrand, Charles E. Mentioned.. 248
Farrar, F. H., jr. Mentioned.. 633,652
Farrington, Madison J. Mentioned 297
Faulkner, W. W. Mentioned 161,195,281,283
Fauntleroy, Charles M.
    Correspondence with Edwin J. Harvie....................................... 841
    Mentioned... 782
Fearing, Benjamin D. Mentioned 112,169
Featherston, W. S.
    Assignments to command.. 846
    Mentioned... 846
Feild, H. R. Mentioned 603
Fentress, Francis. Mentioned.. 297
Ferd. Kennett, Steamer. Mentioned 867
Ferguson, S. W. Mentioned 903
Ferrell, Charles M. Mentioned.................... 144,212,247,341,507
Fight, Major [?]. Mentioned... 755
Fisher, Cyrus W. Mentioned 112,169,173
Fisher, James M. Mentioned.. 344
Fisk, Clinton B.
    Correspondence with
        Curtis, Samuel R.................................. 486,494,504
        McClernand, John A.. 558
    Mentioned................................... 472,494,501,561,562
Fitch, Graham N. Mentioned................... 14,36,37,54–56,140
Fitch, Henry S.
    Correspondence with
        Army Headquarters.. 480
        Sherman, W. T.. 156
    Mentioned............... 159,170,237,243,277,289,345,406,408,426
Fitch, Le Roy. Mentioned.. 886
Fitzgerald, E. Mentioned.. 603
Flash, Henry. Mentioned 639
Fleming, L. J. Mentioned 625
Flood, James P. Mentioned 146,250
Florida. Military departments embracing 624,627,649
Florida Troops. Mentioned.
    Artillery, Light—*Batteries:* Robertson's,* 633.
    Infantry—*Regiments:* 1st, 632.
F. Loring, Steamer. Mentioned 573
Flournoy, T. C. Correspondence with J. H. Lewis.......................... 686
Foard, A. J. Mentioned... 648

* Claimed also for Alabama.

Page.

Font, Captain. Mentioned 525
Foote, Henry S., jr. Mentioned 617
Forbes, James W. Mentioned 499
Force, Manning F. Mentioned 144, 247, 338, 514
Ford, William. Mentioned 146, 517
Forest Queen, Steamer. Mentioned 261, 435, 549, 573
Forest Rose, Steamer. Mentioned 887
Forney, John H.
    Assignments to command 636, 659
    Correspondence with
        Pemberton, John C 768, 773
        Ruggles, Daniel 774
    Mentioned 601, 636, 657, 659, 673, 726, 764
Forrest, A. H. Mentioned 807
Forrest, Jeffrey E. Mentioned 558
Forrest, N. B.
    Correspondence with J. R. Chalmers 838
    Mentioned 15, 399, 400, 405,
        414, 415, 423, 426–428, 431, 432, 435, 441, 443, 456, 457, 463, 467, 474, 475,
        477, 480, 483, 484, 488–492, 494, 495, 497–500, 504, 505, 508, 511, 518, 520,
        523, 524, 530, 532, 538, 558, 652, 727, 755, 765, 807, 811, 813, 817, 823, 835
Forsse, Eric. Mentioned 145
Foster, John S. Mentioned 146, 212, 247, 342, 512, 515
Foster, T. S. Mentioned 598
Fowler, Alexander. Mentioned 340, 514
Fowler, Pleasant. Mentioned 737
Fox, Gustavus V. For correspondence, etc., see Navy Department, U. S.
Fraser, P. A. Correspondence with W. T. Sherman 287
Freeman, H. C. Mentioned 528
Fremaux, L. Mentioned 654
Friar's Point, Miss., Commanding Officer at. Correspondence with U. S.
        Grant 393, 503
Frick, Kilian. Mentioned 435, 538
Frisbie, Orton. Mentioned 212, 338, 350
Frost, D. M. Mentioned 859
Frost, Edward D. Mentioned 770
Fry, Jacob.
    Correspondence with J. C. Sullivan 364, 394, 414, 432
    Mentioned 144, 247, 481
Fuller, Allen C. Mentioned 307
Fuller, John W. Mentioned 248, 339, 436, 492, 498, 531, 538
Fulton, A. S. Mentioned 603
Funke, Otto. Mentioned 509
Gaddy, James E. Mentioned 871, 873
Gaines, Thomas W. Mentioned 517
Galloway Switch, Tenn. Scout to, Oct. 23, 1862. See Memphis, Tenn. Scout
        from, Oct. 21–24, 1862.
Gamble, Hamilton R. Mentioned 279
        For correspondence, etc., see Missouri, Governor of.
Gardner, Franklin.
    Assignments to command 796
    Correspondence with John C. Pemberton 837
    Mentioned 618, 633, 652, 765, 796, 814, 815, 823, 827
Garesché, J. P. For correspondence as Aide-de-Camp, see W. S. Rosecrans.

Page.

Garland, R. R. Mentioned... 568
Garner, George G. Mentioned.............................. 635, 648
    For correspondence as A. A. G., see *Braxton Bragg.*
Gassaway, Henry. Mentioned 591
Gates, Elijah. Mentioned......................... 634, 652, 683, 684
Gay, E. J., Steamer. Mentioned............................... 867
General Anderson, Steamer. Mentioned................. 510, 573
General Bragg, U. S. S. Mentioned 886
General Quitman, Steamer. Mentioned.................. 862
George, J. Z.
    Assignments to command....................................... 745
    Mentioned 745
Georgia. Military departments embracing...................... 624, 627
Georgia Troops. Mentioned.
    Cavalry—*Regiments :* 2d, 835.
    Infantry—*Regiments :* 5th, 633; 40th, 806, 824; 41st, 603, 632, 806; 42d,
      43d, 806, 824; 51st, 806; 52d, 824.
Gholson, Captain. Mentioned.................................... 665
Gibson, William L. Mentioned 81, 84, 146
Giesy, Henry H. Mentioned 523
Gilbert, Alfred W. Mentioned 147, 221
Gilbert, C. C. Mentioned 239
Gilbert, Franklin T. Mentioned.................. 146, 212, 247, 342
Gilbert, Othniel. Mentioned 146
Gile, David A. Mentioned 533
Gillam, Barclay C. Mentioned 339
Gillespie, John W. Correspondence with Earl Van Dorn.......... 771
Gillmore, Robert A. Mentioned............................ 248, 339
Gilmore, J. B. Mentioned....................................... 709
Gladiator, Steamer. Mentioned............. 285, 288, 289, 573, 860
Gladney, Richard Strong. Mentioned 666
Goddard, C. For correspondence as A. A. A. G., see *W. S. Rosecrans.*
Goodell, Lieutenant. Mentioned................................. 403
Gooding, Michael. Mentioned................................... 147
Goodman, M. A. Mentioned...................................... 591
Goodman, W. Mentioned 598, 604
Goodwin, J. W. Mentioned 625, 648
Goodwin, Wilson. Mentioned................................... 418
Gordon, John A.
    Correspondence with Thomas A. Davies...................... 352
    Mentioned.. 146
Gorgas, A. B. Mentioned.. 539
Gorgas, Josiah. Mentioned........................ 686, 700, 749
    For correspondence, etc., see *Ordnance Department, C. S. A.*
Gorman, J. W. For correspondence as A. A. G., see *W. A. Gorman.*
Gorman, Willis A.
    Correspondence with
      Curtis, Samuel R 395, 414, 421, 434, 464, 469, 552, 555, 578
      Grant, U. S.............................. 406, 464, 555, 579
      Hurlbut, Stephen A...................... 496, 522, 526, 548
      McClernand, John A 562
      Sherman, W. T 402, 408, 423, 477, 875, 877
      Steele, Frederick.. 412
    Mentioned 383, 408, 410, 412, 414, 426, 434,
      441, 464, 469, 501, 507, 510, 511, 522, 526, 552, 556, 558, 561, 563, 578, 886

Page.

Gould, Sergeant. Mentioned... **44, 49**

Gracie, A., jr. Mentioned... 765

Graham, G. W. & Co. Mentioned... 350

Graham, John. Mentioned.. 606

Grand Junction, Tenn. Expedition to, Sept. 20–22, 1862. See *Bolivar, Tenn. Expedition from, Sept. 20–22, 1862.*

Grand Junction, Tenn., Commanding Officer at. For correspondence, etc., see *J. McDermott.*

Granger, Gordon.

    Correspondence with

        Army Headquarters.. 139

        Rosecrans, W. S 76, 112, 151, 162–164, 167

        Sheridan, Philip H... 75, 111, 132

    Mentioned.. 41, 52, 62, 86, 106, 111, 139, 144, 148, 152, 162–164, 168, 169, 177, 181, 193, 194, 197–200, 203, 208, 239, 286

Grant, U. S.

    Assignments to command 3, 101, 102, 278, 292, 294

    Controversy with A. Stager. See *Tennessee, Department of the.*

    Co-operation of Curtis with. See

        June 10, 1862–Jan. 20, 1863. *Northern Mississippi. Operations in.*

        Oct. 31, 1862–Jan. 10, 1863. *Mississippi Central Railroad. Operations on the.*

        Dec. 20, 1862–Jan. 3, 1863. *Vicksburg, Miss. Operations against.*

        Jan. 20–July 4, 1863. *Vicksburg, Miss. Operations against.*

    Correspondence with

        Adjutant-General's Office, U. S. A 155

        Allen, Robert... 399, 552

        Army Headquarters 136, 142, 148, 150, 151, 160, 164, 168, 175, 176, 179, 182, 183, 185–189, 191, 194, 197–199, 202, 206, 209, 213, 214, 220, 222, 225, 227, 228, 232–235, 238, 240, 243, 250, 262, 267, 268, 270, 274, 276, 279–281, 283, 290, 296, 298, 302, 303, 308, 318, 377, 386, 425, 461, 503, 530, 542–544, 549, 550, 553, 555, 560, 564, 570, 573

        Asboth, A.. 573

        Bolivar, Tenn., Commanding Officer at 439

        Bowers, T. S 510

        Brayman, M 358, 360, 440, 521, 527

        Buell, Don Carlos 168, 174, 177

        Burke, P. E 270

        Callender, F. D... 536, 537

        Columbus, Ky., Commanding Officer at 293

        Crocker, M. M 190

        Curtis, Samuel R 356, 555, 566, 578

        Davies, Thomas A.............. 303, 309–311, 319, 425, 481, 520, 521, 535

        Davis' Mills, Miss., Commanding Officer at 439

        Dickey, Theophilus Lyle............ 376, 379, 385, 388, 395, 398, 399, 403, 410

        Dodge, Grenville M 184, 194, 235, 327, 353, 355, 372, 377, 388, 399, 400, 403, 411, 427, 436, 457, 482, 488, 489, 497, 524, 530, 532, 543

        Friar's Point, Miss., Commanding Officer at.......................... 393, 503

        Gorman, Willis A 406, 464, 555, 579

        Grierson, Benjamin H 465, 466, 473–475, 483

        Halleck, H. W... 26, 29, 36, 41, 43, 46, 54–56, 60, 67, 79, 82, 83, 87, 88, 90, 108, 114, 130

        Hamilton, C. S 292, 293, 300, 301, 304, 305, 310–312, 315– 318, 320, 325, 326, 329, 330, 342–344, 346, 347, 349, 357, 359, 362, 365–370, 385, 387, 389, 422, 435, 451, 455–457, 473, 509, 518, 524, 525, 530–532, 541, 550, 575

Page.

Grant, U. S.—Continued.
Correspondence with

Hart, James H.. 183

Hatch, Edward.. 442, 466

Haynie, Isham N 257–259, 267, 387, 399, 400, 467

Hillyer, William S.. 457, 531

Holdredge, John C... 128

Holly Springs, Miss., Commanding Officer at 439

Hovey, Alvin P... 98

Humboldt, Tenn., Commanding Officer at............................... 293

Hurlbut, Stephen A 30, 215,
226, 228, 231–234, 238–240, 243, 250, 253, 255, 256, 259, 263, 267–271, 274, 293,
305, 306, 313, 318, 323, 326, 330, 331, 337, 480, 503, 506, 508, 522, 525, 526, 548

Knox, Thomas W 894

La Grange, Tenn., Commanding Officer at............................. 439

Lawler, M. K 509

Logan, John A.. 128–130, 199

Loomis, John M 469

Lowe, William W.. 126, 181, 428, 541

McArthur, John 454

McClernand, John A... 130,
135, 150, 425, 463, 501, 546, 551–553, 559, 561, 563, 567, 574

McDermott, John......................... 379, 386, 439, 458, 459, 464, 467

McPherson, James B..... 293, 294, 300, 301, 306, 307, 313, 314, 317, 324, 327, 328,
331, 376, 389, 423, 428, 435–437, 445, 446, 451, 452, 468, 469, 472–474, 478, 487,
488, 497, 499, 505, 509, 511, 518, 519, 521, 525, 531–533, 545, 554, 557, 558, 569

Marsh, C. Carroll................... 442, 443, 447–450, 454, 455, 468, 472, 484

Memphis, Tenn., Commanding Officer at 480

Mizner, John K 411, 412, 437–439, 443, 448, 472, 484, 493, 498

Murphy, R. C 439, 440, 444

Norton, A. S 370, 416, 483

Ord, E. O. C.. 230, 239

Parsons, L. B.. 355

Pennock, A. M... 426, 530, 541, 544, 550

Porter, David D 356, 380, 404, 426, 551

Pride, George G 380, 434

Quinby, Isaac F.. 107,
123, 153, 179, 184, 203, 236, 353, 354, 357–359, 456, 473, 504, 524, 542

Rawlins, John A.. 299

Reynolds, C. A.. 380

Richardson, R. V 418

Rosecrans, W. S................... 103, 107, 108, 111, 120, 124, 130–132, 139, 148,
151, 162–164, 166, 169, 176, 177, 181, 191, 196, 198, 203, 204, 207, 208, 210, 213–
215, 217–224, 227, 233, 234, 241–243, 251, 252, 254, 275, 276, 283, 291, 301, 400

Ross, Leonard F.. 197

Sherman, W. T.............. 44, 66, 79, 84, 109, 121, 140, 141, 166, 169, 178, 187,
201, 204, 210, 215, 217, 234, 244, 259, 272, 279, 285, 288, 307, 315, 322, 335, 347,
366, 367, 371, 374, 396, 408, 412, 414, 426, 570, 855, 857, 860, 870, 874, 892, 895

Shirk, James W... 318

Smith, John E... 492

Sprague, John W 440

Stager, Anson.. 368, 371

Steele, Frederick.. 392, 410

Sullivan, J. C 357, 358, 360, 371, 396, 398, 400, 405, 413, 415, 423, 429–
431, 436, 458, 464, 465, 477, 483, 489–492, 498, 505, 532, 538, 540, 543, 555, 574

Page,

Grant, U. S.—Continued.
Correspondence with
Thompson, M. Jeff 98
Trenton, Tenn., Commanding Officer at 293
Van Duzer, J. C 230, 378
War Department, U. S 346, 347, 371, 378, 421
Webster, J. D 337
Mentioned 3, 22,
25, 27, 28, 30, 32, 40, 42, 45, 49, 64, 72, 73, 83, 84, 90, 96, 98–101, 121, 122,
142–144, 156, 158, 161, 162, 167, 168, 170–172, 174, 177, 186, 190, 192, 195, 204,
206, 228–230, 245, 246, 253, 258, 262, 269, 270, 274, 278, 280, 282, 284, 286, 287,
298, 299, 301, 307–309, 311, 318, 320, 324, 333, 337, 338, 345, 351, 352, 354–356,
361, 368, 382, 384–386, 392, 394, 397, 398, 401–403, 406, 407, 409, 413, 415, 420–
422, 424, 432, 433, 438, 441, 442, 446, 447, 457–459, 462, 463, 470, 471, 480, 493–
496, 500–503, 505–507, 512, 514, 520, 521, 526–529, 534, 545, 548, 550, 555,
556, 558, 559, 562, 564, 566–568, 575, 576, 580, 582, 585, 588, 591, 665, 667, 691,
708, 732, 758, 766, 768, 771, 800, 801, 806, 807, 809, 811–813, 822, 823, 827, 830,
832, 839, 862, 863, 867, 868, 872, 873, 875–877, 879, 880, 882, 886, 888, 893, 894
Orders in cases of
Abandoned property 156
Church services 30
Coin and U. S. Treasury notes 123
Deserters from Confederate Army 130
Guerrillas 69
Jews 424, 544
Non-combatants 396
Private property 87, 326, 331, 349, 350, 505
Provisions for the poor and destitute 319, 405
Provost-marshals' duties 363
Public property 70
Quartering troops 469, 505
Slaves, etc 115, 396
Trade and intercourse 123, 130, 155, 163, 349, 400, 569, 575
109th Illinois 511, 523, 586
Graves, William H. Mentioned 247, 341, 460, 476, 477, 527
Great Western, U. S. S. Mentioned 887
Green, Galen E. Mentioned 342
Green, Martin E.
Assignments to command 824
Mentioned............ 634, 652, 660, 661, 683, 733, 736, 739, 765, 794, 824, 845
Greene, O. D. Mentioned.. 22
Gregg, John.
Correspondence with John C. Pemberton 827
Mentioned................... 765, 777, 778, 806, 821, 824–826, 828, 829
Grenada, Miss.
Confederate troops at. Organization, strength, etc.
June 14, 1862 600
January 8, 1863 829
Expedition to the vicinity of, Nov. 27–Dec. 6, 1862. Communications from
Adjutant and Inspector General's Office, C. S. A 782
Army Headquarters 320, 327, 382, 401
Curtis, Samuel R 320–323, 382, 383, 395
Griffith, John S 779
Holmes, Theophilus H 766

Page.

Grenada, Miss.---Continued.

Expedition to the vicinity of, Nov. 27–Dec. 6, 1862. Communications from

Jones, E. P 762, 763

Pemberton, John C 763, 770–772, 774, 778, 779

Price, Sterling... 779

Ruggles, Daniel 771, 773, 774

Sherman, W. T 361

Van Dorn, Earl 767, 768, 777–779

See also *Sherman to Rawlins,* p. 408; *Pemberton to Johnston,* p. 784; *Sherman to Grant,* p. 874.

Gresham, Walter Q. Mentioned 145, 247, 339, 515

Greusel, Nicholas. Mentioned 148

Grier, David P. Mentioned.................................... 516

Grierson, Benjamin H.

Correspondence with

Brayman, M... 465

Grant, U. S 465, 466, 473–475, 483

Hamilton, C. S 483

McPherson, James B... 543

Sullivan, J. C.... 468

Mentioned.... 37, 128, 142, 146, 150, 167, 189, 205, 209, 211, 212, 217, 247, 272, 277, 289, 335, 341, 347, 364, 374–376, 396, 402, 403, 409, 412, 437, 439, 448, 455, 457, 461, 472, 473, 475, 476, 478, 507, 509, 512, 513, 516, 533, 578, 588, 855, 861, 870, 874

Griffin, G. G.

Correspondence with Braxton Bragg 625

Mentioned 625

Griffin, R. B. Correspondence with William W. Lowe 126

Griffith, John S.

Correspondence with Earl Van Dorn 779

Mentioned 747, 774, 778, 779, 839

Griffith, Richard R. Mentioned 146, 247

Griffiths, H. H. Mentioned 539

Grimes, S. F. Mentioned 258, 267

Grosskopff, Edward. Mentioned 340

Gulf, District of the. (Confederate.)

Constituted and limits defined 636

Forney, John H.

Assigned to command 636

Relieved from command... 659

Revocation of order relieving from command 659

Jones, Samuel.

Assigned to command 659

Order assigning revoked 659

Gumbart, George C. Mentioned............................ 144, 213, 247, 338, 515

Guerrillas. Treatment of, etc. See *Conduct of the War.*

Guy, W. W. Mentioned 834

Gwin, William. Mentioned..................... 244, 392, 407, 588, 879, 883–885

Haines, Thomas J.

Correspondence with H. W. Halleck................................ 34

Mentioned 507

Haines, William F. Mentioned.................................. 734, 739

Hall, Cyrus. Mentioned 145, 247, 339, 515

Hall, William. Mentioned................................... 249, 340

Page.

Halleck, Henry W.

  Assignments to command.. 90
  Correspondence with
    Allen, Robert 61
    Cates, O. G 91, 92
    Chenowith, B. P 53
    Grant, U. S... 26, 29, 36, 41, 43, 46, 54–56, 60, 67, 79, 82, 83, 87, 88, 90, 108, 114, 130
    Haines, Thomas J... 34
    Hurlbut, Stephen A.. 31, 32, 37
    Johnson, Andrew 14, 22
    Lincoln, Abraham 53, 59, 63, 64, 70, 71, 76, 88, 90, 97, 98
    Lowe, William W... 21
    McClernand, John A.................... 5, 8, 21, 38, 56, 60, 61, 64, 70, 72, 73, 94
    McPherson, James B 78
    Memphis, Tenn., Commanding Officer at.................................... 22
    Myers, William 61
    Nelson, William 21, 23
    Ord, E. O. C... 26
    Pope, John 5, 9, 18, 20
    Quinby, Isaac F 4, 20, 86
    Rosecrans, W. S 14, 24, 26, 34, 42–44, 47, 48, 56, 57, 61, 64, 65, 68, 73, 74, 108
    Sanford, W. W... 94
    Sherman, W. T.... 17–19, 21, 22, 27, 32, 39, 40, 42, 44, 48, 49, 58, 70, 79, 83, 90, 100
    Thomas, George H 24, 77
    War Dept., U. S. 6, 12, 18, 23, 26, 31, 34, 40–42, 43, 45, 52, 59, 60, 67, 76–78, 90, 91, 97
      For correspondence as General-in-Chief, see *Army Headquarters.*
  Mentioned 6, 14, 15,
      19, 20, 25, 27, 29, 31, 32, 38, 40, 44, 48, 66, 72, 73, 77, 79, 84–86, 88, 90, 91,
      93, 95, 107, 108, 122, 167–171, 179, 188, 218, 229, 261, 262, 280, 282, 290, 291,
      309, 318, 320–323, 336, 343, 347, 350, 353, 384, 391–393, 395, 399, 402, 407_
      410, 413, 414, 420, 423–425, 436, 449, 461, 462, 480–482, 494, 500–503, 508,
      520, 526, 528, 529, 531, 534, 544, 545, 566, 595, 598, 642, 665, 868, 876, 892
  Relinquishes immediate command of troops in Department of the Mississippi. 101
  Transfer of, etc., to Washington, D. C. Communications from
    Halleck, H. W.. 64, 88, 90, 91, 98
    Lincoln, Abraham... 76, 90, 97
    Sherman, W. T.. 100
    War Department, U. S 90
      See also *Lincoln to Halleck, p. 63.*

Hallonquist, J. H. Mentioned.. 648, 678
Halstead, M. Correspondence with W. T. Sherman......................... 895
Hamilton, Charles S.
  Assignments to command...................... 297, 298, 364, 553, 565, 569
  Correspondence with
    Army Headquarters.. 574
    Grant, U. S 292, 293, 300, 301, 304, 305, 310–312, 315–
      318, 320, 325, 326, 329, 330, 342–344, 346, 347, 349, 357, 359, 362, 365–370, 385,
      387, 389, 422, 435, 451, 455–457, 473, 509, 518, 524, 525, 530–532, 541, 550, 575
    Grierson, Benjamin H 483
    Lee, Albert L... 207, 369, 373
    McArthur, John 373, 525
    Quinby, Isaac F 524, 548
    Rosecrans, W. S 47, 48, 57, 66, 75, 214, 224, 254, 263, 264
    Smith, John E.. 544
    Whitehurst, Eli.. 306

Page.

Hamilton, Charles S.—Continued.

Mentioned 14, 36, 47–49, 57, 58, 61–66, 68, 74,
84–86, 144, 147, 167, 168, 200, 203, 207, 208, 214, 215, 218, 220–224, 243, 248,
252, 263, 264, 266, 270, 294, 297, 301, 306, 307, 311, 314, 317, 324, 325, 331, 338,
339, 364, 366, 367, 371, 451, 452, 458, 459, 492, 524, 553, 564, 565, 569, 577, 838

Hamilton, Schuyler. Mentioned 41, 52

Hamlen, S. L. Mentioned 878

Hammond, J. H. Mentioned 158, 435, 538, 581
For correspondence as A. A. G., see *W. T. Sherman.*

Hammond, William A. Mentioned 255

Hampton, Wade, jr. Mentioned 782

Hancock, John. Mentioned 249

Handy, Truman. Mentioned 357

Hardee, T. S. Mentioned 639

Hardee, William J.
Assignments to command 635, 636, 639
Correspondence with
Jones, Samuel 660
Wheeler, Joseph 651
Mentioned 29, 140,
423, 600, 618, 619, 628, 633, 635, 636, 639, 641, 648, 651, 652, 656, 657, 659, 765
Staff. Announcements of 639

Harding, Abner C. Mentioned 250, 517, 731, 732

Harding, Chester, jr. Mentioned 145, 249

Hare, Abraham M. Mentioned 145

Harman, B. Desha. Correspondence with Daniel Ruggles 598, 605

Harper, Mr. Mentioned 54

Harrington, Fazilo A. Mentioned 193

Harris, D. B. Mentioned 615

Harris, Isham G. Mentioned 670, 742, 743
For correspondence, etc., see *Tennessee, Governor of.*

Harris, John V. Mentioned 818, 846

Harris, J. W., et al. Correspondence with Jefferson Davis 682

Harris, S. Mentioned 824

Harris, T. H. For correspondence as A. A. G., see *J. C. Sullivan.*

Harris, Thomas W.
Correspondence with J. C. Sullivan 365
Mentioned 146, 181, 247

Hart, Alexander T. Mentioned 540

Hart, James H.
Correspondence with U. S. Grant 183
Mentioned 517

Hart, Levi W. Mentioned 212, 247, 397, 539

Hart, Michael. Mentioned 871, 873

Hartline, B. F. Mentioned 591

Harts, P. W. Mentioned 878

Harvie, Edwin J.
Correspondence with Charles M. Fauntleroy 841
Mentioned 782
Report of inspection of the Army of the Mississippi 841

Hassendeubel, F. Mentioned 539

Hatch, Edward.
Correspondence with U. S. Grant 442, 466
Mentioned 75, 132, 148,
300, 364, 468, 469, 473–475, 478, 484, 487, 488, 498, 499, 505, 509, 516, 521, 534

Page.

Hatchie Bottom, Tenn. Affair at, July 29, 1862. Communications from
L)gan, John A... 136
McClernand, John A... 135
Hatchie River, Miss. Skirmish on the, July 5, 1862. Report of D. M. Caldwell. 73
Hawes, J. M. Mentioned.. 579, 673
Hawkins, Isaac R.
Correspondence with J. C. Sullivan... 444
Mentioned... 174, 341, 394
Hawthorn, A. T. Mentioned... 619, 633, 652
Hayes, Charles S. Mentioned.......................... 145, 248, 293, 339
Haynie, Isham N.
Correspondence with
Carter, James M.. 415
Grant, U. S....................................... 257–259, 267, 387, 399, 400, 467
Lawler, M. K... 192
Logan, John A... 175, 199, 203, 253
McClernand, John A.. 180
Silence, Ned R.. 498
Sullivan, J. C.......... 313, 389, 415, 458, 467, 477, 484, 491, 493, 497, 498
Mentioned.............. 174, 181, 212, 247, 341, 359, 465, 489, 491, 492, 877
Hays, Lieutenant. Mentioned.. 253
Heath, Albert. Mentioned... 340, 514, 523
Hébert, Louis.
Correspondence with
Adams, Wirt... 836
Pemberton, John C.. 812
Price, Sterling.. 720
Mentioned............. 592, 634, 652, 683, 708, 709, 718, 720, 733, 735, 736, 804, 831
Hecker, Frederick. Mentioned... 300
Heg, Hans C. Mentioned.. 35, 147
Heiman, A. Mentioned... 729
Helm, B. H. Mentioned... 181, 233, 765
Henderson, R. J. Mentioned.. 824
Henderson Station, Tenn. Capture of, Nov. 25, 1862. Communications from
Brayman, M.. 359
Grant, U. S... 360
Lawler, M. K.. 360
Sullivan, J. C.. 360, 574
Henley, John W. Mentioned... 591
Henning, Henry R. Mentioned... 338
Henry, Fort, Tenn. Embraced in
Department of the Tennessee... 278
District of West Tennessee... 7
Henry von Phul, Steamer. Mentioned...................................... 573
Hensler, John E. Mentioned.. 146
Hernando, Miss. Expedition to, Sept. 8–13, 1862. See *Memphis, Tenn. Expedition from, Sept.* 8–13, 1862.
Herrick, Thomas P. Mentioned............................... 94, 248, 340, 516
Herrick, Walter F. Mentioned.. 248
Herridge, T. T.
Correspondence with P. D. Roddey.. 605
Mentioned... 605
Herron, Francis J. Mentioned.................... 395, 424, 477, 478, 508, 568
Hescock, Henry. Mentioned.. 147
Heth, Henry. Mentioned... 765

Page.

Heubach, G. R. Mentioned 881

Hewlett, W. A. Mentioned 834, 846

Hiawatha, Steamer. Mentioned 573

Hickenlooper, Andrew. Mentioned 249

Hickory, Tenn. Scout to, Oct. 23, 1862. See *Memphis, Tenn. Scout from, Oct. 21–24, 1862.*

Hickory Valley, Tenn., Commanding Officer at. Correspondence with
 J. C. Sullivan 380

Hicks, Scout. Mentioned 132

Higgins, Edward. Mentioned 792

Hildebrand, Jesse. Mentioned 146, 202

Hill, General. Mentioned 230

Hill, D. H. Mentioned 670

Hill, J. F. Mentioned 592

Hill, L. E.
 Correspondence with
  Beauregard, G. T 593
  Bradfute, W. R 607, 611
 Mentioned 607, 611

Hill, Samuel, Steamer. Mentioned 867

Hill, Sylvester G. Mentioned 517

Hill, W. Mentioned 249

Hillis, David B. Mentioned 248, 339

Hillyer, William S.
 Appointed Provost-Marshal-General of Army of the Tennessee 31
 Correspondence with U. S. Grant 457, 531
 Mentioned 30, 31, 270, 417, 857, 862
  For correspondence as A. D. C., see *U. S. Grant.*

Hindman, T. C. Mentioned 244,
  347, 395, 409, 424, 433, 478, 578, 620, 628, 645, 783, 784, 787, 810, 876

Hinsdill, Charles B. Mentioned 345

Hiriart, E. Mentioned 816

Hitt, Daniel F. Mentioned 247, 515

Hodges, Steamer. Mentioned 828

Hoepner, A. Mentioned 140, 158

Hoffman, William. Mentioned 60

Hoffmann, Louis. Mentioned 539

Hoge, George B. Mentioned 340, 344, 539, 556, 557

Hogg, Harvey.
 Correspondence with John A. Logan 135, 136
 Mentioned 110, 135–138, 146, 153, 161

Hogg, J. L. Mentioned 592

Holdredge, John C. Correspondence with U. S. Grant 128

Holland, Dick F. Mentioned 903

Holloway, William R. Mentioned 310

Holly Springs, Miss.
 Established as main depot for supplies 380
 Expedition to, June 15–18, 1862. Communications from
  Bragg, Braxton 608
  Halleck, H. W 18
  Hurlbut, Stephen A 12
  Ruggles, Daniel 603, 604, 607, 608, 611, 612
  Sherman, W. T 11, 13, 17
   See also *Sherman to Kelton,* p. 27.

                                                                            Page.
Holly Springs, Miss.—Continued.
    Expedition from, July 25–Aug. 1, 1862. Communications from
        Army Headquarters.. 142
        Bragg, Braxton.. 648, 649
        Bryant, George E.. 137, 141
        Dodge, Grenville M... 131, 137
        Hardee, William J... 651
        Hogg, Harvey.. 135
        Logan, John A.. 133–139, 142
        McClernand, John A.................................... 133–138, 150
        Ross, Leonard F...................................... 120, 124–126
     See also *Rosecrans to Sheridan*, p. 139; *Sherman to Quinby*, p. 142; *Grant to Halleck*, p. 150.
    Also
        July 27, 1862. *Toone's Station, Tenn. Affair near.*
           28, 1862. *Humboldt, Tenn. Skirmish near.*
           29, 1862. *Hatchie Bottom, Tenn. Affair at.*
    Scout toward, Sept. 5–6, 1862. See *Sherman to Rawlins*, pp. 204, 870; *Sherman to Pemberton*, p. 872.
    Skirmish near, July 1, 1862. See *Sherman to Rawlins*, p. 84.
Holly Springs, Miss., Commanding Officer at. Correspondence with U. S.
       Grant... 439
Holman, John H. Mentioned... 248, 516
Holmes, Steamer. Mentioned.. 867
Holmes, Samuel A. Mentioned.......................... 147, 248, 339, 516
Holmes, Theophilus H.
    Assignments to command...................................... 655
    Correspondence with
        Adjutant and Inspector General's Office, C. S. A.................. 753,
             757, 765, 768, 782, 783, 786, 787, 793
        Blanchard, Albert G... 766
        Johnston, Joseph E.. 810
        Pemberton, John C....................................... 748, 766
        Ruggles, Daniel... 724
    Mentioned... 244,
       288, 347, 433, 477, 497, 510, 511, 578, 653, 655, 728, 737–739, 747, 748, 751–754,
       756–759, 762, 763, 766–768, 770–772, 777, 780, 781, 785, 801, 827, 859, 874
Holston, John G. F.
    Announced as Senior Medical Officer, Army of the Tennessee............. 30
    Mentioned.. 30, 266
Holt, Joseph. Mentioned.. 892
Home, Steamer. Mentioned....................................... 522, 764
Hooe, Roy Mason. For correspondence as A. A. G., see *Daniel Ruggles.*
Hooker, Joseph. Mentioned... 230
Hopkins, Henry. Mentioned... 147
Horney, Leonidas. Mentioned....................................... 248
Horton, Mr. Mentioned... 17
Hotaling, John R. Mentioned.................................... 176, 342
Hotchkiss, Charles T. For correspondence as A. A. A. G., see *John A. McClernand.*
Hotchkiss, William A. Mentioned.................................. 147
Houghtaling, Charles. Mentioned.................................. 147
House, Captain. Mentioned... 258

Page.

Hovey, Alvin P.
Correspondence with
Curtis, Samuel R 323, 384
Grant, U. S 98
Sherman W. T 856
Thompson, M. Jeff 99
Mentioned 30, 89, 109, 111, 114, 121, 122, 177,
322, 352, 361, 382, 384, 393, 395, 403, 407, 408, 503, 508, 522, 861, 862, 874, 875
Hovey, C. E. Mentioned 539, 549, 581, 584, 891
Howard, O. H. Mentioned 435, 538
Howard, R. A. Mentioned 838
Howe, James H. Mentioned 340, 344, 861
Howe, John H. Mentioned 338
Hoxton, L. Mentioned 639
Hubbard, James M. Mentioned 45
Hubbard, Lucius F. Mentioned 248, 339
Huger, Benjamin. Mentioned 670
Huger, John M. Mentioned 648
Hugunin, James R. Mentioned 249, 516
Humboldt, Tenn. Skirmish near, July 28, 1862. Communications from
Grant, U. S 129, 130
Holdredge, John C 128
Logan, John A 128–130
Humboldt, Tenn., Commanding Officer at. Correspondence with
Grant, U. S 293
Sullivan, J. C 380
Hume, William. Mentioned 730, 731
Humes, W. Y. C. Mentioned 729, 733
Humphrey, Thomas W. Mentioned 515
Hunsaker, J. C. Mentioned 591
Hunt, T. W. Mentioned 639
Hunt, W. R. Mentioned 643
Hunter, David. Mentioned 92
Hunter, William. Mentioned 339, 515
Hurlbut, Frederick J. Mentioned 249
Hurlbut, Stephen A.
Assignments to command 51, 268, 297, 353, 355, 362, 433, 461, 542, 553
Correspondence with
Army Headquarters 470, 496
Curtis, Samuel R 499
Cushman, W. H. W 32
Davies, Thomas A 501, 519
Gorman, Willis A 496, 522, 526, 548
Grant, U. S 30, 215,
226, 228, 231–234, 238–240, 243, 250, 253, 255, 256, 259, 263, 267–271, 274, 293,
305, 306, 313, 318, 323, 326, 330, 331, 337, 480, 503, 506, 508, 522, 525, 526, 548
Halleck, H. W 31, 32, 37
Lauman, Jacob G 228
Logan, John A 231
McClernand, John A 37
McPherson, James B 278, 297, 299, 305
Marsh, C. Carroll 306
Rosecrans, W. S 267
Ross, Leonard F 253, 270, 274

Hurlbut, Stephen A.—Continued.   Page.
Correspondence with
Sherman, W. T... 10, 11, 28, 32, 38, 45, 50, 58, 88, 89
Veatch, J. C... 12
Mentioned. 7-9, 12, 13, 18, 21, 23, 27, 32, 34, 38–40, 42, 44, 48, 49, 51, 55, 58, 60, 72, 73, 79,
84, 85, 96, 99, 100, 106, 109, 114, 118, 119, 121–123, 143, 145, 149, 150, 168, 169,
173, 189, 204, 205, 210, 211, 216, 220, 228, 229, 233, 239, 252, 267–269, 277, 297,
307, 311, 319, 337, 341, 348, 353, 355, 362, 387, 413, 425, 432, 433, 447, 453, 461,
463, 471, 479, 493, 502, 510, 511, 531, 542, 553, 563, 656, 704, 710, 858, 874, 876
Hurlbut, Valeria. Correspondence with W. T. Sherman....................... 860
Hurst, Fielding. Mentioned... 247, 342, 432
Hurt, Lieutenant. Mentioned.. 747
Hurt, R. B. Mentioned.. 620
Hutchens, William D. Mentioned... 146, 486
Hutton, T. H. Mentioned.. 819
Ihrie, George P.
Correspondence with J. C. Sullivan.. 458
Mentioned.. 505
Orders, General, series 1862: No. 1, 876; No. 2, 877.
For correspondence as Aide-de-Camp, see *U. S. Grant.*
Illinois, Governor of. Correspondence with
Army Headquarters.. 298, 303, 309
War Department, U. S... 366
Illinois Troops. Mentioned.
Artillery, Light—*Batteries:* Cogswell's, 146, 212, 247, 341, 514; Cooley's,
341; Vaughn's, 342, 527. *Regiments:* 1st (*Batteries*), A, 146, 212, 247,
341, 519, 539; B, 146, 212, 247, 341, 519, 539; C, 147; D, 89, 144, 213, 247, 331,
338, 342, 514; E, 146, 212, 247, 341; F, 146, 212, 247, 341, 342, 514; H, 146,
212, 247, 341, 397, 519, 539; I, 146, 212, 247, 329, 341, 514; K, 146, 250, 517;
2d (*Batteries*), B, 144, 213, 247, 342; C, 146, 250, 517; E, 144, 213, 247, 338,
515; F, 145, 249, 338, 340, 515; G, 146, 342, 514; H, 146, 203, 250, 517; I,
148, 200; K, 146, 168, 515; L, 145, 247, 339, 514.
Cavalry—*Battalions:* Stewart's, 4, 144, 146, 212, 247, 282, 341, 342, 517;
Thielemann's, 4, 144, 176, 202, 212, 247, 282, 329, 341, 351, 364, 539, 874.
Companies: Carmichael's, 4; Dollins', 4; Ford's, 146, 168, 252, 282, 517;
Jenks', 248; Kane County, 539; O'Harnett's, 4. *Regiments:* 2d, 4, 35,
105, 144, 146, 153, 176, 183, 213, 228, 247, 282, 331, 339, 342, 364, 439, 479, 484,
516, 517; 3d, 539; 4th, 4, 10, 31, 33, 79, 84, 85, 119, 144, 146, 149, 150, 175,
187, 192, 246, 247, 282, 306, 342, 364, 439, 516, 517; 6th, 34, 36, 89, 110, 128,
146, 168, 176, 183, 202, 205, 212, 247, 250, 276, 282, 341, 351, 358, 364, 402, 411,
438, 439, 507, 516, 755, 870–872, 874; 7th, 148, 248, 284, 339, 354, 364, 474, 516;
11th, 4, 41, 47, 128, 144–146, 150, 167, 176, 187, 212, 213, 247, 248, 266, 282,
284, 331, 340, 342, 515; 12th, 146, 212, 247, 331, 342.
Infantry—*Regiments:* 7th, 145, 249, 341, 517; 8th, 134, 144, 212, 247, 275, 318,
323, 338, 514; 9th, 145, 249, 341, 516; 10th, 147; 11th, 134, 144, 150, 160,
182, 250, 275, 515, 590; 12th, 145, 249, 341, 516; 13th, 539; 14th, 145, 247,
275, 339, 515; 15th, 145, 247, 339, 515; 16th, 147; 17th, 144, 213, 247, 275,
338, 417, 515; 18th, 134, 144, 212, 247, 275, 331, 341, 398, 517; 20th, 144,
155, 212, 247, 275, 323, 326, 338, 350, 514; 21st, 22d, 147; 25th, 147, 339;
26th, 147, 177, 248, 339; 27th, 147; 28th, 145, 247, 275, 339, 515; 29th, 134,
144, 155, 212, 247, 331, 341, 387; 30th, 144, 212, 247, 275, 338, 514; 31st, 144,
212, 247, 323, 338, 514; 32d, 145, 247, 339, 515; 35th, 147; 36th, 148; 38th,
147; 40th, 146, 212, 246, 340, 344, 514; 41st, 145, 247, 339, 515; 42d, 147;
43d, 144, 213, 247, 253, 275, 341, 458, 492, 527; 44th, 148; 45th, 144, 156, 212,
247, 338, 514; 46th, 145, 247, 339, 515; 47th, 148, 248, 339; 48th, 144, 212,

Page.

Illinois Troops. Mentioned—Continued.

Infantry—*Regiments:* **48th** (continued), 247, 313, 341, 359, 492; **49th,** 144, 212, 247, 341, 492; **50th,** 145, 249, 341, 517; **51st,** 147; **52d,** 145, 249, 341, 516; **53d,** 31, 145, 247, 282, 339, 515; **54th,** 146, 195, 247, 341; **55th,** 146, 212, 246, 289, 340, 344, 539, 855; **56th,** 147, 248, 339, 516; **57th,** 145, 249, 341, 517; **58th,** 145; **59th,** 147, 181; **60th,** 147; **61st,** 61, 144, 213, 247, 341, 458, 527; **62d,** 34, 146, 247, 341, 479; **63d,** 146, 160, 212, 247, 338, 514; **64th,** 147, 249, 265, 341, 517; **66th,** 145, 249, 341, 517; **71st,** 146, 160, 250; **72d,** 318, 319, 516, 76th, 196, 203, 269, 271, 339, 515; **77th,** 516; **81st,** 250, 337, 338, 514; **82d,** 300; **83d,** 250, 517; **87th,** 372; **90th,** 417, 545; **93d,** 340, 344, 516; **95th,** 300, 307, 331, 515; **97th,** 516; **101st,** 479; **103d,** 300, 307, 339; **106th,** 878; **108th,** 516; **109th,** 323, 341, 511, 523, 586, 590; **111th,** 300, 307, 517; **113th,** 340, 344, 539, 556; **114th,** 340; **116th,** 340, 344, 539; **117th,** 340; **118th,** 372; **119th,** 323, 331; **120th,** 340, 344; **122d,** 341; **124th,** 338, 514; **126th,** 370, 417, 878; **127th,** 340, 344, 539; **128th,** 372; **130th,** 340; **131st,** 372, 516.

Immell, Lorenzo D. Mentioned 248, 340

Indiana Troops. Mentioned.

Artillery, Light—*Batteries:* **6th,** 85, 146, 212, 247, 341, 514; **9th,** 144, 213, 247, 339, 515; **14th,** 144, 213, 247, 331, 342.

Infantry—*Regiments:* **12th,** 514; **16th,** 372; **22d,** 147; **23d,** 72, 144, 213, 247, 338, 514; **24th,** 56; **25th,** 145, 247; **34th,** 31, 89, 146, 881; **41st,** 643; **43d,** 31, 89; **47th,** 31, 56, 121, 122; **48th,** 147, 248, 339, 516; **50th,** 372, 492; **52d,** 20, 33, 40, 44, 145, 146, 168, 201, 205, 211, 215, 271, 517; **53d,** 145, 247, 339, 515; **59th,** 147, 248, 339, 516; **60th,** 372; **63d,** 345; **66th,** 372, 516; **67th,** **68th, 69th,** 372; **83d,** 340, 344, 539; **89th,** 372; **93d,** 340, 344; **97th, 99th,** **100th,** 340, 514; **101st,** 372.

Ingersoll, R. G.

Correspondence with J. C. Sullivan.. 429

Mentioned... 145, 247, 248, 430, 436, 465

Intercourse. See *Trade* and *Intercourse.*

Iowa, Steamer. Mentioned... 573

Iowa Troops. Mentioned.

Artillery, Light—*Batteries:* **1st,** 539; **2d,** 148, 248, 339.

Cavalry — *Regiments:* **2d,** 148, 200, 207, 208, 248, 284, 287, 340, 364, 516, 755; **3d,** 474; **5th,** 4, 110, 146, 250, 282, 517.

Infantry—*Regiments:* **2d,** 145, 249, 341, 516; **3d,** 145, 247, 339, 515; **4th,** 539, 891; **5th,** 147, 248, 339, 516; **6th,** 146, 212, 246, 329, 340, 344, 514; **7th,** 145, 249, 341, 516; **8th,** 145; **9th,** 539; **10th,** 147, 248, 339, 516; **11th,** 145, 213, 249, 340, 515; **12th,** 145; **13th,** 145, 213, 249, 275, 340, 515; **14th,** 145; **15th,** 145, 213, 249, 340, 515; **16th,** 145, 213, 223, 249, 340, 515; **17th,** 147, 248, 339, 516; **25th,** 539, 545; **26th,** 539; **29th,** 486, 495; **30th, 31st,** 539; **32d,** 356; **33d,** 495; **34th,** 539; **35th,** 517; **36th,** 471, 495, 507; **39th,** 430.

Irwin, Captain. Mentioned 285

Irwin, John. Mentioned... 491

Isabella, Steamer. Mentioned... 573

Isbell, R. H. Mentioned 608

Island No. 10, Tenn. Operations about. Communications from

Curtis, Samuel R 356

Davies, Thomas A 356, 479, 481, 880, 881

Gordon, John A... 352

Grant, U. S... 356

Jones, R. B... 881

Montgomery, William A 880

See also *Davies to Halleck,* p. 500; *Hurlbut to Davies,* p. 501; *Hurlbut to Rawlins,* p. 506; *Davies to Hurlbut,* p. 519.

Page

Iuka, Miss. Engagement at, Sept. 19, 1862. Communications from Sterling
  Price 706–709
Iuka, Miss., Commanding Officer C. S. Forces near. For correspondence,
  etc, see *Sterling Price.*
Jackson, Miss.
 Adams, John, assigned to command of post of............................ 826
 Confederate troops at, Jan. 1, 1863. Report of Daniel Ruggles............ 819
 Ruggles, Daniel, relieved from command of post of....................... 826
Jackson, Tenn. Expedition to, July 25–Aug. 1, 1862. See *Holly Springs, Miss.*
  Expedition from, July 25–Aug. 1, 1862.
Jackson, Andrew. Mentioned.. 896
Jackson, Tenn., Commanding Officer at. Correspondence with J. McDer-
  mott 450
Jackson, District of. (Union.)
 Constituted... 297
 Embraced in District of West Tennessee...................................... 565
 Hurlbut, Stephen A.
  Assigned to command 297
  Relieved of command 353, 355
 Sullivan, J. C., assigned to command.. 355
 Tuttle, J. M., assigned to command 353
Jackson, F. F. Mentioned 843
Jackson, John K. Mentioned.............................. 165, 618, 633, 652, 765
Jackson, Thomas J. Mentioned.. 230, 626
Jackson, W. H.
 Assignments to command 729
 Correspondence with
  Pemberton, John C 821
  Ruggles, Daniel 598, 602
  Van Dorn, Earl... 766, 902
 Mentioned 15, 36, 37, 41, 47, 84,
   96, 137, 138, 178, 183, 211, 216, 229, 231, 235, 285, 286, 289, 307, 357, 368, 436,
   439, 440, 443, 444, 450, 460, 595, 596, 598, 604, 611, 614, 638, 688, 711–713, 729,
   743, 746, 756, 772, 812, 814–816, 820, 827, 829, 838, 839, 842, 846, 847, 854, 874
J. C. Snow, Steamer. Mentioned.. 573
Jeffers, W. L. Mentioned.. 505, 579
Jefferson, John W. Mentioned... 248
Jenks, Albert. Mentioned.. 248
Jenney, W. L. B. Mentioned........................ 188, 435, 510, 538, 560
Jennison, C. R. Mentioned.. 91, 92
Jesse K. Bell, Steamer. Mentioned... 573
Jews. Communications from
 Army Headquarters.. 530
 De Wolf & Bros 506
 Grant, U. S... 330, 337, 421, 424, 544
 Kaskell, C. F.. 506
 Kaswell, J. W 506
J. H. Dickey, Steamer. Mentioned 573
J. J. Roe, Steamer. Mentioned 261
Johnson, Abda. Mentioned 824
Johnson, Adam R.[?] Mentioned.. 203
Johnson, Amory K. Mentioned.............. 145, 247, 278, 301, 325, 515, 540, 543

Page.

Johnson, Andrew.
Correspondence with
Halleck, H. W 14, 22
Sherman, W. T 161
Mentioned.. 7, 14, 98, 168, 181, 182, 270, 279
Johnson, B. R.
Assignments to command.. 642
Mentioned... 642, 765
Johnson, Cave.
Correspondence with Jefferson Davis................................... 730
Mentioned... 731, 732
Johnson, W. H.
Correspondence with W. M. Jones...................................... 831, 839
Mentioned 778
Johnston, A. Sidney. Mentioned........................ 172, 641, 673, 715, 859
Johnston, Joseph E.
Assignments to command.. 757
Assumes command of Department of the West........................ 782
Correspondence with
Adjutant and Inspector General's Office, C. S. A 758, 777, 780–782, 826
Banks, A. D 834
Barteau, C. R... 826, 838
Bragg, Braxton... 781, 798, 811, 832, 838
Buckner, S. B... 832, 833
Davis, Jefferson 800, 812, 823, 827, 828, 838
Holmes, Theophilus H 810
Loring, W. W 813, 820
Ordnance Department, C. S. A.. 781
Pemberton, John C.. 780,
   781, 784, 805, 806, 808–811, 813, 815–817, 820, 822, 823, 825, 827, 832, 833
Roddey, P. D... 826
Smith, Martin L.. 800, 804, 828
Van Dorn, Earl.. 808, 822, 833, 835
Geographical command of. See *West, Department of the.*
Mentioned 276, 279, 306, 437, 483,
   488, 518, 526, 642, 652, 727, 757, 758, 765, 786, 801, 813, 819, 833, 843, 846, 859
Staff. Announcements of.. 782
Johnston, Theo.
Correspondence with T. B. Reed....................................... 817, 830
Mentioned... 797, 798, 802
Johnston, T. N. Mentioned.. 819
Johnston, William Preston.
Correspondence with Jefferson Davis 599
Mentioned... 599, 631, 647
Report of operations in Department No. 2—Corinth, etc 647
Johns, W. M. R. Mentioned 603
John Walsh, Steamer. Mentioned................................... 867
John Warner, Steamer. Mentioned................................ 573
Joliat, Francis J. Mentioned 148
Jomini, Henri. Mentioned... 119
Jones, E. P. Correspondence with
Blythe, G. L 762
Pemberton, John C 762, 763
Van Dorn, Earl 762

Page.

Jones, J. P. Mentioned 648, 676, 678
Jones, Paul, Steamer. Mentioned..................................... 867
Jones, Robert B.
    Correspondence with Thomas A. Davies 481, 880, 881
    Mentioned 146, 246, 513, 517, 880, 881
Jones, Samuel.
    Assignments to command 659
    Correspondence with
        Adjutant and Inspector General's Office, C. S. A..................... 705
        Hardee, William J....................................... 660
        Pemberton, John C 734, 742
        Price, Sterling 692, 694, 695
    Mentioned 591, 623, 632, 652, 657, 659, 697, 727, 734
Jones, W. M. Correspondence with W. H. Johnson 831, 839
Jones, W. P. Mentioned.. 603
Jones, W. S. Mentioned 146, 212, 246, 340, 344, 514
Jordan, F. H. Mentioned 648
Jordan, Thomas.
    Correspondence with G. T. Beauregard 640, 669, 679
    Mentioned 107, 648
    For correspondence as A. A. G., see *G. T. Beauregard;* also *Braxton Bragg.*
J. R. Williams, Steamer. Mentioned............................. 573
J. S Pringle, Steamer. Mentioned 573
Judge Torrence, U. S. S. Mentioned............................. 887
Judy, James W. Mentioned..................................... 340
Juliet, U. S. S. Mentioned..................................... 884, 885, 887
J. W. Cheeseman, Steamer. Mentioned.......................... 573
Kallman, Herman. Mentioned 164
Kansas Troops. Mentioned.
    Artillery, Light—*Batteries:* Hopkins', 35, 53, 147.
    Cavalry—*Regiments:* 7th, 53, 54, 66, 91, 94, 111, 112, 131, 148, 200, 204, 208, 222, 248, 284, 287, 340, 364, 439, 476, 516, 575, 755.
    Infantry—*Regiments:* 1st, 34, 67, 146, 247, 249, 340, 515; 8th, 35, 105, 147.
Kaskell, C. F. Correspondence with Abraham Lincoln..................... 506
Kasson, John A.
    For correspondence, etc., see *Post-Office Department, U. S.*
Kaswell, J. W. Correspondence with Abraham Lincoln 506
Keagg,———. Mentioned 854
Kean, Mortimer O. Mentioned.................................. 147
Keane, Mary, Steamer. Mentioned 867
Keith, Stephen. Mentioned.................................... 249
Kelley, D. C. Mentioned...................................... 646
Kelly, John G. Mentioned 637
Kelton, John C. Mentioned 25, 26, 84, 368
    For correspondence as A. A. G., see *Army Hdqrs.;* also *H. W. Halleck.*
Kempton, Solomon D. Mentioned............................... 514, 523
Kennard, George W. Mentioned............................... 350, 514
Kennerly, W. Clark. Mentioned............................... 723
Kennett, Steamer. Mentioned 573
Kennett, Ferd., Steamer. Mentioned.......................... 867
Kennett, H. G. Mentioned 225
    For correspondence as Chief of Staff, see *W. S. Rosecrans.*
Kent, Loren. Correspondence with M. K. Lawler................... 360
Kent, R. B. Mentioned 350

Page.

Kenton, Steamer. Mentioned 522, 526

Kenton, Tenn., Commanding Officer at. Correspondence with J. C. Sullivan 380

Kentucky.

Invasion of, Aug. 16–Oct. 24, 1862.

Communications from

Army Headquarters 179

Beauregard, G. T 660, 690

Bragg, Braxton 653, 655, 656, 658, 662, 675, 677, 682, 688, 690, 706, 713

Grant, U. S 136, 155

Hardee, William J 660

Price, Sterling 683

Quinby, Isaac F 153

Rosecrans, W. S 132, 139

Ross, L. F 152

Van Dorn, Earl 713

See also *Rosecrans to Grant*, p. 131; *Sheridan to Granger*, p. 132; *Grant to Halleck*, p. 160; *Bragg to Adjutant-General*, p. 683; *Bragg to Price*, p. 685; *Bragg to Van Dorn*, p. 897.

Also Oct. 17–Nov. 4, 1862. *Perryville, Ky. Morgan's retreat from.*

Movement of Breckinridge's command. Communications from

Breckinridge, John C 900

Van Dorn, Earl 703

See also *Grant to Halleck*, p. 238; *Sherman to Grant*, p. 244; *Randolph to Van Dorn*, p. 704; *Van Dorn to Price*, p. 706; *Van Dorn to Breckinridge*, p. 897.

Military departments embracing 278, 624, 627

Morgan's second raid in, Dec. 22, 1862–Jan. 3, 1863. See *Dodge to Rawlins*, p. 482.

Operations in. See

June 10, 1862–Jan. 20, 1863. *Western Kentucky. Operations in.*

Aug. 16–Oct. 24, 1862. *Kentucky. Invasion of.*

Dec. 22, 1862–Jan. 3, 1863. *Kentucky. Morgan's second raid in.*

Re-enforcements for. Communications from

Army Headquarters 168, 189, 194, 198, 214

Buell, Don Carlos 168, 174

Grant, U. S 168, 173, 174, 177, 189, 194, 197, 199

Rosecrans, W. S 174, 176, 177, 196, 198, 200, 203

See also *Halleck to Grant*, p. 142; *Grant to Halleck*, pp. 160, 186; *Rosecrans to Grant*, p. 166.

Kentucky Troops. Mentioned. (Confederate.)

Artillery, Light—*Batteries:* Cobb's, 900.

Cavalry—*Companies:* Bolen's, 819, 820; Morehead's, 600; *Regiments:* 1st, 66, 462; Faulkner's,* 141, 142, 161, 164, 281, 289, 352.

Infantry—*Regiments:* 4th, 900; 5th, 326, 900; 6th, 900.

Kentucky Troops. Mentioned. (Union.)

Cavalry—*Battalions:* 15th, 250, 517.

Infantry—*Regiments:* 19th, 516; 22d, 580, 891.

Kerr, Lucien H. Mentioned 146, 167, 212, 342

Ketchum, W. Scott. Mentioned 300

Key, J. J. Mentioned 14

Key, W. O. Correspondence with T. B. Reed 764, 769

Key West, Steamer. Mentioned 573

*Organization completed September 13, 1863.

Page.

Kidd, Meredith H. Mentioned.............................. 144, 213, 247, 342

Kimmel, Daniel. Mentioned... 587

Kimmel, M. M. Mentioned.. 733, 835

      For correspondence as A. A. G., see *Earl Van Dorn.*

King, Ezra. Mentioned... 144

King, Henry. Mentioned.. 350

King, Walter. Mentioned.. 45

Kinney, E. J. Mentioned.. 616

Kinney, Peter. Mentioned... 28, 60

Kirkwood, Samuel J. Mentioned.............. 269, 308, 332, 334, 401

Kitchen, Sol. G.

    Correspondence with Sterling Price.......................... 659

    Mentioned... 662, 666

Kittel, George W. Mentioned 177, 249, 341

Klinck, Leonard G. Mentioned............................... 202

Klutts, Charles. Mentioned................................. 591

Knobelsdorff, Charles. Mentioned 148

Knox, Thomas W.

    Case of.

        Communications from

            Blair, Frank P., jr 582

            Grant, U. S 894

            Knox, Thomas W 580, 893

            Lincoln, Abraham 894

            Sherman, W. T 581, 587, 892, 894, 895

        Court-martial.

           Charges and specifications........................... 890–892

           Proceedings, findings, and sentence................... 889–892

        Correspondence with

           Grant, U. S 894

           Sherman, W. T 580, 893, 894

        Mentioned 581–583, 586–588, 890–892, 894–896

Koyle, Rev. Mr. Mentioned............................... 35

Kroh, P. H. Mentioned.................................. 591

Labor, Lieutenant. Mentioned............................ 819

Lady Jackson, Steamer. Mentioned...................... 573

La Fayette Station, Tenn. Affair near, June 25, 1862.

    Communications from U. S. Grant 36

    Congratulatory orders. (Bragg) 638

    See also *Halleck to Grant,* pp. 46, 67; *Grant to Halleck,* p. 46; *Halleck to Sherman,* p. 48.

Lagow, Clark B. Mentioned 204, 205, 857, 862

La Grange, Tenn. Expedition to, Sept. 20–22, 1862. See *Bolivar, Tenn. Expedition from, Sept.* 20–22, 1862.

La Grange, Tenn., Commanding Officer at. Correspondence with

    Grant, U. S 439

    Richardson, R. V 418

    Sullivan, J. C.. 380

Lamar, T. B. Mentioned.................................. 782

Lamberg, Carl A. Mentioned............................ 147

Landgraeber, C. Mentioned.............................. 539

Landis, John C. Mentioned.............................. 762

Landram, William J. Mentioned................ 513, 516, 589

Lane, James H. Mentioned............................ 91, 92

Page.

Larison, Thomas J. Mentioned 144

Lauman, Jacob G.
Assignments to command............... .... 358, 396
Correspondence with
Hurlbut, Stephen A.. 228
McPherson, James B.............................. 323, 325, 453, 559
Mentioned 118, 169, 204, 228, 231, 232, 268, 317, 348, 358, 361, 385,
396, 397, 429, 446, 461, 468, 472, 512, 515, 540, 545, 554, 558, 559, 569, 577, 874

Lavinia, Logan, Steamer. Mentioned 573

Law, Lieutenant. Mentioned.. 819

Lawler, Michael K.
Correspondence with
Dennis, Elias S 192
Grant, U. S... 509
Haynie, Isham N.. 192
Kent, Loren 360
Logan, John A... 153
Sullivan, J. C....................................... 360, 431, 477
Mentioned... 134, 135, 144, 152, 155, 161, 212, 247, 257, 259, 275, 318, 323, 489, 492, 540

Lawrence, Dr. Mentioned 8, 9

Leake, Frank T. Mentioned 621

Lebo, William B. Mentioned 116

Lee, Albert L.
Assignments to command... 200
Correspondence with
Hamilton, C. S....................................... 207, 369, 373
McArthur, John.... 540
Mentioned 132, 148,
200, 252, 254, 300, 324, 328, 331, 340, 342–344, 346, 348, 357, 359, 364, 366–
369, 391, 429, 448, 455–457, 461, 475, 476, 516, 518, 525, 541, 550, 575, 577

Lee, R. B
Correspondence with G. T. Beauregard 595
Mentioned 620, 623

Lee, Robert E.
Correspondence with Braxton Bragg 619
Mentioned.................................... 230, 261, 619, 642, 738, 749, 823, 840

Lee, Stephen D. Mentioned.................... 558, 765, 805, 821, 825, 831

Leggett, Mortimer D.
Correspondence with
——— 313
Logan, John A... 75
McClernand, John A.. 68, 72, 95
McPherson, James B 446
Ord, E. O. C.. 229
Price, Sterling... 229, 230
Ross, Leonard F 116
Sherman, W. T 72
Mentioned......................... 70, 72, 73, 88, 94–96, 110, 116, 121, 144, 247, 275,
299, 313, 338, 429, 437, 438, 445, 446, 452, 473, 478, 487, 514, 519, 525, 532, 533

Levy, W. M. Mentioned 643

Lewis, James H.
Correspondence with T. C. Flournoy 686
Mentioned... 682

Lewis, James M. Correspondence with Thomas A. Davies 486

                                                                                    Page.
Lewis, S. O. Mentioned 591
Lexington, U. S. S. Mentioned 884, 885, 887, 888
Liddell, St. John R.
    Assignments to command 600
    Mentioned.. 600, 619, 633, 652, 765
Lincoln, Abraham.
    Correspondence with
        Blair, Frank P., jr 350
        De Wolff & Bros 506
        Halleck, H. W 53, 59, 63, 64, 70, 71, 76, 88, 90, 97, 98
        Kaskell, C. F 506
        Kaswell, J. W 506
        McClernand, John A................................... 401, 420, 502, 566, 849
        Mentioned.40–42, 52, 90–93, 158, 159, 165, 169, 262, 284, 334, 382, 384, 386, 401, 402, 410,
            424, 425, 432, 461, 463, 502, 503, 528, 536, 556, 557, 579, 587, 836, 865, 893–897
        Orders, series 1–62: **July 11,** 90; **Nov. 7,** 323.
Lioness, U. S. S. Mentioned... 885, 887
Little, Henry.
    Assignments to command 596, 690
    Correspondence with Sterling Price........... 660, 689, 690, 695, 698, 702, 707, 708
    Mentioned 592, 596, 610, 634, 652, 662, 682–685, 690, 696, 702, 706, 709, 713
Littlefield, Milton S. Mentioned.. 173
Lochbihler, Christian. Mentioned 249, 341, 517
Lockett, S. H. Mentioned 745, 750
Lockland, R. J., Steamer. Mentioned.. 867
Lockwood, Theodore W. Mentioned.. 146
Logan, John. Mentioned 145, 247
Logan, John A.
    Correspondence with
        Bryant, George E 137, 141, 142, 203
        Dennis, Elias S 180
        Dodge, Grenville M...................................... 130, 137, 203
        Dollins, James J.. 125
        Grant, U. S... 128–130, 199
        Haynie, Isham N................................. 175, 199, 203, 253
        Hogg, Harvey.. 135, 136
        Hurlbut, Stephen A....................................... 231
        Lawler, Michael K... 153
        Leggett, Mortimer D... 75
        McClernand, John A................... 6, 38, 76, 128, 129, 133–139, 174
        McPherson, James B.............................. 453, 549, 559
        Nevins, Garrett.................................. 115
        Ozburn, L...................................... 80
        Sanford, W. W 104
        Stevenson, John D 198, 202
        Townes, R. R..................................... 104, 196
        Wallace, M. R. M................................. 80, 89
        Mentioned............ 61, 107, 155, 212, 215, 313, 314, 317, 323, 338, 374, 376, 387, 429,
            437, 446, 451, 461, 472, 512, 514, 544, 545, 548, 557–559, 564, 565, 569, 577, 754
Logan, Lavinia, Steamer. Mentioned 573
Lomax, L. L. Mentioned... 692
Longstreet, James. Mentioned... 230
Loomis, John M.
    Correspondence with U. S. Grant.. 469
    Mentioned... 147, 248, 339

Page.

Loomis, Reuben. Mentioned 516
Looney, Robert F.
Correspondence with John C. Pemberton 743
Mentioned 460
Lord, George P. Mentioned.. 884
Loring, F., Steamer. Mentioned 573
Loring, William W.
Assignments to command.. 824
Correspondence with
Barteau, C. R.. 813
Johnston, Joseph E 813, 820
Pemberton, John C 800,
804, 805, 807, 808, 812, 816, 822, 827, 829, 830, 832, 835, 837, 839, 841
Price, Sterling 807, 845
Withers, H. R 804
Mentioned 806, 813, 815, 820, 822–824
Lothrop, Warren L. Mentioned.................................... 266
Loudon, De Witt C. Mentioned......... 112, 344, 514, 523, 586
Loughborough, James M. Mentioned.............. 637, 654, 664
For correspondence as A. A. G., see *Sterling Price.*
Louis D'Or, Steamer. Mentioned................................. 764
Louisiana.
Military departments embracing.............. 624, 627, 649, 718
Operations in. See *East Louisiana.*
Louisiana, City of, Steamer. Mentioned 573
Louisiana Troops. Mentioned.
Artillery, Heavy—*Battalions:* 8th, 661, 815; 12th, 815. *Regiments:* 1st, 661, 699, 815.
Artillery, Light—*Battalions:* Washington Artillery (*Batteries*), 5th, 632; Boone's, 661, 815; Brown's,* 635, 653; Crescent, 819, 820; Fenner's, 815, 691; Pointe Coupée, 595, 600, 619.
Cavalry—*Battalions:* 9th,† 661. *Companies:* Carroll Dragoons, 661; Daigre's, 815; Jones', 661, 815; Webb's Squadron,‡ 635, 646, 653.
Engineers—*Companies:* Gallimard's, 600, 661.
Infantry—*Battalions:* Confederate Guards Response, 632; Dupeire's Zouaves, 661. *Regiments:* 1st, 618, 633, 652, 657; 3d, 634, 733, 736; 4th, 595, 606, 661; 11th, 595, 632; 12th, 600, 661; 13th, 16th, 632; 17th, 606, 661, 699, 815, 825; 18th, 19th, 632, 657; 20th, 21st, 632; 22d, 815, 825; 25th, 632; 26th, 661, 699, 815, 825; 27th, 661, 699, 815, 831; 29th,§ 661, 699, 815, 825; 30th, 661; 31st, 825; Crescent, 632.
Miscellaneous: Miles' Legion, 661; Stewart's Legion, 661.
Louisville, Steamer. Mentioned................................... 867
Louisville, U. S. S. Mentioned 887
Lovell, Julius. Mentioned 881
For correspondence as A. A. G., see *Thomas A. Davies.*
Lovell, Mansfield.
Assignments to command 697, 711, 729, 787
Correspondence with
Beauregard, G. T 591
Pemberton, John C 744, 786

* Consolidated with Guibor's battery June 30, 1862.
† Sometimes called 1st Regiment Partisan Rangers.
‡ Afterward Company E, 18th Battalion Tennessee Cavalry.
§ Also called 28th.

Page.

Lovell, Mansfield—Continued.
  Correspondence with
    Price, Sterling 745
    Van Dorn, Earl 903
  Mentioned 175, 285, 288, 336, 369, 411,
      599, 602, 607, 614, 616, 624, 697, 711, 713, 714, 717, 718, 720, 721, 724, 729, 733,
      741, 744, 745, 765, 777–779, 786, 787, 814, 815, 829, 842, 843, 847, 854, 855, 867
Lovell, W. S. Correspondence with John C. Pemberton 736
Lowe, William W.
  Correspondence with
    Davies, Thomas A 303
    Grant, U. S 126, 181, 428, 541
    Griffin, R. B 126
    Halleck, H. W 21
    Sullivan, J. C 440, 441
  Mentioned 183, 186, 250, 309, 429, 431, 436, 454, 497, 500, 513, 517, 574, 731, 732
Lower Post Ferry, Tenn. Affair near, July 27, 1862. See *Toone's Station,*
    Tenn.
Lucas, Turner & Co. Mentioned 116
Lum, Charles M. Mentioned 147
Luzerne, Steamer. Mentioned 573
Lyford, S. C. Mentioned 201, 316
Lyman, Charles W. Mentioned 184
Lynch, Alexander W. Mentioned 884
Lynch, John. Mentioned 164
Lynch, J. P. Mentioned 819
Lynch, W. F. Correspondence with
    Pemberton, John C 724
    Ruggles, Daniel 725
Lyndsay, Mr. Mentioned 671
Lyon, H. B. Mentioned 729
Lyon, William P. Mentioned 517
Mabry, H. P. Mentioned 709
McArthur, John.
  Correspondence with
    Grant, U. S 454
    Hamilton, C. S 373, 525
    Lee, Albert L 540
    Ord, E. O. C 235
    Rosecrans, W. S 269
  Mentioned 145, 160, 168, 206, 249, 266, 313, 329, 340, 362, 365, 374,
      385, 387, 422, 423, 446, 451, 455, 461, 509, 512, 515, 545, 549, 557, 564, 565, 577
McBee, J. T. Correspondence with John C. Pemberton 754
McCaa, B. B. Mentioned 606
McCammon, William W. Mentioned 339, 516
McClellan, George B. Mentioned. 43, 49, 52, 55, 56, 68, 70, 82, 83, 85, 100, 186, 261, 627
McClernand, John A.
  Assignments to command 31, 432, 461, 534
  Correspondence with
    Army Headquarters 334, 349, 415, 461, 853
    Bryant, George E 168, 174
    Curtis, Samuel R 545
    Dodge, Grenville M 161, 183
    Fisk, Clinton B 558
    Gorman, W. A 562

Page.

McClernand, John A.—Continued.

Correspondence with

Grant, U. S....... 130, 135, 150, 425, 463, 501, 546, 551–553, 559, 561, 563, 567, 574

Halleck, H. W......................... 5, 8, 21, 38, 56, 60, 61, 64, 70, 72, 73, 94

Haynie, Isham N.. 180

Hurlbut, Stephen A.. 37

Leggett, Mortimer D... 68, 72, 95

Lincoln, Abraham 401, 420, 502, 566, 849

Logan, John A 6, 38, 76, 128, 129, 133–139, 174

Porter, David D 541, 547, 548, 570

Ross, Leonard F.......... 110, 116, 120, 124–126, 152, 155, 161, 163, 167, 182, 183

Sanderson, William L.. 13, 39, 64

Sherman, W. T 40, 534, 537, 560, 562, 563, 568, 571, 572

Stewart, Warren... 125

Wallace, Lew.. 11, 14, 25

War Department, U. S...... .... 274, 277, 300, 302, 308,
310, 332, 345, 348, 349, 371, 375, 391, 401, 413, 420, 461, 462, 503, 528, 579, 866

Directed to organize troops in Indiana, Illinois, and Iowa 282

Mentioned... 10,
11, 19, 31, 32, 37, 38, 40, 42, 45, 49–51, 58, 59, 72, 77, 79, 96, 121, 122, 131, 143,
144, 166, 168, 176, 178, 180, 187, 206, 282, 308, 330, 347, 350, 366, 425, 432, 436,
446, 461, 480, 497, 502, 503, 508, 510, 511, 534–536, 541, 552, 553, 555, 557,
558, 560, 564, 565, 568, 570, 571, 573, 582, 585, 598, 696, 766, 883, 887, 894, 895

Relieved from command of expedition against Vicksburg, Miss........... 555

McClure, Samuel M. P. Mentioned 591

McCook, Alexander McD. Mentioned 604, 613

McCook, Edwin S. Mentioned.. 212

McCown, George W. Mentioned... 617

McCown, John P.

Assignments to command.. 616

Mentioned................................ 592, 626, 631, 634, 635, 651–653, 673, 765

Staff. Announcements of 617

McCown, Joseph B. Mentioned................................... 247, 338, 514

McCoy, James C. Mentioned 409, 435, 538, 875

McCrillis, L. F. Mentioned... 539

McCulloch, H. E. Mentioned....................................... 787, 810

McCulloch, Robert. Mentioned............................... 646, 773, 779

McCullough, William. Mentioned 138, 206, 247, 398

McDaniel, C. A. Mentioned 603

McDermott, John.

Correspondence with

Army Headquarters 386

Grant, U. S 379, 386, 439, 458, 459, 464, 467

Jackson, Tenn., Commanding Officer at........................... 450

Sullivan, J. C................................... 380, 450, 459, 467

War Department, U. S 382

Mentioned.. 145, 249, 340

McDonald, Charles. Mentioned...................................... 586

McDonald, John W. Mentioned 156

McDowell, John A. Mentioned 4,
7, 8, 23, 33, 50, 81, 96, 102, 109, 118, 173, 174, 212, 221, 237, 260, 344, 514, 861

McEntee, Terrence P. Mentioned..................................... 437

McIntosh, John J. Mentioned...................................... 587

McFarland, John. Mentioned.. 788

Mack, Alonzo W. Mentioned.............................. 269, 339, 515

Page.

Mackall, W. W.
Correspondence with Daniel Ruggles.. 799
Mentioned... 765
McKeaig, George W. Mentioned....................................... 340, 344
McKean, Thomas J.
Assignments to command...................... 101, 205, 232, 343, 396
Correspondence with W. S. Rosecrans............................. 256, 263, 264
Mentioned 101, 205, 232, 241, 249, 252, 256, 263–266, 270, 300, 339, 342, 343, 396
McKee, And. W. Correspondence with Braxton Bragg...................... 620
McKelvaine, R. P. Mentioned...................................... 603
McKinney, C. C. Mentioned....................................... 603
McLane, James P. Mentioned..................................... 591
McLean, E. E. Mentioned... 669
Maclean, L. A. Mentioned.. 654
McMahon, Thomas. Mentioned..................................... 515
McMicken, M. B. Mentioned...................................... 648
McMillan, Charles. Mentioned........................ 435, 538, 581, 587
McMullan, B. B. Mentioned...................................... 731
MacMurray, Junius W. Mentioned..................... 147, 340, 516
McMurry, L. P. Mentioned....................................... 603
McNair, E. Mentioned... 765
McNeal, A. T. Mentioned.. 297
McNeil, Quincy. Mentioned.................... 246, 339, 450, 457, 479
McPherson, James B.
Assignments to command 257, 275, 277, 364, 433, 461
Correspondence with
Army Headquarters....................................... 184
Denver, James W..................................... 445, 452, 548
Grant, U. S............. 293, 294, 300, 301, 306, 307, 313, 314, 317, 324, 327, 328,
331, 376, 389, 423, 428, 435–437, 445, 446, 451, 452, 468, 469, 472–474, 478, 487,
488, 497, 499, 505, 509, 511, 518, 519, 521, 525, 531–533, 545, 554, 557, 558, 569
Grierson, Benjamin H..................................... 543
Halleck, H. W.. 78
Hurlbut, Stephen A........................... 278, 297, 299, 305
Lauman, Jacob G.............................. 323, 325, 453, 559
Leggett, Mortimer D...................................... 446
Logan, John A 453, 549, 559
Mizner, J. K... 438
Noble, Silas... 281
Rosecrans, W. S 119, 264
Sherman, W. T 20
Mentioned.................... 21, 22, 47, 78, 120, 257–259,
262, 264–267, 269, 271, 275–277, 299, 312, 315–317, 320, 325, 326, 330, 335, 338,
349, 364–367, 369, 374, 396, 432, 433, 461, 469, 512, 514, 520, 564, 565, 577, 858
McRae, D. Mentioned 592
Madison, Steamer. Mentioned................................... 573
Madison, Relly. Mentioned........................ 144, 213, 342
Magenta, Steamer. Mentioned................................ 862, 867
Magnolia, Steamer. Mentioned................................ 867
Magruder, John B. Mentioned................... 599, 649, 653, 670
Mahan, Dennis H. Mentioned.................................. 119
Mail Facilities. Communications from
Grant, U. S.. 207, 363
Halleck, H. W.. 51

Page.

Mail Facilities—Continued. Communications from
Markland, A. H. 405
Post-Office Department, U. S. 7
Main, Zalmon S. Mentioned 517
Major, ——. Mentioned 22
Major, J. P. Mentioned 713
Malloy, A. G. Mentioned 878
Malloy, F. Mentioned 648
Malmborg, Oscar. Mentioned 340, 344, 539
Maloney, Maurice. Mentioned 146
Maltby, Jasper A. Mentioned 212, 514
Maney, George. Mentioned 603, 618, 632, 643, 644, 652
Manigault, A. M. Mentioned 618, 633, 652
Mann, Charles. Mentioned 145, 247
Mann, Martin. Mentioned 515
Mann, Martin J. Mentioned 527
Mann, P. A. Mentioned 682, 686
Manter, F. H. Mentioned 539
Marigny, M. de. Mentioned 722, 815
Mariner, Steamer. Mentioned 573
Markland, A. H. Correspondence with
Post-Office Department, U. S. 7
Ross, Orlando H. 405
Marks, L. D. Mentioned 699
Marmaduke, John S. Mentioned 579, 619, 633, 652
Marmora, U. S. S. Mentioned 884, 887, 888
Marschner, Berthold. Mentioned 144, 247, 539
Marsh, C. Carroll.
Correspondence with
Grant, U. S 442, 443, 447–450, 454, 455, 468, 472, 484
Hurlbut, Stephen A 306
Mentioned 144, 212, 247, 275, 306, 338, 443, 448, 455, 456, 459, 467, 514
Marsh, Charles J. Mentioned 340
Marsh, E. Mentioned 820
Marshall, Humphrey. Mentioned 688, 696
Marshall, J. W. Mentioned 418, 419
Marshall, Thomas H. Mentioned 828
Martial Law. Mississippi 694
Martin, James S. Mentioned 300, 517
Martin, John A. Mentioned 147
Martin, John D.
Correspondence with G. T. Beauregard 605
Mentioned 267, 683, 709
Martin, W. T. Mentioned 838
Marybugh, Russel W. Mentioned 516
Mary Keane, Steamer. Mentioned 867
Mason, A. P. Mentioned 782, 843
Mason, Rodney. Mentioned 146, 186
Mathes, B. N. Mentioned 617
Mathews, Charles H. Mentioned 516
Mathews, James E. Mentioned 739
Matson, Bellamy S. Mentioned 145, 249
Matteson, Frederick W. Mentioned 147
Matthews, E. W. Mentioned 418

Page.

Matthies, Charles L. Mentioned.. 147, 516
Maurice, Thomas D. Mentioned 147, 248
Maury, Dabney H.
    Correspondence with
        Pemberton, John C 804, 845
        Price, Sterling.. 702, 706
        Van Dorn, Earl 903
    Mentioned 224, 265, 336,
        592, 614, 634, 653, 683–685, 697, 701, 702, 707, 713, 718, 720, 733, 736, 737, 747,
        765, 771, 773, 777–779, 786, 799, 803, 805, 807, 808, 821, 823, 824, 829, 831, 903
Maxey, S. B.
    Assignments to command............................ 796
    Mentioned................................. 603, 618, 632, 643, 652, 765, 796
Maxwell, ——. Mentioned 389
Mayfield, Manning. Mentioned 144
Mayo, George Upshur.
    Correspondence with Jefferson Davis 775
    Mentioned 775, 785
Medon, Tenn., Commanding Officer at. Correspondence with J. C. Sul-
        livan 380
Meigs, Montgomery C. Mentioned....................... 78, 219, 391, 399
Mellon, T. A. Mentioned... 699
Memminger, R. W. Mentioned... 792
        For correspondence as A. A. G., see John C. Pemberton.
Memphis, Tenn.
    Affairs at, generally. Communications from
        Chipman, N. P... 471
        Grant, U. S 29, 30, 41
        Hurlbut, Stephen A.. 506
        McClernand, John A 21, 25
        Quinby, Isaac F.. 13
        Sherman, W. T 109, 110, 112, 116, 118, 121, 127, 140, 169, 178, 187,
            200, 201, 215, 217, 234, 252, 259, 272, 276, 279, 285, 351, 853, 855–857, 860, 869
        Wallace, Lew 14, 25
    Anthony, D. C., appointed and announced provost-marshal for.......... 31, 294
    Asboth, A., relieved from command of post of 542
    Cemetery established at. Communications from W. T. Sherman 278
    Defenses of (immediate). Communications from
        Grant, U. S. ,... 60, 82
        Halleck, H. W.. 56
        Sherman, W. T 221
        See also Halleck to Grant, p. 60; Sherman to Grant, pp. 187, 259; Sherman
            to Kelton, p. 200; Sherman to Rawlins, pp. 201, 215, 217.
    Expedition from, Sept. 8–13, 1862. Communications from W. T. Sherman.. 209
        See also Sherman to Rawlins, pp. 215, 217.
    Hurlbut, Stephen A., assigned to command of post of.................... 353, 362
    Mail facilities... 7
    Naval engagement off, and occupation of, by Union forces June 6, 1862.
            Communications from
        Ellet, Charles, jr.. 9
        War Department, U. S.. 8
    Preservation of order in. Communications from W. T. Sherman . 173, 276, 294, 865
        See also Sherman to Grant, p. 187.
    Provisions for poor and destitute. Communications from W. T. Sherman. 856

Page.

Memphis, Tenn –Continued.

Re-enforcements for. Communications from

Army Headquarters 493, 496

Curtis, Samuel R 499, 500

Hurlbut, Stephen A 470

Scout from, Oct. 21-24, 1862. Communications from W. T. Sherman 289

See also *Sherman to Rawlins*, p. 855.

Sherman, W. T., assigned to and assumes command of post of 99, 110

"Shinplasters," issue of, in. Communications from W. T. Sherman 874

Webster, J. D., appointed commander of the post of 30

Memphis Tenn., Commanding Officer at. Correspondence with

Grant, U. S 480

Halleck, H. W 22

Memphis, District of. (Union.)

Constituted 297

Embraced in District of West Tennessee 565

Hurlbut, Stephen A., relieved from command 542

Sherman, W. T., assigned to command 297

Veatch, James C., assigned to command 542

Memphis, Tenn., Mayor of. Correspondence with W. T. Sherman 127, 252

Memphis, Tenn., Mayor and Council of. Correspondence with W. T. Sherman 874

Mercer, Colonel. Mentioned 755

Mersy, August.

Correspondence with

Burke, Patrick E 427

Dodge, Grenville M 403, 404, 457

Mentioned 145, 249, 341, 404, 428, 516

Merwether, Lizzie A. Mentioned 170

Messinger, G. Mentioned 805

Metcalfe, L. S. Mentioned 86

Meteor, Steamer. Mentioned 573

Metropolitan, Steamer. Mentioned 573

Metropolitan, Steamer, Commanding Officer of Guard on. Correspondence with W. T. Sherman 873

Michigan Troops. Mentioned.

Artillery, Light—*Batteries :* **3d,** 147, 248, 340; **8th,** 89, 146, 168, 338, 514.

Cavalry—*Regiments :* **2d,** 148, 132, 200; **3d,** 57, 63, 124, 148, 242, 248, 265, 284, 287, 340, 364, 367, 439, 455, 465, 474, 483, 521.

Infantry—*Regiments :* **10th,** 147; **12th,** 61, 144, 213, 247, 341, 454, 476, 492, 527; **14th,** 147; **15th,** 145, 249, 340, 365.

Middleburg, Tenn., Commanding Officer at. Correspondence with J. C. Sullivan 380

Middle Tennessee.

Forrest's raid in, July 9-24, 1862. See *Bragg to Smith*, p. 651.

Operations in.

June 10-Oct. 31, 1862. Communications from Sterling Price 714

See also *Clarksville, Tenn. Surrender of, Aug.* 18, 1862.

Nov. 1, 1862-Jan. 20, 1863. Communications from

Army Headquarters 290

Bragg, Braxton 743, 744

Dodge, Grenville M 377, 489

Grant, U. S. 377

Rosecrans, W. S 290, 301

War Department, U. S 291

Page.

Middle Tennessee—Continued.
Operations in.
Jan. 21–Aug. 10, 1863. Communications from
Banks, A. D 834
Johnston, Joseph E 808, 825, 826, 832, 833 835, 838
Pemberton, John C.. 833, 834
Van Dorn, Earl 833, 835
Mignault, Napoleon. Mentioned....................................... 878
Miles, Jonathan R. Mentioned 147, 193
Milikin, Jacob A. Mentioned....................................... 591
Military Railroad Transportation, Officer in charge. Correspondence with
Braxton Bragg.. 609
Militia. Calls for, etc 599, 617, 664, 674, 682
Miller, Pitser. Mentioned... 297
Miller, Wiley. Mentioned.. 104
Miller, William H. Mentioned...................................... 45
Millington, Dr. Mentioned 417
Millington, Mrs. Mentioned.. 416
Mims, L. Correspondence with
Pemberton, John C 805, 808
Reed, T. B... 777
Miner, Phineas R. Mentioned 144, 516
Minnehaha, Steamer. Mentioned 522, 527
Minnesota Troops. Mentioned.
Artillery, Light—*Batteries:* 1st, 145, 249, 340, 515; 2d, 147.
Infantry—*Regiments:* 4th, 147, 248, 339, 516; 5th, 147, 248, 339.
Mintrow, Jesse. Mentioned.. 418
Misenheimer, Abram L. Mentioned.................................... 591
Misenheimer, Joshua. Mentioned..................................... 587
Mississippi.
Affairs in, generally. Communications from
Pemberton, John C 766
Phelan, James 788
Conscription act. Enforcement of, in 681, 737, 738, 748, 790
Martial law 694
Militia. See *Mississippi State Troops.*
Military departments embracing.............. 101, 278, 624, 627, 649, 718
Operations in. See
April 29–June 10, 1862. *Corinth, Miss. Advance upon and seige of.*
May 18–July 27, 1862. *Vicksburg, Miss. Operations against.*
June 10, 1862–Jan. 20, 1863. *Northern Mississippi. Operations in.*
Dec. 20, 1862–Jan. 3, 1863. *Vicksburg, Miss. Operations against.*
Jan. 20–July 4, 1863. *Vicksburg, Miss. Operations against.*
Mississippi, Army of the.* (Confederate.)
Beall, W. N. R., relieved from command of cavalry 610
Bragg, Braxton, relinquishes command 639
Brigade organization of First Division announced...................... 643
Chalmers, James R., relieved of command of cavalry of the, and ordered
to rejoin his infantry brigade.................................... 650
Corps of, designated "divisions".................................... 636
Hardee, William J., assigned to and assumes command................ 636, 639
Johnson, B. R., assigned to command of Third Brigade, Third Division.... 642
Jones, Samuel.
Relieved from duty in... 659
Revocation of order relieving from duty in........................ 659

*Of the Western Department.

Page.

Mississippi, Army of the. (Confederate)—Continued.

Liddell, St. John R., assigned to command of First Brigade, Third Army
Corps.. 600

Orders, General, series 1862: **No. 19,** 623; **Nos. 22, 23,** 639; **No. 31,** 647;
Divisions **(Cheatham), No. 1,** 643; Second Brigade, Reserve
Corps, **No. 61,** 629.

Orders, Special, series 1862: **No. 59,** 642; First Corps (Polk), **No. 75,** 622.

Organization, strength, etc.

June 12, 1862.. 596
June 15, 1862.. 603
June 22, 1862.. 618, 619
June 30, 1862.. 631–633, 635
July 16, 1862.. 648
July 20, 1862.. 652
January 14, 1863.. 835

Smith, R. A., assigned to command of Second Brigade, Reserve Corps.... 629

Wheeler, Joseph, assigned to command of cavalry of the.................. 650

White, T. W., relieved of command of Second Brigade, Reserve Corps.... 629

Wood, S. A. M., assigned to command of Third Division................... 642

Mississippi, Army of the.* (Confederate.)

Bowen, John S., assigned to command of a brigade....................... 824

Brigade, corps, and division organizations announced............... 787, 824

Constituted.. 787

Corps of, designated "divisions".. 824

Green, Martin E., assigned to command of a brigade...................... 824

Inspection of the. Report of Edwin J. Harvie............................. 841

Loring, W. W., assigned to command of First Division.................... 824

Orders, General, series 1862: **No. 7,** 801.

Orders, General, series 1863: Cavalry Division (Van Dorn), **No. 1,** 835.

Orders, Special, series 1862: **No. 7,** 799; **No. 12,** 803; Second Corps
(Price), **No. 82,** 794.

Orders, Special, series 1863: Cavalry Corps (Van Dorn), **No. 3,** 838.

Organization, strength, etc. See *Mississippi and East Louisiana, Department of.*

Price, Sterling.

Assigned to command of Second Corps................................. 787
Assigned to command of Second Division.............................. 824

Reorganization of... 824

Tilghman, Lloyd, assigned to command of Baldwin's brigade.............. 824

Van Dorn, Earl.

Assigned to command of First Corps.................................. 787
Assigned to temporary command of................................... 792
Assumes command of cavalry of..................................... 835

Mississippi, Army of the. (Union.)

Address to soldiers of. Rosecrans....................................... 71

Brigade and division organizations announced........................... 86

Discontinued as a separate army.. 297

Elliott, W. L., relieved from duty with................................. 163

Hamilton, C. S., assigned to and assumes command of............... 297, 298

Lee, A. L., assigned to command of the Second Brigade, Cavalry Division. 200

Mitchell, R. B., assigned to command of First Brigade, Fourth Division.. 105

Mizner, J. K.

Announced as chief of cavalry of.................................... 245
Assigned to command of the Cavalry Division........................ 200

Page.

Mississippi, Army of the. (Union)—Continued.
Orders, General, series 1862: Sept. 4, 200; **No. 83,** 71; **No. 86,** 86; **No. 92,** 97; **No. 128,** 240; **No. 131,** 245; **No. 143,** 291; **No. 151,** 297; **No. 153,** 298.
Orders, Special, series 1862: **No. 185,** 105; **No. 211,** 174; **No. 212,** 176; **No. 225,** 193; **No. 239,** 225; **No. 252,** 265.
Organization, strength, etc.
July 31, 1862 .... 144, 147, 148
September 30, 1862 .... 246, 248
Paine, E. A., relieved from command of First Division 193
Palmer, J. M., assigned to command of First Division 193
Pope, John, ordered to assume command of 3
Quinby, Isaac F., assigned to command of Third Division 298
Rosecrans, W. S., relinquishes command 297
Sheridan, Philip H., relieved from command of the Second Brigade, Cavalry Division 200
Mississippi, Army of the. * (Union.)
Army Corps, 1st, designation changed to Thirteenth Corps 564
Army Corps, 2d, designation changed to Fifteenth Corps 556, 564
Brigade and division organization of Second Corps of, announced 538–540
Constituted 534, 535
McClernand, John A., assumes command 534
Morgan, G. W., assigned to command of 1st Corps 534
Orders, General, series 1863: **No. 1,** 534; **No. 9,** 564; **No. 11,** 572; **Army Corps, 2d (Sherman), No. 1,** 538.
Orders, Special, series 1863: **Army Corps, 2d (Sherman), No. 5,** 549.
Sherman, W. T., assigned to and assumes command of Second Corps 534, 538
Mississippi, Department of the. (Union.)
Halleck, H. W., relinquishes immediate command of troops in 101
Mail facilities 51
Orders, Special (Field), series 1862: **No. 90,** 3; **No. 140,** 68; **No. 160,** 99; **Nos. 161, 162,** 101.
Orders, General, series 1862: **No. 33,** 7; **No. 38,** 51.
Sanitary condition of troops in. Communications from H. W. Halleck... 31, 34
Mississippi, District of. (Union.)
Embraced in the District of West Tennessee............................. 101, 102
Limits extended 211
Merged into Fourth Division, District of West Tennessee 237
Quinby, Isaac F., assigned to command of 211
Mississippi, District of the. (Confederate.)
Confederate troops in. Organization, strength, etc.
July 31, 1862 .... 661, 662
September 10, 1862 699
Constituted, and limits defined 636
Designated Department of Mississippi and East Louisiana 718
Lovell, Mansfield, assigned to the command of First Division 697, 711
Orders, General, series 1862: **No. 38,** 681; **Nos. 46, 47,** 694; **No. 50,** 711.
Orders, Special, series 1862: **No. 58,** 691; **No. 59,** 692; **No. 61,** 697; **No. 74,** 710.
Pillow, Gideon J.
Relieved from duty in.. 691
Reports for duty in 710
Ruggles, Daniel, assigned to temporary command........................ 694
Rust, Albert, assigned to duty in....................................... 697

* So styled by McClernand.

Page

Mississippi, District of the. (Confederate)—Continued.
Van Dorn, Earl.
  Assigned to command 636
  Relieved of command 716
Mississippi, Governor of. Correspondence with
  Davis, Jefferson 612, 622, 655, 686, 700, 713, 716
  Price, Sterling 664, 666
  Ruggles, Daniel 607, 612
Mississippi and East Louisiana, Department of.
Affairs in, generally. Communications from
  Adjutant and Inspector General's Office, C. S. A 724, 738
  Davis, Jefferson 726, 727
  Pemberton, John C 724, 728, 739, 740
  War Department, C. S 716, 727
Confederate troops in. Organization, strength, etc.
  December 31, 1862 .... 814, 815
  January 2, 1863 824
  January 3, 1863 825
  January 10, 1863 831
  January 11, 1863 833
  January 20, 1863 .... 846, 847
Constituted, and limits defined 718
Gardner, Franklin, assigned to duty in 796
List of ordnance and ordnance stores ordered to 775
Maxey, S. B., assigned to duty in 796
Orders, Circulars, series 1862: **Dec. 12**, 794.
Orders, General, series 1862: **No. 1**, 728; **No. 3**, 734; **No. 17**, 787; **No. 19**, 797.
Orders, General, series 1863: **No. 5**, 824; **No. 33**, 847.
Orders, Special, series 1862: **Nov. 30**, 772; **Dec. 1**, 773; **Dec. 9**, 792; **No. 24**, 827.
Pemberton, John C.
  Assigned to and assumes command 716, 718, 728
  Instructions to 716
Subdivisions of.
  First District.
    Constituted, and limits defined 734
    Orders, Special, series 1863: **No. 1**, 827; **No. 3**, 846.
    Ruggles, Daniel, assigned to command 734
  Second District.
    Constituted, and limits defined 734
    Limits extended 748
    Orders, Special, series 1862: **No. 33**, 778.
    Smith, Martin L., assigned to command 734
  Third District.
    Beall, W. N. R., assigned to command 734
    Constituted, and limits defined 734
Mississippi Central Railroad. Operations on the.
Aug. 30–Sept. 1, 1862. Communications from
  Armstrong, Frank C 682, 687–689, 693
  Crocker, M. M 190
  Dennis, E. S 192
  Dodge, Grenville M 192, 194, 195
  Grant, U. S 190, 197
  Lawler, Michael K 192

Page.

Mississippi Central Railroad. Operations on the—Continued.

  Aug. 30–Sept. 1, 1862. Communications from

    Price, Sterling... 689, 690, 693
    Quinby, Isaac F 196
    Ross, Leonard F 197
    Sherman, W. T 189
    Townes, R. R 196

    See also *Sherman to Kelton,* p. 200; *Sherman to Rawlins,* p. 204; *Jordan to Van Dorn,* p. 656; *Price to Van Dorn,* pp. 687, 690.

  Oct. 31, 1862–Jan. 10, 1863.

    Communications from

      Adams, John 758
      Adjutant and Inspector General's Office, C. S. A 777, 782
      Army Headquarters 318
      Barteau, C. R 746, 747, 750, 751, 754, 813
      Blythe, G. L 762, 763
      Bowers, T. S 510
      Buckner, C. B 763
      Davies, Thomas A 479
      Denver, James W 484
      Dickey, Theophilus Lyle 391
      Grant, U. S 296, 311, 312, 314–318, 320,
        322, 324, 328–331, 335, 342, 343, 346, 347, 349, 353, 359, 362, 364–367, 370, 371,
        374, 376, 379, 380, 385, 387, 389, 396, 398, 422, 423, 428, 435, 436, 442, 445, 451,
        454–456, 463, 469, 473, 478, 483, 487, 503, 508, 509, 511, 519, 523, 531–533, 545
      Hamilton, C. S 312,
        313, 316–318, 325, 326, 329, 330, 342–344, 346, 347, 357, 367–369, 373, 455, 509
      Jackson, W. H 766, 902
      Johnston, Joseph E 780, 781, 811–813
      Jones, E. P 762
      Loring, W. W 804, 807, 812, 813
      Lovell, Mansfield 745, 786, 903
      McBee, J. T 754
      McPherson, James B 313, 314, 317, 323, 325, 327, 328, 331, 428, 445,
        446, 452, 478, 487, 497, 509, 518, 519, 521, 525, 532, 533, 540, 543, 548, 549, 554
      Maury, Dabney H 903
      Mizner, J. K 411
      Morris, John B 761
      Pemberton, John C 742,
        743, 745–748, 750, 754–757, 763, 767, 770–774, 778–781, 784–786, 803, 902
      Pride, George G 373
      Quinby, Isaac F 354
      Ruggles, Daniel 771, 773
      Sherman, W. T 344, 358, 361, 368, 374, 381, 385
      Shirk, James W 318
      Starke, P. B 747
      Van Dorn, Earl 740–747, 750, 751, 756, 768, 769, 772, 773, 777, 778, 785
      Waddy, J. R 762
      Withers, H. R 804

    See also *Grant to McPherson,* p. 557; *McPherson to Grant,* p. 558; *Pemberton to Cooper,* p. 766.

  Co-operation of Curtis with Grant 179, 336, 361, 478, 496, 503

  See also

    Dec. 5, 1862. *Coffeeville, Miss. Engagement at.*

Page.

Mississippi Central Railroad. Operations on the—Continued.
> Oct. 31–Jan. 10, 1863.
> Also
>> Dec. 14–19, 1862. *Mobile and Ohio R. R., Miss. Expedition against the.*
>> 20–28, 1862. *Van Dorn's raid. Operations against.*

Mississippi River.
> Operations on. See *Memphis, Tenn. Naval engagement off, and occupation of, by Union forces, June 6,* 1862.
> Resolutions of C. S. Senate. Free navigation of the 712

Mississippi State Troops.
> Calls for 664
> Ordered into active service... 599, 617
> Orders, Special, series 1862: **No. 5,** 599.

Mississippi Troops. Mentioned.
> Artillery, Light—*Battalions:* 14th, 600, 661, 831. *Batteries:* **Brookhaven,** 661; **English's,** 661, 815; **Seven Stars,** 661; **Smith's,** 603, 632, 644; **Stanford's,** 603, 632, 643; **Warren Light,** 633. *Regiments:* 1st,* 661, 699, 815, 825; (*Batteries*), **D,** 815; **H,** 661; **L,** 818.
> Cavalry—*Battalions:* **Baxter's,** 844, 847; **Brewer's,**† 63, 66, 606; **Garland's,** 815; **Hughes',** 815, 838, 845. *Companies:* **Confederate Rangers,**‡ 634; **Henderson's Scouts,** 832, 838; **Hill's, A. P.,** 815, 825; **Hill's, L. E.,** 646, 650; **Magruder Partisans,** 661; **Mitchell's Partisans,** 387; **Norman's,** 661; **Roddey's,** 594, 708; **Terrell Dragoons,** 661. *Regiments:* **1st Partisan Rangers,** 211, 257, 364, 661, 718, 838, 845; **1st,** 47, 137, 205, 216, 217, 610, 649, 661, 844, 846; **4th,** 675, 815, 818, 844, 846; **28th,** 661, 699, 738, 815, 825, 844, 846; **Ballentine's,** 161, 181, 216, 600, 661, 844, 846; **Wirt Adams',** 63, 66, 648, 654, 675, 806, 815, 817, 825, 831, 834, 844. **State.** *Battalions:* **Blythe's,** 738, 747.
> Infantry—*Battalions:* 6th, 661, 699; 7th, 733. *Companies:* **Lewis' Partisans,** 661. *Regiments:* 1st, 729, 733, 737; 3d, 661, 699, 815, 825; 4th, 726, 825; 5th, 633; 6th, 829; 7th, 9th, 10th, 633; 14th, 729; 15th, 829; 20th, 600, 661; 22d, 829; 24th, 603, 632, 643; 29th, 633; 30th, 632; 32d, 633; 33d, 600, 633, 661; 35th, 267, 634, 733; 36th, 733; 37th, 632, 733; 38th, 733; 39th, 661; 40th, 733; 41st, 632; 43d, 669, 733; 44th, 633; 46th, 815, 825.829; **Harman's,** 600. **State.** *Battalions:* 3d, 817, 825, 846. *Regiments:* 5th, 817, 818, 846.

Missouri.
> Operations in. See *Southeastern Missouri.*
> Price's address to soldiers of 794

Missouri, Governor of. Correspondence with O. G. Cates 92

Missouri State Guard.
> Ordered to return to Trans-Mississippi Department........................ 646
> Relieved from duty with the Army of the West............................. 609, 610

Missouri Troops. Mentioned. (Confederate.)
> Artillery, Light—*Batteries:* **Barret's,** 632; **Bledsoe's,** 634, 834; **Clark,** 634; **Guibor's,** 635, 653; **Landis',** 635, 653, 762; **Saint Louis,** 634; **Wade's,** 634.
> Cavalry—*Battalions:* **McCulloch's,**§ 635, 646, 650, 653, 659. *Companies:* **Reves' Scouts,** 634; **Savery's,** 635, 650, 653; **Smith's,**‖ 635, 653, 718. *Regiments:* 1st, 634, 733, ´36; 2d, 718, 838, 844–846; 3d, 634, 733, 736.
> Infantry—*Regiments:* 1st, 729, 733, 736; 2d, 3d, 4th, 5th, 6th, 634, 733, 736.

---

* Batteries designated when practicable.
† Composed of Alabama and Mississippi companies.
‡ Subsequently assigned as Company A, 9th Mississippi Cavalry.
§ Became 2d Regiment Aug. 17, 1862.
‖ Became Company I, 2d Cavalry, Aug. 17, 1862.

974 INDEX.

Missouri Troops. Mentioned. (Union.)

Artillery, Light—*Batteries:* Landgraeber's,* 539. *Regiments:* 1st,† 145 248, 341,517; (*Batteries*), **A**, 495; **C**, 145,247,339,515; **G**, 147,200; **I**, 147; **M**, 147,340,516; **2d**, 471.

Cavalry—*Regiments:* **1st**, 148; **5th**, 148,248,340,516; **10th**, 486,495,539.

Engineers—*Regiments:* Bissell's, 129,146,246,249,314,315,326,341,373,443, 517,578.

Infantry—*Regiments:* **2d U. S. Reserve Corps**, 148,162,164; **2d**, 148; **3d**, 539,574; **5th**, 146; **6th**, 146,212,246,329,340,344,539; **7th**, 144,168,212, 247,275,338,514; **8th**, 61,146,212,246,275,340,344,539; **10th**, 147,248, 339,516; **11th**, 147,218,248,339; **12th**, 539,574; **14th**, 145,249,341,517, 755; **15th**, 148; **17th**, 539,574; **18th**, 145,249,340,517; **21st**, 145,249, 495; **24th**, 248,339,516; **25th**, 145,249; **26th**, 147,248,339,516; **29th**, **30th**, **31st**, **32d**, 539; **33d**, **35th**, 495; **Mississippi Marine Brigade**, 406.

Mitchel, Ormsby M. Mentioned 67
Mitchell, Greenville M. Mentioned 341
Mitchell, Joseph W. Mentioned 249,340,515
Mitchell, Robert B.
  Assignments to command... 105
  Mentioned........................ 35,53,54,77,91,105,151,152,167,176,177
Mizner, John K.
  Assignments to command.. 200,245
  Correspondence with
    Dickey, Theophilus Lyle 391
    Grant, U. S.............. 411,412,437–439,443,448,472,484,493,498
    McPherson, James B 438
    Rosecrans, W. S.. 154,271
  Mentioned....... 61,62,76,77,106,148,167,191,193,197,200,221–224,227,245,248, 265,266,301,364,429,435,437,438,440,442,443,447,448,455,521,540
Mobile, C. S. S. Mentioned.. 724,725
Mobile, Ala. Defenses of (immediate). Communications from
  Bragg, Braxton 657,659
  Davis, Jefferson... 659
Mobile and Ohio Railroad.
  Expedition against, Dec. 14–19, 1862. Communications from
    Adams, John 796–799
    Barteau, C. R... 796,799
    Grant, U. S............................. 388,395,399,403,410,411
    Johnston, Joseph E 798
    Mizner, J. K 412
    Pemberton, John C.. 798
    Ruggles, Daniel.. 797,799
  Raid on, Dec. 13–19, 1862. Communications from
    Dodge, Grenville M....................................... 403,404
    Grant, U. S 399,403,410,411
    Mersy, August 457
Mohrstadt, John C. Mentioned.................................... 340
Molinard, A. S. Mentioned....................................... 340
Monarch, U. S. S. Mentioned.................................. 887,888
Montague, A. W. Mentioned 419
Montgomery, Frederick. Mentioned 866
Montgomery, William A. Correspondence with Thomas J. Newsham....... 880

*Also called 1st Horse. Became Battery F, 2d Artillery, in September, 1862.
† Batteries designated when practicable.

Page.

Moore, David. Mentioned 145 249, 254, 495
Moore, Francis T. Mentioned 517
Moore, Frank. Mentioned.. 513, 517
Moore, John C. (Colonel.) Mentioned....................................... 639
Moore, John C. (General.)
   Assignments to command...................................... 705
   Mentioned.............................. 267, 592, 634, 653, 684, 701, 705, 733, 765, 831
Moore, Jonathan B. Mentioned... 340, 515
Moore, P. W. Mentioned 418
Moore, Risdon M. Mentioned 340
Moore, S. P. Mentioned... 749
Moore, Thomas O. Mentioned 620, 820, 828
Moore, W. H. Correspondence with Sterling Price......................... 669
Morgan, George W.
   Assignments to command 534, 564
   Mentioned....... 403, 409, 425, 434, 441, 461, 496, 497, 510, 534, 535, 537, 552, 560, 563,
      564, 568, 573, 574, 576, 580, 581, 583, 584, 589, 590, 670, 677, 688, 879, 891, 897
Morgan, James D.
   Correspondence with W. S. Rosecrans 119, 126, 152, 154
   Mentioned 102, 105, 106, 108, 114, 119, 120, 124, 144, 147, 148, 151, 152, 154
Morgan, John H. Mentioned 168, 303, 304, 309, 310, 444, 482, 522, 530, 682, 861
Morgan, William H. Mentioned 145, 247, 339, 472
Moro, Francis. Mentioned 146, 212
Morray, James B. Mentioned 250
Morrill, John. Mentioned.. 341, 517
Morris, John B.
   Correspondence with John C. Pemberton 761
   Mentioned.. 674
Morris, T. E. Correspondence with J. C. Sullivan 373
Morrison, J. H. For correspondence as A. D. C., see *John C. Pemberton.*
Morrison, William R.
   Correspondence with
      Dodge, Grenville M 450
      Sullivan, J. C... 432, 459
   Mentioned................................... 247, 341, 415, 432, 457, 460
Morton, Charles A. Mentioned 345, 435, 538
Morton, George H. Mentioned... 659, 660
Morton, O. P. Mentioned............................ 308, 310, 332, 334, 401, 550
Morton, Thomas. Mentioned.. 145, 249, 341
Moses, G. A. Mentioned 844
Moss, Stephen. Mentioned.. 884
Mound City, U. S. S. Mentioned 30, 887
Mower, Joseph A.
   Correspondence with W. S. Rosecrans 220, 223
   Mentioned................................ 147, 208, 214, 219–221, 224, 227, 257
Moyers, Gilbert. Mentioned.. 340, 454
Mudd, John J. Mentioned 314, 317, 418, 499, 516
Mueller, Alexander L. Mentioned 248
Mueller, Michael. Mentioned 146, 212, 247, 341, 514
Mungen, William. Mentioned................. 96, 146, 212, 246, 340, 344, 539, 568
Munitions of War. Supplies of, etc. Communications from
   Allen, Robert.. 397, 399, 402
   Asboth, A.. 573
   Banks, A. D 834

Page.

Munitions of War. Supplies of, etc.—Continued. Communications from

Beauregard, G. T 595, 599
Bragg, Braxton 620, 638, 650, 672, 678, 680
Callender, F. D 537
Cuney, R. H 752, 753
Davies, Thomas A 535
Davis, Jefferson 612, 622, 686, 713, 802
Dodge, Grenville M 184
Gillespie, John W 771
Grant, U. S 108, 304, 380, 433, 465, 485, 490, 492, 536
Halleck, H. W 22, 83
Hamilton, C. S 301
Johnson, W. H 831, 839
McPherson, James B 472
Maury, Dabney H 845
Mayo, George Upshur 775
Morgan, James D 119
Oladowski, H 627, 643, 775
Ordnance Department, C. S. A 700, 749, 775
Parsons, L. B 441
Pemberton, John C 741, 748, 749, 755, 770, 785, 797, 808
Price, Sterling 676, 680, 695, 711
Price, Thomas H 723
Quinby, Isaac F 354
Reed, T. B 764, 769, 776, 777, 782, 792, 800, 802, 817, 830
Rosecrans, W. S 105, 108, 119, 120, 154, 187, 281, 284, 287
Sherman, W. T 3, 18, 83
Smith, Joseph B 837
Smith, Martin L 755, 778, 805
Tilghman, Lloyd 700
War Department, C. S 700, 749
War Department, U. S 282–284, 290

See also *Hammond to Hurlbut,* p. 45; *Sherman to Hurlbut,* p. 45; *Sherman to Rawlins,* p. 141; *Hurlbut to Rawlins,* p. 506; *Bragg to Cooper,* p. 627; *Cooper to Bragg,* p. 654; *Snead to Falkner,* p. 668; *Bragg to Price,* p. 682; *Van Dorn to Randolph,* p. 697; *Van Dorn to Price,* pp. 706, 711; *Tilghman to Price,* p. 706; *Snead to Tilghman,* p. 709; *Van Dorn to Pemberton,* p. 734; *Johnston to Davis,* p. 823; *Stevenson to Thompson,* p. 829; *Harvie to Fauntleroy,* p. 841.

Murphy, Robert C.
Correspondence with U. S. Grant 439, 440, 444
Mentioned 48, 57, 58, 147, 174, 479, 507, 586
Myers, A. C. Mentioned 775
Myers, William.
Correspondence with H. W. Halleck 61
Mentioned 61
Nale, John H. Mentioned 515
Napier, T. Alonzo. Mentioned 426, 428, 431, 432, 440
Naron, L. N. Mentioned 233
Nashville, Tenn. Affairs in, generally. See *Johnson to Halleck,* p. 14; *Halleck to Johnson,* p. 22.
Natchez, Steamer. Mentioned 862, 867
Naval Vessels. Construction of, etc. Communications from Jefferson Davis. 682
See also *Arkansas, C. S. S.*

Page.

Navy, U. S. Co-operation with Army. Communications from

Halleck, H. W 34

Sheiman, W. T 867

War Department, U. S 40

See also

May 18–July 27, 1862. *Vicksburg, Miss. Operations against.*

June 10, 1862–Jan. 20, 1863. *West Tennessee. Operations in.*

Dec. 15, 1862–Jan. 3, 1863. *West Tennessee. Forrest's expedition into.*

20, 1862–Jan. 3, 1863. *Vicksburg, Miss. Operations against.*

Jan. 4–17, 1863. *Arkansas Post, Ark. Expedition against.*

13–19, 1863. *White River, Ark. Expedition up the.*

20–July 4, 1863. *Vicksburg, Miss. Operations against.*

Also order of Grant, p. 575.

Navy Department, U. S. Correspondence with

Army Headquarters 349, 422

Porter, David D 321, 422, 883, 884, 887, 888

War Department, U. S 320

Nebraska Troops. Mentioned.

Cavalry—*Regiments:* 1st, 4.

Neeley, George W. Mentioned 516

Neely, J. C. Mentioned 221, 345, 510, 538

Neely, J. J., sr. Mentioned 297

Negley, James S.

Correspondence with War Department, U. S 29

Mentioned 5

Neil, Henry M. Mentioned 248

Nelson, Horatio C. Mentioned 73, 148, 354

Nelson, William.

Correspondence with H. W. Halleck 21, 23

Mentioned 14, 23, 24, 239, 261, 593, 604, 611, 613, 677

Nevins, Garrett.

Correspondence with John A. Logan 115

Mentioned 515

Newell, Cicero. Mentioned 860

New Era, U. S. S. Mentioned 486, 500, 520, 886

New Era, U. S. S., Commanding Officer of. Correspondence with Thomas

A. Davies 487

New Madrid, Mo. Evacuation of, by Union forces, Dec. 28, 1862. See *Davies to Halleck*, p. 500 ; *Davies to Curtis*, p. 501.

Newsham, Thomas J. Correspondence with William A. Montgomery 880

Newspaper Correspondents. See *Thomas W. Knox.*

Niles, Nathaniel. Mentioned 340

Nimmo, Alexander J. Mentioned 341, 590

Nixon, John W. Mentioned 724

Noble, Silas.

Correspondence with James B. McPherson 281

Mentioned 231, 247, 513, 517

Nodine, Richard H. Mentioned 147

Non-combatants. Action touching 368, 396

North, J. M. Mentioned 350

Northern Alabama.

Operations in, June 10, 1862–Jan. 20, 1863. Communications from Bragg.. 657

Re-enforcements for. Communications from Samuel Jones 692

Northerner, Steamer. Mentioned 573

Northern Mississippi.　　　　　　　　　　　　　　　　　　　　　　Page.

Operations in, June 10, 1862–Jan. 20, 1863.

　Communications from

　　Adams, Wirt 836
　　Adjutant and Inspector General's Office, C. S. A 774
　　Armstrong, Frank C 675
　　Army Headquarters 142, 214, 222, 225, 234
　　Barteau, C. R 740, 766, 769, 838
　　Beauregard, G. T 591, 593–595, 597–599, 601, 602, 623
　　Bowen, John S 734, 898
　　Bradfute, W. R 597, 607, 611
　　Bragg, Braxton 594, 610, 614–
　　　616, 619, 622, 629, 635, 636, 638, 642, 646, 655, 656, 662, 667, 675, 677, 713, 897
　　Breckinridge, John C 898–900
　　Brown, Isaac N 615
　　Davis, Jefferson 599, 614, 698, 700, 707, 715, 716, 733
　　Dodge, Grenville M 235, 389, 391, 482
　　Edmondson, J. H 602
　　Flournoy, T. C 686
　　Granger, Gordon 112, 163, 164
　　Grant, U. S 87,
　　　102, 112, 136, 148, 150, 173, 175, 209, 213, 214, 218, 227, 232, 240, 243, 276,
　　　290, 292–294, 296, 301, 302, 304–306, 327, 355, 372, 499, 524, 530–532, 543, 544
　　Halleck, H. W 6, 9, 14, 23, 24, 26, 45, 48, 49, 56, 65, 68, 73, 74, 77
　　Hamilton, C. S 47,
　　　57, 224, 292, 293, 300, 301, 304, 310, 524, 525, 530, 531, 544, 550, 574
　　Harman, B. D 605
　　Hill, L. E 593, 607, 611
　　Hurlbut, Stephen A 58, 305
　　Johnston, Joseph E 780, 820, 822, 823, 825, 838
　　Jones, Samuel 694, 705
　　Lee, Albert L 207, 540
　　Leggett, Mortimer D 72
　　Loring, W. W 829, 839
　　McClernand, John A 73
　　McPherson, James B 293
　　Mower, J. A 220, 223
　　Negley, James S 29
　　Pemberton, John C 734–
　　　736, 738–740, 744, 820, 821, 826, 827, 832, 834, 835, 839, 841
　　Pope, John 5, 9
　　Price, Sterling 642, 659, 660, 662–669, 674,
　　　678, 682, 687, 689, 690, 692, 695–700, 702, 703, 705, 707, 709, 710, 714, 737, 845
　　Roddey, P. D 605
　　Rosecrans, W. S 14,
　　　24, 26, 27, 35, 36, 39, 42–44, 47, 48, 57, 61, 64–66, 73–76, 103–105, 107, 108, 111,
　　　124, 126, 130, 131, 139, 148, 151, 152, 154, 162–164, 167, 169, 174, 175, 177, 181,
　　　191, 204, 207, 208, 210, 213–215, 217–225, 227, 233, 234, 241–243, 271, 276, 286
　　Ross, Leonard F 163, 182
　　Ruggles, Daniel 594, 602, 613, 614, 617, 619, 620, 726, 846
　　Sanford, W. W 543
　　Schmitt, William A 193
　　Sheridan, Philip H 65, 75, 111
　　Sherman, W. T 49–51,
　　　58, 66, 70, 72, 79, 149, 166, 204, 229, 244, 288, 329, 854, 874, 875

Page.

Northern Mississippi—Continued.
   Operations in, June 10, 1862–Jan. 20, 1863.
      Communications from
         Smith, John E 558
         Sullivan, J. C 540, 543
         Tupper, T. C 599
         Van Dorn, Earl 592, 613, 675, 691, 692,
           694–697, 701, 703, 705, 706, 710, 711, 713, 714, 727, 728, 732, 734–736, 838, 897
         Waddy, J. R 829
         Walker, F. M 898
         War Department, C. S 697, 699, 704, 707, 715
         Whitehurst, Eli 306
         Williams, J. T 604, 613
      See also *Sherman to Rawlins*, pp. 84, 201, 279, 285, 855, 857; *Grant to Halleck*, pp. 114, 160, 220; *Sherman to Grant*, pp. 178, 860; *Grant to Kelton*, p. 206; *Hillyer to Sherman*, p. 307; *Bragg to Price*, pp. 685, 688; *Johnston to Davis*, pp. 823, 827.

      Also
         June 15–18, 1862. *Holly Springs, Miss. Expedition to.*
         July   1, 1862. *Booneville, Miss. Action near.*
                           Holly Springs, Miss. Skirmish near.
             5, 1862. *Hatchie River, Miss. Skirmish on the.*
         27–29, 1862. *Ripley, Miss. Expedition to.*
         Sept.   5– 6, 1862. *Holly Springs, Miss. Scout toward.*
             8–13, 1862. *Memphis, Tenn. Expedition from, to the Cold-water and Hernando, Miss.*
             19, 1862. *Iuka, Miss. Engagement at.*
                        Queen of the West. Attack on the, near Bolivar, Miss.
         Oct.   3–12, 1862. *Corinth, Miss. Battle of, October 3–4, and pursuit of Confederate forces from, October 5–12.*
             31, 1862–Jan. 10, 1863. *Mississippi Central Railroad. Operations on the, from Bolivar, Tenn., to Coffee-ville, Miss.*
         Nov.   27–Dec. 6, 1862. *Grenada, Miss. Expedition to vicinity of.*
         Dec. 13–19, 1862. *Mobile and Ohio Railroad. Raid on, from Corinth to Tupelo, Miss.*
             24, 1862. *Tallahatchie River, Miss. Expedition to.*
      Co-operation of
         Curtis with Grant 179,
           216, 225, 229, 232, 234, 235, 241, 243, 244, 262, 307, 308, 351, 352, 877
         Van Dorn and Price 656,
           663–666, 675–677, 687, 688, 690–693, 696–699, 701–707, 709–711, 714
   Re-enforcements for. Communications from
      Army Headquarters 283, 298, 303, 308, 309
      Grant, U. S 232
      McClernand, John A 310
      Pemberton, John C 738
      Ruggles, Daniel 724, 726
      Tuttle, J. M 269
      War Department, U. S 310
      Wright, H. G 299 309
      See also *Halleck to Grant*, pp. 234, 268; *Hillyer to Sherman*, p. 307.
Northern Virginia, Army of. Orders, Special, series 1863; **No. 19**, 846.
Northrop, Charles. Mentioned 147

Page.

Northrop, Lucius B. Mentioned 628,713
Norton, Addison S.
    Correspondence with
        Grant, U. S 370, 416, 483
        Richardson, R. V... 418, 419
        Sullivan, J. C... 376, 387, 390, 400
    Mentioned 247, 338, 515
Nott, J. C. Mentioned... 648
Noyes, Edward F. Mentioned... 248, 339
Nugent, Edward B. Mentioned... 437
O'Bannon, L. W. Mentioned... 638, 648
O'Brien, Steamer. Mentioned... 352, 481, 880, 881
Ogden, Fanny, Steamer. Mentioned... 573
Oglesby, Richard J. Mentioned... 145, 258, 270
O'Hara, Thomas. Mentioned... 429
O'Harnett, Morison J. Mentioned... 144
Ohio, Army of the.
    Buell, Don Carlos, ordered to resume command of... 3
    Sherman, T. W., assigned to duty in... 3
    Thomas, George H., ordered to resume command of his division 3
Ohio Belle, Steamer. Mentioned... 573
Ohio Troops. Mentioned.
    Artillery, Light—*Batteries:* **3d,** 145, 213, 247, 249, 338, 514; **4th,** 539, 574;
        5th, 145, 249, 340, 515; **7th,** 145, 247, 339, 515; **8th,** 146, 212, 247, 341, 539;
        10th, 145, 249, 340, 515; **11th,** 147, 248, 340, 516; **14th,** 144, 213, 247, 331,
        342; **15th,** 145, 247, 339, 342, 515.
    Cavalry—*Companies:* **4th,** 146, 168, 212, 247, 326, 331, 342, 512, 515. *Regi-*
        ments: **1st,** 4, 26; **5th,** 4, 28, 144, 145, 150, 176, 189, 205, 247, 248, 282, 287,
        317, 339, 341, 342, 364, 414, 457, 516, 517.
    Infantry—*Regiments:* **16th,** 580, 891; **20th,** 144, 213, 247, 338, 514; **22d,**
        145, 249, 341, 516; **27th,** 147, 248, 339; **39th,** 147, 221, 248, 339; **43d,** 147,
        248, 339, 527; **46th,** 27, 33, 146, 212, 246, 280, 340, 344, 514; **48th,** 146,
        212, 246, 340, 344, 516; **50th,** 33; **53d,** 146, 212, 246, 340, 344, 514; **54th,** 40,
        146, 212, 246, 340, 344, 539; **56th,** 28, 40, 44; **57th,** 70, 146, 212, 246, 340, 344,
        539, 568; **58th,** 539; **63d,** 147, 248, 339; **68th,** 144, 213, 247, 338, 514; **70th,**
        31, 146, 212, 246, 340, 344, 514; **71st,** 146, 183, 186, 250, 517; **72d,** 146, 212,
        246, 329, 340, 344; **76th,** 539, 574; **77th,** 146, 202, 211, 244, 260; **78th,** 144,
        213, 247, 275, 338, 479, 514; **80th,** 147, 248, 339, 516; **81st,** 145, 249, 341, 516.
Ohr, Simon P. Mentioned... 341
Oladowski, H.
    Correspondence with
        Bragg, Braxton 627
        Champneys, J. T... 643
        Ordnance Department, C. S. A 775
    Mentioned... 648, 775
Oliver, John M. Mentioned... 249
Oliver, William S. Mentioned... 212, 338, 514
Omaha, Steamer. Mentioned... 568, 573
Ord, E. O. C.
    Assignments to command 153, 167, 237, 268
    Correspondence with
        Grant, U. S... 230, 239
        Halleck, H. W 26
        Leggett, Mortimer D... 229
        McArthur, John... 235

Page.

Ord, E. O. C.—Continued.
Mentioned 112, 124, 136, 143, 145,
     153, 167, 206, 218, 227, 229, 230, 237, 239, 240, 245–247, 253, 263, 264, 268, 708

Ordnance Department, C. S. A. Correspondence with
Adjutant and Inspector General's Office, C. S. A 749
Bragg, Braxton 678
Johnston, Joseph E 781
Oladowski, H 775
Pemberton, John C 748, 770
War Department, C. S 700, 749, 775

O'Reilly, T. Mentioned 885
Orr, J. A. Mentioned 273
Osband, E. D. Mentioned 31, 175, 176, 246
Osterhaus, P. J. Mentioned 573, 574, 783, 874
Otey, John M. Mentioned 648
Oxford, Miss. J. Z. George assigned to command at 745

Ozburn, Lyndorf.
Correspondence with John A. Logan 80
Mentioned 80, 89, 144, 212, 247, 338, 514

Paige, C. L. Mentioned 350

Paine, E. A.
Assignments to command 193
Mentioned 86, 168, 174, 176, 177, 193

Pallen, M. A.
Correspondence with Earl Van Dorn 901
Report of sanitary condition of Army of West Tennessee 901

Palmer, John M.
Assignments to command 193
Mentioned 193

Palmerston, Lord (Henry John Temple). Mentioned 671
Pargoud, J. F. Correspondence with Martin L. Smith 804
Park, John. For correspondence, etc., see *Memphis, Tenn., Mayor of.*
Parker, F. S., jr. Mentioned 648
Parrott, Marcus J. Mentioned 35, 53

Parsons, L. B.
Correspondence with
  Army Headquarters 413, 441, 496
  Grant, U. S 355
  Pride, George G 352
Mentioned 355, 421, 426, 536

Parsons, Moseby M. Mentioned 596, 610, 646, 677
Patrick, Matthewson T. Mentioned 146, 250, 517
Paul Jones, Steamer. Mentioned 867
Payne, Captain. Mentioned 746
Payone, M. S. Mentioned 418
Pearce, Mr. Mentioned 812
Pearce, E. T. Mentioned 329
Pease, Phineas. Mentioned 212
Peckham, James. Mentioned 586
Pegram, John. Mentioned 648, 765

Pemberton, John C.
Assignments to command 716, 718, 728
Correspondence with
  Adams, John 740, 758, 826
  Adams, Wirt 803

Pemberton, John C.—Continued.

   Page.

  Correspondence with

    Adjutant and Inspector General's Office, C. S. A 724,
       740, 742, 745, 749, 753, 757, 762–764, 766, 768, 770, 774, 779, 786, 833

    Barteau, C. R 740, 746, 747, 750, 751, 754, 766, 769, 832

    Bragg, Braxton 743, 744, 754, 755, 769, 771, 778

    Brown, Isaac N 788

    Buckner, C. B 763

    Clark, M. R 829

    Connell, W. M. M 808

    Cuney, R. H 755

    Davis, Jefferson 767, 772, 786

    Dillon, Edward 762

    Fall, Phillip 804

    Forney, John H **768, 773**

    Gardner, Franklin 837

    Gregg, John 827

    Hébert, Louis 812

    Holmes, Theophilus H 748, 766

    Jackson, W. H 821

    Johnston, Joseph E 780,
       781, 784, 805, 806, 808–811, 813, 815–817, 820, 822, 823, 825, 827, 832, 833

    Jones, E. P 762, 763

    Jones, Samuel 734, 742

    Looney, R. F 743

    Loring, William W 800,
       804, 805, 807, 808, 812, 816, 822, 827, 829, 830, 832, 835, 837, 839, 841

    Lovell, Mansfield 744, 786

    Lovell, W. S 736

    Lynch, W. F 724

    McBee, J. T 754

    Maury, Dabney H 804, 845

    Mims, L 805, 808

    Morris, John B 761

    Ordnance Department, C. S. A 748, 770

    Price, Sterling 741, 744, 770, 774, 779, 803, 902

    Ruggles, Daniel 797–799

    Sherman, W. T 871, 872

    Shields, Thomas 834

    Smith, Martin L 738,
       748, 751, 754, 762–764, 767, 770, 771, 774, 780, 793, 794, 803, 817, 829

    Starke, P. B 738, 745, 747

    Stevenson, C. L 814, 815, 821, 824, 826, 828, 829, 831, 837

    Tracy, E. D 821

    Van Dorn, Earl 728, 732, 734–740, 742–
       744, 746, 747, 750, 751, 754–757, 767–770, 777–779, 785, 793, 812, 813, 833, 834

    Waddy, J. R 762, 763, 767, 785, 797, 805, 806, 826, 829

    War Department, C. S 716, 727, 737, 739, 751, 759, 828, 839

    Whitfield, George 822

    Whitfield, John W 814

  Instructions to 716

  Mentioned 279, 280, 285, 286, 289, 290, 304, 310, 327, 331, 335, 336, 357,
    411, 493, 527, 574, 716, 718, 726–728, 733, 738, 743, 752, 755, 758, 762, 764–766,
    768, 770, 771, 773–777, 780–783, 786–789, 796, 798, 800, 802, 814, 815, 817–819,
    822, 823, 826, 833, 834, 846, 847, 854, 855, 857, 866, 867, 870, 871, 873, 874, 903

Page.

Pemberton, John C.—Continued.
Staff. Announcements of 728
Pembina, Steamer. Mentioned 573
Penninger, George W. Mentioned 587
Pennock, A. M.
Correspondence with U. S. Grant 426, 530, 541, 544, 550
Mentioned 886
Peoria Belle, U. S. S. Mentioned 573
Perczel, Nicholas. Mentioned 147
Perkins, Mr. Mentioned 57
Perkins, Scout. Mentioned 400
Perkins, S. H. Mentioned 639
Perrine, Thomas M. Mentioned 590
Perryville, Ky. Morgan's retreat from, Oct. 17–Nov. 4, 1862. Communications from
Davies, Thomas A 303, 304, 309
Grant, U. S 303, 310
Peterson, S. G. W. Mentioned 516
Petri, Charles. Mentioned 147
Pettus, J. J. Mentioned 614, 663, 665, 674, 677, 700, 710, 712, 719, 726, 818
For correspondence, etc., see *Mississippi, Governor of.*
Peytona, Steamer. Mentioned 867
Pfaender, William. Mentioned 145
Phelan, James. Correspondence with Jefferson Davis 726, 788
Phelps, S. L. Mentioned 30, 244, 392
Phifer, Charles W.
Assignments to command 728
Mentioned 591, 635, 653, 684, 713, 728
Phillips, C. D. Mentioned 824
Phillips, E. D. Mentioned 341, 517
Phillips, Jesse J. Mentioned 516
Phul, Henry von, Steamer. Mentioned 573
Pickett, W. D. Mentioned 639
Pike, Albert. Mentioned 55
Pile, William A. Mentioned 147
Pillow, Gideon J.
Assignments to command 691, 710
Correspondence with
Sherman, W. T 172
Van Dorn, Earl.. 715
Walker, Samuel P 171
War Department, C. S... 716
Mentioned 170, 253, 269, 691, 710, 713, 859
Pinney, Oscar F. Mentioned 147
Pinson, R. A. Mentioned 84
Pipe, George. Mentioned 249
Pirtle, John B. For correspondence as A. A. A. G., see *F. M. Walker.*
Pittsburg, U. S. S. Mentioned 886
Pitzman, Julius. Mentioned... 435, 538
Planet, Steamer. Mentioned 573
Plummer, E. S., et al. Correspondence with W. T. Sherman............... 114
Polar Star, Steamer. Mentioned 573
Polignac, C. J.
Correspondence with Braxton Bragg 609
Mentioned 648

Polk, Leonidas.   **Page.**

   Assignments to command 636

   Mentioned 29, 165, 495, 596, 603, 618, 632, 636, 652, 765, 859

Polk, Thomas, Mrs. Mentioned 836

Polk, Trusten. Mentioned 859

Pollard, E. A. Mentioned 680

Poole, D. H. Mentioned 639

Pope, John.

   Assignments to command 3, 40

   Correspondence with

      Asboth, A 5

      Halleck, H. W 5, 9, 18, 20

      War Department, U. S 17, 18

   Mentioned 3, 40, 41, 52, 92, 162, 164, 186, 330, 605, 662, 670, 671, 731, 732

   Transfer of, to Army of Northern Virginia. Communications from

      Halleck, H. W 20, 52

      Pope, John 18

      War Department, U. S 17, 41

Porter, Daniel A. Mentioned 144

Porter, David D.

   Correspondence with

      Grant, U. S 356, 380, 404, 426, 551

      McClernand, John A 541, 547, 548, 570

      Navy Department, U. S 321, 422, 883, 884, 887, 888

      Sherman, W. T 392, 862, 867, 878–880, 882, 889

   Mentioned 320, 323, 349, 351, 352, 409, 422, 424,

      426, 447, 477, 487, 529, 536, 546, 551, 552, 560–563, 582, 585, 589, 876, 877, 879

Porter, Edward E.

   Correspondence with Braxton Bragg... 621

   Mentioned 99, 161

Porter, Jacob M. Mentioned 212, 247

Porter, W. D. Mentioned 175

Port Hudson, La.

   Defenses of (immediate). Communications from

      Pemberton, John C 833

      Ruggles, Daniel.. 719

      See also *Pemberton to Cooper*, p. 749; *Pemberton to Johnston*, p. 784.

   Re-enforcements for. Communications from

      Pemberton, John C 820, 826, 827

      Stevenson, C. L.. 828

      Van Dorn, Earl 717

Post, P. Sidney. Mentioned... 147

Post Office Department, U. S. Correspondence with A. H. Markland...... 7

Potter, Joseph A. Mentioned 355

Potts, R. Mentioned 749

Powell, Albert M. Mentioned... 516

Powell, John W. Mentioned... 145

Powers, E. B. Mentioned 418

Pratt, F. G. Correspondence with W. T. Sherman 868

Prentice, George D. Correspondence with W. T. Sherman...................... 858

Prentiss, B. M. Mentioned 641

President, C S. See *Jefferson Davis*.

President, U S. See *Abraham Lincoln*.

Page.

Preston, William.
Correspondence with
Bragg, Braxton 608, 616
Ruggles, Daniel 621, 622
Mentioned 610, 630, 765
Preston, Zenas. Mentioned 831
Price, Edward. Mentioned 279
Price, Sterling.
Address to the Soldiers of Missouri 794
Assignments to command 636, 654, 657, 729, 787, 824
Co-operation with Van Dorn. See *Northern Mississippi.* *Operations in, June*
10, 1862–*Jan.* 20, 1863.
Correspondence with
Adams, John 666, 669, 695
Alabama, Governor of 674
Armstrong, Frank C .. 646, 650, 662, 666, 675, 682, 687–689, 693, 697, 699, 702, 708
Baxter, George L 667
Bragg, Braxton 657,
662, 663, 666, 667, 675, 677, 678, 682, 683, 685, 688, 690, 696, 703, 706
Commanding Officer Forty-second Alabama 700
Falkner, W. C 668
Hébert, Louis 720
Jones, Samuel 692, 694, 695
Kitchen, Sol. G 659
Leggett, Mortimer D 229, 230
Little, Henry 660, 689, 690, 695, 698, 702, 707, 708
Loring, W. W 807, 845
Lovell, Mansfield 745
Maury, Dabney H 702, 706
Mississippi, Governor of 664, 666
Moore, W. H 669
Pemberton, John C 741, 744, 770, 774, 779, 803, 902
Price, Thomas H 723
Rosser, Thomas H 682
Tennessee, Governor of 714
Tilghman, Lloyd 695, 704, 706, 709
Van Dorn, Earl 663, 665, 675, 680, 687, 690–
692, 695, 696, 698, 701–703, 705–711, 714, 717–721, 723, 737, 741, 743, 744, 747
War Department, C. S 668, 676, 683, 759
Mentioned 14,
23, 29, 34, 37, 47, 58, 103, 107, 114, 132, 136, 139, 148, 163–165, 178, 192, 195,
197, 199, 207–210, 213, 214, 217, 218, 220, 222–224, 227, 228, 230, 233, 234, 238,
241–243, 250, 251, 253, 256, 258, 259, 261, 265, 267, 273, 279, 285, 286, 288, 291–
294, 301, 302, 304, 306, 307, 316, 318, 323, 325, 326, 331, 335, 336, 357, 369, 411,
454, 526, 543, 592, 596, 645, 648, 654, 656, 657, 669, 673, 676, 683, 686, 690, 695–
697, 699–705, 707, 709, 713, 715, 717, 726, 727, 729, 733, 739, 740, 757, 759, 765,
785–787, 800, 808, 814, 815, 818, 823, 824, 829, 840, 842, 843, 857, 862, 874, 897
Staff. Announcements of 637, 654
Transfer of command of, to Trans-Mississippi Department 759–761, 794–796
Price, Thomas H.
Correspondence with Sterling Price 723
Mentioned 637, 654
Pride, George G.
Appointed chief engineer of military railroads in Department of the Ten-
nessee 315

Page.

Pride, George G.—Continued.

   Correspondence with

      Grant, U. S 380, 434

      Parsons, L. B 352

      Sullivan, J. C 373

   Mentioned 262, 297, 315

      For correspondence as Aide-de-Camp, see *U. S. Grant.*

Prima Donna, Steamer. Mentioned 573

Prime, Frederick E. Mentioned 122, 140, 188, 200, 201, 217, 221, 304, 507

Prince, Captain. Mentioned 525

Prince, Edward. Mentioned 74, 248, 339, 516

Pringle, J. S., Steamer. Mentioned 573

Prisoners of War.

   Paroled and exchanged. Communications from

      Davis, Jefferson 700

      Grant, U. S 464

      Price, Sterling 676

      Ruggles, Daniel 827

      Tilghman, Lloyd 704, 706

      War Department, C. S 699, 704

     See also *Bragg to Price,* p. 682; *Van Dorn to Secretary of War,* p. 697; *Randolph to Davis,* p. 697; *Davis to Randolph,* p. 698.

   Treatment, exchange of, etc. Communications from

      Army Headquarters 268

      Bragg, Braxton 680

      Dutton, Carlos 495

      Grant, U. S 388, 566

      Halleck, H. W 9, 67

      Hurlbut, Stephen A 270

      McClernand, John A 561

      Pope, John 9

      Rinaker, John I 388

      Rosecrans, W. S 219

      Sherman, W. T 873

     See also *Halleck to Grant,* p. 60; *Sherman to Kelton,* p. 200; *Burke to Grant.* p. 270; *Rosecrans to Grant,* p. 283; *Gordon to Lovell,* p. 352; *Dodge to Rawlins,* p. 482; *Grant to Dodge,* p. 482; *Curtis to Grant,* p. 578; *Sherman to Rawlins,* pp. 855, 870; *Pemberton to Sherman,* p. 871; *Sherman to Pemberton,* p. 872.

Pritchett, James M. Mentioned 885

Private Property. Action touching. Communications from

   Adjutant-General's Office, U. S. A 91

   Adjutant and Inspector General's Office, C. S. A 598

   Beauregard, G. T 601

   Bowen, John S 739

   Bragg, Braxton 621, 646

   Cates, O. G 91, 93

   Chenowith, B. P 53

   Grant, U. S 87, 326, 331, 349, 505, 575

   Halleck, H. W 77, 91, 92

   Hamilton, C. S 321

   McClernand, John A 571

   Missouri, Governor of 92

   Norton, A. S 416

Page.

Private Property. Action touching—Continued. Communications from
Pemberton, John C 793, 801
Polk, Leonidas 622
Rosecrans, W. S 271
Ruggles, Daniel 598, 601, 602, 611
Sanford, W. W 94
Sherman, W. T 13, 16, 23, 81, 390, 556, 572, 858
Van Dorn, Earl 729

See also *Deitzler to Quinby*, p. 34; *McClernand to Halleck*, p. 60; *Tresilian to Ozburn*, p. 80; *Logan to Wallace*, p. 80; *Ihrie to McPherson*, p. 324; *McPherson to Lauman*, p. 325; *Edmondson to Ruggles*, p. 602; *Ruggles to Shelby*, p. 604; *Ruggles to Edmondson*, p. 613; *Garner to Chalmers*, p. 642; *Snead to Falkner*, p. 668; *Johnson to Davis*, p. 730; *Sherman to Grant*, p. 860; *Orders of, McClernand*, p. 534, *Van Dorn*, p. 745.

Also *Slaves and Slave Property*.

Proctor, Stephen R. Mentioned 601, 641
Provence, David. Mentioned 737
Pryor, J. P. Mentioned 693
Public Property. Communications from U. S. Grant 70
Pugh, Isaac C. Mentioned 145, 247, 323, 515
Purcell, William. Mentioned 249, 340, 515
Putnam, Holden. Mentioned 340, 516
Putnam, J. F. Mentioned 539
Quarles, W. A. Mentioned 729, 733, 737
Queen of the West, U. S. S.
Attack on, near Bolivar, Miss., Sept. 19, 1862. Communications from Alfred W. Ellet 277
Mentioned 242, 277, 884, 885, 887, 888
Quinby, Isaac F.
Assignments to command 211, 237, 298
Correspondence with
Army Headquarters 196, 198
Deitzler, George W 34
Dodge, Grenville M .. 66, 81, 104, 107, 109, 110, 123, 131, 180, 192, 194, 195, 199, 206
Grant, U. S 107, 123, 153, 179, 184, 203, 236, 353, 354, 357–359, 456, 473, 504, 524, 542
Halleck, H. W 4, 20, 86
Hamilton, C. S 524, 548
Sherman, W. T 142
Slack, James R 13
Mentioned 12, 19, 38, 42, 54, 56, 59, 64, 77, 101, 102, 143, 146, 168, 176, 185, 211, 237, 238, 242, 246, 250, 292, 298, 313, 325, 326, 328–331, 339, 342–344, 349, 362, 368, 374, 380, 385, 435, 451, 455, 456, 461, 485, 499, 501, 506, 507, 513, 516, 518, 520, 522, 524, 564, 565, 577
Quinn, Francis. Mentioned 144
Quitman, General, Steamer. Mentioned 862
Rafferty, James L. Mentioned 67
Rains, James E. Mentioned 765
R. Allen, Steamer. Mentioned 573
Randolph, Tenn. Burning of, Sept. 25, 1862. Communications from W. T. Sherman 235
Randolph, George W. Mentioned 614, 619, 624, 644, 647, 694, 715, 716, 723, 727, 738, 749, 790
For correspondence, etc., see *War Department, C. S.*

Page.

Raney, J. E. Mentioned 418
Rankin, John W. Mentioned 147
Ransom, T. E. G.
　　Correspondence with Thomas A. Davies 304
　　Mentioned................................ 144, 250, 275, 303, 309, 515
Rattler, U. S. S 526, 527, 887
Raum, Green B. Mentioned 248, 339, 516
Rawlins, John A.
　　Correspondence with U. S. Grant 299
　　Mentioned.................................... 142, 397, 463, 558

　　　　For correspondence as A. A. G., see *U. S. Grant.*

R. Campbell, jr., Steamer. Mentioned 573
Read, Charles W. Mentioned 175
Reagan, John H. Mentioned.. 673, 674, 685
Reed, T. B.
　　Correspondence with
　　　　Cuney, R. H 752, 753, 776, 782, 800
　　　　Johnston, Theo 817, 830
　　　　Key, W. O 764, 769
　　　　Mims, L 777
　　　　Smith, Martin L............................. 755, 792, 802, 805
　　Mentioned 755
Reeder, George M. For correspondence as A. A. A. G., see *G. M. Dodge.*
Reese, Elias. Mentioned 884
Reichard, August. Mentioned............................... 618, 632, 652
Reid, Hugh T. Mentioned.................................. 145, 249, 515
Reid, John. Mentioned 637, 654
Reid, T. G. Mentioned 679
Rew, R. Y. Mentioned 605
Reynolds, Private. Mentioned 418
Reynolds, A. E. Mentioned 729
Reynolds, A. W. Mentioned.................................... 821, 831
Reynolds, C. A.
　　Correspondence with U. S. Grant 380
　　Mentioned.. 434, 565, 566
Reynolds, Joseph J. Mentioned 836
Reynolds, Thomas. Mentioned.......................... 249, 340, 515
Rhett, T. S. Mentioned.. 749
Rhoads, Frank L. Mentioned 133, 144, 212, 247
Rhoyal, Robert. Mentioned.. 884
Rice, Elliott W. Mentioned 145, 249, 341, 516
Rice, Lafayette M. Mentioned 248
Rich, John M. Mentioned 586
Richardson, Robert. Mentioned 699
Richardson, Robert V.
　　Correspondence with
　　　　Grant, U. S... 418
　　　　La Grange, Tenn., Commanding Officer at................... 418
　　　　Norton, A. S... 418, 419
　　Mentioned 359, 416, 525, 526, 541, 555, 575
Richmond, Jonathan.
　　Correspondence with J. C. Sullivan.................. 444, 451, 460
　　Mentioned 466, 468, 472, 483
Ricker, Elbridge G. Mentioned 32, 38

Page.

Riggin, John. Mentioned 346, 347, 377–379

Rinaker, John I.
    Correspondence with J. C. Sullivan 388
    Mentioned 341

Ripley, Miss. Expedition to, July 27–29, 1862. Communications from
    Grant, U. S 130
    Rosecrans, W. S 124, 130
    Sheridan, Philip H 132
               See also *Rosecrans to Grant*, p. 131.

Ripley, Miss., Commanding Officer at. Correspondence with W. S. Rose-
    crans 271

Rising Sun, Tenn. Skirmish at, June 30, 1862. Congratulatory orders. (Bragg) 639
              See also *Halleck to Lincoln*, p. 64.

Ritter, Richard. Mentioned 515
Rivers, Mr. Mentioned 575
R J. Lockland, Steamer. Mentioned 867
Roach, Ben. Mentioned.. 793
Roane, J. S. Mentioned 592
Robb, U. S. S. Mentioned 5, 6
Robbins, George W. Mentioned 147, 339
Roberts, James. Mentioned.. 8, 9
Robertson, Captain. Mentioned 488
Robinson, ——. Mentioned... 301
Robinson, T. T. Mentioned 591
Rob Roy, Steamer. Mentioned... 352
Rochester, M. Mentioned.. 77
        For correspondence as A. A. G., see *Isaac F. Quinby*.

Roddey, P. D.
    Correspondence with
        Herridge, T. T 605
        Johnston, Joseph E 826
        Williams, J. T 604, 613
    Mentioned 213, 306, 389, 391, 399, 400, 478, 482, 530, 532, 543,
        657, 658, 612, 649, 662, 692, 796, 798, 811, 813, 817, 823, 826, 832, 833, 844, 847

Rodgers, Benjamin F. Mentioned.. 146, 515
Roe, J. J., Steamer. Mentioned 261
Rogers, George C. Mentioned.. 339, 515
Rogers, Henry A. Mentioned 144, 213, 247, 342, 514
Rogers, John A. Mentioned 247, 878
Romeo, U. S. S. Mentioned 884, 885, 887

Rosecrans, W. S.
    Address to soldiers of Army of the Mississippi 71
    Assignments to command.............................. .... 237, 240, 292
    Correspondence with
        Army Headquarters. 139, 154, 175, 187, 239, 251, 286, 287, 290
        Asboth, A 27, 35, 62, 63, 74, 104
        Callender, F. D.. 105
        Davies, Thomas A 264
        Davis, Jefferson C... 36, 152
        Elliott, W. L... 62
        Granger, Gordon..................... 76, 112, 151, 162–164, 167
        Grant, U. S 103, 107, 108, 111, 120, 124, 130–132, 139, 148,
        151, 162–164, 166, 169, 176, 177, 181, 191, 196, 198, 203, 204, 207, 208, 210, 213–
        215, 217–224, 227, 233, 234, 241–243, 251, 252, 254, 275, 276, 283, 301, 391, 400

INDEX.

990

Page.

Rosecrans, W. S.--Continued.

Correspondence with

Halleck, H. W 14, 24, 26, 34, 42–44, 47, 48, 56, 57, 61, 64, 65, 68, 73, 74, 108

Hamilton, C. S 47, 48, 57, 66, 75, 214, 224, 254, 263, 264

Hurlbut, Stephen A 267

McArthur, John 269

McKean, Thomas J 256, 263, 264

McPherson, James B 119, 264

Mizner, John K... 154, 271

Morgan, James D....................................... 119, 126, 152, 154

Mower, Joseph A 220, 223

Ripley, Miss., Commanding Officer at.................................. 271

Schmitt, William A 193

Sheridan, Philip H... 65, 139

Sherman, W. T 854

Stanley, D. S 251, 254–257, 264, 265

Sullivan, J. C.. 423, 441

Thomas, George H 39

Van Dorn, Earl... 265

War Department, U. S 190, 281–284, 286, 290, 291,

Mentioned 23, 25, 27, 38, 42, 44, 45, 50, 77,

101, 102, 136, 144, 147, 160, 173, 175, 189, 206, 214, 218, 227, 237, 239, 246, 248

253, 255–259, 262, 265, 267, 268, 270, 276, 286, 290, 297, 300, 301, 307, 312, 343,

347, 355, 400, 422, 424, 441, 465, 482, 518, 522, 540, 541, 545, 552, 558, 568, 662,

665, 675, 678, 688, 690, 691, 693, 694, 696, 698, 701–706, 709, 717, 801, 858, 859,

Orders in cases of

Flags of truce 291

Slaves and slave property 97

Ross, Leonard F.

Assignments to command 329, 343

Correspondence with

Dodge, Grenville M 198

Grant, U. S.. 197

Hurlbut, Stephen A 253, 270, 274

Leggett, Mortimer D 116

McClernand, John A 110, 116, 120, 124–126, 152, 155, 161, 163, 167, 182, 183

Mentioned 133, 134, 175, 196,

215, 221, 222, 226, 227, 234, 255, 256, 263, 269, 271, 274, 275, 313, 314, 329, 343,

362, 385, 398, 435, 450, 451, 455, 461, 473, 478, 485, 492, 538, 541, 708, 711, 712

Ross, Orlando H.

Announced as agent and general superintendent of military mails for Department of the Tennessee 363

Correspondence with A. H. Markland 405

Mentioned 363

Rosser, Thomas H.

Correspondence with Sterling Price 682

Mentioned 674

Rowett, Richard. Mentioned.................................. 249, 517

Rowley, William R. Mentioned................................... 391

For correspondence as Aide-de-Camp, see *U. S. Grant.*

Roy, T. B. Mentioned.. 639

For correspondence as A. A. G., see *William J. Hardee.*

Ruggles, Daniel.

Assignments to command 694, 734

Page.

Ruggles, Daniel—Continued.

Correspondence with

Adams, John... 796–799

Adjutant and Inspector General's Office, C. S. A............ 721, 726, 771, 773

Beauregard, G. T.. 595, 597, 598, 601–603

Bragg, Braxton.. 608, 611, 614, 619

Brown, Isaac N.. 615

Edmondson, J. H.. 602, 613

Forney, John H.. 774

Harman, B. D.. 598, 605

Holmes, Theophilus H.. 724

Jackson, W. H.. 598, 602

Lynch, W. F.. 725

Mackall, W. W.. 799

Mississippi, Governor of.. 607, 612

Pemberton, John C... 797–799

Preston, William.. 621, 622

Shelby, W. B.. 604

Smith, Martin L... 709

Thompson, M. Jeff... 620

Van Dorn, Earl... 619, 719, 726

Villepigue, John B.. 611, 614, 617

Mentioned.. 279, 285,
595, 599, 607, 609, 622, 658, 662, 678, 694, 713, 765, 770, 774, 785, 814, 815, 826

Orders, General, series 1862: No. 9, 617.

Relieved from command of post of Jackson, Miss............................ 826

Report of Confederate troops at Jackson, Miss., Jan. 1, 1863............... 819

Russell, D. R. Mentioned.. 729

Russell, R. M. Mentioned.. 618, 632, 652

Rust, Albert.

Assignments to command... 697, 898

Mentioned........ 233, 250, 251, 336, 592, 697, 711, 713, 744, 765, 824, 841, 843, 898, 899

Rutherford, Friend S. Mentioned.. 516

Rutherford, John A. Mentioned.. 418

Rutherford, Tenn., Commanding Officer at. Correspondence with J. C.
Sullivan... 380

Ryan, R. E. Mentioned... 418

Saffarans, John L. Mentioned... 622

Saint Louis, U. S. S. Mentioned....................................... 187

Sale, John B. Mentioned.. 792

Saline, Steamer. Mentioned... 178

Sallie Wood, Steamer. Mentioned.. 140

Sampson, Ezekiel S. Mentioned..................................... 248, 339

Samson, U. S. S. Mentioned... 887

Samuel Hill, Steamer. Mentioned.. 867

Sanborn, John B. Mentioned................................... 147, 227, 248

Sanders, Addison H. Mentioned... 346

Sanders, E. J. Mentioned... 682, 689

Sanderson, William L.

Correspondence with John A. McClernand......................... 13, 39, 64

Mentioned.. 10, 72, 144, 247

Sandidge, L. D. Mentioned... 719

Sands, Frank C. Mentioned................................... 147, 340, 516

Page.

Sanford, William W.
  Correspondence with
    Halleck, H. W 94
    Logan, John A 104
    Sullivan, J. C 543
  Mentioned 212, 313
Sanger, W. D. Mentioned 435, 538
Savage, J. H. Mentioned 603
Sawyer, R. M. For correspondence as A. A. G., see *C. S. Hamilton.*
Sawyer, Samuel. Correspondence with W. T. Sherman 116
Saylor, Thomas. Mentioned 454
Scates, Walter B. Mentioned 332, 334
    For correspondence as A. A. G., see *John A. McClernand.*
Schadt, Otto. Mentioned 539
Schaefer, Frederick. Mentioned 148
Schaumburg, W. C. Mentioned 733
Schenck, Robert C. Mentioned 239
Schermerhorn, Edward. Correspondence with Anson Stager 385
Schmidt, Charles H. Mentioned 146, 341
Schmitt, William A. Correspondence with W. S. Rosecrans 193
Schofield, John M. Mentioned 162, 164, 279, 477, 508, 553, 784, 859, 861
Schultz, ——. Mentioned 526
Schwartz, A. Mentioned 528
    For correspondence as A. A. A. G., see *John A. McClernand.*
Scott, Dr. Mentioned 283
Scott, Jefferson K. Mentioned 248, 516
Scott, John. (Acting Master.) Mentioned 885
Scott, John. (Colonel.) Mentioned 495, 505
Scott, Joseph T. Mentioned 654
Scott, Robert K. Mentioned 144, 247, 514
Scott, Thomas M. Mentioned 773
Scott, W. L. Mentioned 603
Seale, ——. Mentioned 352
Sears, William S. Mentioned 350
Seddon, James A. Mentioned 787
    For correspondence, etc., see *War Department, C. S.*
Sells, Miles. Mentioned 878
Semple, H. C. Mentioned 659
Shane, John. Mentioned 249, 340, 515
Sharp, B. W. Correspondence with W. T. Sherman 865
Shaw, Edward. Mentioned 885
Shearon, Thomas R. Mentioned 603
Shelby, W. B.
  Correspondence with Daniel Ruggles 604
  Mentioned 603, 608
Shelby Depot, Tenn. Scout to, Oct. 22, 1862. See *Memphis, Tenn. Scout
    from, Oct.* 21–24, 1862.
Sheldon, Charles S. Mentioned 517
Shelton, George P. Mentioned 29
Shepard, Isaac F. Mentioned 539
Shepardson, G. J. Mentioned 418, 419
Sheridan, Philip H.
  Assignments to command 200

Sheridan, Philip H.—Continued.
Correspondence with
Asboth, A 61, 62, 65
Granger, Gordon.. 75, 111, 132
Rosecrans, W. S.. 65, 139
Mentioned.. 24, 39,
57, 62, 63, 65, 66, 68, 73–77, 104, 124, 130–132, 136, 139, 148, 169, 175, 200, 207
Sherman, Ellen E. Mentioned 896
Sherman, John. Mentioned 582, 882
Sherman, Thomas W.
Assignments to command 3
Mentioned.. 3
Sherman, William T.
Address to soldiers of First and Third Divisions, Army of the Tennessee.... 397
Assignments to command 99, 110, 237, 297, 364, 433, 461, 534, 538, 564
Correspondence with
Anthony, D. C.. 853
Army Headquarters... 186, 200, 351
Blair, Frank P.. 581, 582, 587, 588
Curtis, Samuel R.. 407, 433, 859
Davies, Thomas A 406
Denver, James W... 10, 13, 19
Fitch, Henry S 156
Fraser, P. A 287
Gorman, W. A..................................... 402, 408, 423, 477, 875, 877
Grant, U. S 44, 66, 79, 84, 109, 121, 140, 141, 166, 169, 178, 187,
201, 204, 210, 215, 217, 234, 244, 259, 272, 279, 285, 288, 307, 315, 322, 335, 347,
366, 367, 371, 374, 396, 408, 412, 414, 426, 570, 855, 857, 860, 870, 874, 892, 895
Halleck, H. W..... 17–19, 21, 22, 27, 32, 39, 40, 42, 44, 48, 49, 58, 70, 79, 83, 90, 100
Halstead, M 895
Hovey, Alvin P.. 856
Hurlbut, Stephen A 10, 11, 28, 32, 38, 45, 50, 58, 88, 89
Hurlbut, Valeria.. 860
Johnson, Andrew 161
Knox, Thomas W... 580, 893, 894
Leggett, Mortimer D.. 72
McClernand, John A............... 40, 534, 537, 560, 562, 563, 568, 571, 572
McPherson, James B... 20
Memphis, Tenn., Mayor of 127, 252
Memphis, Tenn., Mayor and Council of 874
Metropolitan, Steamer, Commanding Officer of Guard on............ 873
Pemberton, John C 871, 872
Pillow, Gideon J 172
Plummer, E. S., *et al*.. 114
Porter, David D.................. 392, 862, 867, 878–880, 882, 889
Pratt, F. G 868
Prentice, George D 858
Quinby, Isaac F 142
Rosecrans, W. S 854
Sawyer, Samuel 116
Sharp, B. W.. 865
Smith, Morgan L.. 11, 209
Steele, Frederick 229, 361, 875, 878
Swayne, John T 863

Sherman, William T.—Continued.

Page.

Correspondence with
Tagg, Joseph 869
Walcutt, Charles C 235
Wallace, Lew 9
Mentioned............... 13, 18, 25, 31, 32, 36, 37, 45, 47, 48, 55, 56, 58, 60, 61, 68, 70, 72,
73, 79, 99, 114, 116, 142, 143, 145, 146, 149, 150, 153, 168, 171, 175, 176, 189, 199,
206, 212, 215, 226, 228, 235, 237, 241, 245, 246, 276, 297, 311, 316–318, 320, 330,
337, 340, 353, 362, 364–366, 376, 384, 393, 397, 407, 410, 421, 425, 432–435, 441,
461, 464, 470, 471, 480, 487, 496, 497, 502, 507, 508, 510, 511, 520, 522, 526–532,
534, 536–539, 542–546, 548–552, 555, 556, 560, 561, 563, 564, 566, 567, 573, 574,
576, 619, 656, 688, 691, 696, 704, 756, 766, 768, 771, 823, 884–888, 891, 894, 896

Orders in cases of
Abandoned property 112, 156, 158
Absentees 165
Bribery and corruption.. 158
Captured property... 106, 219
Cemetery at Memphis, Tenn............................... 278
Conduct of the war.. 240, 280, 289
Non-combatants 368
Preservation of order in Memphis, Tenn. 173, 276, 294
Private property... 16, 23, 81, 390, 556
Slaves and slave property.................................. 15, 106, 113, 158, 294
Trade and intercourse.. 117, 163
Staff. Announcements of.. 435, 538
Relinquishes command of the right wing, Army of the Tennessee 535
Shields, Thomas. Correspondence with John C. Pemberton 834
Shipman, A. W. Mentioned.................................... 871, 873
Shirk, James W.
Correspondence with U. S. Grant 318
Mentioned 392, 885
Shorter, John Gill. Mentioned............................ 682, 692, 790, 791
Sibley, H. H. Mentioned................................... 767, 768, 784, 837
Signal, U. S. S. Mentioned.............................. 884, 885, 887
Silence, Ned. R.
Correspondence with Isham N. Haynie 498
Mentioned 498
Silfversparre, Axel. Mentioned.................... 146, 221, 222, 341
Simmons, Samuel. Mentioned............................ 227
Simonton, J. M. Mentioned............................. 729, 733, 737
Simpson, Samuel P. Mentioned 539
Sims, W. B. Mentioned 592
Sinclair, Robert P. Mentioned.......................... 147
Sinon, J. H. Mentioned 418
Sinon, Thomas. Mentioned.............................. 418
Sioux City, Steamer. Mentioned 573
Skylark, Steamer. Mentioned........................... 202
Slack, James R.
Correspondence with Isaac F. Quinby...................... 13
Mentioned 15, 21, 31, 116
Slaughter, J. E. Mentioned 648, 679, 680, 765
Slaves and Slave Property.
Action touching. Communications from
Dodge, Grenville M 66
Grant, U. S 115, 396

Slaves and Slave Property—Continued.

  Action touching. Communications from

    Halleck, H. W 21
    Pillow, Gideon J 171
    Rosecrans, W. S 97
    Ruggles, Daniel... 638
    Sherman, W. T 10, 15, 106, 172, 858, 863

  See also *Chenowith to Halleck*, p. 53; *Sherman's order*, p. 294; *Memminger to Adams*, p. 740.

  Employment of, as laborers. Communications from

    Army Headquarters... 149
    Beauregard, G. T 605
    Grant, U. S.. 115, 371
    Halleck, H. W 56
    Pemberton, John C 756
    Sherman, W. T 113, 158

  See also *Grant to Halleck*, pp. 60, 82; *Sherman to Rawlins*, pp. 121, 140, 169, 201, 215; *McClernand to Grant*, p. 150; *Elliott to Morgan*, p. 154; *Grant to Quinby*, p. 354; *Ruggles to Shelby*, p. 604; *Ruggles to Smith*, p. 709; *Johnson to Davis*, p. 730; *Waddy to Smith*, p. 738; *Van Dorn to Pemberton*, pp. 750, 756; *Sherman to Hovey*, p. 856.

Slemons, W. F. Mentioned 773, 902
Sloan, Thomas J. Mentioned 514
Small, William E. Mentioned 248, 339, 516
Smith, Mr. Mentioned 10
Smith, Telegraph operator. Mentioned..................................... 72
Smith, Major. Mentioned.. 152
Smith, Major. Mentioned.. 431
Smith, Albert J. Mentioned 648, 668
Smith, Andrew J. Mentioned 403, 409, 425, 434, 441, 461, 485, 496, 497, 510, 563, 573, 580, 581, 583, 587, 589, 590, 878, 890, 891
Smith, Arden R. Mentioned 891
Smith, E. Kirby.
  Correspondence with Braxton Bragg 610, 651
  Mentioned............................... 216, 518, 519, 522, 543, 610, 626, 655, 656, 670, 674, 675, 677, 682, 688, 696, 707, 712, 765, 801, 827, 861, 897
Smith, Francis M. Mentioned 144
Smith, Fred. W. Mentioned 161
Smith, Giles A. Mentioned 146, 212, 246, 340, 344, 526, 539, 549
Smith, Gus. Mentioned 479, 482
Smith, James M. Mentioned... 145
Smith, Jason B. Mentioned 146, 517
Smith, J. Condit. Mentioned... 345, 435, 538, 557
Smith, John B. Mentioned 339
Smith, John E.
  Assignments to command.. 492
  Correspondence with
    Blair, Frank P., jr 558
    Grant, U. S.. 492
    Hamilton, C. S 544
  Mentioned.. 144, 247, 338, 478, 492, 509
Smith, Joseph B. Report of subsistence stores on hand at Vicksburg, Miss., Jan. 15, 1863... 837
Smith, Joseph C. Mentioned 517

Page.

Smith, Joseph L. Kirby. Mentioned...... .... 147, 174, 176
Smith, Martin L.
    Assignments to command.. 734
    Correspondence with
        Johnston, Joseph E..... .... 800, 804, 828
        Pargoud, J. F 804
        Pemberton, John C 738,
            748, 751, 754, 762–764, 767, 770, 771, 774, 780, 793, 794, 803, 817, 829
        Reed, T. B.. 755, 792, 802, 805
        Ruggles, Daniel 709
        Van Dorn, Earl 900
    Mentioned 612, 678, 699, 713, 719, 721, 762, 764, 765,
        775, 777, 797, 801, 803, 810, 814, 815, 817, 825, 828, 830, 831, 833, 845, 866
Smith, Melancthon. Mentioned.. 603
Smith, Milo. Mentioned... 539
Smith, Morgan L.
    Correspondence with W. T. Sherman 11, 209
    Mentioned. 4, 7, 11–13, 23, 25, 27, 33, 47, 50, 81, 102, 109, 116, 118, 119, 122, 149, 150, 169,
        204, 206, 211, 212, 216, 217, 260, 275, 340, 344, 345, 358, 361, 374, 385, 397, 408,
        425, 434, 441, 461, 496, 497, 510, 526, 531, 556, 559, 563, 568, 581, 583, 589, 874
Smith, Preston. Mentioned 603, 643, 644, 765
Smith, R. A.
    Assignments to command... 629
    Mentioned 618, 629
Smith, Robert P. Mentioned 885
Smith, R. W. Correspondence with Braxton Bragg.......................... 609
Smith, Thomas. Mentioned 884
Smith, T. Kilby. Mentioned 146, 212, 246, 340, 344, 539, 549, 581, 587
Smith, William I. Mentioned 527
Smith, William S. Mentioned...... 611
Smoote, George T. Mentioned 617
Smyth, William. Mentioned 539
Snead, Thomas L. Mentioned 637, 654
        For correspondence as A. A. G., see Sterling Price.
Snook, John S. Mentioned 338
Snow, J. C., Steamer. Mentioned.. 573
South Carolina Troops. Mentioned.
    Infantry—Regiments : 10th, 19th, 633.
Southeastern Missouri. Operations in. See New Madrid. Evacuation of, by
        Union forces, Dec. 28, 1862.
Southern Mississippi and East Louisiana, Department of.
    Beall, W. N. R., assigned to duty in 616
    Designated District of the Mississippi 636
    Orders, General, series 1862 : First District (Ruggles), No. 4............. 638
    Van Dorn, Earl, assigned to command of...................................... 613, 616
Southwester, Steamer. Mentioned... 573
Sovereign, U. S. S. Mentioned... 887
Sparrestrom, Frederick. Mentioned.................................... 146, 342, 514
Spaulding, Zeph. S. Mentioned.................................. 147, 248, 251, 339
Spear, Edward, jr. Mentioned 145, 247, 339, 342, 515
Spears, Mr. Mentioned 491
Spencer, George E. Mentioned.. 558
        For correspondence as A. A. G., see Grenville M. Dodge.
Sperry, Isaiah M. Mentioned 250

Page.

Spooner, Benjamin J. Mentioned 340, 344, 539
Spoor, Nelson T. Mentioned 148
Sprague, John W.
  Correspondence with
    Grant, U. S 440
    Sullivan, J. C 444, 460
  Mentioned 147, 440
Sprague, William. Mentioned 76, 88
Spread Eagle, Steamer. Mentioned 568, 573
Stacy, James D. Mentioned 870
Stager, Anson.
  Circular to telegraph operators 379
  Controversy with U. S. Grant. See *Tennessee, Department of the.*
  Correspondence with
    Bruch, Samuel 394, 499
    Grant, U. S 368, 371
    Schermerhorn, Edward 385
  Mentioned 346, 347, 377–379, 386, 387
Stanford, T. J. Mentioned 603
Stanley, David S.
  Assignments to command 343
  Correspondence with W. S. Rosecrans 251, 254–257, 264, 265
  Mentioned 86, 139, 144, 147, 168, 174, 176, 177, 193, 197, 222,
      223, 227, 234, 241–243, 248, 251, 252, 264, 266, 313, 325, 329, 339, 343, 344
Stanton, Edwin M. Mentioned 6, 18, 20, 31, 60, 63, 100, 149, 150,
   185, 189, 276, 334, 347, 372, 378, 379, 386, 415, 463, 502, 563, 564, 567, 853, 858
    For correspondence, etc., see *War Department, U. S.*
Starke, P. B.
  Correspondence with
    Blythe, G. L **763**
    Pemberton, John C 738, 745, 747
  Mentioned 699, 746, 747, 750, 754
Starring, Frederick A. Mentioned 516
Steele, Frederick.
  Correspondence with
    Curtis, Samuel R 395
    Gorman, W. A 412
    Grant, U. S 392, 410
    Sherman, W. T 229, 361, 875, 878
  Mentioned 216, 225, 228, 232, 234, 241, 244, 262, 273, 327, 367, 368, 374, 382–
     384, 401–403, 406, 407, 409, 412, 414, 425, 426, 441, 453, 461, 496, 497, 510, 539,
     549, 560, 563, 573, 576, 581, 582, 585–590, 783, 859, 861, 874, 876, 878, 880, 891
Steems, Adam. Mentioned 418
Stenbeck, Andrew. Mentioned 146, 250
Stephenson, W. J. Correspondence with J. C. Sullivan 460
Stevens, Victor H. Mentioned 350
Stevens, W. J. Mentioned 185
Stevenson, Carter L.
  Correspondence with John C. Pemberton .. 814, 815, 821, 824, 826, 828, 829, 831, 837
  Mentioned 765, 800, 809, 820, 821, 823, 826, 831
Stevenson, John D.
  Correspondence with John A. Logan 198, 202
  Mentioned 144, 247, 257, 318, 323, 326, 330, 331, 338, 497, 514
Stewart, A. P. Mentioned 603, 618, 632, 643, 652, 765

Page.

Stewart, Warren.

  Correspondence with John A. McClernand 125

  Mentioned.. 125, 135–139, 247, 562, 563

    For correspondence as Chief of Staff, see *John A. McClernand.*

Stockton, Philip. Mentioned 700, 775

Stokes, John. Mentioned 587

Stokes, Morgan. Mentioned 591

Stolbrand, Charles J. Mentioned 213, 342, 514

Stone, B. W. Mentioned 592

Stone, George A. Mentioned 539

Stone, George H. Mentioned 145, 248, 341, 517

Stout, Brand. Mentioned 196

Strahl, O. F. Mentioned... 603

Strickland, William M. Mentioned 842, 843

Strickland, William T. Mentioned 513, 517

Strong, W. K.

  Assignments to command 415

  Mentioned.. 101, 102, 143, 146, 415

Stuart, David. Mentioned.. 146, 169,

  212, 246, 289, 336, 340, 344, 345, 539, 549, 560, 573, 576, 581, 582, 585–587, 890

Stuart, J. E. B. Mentioned... 861

Stull, Homer H. Mentioned 144, 213, 247, 342

Sturgess, Robert H. Mentioned 212, 338, 514

Subsistence Stores. Supplies of, etc. See *Munitions of War.*

Sucker State, Steamer. Mentioned 573

Sugg, C. A. Mentioned 729

Sullivan, J. C.

  Assignments to command.. 355

  Correspondence with

    Army Headquarters.. 139

    Bolivar, Tenn., Commanding Officer at 380

    Brayman, M............................ 357, 359, 440, 444, 457, 458, 466, 475–477

    Carroll, Tenn., Commanding Officer at................................. 380

    Coldwater, Miss., Commanding Officer at............................. 380

    Crockett, Tenn., Commanding Officer at 380

    Davies, Thomas A... 415

    Davis' Mill, Miss., Commanding Officer at 380

    Dodge, Grenville M 389, 391, 414, 431, 432, 458, 488, 555

    Dyer, Tenn., Commanding Officer at................................. 380

    Fry, Jacob... 364, 394, 414, 432

    Grant, U. S....... .... 357, 358, 360, 371, 396, 398, 400, 405, 413, 415, 423, 429–

      431, 436, 458, 464, 465, 477, 483, 489–492, 498, 505, 532, 538, 540, 543, 555, 574

    Grierson, Benjamin H... 468

    Harris, Thomas W 365

    Hawkins, Isaac R 444

    Haynie, Isham N............ 313, 389, 415, 458, 467, 477, 484, 491, 493, 497, 498

    Hickory Valley, Tenn., Commanding Officer at....................... 380

    Humboldt, Tenn., Commanding Officer at............................. 380

    Ihrie, George P.. 458

    Ingersoll, R. G 429

    Kenton, Tenn., Commanding Officer at............................... 380

    La Grange, Tenn., Commanding Officer at........................... 380

    Lawler, Michael K.. 360, 431, 477

    Lowe, William W.. 440, 441

    McDermott, John 380, 450, 459, 467

Page.

Sullivan, J. C.—Continued.

Correspondence with

Medon, Tenn., Commanding Officer at 380

Middleburg, Tenn., Commanding Officer at 380

Morris, T. E 373

Morrison, William R 432, 459

Norton, A. S 376, 387, 390, 400

Pride, George G 373

Richmond, J 444, 451, 460

Rinaker, John I 388

Rosecrans, W. S 423, 441

Rutherford, Tenn., Commanding Officer at 380

Sanford, W. W 543

Sprague, John W 444, 460

Stephenson, W. J 460

Toone's, Tenn., Commanding Officer at 380

Trenton, Tenn., Commanding Officer at 380

Troy, Tenn., Commanding Officer at 380

Union City, Tenn., Commanding Officer at 380

Mentioned.......................... 74, 147, 227, 346, 347, 355, 360, 427, 436, 451, 454,

457, 461, 467, 478, 481, 488, 492, 511, 518, 523, 525, 531, 532, 541, 544, 570, 577

Sullivan, Peter J. Mentioned 146, 212, 246, 340, 344

Sullivane, Clement. For correspondence as A. D. C., see *Earl Van Dorn.*

Sunny South, Steamer. Mentioned 573

Sutherland, E. W. Mentioned 885

Swain, James A. Mentioned 345

Swallow, Steamer. Mentioned 535

Swanwick, Francis. Mentioned 147

Swarthout, William. Mentioned 249

Swayne, John T.

Correspondence with W. T. Sherman 863

Mentioned 866, 869

Swayne, Wager. Mentioned 147, 339, 527

Sweeny, Thomas W. Mentioned 249, 341, 516

Switzerland, U. S. S. Mentioned 887

Swords, Thomas. Mentioned 556

Szymanski, Ig. Mentioned 828

Tagg, Joseph. Correspondence with W. T. Sherman 869

Tallahatchie Bridge, Miss. Skirmish at, June 18, 1862. See *Holly Springs, Miss. Expedition to, June* 15-18, 1862.

Tallahatchie River, Miss. Expedition to the, Dec. 24, 1862. Communications from

Gorman, W. A 464, 496

Loring, W. W 807

See also *Gorman to Sherman*, p. 477; *Hurlbut to Rawlins*, p. 506.

Tate, Samuel. Correspondence with Braxton Bragg 637

Tatum, G. W. Mentioned 418

Taylor, B. M. Mentioned 730

Taylor, Charles. Mentioned 350

Taylor, D. G., Steamer. Mentioned 573

Taylor, Ezra. Mentioned 33, 81, 221, 236, 237, 281, 435, 538

Taylor, H. Clay. Mentioned 637, 654, 700

Taylor, J. C. For correspondence as A. D. C., see *John C. Pemberton.*

Taylor, John T. Mentioned 435, 538

Taylor, J. W. Mentioned 86, 200

Page.
Taylor, Richard. Mentioned 670, 691, 713, **717**, 765, **768**, 784
Taylor, Thomas H. Mentioned............................. 765, 821, 831
Taylor, W. H. Mentioned 610
Taylor, W. H. H. Mentioned............................ 145, 247, 342, 414
Tecumseh, Steamer. Mentioned.............................. 573
Telegraph Lines., etc.
 Control of, by Post-Office Department, C. S. Communications from
  Adjutant and Inspector General's Office, C. S. A 685
  Bragg, Braxton................................... 673, 683, 685
  Davis, Jefferson.................................... 700
   See also *Price to Bragg*, p. 683.
 Controversy between Grant and Stager. See *Tennessee, Department of the.*
Telegraph Operator. Correspondence with Marcellus M. Crocker 524
Telegraph Operators. Circular to, of Anson Stager 379
Tennessee.
 Affairs in, generally. Communications from
  Halleck, H. W 22
  Johnson, Andrew 14
 Military departments embracing 7, 278, 624, 627
 Operations in. See
   East Tennessee.
   Middle Tennessee.
   Mississippi River.
   West Tennessee.
Tennessee, Army of the. (Confederate.)
 Gardner, Franklin, relieved from duty...................... 796
 Maxey, S. B., relieved from duty 796
Tennessee, Army of the. (Union.)
 Address to soldiers. (W. T. Sherman) 397
 Brigade and division organization announced 344
 Cadwalader, George.
  Assigned temporarily to command of Second Division.............. 153
  Relieved from duty in.................................. 167
 Cavalry Brigade.
  Organization announced 4
  Revocation of order organizing........................... 20
 Dickey, T. Lyle.
  Assigned to command a brigade of cavalry in the.................. 4
  Assigned to command of cavalry in....................... 30
  Assumes command of Cavalry Division 363
  Order assigning to command a brigade of cavalry revoked............. 20
 Dodge, Grenville M., assigned to command of Davies' division............. 310
 Grant, U. S., ordered to resume command........................ 3
 Hamilton, Charles S., assigned to command of left wing.............. 364
 Hillyer, William S., appointed provost-marshal-general................ 31
 Holston, John G. F., announced as senior medical officer............. 30
 Lauman, J. G.
  Assigned to command of Third Division 358
  Assigned to command of Fourth Division 396
 McClernand, John A., assigned to command in the................. 31
 McKean, Thomas J.
  Assigned to duty in the................................ 205
  Assigned to command of Sixth Division..................... 232
  Assigned to command of Fourth Division, right wing 343
  Relieved of command of Fourth Division..................... 396

Page.

Tennessee, Army of the. (Union)—Continued.

McPherson, James B.

Assigned to command of Provisional Division of...................... 257

Assigned to command of center 364

Relieved from command of Provisional Division 275

Orders, Circulars, series 1863: Jan. 2, 523; Jan. 7, 544.

Orders, Field, series 1862: *Divisions:* 5th (Sherman), **No. 36**, 3; **No. 37**, 4; **No. 39**, 7; **No. 40**, 8; **No. 43**, 15; **No. 44**, 16; **No. 45**, 23; **No. 46**, 33; **No. 48**, 50; **No. 49**, 81; **No. 52**, 96; **No. 53**, 102; **No. 54**, 106; **No. 55**, 109; **No. 56**, 110; **No. 57**, 111; **No. 58**, 112; **No. 60**, 113; **No. 61**, 117; **No. 62**, 118.

Orders, General, series 1862: **No. 14**, 461; **No. 54**, 4; **No. 56**, 20; **No. 57**, 30; **No. 60**, 69; **No. 61**, 70; **No. 62**, 102; **No. 64**, 123; **No. 65**, 130; **No. 69**, 155; **No. 83**, 237; **No. 84**, 240; **No. 87**, 255. *New Series:* **No. 1**, 294; **No. 2**, 297; **No. 4**, 319; **No. 10**, 363; **No. 11**, 424. *Divisions:* 4th (Hurlbut), **No. 108**, 251; 5th (Sherman), **Nos. 66, 67**, 158; **No. 68**, 163; **No. 70**, 165; **No. 72**, 173; **No. 82**, 219; **No. 88**, 278; **No. 90**, 294; **No. 93**, 344; **No. 94**, 358; **No. 97**, 361; Cavalry (Dickey), **No. 1**, 363. *Right Wing:* (Sherman), **No. 2**, 390; **Nos. 3, 5**, 397; **No. 9**, 434; **No. 10**, 435. *Left Wing:* (Hamilton), **No. 2**, 321.

Orders, General, series 1863: **No. 5**, 569; **No. 7**, 575; **No. 12**, 586; **No. 13**, 889. Right Wing (Sherman), **No. 12**, 535. *Corps:* 15th, **Nos. 2, 3**, 556; **No. 4**, 560.

Orders, Special, series 1862: **No. 118**, 30; **No. 123**, 51; **No. 133**, 87; **No. 134**, 89; **No. 136**, 102; **No. 141**, 112; **No. 142**, 115; **No. 143**, 117; **No. 154**, 153; **No. 160**, 163; **No. 161**, 166; **No. 162**, 167; **No. 163**, 173; **No. 165**, 175; **No. 187**, 207; **No. 190**, 211; **No. 195**, 218; **No. 199**, 232; **No. 206**, 242; **No. 210**, 257; **No. 214**, 268; **No. 218**, 275; **No. 221**, 277. *New Series:* **No. 5**, 315; **No. 15**, 343; **No. 21**, 353; **No. 23**, 355; **No. 30**, 363; **No. 31**, 365; **No. 44**, 400; **No. 53**, 492; **No. 58**, 511. *Divisions:* 3d (Hamilton's), **No. 5**, 310; **No. 7**, 313; **No. 11**, 329; 5th (Sherman), **No. 98**, 20; **No. 101**, 33; **No. 107**, 51; **No. 111**, 81; **No. 130**, 96; **No. 147**, 128; **No. 156**, 149; **No. 177**, 167; **No. 210**, 189; **Nos. 227, 228**, 204; **No. 243**, 221; **No. 250**, 237; **No. 254**, 240; **No. 255**, 242; **No. 273**, 276; **No. 283**, 280; **No. 285**, 289; **No. 311**, 329; **No. 332**, 362.

Orders, Special, series 1863: **No. 2**, 523; **No. 6**, 542; **No. 10**, 553; **No. 11**, 554; **No. 12**, 556, 568; **No. 15**, 565; (McPherson), **No. 2**, 540; (Sherman), **No. 3**, 536.

Orders, Special Field, series 1862: **No. 1**, 326; **No. 2**, 331; **No. 6**, 349; **No. 7**, 364; **No. 18**, 396; **No. 19**, 398; **No. 21**, 405; **No. 27**, 433; **No. 32**, 469; **No. 34**, 485; **No. 35**, 505. *Right Wing* (Sherman), **No. 2**, 368; **No. 6**, 381; **No. 9**, 385; **No. 19**, 419; **No. 30**, 453; **No. 32**, 485; **No. 38**, 509; (A. J. Smith) Jan. 1, 519.

Organization, strength, etc.

July 31, 1862 143–146

September 10, 1862 .... 212, 213

September 30, 1862 .... 245–247, 249

October 31, 1862 311

November 10, 1862 337–342

December 31, 1862 512–517

January 3, 1863 527

January 20, 1863 576–578

Page.

Tennessee, Army of the. (Union)—Continued.
    Ord, E. O. C.
        Assigned to command of Second Division 167
        Relieved temporarily of command of Second Division 153
        Reserve Corps of, dissolved... 31
    Ross, Leonard F.
        Assigned to duty in... 329
        Assigned to command Stanley's division, left wing 343
    Sherman, W. T.
        Assigned to command of right wing 364
        Relinquishes command of right wing 535
    Smith, John E., assigned to command Eighth Division, left wing 492
    Strong, W. K., assigned to duty in 415
    Todd, J. B. S., relieved from duty 117
Tennessee, Departme t of the. (Union.)
    Affairs in, generally.   Communications from
        Adjutant-General's Office, U. S. A 278
        Army Headquarters.. 279
        Grant, U. S................................ 279, 294, 297, 307, 542, 553, 554
        Rosecrans, W. S 283, 286, 291
    Constituted, and limits defined 278
    Controversy between Grant and Stager.   Communications from
        Army Headquarters... 386
        Bruch, Samuel 394
        Grant, U. S................................ 347, 368, 370, 371, 377–379, 386
        McDermott, J 386
        Schermerhorn, Edward... 385
        Stager, Anson.. 379
        Van Duzer, J. C.. 394
        War Department, U. S 346, 347, 371, 378, 382
    Grant, U. S., assigned to and assumes command......................... 278, 294
    Jews.   Expulsion of, from 424, 506, 530
    Limits extended (temporarily).   See *Curtis to Grant,* p.578.
    Mail facilities.. 363, 405
    Orders, General, Special, etc.   See *Tennessee, Army of the.* (*Union.*)
    Pride, George G., appointed chief engineer of military railroads........... 315
    Provisions for the poor and destitute. Communications from U. S. Grant. 319, 405
    Ross, Orlando H., announced as superintendent of mails................... 363
    Subdivisions of.   See
        Columbus, District of.   *Jackson, District of.*
        Corinth, District of.   *Memphis, District of.*
    Wallace, Lew., assigned to duty in 308
    Webster, J. D., appointed superintendent of military roads............... 315
Tennessee, District of the. (Confederate.)
    Constituted, and limits defined... 654, 657
    Moore, John C., assigned to duty in....................................... 705
    Orders, General, series 1862: **No. 1,** 654; **No. 35,** 705.
    Price, Sterling, assigned to and assumes command 654, 657
Tennessee, Governor of.   Correspondence with Sterling Price............... 714
Tennessee River.   Capture of steamboats on, Aug. 18, 1862.   Communica-
        tions from U. S. Grant... 182, 202
Tennessee Troops.   Mentioned. (Confederate.)
    Artillery, Heavy—*Battalions:* **1st,** 806, 825.   *Batteries:* **Johnston's,** 818;
      Lynch's, 818; **Rice's,** 815, 818.   *Regiments:* **1st,** 661, 815.

Page.

Tennessee Troops. Mentioned. (Confederate)—Continued.

Artillery, Light—*Batteries:* Bankhead's, 603, 632, 644; Baxter's, 633; Carnes', 603, 632, 643; Eldridge's, 603, 632, 643; Hoxton's, 635, 653; McClung's, 899, 900; White's, 835; Humes', 716.

Cavalry—*Battalions:* Barteau's,* 646, 650, 659, 797, 798, 845; Baxter Smith's,† 835; Cox's, 399, 462; Napier's, 500; 17th, 708, 844, 847; 18th, 66, 844, 846. *Companies:* Forrest Guards, 462; Haywood's Partisans, 195; Mann's,‡ 210, 689; Sanders',‡ 646, 650, 689, 693. *Regiments:* Biffle's, § 399, 414; Dibrell's, 462; Forrest's, 42, 462, 613, 635, 646, 650, 653; Jackson's, 47, 55, 66, 68, 75, 80, 88, 94, 95, 107, 110, 135–138, 153, 183, 205, 211, 217, 364, 595, 608, 619, 638, 639, 649, 661, 838, 844, 845; Murray's, 835; Richardson's, 400, 518, 521; Starnes', 462; Stewart's, 418; Wheeler's,‖ 654, 844, 846.

Infantry—*Companies:* Edmondson's Sharpshooters, 644. *Regiments:* 1st, 603, 632; 2d, 633; 3d, 806, 825; 4th, 5th, 603, 632, 643; 6th, 603, 632, 644; 8th, 603, 632, 643; 9th, 603, 632, 644, 737; 10th, 806, 825; 12th, 13th, 603, 632, 644; 14th, 730; 15th, 16th, 603, 632, 643; 17th, 633; 19th, 20th, 900; 21st, 633; 22d, 603; 23d, 633; 24th, 633, 643; 25th, 633; 27th, 603, 632, 644; 28th, 900; 29th, 633; 30th, 806, 825; 31st, 33d, 603, 632, 643; 35th, 37th, 633; 38th, 632; 41st, 806, 825; 42d, 729, 733, 737; 44th, 633; 45th, 900; 46th, 737; 47th, 603, 632, 644; 48th, 633; 49th, 730, 737; 50th, 730, 806, 825; 51st, 603, 632, 643, 806, 825; 53d, 55th, 737; 60th,¶ 61st,** 62d,†† 806, 815; 154th, 603, 632, 644.

Tennessee Troops. Mentioned. (Union.)

Cavalry—*Regiments:* 6th,‡‡ 212, 247, 317, 342, 458, 527; 7th,§§ 341, 342, 414, 429, 432, 878.

Infantry—*Regiments:* 7th,‖‖ 247, 878.

Tennison, Otto M. Mentioned 247, 249, 340, 515

Terry, W. B., Steamer. See *W. B. Terry, Steamer.*

Texas Troops. Mentioned.

Artillery, Light—*Batteries:* Good's, 634.

Cavalry—*Regiments:* Andrews', 634; 3d, 66, 634, 733, 844, 847; 6th, 592, 635, 733, 844, 847; 8th, 835; 9th, 592, 635, 733, 844, 847; 10th, 11th, 14th, 634; 27th, 634, 733, 844, 847.

Infantry—*Regiments:* 2d, 267, 634, 733; 9th, 603, 632, 643.

Miscellaneous: Waul's Legion, 711, 712, 773, 824, 838, 845.

Thayer, John M. Mentioned 539, 549, 581, 584, 890–892, 894, 895

Thielemann, Christian. Mentioned 212, 341

Thielemann, Milo. Mentioned 144

Thom, George. Mentioned 14, 28

Thomas, Allen. Mentioned 699

Thomas, D. C. Mentioned 340, 344

Thomas E. Tutt, Steamer. Mentioned............................. 573

Thomas, George H.

  Assignments to command 3

  Correspondence with

    Halleck, H. W 24, 77

    Rosecrans, W. S... 39

  Mentioned............. 3, 4, 23, 24, 74, 84, 100, 102, 103, 105, 114, 120, 124, 126, 154, 665

---

*Called also 2d Battalion.
†Called also 4th and 8th Tennessee.
‡Merged into 17th Battalion in September, 1862.
§Called also 9th and 19th Tennessee.
‖Called also 1st and 6th Tennessee.
¶Called also 79th Regiment.

**Called also 81st Regiment.
††Called also 80th Regiment.
‡‡Called also 1st West Tennessee Cavalry.
§§Called also 2d West Tennessee Cavalry.
‖‖Called also 1st West Tennessee Infantry.

Thomas, Lorenzo.

    Mentioned 117, 160, 165, 262, 268, 482, 732

    Orders in case of the 109th Regiment Illinois Volunteers 590

        For correspondence, etc., see *Adjutant-General's Office, U. S. A.*

Thompson, Judge. Mentioned 132

Thompson, Captain. Mentioned 878

Thompson, A. P. Mentioned 662

Thompson, Charles R. Mentioned 225

        For correspondence as Acting Aide-de-Camp, see *W. S. Rosecrans.*

Thompson, J. For correspondence as A. A. G., see *John C. Pemberton.*

Thompson, M. Jeff.

    Correspondence with

        Grant, U. S 98

        Hovey, Alvin P 99

        Ruggles, Daniel 620

    Mentioned 41, 47, 98, 178, 505, 579, 613, 617, 619

Thompson, Noah S. Mentioned 213

Thomson, P. H. Mentioned 637

        For correspondence as A. A. G., see *Braxton Bragg.*

Thornton, Gus. F. Mentioned 617

Thrall, Homer. Mentioned 516

Tigress, Steamer. Mentioned 510, 511, 536, 572, 573

Tilghman, Lloyd.

    Assignments to command 824

    Correspondence with

        Price, Sterling 695, 704, 706, 709

        War Department, C. S 700

    Mentioned 290, 336, 385, 697, 698, 713, 715, 726, 729, 824, 847, 874, 902

Tillson, John. Mentioned 147

Tinkham, Charles J. Mentioned 177

Tobin, Thomas F. Mentioned 283

Tod, David. Mentioned 550

Todd, A. H. Mentioned 181

Todd, J. B. S.

    Assignments to command 117

    Mentioned 61, 117

Toler, Josiah. Mentioned 591

Toler, Silas C. Mentioned 147

Toombs, Robert. Mentioned 670

Toone's Station, Tenn. Affair near, July 27, 1862. Communications from

    Logan, John A 125

    McClernand, John A 125

    Ross, Leonard F 125

Toone's, Tenn., Commanding Officer at. Correspondence with J. C. Sullivan 380

Topp, Thomas M. Mentioned 819, 834

Torrence, Judge, U. S. S. Mentioned 887

Tourtellotte, John E. Mentioned 339, 516

Townes, R. R. Correspondence with John A. Logan 104, 196

        For correspondence as A. A. G., see *J. A. McClernand* and *J. A. Logan.*

Townsend, Captain. Mentioned 124

Townsend, E. D. For correspondence as A. A. G., see *Adjutant-General's Office, U. S. A.*

Page.

Trabue, R. P.
Assignments to command 900
Mentioned 900
Tracy, E. D.
Correspondence with John C. Pemberton 821
Mentioned 765, 821, 824, 825, 831
Trade and Intercourse. Communications from
Army Headquarters 179, 185, 186, 189
Dodge, Grenville M 123
Grant, U. S 123, 130, 155,
    163, 188, 296, 330, 335, 337, 349, 354, 357, 396, 400, 421, 424, 522, 569, 575
Halleck, H. W 21
Norton, A. S 416
Pemberton, John C 794
Quinby, Isaac F 123, 179, 353, 542
Rosecrans, W. S 151
Ross, Leonard F 120
Sherman, W. T 117, 163, 868
War Department, C. S 839
    See also *Grant to Halleck*, p. 41; *Halleck to Stanton*, p. 59; *Halleck to Grant*,
        pp. 60, 150; *Sherman to Rawlins*, pp. 121, 140, 169, 855; *Elliott to
        Morgan*, p. 154; *Sherman to Grant*, pp. 178, 187, 259, 272, 860;
        Sherman to Kelton, p. 200; *Quinby to Grant*, p. 236; *McClernand
        to Stanton*, p. 332; *Gordon to Lovell*, p. 352; *Hurlbut to Rawlins*, p.
        506; *Snead to Falkner*, p. 668.
Trans-Mississippi Department.
Affairs in, generally. Communications from
    Adjutant and Inspector General's Office, C. S. A 653, 655
    Bragg, Braxton 649, 653
Holmes, Theophilus H., assigned to command 655
Missouri State Guard ordered to return to 646
Transfer of Price's command to. Communications from
    Price, Sterling 759, 794
    War Department, C. S 759
Transportation. (Railroad and Water.) Communications from
Adjutant and Inspector General's Office, C. S. A 644, 770
Allen, Robert 189, 355, 399, 402, 421, 552, 556
Army Headquarters 190, 194, 276, 355, 433, 447
Bragg, Braxton 609, 612, 615, 624, 625, 627, 637
Davies, Thomas A 493, 535
Davis, Jefferson 653
Dodge, Grenville M 81, 199
Dutton, Carlos 495
Grant, U. S.. 79, 176, 194, 262, 268, 315, 380, 434, 483, 488, 492, 499, 504, 525, 543, 545
Griffin, G. G 625
Halleck, H. W 4, 12, 19, 20, 22, 26, 52, 55, 67, 68, 78, 83, 86
Hurlbut, Stephen A 326
McClernand, John A 8, 25
McPherson, James B 78, 184, 314, 446, 559
Marsh, C. C 454
Parsons, L. B 355, 413, 496
Pemberton, John C 774, 794
Pride, George G 352, 373
Quinby, Isaac F 524

Page.

Transportation. (Railroad and Water)—Cont'd. Communications from

Rosecrans, W. S 119, 126, 176, 177, 191, 193, 196, 198

Sanderson, W. L.. 13

Sherman, W. T 4, 9, 10, 17–21, 23, 27, 32, 33, 40, 45, 79, 81, 96, 111, 229, 234, 244

Wallace, Lew.. 25

War Department, C. S 627, 629

See also *Wallace to Hotchkiss*, p. 14; *Halleck to Stanton*, pp. 18, 45; *Grant to Halleck*, p. 41; *Sherman to Rawlins*, pp. 84, 426; *Grant to Sherman*, p. 335; *McPherson to Denver*, p. 445.

Trapier, James H. Mentioned 673

Trenton, Tenn., Commanding Officer at. Correspondence with

Grant, U. S.. 293

Sullivan, J. C.. 380

Tresilian, Stewart R. For correspondence as A. D. C., see *John A. Logan*.

Trevesant, John P. Mentioned 252

Trezevant, E. B. Mentioned 662

Trinity, Ala. Operations at and in the vicinity of, July 25, 1862. See *Courtland and Trinity, Ala.*

Tripp, Stephen S. Mentioned...................................... 340

Troy, Tenn., Commanding Officer at. Correspondence with J. C. Sullivan. 380

True, James M. Mentioned................................. 146, 247, 341

Tucker, John. Mentioned 78, 86

Tunison, John. Mentioned 350

Tupper, Nathan W. Mentioned............................. 340, 344, 539

Turner, George A. Mentioned 841

Turner, Thomas J. Mentioned 145, 247

Tutt, Thomas E., Steamer. Mentioned 573

Tuttle, James M.

Assignments to command 166, 353

Correspondence with Army Headquarters.......................... 269

Mentioned 135, 166, 182, 197, 211, 309, 341, 353, 394, 494, 513, 517

Tweeddale, William. Mentioned 314

Tyler, U. S. S. Mentioned 885, 887

Tyler, John, jr. Mentioned 674

Tyler, R. C. Mentioned 603

Tyree, Emily. Mentioned.. 54

Union Bank of Tennessee. Affairs of Memphis Branch of. Communication from W. T. Sherman 161

Union City, Tenn., Commanding Officer at. Correspondence with J. C. Sullivan 380

Union Troops.

Halleck, H. W., assigned to command as General-in-Chief of land forces of the United States 90

Mentioned. (Regulars.)

Artillery, Light—*Regiments*: **2d** (*Batteries*), F, 147, 248, 340.

Cavalry—*Regiments*: **2d**, 248, 287; **3d**, 336, 507.

Infantry—*Regiments*: **1st**, 148, 249, 265, 341, 517; **13th**, 116, 202, 211, 218, 244, 260, 285, 340, 344, 397, 539; **15th**, 116, 146, 517; **16th**, 146, 517.

For Volunteers, see respective States.

Organization, strength, etc.

Bolivar, Tenn., Post of....................................... 527

Mississippi, Army of the........................... 144, 147, 148, 246, 248

Tennessee, Army of the....................................... 143–

146, 212, 213, 245–247, 249, 311, 337–342, 512–517, 527, 576–578

West Tennessee, District of 143–148, 245–250

Page.
Union Troops—Continued.
  Recruitment, organization, etc. **Communications from**
    Adjutant-General's Office, U. S. A 262, 432
    Army Headquarters.. 187. 251, 262, 425, 503
    Asboth, A.. 139
    Dickey, T. Lyle 363
    Ellet, Alfred W 406
    Elliott, W. L 139
    Granger, Gordon 139
    Grant, U. S...................... 4, 89, 108, 151, 191, 267, 364, 398, 425, 461, 480
    Lincoln, Abraham... 502
    McClernand, John A.. 277, 300, 308, 332, 334, 371, 375, 401, 415, 560, 562, 564, 853
    Rosecrans, W. S..................................... 86, 108, 139, 190, 191, 239
    Sherman, W. T 344, 538
    Sullivan, J. C.. 139
    War Department, U. S 282, 300, 302, 308, 391, 420, 502
  See also *Bryant to McClernand*, p. 168; *Halleck to Grant*, p. 182; *Grant to Sherman*, p. 322; *Sherman to Grant*, p. 860.
Universe, Steamer. Mentioned 573
Urquhart, D. Mentioned.. 648
Van Arman, John. Mentioned 340, 539
Vance, Zebulon B. Mentioned 791
Vandever, William. Mentioned 324
Van Dorn, Earl.
  Assignments to command 613, 616, 636, 715, 727, 787, 792, 835
  Co-operation with Price. See *Northern Mississippi*. *Operations in, June* 10,
    1862–*Jan.* 20, 1863.
  Correspondence with
    Adjutant and Inspector General's Office, C. S. A.......................... 591
    Beauregard, G. T.. 592, 594
    Bradfute, W. R.. 597, 607, 611
    Bragg, Braxton 613, 656, 675, 688, 713, 897
    Breckinridge, John C... 897
    Davis, Jefferson.. 596, 686, 700, 715, 733
    Gillespie, John W... 771
    Griffith, John S... 779
    Jackson, W. H.. 766, 902
    Johnston, Joseph E... 808, 822, 833, 835
    Jones, E. P.. 762
    Lovell, Mansfield.. 903
    Maury, Dabney H... 903
    Pallen, M. A.. 901
    Pemberton, John C.. 728, 732, 734–740, 742–
      744, 746, 747, 750, 751, 754–757, 767–770, 777–779, 785, 793, 812, 813, 833, 834
    Pillow, Gideon J.. 715
    Price, Sterling.. 663, 665, 675, 680, 687, 690–
      692, 695, 696, 698, 701–703, 707–711, 714, 717–721, 723, 737, 741, 743, 744, 747
    Rosecrans, W. S... 265
    Ruggles, Daniel.. 619, 719, 726
    Smith, Martin L.. 900
    War Department, C. S. 681, 697, 699, 701, 703, 704, 707, 713, 715, 717, 726, 727, 735
  Mentioned 14, 29, 34, 37, 58, 140, 141, 181, 191, 207–209, 213, 220,
    222–224, 229, 233, 243, 244, 250, 253, 259, 265, 269, 270, 273, 279, 285, 286, 288,
    300, 304, 307, 368, 411, 443, 444, 448, 450, 454–457, 459, 463, 470, 473, 478, 482–

Page.

Van Dorn, Earl—Continued.

Mentioned. 484, 487–491, 493, 494, 498, 499, 501, 519, 521, 523–525, 530, 532, 533, 541, 575, 588, 609, 610, 612, 614–616, 619–622, 628, 630, 636, 645, 656, 658, 661, 663, 666. 673, 675, 677, 678, 682, 684, 685, 688, 693, 695, 696, 698, 707, 711, 714–716, 719, 721, 724–727, 734, 742, 744, 745, 747, 757, 762, 765, 785, 787–789, 792, 807, 808, 811–813, 816, 823, 832, 838, 839, 844–846, 854, 855, 857, 867, 872, 874, 897, 903

Orders in cases of

Martial law 694

Private property 729, 745

Recruitment, etc 681

Van Dorn's Raid. Operations against, Dec. 20–28, 1862. Communications from

Barnum, W. L 457

Brayman, M 440, 458, 465, 466, 475–477

Dodge, Grenville M 488

Grant, U. S 437,

439, 440, 442, 443, 448–450, 455–457, 459, 463–468, 472–474, 482, 488–490

Grierson, Benjamin H 465, 466, 468, 473–475, 483

Hamilton, C. S 455, 456

Hatch, Edward 466

Haynie, Isham N 484

Hillyer, William S 457

Loring, W. W 808

McDermott, J 450, 458, 459, 467

McPherson, James B 437, 468, 469, 473, 478, 505

Marsh, C. C 442, 443, 447–449, 454, 455, 468, 472, 484

Mizner, J. K 437–439, 443, 448, 472, 484, 493, 498

Morrison, William R 450, 459

Murphy, R. C 440, 444

Richmond, J 444, 451, 460

Sprague, John W 444, 460

Stephenson, W. J 460

Sullivan, J. C 464

Van Duzer, J. C.

Correspondence with

Bruch, Samuel 394

Grant, U. S 230, 378

Mentioned 368, 370, 371, 377–379, 382, 386, 394

Vaughan, A. J., jr. Mentioned 603

Vaughn, John C. Mentioned 765, 773, 797, 799, 803, 806, 814, 815, 821, 824, 831

Vaughn, Thomas F. Mentioned 342, 527

Veatch, James C.

Assignments to command 542

Correspondence with Stephen A. Hurlbut 12

Mentioned 27, 29, 118, 189, 202, 205, 268, 271, 325, 542, 570, 576

Venable, C. D. Mentioned 603

Vessels. See *Naval Vessels.*

Vicksburg, Miss.

Canal across Burey's Point. Communications from

Halleck, H. W 43

War Department, U. S 26

Confederate troops at. Organization, strength, etc.

January 2–3, 1863 .... 824, 825

January 8, 1863 829

January 10, 1863 831

Page.

Vicksburg, Miss.—Continued.
   Defenses of (immediate). **Communications from**
      Davis, Jefferson 802
      Pemberton, John C 736
      Ruggles, Daniel 709, 719, 721
      Smith, Martin L 900
      Stevenson, C. L 829, 831
             See also *Pemberton to Cooper,* p. 749.
   Operations against.
     May 18–July 27, 1862.
      Communications from
        Beauregard, G. T 613
        Bragg, Braxton 613, 630, 644, 897
        Davis, Jefferson 596, 599, 897
        Halleck, H. W 97
        War Department, U. S 97
        See also *Sherman to Rawlins,* p. 140; *Ellet to Brooks,* p. 148; *Halleck*
          to Ellet, p. 149; *Bragg to Smith,* p. 651.
      Co-operation of Navy, U. S., with Army 43, 97
     Dec. 20, 1862–Jan. 3, 1863.
      Communications from
        Adams, Wirt 803
        Allen, Robert 421
        Army Headquarters 187,
           335, 349, 376, 401, 424, 425, 433, 441, 461, 503, 542
        Barton, S. M 824
        Connell, W. M. M 808
        Curtis, Samuel R 383, 395, 433, 434, 463
        Dillon, Edward 762
        Fall, Phillip 804
        Fitch, Henry A 480
        Gorman, W. A 406, 412, 414, 421, 464, 522
        Grant, U. S 392, 393, 412, 414, 425, 451, 463, 480, 531, 563
        Hébert, Louis 812
        Hurlbut, Stephen A 522, 526
        Illinois, Governor of 366
        Johnston, Joseph E 800, 804, 806, 809, 813, 816, 817, 825, 826
        Jones, E. P 762, 763
        Lincoln, Abraham 350, 502
        Loring, W. W 805, 807, 830
        McClernand, John A 274, 277, 300, 308, 332, 334,
          345, 371, 375, 401, 415, 420, 461, 501, 528, 534, 566, 567, 849, 853, 866
        McPherson, James B 453
        Navy Department, U. S 320
        Pargoud, J. F 804
        Parsons, L. B 413, 441, 496
        Pemberton, John C 763,
          774, 804–806, 808–810, 812, 814, 816, 821, 822, 828
        Porter, David D 321, 356, 882–884, 887, 888
        Sherman, W. T 392, 396, 397, 402, 406–
          408, 419, 423, 426, 434, 435, 453, 485, 509, 588, 862, 875, 877–880, 882, 889
        Smith, A. J 519
        Smith, Martin L 764, 767, 771, 803, 825
        Steele, Frederick 410

Page.

Vicksburg, Miss.—Continued.
Operations against.
Dec. 20, 1862–Jan. 3, 1863.
Communications from
Stevenson, C. L 814, 815, 821, 824, 826
Tracy, E. D 825
Van Dorn, Earl 813
Waddy, J. R 762, 797
War Department, U. S 282,
300, 302, 308, 348, 349, 391, 413, 420, 462, 502, 503
See also *Grant to Sherman*, p. 347; *Pemberton to Cooper*, p. 766;
Johnston to Davis, pp. 823, 827.
Co-operation of
Curtis with Grant 392–395, 401–403,
406–410, 412–414, 421, 423, 424, 426, 433, 434, 441, 453, 463, 464, 471, 877
Navy, U. S., with Army 320,
321, 347, 349, 356, 380, 392, 402, 407, 409, 862, 863, 876–880, 882–889
McClernand, John A., assumes command of expedition............ 534
Jan. 20–July 4, 1863.
Communications from
Army Headquarters........................ .... 542, 545, 550, 555, 578
Boyle, J. T 550
Curtis, Samuel R 555, 578
Fisk, Clinton B... 558
Grant, U. S 543–
545, 548–551, 553, 555–557, 559, 560, 564, 565, 568, 570, 573
Hamilton, C. S.. 548
Hurlbut, Stephen A... 548
McClernand, John A 561–563, 570, 572–574
McPherson, James B........................... 548, 549, 558, 559, 569
Pennock, A. M 550
Sherman, W. T 560, 568, 570
War Department, U. S 579
Wright, H. G 545
Co-operation of
Curtis with Grant 542, 552, 553, 555, 578, 579
Navy, U. S., with Army... 544, 550–552, 560, 561, 570, 762–764, 767, 771
McClernand, John A., relieved from command of.................. 555
Re-enforcements for. Communications from
Adjutant and Inspector General's Office, C. S. A. 753, 765, 767, 768, 777, 786, 793
Bragg, Braxton 755, 769, 800
Davis, Jefferson... 767, 786
Dillon, Edward 762
Forney, John H.. 768, 773
Holmes, Theophilus H 757, 782, 783, 787, 810
Johnston, Joseph E 780, 781, 809, 827, 828
Loring, W. W... 807
Pemberton, John C.. 757,
762, 764, 767, 771, 793, 794, 800, 803, 808, 809, 811, 817, 826
Preston, W 621
Ruggles, Daniel... 622, 771, **774**
Smith, Martin L 762, 793
Van Dorn, Earl... 756
See also *Pemberton to Johnston*, p. 784.

Page

Vicksburg, Miss.—Continued.

Subsistence stores on hand. List of.

December 15, 1862 797

January 15, 1863. 837

Supplies for..752, 753, 755, 764,

769, 776–778, 782, 792, 793, 797, 798, 800, 802, 805, 817, 823, 830, 831, 837, 839

Villepigue, John B.

Assignments to command... 622

Correspondence with

Bragg, Braxton 622

Ruggles, Daniel 611, 614, 617

Mentioned................ .... 57, 139, 140, 163, 166, 178, 182, 197, 205, 216, 231, 233,

234, 243, 250, 251, 253, 322, 336, 595, 600–602, 608, 610, 611, 614, 648, 649,

656, 676, 678, 687, 688, 693, 697, 701, 704, 711, 713, 854, 855, 857, 866, 899

Virginia. Re-enforcements for. Communications from

Grant, U. S 55, 56

Halleck, H. W... 52, 55, 56, 58–61, 71

Lincoln, Abraham 53, 63, 70

McClernand, John A 60

War Department, U. S 42, 52

See also *Halleck to Grant*, pp. 60, 82; *Lincoln to Halleck*, p. 76.

Virginia, Army of. (Union.)

Elliott, W. L., assigned to duty in 163

Pope, John, assigned to command of.................................... 40

Virginia Troops. Mentioned. (Confederate.)

Artillery, Light—*Batteries:* Botetourt, 824.

Vowles, Newton. Mentioned 598

Waddy, J. R.

Correspondence with John C. Pemberton .. 762, 763, 767, 785, 797, 805, 806, 826, 829

Mentioned 728, 820

For correspondence as A. A. G., see *John C. Pemberton*.

Wadsworth, David D. Mentioned 350

Walcutt, Charles C.

Correspondence with W. T. Sherman.................................. 235

Mentioned................................ 169, 212, 246, 280, 281, 285, 340, 344, 514

Walker, C. H. Mentioned 729

Walker, F. M.

Assignments to command 900

Correspondence with John C. Breckinridge 898

Mentioned 900

Walker, John G. Mentioned 884

Walker, John J. Mentioned 623, 648

Walker, Samuel P.

Correspondence with Gideon J. Pillow............................... 171

Mentioned 170, 172

Walker, W. H. T. Mentioned 618, 632, 652

Wallace, Lew.

Assignments to command... 308

Correspondence with

McClernand, John A................................... 11, 14, 25

Sherman, W. T... 9

Mentioned 8, 10,

11, 19, 21, 28, 30, 31, 37, 43, 46, 55, 56, 58–61, 121, 122, 168, 239, 308, 327, 598

Page.

Wallace, M. R. M.
Correspondence with John A. Logan 80, 89
Mentioned 80, 135, 136, 144, 516
Walling, Daniel P. Mentioned 248, 339
Walsh, E., Steamer. Mentioned 573
Walsh, John, Steamer. Mentioned 867
Walter, H. W. Mentioned 648
Wangelin, Hugo. Mentioned 539
War Department, C. S. Correspondence with
Adjutant and Inspector General's Office, C. S. A 732
Beauregard, G. T 598
Bragg, Braxton 612, 619, 625, 627, 629, 630, 673
Davis, Jefferson 697, 698, 731, 732, 802
Ordnance Department, C. S. A 700, 749, 775
Pemberton, John C 716, 727, 737, 739, 751, 759, 828, 839
Pillow, Gideon J 716
Price, Sterling 668, 676, 683, 759
Tilghman, Lloyd 700
Van Dorn, Earl 681, 697, 699, 701, 703, 704, 707, 713, 715, 717, 726, 727, 735
War Department, U. S.
Correspondence with
Adjutant-General's Office, U. S. A 91
Allen, Robert 397
Cates, O. G 93
Denver, James W 484
Ellet, Alfred W 241, 277, 282
Ellet, Charles, jr 8, 9
Grant, U. S 346, 347, 371, 378, 421
Halleck, H. W . 6, 12, 18, 23, 26, 31, 34, 40–42, 43, 45, 52, 59, 60, 67, 76–78, 90, 91, 97
Illinois, Governor of 366
McClernand, John A 274, 277, 300, 302, 308,
310, 332, 345, 348, 349, 371, 375, 391, 401, 413, 420, 461, 462, 503, 528, 579, 866
McDermott, John 382
Navy Department, U. S 320
Negley, James S 29
Pope, John 17, 18
Rosecrans, W. S 190, 281–284, 286, 290, 291
Orders, series 1862: **July 31,** 165; **Oct. 21,** 282, 502.
Ward, Lyman M. Mentioned 146, 340, 515
War Eagle, Steamer. Mentioned 573
Warner, John, Steamer. Mentioned 573
Warner, John. Mentioned 339, 516
Warren, Private. Mentioned 419
Warren, Joseph. Mentioned 15
Warsaw, Steamer. Mentioned 573
Washburn, C. C. Mentioned 384, 408, 409, 496
Washington, J. Barroll. Mentioned 782
Waterhouse, Allen C. Mentioned 146, 212, 341
Watson, P. H. Mentioned 284, 378
For correspondence, etc., see *War Department, U. S.*
Watts, W. O. Mentioned 723
Waul, T. N. Mentioned 824, 854–856
Waverly, Tenn. Expedition to, Jan. 16, 1863. Communications from A.
Asboth 573

Page.

W. B. Terry, Steamer.
  Capture of, Aug. 31, 1862. Communications from U. S. Grant 202
  Mentioned 182, 202
Weaver, James B. Mentioned 249, 341, 516
Webb, Dr. Mentioned 687, 689
Webb, J. Y. Mentioned 646
Webber, William W. Mentioned 369
Weber, Andrew J. Mentioned 248, 339
Webster, J. D.
  Appointed commander of the post of Memphis, Tenn 30
  Appointed superintendent of military railroads in the Department of the
    Tennessee 315
  Correspondence with U. S. Grant 337
  Mentioned 30, 82, 183, 315, 360, 476, 483, 491
    For correspondence as Chief of Staff, see *U. S. Grant.*
Welles, Gideon. Mentioned 97, 882
    For correspondence, etc., see *Navy Department, U. S.*
Wells, Lieutenant. Mentioned 660, 689
West, Army of the. (Confederate.)
  Armstrong, Frank C., assigned to command of cavalry of 642
  Beall, W. N. R.
    Assigned to duty in 610, 614
    Relieved from duty in 616
  Little, Henry.
    Assigned to command of Price's division 596
    Assigned to command of cavalry of 690
  McCown, J. P., assumes temporary command 616
  Merged into Army of West Tennessee 715, 727, 729
  Missouri State Guard relieved from duty with 609, 610
  Orders, General, series 1862: (McCown), No. 1, 616; No. 2, 617; (Price),
    No. 6, 636; No. 7, 637; No. 8, 642; (Van Dorn), No. 47, 616.
    Divisions: (Bowen), No. 4, 736; No. 10, 739.
  Orders, Special, series 1862: No. 112, 596; No. 117, 610; No. 118, 613.
    Divisions: (Bowen), No. 1, 734.
  Organization, strength, etc.
    June 30, 1862 .... 631, 634, 635
    July 16, 1862 648
    July 20, 1862 .... 652, 653
    October 1, 1862 718
    October 20, 1862 733
    October 22, 1862 736
  Price, Sterling, assumes command 636
  Reorganization of ....(Note).. 733
  Van Dorn, Earl, relinquishes command temporarily 616
West, Department of the.*
  Affairs in, generally. Communications from
    Johnston, Joseph E 758, 782, 800, 815, 822, 823, 827
    War Department, C. S 757
  Constituted, and limits defined 757
  Featherston, W. S., assigned to duty in 846
  Johnston, Joseph E., assigned to and assumes command 757, 782
  List of General Officers in 765
  Orders, General, series 1862: No. 1, 782.
  Re-enforcements for. See *Johnston to Davis,* p. 823.

---

*Joseph E. Johnston's geographical command.

Western Department. (Confederate.)

    Addresses to soldiers of. (Bragg)... 626

    Affairs in, generally. Communications from

        Adjutant and Inspector General's Office, C. S. A...................... 624, 649

        Beauregard, G. T.. 606

        Bragg, Braxton 606, 626, 636, 644

        Jordan, Thomas 640, 669, 679

    Beauregard, G. T., relinquishes command (temporarily) of 606

    Bragg, Braxton.

        Assigned to and assumes command of............................... 626, 636

        Assumes command (temporarily) of.................................. 606

    Confederate troops in. Organization, strength, etc.

        July 1, 1862.. 631–635

        July 16, 1862... 648

        July 20, 1862... 652, 653

    Hardee, William J., assigned to command at Tupelo, Miss., and environs.. 635

    Inspection of, July 15, 1862. Report of W. P. Johnston................... 647

    Limits extended 624, 627, 636, 649

    Missouri State Guard transferred to Trans-Mississippi Department........ 646

    Orders, General, series 1862: **No. 72,** 599; **Nos. 74, 75, 76,** 606; **No. 78,**
        616; **No. 80,** 623; **No. 86,** 635; **Nos. 87, 89,** 636; **Nos. 92, 93,**
        638; **No. 98,** 646; **No. 100,** 648; **No. 101,** 650; **No. 103,** 658;
        No. 104, 663; **No. 109,** 672; **Nos. 114, 117,** 680.

    Orders, Special, series 1862: **No. 3,*** 654; **No. 4,*** 656; **No. 6,*** 657; **No.**
        62, 796; **No. 66,** 800; **No. 80,** 595; **No. 82,** 600; **No. 85,** 606;
        No. 86, 610; **No. 88,** 615; **No. 96,** 626; **No. 105,** 638; **No. 123,**
        648; **No. 125,** 650; **No. 131,** 658; **Nos. 133, 134,** 659.

    Polk, Leonidas, announced as second in command 636

    Subdivision of. See *Gulf, District of the; Mississippi, District of the.*

    Villepigue, John B., assigned to command of sub-department in........... 622

Western Kentucky. Operations in, June 10, 1862–Jan. 20, 1863. Communi-
    cations from

    Griffin, R. B 126

    Lowe, W. W.. 126

Western Kentucky, District of. Orders, Special, series 1863: **No. 8,** 550.

Western Rivers. Floating defenses for. Communications from

    Army Headquarters.. 398

    Ellet, Alfred W.. 148, 241, 406

    Ellet, Charles, jr... 9

    Lincoln, Abraham 323

    War Department, U. S.. 8, 282

West Louisiana. Re-enforcements for. Communications from

    Adjutant and Inspector General's Office, C. S. A........................ 768

    Pemberton, John C 837

    Van Dorn, Earl 691

Westmoreland, Steamer. Mentioned 549, 573

West Tennessee.

    Forrest's expedition into, Dec. 15, 1862–Jan. 3, 1863.

        Communications from

        Army Headquarters... 422, 462, 486

        Barnum, W. L... 457

        Bragg, Braxton.. 755

        Brayman, M 440, 444

---

* Headquarters of the forces.

Page.

West Tennessee—Continued.

Forrest's expedition into, Dec. 15, 1862–Jan. 3, 1863.

Communications from

Bruch, Samuel 499

Burke, P E 427

Carter, James M 415

Davies, Thomas A 415, 441, 453, 462, 493, 494, 505

Dodge, Grenville M 427, 428, 431, 432, 457, 458, 488

Fisk, Clinton B 486

Fry, Jacob 432

Grant, U. S .. 400, 404, 426–431, 435, 436, 458, 463, 477, 478, 488–490, 492, 497

Hawkins, Isaac R 444

Haynie, Isham N 415, 458, 467, 477, 491, 493, 497, 498

Ihrie, George P 458, 876, 877

Ingersoll, R. G 429

Lawler, Michael K 477

Lowe, W. W 440, 441

Morrison, William R 432, 450

Navy Department, U. S 422

Pennock, A. M 426

Porter, David D 404, 422

Rosecrans, W. S 400, 423, 441

Silence, Ned R 498

Sullivan, J. C 405,
415, 423, 429–431, 436, 456, 464, 465, 483, 489, 491, 492, 498, 505

See also *Davies to Rawlins*, p. 481; *Hurlbut to Davies*, p. 501; *Fisk to Curtis*, p. 504; *Grant to Hurlbut*, p. 508; *Grant to Hamilton*, p. 518; *Rawlins to Hurlbut*, p. 522.

Also *Columbus, Ky. Operations about.*

Island No. 10, *Tenn. Operations about.*

Co-operation of Navy, U. S., with Army 404,
422, 426, 431, 447, 486, 487, 497, 505, 518

Operations in, June 10, 1862–Jan. 20, 1863.

Communications from

Army Headquarters 182, 198

Brayman, M 357, 521, 527

Breckenridge, W. K. M 564

Bryant, G. E 168, 174

Deitzler, George W 34

Dodge, Grenville M .. 104, 105, 107, 109, 110, 161, 180, 183, 198, 199, 206, 414

Fry, Jacob 364, 394, 414

Grant, U. S 36, 41, 43, 46, 79,
182, 183, 199, 233, 239, 304–307, 309, 313, 318, 319, 357–359, 518, 530, 541, 565

Halleck, H. W 5, 6, 19, 22, 32, 34, 38, 45, 46, 56, 60, 67, 82, 99, 100

Hamilton, C. S 518, 525

Harris, Thomas W 365

Hart, J. H 183

Haynie, Isham N 175, 180, 199, 203, 313, 387, 389, 399, 400

Hurlbut, Stephen A 31, 32, 37, 38,
50, 89, 215, 226, 232–234, 238, 240, 243, 274, 278, 297, 306, 323, 326, 331, 337

Jackson, W. H 598

Lawler, Michael K 153, 509

Leggett, Mortimer D 68, 75, 95, 116

Logan, John A 76, 80, 89, 104, 115, 180

Page.

West Tennessee—Continued.

Operations in, June 10, 1862–Jan. 20, 1863.

Communications from

Lowe, W. W 181

McClernand, John A 6, 8 11, 21, 25, 38, 39, 64 70, 72, 94, 155, 174, 180

McPherson, James B 281, 299, 300, 301, 559

Morris, T. E 373

Norton, A. S... 376, 387, 390, 400

Pennock, A. M 541

Quinby, Isaac F 107, 203, 236, 357

Rawlins, John A.. 299

Ross, Leonard F 110, 116, 152, 155, 161, 167, 183

Ruggles, Daniel 598

Sanderson, W. L.. 64

Sanford, W. W 104

Sherman, W. T 7–10, 17, 19–21, 23, 27, 28, 32, 33, 39, 40, 42, 44, 45,
50, 51, 79, 83, 84, 88, 96, 102, 106, 109, 128, 141, 142, 149, 167, 204, 210, 237, 242

Stevenson, J. D... 198, 202

Sullivan, J. C................................... 380, 398, 413, 538, 540, 555

Townes, R. R. 104

Wallace, Lew.. 14, 25

See also *Grant to Halleck,* pp. 114, 160, 220; *Sherman to Rawlins,* pp.
121, 140, 169, 201, 215, 279, 285; *Sherman to Grant,* pp. 178, 187, 244,
272, 860; *Grant to Kelton,* p. 206; *Hurlbut to Grant,* p. 526.

Also

June   25, 1862. *La Fayette Station, Tenn. Affair near.*

        30, 1862. *Rising Sun, Tenn. Skirmish at.*

July   25–Aug. 1, 1862. *Holly Springs, Miss. Expedition from, to
        Bolivar and Jackson, Tenn.*

Aug.   18, 1862. *Tennessee River. Capture of steamboats on.*

        30–Sept. 1, 1862. *Mississippi Central R. R. Operations on
        the.*

        31, 1862. *W. B. Terry, Steamer. Capture of.*

Sept.   5, 1862. *Burnt Bridge, Tenn. Skirmish at, near Humboldt.*

        20–22, 1862. *Bolivar, Tenn. Expedition from, to Grand Junc-
        tion and La Grange, and skirmish.*

        25, 1862. *Davis' Bridge, Hatchie River, Tenn. Skirmish at.
        Randolph, Tenn. Burning of.*

Oct. 21–24, 1862. *Memphis, Tenn. Scout from, to Colliersville,
        Shelby Depot, Hickory, and Galloway Switch.*

        31, 1862–Jan. 10, 1863. *Mississippi Central Railroad. Opera-
        tions on the, from Bolivar, Tenn., to Coffeeville,
        Miss.*

Nov.   25, 1862. *Henderson's Station, Tenn. Capture of.*

Dec.   15, 1862–Jan. 3, 1863. *West Tennessee. Forrest's expedition
        into.*

        16, 1862. *Waverly, Tenn. Expedition to.*

Co-operation of Navy, U. S., with Army 237, 530, 541

West Tennessee, Army of. (Confederate.)

Constituted.. 715, 727, 729

Denominated Army of the Mississippi 787

Jackson, W. H., assigned to command of cavalry 729

Lovell, Mansfield, assigned to command a corps of 729

Orders, General, series 1862: **No. 52,** 727; **No. 54,** 729; **No. 67,** 772.

Orders, Special, series 1862: **No. 53,** 728; **No. 99,** 745; **Dec. 1,** 773.

West Tennessee, Army of—Continued. (Confederate.)

Price, Sterling, assigned to command a corps of 729
Sanitary condition of. Report of M. A. Pallen 901
Van Dorn, Earl, assigned to and assumes command of 715,727

West Tennessee, Army of. (Union.) See *Tennessee, Army of the.*

West Tennessee, District of. (Union.)

Affairs in, generally. Communications from
Army Headquarters 164,238
Grant, U. S 114,160,168,186,206,220,235,237,238,240,255,268,275
Rosecrans, W. S 166,275
Dodge, Grenville M., assigned to temporary command of Fourth Division . 242
Grant, U. S., assigned to and assumes command of 101,102
Hurlbut, Stephen A., assigned to command Second Division 268
Limits extended 7,101
Location of troops in, August 14, 1862 168
McPherson, James B., assigned to command of forces at Bolivar, Tenn ... 277
Merged into Department of the Tennessee 278
Ord, E. O. C.
Assigned to command Second Division 237
Relieved from command of Second Division 268
Orders, General, Special, etc. See *Tennessee, Army of the.* (*Union.*)
Quinby, I. F., assigned to command Fourth Division 237
Rosecrans, W. S.
Assigned to command Third Division 237
Assumes command of Third Division 240
Sherman, W. T., assigned to command First Division 237
Subdivisions of, announced 237
Union troops in. Organization, strength, etc.
July 31, 1862 143–148
September 30, 1862 245–250
Wirtz, Horace R., announced as chief medical director 255

West Tennessee, District of.* (Union.)

Constituted, and limits defined 565
Hamilton, C. S., assigned to, and assumes command 565,569
Orders, General, series 1863: **No. 1**, 569.

West Wind, Steamer. Mentioned 573
Wever, Clark R. Mentioned 516
Wharton, John A. Mentioned 765,835
Wheeler, Joseph.
Assignments to command 650
Correspondence with William J. Hardee 651
Mentioned 558,650,663,665,666,765,823
Wheeler, J. T. Mentioned 661,902
White, Captain. Mentioned 522
White, D. G. Mentioned 639
White, Hamilton B. Mentioned 249,515
White, T. W. Mentioned 629,737
White, William H. Mentioned 870–873
White, William H., Mrs. Mentioned 872
Whitehurst, Eli. Correspondence with C. S. Hamilton 306
White River, Ark.
Expedition up the, Jan. 13–19, 1863.
Communications from
Gorman, W. A 552,579

Page.

White River, Ark.—Continued.
 Expedition up the, Jan. 13–19, 1863.
  Communications from
   Loring, W. W 837
   Pemberton, John C 837
     See also *McClernand to Sherman*, p. 563.
   Co-operation of Navy, U. S., with Army............................... 477
  Operations on the, June 10–July 14, 1862. Communications from U. S.
   Grant 54
     See also *Quinby to Slack*, p. 13; *Grant to Halleck*, pp. 55, 56.
Whitfield, George. Correspondence with J. C. Pemberton.................. 822
Whitfield, John W.
  Correspondence with John C. Pemberton................................. 814
  Mentioned 709
Whiting, Jasper S. For correspondence as A. A. G., see *Adjutant and In-
     spector General's Office, C. S. A.*
Whittemore, Henry C. Mentioned 876, 878
Wickersham, ——. Mentioned 858
Wicks, M. J. Mentioned... 639
Wigfall, Louis T. Mentioned...................................... 767
Wilcox, John S. Mentioned.. 249
Wilder, W. C. Mentioned.. 539
Wiles, William M. Mentioned...................................... 86
Wilkenson, Theodore. Mentioned 418
Wilkins, W. W. Mentioned 639
Willard, Charles M. Mentioned 294
Willard, Elijah A. Mentioned 586
Willcox, Lyman G. Mentioned..................................... 248
Willetts, N. B. Mentioned 884
Williams, George. Mentioned..................................... 831
Williams, George A. Mentioned.............. 144, 148, 249, 339, 876, 878
Williams, George C. Mentioned 145
Williams, Henry W. Mentioned 668
Williams, J. R., Steamer. Mentioned............................. 573
Williams, J. T. Correspondence with P. D. Roddey................ 604, 613
Williams, Nelson G. Mentioned................................... 145, 247
Williams, William S. Mentioned 145, 213, 338, 514
Williamson, George. Mentioned................................... 680
Williamson, J. A. Mentioned 539
Wilson, James. For correspondence as A. A. A. G., see *M. M. Crocker.*
Wilson, James H. Mentioned 275, 278, 300, 399, 403
Wilson, M. R. Mentioned... 737
Wintter, D. Mentioned 699
Wirtz, Horace R.
  Announced as chief medical director District of West Tennessee.......... 255
  Mentioned 255
Wisconsin, Steamer. Mentioned................................... 573
Wisconsin Troops. Mentioned.
 Artillery, Light—*Batteries:* **5th,** 147; **6th,** 148, 200, 248, 340, 516; **7th,** 34,
   146, 247, 342; **8th, 10th,** 147; **12th,** 248, 340, 516.
 Infantry—*Regiments:* **8th,** 147, 218, 248, 339; **12th,** 146, 247, 269, 271, 339,
   515; **13th,** 146, 203, 250, 309, 517; **14th,** 146, 249, 340, 515; **15th,** 35, 105,
   146, 147, 517; **16th,** 145, 249, 340, 515; **17th,** 145, 249, 257, 340, 515; **18th,**
   145, 249, 340, 515; **28th,** 486; **32d,** 329, 340, 344, 861; **33d,** 340, 515.

Page

Wise, Lieutenant. Mentioned 42
Withers, H. R.
  Correspondence with W. W. Loring 804
  Mentioned... 804
Withers, Jones M. Mentioned.. 131,
                    136, 423, 482, 618, 623, 629, 633, 635, 638, 652, 657, 765
Withers, W. T. Mentioned 699, 792
Wolcott, C. P. For correspondence, etc., see *War Department, U. S.*
Wolfe, Edward H. Mentioned 20
Wood, Oliver. Mentioned.................................... 249, 341, 555
Wood, Peter P. Mentioned 146, 212, 247, 341, 539
Wood, Robert C. Mentioned 637, 654, 690, 691
Wood, Sallie, Steamer. Mentioned 140
Wood, S. A. M.
  Assignments to command... 642
  Mentioned............................... 619, 633, 642, 652, 657, 765
Wood, Thomas J. Mentioned................................. 5, 604, 613
Woods, Charles R. Mentioned..................... 109, 539, 574
Woods, Lewis & Co. Mentioned.................................... 731
Woodward, T. G. Mentioned 183
Woolley, Mr. Mentioned 50
Wooster, Captain. Mentioned 459
Wooten, Thomas D. Mentioned..................... 637, 654
Worthington, Thomas. Mentioned 146
Wright, Benjamin T. Mentioned.................................. 145
Wright, Horatio G.
  Correspondence with Army Headquarters............. 298, 299, 309, 335, 545 550
  Mentioned............ 186, 198, 200, 211, 213, 214, 244, 260, 261, 269, 286, 309, 550, 551
Wright, M. H. Mentioned.. 775
Wright, Uriel. Mentioned............................. 696, 698, 701, 859
Wyman, John B. Mentioned........................... 522, 526
Yandell, D. W. Mentioned... 639
Yates, Richard. Mentioned.............. 187, 269, 298–300, 308, 332–335, 401, 550
                    For correspondence, etc., see *Illinois, Governor of.*
Yazoo, Steamer. Mentioned 867
Yazoo River, Miss. Defenses of. Communications from
  Brown, Isaac N.. 788
  Pemberton, John C.. 738
  Lynch, W. F 724, 725
Yoeman, S. B. Mentioned 539
Young, Captain. Mentioned.................................... 168, 174
Young, W. H. Mentioned 603
Yowell, J. E. Mentioned 47
Zakrzewski, Herman. Mentioned................................. 148
Zickerick, William. Mentioned................................. 516

O